Silent Victory

BOOKS BY CLAY BLAIR, JR.

NONFICTION

The Atomic Submarine and Admiral Rickover
Beyond Courage
Diving for Pleasure and Treasure
The Strange Case of James Earl Ray
Survive!
Silent Victory: The U.S. Submarine War Against Japan
The Hydrogen Bomb, *with James R. Shepley*
Nautilus 90 North, *with Commander William R. Anderson*
Always Another Dawn, *with A. Scott Crossfield*

NOVELS

The Board Room
The Archbishop
Pentagon Country

Silent Victory

THE U.S. SUBMARINE WAR AGAINST JAPAN

by Clay Blair, Jr.

J. B. Lippincott Company
Philadelphia and New York

MAPS BY ELIZABETH NICOLL FELTON

All photographs courtesy United States Navy; Submarine Force Library and Museum; Rear Admiral Lewis S. Parks, U.S.N. (Ret.); United States Naval Institute.

The schematic cutaway of a fleet boat is reproduced from *United States Submarine Operations in World War II* by Theodore Roscoe by permission of Fred Freeman.

The excerpts from *Submarine!* by Commander Edward L. Beach, U.S.N., are reprinted by permission of the publishers, Holt, Rinehart and Winston, Inc.

The excerpts from the article "Unlucky in June: *Hiyo* Meets *Trigger*," by Commander Edward L. Beach, U.S.N., are reprinted by permission from *Proceedings*; copyright © 1957 U.S. Naval Institute.

The excerpts from *War Fish* by George Grider and Lydel Sims (copyright © 1958 by George Grider and Lydel Sims) are reprinted by permission of Little, Brown and Co.

The excerpts from *The Codebreakers* by David Kahn (copyright © 1967 by David Kahn) are reprinted by permission of Macmillan Publishing Co., Inc.

The excerpts from *Sink 'Em All* by Charles A. Lockwood are reprinted by permission of Mrs. Charles A. Lockwood.

The excerpts from *Wake of the Wahoo* by Forest J. Sterling (copyright © 1960 by the author) are reprinted with the permission of the publisher, Chilton Book Company, Radnor, Pa.

U.S. Library of Congress Cataloging in Publication Data

Blair, Clay, birth date
  Silent victory: the U.S. submarine war against Japan.

  Bibliography: p.
  1. World War, 1939–1945—Naval operations—Submarine.
  2. World War, 1939–1945—Naval operations, American.
  3. World War, 1939–1945—Pacific Ocean.   I. Title.
  D783.B58   940.54′51   74–2005
  ISBN–0–397–00753–1
  ISBN–0–397–01089–3 (Deluxe Edition)

Copyright © 1975 by Clay Blair, Jr.

All rights reserved

Second printing

Printed in the United States of America

To Joan—again

Acknowledgments

Countless people contributed to this book in countless ways. I would like to thank:

My wife, Joan. She worked side by side with me in the archives and libraries for many months, traveled around the United States helping to conduct the scores of interviews, transcribed the tapes of those interviews and then indexed the material by subject matter, typed the manuscript twice, drew up the patrol charts and other material listed in the appendix, and helped with the correspondence, the endless filing and refiling, and a hundred other tasks. Without her cheerful assistance and unwavering faith through three years, this book could not have been written.

Peg Cameron and Janet Baker, Lippincott editors, whose work was brilliant, persevering, thoughtful, and to the point.

Many people in the U.S. Navy, beginning with the director of the division of history, Vice Admiral Edwin Bichford Hooper, U.S.N. (Ret.). Particular thanks to Dr. Dean C. Allard, Head, Operational Archives Branch, and his assistants, especially Mrs. Katherine Lloyd; W. B. Greenwood, Librarian, Navy Library; and Commander R. E. Hurd, Head of Ships' Histories division. In addition, special thanks to Thomas J. Stebbins, QMCM (SS), Director of the Submarine Force Library and Museum, Naval Submarine Base, New London, Groton, Connecticut; and to Bernardine Kimmerling and Betty W. Shirley and Judy L. Parker of the Biographies Branch, Office of

Information, Department of the Navy; and to Captain Roger Pineau, friend, naval historian, and Director of the Navy Museum.

I am especially grateful to another friend, naval historian and distinguished submariner Captain Edward L. Beach, U.S.N. (Ret.). In the preparation of the book, Beach kindly granted two long and helpful interviews, later responded to lengthy queries, and finally volunteered to read galleys on the finished book, an enormous task which he carried out with dispatch and thoroughness. He found errors, challenged many assertions, and suggested improvements.

In addition to Beach, I am indebted to the scores of World War II submarine skippers and staff officers who granted interviews or responded to queries; without their cooperation, this book would not have been possible. Particular thanks go to Vice Admiral Ralph W. Christie, U.S.N. (Ret.). A description of his contributions and the names of the other staff officers and skippers who helped appear in the section of Sources given at the back of the book.

Finally, I wish to thank many who contributed to this book in ways other than research or editorial: The Honorable William R. Anderson, former Congressman from Tennessee, and his staff, especially Al Wise and Judy Miller; Julie and Ted Drury, Linda and George Henshaw, Iola and Elmer Hintz, DuBos and Trevor Armbrister of Washington, D.C.; Marybelle and Don Schanche of Larchmont, New York; Barbara and Zen Yonkovig of Greenwich, Connecticut; Rust Hills of Stonington, Connecticut; Susie and Tad Rutledge of Lake Bluff, Illinois; Dr. John Shields and Anne Rutledge Shields of Springfield, Illinois; Captain William Cauldwell, U.S.A.F., and Jean Cauldwell, Yuba City, California; Eleanor and Frederic Sherman and Ms. Evelyn Watt, Key Biscayne, Florida; and Hank Walker of Miami.

Clay Blair, Jr.

Washington–Key Biscayne
1970–74

Contents

Introduction   17

Part I
  1. Background for War   23
      Early Developments—Progress in Europe—Submarines in World War I—Submarines and Politics I—Secret Enterprises—Submarines and Politics II—New Deal for the Navy—War in Europe—The Main Enemy—Plans in the Far East—Intercepted Mail

Part II
  2. Pearl Harbor, December 1941   97
      The Japanese Attacks on Pearl Harbor and Midway—First Patrols to Empire Waters—First Patrols to the Marshalls—The Sinking of I-173—Results of the First Patrols—The Japanese Attack on Wake Island

  3. Manila, December 1941   127
      The Japanese Attack on Clark Field—The Japanese Attacks on Cavite and Manila—The First Patrols from Manila—The "Battle" of Lingayen Gulf—The Loss of Manila

Part III

4. Java and Australia, January through April 1942   163
   The Japanese Drive to the Malay Barrier—Special Submarine Missions—The "Defense" of Java—Retreat to Australia—Evaluation and Decision

5. Pearl Harbor, January through March 1942   204
   January Departures—February Departures—March Departures

6. Brisbane, April and May 1942   217
   Arrival of More S-Boats—The Battle of the Coral Sea

7. Pearl Harbor, April through June 1942   223
   April Departures—The Hunt for "Wounded Bear"—The Battle of Midway—June Departures

8. Washington, June and July 1942   256
   The Midway Security Leak—Changes in the Codebreaking Operation—H.O.R. Engine Problems

9. Alaska, 1942   267
   Japanese Landings on Kiska and Attu—Submarine Patrols in Alaskan Waters

10. Fremantle, April through August 1942   273
    Torpedo Tests and Experiments—Personnel Changes—Departing Patrols

11. Brisbane, May through September 1942   294
    The Battle of Savo Island—May, June, and July Departures—Battle of the Eastern Solomons—August and September Departures

12. Pearl Harbor, July through December 1942   307
    July, August, and September Patrols to Truk—Patrols to Empire, East China Sea, and Alaskan Waters, July through October—Subversive Literature—Battles of Esperance and Santa Cruz—October, November, and December Patrols to Truk—November and December Patrols to Empire and East China Sea Waters

CONTENTS

13. Brisbane, October through December 1942 — 338
    The Battle of Guadalcanal—Submarine Patrols—Changes in Personnel

14. Fremantle, September through December 1942 — 349

15. Summary, 1942 — 359

Part IV

16. Submarine Command, January 1943 — 365

17. Brisbane, January through May 1943 — 369
    The Death of Admiral Yamamoto—"Playing Checkers" with Submarines—Wahoo's January Patrol—The Palau-Rabaul Convoy Route

18. Fremantle, January through July 1943 — 389
    Experiment at Exmouth Gulf—Patrols and Losses

19. Pearl Harbor, January through March 1943 — 398
    The Casablanca Conference—Submarine Command Credits and Debits—Departing Patrols

20. Alaska, 1943 — 416
    The U.S. Invasions of Attu and Kiska—Patrols from Dutch Harbor

21. Pearl Harbor, April through August 1943 — 422
    Additions to the Pacific Fleet—Ultra-directed Patrols—Final Isolation of the Mark XIV Torpedo Defects—The H.O.R. Boats—Some Good Patrols, and Some Bad Ones—First Forays into the Sea of Japan

22. Brisbane, June through December 1943 — 472
    Surface-Force Engagements in the Solomons—More Boats for Australia—Single Patrols—Cooperative Efforts

23. Fremantle, August through December 1943 — 486
    Tankers as Targets—More Cooperative Efforts—Crevalle's First Two Patrols—Mixed Bags and Special Missions—Puffer's First Patrol—Loss of Capelin *and* Cisco *—Final Deactivation of the Mark VI Exploder*

24. Pearl Harbor, September through December 1943   505
The U.S. Invasion of the Gilbert Islands—Improvements in Submarine Weapons and Strategies—Wahoo's Last Patrol—Ultra-directed Patrols—Davenport, Dornin, and Cutter—Special Missions—More Ultra Information—Patrols Good and Not So Good—The First Three Wolf Packs—Changes in Command

25. Summary, 1943   551

Part V

26. Pearl Harbor, January through April 1944   557
The U.S. Invasion of the Marshall Islands—Interceptions in the Marshalls and Other Missions—Action During the Palaus Air Strike—Transfers to Fremantle—Empire and East China Sea Patrols—The Polar Circuit—Wolf Packs Four and Five—Patrols to the Marianas—Patrols to Okinawa

27. Australia, January through March 1944   606
Codebreaking and the New Guinea Campaign—Patrols from Fremantle

28. Australia, April through June 1944   620
Showdown in the Marianas—The Joint Strike on Surabaya—Patrols to Tawi Tawi and Davao—The Japanese Reinforcement of Biak

29. Pearl Harbor, May and June 1944   642
Patrols to the Marianas—The Battle of the Philippine Sea

30. Pearl Harbor and Australia, June to July 1944   664
The Fight for Saipan—Patrols from Pearl Harbor—Search for the Nickel Ship—Wolf Packs in Luzon Strait—Patrols in the East and South China Seas

31. Washington, Summer 1944   689

32. Pearl Harbor and Australia, July and August 1944   693
Debate over Pacific Strategy—Patrols from Pearl Harbor—Four Wolf Packs in Luzon Strait—Patrols from Australia—The Loss of Harder

CONTENTS

33. Pearl Harbor and Australia, September to October 1944   722
    The U.S. Invasions of the Palaus and Morotai—Pearl Harbor Support of the Landings—Wolf Packs from Pearl Harbor—Single Patrols from Pearl Harbor—Australian Support of the Landings

34. Pearl Harbor and Australia, October to November 1944   744
    Air Strikes on Formosa and the Philippines—The U.S. Invasion of Leyte—The Battle of Leyte Gulf—Patrols from Pearl Harbor—Patrols from Australia

35. Pearl Harbor and Australia, November and December 1944   787
    New Inventions for U.S. Boats—Burt's Brooms—The U.S. Invasions of Mindoro and Luzon—Patrols from Australia—Patrols from Pearl Harbor

36. Submarine Command, December 1944   812

37. Summary, 1944   816

Part VI

38. Pearl Harbor and Guam, January through March 1945   823
    The U.S. Invasions of Iwo Jima and Okinawa—Patrols from Guam—Attacks from the Air—Tirante's First Patrol

39. Fremantle and Subic Bay, January through August 1945   845
    The Move to Subic Bay—Pursuit of Ise *and* Hyuga—*The Remaining Targets:* Isuzu, Haguro, Ashigara, *and* Takao

40. Pearl Harbor and Guam, April through August 1945   857
    New Forays in the Sea of Japan—Rescues and Targets—The Japanese Surrender

Part VII

41. After the War   877

Appendixes

 A. World War II Submarine Squadron Commanders, Pacific   889
 B. World War II Submarine Skippers Selected to Flag Rank   890
 C. Postwar Commanders of Submarines Atlantic Fleet   892
 D. Postwar Commanders of Submarines Pacific Fleet   892
 E. Submarine War Patrols, Atlantic   893
 F. Submarine War Patrols, Pacific   900
 G. Top Skippers of World War II   984
 H. Best War Patrols by Numbers of Ships Sunk   988
 I. Best War Patrols by Tonnage of Ships Sunk   988
 J. Top Submarines by Number of Ships Sunk   989
 K. Top Submarines by Tonnage of Ships Sunk   990
 L. Submarine Losses in World War II   991

Sources   993

Index   1007

About the Author   1072

Photograph sections follow pages 160 and 544.

Maps

By Elizabeth Nicoll Felton
(Surface-force tracks and submarine positions are approximate)

Japanese Approaches to Pearl Harbor, Midway, and Wake Island	93
Japanese Attacks on Pearl Harbor and Midway	103
Japanese Invasion of Wake Island	124
Japanese Invasion of Luzon	133
U.S. Submarine Deployment, December 8–15, 1941	142
"Battle" of Lingayen Gulf	152
Japanese Invasion of Borneo and Celebes	167
Japanese Invasion of Java	182
Battle of the Coral Sea	221
Retreat of "Wounded Bear"	232
Movements Against Midway and the Aleutians	235
Battle of Midway	240
Blockade of Truk	311
Recapture of Attu and Kiska	419
Sea of Japan I, Summer 1943	465
Allied Counteroffensive, Summer–Fall 1943	473
Invasion of the Gilberts	507
Invasion of the Marshalls	559
Air Strike on Truk	566
Air Strike on the Marianas	572

Air Strikes on the Palaus	578
Reconquest of New Guinea	608
Strike on Surabaya	628
Invasion of Biak	635
Invasion of the Marianas	648
Battle of the Philippine Sea	656
Ozawa's Retreat, June 20–24, 1944	661
Invasions of the Palaus and Morotai	726
Invasion of Leyte	750
Battle for Leyte Gulf	760
Ozawa's Retreat, October 25–29, 1944	763
Invasions of Mindoro and Luzon	793
Invasion of Iwo Jima	826
Invasion of Okinawa	828
Yamato Sortie	831
Escape of *Ise* and *Hyuga*	848
Sea of Japan II, June 1945	862

Introduction

During the naval conflict in the Pacific between the United States and Japan, 1941–1945, there was a little-known war-within-a-war: the U.S. submarine offensive against Japanese merchant shipping and naval forces. A mere handful of submariners, taking a small force of boats on 1,600-odd war patrols, sank more than 1,000 Japanese merchant ships and a significant portion of the Japanese navy, including one battleship, eight aircraft carriers, three heavy cruisers, and eight light cruisers.

A strong merchant marine was vital to the economy and warmaking potential of the island nation of Japan. Its ships imported oil, iron ore, coal, bauxite, rubber, and foodstuffs; they exported arms, ammunition, aircraft, and soldiers to reinforce captured possessions. When submarines succeeded in stopping this commerce, Japan was doomed.

After the United States recaptured Guam and Saipan in the summer of 1944, U.S. submarines basing from those two islands imposed a virtual blockade against Japan. Few ships entered or left Japanese waters without being attacked by submarine; most that attempted it were sunk. Japan ran out of oil for her navy; gasoline for her aircraft, trucks, and automobiles; steel, aluminum, and other metal for her industry; and food for her teeming population. After the war, when the full impact of the submarine blockade became known, many experts concluded that the invasions of the Palaus, the Philippines,

Iwo Jima, and Okinawa, and the dropping of fire bombs and atomic bombs on Japanese cities, were unnecessary. They reasoned that despite the fanatical desire of some Japanese to hang on and fight to the last man, the submarine blockade alone would have ultimately defeated that suicidal impulse.

In the prosecution of the undersea war, the U.S. submarine force took a secret weapon into battle: from 1941 to 1945 U.S. Navy codebreakers "read the Japanese mail" with comparative ease. Because codebreakers supplied the submarine force with precise information on the sailing dates, course, speed, and routing of most Japanese convoys and naval formations, U.S. submarine force commanders could direct their boats to the proper intercept positions to lie in wait for the oncoming enemy forces. Although no precise accounting has ever been made, the codebreakers assisted, directly or indirectly, in the sinking of perhaps half of all Japanese vessels destroyed by U.S. submarines. The Japanese were unaware of this weapon.

Even so, it was no easy victory. Before the attack on Pearl Harbor, the United States had sworn in various international treaties never to engage in "unrestricted submarine warfare," that is, submarine surprise attacks against merchant vessels. During peacetime years, U.S. submariners who hoped to become part of the U.S. battle fleet mostly concentrated their training on tactics aimed at sinking important enemy men-of-war—carriers, battleships, cruisers—and their boats, known as fleet submarines, were designed with this goal in mind. After December 7, 1941, however, the United States abandoned its high-minded moral position and ordered unrestricted submarine warfare against Japan. By an accident of history, the fleet submarine proved to be the ideal weapon for war against the Japanese merchant marine. However, the shift in missions caught the submarine force flat-footed. It required new strategy and tactics. Many months went by before the submarine force got the hang of this new role.

There were other problems. Peacetime exercises, most of them unrealistic and artificial, had led submariners to believe that aircraft, sonar gear, and powerful depth charges made the submarine highly vulnerable to enemy counterattack. This belief in turn had led to extreme caution in the submarine force. The best way to survive, the peacetime submarine commanders believed, was to make an attack from deep submergence, using sonar apparatus. The daylight periscope attack, the night periscope attack, and the night surface attack

INTRODUCTION

were considered hazardous, and for a submarine to operate on the surface within 500 miles of an enemy air base was considered fatal. Too many months went by before submariners discovered these preconceptions to be wide of the mark.

The cautious peacetime training led to serious personnel problems in wartime. In peacetime bold, reckless, innovative skippers who were "caught" in war game maneuvers were reprimanded, and older, conservative, "by-the-book" officers, who were strict disciplinarians and conscientious with paperwork, rose to command. When war came, too many of these older men failed as skippers. During the first year and a half of the war, dozens had to be relieved for "lack of aggressiveness" (a disaster, both professionally and emotionally, for the men involved) and replaced by brash devil-may-care younger officers, some of whom would never have attained command in peacetime. This general changeover took months to accomplish, and many valuable opportunities were lost before it became effective.

The failure in leadership extended to the highest levels of the submarine force. When the war began, the forces were commanded by officers who had risen to the top by the safest and most cautious routes, who did not understand the potential of the submarine. They placed a premium on caution; bring the boat back. Yielding to higher authority, they allowed their forces to be fragmented and employed in marginal, fruitless diversions. At least a year and a half went by before these command problems were ironed out and men with a good grasp of how submarines could be most profitably employed took over the top jobs.

The product of codebreaking turned out to be a two-edged sword. On the one hand, it provided marvelous intelligence on enemy naval and merchant marine movements. On the other hand, its secret nature and glamour led submarine force commanders to divert far too many boats from the war against merchant shipping to pursue the dramatic "big kill" that would look good in the dispatches—Japanese battleships, carriers, and cruisers. Countless times, U.S. submarine captains were vectored to such targets only to find that, because of navigational errors on the part of the Japanese or themselves, these high-speed prizes passed just beyond attack range and could not be overtaken. Months went by before it dawned on the force commanders that a Japanese tanker—easier to find and sink—was as valuable to the overall war effort as a light cruiser.

Last—but by no means least—the submarine force was hobbled by defective torpedoes. Developed in peacetime but never realistically tested against targets, the U.S. submarine torpedo was believed to be one of the most lethal weapons in the history of naval warfare. It had two exploders, a regular one that detonated it on contact with the side of an enemy ship and a very secret "magnetic exploder" that would detonate it beneath the keel of a ship without contact. After the war began, submariners discovered the hard way that the torpedo did not run steadily at the depth set into its controls and often went much deeper than designed, too deep for the magnetic exploder to work. When this was corrected, they discovered that the magnetic exploder itself was defective under certain circumstances, often detonating before the torpedo reached the target. And when the magnetic exploder was deactivated, the contact exploder was found to be faulty. Each of these flaws tended to conceal the others, and it was not until September 1943, twenty-one months after the attack on Pearl Harbor, that all the torpedo defects were corrected.

Had it not been for these command weaknesses, misconceptions, and technical defects, the naval war in the Pacific might have taken a far different course. Intelligently employed, with a workable torpedo, submarines might have entirely prevented the Japanese invasion of the Philippines and the Netherland East Indies. Skippers emboldened by swift and certain torpedo success, instead of puzzled and dismayed by obvious torpedo failure, might have inflicted crippling damage on the Japanese navy much earlier. The war in the Pacific might have been shortened by many, many months.

Part I

1
Background for War

Early Developments

For centuries militarists recognized that a submarine's invisibility provided it with two distinct military advantages: surprise and the ability to retreat with relative impunity from counterattack. Archimedes laid down the physical principles of submersion in the third century B.C., and from then on men built all manner of submersible vehicles for war, exploration, or amusement. But it was not until 1775 that anybody managed to build a combatant submarine that really worked. The man who did it was an American colonial named David Bushnell; his aim—sink British warships in New York Harbor during the Revolutionary War.

Bushnell's primitive little craft, *Turtle*, was a one-man hand-propelled diving chamber which looked like an egg standing on end. She was designed to creep up submerged on an enemy ship, leave a time bomb screwed to the hull, and withdraw to safety before the explosion. Three times during the Revolutionary War *Turtle* sallied forth to destroy British warships, including Admiral Lord Howe's flagship, *Eagle*. Each time the attacks went awry, but later George Washington was moved to comment, "I thought it was an effort of genius."

The next American on the submarine scene was Robert Fulton,

inventor of the steam engine. In 1800 he designed a hand-propelled combat submarine that was larger and better than Bushnell's. The United States was not then at war and showed no interest, so, looking for backers, Fulton went to Europe, where he became involved in all kinds of international intrigue. In France, Napoleon gave him enough money to build one test model, called *Nautilus*. In a demonstration, Fulton bravely and successfully sank a hulk placed at his disposal. Napoleon said *Nautilus* was dishonorable and wouldn't buy, but his real aim was to copy the boat without paying for it. Upshot: Fulton destroyed *Nautilus*.

Fulton then took his plans to England, where he generated interest with a government committee headed by Prime Minister William Pitt, who put up some money. But Earl St. Vincent, First Lord of the Admiralty, snorted when he heard of Pitt's interest in the Fulton submarine. "Pitt is the greatest fool that ever existed to encourage a mode of war which those who command the sea do not want and which, if successful, will deprive them of it." This statement of hostility became official Admiralty submarine policy for the next hundred years. Realizing that the British had no intention of building his boat, Fulton returned home in disgust and turned his talents to building the first steamship, *Clermont*.

When the Civil War divided the United States, both sides built submarines for combat. The South was more successful. A sugar broker named Horace L. Hunley talked some friends into joining him in putting up money, and after failing with two earlier models, the Southerners built a 40-foot steel submersible craft, C.S.S. *H. L. Hunley*. Propelled by a crew of eight men who, laboring like galley slaves, turned hand cranks on the propeller shaft, *Hunley* was designed to sneak up and attack enemy ships by towing a powder charge (on a long wire) which was supposed to detonate when it connected with the keel of the enemy vessel.

Hunley was a jinxed boat. She accidentally sank at least twice and maybe more—the records are not clear—during training exercises or in vain attempts to reach Union ships. On each of these sinkings, she lost all or most of her crew. In one disaster, Hunley himself was drowned in the boat. But people kept raising her again and recruiting new crews. *Hunley*'s time finally came on the night of February 17, 1864, when she managed to creep, decks awash, hatches open, into Charleston Harbor and hole the Union's 1,200-ton, 11-gun screw sloop *Housatonic*, which sank slowly. This was the first time a submarine sank an enemy man-of-war. *Hunley*'s crew, unfortunately,

EARLY DEVELOPMENTS

did not live to celebrate. The unlucky craft was caught in the explosion wave, which flooded her open hatches, and she went down with all hands for the last time.

A few years later the submarine got a shove forward from two sources, the first being what would now be called a public relations breakthrough. In 1870 the French author Jules Verne published a book called *Twenty Thousand Leagues Under the Sea*, an exciting account of a fictional submarine, *Nautilus*, and her skipper, Captain Nemo. The book was a hit worldwide. It bestowed an enviable image on submarines and submarining and encouraged the idea of a submarine being a truly feasible combat weapon.

The second shove was technical, the nearly simultaneous appearance of two scientific devices: the self-propelled torpedo and the electric storage battery.

Originally, free-floating or moored mines were called "torpedoes." *
When Admiral Farragut gave his legendary order in Mobile Bay, "Damn the torpedoes, full speed ahead," he was referring to what are now called mines. The idea for a self-propelled torpedo which could be launched submerged by an "air gun" (ejected by compressed air) originated with an Austrian naval captain named Giovanni Luppis. In 1864 he took a plan for such a device to Robert Whitehead, an Englishman who was superintendent of the ironworks in Fiume, Yugoslavia. Two years later, Whitehead produced the first working model. It was 14 feet long and 14 inches in diameter and weighed 300 pounds, including an 18-pound dynamite charge in the nose. It was powered by a compressed-air engine which turned a small propeller, and had a speed of 6 knots and a maximum range of 700 yards. Later, another Austrian, M. Ludwig Obry, adapted the gyroscope for use in torpedoes to control a rudder which gave the weapon directional control. Other improvements came with the passing years (extending range, speed, control, and explosive power) but for about five decades the Luppis-Whitehead torpedo, which was offered for sale to anybody who wanted one, remained the basic model.

The most formidable technical problem for the submarine designer was—and had always been—propulsion. Hand-cranking a propeller shaft was surely not the solution; it was hard work, and the huffing man or men doing the cranking quickly burned up what little oxygen there was in the boat. In 1863 the French built a submarine with a compressed air engine, but it was too slow and too limited in range.

---

* Probably derived from *Torpedo nobiliana*, an electric ray fish inhabiting the Atlantic Ocean.

Several European designers built submarines with steam engines, some of which could be supplied with "air" for submerged operations from bottles of compressed air. But the steam engine generated too much heat for the small confines of the submarine, and the crews were nearly roasted.

In 1870, about the time Whitehead perfected the self-propelled torpedo, the electric storage battery, long in development in various countries, emerged as a practical device. It seemed a promising answer to the submarine propulsion problem. The battery power could be used to turn a motor which could turn the propeller shaft. The battery required no "air." It could be utilized submerged as well as on the surface. It generated little heat.

All over Europe—in France, Germany, Spain, Russia, and Britain— privately financed submarine designers seized on the storage battery and began building submarines. Some of these were powered only by batteries; some were powered by steam engines on the surface and batteries submerged. The early batteries were not very powerful and soon exhausted themselves, thereby severely limiting the endurance of the submarine, but at least the idea worked. By 1880 there were forty-two separate submarine projects under way in various nations, fifteen of which led to finished boats.

In the United States, the true submarine genius of the century was just then emerging from obscurity. He was an Irish immigrant schoolteacher, John Philip Holland, a slight, shy, mild-mannered eccentric. At an early age, Holland had been entranced by the accounts of *Turtle*, *Hunley*, *Nautilus*, and the European submarines. He sketched plans and dreamed, studying steam power plants, electric storage batteries, air guns, and the torpedo. But what excited him most was the work of George Brayton, who in 1874 produced America's first successful petroleum-burning internal combustion engine. It was compact, relatively powerful, and did not generate much heat. If Brayton's primitive little engine could be adapted to the submarine for surface propulsion and the electric storage battery for submerged propulsion, Holland would have the perfect combination of motive power. If he could build such a submarine and sell it to the navy, he might become a rich man.

Holland's effort to make his dream a reality is the saga of most inventors. There followed hope, failure, new hope, another failure; desperate measures to raise money; indifference and ridicule; resourceful, ingenious solutions to seemingly hopeless problems; competition from rivals; lawsuits over patents; sleepless nights and shattered nerves. In the ten years between 1878 and 1888, Holland built four submarines with the internal-combustion-plus-electric-battery propulsion system. Each, for various reasons, failed. But with each failure Holland gained experience and stockpiled knowledge.

The U.S. Navy was no help. Naval officers were then absorbed by the doctrines of Captain Alfred Thayer Mahan, an obscure professor at the Naval War College in Newport, Rhode Island, who had conceived—and packaged in a series of writings—what might be called a general theory of sea power and national destiny. His doctrine was bluntly imperialistic. He held, in essence, that a nation that did not constantly expand economically through foreign trade soon withered and died. Mahan urged the United States to shake off its isolationism and build the largest merchant marine in the world. To protect these trading vessels—and the United States—which would inevitably be challenged by a competing foreign power, the United States should also build a navy equal to any existing in the world, together with a network of oversea bases for its support. If an enemy threatened the United States, its big battle fleet would steam out offensively and destroy it in mid-ocean in a single decisive battle. The United States embraced the Mahan philosophy and began building a large merchant marine and navy.

During the ten years Holland was working on his first four submarines, the navy contributed neither money nor encouragement. Holland's boats did not fit the Mahan strategy. They had a maximum range of about 4 miles. They couldn't go with the fleet on the high seas; they were frail and undependable, unable to stand against a heavy sea. Answered Holland, "The navy doesn't like my boats because they have no decks to strut on."

It was France, home of Jules Verne, that probably indirectly helped John Holland most. The French embraced the submarine with a passion. Unlike Britain, an island empire, France had extensive land borders contiguous to potential enemies. To protect herself, she required a substantial standing army. She could not afford to maintain a large army *and* a large navy. To defend herself in a possible sea war with Britain, then the major sea power, the French naval staff conceived a strategy that would not require France to match Britain ship for ship. In event of war with England, France would wage a form of *guerre de course*—commerce raiding—aimed at starving Britain into submission. She would attack Britain's vital merchant ships with relatively cheap, light cruisers. Backing up the cruisers would be a small French battle fleet, which would be held "in being" in port. If the British dared disperse or divide their main fleet to pursue France's marauding cruisers, the French fleet would attack the remaining weaker British fleet and destroy it.

There was one big gap in this strategy. What if the British blockaded the French coast, thereby preventing the cruisers from getting to sea? The answer to that gap, the French decided, was the submarine. If France could develop reliable submarines of limited range and powerful armament, they could break a British blockade and get the cruisers to sea. Thus was born the concept of the submarine as a coastal defense weapon. In 1886, the French navy encouraged French submarine designers and soon began ordering large numbers of submarines. In this way, as British submarine historian Arthur Hezlet states, France became the first nation to put the resources of the state into systematic development of the submarine to meet a specific strategic need.

The U.S. Navy eyed the French submarine buildup first with incredulity and then with interest. Perhaps these little gadgets might be useful after all—to defend the coastline in case part of the enemy fleet to be met in mid-ocean sneaked by undetected. They would serve, in effect, as mobile extensions of coast artillery and as scouts to warn of the approaching enemy. With this limited role in mind, in 1888 the navy announced a competition for one small submarine for coast defense purposes. John Holland won the competition against six other bidders.

Holland worked on the design of this submarine—called *Plunger* —for seven years. (The contract was let in 1895, the keel laid in a yard in Baltimore in 1896.) On every side he was harassed, delayed, and frustrated. His competitors generated political intrigue within the Navy Department and Congress. He was caught up in an endless series of executive power struggles in his various corporations, which finally emerged as the Electric Boat Company. Navy bureaucrats placed impossible technical demands on the project, insisting—over Holland's objections—that the boat be powered by a steam engine for cruising on the surface, even though this concept had already been proved impractical by European submarine builders. Holland became so exasperated at the navy's meddling in his design work that he cried in despair, "What will the navy require next? That my boat should be able to climb a tree?"

Meanwhile, with privately raised funds, Holland began work at a yard in Elizabeth, New Jersey, on his sixth submarine, powered by a gasoline engine developed by Nikolaus Otto, a German engineer, which was better than the Brayton. This boat, called *Holland VI*— 54 feet long with one torpedo tube—was the inventor's masterpiece. Denouncing the navy-sponsored steam submarine as a "monster," Holland proudly showed off *Holland VI* to businessmen, naval officers, and the press. He offered it to the navy but it was turned down, in spite of a strong letter of support from Assistant Secretary of the Navy Theodore Roosevelt.

Holland was not easily discouraged. He towed his submarine from New Jersey to Washington for a promotional demonstration on the Potomac River, right under the noses of the Navy Department and Congress. His supporters argued convincingly that during the Spanish-American War, just concluded, the U.S. coastline had been stripped of all naval vessels to fight the Spanish. Any of the European powers opposed to U.S. intervention in Cuba (there were many among the monarchies) could have raided—or invaded—the country. The same situation might recur in the future. If so, the navy—in spite of Mahan's strategy—should have Holland boats to defend its major harbors and bases.

During the course of the demonstration, two important naval personages took rides in *Holland VI*. One was Admiral George Dewey, hero of the battle of Manila Bay. After his ride, he declared, "If the Spanish had had two of those things in Manila, I could never have held it with the squadron I had." The other was the superintendent of the Naval Academy. After his ride he said, "She will never revolutionize modern warfare . . . but for coast defense purposes she is of inestimable value."

With those ringing endorsements, Holland finally sold the navy. In the deal, he agreed to give the navy *Holland VI* and substitute a similar boat for the steam-powered *Plunger*, which had been abandoned. Later, largely owing to the support of Admiral Dewey, who urged the purchase of twenty submarines, the navy entered into a second deal to buy six more submarines in addition to the aforementioned two. On October 12, 1900, *Holland VI* was formally commissioned U.S.S. *Holland* by the navy and designated Submarine Hull

No. 1. The seven succeeding Holland-designed boats were 64 feet long and mounted one torpedo tube.*

Thus the United States became the second nation—after France—officially to buy submarines for a specific military purpose. By 1910, the navy had commissioned eleven more gasoline-battery submarines built by Holland's corporation, the Electric Boat Company, from which he had been ousted after many disagreements in the executive suites. Three were 82-foot boats mounting two torpedo tubes.† Five were 105-foot boats mounting two torpedo tubes.‡ Three were 135-foot boats mounting four torpedo tubes.§

Most of these primitive boats were deployed overseas in coastal defense roles, protecting U.S. outposts. Six A-boats (*A-2* to *A-7*) and all three Bs were loaded on ships and transported to Manila Bay. The five Cs steamed on their own power to Guantanamo Bay, Cuba, and then, in what was considered an epic feat, 700 miles across open ocean to the newly built Panama Canal. The remaining five boats, *Holland*, *A-1*, and the three Ds, remained in U.S. waters engaged primarily in training new submariners.‖

Meanwhile, the torpedo—crucial to the effectiveness of the submarine as a combat weapon—was steadily improving. Within the U.S. Navy, the job was delegated to the Bureau of Ordnance, or the "Gun Club," as it was derisively called by its detractors, a clannish group of officers and technicians. It performed like most military bureaucracies: slowly, cautiously, unimaginatively, and, at times, stupidly. As a result, for three decades the U.S. Navy depended mostly on foreign ingenuity and sources for its torpedoes.

Around the turn of the century, technicians at Vickers, Limited, a British firm that had acquired Whitehead's patents and made most of the torpedoes for the U.S. Navy, came up with a revolutionary im-

---

* They were: *Plunger, Adder, Grampus, Moccasin, Pike, Porpoise*, and *Shark*, later redesignated *A-1* to *A-7*.

† *Viper, Cuttlefish*, and *Tarantula*, later redesignated *B-1, B-2, B-3*.

‡ *Octopus, Stingray, Tarpon, Bonita*, and *Snapper*, later redesignated *C-1* to *C-5*. (*Bonita*, named for the bonito fish, was inadvertently misspelled.)

§ *Narwhal, Grayling*, and *Salmon*, later redesignated *D-1, D-2, D-3*.

‖ The submarine branch was not a sought-after billet, and submarines were originally called "pigboats" because, before periscopes were used, they had to attack with an up-and-down bobbing motion like that of a porpoise, or "sea pig." Surface-ship sailors ridiculed pigboat sailors with an indelicate ditty:

> Submarines have no latrines,
> The men wear leathern britches.
> They hang their tails out o'er the rails
> And yell like sons-o'-bitches.

provement in the torpedo propulsion system. They found that by mixing pure alcohol and water with the compressed air in a combustion chamber they could generate a type of high-pressure "steam" which could be channeled to turn a turbine connected to the propeller shaft. This breakthrough enabled Vickers to build a torpedo with a large warhead that could travel at a high rate of speed for long distances. Its main weakness was that it left a wake as the expended steam and air bubbled to the surface, enabling the enemy to follow its oncoming trail. No matter. The navies of the world seized on this new marvel, and the torpedo-firing destroyer became an integral part of every major fleet. The early U.S. submarines used this same torpedo.

In 1907, the U.S. Navy built a torpedo factory at Newport, Rhode Island, to manufacture the British steam torpedo. The few torpedo experts there (who had been engaged in fruitless experimental torpedo work) were absorbed by the factory to train the new, poorly educated, unskilled workers hired from the small local population. In deference to cranking up a production line, all research was laid aside. Within the factory (as within all government arsenals) there soon grew a civil service bureaucracy in which seniority, not talent, counted most. Isolated from the outside industrial world, where commercial pressure and new ideas bring improvement in cost-cutting and production techniques, the Newport Torpedo Station entered the twentieth century at its own leisurely, unimaginative pace.

The factory became the mainstay of the Newport economy, which heretofore had depended on employment in the fabulous summer "cottages" of the Vanderbilts and Astors. It was jealously watched over by Rhode Island politicians in Congress. If a naval officer commanding the station summoned sufficient courage to fire an incompetent or insubordinate worker, the Secretary of the Navy soon got a visit from the Rhode Island delegation, demanding his reinstatement. The delegation also resisted any attempt to build a competing facility elsewhere. The end result was monumental inertia, a thin trickle of finely machined steam torpedoes, resistance to change, and only minor refinements in the basic British torpedo and exploder design.

Progress in Europe

Abroad, during this first decade of the century, submarine construction easily outdistanced that in the United States. French naval officers, preparing their naval strategy of *guerre de course*, encouraged submarine designers with lucrative government contracts and public accolades. In 1900, the year the U.S. Navy accepted its first submarine, France laid the keels for dozens of new boats, and by 1907 the French navy had no less than eighty-five submarines, the largest force in the world. In well-publicized naval exercises, French submarines, playing out their coastal defense roles against French battleships posing as British blockade runners, performed beyond all expectations.

The British Admiralty, home office of the largest navy in the world, reluctantly agreed to build five submarines for experimental purposes. In 1901 it entered into a licensing agreement with the Electric Boat Company for five Holland-designed submarines, roughly identical to the U.S. Navy's A-class boats. By 1904 these submarines were in service and took part in British naval maneuvers. One, the British *A-1*, was accidentally rammed and sunk, but despite this tragedy a few British naval experts foresaw potential for the submarine.

One of these was Sir John Fisher, who became First Sea Lord in that same year. He set down his views in an exuberant memo:

It is astounding to me, perfectly astounding, how the very best amongst us failed to realize the vast impending revolution in naval strategy that the submarine will accomplish. . . . I have not disguised my opinion in season and out of season as to the essential, imperative, immediate, vital, pressing, urgent (I cannot think of any more adjectives) necessity for more submarines at once—at the very least 25 in addition to those now ordered and building and 100 more as soon as practicable.

With this push from the top, the Admiralty, in a joint venture with Vickers, carried forward submarine development on a high priority. The British B-type and C-type, included in the 1905–6 shipbuilding program, were substantially larger and more reliable boats than the A-type and mounted two torpedo tubes. By 1910, Britain had about fifty submarines in commission—fewer than France but more than twice as many as the United States.

None of the submarine designers—or operators—was satisfied with the gasoline engine for surface propulsion. Gasoline was too volatile. During the first ten years of submarine operations, there were many disastrous and near-disastrous explosions on board gasoline-powered submarines. Sometimes during submerged operations while running on the battery, gasoline fumes seeped into the hull and intoxicated the crew to a dangerous degree. There was clear need for an internal combustion engine which burned less dangerous fuel.

The answer seemed to be "heavy oil." The leading designer of heavy-oil engines was a German, Rudolph Diesel, who had a small shop in Augsburg. By 1895 Diesel had perfected his first crude heavy-oil engine, and during the succeeding ten years other inventors copied his engine or developed their own models. In 1904 Vickers engineers began work on a heavy-oil engine. In 1908 they installed a small primitive test model in the British submarine *A-13*. The Italians followed with a heavy-oil submarine in 1909. That same year, the British launched a new and larger submarine, *D-1*, powered by a heavy-oil engine. Thereafter, all British submarines were diesel-powered.

Of the major European naval powers, Germany was the last to accept the submarine as a combat vehicle. There were several reasons. Admiral Von Tirpitz, the power in the German navy, was then embarked on a program of building a large German battle fleet. A submarine force would be much cheaper than a battle fleet, as France had demonstrated, and might be preferred by the Reichstag. Von Tirpitz wanted nothing to interfere with his battle fleet plans, so he played down the submarine. With some justification, he said the gasoline engines then available were not sufficiently advanced or safe enough to build a reliable underwater boat. Beyond that, he asserted, the waters along the German coast were too shallow to use them effectively.

The real impetus for German submarine building came from private enterprise. In 1902 the Krupp arms firm built the tiny submarine *Forel*, based on a foreign design. It failed to impress Von Tirpitz, but Krupp sold it to the Russians. In 1904, when Russia and Japan went to war, Russia ordered three more submarines from Krupp—*Karp*, *Karas*, and *Kambala*—which were larger and powered by paraffin (akin to kerosene) engines developed by the German firm, Körting Brothers. These three boats, delivered to Russia, marked the real beginning of German submarine technology.*

* During the Russo-Japanese war, John Holland sold the Japanese navy plans for two advanced-type submarines and went to Kobe to oversee their construction; Elec-

In 1905 the German Naval Staff, having been impressed by *Karp* and the Körting engine, authorized the first German submarine, *U-1*. In effect a copy of *Karp*, it was 139 feet long, mounted a single torpedo tube in the bow, and was powered by Körting paraffin engines. *U-1* was completed in December 1906. In the following two years, the German navy built three more boats: *U-2*, *U-3*, and *U-4*. Each was larger than its predecessor and more heavily armed; *U-3* and *U-4* had two bow- and two stern-mounted torpedo tubes.

The German Naval Staff was far from satisfied with these crude beginnings; it wanted a big oceangoing submarine capable of taking offensive action against the British fleet. In late 1907 it formulated its objectives: a submarine capable of cruising 2,000 miles at high speed (13 to 15 knots), manned by a crew of twenty officers and men, armed with two bow and two stern torpedo tubes. To meet these objectives, German submarine designers produced a 500-ton submarine powered by four Körting engines. The German navy authorized fourteen of these boats, *U-5* to *U-18*.

While these first eighteen U-boats were under construction, heavy-oil engine technology advanced rapidly in Germany. In 1906–7, Krupp designed and built the first diesel engine for submarine propulsion. At the same time, another German firm, Maschinenfabrik-Augsburg-Nürnberg (M.A.N.), produced a competing submarine diesel engine which in many respects was superior to the Krupp engine. However, years dragged by before these engines were reliable. Four U-boats—*U-19* to *U-22*, launched in 1913—were powered by M.A.N. diesel engines. The four that followed—*U-23* to *U-26*, launched in 1914—were powered by Krupp diesels.

The U.S. Navy was the last of the major naval powers to adopt the diesel engine for the submarine. Since there was no diesel technology in the United States, the navy was forced to turn to the British and the Germans for help. Electric Boat Company formed a corporation known as New London Ship and Engine Company (NELSECO), through which it arranged a licensing agreement with the British Vickers firm and the German M.A.N. to build submarine diesels. During the years 1911–14, the navy built seventeen new submarines powered by NELSECO engines.

---

tric Boat sold the Japanese five A-types which were also assembled in Kobe. One of Holland's American competitors, Simon Lake, sold the Russians six (or eight) submarines. Electric Boat sold six to Russia. None of these boats was finished in time to see action, but by 1909 Russia, with twenty-nine submarines, had the third largest submarine force, after France and Britain.

The first of these diesel-powered boats were *Skipjack* and *Sturgeon*.*
Skipjack was placed in commission by a young submariner, Chester William Nimitz, who had previously commanded the gasoline-powered boats *Plunger* and *Snapper*. Nimitz soon became the navy's leading authority on diesel engines. After his tour on *Skipjack*, he visited Rudolph Diesel's engine shops in Belgium and Germany and then took charge of installing the first diesel engines in a U.S. Navy surface ship, the tanker *Maumee*.

The next four U.S. submarines to receive diesel engines were *Carp, Barracuda, Pickerel,* and *Skate*.† These four boats were ill-designed and poorly constructed. When completed in 1912, they were towed to Hawaii for coastal defense use. *Skate*, an unlucky vessel which almost sank during her trials, suffered a battery explosion and, two weeks later, sank in 300 feet of water, drowning all twenty-one of her crew. The boat was raised; her troubles were attributed to a design fault. Later, during a training exercise, *Pickerel* rammed *Carp*, which plunged to the bottom in 600 feet of water, drowning nineteen of her twenty-four-man crew.

The next three diesel boats were *Seawolf, Nautilus,* and *Garfish*.‡ Although better designed than their predecessors, the three boats had a bad run of luck. *Seawolf* ran aground off Santa Margarita Island, California, drowning her skipper and three men. After she had been pulled off, she sank in 50 feet of water and was never raised. *Garfish*, while operating off the coast of California, ran aground near Eureka. The crew was rescued by Coast Guard breeches buoy, but the cruiser *Milwaukee* was stranded trying to pull *Garfish* off the beach. *Milwaukee*'s crew was also saved, but before the ship could be salvaged it was destroyed by a storm.

The last of the seventeen new diesel-powered submarines, launched in 1914, were exceptionally well-designed boats called the K class. They were 500-ton craft with four torpedo tubes. In all, eight K-boats were commissioned. The first four, *K-1* to *K-4*, had names: *Haddock,*

---

* Redesignated *E-1* and *E-2*.
† Redesignated *F-1* to *F-4*.
‡ Redesignated *H-1, H-2,* and *H-3*. In between the Fs and Hs were four Gs, all highly experimental in nature. *G-1* (*Seal*), *G-2* (*Tuna*), and *G-3* (*Turbot*) were designed and built by Simon Lake; *G-4* (*Thrasher*) by an Italian, Laurenti. *G-1, G-2,* and *G-4* were gasoline-powered. *G-3* was diesel-powered. The boats had curious innovations such as deck-mounted torpedo tubes, a five-ton droppable keel for emergencies, airlock hatches to enable divers to leave and enter the boat submerged, and wheels on the keels for "driving" along the sea bottom. All four were found wanting as combat vessels and were used primarily for training new submariners.

Cachalot, Orca, and *Walrus.* After that, the U.S. Navy gave up naming submarines for many years, preferring to designate them by letter and number, each new letter representing a new and better design class. Assistant Secretary of the Navy Franklin D. Roosevelt took a dive in *K-7.* Four K-boats went to Hawaii to replace the ill-fated F class.

On the eve of World War I, August 1914, there were about 400 submarines in the navies of the world. Most of these were old gasoline-powered boats considered unsafe for combat. France, who had pioneered in combatant submarine construction, still led in numbers with 123, but her diesel technology lagged badly and her submarine force had deteriorated. Britain came second with 72 boats, of which 17 were new diesel-powered oceangoing submarines. Russia, with 41 boats, ranked third, but all of these were inferior in design. The United States was fourth in numbers with 34, of which 12 were diesel-powered. Germany ranked fifth with 26 submarines. About 14 of these were smoky Körting-powered boats; 12 were new diesels, many still undergoing shakedown.

Submarines in World War I

After the outbreak of World War I, the British imposed a naval blockade against Germany and the Central Powers. Under international law governing naval warfare, British warships had the right to capture or sink any enemy merchant or passenger vessel attempting to run the blockade, having first removed and cared for the passengers and crews. The same set of laws gave the British the right to "visit and search" vessels flying neutral flags to make certain they were not in fact enemy vessels disguised as neutrals.

Germany was powerless to prevent the blockade; its navy, while strong, was inferior to that of Britain. Lacking the ability to apply naval force, the Germans denounced the blockade as illegal and appealed to neutral nations such as the United States, whose ships were being harassed by the British, to help persuade the British to remove the blockade. These appeals failed; the blockade continued.

Early in the war, the German Naval Staff decided to send its small submarine force to sea on offensive patrol, to attack British warships deployed for the blockade. On August 6, 1914, ten old Körting-powered U-boats set off on the first offensive submarine sweep in the history of naval warfare. Two were lost. The remaining eight returned August 12 without having achieved notable results beyond mere survival.

The Naval Staff ordered further submarine sweeps. On the morning of September 22, with the war only forty-seven days old, *U-9*, commanded by Lieutenant Otto Weddigen, came upon three old 12,000-ton British cruisers steaming a steady course at 10 knots without destroyer escorts. Weddigen fired two torpedoes at the first cruiser, *Aboukir*. Both hit with a resounding explosion. In less than half an hour, *Aboukir* rolled over and sank. Believing *Aboukir* had struck a mine, the other two cruisers, *Cressy* and *Hogue*, stopped to lower boats and rescue *Aboukir*'s survivors. Weddigen maneuvered *U-9* into position and shot two torpedoes each at *Cressy* and *Hogue*. All torpedoes went home. *Cressy* and *Hogue* sank quickly, the total loss of life, 1,400 men.

In the wake of this triumph, a faction of the German Naval Staff argued that Germany should counter the British blockade with a U-boat blockade of Britain. Von Tirpitz, who was now secretary of the German navy, was not sure it would work. There were still only about two dozen U-boats in commission, too few, he believed, to accomplish so vast an undertaking. There were tactical problems: to "visit and search" a neutral vessel to make sure it was not an enemy in disguise would expose the submarine to undue risk. Moreover, he asserted, a submarine blockade was a new kind of war. It raised certain moral, legal, and psychological questions that should be carefully studied. He suggested a limited and cautious approach, a blockade at the mouth of the Thames River.

The debate in the German Naval Staff dragged on for many weeks. Ultimately the advocates of the blockade—who held that a German blockade would force Britain to lift her own blockade within six weeks —won out. On February 4, 1915, Germany announced that a "war zone" would be established around the whole of the British Isles and that all hostile ships found within it would be destroyed. Care would be taken to spare clearly identifiable neutrals, but these neutrals would sail the waters at their own peril. To the U-boat skippers, the Kaiser said, "If in spite of the exercise of great care mistakes should be made, the commander will not be made responsible."

The enterprise was less than successful. In the first three months of the blockade, U-boats sank a mere thirty-three ships—100,000 tons— barely a dent in the massive flow of merchant shipping to and from

Britain. Then U-boats sank without warning two British passenger liners, *Lusitania* and *Arabic* (nearly 1,200 men, women, and children, including 126 Americans, were lost on *Lusitania*). Following these sinkings, which raised cries of outrage the world over, the Kaiser imposed such severe limitations on the U-boat skippers that the German Naval Staff was forced to abandon the campaign.

The Admiralty, meanwhile, embarked on a dozen priority projects to counter the U-boat. By far the most important was radio intelligence. Early in the war, the British established a secret organization to break German naval codes. This effort—which has never been officially described—was eminently successful. The less sophisticated U-boat codes were easy to break. By eavesdropping on the many messages to and from U-boats, the British were able to glean much tactical information. In addition, the British established a series of radio direction finding (RDF) stations to home in on U-boat radio transmissions. When two or more of these stations picked up a U-boat broadcast, it was possible to obtain an exact fix on the U-boat's location.

This information, plus location reports of sightings and attacks at sea, was funneled to a central plotting room at the Admiralty. "The British had a vast amount of intelligence data relating to enemy submarines," U.S. naval historian Carroll Storrs Alden reported after the war.

They knew almost every time a boat left a German base and often who was the commanding officer.... [They could] determine what course the Germans were following in going to and from their billets, the number of days each stayed out, and the characteristic activities of each, e.g., certain ones used only torpedoes, others preferred to sink ships by gunfire and bombs, others laid mines.

Knowing where a U-boat might be was one matter; destroying it was another. Immense resources were channeled into the effort: destroyers, submarines, subchasers, and blimps; hundreds of ex-yachts and fishing trawlers; and innocent-looking merchant vessels that were in fact heavily armed, known as Q-ships. British scientists and engineers produced a crude underwater listening device, known as a hydrophone, and a bomb that would detonate at a preset depth in the water, known as a depth charge. In time, the Admiralty armed many British merchant ships.

It would not, however, adopt the convoy system. The convoy limited all ships to the speed of the slowest and concentrated targets for the U-boat. The Admiralty doubted that merchant ship captains could maintain proper military station.

In the early months of 1916, the German military staffs argued for a resumption of the U-boat blockade of Britain. There was no immediate prospect of a land victory for Germany. What was needed, the staffs held, was a blow that would knock Britain out of the war. The U-boat war should be waged ruthlessly and without restrictions. Germany had many new boats—larger, more powerful, and seaworthy—and more were coming off the ways every month.

The Kaiser doubted, wavered, then gave his approval. In March 1916 the U-boats put to sea for the second phase of the blockade. The new campaign was just launched when a U-boat, without warning, attacked the French cross-channel packet *Sussex*, carrying 436 men, women, and children, including a few Americans. Although *Sussex* did not sink, 50 people were killed by the explosion. Again cries of moral indignation rose from around the world. President Woodrow Wilson presented the Kaiser with what was, in effect, an ultimatum: if U-boats continued to attack passenger ships and freighters, the United States would sever diplomatic relations with Germany.

In the face of this threat, the Kaiser backed down a second time and ordered the U-boats recalled. For the next few months they were used only sparingly against commerce in a vacillating on-again-off-again campaign with severe—and often conflicting—rules that angered and frustrated the U-boat captains. As with Phase One, Phase Two of the U-boat campaign ended with murky results.

The sea war in Europe profoundly influenced naval policy in the United States. President Wilson pronounced that the only way to keep out of the war was to make America so strong militarily that no one would dare attack her. He directed the navy's General Board —a group of senior admirals acting somewhat in the role of a board of directors for the navy—to study the situation and tell him what to do. In 1915, the General Board advised Wilson that the United States should build a navy "ultimately equal to the most powerful maintained by any nation of the world." This policy statement, which became popularly known as "A Navy Second to None," was accompanied by specific recommendations for a huge buildup of battleships, battle cruisers, scout cruisers, destroyers—and submarines.

By the time this recommendation was handed down, the navy had money for nineteen submarines beyond the K class. These were *L-1* to *L-11*, *M-1*, and *N-1* to *N-7*. The Ls were similar to but slightly larger than the Ks; the *M-1*, an experimental type not followed up, even larger yet. The Ns were a throwback, smaller than the Ks. Like all their predecessors, Ls, Ms, and Ns were designed strictly for coastal defense. Each had four bow torpedo tubes and carried a total of eight torpedoes.

Following the recommendation of the General Board to build a navy second to none, Congress approved funds for the purchase of about one hundred submarines beyond the N class. These consisted of forty-three O- and R-class boats and fifty-one S-boats, plus several experimental types. The O and R classes were merely slight improvements over the K-L class. The S class was a notable advance. It was 230 feet long, displaced 800 tons, and carried twelve torpedoes. Electric Boat, or its subsidiaries, built the lion's share of these boats at Quincy, Massachusetts, and San Francisco; Simon Lake received contracts for about twenty boats, which were built at Bridgeport, Connecticut; the Portsmouth (New Hampshire) Naval Yard built about ten.

There was a fundamental design difference between the Electric Boat and the Simon Lake S-boats. The Electric Boat submarines, popularly called Holland S-boats, had internal ballast tanks (inside the pressure hull) and were therefore "single-hull" boats. The Lake S-boats had external ballast tanks, humped on the pressure hull like saddles, and were therefore "double-hull" boats. Electric Boat designed its boats to dive on an angle and sought maximum submerged performance. Lake designed his boats to dive with little or no angle and sought maximum surface performance. In the years following, submarine design was hobbled by this dichotomy; nobody could decide which was better. Gradually, however, the Bureau of Ships, which controlled submarine design and money, leaned to the Simon Lake concept—that is, double-hull construction with priority given to surface performance over submerged performance.

To train the hundreds of men required to man these new submarines, the navy established a formal Submarine School at New London, Connecticut. The base quickly grew into a permanent city with red brick classrooms, barracks, mess halls, and other facilities, as well as finger piers, machine shops, and drydocks along the riverbank. From 1916 onward, the New London Submarine Base was "home from the sea" for all submariners in the U.S. Navy.

To meet the demand for torpedoes—both for surface craft and submarines—the Bureau of Ordnance expanded the Newport torpedo factory and created a second source of supply in Alexandria, Virginia. The technicians at these two installations produced a new and reliable torpedo, called the Mark X, for boats of the new R and S class. Based on the "steam"-powered British Whitehead, the Mark X delivered a warhead of 500 pounds of TNT to a range of 3,500 yards at 36 knots.

In early 1917, with the war situation everywhere growing more grave for Germany, the military staffs again pressed the Kaiser to lift all restrictions on the U-boats. America be damned, the Naval Staff said. If she came into the war, the U-boats would sink all her troop and supply ships before they reached Europe; Britain would be forced to give up before U.S. support could possibly become effective. Again the Kaiser gave his consent. Moreover, this time he ordered the entire German navy to reorganize itself in support of the U-boat. The main task for the surface navy, he decreed, was to get the U-boats in and out of port safely. "To us," he said, "every U-boat is of such importance that it is worth using the whole available fleet to afford it assistance and support."

This third phase of the U-boat campaign, which would continue unabated to the end of the war, began on February 1, 1917, when the German Naval Staff sent fifty-seven U-boats to sea. In the ensuing months, it kept an average of thirty-five to forty boats on station at all times.

The initial results were devastating. In the first three months of the new campaign, U-boats sank 1,000 Allied merchant and passenger ships: in February the tonnage sunk was 540,000, in March 593,000, and in April 800,000. The sinkings continued at these high levels for another four months, into September. The British Isles were nearly shut off from the outside world. U.S. Ambassador Walter H. Page said, "The submarine is the most formidable thing the war has produced—by far. The submarine menace of 1917 threatened us with absolute and irremediable disaster."

With the exception of a small minority of die-hard pacifists, Americans reacted violently to the new U-boat war. On the third day of the campaign, February 3, 1917, President Wilson broke diplomatic relations with Germany. On February 26, he ordered the arming of U.S. merchant ships. Six weeks later, April 6, 1917, at the peak of the

U-boat offensive, Wilson, stating "the world must be made safe for democracy," asked the Congress to declare war on Germany.

For many years, U.S. naval strategists had been preparing a contingency plan for war with Germany known as Plan Black. It assumed that the powerful German battle fleet would steam into the waters of the United States or the Caribbean, attempt to destroy the U.S. Fleet, and then land an invasion force on the mainland. According to Plan Black, when the United States received word that the German navy was under way, the U.S. Fleet would assemble in the Chesapeake Bay on a specified "M" day and then steam out—Mahan style—and aggressively destroy the Germans in mid-ocean in a single decisive battle. For years most of the training exercises of the Atlantic Fleet had been built around Plan Black.

Now the United States was at war with Germany. Clinging to the basic tenets of Black, the admirals began mobilizing the Atlantic battle fleet for a major naval engagement with the Germans on the high seas. In addition, they took steps to counter an expected U-boat assault in waters along the East Coast. Battleships, cruisers, destroyers, and patrol craft that had been decommissioned were ordered back in service. All along the coast, destroyers and submarines put to sea as scouts, looking for the German fleet or the hordes of U-boats.

In Britain, the highest ranking U.S. naval officer on the scene, Admiral William S. Sims, was first to perceive that the navy was preparing for the wrong kind of war. There was no danger of the Germans attacking the U.S. Fleet, he concluded; they were bottled up in the North Sea by the British. The threat from the sea was the U-boat, not in American waters but close to Britain, blasting away at merchant ships trying to bring in war matériel. If this war of attrition was not stopped—and stopped soon—Sims cabled Washington, the Allies were sure to be defeated within a few months. Sims urged the navy to shelve Plan Black, send as many destroyers as possible to European waters to hunt down the U-boat, and organize the merchant and troop ships into heavily guarded convoys to make the U-boats' job more difficult.

Most U.S. admirals were incredulous when they read these dispatches. Sims had either lost his judgment or had been brainwashed by the British. Everything he proposed ran counter to the Mahan offensive strategy of the single decisive battle; he was proposing a *defensive* strategy. The U-boat situation could not possibly be that serious.

Although they condescended to send a token force of six destroyers to Europe, more or less as a goodwill measure, the admirals clung to Black. The German fleet *might* steam out and sweep the British fleet off the sea while the German army overran Europe. That would leave the United States standing alone. The admirals would not strip the fleet of any more destroyers for anti-U-boat duty in Europe or for convoy duty. In place of convoys, the admirals urged that the arming of merchant vessels be speeded up. Nobody wanted to get entangled in the dull and defensive chore of escorting merchant ships to Europe.

Weeks went by. There was no sign of the German fleet, no hordes of U-boats in American waters. Meanwhile, hundreds of thousands of tons of merchant shipping went to the bottom in British waters. Finally the admirals conceded that Sims was right.

When the dawn came, the navy shifted gears quickly and skillfully. It canceled construction and recommissioning of battleships and concentrated on building destroyers and antisubmarine patrol craft. It persuaded the British to introduce a convoy system. It sent dozens of destroyers to Europe to work with the British, tracking down the U-boat in its prime operating areas, and sent a detachment of battleships to serve with the main British fleet checking the German fleet in the North Sea.

In London, Admiral Sims, impressed by the successes of British submarines against the U-boat, proposed that the United States send a contingent of submarines to the war zone. The Navy Department approved the idea and appointed Captain Thomas Charles Hart, a torpedo expert and strict disciplinarian with submarine experience, to lead the expedition. Chester Nimitz, the diesel expert, was ordered to help Hart get the boats in shape for overseas movement.

Hart and Nimitz were hard pressed to find enough combat-worthy submarines to form the contingent. In early summer of 1917, when the idea was broached, the United States still had only forty-six submarines in commission, half of them ancient gasoline-powered boats stationed in Manila, Panama, and at the New London Submarine School. The best of the diesel boats then in commission were eight Ks and seven Ls. However, four of the Ks were based in Hawaii. That left four Ks and seven Ls, a total of eleven. To these, Hart added Nimitz's old command, *Skipjack (E-1)*, the navy's first diesel-powered submarine, then serving as a school boat in New London.

All twelve boats were sent to navy yards for extensive overhauls and then divided into two divisions, 4 and 5, and sent to the Azores and southwest Ireland respectively.* Although, in the months that followed, Division 5 in Ireland made twenty-one contacts with enemy submarines (Division 4 in the Azores made none), neither division sank any enemy ships. What the American submariners did accomplish was to note, and learn from, the superiority of British and German submarine technology. British and German submarines were more advanced in speed, range, and toughness. They dived faster and handled better submerged. Their engines, periscopes, torpedoes, guns, sonar, and other gear were far superior to the best produced in the United States. The Americans borrowed freely, both technically and operationally, from the British and, later, the Germans.

When U-boats were reported in U.S. waters, the remaining available U.S. submarines—*E-2*, the new Ns, and the other four Ks, transferred from Hawaii to the Caribbean—were pressed into anti-U-boat patrols, basing out of New London, Key West, and other East Coast ports. None of these patrols resulted in destruction of the enemy.

Toward the end of the war, the United States sent a second contingent of submarines to the war zone. It consisted of Division 6, composed of *L-5, L-6, L-7,* and *L-8,* and Division 8, composed of seven new O-class boats, *O-3* to *O-10.* Division 6 reached the Azores on November 7, 1918, four days before the Armistice. Division 8 sailed from Newport on November 2. It was on the high seas, en route to Europe, on November 11 and was recalled.

It was radio intelligence (codebreaking and radio direction finding) plus the dull defensive convoy system that finally neutralized the U-boat. Sailing in tight formation, zigzagging, escorted by destroyers and other antisubmarine vessels, and routed around known positions of U-boats, merchant ships and troop transports crossed the Atlantic by the hundreds, carrying supplies and men to Europe. Figures tell the tale. After the convoy system was organized, Allied shipping losses fell from 800,000 tons per month to 300,000. In the first three months of 1917, the Allies lost 1,000 ships. In the nine months of the war in 1918, the Allies lost 1,133 ships, 999 of them sailing alone. Only 134 were lost in convoy.

After the war ended, statisticians worked up the figures on total Allied losses to the U-boat. In the warship category, U-boats sank ten

* Division 4 consisted of *K-1, K-2, K-5, K-6,* and *E-1.* The four Ks got under way in October 1917, escorted by Hart's flagship *Bushnell.* Division 5—*L-1, L-2, L-4, L-9, L-10,* and *L-11*—plus *E-1,* sailed in December, again escorted by *Bushnell.* Bad weather plagued them, and it was not until February that all seven Ls reached Bantry Bay in Ireland.

battleships, eighteen cruisers, twenty-one destroyers, and nine submarines. In the merchant-ship category, U-boats sank 5,708 Allied vessels, totaling about 11 million tons. About half the merchant ships were British.

The U-boat was neutralized, not defeated. During the war, the Germans built about 373 U-boats. In the first two years, casualties were light. In the last two years, when intelligence-gathering methods improved and the convoy system was put into effect, losses rose to about an average of seven boats per month. But the German shipyards were turning out new and improved U-boats faster than the losses. When the war ended, there were 179 U-boats in commission and 224 on the building ways. The plan for 1919 was to build thirty a month. In all, the Germans lost 178 submarines and about 5,000 officers and men. But for every U-boat lost, thirty-two Allied ships went to the bottom.

The single most effective offensive weapon against the U-boat—statistically—turned out to be the submarine. During the war, there were an average of 35 Allied submarines on full-time patrol against the U-boat. This small force sank 18 U-boats—twice as many as the celebrated decoy Q-ships and three times as many as the 625 aircraft and blimps assigned to antisubmarine warfare. The 4,000 various auxiliary vessels which the British pressed into service accounted for 32. The 300 destroyers, sloops, and subchasers assigned exclusively to hunt the U-boat sank 41. Mines and other causes accounted for the rest.

The submarine, designed originally for coastal defense, employed in a *guerre de course*, had brought on what official British historian Sir Julian Corbett described as "the greatest sea fight in history." Merely to neutralize the U-boat had required the efforts of a million Allied sailors, thousands of offensive vessels and aircraft, and untold hundreds of millions of dollars.

The emergence of the submarine demanded a whole new range of naval planning. Contrary to doctrine of the past, the *guerre de course* would now have to be considered a potentially decisive method of waging war. In the future, any power desiring to command the sea would not only have to deploy a superior surface fleet but also have to have in hand a vast armada to counter the submarine menace of an enemy power. If it depended upon the sea for supplies, as did Britain, it must also be certain that if war came, it had shipping—or the capability of building shipping—to offset the inevitable losses to submarines.

Submarines and Politics I

After the German navy had been defeated and World War I was over, the next likely naval threat of consequence to the United States seemed to be Japan. For decades after Commodore Perry's visit, the two countries had been friends and good neighbors. During the Russo-Japanese War, American public opinion favored the Japanese; the United States and Japan had been allies in World War I. Yet there were signs that this long-term goodwill was running thin. The army had become a powerful faction in the Japanese power structure, and some elements of the army advocated expansionism and the conquest of China, which ran counter to U.S. policy in the Far East and the general sentiment of the nation.

For a decade the Japanese navy, generally considered to be dominated by the Japanese army, had been growing steadily in size and quality. In return for helping Britain fight the U-boat in the Mediterranean, Japan, under the terms of the peace treaty, had been awarded German island possessions in the Pacific: the Marianas (less Guam, a U.S. possession), the Carolines, and the Marshalls. All these lay athwart the U.S. sea line of communications to the Philippines. If they were developed as naval bases, the islands, in effect, would enhance the power and mobility of the Japanese fleet.

Since the turn of the century, the U.S. Navy—influenced by Mahan—had on paper a war plan known as Orange for the naval defeat of Japan. Plan Orange, revised repeatedly over the years, assumed a Japanese attack against the United States would begin in the most vulnerable area, the Philippines. In such an event, according to Orange, the small army garrison in the Philippines and the Asiatic Fleet would blunt the initial attack, then fall back to the Bataan peninsula and the island citadel at the mouth of Manila Bay, Corregidor. Meanwhile, the U.S. Fleet would form up in U.S. waters, proceed westward via the Panama Canal, stop in Hawaii and Guam to secure those forward bases and refuel, and then steam onward to the Far East to engage the Japanese in a single decisive battle, still according to the precepts of Mahan. After crushing the Japanese, the U.S. Fleet would then cruise to Japanese waters and blockade the home islands until Japan sued for peace. Meanwhile, transports coming behind the U.S. Fleet would convoy American troops to relieve the garrisons on Bataan and Corregidor and wipe out the vestiges of Japanese troops.

Plan Orange, a key "problem" for all senior naval officers attending the War College in Newport, was considered doctrine. In the early part of the century, when the fleet was faced with going "round the Horn" to reach the Pacific, Orange had influenced Theodore Roosevelt's decision to dig the Panama Canal. Orange dictated characteristics for fleet vessels—speed, range, sea-keeping ability. Most fleet problems rehearsed a portion of Plan Orange. After World War I, Orange dominated all U.S. naval thinking and planning.

During the immediate postwar period, the U.S. submarine force grew substantially in size and prestige. Forty-three O- and R-boats were commissioned; the fifty-one larger S-boats were coming off the building ways slowly but steadily. Many able naval officers, attracted by the opportunity for early command, were drawn to submarines.

Despite this influx, the force still remained a thing apart, a navy within a navy, but it was a fiercely proud service. It was—and would always be—an elitist group, mostly made up of volunteers. The officer corps knew one another intimately. Its members married sisters or daughters of fellow submariners. In comparison with other military services, it was a small group in which everyone knew everybody else's business.

Until World War I the submarine had been considered primarily a defensive weapon in the U.S. Navy, an adjunct to coastal artillery. With the war, U.S. submariners believed it had earned a larger role. German U-boats had sunk those twenty-eight Allied capital ships—battleships and cruisers. Both the British and Germans had employed the submarine—in limited fashion—in fleet actions. The submarine, they argued, could be a useful offensive adjunct to the U.S. fleet, not only as a forward scouting screen but for attacking large enemy warships.

After the first S-boats were commissioned, the navy experimented with this concept. But the tests were unsatisfactory. Boats of the S class—especially those built by the government at Portsmouth—proved to be too slow, short-legged, and fragile for extended operations with the fleet. In 1921 Captain Hart led a group of new S-boats *
from the East Coast to Manila, simulating a movement in accordance with Plan Orange. The voyage took seven months. After that and further tactical exercises with the fleet, the S class was returned to

* *S-2, S-3, S-4, S-6, S-7, S-8, S-9, S-14, S-15, S-16,* and *S-17.*

square one—it was consigned to coastal defense roles guarding Manila, Hawaii, Panama, and the east and west coasts of the United States.

It was clear that if submarines were to be integrated into the fleet, the United States would need a far larger, longer-ranged submarine. Such a submarine would have to have a huge fuel capacity. It would have to carry a large number of torpedoes within its hull. It would have to have good sea-keeping qualities. It would have to be mechanically reliable. Its average speed would have to match the fleet's, set by Plan Orange at 17 knots. In sum: Orange dictated a large high-speed fleet boat with immense fuel capacity and powerful, reliable diesel engines.

Large submarines were not unknown. During the war, the Germans had built many, notably six enormous *Deutschland* "commercial" boats of 2,000 tons, with a range of 13,000 miles. These slow, clumsy boats were later converted to combatant vessels (*U-151* to *U-157*) with two huge 5.9-inch guns; they routinely patrolled for three months at a stretch. Toward the end of the war, the Germans had under construction a much-improved large submarine known as a "cruiser." These boats (*U-142* to *U-150*) were to be 2,700-ton giants with a surface speed of 17 knots and a range of 5,000 miles.

The United States, too, had experimented with large submarines. During the war it gave Electric Boat a contract to build three—known as the T class—which on paper were similar to but smaller than the German "cruiser" class. The Ts were to be 268 feet long, displacing about 1,100 tons. They would have a speed of 20 knots, a very long range, and be capable of carrying sixteen torpedoes. The Ts were eventually finished and commissioned, but in almost every respect they were failures: slow, clumsy, dangerous.

The overwhelming technical problem, as always, was propulsion. Although the Germans had raised the level of building diesels to a fine art, the United States still had not got the hang of it. The diesel engines on the Ts were heavy, weak, and unreliable. The navy salvaged some M.A.N. engines from a German U-boat and substituted them in *T-2*. However, they were too big; the attempt was likened to "trying to fit an elephant into a pony's stall." After that, the Ts were abandoned.

But the submarine force was still determined to make a place for itself with the fleet. When all the German submarine and diesel technology was in hand, it proposed to the General Board a fleet boat based on the German "cruiser" class but powered by new diesels to be manufactured by a St. Louis firm, Busch-Sulzer. They would be enormous: 342 feet, 2,000 tons. The board authorized three of these, to be known as the V class (the U was skipped, for obvious reasons). The keels for these boats were laid at the naval shipyard at Portsmouth, New Hampshire, in late 1921. Completion of the three, however, took nearly four years—not entirely because of technological problems but because of political snags.

For while submarine duty had grown in popularity within the navy by this time, to those outside the service the U-boat campaign against merchant shipping had given the submarine a reprehensible image. By war's end, it was almost universally loathed. Many notable persons in both Europe and the United States argued that the submarine was immoral and, like poison gas, should be outlawed.

The British Admiralty supported this position. During the peace treaty negotiations (after the surviving U-boat force had been destroyed), the British offered to abolish their submarine force if other powers would do likewise. There were several reasons behind the British proposal. Britain was still an island empire, dependent on sea commerce for survival. She had suffered enormously from the submarine and might again suffer in the future. Her navy was still the largest. It too had suffered serious damage from the submarine. It could happen again.

The British proposal evoked a hot debate in U.S. naval circles. Some admirals believed the aircraft carrier * and ASDIC, a new and remarkable British-developed underwater listening device which precisely located the submarine, had rendered all submarines obsolete. The U.S. Chief of Naval Operations, Admiral William Shepherd Benson, agreed with the British proposal and tried to persuade his colleagues in the Navy Department that the submarine was a dodo. He was strongly opposed by many officers, including Thomas Hart, then head of the Office of Naval Operations, Submarine Section. In a memo to the Naval Planning Session in 1919, Hart stated that Benson's attitude reflected a "big ship conservatism and reluctance to deal with anything that may upset the old order."

The public mood intruded next. In 1920, Warren Harding was elected President of the United States on a "return to normalcy" campaign slogan. By then, the nation had turned strongly pacifist. When the economy slipped into a sharp depression in 1921, many citizens

* The collier *Jupiter* was converted to the first U.S. aircraft carrier in 1920-21 and commissioned in early 1922.

asked why the government was spending so much precious money building a navy "second to none." We would never fight the British, they argued. There was no significant French or Italian fleet. The U.S. Fleet was already larger than Japan's. Moreover, U.S. Air Corps zealot General William ("Billy") Mitchell was ready to "prove" navies obsolete by sinking battleships with cheap land-based aircraft.

The Admiralty followed this debate with keen interest. Although most British admirals believed a war with the United States unthinkable, they opposed a continuing buildup of the U.S. Navy which they were then unable, economically, to match. In the past, Britain's allies had often turned out to be her future enemies; it was the duty of the Admiralty to weigh the capabilities—not the intentions—of competing foreign naval powers. To head off the buildup, in late 1921 the British proposed a naval arms limitation conference. President Harding, seeking a gesture of peace and "normalcy," agreed at once. In the opening session held in Washington, Secretary of State Charles Evans Hughes stunned the conference—and the world—by announcing that the United States was prepared to scrap its naval building program if all other powers would follow suit.

During this historic conference, the future of the submarine again hung in perilous balance. Before his delegates left for Washington, King George V of Britain told the Admiralty in a note that "we should press hard for the abolition of submarines." At the conference, the British delegate offered to scrap "the largest, most modern, most efficient submarine fleet in the world, and to disband our personnel . . . if other powers will do the same and desist from building."

Neither the French nor the U.S. delegates agreed. The French, a weaker naval power, still held the submarine in high regard and declared its abolition "contrary to good sense." In regard to submarines then in being—the Os, Rs, and Ss—the navy's General Board stated that as a "defensive" craft the submarine was "a weapon of peculiar value to the U.S. for protecting our interests in the West Indies and the Philippines and along our extensive coastline." The United States and France countered the British proposal with a suggestion that a limit of 90,000 tons be placed on submarine tonnage in all navies. That figure was sufficient to cover U.S. submarines then in service or projected; it more than covered the French.

Pressing hard for total abolition, the British delegate threw the conference into turmoil by accusing the French of favoring "unrestricted" submarine warfare. He quoted a high-ranking French naval officer as saying the Germans were "absolutely justified" in the way they had employed the U-boat in World War I. Although the French delegates piously denied that the French navy favored unrestricted submarine warfare, word of the charge and countercharge leaked to the press, touching off a storm of controversy in the major capitals. As a result, the conferees were then forced to deal not only with the question of submarine tonnage but also with the moral question of submarine warfare.

Many outsiders jumped into this debate, including U.S. Senator Elihu Root, who proposed a series of resolutions which would greatly restrict the use of submarines in time of war. In essence, he argued for a return to the old rules of sea warfare, requiring "visit and search" before a submarine seized or destroyed an enemy vessel. The navy's General Board—sounding much like the German Naval Staff during World War I—stoutly opposed the Root resolution, arguing that the submarine was "an effective and legitimate weapon of warfare" and that the Root proposals placed "inequitable restrictions upon the use of submarines" and introduced "ambiguities in the rules governing their use."

The Washington naval conference dragged on for many weeks, with much wrangling and horse trading on many levels. In February 1922 the conferees finally reached agreement. They set a 5:5:3 ratio in battleship and aircraft carrier tonnage between Britain, America, and Japan, respectively. In addition, they agreed to a ten-year "holiday" on building capital ships (battleships and carriers) and restricted battleships to 35,000 tons. In order to obtain Japan's signature on the document, the United States agreed not to strengthen, in a military sense, any of her Pacific bases west of Hawaii (i.e., Guam or the Philippines). Taking into account the Japanese acquisition of the many German islands in the Pacific and the fact that the United States had two oceans to defend and the British three, many naval experts felt that the agreement actually reversed the 5:5:3 ratio to favor Japan. It also significantly complicated—and weakened—the navy's Plan Orange.

Even so, the United States cheered the conference as a victory for peace. Great battleships and battle cruisers, on which the United States had already spent hundreds of millions, were broken up in the building yards. In the ensuing years, the navy shrank to a mere 7,000 officers and 100,000 enlisted men. Its representatives were forced to beg Congress for sufficient funds to keep ships already in commission operating. Meanwhile, the nation marched off into the Jazz Age—bootlegging, fancy automobiles, and madcap fads; wild speculations in the stock market and in Florida land. The new heroes would be aviators: Billy Mitchell, Charles Lindbergh, Wiley Post, Amelia Earhart.

The submarine questions raised at the Washington conference were never explicitly settled. The French refused to ratify that portion of the treaty which contained the Root resolution, leaving the moral question moot. The British proposal to abolish all submarines was resoundingly voted down. The various substitute proposals to limit total submarine tonnage appealed to no one, and none was adopted. When the conference broke up, all nations were legally at liberty to build as many submarines as they pleased and to employ them in wartime however conscience dictated.

However, the general deemphasis of things naval following the conference seriously retarded submarine development in the U.S. Navy. The projected S-boat building program was "stretched out" to 1925. The three V-type fleet boats were retained, but these too were delayed by a pinchpenny Congress.

Secret Enterprises

During the conference, two secret enterprises were set in motion that would ultimately prove immensely valuable to the U.S. Navy and the submarine force. Both aimed at breaking the Japanese diplomatic and naval codes.

The first was led by a flamboyant eccentric named Herbert Osborne Yardley, the foremost cryptologist in the United States. During World War I, Yardley had headed the army's codebreaking section. After the war, he established what came to be known as the Black Chamber in New York City. Supported by the army, the navy, and the State Department, Yardley was directed to concentrate on Japanese diplomatic codes. By the time the conference met, Yardley and his team could read Japanese diplomatic dispatches with ease. During the conference, the Black Chamber supplied Washington with about 5,000 decoded Japanese messages.

The second enterprise was strictly naval. An espionage unit composed of operatives from the Office of Naval Intelligence (ONI), men from the city Detective Bureau, and agents of the Federal Bureau of Investigation broke into the Japanese Consulate in New York, made photographic copies of Japanese navy codebooks, and then replaced the originals. Since no one in the navy was skilled in the Japanese language, a former Quaker missionary to Japan, Dr. Emerson J. Haaworth, was hired to translate the books. During this three-year task, Dr. Haaworth kept his translations in a red binder. The code, therefore, came to be known—informally—as the Red Code.

To remedy the lack of Japanese-language specialists in the U.S. Navy, ONI launched a Japanese language course. Each year, two officers were sent to the American Embassy in Tokyo as assistant naval attachés. They remained there three years, studying Japanese history, culture, and the language, with emphasis on naval terminology. Almost without exception, those language officers were funneled into codebreaking.

When Dr. Haaworth was winding up his work, it became clear to ONI that the acquisition of the Red Code was not the end but the beginning of an enterprise that must continue and expand. Any day the Japanese navy might change its code. Naval Intelligence could not count on espionage alone. It needed its own staff of codebreakers and radio intercept stations to provide the codebreakers with a high volume of encoded Japanese navy traffic.

To meet this need, in 1924 the navy established what was called a Research Desk in the Office of Naval Communications. The first man to command this desk was a young lieutenant, Laurence Frye Safford, coincidentally a submariner, who had been executive officer (second in command) of S-7 on the voyage to Manila in 1921. Safford, like most codebreakers, was an intense eccentric with little regard for navy routine and protocol. He founded a codebreaking school and set up radio intercept stations on Guam and in the Far East.

Assisting Safford was a remarkable woman, Mrs. Agnes Meyer Driscoll. Mrs. Driscoll, a codebreaking genius, had formerly worked for the army's leading codebreaker, William Frederick Friedman but had had a falling out with Friedman—common among codebreakers— and volunteered her services to the navy. For years Mrs. Driscoll was the foremost authority on Japanese naval codes and the navy's most talented—and underpaid—codebreaker. She passed on her expertise to Safford, who was more electronic gadgeteer than codebreaker, and to his successors on the Research Desk and the students in the codebreaking school.

While the three V-class fleet boats were under construction at Portsmouth Navy Yard, the Bureau of Ordnance carried forward experimental work on torpedoes. The goal was to build a more powerful and sophisticated instrument for the fleet boats. Most of the research was conducted at the Newport Torpedo Station; in the postwar years the navy had closed down the Alexandria facility because of pressure from Rhode Island politicians.

Much of the important torpedo research in the 1920s—restricted by an acute shortage of money—was conducted by a lieutenant from the class of 1915, Ralph Waldo Christie. Christie, tall and handsome, had been attracted to submarines during the war and was one of the first graduates of the new Submarine School at New London. He had commanded the gasoline-powered *Octopus* (*C-1*) in Panama, *R-6*, and *S-1*, an experimental boat designed to launch an aircraft.* He took a postgraduate course in ordnance engineering, receiving an M.S. degree in Mechanical Engineering from the Massachusetts Institute of Technology in 1923. Thereafter, Christie divided his career between submarine duty and torpedo research—or the "Gun Club."

In the never-ending cycle of weapon and counter weapon, torpedo experts of the early 1920s faced a new and formidable problem. Since the war, the navies of the world had been beefing up the sides of their major warships with armor plating. So intense and thorough was this work that by 1922 it was considered improbable that a torpedo striking the side of such a vessel would seriously cripple or disable it. It was now imperative to develop an exploder that would set off the torpedo *beneath* the vessel, where there was—as yet—no armor plating.

The most promising idea involved a device the Germans had developed during the war to explode their mines called a "magnetic pistol." A ship, or any mass of iron or steel, carries its own considerable magnetic field. Seamen had known for years, for example, that when a magnetic compass was mounted on a steel ship it was likely to go berserk; it had to be carefully mounted and then adjusted to operate accurately within the magnetic field of the ship. The Germans installed magnetic compasses on their mines, connected to a detonator. When an enemy ship came near, its magnetic field disturbed the compass on the mine and made the needle swing, touching off the detonator—hence "magnetic pistol."

The compass pistol would not be practical on a torpedo moving

---

* The aircraft, a small seaplane, was stored in a knocked-down condition in a round cylinder on deck and assembled after the submarine surfaced. The idea was that *S-1* would scout ahead of the fleet, and the aircraft would vastly expand her scouting ability. However, the experiment was a failure, owing to the extreme difficulty of assembling, launching, and recovering the plane at sea.

through a heavy sea, but the idea of utilizing the magnetic field of the enemy ship to explode some kind of electronic device seemed worth exploring. In the summer of 1922, when Christie was shuttling between the torpedo lab at M.I.T. and the Newport Torpedo Station, the Bureau of Ordnance appropriated $25,000 to the station with orders to produce an "influence" exploder on the highest possible priority. The work—known as project G-53—was carried forward behind the tightest veil of secrecy the navy had ever created. Only a handful of people in the bureau with a "need to know" were aware of the project, and none in the fleet.

The concept that gradually emerged was a magnetic exploder that was actuated by a combination of the forces within both the magnetic field of the earth and the magnetic field of the enemy vessel. The theoretical problems were considerable. Very little was known about the magnetic fields of ships, as seen from beneath the keel. The magnetic field of the earth varies in intensity from pole to equator to pole. The device would have to compensate for these variations, since a naval war might be fought at any place on the globe a ship could float. The system itself would require electronic tubes rugged and simple enough to withstand a rough ride to the target without causing a premature explosion. Some method would have to be devised to arm the torpedo after it was well away from the magnetic field of the submarine; otherwise it might blow up its own launcher.

Christie was one of the insiders present at the birth of this promising idea. He was fascinated by it and believed that, if brought to fruition, it would be one of the most valuable weapons in the history of naval warfare. In the coming years, it would become one of his pet projects, and his technical contribution to it would be substantial.

The technicians at the Newport Torpedo Station made gratifying progress with hand-built prototypes of the magnetic exploder. In early 1924 they wrote the Bureau of Ordnance that they were ready for a live test with a real warhead. They requested that extensive surveys be made to determine, precisely, the characteristics of the magnetic fields of surface vessels, and that one of the battleships to be scrapped under the terms of the Washington conference be made available as an experimental target.

The Bureau of Ordnance pompously denied these requests for three reasons: (1) since the bureau, in cooperation with the Carnegie Institute, had already conducted magnetic field surveys on two battleships in the Norfolk Navy Yard, further surveys were considered "unessential"; (2) the bureau believed a forthcoming test in which the battleship *Washington* was to be sunk by a mine submerged beneath her bottom would demonstrate equally well the explosive efficiency of a torpedo; and (3) the bureau doubted that the magnetic exploder was far enough along to "permit sufficient surety of safety to the firing vessel to warrant use of a live warhead."

All during the year 1925, Newport—then commanded by Captain Thomas Hart—bombarded the bureau with repeated requests for a target "whose complete destruction can be tolerated as the only practical means of obtaining the concrete information desired." The bureau yielded—slightly. It made available an obsolete tugboat, scheduled for scrapping. Newport was not satisfied, replying that "apprehension was felt at the Station that this target vessel would be unsatisfactory due to its small displacement." Finally, in December 1925, the Navy Department yielded further and provided Newport with the hulk of the old submarine *L-8*, also due for scrapping. Newport was still not satisfied—*L-8* was far from being the battleship for which the exploder was intended—but it accepted these crumbs from the bureau with thanks.

On May 8, 1926, amid greatest secrecy, Newport prepared for this historic first test of the magnetic exploder. For safety reasons, the torpedo would not be fired from a submarine but from a "dummy tube" mounted on the test range. Hart and the other officials at Newport gathered at the range to watch. The first shot missed, running deep under the target. The second was perfect; *L-8* exploded in a vast column of fire and water. Hart got off a letter to the Bureau of Ordnance stating that the May 8 test was "the opening of a new phase of torpedo warfare which gives the United States a tremendous advantage over any prospective enemy."

The submarine force, meanwhile, encountered further disappointments and setbacks. In 1925–26, the second generation of fleet boats, three long-delayed V-class boats—*V-1*, *V-2*, and *V-3*, later designated *Barracuda*, *Bass*, and *Bonita* *—were completed and commissioned. They proved to have many shortcomings. The Busch-Sulzer diesels failed to generate design power and were unreliable. The fuel tanks

---

* *Barracuda* and *Bonita* were named for submarines (*F-2* and *C-4*) which had been scrapped, beginning a custom that continues to the present. The misspelling of *Bonita* was not corrected.

leaked, leaving a telltale oil slick on the water. None of the boats reached design speeds of 21 knots surfaced and 8 knots submerged. They were slow in diving and unwieldy in submerged maneuvers.

When it became clear that the first three Vs were failures, submariners believed the design solution lay in the direction of larger and more powerful diesel engines—hence a much larger submarine. The General Board approved a limited move in this direction, authorizing three enormous boats 371 to 381 feet long, displacing 2,700 tons. These were *V-4*, *V-5*, and *V-6*, redesignated *Argonaut*, *Narwhal*, and *Nautilus*.* Through a licensing arrangement with M.A.N., the engines were built at the New York Navy Yard.

This second generation of V-boats was commissioned in the late 1920s. Although wonders to behold, the boats were also flops. The navy-built M.A.N. engines failed to produce design power; some developed dangerous crankshaft explosions. Neither *Narwhal* nor *Nautilus* could maintain the average fleet speed of 17 knots, and their cruising speed was much less. They were slow in diving and, once submerged, were unwieldy and slower than designed (6 and a fraction knots top speed instead of 8). They presented surface-ship sonar with a massive target and had a large turning circle.

After studying these boats and their performances, the General Board recommended that the idea of incorporating the submarine into the fleet be abandoned. The boats were clearly inadequate and unreliable, incapable of the prolonged voyages contemplated under Plan Orange. With the diesel engines then available, there seemed no way to achieve the necessary size and torpedo storage and still make fleet speed of 17 knots. Further advances in aircraft, aircraft carriers (the new *Saratoga* and *Lexington*), and sonar appeared conclusively to have rendered the submarine too vulnerable.

This recommendation was a bitter pill for the submarine force, which had worked for ten years to create a respectable place for itself. However, submariners were not about to give up. With the inadequate tools at hand, they sought again and again in exercises with the fleet to prove that the submarine could be useful in spite of all the

---

* *Narwhal* and *Nautilus*, designed as fleet boats, were virtually identical. Each had six torpedo tubes, four forward and two aft, plus four torpedo tubes and two 6-inch guns on deck. *Argonaut*, designed primarily as a minelayer—the first and only such experiment—had four torpedo tubes forward and two minelaying tubes aft, plus two 6-inch guns on deck. All three had a fuel capacity of about 180,000 gallons— twice that of *Barracuda*, *Bass*, and *Bonita;* four times that of the S class; nine times that of the O and R classes.

odds. No real decision was ever made; the question was left moot.

In addition, submariners evolved a new mission for their boats: very long-range scouting and intelligence gathering for the fleet. Under this concept, submarines operating alone would sail from Pacific bases (Pearl Harbor, Hawaii; Dutch Harbor, Alaska) and take up stations off key Japanese naval bases in the Mandates and Empire (Japanese homeland) waters. The primary mission would be to keep the commander in chief of the U.S. Fleet advised by radio on movements of Japanese capital ships. In event of war—it was assumed war would be properly and formally declared—these same submarines, if lucky, could attack enemy ships leaving Japan to engage the U.S. Fleet. The boats would remain at sea for long periods: seventy-five days. They might travel up to 12,000 miles.

All these factors radically altered submarine design. In 1929, the navy produced plans for an experimental fleet boat much smaller than *Argonaut, Narwhal,* and *Nautilus.* This boat, *V-7*, later redesignated *Dolphin,* was not a new design from the keel up but rather a scaled-down version of her forerunners. She was powered by M.A.N. engines built at the New York Navy Yard, similar to those in the previous class but less powerful. She had six torpedo tubes, four forward and two aft. Her keel was laid in June 1930.

Submarines and Politics II

Since the Washington Naval Arms Limitation Treaty, signed in 1922, was due to expire in 1936, the five principal naval powers met in London in 1930 to try to reach agreement on what should follow. Although most of the debate centered on surface craft, the question of the submarine was discussed at length. For the first time in history, certain specific limitations were imposed on submarine development and warfare which influenced submarine design.

The five major naval powers attending the conference were the United States, Britain, Japan, France, and Italy. By then the United States, with 81 submarines in commission, had the largest number, but none was free of serious shortcomings. Japan was second with 72 submarines, half of which were obsolete, but she led the world in terms of reliable oceangoing boats suitable for operating in the broad reaches of the Pacific. France, with 66 submarines, was third, two thirds of which were big oceangoing types; she had another 41 on the building ways which, when completed, would put her in first place. Britain, with 53 submarines (half as many as in 1922), ranked fourth, and some of her newest boats were unwieldy monsters like the Vs. Italy with 46 submarines, mostly obsolete coastal submarines, came last, but she had 21 of a new type then under construction.

As in 1922, the British again proposed abolition of the submarine. Prior to the conference, the U.S. Navy—to the dismay of the submarine force—had privately agreed to support the British position. At the same time, the navy expressed doubt that Japan, France, or Italy—the weaker naval powers—would agree. This proved to be the case, and once again the British proposal to abolish the submarine outright went down to defeat.

Next, the conferees again discussed limitations on total submarine tonnage for each navy. After much wrangling, the United States, Britain, and France agreed to limit their submarine force to 52,700 tons each and to build no submarine larger than 2,000 tons or with secondary armament larger than a 5-inch gun. Neither the French nor the Italians would sign this document, but they each agreed not to build a submarine force larger than that in existence or under construction. Since the French program envisioned a total tonnage of 82,000, she shortly became the leading submarine power in the world.

In actual fact, the limitations agreed to by the United States, Britain, and Japan were hollow concessions. Nobody ever again wanted to build a diesel submarine larger than 2,000 tons, and it would be impractical to mount a gun larger than 5 inches on a submarine 2,000 tons or smaller. The upper limit of 52,700 tons meant that the United States and Japan would have to pull back by about 20,000 tons apiece, but this merely meant scrapping or decommissioning a dozen or so obsolete boats.* From the standpoint of combat effectiveness, none of the submarine forces of the three major naval powers was significantly curtailed.

During the conference, the question of limitation on the submarine in time of war came up again. The old Root resolution of 1922—which, in effect, outlawed unrestricted submarine warfare—was resur-

* In 1930 and 1931, in response to the new limitation, the navy struck the following boats from the commission list: H-2 and H-3; K-1 to K-8; L-2, L-3, L-9, L-11; T-1, T-3; N-1, N-2, N-3. In addition, it retired and sold thirteen Lake-built Os and Rs: O-11 to O-16 and R-21 to R-27. S-2 to S-10 were stricken between 1930 and 1937. During the 1930s, *Barracuda, Bass,* and *Bonita* and some O-, R-, and S-class boats were mothballed. By special agreement, the three V-boats, *Narwhal, Nautilus,* and *Argonaut,* were exempt from the submarine tonnage and armament limitations, as were some British and French monsters.

rected and incorporated into the final agreement signed by the United States, Britain, and Japan. The specific language, Article 22, was as follows:

(1) In their action with regard to merchant ships, submarines must conform to the rules of International Law to which surface vessels are subject.

(2) In particular, except in the case of persistent refusal to stop on being duly summoned, or of active resistance to visit or search, a warship, whether surface vessel or submarine, may not sink or render incapable of navigation a merchant vessel without having first placed passengers, crew and ship's papers in a place of safety. For this purpose the ship's boats are not regarded as a place of safety unless the safety of the passengers and crew is assured, in the existing sea and weather conditions, by proximity of land or the presence of another vessel which is in a position to take them on board.

Immediately after the conference, the navy received money for two additional submarines. This time, the General Board ruled, any new boat should be redesigned from the keel up, a prototype for future submarine development. The submarine force argued for a 17½-knot, 1,200-ton boat, hoping it would prove capable of operating with the fleet as well as conducting long-range independent reconnaissance. Others, including the Naval War College, argued for smaller boats— about 1,000 tons—so that more submarines could be built within the treaty limitation of 52,000 tons.

The outcome was a compromise. The two boats *V-8* and *V-9*, redesignated *Cachalot* and *Cuttlefish*, were 1,100 tons. They were powered by M.A.N. engines built at the New York Navy Yard, scaled-down versions of those in *Narwhal*, *Nautilus*, and *Dolphin*. Neither boat had speed enough to keep up with the fleet, but both were designed for a theoretical endurance of seventy-five days and 13,000 miles.

These two boats, plus the other smaller V-boat, *Dolphin*, proved disappointing, mainly because the navy-built M.A.N. engines were unsatisfactory. They failed to generate the power specified in their design, were unreliable, and were much too large for the cramped hull of these smaller submarines. As a result, all the boats were too slow and spent too much time in navy yards repairing engines. *Cachalot* and *Cuttlefish* were out of commission with engine problems so often they were facetiously named "Breakdown Division Number One."

It was now clear that if submarines were to remain small—and that was the decision—a smaller, more powerful, and reliable diesel engine was needed. To help solve this problem, the navy turned to private industry, putting up several hundred thousand dollars for development of a reliable lightweight (half the weight per horsepower) high-speed diesel engine for submarines. The money was divided among five manufacturers, among them the Winton Engine Company (later absorbed by General Motors) and Fairbanks-Morse Company. The firms were willing to enter the competition for peanuts because they realized that a diesel engine that would fit into a small submarine hull would also fit into a railroad locomotive. On the insistence of the navy's diesel expert, Dr. E. C. Magdeburger, an additional $100,000 was put up to continue development of an extremely sensitive but high-performance diesel engine based on one of the M.A.N. designs. This money went to Hooven-Owens-Rentschler (H.O.R.), the U.S. licensee for M.A.N.

The trend toward smaller submarines likewise called for a smaller, more powerful, and rugged torpedo. The work on this new torpedo was carried out at the Newport Torpedo Station under the direction of Ralph Christie. What emerged was the Mark XIV, a steam torpedo with a 500-pound warhead. It could be fired at two speeds, low and high. At high speed the Mark XIV traveled at 46 knots for a maximum distance of 4,500 yards; at low speed, 31.5 knots for 9,000 yards.

The Mark XIV torpedo was designed for the very secret Mark VI magnetic exploder. By then the Mark VI, after several redesigns, was being produced in limited quantity (30 units for $30,000) by the GE lab in Schenectady. It had been tested in artificially created magnetic fields in the Newport lab and in a limited field test with the cruiser *Raleigh* in southern latitudes, but there was still insufficient data on the magnetic fields of ships and the interrelated magnetic field of the earth.

At Christie's urging, the Navy Department consented to make ships available for a larger, more comprehensive field test. The new 10,000-ton cruiser *Indianapolis* and two destroyers reported to Newport. Amid greatest secrecy, the ships took on personnel, torpedoes, and Mark VI exploders and sailed to the equator, off the west coast of South America. There, over a hundred torpedo shots were fired beneath *Indianapolis* in various locations along the equator or between 10 degrees north and south latitude. The dummy warheads were ingeniously fitted with a new photoelectric device known as the electric eye. As the torpedo passed beneath the cruiser, the eye, mounted in a window in the warhead, caused the shadow of the ship to be recorded on film. The tripping of the magnetic exploder was indicated by burning a wisp of guncotton. During the tests, the technicians made over 7,000 readings on magnetic fields. All in all, Christie said later, "the exploder performed very well and a considerable quantity of new information on magnetic fields was accumulated."

Back in Newport, meanwhile, Christie (who did not go with the test group) and his associates were trying to persuade the navy to provide another obsolete hulk for a live test for the redesigned exploder. After much correspondence, the Chief of Naval Operations agreed to make available a decommissioned destroyer, *Ericsson*, but, perhaps quixotically, he prohibited the firing of a "loaded warhead" against her. He further insisted that if *Ericsson* were sunk by mistake, Newport should be prepared to raise and repair her. Since Newport was in no position to assume this large responsibility and the main purpose in asking for the ship had been for a live test, the offer was declined. No live test of the redesigned Mark VI was ever conducted—an inexplicable and scandalous lapse, as time would prove.

After the *Indianapolis* field test was completed, Newport proclaimed the Mark VI ready for production. For security reasons, it was produced at Newport. The finished exploders were stored away under strictest security regulations, and a dummy contact exploder, the Mark V, was issued to the fleet. When—or if—war came, the Mark VI could be quickly substituted for the Mark V. A manual for adjusting, firing, and maintaining the Mark VI was written—but, for security reasons, not printed—and locked in a safe.

Over the years, the navy's codebreaking unit had been expanding and growing in sophistication. Up to the London Naval Conference in 1930, two dozen men and women had completed the codebreaking school and another dozen had gone through the Japanese language course in Tokyo. The radio intercept stations in the Far East eavesdropped on Japanese navy transmissions twenty-four hours a day, and the codebreakers read these messages, building up a vast knowledge of the Japanese navy.

About the time of the London Naval Conference, the codebreakers received a jolt: the Japanese changed the diplomatic and naval codes, and the new codes were much more difficult. When this change occurred, the father of navy codebreaking, Laurence Safford, was absent on sea duty. The man in charge of the Research Desk was Thomas Harold Dyer. Dyer was an exceptionally able codebreaker and a stable administrator. He and Mrs. Driscoll tackled the new Japanese navy code, which they called Blue, assisted by the many new people in the section. By then, the IBM Company had developed its first punch-card system, and Dyer acquired some of this new equipment. By 1933, when Dyer returned to sea duty, the Blue code had been solved and the navy was once again reading Imperial Japanese Navy traffic.

While Dyer and Mrs. Driscoll worked on the Blue code, another codebreaker with a gift for machines, Jack Sebastian Holtwick, worked on a new code employed by Japanese naval attachés, less complex than the Blue code. After it had been broken, Holtwick built an ingenious device known as the Red machine which could read the code automatically. For the next six years, the navy eavesdropped on Japanese naval attaché traffic. It proved to be an invaluable source of intelligence.

One of the facts turned up in decoded Japanese navy messages was that Japan had developed a reliable and accurate radio direction finding system in the Pacific. The Japanese navy was tracking—and pinpointing the location of—U.S. Navy ships. The United States had no such system.

When Laurence Safford returned to Washington from sea duty, he looked into this deficiency and found the U.S. Navy far behind the rest of the world in RDF technology. In cooperation with a navy radio expert, Dr. A. Hoyt Taylor, Safford pushed through the design of a new RDF unit at the Navy Research Laboratory. The first samples of these were shipped to the Philippines. The second group went to Pearl Harbor, Dutch Harbor, and Samoa, a U.S. island in the South Pacific. After these RDF units went into operation, they were useful to the codebreakers for tracking Japanese navy vessels.

New Deal for the Navy

In 1933 the fortunes of the navy took a dramatic turn for the better, owing partly to new dangers on the international horizon, partly to the arrival of pro-navy leadership in Washington, and, ironically, partly to the Depression.

In the Far East, Japan invaded Manchuria and declared that, as far as she was concerned, the naval limitations agreements would expire in 1936. In Europe, Adolf Hitler came to power and almost immediately launched secret negotiations with the British which would enable him to build U-boats. In Washington, the navy's best friend in Congress, Representative Carl Vinson, moved up to be Chairman of the House Naval Affairs Committee; and President Franklin Roosevelt, concluding that a new naval building program was not only imperative for the defense of the nation but would also help eliminate unemployment in certain areas, recommended a large naval construction program as a part of the National Industrial Recovery Act.

Congress agreed to the recommendation and immediately voted $238 million for the construction of new naval vessels. More money came the following year. The long-range plan was to build 3 more aircraft carriers (*Yorktown, Enterprise,* and *Wasp*), 7 battleships, 11 cruisers, and 108 destroyers.

As part of the buildup, the submarine force received money for construction of 26 new submarines over the next several years. These boats, commissioned between 1935 and 1939, fell into two categories: P class * and *Salmon* class.† All were similar to, but larger than, the *Cachalot-Cuttlefish* design. All were powered by the new lightweight high-performance diesel engines developed by private enterprise: sixteen by General Motors' Winton, eight by Hooven-Owens-Rentschler, and two by Fairbanks-Morse. The P class had four torpedo tubes forward and two aft; the *Salmon* class had four tubes forward, four aft. All had 3-inch deck guns. All dived within sixty seconds.

In most of the boats, the power plant arrangement was a new sys-

---

* *Porpoise, Pike, Shark, Tarpon, Perch, Pickerel, Permit, Plunger, Pollack,* and *Pompano.* P-boats were 300 feet, displacing 1,300 tons. The design depth was 250 feet. Fuel capacity was 90,000 gallons.

† *Salmon, Seal, Skipjack, Snapper, Stingray, Sturgeon, Sargo, Saury, Spearfish, Sculpin, Squalus, Swordfish, Seadragon, Sealion, Searaven,* and *Seawolf. Salmon*-class boats were 308 feet, displacing 1,450 tons. The design depth was 250 feet. Fuel capacity was 110,000 gallons.

The Ps started out being called *P-1, P-2,* etc.; *Pompano,* for example, was *P-10.* In the same way, *Salmon* began as *S-1,* and *Seal* was *S-2.* Then someone awoke to the absurdity about to take place—confusion of this class with the older S-boats—and names were substituted. There were many differences between and within classes. *Porpoise* and *Pike,* for example, had riveted hull construction, but beginning with *Shark* the navy turned to all-welded construction. The four "Sea" boats were the most satisfactory of the lot.

tem known as "diesel-electric" drive. Each of the four engines turned a generator. The four generators could be arranged to supply power to electric motors which turned the propeller shaft or to charge batteries. The system gave the submarine commander great flexibility. He might use two engines for cruising and two for charging batteries at the same time, or one for cruising and three for charging, or he might put all four on the line for maximum speed.

For submerged operations, the Ps and *Salmons* had a new, more powerful battery, manufactured either by Exide Storage or by Gould Battery Company. The battery—containing about 250 large cells—was located beneath the main deck inside the pressure hull in two compartments. It supplied power directly to the electric motors which turned the propeller shaft. Theoretically, a fully charged battery could propel a submerged P or *Salmon* at 2 knots for forty-eight hours or at maximum speed for about one hour.

These Ps and *Salmons* were also equipped with a firepower-control device, first tried out on *Cachalot*, known as the Mark 1 Torpedo Data Computer (TDC), manufactured by the Arma Corporation. Receiving data from the periscope or sonar on the enemy's bearing, range, and angle on the bow (the relative bearing of the submarine to the enemy), the TDC automatically plotted the course of the enemy relative to the course of the submarine and computed and set the proper gyro angle in the torpedo to intercept him. The data were displayed on dials, giving the submarine commander a continuous visual picture of the battle.

The Ps and *Salmons* were air-conditioned. This served two purposes: it made the boats livable in tropical waters where inside-hull temperatures sometimes rose to 110 degrees or more, and it reduced humidity and condensation which collected on the inside of the pressure hull and caused electrical shorts. Air conditioning had drawbacks: it added weight and took up room inside the cramped hull. Many believed it to be an unnecessary luxury.

Finally, the Ps and *Salmons* were equipped with several new safety features. Each carried a supply of Momsen Lungs, an oxygen rebreather developed by a submariner, Charles Bowers Momsen. By flooding the forward or after torpedo rooms, equalizing sea pressure and torpedo room pressure, men wearing Momsen Lungs could leave the submarine through escape hatches from a depth of 100 feet or more. The forward and after torpedo room hatches were also fitted with devices to lock on the McCann Rescue Chamber, a diving bell developed by another submariner, Allan Rockwell McCann. In addition, all the boats had buoys containing telephones. In case of disaster, the crew could let the buoy rise to the surface, marking the position of the stricken submarine, while the telephone enabled rescuers to talk with the entrapped crew.

In the fall of 1936, the first of these new boats—the P-class *Pike, Porpoise, Shark,* and *Tarpon*—were assigned to Submarine Division 13, commanded by Charles Andrews Lockwood, Jr., class of 1912. Lockwood, a short energetic officer with a warm and friendly air, had served in submarines since 1914. An unwilling submariner in the beginning, he had grown fond of life in the boats. He had spent most of World War I in Manila, commanding the aging gasoline-powered *Adder* (*A-2*) and *Viper* (*B-1*). During the closing days of the war he had been transferred to the Submarine School in New London and thereafter served as commander of *Seal* (*G-1*), *N-5*, and *R-25* in Panama, *S-14* on its voyage to Manila, and the V-boat *Bonita*. He had turned down further schooling—important to a navy career—in favor of submarine sea duty and was a thoroughly competent seaman with a knack for things mechanical. For years he had actively urged improvements, refinements, and new designs.

Long a believer that the submarine should be incorporated into the fleet, Lockwood led his new boats in Fleet Exercises and Problems. He found them to be a great improvement over his old *Bonita* and the later V class, yet he was not satisfied. The new engines—particularly the H.O.R.s—were full of bugs. Pistons seized, connecting rods broke, generators sparked dangerously, heavy exhaust smoke revealed the submarine's position. Lockwood wanted more torpedo tubes—six forward and four aft, like the boats the British were building. He wanted a larger deck gun—at least a 5-incher, like the one he had had on *Bonita*. He wanted longer periscopes with thinner tops, more fuel and freshwater capacity, better radio and sonar gear, an improved TDC, and more surface speed.

As in all the artificial fleet problems since 1927, when the fleet boats had first participated, Lockwood's seemed to reveal major submarine vulnerability: aircraft were a dangerous threat to any submarine remaining on the surface in the vicinity of carriers or air bases, day or night, and destroyers equipped with "active" (pinging) sonar were mortal enemies. One division of destroyers became so proficient at hunting down Lockwood's fleet boats that the commander concluded his ships could detect and destroy 70 percent of all submarines attempting to penetrate his lines.

Added to these hazards was another, which to a large extent dominated skipper performance. If a skipper were "caught" during a Fleet Problem, Tactical Exercise, or torpedo practice, he might receive a severe dressing down. For this reason the submarine navy developed a well-entrenched habit of extreme caution in its tactics. Because boats at periscope depth were visible to aircraft, this method of attack was believed to be too dangerous. Submarine captains were encouraged to make "sonar attacks" from a depth of 100 feet, where layers of cold water sometimes deflected sonar pinging and where they would be safe from detection by aircraft. Attacks from that depth compounded the difficulties of hitting the target. Altogether, Lockwood's Fleet Exercises and Problems revealed or confirmed that the fleet submarine as an efficient instrument of war still had a long way to go.

The *Salmon*-class boats which followed the Ps into service had still another weakness that no one suspected until a tragedy occurred. The lid on the main induction—the large air line which supplied air for the four diesel engines while running on the surface—sometimes failed to shut during the dive. This happened to *Snapper* and *Sturgeon*, without loss of life, and to the new *Squalus*, with tragic results. Commanded by Oliver Francis Naquin, on her eighteenth dive, May 23, 1939, *Squalus* partly flooded and sank in 243 feet of water. The telephone buoy popped up as designed, and a sister ship, *Sculpin*, found *Squalus*. Twenty-three men died in the flooding; the other thirty-three, including Naquin, were rescued by a McCann Rescue Chamber. *Squalus* was raised, refurbished, and renamed *Sailfish*.

Submarine designers responded favorably to Lockwood's criticisms of the fleet boat. They drew up plans for a new design known as the *Tambor* class. These boats would be slightly larger than the *Salmon* class: 310 feet, 1,500 tons. They would be powered by the best of the new engines, the General Motors Winton. They would have ten torpedo tubes—six forward, four aft—and carry a total of twenty-four torpedoes. They would be equipped with a new TDC,* the new high-

---

* The second model of the TDC, the Mark 2, was developed by the Ford Instrument Company on Long Island. The third and best version, the Mark 3, was developed by the Arma Corporation. The Mark 3 became standard fleet boat equipment. Thereafter, Ford Instrument concentrated on firepower control gear for surface ships.

capacity Kleinschmidt fresh-water distiller, a 5-inch gun, and longer, thinner periscopes. They would be capable of cruising at fleet speed for about 12,000 miles.

However, before this new class of submarines was approved, a new and serious problem arose. Thomas Hart, then a sixty-year-old admiral, was named chairman of the navy's General Board. Hart was staunchly opposed to further development and construction of fleet submarines. He believed them to be too large and impractical, too full of gadgets (TDC) and luxuries (air conditioning). He preferred a small simple submarine about half the size of *Tambor*—about 800 tons, six tubes (four forward, two aft)—comparable to the medium-sized U-boats of World War I and the U.S. *S* class.

In the fall of 1937, Lockwood was transferred to shore duty in Washington to run the "submarine desk" and to chair the Submarine Officers' Conference. As such, Lockwood became "Mr. Submarine" in the Navy Department. He immediately locked horns with Admiral Hart.

The showdown came on May 24, 1938, when the General Board met to lay down submarine characteristics for the 1940 building program. To assist him, Lockwood called on an old boss and friend, Captain Richard Stanislaus Edwards, then commanding the Sub Base in New London. Edwards was a much-respected tactician and strategist. With his help, Lockwood and the other submariners attending the meeting worked out a compromise. In 1940, the navy would build six *Tambors* * and two small submarine prototypes, *Mackerel* and *Marlin*.† Lockwood won most of his points for the *Tambor* design, including air conditioning. However, at Hart's insistence, the 5-inch deck gun was disapproved.

Lockwood and the others had won a victory of sorts in the General Board, but they had been so preoccupied with technical details they overlooked a larger point that would shortly return to haunt them. A request for a mere six new fleet submarines for 1940 was an absurdly low figure. Had the submariners asked for three or four times that figure, and had the request been granted, they would have been far better prepared for the responsibilities that would soon befall them. However, no one pushed for larger numbers; the submarine force, so long

---

* *Tambor, Tautog,* and *Thresher* with Winton engines; *Triton, Trout,* and *Tuna* with Fairbanks-Morse engines.

† They were S-boat size: 238 feet, 800 tons. They had four tubes forward, two aft, and a total torpedo capacity of twelve.

conditioned to getting by on half a loaf, considered six new submarines sufficient.

An important ally in that conference of May 1938 was Ralph Christie, then working in the Bureau of Ordnance as head of the Torpedo Section. In the Navy Department, he was "Mr. Torpedo." Christie had been involved in the study and planning for the *Tambor* class. He was a strong and articulate advocate of the *Tambor* as the primary weapon for the submarine force.

As head of the Torpedo Section, Christie was then besieged by a hundred other major problems. The most pressing was the matter of torpedo production. The buildup of the navy had brought with it a huge demand for surface ships, submarine, and aircraft torpedoes. Navy policy then was that for every destroyer torpedo tube there should be three torpedoes, for every submarine tube six torpedoes, and for every torpedo plane five torpedoes. To meet this demand, the Newport factory, still the sole source of torpedoes, had been expanded from 1,000 workers in 1933 to 3,000 in 1937, operating on a three-shift, twenty-four-hour, five-day-week schedule. The bureau had recently spent $1.25 million (considered a huge sum) for new production lines and machine tools. Even so, the production rate was only about two and a half torpedoes each working day (591 were turned out in 1937), and the backlog of orders had risen to $29 million. At the going production rate, Christie had calculated, by 1942 the navy would be short 2,425 torpedoes.

Obviously something had to be done to increase production. What was needed, Christie concluded, was a second and possibly a third source of supply. The mothballed torpedo factory in Alexandria, Virginia, was one obvious prospect. After promising the Rhode Island Congressional delegation, led by Congressman Aime J. Forand, that the Newport factory would be expanded, Christie got permission to reopen the Alexandria factory and obtained money to establish a third source at Keyport, Washington. However, as time would prove, all these measures were far too little and much too late.

War in Europe

While U.S. submariners dealt with their problems, fascism was on the march the world over. In the Far East, Japan broadened her conquest of Manchuria to all of China, weakened by the warring factions of the reactionary Chiang Kai-shek and the Communist Mao Tse-tung. Firebrands in the Japanese government urged that all the Far Eastern colonies of the imperialistic white man—India, Burma, Thailand, Indonesia, Indochina, and the Philippines—be brought under Japanese hegemony. Having renounced the Naval Arms Limitation Treaty, Japan embarked on a huge buildup of her navy and strengthened her bases in the Marianas, the Carolines, and the Marshalls.

To deter the Japanese, President Roosevelt ordered that the United States Fleet shift its base from West Coast ports to Pearl Harbor, Hawaii. The fleet commander, Admiral James Otto Richardson, objected. Pearl Harbor lacked the facilities to support the fleet. The officers and men would be separated from their families—and the good liberty in West Coast ports. Pearl Harbor was too exposed to surprise attack by the Japanese. To ensure the safety of the fleet, Richardson would have to maintain constant long-range air patrols, a tedious and boring procedure that wore out pilots and airplanes. Roosevelt held firm and began looking for a more tractable fleet commander.

In Europe, Adolf Hitler, culminating a series of bloodless coups, attempted to grab Poland. Two days later, September 3, 1939, England and France, allying with Poland, declared war on Germany.

The German navy was not prepared for war. During its short buildup, Admiral Erich Raeder had concentrated on 12,000-ton "raiders" (*Deutschland, Admiral Scheer, Admiral Graf Spee*), capable of operating at sea for long periods. Raeder did not believe Germany would go to war with England. The most likely enemy was France. The raiders were designed primarily to force France into using most of its fleet for escort duty, thereby making the Baltic and North seas and the North Atlantic safe for German shipping.

The hands-off-England policy had also retarded submarine development. If there was to be no war with England, why build submarines? When war came, the German submarine force, commanded by Captain Karl Doenitz, numbered only fifty-seven U-boats, of which a mere twenty-two could be classed as oceangoing; the rest were small training boats or medium-size experimental types. After the war, Doenitz said, "The war was, in one sense, lost before it began. Germany was never prepared for a naval war against England . . . a realistic policy would have given Germany a thousand U-boats at the beginning."

Prior to the outbreak of hostilities, Doenitz had deployed all available boats at sea. Because Germany had signed the London Submarine Agreement, the force, in theory, was to operate under the "restricted" and "visit and search" rules that had also been adopted by England, Japan, and the United States. However, on September 3, *U-30* sank without warning the passenger liner *Athenia*, with more than 1,400 men, women, and children embarked. The British cried "atrocity"; the Nazis claimed "sabotage." One point was clear to the Admiralty: the quaint rules of war at sea were not going to work.

Britain immediately instituted the U-boat countermeasures developed in World War I. First, the convoy system was put in force—this time without delay. Merchant ships were armed and ordered to fire or ram an attacking U-boat and get off a radio report. British radio intelligence experts cranked up the RDF system, and codebreakers tackled the German naval codes. But Britain had neglected her antisubmarine ships. When war came, there were only 220 vessels equipped with the secret sonar device ASDIC: 165 destroyers, 35 sloops, frigates, and corvettes, and 20 trawlers, not nearly enough to protect the British fleet and convoys and also aggressively hunt down independent U-boats. In addition, the British Coastal Command was short of antisubmarine aircraft.

During the first few weeks, while Hitler was attempting to come to terms with England and France through diplomacy, he held his U-boats in partial check. When diplomacy failed, he unleashed the boats in total unrestricted submarine warfare that would continue throughout the war. In the first two months, U-boats, few in number, sank the British carrier *Courageous* and the battleship *Royal Oak* and very nearly got the carrier *Ark Royal*. However, merchant ship sinkings were slim compared to 1917–18: in October 1939 a mere 136,000 tons, even less in November and December.

During the peacetime years, both the British and the Germans had developed in secret a magnetic exploder for their submarine torpedoes similar to the U.S. Navy's Mark VI. After hostilities began, both submarine forces found the exploder less than satisfactory, so they deactivated the device and reverted to the simple, reliable contact exploder. U.S. observers in Britain reported these failures to the Bureau of Ordnance, but the bureau took no action to test its own magnetic exploder under wartime conditions against real target. The attitude seemed to be: theirs might not work, but ours will.

Lacking numbers, a reliable torpedo, and experience, the first year of the U-boat war was less than effective. However, by the fall of 1940, Doenitz, now an admiral, had many more boats operating from advance bases in occupied France. He directed them by radio in what he called *die rüdetaktik*—wolf packs which made night surface attacks against convoys.

The results were devastating. With a mere six boats at sea, on the average, Doenitz drove the shipping loss to 300,000 tons in September. In October, U-boats sank 346,000 tons. In one convoy, twenty out of thirty-four ships went to the bottom. Oil imports to England fell by 50 percent. Prime Minister Winston Churchill, who saw the danger clearly, ordered his governmental departments to explore every conceivable technical and operational means of combating the sea menace.

In addition to the RDF stations scattered around the British Isles, the most promising technical innovation for detecting the presence of a U-boat was radar. Radar in primitive form had been under development in both the United States and Britain for about a dozen years. The basic principle was simple: to send out an electrical impulse that would "bounce" from an object and return to the sending set, giving exact range and bearing to the object. However, it was a large step from the drawing board to a practical device that could be based on shore or carried in an aircraft. Under pressure of war, Britain led the United States in bringing radar into practical use. In late 1940 a few sets became available for antisubmarine patrol planes.

With Japan on the move in the Far East and Britain besieged by the blitz and the U-boat, the United States drastically stepped up its naval preparations. Treaty limitations—including limitations on submarine tonnage—were abandoned. In July 1940 Congress voted $4 billion to create a "Two-Ocean Navy," one for the Atlantic and one for the Pacific. President Roosevelt established a Neutrality Patrol in the Atlantic to discourage U-boats from entering U.S. and Caribbean waters. He worked out a deal with Britain to exchange fifty World War I destroyers in return for the right to build U.S. naval bases on British soil in the Caribbean and South America.

In addition to carriers, battleships, cruisers, and destroyers, the Two-Ocean Navy bill contained more money for new *Tambor*-class fleet boats, but again, as time would prove, too few were ordered. Belatedly, the navy enlarged submarine-building facilities at Electric Boat Company in Groton and the navy yards at Portsmouth, New Hampshire, and Mare Island, near San Francisco. In addition, the navy gave submarine construction contracts to the Manitowoc Shipbuilding Company in Manitowoc, Wisconsin, the Cramp Shipbuilding Company in Philadelphia, and the Boston Navy Yard.

The bill also provided money for demothballing many older submarines that had been placed in reserve status. In all, nineteen Os and Rs, sixteen Ss, and *Barracuda*, *Bass*, and *Bonita* were refurbished and recommissioned, adding thirty-eight more submarines to the active list.* The Os and Rs were used for training purposes. The Ss, plus *Barracuda*, *Bass*, and *Bonita*, were prepared for combat. The demothballing programs took money from the new submarine building program and tied up building facilities that could have been used for new construction.

The Main Enemy

Within U.S. naval circles, the main enemy was still Japan. For this reason, the growing band of navy codebreakers concentrated on Japanese codes. During the years 1937–40, their job became increasingly difficult as the Japanese changed to infinitely more complex systems.

The first problem occurred in mid-1937, when the Japanese switched both diplomatic and naval codes again. To regain those codes, Laurence Safford's unit joined forces with William Friedman and the army codebreakers in a display of interservice harmony and cooperation rare for those days. The assault on the Japanese diplomatic code—known as Purple—received the highest priority; William Friedman and the army took on that chore. Safford's group provided support by supplying intercepted messages and money and by processing all other Japanese systems through the calendar years 1939 and 1940, leaving the Friedman group free to concentrate its entire facilities, energy, and thought on Purple.

The navy also contributed, indirectly, by supplying the army with the standard solution and techniques for the older Red machine. There was enough similarity between Red and Purple that the standard solution for Red produced a partial solution for Purple—that is, about 25 percent. But the remaining 75 percent stopped Friedman cold for about nineteen months. The final solution was provided by the genius

---

* Actually thirty-seven. During trials, one of the recommissioned boats, *O-9*, sank in deep water off Portsmouth with the loss of all thirty-three hands.

of one of Friedman's team, Harry Lawrence Clark. The result was a little hand-built Purple machine, a maze of wiring, stepping switches, and rotors with a typewriterlike keyboard, which whizzed and occasionally spewed sparks. But it produced what was required. (With the job done, Friedman suffered a nervous collapse.)

Navy codebreakers, meanwhile, concentrated on the new Japanese navy code, which they called Black. The initial break was achieved by Wesley Arnold ("Ham") Wright, working with Mrs. Driscoll, who was then recovering from a near-fatal automobile wreck. However, there was something wrong with Wright's break; it wouldn't fit together. Tom Dyer examined Wright's work, found an error, made a correction, and by 1940 navy codebreakers could read the Black code about 50 to 60 percent.

After this contribution, Dyer was transferred to Pearl Harbor to become communications officer for the 14th Naval District. He secretly took along codebooks and some IBM equipment, which he stored in a vault. In his spare time, he worked on the Black code. Little by little, he acquired additional help—including some Japanese-language officers—and unofficially began building a codebreaking unit, which was called Hypo—the Navy's prewar phonetic designation for the letter H—for Hawaii. (The Washington operation was called Negat, or N for Navy Department.)

A year or so later, the navy established a second Pacific codebreaking unit at the small Philippine naval base Cavite, on Manila Bay. It was called Cast, the prewar phonetic letter for C, or Cavite. It was initially put into operation by a Japanese-language officer, Redfield ("Rosey") Mason, who also served as intelligence officer on the staff of the commander in chief of the Asiatic Fleet.

In June 1940 the Japanese navy again changed its codes. This time, two codes replaced the all-purpose Black. One, very difficult, was called the Japanese Flag Officers' code. The other, infinitely easier, was called by some JN-25 (the twenty-fifth variation of the Japanese navy code since its acquisition by espionage in the early 1920s). The most capable codebreakers, Mrs. Driscoll, Tom Dyer, and Ham Wright, concentrated on the Flag Officers' code. They couldn't break it and never would; it was seldom used, and the codebreakers lacked a sufficient volume of messages to work on. The younger team worked on JN-25. Within three months they had cracked it, turning in the first solid translations in September 1940. Three JN-25 codebooks were laboriously hand printed: one for Negat, one for Hypo, and one for Cast.

About this time, Army Chief of Staff George Catlett Marshall and Chief of Naval Operations Harold Raynsford Stark decided—with Roosevelt's unofficial approval—that Britain, whose interests in the Far East were no less than those of the United States, should be let in on the secrets of Japanese codebreaking. Accordingly, a special mission composed of army and navy officers traveled to London to make arrangements.

When word of this proposed transaction trickled down to U.S. codebreakers—who had not been consulted—they were angry for several reasons. First, they feared that word would leak out of London to the Germans or Japanese and all their work would be for naught. Second, they objected to the one-sidedness of the deal. The United States had not asked for a quid pro quo. It was to be a giveaway, with no British codebreaking secrets furnished the United States. U.S. codebreakers knew that the British then possessed German Enigma machines, captured in North Africa and salvaged from a U-boat. At the very least, they believed, the British should turn over an Enigma machine.

Although both Marshall and Stark insisted that the United States honor its commitment, they consented to a bargaining session to see what could be obtained from the British in return for Purple. After much haggling, the parties agreed to a full exchange of cryptographic systems, cryptanalytic techniques, direction finding, radio interception, and other technical communication matters pertaining to Germany, Italy, and Japan. In the agreement, which was reduced to writing, Britain promised to turn over an Enigma machine.

The United States accordingly gave to Britain the second and third Purple machines built,* two Red machines, consular codes and other minor diplomatic systems, two of the three laboriously hand-printed JN-25 codebooks, two merchant marine codebooks, the naval attaché ciphers, a list of current call signs, and other miscellaneous data. Safford had strongly objected to releasing the Japanese naval codebooks to Britain before they had been sent to Cavite or Pearl Harbor, but he was overruled by higher authority. His men set to work making two more copies.

In return, the British gave the United States their latest Marconi-

---

* Eight had been ordered initially: six for Washington, one for Cast at Cavite, and one for Hypo at Pearl Harbor.

Adock high-frequency direction finder, much superior to any RDF gear then in existence in the United States, and some radar technology. But they reneged on the Enigma machine, stating that Enigma had not been part of the bargain. Moreover, they said they had not requested the Japanese naval code, did not expect it, didn't even know the United States had broken it, and had no use for it in London. In spite of this, the United States agreed to furnish the British yet another Purple machine, the eighth and last, scheduled for shipment to the Hypo unit at Pearl Harbor.

After the fall of France in 1940, Japan, influenced by War Minister General Hideki Tojo, entered into a Tripartite Pact with Germany and Italy, then forced the weak Vichy government to allow Japanese troops into Indochina to build air bases and close off the railroad to China. This was the first big Japanese advance beyond the borders of China. When it came, most U.S. naval officers believed war with Japan was inevitable. The fleet at Pearl Habor went on full war alert for a while, then relaxed.

Most of the new fleet boats coming into the submarine force—the Ps and *Salmons*—were based close to the fleet either in San Diego or Pearl Harbor. In 1939 and 1940, they were commanded by Rear Admiral Wilhelm Lee Friedell. Charles Lockwood, then a captain, served as his chief of staff. Ralph Christie was commander, Division 15.*

Lockwood had not yet given up his battle to persuade the navy to include fleet submarines in the main battle fleet, and he trained the boats with that goal in mind. However, when the new boats did exercise with the fleet, they did little better than the old. One result was that under Plan Orange (renamed in its latest version Rainbow Five) the fleet boats were finally excluded from direct—and close—operation with the fleet. They would serve as long-range scouts in distant Japanese waters and off the exposed islands of Midway and Wake and the Japanese-held Marshalls, serving to report Japanese fleet movements, to attack enemy capital ships and other targets, and to perform special missions as directed by the commander in chief of the U.S. fleet.

A major weakness in Rainbow Five was the pitifully inadequate Asiatic Fleet, which was detailed to blunt the Japanese invasion forces in the Philippines. It was composed of not much more than the heavy

---

* *Salmon, Seal, Skipjack, Snapper, Stingray,* and *Sturgeon.*

cruiser *Houston*, the light cruiser *Marblehead*, thirteen aged destroyers, and six ancient S-boats plus their tender, *Canopus*.

In October 1939 Admiral Stark made the first real effort to reinforce the Asiatic Fleet. He ordered that Submarine Division 14, commanded by John Wilkes and composed of the first seven P-class boats—*Porpoise, Pike, Shark, Tarpon, Perch, Pickerel,* and *Permit*—be transferred from San Diego and Pearl Harbor to Manila, augmenting the six S-boats. Together the P-boats and S-boats (less *Shark*, which was delayed a full year with engine problems) were reorganized into Submarine Squadron Five, Wilkes commanding. This squadron of thirteen boats was—potentially—the most lethal arm of the insignificant Asiatic Fleet at the time.

After the Japanese incursions into Indochina in the summer of 1940, Admiral Stark named Admiral Thomas Hart, then sixty-three years old, to command the Asiatic Fleet. Hart's land-based partner was General Douglas MacArthur, then sixty, who had been serving as military adviser to Philippine President Manuel Quezon since stepping down as chief of staff of the U.S. Army in 1935. For some years, MacArthur had been training Filipino troops with the hope that by 1946, when the Philippines were due to be granted independence, the government could defend itself from outside attack.

When Hart arrived in Manila in October 1940, he was convinced that a Japanese attack on the Philippines was imminent, and he was not much impressed by the U.S. Navy's establishment there. He received little shore support from the Commandant, 16th Naval District. Traditionally, Manila had been a sinecure for infirm senior naval officers serving out final tours. They were "not up to the quality that conditions called for," Hart reported. The commandant on duty when he arrived was in "unsatisfactory mental and nervous state" and returned to the States. After six months, his replacement was likewise invalided home. The various machine shops and shipyard facilities at Cavite and elsewhere were "inadequate" for maintaining the Asiatic Fleet in a combat-worthy state.

Hart took over with an iron fist. He found the ships of the Asiatic Fleet scattered all over: in China, Hong Kong, Singapore. His first step was to recall most of these units to Philippine waters. Then he ordered that some 2,000 navy dependents be returned to the States, an order that caused great bitterness. After it had been carried out, Hart began to exercise his small force in maneuvers.

One month after taking over, Hart requested that the Navy Department send him reinforcements. Admiral Stark responded by ordering Submarine Division 17 * to Manila. Three of the four boats departed on twenty-four-hour notice. A month later, the fourth, *Seawolf*, together with *Shark*, finally seaworthy, joined the force in Manila. By December 1940, Admiral Hart's Asiatic Fleet submarine force, John Wilkes commanding on the tender *Canopus*, consisted of the original six S-class and eleven fleet boats.

The transfer of these submarines to Manila was a further blow to Lockwood and other submariners. Little by little most of the available fleet submarines were being siphoned off to carry out a mission for which they were not designed, coast defense of the Philippines. In terms of naval strategy, the idea was a throwback to pre-World War I days. Yet Admiral Hart complained further to his staff and to Wilkes, saying that the navy should have followed his thinking and built smaller submarines with fewer gadgets to go wrong. Smaller submarines, he believed, could better defend the Philippines.

In early January 1941, the U.S. and British military staffs launched secret discussions over command and strategy, should the United States be drawn into the war. The staffs reached this conclusion: "Since Germany is the predominant member of the Axis powers, the Atlantic and European war is considered to be the decisive theater. The principal United States military effort will be exerted in that theater, and operations of United States forces in other theaters will be conducted in such manner as to facilitate that effort."

This conclusion, in effect, was a turnabout in U.S. strategy. Germany—not Japan—now loomed as the prime threat. Every effort would be made to deter Japan from further aggression. However, if she entered the war against the Allies, the Pacific strategy would be "defensive" until Hitler and Mussolini were defeated.

In line with this strategy, on February 1, 1941, President Roosevelt took steps to strengthen U.S. naval power in the Atlantic Ocean. On that date, he divided the United States Fleet into two forces—the Pacific Fleet, to remain at Pearl Harbor, and the Atlantic Fleet, to be based in ports on the East Coast. The Atlantic Fleet would be composed of some units that could be spared from the Pacific Fleet, existing vessels in the Atlantic, and new ships coming off the ways. To command the newly designated Atlantic Fleet, the President

---

* Commanded by Willis Merritt Percifield, and consisting of *Seadragon, Sealion, Searaven,* and *Seawolf.*

named Admiral Ernest Joseph King. To command the Pacific Fleet, Roosevelt named Admiral Husband Edward Kimmel. The puny Asiatic Fleet remained under command of Admiral Hart.

The primary task of the Atlantic Fleet was to protect sea communications between the North American continent and the British Isles against Doenitz's U-boats. Although the United States had not yet declared war against the Axis, Roosevelt decided that Atlantic Fleet vessels, in addition to maintaining the already existing Neutrality Patrol, would escort Britain-bound convoys across the extreme North Atlantic. To support this objective, a base was built at Argentia, Newfoundland, and destroyers were detached from regular fleet duties for intense training in antisubmarine operations.

When U.S. naval planners got down to implementing this decision, it was clear that there was a critical shortage of escort vessels suitable for operations against the U-boat. Many of the few available were old, ill-equipped, and thinly manned. Somewhat belatedly—the U-boat war had been in progress for a year and a half—the United States launched a crash program to build escorts for herself, Britain, and Canada. But it would be another year and a half before these vessels began coming down the ways in substantial numbers. Meanwhile, Admiral King told his commands, "We must do all that we can with what we have."

Under the terms of the secret Anglo-American agreements, it was also decided that when, as, and if the United States entered the war against the Axis she would send a contingent of submarines, plus supporting facilities, to European waters. According to the war plan, they would operate under British command against the U-boats from bases in England and Gibraltar. To prepare this force, Admiral King chose Richard Edwards, whom he named Commander, Submarines Atlantic Fleet. For his tactical commander, Edwards chose Ralph Christie, recently promoted to captain. Charles Lockwood, then naval attaché in London, worked out the details for basing the submarines.

By that time, the first six *Tambor* fleet boats had been placed in commission. In trials, *Tambor* had exceeded the highest expectations. She made 21 knots on the surface, 10 knots submerged. She could crash dive to periscope depth (60 feet) in thirty-five seconds. She responded to the helm and planes "like a dream." Her improved Winton and Fairbanks-Morse engines, TDC, and sonar gear were more reliable than any heretofore. She had good sea-keeping qualities, and (as live tests had proven) her hull was sturdy against depth charge attack. With her air conditioning, Kleinschmidt fresh-water distillers, fine mess hall, galley, and crew sleeping compartment, she was considered to have excellent habitability for long cruises. After twenty years of trial and error, U.S. submarine designers had finally built a fleet boat unmatched by that of any other nation.

Edwards and Christie wanted to form their proposed European submarine force around the division of six new *Tambors* or their successors, but Admiral Stark said no. The Pacific submarine force had already been severely depleted by the transfer of eleven fleet boats to Admiral Hart in Manila. The six new *Tambors* and their successors would be sent to Pearl Harbor.

What then would comprise the European submarine force? Counting those recently demothballed, there were then a total of thirty-eight of the original fifty-one S-class.* Of the thirty-eight, six were in Manila and six were in Panama. That left twenty-six, of which twenty-two were deemed combat-worthy. These twenty-two S-boats—all over sixteen years old and most nineteen or twenty years old—plus *Barracuda*, *Bass*, and *Bonita* were selected for the European submarine force and placed under Christie's command.

Christie was not happy at the thought of sending these ancient tubs into combat. The worst of the lot were *Barracuda*, *Bass*, and *Bonita*. After seeing them in operation, Christie sent them to Panama to join the S-boats guarding the canal.

As part of their training for overseas deployment, in mid-1941 Christie began sending his boats on limited patrols from new submarine bases in Bermuda, the Virgin Islands, and Guantanamo Bay, Cuba. If a skipper sighted a U-boat, his orders were not to shoot but to trail and report by radio in "plain language." In the fall of 1941, after the U.S. destroyer *Greer* had been fired upon by a U-boat and Roosevelt gave orders to shoot to kill, Christie placed his boats on a total war footing.

In late 1941, when Admiral Doenitz deployed his U-boats in force off Newfoundland to intercept Britain-bound convoys at the point of origin, Admiral King ordered Edwards and Christie to launch a counterattack. The two men boarded the new tender *Griffin* and proceeded to the base at Argentia, in company with a force of seven submarines—six S-class plus *Mackerel*, then only a few months in commission. As did other U.S. submarines patrolling the Atlantic in 1941, they found poor hunting.

* Three had sunk; ten had been scrapped.

Plans in the Far East

The naval plan for the defense of the Philippines changed from month to month. When Admiral Hart first arrived in Manila, the plan was that the submarines would engage the oncoming Japanese while the feeble surface forces retreated southward to Singapore and the Malay Barrier, joining with British and Dutch naval forces (the Australian and New Zealand navies had made it clear they would remain in home waters) and mounting a counteroffensive, or at least trying to stop the Japanese short of the Malay Barrier. However, Hart was never able to formulate joint war plans with the British and Dutch or hold joint maneuvers and work out a communications plan.

In January 1941, U.S. naval planners came to Manila announcing a decision to reinforce the Asiatic Fleet with additional surface craft: an aircraft carrier, a cruiser division, and a squadron of destroyers. The British would maintain the bulk of their fleet in the Atlantic and Mediterranean. Hart would probably command the combined naval forces in the Far East.

A month or so later this plan was reversed. There would be no surface reinforcements for Hart, but British naval forces in Singapore would be "heavily reinforced" with battleships and cruisers. The British would probably take command of the combined forces in event of war. However, there was still no joint planning.

In the spring of 1941, Hart was certain the Japanese were ready to attack and withdrew from Manila all U.S. naval forces, including submarines, to the southern Philippine islands where they would be safer from enemy air attack. When no attack materialized, Hart returned his fleet to Manila Bay.

In June 1941, still another war plan began to emerge. General MacArthur, who assumed command of all U.S. Army ground forces as well as the Filipino army, argued for an aggressive defense, a "stand and fight" policy. He believed that, given six months to train a Filipino army of 200,000 men, plus U.S. Army ground reinforcements, 100 fighter planes, and 100 long-range B-17 "Flying Fortresses," and with help from Admiral Hart, he could hold the Philippines until the Pacific Fleet arrived to do battle with the Japanese fleet, as originally envisioned in Plan Orange. MacArthur's was a "positive" plan which seemed reasonable. It was approved by General Marshall, who ordered the planes and limited ground reinforcements, with weapons and ammunition, shipped to the Philippines.

In line with MacArthur's new—and aggressive—plan to stand and fight in the Philippines, Admiral Stark decided to send Admiral Hart more submarines. In October 1941 he ordered that Division 15, commanded by Stuart Shadrick ("Sunshine") Murray, and Division 16, commanded by Joseph Anthony Connolly and composed in total of twelve *Salmons*,* be transferred in two contingents from Pearl Harbor to Manila. Known as Squadron Two, this expedition included the tender *Holland*, with Captain Walter Edward ("Red") Doyle aboard to relieve John Wilkes as Commander, Submarines Asiatic. For his chief of staff, Doyle chose James Fife, Jr., a teetotaler, strict disciplinarian, and longtime submariner who had commanded the fleet boat *Nautilus* and the Submarine School.

With the arrival of *Holland* and her submarine escort, the Asiatic submarine force swelled to twenty-nine submarines: six S-class, seven P-class, and twelve *Salmons*.†

Admiral Hart expected a Japanese attack at almost any hour. His staff was divided about what to do: remain in Manila Bay and fight from there or withdraw to the south. Hart, a feisty sailor who believed that MacArthur's newly arrived fighter planes and bombers would afford his naval units protection, preferred to remain in Manila Bay. His chief of staff—and the Navy Department—wanted him to withdraw to the south. Complying with Navy Department orders, Hart withdrew his surface units but, on his own initiative, made the decision to keep the twenty-nine submarines and the tenders *Canopus*, *Holland*, and *Otus*, a former merchant ship being converted for submarine duty, in Manila Bay.

The shifting of submarines to Manila again left the Pearl Harbor force seriously depleted. After the departure of Doyle and the twelve *Salmons* there remained two squadrons, Four and Six. Squadron Four,

---

* *Salmon, Seal, Skipjack, Snapper, Stingray, Sturgeon, Sargo, Saury, Spearfish, Sculpin, Sailfish,* and *Swordfish.*

† Division 21	Division 22	Division 201	Division 202	Division 203
Salmon	*Snapper*	S-36	*Seadragon*	*Permit*
Seal	*Stingray*	S-37	*Sealion*	*Perch*
Skipjack	*Sturgeon*	S-38	*Searaven*	*Pickerel*
Sargo	*Sculpin*	S-39	*Seawolf*	*Porpoise*
Saury	*Sailfish*	S-40		*Pike*
Spearfish	*Swordfish*	S-41		*Shark*
				Tarpon

PLANS IN THE FAR EAST

commanded by Freeland Allan Daubin, was made up of Division 42, commanded by Clifford Harris ("Stony") Roper and composed of six old V- boats,* and Division 43, commanded by Norman Seaton Ives, composed of three of the latest P-boats.† Squadron Six, commanded by Allan McCann, inventor of the rescue bell, with his flag in a new tender, *Pelias*, consisted of Division 61, commanded by Charles Dixon ("Shorty") Edmunds and composed of six new *Tambors*,‡ and Division 62, commanded by Forrest Marmaduke O'Leary and composed of six follow-on *Tambors*.§

In the fall of 1941, these Pearl Harbor submarines were commanded by Rear Admiral Thomas Withers, Jr., who had relieved Admiral Friedell. Withers, then fifty-five years old, was a soft-spoken, kindly officer who had qualified in submarines in World War I. Withers had commanded a division of K-boats and a division of S-boats, but his experience with fleet boats was limited. His chief of staff was Charles Wilkes ("Gin") Styer. Styer had placed *Cuttlefish* in commission and had commanded a division of *Salmons*.

On paper, Withers commanded twenty-one fleet boats. But in November 1941 only ten of them were actually in Pearl Harbor.ǁ Nevertheless, he worked hard to place this small force on a war footing. He ordered his submarines to practice deep diving. Up to then, submarines rarely descended to 100 feet. The new orders were to submerge to 100 feet on the first dive and go to test depth at least once during every trip to the operating areas. (Test depth was the so-called design depth, or depth considered absolutely safe. In official Acceptance Trials, and following major navy yard overhaul, all submarines were submerged to test depth to check for leaks and weaknesses. Such dives were considered an event. The test depth of the *Salmon-Tambor* class was 250 feet. However, under emergency conditions they could go much deeper.)

In addition, Withers hammered home the danger of aircraft, tak-

---

* *Argonaut, Nautilus, Narwhal, Dolphin, Cachalot,* and *Cuttlefish.*
† *Pompano, Pollack,* and *Plunger.*
‡ *Tambor, Triton, Thresher, Trout, Tautog,* and *Tuna.*
§ *Grenadier, Gar, Gudgeon, Grayling, Grampus,* and *Grayback.*
ǁ Five of the nine boats of Squadron Four—*Nautilus, Cuttlefish, Pompano, Plunger,* and *Pollack*—were at Mare Island, California, for overhaul and modernization. Six of the boats of Squadron Six—*Tuna, Gar, Grenadier, Grayling, Grampus, Grayback*—were also in the States, either in a navy yard for repairs or on shakedown cruises. That left Withers with the following fleet boats:
  Squadron Four: *Argonaut, Narwhal, Dolphin,* and *Cachalot.*
  Squadron Six: *Tambor, Tautog, Thresher, Triton, Trout,* and *Gudgeon* (in Hawaiian waters on shakedown).

ing his skippers aloft in airplanes to show that, under some circumstances, a submarine was clearly visible from the air while cruising at 125 feet. When some skippers expressed doubt, Withers got the planes to drop small "firecracker" bombs on the submarines. After that, "all doubts were answered." More than ever before, the sonar attack was emphasized over the periscope approach. The night surface attack then being used so effectively by Doenitz in the Atlantic was not adopted by the Pacific submarine force.

Although Admiral Doenitz was deploying his U-boats in wolf packs in the Atlantic, Withers—and most other submariners—opposed this concept also. Wolf-packing brought with it a built-in need for close and frequent communications between boats and headquarters. The codebreakers and RDF experts in the Atlantic were gathering valuable intelligence on the U-boats because of this constant "talking." This fate would not befall U.S. submarines. They would operate alone with strict radio silence.

Beginning in October, Withers began limited rehearsals of a portion of Rainbow Five. He sent two submarines, *Dolphin* and *Narwhal*, on a forty-five-day simulated patrol off Wake Island. These patrols provided useful information and experience on food and fresh-water consumption, the psychological effects of prolonged confinement, and some indication of how the machinery would hold up. After their return, Withers was convinced that submarine crews—provided sufficient water and food—could patrol for sixty days without cracking up and that after a three-week machinery refit the submarine would be ready for another patrol.

About the time Withers began these practice patrols, the submarine skippers—and a few select torpedo officers—were briefed for the first time about the secret Mark VI magnetic exploder. The boats going on patrol substituted the Mark VI for the Mark V contact exploder. Everyone was amazed to learn of this secret weapon and its potential. Yet there was very little information on how to adjust the device or repair it. The skippers were instructed to set the torpedo to run deep beneath the keels of the enemy; the exploder would take care of the rest. The submarine force placed blind faith in the Gun Club. No live tests of the torpedo were conducted.

In November, Withers sent four more boats on simulated war patrol. *Tambor* and *Triton* relieved *Narwhal* and *Dolphin* at Wake Island. *Argonaut* and *Trout* took up station at Midway. Withers did not rehearse one main feature of Rainbow Five, however, the stationing of submarines off key positions in the Japanese home islands. That voyage was considered too arduous, risky, and possibly provocative.

In Tokyo, Tojo, now Prime Minister, made the decision to widen the Asian war. Japanese forces would strike or invade the Philippines, Hong Kong, Singapore and the Malay Peninsula, Thailand, and Java, where there were rich deposits of oil. It was to be a "quick" war that would leave Japan in complete control of the land masses, islands, and seas of the entire Far East.

A key element in the plan was the total destruction of United States, British, and Dutch naval forces in the Pacific by the Japanese navy and land-based air power. The burden of responsibility for this task fell to the chief of the Japanese navy, Fleet Admiral Isoroku Yamamoto. Like many other Japanese naval officers, Yamamoto was opposed to widening the war and, for a period, actively talked against it. However, when he was finally overruled and ordered to come up with a plan, he set about the task with diligence and thoroughness.

The prime naval target was the U.S. Pacific Fleet, based at Pearl Harbor. Yamamoto, influenced by the views of Mahan—and the British—believed that it should be destroyed in a single decisive battle from which the United States could not recover in time to mount a counteroffensive in the Far East and would ultimately concede to Japan all that she had conquered. To accomplish this, most of Yamamoto's planners believed the fleet should be lured into the Far East, where land-based air power could assist in the knockout blow. However, Yamamoto conceived the bold—and risky—idea of a surprise attack on the fleet while it was anchored in Pearl Harbor. He held to this concept despite the objections of many of his planners, and by January 1941 he had worked out most of the details.

The Japanese navy at that time was superior in strength to the combined U.S. Pacific and Asiatic Fleets; it had 10 aircraft carriers, 10 battleships, 35 heavy and light cruisers, and 111 destroyers. The combined United States naval force numbered 3 aircraft carriers, 8 battleships (all at Pearl Harbor), 24 heavy and light cruisers, and 80 destroyers.

In addition, the Japanese navy had a substantial submarine force, comprising sixty boats in four broad categories: fourteen 800-ton "coastal" submarines, similar to but newer than the S-class; four minelayers, each capable of planting forty-two mines; twenty fleet boats, comparable in size and range to the *Salmon* class; and twenty-two "special" submarines, almost the size of *Narwhal-Nautilus*, most of them equipped to carry either a midget submarine or a reconnaissance aircraft. The coastal submarines were designated RO-class, all others I-class.

Of all the Japanese submarines, the most interesting—and original— were the five I-class equipped to carry the midget submarine. The midgets were about the size of the first U.S. A-class boats. Powered only by battery, they could travel for fifty minutes at a speed of 19 knots—or at a slower speed for a longer time. Each had a crew of two men and was armed with two torpedoes in separate tubes in the bow. Conceived and built in 1934, they were originally intended to be launched from surface craft, the seaplane tenders *Chitose* and *Chiyoda*, each of which could carry twelve midgets into battle. Two months before the Pearl Harbor attack, Yamamoto ordered the five I-class converted to take the midgets, which were to cruise right into Pearl Harbor during the attack and launch their torpedoes at U.S. battleships.

The main Japanese force that would attack Pearl Harbor left Japan in dribs and drabs about mid-November, assembling in Tankan Bay in the Kurile Islands. It consisted of six of the newest and largest aircraft carriers, carrying 423 combat planes; a screen of one light cruiser and nine destroyers, plus a support force of two battleships and two cruisers; a supply train of eight tankers; and three I-class fleet submarines which would patrol ahead as scouts. All during its absence from Japanese home waters, the strike force maintained absolute radio silence. On November 27, it left for Pearl Harbor.

The main submarine force, consisting of the five midget carriers plus twenty regular submarines, mostly fleet boats, did not assemble with the fleet in the Kuriles. It sailed independently from Kure and Yokosuka about November 19, stopping at Kwajalein to refuel, arriving off Pearl Harbor on the sixth of December. At midnight, the five I-class midget carriers launched their baby submarines, which were to be recovered the following evening after sunset at a prearranged rendezvous. The other twenty submarines took up station in an arc off the mouth of Pearl Harbor. Their mission was to sink any ships that might flee from the harbor.

Intercepted Mail

As war drew ever closer in the Far East, the navy's codebreaking organization expanded and broadened its operations.

In Washington, Laurence Safford's Negat unit grew to a team of about three hundred men and women. They read JN-25 and stood watch and watch with the army on the Purple machine, over which the Japanese were then sending a huge volume of traffic. In addition, Safford improved the security of U.S. Navy codes and oversaw the operations of his two outlying units, Hypo and Cast.

The output of the Purple machine, known as Magic, was translated by a team of Japanese-language specialists and then circulated to a limited group which included, among others, President Roosevelt, General Marshall, and Admiral Stark. Until about mid-1941, Admiral Kimmel also received, verbatim, most of the Magic output. However, in the fall this practice was abandoned for security reasons. If the Japanese broke the U.S. Navy code, they would see that the United States was reading Purple. Thereafter, Admiral Kimmel received only infrequent gists of Magic, with only occasional—and guarded— indications as to the source.

The output of JN-25, considered strictly navy business, was limited mostly to Admiral Stark and officers in ONI. Pertinent information on major Japanese fleet movements was also passed along to Hypo and Cast. These messages, known as Ultra (short for Ultra Secret), were in turn routed to Admiral Kimmel and Admiral Hart.

Until about mid-1941, Negat was also reading the Japanese merchant marine codes. An unfortunate incident closed down that source of information.

On May 28, 1941, the huge Japanese whaler *Nisshin Maru* put into San Francisco for refueling. Under terms of the U.S. Neutrality Act, the Customs Service routinely inspected all visiting foreign vessels for contraband, gun mounts, etc. The local representative of ONI, "with all the finesse of a drunken elephant," prodded a customs agent into seizing the secret codebooks from the whaler so he could copy them. The agent found the codebooks in the radio shack and—over the violent protests of the Japanese captain—whisked them ashore and made copies of them, returning the package to the Japanese captain in an "obviously opened condition."

Not long afterward, Radio Tokyo began broadcasting merchant

marine messages in a brand new code, which Negat could not read. Because Negat, Hypo, and Cast were already overtaxed, men and resources could not be spared to tackle the new merchant marine code. It would remain unreadable a long time.

In Pearl Harbor, Hypo now had a new boss, Joseph John Rochefort, a former enlisted man, not a Naval Academy graduate. Rochefort, a graduate of the Japanese language course in Tokyo, had been one of Safford's first—and most promising—recruits in the late 1920s. For sixteen years, he had alternated between codebreaking and sea duty. Of all the codebreakers, he was the most irascible and temperamental.

Rochefort supervised a team which included the navy's most talented codebreakers: Tom Dyer, Jack Holtwick, who had developed the Red machine, and Ham Wright. In addition, he fell heir to a half dozen superior Japanese-language experts, recently withdrawn from the embassy in Tokyo. Finally, he had Wilfred Jay ("Jasper") Holmes, a retired submariner recalled to active duty to prepare detailed charts and maps to keep track of all ship movements—including those of Imperial Japanese Navy vessels—in the Pacific Ocean.

Jasper Holmes was in many ways a remarkable naval officer. In addition to spending long years on various submarines, he had obtained a master's degree in Electrical Engineering. A gifted writer, in 1934 he won a Naval Institute essay prize. After retiring from the navy for physical disability (arthritis) in 1936, while commanding S-30 in Hawaii, he taught at the University of Hawaii and wrote submarine yarns as a sideline for the *Saturday Evening Post* under the pen name of Alec Hudson. These stories had encouraged many young naval officers to join the submarine force. Once again on active duty, his contribution to the force—carried forward in spite of old and new physical informities—would be enormous.

Because of the giveaway to Britain, Hypo had neither Purple machine nor JN-25 codebook. Pending the arrival of a codebook, Hypo was ordered to concentrate on the difficult and seldom-used Japanese Flag Officers' code. Rochefort, Dyer, Holtwick, and Wright devoted most of their efforts to this near-hopeless task, while some others at Hypo concentrated on minor codes that revealed little of interest. In fact, Hypo depended completely on Negat for information on Japanese intentions and fleet movements derived from the Purple machine, JN-25, and other sources. All the high-price talent at Hypo was, in effect, wasted.

In the Philippines, in Cast, the youngest and least experienced of the codebreaking units, there had also been changes. Created by Rosey Mason, who also served as Admiral Hart's overall intelligence officer, it was taken over by another Japanese linguist, Spencer August Carlson. After seeing Carlson in action, Mason became disenchanted and recruited a communications specialist, Rudolph Joseph Fabian, five years junior to Carlson, to head the outfit. Fabian's chief codebreaker was John Marion Lietwiler, assisted by Gill MacDonald Richardson. They presided over a staff of talented enlisted men.

By 1941, Cast had Purple and Red machines but no JN-25 codebooks. The primary output from Cast was Magic from the Purple machine, which was given to Admiral Hart and General MacArthur and a few others, along with information on Japanese fleet movements obtained from Negat. In midyear, when the language students were evacuated from Tokyo, Fabian also fell heir to some of these, notably Rufus Lackland Taylor. In September, Admiral Hart ordered Cast to shift its location from Cavite to a tunnel on Corregidor. All in all, MacArthur and Hart had much better intelligence—the complete output of the Purple machine—than did Admiral Kimmel in Pearl Harbor.

In the fall of 1941, the flow of Magic (and other decoded messages) indicated that Japan was preparing for a major war. It would later be argued through countless volumes of testimony in Congressional hearings that Washington was well aware of this attitude but never suspected it would begin with an attack on Pearl Harbor. However (as Kimmel would argue later), there were numerous messages pointing a finger at Pearl Harbor. On October 9 and 10 the codebreakers decoded and translated two dispatches from Japan to Japanese agents in Honolulu, ordering them to make precise reports on the exact location of U.S. naval vessels in Pearl Harbor based on a grid system furnished the agents. On November 15 a message was decoded and translated, ordering the agents to report these locations irregularly, but at least twice a week, and to take extraordinary security precautions. On November 18 Japan requested specific information on ships anchored in specific areas at Pearl Harbor.

None of these messages was sent along to Admiral Kimmel. He said later, "Knowledge of these . . . dispatches would have radically changed the estimate of the situation made by me and my staff. . . . Had they been supplied to the Hawaiian Commanders the result of the attack would have been far different, if indeed the attack would ever have been made." Those who saw the messages either failed to recognize their significance or felt that Kimmel had already been sufficiently warned.

While Admiral Yamamoto was gathering his fleet for the attack on Pearl Harbor, the Japanese government made a last-ditch diplomatic effort to cool tensions and gain concessions in the Far East. While the Japanese emissaries were in Washington, the codebreakers read their dispatches back to Tokyo on the Purple machine. Most of these expressed doubt that the mission would be successful. Tokyo set a deadline for breaking off the talks, November 25, then postponed and reset the deadline.

The one message that intrigued the codebreakers most was called the "winds" message, sent on November 19 to all embassies and consulates and intercepted, decoded, and translated as follows:

Regarding the broadcast of a special message in emergency. In case of emergency (cutting off of diplomatic relations) and the cutting off of international communications, the following warning will be added in the middle of the daily Japanese language short-wave news broadcast:

1. In case of Japan–U.S. relations in danger: "East wind, rain."
2. In case of Japan–USSR relations in danger: "North wind, cloudy."
3. In case of Japan–British relations in danger: "West wind, clear."
This signal will be given in the middle and at the end as a weather forecast and each sentence will be repeated twice. When this is heard please destroy all code papers, etc. This is as yet to be a completely secret arrangement. Forward as urgent intelligence.

All three codebreaking units, Negat, Hypo, and Cast, set up a twenty-four-hour watch on the Japanese news broadcasts. At Cast, a junior language officer fresh from Tokyo, Thomas Robert Mackie, while reading a long dull economic report from Radio Tokyo, came across the Chinese characters TOOFUUUU,* set off by double parentheses. In translation it meant "East wind, rain." He believed it was the message he had been detailed to find. Mackie took his translation to his superiors, but they gave it no credence. They argued that the

---

* Both Chinese and Japanese characters are sent in Morse code, using complicated combinations of our own letters.

signal would certainly be sent in Japanese (*Higashi no kaze ame*), not Chinese. No alert was sent to Washington.

Mackie was furious and brooded over the lapse for years. He believed that had an alert been sent, Washington might have more forcefully warned Admiral Kimmel of danger, thus preventing the Pearl Harbor attack.*

As the situation deteriorated diplomatically, Admiral Stark did, in fact, send two "war warnings" to Admirals Kimmel and Hart, but both pointed the finger at the Philippines and elsewhere—not Pearl Harbor. On November 24 he cabled:

CHANCES OF FAVORABLE OUTCOME OF NEGOTIATIONS WITH JAPAN VERY DOUBTFUL. THIS SITUATION, COUPLED WITH STATEMENTS OF JAPANESE GOVERNMENT AND MOVEMENTS THEIR NAVAL AND MILITARY FORCES, INDICATE IN OUR OPINION THAT A SURPRISE AGGRESSIVE MOVEMENT IN ANY DIRECTION INCLUDING ATTACK ON THE PHILIPPINES OR GUAM IS A POSSIBILITY.

Three days later, November 27, he sent another message:

THIS DISPATCH IS TO BE CONSIDERED A WAR WARNING. NEGOTIATIONS WITH JAPAN HAVE CEASED . . . AND AN AGGRESSIVE MOVE BY JAPAN IS EXPECTED WITHIN THE NEXT FEW DAYS . . . AGAINST EITHER THE PHILIPPINES, THAI OR KRA PENINSULA OR POSSIBLY BORNEO. EXECUTE APPROPRIATE DEFENSIVE DEPLOYMENT.

The codebreakers and radio intelligence experts endeavoring to keep track of the Japanese fleet were bedeviled by a number of obstacles. On November 1, the Japanese changed all the encoded call signs of ships, shore facilities, and administrative headquarters. (This change was made routinely about every six months.) Radio intelligence men worked feverishly to reidentify the 20,000 new calls. They were making some progress when, on December 1, the Japanese abruptly changed them again. This new switch made Joe Rochefort suspicious. He informed Admiral Kimmel, "The fact that service calls lasted only one month indicates an additional progressive step in preparing for active operations on a large scale."

There was another puzzle. After November 16, all the traffic be-

---

* Mackie was also perplexed that Fabian had not recruited the services of William Ritchie ("Ike") Wilson, who had been a language student in Tokyo with Mackie in 1938–41. Wilson, one of the best linguists the program produced, was then serving on the destroyer *Pope* in the Asiatic Fleet. (Later, *Pope* was sunk by the Japanese, and Wilson spent the war as a POW.)

tween Tokyo and the Japanese aircraft carriers ceased. In the past when the Japanese carriers stopped transmitting, it was usually an indication they were in home ports. Rochefort assumed this to be the case once more and so reported to Admiral Kimmel.

Then came the real blow. On December 1, the Japanese navy changed the keys to JN-25. Until the keys could be recovered, no one could read the code.

Joe Rochefort's log of December 2 stated, "Almost a complete blank of information on the carriers today." The next day he reported, "No information on submarines or carriers." The continued silence of the Japanese carriers was worrisome to Admiral Kimmel. He remarked to his staff intelligence officer, Edwin Thomas Layton, only half jokingly, "What, you don't know where the carriers are? Do you mean to say they could be rounding Diamond Head and you wouldn't know it?"

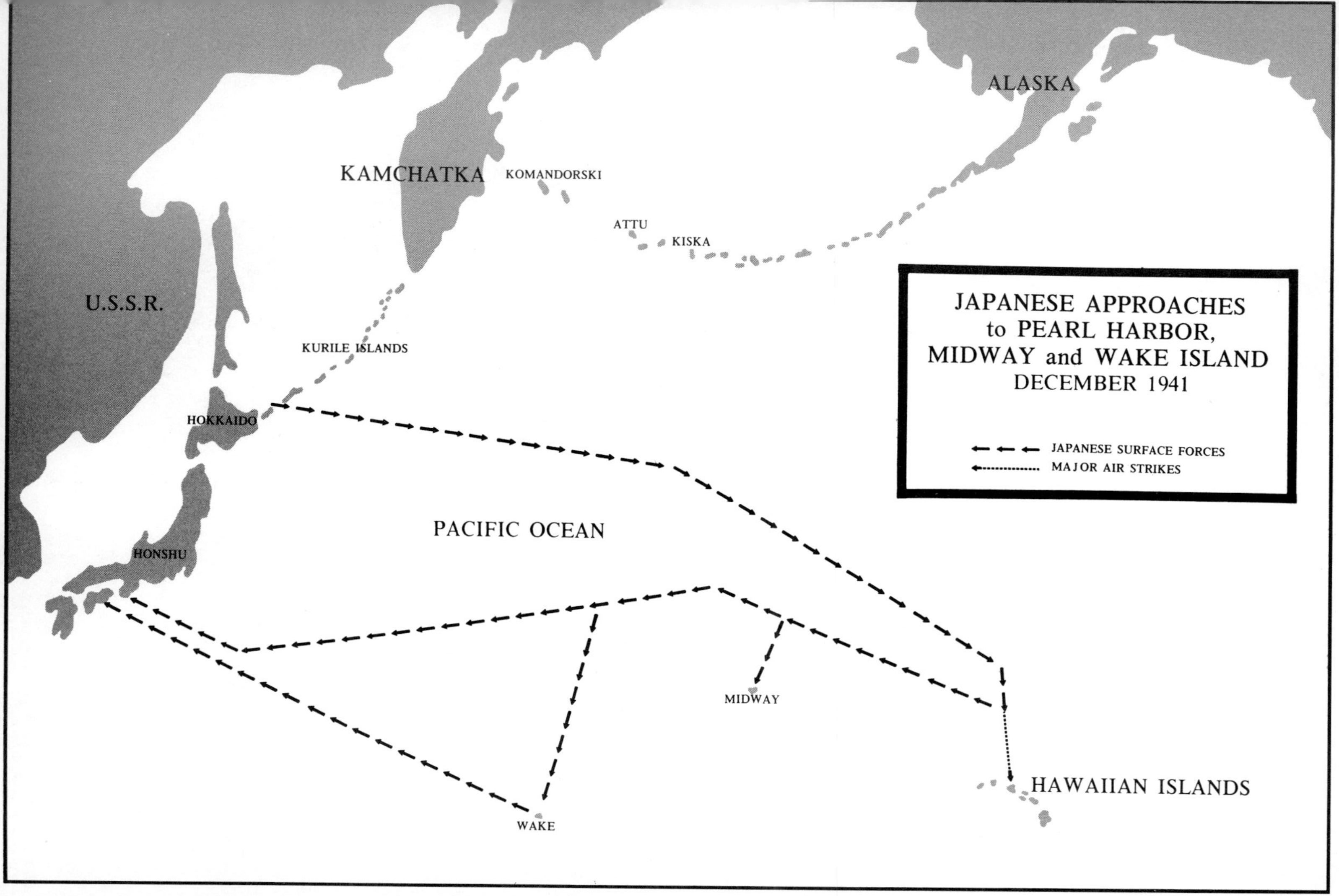
JAPANESE APPROACHES
to PEARL HARBOR,
MIDWAY and WAKE ISLAND
DECEMBER 1941
JAPANESE SURFACE FORCES
MAJOR AIR STRIKES
ALASKA
KAMCHATKA
KOMANDORSKI
ATTU
KISKA
U.S.S.R.
KURILE ISLANDS
HOKKAIDO
HONSHU
PACIFIC OCEAN
MIDWAY
WAKE
HAWAIIAN ISLANDS

Part II

2

Pearl Harbor, December 1941

The Japanese Attacks on Pearl Harbor and Midway

At about eight o'clock on the morning of December 7, Charles Warren Wilkins, commanding officer of the huge old V-class boat *Narwhal*, was lying in bed at his home on Black Point, Honolulu, reading a magazine. Wilkins, ironically nicknamed "Weary" because of his surplus of nervous energy, had just returned from one of Tommy Withers's "realistic" practice war patrols off Wake Island.

It had been the longest patrol to date, thirty days on station plus travel time. *Narwhal*, and the smaller V-boat *Dolphin*, patrolling with her, had remained submerged from dawn to dusk, with no contact with the friendly forces on the island. Since it was believed that a Japanese attack could begin with an assault on Wake, the boats had maintained a warlike footing, with live warheads in the tubes and the secret Mark VI magnetic exploder in the warheads. But they were not to shoot unless the enemy was unambiguously taking offensive action against the island.

During the patrol, both these old boats had developed serious matériel deficiencies. *Narwhal* had leaked oil in prodigious quantities —20,000 gallons. Wherever she went, she left a telltale oil slick visible from the air. Wilkins had been thankful when *Tambor* and *Triton* relieved *Narwhal* and *Dolphin* on patrol station. Now, back at Pearl Harbor, *Narwhal* was scheduled to go into the navy yard the following day to weld the rivets in the leaky oil tanks and receive other repairs.

The telephone rang. It was Virginia Rainer, wife of *Dolphin*'s skipper, Gordon Benbow ("Dizzy") Rainer. Mrs. Rainer said excitedly, "Weary! There's something going on at Pearl Harbor. Diz and I can hear noise and see flak."

Wilkins reassured her. It was probably just another interminable drill, probably the army. He told her not to worry and hung up, returning to his magazine. But a few minutes later, Mrs. Rainer called again. "It's real," she insisted. "The Japs are bombing Pearl Harbor. I heard it on the radio."

Wilkins jumped out of bed and put on a uniform. Tearing through Honolulu in his car, he no longer doubted; he could see and hear the Japanese planes and bombs. He was grateful for the alert from Virginia Rainer. Then a single thought fixed in his mind. The day before, the commanding officer of an oil barge had asked permission to moor alongside *Narwhal*. Wilkins had said yes. If a Japanese plane hit that oil barge, Wilkins thought, *Narwhal* would probably be blown sky high.

When the first bombs began to fall, the submarine force duty officer at Submarine Headquarters, located on the second floor of the supply building over the torpedo shop, got on the telephone. His first call—at 7:55—was to Withers's chief of staff, Gin Styer, who was at home. Styer immediately called Withers to inform him of the attack and then rushed to Pearl Harbor.

The duty officer next called Freeland Daubin, commanding Submarine Squadron Four and the Submarine Base. Daubin and Withers lived in a house at Makalapa—a new housing development on the hill behind Pearl Harbor—a few doors down from Admiral Kimmel. Daubin dressed hurriedly and raced out of the house, just as Kimmel's official car arrived from the base to pick up the admiral. Kimmel ran from his house, adjusting his tie. Daubin jumped on the running board of Kimmel's car and hung on for the five-minute drive to the sub base, where Kimmel had set up temporary headquarters down the hall from Withers. (Admiral Kimmel's flagship, the battleship *Pennsylvania*, was in drydock.)

On the tender *Pelias*, moored in a backwater at the sub base, Al McCann, commanding Submarine Squadron Six, was in his stateroom in his pajamas performing Gene Tunney exercises when the alert came. He raced to the bridge in his pajamas. What he saw, he said later, "turned my stomach upside down." It was "unbelievable . . . shabby . . . absurd." Battleship row—*California, Oklahoma, Maryland, West Virginia, Tennessee, Arizona,* and *Nevada*—was under severe air attack. The noise was deafening. There was smoke and flame all over the harbor.

Pelias was not yet fitted with her full complement of antiaircraft weapons. McCann did not fire those he had, lest his gunners hit friendly ships, but watched in disbelief as the bulk of the Pacific Fleet crumpled under the weight of the attack. For a while, he considered getting under way and standing out of the harbor, but his path was blocked by flaming and exploding ships. When a wave of torpedo planes came over, McCann was certain they were headed for *Pelias*, but they overflew the tender and attacked Hickam Field. (*Pelias*, having only arrived November 25, was not on the Japanese target list, and only one crewman was injured: he lost his footing and fell off the gangplank while craning for a better look at the holocaust.)

That morning there were four submarines in Pearl Harbor. In addition to Wilkins's *Narwhal* and Rainer's old *Dolphin*, there was one other old V-boat, *Cachalot*, and the new Tambor-class *Tautog*, just returned from a long patrol off Midway. *Narwhal, Dolphin,* and *Tautog* were moored at the sub base finger piers. *Cachalot* was in the navy yard undergoing overhaul.

When the first Japanese planes appeared, the crews on all four boats ran to battle stations, setting up .30- and .50-caliber machine guns. When a Japanese plane came low over *Tautog*, the duty officer, William Bernard ("Barney") Sieglaff, coolly directed enlisted gunners manning a .50-caliber machine gun. The tracers climbed upward into the fuselage, and the plane burst into flame and crashed into the water, 50 yards off the sub base piers. *Tautog* was the first U.S. submarine to destroy anything Japanese.

At the navy yard, gun crews on *Cachalot* hammered away at Japanese planes with machine guns but got no positive hits. During the battle, a Japanese plane headed for larger game strafed the boat, hitting Seaman Second Class G. A. Myers in the right lung. Myers was rushed to the sub base dispensary where, in time, he recovered. Myers was the first submarine force casualty of World War II and the only submarine casualty at Pearl Harbor.

Outside Pearl Harbor in nearby waters, that morning, were five submarines. One of these, *Gudgeon*, was at Lahaina Roads, a "sanctuary" for practice submarine operations. *Gudgeon*'s skipper was Elton Watters ("Joe") Grenfell. At 8 A.M. on December 7, *Gudgeon* was practicing recognition signals with navy patrol planes. When the planes came over, Grenfell flashed a signal with a blinker tube. They were working out a nonradio system whereby navy planes—in event of war—would not accidentally attack U.S. submarines.

While so engaged, *Gudgeon*'s radioman picked up a plain-language radio broadcast: AIR RAIDS ON PEARL HARBOR. THIS IS NOT DRILL.*

Upon hearing the message, Joe Grenfell said, "They're crazy." But after a few minutes in the radio shack he was satisfied it was the truth. He rushed topside to transmit the news to the patrol plane by blinker tube. It took him fifteen minutes. The planes returned to base.

Grenfell then radioed Tommy Withers for instructions. The admiral told him to remain where he was and submerge. There were three more fleet boats arriving from overhaul in the States at Mare Island: *Pompano*, *Pollack*, and *Plunger*. Grenfell should rendezvous with those old P-boats and await further orders. (Another boat, the old *Cuttlefish*, had departed Mare Island with the group but was forced to return after a mechanical failure.)

At about 8:40, the radioman on *Plunger* received the plain-language alert of the Japanese attack. *Plunger* and the other two had originally been scheduled to arrive off Pearl Harbor at 8 A.M. that morning, but they had been slowed by bad weather and were still about 125 miles northeast of Oahu. On board was SubDiv 43 commander Norman Ives.

When *Plunger*'s duty officer on the bridge, David Hayward McClintock, learned of the message, he gave orders to rig ship for dive. *Plunger*'s skipper, David Charles White, came to the bridge and moments later spotted what both men believed to be a Japanese scout

* Professors James H. and William M. Belote of the U.S. Naval Academy have established that "not" rather than "no" was the actual word transmitted.

THE JAPANESE ATTACKS ON PEARL HARBOR AND MIDWAY 101

plane coming from the direction of Pearl Harbor. After flashing the alarm to *Pompano* and *Pollack*, all three submarines submerged. But Ives was not convinced the aircraft was Japanese. He ordered White to surface. When *Plunger* came up, the plane roared in at 200 feet, strafing with machine guns but missing the mark. Then it continued on in a steady northerly course, visible for about ten minutes.

White assumed that the Japanese plane was returning to the enemy task force that had launched the attack on Pearl Harbor. Here was valuable information for the fleet there. But Ives still doubted the plane was Japanese. "That was probably just one of our planes trying to signal us," he told White. When White asked permission to send off a report, Ives said no. White begged but was still turned down. Why clutter up the airways, Ives said, when the Japanese were probably being annihilated?

Shortly after noon, Tommy Withers sent an order for *Plunger*, *Pollack*, and *Pompano* to proceed cautiously—and submerged—to Lahaina Roads to join up with Grenfell's *Gudgeon* and await further orders. When the three Ps arrived that evening there was a tense and garbled exchange of signals by flashlight. The plan worked out was that all four boats would form a submerged scouting line, going east and west. Instead, the three Ps steamed north-south while Grenfell in *Gudgeon* went east-west, many times crossing the paths of the other boats. "It's a miracle we didn't collide," Grenfell recalled.

The following morning the four boats—still waiting for orders—were seen by U.S. Army Air Corps planes, who reported the contact to Admiral Kimmel. Kimmel, believing the submarines to be Japanese, immediately ordered them bombed. Fortunately Withers heard about the order and stopped it at the last moment.

Fifty miles to the northwest of Pearl Harbor the *Tambor*-class *Thresher,* commanded by William Lovett Anderson, returning from her long patrol off Midway, had just picked up an old four-stack destroyer escort when word of the attack came over the radio. Anderson was in a hurry to reach port. That morning, on the surface, a heavy sea had swept the bridge, catching one of the lookouts in the periscope shears and hurling him to the deck. He was in critical condition with a broken leg and serious internal injuries.

Coming in, *Thresher* and the destroyer passed a U.S. task force steaming out to find the Japanese. The destroyer left *Thresher* to join the task force, while Anderson planned to submerge until dark and then make his way to port on the surface alone.

As *Thresher* was going under, however, she received a message from Tommy Withers not to separate from her escort under any circumstances. After breaking the encoded message, Anderson poked up his vertical antenna and radioed the escort to come back and meet *Thresher* at the point she submerged. After a while, Anderson saw a four-stack destroyer through the periscope, exactly at the rendezvous point. He surfaced.

It was not the escort but a different U.S. four-stacker. Thinking *Thresher* was a Japanese submarine, it turned bow on and commenced firing with the forward gun. With 5-inch shells falling all around and the destroyer coming in to ram, Anderson made a record dive to 250 feet and rigged for depth charge. As Anderson evaded, the destroyer thundered overhead but—fortunately—dropped no depth charges. Anderson's attempt to establish contact by sonar failed.

When the destroyer was gone, Anderson again poked up his radio antenna and informed Withers of the attack. Withers tried to set up new rendezvous with several other escorts, but they all fell through. That night, desperately trying to reach port so that the injured man could receive medical attention, Anderson threaded *Thresher* through a throng of friendly surface craft, twisting and dodging to avoid being sighted. "We had no friends," one of his junior officers recalled.

The following morning Withers informed *Thresher* that the Pearl Harbor entrance net would be opened at a specified time and to proceed homeward, but each time Anderson approached he was driven off by friendly forces. Withers, informed of this, then directed *Thresher* to a sanctuary where the boat was to remain submerged, but once there *Thresher* was driven down many times by friendly destroyers and bombed by U.S. Army Air Corps planes—the first of many U.S. submarines that would be attacked by friendly aircraft in the war. During this perilous waiting period, the injured man died. Shortly thereafter, an escort appeared. After exchanging recognition signals, she took the badly shaken *Thresher* into Pearl Harbor.

When the Japanese attacked Pearl Harbor, there were two fleet boats patrolling off Midway: *Trout*, commanded by Frank Wesley ("Mike") Fenno, Jr., and the ancient, clumsy V-class minelayer *Argonaut*, commanded by Stephen George Barchet, a former football star at the Naval Academy. Mike Fenno heard the radio alarm from Pearl

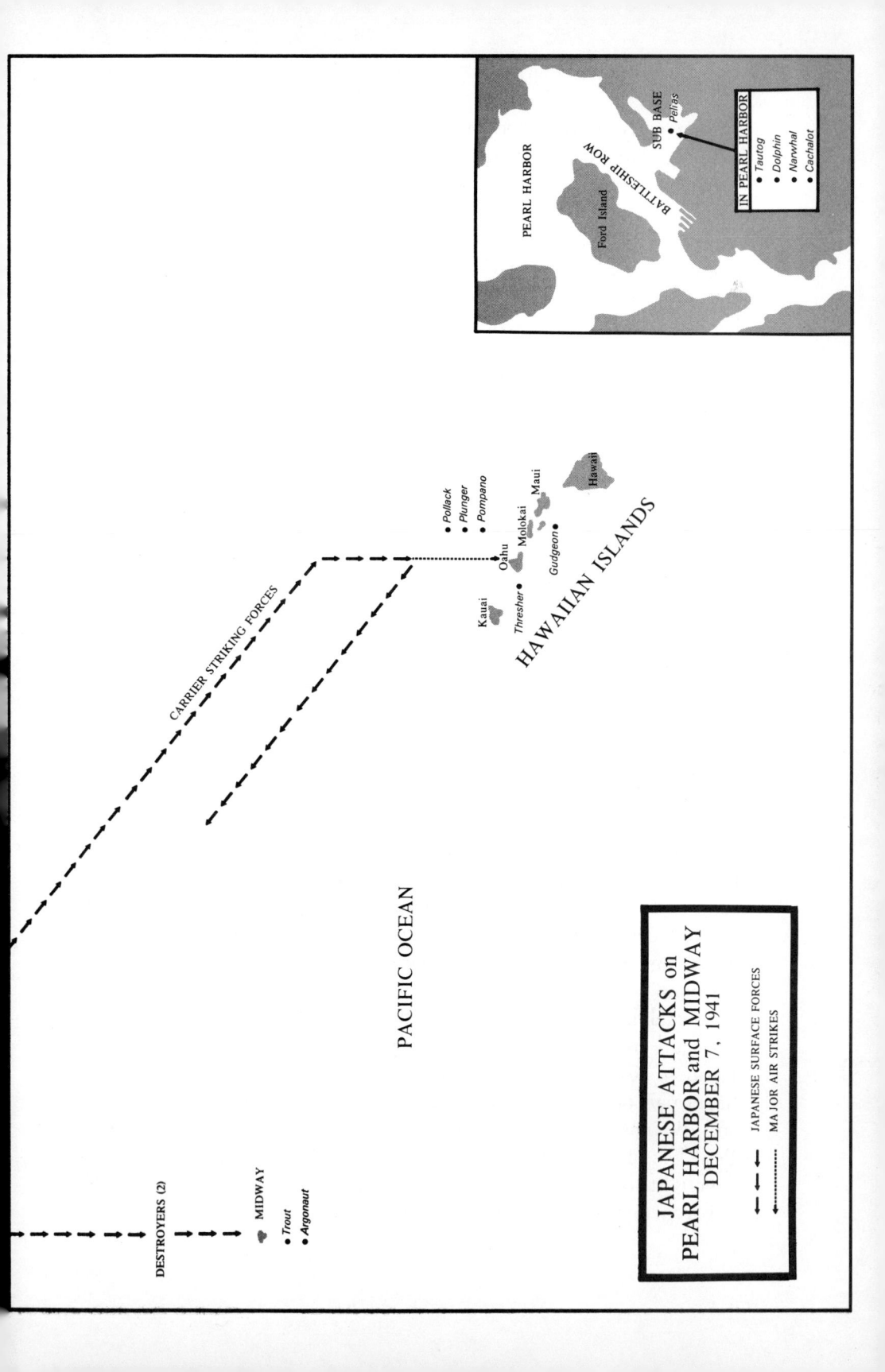

JAPANESE ATTACKS on PEARL HARBOR and MIDWAY
DECEMBER 7, 1941

→ → → JAPANESE SURFACE FORCES
· · · · MAJOR AIR STRIKES

IN PEARL HARBOR
- Tautog
- Dolphin
- Narwhal
- Cachalot

PEARL HARBOR
Ford Island
BATTLESHIP ROW
SUB BASE
· Pelias

PACIFIC OCEAN

CARRIER STRIKING FORCES

HAWAIIAN ISLANDS
- Kauai
- Oahu
- Thresher
- Pollack
- Plunger
- Pompano
- Molokai
- Maui
- Gudgeon
- Hawaii

DESTROYERS (2)
MIDWAY
- Trout
- Argonaut

Harbor early in the morning and went on full alert. Barchet was submerged and did not learn of the attack until he surfaced that night.

After sunset, Fenno and Barchet, both on the surface, discerned naval gunfire at Midway. They assumed—as did Kimmel, Withers, and the U.S. Marine commander on Midway—that the Japanese were landing a large invasion force. Midway had been reinforced by aircraft delivered by the carrier *Lexington* a day or so prior to the Pearl Harbor attack, yet without the fleet to come to its rescue it would easily be overwhelmed, thus providing the Japanese with a staging base for the invasion of Hawaii.

Of the two boats, *Argonaut* was closer to the "invasion force." In accordance with standard peacetime doctrine, Barchet decided to submerge for a sonar approach. He took *Argonaut* deep and went in cautiously.

Argonaut's crew was apprehensive. The night sonar attack was the safest of all possible courses open to Barchet. Yet—and yet and yet. This was not a drill, it was the real thing. The "invasion force" was bound to be screened by half a dozen cruisers and destroyers. Once Barchet fired a torpedo, they would counterattack and there would follow the absolute terror of exploding depth charges. A horrible, sudden death was not merely a possibility but a probability. It was ironic, indeed, that the first real approach of the war fell to clumsy, ancient *Argonaut*, designed not as an attack submarine but a minelayer.

The "invasion force" turned out to be two Japanese destroyers whose mission was to inflict whatever damage they could by shore bombardment. They may have detected *Argonaut*. One passed close by, hunting. Barchet went to 125 feet. Having completed the bombardment (causing severe damage), the Japanese withdrew before Barchet could get organized for another approach. Mike Fenno in *Trout* was too far away and on the wrong side of the atoll to get into position.

A week later, while running submerged at 200 feet, *Argonaut* made a second contact. As determined by sonar, there were three or four Japanese destroyers overhead. Barchet decided that discretion was the better part of valor. He remained deep, tracking the vessels on sonar, and did not attack. *Argonaut's* executive officer, William Schuyler Post, Jr., said to Barchet in a voice heavy with irony, "Don't you think we ought to at least put up the periscope and take a look, Captain?"

Barchet, who had not been pleased with Post as his exec, was

THE JAPANESE ATTACKS ON PEARL HARBOR AND MIDWAY

enraged by this taunt and later sent a letter to higher authority, recommending that Post be disqualified from submarines. Post was transferred to Al McCann's staff.

Far to westward, Guam, flanked by the heavily fortified Japanese islands of Saipan and Tinian, fell immediately. Then the Japanese moved against Wake, the tiny atoll lying about halfway between Midway and Guam. About twenty-four Japanese land-based bombers from the Marshalls pasted the island shortly after the Pearl Harbor attack.

Tambor and *Triton* were nearby on simulated war patrol during this first assault. *Tambor,* commanded by John Williams Murphy, Jr., was patrolling to the north of the island. *Triton,* commanded by Willis Ashford ("Pilly") Lent, patrolled to the south. Both submarines were submerged. They did not learn of the attack on Pearl—or Wake—until they surfaced that night. They saw fires raging on the island, but there was no way the submarines could be of help.

On the night of December 10, Pilly Lent, patrolling south of Wake, spotted a Japanese destroyer—or cruiser—on the horizon. At about that same time, the ship evidently spotted *Triton* and turned toward her, closing rapidly. Lent took *Triton* deep and commenced evasive tactics. But the Japanese dropped no depth charges. Lent remained deep, deciding, like Barchet, to make a sonar approach. From 120 feet he fired all four stern tubes, then went to 175 feet and ran away silently. After fifty-eight seconds, Lent heard "dull explosions." His crew cheered. On the first live shot of the war for Pearl Harbor submarines, Lent believed he had sunk his first target.

John Murphy on *Tambor* was shaken by the news of the attack on Pearl Harbor and Wake. So was his torpedo officer, Edward Dean Spruance, son of Admiral Raymond Ames Spruance, who commanded a cruiser force operating with the carrier *Enterprise.* On the night of December 11, Murphy saw three ships but was unable to gain a firing position. Next day he accidentally shot a torpedo at nothing. In the confusion, and apparently fearing a counterattack, Murphy shut down all machinery and drifted down to 310 feet, where he developed a leak in one of his sonar heads that was serious enough, he believed, to warrant returning to Pearl Harbor.

The defenders of Wake held on valiantly for a long time, but with no help from the submarine force. A few days after *Tambor* left, Pilly Lent also withdrew and returned to Pearl Harbor.

First Patrols to Empire Waters

When the dust and smoke cleared at Pearl Harbor, Tommy Withers found the submarine force had been lucky. The four boats in port, plus the tender *Pelias*, survived intact. (The oil barge had moved away from *Narwhal* before the attack, as Wilkins discovered much to his relief.) The five boats outside finally got in without serious damage from Japanese or U.S. forces. No bombs fell on the sub base itself. The torpedoes and magnetic exploders in storage were not touched. Nor—inexplicably—were the Pearl Harbor tank farms, containing 140 million gallons of diesel oil.

Six hours after the attack, Withers received a message from the Navy Department: EXECUTE UNRESTRICTED AIR AND SUBMARINE WARFARE AGAINST JAPAN. The London Submarine Agreement had been renounced by Washington.

There were no moral qualms at Pearl Harbor. "On the contrary," Weary Wilkins said later, "I was cheered by the order." Said Barney Sieglaff, duty officer on the *Tautog*, "After the carnage at Pearl Harbor—a sneak attack—who could have moral qualms about killing Japanese? Every ship they had, combat or merchant, was engaged in the war effort one way or the other."

In the hours following receipt of the message, Withers, Styer, Daubin, and McCann huddled in conference, drawing up strategy. McCann recalled, "It required a quick adjustment in thinking. Plan Orange was a dead issue. There would be no cruise to the Philippines for a decisive blow against the Japanese fleet. The submarine force was left on its own, to do what it could against the Japanese sea lines of communication. Fortunately the fleet boat was ideally suited for this new and completely unexpected mission."

Admiral Kimmel injected himself directly in the plan for deployment of the first Pearl Harbor submarines. Like many others, he was concerned that the Japanese fleet would return for a second strike, bringing along an invasion force. One theory had it that the Japanese fleet had put into bases in the Marshall Islands, 2,000 miles southwest of Pearl Harbor. From there, the theory went, the Japanese would mount the second assault on Hawaii and Midway. Kimmel ordered

FIRST PATROLS TO EMPIRE WATERS

Withers to send the majority of his submarines to reconnoiter the Marshall Islands and sink what they could find. The others would go to Empire waters, off the Japanese homeland islands.

After a quick survey, Withers determined that seven of the nine submarines at Pearl Harbor could be made ready for patrol within a few days. Four—Dizzy Rainer's *Dolphin*, William Anderson's *Thresher*, *Tautog*, commanded by Joseph Harris Willingham, and Lewis Smith Parks's *Pompano*—would go to the Marshalls. Three—Joe Grenfell's *Gudgeon*, Dave White's *Plunger*, and Stanley Page Moseley's *Pollack*—would go to Empire waters. The remaining two—Waldeman Nichlous Christensen's *Cachalot* and Wilkins's *Narwhal*—were held back for extensive repairs.

On December 11, four days after the attack, Grenfell's *Gudgeon*—still officially on shakedown status—loaded with food and fuel for the 3,400-mile voyage to Japan, got under way, escorted to sea by the destroyer *Litchfield*. Beyond the shambles of Pearl Harbor, on the high seas, at a predetermined point, *Litchfield* turned back, leaving *Gudgeon* to proceed on her own.

Joe Grenfell represented the first offensive strike against Imperial Japan by the U.S. Navy in World War II. In terms of his background and training, he was typical of the average fleet boat skipper in December 1941. Thirty-eight years old, a lieutenant commander wearing two and a half stripes on his sleeve, he received 25 percent extra pay for serving in submarines. (Naval aviators earned 50 percent extra pay, and later in the war submariners also made 50 percent extra.)

Grenfell had graduated from the Naval Academy in 1926.* After a mandatory two-year service in surface ships, he had volunteered for the six-month Submarine School at New London in 1928. After an extra-long tour on *R-4*, he had attended postgraduate school, obtaining a master's degree in Mechanical Engineering, then served two years on *Pickerel* during her commissioning (formal acceptance as a fleet unit), shakedown cruise (a 4,000-mile trip to the Amazon River), and exercises with the fleet in 1938 and 1939. After a shore tour in Wash-

---

* During peacetime, selection to command of submarines (and other vessels) was usually made by "class year"; at a certain period, all members of a certain Naval Academy class would (in the ordinary course of events) become eligible for command of an S-boat or a fleet boat, depending on seniority, and those qualified would move up to command more or less as a group. Of course, there were overlaps; it was not possible to work it as smoothly as the Bureau of Personnel might have wanted. In the year or so before the war, the classes of 1925, 1926, and 1927 had become eligible for command of fleet boats and moved up accordingly.

ington (Bureau of Ships), he had assumed command of *Gudgeon*, placing her in commission in April 1941.

As skipper of *Gudgeon*, Grenfell commanded a normal complement of four other Naval Academy graduates and fifty-five enlisted men—in all, a crew of about sixty. (In addition, on this cruise Grenfell carried two reserve officers for indoctrination purposes.) The second or executive officer was Hyland Benton ("Hap") Lyon, class of 1931. Usually the exec of a fleet boat was fully qualified for command, in case something happened to the skipper. As on surface ships, the exec played an important role in administration, being in charge of most paperwork, ordinary discipline, navigation, morale, and a hundred other day-to-day details. During attacks, he served as assistant approach officer. A good exec enabled his skipper to remain aloof from routine problems so that he could concentrate on the objective of the mission.

The other three regular officers on *Gudgeon* were Robert Edson ("Dusty") Dornin, class of 1935, Richard Marvin ("Dixie") Farrell, class of 1935, and Sigmund Albert Bobczynski, class of 1939. Dusty Dornin, a famous football player at Annapolis (many had entered the submarine service), was the fire control officer—the main torpedo data computer (TDC) operator. *Gudgeon* had not yet been in commission five months, but already Dornin, an extraordinarily able officer, had proved himself one of the best TDC operators in the submarine force. In practice, *Gudgeon* had "sunk" thirty-two out of thirty-three targets—a record. Dixie Farrell was the engineer and diving officer. Young Bobczynski, two and a half years out of the Academy, fresh from Submarine School, was "George"—the low man on the wardroom totem pole who took care of the commissary and other minor duties.

The fifty-five enlisted men, including half a dozen chief petty officers, were mostly experts, with long submarine experience.* First and foremost among them was the senior chief, who was called "chief of the boat." An important man (comparable to an army top sergeant), the chief of the boat generally held sway over all enlisted men and dealt with many of their administrative problems. During battle stations, he usually stood watch at the diving vents. In addition to the

---

* The chiefs on many submarines were quite old and conservative. Reported one submarine skipper, "The average age of my chiefs was up in the fifties, and I even retired my chief electrician during wartime at age sixty-five. I can assure you that at least half these chiefs had no other thought than that the war would soon be over and they would return home safely. They were extremely cautious and only interested in the most cautious operation of the submarine with the utmost safety."

FIRST PATROLS TO EMPIRE WATERS

chief of the boat, there was one yeoman (male secretary), one pharmacist's mate (inevitably "Doc"), and two black or Filipino stewards.* The rest of the crew were torpedomen, machinists, electricians, quartermasters (who helped with navigation and kept the logbooks), cooks, gunner's mates, and seamen and firemen just starting out.

Most hands except Grenfell stood watches—four hours on, eight hours off. The off-watch officers usually had many duties to perform. They slept in staterooms in the forward battery compartment (usually two men to a stateroom). The chiefs slept in a more private space (in the aft end of the forward battery compartment) than the other enlisted men, who slept in a crowded bunk space in the after battery compartment or in bunks rigged over the torpedo storage spaces in the forward and after torpedo rooms. When off watch, the enlisted men worked on machinery or "routined" torpedoes. They sometimes gathered in the crew's mess and passed a few free hours playing poker, cribbage, or acey-deucey or listening to the radio. In keeping with navy tradition, all hands drank gallons of weak coffee and ate hearty, wholesome meals, but, to a man, the whole crew worked very hard indeed.

Withers had told Grenfell to proceed with extreme caution; there might be Japanese submarines all along his route. No one knew what surprises the Japanese might produce. They might have radar or an antisubmarine weapon unknown to the U.S. Navy. The skippers were told that when they were within 500 miles of an enemy air base they were to remain submerged in daytime. At night, they were to run on one engine to conserve fuel. They were to husband their torpedoes, using only one or two against a merchant ship. In spite of what Ralph Christie had done to increase production, there was a critical shortage of submarine torpedoes at Pearl Harbor and no sign that the production facilities would soon catch up. "We can't shoot ourselves out of torpedoes," Withers had said.

All submarines had orders to maintain strict radio silence. If Withers had information or orders for his boats, he sent them messages over the nightly Fox schedules originating from Pearl Harbor. The submarine radio operators "guarded" (i.e., monitored) these broadcasts, watching for their own coded call sign. When it appeared in the long string of messages, they would copy it. The message

---

* Because of the widespread navy belief that blacks had superior night vision, many stewards also stood lookout watches.

would then be decoded by the communications officer or by other officers designated for this task. All messages were repeated three times. Very important messages were repeated on successive nights. Messages were numbered serially. If an operator missed a message because he was submerged when it was transmitted or for other reasons, he had orders to "open up" (i.e., break radio silence) at the earliest opportunity and request that it be repeated.

It took Grenfell about twenty days to reach the vicinity of Japan. It was a slow, tedious, monotonous voyage, carried out cautiously, as Withers had ordered. One officer came down with pneumonia and kept to his bunk for twenty days, until he was pronounced fit. Eight hundred miles off the coast of Japan, running submerged, Grenfell saw a few fishing boats. At about 10 A.M. on December 31, he picked up his first real target: the mast tops of what looked like a freighter. Remaining submerged, Grenfell tried to overtake for twenty-five minutes but could not get closer than 14,000 yards—about 7 nautical miles.*

Grenfell now proceeded with even more extreme caution. During daytime, he remained submerged at about 100 feet, coming up for periodic periscope observations but careful not to expose too much periscope. His sonar men listened carefully for the noise of other ships, especially enemy submarines. After dark, he surfaced to charge batteries. Four lookouts and the officer of the deck kept watch for enemy antisubmarine patrol planes. (They saw none.) Inside the hull, tension ran high. The experience was new and terrifying. "For the first time," recalled Grenfell later, "you realized that you could get killed. We were out there, all alone. Even a serious operational casualty, such as a battery fire, could land us in the hands of the Japanese."

There was another matter, somewhat delicate. In effect, Grenfell was breaking the London Submarine Agreement. Neither the United States nor Japan had publicly abrogated the rules of international warfare. If caught, Grenfell conceivably could be hanged as a pirate. To help him out in such an eventuality, he carried a paper signed by Withers, ordering him to wage unrestricted submarine warfare against Japan.

On January 2, after a voyage of twenty-one and a half days, Grenfell arrived on patrol station off Bungo Suido, the southern entrance to Japan's Inland Sea. He was astonished to find navigational beacons

---

* A nautical mile is about 800 feet longer than a statute mile.

ashore burning brightly and sampans cruising with running lights. On the afternoon of January 4 he sighted a small coastal freighter, closed to 2,600 yards, and fired two torpedoes. Both missed. "It had been the almost perfect approach," Grenfell recalled later. "Dusty Dornin almost wept."

It had long been clear to Joe Grenfell and Dusty Dornin that even with the help of the TDC the firing of torpedoes at an enemy ship would be a complex and difficult business. Now that they had tried it, they knew it for certain. Once the enemy had been sighted, it was not easy to maneuver into proper position with *Gudgeon*'s slow submerged speed. The enemy's range, speed, and "angle on the bow" (the relative bearing of the submarine to the enemy) all had to be estimated from quick periscope observations, during which time the skipper was also sweeping around the horizon, keeping an eye on enemy escorts and a sharp watch for aircraft. To obtain a fairly accurate range estimate, it was necessary to guess accurately the height of the mast of the target vessel, then extrapolate from the horizontal lines in the periscope cross hairs, using a slide rule or a device built in the periscope called a stadimeter.

In peacetime they had trained with high-speed fleet units, such as destroyers, with known masthead heights. Setting up on a slow-moving shallow-draft merchant ship whose masthead height could only be guessed at was a wholly different ball game. Where there were two or more ships involved, or ships were zigzagging, it was even more difficult. The skipper had to keep in his head at all times a picture of what was happening on the surface. The approach party had to guess the zigzag pattern, estimating when the zigs and zags would occur so the submarine did not set up in one place and then find itself far out in left field.

Then there was the question of torpedo "spreads"—how to space the firing of torpedoes to obtain hits. Under ideal circumstances, peacetime exercises had shown, it was best to fire three torpedoes: one forward of the bow, one at the middle of the target (MOT), and one astern. This spread compensated for errors in speed estimates or changes in target speed. If the target was moving faster than estimated, the torpedo fired forward of the bow would actually hit in the forward end of the ship, the MOT torpedo in the stern, with the torpedo aimed at the stern missing. If the target was moving slower than estimated, the one aimed forward of the bow would miss ahead, the MOT would hit in the bow, and the stern shot about the middle of the target. In sum: in a spread of three torpedoes, two would probably hit.

However, the orders from Withers had been not to fire three-torpedo spreads at merchant ships; one or two should suffice, he said. Grenfell and Dornin had to revise spread techniques, aiming torpedoes to hit. This, in turn, meant that the man on the periscope had to estimate with a high degree of accuracy not only the speed and range of the target but also its length.

All these observations, estimates, and calculations had to be carried out with efficiency and coolness under great stress. During the approach, the skipper had also to be thinking of his move immediately after firing, should an escort ship charge down the bubbles and vapor of the torpedo track. The diving officer in the control room had to maintain the boat in precise trim at periscope depth. An error could take the boat too deep to raise the periscope or bring it up so shallow that the periscope shears were exposed.

Although Grenfell had been positioned on what was thought to be the busiest sea lane in Japanese waters, five long days passed before he spotted another target. It was night, and *Gudgeon* was on the surface, charging batteries. Grenfell decided to remain there and make a night surface attack. From 2,500 yards, he fired three torpedoes. On the bridge, Grenfell felt the shock of an explosion. The sonarman reported a hit. Grenfell and Dornin were certain they had sunk a freighter of 5,000 tons.

The second boat to arrive in Japanese waters was Stan Moseley's *Pollack*. Leaving Pearl Harbor on December 13, *Pollack* followed *Gudgeon* westward, slowly and cautiously, arriving in her area at the mouth of Tokyo Bay about December 30 in foul weather. On New Year's Eve, after dark, Moseley made contact with a destroyer, dived, and fired two torpedoes. Both missed, a frustrating experience that led Moseley to take a dim view of the night periscope attack.

Thereafter, targets came thick and fast. On January 3, Moseley attacked a transport in daytime, firing only one torpedo (as Withers had suggested). It missed. On the night of January 5, while on the surface, he abandoned the conservative torpedo doctrine and let fly six torpedoes at a single transport. He heard explosions and was certain of a hit. On January 7, he made a day periscope attack on another freighter, firing two torpedoes which hit. On the night of January 9, in the same location, Moseley fired two bow and two stern torpedoes at another freighter. He was certain the ship sank. Later that same night, he fired *Pollack*'s last torpedo at a destroyer but missed.

Dave White in *Plunger* got off to a frustrating start. On his first dive after leaving Pearl Harbor, he found a serious leak in the pressure hull, a navy yard error undetected until then. With a weakness like that it would be suicidal to go on to Japan. With regret, he radioed Withers word of the casualty, requesting permission to return to Pearl Harbor for a quick fix. White got back to Pearl Harbor on December 13 and left again the following day.

After a long and tedious voyage, White reached his area, Kii Suido, the northern entrance to the Inland Sea, about January 4. In addition to her Mark VI magnetic exploders, *Plunger* carried another secret weapon into combat: a primitive radar set known as the SD. The SD was new. It had extremely limited range, 6 to 10 miles. It was "nondirectional," useful primarily for detecting enemy aircraft. Its mast could be poked up before the boat surfaced.

Like many submarine skippers, White was leery of the SD. In limited tests, he had found it temperamental and unreliable. It gave off a powerful signal which could be picked up by Japanese RDF stations. Unsparing use of the SD, White believed, was tantamount to breaking radio silence. It would make his presence known and reveal his exact location. The Japanese could send antisubmarine vessels or aircraft to attack him and route their shipping well clear of him. White preferred to depend on alert lookouts for spotting Japanese planes.

Shortly after White arrived on station, *Plunger* was seen by a Japanese destroyer which came on using powerful echo-ranging sonar—or "pinging." Hearing the pinging was a jolt. The submarine force had not known for certain, until now, that the Japanese had such gear. The Japanese not only had it, they knew how to use it. The destroyer found *Plunger* and unleashed twenty-four close depth charges. It was a vicious, determined attack, the first for both the hunter and the hunted in Empire waters. It jarred the boat and crew severely. White was thankful that he had put back into Pearl Harbor to repair the weakness in his hull. Had he not, *Plunger* might not have survived.

This unfriendly greeting instilled in White a healthy respect for Japanese antisubmarine operations. He patrolled cautiously off Kii

Suido and saw few targets worth a torpedo until January 18, when the watch picked up a big freighter via periscope. White went to battle stations and fired one torpedo. It hit. To make sure of a kill, White fired a second. He saw his target sink.

First Patrols to the Marshalls

The four boats assigned to reconnoiter the Marshalls were next to leave Pearl Harbor. Withers ordered the first one, Lew Parks's *Pompano*, to go by way of Wake Island and see what was going on. Parks, an amateur photographer, had arranged to have a device fitted to the periscope eyepiece to which he could attach a camera.* His exec was yet another famous football player from the Naval Academy, Slade Deville Cutter, a classmate of Dornin's, who had kicked a field goal to beat Army in 1934. *Pompano* got under way on December 18.

Proceeding westward, with navy surface forces fully briefed on her course, *Pompano* nearly came to grief at the hands of friendly aircraft anyway. On December 20, two days out of Pearl Harbor, a navy antisubmarine patrol plane roared out of the blue and dropped a bomb which fortunately exploded at a fair distance. The plane then radioed an "enemy submarine contact" to the carrier *Enterprise*, which was in the vicinity. At two o'clock that same afternoon, three *Enterprise* dive bombers found *Pompano* and delivered three well-placed bombs. The second bomb struck with a bone-shattering explosion, splitting seams and causing *Pompano*'s fuel oil tanks to leak. Parks shook the attackers—who finally realized he was friendly—and proceeded onward, trailing a telltale oil slick.

On reaching Wake Island, Parks nosed *Pompano* so close to the beach he could see Japanese troops manning gun emplacements. But he saw no sign of Japanese shipping. He continued on to the Marshalls, trailing oil, bedeviled by breakdowns in his temperamental H.O.R. diesel engines.

Soon Parks was raising his periscope close to the beaches in the Marshall Islands. He saw no sign of the Japanese fleet or a possible invasion force, but he found a huge Japanese transport, believed to be the 16,000-ton *Yawata*, anchored in the harbor at Wotje. Parks waited

---

* During peacetime, the technique of periscope photography had been retarded by a navy rule that prohibited cameras on board submarines for security reasons. Even so, Parks had a camera on board *Pompano* and had solved some of the complicated problems of focus, filtering, mounting brackets, and so forth.

patiently for *Yawata* to finish her business and get under way. On January 12, she came out, escorted by a few patrol craft. Assisted by Slade Cutter, Parks swung in, fired four torpedoes, and then went deep to avoid counterattack. Parks was certain of at least two hits. When he returned to periscope depth, he found his target with a heavy sea on the port beam, apparently settling. Parks reloaded torpedoes, preparing to polish her off. Before he could get into position, however, the sonar operator believed he heard "breaking-up noises"—crunching steel plates, rushing water, exploding boilers—and when Parks next raised the periscope there was no sign of *Yawata*. He was certain she had sunk.

Parks had seen the mast tops of other ships in Wotje Harbor, so he waited around to see what else might come out. Five days later, he saw a patrol craft, possibly a destroyer. He went to battle stations and fired two torpedoes. Both detonated prematurely, exploding shortly after leaving *Pompano*'s torpedo tubes, a terrifying jolt. The Japanese vessel turned and charged. Parks coolly made ready two more torpedoes, let the Japanese get within 1,000 yards, then fired both torpedoes "down the throat." The theory of a down-the-throat shot was that if the oncoming ship saw the torpedoes and turned—port or starboard—to avoid them, she would be hit broadside. However, the Japanese did not turn. The torpedoes missed and the ship countered, delivering a frightening but ineffectual depth-charging. Parks evaded and went deep.

All the while, fuel oil was steadily leaking from the tank ruptured by the *Enterprise*'s dive bombers. Parks remained on station as long as possible and then radioed Withers that he was running out of fuel. Withers authorized a return to Pearl Harbor.

The second boat assigned to the Marshalls was old *Dolphin*, commanded by Dizzy Rainer. "In my opinion," submarine skipper Royal Lawrence Rutter, who watched her leave, said later, "she should never have been sent on patrol without an overhaul, which she had not had for six months. She had too many deficiencies." Rainer departed on Christmas Eve.

Reaching the Marshalls, Rainer poked into Arno, Maloelap, Wotje, Jaluit, and Kwajalein, often coming within 500 yards of the beaches. He noticed more traffic at Kwajalein and reported that fact to Withers, confirming the belief that Kwajalein was the principal Japanese base in the Marshalls.

Dizzy Rainer discovered, as did the other skippers, that the psychological strain of making a war patrol was much greater than suspected from peacetime exercises. It was, in fact, nearly overwhelming. The safety of the ship and crew depended almost entirely on the judgment and acuity of the captain, and one mistake could be the last. It required cool nerves and limitless stamina to bear it, week in and week out, with sleep constantly interrupted by reports from the bridge, periscope, sonar, and radio watches. On top of this, Rainer had additional problems: during this first wartime patrol, he counted seventeen major and eighteen minor mechanical failures.

Rainer collapsed under the strain, suffering what was then called a "nervous breakdown." His exec, Bernard Ambrose ("Chick") Clarey, nine years junior to Rainer, informally took command of *Dolphin* for the remainder of the patrol.

On January 24, one month after leaving Pearl Harbor, *Dolphin* sent a message to Withers: RADIO TRUNK IS FLOODED AND USING JURY RIG ANTENNA. VESSEL IS UNABLE TO CARRY OUT ORDERS HAVING REACHED LIMIT OF MATERIEL ENDURANCE. ATTEMPTING TO MAKE REPAIRS. Upon receipt of this message, Withers ordered *Dolphin* back to Pearl Harbor.

Joe Willingham, commanding *Tautog*, got under way for the Marshalls the day after Christmas. On January 9, he reported no enemy activity at Rongelop, Bat, Wotho, and Bikini. On January 11, Willingham saw three Japanese submarines going into Kwajalein, but they disappeared in a rainsquall before he could set up and shoot. On January 13, he attacked a small minelayer, firing three torpedoes. He missed and received a depth-charging. Bedeviled by fogging periscopes and a critical shortage of fresh water, Willingham also cut his first patrol short.

The fourth and final boat to put out for the Marshalls was *Thresher*, commanded by William Anderson. Anderson left on December 30, scouted Majuro atoll, pushed far westward to Truk, and thence up to the Marianas, where he attacked a large freighter at Guam. He fired six torpedoes. Five missed, one hit. Anderson believed the ship had sunk. On the way home, two days out of Pearl Harbor, *Thresher* was bombed by friendly aircraft for the second time since the war started.

The Sinking of *I-173*

While these boats were out on patrol, the codebreakers worked obsessively. Joseph Rochefort at Hypo felt a personal responsibility for the Pearl Harbor disaster. He said later, "We failed to forecast the attack. . . . I failed Admiral Kimmel. . . . I had not done my job. Many, many of my friends were killed at Pearl Harbor."

Rochefort placed Hypo on a twenty-four-hour war footing. Together with Dyer, Wright, Holmes, and the others he rarely got home, sustained by pep pills kept in a bucket on Dyer's desk. On orders from Washington, Hypo abandoned the fruitless work on the seldom-used Japanese Flag Officers' code and concentrated on the much-used JN-25. Dyer's IBM cards whirred away, falling into slots, providing clues. Rochefort, wearing a nonregulation maroon smoking jacket and bedroom slippers (it was cold in the basement quarters), alternately paced and shuffled through the hundreds of incomplete messages piled in great disarray on his desk.

The codebreakers made substantial progress. The keys to JN-25 were recovered. On December 15, the JN-25 codebooks, lost in transit from Washington, turned up at Hypo. By December 20, using all the techniques of communications intelligence—interception, RDF, call sign analysis, traffic analysis, and cryptanalysis—together with Joe Rochefort's incredible "sixth sense," the Hypo group regained their contact with portions of the Japanese fleet blacked out since before Pearl Harbor.

Rochefort and his team gave high priority to tracking the movement of Japanese submarines. This proved to be easier than it seemed at first glance. Japanese submariners were irresponsibly chatty, communicating almost daily to their commanders or home base, in a code that was not difficult to break. They were ordered about by the Japanese submarine commanders, with specific departure and arrival dates, speed of advance, tracks, and "noon positions" to be adhered to. Departing from an assigned area, the submarines often—and stupidly—lobbed a few shells from their deck guns into islands, positively revealing their positions.

A case in point was the three Japanese submarines patrolling off the west coast of the United States. On departure, they fired a few shells into a refinery near Los Angeles. Thus alerted, Joe Rochefort and Jasper Holmes, together with radio intelligence experts Thomas A.

Huckins and Jack Williams, got on the scent. Employing the imperfect RDF gear, they roughly followed the three submarines, intercepting their frequent transmissions as they proceeded back toward their base in Kwajalein on a great circle course. On the night of January 25, the three submarines passed Midway Island, where they paused to fire a few shells.

Alerted by this bon voyage gesture, Rochefort and Holmes plotted their great circle course from Midway to Kwajalein and determined their speed of advance, based on previous observation. It became clear that Joe Grenfell in *Gudgeon*, returning from Japan, was almost in their path. Holmes contacted Withers in guarded language, and soon a coded dispatch was on its way to Grenfell, ordering him to lie in wait for the Japanese submarines.

On January 27, Grenfell remained submerged exactly on the projected point of interception. At 9 A.M., Grenfell's exec, Hap Lyon, was manning the periscope. Sure enough, right on schedule, he spotted a Japanese submarine. "It was coming along, fat, dumb, and happy," Grenfell said later. "The boat was not even zigzagging. The men were lounging on the upper deck, sunbathing and smoking."

Grenfell went to battle stations and fired three torpedoes from the bow tubes. Upon the exit of this great weight forward, the diving officer momentarily lost control. He overcorrected and *Gudgeon* nosed down, dunking her periscope, leaving Grenfell blind. However, at eighty-one seconds, Grenfell thought he heard a dull explosion. When *Gudgeon* got back to periscope depth, there was no submarine in sight and no propeller sounds on sonar.

Had they hit it? Dusty Dornin and Dixie Farrell were doubtful. "I don't think the torpedoes exploded," Dornin said later. "What I think happened was they either saw the torpedo wakes or the torpedoes dudded against the side and they panicked and dived with the hatches open and flooded the boat." Grenfell did not report the submarine as sunk, merely "damaged."

Rochefort and Holmes knew otherwise. After that morning one of the three Japanese submarines, *I-173*, no longer came on the air to chat. It disappeared from radio traffic forever, proof to Rochefort and Holmes, at least, that it was sunk.

I-173 was the first major Japanese man-of-war sunk in World War II [*] and the first vessel to go down as a direct result of radio intelligence. For the remainder of the war, the codebreakers achieved a high

---
[*] Two midget subs had been sunk during the Pearl Harbor attack.

degree of success in tracking the movements of Japanese submarines. The intelligence thus gained enabled naval commanders to route their forces around Japanese submarines and to make many kills. For this reason and others, the Japanese submarine force was almost completely ineffectual.

Results of the First Patrols

One by one, the first eleven boats—the four at Midway and Wake, the seven that left Pearl Harbor—returned to Pearl Harbor. In accordance with procedures developed by Withers in peacetime, the regular crews turned the boats over on docking to relief crews, who would make the necessary repairs while the regular crews rested. In the interim, Withers had rented the plush Royal Hawaiian Hotel on Waikiki Beach for a rest camp.

On return from patrol, each skipper was required to turn in a patrol report containing a day-by-day log, recounting the highlights of the patrol and including special sections for detailed analyses of torpedo attacks, ship and aircraft contacts, matériel failures, and other data. These reports were forwarded in turn to the division commanders, the squadron commander, and Withers. The division and squadron commanders and Withers attached comments to the reports—called "endorsements," whether approving or condemning—summarizing the patrol and its results, with judgments about the way the patrol was conducted, particularly the attacks against enemy ships. The reports, together with the endorsements, were then reproduced and distributed to boats preparing for patrol, to higher headquarters, and to Washington. These endorsements became the principal policy-making documents for the submarine force.

The endorsements also contained a section dealing with damage inflicted on the enemy: ships sunk, ships damaged. These scores were arrived at after detailed personal interviews with the skipper and his senior officers and consultations with Jasper Holmes, at Hypo, who frequently had information from attacked Japanese vessels that reported the results by radio.

The first endorsements handed down by Withers and his staff came as an unpleasant surprise to many submarine skippers, amounting, as they did, to a complete reversal of peacetime training policies. Steve Barchet in *Argonaut* was criticized for making a night sonar approach on the Japanese destroyer at Midway. His division commander believed he should have made a night periscope attack, since the moon was bright and the visibility good. Withers went a step further, suggesting that Barchet might have made a night surface attack, such as the Germans were finding so successful against Allied convoys in the Atlantic. Pilly Lent in *Triton* was upbraided in much the same language. His squadron commander, Al McCann, wrote that Lent should have made a night periscope attack against the destroyer at Wake Island rather than a sonar attack. He further criticized Lent for his tendency to dive "immediately upon seeing or hearing anything." Lent was not credited with sinking—or even damaging—the destroyer. Like Withers, McCann urged skippers to adopt the night surface attack.

Two of the three skippers who patrolled to Empire waters also received a jolt. Although Withers had instructed them to proceed at one-engine speed and submerge when they were within 500 miles of enemy airbases, he carped about the extreme length of time it took to reach station and return. "With efficient lookouts," Withers wrote in the endorsements to Joe Grenfell's report, "more surface cruising could have been done, reducing the terrific overhead in time, a great part of which should have been spent on station." Withers also criticized Grenfell for remaining submerged each day until 9 P.M., stating that *Gudgeon* should have surfaced immediately after dark. Dave White in *Plunger* was knocked for diving when he saw the destroyer that worked him over. Withers believed that White should have made a night surface attack on the destroyer. These criticisms, too, amounted to a turnabout in policy.

Both Grenfell and White were rapped for being profligate with torpedoes. Grenfell had fired two torpedoes at the small freighter on January 4; Withers thought one would have been sufficient. On the January 9 attack on the 5,000-ton freighter, Grenfell had fired three torpedoes. This was "excessive," Withers wrote. "Until the supply of torpedoes is augmented, it is essential to conserve torpedoes for more appropriate targets." He was critical of Dave White for firing a second torpedo at his big freighter on January 18 after the first was seen to hit.

Withers could be forgiven for his concern over torpedo expenditure. There were only 101 reserve torpedoes left in Pearl Harbor. According to the prewar production schedules, he was to receive 192 more by July—about 36 a month. However, his quota had recently been cut to 24 a month. At the rate his boats were expending torpedoes, he would

RESULTS OF THE FIRST PATROLS

need more than 500 to reach July. There was no way the production rate could be drastically increased to meet this demand. Unless his skippers were more conservative, Pearl Harbor would soon run out of torpedoes.

Only Stan Moseley in *Pollack*, who believed he had sunk three ships on his patrol, escaped criticism. His report was extremely brief and exceptionally "modest." His division commander, Norman Ives, wrote, "Getting the Commanding Officer to admit anything that is to his credit is almost as difficult as drawing blood from a turnip."

Withers was otherwise more generous in the actual scorekeeping for these first three Empire patrols. Joe Grenfell received credit for the freighter and the submarine. Moseley was credited with all three of his ships. White received credit for the one ship he claimed.

After the war these credits were found to be wide of the mark through the researches of JANAC, the teams of the Joint Army-Navy Assessment Committee which were sent into Japan to compile, as accurately as possible, Japanese merchant shipping and man-of-war losses from Japanese sources. JANAC also made use of wartime Ultras on record—the intercepts of Japanese messages reporting U.S. submarine attacks and results. In nearly all cases postwar figures reduced claims credited by submarine force commanders. The first three Empire patrols were fairly typical in this respect. White's ship was confirmed. Grenfell's submarine was confirmed but the freighter was disallowed. Moseley's score was cut from three freighters to two. In sum, the three skippers claimed six ships for about 30,000 tons; the JANAC credit was four ships for about 15,000 tons.

Withers also faulted three of the four skippers patrolling the Marshalls. Willingham in *Tautog* was criticized for firing three torpedoes at the small minelayer. Rainer in *Dolphin* was reprimanded for submitting an overly vague patrol report and for not detailing the matériel deficiencies of his ship. "The patrol of *Dolphin*," Withers wrote, "was a series of matériel casualties, many of which were due to the age of the vessel. After talking to the Commanding Officer, I do not feel that the report is a true reflection of the condition of the ship. It does require a lot of work." Anderson in *Thresher* received a stiff blast from his squadron commander, Al McCann: "The percentage of time utilized in productive effort was all too low." He criticized Anderson for being too quick to dive on night contacts, for firing six torpedoes at the freighter off Guam, and for not carrying out orders to reconnoiter Saipan.

These four skippers were also credited with the sinkings they claimed. Lewis Parks received credit for the huge transport *Yawata* believed sunk at Wotje; Anderson got credit for the 4,500-ton freighter believed sunk off Guam. However, neither of these sinkings was credited by JANAC. If the torpedoes had hit and the ships were damaged, the Japanese evidently towed them to port and repaired them. None of the four boats going to the Marshalls actually sank a ship.

Although the overall results turned in by the seven boats going on patrol following the Pearl Harbor attack were disappointing—a total of eight ships credited, later reduced to four—Withers was liberal with awards. Six of the seven skippers received the navy's highest decoration short of the Congressional Medal of Honor, the Navy Cross.* (The seventh, Dizzy Rainer on *Dolphin*, received no award. He was relieved of command and returned to the States, where he wound up in a mental institution and, in 1943, retired from the navy.)

On their return, five of the eleven submarines that patrolled in December and January from Pearl Harbor had to be sent to the navy yard for extensive overhaul: *Argonaut, Dolphin, Plunger, Pompano,* and *Tautog*. While in drydock, *Plunger*'s supporting blocks slipped and she rolled to starboard 60 degrees, smashing her periscopes and shears. The damage was so severe she was out of action for the next four months. With these boats deleted from the ready list, Withers's force was critically reduced in strength.

The Japanese Attack on Wake Island

Measured against the catastrophe that befell the U.S. Navy at Pearl Harbor, the errors and failures of the Pacific Fleet submarine force during the early days of the war were small. The gravest, perhaps, was the failure to help save Wake Island.

---

* These medals for valor in combat could mean much more than a mere ribbon to wear on the left breast beneath the gold dolphin insignia that showed an officer was qualified in submarines. When it came time for selection to the next higher rank, a Navy Cross gave a man a leg up on his competitors. Equally important, for years there had been a law on the books known as the "tombstone promotion." Under its terms, an officer who received a decoration for valor could retire at the next higher rank and receive more retirement pay. In the normal course of events, all these men would be selected for the rank of captain. Those who failed to be selected for rear admiral could nevertheless, under terms of the tombstone law, retire as rear admirals. For those planning a second career (in business, for example), the title "Admiral," although honorary, was more important than "Captain." It was also important to those who had social ambitions in retired life.

THE JAPANESE ATTACK ON WAKE ISLAND 123

Joe Rochefort and the Hypo unit had developed sound radio intelligence on Japanese fleet movements in and around Wake. The initial invasion force consisted of a light cruiser, six destroyers, and two transports, embarking 500 men. After being repulsed on December 11, the Japanese brought up additional ships from the force that had attacked Pearl Harbor. These included two aircraft carriers, *Soryu* and *Hiryu*; two cruisers, *Tone* and *Chikuma*; and two more destroyers, *Tanikaze* and *Urakaze*. Had Pilly Lent in *Triton* and John Murphy in *Tambor* been furnished this intelligence and patrolled Wake more aggressively, they might have inflicted damage on the invasion force.

In addition, Admiral Withers could have sent more submarines to the island. On the way to Empire waters, *Gudgeon, Pollack*, and *Plunger* passed close to Wake at about the time the fierce and final fight was taking place. With a simple radio order, Withers could have diverted them to the scene, reinforcing *Triton* and *Tambor*. In addition, *Trout* and *Argonaut* could have been shifted from Midway. Four, five, six, or seven fleet submarines patrolling aggressively at Wake might have seriously delayed or even stopped the invasion. Some might have got a shot at the two Japanese carriers. At the very least, six or seven submarines could have evacuated the 350 stout-hearted defenders. Apparently no thought was ever given this idea.

In defense of Withers, it should be pointed out that at this point in Pearl Harbor history all was mostly confusion and despair. Admiral Kimmel had been recalled to Washington to face the first of an endless series of committees and courts inquiring into the facts about Pearl Harbor—to become Washington's scapegoat. Admiral William Satterlee Pye, a battleship force commander, had taken temporary charge of what was left of the Pacific Fleet. Before his departure, Admiral Kimmel had formed three task forces grouped around the carriers *Lexington, Saratoga,* and *Enterprise. Lexington* was sent toward the Gilbert Islands; *Enterprise* went out to mill around Midway; *Saratoga* headed for Wake. When Pye took temporary command, he recalled these carrier forces to Pearl Harbor. All might have concentrated at Wake and saved the island. Instead, Pye avoided a fight. This episode, Jasper Holmes wrote, "not 7 December, was the nadir of the Navy."

The second error was in sending four submarines to the Marshall Islands to search for the Japanese fleet or invasion forces. These boats could have been more profitably employed in Empire waters. With the intelligence Hypo had developed, it was clear that those Japanese forces not still at Wake Island had returned to the Empire. Roche-

INVASION of WAKE ISLAND
DECEMBER 23, 1941

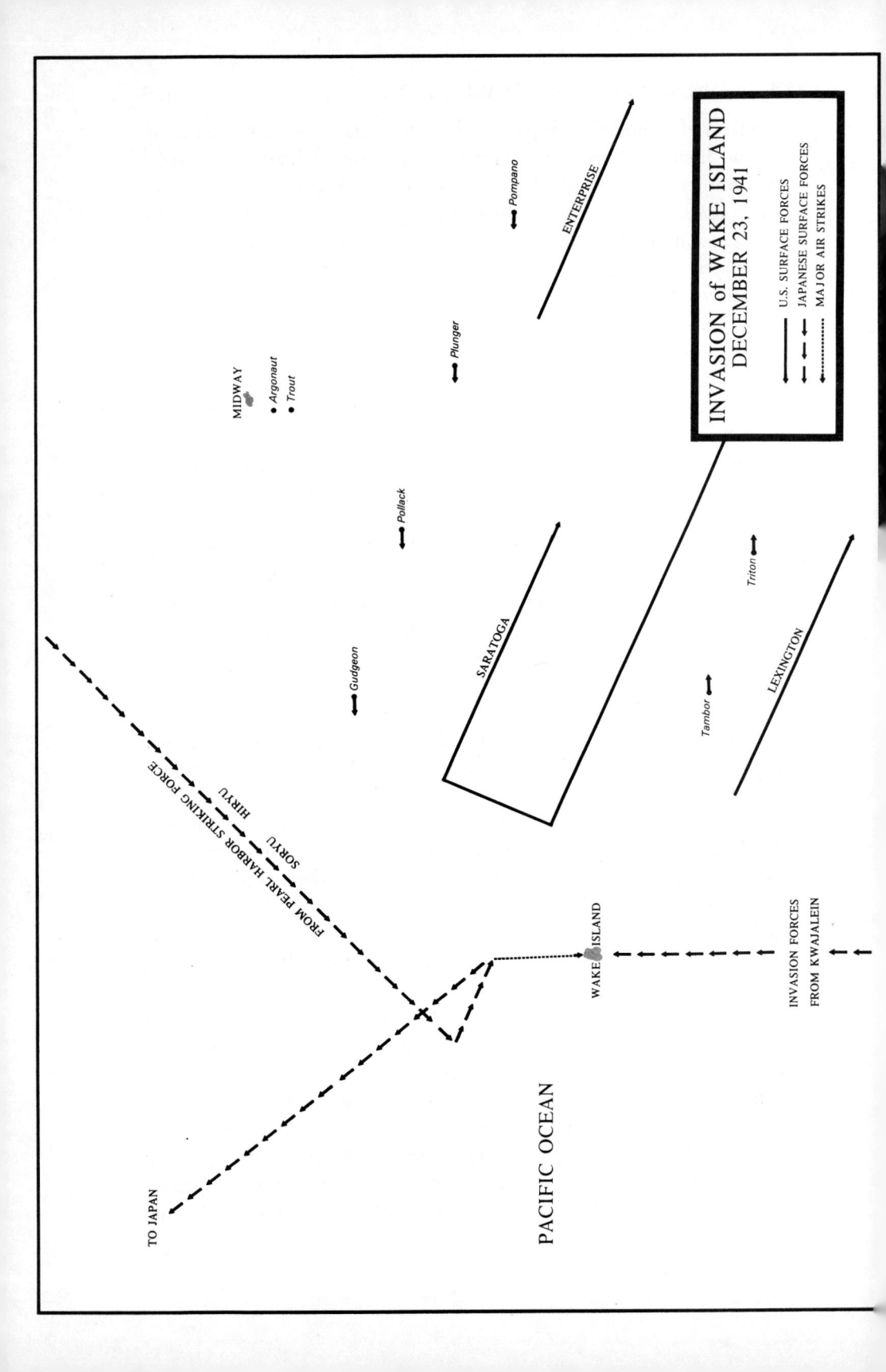

U.S. SURFACE FORCES
JAPANESE SURFACE FORCES
MAJOR AIR STRIKES

fort and Holmes knew in advance that these four submarines would be going on a wild goose chase. However, no one was yet ready to place great confidence in the codebreakers. They had failed to warn of Pearl Harbor. It could happen again.

The other errors could be laid to faulty peacetime concepts and training. In addition to the overstress on the sonar approach and aircraft detection—quickly reversed—perhaps the gravest was the failure to develop wolf-pack tactics and methods of communicating between wolf-packing submarines. Had this been done—or at least tried—the first three boats going to Empire waters could have operated as a mutually supporting pack. Time would prove that wolf-packing was not nearly so dangerous as believed and produced better results. It increased area coverage, brought greater firepower to bear on a given Japanese convoy or fleet unit, and befuddled antisubmarine vessels. It also worked to increase the aggressiveness of submarine skippers. A skipper operating alone could be as cautious as he pleased, avoiding the enemy altogether if he were of that mind. A member of a wolf pack would find it difficult to avoid a fight when his packmates were attacking and exposing themselves to danger. However, it would be a long time before the submarine force even considered wolf-packing.

In the wake of the Pearl Harbor disaster, President Roosevelt made sweeping changes in the navy high command. When word of these changes reached the submarine force, there were cheers. The key people, it seemed, were all submariners.

First, and most important, Roosevelt named Admiral Ernest Joseph King, Jr., to the post of Commander in Chief, United States Fleet, and Chief of Naval Operations, replacing Admiral Stark. King had commanded both the Submarine Base at New London and a division of S-boats and had played a key role in salvaging two sunken submarines in the 1920s, *S-51* and *S-4*. Although King had never commanded a submarine, he wore the dolphin insignia plus his aviator's wings.

Second, King appointed former submariner Chester Nimitz to replace Kimmel (and Pye) as Commander in Chief, Pacific Fleet. After his submarine service before and during World War I, Nimitz had established the Submarine Base at Pearl Harbor and then commanded a division of early fleet boats, including *Barracuda*, *Bass*, and *Bonita*.

King's staff in Washington was laced with submariners. For his deputy chief of staff he named Richard Edwards, then commanding Submarines Atlantic. Edwards, who would eventually become King's right arm, had commanded a squadron of fleet boats, and the Submarine Base at New London and had helped Lockwood fight for the *Tambor* class before the General Board in 1938. For his operations officer, King picked Francis Stuart ("Frog") Low, another submariner. Later, King appointed one-time submariner Charles Maynard ("Savvy") Cooke to be Assistant Chief of Staff for War Plans.

3
Manila, December 1941

The Japanese Attack on Clark Field

Early on the morning of December 8, Manila time, the commanding officer of *Sturgeon*, William Leslie Wright, rolled aboard his boat, moored at a pier in Manila near the tender *Holland*, feeling little pain after an evening ashore. Wright liked to drink whiskey and tell tall sea stories—hence his nickname, "Bull."

Bull Wright woke up his exec, Reuben Thornton Whitaker, and in a drunkenly grave tone stated that in his opinion the United States would be at war "soon." Then he went to his stateroom and collapsed on his bunk. Whitaker went back to sleep.

Two hours later, at about 3:30—8:30 Pearl Harbor time—the duty officer woke Whitaker to inform him that a message had come from Admiral Hart: JAPAN HAS STARTED HOSTILITIES, GOVERN YOURSELVES ACCORDINGLY. Whitaker jumped from his bunk and ran into Wright's stateroom. He shook Wright awake and relayed the message.

"So the little sons of bitches want to fight, do they?" Wright responded sleepily.

"Captain," Whitaker said, "I'm going to get the boat under way and move out into Manila Bay so we can dive if we have to."

Wright fixed Whitaker with a bleary eye. "Hey, Reuben, take care of that for me, will you? I'm going back to sleep."

While Wright went back to sleep, Whitaker took charge. He got *Sturgeon* under way, assisted by the third officer, Chester William Nimitz, Jr., son of the admiral. At 3:45, *Sturgeon* received a second message from Hart: SUBMARINES AND AIRCRAFT WILL WAGE UNRESTRICTED WARFARE. Whitaker dropped anchor far out in Manila Bay and awaited further orders.

The Japanese war plan that was now unfolding with machinelike perfection envisioned the following: (1) destruction of the Pacific Fleet at Pearl Harbor in a surprise attack; (2) the capture of Wake Island; (3) simultaneous strikes against MacArthur's air force in the Philippines and the British base at Hong Kong; (4) an invasion of the Malaya Peninsula, aimed at the capture of the British stronghold of Singapore. After MacArthur's air power had been destroyed, Japanese troops staging from Indochina, Hainan (a large island off the northeast coast of Indochina), Formosa, the Pescadores, and Palau would invade and capture the Philippines and then push southward to capture Borneo, Sumatra, Java, Timor, and New Guinea.

The key to Japanese strategy in the Far East was the destruction of MacArthur's air power and the capture of the Philippines. The first step was to be a surprise attack against MacArthur's airfields by Japanese bombers based in Formosa, timed to coincide with the Pearl Harbor attack. The aim was to destroy MacArthur's air force before it could take to the air. The second step was the invasion itself. Japanese forces were to land at five different points on the east, west, and north coast of Luzon, with the main force going ashore in Lingayen Gulf, a shallow bay in the middle of the western coastline.

However, a hitch developed. On the morning of the eighth, Manila time, there was bad weather over Formosa and the planes could not take off as scheduled. The Japanese were sure that MacArthur, warned by the Pearl Harbor attack, would have his aircraft on full alert. The big Flying Fortresses would be dispersed or airborne; the fighters would be airborne on constant patrol. It would be a tough and costly battle.

To defend the Philippines, MacArthur planned first to launch his "indestructible" B-17 Flying Fortresses against Japanese airfields and naval bases on Formosa, with the aim of neutralizing Japanese air power and naval forces—including any troop convoys assembling for an invasion of the Philippines. If the Japanese invasion forces should escape the bombardment and slip through, he would bomb the ships at sea or when they tried to unload their troops on the Philippine coast.

THE JAPANESE ATTACK ON CLARK FIELD

If the invasion succeeded, he would fight on land until forced to withdraw the U.S. Army and Philippine troops to the "Ultimate Defense Area"—the Bataan peninsula and Corregidor—and hold out until the Pacific Fleet arrived, in accordance with the old Plan Orange.

When MacArthur received word of the Pearl Harbor attack, there were thirty-three B-17s and about ninety pursuit planes in the Philippines. This was far from the full force of a hundred B-17s MacArthur had been promised, yet it was enough to inflict serious—and perhaps decisive—damage on the Japanese forces on Formosa.

For reasons that have never been satisfactorily explained by the many historians who have investigated, MacArthur failed to launch his B-17s against Formosa. There were conflicting explanations from MacArthur's air generals. One said that he urged MacArthur to launch the attack, according to the prearranged battle plan, and that MacArthur turned him down. Another said that first general did not urge the attack. One reason given was that no reconnaissance flights had been conducted over Formosa, and therefore no one knew exactly where to send the bombers. But just why such reconnaissance flights had not been conducted before hostilities broke out has never been explained.

For hours following the alert from Pearl Harbor, MacArthur's air force shunted about in confusion. Fighters were sent aloft on false alarms, hunting mythical Japanese aircraft. Some of the B-17s took to the air for safety. Others were ordered shifted to another base. At about 11 A.M. MacArthur finally gave the go-ahead to bomb Formosa that afternoon, with a second wave scheduled for the following day.

At 11:30, half the B-17s in the Philippines were on the ground at Clark Field, just outside Manila, being readied for the mission. By that time, the weather on Formosa having cleared, the Japanese had launched their delayed attack. When the Japanese bombers reached Clark Field, the crews were amazed—and pleased—to find seventeen Flying Fortresses and dozens of fighters on the ground. In one stroke, they destroyed half of MacArthur's air force and won control of the air in the Philippines.

Admiral Hart was not caught unawares. Since receipt of Admiral Stark's war warning on November 27, the Asiatic Fleet had been on a war footing. The major surface forces had been sent to southern Philippine waters, beyond range of Japanese planes based on Formosa. The shore establishments—designed primarily to support submarines and naval aircraft—were working feverishly to prepare defenses. Antiaircraft units had been placed on five-minute alert. Civilian employees and personnel at the naval installations at Cavite, Mariveles, Olongapo, Sangley Point, and Corregidor were storing torpedoes, mines, spare parts, communications gear, and machinery in casements and tunnels, where they would be safer against air attack. The secret Mark VI magnetic exploder had been issued to the twenty-three fleet submarines.

From the naval point of view, the weight of the defense of the Philippines fell to the submarine force. For as long as MacArthur could provide protection against air attacks, Admiral Hart would stand and fight, with Manila as the main base for the boats. For this reason, the valuable tenders *Canopus*, *Holland*, and *Otus* had not been sent south with the other surface forces. On the morning of the eighth, they were dispersed: *Otus* at Mariveles, the small naval base on the Bataan peninsula, *Canopus* anchored off the Cavite Naval Station, *Holland* behind the breakwater in Manila Harbor.

Admiral Hart's plan for a submarine defense of the Philippines was as follows. Upon the outbreak of hostilities, one third of the force—about eight boats—would immediately be sent on the high seas to "raid Japanese communications" and maintain scouting patrols "in the vicinity of Japanese bases"; one third of the force—another eight boats—would be stationed around the perimeter of Luzon to scout for and intercept invading forces; and one third of the force would be held as a "strategic reserve" to be launched against the main Japanese invasion force, when it was found.

Hart assumed that MacArthur's aircraft would provide intelligence on enemy ship movements, both distant and local, and he would reposition his submarines to take advantage of that information. Hart planned to maintain contact with his submarines by two methods: at night, when they were on the surface charging batteries, he could reach them with ordinary high-frequency radio broadcasts from transmitters at Cavite or Corregidor; during the day, when the submarines were submerged, he could reach them by low-frequency radio (which penetrated underwater to a depth of 50 feet or so) up to a range of about 1,000 miles.

When Hart received word of the attack on Pearl Harbor at his office in the Marsman Building in downtown Manila, he immediately sent off the messages received by *Sturgeon* and the other submarines. Next, he summoned John Wilkes and told him he would not be returning to the States. Wilkes would serve as "special adviser" to Red Doyle, who was then officially commanding Asiatic Submarines. Wilkes had had two years' experience commanding submarines in Asiatic waters; Doyle had none. Wilkes would, in effect, remain as the submarine boss; Doyle would be eased aside. Jimmy Fife would remain as chief of staff. One of the division commanders, Sunshine Murray, was designated operations officer.

While the Japanese were bombing Clark Field, Wilkes called his submarine commanders to his flagship, *Holland*. He and Fife and Sunshine Murray handed out brief operations orders. Each skipper was urged to "use caution and feel his way." Wilkes explained later:

It was felt that this [first] patrol would be the most dangerous and would also be most informative as to enemy methods on formations, convoying, anti-submarine warfare. It was especially desired that this information be obtained and disseminated for the benefit of future operations. For this reason, it was planned that the first patrols would be brief, limited to three weeks . . . so the information would be available as soon as possible.

Sunshine Murray was blunt and direct. "Listen, dammit," he told the skippers. "Don't try to go out there and win the Congressional Medal of Honor in one day. The submarines are all we have left. Your crews are more valuable than anything else. Bring them back."

In addition, the skippers were cautioned to be sparing with torpedoes. The magnetic exploder—the secret weapon—should produce amazing results, Wilkes advised. If possible, sink merchant ships with one torpedo. Use two only if absolutely necessary. For capital ships (aircraft carriers, battleships, cruisers), use what the situation demanded without being profligate. Order of priority: (1) capital ships; (2) loaded transports; (3) light forces, transports, and supply ships in ballast. Shoot on sight. There were no friendly forces north of Manila.

On December 8 and 9, Manila time, eighteen submarines—four S-boats, fourteen fleet boats—put to sea for war patrol.

The Japanese Attacks on Cavite and Manila

Within forty-eight hours of the Japanese attack on Clark Field, it was clear to Hart that his plan for utilizing Manila as a major submarine base must be abandoned. The Japanese had all but wiped out

MacArthur's air forces. Japanese bombers could attack Manila at will. The tenders *Otus, Holland,* and *Canopus*—plus the Cavite Naval Station—would be sitting ducks. On the evening of the ninth, Hart made his decision: Red Doyle would take *Otus* and *Holland*, plus other miscellaneous craft, south to the Malay Barrier or farther. John Wilkes would remain on *Canopus*, which would be anchored in shallow water at the Manila waterfront and camouflaged. The submarines would be supplied and serviced by *Canopus*, Cavite, Mariveles, and Corregidor for as long as possible, submerging in Manila Bay during air attacks.

On December 10, these orders were executed. John Wilkes formally reassumed command of Submarines Asiatic Fleet. In preparation for the journey south, *Otus* was shifted to Cavite to take on a load of submarine torpedoes and spare parts and other gear that would complete her conversion to a full-blown submarine tender. While she was so engaged, Japanese high-level bombers appeared over Manila and prepared "in a leisurely manner" to carry out one of the most devastating air attacks of the war.

The main target that day was the Cavite Naval Station. The first two salvos that fell straddled *Otus*. Her commanding officer immediately got under way and began backing away from the wharf, leaving behind most of the gear *Otus* had come to get. Miraculously, she remained untouched.

Sealion, commanded by Richard George Voge, and *Seadragon*, commanded by William Edward ("Pete") Ferrall, were at that moment in the Cavite shipyard in overhaul. Of the two, Voge's *Sealion* was less ready; her engines were still dismantled. *Seadragon* had been finished in a rush. Ferrall was expecting to leave the yard in three or four days. That day she was being painted. There were dozens of paint cans on her wood-slat deck.

When the air raid alarm sounded, men on *Seadragon* and *Sealion* mounted machine guns topside and prepared for battle. On the first run, a bomb fell on the dock alongside *Seadragon*, blowing up a temporary mess hall. Both submarines hammered away with .50-caliber machine guns, but the bombers were hopelessly high.

Seeing them preparing for a second run, Voge and Ferrall ordered all men below decks. This time, two bombs fell on *Sealion*, one on the cigarette deck (a small deck on the aft end of the bridge where, in peacetime, sailors came topside to smoke and breathe fresh air) and one just over the after engine-room hatch. Fragments of the bomb

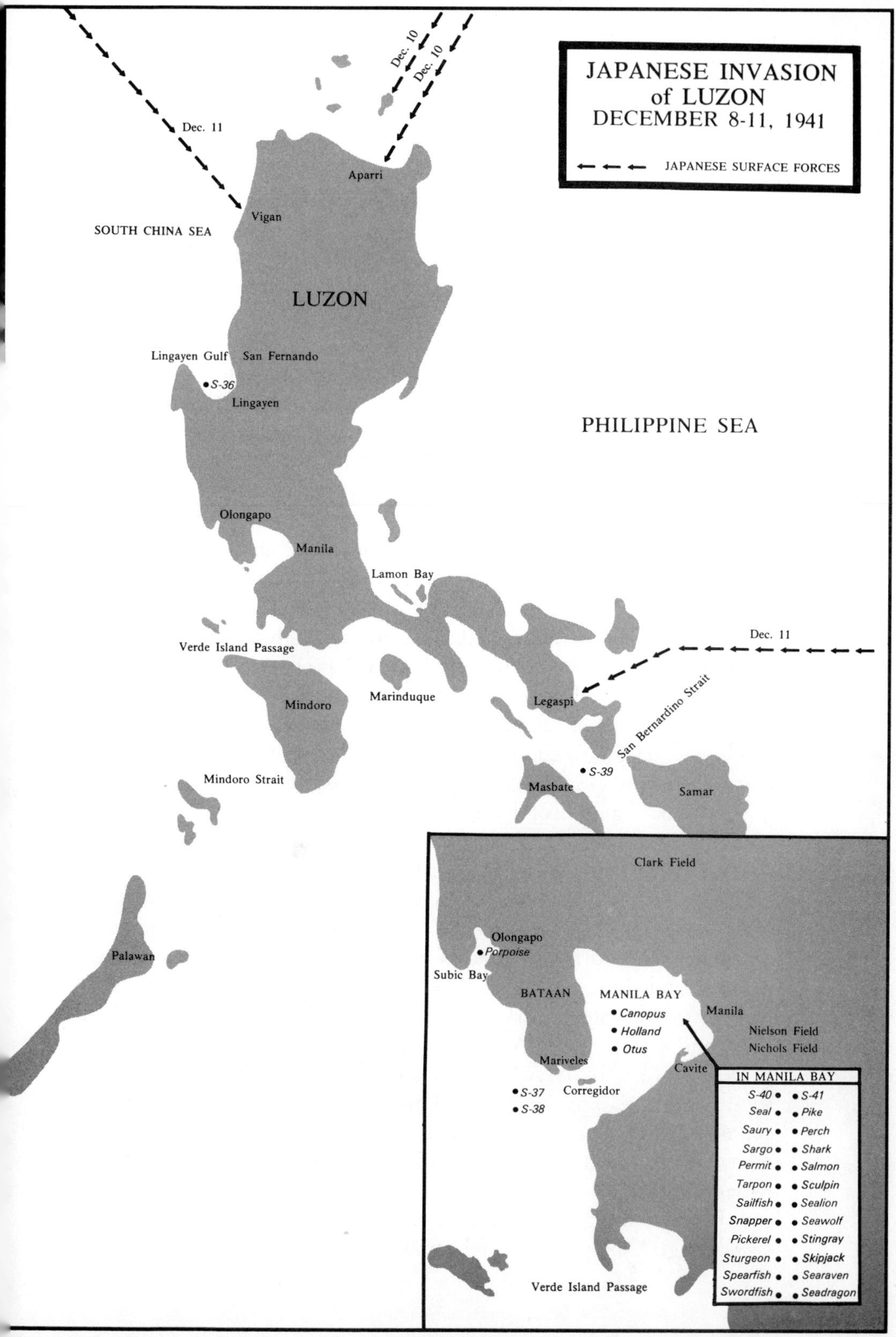
JAPANESE INVASION
of LUZON
DECEMBER 8-11, 1941
JAPANESE SURFACE FORCES
Dec. 10
Dec. 10
Dec. 11
Aparri
Vigan
SOUTH CHINA SEA
LUZON
Lingayen Gulf
San Fernando
S-36
Lingayen
PHILIPPINE SEA
Olongapo
Manila
Lamon Bay
Dec. 11
Verde Island Passage
Marinduque
Mindoro
Legaspi
San Bernardino Strait
S-39
Mindoro Strait
Masbate
Samar
Palawan
Clark Field
Olongapo
Porpoise
Subic Bay
BATAAN
MANILA BAY
Canopus
Holland
Otus
Manila
Nielson Field
Nichols Field
Mariveles
Cavite
S-37
S-38
Corregidor
IN MANILA BAY
S-40
S-41
Seal
Pike
Saury
Perch
Sargo
Shark
Permit
Salmon
Tarpon
Sculpin
Sailfish
Sealion
Snapper
Seawolf
Pickerel
Stingray
Sturgeon
Skipjack
Spearfish
Searaven
Swordfish
Seadragon
Verde Island Passage

and pieces of *Sealion* gashed three holes in the conning tower of *Seadragon*, where half a dozen men were taking cover. Ferrall's fifth officer, Ensign Samuel Howard Hunter, Jr., was killed by the fragments. Four men in the engine room of Voge's *Sealion* were killed by the same bombs. These five were the first U.S. submariners to be killed in the war.

Topside there was chaos. Japanese bombs fell into Cavite by the dozens. The paint shop blew up, spreading fire all over the yard. Then the torpedo repair shop was hit. Air flasks and warheads exploded, spewing lethal fragments. Next to *Seadragon*, the minesweeper *Bittern* burned furiously. A barge carrying forty-eight Mark XIV torpedoes for *Seadragon* and *Sealion* was hit. It capsized, and its valuable cargo rolled overboard. The paint cans on *Seadragon*'s deck blazed. The *Sealion*, mortally holed, listed to starboard, half sunk by the stern. Her crew, including three wounded, ran up the hatches and onto shore.

Receiving word that *Bittern*'s magazines were about to blow, Pete Ferrall ordered *Seadragon* abandoned. Ferrall's exec, Norvell Gardiner ("Bub") Ward, another athlete from the class of 1935, picked up Hunter's body and dragged it topside through the raging inferno to the dock. The *Seadragon* crew joined that of *Sealion* at the Cavite baseball diamond. But on second thought Ferrall refused to abandon his ship. He rushed up to the ball field and ordered his crew back.

The submarine rescue vessel *Pigeon* moved in to lend Ferrall assistance. She threw *Seadragon* a line and, in spite of damaged steering gear and the raging fires, hauled her clear. Later that evening, Ferrall brought *Seadragon* alongside *Canopus* in Manila for repairs. Then she was sent to Surabaya, Java, for further work. *Sealion* was deemed beyond hope. She was stripped of some machinery and then destroyed with three depth charges, leaving Dick Voge without a command.

Cavite was a burning shambles. Five hundred were dead and many more wounded. In addition to the loss of *Sealion*, the submarine force had lost all Cavite submarine repair facilities, the torpedo overhaul shop, and a total of 233 Mark XIV torpedoes, including those on the barge. The low-frequency radio tower for transmitting to submerged submarines was also destroyed. This meant that boats could only be contacted on the surface at night. All the submarine force could salvage from Cavite were about 150 torpedoes and some spare parts which had been stored in casements before the bombing. These were transferred to tunnels on Corregidor.

Although *Canopus* was well camouflaged with netting and painted to resemble the Manila docks alongside which she was moored, Hart did not believe she would escape destruction for long. Accordingly, he ordered John Wilkes and his staff to take up headquarters ashore in a new enlisted men's club. The torpedo overhaul shop on *Canopus* —the only remaining one in the Philippines—was moved to the tunnels of Corregidor. Other stores and supplies were moved ashore in Manila. Each day, all hands on *Canopus* except the gun crews were ordered ashore to slit trenches.

Japanese planes came over Manila daily from noon to 1 P.M., dropping bombs. "You could set your watch by them," Wilkes recalled later. "We even advanced the lunch hour to eleven so we could eat before we dived into the slit trenches."

Every day brought darker news. The British capital ships *Repulse* and *Prince of Wales* were lost to Japanese aircraft near Singapore. The British had failed to repel Japanese landings in Malaya. British troops were retreating to Singapore. Hong Kong was under siege. Wake Island had been overrun. The Pacific Fleet (Hart learned, bit by bit) lay on the bottom at Pearl Harbor. It could not, as planned, reinforce the Philippines and deal the Japanese fleet a decisive blow.

The First Patrols from Manila

Meanwhile, the submarines were at sea. The initial plan for deployment, drawn up in haste by the deposed Red Doyle, Jimmy Fife, and Sunshine Murray and approved by John Wilkes, assumed that there would be ample warning of a Japanese attack, that Japan would declare war in a formal way, and that MacArthur's aircraft would provide a reliable flow of intelligence on Japanese ship movements. None of these assumptions proved valid. The submarine defense plan had to be reorganized on the spot. The idea of a one-third "reserve force," for example, was immediately abandoned.

By December 11, twenty-two of the surviving twenty-eight submarines had gone to sea. Since it seemed most likely that a Philippine invasion force would approach from Japanese bases to the west or northwest of Luzon—Formosa, the Pescadores, Indochina, or Hainan— thirteen boats were sent to western areas. Since Palau, lying to the eastward of Luzon, was also believed to be a heavily fortified Japanese base, five boats were sent to areas off the east coast of Luzon. The remaining four were stationed along the southern approaches to Luzon.

The five boats going eastward were *Seawolf, Sculpin, Skipjack,*

Tarpon, and *S-39*. The four fleet boats went through San Bernardino Strait, then dispersed; *S-39* remained in or near the strait. All five ran into foul December weather on the east side of Luzon.

Tarpon, commanded by Lewis Wallace, was twice "pooped" (swamped by huge waves). She rolled violently and took heavy water down the conning tower hatch. The water rushed into the pump room, a compartment below the control room. Before Wallace got control of the boat, water was waist deep in the pump room and two feet deep in the control room. A great deal of the machinery was flooded out. After Wallace got the damage repaired, he sighted one fair-size Japanese ship sailing alone. He made a sonar approach. It was botched when a torpedoman, distracted by a leak, accidentally fired a torpedo.

Seawolf, commanded by Frederick Burdette Warder, thrashed around in heavy seas and then proceeded northward along the east coast of Luzon to Aparri, where the Japanese landed a small invasion force on December 10. Freddy Warder was a courageous and prepossessing officer, a salty-tongued fighter who was worshiped by his officers and crew. In the immediate prewar days, Warder had stood toe to toe with Admiral Hart in a dispute over one of his enlisted men, wrongly accused in a barroom scuffle. Warder had risked being relieved of command in order to right this wrong, and in the face of Warder's adamant stand Admiral Hart had backed down.

Arriving at Aparri, Warder found a destroyer guarding the mouth of the harbor. Warder eased *Seawolf* around the destroyer—which to his surprise was pinging—and proceeded boldly into the harbor. In brief and careful periscope observations, Warder found a Japanese seaplane tender at anchor. He set up and, from a range of 3,800 yards, fired four bow tubes—two torpedoes set to run at 40 feet, two set to run at 30 feet, so the torpedoes would pass under the keel and actuate the magnetic exploder.

Warder waited. There was no explosion. He had missed a fat target at anchor! Turning to run out of the harbor, Warder set up his four stern tubes, firing from a range of 4,500 yards. Watching through the periscope, Warder saw a plume of water near the waterline of the ship, but there was no explosion, no flame or smoke. If the torpedo hit, the exploder must have failed. Warder was furious. He had penetrated a harbor, fired eight precious torpedoes, achieved zero results. Following this, Warder received orders to round the northern tip of Luzon and proceed down the west coast of Luzon to Manila.

THE FIRST PATROLS FROM MANILA

Sculpin, commanded by Lucius Henry Chappell, patrolled off Lamon Bay. The weather was foul, the visibility abysmal. When Warder was shifted from Aparri, *Sculpin* was directed to take her place. On December 21, Chappell headed northward, leaving Lamon Bay unguarded. Three days later, a large Japanese landing force from Palau steamed into Lamon Bay and put troops ashore. Chappell spotted a ship coming out of Aparri but was unable to get into position to fire. After *Tarpon* was swamped, Chappell requested permission to return south near Lamon Bay. He ran into such foul weather he was unable to attack Japanese shipping going in and out of the bay.

Skipjack, commanded by Charles Lawrence ("Larry") Freeman, proceeded eastward toward the Palaus. During the day, Freeman, following peacetime drills, ran submerged at 120 to 150 feet, maintaining a sonar watch. If the sonarman heard anything, Freeman came up to periscope depth for a look. On Christmas Day, Freeman's sonar picked up fast, heavy propeller beats, indicating a big ship. Freeman surfaced and ran in to 12,000 yards, where he saw his quarry was an aircraft carrier and a destroyer! This—the first time in the war that a U.S. submarine encountered a Japanese carrier—was for a submarine skipper a truly momentous occasion, as it would continue to be throughout the war.

Freeman submerged and began his approach by sonar from a depth of 100 feet. When the sonarman reported a range of 2,200 yards, Freeman fired three of his four bow tubes. (The fourth was out of commission.) After firing, Freeman went deep—to 230 feet—passing up an opportunity for a stern shot. All three torpedoes missed. In the postmortem on the attack, the sonar operator decided he had made a mistake on the range. It was not 2,200 yards but more like 3,000 or 3,500 yards. Freeman noted in his log, "It was not a very Merry Christmas after that."

The five boats going to the east of Luzon thus achieved zero results. Freeman missed an aircraft carrier, Warder missed a seaplane tender at anchor, Chappell missed the landings at Lamon Bay, Wallace almost lost *Tarpon* in heavy seas, and S-39, patrolling San Bernardino Strait, found no targets worthy of attack.

The four boats deployed to the south of Luzon were *Shark*, S-37, S-38, and S-40. *Shark*, commanded by Louis Shane, Jr., went down to the island of Marinduque and anchored in Santa Cruz Harbor. Shane induced the mayor to extinguish the navigation lights but did little else. After ten days of idleness, he was ordered to return to Manila. *S-37*, *S-38*, and *S-40* patrolled Verde Island Passage. On December 12, Wreford Goss ("Moon") Chapple, the much loved but not exceptionally bright officer commanding *S-38*, fired one torpedo at what he believed to be a Japanese ship off the northwest tip of Mindoro and claimed a sinking. However, no Japanese ships were in the area at that time. If Moon did, in fact, sink a ship, it must have been friendly.

On paper, the deployment of the thirteen fleet boats to the west appeared to be a classic solution to the problem confronting Admiral Hart and John Wilkes. Half the boats—seven—were sent to distant points from which the Japanese might launch invasion forces. Two went to the Formosa-Pescadores area, one to the Hong Kong area, one to Hainan Island, and three to the Camranh Bay area in Southeast Indochina. Their missions were to warn of departing Japanese forces and attack these and merchant ships when possible.

The two boats sent to the Formosa area were *Sturgeon* and *Searaven*. Bull Wright in *Sturgeon* got there first. He closed to within 13 miles of the coast, heard two ships pinging, promptly went to 250 feet, and rigged for depth charge. He noted in his log, "This area is too closely patrolled, I believe, to risk staying closer inshore." A few days later, Wright spotted a tanker with a destroyer escort. He did not attack either ship. Next day, December 18, he picked up a large convoy: a *Zinto*-class cruiser and several destroyers escorting five big freighters. In accordance with the stated order of target priority, Wright made an approach on the cruiser. He got within 1,700 yards, but a destroyer came into view and Wright ducked to 200 feet without firing. The destroyer dropped a few depth charges which caused minor damage. On the night of December 21, Wright sighted a ship, remained on the surface, and fired four bow torpedoes. All missed.

Searaven, commanded by Theodore Charles Aylward, reached the Formosa area shortly after *Sturgeon*. Aylward was not in the best of health. For some years, his blood pressure had been climbing. During the patrol, he suffered pains in his chest, dizziness, and headaches. One consequence was that his exec, Francis David Walker, Jr., a classmate of Dusty Dornin and Slade Cutter, assumed much of the command load. Aylward, also fighting very heavy weather, fired at two ships, expending three torpedoes. All missed.

The boat sent to Hong Kong was the old *Pike*, first of the modern

THE FIRST PATROLS FROM MANILA

generation of fleet boats, commanded by William Adolph New. Billy New found plenty of junks and sampans but few targets. On the night of December 17, cruising in bad weather, he sighted a freighter and fired one torpedo from 3,000 yards. It missed. He saw no other targets.

Swordfish, commanded by Chester Carl Smith, a deceptively mild, conservative officer, headed for the island of Hainan. On the way from Manila to station, Chet Smith encountered two separate freighters, sailing alone. He fired two torpedoes at the first with a depth setting of 40 feet. The ship, Smith believed, sank. His two-torpedo salvo at the second ship, set for 40 feet, missed.

Working the south coast of Hainan, Smith found the area teeming with enemy vessels. On December 14, he attacked two separate steamers, one at dawn, one in late afternoon. He fired two at the first, believing he sank her. He fired three at the second with a depth setting of 30 feet. The first torpedo exploded prematurely close aboard, but Smith believed the others hit, sinking the ship, raising his score to three. On December 16, Smith came across an eastbound convoy of six big transports. His position was unfavorable, but he fired three torpedoes from a range of 2,800 yards at the last ship in line. One torpedo exploded prematurely; the other two, Smith believed, hit and sank the ship, bringing his score to four. Later that night, Smith got off a contact report on the convoy to John Wilkes in Manila.

The three boats assigned to patrol near Camranh Bay, Indochina—a big Japanese navy base—were *Pickerel*, *Spearfish*, and *Sargo*. *Pickerel*, commanded by Barton Elijah Bacon, Jr., got there first. The weather was rough and miserable. On December 14, Bacon saw a Japanese submarine coming out of Camranh Bay, its rising sun ensign flapping from a halyard. Bacon started his approach but then saw a destroyer. Believing this to be a superior target, he shifted to the destroyer. In the switch, however, the fire-control party became confused and both targets pulled off unharmed. On December 19, Bacon foolishly let fly five torpedoes at a small gunboat not worth one. All missed. Toward the end of his brief patrol, he noted in his log, "Seventeen days is about proper length for a patrol because twenty-one days is too long. Personnel become weary under constant strain and tempers become touchy."

Spearfish, commanded by Roland Fremont Pryce, arrived next in "mountainous" seas. On December 20, Pryce sighted three Japanese submarines standing out in column. While making the approach, a green helmsman remained on the wrong course for eight minutes before the error was discovered. The approach was botched, but Pryce fired anyway: four torpedoes from 9,000 yards—4½ miles—one of the longest torpedo shots of the war. A little later, Pryce spotted another submarine but could not reach a favorable firing position. After a few days, Pryce was ordered to Hainan Island.

The third boat into the Camranh Bay area was *Sargo*, commanded by Tyrrell Dwight Jacobs, a member of the Gun Club who had spent two years at the Naval Academy doing postgraduate work in ordnance engineering. By the time Jacobs got on station, the codebreakers were tracking some Japanese fleet movements. On December 14, *Sargo* was vectored to intercept three cruisers. They appeared as predicted, but Jacobs was unable to maneuver into position to attack. Assuming the cruisers were escorting troop transports or freighters, Jacobs moved in to intercept. That night he picked up a freighter, and fired one torpedo. Eighteen seconds after shooting, a violent explosion shook *Sargo*. The torpedo had prematured.

The explosion destroyed Jacobs's faith in the Mark VI magnetic exploder. Either there was something drastically wrong, he believed, or the Japanese had devised something to set it off before the torpedo reached its target. After a thorough discussion with his exec and his torpedo officer, Cassius Douglas Rhymes, Jr., Jacobs decided to deactivate the influence feature of the Mark VI and rely solely on contact.

On December 24, Jacobs sighted two fat cargo vessels through his periscope. At a range of about 1,000 yards, he fired two torpedoes at the lead ship and one at the trailing ship, with depth settings of 13 and 16 feet respectively. No explosions. During the attack, the diving officer lost control and *Sargo* broached to 45 feet, exposing her conning tower. The merchantmen saw her and turned away. Jacobs got off two quick shots from his stern tubes at the lead ship, range 1,800 yards, depth setting 10 feet. No hits. On the following day, he spotted two more merchantmen but couldn't get into position to attack.

Later, Jacobs found two more merchantmen sailing together. From a range of 900 yards, he fired two stern torpedoes at the rear ship, depth setting 10 feet. Both missed. An hour later, two more merchantmen came into sight. This time Jacobs, who had now fired eight torpedoes at four separate targets with zero results, was determined to do all in his power to ensure a hit. He dragged out the approach for

THE FIRST PATROLS FROM MANILA

fifty-seven minutes, inviting his exec to alternate on the periscope. The theoretical bearing on the TDC seemed to match the periscope observations perfectly. When he was absolutely certain, Jacobs fired two torpedoes at the lead ship and two at the rear ship, average range about 1,000 yards, depth setting 10 feet. All four torpedoes missed.

Jacobs was angry, baffled—and technically curious. After analyzing all the data on his attacks with Doug Rhymes, he concluded that the Mark XIV torpedo was running *deeper* than prescribed in the manuals. This was so, he reasoned, because the warheads were heavier than the exercise heads they had practiced with in peacetime. Accordingly, Jacobs ordered Rhymes to adjust the rudder throws to make the torpedoes run at a shallower depth.

The next day, an opportunity loomed for Jacobs to test his theory. About dusk, he sighted two more merchantmen. Before he could get off an attack, he lost them in the darkness. He surfaced and regained contact about 10 P.M. However, instead of attacking in darkness, he decided to run ahead, dive, and attack in daylight when he could be absolutely sure of his firing data. He carried this plan forward, but rough seas arose, and when the two ships reappeared Jacobs could not get into firing position. Several days later, he sighted a big slow-moving tanker. Again, the approach was dragged out, with Jacobs and his exec alternating on the periscope. In the thirty-five-minute period, the two men made seventeen unhurried periscope observations. Finally, at a range of 1,200 yards, depth setting 10 feet, Jacobs fired one torpedo. No explosion.

Jacobs was exasperated. He broke radio silence to send Wilkes a message raising serious questions about the reliability of the Mark XIV torpedo. He informed Wilkes that he had deactivated the Mark VI exploder and adjusted the rudder throws to make the torpedo run shallower. Even so, he reported, in six separate attacks during which he fired thirteen torpedoes, none had exploded.

The remaining five boats deployed to westward were stationed along the western coast of Luzon. Wilkes sent *Saury* and *Sailfish* northward to the vicinity of Vigan, S-36 was positioned in Lingayen Gulf, considered for decades the most likely invasion area, while *Perch* and *Permit* were stationed in the south, off Subic Bay.

Sailfish (formerly *Squalus*) was a difficult command. Some superstitious sailors considered her jinxed. If she sank once, she could sink again. Twenty-six men had drowned inside her hull; the memory was not easily erased. A sailor with a morbid sense of humor had

U.S. SUBMARINE DEPLOYMENT
DECEMBER 8-15, 1941

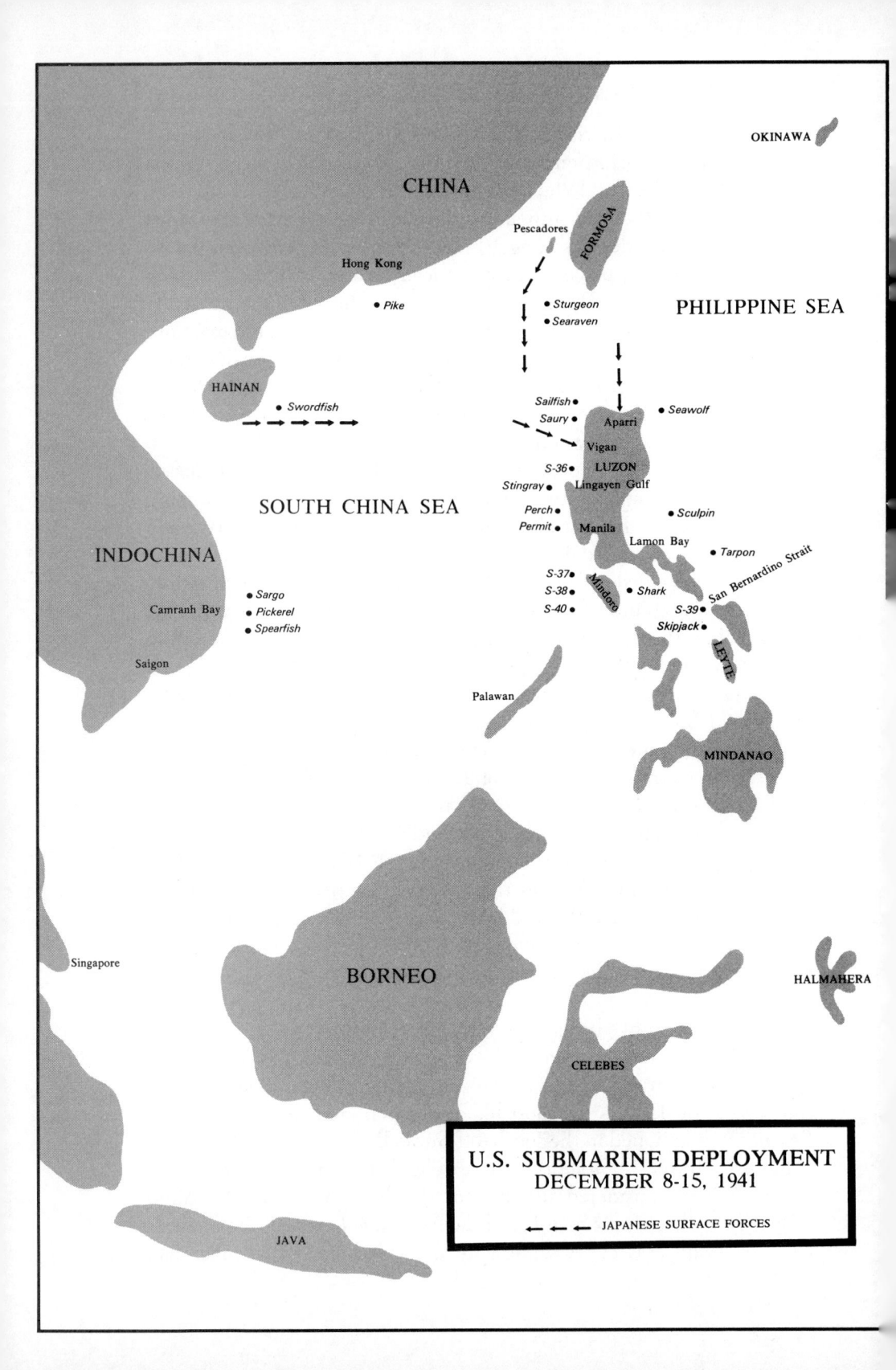

← ←- ←- JAPANESE SURFACE FORCES

THE FIRST PATROLS FROM MANILA

informally christened her "Squailfish." To help improve her image, the navy had hand-picked one of the ablest of the peacetime skippers to command her, Morton Claire Mumma, Jr. Mumma, a strict disciplinarian, had imposed his strong personality on the boat; anyone referring to her as "Squailfish" would be court-martialed. But for all his zeal, competence, and emphasis on spit and polish, the boat remained "different."

On the morning of December 10, the Japanese landed a small force at Vigan. The landings were supported by small naval units, including a cruiser and several destroyers. Mort Mumma in *Sailfish* saw the cruiser and destroyers but was unable to get into firing position. *Saury*, commanded by John Lockwood Burnside, Jr., was cruising farther north and made no contacts with the enemy. The Japanese landed unopposed by U.S. naval forces.*

Three nights later, Mort Mumma sighted two destroyers off Vigan and submerged to make a sonar approach. The destroyers evidently picked up *Sailfish*. Two or three depth charges fell, slightly jarring the boat. Mumma fired two torpedoes from a depth of 100 feet, range 500 yards. Fifteen seconds after firing, *Sailfish* was rocked by an explosion. It was either a premature or another depth charge, no one could tell in the confusion and noise. Mumma preferred to believe one of his torpedoes had hit a destroyer and sunk it. "Following the explosion," he wrote in his report, "no screws were heard." In all probability, the destroyer had stopped to listen, or the force of the explosion and rush of water blanked out noise, or the destroyer had passed overhead to a new position.

Immediately after the attack, the destroyers began depth-charging *Sailfish*. About eighteen or twenty charges fell. During the counterattack, Mort Mumma, like his classmate, Dizzy Rainer in *Dolphin*, went to pieces. He summoned his exec, Hiram Cassedy, ordered him to take command of the boat, and to lock him (Mumma) in his stateroom. Cassedy did as ordered, getting off a radio dispatch to John Wilkes which was picked up and decoded by some other submarines.

---

* MacArthur's dwindling air force attacked the Japanese landing at Vigan, destroying two minesweepers and heavily damaging two transports. One pilot, Colin Kelly, flying a B-17, was sent out to find a Japanese aircraft carrier believed to be in the area. Kelly couldn't find the carrier but sighted what he believed to be the battleship *Haruna* and attacked. *Haruna* was then in Malayan waters; Kelly had attacked the heavy cruiser *Ashigara*. He claimed sinking her, but he was mistaken. While returning to Clark Field, Kelly's plane was attacked and set aflame by Japanese aircraft. Kelly ordered his crew to bail out. They made it; he didn't. MacArthur credited Kelly with sinking a battleship, and he became a national hero.

Reuben Whitaker, Bull Wright's exec on *Sturgeon*, remembers that the message said approximately: ATTACKED ONE SHIP . . . VIOLENT COUNTERATTACK . . . COMMANDING OFFICER BREAKING DOWN . . . URGENTLY REQUEST AUTHORITY TO RETURN TO TENDER.

Wilkes ordered *Sailfish* back to Manila, sending *Seal*, commanded by Kenneth Charles Hurd, to replace her. He then relieved Mumma, giving command of the boat to Dick Voge, who had lost *Sealion* in the Cavite bombing attack. Despite the thin evidence, Wilkes credited Mumma with sinking the destroyer and awarded him a Navy Cross. The citation (perhaps designed to save everybody embarrassment) extolled Mumma's "extraordinary heroism" and concluded, "By his forceful and inspiring leadership [he] enabled the *Sailfish* to complete successfully an extremely perilous mission."

For Mumma—or for anybody else—being relieved of command in peace or war was a shattering professional blow. Command of a combatant ship was the ultimate goal of all naval officers, usually the high point of their professional career. To fail in command usually spelled the end for an officer, denying him an opportunity for good jobs and advancement to flag rank. Mumma's humiliation before his classmates and fellow submariners was further heightened by the fact that he had no way to leave Manila for other duty. He had to remain and face them every morning.

Many officers, especially the younger ones, were appalled by Mumma's conduct in war. No one could understand it. At the Naval Academy, they had been exhorted to "go in harm's way" and give their lives for their country. But they were soon to discover that Mumma was no isolated case. All too many of his contemporaries in the submarine force showed a disinclination to attack the enemy boldly and persistently, an unforeseen circumstance that would plague the submarine force throughout the war.

All the while, S-36, commanded by John Roland McKnight, Jr., maintained a lonely patrol in the shallow waters of Lingayen Gulf. She carried a total of twelve torpedoes, enough for three or four shots at the enemy if, as believed, Lingayen Gulf turned out to be the most likely point to land the main Japanese invasion forces. Why Hart and Wilkes did not position the other five S-boats inside Lingayen Gulf has never been made clear.

On the night of December 11, Wilkes sent a radio dispatch to McKnight. Because of a faulty calibration in S-36's receiver—undetected at the time—McKnight did not receive the message. Wilkes repeated the message again and again that night and on subsequent nights. Fearing that the boat might be in serious difficulty, or perhaps lost, on the night of the sixteenth, Wilkes ordered McKnight to exit Lingayen Gulf and return to Manila. McKnight received that message and pulled out. To replace S-36, Wilkes sent *Stingray*, commanded by Raymond Starr Lamb, a codebreaker who had worked for Tom Dyer at Hypo before the war. *Stingray* would take up station off the mouth of Lingayen Gulf, in deeper waters.

The two boats stationed off Subic Bay were *Perch* and *Permit*. *Permit* was commanded by Adrian Melvin Hurst, a brother-in-law of Gin Styer, Withers's chief of staff. Hurst left for patrol with only two of his four engines in commission. After a few days on station, he and some others developed "Guam blisters" (an extremely uncomfortable form of impetigo), prickly heat, and other minor diseases. On the fifth day out, an electrician caught his hand in some machinery, crushing bones and severing tendons. Hurst returned to Manila on December 20 after a nine-day patrol.

Perch, commanded by David Albert Hurt, guarded Subic Bay alone until December 18, when she was ordered to proceed to Formosa to replace Bull Wright's *Sturgeon*, then Manila bound. Near Formosa on Christmas Day, Hurt sighted a steamer and fired four torpedoes; one broached and circled back toward *Perch*, in what was called a circular run, exploding off her beam. Two days later, Hurt picked up a convoy consisting of a light cruiser, two destroyers, and a tanker. The approach was botched, and a destroyer attacked. Hurt took *Perch* to the bottom in 170 feet of water and lay quiet until the destroyer moved off. It was not the recommended form of evasion. It would have been better if Hurt had maintained his mobility and evaded the destroyer by creeping away.

The "Battle" of Lingayen Gulf

On station off Lingayen Gulf, Ray Lamb in *Stingray*, who had been plagued with leaky pipes for some time, noted a new infirmity in his boat: a small air leak that sent a steady stream of little bubbles to the surface. Believing this would be a dead giveaway to the enemy in a glassy sea, Lamb ordered his crew to fix it. They couldn't. After all efforts failed, Lamb radioed Wilkes, requesting permission to return to Manila for repairs. Wilkes granted the request.

At 5:13 on the afternoon of December 21, Lamb, coming to periscope depth preparatory to surfacing for the trip to Manila, spotted smoke on the horizon. He immediately turned *Stingray* toward the smoke. Moments later, he made out *columns* of smoke. He had sighted a submariner's dream (or nightmare): the main Japanese invasion force, headed in for Lingayen Gulf.

What happened in the following hours brought little credit to Lamb or the submarine force. In Lamb's words:

Turned to approach course but saw it would be impossible to intercept the column. Came to forty-eight feet and sent contact report to Commander in Chief, Asiatic Fleet . . . message sent twice but no receipt heard. . . . At this time heard distinct echo ranging, could no longer make out smoke due to darkness, turned and ran north for several miles to clear echo ranging, as I considered it of primary importance to ensure contact report reached the Commander in Chief. Surfaced, repeated contact report and sent amplifying report. . . . Turned to pursue enemy but could not make him out.

On receiving the message, Wilkes canceled Lamb's orders to return to Manila and told him to attack. For several hours, while the most luscious submarine target of the war approached the gulf, Lamb thrashed about in a manner that led many of his crew to believe him less than aggressive. At about three the following morning, he sighted a light on a Japanese ship. He turned to bring *Stingray*'s stern tubes to bear, but the light went out and he lost the ship in the darkness. Half an hour later, Lamb spotted a destroyer close by. Instead of shooting at it, Lamb, who believed himself to be in the middle of a screen, dived and went to 200 feet to evade. While submerged, Lamb heard echo ranging all around him, but no depth charges fell. When it seemed prudent, he eased away from the destroyers. At dawn, he came to periscope depth and searched the seas. They were empty. The invasion force had slipped past him and landed.

Instead of fighting into the gulf, Lamb turned in the opposite direction, standing out to sea at low speed at a depth of 100 feet. Later he would explain that his crew was "exhausted" and needed a rest. During this crucial period in the history of the Philippines, Lamb remained submerged, far from the Japanese, for 14 hours and 36 minutes, surfacing at about six on the evening of the twenty-second.

That evening, Lamb made a halfhearted attempt to slip by a Japanese destroyer screen which had now taken station at the mouth

THE "BATTLE" OF LINGAYEN GULF

of the gulf. However, when a searchlight—presumably mounted on a destroyer—some 2 miles distant swung toward *Stingray*, Lamb dived and went deep. He heard four distant explosions—depth charges or torpedoes from another submarine, he was not sure. He lay quiet again, then slipped away to seaward. At 10:42 P.M. he surfaced and went farther out to sea to charge his batteries. While so engaged, Lamb found several more leaks that caused him concern.

Later he wrote in third person, "At [that] time the commanding officer believed it would be impossible to remain at deep submergence for a period of time necessary to pass under enemy screen and penetrate Gulf without continuously pumping bilges and leaving oil slicks on surface, therefore request was made to return to Manila for repairs."

Lamb arrived back in Manila without having fired a single torpedo at the enemy. Wilkes relieved him of command.

Upon receiving Ray Lamb's contact report, John Wilkes rushed six boats to the scene: two of the S-boats patrolling Verde Island Passage, S-38 and S-40; *Salmon*; Adrian Hurst's *Permit*, now ready for a second patrol; *Porpoise*, which had been replacing her battery at Olongapo when the Japanese attacked; and Burnside's *Saury*, ordered south from Vigan. Wilkes's orders were explicit: enter Lingayen Gulf and attack the enemy landing forces.

Moon Chapple, another varsity football player (and heavyweight boxer) at the Naval Academy, was patrolling Verde Island Passage in S-38 when the order came. He charged north like a fullback going up the middle. On the morning of December 22, just before dawn, he dived and took his boat inside. The water in the gulf was shallow, full of uncharted reefs and humps. Later Chapple conceded he was "scared," but he gave no hint of his true feelings to his fired-up—and exhausted—crew.

Inside the gulf, just after daybreak, Chapple raised his periscope to find four fat transports standing in. Chapple put his crosshairs on the transports and ordered all four bow tubes made ready. When the ships reached a range of 1,000 yards Chapple fired, confident of his aim, but no explosion followed. The torpedoes had missed! A Japanese destroyer spotted Chapple's torpedo wakes. It charged over S-38, pinging with sonar gear, but dropped no depth charges.

When it moved off, Chapple got under way and moved deeper into the gulf toward the main landing area. While his crew reloaded the four forward tubes, he raised his periscope and saw dozens of ships. This time he picked a big transport that was anchored, a sitting duck. Believing his first four torpedoes had been set too deep, he now set them for 9 feet. He fired two torpedoes from a range of 500 yards. Thirty seconds later, there was a thundering explosion and the target settled to the shallow bottom. It was a 5,445-ton transport, *Hayo Maru*.

Moments later, two destroyers counterattacked. Chapple took S-38 to 80 feet and lay quietly in the water while depth charges exploded hither and yon—none close. After two hours, he got under way, evading. But S-38 went aground, stuck fast in the muddy bottom. Chapple let her stay where she was most of the day, while Japanese ships, small craft, and landing craft buzzed overhead. Later he dislodged the boat from the mud and crept away. That night, well clear of the landing force, he surfaced to air the boat and charge batteries. At dawn, he submerged and lay on the bottom all day to give his crew a rest and reload the empty tubes.

The following morning, Chapple again came to periscope depth to do battle. Almost immediately, he saw a column of six transports standing into the gulf and set up to fire. On the final approach, almost at the moment of firing, the boat was wracked by an awesome explosion. Evidently a Japanese plane had spotted S-38 and dropped a string of bombs. Chapple broke off the attack, went deep—180 feet—and lay on the bottom the rest of the day.

After sunset, he surfaced again. Chapple had been on the bridge only a few moments when he heard a jarring internal explosion. Hydrogen gas in the after battery, which had not been properly ventilated, exploded. Three men were seriously injured, and the after battery was a shambles. Chapple withdrew from the gulf, eluding the screen of destroyers patrolling at the mouth.

All five other boats attempted to penetrate the destroyer screen.

On the night of December 22, Johnny Burnside in *Saury* charged down from Vigan. Off San Fernando—on the north end of the gulf—Burnside ran into what seemed a squadron of Japanese destroyers "all over the place." (Later he wrote, "It is too bad Lingayen Gulf was not mined. We can't foresee everything.") Finding one stopped in the water, Burnside closed to 1,500 yards and fired a torpedo. It missed.

The next night, Burnside tried again to penetrate the screen, but a destroyer picked him up and drove him under. He was worried about his position, fearing he had wandered into the areas reserved for *Permit* and *Porpoise*. But Wilkes ordered Burnside to clear the area and make way for *Salmon*.

Salmon was commanded by Eugene Bradley McKinney, a soft-spoken officer who had taken his postgraduate work in law, earning a degree. McKinney said later, "At first, my crew didn't accept me. They asked why the navy would send a damned lawyer to command a submarine. When we came into Manila from Pearl Harbor, I made the crew put on whites and go on deck. One of the men said scornfully, 'New battleship arriving on Asiatic Station! U.S.S *Salmon*.' When the war came, I guess I wanted to prove to them a lawyer could fight a submarine as well as anybody else."

On the night of December 23, McKinney moved in toward the destroyer screen. He was detected immediately. Coolly remaining on the surface, turning and dodging, McKinney got boxed in. He said later, "I confess I felt a lot like diving. But I was curious. We stayed on the surface and the destroyers came on. I guess the Jap skippers were just as inexperienced and puzzled as I was." When one of the destroyers crossed *Salmon*'s stern, McKinney fired two torpedoes from 2,500 yards. The destroyer turned aside; the torpedoes missed. McKinney's exec, Irvin Swander Hartman, Freeland Daubin's son-in-law, urged McKinney to dive and evade. But McKinney remained on the surface.

One of the destroyers turned toward *Salmon*, coming directly up the stern. McKinney ordered two stern tubes made ready. He would allow the destroyer to come very close, then fire a down-the-throat shot. McKinney let the destroyer come within 1,200 yards and then fired. He and Hartman saw an explosion and believed, like Mumma, that they had sent one enemy destroyer to the bottom.

After firing, McKinney dived. The destroyers charged over, unleashing a barrage of depth charges. The boat shook, the lights went out, the crew hung on in terror. Later, McKinney recalled, "It was awful . . . it went on for hours."

Next to charge the line was Nicholas Lucker, Jr., in *S-40*. Lucker's exec was Thomas Kinkaid Kimmel, younger of two sons of the admiral, both of whom were in submarines. In the dark of night, Lucker boldly crept by the patrolling destroyer screen into the gulf. Later, Kimmel said, "We adjusted speed so we would be able to cross the entrance (which is quite long) at dawn. As soon as it commenced to get light we visually sighted several ships in the gulf and immediately submerged and commenced an approach to gain torpedo attack. It was extremely rough, and as diving officer I had considerable difficulty in maintaining depth control."

Even so, Lucker got into range and set up on a group of ships at 1,000 yards. He fired four torpedoes at one ship. "Just before firing," Kimmel recalled, "there was some discussion as to whether the torpedoes should be spread. Our doctrine called for no spread at a range of one thousand yards. I remember volunteering, 'You'd better spread them,' but the doctrine prevailed." All missed. Later Lucker said, "I couldn't believe it."

After firing, Kimmel lost control of the boat, and she broached in broad daylight, within sight of several escorts. A destroyer charged in; Lucker went "deep" (80 feet) to evade. However, the engine room reported a serious leak in the exhaust valves, a calamity that forced Lucker to make use of his noisy trim pump. The destroyer heard the pump, located *S-40* by sonar, and came over, delivering a shattering depth-charge attack. The boat bounced around like a cork, but Kimmel kept her from broaching again. Lucker evaded and made his way to a small cove outside the gulf. After dark, he surfaced and found much of the superstructure from the engine-room hatch aft blown away. He reported the damage to Wilkes.

Back in Manila, Wilkes had no clear picture of what was going on at Lingayen Gulf. He was unable to establish radio contact with Gene McKinney in *Salmon*. Burnside in *Saury* reported McKinney had taken "about 180" depth charges and was surely lost. There had been no word from Moon Chapple. On the night of December 24, nevertheless, Wilkes issued orders to withdraw to *Saury* and *Salmon*, as well as *S-38* and *S-40*, and ordered *Permit* and *Porpoise* to take their place and penetrate the gulf.

Porpoise, commanded by Joseph Anthony Callaghan, was next to assault the line. He delayed a few hours, finishing a battery charge, then headed in. He was immediately picked up by a destroyer which dropped eighteen depth charges, Callaghan reported, "seeming to explode directly overhead." He went north to "escape" and, upon reflection, decided that a further attempt to penetrate Lingayen Gulf was "impractical at this time." Callaghan's reasons, as listed in his patrol report, were: strong enemy defense at entrance; can't go in submerged; can't go in on surface at night; enemy carrier and cruiser no longer in gulf; reduced number of enemy vessels in gulf; necessity of passing through *Salmon* and *Saury* areas. He concluded, "Believe from general information in dispatches that a true picture at Lingayen

THE "BATTLE" OF LINGAYEN GULF

not known by higher authority." Wilkes ordered *Porpoise* to go to Hainan Island.

The last boat to make the try was *Permit*, commanded by Adrian Hurst. Approaching the gulf submerged in daytime, Hurst sighted two destroyers. From a range of 1,500 yards, he fired two stern tubes. Both torpedoes missed ahead. Hurst went deep—to 200 feet. Fourteen depth charges fell, none close. The next day, Hurst tried to enter the gulf, evading a destroyer and going deep. He received a report that the main induction—the main air line to the engines—had flooded topside. "*Permit*," he wrote, "became heavy at 220 feet, requiring a 12-degree up-angle to keep her from sinking to the bottom." Like Nick Lucker, he had to use a noisy trim pump. He gave up the attempt, writing, "Slightly inside Gulf . . . in view of inability of this vessel to maintain deep depth control and at the same time run silently, the decision was made to leave Gulf, stand out to sea and report." Later he added, "Everybody has been on board since 8th of December under trying conditions and an opportunity to rest and relax in the sunshine is rapidly becoming imperative for maintenance of good health, morale and efficiency." *Permit* returned to Manila after six days, the shortest patrol of the war.

There were at least nine other fleet boats within easy reach of Lingayen Gulf: Hurd's *Seal* off Vigan; Wright's *Sturgeon* and Aylward's *Searaven*, returning from Formosa; Voge's *Sailfish* and Hurt's *Perch*, en route to Formosa to relieve *Sturgeon* and *Searaven*; New's *Pike*, returning from the Hong Kong area; *Snapper*, commanded by Hamilton Laurie Stone, en route to Hong Kong to relieve *Pike*; Bacon's *Pickerel*, returning from Camranh Bay; and Freddy Warder's *Seawolf*, coming around from Aparri to Manila. None was pressed into the battle for Lingayen Gulf.

Thus the boats deployed to the west had no better luck than the boats deployed to the east. Bull Wright and Dave Hurt both missed opportunities to sink cruisers in Formosa waters; Tyrrell Jacobs missed three cruisers near Camranh Bay; Bart Bacon missed a submarine and a destroyer; Roland Pryce missed three submarines; Ray Lamb missed the entire Lingayen Gulf invasion force. Although Mumma and McKinney were each credited with sinking a destroyer off West Luzon, Japanese records failed to confirm these sinkings and they were later withdrawn. Hurst, Callaghan, and Burnside also missed opportunities to sink Japanese destroyers.

"BATTLE" of LINGAYEN GULF
DECEMBER 21-25, 1941

← ← ← JAPANESE SURFACE FORCES

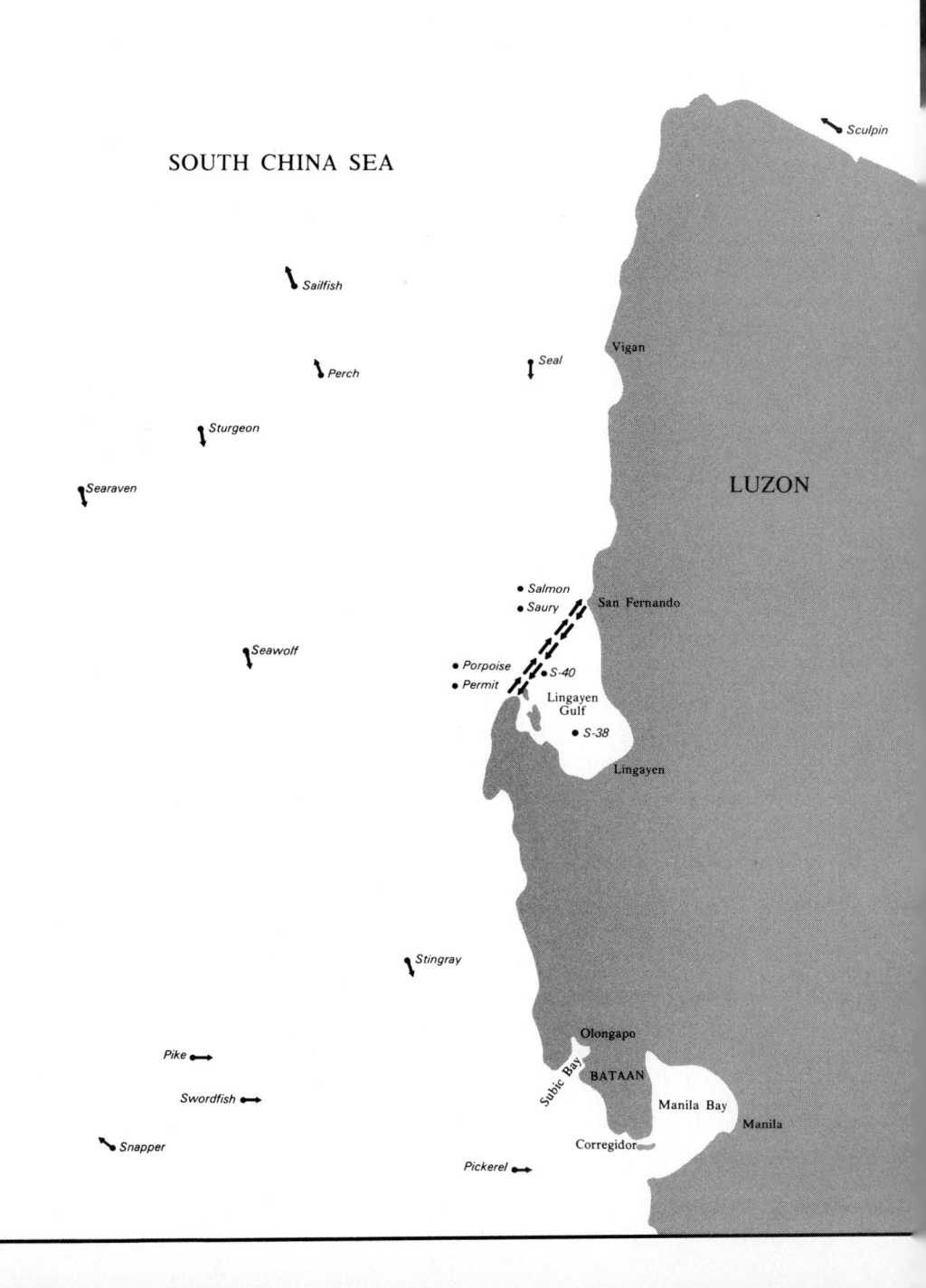

The Loss of Manila

With Japanese troops ashore at Lamon Bay, Aparri, Vigan, Legaspi, and Lingayen Gulf, and MacArthur's air forces reduced to rubble, the Philippines were clearly doomed. On Christmas Eve, MacArthur informed Hart that Manila would be declared an "open city" within twenty-four hours to save it from further destruction. The ground forces would be withdrawn to the Ultimate Defense Area—the Bataan peninsula. MacArthur, Philippine President Manuel Quezon, and U.S. High Commissioner Francis B. Sayre would move to Corregidor.

Admiral Hart had been half expecting this news, but not so soon. He now faced this question: Should he abandon the Philippines as a submarine base, withdrawing the tender *Canopus* and the boats, or leave them to fight on from Bataan and Corregidor? He decided they should fight on for as long as possible. That night he ordered *Canopus* to run down to Mariveles, where, it was hoped, she might find protection under the guns of Corregidor. There was no time to collect the submarine torpedoes, stores, and spare parts that had been off-loaded in Manila. These were abandoned, a loss that would be severely felt later.

Canopus moved in the nick of time. The following day—Christmas—Japanese bombers blasted the Manila waterfront. Some of the bombs fell on submarine headquarters in the enlisted men's club, driving Wilkes and his staff into slit trenches. That afternoon, Hart ordered Wilkes to shift his headquarters to Corregidor. Wilkes, Jimmy Fife, Sunshine Murray—all those who had not boarded *Canopus*—left the Manila waterfront immediately by small boat. Wilkes said later, "We arrived [at Corregidor] late Christmas afternoon and set up our headquarters in a tunnel by pushing over a number of spare-part boxes to make room for a cot, a radio receiver, and one typewriter, this consisting of our sole equipment. We, by that time, were quite portable."

Admiral Hart now faced the question of what to do about himself. Evacuate to Corregidor? Go south to the Malay Barrier where he could better command his surface forces? He decided on the latter course. Originally, he intended to leave the Philippines by navy patrol plane. When the planes were destroyed by Japanese aircraft, Wilkes offered transportation in a submarine, *Shark*. Taking only two staff officers, Hart departed Manila in *Shark* at two on the morning of December 26, bound for the Dutch naval base at Surabaya, Java.

John Wilkes now faced a depressing new situation. Among the orders MacArthur issued for the evacuation of Manila was one calling for the destruction of all diesel oil stocks, military and commercial. The order had been given without consultation with Wilkes and was being carried out "in a highly satisfactory manner" by a young naval lieutenant.

There was no fuel oil at Corregidor, little at Mariveles. Wilkes had intended to move the stocks the lieutenant was systematically destroying to Mariveles on the day following. Hearing that the oil was being destroyed, Wilkes sent one of his staff officers, Willis Percifield, back to Manila to salvage what he could. Three days later Percifield returned from his mission with 300,000 gallons stored in barges and barrels. "This oil was all we had left to operate the twenty-eight submarines on," Wilkes said later. "That in itself made our stay in the Manila area very short."

The oil shortage was merely one hardship. Soon after the submarine staff arrived on Corregidor, Japanese bombers launched the first attack against the "Rock." Thereafter, they came over daily, dropping hundreds of bombs. *Canopus* suffered a direct hit which killed and wounded many men. Because of the incessant air raids, submarines returning from patrols had to remain submerged in lower Manila Bay during daylight hours. Refitting and replenishment was carried out at night by crews already exhausted from the day's tension and fighting. Clearly Corregidor-Mariveles was no place from which to conduct a submarine war.

On New Year's Eve, seven days after shifting to Corregidor, John Wilkes made the decision to abandon the Philippines and withdraw his submarines south to Surabaya. There were then ten boats in port plus *Canopus*, which had been damaged by air attack. She was an old—and slow-moving—ship. If she made a run for it, Wilkes believed, she would probably be discovered by Japanese aircraft and sunk at sea with the loss of all hands. Better, he thought, that she should be left behind.

There were many hundreds of submarine personnel on Corregidor and at Mariveles: refugees from Cavite; the crews of *Sealion*, *Canopus*, and auxiliary craft; hundreds of machinists, optical, torpedo, and compass specialists. It was up to Wilkes to pick who should go and who should stay to become prisoners of war. He decided that each submarine could safely evacuate 25 men, a total of 250 people. "This was a very tough decision to make," Wilkes said later. "And I used

THE LOSS OF MANILA 155

only one guiding principle, whether officer or man. Would the men that we were to take be of value in prosecuting the war no matter where we went?"

Having made his selection, Wilkes then divided his own staff between two submarines, Chet Smith's *Swordfish* and Freddy Warder's *Seawolf*. Wilkes, Percifield, Sunshine Murray, and others boarded *Swordfish*, bound for Surabaya to join Hart. Jimmy Fife, who was promoted to captain on January 1, and other staff officers, including Mort Mumma, boarded *Seawolf* bound for Darwin, Australia, where *Holland* and *Otus* had been sent with Red Doyle.

All the other submarines left Manila in those last days of December. Ray Lamb's *Stingray*, with a new skipper, Raymond John Moore, went west to patrol Hainan Island. Three boats established a patrol off Subic Bay, where yet another Japanese landing was expected. These were Ted Aylward's *Searaven*, returning from Formosa, Nick Lucker's *S-40* (hastily but imperfectly repaired), and *S-41*, commanded by George Michael Holley, Jr. All three boats missed a small Japanese landing force which put ashore there. The remaining eight boats of the Asiatic Fleet—*S-36*, *S-37*, *S-38*, *S-39*, *Pike*, *Pickerel*, *Permit*, and *Sturgeon*—were ordered to patrol southward in the Philippines.*

The submarines left Manila with a feeling of shame and frustration. They had utterly failed to stop the Japanese advances. In December, the Asiatic submarine force had mounted forty-five separate attacks, firing ninety-six torpedoes. Wilkes credited eleven ships sunk —including the two destroyers by Mumma and McKinney—but postwar Japanese records confirmed only three: one big freighter by Chet Smith off Hainan, one very small freighter by Kenneth Hurd in *Seal* off Vigan, and one big freighter by Moon Chapple in Lingayen Gulf.

The loss of Manila—and Luzon—was a greater military tragedy than the loss of and damage to the battleships at Pearl Harbor. The conquest enabled the Japanese swiftly to overrun the Philippines and push farther south, all the while protecting the flank of the southward movement along the mainland of Asia.

Most of the blame must be laid to MacArthur and his air generals.

---

* Pete Ferrall's *Seadragon*, damaged in the December 10 Cavite air raid and repaired at Surabaya, left on December 30 to patrol the Camranh Bay area, replacing Pryce's *Spearfish*, which moved up to Hainan Island to patrol with *Porpoise* and *Stingray*.

They had ample warning, more than eight hours. There was adequate time to mount a strike against air bases on Formosa before the Japanese planes were airborne. There was adequate time to disperse aircraft. Neither was done. The Japanese caught MacArthur's planes on the ground. In two days, his air force was wiped out.

Had MacArthur's air force reacted prudently and intelligently, putting up a stubborn defense, the Japanese would almost certainly have been forced to bring up several carriers for launching air attacks against the Philippines. If so, these might well have become targets for U.S. submarines. The loss of one or two aircraft carriers would have gravely impeded the conquest of the Philippines and knocked the Japanese timetable askew.

The submarine defense of the Philippines was, on the whole, abysmally planned and executed. Eight major errors can be listed.

1. Faulty peacetime training. Most of the peacetime training at Manila was unrealistic, as was the training for submarines at Pearl Harbor and elsewhere. Like Withers, Wilkes considered the aircraft a fatal threat to the submarine and for this reason insisted on the sonar approach. There was little or no training in individual night surface attacks or in wolf-pack tactics. None of the Manila boats had practiced long-range patrolling, such as Withers inaugurated at Pearl Harbor. The skippers were ignorant of the psychological effects of long-term confinement. Many had no idea even about how much food to take along. Said William Thomas Kinsella, a junior officer on *Seawolf*:

We operated very infrequently. When we did, we devoted most time to our own individual training: gunnery and torpedo practice. There were countless days and countless hours spent at sea with the submarine commander [Wilkes] riding the tender and having our three divisions of submarines following astern on the surface by columns of ships by divisions engaging in surface tactics which were ordered by use of signal flags and had to be responded to by individual submarines. In other words, it was the old 'squads-right and squads-left' type of drill. Considering the submarines were of three different classes [S, P, and Salmon], none of which had a common cruising speed, it was just one big bloody mess which never contributed a thing toward improving our readiness. All it did was frustrate us and waste a lot of fuel oil. With such unimaginative thinking as that, how in hell could they ever have thought of a plan to defend the Philippines?

2. Poor upkeep and maintenance. "John Wilkes was never one to place upkeep in high regard," Joseph Callaghan wrote. "I had *Porpoise* in drydock in January 1941 and did not have an overhaul period assigned until the following May. I was due for a battery overhaul, but it was postponed continually."

Many fleet boats suffered countless matériel failures, leaks, and other casualties that would not have occurred with a reasonably efficient program for maintenance. Almost without exception, Asiatic Fleet boats suffered continuous engine breakdowns, especially those powered by the absolutely unreliable H.O.R.s. To have one or two engines out of commission on patrol was the rule rather than the exception for the H.O.R. boats. (The men called the engines "whores.") After *Holland* left Manila, some boats could not obtain spare parts for their engines. To keep running, the skippers cannibalized their own engines for spare parts. After one month at war, it was clear that the H.O.R.s would have to be replaced by Winton or Fairbanks-Morse engines.

When war came, all six S-boats were in miserable condition, much in need of overhaul. George Holley, skipper of *S-41*, recalled some of his major casualties:

Flooding of the starboard main motor through a rupture of its cooler; failure of the JK sound gear right at the start of the first patrol; complete failure of the only radio transmitter; failure of the gyro compass; failure of Number One [attack] periscope, making it useless for about half of the first patrol; failure of the bow plane rigging and tilting mechanism; failure of the starboard main control panel in the engine room; discovery of a hole through the pressure hull into the main drain caused by electrolytic action, which was repaired by drilling, tapping, and insertion of an ordinary pipe plug by the smallest man in the crew, who was lowered head first, after being lathered with grease so we could get him out again; continual trouble with the main engine air compressors, whose third-stage rings and liners wore out at an alarming rate; complete failure of the refrigeration plant at the start of the second patrol, necessitating eating meat like mad until it was too rotten and had to be thrown overboard. And so it went!

3. Basing submarines in Manila. The decision to base tenders and submarines in Manila Bay may have been good for liberty and recreation but it was unwise for war. The safety of these units depended entirely on MacArthur's air power. When the air power was lost, the

tenders and submarines were highly vulnerable to air attack. From December 10 to December 31, when submarines finally evacuated Manila Bay, submarine repair and refit was carried out at great risk.

There had been no need to take those risks. There were many harbors in the southern Philippines ideally suited for a submarine base. During 1941, the submarines had deployed to some of these, notably Tawi Tawi, 500 miles south of Manila. For a fleet submarine, 500 miles was a thirty-hour cruise on the surface, a small addition to patrol time. Submarines basing from Tawi Tawi could reach all the patrol areas assigned without undue inconvenience. The mileage from Tawi Tawi to Camranh Bay is about the same as the mileage from Manila Bay.

4. No initial deployment for war. After Hart received Admiral Stark's war warning on November 27, he gathered all his submarines in Manila Bay. None left for patrol until Clark Field had been bombed. If Hart had sent submarines on war patrol prior to the outbreak of hostilities, to Hainan, Formosa, and Palau, one or several, more likely than not, would have seen the Japanese invasion forces massing for the assault on the Philippines. These submarines could have provided timely warning on the approach of hostile forces, enabling Wilkes to deploy his reserve force accordingly. But by the time the submarines got to these places, the Japanese had already departed.

5. Weak instructions for war. John Wilkes sent his submarines into combat with orders to patrol briefly and cautiously and place survival above inflicting damage on the enemy. Inasmuch as the submarine force constituted the main naval defense of the Philippines, and the Japanese were moving with awesome speed and effectiveness, the orders appear inexplicable. What was required was not caution—the skippers were already prone to caution from years of misguided peacetime training—but a ringing cry to battle. Those skippers who were obviously unfit, and there were all too many at Manila, should have been instantly replaced by younger men with a taste for battle.

6. No defense of Lingayen Gulf. Most military experts—including naval strategists—had believed for four decades that Lingayen Gulf was the logical place for the main amphibious landing in Luzon. The overland route to Manila lay across a broad, fertile plain where tanks and other mechanized vehicles could maneuver. Yet in his war plan Wilkes placed only one S-boat inside the gulf and no fleet boats at sea along its approaches, an inexplicable lapse.

THE LOSS OF MANILA

By December 20, the Japanese were well established at Vigan and moving south. An invasion at Lingayen Gulf seemed a dead certainty to MacArthur and Hart. There was no air power left for reconnaissance purposes. If the Japanese were to be stopped at the gulf, submarines would have to do it. Yet as late as December 21 Wilkes still had only one submarine standing off the gulf, Ray Lamb's *Stingray*. The following day, Lamb picked up the incoming invasion force and got off a report. After that, Wilkes rushed submarines to the gulf, but it was too late. The Japanese were already inside, disembarking troops, with the mouth guarded by a heavy screen of destroyers.

Why had Wilkes left Lingayen Gulf unguarded? The question was evidently never officially raised. In all the after-battle reports submitted by Hart, Wilkes, and others, the matter is glossed over.

Wilkes had time—and resources—to mount a realistic defense of Lingayen Gulf. Counting the submarines going to and from distant stations and those patrolling along the west coast of Luzon, there were fourteen fleet boats in the vicinity of Lingayen Gulf from December 20 to December 25, the crucial period. Had Wilkes placed these boats on an arc about 150 miles to the west and northwest of the gulf, one or several would probably have picked up the force far at sea where there was room to attack offensively and repeatedly. Once contact had been made, the other boats on the arc could have been quickly vectored to the battle. Had the arc been formed and the skippers ordered to fight aggressively, the Japanese invasion force might have been decisively damaged or even turned aside.

The arc might also have snared some larger game. During the Lingayen landings, the Japanese brought the battleships *Kongo* and *Haruna* plus cruiser and destroyer escorts from Malayan waters for support. These battleships were lying off the western coast of Luzon for four or five days.

A submarine victory at Lingayen Gulf might also have done much to put backbone in MacArthur's ground forces. Instead of abandoning Manila and withdrawing to Bataan and Corregidor, MacArthur might have elected to stand and fight. If this had been the case, the whole course of the war might have changed. With continued interdiction by the submarine force against Japanese ships attempting landings in the gulf or supporting aircraft carriers, MacArthur's forces might have held, counterattacked, and driven the Japanese out of Luzon, even without air power.

7. Unnecessary loss of materiel and men. Although most of the

submarine force escaped Manila intact, there were inexcusable losses. The 233 torpedoes lost in the bombing of the Cavite Naval Station should have been dispersed to Corregidor, or even beaches and fields, long before the Japanese attack. The destruction of *Sealion* and the damage to *Seadragon*—and the loss of life on those boats—was unnecessary. The Japanese bombed Clark Field on December 8; Cavite, a logical target, was not bombed until December 10. In the two-day interval, *Sealion* and *Seadragon* could have been towed from the yard to a place of safety or submerged in Manila Bay. The loose gear belonging to these boats—engines, compressors, batteries—could also have been put in a safe place.

The most tragically unnecessary loss to the submarine force was the tender *Canopus* and her skilled technicians, including those from Cavite Naval Station who joined *Canopus* after the bombing. Countless scores of opticians, electricians, machinists, and torpedomen were left behind with *Canopus* to take up guns and help in the futile struggle to save Bataan and Corregidor. Had Wilkes gathered up all these experts and put them on *Canopus* and then ordered her to make a dash for it, she might well have reached Australia safely. In any case, a death at sea would have been no worse than what actually befell them. Many submarine technicians died in battle or in the Death March or in Japanese POW camps. Their loss left a large gap in the Asiatic submarine force for many months to come.

8. Failure to take immediate action to make a live test on the Mark XIV torpedo. Shortly after the war began, the Bureau of Ordnance notified Wilkes (and other S-boat commanders) that the old Mark X torpedo ran 4 feet deeper than designed. Wilkes and others took action to make corrections, and thereafter the torpedo (with a contact exploder) performed well. Many of Wilkes's skippers returning from their first brief war patrols (notably Freddy Warder) insisted that the Mark XIV torpedo was defective—running deep and/or failing to explode as designed by magnetic influence. On *Sargo* Tyrrell Jacobs, a torpedo expert, conducted as careful a seagoing test as could be imagined and risked his own life by breaking radio silence to raise doubts. Yet neither Wilkes nor his chief of staff, Jimmy Fife, saw fit to make a test firing at Manila. A crude test—that might have revealed much—could have been conducted in a single day against one of the ships abandoned in Manila Bay or against fishing nets.

U.S.S. Adder (A-2)

U.S.S. S-20

Preparing to fire torpedo

Readying a torpedo for loading through submarine hatch

Motor machinists adjust diesel in engine room

Planesmen at diving plane controls

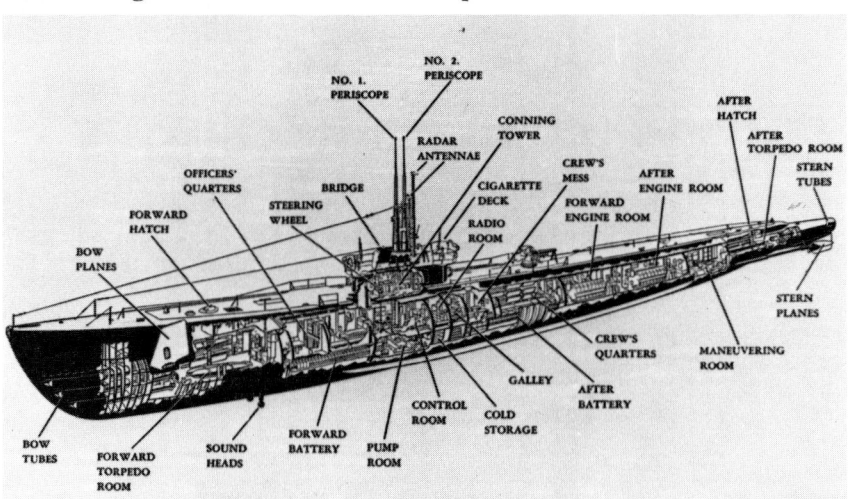

Cutaway of a fleet boat　　　　　　　　　　*Fleet boat (right)*

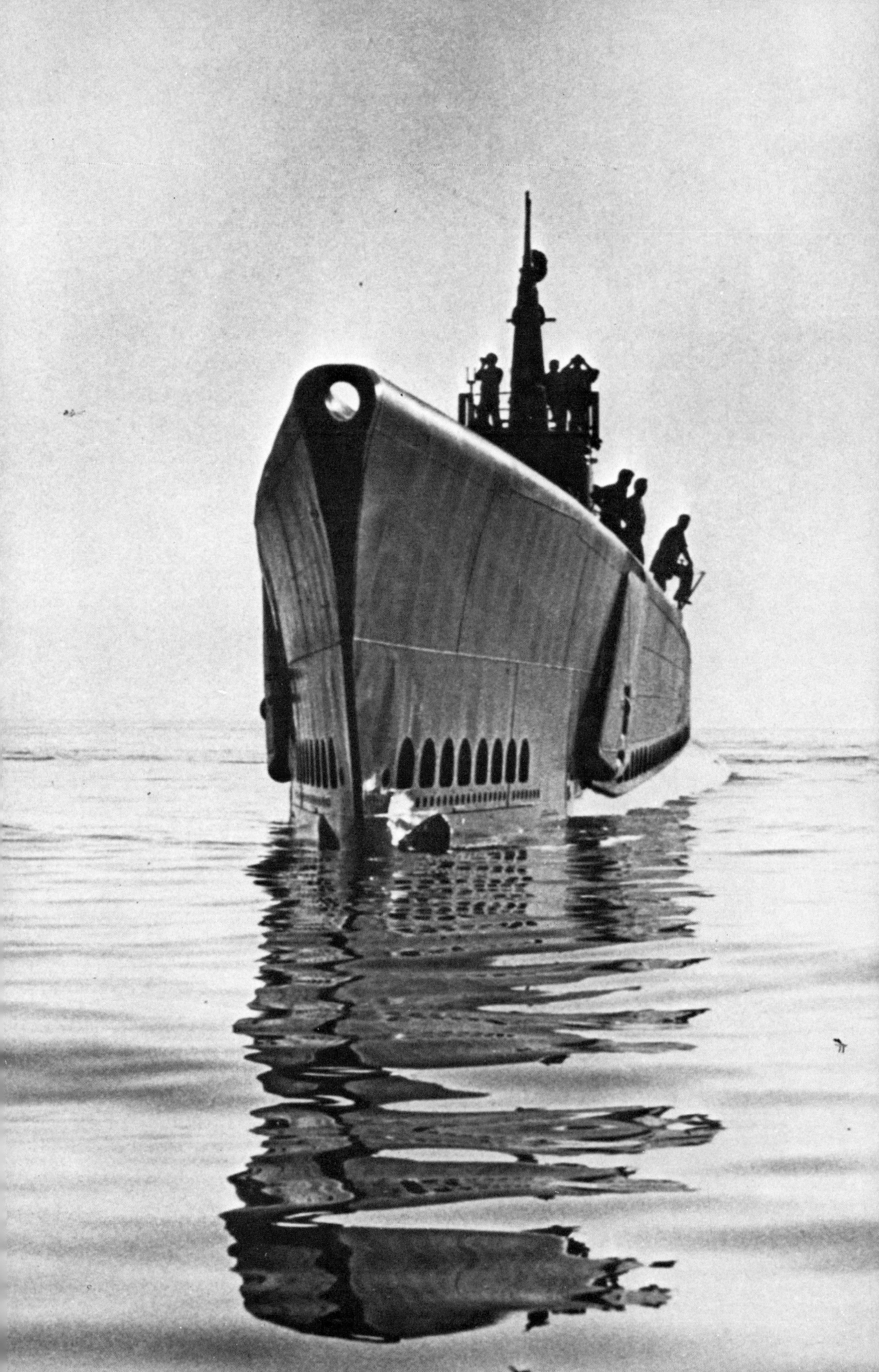

Off-duty enlisted men playing poker and writing reports in crew's mess on a fleet boat

Men at battle stations in conning tower

Radioman in radio shack copies messages from Pearl Harbor

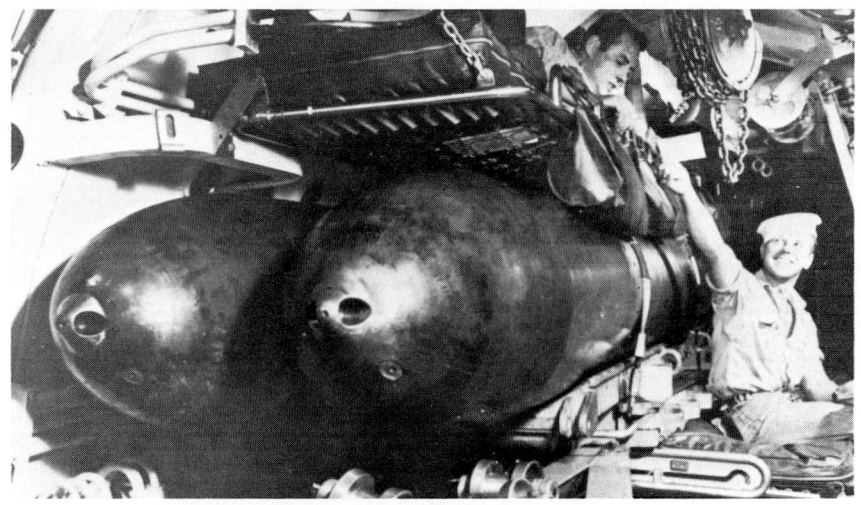

In forward torpedo room, bunk is slung over two torpedoes

Charles Andrews Lockwood, Jr., class of 1912

Ralph Waldo Christie, class of 1915

James Fife, class of 1918

Richard George Voge, clowning in fake glasses and mortarboard at a party

Charles Wilkes Styer

Allan Rockwell McCann

John Wilkes

Freeland Allan Daubin

Philip Gardner Nichols

Thomas Withers

Robert Henry English

Merrill Comstock

Fife (left), Lockwood (center), and Styer (right) in a poker game

Submarine Base, New London

Submarine Base, Brisbane

Submarine Base, Pearl Harbor

Submarine Base, Subic Bay, Philippines

Submarine Base, Fremantle (Bonefish *arriving from war patrol*)

"Bend of the Road"

A spectacular sinking: Puffer *torpedoes* Teiko Maru, *formerly the French liner* D'Artagnan

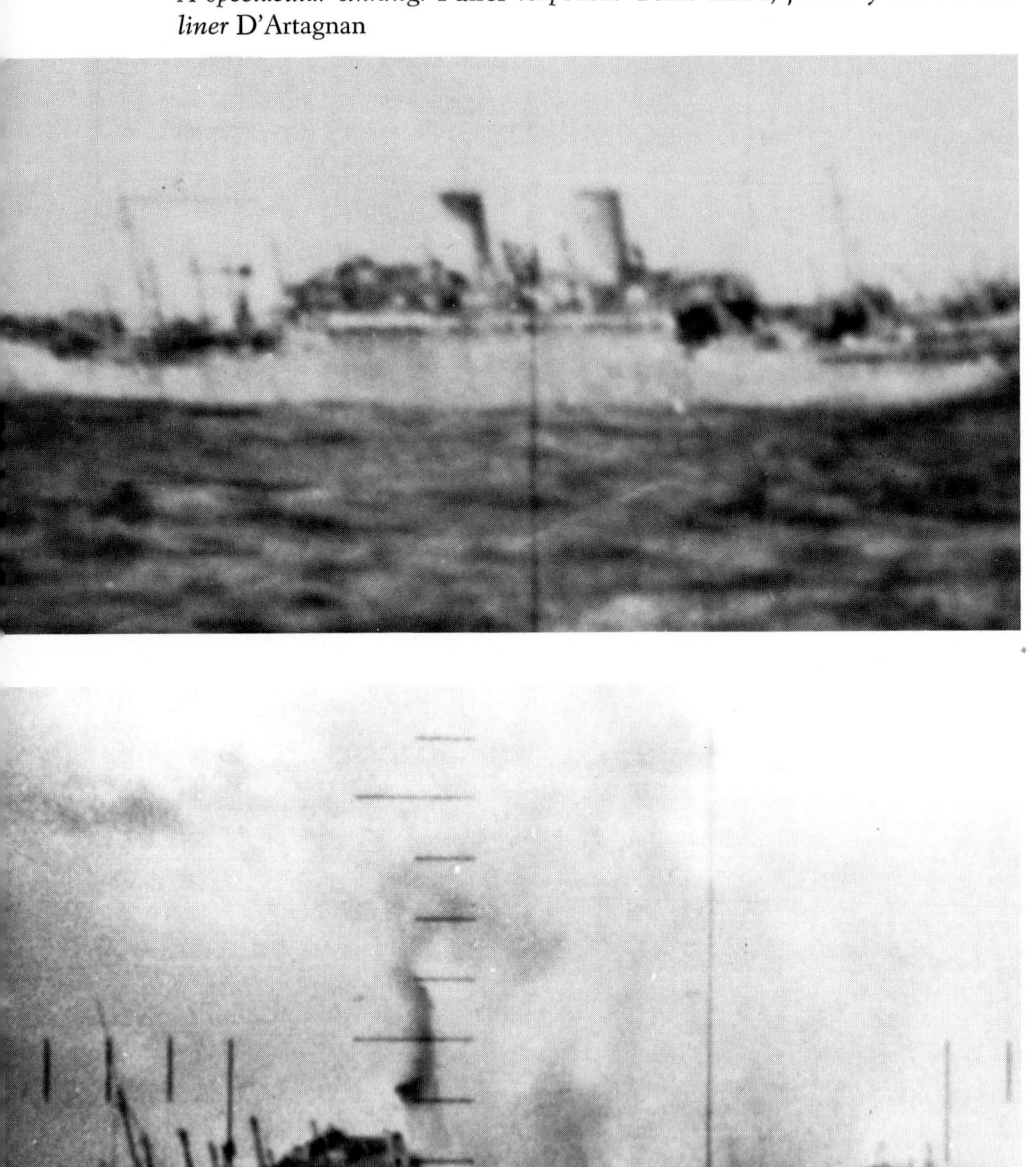

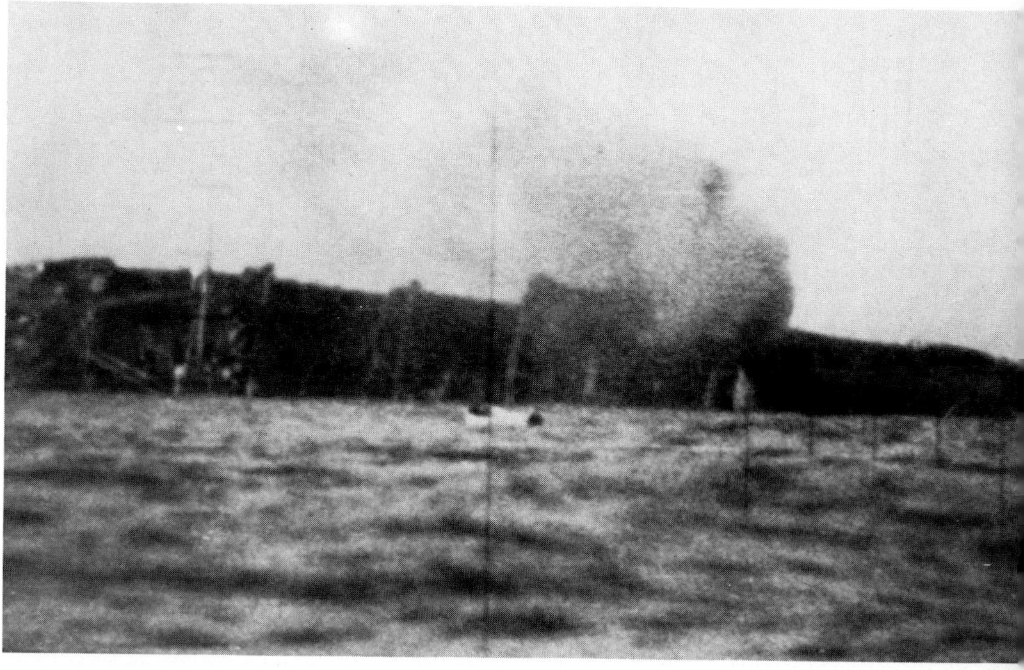

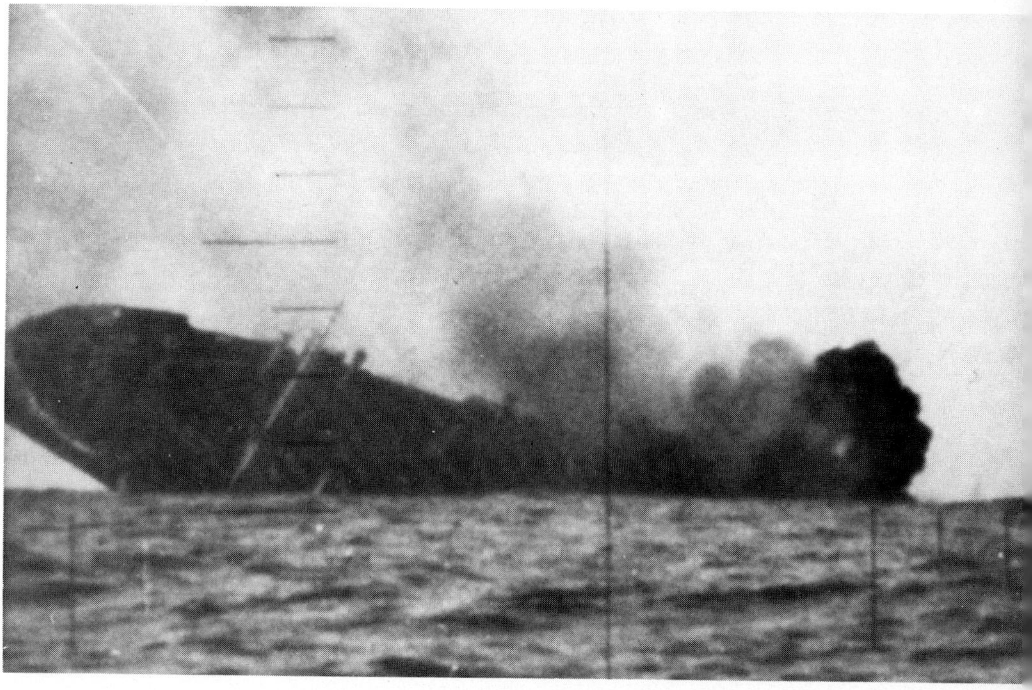

Submarine Base, Guam

Camp Dealey, submarine crew rest area, Guam

Part III

4

Java and Australia, January through April 1942

The Japanese Drive to the Malay Barrier

The Japanese, having driven MacArthur's forces into the Ultimate Defense Area of Bataan and Corregidor, then proceeded to seize key cities, airfields, and ports in the southern Philippine islands. The Gulf of Davao, on the southern tip of Mindanao, became the principal Japanese staging area. From it, the Japanese launched a two-pronged drive toward the Malay Barrier, the western force going down through Makassar Strait, the eastern going down through Molucca Passage. The objectives: capture of Borneo, Celebes, Ambon, Timor, Bali, and Java. Far to the west, Japanese forces staging from Indochina continued to reinforce the drive on the British base at Singapore and prepared to send a force to invade Sumatra and Java.

In Java, Admiral Hart assumed command of all remaining American, British, Dutch, and Australian naval power. (His command was known as ABDA, an acronym based on the initials of the four countries.) His staff, based in a mountaintop headquarters at Bandung, was composed of naval officers from the four nations, most of whom held conflicting views about what to do. The British wanted to pour more troops into Singapore, utilizing the naval power as escorts for the convoys. The Dutch wanted to stop the Japanese drive short of Sumatra and Java. The Australians wanted all forces to retreat below the Malay Barrier and protect their homeland from invasion.

Admiral Hart's strategy—if it can be dignified by that word—leaned to the Dutch view: if possible, the Japanese should be stopped short of the Malay Barrier. He would position his submarines off Davao and Indochina to interdict Japanese invasion forces at the point of origin. Others would be placed in Makassar Strait and Molucca Passage to block those key portals to the south. The handful of surface forces—a few cruisers and old destroyers—would be organized into task forces, to strike at the invasion forces wherever they could.

When Hart gave the order to concentrate the submarines for the defense of the Malay Barrier, the force was scattered far and wide. The tenders *Holland* and *Otus* were in Darwin, Australia, along with two fleet boats, Freddy Warder's *Seawolf*, which had delivered Jimmy Fife and others, and Lew Wallace's *Tarpon*, which had come down from San Bernardino Strait after nearly being lost in the storm. Larry Freeman's *Skipjack* was en route to Darwin. Dave Hurt in *Perch*, who had left Formosa for Hong Kong waters following the surrender of that place on Christmas Day, reported two engines and both periscopes out of commission, so he too was sent to Darwin for overhaul. Other boats were at Formosa, Hong Kong, Hainan, Indochina, Surabaya, and Luzon.

Hart first ordered Wilkes to place a heavy concentration of boats at Davao, the Japanese staging base for the push south. Wilkes sent eleven with an urgent call for aggressiveness: ATTACK. ATTACK. ATTACK. ATTACK. Dick Voge in *Sailfish*, patrolling off Formosa, went there by way of Aparri and down the east coast of Luzon. Ham Stone in *Snapper*, patrolling off Hong Kong, followed Voge's trail to Aparri and then went down east of Luzon. Hurd in *Seal* left Vigan, circled the north end of Luzon, and then went south along the east coast of Luzon. Ted Aylward in *Searaven*, Gene McKinney in *Salmon*, Johnny Burnside in *Saury*, Bart Bacon in *Pickerel*, Adrian Hurst in *Permit*, and Billy New in *Pike* converged on Davao via the Sulu and Celebes seas. Chet Smith in *Swordfish* and Louis Shane in *Shark* left Surabaya for their second patrols and approached Davao by way of the Banda Sea.

These eleven boats—spread across the Celebes Sea from Davao Gulf southward to Molucca Passage—did almost nothing to stop the Japanese invasion forces leaving Davao. By the time most of them reached station, the Japanese had left, the Western Invasion Force going down through Makassar Strait and the Eastern Invasion Force going down through Molucca Passage. U.S. submarines sank only one Japanese ship in this early deployment, a small freighter torpedoed by Bart Bacon in *Pickerel*.

Three boats left station early: Ted Aylward's *Searaven*, Billy New's *Pike*, and Adrian Hurst's *Permit*. Aylward's health had deteriorated further, the dizziness and headaches coming on more frequently. He ran short of food and tobacco, the latter "acutely felt." He went to Darwin, where, according to his exec, Francis Walker, he was ready to turn in his command but could not find a qualified relief. Billy New in *Pike* followed him to Darwin.

Adrian Hurst, who had sixteen extra people on *Permit*, including Ray Lamb from *Stingray* and one of Hart's staff officers, Robert Lee Dennison, also ran out of food. In addition, Hurst wrote in his report that 90 percent of the crew and officers suffered from prickly heat, Guam blisters, boils, carbuncles, ear infections, loss of weight, lack of laundry, and the inability to air bedding. One officer was on the sick list with swollen hands and feet. Hurst went into Surabaya, the crew subsisting on torpedo room emergency rations. When he arrived, Wilkes relieved him of command, turning the boat over to Moon Chapple, who had brought his badly battered S-38 down from Manila.

One of the boats was lost, Louis Shane's *Shark*. Going up through the Banda Sea, *Shark* reconnoitered Ambon in the Moluccas and then continued northward to Molucca Passage. Shane broke radio silence to tell Wilkes about an empty northbound cargo ship he had sighted. Wilkes upbraided him for this, considering the report of little value. That was the last ever heard from *Shark*. She was probably lost to Japanese depth-charge attack in or near Molucca Passage. Fifty-nine officers and men perished with *Shark*, the first boat of the war to be lost to Japanese antisubmarine forces at sea.

Of the eleven boats at Davao and vicinity, Dick Voge in *Sailfish* came closest to inflicting serious damage on the enemy. While patrolling off Halmahera Island, south of Davao, he sighted a *Nachi*-class cruiser and destroyer escort. In a daylight periscope attack, Voge fired four torpedoes. He reported one explosion and believed the cruiser's propellers stopped, indicating damage, for which he received credit.

The Eastern Invasion Force pushed south through Molucca Passage with ease, making landings at Kema on the northeast coast of Celebes, then Kendari on the southeast coast. Chet Smith in *Swordfish*, coming up from Ambon, made a daring assault on the invasion ships already inside Kema and vicinity. He went inside the harbor, where he believed he sank four ships for 20,000 tons; however, postwar Japanese records confirmed only one for 4,000 tons.

Japan's Western Invasion Force, meanwhile, jumped off and headed for Makassar Strait. The first target was Tarakan on the northeast coast of Borneo. Wilkes withdrew Roland Pryce in *Spearfish* from Indochina to take up station off Tarakan, along with *S-37*, commanded by James Charles Dempsey, and George Holley's *S-41*. However, the Japanese landed unopposed; none of the submarines made contact.

The next southward goal in Makassar Strait appeared to be Balikpapan, an oil port on the southeast coast of Borneo. Wilkes deployed seven submarines for this battle. Raymond Moore's *Stingray*, withdrawn from Hainan, was stationed north of the narrow neck of Makassar Strait. Joseph Callaghan's *Porpoise*, withdrawn from Camranh Bay, was stationed in the neck, along with Bart Bacon's *Pickerel*, shifted over from Davao. Bull Wright's *Sturgeon* was positioned just to the south of the neck. Roland Pryce in *Spearfish* was moved south from Tarakan and placed directly off Balikpapan, along with Burnside's *Saury*, withdrawn from Davao, and Nick Lucker's *S-40*.

On January 22, Billy New in *Pike* came in contact with the Western Invasion Force. He counted twenty-six ships escorted by fourteen destroyers. He got off a report to Wilkes but did not attack. "Any torpedo fired," he wrote later, "would have left tracks saying, 'X marks the spot.'" Immediately to the south, Bull Wright in *Sturgeon* picked up New's contact report and went to battle stations.

Up to then, Wright had had a discouraging second patrol. Five nights earlier, on January 17, he had missed a tanker near Tawi Tawi with three torpedoes. *Sturgeon* submerged, awaiting the oncoming force. Soon the sonarman reported destroyers and a "heavy screw ship." Wright and his exec, Reuben Whitaker, and young Chester Nimitz were certain it must be an aircraft carrier. Setting up a cautious sonar approach, Wright passed beneath the destroyer screen. When the target reached 1,400 yards, he fired a spread of four torpedoes. Shortly afterward, the sonarman reported hits and explosions.

Later, they surfaced. Confident of the aim and torpedo performance, Wright got off a message paraphrasing a bawdy song: STURGEON NO LONGER VIRGIN. The message, which soon became famous, was evidently Bull; postwar Japanese records revealed no loss of—or even

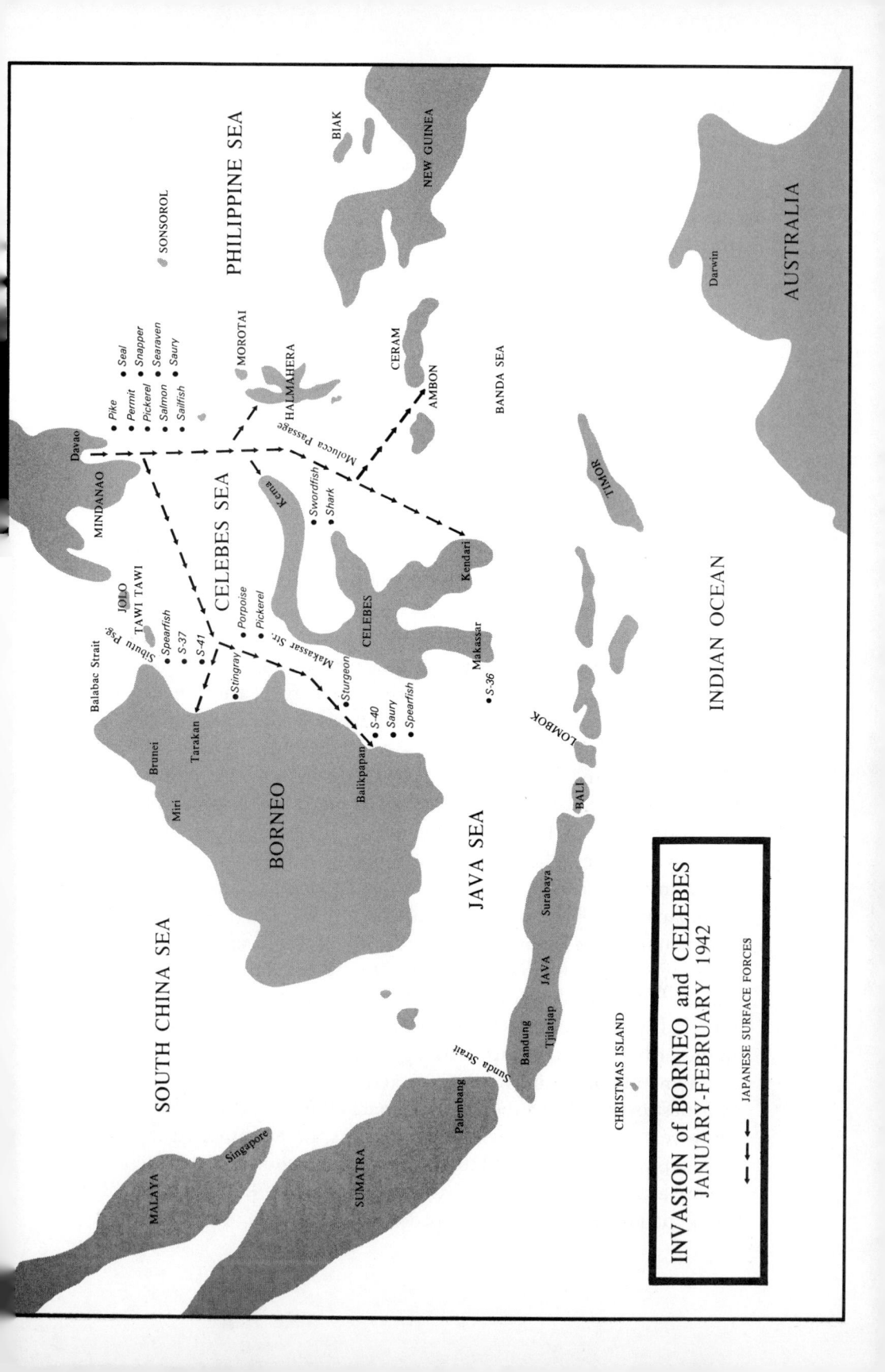

INVASION of BORNEO and CELEBES
JANUARY-FEBRUARY 1942

→ JAPANESE SURFACE FORCES

notable damage to—a carrier at this time and place. The torpedoes must have prematured or otherwise exploded harmlessly. *Sturgeon* was still a virgin.

Wright made two more attacks. The first was against a destroyer. While his exec manned the periscope, he fired four torpedoes from 1,000 yards and claimed a sinking. The second target was a tanker, which Wright claimed he sank with three torpedoes. His total credited score during the battle of Balikpapan was three ships for 20,000 tons. However, JANAC failed to substantiate any of these claims.

Joseph Callaghan in *Porpoise* moved south to patrol off Balikpapan. *Porpoise* had been under way from Manila since December 22—at Lingayen Gulf, Indochina, and now Balikpapan. Callaghan was exhausted. Later he said, "I have always considered that I had all the requisites for being a successful wartime submarine commander except one: stamina. That was my undoing, the lack of it and total exhaustion I experienced may be attributed to it." In addition, he and his exec were at odds.

Off Balikpapan, a cruiser passed *Porpoise* at 4,000 yards. Callaghan was unable to attack. Later that night, while Callaghan was sleeping on the floor of the conning tower, the watch picked up another contact. Coming awake, Callaghan had difficulty adjusting himself "due to fatigue." He ordered a quick stern shot which missed. Another torpedo was fired by mistake. Later, Callaghan wrote in his report that he would have never given the orders to fire if he had been in "full possession of his mental faculties." When Callaghan got into Surabaya, Wilkes relieved him of command.

Johnny Burnside in *Saury* and Roland Pryce in *Spearfish*, lying off Balikpapan, had received the contact reports, but both missed the oncoming Japanese force because they had not been able to get an accurate navigational fix for several days. Burnside later estimated he was 65 miles out of position. Pryce figured he missed by 17 miles and reported with candor, "I failed to make the most of my opportunities in the early part of this patrol through overcautiousness."

Raymond Moore in *Stingray* picked up two transports escorted by two destroyers. He attempted to attack but was driven off by the destroyers. During the next several nights, he encountered this same formation, which appeared to be on a regular shuttle run. Each time Moore attempted to attack, he was driven away. Nick Lucker in *S-40* found no targets worthy of a torpedo.

While this "battle" was in progress, there were four other submarines southbound in Makassar Strait: John McKnight's S-36; S-39, commanded by James Wiggins Coe; Tyrrell Jacobs's *Sargo*; and Lucius Chappell's *Sculpin*. S-36 and S-39 were patrolling from Manila to Surabaya. Jacobs's *Sargo* was returning from her frustrating torpedo-plagued patrol off Indochina. Chappell's *Sculpin* was returning from her patrol off east Luzon, which, like *Sargo*'s, had produced no sinkings. None of these boats took part in the fighting.

Like Burnside and Pryce, McKnight in S-36 found navigation in Makassar Strait difficult. The weather had been foul. He relied mainly on dead reckoning. His charts—like the charts on all the boats—were imprecise and incomplete. As a result, McKnight ran hard aground on Taka Bakang reef at the south end of Makassar Strait. The hull holed, flooding the forward battery. Considering his situation grave, McKnight broke radio silence and sent a plain language message to all U.S. men-of-war: AGROUND TAKA BAKANG SINKING.

Tyrrell Jacobs in *Sargo* picked up McKnight's distress message. Although it was getting light, Jacobs remained on the surface for four and a half hours, relaying the message to Wilkes. When Wilkes acknowledged it, Jacobs proceeded toward S-36 on the surface in broad daylight until 2:15 that afternoon, when he was ordered by Wilkes to submerge. After dark, Jacobs surfaced and soon saw S-36's searchlight.

Wilkes, meanwhile, had mounted a rescue mission. First he sent a navy patrol plane to survey the situation. By the time it buzzed low over S-36, McKnight had changed his mind. With assistance, he radioed, he might save his ship. The next morning a Dutch launch arrived from Makassar City, 60 miles to the east. The launch removed two officers and twenty-eight enlisted men, leaving McKnight and the rest to save the ship. Conditions worsened meanwhile, and when the Dutch ship S.S. *Siberote* arrived that afternoon McKnight decided to abandon the effort. He rigged S-36 for flooding. *Siberote* took off McKnight and the remaining men, and all hands reached Surabaya on January 25. McKnight was not blamed for this episode, the second submarine loss of the war at sea.

When Tyrrell Jacobs got into Surabaya, there was hell to pay. Wilkes conceded that the Mark XIV might be running deep (and ordered all skippers to use shallower settings except against capital ships) but he upbraided Jacobs for deactivating the magnetic exploder. Jacobs pleaded with Wilkes to allow *Sargo* to fire a torpedo through a fishnet to make a test. "The request," his torpedo officer Doug Rhymes wrote later, "was denied—reportedly due to a shortage of torpedoes." Rhymes added:

The Bureau of Ordnance flew a torpedo expert, Lieutenant Commander Walker, all the way out from Washington to investigate Sargo's torpedo problems. He put us through rigorous drills in preparing torpedoes for firing and in routine maintenance procedures. Near the end of our checklist in getting one of the torpedoes ready, Walker interrupted the proceedings, made a couple of checks, then directed me to lock the gyros in place. I looked . . . and noted that he had turned the gyro backwards [a Mark XIV gyro could be locked in a reverse position and result in an erratic run] I turned the gyro to the correct alignment, locked it in place and told Walker that we preferred to attack the enemy ships instead of our own. His face fell half a foot. . . . Walker did not point out a single fault in our preparations and maintenance procedures; nevertheless, [his] report, in summary, placed all the blame for Sargo torpedo problems on Sargo personnel. As a result, the Bureau of Ordnance reaffirmed their position that the Mark XIV torpedoes ran at their set depth.

Meanwhile the Japanese far to the west were pouring down from Indochina to Malaya to reinforce the siege of Singapore. The primary staging area for this effort was Camranh Bay. Only one U.S. submarine could be spared to interdict this flow, Pete Ferrall's *Seadragon*.

Ferrall reached the Camranh Bay area on January 10 and found the seas teeming with enemy ships. As soon as he reached station, he picked up a small destroyer. Although the target was probably not worth a torpedo, Ferrall set up and fired two with a depth setting of 15 feet. Both ran under the target without exploding. Ferrall broke off the attack after deciding the destroyer might be leading a convoy.

It was. At 12:47, eleven troopships escorted by a cruiser and three destroyers came along. Ferrall rang up flank speed but was unable to get closer than 2,500 yards. Even so, he fired two torpedoes at the last ship in the column: no hits. Two destroyers broke off and hunted *Seadragon*, but Ferrall evaded. Later that afternoon, he sighted yet another large steamer but could not get into firing position.

Two days later, Ferrall found more action. In the morning, he sighted seven big ships: five freighters, a tanker, and one steamer.

However, he was unable to reach a favorable firing position on any. In the afternoon, an unseen aircraft dropped a string of bombs on *Seadragon*. Ferrall went deep and slipped out of the area. (When he surfaced that night, Ferrall discovered that the black paint was peeling off the hull and superstructure, exposing the undercoating of red lead. The crew rechristened the boat "The Red Dragon.")

The targets seemed endless. About midnight on January 16, Ferrall picked up two more big ships. Remaining on the surface, he closed to 500 yards and fired two torpedoes: no hits. He set up for a second attack and fired two more torpedoes, from 1,200 yards: again, no hits. Four days later, *Seadragon* found another convoy—five steamers—but Ferrall was unable to get into firing position. On January 23, he picked up a four-ship convoy and fired one torpedo at the lead ship. It hit; Ferrall could see damage. He fired two torpedoes at the second ship but both missed. Then he surfaced and manned the 3-inch gun to polish off the damaged ship. However, after he got off twelve rounds, a plane drove *Seadragon* under. On January 25, he fired two torpedoes at another freighter. No hits. That night he unintentionally tangled with a destroyer, which charged *Seadragon* and delivered a dozen well-placed depth charges.

After that, John Wilkes ordered Ferrall to shift his area from Indochina to the west coast of Luzon. He was relieved by Ted Aylward in *Searaven*, which came from Australia via Molucca Passage, where Aylward believed he had sunk a Japanese destroyer.

In all, Pete Ferrall had sighted a cruiser, thirty large troopships, freighters, tankers, and numerous destroyers. He made eight separate attacks, firing thirteen torpedoes. Only one torpedo had hit, causing damage to one ship. Like Jacobs, who had preceded him to this target-rich area, Ferrall and his exec, Bub Ward, developed grave suspicions about the Mark XIV torpedo.

During the crucial month of January 1942, U.S. submarines at Davao, Molucca Passage, Makassar Strait, and Camranh Bay sank only three ships confirmed in Japanese records: Bacon's small freighter, Chet Smith's large freighter, and a large freighter sunk at Hainan Island by Raymond Moore in *Stingray*. In two months of war patrolling, the twenty-eight Asiatic Fleet submarines had sunk a total of six confirmed ships, all freighters. Two submarines—*Shark* and *S-36*—had been lost at sea, a total of three counting *Sealion*.

Special Submarine Missions

At this critical phase in the Far Eastern campaign, the Asiatic Fleet submarines were called upon to provide a new and wholly unexpected service. General MacArthur and the defenders of Bataan and Corregidor desperately needed ammunition and food. The navy had promised help, but only one or two small surface vessels had reached Corregidor; the rest had been intercepted or sunk by the Japanese. MacArthur requested through Washington that submarines be assigned to bring in supplies.

When this request filtered down to John Wilkes in Surabaya, he was of two minds. His submarines constituted the main fighting power of the Asiatic Fleet. They were needed for the defense of the Malay Barrier. At best, they could transport only a small trickle of supplies to Corregidor, a drop in the bucket. On the other hand, Wilkes felt sympathy for the shipmates he had left behind. Even a small gesture of help might boost morale. Admiral Hart, who considered such missions "diversions" from the main task—stopping the Japanese onslaught—asked Washington that they be "kept to a minimum."

The first mission was assigned to Freddy Warder, whose *Seawolf* was in Darwin. Warder did not like the assignment, but he followed orders. He and his exec, William Nolan Deragon, removed sixteen of *Seawolf*'s torpedoes, leaving only four in the forward tubes and four in the after tubes. They rounded up all the surplus ammunition they could find in Darwin and loaded it in *Seawolf*. It was indeed a drop in the bucket: 675 boxes of 50-caliber machine-gun ammunition and seventy-two 3-inch antiaircraft shells. "The way they were expending ammo up there," Warder recalled, "it amounted to about one day's supply."

On January 16, Warder stood out of Darwin for the 1,800-mile voyage to Corregidor. Off Kema on January 21, he spotted a portion of the Western Invasion Force bound for Balikpapan: a cruiser, six destroyers, and seven transports. Toward dusk, in rainy weather, he made an approach on the cruiser and a destroyer but could not gain firing position.

After a ten-day trip, Warder reached Corregidor early on the morning of January 27. The army gratefully received the 50-caliber ammo but was disappointed with the 3-inch antiaircraft shells. There

SPECIAL SUBMARINE MISSIONS

were plenty of those on Corregidor, and experience had proved that one in three was a dud.

After unloading the ammo, Warder and Deragon proceeded to fill *Seawolf* with as many submarine spare parts as she could hold. In addition, they took aboard sixteen torpedoes by means of an ingenious skid devised by the torpedo officer of *Canopus*, Louis Darby ("Sandy") McGregor, Jr. Lastly, Warder took aboard twenty-five passengers, designated by name, half by Hart in Surabaya and half by MacArthur: a British intelligence officer, twelve army pilots, six navy pilots, five navy enlisted pilots, and one navy yeoman.

Warder returned south through the Sulu and Celebes seas, Molucca Passage, and thence to Surabaya. The submarine spare parts were gratefully received.

Meanwhile, Pete Ferrall in *Seadragon*—shifted from Camranh Bay to Luzon—reached Lingayen Gulf, slipped by the destroyer screen at the mouth, and took *Seadragon* inside—the first fleet boat to make it. He saw a cruiser under way close to the beach but could not get close enough to shoot. He remained inside the gulf most of the day scouting, then withdrew to sea.

In the next two days, Ferrall found good hunting outside the gulf. On February 1, he intercepted a southbound three-ship convoy. He fired one torpedo at the lead ship and one torpedo at the second ship. Both missed. The next day he encountered a five-ship convoy. He fired two torpedoes at the fourth ship in column and one at the fifth. The first torpedoes hit, but the third missed. The ship Ferrall hit, the 6,441-ton transport *Tamagawa Maru*, was loaded with troops and equipment. Ferrall stood off and watched it sink.

While Ferrall was in Luzon waters, Admiral King decided that the Cast codebreaking unit, holed up in a tunnel on Corregidor, should be evacuated by submarine. If the Cast experts were captured by the Japanese, they might be tortured and reveal all their secrets. Wilkes ordered *Seadragon* to put into Corregidor, evacuate as many codebreakers as he could, with gear, and pick up a load of torpedoes and submarine spare parts.

Ferrall arrived off Corregidor on the night of February 4. During the night, working parties—now under artillery fire—stored two tons of submarine spare parts and twenty-three torpedoes in *Seadragon*. In addition, Ferrall evacuated twenty-five people, seventeen of them members of the Cast unit, including the commanding officer, Rudolph

Fabian. They brought along one and a half tons of equipment: the Red and Purple machines, radios, codebooks, and other gear.

Ferrall left for Surabaya the following day.

The next boat sent on a special mission to the Philippines was *Sargo*. Her skipper, Tyrrell Jacobs, was to deliver 30-caliber ammunition to some U.S. Army troops still holding out on western Mindanao. Jacobs was not happy with the assignment either.

Later he said, "Rightly or wrongly, I felt this [mission] reflected a distrust in my ability as a submarine commanding officer and a lack of confidence in me by the high command."

On February 3, Jacobs offloaded all his torpedoes except for eight— those in the torpedo tubes. The following day, he took aboard 666 cases of ammo, a total of one million rounds, weighing about forty tons. On February 5, Jacobs got under way, avoiding the usual sea lanes, bound for Polloc Harbor on the west coast of Mindanao.

Nine days later, *Sargo* nosed submerged into the harbor. Were the Americans still holding out? Yes, Jacobs concluded, after seeing an American flag flapping on a pole near the pier. After dark, he surfaced and made contact with the soldiers by means of blinker tube. By eight o'clock that night, the 666 cases had been loaded on a barge. Jacobs took aboard twenty-four U.S. Army Air Corps enlisted men— B-17 specialists who had been left behind—and carried them back to Surabaya.

Chet Smith in *Swordfish*, winding up his patrol off Davao, was also ordered to Corregidor, arriving on February 19. That night, Smith refueled and took on thirteen torpedoes from Sandy McGregor. The following day he received instructions to evacuate Philippines' President Quezon and party to Panay, 300 miles south.

There were ten people in the Quezon party: Quezon, his wife, and their two daughters and son; Vice President Osmena; the Chief Justice, Santos; and three Philippine army officers. "Quezon was in ill health, suffering from tuberculosis, which was aggravated by the dust generated by the bombs falling on Corregidor," Smith recalled later. "He wore pajamas the whole trip. Quezon's two little girls and Mrs. Quezon were seasick and miserable. But the son, Manuel, had a ball."

Reaching Panay, Smith debarked his load of VIPs. While there, he received orders to return to Corregidor to evacuate U.S. High Commissioner Francis B. Sayre and a party of three, plus more of the Cast codebreakers. When Smith arrived back at Corregidor, the Sayre party came aboard. It consisted of not four but thirteen people, including Mrs. Sayre, their son, and seven members of his staff, of which three were female. With all these people, there was no room for the codebreakers, and Smith simply delivered the Sayre party to Australia.

The "Defense" of Java

By the first week of February 1942, the Japanese were ready for the final assault to push the Westerner out of the Far East. The drive on MacArthur's forces on Bataan and Corregidor was not proceeding as rapidly as planned. However, it was clearly only a matter of time before those troops collapsed or died of starvation. Singapore was surrounded and teetering. The Japanese had consolidated staging bases in Kendari, southeast Celebes, and in Balikpapan, southeast Borneo, for the drive against the Malay Barrier.

At his mountaintop headquarters in Bandung, Java, Admiral Hart, punchy from two unrelieved months of combat, confusion, failure, and retreat, radioed Admiral King requesting to be relieved of command. Hart suggested that the Dutch, who had the greater political and economic stake in Java, be given the opportunity to see if they could do better. King, who distrusted the Dutch, was opposed to the idea, but President Roosevelt decided that Hart should come home. It took a little time for the wheels to turn, but Hart was shortly relieved by Dutch Vice Admiral Conrad E. L. Helfrich, more politician than sailor.*

The question Helfrich faced was: Where would the Japanese strike next? To the west in Sumatra? To the east in Timor and possibly Australia? Java itself?

By that time, the codebreakers at Negat, Hypo, and Cast—together with British and Dutch codebreakers at Bandung—were reading the Japanese naval mail fairly completely, or so they believed. They kept a special ear tuned to the major Japanese fleet units, especially the aircraft carriers. They had tracked Carrier Division One (*Akagi, Kaga*) to Truk Island in the eastern Carolines and then followed it to Palau

---

* Back in Washington, Hart was reappointed to the General Board. He helped with the Pearl Harbor investigations and then retired. In 1945, he accepted an appointment as U.S. Senator from Connecticut, filling out the term of Francis T. Maloney, who died in office, but did not seek reelection. He died in July 1971 at the age of ninety-four.

in the western Carolines. They tracked Carrier Division Two (*Soryu, Hiryu*) from home waters to the Palaus. In addition, they followed the battleships *Kongo* and *Haruna*—which had supported the Lingayen landings—to the Palau Islands.

This great concentration of Japanese naval power at Palau seemed to indicate a thrust against the eastern islands, Timor, perhaps Australia itself. After weighing all the radio intelligence information the codebreakers could assemble, Admiral King informed Admiral Helfrich that the evidence seemed to indicate a main thrust against Timor, 700 miles east of Java.

Other intelligence seemed to bear out Admiral King's assessment of the situation. The RDF experts and codebreakers detected a steady buildup of Japanese naval forces at Kendari, southeast Celebes. The distance from Kendari to Timor was about 300 miles due south. This was an easy jump for the Japanese, who had pushed 1,500 miles straight south since their landing at Vigan, Luzon, December 10.

The submarines still constituted the most formidable fighting arm of the Asiatic Fleet. In early February, there were twenty-six left. As they arrived in Surabaya, they were sent into the small Dutch navy yard for a quick upkeep and replenishment and then went out again on patrol. To facilitate the turn-around time, Wilkes ordered the tenders *Holland* and *Otus* shifted from Darwin to Tjilatjap (pronounced "Chilachap"), a tiny river port on the south coast of Java.

Influenced by King's assessment, Admiral Helfrich ordered Wilkes to deploy the majority of submarines on patrol—or going on patrol—east of Java. These would cover the Flores, Banda, and Molucca seas, with a special concentration off Kendari and Timor. One S-boat would guard Karimata Strait between the South China and Java seas to warn if enemy forces should approach Java from the northwest. Another S-boat would be stationed off Balikpapan in Makassar Strait to give warning should enemy forces approach Java from the north. One boat —Ted Aylward's *Searaven*—would remain off Camranh Bay to interdict Japanese reinforcements of the Singapore campaign.

When Wilkes got down to detailed planning, he discovered that six of his twenty-six submarines would not be available for the impending battle. Two—Smith's *Swordfish* and Jacobs's *Sargo*—had been diverted for the special missions in the Philippines. Four—Stone's *Snapper*, Moore's *Stingray*, Wright's *Sturgeon*, and Ferrall's *Seadragon*—had just arrived in Java from long war patrols and could not be made ready

THE "DEFENSE" OF JAVA 177

in time. Furthermore, it seemed prudent to keep four boats to evacuate submarine staffers and codebreakers from Java should the defense fail.

Counting Ted Aylward's *Searaven* off Indochina, that left a total of twenty submarines. Wilkes sent Jim Coe's *S-39* westward to patrol Karimata Strait and George Holley's *S-41* to the waters off Balikpapan. The other seventeen boats were sent—or prepared to be sent—on patrol eastward of Java. Four of the seventeen—*Skipjack, Tarpon, Perch,* and *Pike*—came over from Darwin; the others left from Surabaya or Tjilatjap.

Lucius Chappell in *Sculpin* took station directly off Kendari. On February 4, he sighted a destroyer patrolling off the port, set up, and fired three torpedoes. Two of these hit, and Chappell believed he had sunk her. He was wrong. Postwar records revealed that he had torpedoed *Suzukaze*, but she grounded on the beach to save herself, was repaired, and lived to fight on.

A few days later, Chappell saw a huge convoy of ships standing out of Kendari. They were escorted by cruisers, destroyers, and what Chappell took to be a carrier. Was this the Timor invasion force? The question was academic to Chappell. He went to battle stations and fired two torpedoes at a cruiser. He believed he had damaged her, but postwar records failed to bear out the claim. Some of the destroyers came over and dropped depth charges on *Sculpin*, holding her down while the convoy cleared Kendari. That night, Chappell got off a contact report but no one received it.

The force leaving Kendari was not the Timor invasion force but one designated to proceed west and capture Makassar City on the southwest coast of Celebes. The codebreakers picked up its movement, and Wilkes quickly repositioned several submarines along its path. However, the codebreaking information contained an error. The force came through twenty-four hours later than predicted, and most of the boats missed it.

One did not. Jim Dempsey in *S-37*, patrolling the Flores Sea, was waiting off Makassar City. Late in the afternoon of February 8, Dempsey's exec, William Hockett Hazzard, standing periscope watch, sighted what appeared to be a broomstick on the horizon. The broomstick grew to be a destroyer. Behind it, he saw a convoy of fifteen ships escorted by four more destroyers.

After dark, Dempsey surfaced and went to battle stations. Unable to get into position to attack the main convoy, he decided to attack the destroyers. He closed to 800 yards and fired four torpedoes, one each at the four destroyers. Three missed, but one struck *Natushie* amidships, instantly warping her deck into an inverted **V**. A cloud of soot mixed with orange flame burst from the funnel; then she settled and sank. It was the war's first confirmed sinking of a Japanese destroyer and the only ship of the Makassar City invasion force to be lost.

Two nights later, Dempsey attacked another destroyer, but the torpedoes were erratic and he missed. Still later his patrol was brought to an end when S-37 ran aground in Lombok Strait and Dempsey subsequently had to bring her back into Surabaya for repairs.

The swift and unexpected invasion of Makassar City was a jolt. The next day came another: The codebreakers detected a force leaving Camranh Bay, bound southeast—toward Sumatra.

Wilkes got off an urgent Ultra to Ted Aylward in *Searaven*, giving the projected track and speed of the enemy. Aylward maneuvered into position, dived, and waited. On the morning of February 11, the force came along right on the dot. Aylward set up at close range and fired two torpedoes each at two heavy cruisers. The seas were rough, and the torpedoes may have run erratically. Whatever the reason, all missed and the force continued on unharmed.

What was this force?

In a day or two the question was answered. On February 14, the Japanese seized Palembang in southeast Sumatra by paratroopers. A few days later, the force Aylward had tried to attack landed large numbers of troops on Sumatra. They linked up with the paratroopers, and that island swiftly fell to the Japanese. On February 15, Singapore surrendered.

Despite these developments to the west, the codebreakers held to the view that the major Japanese forces would attack Timor. The four carriers and two battleships were preparing to depart Palau—southbound toward Timor.

Accordingly, Helfrich and Wilkes made no redisposition of the submarines to westward. *Searaven* and S-39 remained the only two deployed to cover the thousands of square miles of ocean along the western approaches to Java. S-41, the only boat in Makassar Strait, was inexplicably shifted from Balikpapan north to Tarakan. All the others remained deployed to the eastward of Java, with special concentrations off Kendari and Timor. This decision, Wilkes reported later, "resulted in uncovering the entire length of the Makassar Strait."

It was a nightmarish time for the submarine force. Most of the crews had been in combat for well over two months. There had been little time for rest in Surabaya, which, like Manila, was under constant air attack, and little time to repair vital machinery, especially engines. There had been a shortage of everything: spare parts, torpedoes, food. Those boats without air conditioning or with insufficient air conditioning were like ovens; the crews were wilted and listless from the heat and covered with rashes. Everywhere, the skies were thick with Japanese aircraft. On top of this, almost every torpedo attack—which inevitably brought on a severe and unnerving depth-charge attack—failed for one reason or another.

Roland Pryce, commanding *Spearfish*, patrolled off the southwest coast of Celebes at a place called DeBril Bank. On February 12, he sighted two Japanese cruisers, probably from Makassar City. He went to battle stations, fired four torpedoes at 1,700 yards at one cruiser, and then went deep to reload. Coming up to make a second attack, he was depth-charged. He dropped to 260 feet and evaded, and when he returned to periscope depth the cruisers were gone. *Spearfish* put into Tjilatjap for repairs. Pryce was jumpy, bleary-eyed, exhausted. Yet he returned to sea again after one day.

Larry Freeman in *Skipjack*, one of the Australia-based boats, was sent toward Palau. En route, he was turned around and ordered to patrol the north end of Molucca Passage. On the night of February 14, Freeman found a fat tanker. He submerged for a sonar approach and fired two torpedoes from the extreme range of 5,200 yards, 2½ miles. Both missed. A few nights later, he intercepted a big seaplane tender steaming through the same waters. Again, Freeman submerged for a night sonar approach, firing two torpedoes from 2,000 yards. Both missed.

Everywhere it was the same. Dave Hurt's *Perch*, another Australia-based boat, patrolled off Kendari. On February 15, he fired two torpedoes at a freighter. Both prematured. In the northern waters of Makassar Strait, George Holley in *S-41* picked up a transport and fired four torpedoes. He believed the ship sank, but postwar records did not agree; his torpedoes evidently missed. A little north of Kendari, Chappell in *Sculpin* attacked a freighter and destroyer with two torpedoes aimed at each. All missed.

* * *

The Japanese now began playing out the last hand in the conquest of the East Indies. The invasion forces jumped off from Ambon Island and landed on Timor—as expected—on February 17. The following day another force, basing from Makassar City, landed on the southeast coast of Bali in Lombok Strait. Carrier Divisions One and Two and two battleships, plus supporting cruisers and destroyers, came south from Palau. On February 19, carrier-based planes struck Darwin, sinking about fifty ships in the harbor and inflicting such damage on the town and shore installations that they were abandoned. The carriers refueled at Kendari, returned to the waters of Timor, then went south through the Barrier into the Indian Ocean.

All this movement was accomplished without detection by seventeen submarines deployed to the east of Java. Only after the fact did Helfrich and Wilkes order submarines into positions to intercept the carriers in the Indian Ocean and to attack the invasion forces at Bali and Timor.

Freddy Warder's *Seawolf* was one of the boats sent to the southeast coast of Bali to attack the invasion forces there. Warder was aching for a fight. He had now made three war patrols without sinking a Japanese ship. When he reached the landing zone, he almost put *Seawolf*'s bow on the beach. Finding himself trapped in a shallow coral cul-de-sac, Warder surfaced and threaded his way out to deeper water.

The forces at Bali were insignificant: two transports and several destroyers. Warder set up and fired two torpedoes at each of the freighters. He watched the first two miss; then one of the destroyers charged, dropping forty-three close depth charges. "My face was stung with flying cork and paint chips," Warder wrote. "My ears were deafened and my eyes were kept busy watching the gauges and manifolds dance. On one blast the overhead appeared to come in six inches. This ship is strong!"

In spite of Warder's determination, seamanship, and bravery, no Japanese ships were sunk at Bali. The Japanese took the island with ease.

To the east, Wilkes had concentrated three boats near Timor: Lew Wallace's *Tarpon*, Bart Bacon's *Pickerel*, and Billy New's *Pike*. The waters were thick with Japanese ships, but only one boat, New's *Pike*, got off a shot. On the night of February 20, New picked up two light

THE "DEFENSE" OF JAVA

cruisers. He set up and fired two torpedoes at one from 4,000 yards—2 miles. Both missed. Bart Bacon in *Pickerel* sighted several cruisers. When one stopped to recover its scout plane, Bacon maneuvered to attack. "It was a situation of which every submarine officer dreams," he wrote. However, when Bacon closed to 5,000 yards, the cruiser sped off. It returned a little later with a destroyer, and the two ships delivered a depth-charging, forcing Bacon deep.

All three of these boats were shifted around willy-nilly, chasing various Ultra reports and looking for the Japanese carrier forces going from Kendari to the Indian Ocean. On the night of February 23, Wilkes ordered Lew Wallace in *Tarpon* to a position north of the Barrier. Confident of his exec-navigator Richard Victor Gregory, Wallace elected to go through Boling Strait, a little-known and poorly charted area west of Flores Island.

Proceeding northward at 12 knots, *Tarpon* ran aground about midnight. Dismayed, Wallace, Gregory, and the third officer, John Howard Maurer, led the crew in emergency action to get *Tarpon* off the sandbank. They dumped weight, three forward torpedoes and two hundred rounds of 3-inch ammunition; they shifted lube oil aft and blew fuel oil and fresh water to sea; but still *Tarpon* would not budge.

Believing his ship to be lost, Wallace sent an urgent appeal for help. Billy New in *Pike* and Bart Bacon in *Pickerel* were close by. Wilkes ordered them to proceed to *Tarpon*, take off her crew, and destroy the boat if it could not be refloated. However, at flood tide the following afternoon, Wallace got *Tarpon* free and, with his little remaining fuel, limped back to Australia without having fired a torpedo. He was not blamed for the grounding.

The Japanese landed at Timor without losing a ship.

As it turned out, the landings on Bali and Timor were not the Japanese main thrust. They were sideshows, carried out by "light forces." Undetected by the codebreakers, the main thrust had formed up in Indochina and Jolo Island, Philippines, for a direct assault on Java.

The main thrust was a formidable one. The group in Indochina comprised fifty-six transports escorted by a carrier, seven cruisers, and two flotillas of destroyers; at Jolo there were forty transports escorted by four cruisers and fourteen destroyers—in all, ninety-six transports and about forty warships. In addition, the carrier task force from

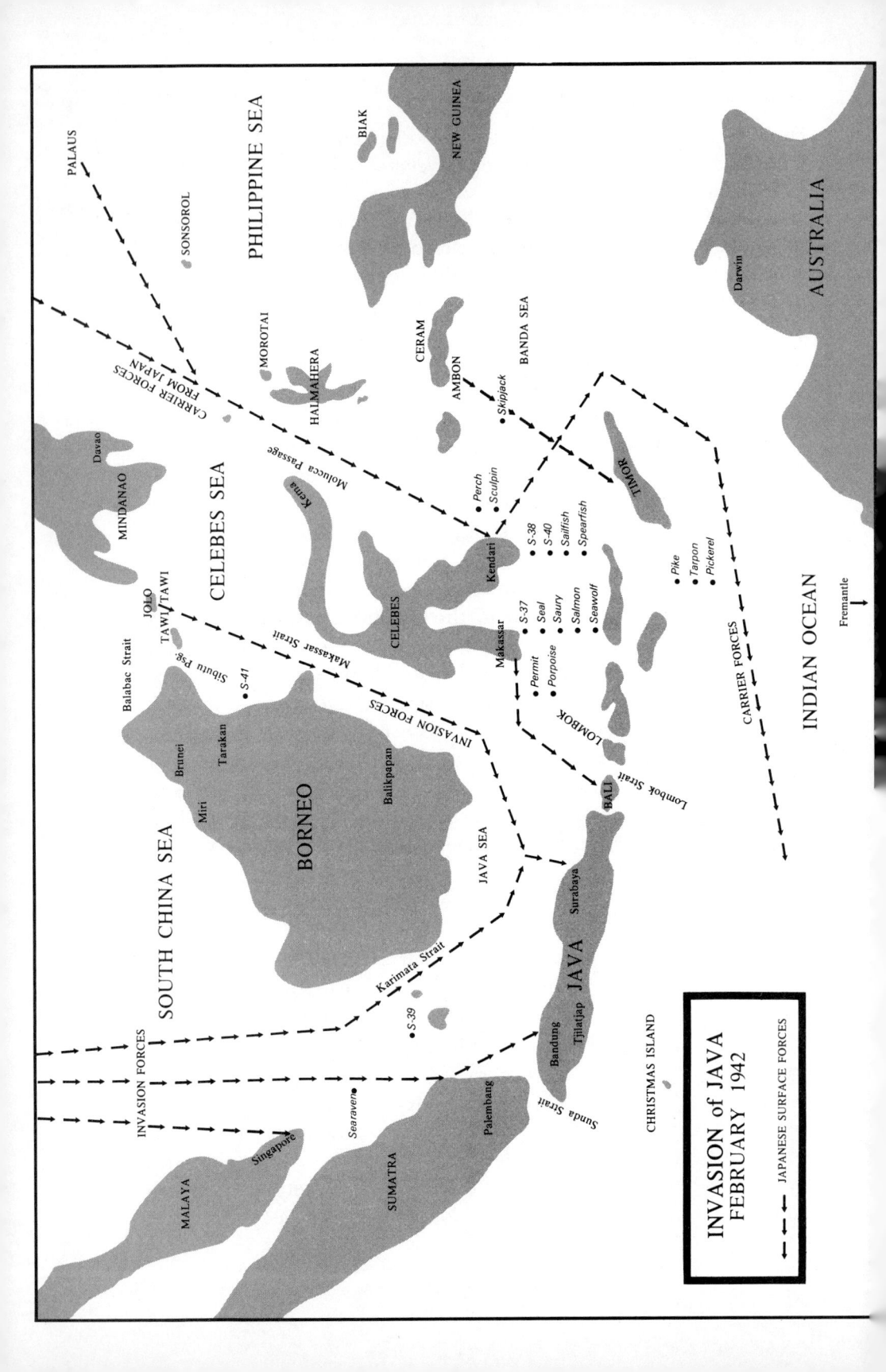

INVASION of JAVA
FEBRUARY 1942

→ JAPANESE SURFACE FORCES

THE "DEFENSE" OF JAVA

Kendari—four carriers, two battleships, and supporting cruisers and destroyers—took station south of Java to lend support.

The main thrust approached Java undetected. The group from Indochina came southeast through Karimata Strait. Neither Ted Aylward in *Searaven* nor Jim Coe in *S-39* saw it. The group from Jolo Island came south through Makassar Strait. George Holley in *S-41*, patrolling close to Tarakan, did not see it. After the invasion of Bali and Timor, the two groups merged off the south coast of Borneo, about 200 miles northeast of Surabaya.

When the main thrust was finally discovered, Admiral Helfrich gave orders for all submarines to converge on Java and mount a last-ditch defense of the island. They would take station south of Makassar Strait and off Surabaya. To speed up their redeployment, Helfrich ordered them to travel on the surface in daylight. When Wilkes protested this order as dangerous, Helfrich became angry. He was scornful of the results achieved by U.S. submarines, implying that if the force took greater risks it might be more effective against the Japanese.

The "defense" of Java was another sorry chapter in the history of the Asiatic Fleet submarine force. For a period of about one week, the Java Sea was dense with Japanese ships. U.S. submarines were not able to send a single one to the bottom.

The stories had a depressing sameness. John Burnside in *Saury*, patrolling north of Lombok on the night of February 24, encountered a large convoy but was driven off when one of the Japanese ships turned a searchlight directly on him. Not far away, Kenneth Hurd in *Seal* attacked two freighters, firing two torpedoes at each. He believed both sank, but postwar records did not bear him out. Dave Hurt in *Perch*, shifted west from Kendari, attacked a ship off DeBril Bank the next night, but the ship drove him off with gunfire. One shell hit the antenna trunk, impairing *Perch*'s ability to transmit radio messages.

Roland Pryce in *Spearfish*, returning to action after his one-day refit in Tjilatjap, also patrolled off DeBril Bank. On February 24, he made contact with a portion of the main invasion force, but a destroyer drove him off and held him down. The next day, Pryce sighted two cruisers, escorted by two destroyers. He fired four torpedoes at one of the cruisers from the point-blank range of 900 yards. All missed. The destroyers attacked, dropping two depth charges almost directly overhead. Pryce again went to deep submergence, failing to follow up the attack, although one cruiser passed directly overhead. Pryce wrote in his patrol report:

I am bitterly disappointed at having failed to make the most of it after having attained a favorable attack position. I feel that my judgment was not normal due to physical and mental strain that resulted in my nervousness at that all-important moment just before firing. . . . I am wasting time, and a submarine's effort when I expose it to attack and then fail to realize the risk. I need rest.

As soon as Wilkes had a chance, he ordered Pryce into Surabaya and relieved him. Pryce wrote later, "I have lived with the complete frustration of those three months for over thirty years, and even the knowledge we all now have that defective torpedoes were my critical problem doesn't alter the anguish I felt at the end of February 1942."

Wilkes gave *Spearfish* to one of the younger men, Jim Dempsey, who had performed well with S-37 off Makassar City. S-37 went to a classmate of Dempsey's, James Richard Reynolds, who had been the division engineer. "That was a lucky break," S-37's exec, Bill Hazzard, said. "The boat was in such miserable condition, it took an engineering genius to keep it afloat."

On February 25, lawyer Gene McKinney in *Salmon* also found two cruisers. McKinney ordered his crew to battle stations in his soft voice, submerged, and went in for a night periscope attack. He closed the range to less than a mile and fired two torpedoes at one cruiser, two at the other. All torpedoes missed. The cruisers continued on unharmed.

That same day, Freddy Warder in *Seawolf* picked up a small force, probably three transports and a destroyer. He came so close to one of the transports he almost collided with it. Then he backed off and fired three torpedoes. He saw one torpedo hit forward of the ship's bridge, throwing up water. "There is not enough of a bang out of these fish to suit me," Warder complained in his patrol report. Swinging around, he fired three torpedoes at the destroyer. He heard explosions and believed he sank the destroyer and possibly the other freighter behind it. However, postwar Japanese records did not bear him out.

Perch, commanded by Dave Hurt, raced west to take position off Surabaya. On the night of February 27, Hurt came across two cruisers and three destroyers. He tried to get off a contact report to Wilkes, but the radio antenna was still damaged from the attack delivered

THE "DEFENSE" OF JAVA

against him on February 25 off Makassar City, and he was never sure the report got through. Hurt tried to maneuver into position to shoot at the cruisers, but the Japanese eluded him.

While this was going on, Wilkes ordered *Holland* to leave Tjilatjap and flee to Australia. Inasmuch as the codebreakers were aware of the Japanese carrier force south of Java, *Holland* was assigned a submarine escort. Five boats carried out this mission: Stone's *Snapper*, Moore's *Stingray*, Jacobs's *Sargo*, Wright's *Sturgeon*, and Ferrall's *Seadragon*. All were jammed with submarine staff. *Snapper* embarked the seventeen codebreakers from Cast which Pete Ferrall had just delivered to Java.

This group was not discovered by the Japanese aircraft carriers. However, *Sargo*, carrying thirty-one extra passengers, was nearly sunk by a Royal Australian Air Force plane which attacked with bombs.

"This was a terrific explosion," Jacobs wrote in his report. "Glass rained down. The power and lighting were lost." Both periscopes were wrecked. Luckily no one was injured, and Jacobs managed to regain control of the boat before it plunged to the bottom.

This episode further demoralized Jacobs, who had been criticized for his first patrol and sent off to Mindanao on a special mission for his second. On arrival in Australia, he asked to be relieved of command of *Sargo*. He said later, "Now I know it was a big mistake, for it shoved me out of the submarine force forevermore." He wound up in a desk job in the Bureau of Ordnance, where he won an award for outstanding work on torpedoes.

Sargo went to Rich Gregory, who had been Wallace's exec on *Tarpon*. Gregory, class of 1932, became the youngest navy officer in command of a fleet boat.

After the submarines had failed to make a dent in the Japanese invasion force, Admiral Helfrich mobilized his surface forces, depleted by the loss of the old cruiser *Marblehead* by air attack,* for a final assault on the enemy. This futile action, which later became known as the Battle of the Java Sea, was the first major engagement of surface men-of-war since the Battle of Jutland in World War I.

The Allied force consisted of the U.S. heavy cruiser *Houston* and a British heavy cruiser, *Exeter*; three light cruisers, Australia's *Perth*, the

---

* *Marblehead* was badly damaged by Japanese aircraft; *Otus* escorted her from Tjilatjap to Ceylon, India.

Dutch *DeRuyter*, and *Java*; plus ten American, British, and Dutch destroyers. Helfrich gave command to Dutch Rear Admiral Karel Doorman. Doorman had no battle plan. The striking force operated as a combined unit for only a few days. Communications were poor. Every order from Doorman had to be laboriously translated.

The force went out to engage the Japanese on the last day of February. Doorman gave a single simple command: "Follow me."

What ensued was a confused, zigzagging battle of four or five hours, with gunfire and torpedoes zinging in every direction. When the smoke had cleared, Doorman had lost two of his light cruisers, *DeRuyter* and *Java*, plus two destroyers. In a subsequent engagement, *Houston* and *Perth* were sent to the bottom. The Japanese lost not a single ship. One destroyer was damaged. The ninety-six ships of the invasion convoy were untouched.

U.S. submarines took no part in this battle. After it, two of the S-boats in the area aided in the rescue of Allied survivors. Henry Glass Munson, who had relieved Moon Chapple on S-38, found fifty-eight survivors of H.M.S. *Electra* in the water, picked them up, and delivered them to Surabaya. James Reynolds in S-37 found sixty survivors (including two U.S. sailors) from *DeRuyter* in a lifeboat. He took the two Americans on board and gave the Dutchmen in the lifeboat rations and water plus directions for reaching Java.

After the Battle of the Java Sea, Java was clearly lost. Jimmy Fife, John Wilkes, and the remaining staff officers left Bandung for Australia, Fife in a patched-up navy patrol plane and Wilkes via Tjilatjap on *Spearfish*, now commanded by Jim Dempsey.

During the entire crucial month of February 1942, the Asiatic submarine force had sunk two ships confirmed in Japanese records: Jim Dempsey's destroyer off Makassar City and Pete Ferrall's troopship off Lingayen Gulf.

When Wilkes departed from Java, he left about a dozen submarines on war patrol to inflict whatever damage they could on the Japanese invasion forces. Two—Warder's *Seawolf* and New's *Pike*—patrolled south of Java, looking for the Japanese carrier force. The others took station directly north of Java, from Lombok Strait west to Sunda Strait, the body of water lying between Java and Sumatra.

The westward-most boat was Jim Coe's S-39. During the battle, Coe had been ordered off on a special mission to rescue a British rear admiral and air marshal who supposedly fled Singapore to the small island of Chebia. At great risk to S-39, Coe landed a party on the island but found nothing; the British had evidently been rescued by someone else. Withdrawing through Sunda Strait for Australia on March 4, Coe sighted a big Japanese tanker. He attacked, firing four Mark X torpedoes with contact exploders. Three hit. Down went *Erimu*, 6,500 tons, confirmed in postwar records. Coe, like two other S-boat captains who had sunk ships, Moon Chapple and Jim Dempsey, became something of a hero.

The other nine boats north of the Barrier, including Ted Aylward's *Searaven* en route home from Indochina, patrolled in the dangerously shallow waters immediately north of Surabaya. They found plenty of targets, including many cruisers. On March 1, Kenneth Hurd in *Seal* fired four torpedoes at a cruiser, two at a destroyer. All missed. That same day, Moon Chapple in *Permit* found a heavy cruiser, two light cruisers, and several destroyers. From the point-blank range of 600 yards, Moon fired three torpedoes at a destroyer and missed. The next day Hank Munson in S-38 fired four torpedoes at a light cruiser and two at a destroyer. He believed he damaged—or sank—the cruiser, but postwar records failed to bear him out. Munson was relentlessly pursued by destroyers and depth-charged for twenty-four hours. Gene McKinney in *Salmon* attacked two cruisers, firing two torpedoes at each. All missed. Three nights later, he fired two more at a light cruiser and believed they hit for damage, but postwar records did not bear out the claim. Ted Aylward in *Searaven*, passing Makassar City, fired two torpedoes at a tanker. Both missed.

A little farther eastward, Dick Voge in *Sailfish* patrolled Lombok Strait. On the night of March 2, he encountered what he thought was the enemy carrier force coming north from the Indian Ocean. He fired two torpedoes at a destroyer, then four at what he believed to be the aircraft carrier *Kaga*. Two of the four torpedoes hit, Voge claimed, inflicting severe damage. After that, destroyers drove Voge off and delivered forty depth charges in the next hour and a half. Voge was credited with damaging *Kaga*, believed then to be the first Japanese carrier of the war to be hit by U.S. submarines, for which he earned great respect and a Navy Cross. However, postwar records changed the results. *Kaga* was not in Lombok Strait that night but still south in the Indian Ocean. What Voge had hit was another important ship, the aircraft ferry *Kamogawa Maru*, 6,440 tons. It sank.

* * *

One of the boats patrolling north of Surabaya, Dave Hurt's *Perch*, was lost. On the night of March 1, *Perch* was on the surface, 20 miles north of Surabaya. Hurt sighted two destroyers and dived, going to battle stations. When the range had closed to about 1,000 yards, the destroyers apparently saw *Perch*'s periscope or picked her up on sonar. They turned toward *Perch* at high speed. Trying to go deep at a place his unreliable charts showed 200 feet, Hurt dug in the mud at 140 feet. The destroyers made three depth-charge attacks, badly damaging the boat. Then they broke off and left.

Early on the morning of March 2, Hurt came to the surface to assess damages. They were severe. Two engines were out of commission. Both periscopes were badly damaged. The hull was dimpled. There was an infinity of leaks. Two hours before dawn, Hurt saw two more destroyers. Simultaneously, they sighted *Perch*. As they came in to attack, Hurt dived again and lay on the bottom, the same tactic he used off Formosa on his first patrol. The first string of depth charges missed. The second, third, fourth, and fifth hit, further damaging *Perch*. Then the destroyers went off. During the day, Hurt lay on the bottom, stopping leaks, making repairs.

After sunset on March 2, Hurt surfaced once again. Only one of his four engines would operate, and its holding bolts were half gone, causing it to vibrate dangerously. Believing escape to be the only prudent course, Hurt headed north at 5 knots. His goal was to get away from the invasion forces and Surabaya and run east through the Flores and Banda seas to Australia. At dawn on March 3, he ordered a dive to see if the boat could be handled submerged. As they started down, the diving officer realized *Perch* was going to plunge to the bottom. He blew all ballast tanks, but *Perch* stubbornly refused to surface completely. She lay there, half submerged, half surfaced, bow jutting up.

While Hurt's men were trying to make repairs, two cruisers and three destroyers appeared, closing fast. The first fired two shells, close. Unable to run, fight, or dive, Dave Hurt gave the command that most saddens a captain's spirits: "Abandon ship, scuttle the boat."

Hurt and his exec, Beverly Robinson Van Buskirk, took the men topside. They wore lifebelts and carried off an "amazing" quantity of personal gear (pictures, razors, soap, combs, socks, wallets) in partially inflated, watertight rubber contraceptives provided by the pharmacist's mate.

Two men were left belowdecks to scuttle the ship, First Lieutenant

Kenneth George Schacht (another officer from the class of 1935 who played on the football team with Dusty Dornin and Slade Cutter) and an enlisted man. Schacht went aft to the engine room, opened some vents, then dashed for the conning tower. When he arrived, he had to fight his way up the hatch through a wall of water. For this work—depriving the Japanese of the secret gear carried by *Perch*—Schacht later received a Navy Cross.

Hurt and his men were picked up almost immediately by one of the Japanese destroyers. "They didn't treat us badly," Schacht wrote later. "In fact they gave us hardtack and tea. And the destroyer skipper offered his condolences to our skipper on the loss of his ship." The Japanese took the crew into Makassar City. From there they went to Japan, where they spent the war working in the mines at Ashio. Nine of the crew died in Japan. Fifty-three, including Hurt, Van Buskirk, and Schacht, who dropped in weight from 195 to about 125 pounds, survived.

The remaining boats peeled off and headed south through the Barrier for Australia, some with orders, some without. John McKnight, who had relieved Joseph Callaghan in *Porpoise*, attacked a convoy near Lombok Strait on March 13, firing four torpedoes at a freighter which he believed he damaged. Then, he wrote, "due to extreme physical exhaustion of crew, physical and nervous exhaustion of myself, together with exhaustion of provisions, I decided to start south by shortest route. Tried to notify headquarters of decision but couldn't reach them." He was ordered to go back, but, he wrote, "I did not think ship able to comply with these orders so I kept on going." Bart Bacon, returning to Australia in *Pickerel*, noted, "Everybody on the boat is exhausted from this continuous patrolling. Everybody's eyes have suffered from strain and soreness. There is a lot of fatigue."

Two more skippers were relieved of command when they reached Australia. One was Larry Freeman in *Skipjack*. In two patrols, Freeman, resolutely holding to the sonar attack, had missed an aircraft carrier, a tanker, and a seaplane tender. *Skipjack* was given to young Jim Coe from S-39. Later, Freeman wrote, "Although I was told that I was being relieved in order to give me a physical and mental rest after exhaustive patrols, I'm sure that the fact that the *Skipjack* had not inflicted any damage on the enemy had a great deal to do with this decision—in fact I think it was the primary reason."

The other skipper who lost his command was Ted Aylward in *Sea-*

raven. Aylward received a Navy Cross for sinking the destroyer in Molucca Passage (not confirmed in postwar Japanese records), but after a medical examination he was relieved. "The stress and strain of submarine patrol duty" had increased Aylward's tendency to high blood pressure, dizziness, and pains in the chest, the doctor wrote. "In view of the above findings, it is recommended that he be relieved of his present submarine duty." *Searaven* was given to Hiram Cassedy, Mort Mumma's exec who had brought *Sailfish* back from her first patrol off Vigan.

The last boat to leave the Java area was Freddy Warder's *Seawolf*. Warder had been patrolling south of the Barrier with Billy New in *Pike*. He was low on food, fuel, and torpedoes. The crew had been reduced to smoking coffee grounds rolled in toilet paper.

While standing off the south exit of Sunda Strait, near the western tip of Java, Warder received word from Wilkes to go due south 200 miles to a tiny dot in the Indian Ocean known as Christmas Island. The Japanese had invaded Christmas; there might be worthwhile targets. Warder turned south.

On the morning of March 31, Warder nosed into Flying Fish Cove submerged (unlike most landing areas utilized by the Japanese, the water in Flying Fish Cove was deep) to find a submariner's dream: four light cruisers in line. He chose the flagship (identified by a pennant) and fired four torpedoes from a range of 1,000 yards. With destroyers alerted and pinging, Warder coolly watched his torpedoes explode against the target. Then he went deep to evade, while the destroyers rocked *Seawolf* with "well-placed" depth charges. That night, he withdrew to sea to charge batteries.

The following morning, with the entire Japanese force alerted to his presence at this tiny island, Warder boldly nosed in submerged for another attack. He was astonished to find a cruiser almost identical to the one he believed he had sunk the day before displaying the same flagship pennant from the main truck. From a range of 1,700 yards, Warder fired a salvo of three torpedoes, then went deep to evade the destroyers. The sonarman heard the torpedoes strike, followed by "convincing" breaking-up noises. Warder withdrew to deep water.

Later that afternoon, a Japanese force came boiling out of Flying Fish Cove. Warder, who had anticipated this move, was in perfect firing position. He picked another cruiser flying the flag of a rear admiral and fired his last two torpedoes from a range of 1,100 yards.

Sonar reported a perfect hit. Warder had no time to check through the periscope; the destroyers were on him within minutes. For the next nine hours, they raked *Seawolf* mercilessly. When Warder finally eased *Seawolf* to the surface an hour past midnight on April 2, his crew was "near the end of their rope," both mentally and physically. Warder set a course due east for Australia.

After this patrol, terminating in Australia, Warder's crew nicknamed him "Fearless Freddy." He was credited with sinking three ships for 14,000 tons, including one cruiser, and damaging five ships for 30,000 tons. However, postwar records did not bear out the sinkings. Warder had only damaged the cruiser *Naka* at Christmas Island; she made it back to port and after a year of repairs was returned to the active list.

In the month of March 1942, Asiatic submarines sank only two ships confirmed in Japanese records, Jim Coe's tanker and Dick Voge's aircraft ferry. The total score for four months of war: ten ships.

Retreat to Australia

The ships and submarines departing Java after its fall set course for Perth-Fremantle, a seaport on the southwest coast of Australia. *Holland* arrived on March 3, *Otus* a week later. John Wilkes and Jimmy Fife set up a temporary submarine base along the docks at Fremantle and paused to catch a breath.

The pause was short-lived. They had no sooner arrived than Admiral King warned of a possible Japanese invasion of Australia, with the initial landings at Darwin. The codebreakers had tracked the carrier task force in the Indian Ocean back to Kendari. Carrier Division Five (*Shokaku, Zuikaku*) had left Empire waters for Kendari. All the evidence seemed to indicate that this large Kendari-based carrier force —six in all—would be employed in support of an invasion of Australia.

The Japanese were, in fact, debating the pros and cons of such an invasion. Admiral Yamamoto favored it; the army was opposed. The conquest of Australia would require an immense number of troops, ships, guns, tanks, and equipment. The army demanded time to study the proposal, weighing its possibility against commitments in China,

Indochina, Burma, and elsewhere, including the Philippines, where MacArthur was still holding out on Bataan and Corregidor.

Believing an invasion of Australia to be next on the Japanese timetable, Wilkes and Fife prepared to employ their submarine force to help turn it. The six submarines that had escorted *Holland* and lifted staff members to Australia were made ready for immediate patrol. Ham Stone in *Snapper* was sent to the Celebes Sea to scout Tarakan and Davao. Lucius Chappell in *Sculpin* was sent back to his old hunting ground off Kendari. The other four—*Seadragon, Sturgeon, Sargo, Stingray*—were sent, initially, to guard the approaches to Darwin. (Lew Wallace's *Tarpon*, badly damaged by flooding during the storm and the grounding in Boling Strait, was ordered to return to the States via Pearl Harbor for complete overhaul.) *Holland* was shifted farther south to Albany. Wilkes remained in Perth-Fremantle; Jimmy Fife went to Albany.

While *Sculpin* was patrolling off Kendari, Carrier Division Five arrived from Empire waters on March 24. The codebreakers picked up the arrival, and Wilkes notified Chappell. Two days later, March 26, the six carriers and two battleships got under way from Kendari and stood out to sea. They were bound for a raid, not on Australia but on India. Chappell missed this sortie, but on the same day he picked up a freighter and fired three torpedoes. All missed. Within the next six days he missed two more freighters with three torpedoes apiece.

Chappell was angry. All these shots had been easy setups. He decided there was definitely something wrong with the torpedoes and requested permission to leave station and return to Fremantle. He wrote, "If the truth must be told, the Commanding Officer was so demoralized and disheartened from repeated misses he had little stomach for further action until an analysis could be made and a finger put on the deficiency or deficiencies responsible and corrective action taken."

Ham Stone in *Snapper*, patrolling near Davao, picked up a fine target on March 31, a large armed tender or auxiliary cruiser estimated at 10,000 tons. Stone, who had missed five ships in previous attacks, was determined to sink this one. Assisted by his exec, Carl Tiedeman, a cool meticulous officer with an analytical turn of mind, Stone closed to point-blank range, 600 yards, and fired two torpedoes. Stone believed he saw two hits; the ship stopped dead in the water. Stone fired a single stern shot to polish her off. Though he claimed a sinking, postwar records failed to bear him out.

After the invasion threat to Australia evaporated, the five boats guarding the approaches to Darwin were released for regular patrol. Pete Ferrall in *Seadragon* headed for his old hunting grounds off Indochina with *Sargo* and her new young skipper, Rich Gregory. Raymond Moore's *Stingray* returned to the Java Sea along with Bull Wright's *Sturgeon*. *Spearfish*, commanded by Jim Dempsey, went up to patrol the west coast of Luzon near Lingayen Gulf.

While these boats had been deploying for combat, General MacArthur had requested further assistance at Corregidor. He wanted at least one submarine to evacuate him and his staff from the Rock.

That mission was assigned to *Permit*. Moon Chapple was withdrawn from patrol station off Surabaya and ordered north to Corregidor. While he was making his way northward, however, General MacArthur and party left Corregidor in four PT boats. Chapple received new orders to rendezvous with the PT boats at a small island west of Panay.

Chapple arrived there on March 13, only to find that MacArthur had gone on to Mindanao, leaving behind one of the PT boats whose engines were crippled. Chapple took the fifteen-man crew of the PT boat aboard, destroyed the craft with his deck gun, and went on to Corregidor, arriving March 15. He off-loaded eight survivors of the PT boat (keeping seven), plus most of the 3-inch and small arms ammunition he had on board.

The senior naval officer present then ordered Chapple to evacuate eight officers and thirty-two men, thirty-six of them codebreakers. (Among them was Thomas Mackie, the young linguist who believed he had picked up the "winds" message.) Counting these forty and the seven men from the PT boat plus his own crew, Chapple had a total of 111 people on board his ship. He received three torpedoes from Sandy McGregor but no spare parts. These were not obtained, Chapple wrote in his patrol report, "because it was found that advance notification was necessary."

Upon leaving Corregidor, Chapple was ordered by the senior naval officer present to conduct an offensive patrol near Marinduque Island, southeast of Manila Bay. Chapple was astonished by these orders. There were 111 people on the boat, many of them codebreakers. If anything should happen to *Permit* during an offensive attack, forcing

Chapple to abandon ship, the codebreakers would in all probability fall into Japanese hands. Yet Chapple did as he was told.

On the night after leaving Corregidor, March 17, Chapple sighted a column of three destroyers coming up astern. He went to battle stations and fired two stern tubes at the overtaking column. Both missed. The destroyers turned toward *Permit*, attacking. Chapple dived. Twelve depth charges fell close aboard, while Chapple's terrified passengers huddled in the torpedo rooms and passageways. The destroyers remained in the vicinity, pinging and dropping an occasional depth charge. Chapple was forced to remain submerged for 22½ hours, bleeding oxygen from storage tanks into the boat to keep his crew and passengers from suffocating.

The next evening, in darkness, Chapple surfaced and escaped. A week later, en route to Australia, he sighted a steamer, fired three torpedoes at her, but missed. On April 7, after a voyage of twenty-three days, Chapple arrived in Australia. In place of a congratulatory handshake for this perilous voyage, he received a royal chewing out. Wilkes later reported officially to Washington, "The Commanding Officer, *Permit*, should have protested the carrying of a total of one hundred eleven persons in his ship."

While Chapple was southbound, Wilkes radioed Stone in *Snapper*, then near Davao, and Ferrall in *Seadragon*, patrolling off Indochina, to put into Cebu, still in friendly hands, and deliver a load of food to Corregidor. Neither skipper received the orders with overwhelming enthusiasm.

On April 3, Ferrall, escorted by a PT boat, nosed into Cebu Harbor. He unloaded ten torpedoes and 250 pounds of 3-inch ammunition. During that night and the following, soldiers loaded *Seadragon* with 30 tons of provisions, rice and flour, in 100-pound sacks. Then Ferrall got under way, passing Stone in *Snapper* coming into the same port. When Stone had moored, he unloaded four torpedoes * and 185 rounds of 3-inch ammunition. Then he took on board 46 tons of food. On April 6, Stone stood out of the channel and headed for Corregidor.

When Ferrall arrived off Corregidor, a small vessel came out to meet him and take off the food. By then, April 6, the situation was deemed "critical" by the local naval commander. The Japanese might overrun the fortress at any moment, he reported to Ferrall. When

---

* The fourteen torpedoes left at Cebu by Ferrall and Stone were never recovered.

the men had unloaded only 7 of the 30 tons of food, he stopped them and ordered Ferrall to clear the area at once. Ferrall evacuated twenty-three people, including an army colonel, *Canopus* torpedo officer Sandy McGregor, two other naval officers, and nineteen navy enlisted men (one of whom was a stowaway). Among these were the last seventeen members of the Cast codebreaking unit, including codebreaker John Lietwiler and linguist Rufus Taylor.

Going out, *Seadragon* was shaken by a violent earthquake that jarred the whole of the Philippines. *Snapper*, headed north from Cebu, making 15 knots on the surface, was rocked by the same earthquake. "The sea changed from dead calm to choppy instantaneously," Stone later reported. "A sudden wind came up from the north and the ship shook violently." Believing he had run aground, Stone backed all engines and brought *Snapper* to a dead stop. A quick inspection revealed no damage. The fathometer indicated 1,200 fathoms beneath the keel.

Stone surfaced off Corregidor on April 9. Bataan was now in enemy hands; most of the U.S. and Filipino troops had surrendered. A small vessel put out in the dark and came alongside *Snapper*. In an hour and a half, the men unloaded 20 tons of food, almost half of Stone's load. Stone took on board twenty-seven passengers and departed. Going out, Stone saw three enemy destroyers. Instead of attacking, he went deep and evaded, a decision that did not sit well with his officers.

Back in Australia, Wilkes ordered three more submarines into the Corregidor relief shuttle. The first of these was Chet Smith's *Swordfish*. Smith removed all his torpedoes except those in the tubes and took abroad 40 tons of food, departing Fremantle on April 1. Next was Hi Cassedy in *Searaven*; he departed April 2 with 1,500 rounds of antiaircraft ammunition. Last to go was Dick Voge in *Sailfish*, who left April 22 with 1,856 rounds of antiaircraft ammunition.

When Bataan fell and the surrender of Corregidor seemed a matter of hours, Wilkes ordered all three of these boats to abandon the mission. "This was all a great big waste of time," Smith recalled. "Even if we had delivered the food, it was just a drop in the bucket. The whole business made me and the crew very bitter. We could have spent our time more profitably sinking Jap ships. An interisland freighter could have done a much better job of delivering food—if it could have got in." Smith returned by way of Java but found nothing worth a torpedo.

Hi Cassedy in *Searaven* was diverted to yet another special mission. He received orders to go to a deserted coast on enemy-held Timor to rescue thirty-one Royal Australian Air Force personnel who had been left behind and were still hiding out with a radio. After spending two arduous nights landing rubber boats on a jungle coastline through heavy surf, Cassedy's men found the Australians—weak from malaria and dysentery—and got them aboard.

Setting off for Fremantle, Cassedy was suddenly confronted with a crisis. A fire erupted in the aft end of the submarine, cutting off the power to the generators and filling the boat with dense smoke. As his men struggled to bring the fire under control, *Searaven* lay helpless on the surface for hours, a perfect target for the Japanese.

When this mishap occurred, Stone in *Snapper*, returning to Australia with his twenty-seven passengers and 26 tons of undelivered food, was slightly south of *Searaven*. Wilkes ordered Stone to reverse course and stand by *Searaven*. Stone found Cassedy the following morning—April 24—and tossed him a tow line. As they moved southward at 6 knots, a navy patrol plane dispatched by Wilkes flew overhead providing "air support." Later that day, an Australian sloop came on the scene to replace *Snapper* as the tow ship. Both Stone and Cassedy returned to Fremantle April 25. Smith returned in *Swordfish* five days later. Dick Voge, patrolling his way home, arrived on May 20 without having fired a torpedo.

The last boat to call at Corregidor was *Spearfish*, commanded by Jim Dempsey, patrolling near Lingayen Gulf. Dempsey had infused *Spearfish* with the same fighting spirit he had given his old command, S-37. On April 17, in the north end of the Sulu Sea, he shot and sank an "unknown" freighter of 4,000 tons, credited in the postwar analysis. A week later, alerted by an Ultra, he sank the 7,000-ton *Toba Maru* coming out of Lingayen Gulf headed for Ambon, loaded with aviation gas and personnel. A few nights later, Dempsey received urgent word from Wilkes: Put into Corregidor, very cautiously, and pick up a load of special passengers for Fremantle. On May 3, Dempsey eased into Manila Bay submerged, dodging a Japanese minesweeper and destroyer. That night a small boat put out from Corregidor with the passengers, the last to leave the Rock before it surrendered.

When Dempsey saw his prospective passengers, he was momentarily nonplussed. There were twenty-five in all, twelve officers and twelve army nurses and the wife of a naval officer. (Later he found he also had two stowaways.) Among the officers was Earl LeRoy Sackett, commanding officer of *Canopus*. They brought along a complete roster of all army, navy, and marine personnel left on Corregidor, plus seventeen foot lockers full of financial records. Dempsey's crew took the passengers and foot lockers on board, passing cigarettes and candy to those on the boat who would be left behind. In twenty minutes the transfer was complete. Dempsey submerged and for twenty-two long, grueling hours threaded his way seaward, again dodging enemy ships.

The following night, after surfacing, Dempsey's radioman picked up the last forlorn navy radio transmission from Corregidor: ONE HUNDRED AND SEVENTY-THREE OFFICERS AND TWENTY-THREE HUNDRED AND SEVENTEEN MEN OF THE NAVY REAFFIRM THEIR LOYALTY AND DEVOTION TO COUNTRY, FAMILIES, AND FRIENDS.

On May 6, about forty-eight hours after Dempsey departed, General Jonathan Wainwright surrendered Corregidor.

Evaluation and Decision

The refugee Asiatic submarine force dug in at Perth-Fremantle and Albany. John Wilkes set up headquarters in downtown Perth in the Colonial Life Insurance Building and established a refit base on the wharves in Fremantle, where *Otus* —still not fully converted to tender status—berthed. For his personal quarters, he obtained a beautiful estate bordering on a lake, known as "Bend of the Road" (and jokingly called "Bend of the Elbow" by the junior officers). Jimmy Fife, a man who preferred the austere, abstemious life, lived aboard *Holland* in Albany.

The first order of business was the usual military one: prepare a report to headquarters setting the record straight about what had happened. During the retreat, there had been little time for stock-taking and writing reports. The only records that survived were the submarine patrol reports, a rough "war diary" kept in a large green-backed ledger, and the personal diaries of both men. With these and firsthand accounts of staff and submarine personnel, Wilkes and Fife spent a full month drafting a book-length document for Admiral King. It contained an operational record of the submarines, a strategic analysis of the campaign interspersed with the lessons learned.

The main lesson was that the Japanese navy was much better than anyone had dreamed. The series of amphibious landings from Luzon to Java and the coordination of major fleet units supporting these operations had been executed with almost flawless timing and expertise. The amphibious forces had been escorted by skilled and well-trained units which had kept their charges in shallow waters where submarines found it hard—if not impossible—to get at them. Contrary to popular belief, the Japanese did not have poor night vision; they were excellent night fighters.* Their antisubmarine vessels were equipped with good sonar gear operated in most cases by experts.

There seemed to be only one flaw. The Japanese depth charge was inexplicably inferior. It was not a powerful charge—perhaps no more than 200 or 300 pounds—and it apparently could not be detonated below 150 feet. Although the charges made a fearful racket when they landed close by, U.S. submarine hulls seemed to withstand the blast with amazing resiliency. To escape its full force, the submarines had merely to go deeper than 150 feet—say, to 200 or 250 feet.

The war had shown some deficiencies in U.S. submarines. The most serious, Wilkes and Fife wrote, were torpedo problems. It was now clear that the Mark XIV was running deeper than set and that the magnetic exploder was not always reliable. The H.O.R. engines had not borne the test of combat well; those boats with H.O.R. engines † would ultimately receive Wintons or Fairbanks-Morses as replacements. Fleet boat silhouettes were too large and would have to be trimmed around the conning tower. A lot of the internal machinery—especially trim pumps—would have to be made to run more quietly. All boats should have beefed-up air conditioning and should be fitted with Kleinschmidt distillers and—when available—radar.

During the campaign, Admiral Hart had clung to his view that the fleet boat was too big, too luxurious, and had too many gadgets. He had radioed Admiral King to the effect that smaller submarines might have inflicted more damage on the Japanese. Wilkes and Fife took issue with Hart. They defended the fleet boat and the gadgets Hart had criticized, such as the torpedo data computer (TDC). Wrote Wilkes, "The present day action against well screened forces such as the vessels of this command have encountered in the majority of

---

* It was learned later that Japanese night vision was considerably enhanced by huge 16-power binoculars.

† McKinney's *Salmon*, Hurd's *Seal*, Coe's *Skipjack*, Gregory's *Sargo*, Burnside's *Saury*, Dempsey's *Spearfish*, and Ferrall's *Seadragon*.

their attacks makes the use of the TDC or a similar instrument almost mandatory."

The submarines had failed to stop the Japanese attack, Wilkes and Fife concluded, because they had been used not offensively, as designed, but in "defensive positions." They wrote:

In all operations to date the enemy have made most effective use of shallow water in preventing our submarines from getting at them, and landing positions were evidently chosen with this in mind. Withdrawal of submarines to defensive positions also had the effect of permitting the enemy to concentrate his anti-submarine forces near his own dispositions instead of being required to disperse them to cover his long lines of communications. . . . It was . . . apparent that our best use of the large submarines could only be on the distant supply lines in the open sea.

Not much was said about the touchy "skipper problem," but in the minds of Wilkes and Fife it loomed large. The war had produced some fine aggressive leaders—Warder, Smith, Voge, McKinney, Ferrall, and others—but it had also uncovered all too many clinkers. "Overcaution" was a command problem unique to submarines. A destroyer skipper, operating in formation with other ships, was not apt to find an opportunity to slink away if he were so inclined. But a submarine skipper, operating far from direct supervision, in absolute command of his ship (and usually manning the periscope during an attack), could be as brave or as cautious as he wished and could fudge patrol reports to cover his actions.

The overcautious skippers were soon found out. When younger officers from the various boats got together over drinks in officers' clubs and rest camps in Surabaya, Darwin, and Fremantle, they freely exchanged appraisals. Those with overcautious skippers were bitter and let their feelings be known. Some younger officers, defying navy tradition and risking their own careers, even went directly to Wilkes or Fife to lodge unofficial complaints or request transfers to boats with more aggressive skippers.

Doug Rhymes, the torpedo officer on *Sargo*, inspired by complaints he had heard about some skippers, wrote a poem:

The Fearless Skipper

The Captain is a rugged guy
With hair upon his chest.

O'er a glass of beer in peacetime
He's at his fighting best.

He scorns far distant danger
With a scornful, scornful leer
And never runs for cover
When everything is clear.

He swings around the periscope
With firm and steady hands;
When the ship is unescorted
He has no fear of cans.

In eyes so gray and piercing
There shines a reckless gleam
As he takes his sip of coffee
And adds a little cream.

With conversational courage
He talks a fearless fight.
He's a rough, tough hombre
When nothing is in sight.

All hazards of navigation
Cause him no loss of sleep.
He cruises along most calmly
In water one mile deep.

His nerves are surely made of steel,
His voice has a confident sound,
And he never gets excited
When danger's not around.*

All kinds of theories were advanced on what kind of men made the best skippers. Some believed that intelligent men who could think out enemy traffic patterns and other complex matters were best. Some believed the dullards, who were thought to be unable to assess the risks they were taking, were best. Many believed that former athletes who had competed in organized sports (such as varsity football at Annapolis) were best. Many of the younger officers believed younger

---

* Quoted with permission of Cassius Douglas Rhymes, Jr., Captain, U.S.N. (Ret.).

and more physically fit men could perform better than older men. A few believed that peacetime misfits, trying to build their records and earn awards, performed best.

However, for every one of these theories, there were glaring exceptions that contradicted it. One example: how to account for the sterling performance of a seemingly cautious, nonathletic lawyer in the upper-age bracket such as Eugene McKinney on *Salmon*?

The truth was, there was absolutely no way to tell in advance whether a new submarine skipper would be aggressive or nonaggressive. What he did, how he performed, was the result of deep inner motivation that could not be quantified or assessed in port or even while he was an exec. An aggressive exec might turn cautious when left alone and handed responsibility for a ship and the lives of sixty men. There was only one solution to the problem: Give everybody who deserved it and was qualified a chance and see how he made out; then, if he failed to perform, relieve him after two patrols.

The Wilkes-Fife report concluded with an optimistic statistical summary of results achieved. In about seventy-five war patrols, the twenty-five surviving Asiatic submarines had made a total of 136 attacks against Japanese men-of-war and merchant ships, firing about 300 torpedoes. Wilkes reported that thirty-six Japanese ships had been sunk. Japanese postwar records reduced this to ten. Wilkes reported that for every Japanese ship sunk, his submarines had expended about ten precious torpedoes. In actual fact, the figure was about thirty.

For his part, Admiral King now faced a decision: whether to leave the submarines in Australia or withdrawn them to Pearl Harbor. King decided to leave them in Australia, ordering Wilkes to conduct offensive submarine warfare against Japanese sea lines of communication in the South China, Celebes, and Java seas and elsewhere.*

At first glance, this seemed a sound decision, and no submariner questioned it. Fremantle appeared to be the ideal place from which to reach the Barrier and Japanese possessions beyond it. In theory and on paper, the Asiatic Fleet still existed. These submarines had been assigned to the Asiatic Fleet; they were there; let them stay and create havoc at Surabaya, Balikpapan, Camranh Bay, Manila, Davao, and elsewhere.

---

* Wilkes's area extended roughly from latitude 10 degrees south to 20 degrees north and from longitude 100 degrees east to 130 degrees east—in all, about three million square miles of ocean.

In retrospect, the decision appears unsound. Wilkes had only nineteen fleet boats capable of patrolling his enormous slice of the Far East. With the vast distances involved, he could only maintain one third—six or seven boats—on station at any given time. The remaining two thirds would always be en route to and from station or in overhaul or refit. The best he could do with so small a force was to cover Camranh Bay, Manila, and three or four additional ports where he hoped to find Japanese traffic, helped when possible by Ultra reports. Each major port was heavily defended by Japanese antisubmarine aircraft and patrol vessels, forcing the submariners to use extreme caution. Being at the tail end of the Pacific pipeline, Wilkes had to operate with a chronic shortage of torpedoes, spares, and manpower and limited overhaul facilities.

In making his decision, Admiral King apparently failed to appreciate the peculiar geography of the Far East. Because of it, the majority of the shipping bound to and from Japan and its newly acquired possessions in the Indies passed through a bottleneck on the northern end of the Philippines known as Luzon Strait, the body of water lying between Luzon and Formosa. It is deep and open, ideal operating water for submarines on offensive patrol. Had the Asiatic submarines been concentrated in these waters rather than trying to cover each individual and heavily defended port in Southeast Asia, they could have shot at the same ships under conditions much more favorable to the submarine.

Years later, one submariner drew this analogy: "Say your objective is to contact all the commuters who live in a town outside New York. The way they went about it would be comparable to going to each individual commuter in his home. The most efficient way to find them is not like that but at the railway station when they're all bunched together, trying to get on the same trains. Luzon Strait was the rail center. They had to go through there, going and coming."

Luzon Strait was a long and difficult way from Fremantle. The voyage required at least two weeks of travel through shallow water close to many Japanese air bases. Once on station, a Fremantle-based boat would be so low on fuel it could stay in the area only a few days. In addition, there were jurisdictional problems: the line separating Withers's area from Wilkes's area ran through the middle of Luzon Strait. If boats operated there, they were to stay clear of the imaginary line lest they cross it by accident and shoot at one another. For these reasons and others, Wilkes did not patrol Luzon Strait.

EVALUATION AND DECISION

Had King ordered the Asiatic boats back to Pearl Harbor, they could have covered Luzon Strait with relative ease—using Midway as a refueling point. The route from Pearl Harbor and Midway to Luzon Strait lay westward across deep open seas free of Japanese air bases. The boats could have traveled all the way on the surface at high speed. With twenty boats refueling at Midway (or the U.S.-held Johnston Island to the south of Midway) Wilkes could have maintained one third of his force—about six or seven boats—in the strait at all times. Operating at night as wolf packs, exchanging information on contacts, they could have mounted a blockade across the main north-south Japanese trade routes at a key bottleneck. As time would prove, this was a much more effective way to sink ships than by lying in wait off heavily fortified ports.

In addition, the consolidation of all submarines at Pearl Harbor under a single commander would have provided other benefits. The complicated and wasteful pipeline to Fremantle could have been eliminated, yielding more torpedoes and spare parts in hand. If the codebreakers had also been consolidated in Hawaii, they could have concentrated their resources on tracking convoys and men-of-war in the limited area of Luzon Strait rather than across the whole three million square miles assigned to Fremantle. Maintenance shops—for torpedoes, engines, batteries—could also have been consolidated at Pearl Harbor, freeing many qualified submariners for duty on the short-handed boats. The two administrative staffs could have been trimmed to one. Being closer to Mare Island Navy Yard, the Asiatic boats would have been "modernized" (with radar, etc.) much sooner, greatly improving their effectiveness.

With King's decision, the opportunity for an imaginative strategic war against Japanese commerce to the south was lost. The Asiatic boats remained in Fremantle, operating under difficult conditions, achieving very little for a long time to come. The two submarine commands grew into independent rival organizations, competing for Japanese shipping rather than cooperating. When General MacArthur was appointed chief of all Allied forces in the Southwest Pacific—including naval forces—the efficiency and results of the Fremantle submarine force was further reduced by insistent demands from MacArthur for more and more special missions to the Philippines.

5

Pearl Harbor, January through March 1942

January Departures

Admiral Chester Nimitz had taken command of what was left of the Pacific Fleet at Pearl Harbor on January 1, 1942, on the deck of a submarine. Nimitz had urged his staff to forget the past—the infamy of the Pearl Harbor attack—and do the best job possible with what they had. It would be at least a year before the Pacific Fleet could expect substantial reinforcements for waging a meaningful offensive against the Japanese. The defeat of Germany was still the primary strategic goal; defeat of Japan was secondary.

The main surface forces left to Nimitz were the three aircraft carriers *Lexington, Saratoga,* and *Enterprise* and some cruisers and destroyers. Following the futile—and disgraceful—nonattempt to save Wake Island, these had been assigned to convoy duty, escorting ships from San Francisco to Pearl Harbor and from Pearl Harbor to Samoa, the U.S. island possession in the South Pacific. On January 11, while engaged in this duty, *Saratoga* was torpedoed by a Japanese submarine and required extensive repairs. Another carrier, *Yorktown,* was shifted from the Atlantic to the Pacific.

During the first three months of 1942, Nimitz directed the three carrier task forces of his command in a series of hit-and-run attacks against Japanese outposts. On February 1, U.S. carrier planes struck

JANUARY DEPARTURES

the island of Kwajalein in the Marshalls, helped in part by intelligence provided by Dizzy Rainer and Chick Clarey on the first patrol of *Dolphin* and by Lew Parks and Slade Cutter in *Pompano*. Afterward they hit Wake Island, Marcus Island, Rabaul, and New Guinea. None of these strikes accomplished much except to lift spirits and give U.S. carrier pilots combat experience.

The raids were carefully engineered to avoid counterattack by the main Japanese carrier forces. In his planning, Nimitz relied on the codebreakers, who were tracking the Japanese carriers. The raids against Wake, Marcus, Rabaul, and New Guinea, for example, were launched when the codebreakers reported the major Japanese carrier forces far away at Kendari and south of Java during the invasion. At no time were U.S. carriers ever in danger of attack by Japanese carrier forces.

Admiral King's operations officer, submariner Frog Low, conceived a more spectacular mission for the Pacific carriers: a bombing raid on Tokyo itself. The problem was to find a way to launch aircraft from sufficiently long range to ensure that the carriers would not be destroyed by land-based aircraft in Japan. Low's solution: use U.S. Army Air Corps B-25s. At Norfolk, the carrier *Hornet* was detailed for the mission. The air corps furnished sixteen B-25s and assigned one of its most famous aviators, Lieutenant Colonel James Doolittle, to head up the force. The planning and training for this strike was carried forward in greatest secrecy.

Meanwhile, Tommy Withers and Gin Styer had prepared the few submarines of the Pearl Harbor command for patrol. *Cachalot* had been hurried out of the Pearl Harbor Navy Yard. *Cuttlefish* and *Tuna* had arrived from the Mare Island Navy Yard, along with a new boat, *Grayling*. *Triton* and *Trout*, which had been patrolling off Wake and Midway when war came, were hastily refitted at Pearl Harbor. These six were all Withers and Styer could send off on patrol in January.

When the boats were ready to shove off, the codebreakers reported the movement of Carrier Division One (*Akagi, Kaga*) to the island of Truk in the eastern Carolines. The presence of this force at Truk increased the speculation that the Japanese were still planning to invade Hawaii from bases in the Marshalls and Carolines. For this reason, Withers sent half the six boats going on patrol to reconnoiter the Marshalls and the Carolines, especially Truk. One, Mike Fenno's

Trout, was detailed to a special mission at Corregidor. Only two went to Japanese home waters: *Tuna* to patrol off the east coast of Japan and *Triton* to explore virgin territory in the East China Sea.

The submarine skippers at Pearl Harbor, like those in the Asiatic submarine force, were developing a distrust for the Mark XIV torpedo and the magnetic exploder. Many believed the torpedo ran deeper than designed and that the magnetic exploder was defective, causing the prematures Lew Parks in *Pompano* had experienced in the Marshalls on his first patrol. Some urged Withers to give orders to deactivate the exploder and fire the torpedoes to run shallow for direct contact hits. Withers said no, absolutely. There was a critical shortage of torpedoes at Pearl Harbor. To sink a ship by contact explosion would require two or three torpedoes, whereas, he said, one torpedo exploding underneath, actuated by the magnetic exploder, would undoubtedly sink the same ship.

Many skippers going on patrol were unhappy with this decision; it did not seem to be based on facts but rather on the shortage of torpedoes. Some skippers decided that once they left Pearl Harbor and reached the combat zone they would deactivate the exploder anyway and shoot for contact, swearing their men to secrecy, doctoring the patrol reports to cover this unauthorized practice, and exaggerating the size of the enemy ship to justify firing more than one torpedo.

This doctoring soon became commonplace, helping to obscure the real facts about the Mark XIV torpedo and the Mark VI magnetic exploder.

Mike Fenno in *Trout* was ordered to deliver antiaircraft shells to the hard-pressed forces on Corregidor. Fenno, eager to sink Japanese ships, liked this assignment no better than had Jacobs, Warder, or Chet Smith. He and his exec, Albert Hobbs Clark, engineered a compromise. *Trout* would deliver the ammunition and then pick up a load of torpedoes and fuel at Corregidor and patrol Formosa Strait and the lower reaches of the East China Sea on the way home. He would not evacuate personnel.

Fenno removed most of his torpedoes and ballast, leaving only eight torpedoes in the tubes. *Trout* was then loaded with 3,517 3-inch antiaircraft shells. Stopping at Midway to top off his fuel tanks, Fenno then went westward to Corregidor, arriving the night of February 3.

During the brief layover in Corregidor, Fenno and Clark—the first

JANUARY DEPARTURES

Pearl Harbor submariners to make contact with Asiatic Fleet submariners since the war began—heard much about the sad performance of Asiatic submarines during the battle for Luzon and the southern areas. They also heard grousing and criticism of the Mark XIV torpedo and the magnetic exploder. They took this word-of-mouth information back to Pearl Harbor.

Meanwhile, working parties unloaded the antiaircraft ammunition. When the job was finished, Fenno drew ten torpedoes from Sandy McGregor's stock and 27,000 gallons of fuel oil. When the weight was totaled, Fenno had a problem. He needed additional ballast to replace that removed in Pearl Harbor. He requested twenty-five tons of sandbags as a substitute, but these were denied; sandbags were a precious commodity on Corregidor. Instead, Fenno was offered twenty tons of gold and silver, which had been removed from Manila banks to Corregidor for safekeeping.

During the night, the gold and silver arrived on flatbed trucks. Fenno formed a bucket brigade. Five hundred and eighty-three gold bars were passed from hand to hand, while a detail of army and navy officers watched carefully, keeping inventory. After the gold had been stacked in the bilges, the men brought eighteen tons of silver coins, packed in heavy sacks. Fenno hastily signed a receipt for the treasure, adding a note at the bottom that he had been unable personally to verify the inventory and would have to accept the word of those who had loaded the cargo.

After leaving Corregidor, Fenno patrolled northward through Formosa Strait. He ran into foul winter weather: gale winds and mountainous seas. Along the north coast of Formosa, Fenno found a freighter and fired three torpedoes. The ship, *Chuwa Maru*, 2,700 tons, blew up and sank. Passing through the Bonin Islands on the way home, Fenno fired another three torpedoes at a small patrol vessel not worth one. A companion ship apparently fired two torpedoes at *Trout* but missed. After that, *Trout* returned to Pearl Harbor.

Admiral Withers hailed Mike Fenno a hero. The rescue of the gold and silver made uplifting newspaper copy at a time when good news was desperately needed. President Roosevelt directed that Fenno be awarded the Army Distinguished Service Cross; everybody else on board got an Army Silver Star Medal. Behind the scenes, however, Fenno had a problem: according to the inventory he had signed, one of the bars of gold, worth $14,500, was missing. After an inch-by-inch search of *Trout*, it was found in the galley. One of the cooks was using it for a paperweight.

John Leslie DeTar, commanding *Tuna* in Empire waters on his first war patrol, was an odd and controversial character. He wore a pistol and slept on a mattress in the conning tower. Although he had two Kleinschmidt distillers on board, he strictly rationed fresh water, denying his crew permission to take showers. He believed some crewmen were carrying out acts of sabotage on the hydraulic system, which constantly malfunctioned.

DeTar had a busy patrol. After reaching station, he spent four fruitless days searching for a convoy reported by the codebreakers en route from Japan to the Bonins. Off Japan, on his first shot of the war, DeTar fired three torpedoes at a freighter from 3,500 yards. They missed and DeTar lost depth control. Later, he deactivated the magnetic exploder and attacked a destroyer and several other ships, sinking a 4,000-ton freighter confirmed in postwar records.

When he returned to Pearl Harbor, DeTar received a Navy Cross for all this and was publicly complimented on an aggressive patrol. However, behind the scenes, Withers was furious that DeTar had deactivated his magnetic exploders and again strictly forbade other skippers to do so. In addition, he criticized DeTar for wasting time going to and from station submerged and for unnecessarily impairing morale by restricting use of fresh water. Skippers at Pearl Harbor critical of the exploders thought DeTar was a fool to admit in writing that he had deactivated those on his torpedoes.

Pilly Lent in *Triton*, assisted by his exec, John Christie Hollingsworth, explored the East China Sea, patrolling off Nagasaki along the sea lanes from Shanghai, Dairen, and Korea. The winter weather—as Mike Fenno had found farther south—was miserable. In all, Lent made fourteen ship contacts and fired twelve torpedoes, sinking two ships confirmed in postwar records. On return to Pearl Harbor, Lent received a Navy Cross for conducting the "most aggressive patrol" to date, yet Withers was carping in his endorsement, criticizing Lent for his "undue" worry about Japanese aircraft, for failing to follow up attacks, and for squandering torpedoes.

The extreme shortage of torpedoes will not allow this high expenditure for the results obtained. One good hit using the magnetic exploder should be sufficient for a 5,000-ton merchant ship. If one hit does not sink a ship of this type, it should be sufficiently damaged to keep her in one spot so the submarine can take up favorable position to finish her off.

Patrolling the Marshalls, Martin Perry ("Spike") Hottel, commanding the old V-boat *Cuttlefish* on his first war patrol, had a run of bad luck. On February 28, he sighted two ships, set up, and fired two torpedoes at one, four at the other. All six torpedoes missed. Then he suffered a calamity. His machinists had brought along cans of carbon tetrachloride for cleaning fluid. When the cans were opened, the powerful fumes seeped through the boat, poisoning the crew. For days after, all hands were violently ill and too weak to do anything except lie in their bunks. Withers was not pleased.

Cuttlefish's sister ship *Cachalot*, commanded by Waldeman Christensen, made the longest war patrol to date—sixty-six days—through the Marshalls and Carolines. Christensen proved to be an extremely cautious skipper; he managed only one attack. It failed.

Eliot Olsen, commanding *Grayling*, patrolled off Truk. By the time he reached the area, the codebreakers reported Carrier Division One ready to sail for the Palaus. Olsen took station on the Truk-Palau route, but both *Akagi* and *Kaga* got by him undetected. Later he received an Ultra informing him that another aircraft carrier, the smaller *Hosho*, was arriving at Truk from Japan. Olsen maneuvered into position to intercept.

Shortly after 1:30 P.M. on February 18, while Olsen was running at deep submergence, the sonar operator picked up heavy screws. Olsen came up to periscope depth. He saw *Hosho* right on schedule, no planes on deck, none flying overhead, funnels down, ensign flapping in the breeze. There was a single escort, a destroyer, some distance away. Olsen ordered all torpedo tubes made ready. But by then it was too late. The carrier was too far away; there was no time to close or shoot. It went by untouched, a "sad blow to morale."

When Olsen returned to Pearl Harbor, having missed Carrier Division One, then *Hosho*, and a small freighter as well, he received a blistering dressing-down from Withers and scathing endorsements to his patrol report.

Grayling was never nearer to [Truk] than ten miles and then on only one occasion. It is impossible to observe any activity submerged from this distance. The failure to fire at Hosho *is attributed to unnecessary deep submerged running or . . . too infrequent periscope observations resulting in practically no coverage of the area. Having picked up the carrier at approximately 5,000 yards, the failure to have tubes ready for firing is inexcusable.*

Olsen's division commander, Forrest Marmaduke O'Leary, criticized him for wasting three torpedoes on the small freighter, for spending too much time submerged, for relying too greatly on sonar, and for running deep "in spite of intelligence reports previously received" on *Hosho*. "Had the making-ready of torpedoes been expedited," O'Leary said, "it is probable that firing could have been accomplished while the target was within effective range."

Olsen had not conducted a heads-up patrol. On the other hand, Withers and others at Pearl Harbor greatly underestimated the difficulty of capitalizing on Ultra information. Navigation was a problem. As in the case of *Hosho*, the codebreakers often provided an exact interception point. However, if the Japanese navigator or the submarine navigator was off in his calculations by a mile or so—not unusual when weather was bad—the submarine might find itself out of position by 5,000 or 6,000 yards—that is, close, but not close enough to shoot. If the intercept was bungled in daylight, as in the *Hosho* case, there was no way for the submarine to pursue at surface speed without being detected. Withers could be faulted for not rehearsing his submarines in simulated Ultra intercepts before they left for patrol, for failing to encourge interceptions of these contacts in darkness rather than in daylight, and for failing to develop a scientific method of search along the expected track.

February Departures

By February, the other boats of Al McCann's Squadron Six reported to Pearl Harbor. With the addition of these, and Weary Wilkins's big *Narwhal*, which completed her overhaul, Withers sent a total of seven submarines on patrol. Two went to the Carolines and Marshalls, four to Empire waters, and one to Formosa Strait.

En route to patrol in Empire waters, Joe Grenfell in *Gudgeon*, like *Thresher*, *Sargo*, and *Pompano*, was bombed by friendly aircraft. On the afternoon of March 4, while running on the surface near Marcus Island, lookouts spotted a dive bomber roaring in. Grenfell dived instantly. At 80 feet, a 500-pound bomb exploded, luckily inflicting "no damage whatsoever," Dusty Dornin later recalled. When he returned from patrol, Grenfell learned the dive bomber, like those that hit Lew Parks and Slade Cutter in *Pompano*, came from the carrier *Enterprise*. The pilot evidently had not been briefed that a friendly submarine was in the area.

While these boats were on patrol, the codebreakers picked up important information of Japanese carrier movements, and on February 25 Withers made a vigorous attempt to reposition his submarines to intercept a Japanese carrier, damaged by a coral reef, that was returning from the Palaus to Japan for repairs. Stan Moseley's *Pollack*, Donald McGregor's *Gar*, and Weary Wilkins's *Narwhal* spent several days lying in wait along the expected track. Wilkins found the carrier on the night of March 9 and fired two torpedoes. Both missed. Two escort destroyers prevented Wilkins from making a second attack.

A week later, the codebreakers picked up information that Carrier Division Five (*Shokaku, Zuikaku*) was leaving Japan for Kendari. On March 8, Withers alerted his submarines, providing very specific information in the days following. *Narwhal, Gar, Gudgeon, Pollack*, and *Grenadier* were within reach of the southbound track, but none intercepted. The force reached Kendari untouched.

Grenadier, commanded by Allen Raymond Joyce, had an unhappy patrol off Tokyo Bay. En route to his area, Joyce suffered a major casualty: a main generator went out of commission. By the time he reached his patrol area, it had been fixed. However, on station *Grenadier* took a large quantity of water down the conning tower hatch and into the pump room beneath the control room, flooding out the trim and drain pumps, the low pressure blowers, the main hydraulic pump, and one air compressor. This casualty, Joyce reported, was a "physical and mental problem for crew and officers."

On the afternoon of March 7, while submerged off Tokyo Bay, the watch spotted a freighter. Joyce went to battle stations and fired four torpedoes, one of which he believed hit. However, when the ship did not sink, Joyce fired two more torpedoes. Still it didn't sink. Joyce left station early and returned to Pearl Harbor. A day or two later, Withers sent the Ultra on the movement of Carrier Division Five which *Grenadier* might have intercepted.

When Joyce put into port, Al McCann and Marmaduke O'Leary drafted blistering endorsements for his patrol report. O'Leary, judging the patrol a "total failure," pointed out that Joyce could have remained on station off Tokyo another "ten to fourteen days" but that he returned to base because "he was tired." Commented O'Leary, "Commanding Officers must have confidence and place responsibility in the hands of their juniors so that they will never get tired." McCann was critical of Joyce for firing six torpedoes at the freighter: "The torpedo supply does not warrant such a prodigal use of torpedoes." Withers grumped, "Three . . . lights sighted were not investigated at all; in fact, one was deliberately avoided."

Withers relieved Joyce of command, and he left submarines for good.

Although the seven submarines leaving for patrol in February missed the big game, the carriers, all but *Grenadier* sank at least one ship confirmed in Japanese records. Stan Moseley, patrolling the Formosa Strait in *Pollack*, sank one by torpedo and then surfaced to damage another with his 3-inch deck gun, making the second recorded gun attack (after Ferrall's in *Seadragon*). Willard Arthur Saunders, commanding *Grayback* in the Marianas, let his exec, Bruce Eastman Wiggin, conduct an attack; Wiggin sank a freighter. Edward Shillingford Hutchinson, patrolling off Truk in *Grampus*, sank an 8,600-ton freighter. Weary Wilkins in *Narwhal* sank one and evaded destroyers. Joe Grenfell and Dusty Dornin in *Gudgeon* got two ships. In return, they received a fearful eight-hour depth-charging from what they believed to be a Q-ship, a heavily armed merchant ship used as a decoy. During this ordeal, Grenfell reported later, "the Diving Officer got so excited he lost control of the boat and we plunged to 425 feet."

When he returned from this patrol, Grenfell had an adventure that was almost as grim. Withers decided that *Gudgeon* would get her final shakedown repairs at the navy yard in Pearl Harbor. Grenfell received permission to make a quick flight to the States to see his family and found a seat on a big navy seaplane, crowded with twenty passengers and a crew of ten. While taking off, the plane lost an engine and made a forced landing. It struck a dock opposite the sub base and half sank in 30 feet of water. Floundering around inside the sunken plane, Grenfell found a hole in the fuselage and struggled out with a badly injured leg. He was sent to the hospital and then to the States—by ship. "And that's how I lost command of the good ship *Gudgeon*," Grenfell said later.

March Departures

In March, there was an important shake-up in the submarine hierarchy at Pearl Harbor. Freeland Daubin, commanding Squadron Four and the Submarine Base, was promoted to rear admiral and ordered to command Submarines Atlantic. He was replaced by a tough-minded, coolly aloof officer, Robert Henry English, a onetime submariner who had commanded the cruiser *Helena* during the attack on Pearl Harbor. In peacetime years, English had headed the "submarine desk" in Washington and served as chief of staff to Commander Submarines Pacific.

About that same time, English received two new division commanders: John Meade Haines took command of Division 42 and George Clifford ("Turkey Neck") Crawford took command of Division 43. Haines, who commanded *Narwhal* in peacetime, had been exec of the battleship *Maryland* during the Pearl Harbor attack. Crawford, who commissioned *Perch*, had, like Jimmy Fife, served as head of the Submarine School, where he tried unsuccessfully to establish a stiff policy of "bilging" the lower 30 percent of the class. He had then served, like Fife, as a naval observer in London. Returning from Europe, Crawford's ship, *Empire Celt*, had been torpedoed by a U-boat. He was rescued off the stern by a minesweeper.

After arriving in Pearl Harbor, Crawford, who knew that the Germans and British had long since given up on the magnetic exploder, instructed his skippers to deactivate the Mark VI. When Tommy Withers heard this, he "went through the overhead," Crawford recalled. He ordered Crawford on the carpet and said, "You tell those skippers to use the magnetic exploder. I *know* it works. I was at Newport when it was tested. I don't want to hear any more discussion about it. If I hear one more word from you on the subject, I'm going to send you to general service."

Four boats left for patrol in March: *Trout, Thresher, Grayling,* and *Tambor*. The codebreakers reported no Japanese carriers or other capital ships in the Marshalls or Truk. They were then at Kendari, in the Indian Ocean, or in home waters. Withers sent only one boat, *Tambor*, to the Marshalls. The other three went to Empire waters.

Mike Fenno, patrolling in *Trout* off Kii Suido, turned in what seemed to be a spectacular performance. This was Fenno's third patrol, and his first opportunity to get at the Japanese unencumbered by gold and silver ballast. He nosed *Trout* to within a mile or two of the beach and remained there for almost thirty days, firing away at targets. Fenno obeyed orders and relied on the magnetic exploder, setting his torpedoes to run at 35 to 40 feet even against smaller merchant ships.

In all, Fenno made twelve attacks, fired twenty-one torpedoes at seven or eight different ships, and obtained many hits, he believed. When he returned to Pearl Harbor, the high command was ecstatic. It credited him with sinking five ships for 30,000 tons and damaging one for 15,000 tons. Bob English wrote, "This patrol is the most successful one conducted by a submarine of this force to date and reflects great credit on the commanding officer and all officers and men."

Fenno's apparent success with the magnetic exploder reinforced the belief in the Pearl Harbor submarine command that it was a reliable device and that those skippers who were having difficulty must be doing something wrong: they were not properly maintaining their torpedoes on patrol or the fire-control party was not well trained. However, postwar records indicated that Fenno, too, had torpedo problems. Only two ships actually sank: *Uzan Maru*, 5,000 tons, and *Kogosan Maru*, 2,000 tons, for a total of 7,000, not 30,000 tons.

Thresher, commanded by William Anderson, patrolled off Tokyo Bay with orders to conduct a special mission: support the Doolittle raid on Tokyo by furnishing weather reports.

While waiting for *Enterprise* and *Hornet* to arrive off the coast of Japan from San Francisco, Anderson had a busy—and harrowing—time. He received an Ultra reporting that at least four Japanese submarines were operating off Tokyo Bay. Though he took precautions, one of the subs found *Thresher* and fired two torpedoes, which fortunately missed. In the ensuing days, Anderson attacked three freighters, firing three torpedoes at the first two, which missed, and one at the third. The third freighter, *Sado Maru*, 3,000 tons, sank.

Immediately after sinking *Sado Maru*, Anderson was counterattacked by enemy patrol vessels. Three or four pinned *Thresher* down from noon to midnight, delivering one of the worst depth-chargings of the war. During the attack, Anderson lost control of the boat and plunged to 400 feet. The boat was badly damaged, and Anderson considered returning to Pearl Harbor immediately. However, he stayed to support the Doolittle raid.

That naval force, commanded by William Frederick ("Bull") Halsey, Jr., was bearing down on Japan. Halsey planned to launch the planes from a point 500 miles off the coast. But on the morning of April 18, while still 650 miles out, the carriers were sighted by a Japanese patrol boat which Halsey logically believed had flashed a warning to Tokyo. (If there was a warning, it was not received.) Halsey and Doolittle agreed it was now or never and launched the sixteen bombers. In spite of Halsey's fears, the raid achieved complete surprise.

The physical damage to Japan was insignificant. Yet psychologically the raid—hailed by Halsey as "one of the most courageous deeds in all military history"—was important. It shored up sagging morale in the United States and caused the Japanese to lose face. Every available warship and submarine was mobilized to go after *Enterprise* and *Hornet*, but Halsey got away.

Doolittle and his crews did not fare as well. They were supposed to overfly Japan and land at bases in China. However, the decision to launch early, from a longer range, upset this plan. Flying through darkness and bad weather, fifteen of the bombers either crash-landed in China, short of the bases, or the crews bailed out. One plane landed in Vladivostok. Doolittle and most of his men wound up in friendly Chinese hands. But the Japanese caught eight men (of whom three were executed and one died of starvation), and the crew that landed in Vladivostok was interned for a year before being released.

Anderson and *Thresher*, in fact, contributed little to the Doolittle raid. When Anderson returned to Pearl Harbor, he stepped down from command and went to be submarine repair superintendent at the Mare Island Navy Yard. The badly damaged *Thresher* was sent to the yard for extensive repairs.

Eliot Olsen patrolled in *Grayling* off Bungo Suido. On April 13, the only time Olsen fired torpedoes on this patrol, he sank the 6,243-ton *Ryujin Maru*. Returning to Pearl Harbor, Olsen claimed one sinking for 6,000 tons, which was the most accurate—and conservative—claim by any skipper thus far. In contrast to his first patrol off Truk, when he missed the carrier *Hosho*, the second was described as "aggressively conducted."

John Murphy in *Tambor* (with young Spruance embarked) patrolled to Rabaul and back, finding many targets. He made nine aggressive attacks against Japanese ships, firing a total of eighteen torpedoes. However, headquarters was not at all pleased with Murphy's shooting. "There was an excessive expenditure of torpedoes," his cool patrol report endorsement stated. "With the supply of torpedoes available, such unproductive expenditure cannot be justified." Murphy blamed his bad luck on torpedo performance and recommended—like many of his contemporaries—that they be set to run shallower. His boss, Al McCann, wrote sternly, "The Squadron Commander does not concur in the *Tambor*'s recommendation regarding depth setting of torpedoes. Specific instructions in this regard have been issued and must be followed." Murphy was credited with sinking one ship, but it was not confirmed by postwar records.

Altogether, Tommy Withers was able to mount only seventeen war patrols from Pearl Harbor during the first three months of 1942. The skippers were credited with sinking twenty-two ships, reduced in postwar accounting to fifteen. After four months of operation, there was still no submarine "strategy." The boats were sent to random spots, usually to places where Japanese antisubmarine effort was most heavily concentrated and where it was hoped there might be traffic. Many dozens of patrol days were expended in fruitless pursuit of the glamorous Ultra information, with no return for the effort. Ten of the twenty-four war patrols mounted since the Pearl Harbor attack were directed to the Marshalls, Carolines, and Marianas. These ten—42 percent of the total Pearl Harbor effort—had accounted for two ships, 10 percent of the confirmed sinkings. Except for *Trout*, leaving Corregidor with her load of gold and silver, no Pearl Harbor boats had entered the traffic bottleneck in Luzon Strait.

By the end of March, almost every Pearl Harbor submariner who had fired a torpedo in anger believed that the Mark XIV torpedo or the Mark VI exploder—or both—was defective. There were insistent reports from Asiatic skippers that the torpedoes and exploders were defective. Turkey Neck Crawford had brought word from Europe that the British and Germans had abandoned the magnetic exploder. That Withers, McCann, English, Styer, and the other desk-bound staffers refused to listen to suggestions and criticisms from those they had sent into combat with this weapon seems, in retrospect, incomprehensibly stubborn and stupid. At the very least, Withers could have expended a few days conducting live tests against an expendable target—shortage or no shortage.

6
Brisbane, April and May 1942

Arrival of More S-Boats

Admiral King—influenced by Admiral Hart's criticism of the fleet boat—decided to send more S-boats from the Atlantic to the southwest Pacific to augment the force that survived the Manila-Java campaign. They would be stationed in Brisbane, on the east coast of Australia, their mission to defend the coasts of Australia against a possible Japanese invasion.

Ralph Christie, commanding the majority of Atlantic-based S-boats, was selected to lead this expedition to Australia. Originally, Christie planned to sail with three divisions, about eighteen boats.* However, when Christie arrived in Panama, he decided the "20" boats were not up to the voyage, and they were deleted.† At the eleventh hour, Admiral King also deleted the "30" boats, diverting them to Alaska for patrol under command of Submarines Pacific.

On March 5 Christie, reduced to the six "40" boats, got under way

---

* Division 51 consisting of the "20" boats (S-20, S-21, etc.); Division 52, composed of the "30" boats (S-30, S-31, etc.); Division 53, consisting of the "40" boats (S-42, etc.).

† S-1, Christie's old command, S-21, S-22, S-24, S-25, and S-29 were loaned to Britain, freeing up an equal number of British submarines for combat. S-21, S-22, S-24, and S-29 were returned after the war. S-25 was recommissioned HMS P-551. Later, the British loaned her to Polish Free Forces. Rechristened *Jastrazab*, she was sunk accidentally by Allied forces off the coast of Norway on May 2, 1942. S-26 was lost in a collision with an escort at Panama, January 24, 1942.

from Panama in his tender *Griffin*. *Griffin*, loaded with a valuable cargo consisting of Mark XIV torpedoes for the Fremantle submarines, radar for surface ships, and tons of spare parts and Mark X torpedoes for her S-boats, was escorted by two destroyers. Together with S-42 through S-47, they sailed westward across a calm peaceful ocean at about 9½ knots, cruising speed for the S-boats, making one stop for fuel at Bora Bora in the Society Islands.

Until the last day the voyage, in the words of one skipper, was "uneventful," with a tail wind and "fairly easy cruising." On the night before they were due to enter Brisbane, however, a violent storm arose. The wind climbed to 60 knots and churned the seas. Large hailstones pelted the boats, and waves swept over the stern. *Griffin* and her six charges milled about, keeping clear, and entered Brisbane harbor April 15, after a voyage of about forty-three days.

Meanwhile, the five S-boats from Manila-Java-Fremantle came around the southern side of Australia, via Melbourne. With the addition of these, Christie then commanded a force of eleven S-boats. He moored *Griffin* at New Farm Wharf and began building a fairly elaborate submarine facility.

The Battle of the Coral Sea

The military command structure in the Australia–New Zealand area (ANZAC), in flux during the retreat from Manila, had only recently been determined. General MacArthur, named Supreme Allied Commander, set up headquarters in Melbourne. On the navy side, directly under MacArthur, the top commander, also located in Melbourne, was Vice Admiral Herbert Fairfax Leary. In Brisbane, the senior American naval officer was Rear Admiral Francis Warren ("Skinny") Rockwell, a refugee from Manila, where he had been commandant of the 16th Naval District. The senior naval officer on the west coast of Australia was then Rear Admiral William Reynolds ("Speck") Purnell. Rockwell commanded the submarines in Brisbane through Christie; Purnell commanded the submarines in Fremantle through Wilkes.

The seventy-five men of the Cast codebreaking unit, evacuated from Corregidor in *Permit* and *Seadragon* (two loads), had also arrived in Melbourne by various means. Still commanded by Rudolph Fabian, the unit moved temporarily into Australian army quarters,

Victoria Barracks, and then to a recently completed red brick apartment known as the Monterey Building, where Australian Navy Intelligence was setting up new quarters. The Cast unit was soon operational, exchanging data with Joe Rochefort's Hypo and Laurence Safford's Negat and producing further valuable information on Japanese intentions.

In Japan, Admiral Yamamoto, heady with success, pushed the Japanese high command into adventures exceeding the original "quick war" plan. With his idea for the invasion of Australia denied, he urged further expansion into the islands northeast of Australia—the Solomons, Samoa, Fiji, and New Caledonia. He also proposed the capture of Port Moresby, a strategic post on the southeast coast of New Guinea, only 270 miles from Australia. Securing these strongholds, Yamamoto argued, would enable the Japanese navy to cut the vital supply lines between Hawaii, Panama, and Australia.

At the same time, Yamamoto proposed that the Japanese capture the island of Midway and invade the Aleutians. The capture of Midway, Yamamoto believed, would deny the United States an important forward base for refueling submarines and surface vessels and would provide the Japanese an air base from which they might launch long-range bombing attacks against Pearl Harbor. Most important, a Japanese invasion of Midway might draw the remaining U.S. sea power in the Pacific into the long-sought "decisive naval engagement." If all its sea power in the Pacific were finally destroyed, Yamamoto believed, the United States would probably abandon its efforts to take back what the Japanese had captured and enter into a cease-fire. This would enable the Japanese to consolidate and capitalize, economically, on their conquests.

The Yamamoto plan for Midway and the Aleutians was coolly received. Japanese naval forces, on the move since mid-November 1941, were bone-tired. The ships needed docking and repair. The aircraft were wearing out from incessant missions. How would Japan defend—and support—Midway, 2,300 nautical miles from the Empire? Yamamoto was piqued by these objections. It was either Midway or his resignation, he responded.

Yamamoto got his way. Tokyo authorized the invasion of Midway but set no firm date. The navy would first spearhead the drive to the Solomons and Port Moresby.

* * *

The Cast codebreakers, in what Joe Rochefort would later describe as a "fantastic piece of work," detected the proposed Port Moresby invasion plans almost immediately. In early April, they predicted that the invasion force would be escorted by Carrier Division Five (*Shokaku, Zuikaku*) and the light carrier *Shoho*, plus many cruisers and destroyers. At the time Cast provided this information, Nimitz had four operational carriers in the Pacific: *Yorktown, Enterprise, Lexington*, and *Hornet*. (*Saratoga* was still in the States undergoing repairs from the January torpedo damage.) *Hornet* and *Enterprise* were then committed to the Doolittle raid on Tokyo. That left only *Yorktown* and *Lexington*, plus their escorting cruisers and destroyers. After study, Nimitz concluded that with the help of land-based army aircraft from Australia and Samoa, the United States might engage this Japanese force on a more or less equal footing and prevent the invasion of Port Moresby.

Working with this invaluable intelligence, Nimitz prepared his forces. The *Yorktown* Group, commanded by Rear Admiral Frank Jack Fletcher, was already in the area. In mid-April, Nimitz sent the *Lexington* Group speeding south. On May 3, after the Japanese occupied Tulagi in the Solomons, Fletcher, in *Yorktown*, retaliated with an air strike on the harbor, achieving small results.

As the two fleets maneuvered warily in the Coral Sea, land- and carrier-based aircraft on each side sought to find the other. On the morning of May 7, U.S. carrier-based planes located a portion of the Japanese invasion force, including the light carrier *Shoho*, and sank *Shoho* within fifteen minutes. Meanwhile, Japanese carrier planes found the U.S. destroyer *Sims* and the tanker *Neosho*. Mistakenly reporting this as a "United States carrier force," which confused the Japanese admirals, the planes attacked, sinking *Sims* and critically damaging *Neosho*.

On the following day the Battle of the Coral Sea, the first engagement of carriers in naval history, reached a climax. Aircraft from both sides found the opposing forces at about the same time. In the exchange, U.S. planes damaged *Shokaku* with six bombs but missed *Zuikaku*; the Japanese damaged *Yorktown* and *Lexington*. *Lexington*, soon swept by uncontrollable fires, was abandoned and finally sunk by U.S. destroyers.

Ralph Christie had arrived in Brisbane in the midst of preparations for the Coral Sea battle. He managed to get four boats to sea prior

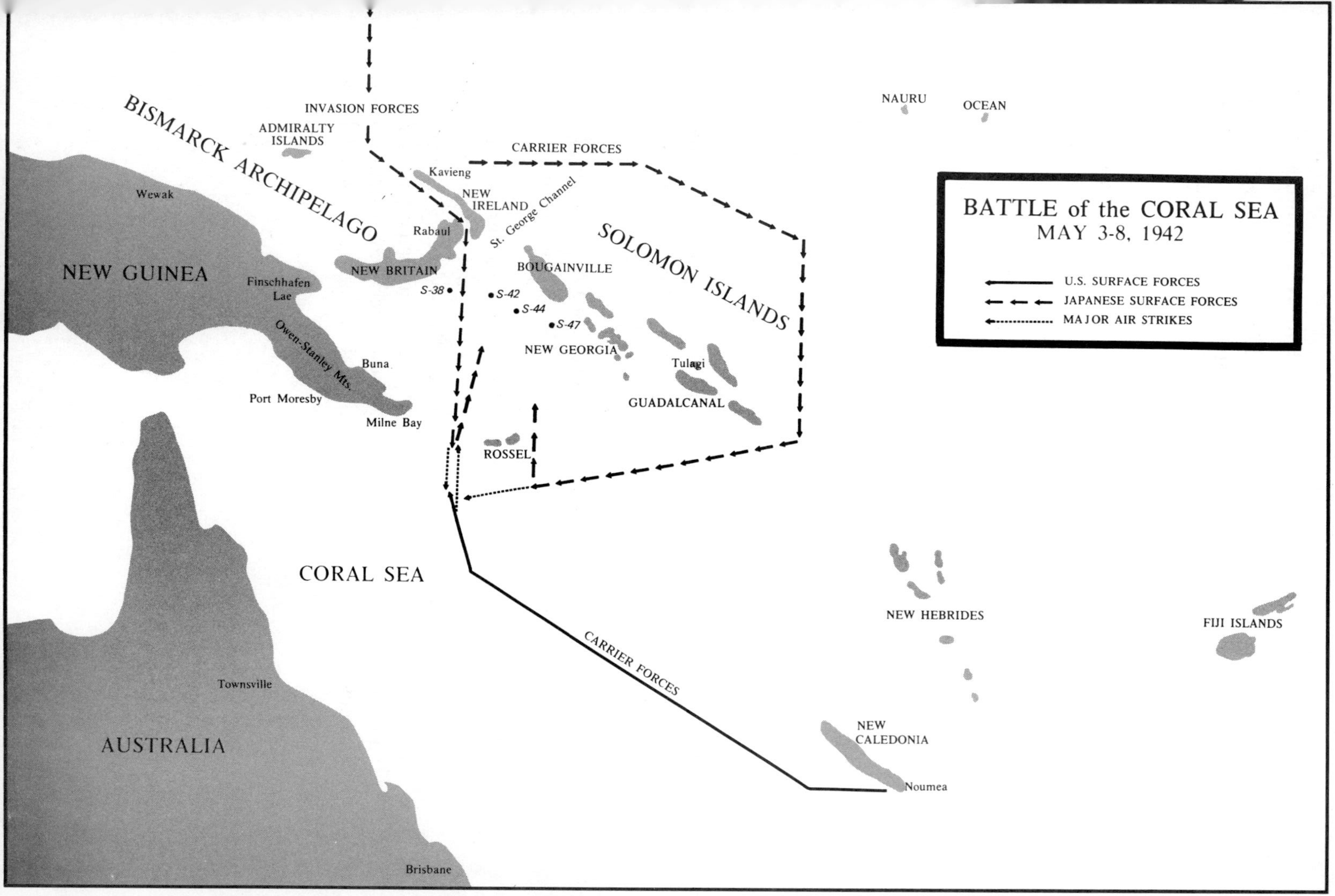
BATTLE of the CORAL SEA
MAY 3-8, 1942
U.S. SURFACE FORCES
JAPANESE SURFACE FORCES
MAJOR AIR STRIKES
INVASION FORCES
ADMIRALTY ISLANDS
BISMARCK ARCHIPELAGO
CARRIER FORCES
Kavieng
NEW IRELAND
St. George Channel
Rabaul
NEW BRITAIN
Wewak
NEW GUINEA
Finschhafen
Lae
Owen-Stanley Mts.
Buna
Port Moresby
Milne Bay
S-38
S-42
S-44
S-47
BOUGAINVILLE
SOLOMON ISLANDS
NEW GEORGIA
Tulagi
GUADALCANAL
ROSSEL
NAURU
OCEAN
CORAL SEA
CARRIER FORCES
NEW HEBRIDES
FIJI ISLANDS
NEW CALEDONIA
Noumea
Townsville
AUSTRALIA
Brisbane

to it: one of the original Manila boats, Hank Munson's S-38, and three "40" boats he brought from the States, S-42, S-44, and S-47. The four boats made a combined total of five attacks on the periphery of the battle. Oliver Grafton Kirk, commanding S-42, was the only one to achieve a confirmed sinking. Off the south coast of New Britain, he torpedoed and sank the Japanese minelayer *Okinoshima*, 4,400 tons, which had been damaged by planes from *Yorktown* when she raided Tulagi.

In tactical terms, the U.S. Navy lost the Battle of the Coral Sea. However, in a strategic sense, it won a victory. For the first time in the Pacific war, a Japanese invasion by sea had been stopped cold. Moreover, *Shokaku* was too badly damaged to be made ready in time for Yamamoto's planned invasion of Midway. *Zuikaku* had lost so many planes she could not be made ready in time either. The Coral Sea battle left the Japanese with only four big carriers in ready status.

In the days following the battle, the Cast unit decoded another valuable Japanese message. It was a long one, on which linguist Thomas Mackie worked relentlessly and, when finished, appended a note to call attention to its importance. It revealed that the Japanese had given up taking Port Moresby by amphibious operation. The next attempt would be made overland by the Japanese army, using the Buna-Moresby trail crossing the towering Owen-Stanley Range. The Japanese engineers would widen the trail into a road over which trucks could travel and troops could march.

Mackie's message, later described by a senior codebreaker as "one of the three most important to be decoded in the war," gave MacArthur time to plan a land defense of Port Moresby which later proved to be successful. The message was also an important signal to Nimitz that the remaining big Japanese carriers required to support a second Japanese amphibious assault against Port Moresby might be employed on another mission.

7

Pearl Harbor, April through June 1942

April Departures

While the Coral Sea battle was shaping up, Admiral Nimitz decided to make another important change in the Pearl Harbor submarine hierarchy. He named Bob English, only recently appointed to command Squadron Four, to succeed Tommy Withers as Commander Submarines Pacific. Withers returned to the States to command the Portsmouth Navy Yard, engaged in turning out new fleet boats. English was replaced in Squadron Four by a huge and likable character, a former Naval Academy football star and coach, John Herbert ("Babe") Brown.

About the time this changeover took place, the first boats of a new squadron—Eight—began arriving in Pearl Harbor with a new tender, *Fulton*. The new squadron was commanded by Stoney Roper, who had been commanding Division 42 at Pearl Harbor when the Japanese attacked.

Inasmuch as Fremantle had no drydock or facilities for extensive overhauls, English and Wilkes worked out a deal for a gradual exchange of submarine squadrons—Squadron Two for McCann's Squadron Six. Under the agreement, Wilkes would send one or two Squadron Two boats to the Pearl Harbor command for overhaul, and English would replace them with Squadron Six boats fresh from overhaul. In time, McCann's tender, *Pelias*, would replace *Holland*. On the way to and from Australia, the boats would patrol off various Japanese-held islands: the Marianas, the Carolines, the Marshalls.

The buildup of submarines basing at Pearl Harbor was retarded by this arrangement. It would take months to overhaul and modernize the Asiatic boats back at Mare Island. The patrols to and from Australia—like regular Pearl Harbor patrols to the same islands—produced few sinkings compared to patrols in Empire waters. Generally, the deal favored the Fremantle command, which was trying unsuccessfully to cover the far-flung ports in the Southwest Pacific.

With the reinforcements of Squadron Eight plus boats returning from overhaul, Pearl Harbor was able to send fourteen boats on patrol in April, well over twice the monthly average during the January–March period. Three of the fourteen—*Gar*, *Grampus*, and *Tautog*—were sent to Fremantle, patrolling the Marshalls and Carolines along the way. In addition, *Greenling* went to Truk, *Cuttlefish* to the Marianas, and *Gato* to the Marshalls. Eight went to Empire waters, five of them off the east coast of Japan and three to the East China Sea.

Three of the older boats got off to halting starts. *Cachalot*, *Cuttlefish*, and *Pollack* all broke down, and though the last two ultimately completed their patrols (*Cachalot* went to the Pearl Harbor Navy Yard and her skipper, Waldeman Christensen was relieved of command), they accomplished nothing. Commands were shifted among a number of the boats, causing considerable ill will in wardrooms. Pilly Lent was moved from *Triton* to *Grenadier*, and command of *Triton* was given to Charles Cochran Kirkpatrick, bypassing *Triton*'s exec, John Hollingsworth, a classmate of Kirkpatrick's; Hollingsworth left in anger for other duty.

Kirkpatrick (class of 1931) was the youngest skipper yet to get command at Pearl Harbor. "They told me to go out there and raise hell," Kirkpatrick said later. "Believe me, considering I was sort of a 'youth experiment,' had made no war patrols, plus the unpleasant Hollingsworth business, I was really determined to show them I could cut the mustard." To fill out his wardroom, Kirkpatrick drew a man from the class of 1935, John Holbrook Eichmann, for his exec and Jack Randolph Crutchfield from *Plunger* (still in the navy yard) for his third officer.

Triton and *Grenadier*, plus Lew Parks in *Pompano* and Johnny

DeTar in *Tuna*, were sent to the East China Sea. Kirkpatrick found action a few days later. Passing north of Marcus Island, he was astonished to find a Japanese ship lying to, all alone and brightly lighted. He went to battle stations and fired one torpedo at point-blank range. It missed. Coming about, Kirkpatrick fired a second: another miss. On close inspection, the ship turned out to be a small trawler, not worth a torpedo. Angry at this misjudgment, Kirkpatrick ordered his crew to man the 3-inch deck gun. Within the space of eighteen minutes, *Triton* fired nineteen rounds plus a hurricane of small-arms fire. The trawler, estimated to be 2,000 tons—the first Japanese vessel to be sunk by deck gun—went down.

Pressing on to his patrol station in "Tung Hai," as sailors call the East China Sea, Kirkpatrick found glassy, shallow waters, poor sonar conditions. On May 1, a six-ship convoy with a single small escort came into view. Manning the periscope, Kirkpatrick closed and unhesitatingly attacked, firing two torpedoes at two freighters. The first two hit, the second two missed, leading Kirkpatrick to believe—generally—that the torpedoes were running deep. *Taei Maru*, 2,200 tons, sank. Shifting targets, Kirkpatrick fired a single torpedo at another freighter. It ran under without exploding, but a second single, set at a shallow depth and aimed at another freighter, exploded, breaking the back of the vessel, the *Calcutta Maru*, 5,300 tons.

A few nights later, Kirkpatrick, cruising on the surface amid swarms of junks and sampans, came upon another convoy. He fired two torpedoes at a trailing ship, both set for shallow depth. One sank upon leaving the tube; the other went ahead of the target. Kirkpatrick launched a second attack against this same ship, firing two shallow-set torpedoes from 1,200 yards. One hit, blowing up *Taigen Maru*, 5,660 tons. Later, Kirkpatrick fired two torpedoes at two more ships in this convoy. One of the torpedoes hit the first ship, the second ship evaded, and a destroyer charged in, forcing Kirkpatrick to break off the attack.

Both Johnny DeTar in *Tuna* and Lew Parks in *Pompano* had frustrating patrols. *Tuna*, patrolling south of Korea, made six separate attacks, fired seventeen torpedoes, and made one hit that sank a ship—for 8,000 tons, DeTar believed, but postwar accounting reduced it to 800. DeTar's division commander was critical of his torpedo expenditure.

Cruising off Formosa, Lew Parks and Slade Cutter found the

hunting disappointing. After two weeks of empty seas, Parks finally spotted a target, a small tanker. Parks dived but could not gain firing position. He surfaced in broad daylight and chased after the ship, trying to gain a position ahead, a tactic that became known by the football term "end around." A fire temporarily disabled one main generator, slowing him down. A Jap plane drove *Pompano* under, causing a further delay. But after a seven-hour chase—a chase that earned him high praise—Parks put two torpedoes into the ship, *Tokyo Maru*, 900 tons. It exploded and sank immediately. Because of the shortage of Mark XIV torpedoes, Parks was carrying the old Mark X torpedoes with contact exploders.

A few days later, Parks found a big transport, escorted by a single destroyer. He skirted the destroyer at 300 yards, closed to the point-blank range of 750 yards, and fired two Mark X torpedoes. The 7,983-ton *Atsuta Maru* went to the bottom. In Pearl Harbor, Parks received glowing endorsements and a Navy Cross.

To the north of *Triton*, Pilly Lent in *Grenadier* came across a beautiful target: a convoy of six freighters, plus one magnificent passenger vessel Lent recognized as *Taiyo Maru*, 14,500 tons. He went to battle stations, firing four torpedoes at *Taiyo*, one to explode on impact, two to run under and explode by magnetic influence, the last to explode on impact. The two torpedoes set to run under failed to explode. The other two hit and *Taiyo* went down, carrying about 1,000 Japanese oil technicians, scientists, and engineers who were en route to Java and Sumatra to restore the Dutch oil fields to full production.

Lent did not see *Taiyo* sink. Two minutes after firing, a string of bombs exploded over *Grenadier*. Then came destroyers, which dropped a total of thirty-six depth charges over the next four hours. Lent stayed deep—below 250 feet—and the charges did no damage. But the destroyers kept him from taking another shot at this valuable convoy. The surviving ships presumably picked up most of the oil technicians and continued on their way.

Back at Pearl Harbor, Lent complained bitterly about torpedo performance. Two of his torpedoes set to run deep under *Taiyo Maru* and actuate the magnetic exploder had failed to go off. Something was obviously wrong. His division commander, Marmaduke O'Leary, agreed, pointing out that three other skippers of his division had reported magnetic exploder failures. He recommended that the Mark

XIV torpedo be set to run at a much shallower depth, barely beneath the keel (as C. C. Kirkpatrick in *Triton* had done).

Bob English did not agree at all. Stubbornly following the policy of his predecessor—and the Gun Club line—English unstintingly supported the torpedo and exploder. Like Withers, he refused to take time out for a live test, blaming most torpedo failures on skippers and crews. He gave eight possible reasons for failures—including errors in estimated range, speed, and course of enemy target; inexperience with TDC; "guess and snap decisions"; and "physical condition" of the skippers—and concluded, "Commanding Officers will continue to set torpedoes at a depth not less than five feet greater than the maximum draft of the target." In other words, continue to rely on the magnetic exploder.

Two new boats, *Drum* and *Silversides*, patrolled off the east coast of Honshu and racked up impressive scores. *Drum*, commanded by Robert Henry Rice—son-in-law of Admiral King's chief of staff, Russell Willson—arrived off Nagoya, south of Tokyo Bay, about May 1.*
One of his officers was Manning Marius Kimmel, son of the admiral and brother of Thomas Kimmel on *S-40*. Like his brother, Manning was eager for blood—to help clear the family name.

Rice, like Mike Fenno, was a bold and aggressive skipper. Guided by an Ultra, shortly after midnight, Rice spotted a ship "with considerable top hamper" and immediately fired two torpedoes. One hit; one missed. A destroyer charged out of the darkness. Rice crash-dived, firing a torpedo at the destroyer on the way down. It missed. Hearing no depth charges, Rice cautiously came to periscope depth. The destroyer was lying to, 1,500 yards distant, probably listening on passive sonar. Rice fired three more torpedoes at it. All missed.

Later, Rice's division commander gave him credit for damaging the ship he first shot at, calling it "medium-sized." However, one of Joe Rochefort's men at Hypo had been eavesdropping on the Japanese radio report of this attack. He knew—and passed word through Jasper Holmes—that the ship Rice had hit with one torpedo had sunk. It was not a "medium-sized" freighter but a major Japanese naval vessel, the seaplane carrier *Mizuho*, 9,000 tons, the largest Japanese combatant vessel sunk by submarines up to that time.

A week later, Rice made a day periscope attack on a ship he believed

---

* *Drum* and two other new boats, *Flying Fish* and *Greenling*, were all bombed by friendly aircraft when leaving the United States.

to be a naval auxiliary of perhaps 6,000 tons. It was loaded and "exceptionally neat and new looking." Rice fired four torpedoes. There was a violent explosion. The identity of this ship was never determined, but Rice was credited with an "unknown maru" of 4,000 tons. Four days later he sank 5,000-ton *Shonan Maru* with a single torpedo and, two weeks later, 2,300-ton *Kitakata Maru*, also with one torpedo. On May 28, he sighted a large auxiliary or merchant ship, fired five torpedoes, and missed. Rice's score for the patrol, confirmed by postwar records: four ships for 20,000 tons. This was the most productive patrol so far by any submarine.

Silversides was commanded by a classmate of Rice's, Creed Cardwell Burlingame. Burlingame was one of the more colorful skippers, swashbuckling and devil-may-care. His exec, Roy Milton Davenport, was an oddity in the submarine force, a teetotaler and devout Christian Scientist who played a trombone (badly). Burlingame kidded Davenport about his religious zeal and took along a buddha which he "worshiped" ostentatiously.

Burlingame cruised most of the way to Japan on the surface. Six hundred miles from the coast, *Silversides* found herself embroiled in the tail end of a typhoon. About that time, a Japanese trawler came into view. Burlingame attacked in pitching seas with his deck gun. The trawler returned fire and killed an enlisted man, Michael Harbin, the first man to die in a submarine gun action. A few days later, Burlingame spotted a Japanese submarine. He fired one torpedo—with Harbin's name chalked on the side—heard an explosion, and claimed a hit, but postwar records failed to verify the loss of a Japanese sub at this time and place.

In action off the coast of Japan during the next few weeks, Burlingame seemed fearless. On May 17, while threading his way through an armada of sampans laying out fishing nets, Burlingame found a small convoy. Making an approach, *Silversides* got enmeshed in one of the nets, buoyed by a glass ball with a Japanese flag attached. Trailing the Japanese flag, Burlingame went on, firing at a freighter. It came apart in a massive explosion of fire and flames and sank. He fired at a second but missed. Later he damaged another freighter and a tanker. After the last attack, *Silversides* was pinned down by a destroyer, which dropped thirteen depth charges.

"During the depth-charging," Burlingame recalled, "I rubbed the belly of the buddha. Roy Davenport put his faith in the Lord, claiming He had placed an invincible shield between the boat and the

Japanese. Afterward, I needled him. 'Roy, who do you think got us out of that one, Buddha or Mary Baker Eddy?' "

Five boats patrolled the Marshalls and Carolines during April and May, including three going to Australia—*Gar*, *Grampus*, and *Tautog*.

En route to the Marshalls, Joe Willingham's *Tautog* was nearly sunk by a Japanese submarine. At about 10 A.M. on April 26, while proceeding on the surface, *Tautog*'s officer of the deck sighted a periscope "opening out, preparatory to firing." With fine presence of mind, the OOD ordered hard left rudder and called the crew to battle stations. When the stern torpedo tubes came into position, Willingham fired a single torpedo. It either hit or exploded magnetically *above* the Japanese submarine. Willingham flashed a passing patrol plane to investigate. The pilot reported boxes, cushions, and other debris. *RO-30*, a 1,000-ton submarine, was stricken from the Japanese navy list.

Henry Chester Bruton, commanding the new boat *Greenling*, was, like Gene McKinney on *Salmon*, a seemingly mild-mannered lawyer. Reconnoitering Eniwetok en route to Truk, Bruton had a maddening experience. Late in the afternoon of April 20, he sighted a big ship and submerged and went to battle stations, firing four torpedoes. All missed. He surfaced, trailed, and six hours later fired another two torpedoes. Both missed. Moreover, the target fired back with a deck gun. Bruton responded in kind, manning his own deck gun, firing ten rounds. When a shell from the enemy landed close, ricocheting over the heads of his gun crew, Bruton ended his gun attack. At dawn, he let fly two more torpedoes, one of which prematured, one of which missed.

Later English criticized this, Bruton's first attack. "The expenditure of eight torpedoes in three attacks upon a 7,100-ton armed merchantman is considered unjustified, particularly so when all these torpedoes failed to hit. The tenacity and persistence with which this contact was held would have been most commendable if the target had been more important . . . chance shots at long range are deplored."

A few days later, patrolling off Truk, Bruton had better luck—and aim. He sighted a ship and fired one torpedo. The ship broke in two and sank in three minutes. It was *Kinjosan Maru*, 3,200 tons.

William Girard Myers, commanding *Gato*, patrolled Kwajalein, his assigned station in the Marshalls. On May 3, off Roi Island, having been alerted by an Ultra, he sighted a fast and large Japanese merchant ship that had been converted to a light aircraft carrier. Going to battle stations, Myers fired five torpedoes at the vessel, now named *Taiyo (Otaka)*,* believing he had obtained at least two hits. The following day, however, he saw the ship, undamaged, anchored inside the reef with five cargo vessels and two destroyers clustered around her. While Myers attempted to maneuver into better position, a destroyer attacked with depth charges. *Gato* withdrew to safer territory, having inflicted no damage on these valuable targets. In the postmortem, Myers figured he had misjudged the speed of *Taiyo (Otaka)*.

Gar, commanded by Don McGregor, also patrolled off Kwajalein on the way to Australia. McGregor fired at a freighter off Kwajalein, believing he had scored hits, but the ship did not sink. McGregor's exec, John Allison Fitzgerald, was dissatisfied with the patrol. He urged McGregor to accept greater risks—go closer to the beach and stay nearer the surface—but McGregor was captain and did what he believed best to ensure the safety of his ship.

The Hunt for "Wounded Bear"

While thirteen boats were out patrolling their areas, the Battle of the Coral Sea took place in southern waters. The light carrier *Shoho* had been sunk and the big carrier *Shokaku* badly damaged. After the battle, the codebreakers tuned in on *Shokaku* and her sister ship in the battle, *Zuikaku*. Both, they learned, would return to Japan by way of Truk.

These two carriers, especially the damaged *Shokaku*, were obviously prime targets for submarine torpedoes. Having got the information on May 7 (May 8, Coral Sea time), Pearl Harbor alerted the submarines on patrol to lie in wait for them, code-naming *Shokaku* "wounded bear."

Phase One of this intercept mission was played out at Truk, first stop for the carriers. Four submarines were ordered to intercept: *Greenling*, *Gar*, *Grampus*, and *Tautog*. Chester Bruton's *Greenling*

---

* Originally *Kasuga Maru*, she was one of five Japanese merchantmen so converted. After conversion, she was renamed *Taiyo* (not to be confused with the passenger ship *Taiyo Maru* Pilly Lent sank in the East China Sea). The codebreakers confused the carrier *Taiyo*'s call sign, erroneously naming her *Otaka*, which, in effect, gave the Japanese another carrier, causing more confusion.

THE HUNT FOR "WOUNDED BEAR"

was already off Truk when the word came; *Gar, Grampus,* and *Tautog* had to hurry from the east.

Pearl Harbor, believing *Shokaku* to be more badly damaged than she actually was, underestimated her speed and rate of advance. *Gar, Grampus,* and *Tautog* were all too late; "wounded bear" was already safely inside the Truk lagoon. Bruton in *Greenling* was patrolling the north side of the island and couldn't see her arrive.

Joe Willingham on *Tautog* remained on station south of Truk to intercept other Japanese forces returning from the Battle of the Coral Sea. He fired two torpedoes at *Goyo Maru,* one of the ships of the invasion force. One torpedo hit; one made a circular run toward *Tautog,* driving Willingham deep to avoid. *Goyo Maru* beached to save herself. Two days later, Willingham was alerted by Ultra that four Japanese I-class submarines were also returning from the battle. Of the three he sighted, the first caught him by surprise and he had no time to shoot. He fired two torpedoes at the second, believing he had hit, but postwar records failed to confirm him. Willingham also fired two torpedoes at the third, *I-28,* obtaining one hit, then closed the range and fired one more. Simultaneously, *I-28* fired two torpedoes at *Tautog,* and Willingham went deep to avoid. The Japanese torpedoes missed, but Willingham's third shot hit and *I-28* went down.

The "wounded bear," *Shokaku,* remained at Truk only briefly. She got under way for Japan about May 11 or 12, unseen by any U.S. submarine. However, it was not long before the codebreakers had obtained her track and speed. Pearl Harbor alerted *Cuttlefish* in the Marianas, but *Shokaku* went wide of *Cuttlefish* and continued on toward Japan.

Having missed the carrier at both Truk and Guam–Saipan, Pearl Harbor now began to shift submarines in the Empire area to intercept. Bob Rice in *Drum* was ordered to guard Kii Suido, the north entrance to the Inland Sea. Pilly Lent in *Grenadier* was ordered to take station off the south entrance, Bungo Suido. Stan Moseley in *Pollack,* approaching Empire waters, was ordered to intercept. Again, Pearl Harbor underestimated the "wounded bear's" speed. All three boats got into position too late.

Young Kirkpatrick in *Triton,* patrolling off Okinawa, was intercepting and reading the messages about *Shokaku* with intense interest. Although none were directed to him for action, he laid out the track of the oncoming carrier and figured that by running on the surface

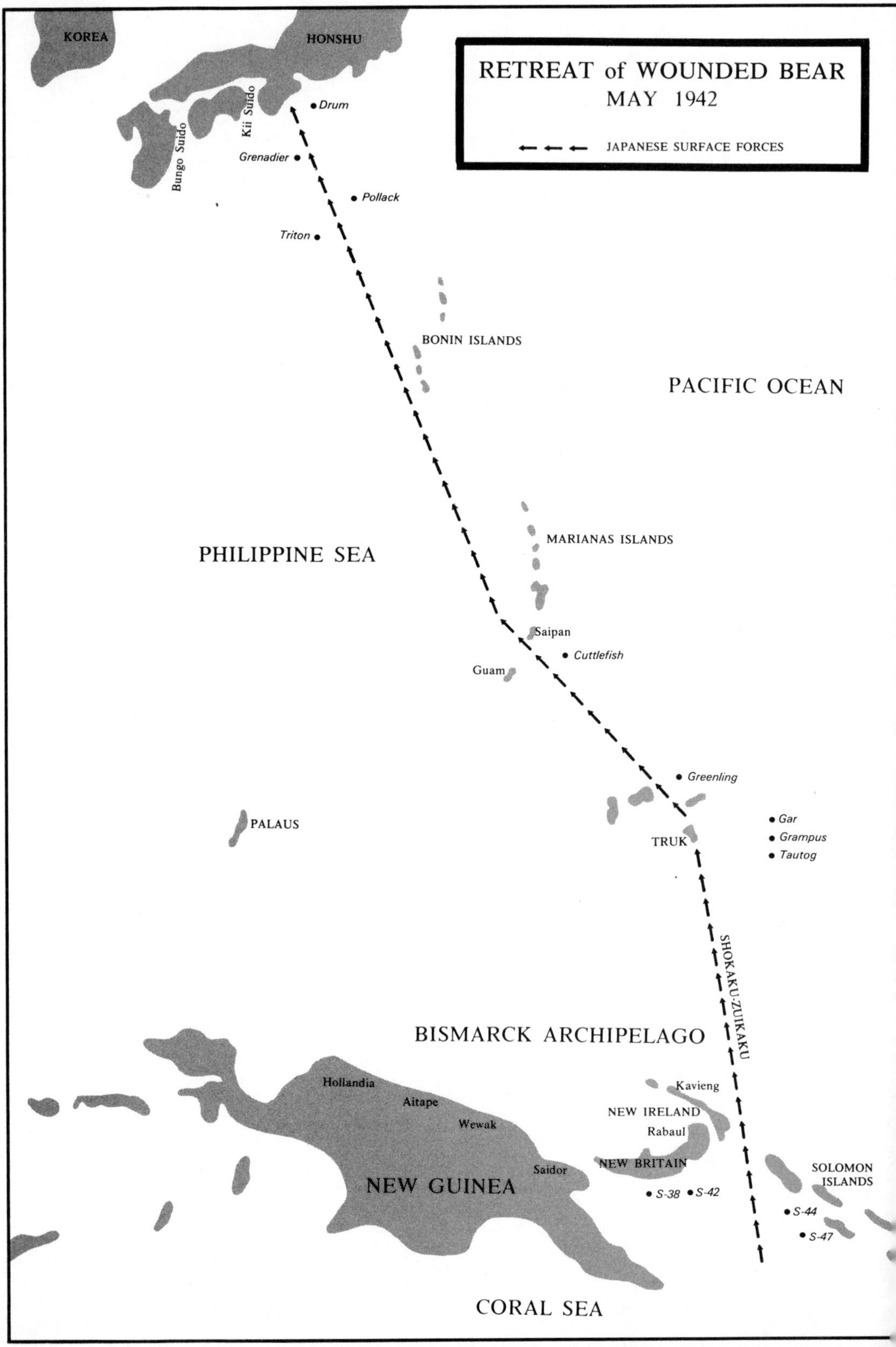

RETREAT of WOUNDED BEAR
MAY 1942
JAPANESE SURFACE FORCES
KOREA
HONSHU
Bungo Suido
Kii Suido
Drum
Grenadier
Pollack
Triton
BONIN ISLANDS
PACIFIC OCEAN
MARIANAS ISLANDS
PHILIPPINE SEA
Saipan
Cuttlefish
Guam
Greenling
PALAUS
TRUK
Gar
Grampus
Tautog
SHOKAKU-ZUIKAKU
BISMARCK ARCHIPELAGO
Hollandia
Aitape
Wewak
Kavieng
NEW IRELAND
Rabaul
NEW BRITAIN
Saidor
NEW GUINEA
S-38
S-42
SOLOMON ISLANDS
S-44
S-47
CORAL SEA

THE HUNT FOR "WOUNDED BEAR" 233

he might possibly intercept. On May 16 he arrived at what he believed to be the proper position and dived, calculating that his target would come by at 3:15 that afternoon. At 3:20 he sighted a destroyer, then the "bear," making 16 knots on a northerly course, range 6,700 yards.

Kirkpatrick was not in the most favorable attack position. One torpedo was left forward, four aft. He turned to an approach course, trying to bring his stern tubes around, but the carrier opened the range. Seeing it was hopeless, Kirkpatrick waited a while, then surfaced and pursued at full power (19½ knots), but he could not catch up. *Shokaku* entered port on May 17, having eluded seven or eight submarines.

That same day, May 17, while returning submerged to his regular patrol area, Kirkpatrick made one of the luckiest finds of the war: a Japanese submarine surfaced right in his path. Kirkpatrick fired his one remaining bow torpedo, and *I-64*, 1,600 tons, bound from Sasebo to Kwajalein, went to the bottom, stern first, with all hands. Counting *Tautog*'s *I-28*, sunk that same day, it was the fourth Japanese submarine destroyed by Pacific submarines.

Back at Truk, meanwhile, Chester Bruton in *Greenling* (who had not seen *Shokaku* leave Truk) had been shifted from the North Pass to the Northeast Pass. On May 16, the carrier *Zuikaku*, trailing *Shokaku* by several days steamed majestically out of North Pass, escorted by four destroyers. Bruton tried to maneuver into firing position, but the carrier was too far away and moving too fast. "It was an erroneous concept to rigidly station us so close to the island passes like that," Bruton said later. "If I had had flexibility, I would have been in a better position and maybe could have intercepted the carrier. The problem was, we were being given instructions by people at Pearl Harbor who had never been on war patrol."

Zuikaku proceeded on a northerly course, tracked by the codebreakers. Stan Moseley in *Pollack*, patrolling off the southern Empire islands, was moved into position to intercept. In the early hours of the morning of May 21 he picked her up, believing at first that she was a slow-moving merchant ship on a parallel course. He set up quickly, firing four torpedoes from 2,000 yards range. However, he underestimated *Zuikaku*'s speed, and all four torpedoes missed.

She put into port a day or so later, unharmed.

The Battle of Midway

In Tokyo, immediately following the Battle of the Coral Sea, Admiral Yamamoto pushed the button to begin the bold thrust at Midway and the invasion of the Aleutians. Joe Rochefort's Hypo codebreakers intercepted the large number of orders flowing from Imperial Naval Headquarters to the fleet, ordering the campaign. Although there were some agonizing gaps in the messages, Rochefort, with his incredible sixth sense, rightly judged that Midway would be the prime target, with a diversionary thrust into the Aleutians.

In the Japanese messages, the interior code designating the primary objective was "AF." Not everyone agreed with Rochefort that AF meant Midway. Admiral King thought it might be Hawaii. The army thought it might be California. To help resolve the doubt, Rochefort engaged in a rare bit of radio deception. He instructed Midway on a closed-circuit underwater cable to send out a plain-language message stating the fresh-water evaporators had broken down and there was only a limited supply of fresh water. It worked. "In the next twenty-four or thirty-six hours," Rochefort said later, "our counterpart in Japan, the Owada Communications Group, sent a message to Admiral Yamamoto stating that AF was short of fresh water. That trick helped convince most of the doubters."

Upon receiving this information, which included the exact Japanese order of battle, Nimitz concluded that by combining his three available carriers with land-based aircraft from Midway, the U.S. Navy might be able to deal the Japanese a decisive blow. Accordingly, he ordered Jack Fletcher in *Yorktown* to proceed from the Southwest Pacific at best speed and repair her damage at Pearl Harbor. *Enterprise* and *Hornet*, having returned to Pearl Harbor from the Doolittle raid on Tokyo, were made ready, together with every available surface craft, some eight cruisers and fourteen destroyers. Bull Halsey, hospitalized with shingles, was replaced by Admiral Raymond Spruance.

In addition, Nimitz ordered Bob English to prepare every submarine in the Pacific for battle. The plan worked out by English, his chief of staff, Gin Styer, and Operations Officer Edward Keith Walker was as follows:

One force of submarines would be stationed on a fanlike arc to the

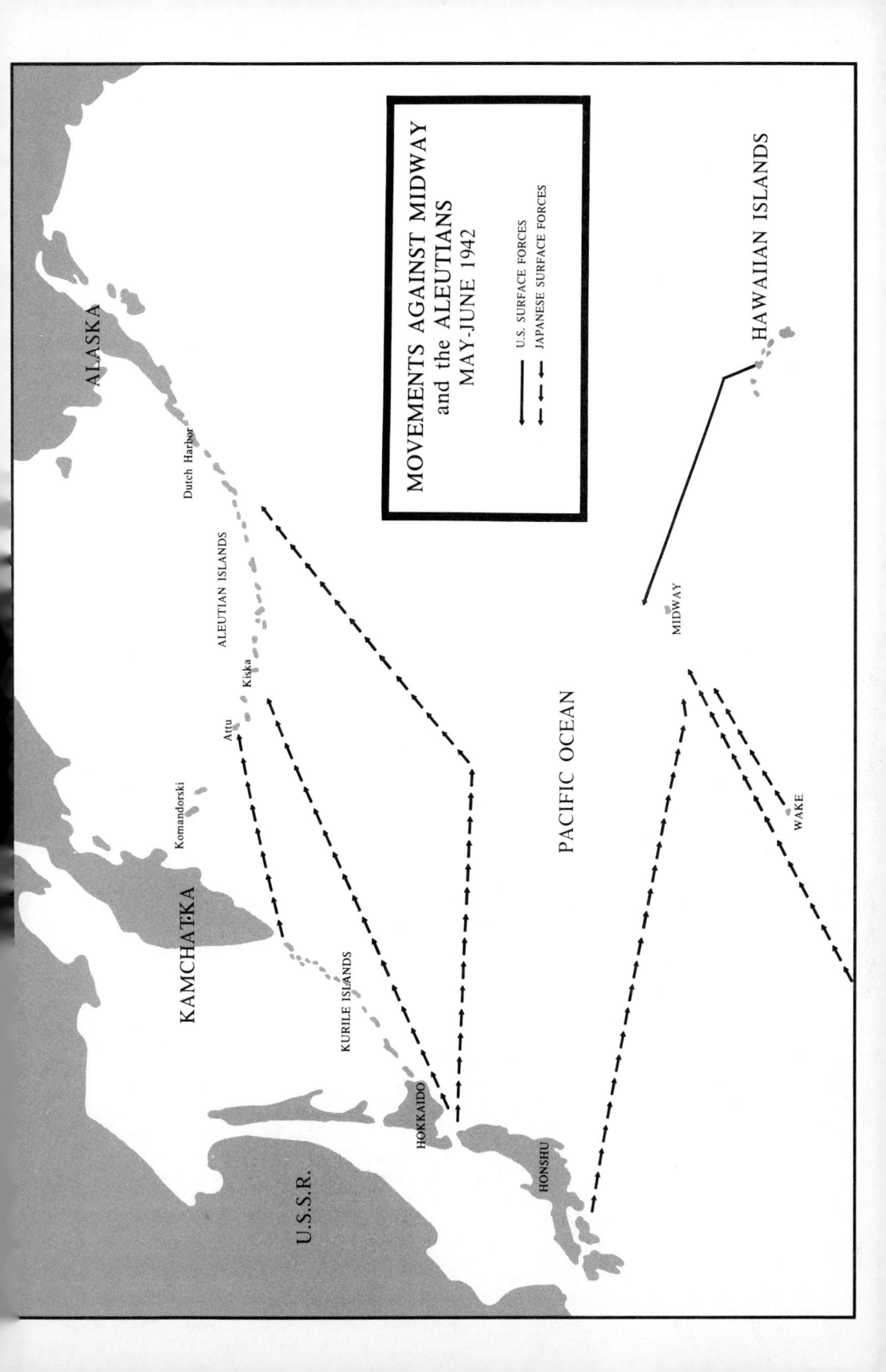

MOVEMENTS AGAINST MIDWAY
and the ALEUTIANS
MAY-JUNE 1942

→→→ U.S. SURFACE FORCES
--→ JAPANESE SURFACE FORCES

southwest, west, northwest, and north of Midway, distance 150 to 200 miles. Their mission was to defend Midway from invasion and to attack capital ships if they came within the assigned areas. A second and smaller force would be positioned between Midway and Hawaii to intercept, report, and attack any Japanese fleet units that might slip around U.S. surface forces and head for Hawaii. A third force would be stationed to the north of Oahu, to attack any enemy force bearing down on Pearl Harbor.

English then had a total of thirty fleet boats under his command: of these, two were in overhaul, five had left for routine patrol in May, eleven were on distant patrol or returning from patrol, and twelve were in Pearl Harbor.

Four of the five boats on routine patrol were recalled and rerouted to stations near Midway. Nine of the eleven boats on distant patrol were ordered to converge on Midway, if fuel and torpedo supply warranted. The twelve boats in Pearl Harbor were fueled, armed, and ordered to sea.

The Midway defense force, in position by June 3, was composed of twelve submarines. One was 700 miles due west of Midway. Nine were stationed on the fanlike arc southwest to north of the island. Two others were placed inside the 150-mile arc, like linebackers.*

The Hawaii defense force consisted of seven boats, all from Pearl Harbor. They were disposed in two groups, three 600 miles away, between Midway and Hawaii,† and four 300 miles north of Hawaii.‡ Much farther to the west of Midway were the other boats returning from patrol stations.§ The tender *Pelias,* preparing to leave for San Francisco to load up for her trip to Fremantle, was sent on her way

---

* The boats composing the Midway force and their origins were:

From Pearl Harbor:	Recalled from patrol:	Returning from patrol:
1. *Gudgeon* (Lyon)	6. *Grouper* (Duke)	10. *Cuttlefish* (Hottel)
2. *Nautilus* (Brockman)	7. *Cachalot* (G. A. Lewis)	11. *Grenadier* (Lent)
3. *Trout* (Fenno)	8. *Dolphin* (Rutter)	12. *Gato* (Myers)
4. *Grayling* (Olsen)	9. *Flying Fish* (Donaho)	
5. *Tambor* (Murphy)		

† *Plunger* (White), *Narwhal* (Wilkins), and *Trigger* (Lewis).
‡ *Growler* (Gilmore), *Finback* (Hull), *Pike* (New), and *Tarpon* (Wallace).
§ *Greenling* (Bruton), *Drum* (Rice), *Pollack* (Moseley), *Tuna* (DeTar), *Pompano* (Parks), and *Porpoise* (McKnight—from Australia).

THE BATTLE OF MIDWAY 237

prematurely—to get her out of Pearl Harbor. The other tender, *Fulton*, remained.

At 9 A.M. on June 3, a Midway patrol plane spotted the Japanese invasion force 700 miles west of the island, not far from *Cuttlefish*. Air Force B-17s, basing out of Midway, made a bombing attack on the force that afternoon, but their aim was off; they got no hits. In the early hours of June 4, torpedo planes based on Midway also attacked the invasion force, damaging one ship slightly.

Shortly after that attack, Hottel in *Cuttlefish* sighted what he believed to be a tanker and sent off a report to English—the first contact between U.S. submarines and the Japanese in the Battle of Midway. Believing the tanker to be a unit of the invasion force, English ordered Hottel to stalk it and send in position reports, a key assignment.

Hottel was uneasy. His lookouts believed they saw aircraft. Dawn was coming up fast. There was no way he could trail in broad daylight. The aircraft—friend or foe—would attack, he was certain. He had already performed his primary task, reporting the oncoming enemy. There was no way he could pull ahead and make an attack without being detected.

Hottel dived, losing contact with the enemy.

While this skirmish was in progress, on June 4, the Japanese striking force, composed of Carrier Divisions One (*Akagi, Kaga*) and Two (*Soryu, Hiryu*), all veterans of the Pearl Harbor attack, reached its assigned position undetected, about 150 miles northwest of Midway, and launched planes against the island. Meanwhile, planes on Midway took off to find the Japanese. At 6:35 A.M., Japanese planes attacked Midway. At 7:05, Midway planes attacked the striking force. Neither side inflicted decisive damage.

The Japanese had backup planes on the carrier decks armed with torpedoes in case U.S. naval vessels were sighted. None of the Japanese planes, as yet, had spotted any U.S. ships. Believing them to be elsewhere, the Japanese now ordered the backup planes rearmed with bombs for a second strike against Midway. While this work was in progress, Midway-based dive bombers and B-17s attacked the Japanese again, doing little damage but causing much distraction. In the midst of this attack, a Japanese plane reported sighting a U.S. carrier to the northeast. The Japanese again changed plans, ordering the backup planes reloaded with torpedoes instead of bombs.

Meanwhile, all three U.S. carriers had launched air strikes against the Japanese carriers. *Hornet*'s dive bombers and fighters made a wrong turn, headed south, and never found the enemy. But her torpedo planes, together with torpedo planes from *Enterprise* and *Yorktown*, found the Japanese force and attacked at 9:28. Altogether there were forty-one torpedo planes. Of these, thirty-five were shot down by the Japanese. Not a single torpedo found the mark.*

The Japanese were jubilant. The striking force seemed invincible. They had beaten off everything the Americans had thrown at them—land-based and carrier-based torpedo planes, high-level bombers. Now they prepared to launch a strike against the American carriers and bring to a conclusion what was certainly to be the greatest Japanese naval victory in all history.

At that moment, 10:24, dive bombers from *Enterprise* and *Yorktown* pushed over and attacked the striking force, finding *Akagi*, *Kaga*, and *Soryu* in their sights. (The fourth carrier, *Hiryu*, was to the northward, somewhat detached from the main group.) "Within three minutes," as Jasper Holmes wrote later, "what had been a Japanese victory became a Japanese disaster." *Akagi*, *Kaga*, and *Soryu*, shuddering under the impact of dive bombers, burst into uncontrollable flames.

Hiryu, off to herself, was not bombed in this assault. She launched her dive bombers against the American carriers. They found *Yorktown* and disabled her with two bombs. In a second attack, later in the day, *Hiryu*'s torpedo planes, fighting through a withering wall of antiaircraft fire that destroyed half their number, managed to fire four torpedoes against the damaged *Yorktown*, two of which hit. With *Yorktown* listing and fires raging, her captain gave the order to abandon ship. At about the same time, dive bombers from *Enterprise* and *Yorktown* found *Hiryu* and hit her with four bombs. She was left a flaming wreck.

Sixteen Japanese submarines were assigned to the Battle of Midway, disposed in two groups. Ten were stationed to the northeast of Midway and four between Midway and Pearl Harbor, considerably south of the three submarines English had placed between the two islands. For various reasons, all the Japanese submarines arrived on

---

* The aerial torpedoes had all the defects of the Mark XIV submarine torpedoes, plus others.

station late and therefore missed making contact with the U.S. carrier task forces.

Rochefort and the Hypo unit tracked the Japanese submarines by means of codebreaking and RDF, relaying reports to English, who in turn relayed information to his submarines. On June 4, the day of the major engagement, English informed his submarines that a Japanese submarine tender was servicing Japanese submarines 700 miles west of Midway. Four times in the next three days, English sent further information on the position of Japanese subs.

Knowing the position of the Japanese submarines enabled Nimitz to make what otherwise might have been a risky, even reckless move. After *Yorktown* had been abandoned, her men were recovered by escorting cruisers and destroyers. These ships were encumbered by the survivors. On the afternoon of June 4, Nimitz ordered the tender *Fulton* to get under way and bring back the survivors, thus freeing the other ships for further combat. *Fulton*, alerted to known positions of Japanese submarines, raced to the rescue. She returned to Pearl Harbor on June 8 with 2,025 survivors of *Yorktown* and other U.S. vessels.

In spite of all the codebreaking and RDF-ing, one Japanese submarine, *I-168*, scored a victory. She had left Japan behind the others, delayed by overhaul. Maintaining radio silence as she cruised more or less independently of the main Japanese submarine force, on June 5 she bombarded Midway, until driven down by U.S. destroyers. Later that night she picked up a report on the damaged *Yorktown* and headed for her position.

On the morning of June 6, *I-168* found *Yorktown*. By then the carrier's fires had been brought under control and a tug, *Vireo*, was attempting to tow her back to Pearl Harbor. The U.S. destroyer *Hammann* was alongside, supplying electric power. *I-168* fired four torpedoes at this overlapping formation. One torpedo hit *Hammann*. The destroyer broke up and sank immediately. Two torpedoes hit *Yorktown*. Added to her other damage, this was enough to send the carrier to the bottom. *I-168* was heavily counterattacked by other U.S. destroyers, but she managed to evade and limp back to Japan, having made the biggest kill yet by any submarine in the Pacific.

The role played by U.S. submarines in the Battle of Midway was one of confusion and error.

On June 4, Midway-based aircraft had spotted and reported the

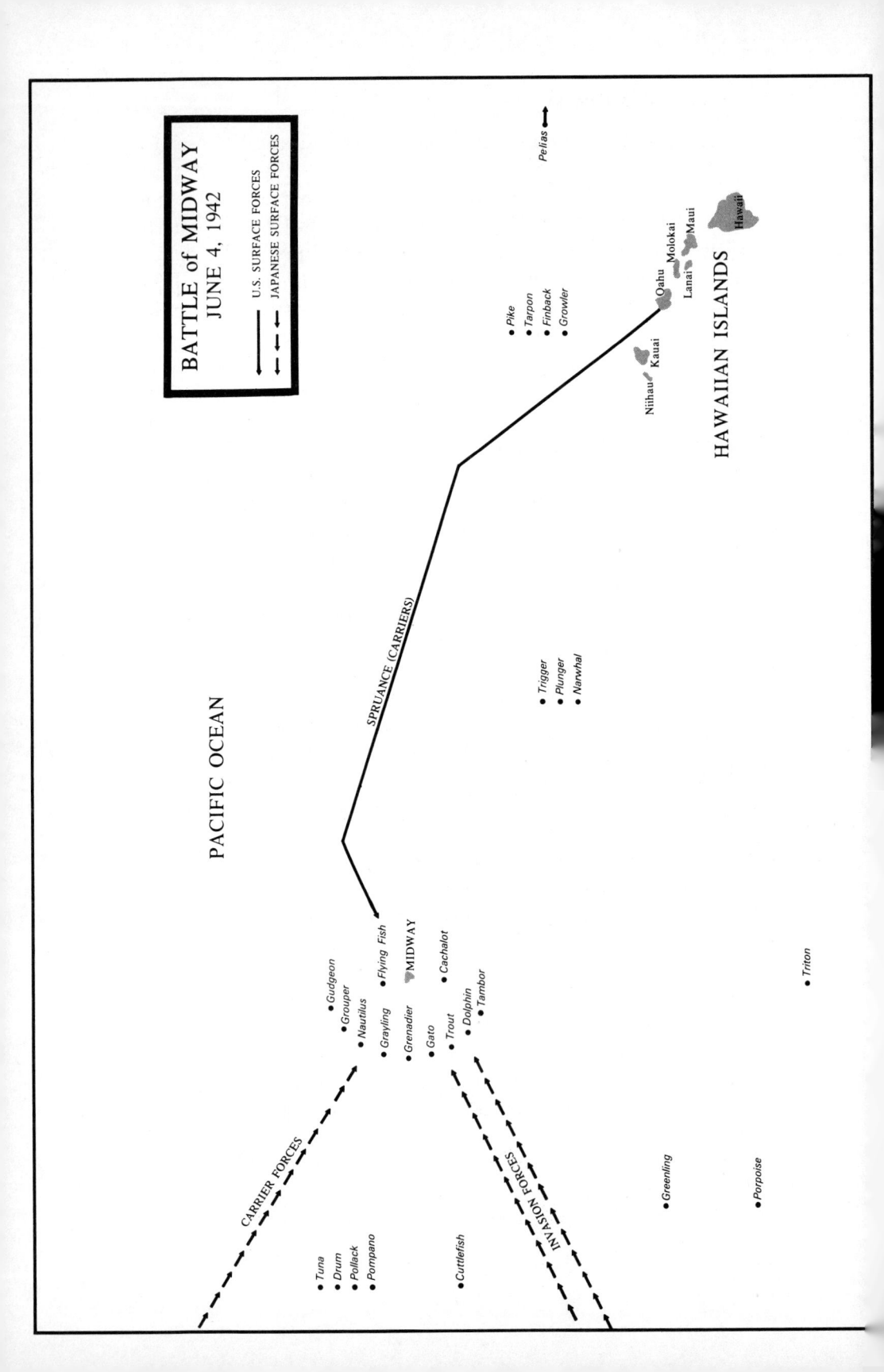

BATTLE of MIDWAY
JUNE 4, 1942

U.S. SURFACE FORCES →
JAPANESE SURFACE FORCES ⇢

PACIFIC OCEAN

HAWAIIAN ISLANDS

- Niihau
- Kauai
- Oahu
- Molokai
- Lanai
- Maui
- Hawaii

• Pelias

• Pike
• Tarpon
• Finback
• Growler

SPRUANCE (CARRIERS)

• Trigger
• Plunger
• Narwhal

• Tuna
• Drum
• Pollack
• Pompano

• Cuttlefish

• Gudgeon
• Grouper
• Nautilus
• Grayling
• Flying Fish
▼ MIDWAY
• Grenadier
• Gato
• Trout
• Cachalot
• Dolphin
• Tambor

CARRIER FORCES

INVASION FORCES

• Greenling

• Triton

• Porpoise

position of the Japanese striking force at 5:45 A.M. Thereafter, a flood of contact reports giving the location, range, speed, and course of the striking force filled the airways. English sent his submarines a report at 7:15 A.M. indicating a contact with an enemy carrier, giving a range and bearing from Midway. Some of the submarines deployed at Midway intercepted these reports and began moving toward the enemy on their own initiative. But *four hours* went by before English actually ordered nine of his twelve submarines (less *Cuttlefish* and the linebackers, *Flying Fish* and *Cachalot*) to close the enemy. This was shortly after the carrier-based torpedo planes attacked the striking force and long after the initial attack from the Midway-based aircraft.

The submarines nearest to the reported position of the striking force were Hap Lyon's *Gudgeon*, William Herman Brockman, Jr.,'s *Nautilus*, and Claren Emmett Duke's new boat, *Grouper*, all to the north or northwest of Midway.

Duke intercepted English's 7:15 A.M. contact report. He turned toward the reported position on the surface, going to battle stations at 7:26. Five minutes later, he sighted planes on the horizon that appeared to be taking off from a carrier. Duke dived and went in, but, he reported later, he was frustrated by the enemy. At 7:51, a plane machine-gunned and bombed his periscope. This attack, Duke reported, was followed up by a destroyer attack with depth charges over the next few hours. Duke fired two torpedoes from a deep depth, inflicting no damage on the destroyer.

While Duke stayed deep, important time passed by. At 11:40 he inched back to periscope depth. Sighting smoke pouring from what he believed to be two burning carriers, Duke again went deep, inching toward the targets. At 1:14 P.M., he heard several heavy explosions. Thinking that one of the carriers might be exploding overhead and might sink on *Grouper*, he went deep again and evaded.

In the hours following, Duke and *Grouper* were very nearly lost, not to enemy forces but by bad luck. During a quick dive to escape an aircraft, Duke lost depth control and *Grouper* plunged downward at a terrifying angle. As the officers and men struggled to bring her out of her fatal-seeming dive—blowing tanks, backing "emergency" (full power astern)—the depth gauge needle swung past 200 . . . 300 . . . 400 . . . 500 feet, far below *Grouper*'s test depth. At 600 feet, deeper than any fleet boat had ever gone, Duke pulled her out and climbed back to a normal depth. A large quantity of water had leaked in through the stern tubes, Duke reported, "and everyone had a few more gray hairs."

Later, Duke's division commander, Willard Merrill Downes, wrote:

From the report, it is evident that many golden opportunities to inflict severe damage on the enemy were missed. The Commanding Officer chose in many instances to use evasive tactics rather than aggressive tactics. It is unfortunate that an unseasoned ship, so far as combat is concerned, should get its baptism of fire in an engagement of the magnitude of the Battle of Midway. It is felt that this initial introduction to combat together with the inadvertent deep dive of Grouper *colored the decisions of the Commanding Officer throughout the patrol.*

English added, "It is regretted that the attack on two burning carriers [at Midway] was not pressed home. It hardly seems conceivable that 100 depth charges [the number reported by Duke] were dropped on *Grouper* on the morning of June 4 and another 60 to 70 that afternoon."

When Hap Lyon in *Gudgeon* got the 7:15 contact report, he was not far from the Japanese. He turned south to run on the surface. "He was no chicken," said Dusty Dornin, who had moved up to be *Gudgeon*'s exec. "The problem was, Hap was blind as a bat." At 8:42, *Gudgeon* picked up the "pagoda masts" of two battleships on the horizon. Whether Lyon or Dornin sighted these masts is not clear. Dornin said he saw them and that Lyon "couldn't see a damned thing." In his patrol report, Lyon said, "The Commanding Officer alone sighted these vessels," and then he discounted them as doubtful sightings, adding, "The Commanding Officer has had a long history of defective vision which has grown progressively worse with each patrol until now he has difficulty recognizing his friends beyond 30 paces. He therefore views with suspicion anything he sees himself which is not verified."

Hap Lyon turned *Gudgeon* toward the targets and remained on the surface, going in. Dornin, who had already proved himself to be one of the most courageous men in the submarine force, said later, "Frankly, I urged Hap to dive. God! There were planes all around. There's a line between bravery and recklessness. You have to draw that line."

Lyon dived, closing at top speed. He remained on a normal approach course for forty-five minutes. When he raised the periscope, the battleships were nowhere in sight. There were Japanese planes overhead, so he decided to remain where he was, believing he must be on—or near—the rendezvous point for the Japanese carriers. He waited two hours but saw no carriers. He wrote in his patrol report, "Felt I should proceed to a better station but had no idea where to go." He waited on station until 4 P.M., hoping to see the Japanese carriers, but he had no further contact with enemy ships. At dusk, he poked up his radio antenna to see if English had any new instructions, but a plane (Japanese or U.S.) bombed *Gudgeon* and Lyon went back down.

William Brockman in old *Nautilus* picked up a contact report from U.S. aircraft at 5:44 A.M. He plotted the position and concluded that if the report were accurate the Japanese striking force was close by, on the northern boundary of his sector. Remaining submerged, he guided slow, clumsy *Nautilus* toward the position.

At 7:55, Brockman saw masts on the horizon. While making this observation, his periscope was strafed by an aircraft. At 8 A.M. he sighted a formation of four ships: a battleship and a cruiser in column with two "cruisers" on the bow, escorting. (The "cruisers" were probably destroyers; many submarine skippers confused destroyers for cruisers in the early days of the war.) Before Brockman could get off a shot, one of the destroyers turned and attacked, dropping twenty depth charges and forcing *Nautilus* deep.

Twenty-four minutes later, Brockman was back at periscope depth, taking another look. As he wrote later:

The picture presented on raising the periscope was one never experienced in peacetime practices. Ships were on all sides moving across the field at high speed and circling away to avoid the submarine's position. Ranges were above 3,000 yards. The cruiser had passed over and was now astern. The battleship was on our port bow and firing her whole starboard broadside battery at the periscope. Flag hoists were being made; searchlights were trained at the periscope.

Brockman coolly fired two torpedoes at the battleship, which was now evading at high speed. One torpedo failed to fire; the other missed.

The destroyer charged in again, pinging. Brockman dropped to 150 feet, with depth charges exploding all around. When the Japanese broke off the attack, he came back to periscope depth, astonished to find a Japanese carrier barreling along on a converging course. As he was looking, the destroyer charged in again. Brockman set up and fired one torpedo at the destroyer, forcing it to change course, but it returned in a moment, dropping eight more charges. Brockman took *Nautilus* deep, creeping along the converging course for the carrier. When the depth-charging stopped, he promptly returned to periscope depth. The seas were empty.

Half an hour later, at 10:29, Brockman spotted four "large clouds" of smoke on the horizon. This was five minutes after navy dive bombers had hit *Akagi*, *Kaga*, and *Soryu*. At the same time, he picked up a message that a carrier had been damaged. Brockman turned toward the smoke, which he estimated to be about 10 or 11 miles distant. At 11:45, he saw clearly the smoke was coming from a burning carrier, range 8 miles. He continued on submerged at 3 to 4 knots. The burning carrier seemed to be motionless.

As they came up on the target, Brockman's exec, Roy Stanley ("Ensign") Benson, and others had a good look through the periscope. They compared the carrier silhouette to recognition pictures of Japanese ships pasted on the bulkhead in the conning tower and decided the carrier was *Soryu*. Its fires seemed to be under control; two cruisers (or destroyers) stood by. Men in whaleboats were apparently trying to pass a tow line.

Brockman ordered four torpedo tubes made ready. In the six minutes between 1:59 and 2:05, he fired four carefully aimed torpedoes. Three functioned; one failed to leave the tube. At the periscope, Brockman watched the torpedoes streak 2,700 yards toward the carrier. "Red flames," he reported, "appeared along the ship from bow to amidships . . . many men were seen going over the side." All five officers in the conning tower took turns looking through the periscope at the target. Then the destroyers charged *Nautilus*, and Brockman, satisfied he had sunk a damaged carrier, went to 300 feet. "The Commanding Officer believes that she was destroyed at this time by fire and internal explosions," Brockman later wrote. "He did not, however, acutally see her sink."

Brockman's performance on June 4, in terms of courage and persistence, was outstanding, and he received a Navy Cross. Credited with sinking *Soryu*, Brockman was later to be denied. In a careful postwar analysis, the U.S. Navy determined, after comparing position reports of *Nautilus* and the Japanese forces, that the carrier Brockman shot at was not *Soryu* but *Kaga*. Japanese survivors provided proof. Three rescued from *Kaga* reported seeing three torpedoes fired from a submarine at 2:10, about the time Brockman fired. Two of the tor-

THE BATTLE OF MIDWAY

pedoes missed. The third struck amidships but failed to explode. It shattered, throwing loose the air flask, which floated free and served for a while as a life preserver for several of *Kaga*'s crew. Survivors of *Soryu* reported no submarine torpedoes fired at that vessel.

The eight other submarines patrolling close by Midway that day were too far removed to close the enemy. Pilly Lent in *Grenadier*, patrolling in the sector south of *Nautilus*, intercepted a contact report at 6:15 A.M. After a quick plot, Lent realized the force "was already beyond us." At 8:37 he surfaced and proceeded toward Midway, "hoping to intercept retiring enemy units." A plane drove him down at 8:55. After a few minutes, he again surfaced and continued on.

To the south of *Grenadier*, even farther from the striking force, Eliot Olsen in *Grayling* had little chance at making an attack. He milled around, hoping to intercept something worthwhile. While so doing, he unwittingly became a target for U.S. aircraft.

On the afternoon of June 7, a formation of twelve B-17s based on Midway caught *Grayling* cruising on the surface. The bomber pilots —all green—believed they had found a retreating Japanese cruiser. Although Olsen flashed a proper recognition signal with his searchlight, the three leading B-17s dropped a string of twenty 1,000-pound bombs. Olsen immediately crash-dived. When the B-17 pilots returned to Midway, they triumphantly reported sinking "one Japanese cruiser which went down in fifteen seconds."

To the south of *Grayling*, the remaining four boats—Myers's *Gato*, Fenno's *Trout*, Rutter's *Dolphin*, and Murphy's *Tambor*—were frustrated and ineffectual. While trying to run on the surface toward the enemy force, they were machine-gunned or lightly bombed by enemy (or friendly) aircraft. They dived to avoid being hit. None was able to make enough distance to meet the enemy.

After the June 4 battle, there remained a huge Japanese naval force somewhere on the seas to the west of Midway: the main body of battleships, some light carriers, many cruisers and destroyers, plus the invasion force.* Nimitz did not believe the Japanese would now

---

* This force included an extraordinary vessel, *Yamato*, the largest warship ever built. She and two sister ships, *Musashi* and *Shinano*, were designed by Japanese naval architects in 1935, after Japan renounced the arms limitation agreement. Each ship was to be about 59,000 tons, mounting nine 18-inch guns—more firepower than any ship in history. Built in secret, *Yamato* was completed in December 1941, after Pearl Harbor. *Musashi* came later. Before *Shinano* was completed, the Japanese

attempt the Midway landing, but the possibility could not be disregarded.

At 2:15 A.M. on June 5, John Murphy in *Tambor*, 90 miles to the west of Midway, made contact with a group of ships. It was dark. Neither Murphy nor his officers (including young Spruance) was certain what they had found. Murphy got off a vague contact report to Bob English, mentioning "many unidentified ships," but did not give a course.

This message actually led to a major mistake in the Battle of Midway. Admiral Spruance assumed the "many unidentified ships" must be the Japanese invasion force and that the invasion was still on. The carrier forces redeployed to the north of Midway to gain a favorable position to attack the invasion force as it closed. Bob English ordered his Midway submarines to fall back to a 5-mile radius from the island and repel landing forces. He also ordered the three boats standing by between Midway and Hawaii—*Trigger*, *Plunger*, and *Narwhal*—to join the Midway force.

In fact, however, Yamamoto had given up the attempt and had ordered his forces to fall back, regroup, and leave the area. The "many unidentified ships" that Murphy had sighted were merely four cruisers and two destroyers which had been previously ordered to bombard Midway. About forty minutes after Murphy sent off his report, Yamamoto ordered them to rejoin the retreating forces. When they turned to do so, a Japanese lookout sighted *Tambor* and gave the alarm. In maneuvering to avoid, two of the cruisers, *Mogami* and *Mikuma*, collided. *Mogami* severely damaged her bow; *Mikuma* trailed oil from a ruptured fuel tank. The other two cruisers retired to the northwest, leaving *Mogami* and *Mikuma* and the destroyer escort proceeding on a westerly course, speed reduced to 17 knots.

Although Murphy had been in visual contact with the cruisers and destroyers for two hours, he had not got off a torpedo. He was afraid, he said later, that they might be friendly forces, reported to be in the area. However, at 4:12 A.M., with visibility increasing, he recognized the ships as Japanese and saw that *Mogami* was badly damaged. With dawn coming on, Murphy submerged. He was unable to gain attack position, but at about six he got off another contact report, this time

---

decided to convert her to an aircraft carrier—the world's largest. All three ships had heavy armor plating and were considered, by the Japanese, unsinkable. The codebreakers did not know about them.

THE BATTLE OF MIDWAY 247

correctly identifying the vessels as two *Mogami*-class cruisers on a westerly course.

Four valuable hours had gone by between *Tambor*'s first and second reports. During that time Admiral Spruance, anticipating an invasion, had moved about 100 miles to the northeast of Midway, and the submarines had pulled back eastward to stations about 5 or 10 miles from Midway. During the same four hours, Yamamoto's major forces had moved about 100 miles farther west and were increasing the gap by about 25 miles every hour. Two or three more confused hours went by before land-based Midway planes reported positively that there was no sign of an invasion. On the contrary, every contact they found indicated the Japanese forces in full retreat.

Thus Murphy's report sent all U.S. forces capable of pursuing and attacking the badly disorganized Japanese forces *in the wrong direction.* Aircraft sank the limping *Mogami*, badly damaged *Mikuma*, and unsuccessfully attacked a destroyer, *Tanikaze*. But the rest of the Japanese force got clean away, withdrawing toward Wake, where Japanese land-based aircraft could provide protection. Now low on fuel and aware of Japanese planes concentrating on Wake, the U.S. carriers broke off the chase, and the opportunity to inflict a coup de grace on the Japanese navy was irretrievably lost.*

On the brand-new *Trigger*, commanded by Jack Hayden Lewis, there was a tremendous surge of excitement as she raced to engage the landing force supposedly bearing down on Midway. In the early hours of June 6, with the lights of Midway visible on the horizon, Edward Latimer ("Ned") Beach had the watch. "We got orders to change course," said another officer, reservist Richard S. Garvey. "Ned reported land ahead and sent for the skipper. After a few minutes, Lewis came from the bridge to study a chart wearing red goggles, the new invention to preserve night vision. There were some reefs on the chart marked in red. We weren't experienced with night-adaptation goggles then. We didn't realize that red goggles blanked out the red on the chart."

Having studied the chart, Lewis went back to the bridge to conn

---

* Some naval historians make the case that this was a lucky break for Admiral Spruance. The codebreakers had no knowledge of the superbattleship *Yamato*. Had Spruance pursued instead of retiring, it is possible that he would unwittingly have brought his two remaining carriers, *Enterprise* and *Hornet*, within range of *Yamato*'s 18-inch guns in darkness, when he was unable to launch planes. *Yamato* might well have sunk both carriers, turning the Midway victory for the United States into a draw.

the ship into its proper position. "The next thing you know," Garvey said, "Somebody yelled down that we were either running into land or the wake of a huge ship."

In fact, *Trigger* was going aground. Beach later described the moment: "suddenly, catastrophically, with a horrible, shattering smash, *Trigger* ran head on into a submerged coral wall! Her bow shot skyward. Her sturdy hull screamed with pain as she crashed and pounded to a stop . . . here poor *Trigger* lay, bruised, battered, and hors de combat."

Below decks, all was turmoil. "I was sleeping in the wardroom with Willie Long, another officer," Garvey recalled. "There was a terrific crash. Long and I were thrown out of our bunks. All the lights went out. The collision alarm went off. The watertight doors slammed shut. We were sealed in the compartment. I thought we had been torpedoed. Long said, 'Hell, we can't do anything about it. We may as well go back to bed.' "

Lewis, dismayed, surveyed his ship. *Trigger* was stuck fast, with the Japanese invasion fleet expected any moment. Feverishly, the crew lightened ship, emptying the trim tanks and dumping fuel. After a call for help, a tug came from Midway. Backing emergency, and with the tug straining, *Trigger* broke free and refloated. There was a "gaping hole" in a ballast tank, the sonar heads had been wiped away, but *Trigger* was still seaworthy. She took up her patrol station.

For the next several days, English shifted his boats here and there, trying to intercept various Japanese vessels, damaged and otherwise. Most of the submarines returning from distant patrol were pressed into this elusive hunt. They had various minor adventures. *Cuttlefish* was bombed by planes; *Grouper* fired a torpedo at a "submarine periscope" but missed; *Greenling* tried to find two cruisers returning to Wake Island; *Drum* was sent to find a "burning battleship" and "damaged cruiser" retreating to the west. None did any damage to the Japanese.

So ended what was later to be called the "incredible victory." Yamamoto had failed abjectly. He had drawn Nimitz into a decisive battle which the United States, not the Japanese, won. Credit for the outcome was largely due Rochefort and the Hypo unit.

Years later, Chester Nimitz, in collaboration with Professor E. B. Potter of the U.S. Naval Academy, wrote in *The Great Sea War:*

JUNE DEPARTURES

Midway was essentially a victory of intelligence. . . . Since the United States was intercepting and reading Japanese coded messages, American intelligence of the enemy's plans was remarkably complete. Nimitz's information indicated the Japanese objectives, the approximate composition of the enemy forces, the direction of approach, and the approximate date of attack. It was this knowledge that made the American victory possible.

Indeed it was. And after the battle, the Hypo unit celebrated with an epic three-day party. Joe Rochefort, ordinarily a restrained drinker, let himself go—three sheets to the wind.

The submariners, certainly, had nothing of their own to celebrate. Only two or three got off a torpedo, and none hit anything. One sent an incomplete contact report that misled Admiral Spruance and prevented the possible sinking of more major Japanese ships. The skippers blamed Bob English's plan; Bob English blamed the skippers.

June Departures

After the Battle of Midway, and fearing Nimitz might relieve him on account of the poor showing of his submarines, English made wholesale changes in his staff and submarine skippers.

First came his staff. English's second-in-command, Gin Styer, was relieved by John Bradford Griggs, Jr., a big happy-go-lucky officer with a cheerful, optimistic air; Styer returned to the States to command a new squadron, Ten, then forming up with a new tender, *Sperry*. Operations Officer Edward Walker, long on the job and due for relief, left submarines for good, returning to the States to command a destroyer, *Mayrant*, on which Franklin Delano Roosevelt, Jr., was gunnery officer. English requested Dick Voge, then commanding *Sailfish* in Fremantle, for Walker's relief. While waiting for Voge to return from the Southwest Pacific, English gave the job temporarily to John Huston Brady, operations officer for Babe Brown in Squadron Four.

Then it was time for the skippers. Four of the old hands who had performed well—Mike Fenno, Lew Parks, Stan Moseley, and Pilly Lent—moved on to staff jobs or returned to the States for new construction—that is, to put a new boat in commission and train the new crew for combat. Hap Lyon on *Gudgeon*, who had expressed concern about his eyesight, was relieved for physical reasons. Three skippers suffered the humiliation of being relieved for cause: Johnny DeTar on *Tuna* for general all-round inability; Spike Hottel on *Cuttlefish* for failing to produce; John Murphy on *Tambor* for his poor torpedo shooting on patrol and the incomplete contact report on the Japanese forces that had misled Spruance in the Battle of Midway. Spike Hottel, a torpedo expert, later wrote:

Admiral English had adopted the British practice of relieving unproductive skippers, and unfortunately I was in that category. During my interview with him, I was able to convince him that there were ameliorating circumstances and on his part he convinced me that my particular talents [torpedoes] were badly needed in [the tender] Fulton and promised that as soon as I had done the job there he would see that I got another command.

Wrote John Murphy:

I think I had bad luck to the extent that some warheads didn't explode as they were designed to do. I also think that some of my attacks were not well conducted and that my judgment was faulty more than once. However, I believe that the principal reason I was not kept on . . . was that Tambor's report of contact in darkness with Japanese cruisers and destroyers at the start of the Battle of Midway was misinterpreted as a report of contact with the Main Body. . . . We should have made an opportunity . . . to amplify our initial report, but we didn't. I was told that Admiral Spruance directed Admiral English to have me transferred because of this incident. I really cannot find much fault with the decision.

The fact that Admiral Spruance's son was on *Tambor* during the battle was evidently no help to Murphy.

Now that the Japanese had lost four heavy carriers and another major move against Midway seemed out of the question, English requested permission from Nimitz to build a major submarine base at the island. A base on Midway, English pointed out, would reduce the round-trip voyage to Empire waters—or anywhere westward—by about 2,000 miles, enabling the boats to remain on patrol station longer. Nimitz disapproved a major submarine base but gave the green light to move Stoney Roper's Squadron Eight tender *Fulton* and her refit crews there. The move, which considerably reduced the overhead in travel time about which Withers had complained repeatedly, could well have been accomplished many months earlier.

That done, English then set about re-establishing the cyclic patrols to Empire waters—completely interrupted by the Battle of Midway—and the exchange of submarines with Fremantle. Immediately following the battle, English ordered six boats to put into Midway to refuel and then proceed to Empire waters. *Cachalot*, *Dolphin*, and *Nautilus* would patrol the east coast of Japan. *Plunger*, *Grouper*, and *Flying Fish* would patrol the East China Sea. In addition, English sent *Thresher* to Fremantle.

Cachalot's second patrol, under George Alexander Lewis, was a great disappointment (upon her return from the east coast of Japan Lewis was relieved on grounds that his patrol was "not aggressively conducted"), and old *Dolphin*'s patrol off Bungo Suido was no better, marked as it was by a disabling fuel leak and the later hospitalization of her skipper, Royal Rutter, with bronchial pneumonia. *Dolphin* was turned over for repairs to a Squadron Four relief crew skipper, Dudley Walker ("Mushmouth") Morton, who had commanded *R-5* in the Atlantic.

Morton ran into trouble. *Dolphin*, he believed, was beyond repair and should never again be sent on patrol. When Carter Lowe Bennett, a Gun Clubber who had been at M.I.T. for a postgraduate course in ordnance when the war broke out, reported as Morton's exec, Morton told him, "The *Dolphin* is a death trap. I'm going to try to get off her. I advise you to do the same."

Morton got his way, but perhaps not in the manner he planned. When he took the repaired *Dolphin* to sea on trials, the division commander, John Haines, was far from satisfied. "He said the boat was filthy and Morton was incompetent to fix it," recalled John Brady. Haines relieved Morton of command and was prepared to send him to surface duty.

As Brady recalled the story, he intervened, going to Haines's boss, Babe Brown, for help. "Brown said, OK, he would talk to Morton," Brady said. "The two of them got together. Morton had been a star football player at the Academy, and that counted for a hell of a lot with Brown. He said to me later, 'I like the way Morton shakes hands.' The upshot was, Brown rescued Morton and sent him back to the PCO [Prospective Commanding Officer] pool." * Carter Bennett went to *Cuttlefish*.

---

* The PCO pool was established early in the war. It consisted of officers, qualified for command, who were waiting for a billet to open up. Before being assigned to the pool, most officers made a "PCO cruise"—that is, went on war patrol on a submarine

With Morton gone, *Dolphin* was once more skipperless. By that time, Rutter was back in good health. Brown ordered him to reassume command of *Dolphin* and get ready for another patrol.

To Bill Brockman on *Nautilus*, a hero for his aggressive attack on *Soryu*, English made a startling proposal. *Nautilus* had two fine six-inch guns, one forward, one aft. At Hayama, on the east coast of Honshu, not far from the entrance to Tokyo Bay, was a Japanese summer palace. Emperor Hirohito might even be in residence there. Would it not be sensational—and uplifting for the American people— if Brockman bombarded the summer palace with his guns?

English had detailed charts of the area and surrounding waters. Brockman studied them carefully—and somewhat skeptically. To get within range of the summer palace, he would have to transit shallow waters, filled with islands and rocks and probably teeming with Japanese antisubmarine vessels. To take clumsy, huge *Nautilus* into the area would be near-suicidal. Yet he assured English that he would discuss the proposal with his officers and do what he could.

Some submariners would fault English for urging this mission on Brockman. To them, it appeared to be a stunt, like the Doolittle raid on Tokyo, with no military significance. The odds against hitting the palace were a thousand to one. The odds on killing Brockman and *Nautilus* were very, very good. The submarine force had fallen on its face in the Battle of Midway, they believed, and English was merely looking for something sensational to restore its image.

Off Tokyo, Brockman wisely decided against bombarding the emperor's palace, but he found plenty of targets. On June 22, he fired two torpedoes at a destroyer, claiming a kill. On June 25, he attacked a tanker in convoy, missed, and received twenty-one depth charges from the escorts. After dawn, Brockman attacked another destroyer with two torpedoes. They hit, and *Yamakaze* went to the bottom slowly. On June 27, he attacked a larger freighter with three torpedoes and missed. A cruiser (or destroyer) counterattacked with depth charges, shaking *Nautilus* badly. Brockman, feeling *Nautilus* could not withstand another depth-charging without repairs, cut short the patrol and came home.

---

commanded by another officer in order to gain combat experience. Owing to the acute shortage of qualified skippers, the PCO pool was often merely theoretical, containing, at most, one or two men (sometimes none). Those in the PCO pool sometimes worked in the refit crews, serving as temporary commanding officers while the ship was in drydock or alongside a dock in refit.

When Brockman reached Pearl Harbor, English was on the dock to greet him. His first question was: Did you bomb the palace? Brockman replied no. English, Brockman remembers, was disappointed. But Brockman provided something almost as good. He had obtained a periscope picture of the destroyer *Yamakaze* going down by the stern. Elated, English released it to the press and it was published as *Life's* Picture of the Week. English made copies and gave them out to everyone who called at his office with the comment, "This is the way it's supposed to be done." In addition, he recommended Brockman for another Navy Cross, his second in about five weeks, a speed record for medals never again equaled in the submarine force.

Of the three patrols in the East China Sea, Claren Duke's on *Grouper* resulted in damage to two ships and was officially judged successful (though no sinkings resulted), but he was unable to make up for his performance during the Battle of Midway (where, according to his division commander, he had used "evasive" rather than "aggressive" tactics), and he was relieved of command and sent to surface forces.

Glynn Robert ("Donc") Donaho, a strange and difficult character, was reasonably aggressive in *Flying Fish*, but he was considered unreasonably spendthrift of torpedoes (in view of the shortage) and got zero score. Donaho, who stood near the bottom of the class of 1927, was considered machinery-oriented and bad at handling people by his classmates, a judgment exemplified on this patrol when he forced his enginemen to make a routine overhaul of all engines, a task normally conducted during refit.

Dave White, making his second patrol in *Plunger*, turned in the most aggressive performance. White carried a full load of Mark X torpedoes with contact exploders. In nine separate attacks, he fired sixteen torpedoes and obtained five good hits. He was credited with sinking two ships for 19,000 tons and damaging two for 10,000 tons, reduced in postwar accounting to two ships sunk for 6,300 tons, plus damage. English gave White full marks for aggressiveness but was critical of him for firing too many torpedoes on "snap estimates from the bridge without TDC help" and urged all his skippers to shoot with more care.

While on this patrol, White nearly sank a ship by accident that would have caused an international uproar. Through diplomatic channels, President Roosevelt had arranged an exchange of political prisoners trapped in the United States and Japan by the outbreak of war, including U.S. Ambassador to Japan Joseph C. Grew. They were put aboard the neutral vessels *Asama Maru* and S.S. *Conte Verde* for transfer from Japan to the United States.* They were to sail with lights and other markings on a prearranged route, as would the vessels returning the Japanese.

On June 5, English had sent instructions to his submarines, describing these ships, the routes, and the markings. Later, on June 25, when the vessels actually got under way, English sent further messages, designed to assure immunity from submarine attack. Dave White failed to receive these messages. In the early morning hours of June 30, he picked up *Conte Verde* and began an approach, somewhat astonished to find a ship all lighted up.

Back at Pearl Harbor, Turkey Neck Crawford was on duty that night in submarine headquarters. "The Communications Officer," Crawford remembered, "came in to see me and wanted to send the immunity message again. I checked through the files and discovered that we had sent it four nights in a row. I questioned the need to send it again. However, the Communications Officer thought it might be a good idea, so, somewhat reluctantly, I put it on the air."

On *Plunger*, White had *Conte Verde* fixed in his periscope hairs and the crew at battle stations when his communications officer, having picked up and just decoded this fifth immunity message, rushed up into the conning tower. White broke off the attack at the last minute, settling for a photograph taken through the periscope from a range of 800 yards.

The strategic war against Japanese shipping by Pearl Harbor submarines—interrupted by the fruitless recall and deployment at Midway—produced relatively little damage during April, May, and June of 1942. In all, there were twenty-one regular patrols, resulting in the sinking of twenty-two confirmed ships. The standout skippers were Bob Rice on *Drum*, who sank four ships on one patrol for 20,600 tons, and young C. C. Kirkpatrick on *Triton*, who sank five ships for 15,800 tons on his first patrol.

After the Battle of Midway, Bob English had relieved a total of

---

* *Asama Maru* left Tokyo June 25, 1942, and stopped at Shanghai, Hong Kong, and Singapore, collecting internees. She proceeded through Sunda Strait to the Indian Ocean and thence to Mozambique, where Americans were transferred to the Swedish liner *Gripsholm*, which arrived in New York August 25.

twelve of his skippers—good or mediocre or unproductive. Because he was impressed by the success of the "youth experiment" with C. C. Kirkpatrick, two thirds of the men he named as replacement skippers were about six years younger than their predecessors—class of 1930 or younger. Five of the twelve were Kirkpatrick's classmates from 1931.

Many submariners basing at Pearl Harbor did not think English had gone far or fast enough in reaching down for youth. They believed that execs such as Dusty Dornin and Slade Cutter and others from 1935, men who had not been imbued with cautious peacetime habits, should be fleeted up to command, and the sooner the better. English, however, proud of Pearl Harbor's record of not having lost a single boat in combat, was not ready to be pushed that far.

8

Washington, June and July 1942

The Midway Security Leak

During the Battle of Midway, there was a serious leak in the codebreakers' tight security system. The leak led to the publication of newspaper stories which—in many eyes—revealed to the Japanese that the U.S. Navy was reading the Japanese navy code. The newspaper stories, in turn, led to official investigations and a complete reorganization of the administrative structure of the codebreakers. In the power struggles which ensued, many men, including Hypo's Joe Rochefort, were bloodied and professionally ruined.

These events began unfolding on May 8 at the Battle of the Coral Sea, when the Japanese hit the carrier *Lexington* and caused her to be abandoned. On board *Lexington* during the battle was an Australian newspaperman, Stanley Johnston, who was then an employee of the *Chicago Tribune*. Johnston, a tough, capable reporter, had earned the respect of *Lexington*'s skipper, Captain Frederick Carl Sherman, and shared his cabin. He was especially close to the exec, Morton Tinslar Seligman, then one of the navy's top aviators.

When *Lexington* went down, Johnston conducted himself with distinction. He was among the last to leave the ship. A strong swimmer, he helped to get many *Lexington* crewmen, who were thrashing in the oily water, into a lifeboat. Sherman and Seligman were so

THE MIDWAY SECURITY LEAK

impressed they recommended the reporter for a navy citation for heroism and conduct far beyond his call as a newspaperman. The drama of the disaster drew Johnston and Seligman even closer.

While the *Lexington* survivors, including Seligman and Johnston, were being returned to the States on a transport, Admiral King sent Vice Admiral Robert Lee Ghormley to the Southwest Pacific to command U.S. naval forces. Ghormley was not a part of "MacArthur's Navy" but rather a subcommander for Nimitz. He established his headquarters on Noumea, a Free French island northeast of Brisbane.

While Ghormley was on Noumea, the Battle of Midway was shaping up. Somehow Ghormley obtained—the source is not clear—the Ultra dispatch on the Japanese Order of Battle for Midway. He then rebroadcast this information to ships under his command in a lesser code known as "Cupid," which every ship could read.

The broadcast was picked up on the transport taking the *Lexington* survivors to the States, which had stopped a few days in Noumea. Among those who read it was Mort Seligman. Seligman showed the message to Stanley Johnston.

Stanley Johnston ultimately left the transport and caught a plane to Chicago, arriving on the eve of the Battle of Midway. His mind was naturally fixed on the dramatic events he had lived through— *Lexington* and her heroic fight against the Japanese. On the way back to the States, he had been roughing out a story, with Fred Sherman and Mort Seligman and the crew of *Lexington* cast in the role of heroes. When he got to Chicago, he joined forces with another *Chicago Tribune* reporter, Wayne Thomis, and together they shaped Johnston's reportage into a book entitled *Queen of the Flat-Tops, the U.S.S. Lexington and the Coral Sea Battle*.

Meanwhile, the Japanese and U.S. navies met at Midway. On Sunday, June 7, as the battle was still in progress, a story appeared on the front page of the *Chicago Tribune* and in other newspapers that subscribed to the *Chicago Tribune* news wire. The lead:

The strength of the Japanese forces with which the Navy is battling somewhere west of Midway Island in what is believed to be the greatest naval battle of the war was well known in American naval circles several days before the battle began, reliable sources in naval intelligence disclosed here tonight.

The Navy learned of the gathering of the powerful Japanese units soon after they put forth from their bases, it was said. Altho their purpose was not specifically known, the information in the hands of the Navy Department was so definite that a feint at some American base, to be accompanied by a serious effort to invade and occupy another base, was predicted. Guesses were even made that Dutch Harbor and Midway might be targets.

The story went on to list the Japanese Order of Battle in detail. It named the four carriers of the striking force and even the names of the four cruisers supporting the invasion force. Near its conclusion, the story stated, "When it [the Japanese fleet] moved, all American outposts were warned. American naval dispositions were made in preparation for the various possible attacks the Japs were believed to be planning."

The story was datelined WASHINGTON and carried no by-line. According to Wayne Thomis, he had written it himself in Chicago. He denied having had help from his fellow author, Johnston, saying, "I got out *Jane's Fighting Ships* and got the list of Japanese carriers and battleships and cruisers. The split-up of forces was an educated guess on the way the Japanese might do it."

To the codebreakers in the Navy Department reading the story in stunned disbelief, it seemed more than "an educated guess." For example, why were *Shokaku* and *Zuikaku*, normally part of the striking force, missing from the *Chicago Tribune* lineup? The navy called Thomis and Johnston to Washington to deplore publication of the story and to ask questions. It did not take long for the admirals to learn that Johnston had been close to Sherman and Seligman on *Lexington*. The codebreakers, meanwhile, waited with bated breath. Although there had been no specific mention of codebreaking, they were sure the Japanese would deduce it from the story and shortly change their codes.

The story of the leak shot up through channels to Admiral King; then to Secretary of the Navy Frank Knox, formerly publisher of the *Tribune*'s rival *Chicago Daily News*; then to President Roosevelt. Roosevelt had no love for *Chicago Tribune* publisher Colonel Robert R. McCormick, an arch-conservative anti-New Dealer. Perhaps this security leak seemed to be a chance to get McCormick. Roosevelt had the Justice Department appoint a special prosecutor, William L. Mitchell, to direct a grand jury in Chicago to ascertain if the *Chicago Tribune* had violated security laws. Johnston, Thomis, and *Tribune*

Managing Editor J. Loy "Pat" Maloney testified, but after five days of investigation the grand jury failed to return a true bill.

One reason the proceedings may have ground to a halt was that common sense finally prevailed in Washington. If the grand jury had indicted, a public trial would have followed. Inevitably, evidence would have been introduced by the navy to the effect that the information of the Japanese Order of Battle had been obtained via codebreaking and that its publication compromised or tended to compromise codebreaking secrets. The trial might thus have drawn more attention—and gone into more specific details—than the news story.

It had all been hurriedly brushed under the rug when yet another indiscretion occurred. On August 31, Congressman Elmer J. Holland of Pennsylvania, a freshman Democrat and New Dealer, rose to denounce the *Tribune* for "unthinking and wicked misuse of freedom of the press." Holland went on to say that "American boys will die . . . because of help furnished our enemies." What help? Holland said, "Somehow our Navy had secured and broken the secret code of the Japanese Navy." Holland's speech was thoughtlessly printed by some editors.

Again the codebreakers waited with bated breath. However, the Japanese either missed all this or failed to guess its import. Neither the *Chicago Tribune*'s story nor Holland's speech led the Japanese to change their codes.

The chief result was that procedures for handling Ultra were tightened and its distribution even more sharply limited. Those involved, including all submarine skippers, were required to sign an oath vowing never to reveal details of Ultra as long as they lived. On board submarines, when an Ultra was received—identified by the first word in the dispatch—junior officers decoding messages on the submarine were required to stop with that first word. On most boats, the message was decoded only by the commanding officer, after which the cipher strips were burned. The commanding officer was charged never to mention the word Ultra or discuss an Ultra message in any form. In most cases, as far as the crew knew, when an Ultra-produced enemy contact was made, it was merely happenstance.*

Behind the scenes in the Navy Department, Admiral King's investigation traced the leak back through Johnston to Seligman to Ghorm-

---

* Usually results of Ultra contacts and attacks were detailed in a separate and more highly classified annex to the patrol report, but occasional slips were made and some Ultra contacts were listed as such in the regular report.

ley. Ghormley was not officially punished. It had been stupid to retransmit Ultra information in a lower code, but it was not a violation of law or Navy Regulations. However, Seligman *was* punished. Following the award of a second Navy Cross for heroism while on board *Lexington*, he was sent to shore duty and retired from the navy. Stanley Johnston's Navy Citation was "killed at the White House level," according to Thomis. Johnston continued as a *Tribune* reporter for many years.

Changes in the Codebreaking Operation

Coincidental with the leak, perhaps in part because of it, there was a shake-up in the Washington codebreaking operation that would have profound consequences for Joe Rochefort and many others.

For years Safford's Negat unit had occupied a hazy position in the Navy Department organization. It was more or less an entity of its own—a small private fiefdom working in total secrecy, lying midway between the Office of Naval Intelligence and the Office of Naval Communications. It depended on ONI for translators and administrative assistance; it depended on ONC for technical assistance such as radio intercept and RDF gear.

In peacetime, this loose informal arrangement and Safford's erratic management style went virtually unnoticed by higher-ups. But now, with war raging, Negat, which was also charged with the increasingly important function of intercepting and breaking German U-boat codes, was growing by leaps and bounds. It was also clearly growing in power. Little noticed in peacetime, Negat and its outlying posts, Hypo and Cast, had now become a chief source of intelligence.

In any bureaucracy, a powerful element like Negat not nailed down in the chain of command soon becomes a prize to be seized. In February 1942, Joseph Reasor Redman had become Director of Naval Communications. Although he was in poor health, Joe Redman was an active and shrewd bureaucrat. He did not like Safford's informal—and disorganized—working style and launched a campaign to bring Negat under control of ONC. He was assisted by his younger brother, John Roland Redman, who also had a background in naval communications and was then serving in a vague job on the Interdepartmental Communication Liaison Division, Office of Chief of Naval Operations.

The Office of Naval Intelligence, then commanded by Theodore

CHANGES IN THE CODEBREAKING OPERATION

Stark Wilkinson, reacted at once to the "Redman Brothers' campaign." Wilkinson and his director of Far East Intelligence, Arthur Howard McCollum, a Japanese linguist and close friend of Safford's and Rochefort's, launched a counterattack. If anyone should control Negat, they argued, ONI should. There had always been a closer relationship between Negat and ONI than Negat and ONC. "The NavCom people such as the Redman brothers didn't know anything about codebreaking," McCollum said later. "We did. We were intimately involved. We provided the translators. Negat provided intelligence, one source of many—albeit the most important—in a vast network controlled by ONI. It was logical that Negat come under our jurisdiction." Safford and Rochefort agreed. Both detested the Redman brothers.

The bureaucratic tug-of-war dragged on through the spring of 1942 to the Battle of Midway. After that battle, there was a showdown in Washington, a big meeting to decide the winner. It was presided over by Frederick Joseph Horne, one of King's vice chiefs of naval operations. "Jack Redman had done his work well," a codebreaker said later. "Horne heard all the arguments. Then he ruled that Negat should fall under the Office of Naval Communications. Admiral King approved."

With Joe Redman in charge, Negat, and its allied agencies, continued an orderly expansion. It moved from the Navy Department Building on Constitution Avenue into the red brick buildings of a former girls' school located in a northwest residential area of Washington, near the circle at the intersection of Nebraska and Massachusetts avenues. In the new quarters—guarded by a detachment of marines—Safford was pushed to one side, relegated primarily to "tinkering with gadgets." Arthur McCollum, feeling a wall growing between himself and the codebreakers, asked for sea duty but was turned down for the time being. Rosey Mason, who had returned from Australia, Joseph Numa Wenger, and others rose to high positions in the revamped organization.

In Pearl Harbor Joe Rochefort, fatigued from his work prior to and during the Battle of Midway, grew more arrogant and irascible. When the Redman brothers in Washington asked what they could do to help, Rochefort replied, "Send me more people, but leave me alone." He railed about the Redmans and talked of "seceding" from the Office of Naval Communications, under which his Hypo unit had been placed. The Redman brothers naturally resented these intemperate statements.

A new element of controversy then intruded. Admiral David Worth Bagley was named commandant of the 14th Naval District, under which the Hypo unit served administratively. Bagley was anxious to reward the deserving people in Hypo for the job they had done at Midway. He called Rochefort in and asked for a list. Rochefort formed a "committee" of Hypo personnel, including many Naval Reservists. They drew up a list with Rochefort's name at the top.

"I didn't have any part of it," Rochefort said later. "How could I officially submit a list with *my* name on the top? I never even saw the list as it was finally submitted by the committee."

Admiral Nimitz, too, was anxious that Rochefort and Hypo receive due credit. What he and Bagley finally arrived at was a recommendation that Rochefort be awarded a Distinguished Service Medal, the U.S. Navy's highest award for men who have not been in combat. The recommendation went forward to Washington with strong endorsements from both Bagley and Nimitz.

This piece of paper touched off a furor in the Navy Department. "The Negat people and the Redman brothers," Rochefort said later, "had taken the position that the solving of the key message at the Battle of Midway had been a joint effort, a team effort by Negat, Hypo, and Cast, and that no single person should receive credit. In reality, the Negat people had taken most of the credit themselves. They had convinced Admiral King that they had done the bulk of the work."

As the recommendation worked its way through channels, it accumulated fourteen endorsements, mostly negative; the final one, as a codebreaker recalled, said in effect that Rochefort not only did not deserve any credit but should probably not be kept in the Hypo unit at all.

Joe Rochefort never received a medal, and in time the roof fell in on him. The "Washington crowd"—the ONC people now in charge of codebreaking—ordered him relieved of command and returned to Washington. "The proposed medal had much to do with it," a codebreaker said. In Washington, Rochefort was invited to join the operation there. He declined. "He wanted no part of Washington," said a codebreaker. "He was deeply hurt and burned out." Rochefort requested sea duty.

Washington replaced Rochefort at Hypo with an ONC man, William Bernard Goggins. When war broke out, Goggins had been exec of *Marblehead* in the Philippines–Java area and was badly burned during the Battle of the Java Sea when *Marblehead* was crippled.

The younger Redman brother, John, went to Pearl Harbor to serve as Nimitz's communications officer. A classmate of Goggins's, Roscoe Henry Hillenkoetter, arrived to establish an overall intelligence center, composed of the intelligence units of the 14th Naval District, the Pacific Fleet, and the U.S. Marine Corps. The unit became known as ICPOA, an acronym for Intelligence Center, Pacific Ocean Area. In time, it became a massive organization, staffed by thousands, of which the Hypo unit (renamed FRUPAC for Fleet Radio Unit, Pacific) was a large and important part.

Meanwhile Rochefort was serving at sea—on a dry dock. Following his request for sea duty, he was ordered to the Floating Drydock Training Center, Tiburn, California, assigned to fit out and command the floating drydock U.S.S. *ABSD No. 2*.

"That was Joe's first and only command," a codebreaker said. "A drydock—Joe's reward for providing the most important intelligence in the history of naval warfare."

H.O.R. Engine Problems

The shortage of fleet boats in the Pacific was compounded by a political decision in Washington and an unforeseen technical problem.

During the summer of 1942, Churchill requested that Roosevelt order U.S. fleet submarines into the battle against the U-boat in the Atlantic, replacing the original European submarine force Ralph Christie had taken to Brisbane. Admiral King was opposed on the sound ground that every available fleet submarine should be sent to the Pacific. Roosevelt overruled King and—primarily as a political gesture—ordered a squadron of six new fleet boats to operate from Scotland. The squadron was designated Fifty and assigned to Norman Ives, who had been serving as Chief of Staff to Commander Submarines Atlantic Freeland Daubin.

While Ives was preparing his squadron for movement to Scotland, the decision was made to launch Operation Torch, the Allied invasion of North Africa. The six boats of Squadron Fifty were assigned to assist in the invasion and then return to base in Roseneath, Scotland, for regular patrols in the Bay of Biscay and elsewhere. The ancient tender *Beaver*, commissioned in 1918 but since modernized, was designated to serve as mother ship for Squadron Fifty.

In New London, Norman Ives was hard pressed to find six boats to make up his squadron, but eventually he formed it with *Barb*, *Blackfish*, *Shad*, and *Herring*, plus two boats, *Gurnard* and *Gunnel*, that were units of Squadron Twelve, scheduled for duty in Pearl Harbor.

There was a serious problem with the Squadron Twelve submarines. They were powered by "second-generation," lightweight, high-performance H.O.R. engines which the Bureau of Ships believed held great promise. In shakedown trials, the engines had proved to be even more unreliable than the first-generation H.O.R.s. The trouble seemed to be in the gear train. The teeth chipped off, feeding an excessive load back to the crankshaft and setting up torsional vibration which caused twisting and eventual breakage.

When word of this reached the chief engineer at H.O.R. in Hamilton, Ohio, a "young, capable, and sincere individual," he had a stroke and died a few days later. H.O.R. was making engines not only for the twelve submarines of Squadron Twelve, but also for about one hundred urgently needed 135-foot navy subchasers. In addition, more fleet boats were scheduled to get the H.O.R. in 1943 and 1944. The Navy and H.O.R. brought in engineer Robert P. Ramsey as a troubleshooter.

"At that time," Ramsey said later, "I had never seen an H.O.R. submarine engine. I was delegated to go to New London, meet with the Navy Board, and explain what happened. I did not have the faintest idea. With the great help of Professor Frank Lewis of M.I.T., a torsional vibration expert, it was finally found that all of the gears in those twelve submarine engines came from a batch of Navy-inspected steel which had undergone something that would not have happened once in a million times by chance. The steel was perfect from a chemical standpoint, as specified, but the whole batch had cooled too rapidly in the bloom at the steel mill, causing the formation of what is known as 'snowflakes,' a complete cleavage of internal integrity in the steel. You could not get steel at that time for anything but an aircraft, so a decision was made by the navy that we utilize the 100 percent spares shipped with the engines and flame-harden them."

The investigation of the H.O.R. engine failure took many weeks. Meanwhile, Squadron Fifty left for North Africa, Norman Ives commanding from the cruiser *Augusta*. Only five of the six boats made it;

H.O.R. ENGINE PROBLEMS

Gurnard was held up with engine problems and went directly to Roseneath.

The five submarines involved in Torch had a nightmarish time. The confined area of the North African landings was infested with U-boats. Vichy French submarines and naval units at Dakar might sortie at any time. British submarines and surface forces were zipping to and fro, plus U.S. surface forces conducting the first major amphibious assault in U.S. history. The weather was bad and recognition signals were mixed up. *Gunnel* was bombed by an Army aircraft. *Shad* was heavily depth-charged by a friendly destroyer. None of the boats made a noteworthy contribution to the landing.

Throughout the operation, *Gunnel,* commanded by John Sidney McCain, Jr., son of Rear Admiral John Sidney McCain, then commander of naval aircraft in the South Pacific, had ceaseless problems with her H.O.R. engines. On the way home, the entire drive gear trains on all four main engines carried away when McCain was 1,000 miles from the base at Roseneath. He sent out a call for help and proceeded toward Scotland on his auxiliary ("dinky") engine, making 85 miles a day. A British escort met him and took him into Falmouth. After that, McCain returned *Gunnel* to the States for extensive engine repairs.

Meanwhile, *Gurnard,* commanded by Charles Herbert Andrews, who had a master's degree in engineering, reached Scotland. From there, he was ordered to patrol the Bay of Biscay. Said Andrews later, "We had lousy rules. We couldn't surface in daytime. If we spotted a ship over 5,000 tons, we had to first report it by radio, obtain permission from the British, and then try to sink it. . . . We chased over forty ships. . . . Most were flying a Spanish or Irish flag. . . . We never fired a torpedo."

Andrews's exec was Robert Elwin McCramer Ward, who had survived the sinking of S-26 in January in the Gulf of Panama. Andrews was a reticent, modest, almost self-effacing officer, who ran a fine boat and always insisted that the machinery work properly. Ward, a perfectionist, liked Andrews immensely. "I learned more from Herb Andrews about what to do right than any other officer in the navy," he said later. Said Andrews, "Ward was amazing. He always seemed to know ahead of time what I wanted to talk about and had prepared himself thoroughly. Then I found out why: he'd peep in and take a look at my calendar, on which I jotted down items for future discussion."

During this patrol, Andrews used his H.O.R. engines sparingly and never at full power, fearing that the vibration would tear them apart. "I only used three," he said later, "saving the fourth for a spare. When two of them broke down in the Bay of Biscay, I cut the patrol short and limped back to Scotland." From there, he followed McCain in *Gunnel* back to the States for extensive engine repairs.

The remaining four boats of Squadron Fifty—*Barb, Shad, Blackfish,* and *Herring*—had either Fairbanks-Morse or General Motors Winton engines which were relatively trouble-free. All four boats made four war patrols in the Bay of Biscay or in waters off Norway. In April 1943, two other H.O.R.-powered boats from Squadron Twelve, *Haddo,* commanded by Pilly Lent, and *Hake,* replaced *Gunnel* and *Gurnard,* making two war patrols each. Some skippers who had been shifted from the Pacific—Nick Lucker, Roland Pryce, Eliot Olsen—served as relief skippers, making one patrol each.

In all, the Squadron Fifty boats conducted twenty-seven war patrols, including the deployment for Operation Torch. Although one or two of the boats tangled with U-boats and several shot at Axis merchant ships, postwar records credited no positive sinkings.

In mid-1943, the boats were withdrawn and sent to the Pacific. No more fleet boats were sent to Europe.

In New London, meanwhile, the twelve boats of Squadron Twelve were delayed several months while the H.O.R. engines were repaired by troubleshooter Ramsey. The delay was a bitter pill for the Pacific submarine force commanders. Counting the four boats diverted to Scotland, it meant that a total of sixteen fleet boats had been denied the Pacific submarine force in late 1942 and early 1943.

After the experiences of Andrews and McCain with *Gurnard* and *Gunnel,* submariners developed a complete distrust for the new H.O.R. engines. A rumor went around that the engines had been deliberately sabotaged on the drawing boards by the German parent company, M.A.N. No more H.O.R.s were ever installed in fleet boats.

9
Alaska, 1942

Japanese Landings on Kiska and Attu

The Pacific war plan, Rainbow Five, included a provision that two submarines of the Pearl Harbor force be dispatched to Dutch Harbor, Alaska, upon outbreak of hostilities with Japan. Their mission would be to provide information on Japanese fleet movements in Alaskan waters to the Commander in Chief, Pacific Fleet, and defend that tiny, barren, frigid outpost from Japanese attack.

After the Pearl Harbor attack, Tommy Withers had sent two S-boats to Dutch Harbor from the West Coast. These were S-18, commanded by William John ("Moke") Millican, and S-23, commanded by John Reeves Pierce. In February, both these boats made brief patrols.

"The conditions those boats endured up there," said Frederick Joseph ("Fritz") Harlfinger II, who served on S-boats in Alaska, "are simply indescribable. It was God awful. Cold. Dreary. Foggy. Ice glaze. The periscopes froze. The decks and lifelines were caked with ice. Blizzards. You could never get a navigational fix."

An entry in Pierce's log for February 13 gives a further hint of what it was like:

Shipped heavy sea over bridge. All hands on bridge bruised and battered. Officer of Deck suffered broken nose. Solid stream of water down hatch for 65 seconds. Put high pressure pump on control room bilges; dry after two hours. . . . Barometer 29.60; thirty knot wind from northwest.

Beginning in April, the six "30" boats that Admiral King had split from Ralph Christie's Brisbane-bound force began to arrive.* Then came two more, S-27 and S-28, bringing the total at Dutch Harbor to ten. This force was commanded by a navy lawyer, Oswald Symister Colclough, who was, technically, a "subordinate command" of the Pearl Harbor submarine force. In reality, Colclough was an independent commander, reporting to the senior naval officer in the area, Rear Admiral Robert Alfred Theobald.

The Japanese diversionary force sent to Alaska during the assault on Midway had two objectives: first, to launch a carrier strike against Dutch Harbor in hopes of drawing Nimitz's three carriers to those waters and away from Midway, and second, to occupy Kiska, Adak, and Attu. The force consisted of Carrier Division Four (the light carriers *Ryujo* and *Junyo*), plus seven cruisers and many destroyers, submarines, transports, and auxiliaries. To oppose this force, Admiral Theobald had six cruisers, eleven destroyers, and Colclough's flotilla of ten S-boats, plus other miscellaneous craft.

The U.S. defense of the Alaskan area was a fiasco from start to finish. Admiral Theobald did not believe the intelligence produced by Rochefort; he thought it had been planted. He deployed his forces—which included six of his ten S-boats—close to Dutch Harbor and made no effort to intercept or engage the Japanese forces. Japanese planes from *Ryujo* and *Junyo* struck Dutch Harbor on June 3 and 4, causing considerable damage on the second day in spite of foul weather. The Japanese landed unopposed on Kiska and Attu, having canceled the Adak landing after their own fiasco at Midway.

U.S. submarines in Alaskan waters contributed nothing. The S-boats, groping about in fog and cold rain, had all they could do to survive. One did not. On his first patrol, Herbert Lollis Jukes, commanding S-27, ran aground on Amchitka Island June 19. Jukes tried every imaginable way to dislodge the boat, but she was stuck fast. High seas broke over the conning tower. Jukes sent out distress messages, but there was no one to come to the rescue. He abandoned ship in rubber boats, taking refuge on the deserted island. Six days later, a

---

* S-30, S-31, S-32, S-33, S-34, and S-35.

navy search plane found the crew, hungry and cold. They were rescued and returned to Dutch Harbor.

"Jukes came in under a cloud," said Walter Deane Innis, an aviator classmate based at Dutch Harbor. "They were going to court-martial him. But I guess sanity prevailed, finally. They realized you couldn't really blame him, in that weather, with that old boat. He saved his crew without a single injury or case of illness and got them rescued." *

Submarine Patrols in Alaskan Waters

After the Battle of Midway, Admiral Yamamoto sent a third carrier to Alaskan waters, *Zuiho*, a small one that had originally been detailed to support the landing forces at Midway. *Zuiho* split off from the retreating Japanese forces on June 9 and went directly to Alaska. Then on June 20, the large carrier *Zuikaku*, which had participated with *Shokaku*, the "wounded bear," in the Coral Sea, left Japan for Alaskan waters.

With four carriers, seven cruisers, and many transports and destroyers plying Alaskan waters and the routes to and from northern Japan, the area appeared to be ripe hunting grounds for fleet submarines. In mid-June, after the Midway battle, Nimitz ordered Bob English to send as many boats as he could spare to the area to operate more or less under the tactical control of Ozzie Colclough. Over the next few weeks, English sent seven: *Growler, Triton, Finback, Grunion, Trigger, Tuna,* and *Gato*.

The codebreakers provided these fleet boats with much information on the movements of the carriers and other vessels. Even so, the boats turned in a disappointing performance. They were operating in strange waters infested with Japanese submarines, and they were bedeviled by foul weather and poor charts. They found no major Japanese vessels. Most of the attacks made were against Japanese destroyers or patrol vessels. One fleet boat was lost.

One of the seven submarines, *Growler*, was a new one commanded by a remarkable officer, Howard Walter Gilmore, an enlisted man who took a competitive examination to enter the Naval Academy. He

* One S-boat skipper, Thomas Fort Williamson, commanding *S-31*, was killed by an emergency flare.

had graduated in 1926, standing 34 in a class of 456. In peacetime, Gilmore had served as exec of *Shark*. During *Shark*'s shakedown cruise, Gilmore and Charles Otto Triebel, then a junior officer on *Shark*, had very nearly been killed in Panama by a gang of hoodlums. Both officers had their throats cut; both bore scars from the encounter. Gilmore had been plagued by other troubles too. His first wife died of polio, and just before *Growler* left for the Pacific his second wife had fallen down a stairway and seriously injured herself. She was still unconscious when Gilmore left. "Howard was one of the finest men I ever knew," Triebel said later, "but he was born under an unlucky star."

Gilmore was first to reach Alaska. In combat, he seemed to be without fear. Off Kiska, he found three destroyers at anchor. They had just escorted a transport and a seaplane tender, *Chiyoda*, into the port. In this, his first attack of the war, Gilmore fired simultaneously at *all three* anchored destroyers. One fired back, and as Gilmore went deep the crew could hear the whine of two torpedoes passing the boat. Gilmore claimed the sinking of the three destroyers, English credited him with two, but postwar analysis gave him credit for only one, *Arare*. The other two, *Kasumi* and *Shiranuhi*, were severely damaged but were towed back to Japan for repairs and fought again. A few days later, Gilmore tangled with another destroyer, this one patrolling. *Growler* was aggressively pursued and severely depth-charged.

Young C. C. Kirkpatrick in *Triton*, going on his second patrol, arrived next. On July 4, he staged an appropriate show of fireworks to celebrate Independence Day. Patrolling off Agattu, Kirkpatrick found another destroyer, *Nenohi*. He tracked her for ten hours, in and out of fog banks, until he could gain favorable firing position, and then fired two torpedoes to hit. One did. *Nenohi* blew up and sank in five minutes, taking down 200 of her crew. Later, Kirkpatrick fired another four torpedoes at a target which disappeared into the fog. Still later, he put into Dutch Harbor, picked up a contingent of twenty-four army soldiers, and landed them on Adak Island.

At least two other fleet boats tangled with Japanese destroyers. Jesse Lyle Hull, commanding the new boat *Finback*, attacked two and received a brutal working over afterward. Hull believed he sank one and damaged the other. English credited damage to one. Later Hull conducted two reconnaissance missions, one at Kiska and one at Tanaga Bay, boldly taking *Finback* submerged into enemy waters.

The other boat was another new one, *Grunion*, commanded by Mannert Lincoln Abele. On the way from New London to Panama, *Grunion*—maneuvering in a heavy gale—had rescued sixteen men in a lifeboat from a merchant ship torpedoed by a German U-boat, dropping them in Panama. One of the survivors, George F. Drew, the ship's engineer, later wrote, "I have never seen such wonderful seamanship as Abele executed when he rescued us." From Panama, *Grunion* went to Pearl Harbor, received prepatrol training, and left for Alaska.

Patrolling off Kiska on July 15, Abele attacked a destroyer, firing three torpedoes which missed. Later that same day he attacked three ships he believed to be destroyers. English credited Abele with sinking three destroyers, but postwar analysis showed they were patrol craft of about 300 tons each, only two of which sank. On July 28, *Grunion* attacked an unidentified ship, fired two torpedoes, and missed. On July 30 off Kiska, Abele reported heavy antisubmarine activity and said he had ten torpedoes remaining. Colclough ordered him back into Dutch Harbor.

Nothing more was ever heard from *Grunion*. She disappeared without a trace, like *Shark*.*

The remaining three fleet boats achieved little. *Trigger*, commanded by Jack Lewis, had repaired her damage from the unfortunate grounding at Midway and set off for Alaska. During her long patrol, she spotted six destroyers, one patrol boat, and three freighters, but Lewis made no attacks at all. *Tuna* had a new skipper, Arnold Henry ("Ike") Holtz, another young officer from the class of 1931, who had replaced Johnny DeTar; *Tuna* landed an army party on an island but then missed a chance to sink a Jap sub. William Myers, going on his second patrol in *Gato*, believed he sank a 9,000-ton freighter, but postwar analysis denied him; upon return to port, Myers went to Bob English's staff as Force Engineering Officer.

English credited these seven fleet boats with sinking six destroyers and damaging one. When the reports reached Nimitz, he put out a

* Some believed she had been sunk by a Japanese submarine, *I-25*, which reported sinking a submarine in the area. Subsequently it was learned that *I-25* sank a Russian submarine, one of four en route from Vladivostok to Mare Island for a lend-lease overhaul.

colorful press statement: "When subs hit 'em, they go down for the full count." As postwar records revealed, this was not entirely accurate. The fleet boats had actually sunk two destroyers and two small patrol craft and seriously damaged two other destroyers. Two submarines, S-37 and *Grunion*, had been lost. The big game—four aircraft carriers, seven cruisers, many transports and auxiliaries—had again eluded the Pearl Harbor submarines. Based on average returns, the seven boats would have done far more damage in Empire waters.

The force of nine remaining S-boats continued patrolling from Dutch Harbor in the face of terrible hardships. One more boat, S-35, commanded by Henry Stone Monroe, was almost lost. On December 21, while patrolling off Amchitka in foul weather, S-35 took heavy seas down the conning tower hatch which tore insulation from electrical cables and started a bad fire. Monroe, who had sprained an arm and leg on the bridge when hit by a huge wave, left his bunk to help direct fire-fighting procedures. The fire raged out of control, twice forcing all hands to the pitching deck topside. Finally, Monroe got the fire out and limped back to Dutch Harbor. That he returned at all was considered amazing.

In all of 1942, the brave S-boat sailors sank only one ship confirmed in postwar Japanese records. She was a 2,894-ton freighter sent to the bottom by Robert Frederick Sellars in *S-31* on October 26.

10
Fremantle, April through August 1942

Torpedo Tests and Experiments

John Wilkes and the Asiatic submarine force in Fremantle were in despair. In April, although Wilkes managed to get seven boats on patrol, two of the seven, *Pike* and *Porpoise*, returned to Pearl Harbor for overhaul; three, *Swordfish*, *Sailfish*, and *Searaven*, had been assigned to special missions to Corregidor and Timor; and only one boat, *Skipjack*, commanded by Jim Coe, achieved any success. Off Camranh Bay, Coe sank three confirmed ships for 12,800 tons. In terms of confirmed ships sunk, this was the best score achieved on a single patrol by any Asiatic skipper. All the others turned in zero results.

While the April boats were out, Wilkes, who was long overdue for rotation to the States, received a radio dispatch stating his replacement was on the way. As was the custom, the message did not name his relief but referred to the officer only by his signal number—a number permanently assigned to each naval officer. There had been a mixup in the number. Fremantle got the impression that the officer on the way was Palmer Hall ("Crow") Dunbar, Jr., an officer who had pushed the McCann Rescue Chamber to its successful conclusion. He was an engineering type, hardly the flaming leader needed to charge up the demoralized submariners in Fremantle.

"When we saw that message and that signal number," Sunshine

273

Murray recalled, "it was another blow." The man who showed up, however, was not Dunbar but Charles Lockwood, recently detached from the job of naval attaché in London and promoted to rear admiral.

After the usual ceremonial inspection tour, Lockwood relieved Wilkes in a formal ceremony.* At the same time, he also relieved Rear Admiral Speck Purnell, who commanded all Allied naval forces basing in West Australia.†

Lockwood, an eternal optimist and man of good cheer, was almost overcome by the depression and fatigue he found all through the command. He buzzed here and there, giving pep talks. He leased two small hotels for submarine rest camps, the Ocean Beach at the seashore and the King Edward in downtown Perth. Then he launched an informal inquiry to find out why Asiatic submarines had not done a better job of stopping the Japanese in the Philippines and Java, summarizing his findings in a personal letter to his old friend Richard Edwards, then Admiral King's right-hand man.

The boys here [Lockwood wrote] have had a tough row to hoe in the last four months. Why they didn't get more enemy ships is a highly controversial point but my reading of all war diaries thus far submitted has convinced me that among the causes are: (a) bad choice of stations in that most likely invasion points were not covered soon enough nor heavily enough, (b) bad torpedo performance, in that they evidently ran much too deep and had numerous prematures . . . , (c) buck fever—firing with ship swinging when he thought it was on a steady course; set up for one target and firing at a totally different one, (d) lack of or misunderstanding of aggressiveness; many evaded destroyers in the belief that they should save torpedoes for convoy following; one said he thought a sub should never "pick a fight with a destroyer."

Shortly after Lockwood arrived in Fremantle, Coe in *Skipjack* returned from his fifty-day patrol off Camranh Bay. Coe, a methodical as well as a courageous officer, submitted a careful analysis of Mark XIV torpedo performance for his patrol. There was every indication,

---

* John Wilkes received a Distinguished Service Medal (DSM) "for exceptionally meritorious and distinguished" service during the retreat from Manila to Fremantle and then returned to the States to commission and command a new cruiser, *Birmingham*. Fife also received a DSM for his services as Wilkes's chief of staff.

† Then known as Task Force 51. Technically, Lockwood became commander of Task Force 51 and wore two hats, submarine commander and surface-ship commander.

TORPEDO TESTS AND EXPERIMENTS 275

he said, that torpedoes were running much deeper than set. He added a bitter postscript. "To make a round trip of 8,500 miles into enemy waters, to gain attack position undetected within 800 yards of enemy ships only to find that the torpedoes run deep and over half the time will fail to explode, seems to me to be an undesirable manner of gaining information which might be determined any morning within a few miles of a torpedo station in the presence of comparatively few hazards."

After reviewing Coe's report, Lockwood decided to take action beyond his letter to Edwards. His first official action was within proper channels; he inquired of the Bureau of Ordnance if there was any information or recent tests to indicate deep-running in the Mark XIV or defects in the exploder. He received in reply a prompt—and lofty—pronouncement which, in effect, accused the skippers of using torpedo defects as an alibi for poor marksmanship. Receiving this, Lockwood was enraged. "I decided to take matters into my own hands," he wrote later.

Lockwood chose to conduct his own tests, as Tyrrell Jacobs in Surabaya, had proposed. Wilkes and Fife had been in Australia for almost three months, and still this had not been done. "All the skippers wanted to make the tests," a submariner said. "But you have to remember that the Bureau of Ordnance was a mighty bureaucracy. A naval officer, conditioned to believe the bureau's word was infallible in matters of ordnance, did not lightly challenge it. They could snow you with technical data, incomprehensible to the average line officer. It took Charlie Lockwood—plus flag rank—to take that bull by the horns."

Lockwood got in touch with Jimmy Fife, who was still based in Albany with *Fulton*, refitting submarines after patrol. The two men discussed the possibility of a test. Fife suggested that he obtain a fishnet from one of the many Portuguese fishermen working from Frenchman's Bay, Albany, and fire some of Coe's remaining torpedoes into it. Lockwood agreed.

This test—considered historic by many submarine skippers—was conducted on June 20, 1942, more than six months after the Japanese attack on Pearl Harbor. By that time, the three submarine commands had fired over eight hundred torpedoes in combat. Not one had been fired in a controlled test.

Under Fife's direction, the net was submerged in the calm, quiet waters of Frenchman's Bay. Ted Aylward (ex-*Searaven*), who had served a tour at Newport in 1928 and was now torpedo officer of *Holland*, was an official witness. Coe brought *Skipjack* to within 850 yards of the net and submerged to periscope depth. His torpedomen had loaded into a tube one of the Mark XIV torpedoes Coe had carried for the last seventy days. It was fitted with an "exercise head," weighted with calcium chloride solution to approximate the weight of a live warhead. They set the torpedo to run at 10 feet.

On signal from Fife, Coe fired. The torpedo swished from the tube, bearing down on the net. When it had been recovered, its built-in depth recorder showed that it had run at a depth of 25 feet. When the net was hauled up, there was a ragged hole punched in it at a depth of 25 feet. Both sets of data showed the torpedo (which follows a porpoising path) had run 15 feet deeper than set.

This test proved what most skippers had suspected. But the professorial Fife was not satisfied. One test was not a "scientific sample." On the following day, with Fife officiating, Coe fired two more torpedoes at the net. The first, set again for 10 feet, was fired from a shorter range, 700 yards. It cut the net at 18 feet. The second torpedo was set for zero feet and also cut the net at 18 feet. After taking ranges, the porpoising track of a torpedo, and other factors into account, the three tests indicated to Fife that the Mark XIV ran an average 11 feet deeper than set. On the day following the second test, June 22, Lockwood sent off a message to the Bureau of Ordnance, describing the tests and the results.

In Pearl Harbor, Bob English, who monitored Lockwood's transmissions, must have been startled to read the message to BuOrd, going over the air as it did only four days following English's own message on torpedo policy (listing eight reasons for torpedo failure, most of them the fault of skippers or crews). After he read Lockwood's message, English did a complete about-face. He informed BuOrd that some of his skippers reported deep-running torpedoes and inquired, HAVE NET TESTS INDICATED THAT TORPEDOES RUN GREATER THAN FOUR FEET BELOW SET DEPTH?

The Bureau of Ordnance responded to Lockwood on June 30. "Instead of thanking us," Lockwood wrote, "they scorned our inaccurate approach to obtain these findings." Specifically, BuOrd stated "no reliable conclusions" could be drawn from Lockwood's tests "because of improper torpedo trim conditions introduced." Lockwood, privately furious, reported that he would repeat the tests with proper trimming.

TORPEDO TESTS AND EXPERIMENTS

He also asked that the bureau request Newport to make its own test and inform him of results by urgent dispatch.

Lockwood then set up another, "more scientific" field test. In Albany, Jimmy Fife made arrangements to restring the fishing net. On July 18, *Saury*, in Albany for refit, fired four Mark XIV torpedoes at the net from a range of 850 to 900 yards. The first shot was wasted; the fishing net had been carried away during the night. After the net was reset, the other three torpedoes were fired, set to run at 10 feet. All three punched holes in the net at 21 feet. Fife concluded, as in the first test, that the torpedoes ran an average of 11 feet deeper than designed.

Lockwood considered this second series of tests conclusive. Two days later, he sent off a dispatch to the Bureau of Ordnance, reporting the results. In addition, he wrote another personal letter, this one to William Henry ("Spike") Blandy, then chief of the Bureau of Ordnance. Blandy was a year junior to Lockwood and an old friend. Lockwood told him, "We haven't gotten very far in our exchange of punts and I am very desirous not to start a radio controversy with your Bureau. Please lend us a hand to clear the air and give us the dope we need." He asked Blandy to devote some of his "valuable time" to the project and request that Newport make backup tests.

Admiral King and Admiral Edwards, meanwhile, were making a special effort to help the submarine force solve its torpedo problems. Roland Pryce (ex-*Spearfish*) returned to Washington and, working with Edwards, prepared an analysis of all torpedo attacks to date. "Our conclusion," he said later, "was that no matter what blame the Commanding Officer assumed, or what questionable claims were made, we should have had about 100 percent more hits."

On the day after Lockwood radioed the results of the test, Admiral King, who received a copy of the dispatch, lit a blowtorch under the Bureau of Ordnance. In a letter to Blandy, King requested that the Bureau proceed immediately to recheck the tactical data for all torpedoes. King stressed that "it was of utmost importance not only to supply submarine personnel with correct data but in addition to take steps to restore their confidence in the reliability and accuracy of the performance data furnished them."

In Pearl Harbor, Bob English, who had also received a copy of Lockwood's latest dispatch, officially informed his skippers that the

Mark XIV torpedoes ran 11 feet deeper than set. He ordered his boats to continue to rely on the Mark VI magnetic exploder but to subtract 11 feet to obtain the correct depth setting.

With this convergence of pressure, Spike Blandy was moved to action. Newport ran a new series of tests, this time firing from a submerged submarine, *Herring*, rather than from a "torpedo barge." On August 1, almost eight months after the Pearl Harbor attack, Newport conceded that the Mark XIV ran 10 feet deeper than set. In a follow-up memo six weeks later, Newport admitted that its depth-control mechanism had been "improperly designed and tested" and passed along instructions for making modifications so that the Mark XIV torpedo could be "trusted" to run within 3 feet of the actual depth settings.

In one sense, all this was immensely gratifying to Lockwood and his skippers. They had browbeaten the Bureau of Ordnance into conceding, officially, what was already known, and all skippers could now fire torpedoes at a uniform depth without fudging their official reports. Yet those who had already been setting torpedoes to run much shallower than authorized were far from satisfied. They believed the magnetic exploder to be defective as well, and they urged further tests to determine what caused prematures, duds, and other erratic torpedo behavior.

Here Lockwood, like Bob English, demurred. He believed that the deep-running fault had been the major cause of the apparent failure of the magnetic exploder. The torpedoes had been running too deep to enter the magnetic field of the target, and so they failed to explode. Now that torpedoes would be set to run shallower, the magnetic exploder—potentially a marvelous device—would work. Lockwood held to this view even though he knew, like Turkey Neck Crawford and others, that the British and Germans had discarded their magnetic exploding devices.

One overriding reason for holding to the magnetic exploder was that the warheads on the Mark XIV torpedo were relatively puny; 500 pounds. If the force relied solely on contact exploders, it could never hope to penetrate the armor of the glamorous targets: battleships and aircraft carriers. Moreover, one 500-pound warhead was not likely to finish off even a sizable merchantman. A positive sinking would require at least two or three torpedoes—perhaps four—an unacceptable expenditure, considering the acute shortage and the slow production rate in the United States. Finally, the contact exploder was not the best to use against shallow-draft vessels—destroyers, for example. The torpedo would have to be set to run so shallow it might broach and run erratically, perhaps even circling back to the submarine that fired it.

While this was going on, the submarine force received some *encouraging* torpedo news. Back in the States the Bureau of Ordnance was proceeding with two radically different types of torpedoes, an "oxygen" torpedo and an "electric" torpedo.

The oxygen torpedo was the ultimate extension of the "air" (or steam) torpedo; the oxygen would be carried in its most compressed state, as a liquid, hydrogen peroxide. In the 1920s and 1930s, Ralph Christie, working with the Ordnance Laboratory in Alexandria, Virginia, had carried out experimental work on an oxygen torpedo which was called the G-49 project or "Navol." In theory, the use of hydrogen peroxide greatly increased the speed and range of the torpedo. On paper, Christie's Navol could propel a 500-pound warhead at a speed of 50 knots to a range of 15,000 yards.

When presented with the concept, the operating forces had been unanimously negative. For decades they had resisted the carrying of highly volatile fuels (such as gasoline or hydrogen peroxide) on shipboard. If mishandled or caught in a fire, such fuels might explode, destroying the ship. During combat, an enemy shell could hit the storage tanks (or even the weapon), causing fatal damage. For these reasons, oxygen torpedo development received little encouragement.

Even so, the Bureau of Ordnance continued to tinker with it, even giving the Navol torpedoes numbers—Mark XVI for submarines, Mark XVII for surface ships. In the mid-1930s, the bureau fitted a Mark XIV with a hydrogen peroxide engine and conducted a test with a 500-pound warhead. The torpedo ran nearly as designed: 16,500 yards at 46 knots. Subsequently, the bureau authorized the building of fifty test Mark XVII torpedoes for surface ships. By the time the Japanese attacked Pearl Harbor, six of these had been completed. The work on both surface-ship and submarine Navols was proceeding.*

The second torpedo, the "electric," was, Admiral King believed,

---

* It did not get far. Admiral King, who believed it would interfere with the production of desperately needed regular torpedoes, gave it bottom priority. Long before Pearl Harbor, the Japanese had developed oxygen torpedoes for both surface ships and submarines. The surface-ship torpedo, called the "Long Lance," was a 24-inch torpedo which could carry a 1,078-pound warhead for 22,000 yards at 49 knots or 40,000 yards at 36 knots. The best U.S. surface-ship torpedo, the Mark XV, was a 21-inch torpedo that could carry a 780-pound warhead for 6,000 yards at 45 knots or

more encouraging. The electric, powered by batteries, would leave no smoky trail—the deadly arrow pointing to the launching submarine. Although it would be slower than the steam torpedo and have a shorter range, the odds on the enemy spotting it and evading would be much smaller. It would be the ideal weapon for daylight periscope attack.

The bureau's effort to develop an electric torpedo was another long and sad story. Initial work had begun during World War I, when the bureau gave a small contract to the Sperry Gyroscope Company in 1915. Nothing came of this, but the experimental work had been carried forward on a spare-time basis by one technician at Newport during the 1920s. He finally got one made—called the Mark I—but it was lost during a test firing. The project lay dormant until 1941, when Newport, in cooperation with the Electric Storage Battery Company (Exide) and the General Electric Company, began work on what was called the Mark II.

The real impetus for an electric torpedo came from Admiral Doenitz, whose U-boats, employing electrics, had wreaked such carnage off the East Coast in early 1942. Several of these German electrics ran up on the beach and fell into the hands of the Bureau of Ordnance. Admiral King was much impressed and urged BuOrd to provide U.S. submarines with an electric. BuOrd, in turn, instructed Newport to hurry up with the Mark II development or shelve it and copy the German model. "Every emphasis was placed on an early accomplishment and only minimum military characteristics established as an aid toward expediting the project," a BuOrd historian wrote later. In other words: Turn out a cheap, quick model.

Newport, typically, preferred its own finely machined project to the German. A small unit was established within the Newport design department to expedite the Mark II. It drew up plans to convert five Mark XIV and five Mark X submarine torpedoes to electric models. These torpedoes were to have a speed of 33 knots and a range of about 3,500 yards with a regulation 500-pound TNT warhead. However, there was a serious hitch: GE was unable to take over production of electric torpedoes, and there was no room at Newport, where three

---

15,000 yards at 26.5 knots. The Japanese oxygen torpedo for submarines—standard issue at the time of Pearl Harbor—was called the Type 95, Mod-1. It was 21 inches and could carry a 900-pound warhead 10,000 yards at a speed of 49 knots or 13,000 yards at 45 knots. A later version, Mod-2, carried a 1,210-pound warhead to 6,000 yards at 49 knots or 8,200 yards at 45 knots. After the war, the Japanese reported no shipboard accidents and generally considered the oxygen torpedo superior to the "air" torpedo.

shifts were working around the clock to turn out steam torpedoes for the fleet and falling critically behind schedule nevertheless.

The Bureau of Ordnance, forced to turn to another outside source for help, chose the Westinghouse Electric & Manufacturing Company. On March 10, 1942, BuOrd and Westinghouse representatives held a meeting. A week later, Westinghouse representatives visited Newport to collect all the data and design work to date on electric torpedoes. The result was that Westinghouse decided the best and quickest way to turn out an electric torpedo was to copy the German model as closely as possible, without any help from Newport. The decision was approved by the Bureau of Ordnance. The Westinghouse Electric Torpedo was designated the Mark XVIII. Newport could continue development of the Mark II at its own leisurely pace.

Westinghouse engineers went to work with a speed and fervor that was dazzling. By mid-April they had completed the general design of the copy. On May 2 the Bureau of Ordnance issued a letter of intent for the manufacture of 2,000 Mark XVIII torpedoes, 2,020 warheads, 543 exercise heads, tools, spare parts, and workshop equipment, plus other manufacturing gear. In the last week of June—only fifteen weeks after Westinghouse entered the picture—the first test models were delivered to Newport. "It was the single most dramatic chapter in the whole history of torpedo development," said a submariner. "And it proved the value of bringing in outside competition and the profit motive."

An officer in Washington, seeking to buck up the submarine force, optimistically predicted in June that the force would have the first electrics "within a few weeks." However, the Westinghouse project encountered a series of disappointments and setbacks. The first test shot was a failure; something went wrong with one of the electrical circuits. Subsequent testing was difficult. There were manufacturing bugs. The batteries fell short of expectations and gave off too much hydrogen gas. Some of the machinery failed because Westinghouse— the BuOrd historian wrote later—was not used to the "close tolerances" required and was forced to employ unskilled Rosie the Riveter workers. After a flashy start, the project bogged down. Newport offered no help but continued to work on its competitive design, the Mark II. It would be a long time before the submarine forces received an electric torpedo.*

---

* The Japanese had developed an electric torpedo in 1934 known as the Type 92, Mod-1, that propelled a 660-pound warhead 7,660 yards at a speed of 28 to 30 knots. When the Type 95 oxygen torpedo was developed for Japanese submarine issue, the

Personnel Changes

After the torpedo tests, Lockwood turned his attention to staff and personnel problems. John Wilkes had abolished the "squadron echelon" in Manila, wiping out the squadron and division commanders and taking direct control of the boats himself. Lockwood, who considered this a bastard organization, took steps to make it conform to the organization at Pearl Harbor. He reorganized the original Manila fleet boats into Squadron Two, appointing Jimmy Fife to command it. He shifted Sunshine Murray from operations officer to replace Fife as chief of staff.

Shortly thereafter, Al McCann, commanding Squadron Six, arrived from San Francisco in the tender *Pelias* and was integrated into the command. Two officers who hitched a ride out on *Pelias* became key executives in the Lockwood organization: Heber Hampton ("Tex") McLean replaced Sunshine Murray as operations officer and John Mylin ("Dutch") Will became Lockwood's engineering and repair specialist.

It was like old home week; these men had been close friends and associates for years. When Lockwood had commanded Division 13 in San Diego in 1935–37, Jimmy Fife, commanding *Nautilus*, had been one of his skippers. Sunshine Murray and Tex McLean had commissioned *Porpoise* and *Pike* respectively and served in Division 13 under Lockwood. Dutch Will had relieved Sunshine Murray as commander of *Porpoise* and then served as engineering officer on Admiral Friedell's staff at Pearl Harbor when Lockwood was Friedell's chief of staff.

Not all the operating submariners shared Lockwood's views about the squadron echelon. They had high opinions of Murray, Fife, Will, McLean, and McCann, but they believed the many division commanders and their big staffs constituted unnecessary layers of officialdom between the boats and the force commander and his own staff, adding more red tape and paperwork. "Lockwood had a bad habit of gathering a lot of his old peacetime cronies around him," Reuben

---

electric was pushed into the background. After the war began, however, the Japanese produced electrics in quantity to supplement oxygen torpedoes. The Germans gave the Japanese ten of their electrics (together with plans), but the Japanese did not build them owing to a shortage of personnel and facilities. Generally speaking, with the oxygen and electric torpedo in hand at the war's beginning, the Japanese were vastly ahead of the United States in submarine and surface-ship torpedo development.

Whitaker, exec of *Sturgeon*, said later. "Many of them were just so much dead wood trying to find something to do. They got in the way."

About the time Lockwood got his organization the way he wanted it, he was relieved of one of his hats. In early July, Arthur Schuyler ("Chips") Carpender, who had been serving in the Bureau of Personnel, arrived in Melbourne, reporting to MacArthur's navy chief, Admiral Leary. Leary sent Carpender to relieve Lockwood as overall navy commander on the west coast of Australia (Task Force 51), a job comparable to that of Carpender's classmate, Skinny Rockwell, on the east coast. Lockwood was relegated to the position of submarine commander. In his personal diary Lockwood wrote optimistically, "Now I can work on subs alone . . . it's a huge relief to get from under all sorts of extraneous matters."

That was not to be. Submarines comprised the only real naval fighting force on the west coast of Australia, and Carpender injected himself totally in submarine operations. After only a few days on the job, he began to criticize everything Lockwood and his men were doing. He objected to the location of the rest camps, preferring them inland, away from the bright lights—and girls—of Perth. He criticized the ordering of beef from the States for the submarines instead of using Australian mutton. He disapproved of slang in the patrol reports—the use of "fish" when "torpedo" was meant. He got into details of how submarines should be deployed off enemy harbors. He questioned Lockwood's decision to restore the squadron echelon. He accused the skippers of not being sufficiently aggressive.

This was no minor bureaucratic squabble. "They detested one another," an officer said later. Lockwood himself was demoralized. Through the coming weeks, his personal diary was one long cry of anguish at the situation he found himself in. He wrote in July, for example:

Large day, mostly filled with arguments with Carpender. Must admit I get a bit discouraged when it appears that we are fighting this war all wrong. I had no idea this boy could be so damned fussy about details which contribute nothing to licking the Japs. . . . How long will it be before I lose my temper and get put under hack? . . . The most minute details must be discussed hour after hour and the most elementary things explained. . . . I've heard about how they run things in the Atlantic Fleet so often that I'm ready to shoot any Atlantic sailor on sight—and they, after all, haven't done much to write home about.

"It got to the point where they couldn't speak to one another," Sunshine Murray recalled. "I had to be the emissary most of the time. When it came time for a conference with Carpender, Lockwood would find some excuse to run down to Fremantle and inspect the base. Carpender's offices were on the second floor, the submarine staff on the third. For a long time, it seemed as though I spent half my time on the stairway, going up or coming down."

Lockwood also avoided Carpender by absorbing himself in petty details. One project that removed Lockwood from Carpender's presence was a plan for an advance base such as English had established at Midway. Patrolling Indochina from Fremantle meant a 6,600-mile round trip, comparable to patrolling the coast of Germany from New London, Connecticut. Lockwood pored over charts of northwest Australia, a desolate, primitive landscape, studying possibilities.

At first, Darwin seemed the logical answer, and in June Lockwood flew there for an inspection. He arrived the day after the Japanese had bombed the port for the fourth time, staging from the island of Timor, only 360 miles away, so Lockwood crossed Darwin off the list —at least until MacArthur had recaptured Timor. On the way home, he stopped at Exmouth Gulf, 750 miles north of Fremantle.

Exmouth Gulf seemed a possibility. A base there would be safe from Japanese bombers, would save two days' fuel, and would extend time on station by two days. Yet the place was desolate and deserted, except for a few navy patrol planes and their tenders. And from September to April the gulf was roughed by northwest winds that would make it difficult for a submarine to moor alongside a tender. "Willy-willies"—dreaded windstorms—often swept across the flat plains and flattened the pearl-fishing villages along the coast. Sunshine Murray tactfully pointed out that submarine crews might not be overjoyed at the prospect of a "rest" in temporary Quonset huts set in a sea of mud, assaulted by "ten million" flies, and minus the greatest assets of Perth—girls and pubs.

Lockwood's answer was to propose using the ex-yacht, ex-Yangtze gunboat *Isabel* as a ferry between Exmouth Gulf and Fremantle so the crews could spend their liberties in Perth. Chet Smith thought *Isabel* too slow and small for the purpose and the whole idea a bad one.

But Lockwood was determined. He gave the plan a code name—Potshot—and pursued it obsessively, as vigorously as he had the torpedo defects. Admiral Leary approved the move north, but Lockwood's staff officers conferred halfheartedly with the Australians and delayed the project time and again with "studies."

Departing Patrols

During the four-month period May–August 1942, Lockwood's submarine force consisted of twenty boats. Four arrived from Pearl Harbor: *Gar*, *Grampus*, *Grayback*, and *Tautog*. Three returned to Pearl Harbor for overhaul: *Pickerel*, *Stingray*, and *Permit*. In all, Lockwood mounted twenty-eight patrols from Fremantle, spreading his small force thin at Indochina, Manila, Davao, Java, Borneo, and other areas conquered by the Japanese. The results were—predictably—very poor. One reason: Carpender's assertion that the skippers lacked aggressiveness appeared to be correct in all too many cases.

Snapper, commanded by Ham Stone, was a troubled boat. The exec, Carl Tiedeman, and the junior officers, including William Grizzard Holman, Raymond Francis DuBois, and a young reservist, James W. Liddell, who had been an all-American football player at Northwestern University, were unhappy. On May 27, Lockwood made an entry in his personal diary: "Investigated *Snapper* most of the morning and was very sorry to tell her skipper that I am going to relieve him of command. No other solution possible."

To replace Stone, Lockwood picked Harold Edward Baker, then only thirty-three and the second youngest officer to be chosen to command a fleet boat (after his classmate of 1932, Rich Gregory in *Sargo*). Baker had stood 8 of 421 in his class and had been literary editor of *The Log*. He had been exec of *Permit* under Adrian Hurst and Moon Chapple.

Young Baker took *Snapper* on her third patrol to the Celebes Sea. The cruise was a bust. During the forty-nine days at sea, *Snapper* sighted only small Japanese patrol vessels and returned to port without having fired a torpedo. The next time out, Baker went to the South China Sea and was on patrol for seventy-nine days. He fired two torpedoes at a freighter and missed. On the way back to Fremantle, *Snapper* was bombed by a friendly navy patrol plane.

Lockwood had adopted the Pearl Harbor custom of appending endorsements to the patrol reports. Baker's endorsements for this patrol were scathing. Jimmy Fife wrote, "The past two cruises of *Snapper* have been devoid of aggressive hunting for the enemy. This submarine had not been fought to expected effectiveness." Lockwood wrote in his personal diary that he "met *Snapper* . . . and was depressed by her showing. We'll have to pull out skipper." Next day, after lunch with Baker, Lockwood noted, "Told him . . . I'd have to relieve him because he hasn't done a proper job."

Baker returned to the States for further assignment. *Snapper* sailed on into an unhappy future.

Baker's classmate, young Rich Gregory on *Sargo*, was not doing much better. On his second patrol in command of *Sargo*, he patrolled the South China Sea. In his only attack, he fired three torpedoes at a freighter and missed. Fife wrote in the endorsement, "It is evident that three torpedoes were wasted. This is particularly censurable considering current shortage."

Tex McLean, Lockwood's operations officer, requested permission to make a patrol with Gregory on *Sargo*. This was a radical idea; no senior officer in Pearl Harbor or Fremantle had ever made a regular war patrol on a submarine. Lockwood gave the proposal a "fair breeze." It would not only give McLean an opportunity to observe Gregory, it would also provide McLean with combat experience that might be helpful in planning future operations.

Gregory made his third patrol in the South China Sea. McLean was not impressed. Later he said, "Gregory was a hell of a fine guy, personally. But he was more the engineering type." Under the watchful eye of McLean, Gregory fired two torpedoes at a freighter. When it did not sink, he fired three more torpedoes, which missed. One circled back at *Sargo* and exploded close by the stern. Gregory then surfaced and pumped thirty-five rounds of 3-inch ammunition at the ship. Finally, *Teibo Maru*, 4,472 tons, went down.

When *Sargo* returned from patrol, McLean recommended that Gregory be relieved of command. To Lockwood he said privately, "You ought to give the *Sargo* cook a medal. He's the best morale builder on the boat." Lockwood agreed. He wrote, "*Sargo*'s patrol was not conducted with sufficient aggressiveness. Torpedoes were wasted, opportunities were lost to inflict damage on the enemy indicating a lack of basic training."

Gregory was relieved of command and assigned to the Submarine Repair Unit, Fremantle.

One of the exchange boats, *Grampus*, commanded by Ed Hutchinson, made its third patrol off Manila Bay. When Hutchinson arrived on station, he found a full moon shining brilliantly, making *Grampus* a good target for antisubmarine vessels. Without asking Fremantle, Hutchinson shifted to Lingayen Gulf, where he found the weather bad. He then withdrew westward 60 miles—into open ocean. During the course of the patrol, many of his crew became ill with catarrhal fever and suffered from food and water poisoning. Hutchinson sighted several juicy targets—including a seaplane ferry and a tanker—which he fired at but missed.

Hutchinson's patrol report endorsements were also harsh. His division commander, Shorty Edmunds, said, "The Commanding Officer's reasoning in conducting the patrol off Lingayen Gulf instead of Manila Bay is not understood." His squadron commander, Al McCann, wrote, "Of six contacts reported only two attacks were made; approaches on the others were broken off because the range could not be closed sufficiently while submerged for an attack. In no case was an attempt made to gain a firing position by using high speed on the surface." Lockwood added the final chilly note. "This patrol of *Grampus* was not conducted in a sufficiently aggressive manner."

Also relieved of command, Hutchinson returned to the States for new construction. But he would be heard from again.

Willard Saunders, commanding another exchange boat, *Grayback*, patrolling off Camranh Bay, also conducted a less than distinguished patrol. Saunders found five targets. He was unable to close two, but on August 7 he fired two torpedoes at a small trawler from a range of 2,050 yards. On August 12, he fired three more at another target. None of the torpedoes hit. Saunders cut his patrol short and came home.

Grayback's patrol report endorsements were not glowing. Shorty Edmunds wrote, "The Commanding Officer and the Executive Officer showed marked symptoms of physical fatigue on return to port." Al McCann wrote, "The Commanding Officer states that physical endurance of officers and crew was heavily taxed by this patrol, and discontinued the patrol a few days early on this account." Lockwood admonished Saunders for not patrolling closer to the coast and said,

"The decision to fire torpedoes at a small armed trawler was not sound."

Saunders was relieved. He returned to the States for new construction.

Chet Smith, taking *Swordfish* on her fourth patrol, cruised in the South China Sea and Gulf of Siam. Smith, as usual, conducted an extremely aggressive patrol, sinking two confirmed ships for 6,500 tons. However, he came down with a bad cold, and when he returned to Fremantle he asked Lockwood to let him remain in port during *Swordfish*'s next patrol.

To replace Smith for this one patrol, Lockwood picked Albert Collins ("Acey") Burrows, a lawyer like Gene McKinney and Chester Bruton. Burrows, who had made one war patrol on Hurd's *Seal* as a PCO, took *Swordfish* to the Celebes Sea. He fired eleven torpedoes, achieving no damage. All officers and about 90 percent of the crew came down with an acute stomach disorder which was thought to be caused by food poisoning but was later traced to bad drinking water.

On return to Fremantle, Burrows was severely criticized. Jimmy Fife fumed over the profligate expenditure of torpedoes, resulting in zero damage, complaining that Burrows "allowed four valuable targets to escape." Lockwood grumped that Burrows spent time submerged "in the wrong area" and that Burrows's conduct of the patrol showed "lack of experience and seasoned judgment."

Burrows returned command of *Swordfish* to Chet Smith and reported for duty on Lockwood's staff. Burrows, too, would be heard from again—in spectacular fashion.

John Burnside in *Saury* had a difficult time on his third patrol. Setting off in late April, he was forced to return to Fremantle to repair a broken tank. He got under way again in early May to patrol off Manila. His exec was Harry Meakin Lindsay, Jr. Bill Hazzard, who had left S-37 to join *Saury*, believed Lindsay to be a detriment to Burnside. "Off Manila," Hazzard said later, "Lindsay fudged the navigation to make it look as though we were closer to shore than we were. Lindsay thought Burnside was rash to get in too close. In the hands of a better exec, Burnside might have done much better."

Returning from Manila, Burnside received an Ultra on an aircraft ferry carrying planes and aviation stores to Kendari. Burnside planned to intercept off Davao Gulf. On station, he ordered periscope looks every fifteen minutes. On one of these looks, Bill Hazzard spotted the ship. After a brief approach, Burnside fired but then lost depth control, exposing the periscope shears. "We were too far off the track and too late," Hazzard said. "An aggressive exec would have insisted on more frequent looks."

On return to Fremantle, Burnside was relieved. He went to surface forces and then was stricken by Hodgkin's disease, spent most of the war in hospitals, and died October 9, 1946.

Lockwood appointed Leonard Sparks ("Tex") Mewhinney, an enthusiastic Texan, to replace Burnside, and *Saury* got tougher. Mewhinney, another lawyer, had served on S-boats in peacetime and had gone along on Burnside's last patrol as a PCO. He took *Saury* back to the Manila area, keeping Lindsay for his exec—temporarily. (Lindsay was later sent to general service.) Off Manila, Mewhinney bungled an attack on a huge fast-moving tanker. He fired two torpedoes, hitting the tanker's propellers. The tanker stopped dead, but Mewhinney, fearing an air attack, went deep, and when he returned to periscope depth the tanker was gone.

Mewhinney made up for the bungle on the way home. One night, while *Saury* was cruising on the surface in Makassar Strait, the bridge watch picked up a target. Bill Hazzard, who had good night vision and saw the target, urged a night surface attack. As Hazzard recalled, Mewhinney demurred. His night vision was poor; he preferred a periscope. However, time ran out. Mewhinney "grudgingly" shot quickly, on the surface, in darkness, firing three torpedoes. Moments later, there was an awesome explosion. Flames shot 1,000 feet straight up into the air as the aircraft ferry *Kanto Maru*, 8,600 tons, filled with aviation gasoline, blew up and sank.

Even old hands who had demonstrated no lack of aggressiveness came in for criticism.

Gene McKinney took *Salmon* on her third patrol off Indochina, where he nailed two handsome targets—his first confirmed ships. The first vessel he believed to be the light cruiser *Yubari*; it turned out to be even better, the repair ship *Asahi*, 11,400 tons, one of the largest ships sunk by any submarine up to that time. The second was a transport, *Ganges Maru*, 4,400 tons.

On his next patrol, McKinney was not so lucky. Cruising northeast of Borneo in Palawan Passage, he intercepted a huge converted whale factory,* set up, fired—and missed. When he returned to Fremantle, Jimmy Fife's endorsement was frosty, blaming the miss on "personnel failure in the operation of the TDC, which caused torpedoes to go out on the wrong gyro angle and pass astern of the target."

Freddy Warder, taking *Seawolf* on her fifth patrol, cruised off Manila Bay, near Corregidor. Ever aggressive, Warder made seven separate attacks against seven ships, including an armed merchantman and a destroyer. Even so, Lockwood was critical of the patrol, suggesting that Warder might have gained better firing position on these ships if he had not patrolled *so close in*. He refused to credit Warder with a sinking, but postwar Japanese records gave Warder one small freighter of 1,200 tons. This was the first confirmed ship sunk by Warder.

On the next patrol, Warder took station near Borneo. He made six attacks and was credited with sinking two ships, confirmed in postwar records, and damaging one. Both Fife and Lockwood were again critical. "*Seawolf* obtained two hits out of seventeen torpedoes fired," Fife complained. "This is far below the expected standard of performance." Lockwood bore down harder. "The failure of *Seawolf* to inflict greater damage on the enemy can be attributed principally to improper solution of fire-control problems. Decisions to fire were made when excessive ranges existed [and] when lack of reliable data indicated that only a bare possibility of hitting would result." To all this, Warder later responded, "The goddamned torpedoes were no damned good. That was the problem."

Moon Chapple in *Permit*, patrolling in the Java Sea off Surabaya and northward in Makassar Strait, had a luckless time. He was directed by two separate Ultras to intercept tankers coming into Tarakan and Balikpapan but missed both and ran *Permit* aground on DeBril Bank. He returned to port without having fired a torpedo.

On the next patrol, Chapple took *Permit* to Pearl Harbor for overhaul by way of Davao Gulf. Again, no attacks. Bob English, who wrote the endorsement in Pearl Harbor, criticized Chapple for remaining submerged too much and for failing to make more frequent periscope observations.

Kenneth Hurd took *Seal* on her third and fourth patrols in the waters off Indochina. On the third patrol, he sank one small freighter

---

* Before the war, the Japanese whaling industry processed its catch in big factory ships. When war began, these ships (usually around 19,000 tons) were converted to tankers. They were a special class.

for 2,000 tons; on the fourth, he made eleven contacts but managed to damage only one, a freighter estimated at 4,000 tons. Both Fife and Lockwood were critical. "More damage," Lockwood wrote, "should have been inflicted on the enemy." Hurd had declined to attack a destroyer. Lockwood called this a mistake and urged all skippers to take on destroyers.

Pete Ferrall returned *Seadragon* to the Indochina coast for her third patrol. It was a good one. In six attacks, Ferrall sank three ships for 16,000 tons, all confirmed in Japanese records. Both Fife and Lockwood wrote approving endorsements. Ferrall had topped Jim Coe's record, set in *Skipjack* in May, of three ships for 12,800 tons.

On the fourth patrol, Ferrall returned to the same area. He made contact with eighteen enemy ships, including two heavy cruisers, attacked five ships, and claimed two sunk. However, this was reduced in postwar records to one for 2,500 tons. Lockwood was not pleased with *Seadragon*'s performance, noting, "With targets as scarce as they are, submarines must take what comes rather than wait for something better, and must relentlessly pursue all contacts." He was particularly critical of Ferrall's attack on the two heavy cruisers, which resulted in no damage. Ferrall blamed it on faulty magnetic exploders, but Fife disagreed, stating that Ferrall had made a mistake in the speed estimate.

One episode on this patrol became submarine legend. While off Indochina, one of Ferrall's crewmen, Seaman First Class Darrell Dean Rector, fell to the deck unconscious. The ship "doctor," Pharmacist's Mate First Class Wheeler B. Lipes, diagnosed Rector's malady as appendicitis—a bad case.

What to do? The prescribed procedure was to put the man in bed, pack him with ice, and keep him on a strict liquid diet until the submarine returned from patrol. Saunders on *Grayback* had had a case of appendicitis on his last patrol and had done just that. But Lipes did not think Rector could last. In his opinion, there was only one way to save him—operate.

Ferrall was torn. Lipes was no doctor. He had never operated on anyone for appendicitis. Yet Rector was in agony. Lipes said to Rector, "I can do it, but it's a chance. If you don't want me to go ahead..."

"Let's go," Rector said.

That settled it. Ferrall gave his approval and ordered preparations. He took *Seadragon* to 120 feet to ensure a smooth platform. The wardroom was converted to an operating room. Ferrall's exec, Bub Ward, served as Lipes's chief assistant. Other *Seadragon* officers stood by. Lipes devised surgical instruments from the wardroom silverware—bent spoons for muscle retractors, for example—sterilized in torpedo alcohol.

There followed a tense two and a half hours in *Seadragon*'s wardroom. Devising a mask from a tea strainer, Lipes knocked Rector out with ether. Then he operated, following instructions and diagrams in his medical books. He removed the appendix, stitching up the incision with catgut. Rector not only lived; he recovered fully.*

When Ferrall reported the operation in Fremantle, the squadron medical officer was appalled. Jimmy Fife's endorsement was typically unenthusiastic. "While this had a happy ending, it is hoped that his success on this occasion will not encourage others to take unnecessary risks."

In sum, the twenty-eight war patrols mounted from Fremantle during the period May through August 1942 produced a total of seventeen sinkings—little better than half a Japanese ship per war patrol, a miserable return. There was no great upsurge in kills after the deep-running defect of the Mark XIV torpedo was positively confirmed. The nine boats going on patrol in May—before the tests—accounted for seven enemy ships in thirty attacks. The ten boats going on patrol in July—after the tests—accounted for four enemy ships in fifteen attacks. Success still depended on many factors: position, sea conditions, depth control, coolness and skill at the periscope and TDC, torpedo maintenance—and the performance of the magnetic exploder.

In his management and deployment of Fremantle submarines, Lockwood displayed no more imagination or resourcefulness than his predecessor, Wilkes. He followed the procedure, already established, of positioning boats off the most likely (and heavily defended) traffic points, supplying them with Ultras when available. He made no special effort to blockade the oil exports from Borneo and Sumatra or any other specific strategic raw materials. It was "catch as catch can," with much hope and wishful thinking involved. As Lockwood's

---

* Before the attack on Pearl Harbor, Freeland Daubin, fearing that some of his submariners might come down with appendicitis at sea, had proposed that all men in Squadron Four have their appendixes removed. At the time, the idea seemed absurd. Considering the large number of appendicitis attacks that occurred during the war, however, some with near-fatal consequences, the idea, in retrospect, had merit.

patrol report endorsements of the period reveal, most of his effort was expended in finding ways to improve the courage and shooting skill of the officers and crews so they would sink more shipping when—or if—the opportunity presented itself. None of his boats explored the bottleneck in Luzon Strait.

11
Brisbane, May through September 1942

The Battle of Savo Island

Despite the disastrous defeat at Midway, the Japanese continued their offensive drive deep in the South Pacific. The purpose, generally, was to establish bases near the northeast tip of Australia from which the Japanese could interdict the flow of men and equipment from the United States. A significant interruption of this flow could delay and frustrate General MacArthur's buildup for the recapture of occupied territory.

In July 1942 the principal Japanese objective was still Port Moresby, New Guinea. As the codebreakers predicted, the second assault came by land. Japanese troops hacked their way over the Owen-Stanley Range and prepared to attack Port Moresby from the rear. Having been forewarned, MacArthur sent troops and aircraft from Australia to defend Port Moresby and moved his headquarters from Melbourne forward to Brisbane. The Cast codebreaking unit, renamed Fleet Radio Unit, Melbourne (FRUMEL) to conform to the organizational changes in Washington, remained behind in Melbourne.

Where else would the Japanese strike?

The codebreakers provided the answer. In late June they picked up and decoded a Japanese radio message stating that the "Guadalcanal landing"—designated "AN Operation"—would take place on July 4.

THE BATTLE OF SAVO ISLAND 295

The force would consist of a naval landing party plus the 11th and 13th Pioneer Forces. (The latter was a construction outfit like the U.S. Navy Seabees which specialized in building airfields.)

Guadalcanal? Nobody had ever heard of the place. It was not even on most navy maps and charts of the South Pacific. Finally the geography experts found it, a small island in the chain known as the Solomons, a British protectorate 750 miles due east of Port Moresby and 1,000 miles northeast of Townsville, Australia. A Japanese airfield on Guadalcanal would dominate shipping lanes from the United States and Hawaii. Japanese bombers could reach U.S. bases in New Caledonia and New Hebrides; Guadalcanal could provide a jumping-off place for an invasion of those places.

Reading the intercepted message in Washington, Admiral King proposed that the U.S. Navy and Marines commanded by Admiral Ghormley, from Noumea, launch a counteroffensive against Japanese operations aimed at Guadalcanal. It was a new strategy—the existing war plan was merely to contain the Japanese, not to go on the offensive—and, considering the few naval forces then available to Ghormley, a bold concept. However, when MacArthur got wind of this proposal he was angry—not by the plan itself but that it was proposed as an all-navy show. He radioed Washington: IT IS QUITE EVIDENT . . . THAT NAVY CONTEMPLATES ASSUMING GENERAL COMMAND CONTROL OF ALL OPERATIONS IN THE PACIFIC THEATER, THE ROLE OF THE ARMY BEING SUBSIDIARY AND CONSISTING LARGELY OF PLACING ITS FORCES AT THE DISPOSAL AND UNDER COMMAND OF NAVY OR MARINE OFFICERS.

The MacArthur response touched off a flap in Washington and made many naval officers implacably hostile to the general forevermore. Army Chief of Staff Marshall agreed in spirit with MacArthur, yet he saw the strategic and propaganda advantages of a limited counteroffensive in the South Pacific. In a frosty meeting with Admiral King, the two men worked out a compromise. Ghormley and the naval forces would seize Guadalcanal and a small Japanese base northeast of Guadalcanal, Tulagi. In addition to stopping the Japanese at Port Moresby, MacArthur would assume overall responsibility for future moves in the Solomons: Rabaul, New Guinea, and New Britain.

While all this was being hashed out, the Japanese landed on Guadalcanal. Working in feverish haste to mount a counteroffensive before the Japanese could build an airfield, Admiral Ghormley got together almost every available naval vessel in the Pacific. The force consisted, finally, of the three aircraft carriers *Enterprise*, *Wasp*, and

Saratoga plus supporting cruisers and destroyers and an invasion force of 19,000 marines. Washington code-named the proposed assault Operation Watchtower. Ghormley unofficially dubbed it Operation Shoestring.

All this took time—during which the Japanese built the airfield. On August 7, Ghormley's marines went ashore on Guadalcanal virtually unopposed, and by late afternoon they had captured the airfield. A larger force landed at Tulagi, meeting small resistance. By August 8, Tulagi was "practically secure." Ghormley and his admirals and generals congratulated themselves on a job well done.

The celebration did not last long. At Rabaul, the Japanese reacted swiftly and efficiently. They sent off land-based aircraft to attack U.S. forces at Tulagi and Guadalcanal and to seek out the carriers. They organized a task group of heavy cruisers and destroyers to attack the transports unloading marines and supplies at Guadalcanal and then a convoy of reinforcements for both Tulagi and Guadalcanal.

The ensuing naval engagement—known as the Battle of Savo Island—was the worst defeat ever inflicted on the United States Navy at sea. Ghormley lost four heavy cruisers, *Canberra*, *Quincy*, *Vincennes*, and *Astoria*. *Chicago* was severely damaged and only barely made it to port. Nearly 1,500 officers and men were killed. The Japanese lost no vessels. The skipper of *Vincennes*, Captain Frederic Louis Riefkhol, was "broken in spirit" by the loss of his vessel; Captain Howard Bode, skipper of *Chicago*, committed suicide. The official blame was spread around evenly, but Ghormley, no favorite of King's, fell into disfavor.

This initial engagement was merely a prelude to a prolonged seesawing series of naval battles that would rage off and on in the Solomons for the next four months. "It opened a bloody and desperate campaign for an island," wrote naval historian Samuel Eliot Morison, "that neither side really wanted but which neither could afford to abandon to the enemy."

May, June, and July Departures

Since his arrival at Brisbane in April, Ralph Christie, maintaining headquarters on the tender *Griffin*, had been sending his force of eleven S-boats on war patrols. After the initial deployment of four submarines in April for the Battle of the Coral Sea, he sent off six in

May and five in June. The primary areas were the Japanese bases at Rabaul and Kavieng and smaller bases in Bougainville, Tulagi, and elsewhere.

The S-boat patrols from Brisbane were, like the S-boat patrols in the Aleutians, nightmares that no one would ever forget. The equatorial heat was intense; the temperature inside the submerged boats ranged from 105 to 120 degrees. Only one of the eleven boats—S-44— had air conditioning, a makeshift unit bought in Philadelphia with private funds and installed by the crew.

William James Ruhe from the class of 1939, an artist and musician then a junior officer on S-37, later described the life:

The bunks beyond the wardroom are filled with torpid, skivvy-clad bodies, the sweat running off the white, rash-blistered skin in small rivulets. Metal fans are whirring everywhere—overhead, at the ends of the bunks, close to my ear. . . . I am playing cribbage with the skipper, mainly because I don't like to wallow in a sweat-soaked bunk most of the day. I have my elbows on the table near the edge and I hold my cards with my arms at a slight angle so the sweat will stream down my bare arms . . . without further soaking the pile of cards in the center. . . . Overhead is a fine net of gauze to catch the wayward cockroaches which prowl across the top of the wardroom and occasionally fall straight downward . . . they live in the cork insulation which lines the insides of the submarine's hull . . . we've killed over sixteen million cockroaches in one compartment alone. . . . The deck in the control room is littered with towels, used to sponge up the water dripping off the men and the submarine itself. . . . The food is routine —something canned. The dehydrated potatoes, powdered onions, and reconstituted carrots have the same general taste—like sawdust.

The boats had countless mechanical failures. (S-45 was plagued with engine trouble; S-46 experienced a main motor failure at sea.) All had electrical problems, intensified by the tropical humidity; most leaked oil from the riveted tanks. The diving planes were noisy, the sonar gear inadequate. S-37, which had been "saved" on the retreat from Manila by the engineering talent of James Reynolds, was almost a complete wreck, the worst of the eleven boats. On arrival in Brisbane, she spent six weeks in overhaul. At sea, someone accidentally punched another hole in her fragile hull.

Three skippers overcame these hardships and delivered attacks on the Japanese: John Raymond ("Dinty") Moore on S-44, his successor

Reuben Whitaker, and Hank Munson on *S-38*. Moore, who had sunk a ship on his first patrol in April, was something of a character. "He was born in Tennessee," said a submariner, "and affected a hayseed front. But underneath he was very intelligent—he stood thirty-three in a class of two hundred and forty—and a very no-nonsense type of guy." Moore was helped considerably by his exec, Thomas Slack Baskett, with whom Moore worked in close harmony. Baskett, who stood 8 out of 422 in the class of 1935, was an urbane, low-key, thoroughly competent officer, no less aggressive than Moore.

Moore sank his second ship on his second patrol, north of Guadalcanal. It was a nerve-shattering adventure. He fired from close range and then stayed at the periscope to watch the results. The ship, converted gunboat *Keijo Maru*, 2,262 tons, sank with her stern high in the air. Moore could see people running along the slanting deck, jumping into the water. He took a final look and ordered *S-44* deep.

As the boat was going down, there was a sudden cataclysmic explosion overhead. Apparently *Keijo Maru* blew up just as Moore was sliding beneath her. Inside *S-44* there was terror and chaos. Glass gauges shattered. The spare torpedoes were torn from their racks, the small conning tower flooded. All through the hull the men could hear the nightmarish sounds of the ship they had torpedoed breaking apart and sinking—presumably on top of them. But Moore maneuvered *S-44* away, turning and diving deep, escaping without further damage.

On his third patrol, off Kavieng, Moore got his third ship—a big one. On the morning of August 10, four of the Japanese cruisers that had decimated the U.S. Navy in the Battle of Savo Island came into view, returning home. Moore, with a new exec, Clifton W. ("Barney") Flenniken, Jr., set up on the last cruiser in line, opened the range to get a better shot, and fired four torpedoes at 700 yards. Thirty-five seconds later the first torpedo hit with a shattering explosion.

"Evidently all her boilers blew up," Moore said later. "You could hear hideous noises that sounded like steam hissing through water. These noises were more terrifying to the crew than the actual depth charges that followed. It sounded as if great chains were being dragged across the hull, as if our own water and air lines were bursting."

The Japanese heavy cruiser *Kako*, 8,800 tons, plunged to the bottom. Although Warder, Brockman, Wright, Voge, McKinney, and others had already been given credit for sinking major Japanese men-of-war, *Kako* was, in fact, the first major combatant ship lost to U.S.

submarines in the war. When Moore returned to Brisbane, he was awarded a Navy Cross and Flenniken a Silver Star. By sinking one ship on each of his three patrols, Moore had created an S-boat record that would never be equaled, let alone beaten.

After that patrol, command of *S-44* went to Reuben Whitaker, who had been Bull Wright's exec on *Sturgeon*. Whitaker proved to be a fitting choice to command the hottest S-boat in Brisbane. On his first —and only—patrol as an S-boat skipper, Whitaker fearlessly attacked a column of three Japanese destroyers off New Georgia. He fired three torpedoes at one and believed he sank it. Afterward, *S-44* received a brutal depth-charging. Whitaker was credited with a kill, but JANAC denied him credit.

Hank Munson on *S-38* got his ship in St. George's Channel near Bougainville after the initial American landing on Guadalcanal. About midnight on August 8, while on the surface, Munson picked up a Japanese convoy—six transports, plus escorts—steaming down to Guadalcanal. Munson chose a target, a large freighter escorted by a destroyer. He submerged, underran the destroyer, and fired two torpedoes from deep submergence.

It was, Munson said later, a lucky shot. Both torpedoes hit the 5,600-ton *Meiyo Maru*, a key vessel of the Japanese expeditionary force. With the loss of this ship, the Japanese temporarily recalled the other five transports, giving the marines on Guadalcanal a little more time to consolidate their defenses.

Ralph Christie also believed that some of his skippers were not putting forth their best effort. Three were relieved for "not producing," as Christie wrote Lockwood—Nick Lucker on *S-40* (who missed a good target off Savo Island), George Holley on *S-41*, and Edward Robert ("Irish") Hannon on *S-43*—and James Reynolds on *S-37*, who sank a 2,800-ton ship off New Ireland, said later that he requested his own relief.

Later, Lucker wrote, "I felt that I would never accomplish much on *S-40*, as most of our time was spent in trying to keep the ship running, and . . . I believe I was completely worn out." Wrote George Holley, "I rather suspect that I may have been criticized for lack of aggressiveness. . . . No excuse can be offered." Wrote Hannon, "The mental strain and worry over not being able to rely on the engines [on *S-43*] to charge the batteries each night apparently took their toll, for when the *S-43* returned from its second patrol I was simply exhausted."

Not everybody thought Christie should relieve these men. Excessive caution on a fleet boat was reprehensible, but caution on these old buckets of bolts was not only condoned but forgiven. Said Thomas Kimmel, who was on *S-40*, "Nick Lucker was an intelligent competent submariner. . . . I believe [he] was a good submarine commanding officer who was one of those victimized by the frustration of the early part of the war."

One S-boat was lost during this period: *S-39*, commanded by Francis Elwood Brown. Leaving Brisbane, Brown twice suffered major breakdowns and was forced to return for repairs. When *S-39* finally got to sea and seemed well on her way, her exec came down with pneumonia. Brown radioed Christie for instructions. Christie told him to put the exec ashore in Townsville. After this was done, Brown proceeded toward his patrol area north of Guadalcanal.

Three nights later, while *S-39* was traveling on the surface minus one executive officer, she ran aground on a reef off Rossel Island. Jolted up and down by heavy seas breaking over the afterdeck, the boat immediately took a 35-degree list to port. Brown blew his ballast tanks dry, dumped fuel, and backed emergency, but *S-39* was stuck fast.

During the next twenty-four hours, Brown and his crew did everything possible to save the ship, including dumping more fuel and deactivating and firing the four bow torpedoes. Meanwhile, the boat was twisted sideways to the sea and pounded fiercely. Brown sent a call for help. The Australian naval vessel *Katoomba* responded.

On the morning of August 15, when *S-39* was thrown violently on her side, Brown passed the word that anyone who wanted to abandon ship and swim through the crashing surf to a nearby reef might do so. No one did. Then a young lieutenant volunteered to swim to the reef with lines. Joined by one of the enlisted men, he made it and tied the lines to one of the jettisoned torpedoes which had lodged on the reef. Using these lines, thirty-two of the crew transferred to the reef. The remaining twelve stayed on board, awaiting rescue by *Katoomba*.

Katoomba appeared, and by ten the following day all hands had been rescued from the reef or the stricken sub. The codebooks and other classified material were removed or destroyed. Satisfied that *S-39* would soon be torn to pieces on the rocks, Brown did not request that

Katoomba destroy her by gunfire. He and his crew were dropped in Townsville, from where they made their way back to Brisbane. Meanwhile, Christie sent aircraft out to ensure *S-39*'s destruction by bombing.

Christie was impressed by Brown's coolness and his efforts to save his ship. Although some on his staff (and higher up) suggested a court-martial, Christie headed them off and gave Brown command of Irish Hannon's *S-43*.

Battle of the Eastern Solomons

The battles for Guadalcanal—and the Solomons—quickly became the focal point of the naval war in the Pacific. By mid-August, the marines were operating aircraft from the captured air base—which they named Henderson Field—and Admiral Ghormley was gamely hanging on. The Japanese, on the other hand, were determined to drive the U.S. forces from Guadalcanal. They threw the whole weight of the Japanese navy, including the surviving heavy carriers *Shokaku* and *Zuikaku*, the light carrier *Ryujo*, and eight battleships, into the South Pacific.

The war continued to go badly for the U.S. Navy. After the disaster of Savo Island came the Battle of the Eastern Solomons. The three Japanese carriers (*Shokaku*, *Zuikaku*, and *Ryujo*), supported by eight battleships plus nine cruisers, thirteen destroyers, and thirty-six submarines, steamed to meet Ghormley's force of three carriers (*Enterprise*, *Wasp*, and *Saratoga**), one battleship (*North Carolina*), four cruisers, and ten destroyers. Just before the forces met, Ghormley was misinformed by the codebreakers on the location of the Japanese force and sent *Wasp* off to refuel, thinking it had plenty of time to get back into battle.

The two forces met on August 25. The Japanese lost the light carrier *Ryujo*, a transport, and a destroyer. Two ships were badly damaged, one of them the cruiser *Jintsu*, which Freddy Warder believed he had sunk at Christmas Island. The United States lost no ships, but *Enterprise* was severely damaged by dive bombers, and a few days later, in an epilogue to the battle, *Saratoga* was torpedoed for the second time by a Japanese submarine and put out of action for

---

* The fourth U.S. carrier in the Pacific, *Hornet,* was en route from Pearl Harbor but arrived too late for the battle.

three crucial months. Because his forces had sunk the light carrier *Ryujo*, Ghormley claimed a victory. But her loss was less serious than the operational losses of *Enterprise* and *Saratoga* due to damage.

The worst was yet to come. Two weeks after *Saratoga* was hit, Japanese submarines struck again. On September 15, *I-15* and *I-19* found *Wasp* and the recently arrived *Hornet* and their support groups in the Coral Sea, south of Guadalcanal, bringing reinforcements to the island. *I-19* fired four torpedoes at *Wasp*. Three hit. *Wasp* burst into flames and was abandoned; a U.S. destroyer polished her off. *I-15* fired at *Hornet* but missed. However, one of her torpedoes hit the battleship *North Carolina*, tearing a 32-foot gash in her hull. Another blew off the bow of the destroyer *O'Brien*. *North Carolina* survived; *O'Brien* limped into Espiritu Santo for temporary repairs but foundered on the way to California.

After September 15, the United States had only one operational fleet carrier left in the Pacific—*Hornet*—and one undamaged battleship—*Washington*. Taken together, the naval actions in the Solomons over the three-week period August 25–September 15 amounted to another severe defeat for the U.S. Navy.

The only good news came from Port Moresby. General MacArthur's ground forces beat off the Japanese troops that crossed the Owen-Stanley Range to attack from the rear. This victory was the first positive Allied success against Japanese troops. It was due, in large measure, to the codebreakers.

August and September Departures

With all this Japanese naval power concentrated in the Solomons, the area seemed ripe for U.S. submarines. The S-boats were obviously ineffectual, as Christie wrote Admiral Leary. "These vessels are twenty years old," he said. "The character of service in this theater is beyond the capability of S-boats." He suggested that they all be returned to the States for overhaul and reassigned to "areas where heavy antisubmarine measures may not be met." Leary agreed. He ordered that the S-boats, plus the tender *Griffin*, be prepared for return to the States. Jimmy Fife's Squadron Two, with tender *Holland*, basing in Albany, were ordered to replace them.

About the time Leary gave that order, he was transferred to other duty. His replacement was Lockwood's nemesis, Chips Carpender.

By the time Carpender left Fremantle, he and Lockwood were on the verge of committing mayhem. One of Lockwood's staff said later, "If Carpender had not been sent to MacArthur's staff, *both* Lockwood and Carpender would have been pulled out" and sent to other duty.

The order to shift Squadron Two and *Holland* from Albany on Australia's southwest coast to Brisbane on the eastern coast devastated Lockwood. It left him with *Pelias* and Squadron Six, about eight submarines to cover his huge area. In his diary, he called the redeployment a "theft" and shot off a protest to Chips Carpender in which he described the difficulty of waging a submarine war against Japanese shipping with so small a force. But it was to no avail. The orders stood. In August, the first three Squadron Two boats—Voge's *Sailfish*, Bull Wright's *Sturgeon*, and Chappell's *Sculpin*—went to Brisbane by way of southern Australia.

In Brisbane, close to the many thrones there, Christie inched up in power and prestige. "From *Griffin*, where I lived, it was only a fifteen-minute drive downtown to MacArthur's and Carpender's headquarters," he said later. "I went down every morning to pick up Ultra messages and to visit." Carpender and Christie cultivated a close working relationship and mutual respect. Christie, who often saw and spoke with General MacArthur, developed an overwhelming admiration for him. "He was one of the truly great men in history," Christie said later.

In faraway Perth-Fremantle, Lockwood, having lost the battle to prevent the shift of Squadron Two, launched a campaign to have himself transferred to Brisbane to command it in the Solomons. He flew to Brisbane to engineer this change but met with a cool reception from Carpender and from Christie, whom Lockwood would, in effect, displace. On return to Perth, Lockwood put his views in writing to Carpender. "My proper station at this time should be in Brisbane even if only temporarily in order to better carry out my responsibilities. . . . I hope that you will give the matter consideration as the operation of Task Force 51 at the moment is not of great importance." Carpender responded coldly—"I frankly do not concur and wish you to remain at Fremantle"—and gave the responsibility of commanding Squadron Two to Ralph Christie, a slap at Lockwood, who was three years senior.

During the course of all this shifting and politicking, General MacArthur, perhaps as a psychological gesture, moved his headquarters from Brisbane to Port Moresby. Carpender, who wanted to remain in

Brisbane near his Australian-based naval units (mainly Christie's submarines), did not move to Port Moresby with MacArthur. Instead, he hand-picked a "personal representative" as a stand-in. That representative turned out to be Jimmy Fife. When Carpender sent for Fife, the orders went directly to Fife, bypassing Lockwood, another insult.

One of Fife's primary duties in Port Moresby was to protect the Ultra dispatches. Carpender did not want a leak like the one that had occurred in Ghormley's command. In Port Moresby, Fife received Ultra on navy radio channels, then took it directly to General MacArthur and his chief of staff, General Richard Southerland. Following Carpender's orders, Fife refused to give the messages to MacArthur's intelligence chief, Charles A. Willoughby, or to his communications specialist, General Spencer B. Akin. Returning from MacArthur's office, Fife burned the messages in a bucket near Willoughby's desk. Willoughby was much annoyed—both by the exclusion from the secrets and the smoke.

When the first three Squadron Two boats reported to Brisbane from Albany in late August, Christie, with Lockwood's blessing, made some changes in command. Dick Voge on *Sailfish* had long-standing orders to report to Bob English to become Pearl Harbor's operations officer, so Christie gave the boat to Dinty Moore as a reward for his outstanding performance on *S-44*. Bull Wright on *Sturgeon* returned to the States to command a new division of Manitowoc-built boats. Christie gave *Sturgeon* to a fellow Gun Clubber with an M.A. in ordnance engineering and a nearly unpronounceable surname: Herman Arnold Pieczentkowski. "Pi," as he was called, had made one war patrol as Dick Voge's exec. Chester Nimitz, Jr., moved up to be Pi's exec. These two, plus Lucius Chappell's *Sculpin*, joined five S-boats for war patrols in the Solomons.

Up to then Ralph Christie, torpedo expert, father of the magnetic exploder, had had no wartime experience with the Mark XIV torpedo. His S-boats used the old Mark X with the contact exploder, which worked fine. Some of the skippers and crews on the fleet boats arriving from Fremantle raised questions about the Mark XIV torpedo and the exploder, but Christie would hear none of it. He believed (like English) that—apart from the now-corrected deep running—any defects in Mark XIV torpedoes could be laid to poor maintenance, improper settings, or errors by the skipper or the TDC team. All fleet submarines under his command would continue to use the magnetic exploder.

Before the boats left for patrol, Christie inspected them. "I found the torpedoes in appalling condition," Christie said later. "Afterbody syphons uncapped. Exploder mechanisms frozen. Scoops plugged with grease. Reversed torpedo locks. Many of the torpedo officers and men had not been properly trained. From that time on, there was conscientious maintenance of torpedoes—according to the book."

The three pioneer fleet boats at Brisbane turned in mixed results. Lucius Chappell, patrolling in *Sculpin* off New Britain and New Ireland in confined waters swarming with enemy destroyers, made five aggressive attacks. He believed he had sunk three ships for 24,000 tons, but postwar records credited him with two ships for 6,600 tons. Toward the end of the patrol, he attacked the light cruiser *Yura* but failed to inflict serious damage.

Pi, in *Sturgeon*, made three attacks and sank one ship; it was *Katsuragi Maru*, 8,000 tons, an aircraft ferry. Following that attack, *Sturgeon* received a vicious depth-charging.

Dinty Moore, in *Sailfish*, evidently had a tough time shifting from his S-boat to a fleet boat. Getting under way, he bent a propeller, delaying his start. Patrolling the Solomons, he sighted at least twenty Japanese destroyers, perhaps more, plus a seaplane tender. He made one attack against a minelayer, firing three torpedoes. All missed. The minelayer responded with a depth-charge attack, dropping eleven well-placed missiles. Moore wrote in his report, "The large number of contacts with no results is disappointing. Lack of results may be attributed to strong antisubmarine measures, many glassy calm days, bad management and bad luck. Just how much to one and just how much to the other, I can't say."

On their August and September patrols, none of the S-boats scored sinkings. One by one, as the fleet boats reported for duty, the Ss were pulled from combat and returned to the States for other duty. Many of their skippers and execs went on to commission new fleet boats.

In his deployment of the fleet boats, Christie displayed little imagination and ingenuity. By September, when the first three left Brisbane, it was clear from codebreaking information and other intelligence that the Japanese were using Palau and Truk as bases for operations in the Solomons. There was heavy traffic—both men-of-war and merchant shipping—between those islands and Rabaul and Kavieng. Rather than attack this traffic on the high seas, with open water and plenty of leg room, Christie chose to position the boats off the terminal points, where air and sea antisubmarine measures were heaviest. As a result, the skippers were forced to remain submerged a great deal of the time in shallow and dangerous waters, wasting two prime assets of the fleet boat: speed and mobility.

In making his decisions on deployment, Christie was influenced by the existing target priority established by Admiral King in Washington. Japanese carriers, battleships, cruisers, and other major combatant units were still top, with merchant ships, tankers, destroyers, and auxiliaries taking second place. The waters were teeming with Japanese aircraft carriers, battleships, and cruisers, most of them being tracked by the codebreakers. In his eagerness to help the beleaguered and thin U.S. surface forces, Christie constantly shifted his boats to intercept these prime Japanese targets. However, it was all wasted effort. Except for Chappell's inconclusive shot at the light cruiser *Yura*, none of the boats found or attacked major Japanese units.

12

Pearl Harbor, July through December 1942

July, August, and September Patrols to Truk

On the heels of the Alaskan foray, Admiral Nimitz ordered Bob English to send a contingent of Pearl Harbor submarines to the Japanese staging base, Truk. The boats had a twofold mission: first, to intercept and sink capital ships and troop and supply ships headed for the Solomons, and secondly, to provide intelligence on capital-ship movements so that Admiral Ghormley and his hard-pressed surface forces would know what to expect next.

By the time English received these orders in July 1942, his submarine force had acquired added strength. Stoney Roper in *Fulton* had finished the advance base at Midway. Some boats had been ordered there for refit, reducing travel-time overhead. Many others had stopped there, going and coming from patrol, to top off fuel tanks. The first boats of Gin Styer's Squadron Ten had reported to Pearl Harbor for duty.

There was also an important change in English's staff: Dick Voge arrived from Brisbane to relieve John Brady as operations officer. Voge, having made four long and arduous war patrols in *Sailfish*, was the first officer who had taken a submarine into combat to assume an important position in any of the three submarine commands.

Voge proved to be a staff officer with unusual gifts. He was exceptionally bright and analytical, dedicated, articulate, intense, and tough-minded. In peacetime on *Sealion* and in wartime on *Sailfish*, he had passed his off-duty hours working out solutions to torpedo spreads and other complex mathematical problems. Having been a recipient of Ultra on *Sailfish*, he had an appreciation of its value and as-yet-unrealized potential. Shortly after arriving at Pearl Harbor, he established a close working relationship with FRUPAC's Jasper Holmes, an old friend and fellow S-boat commander. Holmes, who admired and trusted Voge, gave him more Ultra information than he had given Brady. Eventually, the two men had a hot line laid between their two offices.

As the weeks and months rolled on, Dick Voge, in fact, became one of the most valuable officers in the submarine force, a sort of genius at his job. He had an uncanny knack for sniffing out Japanese moves and for sending the right skipper and boat to the right place. Having been whipsawed around at sea, chasing repeated Ultras, he gave the skippers much more freedom to pursue these contacts by their own devices—and achieved better results. Best of all, he possessed a sense of humor and compassion. His nightly Fox schedules contained not only operational orders and information on Japanese movements but also personal messages to officers and men. "Sometimes you got awfully lonely out there," a submarine skipper remembered. "Then here would come Voge's newsletter about so-and-so's wife having a baby, all's well at home, and so on, and you got the feeling Voge really cared about you, that he was looking out for your best interests every waking minute."

In response to the Nimitz order, Bob English sent eleven boats to Truk during the period July through September. Six of these were Pearl Harbor boats that returned to Pearl Harbor or Midway. Five were exchange boats on the way to Australia. In addition, two submarines—*Nautilus* and *Argonaut*—landed commando parties on Makin Island in the Gilbert chain, a feint designed to draw Japanese naval forces from the Solomons and reduce pressure on Ghormley.

In general, the operation was, like the sortie to Alaskan waters, another failure for Pearl Harbor submarines. The eleven boats at Truk, operating independently of one another and close to the island, where antisubmarine activity was intense, sank only eight confirmed ships. Many boats were badly bombed or depth-charged. On at least three occasions, the submarines attacked major Japanese carriers or battleships, but for one reason or the other the attacks resulted in no sinkings. On other occasions, a battleship and carriers were sighted but no attacks could be made. The *Nautilus-Argonaut* raid on Makin was a fiasco.

The first wave of six boats left for Truk in July. Bob Rice in *Drum*, who had scored heavily on his first patrol in Empire waters, was one of the earliest. He had a miserable patrol. He missed one freighter—perhaps due to erratic torpedo performance—and damaged another. While he was preparing a second attack on the damaged ship, Japanese aircraft delivered a bombing attack on *Drum*, forcing him to break off. English, who had praised Rice's aggressiveness on his first patrol, criticized him this time for failing to follow up.

Eliot Olsen in *Grayling*, who had been roasted for missing the carrier *Hosho* at Truk in February and had made a lively second patrol in Empire waters, had an experience at Truk similar to Rice's. He fired at a ship, perhaps a submarine tender, achieving two hits. When he tried to follow up the attack, he was bombed by aircraft. Bedeviled by a squealing port shaft, air leaks, and other matériel failures, Olsen terminated the patrol early, returning to Pearl Harbor after forty-three days. English criticized Olsen for not following up the attack on the supposed submarine tender and sent *Grayling* to a long navy yard overhaul. Olsen went to duty in the Atlantic.

Greenling, commanded by lawyer Chester Bruton, whom English had rebuked for his performance on his first patrol off Truk, seemed destined at first to rack up more failures. On his first attack against a group of enemy vessels, Bruton fired three torpedoes; all missed. An escort counterattacked; Bruton fired; another miss. He found a tanker and fired four torpedoes; all misses. The score was nine torpedoes, no hits.

This pattern changed dramatically for Bruton on the night of August 4. While running on the surface, he saw what he believed to be an aircraft carrier. He set up fast and fired four stern torpedoes, all apparent misses. He continued tracking, hiding in rainsqualls. Four hours later, he made a second night surface attack, firing three bow tubes and achieving two solid hits. The target fired a deck gun at *Greenling*, then sank swiftly.

Running through the wreckage, Bruton picked up a survivor. He told Bruton the ship was not an aircraft carrier but the huge 12,000-ton *Brazil Maru*, which had been carrying 600 passengers, 400 of them soldiers bound for the Solomons. *Brazil Maru*, the largest ship sunk to date by any U.S. submarine, had been scheduled for conversion to a light aircraft carrier on her return to Japan. The survivor also reported to Bruton that earlier that night the ship had been struck by torpedoes that had failed to go off.

With this and subsequent successes, Bruton's aim improved considerably. The next night he spotted another ship, *Palau Maru*, 5,000 tons. He closed to point-blank range—800 yards—and fired three torpedoes for three hits. The ship sank. Later, he sighted and closed other ships but was driven off by escorts and aircraft. On return to Pearl Harbor, English credited Bruton with two ships for 24,000 tons (later reduced to 17,000) and gave him a Navy Cross, but his endorsement was, on the whole, lukewarm. He criticized Bruton for overcautious use of the periscope, for remaining deep on one attack when he might have followed up, and other matters.

Three exchange boats routed to Fremantle by way of Truk all had new skippers. *Gudgeon* was commanded by William Shirley Stovall, Jr., who had been a classmate of Bob Rice's wife, Eunice Willson, in codebreaking school in 1936. After that, Stovall had rotated to sea, serving on S-boats. It was foolhardy in the extreme to send a man with Stovall's intimate knowledge of codebreaking into Japanese-held waters, but English, like Lockwood and Christie, had a critical shortage of qualified submarine skippers. Dusty Dornin, who remained as Stovall's exec, could have commanded *Gudgeon*, but English was not yet ready to give that responsibility to a Naval Academy graduate of the class of 1935.

Stovall and Dornin had a furiously active patrol. The first target was a small patrol craft at which Stovall fired three torpedoes. All missed. A few nights later, he made a night surface approach on a convoy of two destroyers and three tankers. Before he could get off a shot, one of the destroyers sighted *Gudgeon* and charged, firing a torpedo. Stovall went deep. *Gudgeon* took twelve depth charges, none close. A week later, Stovall made a night surface attack on a cargo vessel escorted by a single destroyer, firing three torpedoes, two of which seemed to hit. Stovall escaped on the surface. On August 3, Stovall made a day periscope attack on an unescorted merchantman, firing three torpedoes, scoring two hits.

The climax of *Gudgeon*'s busy patrol came on August 17, when Stovall found two large transports and two destroyers, escorted by a screen of three aircraft from Truk. Making a day periscope attack, he

BLOCKADE of TRUK
AUGUST-OCTOBER 1942

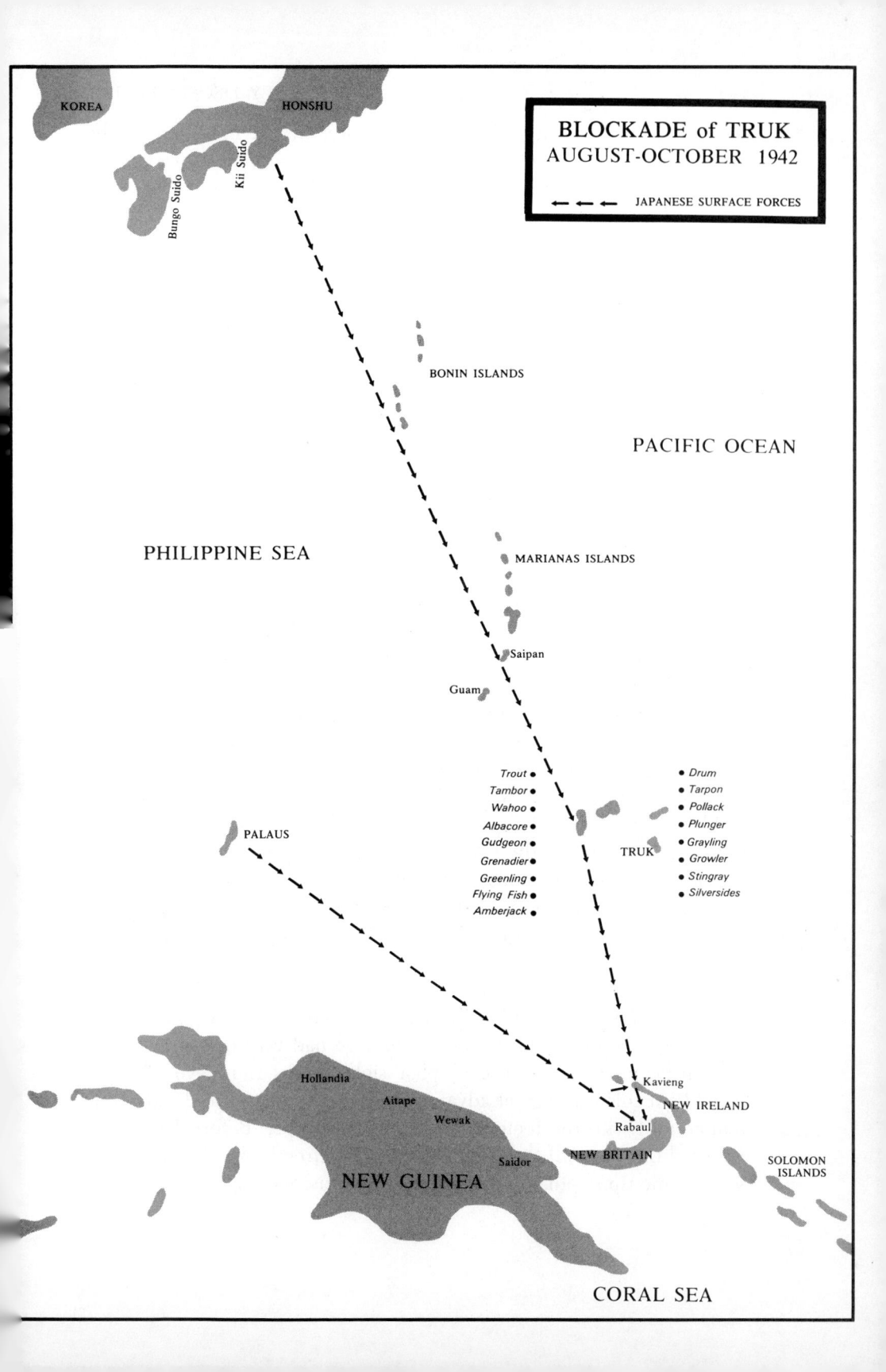

← ← ← JAPANESE SURFACE FORCES

fired three torpedoes at each transport. Three hit the first, two hit the second. Then the destroyers counterattacked, dropping no less than sixty depth charges, many close. "Minor leaks occurred throughout the boat," Dornin reported later with understatement, and "the crew was shaken up considerably."

When *Gudgeon* reached Fremantle, Lockwood credited Stovall with four ships sunk for 35,000 tons, one of the best performances of any submarine to date. There were many congratulations all around. However, JANAC trimmed the actual sinkings to one, the 4,858-ton cargo vessel *Naniwa Maru*. Said Dornin later, "It was the same old defective torpedo story all over again."

Stovall, shaken by the depth charges and the heavy responsibilities of command, requested that Lockwood relieve him. Lockwood noted in his diary, "Very poor story. Skipper cracked up and asks to be relieved." However, after a rest in Perth, Stovall changed his mind and got ready for another patrol.

Of the other two new skippers on the exchange boats, Stephen Henry Ambruster on *Tambor* and Bruce Lewis Carr on *Grenadier*, Ambruster conducted the more aggressive patrol. Lockwood credited him with sinking two big freighters for 12,000 tons (although Japanese postwar records cut the total tonnage in half). Carr was credited with sinking a tanker (denied postwar), but Lockwood criticized him for missing a number of other opportunities.

The second wave of five boats left in August and September and prowled Truk during the heaviest movement of major Japanese ships to and from the Solomons. Though all five found major Japanese vessels, aircraft carriers and battleships, the results were disappointing. Nevertheless, two of them could claim "firsts."

Mike Fenno's *Trout* was now commanded by Lawson Paterson ("Red") Ramage, another member of the class of 1931. Ramage had made one war patrol with Pilly Lent on *Grenadier*. A genial backslapper and popular with his crew, Ramage had very nearly failed his submarine physical because of poor sight in his right eye. "But it turned out this was a great advantage," he said later. "I didn't have to fool around with the focus knob on the periscope. Before I raised it, I turned the knob all the way to the stop [extreme focus]. When the scope came up, I put my bad eye to the periscope and could see perfectly."

JULY–SEPTEMBER PATROLS TO TRUK 313

Alerted by an Ultra, on August 28 Ramage intercepted a Japanese task group consisting of the light carrier *Taiyo* (*Otaka*), plus cruisers and destroyers. Relentlessly aggressive, Ramage closed to short range and fired five torpedoes at the carrier. He believed some of the five hit, reporting, "A large volume of smoke was pouring out of the starboard side near the waterline and pouring up and over the flight deck." Postwar Japanese records confirmed that *Taiyo* (*Otaka*) suffered medium damage from a submarine attack on the day and at the place Ramage claimed. It was the first hit any U.S. submarine had actually scored on a Japanese aircraft carrier; had the warheads been more powerful, *Taiyo* (*Otaka*) might have sunk.

A few days later, while making a periscope navigational fix, *Trout* was caught by Japanese aircraft. A tremendous explosion shook her from stem to stern. One man was thrown from his bunk. Others froze in shock. Ramage went deep, where he found the bomb had wrecked both periscopes. He cut his patrol short and set a course for Brisbane to have the periscopes replaced.

On the same day Ramage attacked *Taiyo* (*Otaka*), Donc Donaho in *Flying Fish* spotted a battleship of the *Kongo* class, escorted by two destroyers and aircraft from Truk. Assisted by his exec, Enrique D'Hamel Haskins, Donaho moved in to attack, planning to fire four bow tubes at the battleship and two bow tubes at a destroyer. The four bow torpedoes streaked toward the battleship. Donaho, manning the periscope, saw two hits, the first for the submarine force on a Japanese battleship. He believed he saw fire along the waterline and later reported to English: SET ON FIRE, ONE BATTLESHIP. Before he could fire at the destroyer, one of the aircraft escorts attacked *Flying Fish* with a bomb which fell close and forced Donaho deep. Four destroyers or patrol craft attacked with depth charges.

Two hours later, Donaho shook the destroyers and returned to periscope depth for a look. While he was searching the horizon, a "nervous torpedoman" in the after torpedo room accidentally fired a torpedo in Number 7 tube with the outer door closed. As the report of that accident reached Donaho, another Japanese bomb fell close aboard, forcing *Flying Fish* deep again. Number 7 torpedo was jammed in the tube. Donaho could not open the outer door to get rid of it. Two engines flooded due to leaky exhaust valves.

When the sun set, Donaho returned to periscope depth. He found two destroyers close by and prepared torpedo tubes forward. Working quickly—perhaps too quickly—Donaho set up and fired three torpedoes at one of the destroyers. All missed. He did not follow up. After dark, Donaho surfaced. One of the destroyers charged at *Flying Fish*, forcing Donaho deep again, and dropped eleven close depth charges. Later, Donaho surfaced again, saw the two destroyers 1½ miles astern, and dived. He did not attack.

After midnight, he surfaced and left the area. For the next two days he remained at sea, trying to get rid of Number 7 torpedo. His men were finally able to pull it back inside the after torpedo room, but in the process they partially flooded the compartment.

On September 2, with all machinery back in commission, Donaho returned to the Truk area for more combat. Finding a patrol vessel, he fired two torpedoes from 700 yards. Both missed. The patrol boat charged at *Flying Fish*, dropping eight charges very close and causing serious damage. The next night, Donaho played tag with the patrol boat, firing two torpedoes at it, achieving one hit. "We watched it sink," Donaho reported. On the morning of September 4, at dawn, Donaho closed another patrol boat on the surface. It opened fire on *Flying Fish* with a 3-inch gun. Donaho cleared all personnel from the bridge, then closed to 600 yards and fired a torpedo. It missed. As the patrol boat charged in, Donaho dived. *Flying Fish* went down with a terrific angle. The patrol boat dropped eight charges, all close.

Two destroyers joined in the hunt. They pinned *Flying Fish* down for four and a half hours, dropping fifty-four depth charges, many of them very close. Donaho went deep—to 350 feet. In order to maintain depth, he held the damaged *Flying Fish* at an 18-degree up-angle, making standing almost impossible. Finally, he shook the destroyers and slipped off into the darkness, having survived one of the worst depth-chargings of the war. Donaho requested permission to leave station early. It was granted.

On return to Pearl Harbor, English gave Donaho a hearty "well done" and a Navy Cross. He credited Donaho with two hits on a battleship but picked nits in the endorsement, criticizing Donaho for firing not six but four torpedoes at the battleship and for failing to fire at the two destroyers when he surfaced later that night. Enrique Haskins, who won a Silver Star for this patrol, left the boat, returning to the States to command the school boat *R-10*. He was replaced by another *Flying Fish* officer, John Franklin Walling.

* * *

Wahoo was a new boat with a new skipper, Marvin Granville ("Pinky") Kennedy. He patrolled Truk after *Flying Fish*. Kennedy, who had been exec to Weary Wilkins on the first patrol of *Narwhal*, had a fine wardroom. His exec was Richard Hetherington O'Kane, and the third officer was George William Grider.

Like Donc Donaho, Pinky Kennedy ran a taut ship. He was a "perfectionist and a slave driver," Grider wrote later. After commissioning and shakedown, Kennedy had trained his crew relentlessly. "We were on the fine edge of exhaustion all around," Grider wrote, "training all day and working all night." To complicate matters, Kennedy did not have complete faith in O'Kane. O'Kane struck Grider, and possibly Kennedy, as a young man who was "overly garrulous and potentially unstable."

Off Truk, Kennedy's first target was a lone freighter. He fired three torpedoes, missed, and, in Grider's words, "kept going," fearful of a counterattack from the air. "After the exhausting months of drills," Grider wrote, ". . . it was demoralizing to creep away submerged from that first target." A week later, while on the surface at night, Kennedy found his second target—another lone freighter. He chose to make a cautious submerged periscope attack and fired four torpedoes, one at a time. The first three missed; the last hit. Kennedy claimed a freighter of 6,400 tons. English later credited it, but postwar analysis showed no sinking at this time and place.

A short time later, Kennedy missed two of the best targets of the war. The first was the aircraft tender *Chiyoda*, which came along without an escort. "The Japs were just begging someone to knock off this tender," Kennedy later wrote, "but it was not our lucky day"; Kennedy did not have time to get into position to shoot. The next was an aircraft carrier which Kennedy believed to be *Ryujo*, sunk six weeks earlier in the Solomons. Whatever it was, it came into sight, escorted by two destroyers. Kennedy later wrote in his report:

Made approach which, upon final analysis, lacked aggressiveness and skill . . . watched the best target we could ever hope to find go over the hill untouched. . . . Had I but required a more rigorous and alert watch we might have picked it up sooner. Had I correctly estimated the situation and made a more aggressive approach we could have gotten in a shot.

When *Wahoo* returned to Pearl Harbor, English was furious. "Opportunities to attack an enemy carrier," he wrote in Kennedy's patrol report endorsement, "are few and must be exploited to the limit with due acceptance of the hazards involved."

Richard Cross Lake patrolled Truk in *Albacore*, another new boat, and he too missed opportunities to attack Japanese men-of-war. The first was a small Japanese submarine, which turned directly toward *Albacore* at the last minute. The second—and the heart-stopping one—was a *Zuikaku*-class carrier picked up on October 9, escorted by one heavy cruiser and a destroyer. Lake closed to 8,000 yards, but he was detected. The cruiser and destroyer pinned *Albacore* down, dropping eleven close depth charges which badly shook the boat. Lake prepared a sonar attack from deep submergence, but exploding depth charges and screws from the cruiser and destroyer "spoiled" the sonar bearings and he withheld fire.

Amberjack, commanded by another new skipper, John Archibald Bole, Jr., patrolled the sea lanes south of Truk, dropping down as far as Rabaul and Kavieng. Guided by a flow of Ultras, Bole and his exec, Chick Clarey (ex-*Dolphin*), picked up a battleship escorted by a cruiser. In a night periscope attack, Bole fired four torpedoes at the cruiser and then got set to swing the boat and fire four stern tubes at the battleship. But Bole had "badly underestimated" the speed of the cruiser, and all torpedoes missed. Alerted, the battleship turned a searchlight on *Amberjack*'s periscope. Believing the battleship would zig away before he could fire his stern tubes, Bole fired his last remaining other two bow tubes at the battleship. Both missed.

Continuing this extremely aggressive patrol, Bole later sank a 2,000-ton transport. Then, off Kavieng Harbor, Bole fired four torpedoes at long range into the anchorage. One damaged a freighter; others sank the huge 19,000-ton whale factory, *Tonan Maru II*, the largest ship sunk by a U.S. submarine to date. (However, she sank in shallow water and was salvaged, towed to Japan, and returned to service.) Low on fuel and torpedoes, Bole followed *Trout* into Brisbane for refit and replenishment. Christie, who endorsed the patrol report, gave Bole high marks.

While these boats were patrolling Truk, Nimitz ordered the diversionary commando raid on Makin Island. The troops picked for the raid were all marines, Companies A and B of the 2nd Raider Battalion, commanded by Colonel Evans F. Carlson. (One of his officers was

Major James Roosevelt, son of the President.) In all, the marines totaled 211—13 officers and 198 men. Their transportation would be Bill Brockman's *Nautilus* and *Argonaut*, recently arrived from her modernization at Mare Island, now commanded by Jack Pierce, who had made two pioneering Alaskan patrols commanding S-23. The two huge submarines were temporarily converted to "troop transports" by removing all torpedoes except those in the tubes and installing extra air conditioning and tiers of bunks. They were formed into a task group commanded by their division commander, John Haines.

Everything was thrown together in great haste, and *Nautilus* and *Argonaut* got under way for Makin on August 8, the day after the Guadalcanal landing. Living conditions were far from satisfactory. The air conditioning was not adequate. Belowdecks it was sweltering, and the marines were either wilting or seasick. To keep them in shape, Haines permitted them to go topside in small batches for ten-minute basks in the sun.

The submarines arrived off Makin August 16, and the following morning at about three o'clock, Carlson launched his marines in rubber boats. Though they had rehearsed it before leaving Pearl Harbor, the debarkation was a fiasco. Seas swamped the boats, drowning most of the outboard motors. The few boats that ran towed the others as best they could, abandoning their carefully conceived landing pattern. In the darkness, Colonel Carlson lost sight of his "flag boat" and had to go ashore in someone else's. Somehow, the Japanese had been forewarned or were exceptionally alert, perhaps because of the U.S. attack on Guadalcanal. There were snipers hiding in trees. Cascading through the surf, the Raiders got ashore in helter-skelter formation, in front of the Japanese rather than behind as planned. The reception was warm. Communications between the marines and the submarines was primitive and sporadic.

While the marines were fighting ashore, Brockman, on request, used *Nautilus*'s two huge guns to advantage, lobbing 65 rounds blind into the harbor, 7 miles away. By great fortune, his shells struck two Japanese ships, one freighter and one small patrol craft. They were in the harbor and in maneuvering to avoid his fire had steamed directly into it. Although marines saw these ships destroyed, postwar analysis did not credit Brockman with any sinkings at Makin Island.

That night, Brockman and Pierce attempted to recover the marines. The recovery was a disaster also. The short-cycle surf overturned the boats and ripped weapons from the men's hands. Only seven of nineteen boats made it. Many men were severely wounded. The wardrooms of *Nautilus* and *Argonaut* became operating rooms. Brockman and Pierce spent the whole night trying to find the rest of the landing party. When dawn came, they remained on the surface and moved in close to the beach, recovering two or three more boats and sending another in with five marines and a line for throwing guns and arms ashore. At that point Brockman and Pierce were driven under by Japanese aircraft. The rescue boat was strafed and its five volunteer marines were killed.

The two submarines waited submerged all day, pinned down by aircraft. After dark, guided by signal light from Carlson, they inched in toward the beach again. By midnight, all but thirty marines were accounted for. These, it was believed, were dead. (In fact, nine were still alive. They were captured and beheaded.)

The Makin raid was acclaimed a great "victory" and a "brilliant exploit" by the U.S. Navy and Marine Corps public relations machinery. Medals were handed out left and right. John Haines—the oldest submariner yet to make a war patrol—received a Navy Cross. For a time, Colonel Carlson and Major Roosevelt were household names. Haines later boasted that because of the raid a task force of Japanese carriers, transports, and destroyers going to reinforce Guadalcanal were diverted to the Gilberts, thus achieving the primary objective of the mission. However, Jasper Holmes, who knew the location of most Japanese naval vessels, wrote, "It is doubtful that any Japanese forces were diverted from Guadalcanal."

As Jasper Holmes also pointed out, the raid, in the long run, was deleterious to the Pacific war effort. In subsequent months, the Japanese, having been presented with a dramatic demonstration of how weak their defenses in the Gilberts actually were, took steps to remedy that gap. Later, when the U.S. Marines stormed ashore at Tarawa, another island in the Gilberts slightly to the south, they met near disaster. In a ghastly beachhead slaughter, over 1,000 marines and sailors were killed and twice that number wounded.

Patrols to Empire, East China Sea, and Alaskan Waters, July through October

The diversion of forces to Truk seriously impeded the submarine war against Japanese shipping. During the four-month period July

EMPIRE, EAST CHINA SEA, AND ALASKAN PATROLS 319

through October, English could mount only twenty war patrols to Empire, East China Sea, and Alaskan waters. Six of them were conducted by the antiques of Squadron Four, feeling the strain of war.

Narwhal, commanded by Weary Wilkins making his third patrol, was no longer leaking oil, but she was seriously in need of modernization. Nevertheless she went to heretofore unexplored territory: the island of Etorofu, northeast of Hokkaido, the northernmost of the main Japanese home islands.

Aided by his exec, Frank De Vere Latta, Wilkins conducted a most aggressive patrol. Penetrating the Sea of Okhotsk, he boldly sank two small interisland freighters and shifted southward to patrol off northeast Honshu, where the waters were dense with shipping. Wilkins fired at one juicy target, but a torpedo prematured twelve seconds after leaving the tube, badly jarring *Narwhal* and alerting the target, which immediately evaded. An hour later, Wilkins sank the 3,000-ton *Meiwa Maru* and fired at another ship. Aircraft and surface vessels counterattacked. Wilkins counted—and logged—124 depth charges, a record; one of his crewmen, unnerved by the charges, finally went berserk. A week later, Wilkins sank the 2,500-ton passenger freighter *Bifuku Maru*. He was attacked by a group of Japanese destroyers but managed to evade. Back at Pearl Harbor, English sent *Narwhal* off for a long period of modernization, while Wilkins went to a job in the Bureau of Personnel.

Pompano remained skipperless for a while after Lew Parks went to English's staff. Then, who should arrive but Willis Manning Thomas, class of 1931. In prewar days, Thomas had served on *Pompano* as exec to Parks and then, like many other submariners, had gone off to recommission one of the fifty old destroyers loaned to Britain. Now he was back. Even though Thomas had made no war patrols, both Slade Cutter and *Pompano*'s third officer, David Rikart Connole, were "absolutely delighted" to have him for skipper.

This third patrol for *Pompano* was conducted off Honshu, where the old boat very nearly came to grief. On August 9, she was caught on the surface by a destroyer, which promptly opened fire. Thomas crash-dived, and the destroyer closed for a savage depth-charge attack. An engine exhaust valve sprung loose. Seawater poured in. *Pompano* sank below 250 feet, with water rising over the engine-room floor plates. Thomas put on more speed and started the pumps. The noise brought on another savage depth-charging. Minutes later, *Pompano* ran aground submerged, wiping off her sonar heads.

Thomas believed that his ship was doomed. Like Dave Hurt's *Perch*, she seemed trapped in shallow water with no hope of getting away. Thomas called Cutter and Connole separately to his cabin and told them quietly to prepare the boat for scuttling.

Cutter and Connole did not want to give up the ship without a last fight, and so they prevailed on Thomas to cancel the scuttling and make one more try. It was successful. Surfacing the boat a mere 1,000 yards from the Japanese coast, Thomas was able to clear the area and elude the destroyer.

The third antique to put to sea was Spike Hottel's *Cuttlefish*, now commanded by Elliott Eugene ("Steam") Marshall, another of the class of 1931. He wound up with two execs, Carter Lowe Bennett and John Day Gerwick, who had been on *Argonaut*'s first patrol off Midway. Bennett and Gerwick shared a bottle of bourbon one night and divided the duties: the senior man, Bennett, to be exec and navigator, Gerwick to be engineering officer.

Off Japan, Steam Marshall's first contact with the Japanese came in a near collision with a destroyer. The two ships met, nose to nose, about midnight. Marshall crash-dived. On the way down, the conning tower hatch failed to close properly. Carter Bennett and the quartermaster, Richard F. Breckenbridge, fought their way through a stream of water; by the time they got the hatch shut there was three feet of water in the conning tower.

Later, Marshall, bedeviled by heavy seas, attacked two ships, the first a 10,000-ton steamer and the second a 19,600-ton *Tonan Maru*-type whale factory, converted to a tanker. Marshall fired three torpedoes at the steamer and was certain it sank, but to make sure, he shot an extra torpedo. He believed he sank the whale-factory tanker. On return to Pearl Harbor, English credited Marshall with both ships, totaling 29,600 tons, but postwar records confirmed neither of the big sinkings.

English was generous with awards. Marshall received a Navy Cross, Bennett and Gerwick Silver Stars. In addition, Quartermaster Breckenbridge received a Navy Cross for "extraordinary heroism" in remaining in the conning tower and helping Bennett close the hatch. This was one of three Navy Crosses awarded to enlisted men in submarines during World War II.

Cuttlefish returned from this third patrol in atrocious mechanical shape. As was her sister ship *Cachalot*, the fourth antique, which had made a luckless patrol in the Aleutians, she was withdrawn from combat service and sent to New London to serve as a school boat. Marshall and Gerwick went to new construction, while Bennett, whom Marshall had qualified for command, went to the PCO pool.

The fifth antique, *Dolphin*, again commanded by Royal Rutter, followed *Cachalot* into Alaskan waters. On the way, she encountered a terrifying North Pacific storm and for days was buffeted by huge seas. Going into Dutch Harbor for voyage repairs, Rutter was galvanized by a cry over the PA system, "Torpedoes dead ahead!" Rutter said later, "I hit the bridge just in time to see two parallel torpedo tracks.... We thread-needled them and got out fast."

Rutter made a long patrol in the Sea of Okhotsk, where Wilkins had taken *Narwhal* some weeks earlier, but found nothing worth a torpedo. On return to Pearl Harbor, *Dolphin* was assigned to training duty at Pearl Harbor and later followed *Cachalot* and *Cuttlefish* to New London. Royal Rutter went to the PCO pool.

The sixth antique, *Nautilus*, having been reconverted for combat following the Makin raid, patrolled off the east coast of Japan. Her skipper, Bill Brockman, ever aggressive, launched his cruise by blasting two fishing trawlers off the face of the sea with his huge deck guns. On the night of September 27, he attacked a six-ship convoy, firing both torpedoes and deck gun into the Japanese force. When one freighter turned to ram, Brockman, still on the surface, countered with gunfire and torpedo fire, sinking the ship, *Ramon Maru*, 5,000 tons. In the ensuing days he sank two more big freighters, totaling 7,500 tons. All three ships were confirmed in postwar records.

On return to Pearl Harbor, English decided that *Nautilus* and her sister ships *Narwhal* and *Argonaut* were too big and clumsy for war patrol in Empire waters. From then on the three old boats were reserved for special missions like the Makin raid and for landing guerrillas, spies, ammunition, and supplies in the Philippines.

The other fourteen patrols from Pearl Harbor to Empire and East China Sea waters during July through October were conducted by the newer boats. One of these, *Haddock*, commanded by Arthur Howard Taylor, was equipped with a new type of radar known as the SJ. The first radar set carried by U.S. submarines—the SD—was nondirectional, purely an aircraft warning device. The SJ, a major improvement technically, was a "surface search" radar, designed specifically for picking up enemy shipping. It provided exact range and bearing, enabling the submarine to "see" at night or in rain, fog, or snow.

For a historic trial of submarine radar, English sent Taylor to the lower East China Sea. The radar helped him sink two Japanese ships. Off Formosa on August 12, Taylor made a conventional daylight periscope attack against a large freighter, inflicting damage. That night, he tracked the damaged ship by radar, made an end around and carried out a successful night surface attack. The ship was never identified, but Taylor was credited with 4,000 tons. Two weeks later, in the Formosa Strait, Taylor's radar picked up another ship. He made another end around and waited. When the ship caught up, Taylor fired four torpedoes. All missed. He fired two more, sinking *Teishun Maru*, 2,250 tons. On return to Pearl Harbor, English credited Taylor with sinking three ships for 24,000 tons, but postwar analysis reduced this total to two ships for 6,251 tons.

This was not an overwhelming score. However, during much of the patrol the SJ was out of commission or calibration. Nor had they had much time to practice with the set. Even though it had not performed consistently, Taylor was enthusiastic. The SJ had obvious potential, both for attack and for navigating in tricky enemy waters. As fast as SJ radar became available to the submarine force it was installed in the boats, and extra technicians, skilled in radar repair, were added to the ship's table of organization.

Of the skippers departing Pearl Harbor in August on first patrol, one was destined to win instant fame and glory. This was mild-mannered, soft-spoken Thomas Burton Klakring, commanding a new boat, *Guardfish*. Klakring's exec was Herman Joseph Kossler, a big, affable officer, Klakring's opposite in temperament. The two men got along famously.

On the way out to Pearl Harbor, *Guardfish* nearly came to grief, Klakring remembered. "In Panama, at Cristobal on the Atlantic side, there was a minefield with a narrow gate, maybe 150 feet wide, operated by the army. When you gave a certain signal, the army opened the gate for a brief period. Very brief. Then you barreled through. I gave the proper signal and rang up flank speed. Something malfunctioned. The gate didn't open. At the last minute, I backed full on both engines to avoid hitting the gate. The bow swerved. The next thing I knew, we were backing into the minefield. Before we could get out of there, we sliced a mine in half with the port propeller. For some inexplicable reason, it didn't explode. The force of the blow even bent the propeller. It was a terrible, terrifying experience."

English assigned Klakring to the northeast coast of Honshu; it was dense with shipping of all kinds. Nosing into the area, Klakring picked up a large naval auxiliary with an escort and fired three torpedoes. All missed. An escort held *Guardfish* down with a desultory, ineffectual depth-charging until the auxiliary was beyond range. Klakring then engaged two fishing trawlers with his deck gun and sank them both.

In the days following, Klakring seemed to spot a ship nearly every day—or hour. One reason was that he maneuvered *Guardfish* extremely close to shore in order to get between the beach and the close-in shipping lanes.

"This was a difficult technique to master," Klakring said later. "In the early morning, after we got our battery charge in, we made a high-speed run at the beach, sort of groping toward the mountainous coast in the pitch dark. There were tricky currents—some northbound, some southbound. We got so we could time it just right. Get right in there on the beach just about daybreak when we had to submerge. Then we were in ideal position."

Within a space of eleven days, Klakring believed he sank six fat vessels. Four of these, he thought, went down in one day, September 4. One was a freighter anchored inside a harbor. Klakring fired from a range in excess of 7,500 yards. It was the longest shot of the war that resulted in a sinking.

When *Guardfish* returned to Midway for refit, Bob English was ecstatic. Klakring, considered by most an engineering specialist of modest promise, had turned out to be a submarine force commander's dream. English gladly and uncritically credited him with what he claimed, six big ships for 50,000 tons—four of these (34,000 tons) sunk in a single day. From a tonnage standpoint, this bag was nearly twice that achieved by any submarine in any of the three forces: Pearl Harbor, Brisbane, or Fremantle. No one had sunk six ships on a single patrol; no one had sunk four in a single day. Klakring received a Navy Cross, Kossler a Silver Star.

In addition, English authorized a rare event for the submarine force, a press conference. War correspondents regularly went to sea and interviewed surface-ship officers and men, but up to then they had been more or less barred from the submarine force, which they had dubbed "The Silent Service." There were two reasons. First was security: the submarine force, fighting in Japanese waters, did not want inadvertently to reveal operational or technical secrets; in particular, submariners wanted to safeguard the secrets of Ultra, the magnetic exploder, and the fact that Japanese depth charges were set to explode too shallow. The second reason was political: nobody wanted the press digging deep into submarine force problems—nonaggressive skippers, malfunctioning and scarce torpedoes, and the failure to stop the Japanese forces at Manila, Java, Midway, and the Solomons.

The press conference—heavily censored—gave rise to another submarine legend that died hard. Herman Kossler remembered its origin. "One Sunday, we came in very close to the Japanese coast. On the chart, we saw a notation: 'race track.' Through the periscope, we saw a train crossing a trestle. We could see people on the train, all dressed up as if they were off on a picnic. Somebody in the conning tower made a feeble joke: 'Maybe they're going to the races.'"

During the press conference, Klakring, having a little fun, recalled the race track and told reporters that the officers on *Guardfish* "placed some bets on the ponies." Said Kossler, "I could have killed him for saying that . . . but, what the hell! We'd had a great patrol. He was entitled to spin a sea story if he wanted to. It was a good story—good for the morale back home." English was pleased. It was almost as good a stunt as shelling the Emperor's summer palace.

Guardfish thereafter became famous as the submarine that "watched the horse races." As the story was told and retold, it grew in drama and dimension. In the final version, it was said that *Guardfish* entered Tokyo Bay and watched horse races from there. The New York State Racing Commission appointed Klakring an honorary member. There was a "Klakring Day" at Pimlico racetrack. Stuck with the story, the *Guardfish* crew tired of denying it—or perhaps even came to believe it.*

The tonnage *Guardfish* sank was also exaggerated with the telling.

---

* When *Guardfish* arrived in New Orleans after the war, the *New Orleans States* newspaper headline read SUB WHOSE CREW SAW JAP HORSE RACE ARRIVES HERE. In the body of the story, a *Guardfish* crewman, Torpedoman Eugene Brewer, was quoted. "We were laying three or four miles off the coast of Honshu . . . and I was watching things through the periscope. There on the beach I saw horses running along, as in a race. We were that close."

Life magazine added 20,000 tons to what Klakring had claimed and published a long article on his first patrol under the subtitle, "U.S. sub patrols the Jap coast, watches Jap horse races and sinks 70,000 tons of shipping." In the postwar analysis, Klakring's tonnage score was reduced by about two thirds, to five ships for 16,600 tons.

Another Pearl Harbor boat operated close to the Japanese shores during the fall of 1942. Because of the torpedo shortage, John Behling Azer, commanding the new boat *Whale*, was ordered to lay mines off Kii Suido. It was the first such mission for any Pearl Harbor skipper, and it turned out to be a spine-chilling assignment.

The orders were to lay the mines 20 miles offshore, in fairly deep water. But Azer's exec, Fritz Harlfinger, who had come from S-32 in the Aleutians, observed that enemy ships were running close to shore and suggested that Azer plant the mines as far in as possible. Azer was hesitant, as would be any prudent man making his first submarine war patrol within spitting distance of the Japanese beach. Harlfinger pressed; Azer gave his consent. "We were a bunch of wild Indians in that wardroom," Harlfinger said later.

Whale planted her minefield very close to the beach—by moonlight. The next day they saw a convoy. Azer attacked, hoping to sink ships with his torpedoes or drive them into the minefield. As he was attacking, an escort charged in. Bedlam followed, with torpedoes, mines, and depth charges all going off at once. In the ensuing days, Azer and Harlfinger believed they had accounted for four freighters, and so radioed English. But postwar analysis discredited the entire claim.

On the way home, *Whale* was viciously attacked by a patrol craft and almost lost. The first salvo opened valves, flooding part of the boat and standing her on her tail with a tremendous up-angle. Said Harlfinger, "We barely held our own with the leaks. All available spare men were sent to the forward part of the boat in a desperate effort to regain an even keel. Charge after charge was dropped. We were pursued by the patrol boat for seventeen hours."

Finally, *Whale* got away.

Some of the old hands making second and third patrols turned in excellent results. Lawyer Bruton in *Greenling*—perhaps reacting to the criticism of his first two patrols—sank four confirmed ships for 20,000 tons and damaged a light carrier for 22,000 tons. Howard Gilmore in *Growler* sank four ships for 15,000 tons. Jesse Hull in *Finback* sank three ships for 22,000 tons and damaged two others for 14,000 tons. Bob Rice in *Drum* sank three for 13,000 tons.

On the whole, the newer boats going to Empire waters or the East China Sea on regular patrols sank twice as many ships as the boats going to Truk. There were more targets and—with experience—the skippers had learned where to look for them. Skippers felt more confident with Dick Voge handling operations. Antisubmarine measures near Japan were less intense. The deep-running defect in the Mark XIV had been cured. Now, when a torpedo was fired, it usually ran as directed. If the magnetic exploder worked (or if a skipper violated orders and set for contact hit), there was a good chance for a sinking.

Subversive Literature

Bob English had not distinguished himself in command of Submarines Pacific. He failed to organize a hardheaded and persistent strategic war against Japanese shipping in the home islands, allowing his submarines to be shunted to Alaska, Truk, and elsewhere on missions that produced little. He had ignored the Mark XIV torpedo problem, leaving it for Lockwood, a newcomer to the Pacific, to solve. His management of submarines during the Battle of Midway had been less than professional.

Few of his skippers respected him. One reason was that English continued to write negative and harsh endorsements for patrols—such as those conducted by Chester Bruton, Donc Donaho, and Bob Rice at Truk—that were aggressive yet unlucky or bedeviled by torpedo failures. The skippers resented being second-guessed by a man who had little understanding of the fleet submarine and who had never been on one in combat.

Art Taylor, the bright and aggressive skipper of *Haddock*, which had taken the first SJ radar into combat, was one submariner who could not contain his resentment. During his first war patrol, Taylor, like Doug Rhymes in Australia, wrote a poem.

Squat Div One

They're on their duff from morn till nite;
They're never wrong, they're always right;
To hear them talk they're in the fight—
Oh, yeah?

> A boat comes in off a patrol,
> The skipper tallies up his toll
> And writes it up for all concerned.
> He feels right proud of the job he's done,
> But the staffies say he shoulda used his gun!
> Three fish for a ship of two score ton?
> Outrageous! He should have used but one!
> A tanker sunk in smoke and flame—
> But still he's open wide to blame.
> His fish were set for twenty right—
> That proves he didn't want to fight!
> Oh, yeah?
>
> The freighter he sunk settled by the stern—
> With depth set right she'd split in two!
> So tell me, what is the skipper to do?
> He's on the spot and doing his best,
> But that's not enough by the acid test.
> The staff must analyze his case
> And pick it apart to save their face.
> Just because you sink some ships
> Doesn't mean you win the chips—
> You've got to do it according to Plan;
> Otherwise you're on the pan!
>
> So here's to the staff with work so tough
> In writing their endorsement guff—
> Whether the war is lost or won
> Depends entirely on "Squat Div One."
> Oh, yeah? *

Taylor made a typed copy of his poem, and it began to circulate slowly. First to read it was Bernard Francis McMahon, a tall handsome officer who was making a PCO cruise with Taylor. When *Haddock* returned to Midway for refit alongside *Fulton* (Squadron Eight), Taylor showed a copy to one of English's staff officers who was in Midway. The officer requested a copy. Taylor sent it via John Murphy, whom English had relieved on *Tambor* and who was then operations officer of Squadron Eight. Spike Hottel, whom English had relieved on *Cuttlefish* and who was then torpedo officer of Squadron Eight, received a copy and directed a yeoman to have it mimeographed. One of these went to Bob Rice on *Drum*. Another

---

* Quoted by permission of Arthur Howard Taylor, Rear Admiral, U.S.N. (Ret.).

copy went to Stoney Roper, commanding Squadron Eight. He did not think it funny but took no action to suppress it.

Eventually, copies of the poem wound up in submarine headquarters in Pearl Harbor. When Bob English read it, he was enraged. He immediately addressed this classified letter to the commanders of Squadrons Four (Babe Brown), Eight (Roper), and Ten (Gin Styer):

Subject: *Subversive Literature*
Enclosure: *(A) Copy of piece of subversive literature*

1.   The enclosure represents either a misdirected sense of humor or a state of morale on the part of the author which reflects discreditably on submarine standards. It is as damaging to discipline as any piece of subversive literature which has appeared for distribution in a naval organization, particularly since it evidently was prepared by a member of the naval service having access to confidential correspondence.

2.   The origin of the enclosure is not known, but from its text it would appear that it came from someone in the Submarine Force, Pacific Fleet. Whatever its origin, it was found in circulation in this force and its introduction indicates a sympathetic attitude to it on the part of some officers. It is needless to say that propaganda of this nature, if allowed to generate and grow, will eventually undermine the high state of morale and discipline of the Submarine Force.

3.   Squadron commanders are directed to investigate the source and intent of the subject enclosure, the extent of its distribution, and report the conclusions to the Commander, Submarine Force, Pacific Fleet.

When this demand for an official investigation landed on Roper's desk, he immediately launched one. A week later, he returned a nine-page single-spaced report to English, naming Taylor as the culprit, detailing the roles of Murphy and Hottel, and containing written statements from all three officers. Roper concluded that while Taylor committed a serious error in judgment, the error came from a misdirected sense of humor. Hottel, he said, had helped distribute the poem because he resented having been relieved of command. Murphy, Roper went on, made a grave mistake in not keeping him [Roper] fully informed as to how extensively the poem had been distributed.

Upon receipt of Roper's report, English ordered Roper to relieve Taylor of command of *Haddock*. Taylor recalled later, "Captain

Roper, God bless him, really carried the torch for me in a series of messages back and forth with Admiral English. Just two days before *Haddock* was due to sail he told me he was happy to tell me I would keep my command."

Soon after the investigation, Roper himself was returned to the States to command the heavy cruiser *New Orleans*. Willard Downes fleeted up to command Squadron Eight. But in all this foolishness Bob English was the real loser.

Battles of Esperance and Santa Cruz

None of the submarine activity at Truk had made an appreciable dent in the Japanese reinforcements bound for the Solomons. Except for the light carrier *Taiyo (Otaka)* damaged by Red Ramage, carriers, battleships, cruisers, and most of the troop transports and freighters got by unscathed.

On October 11–12, the Japanese and U.S. naval surface forces met again in the Solomons in what would be known as the Battle of Esperance. Naval historian Morison wrote that "it might have been called the Battle of Mutual Errors." In the darkness, both sides became confused, misidentified ships, gave orders to fire, and then gave orders to withhold fire. The Japanese lost the heavy cruiser *Furutaka* and the destroyer *Fubuki*, and the heavy cruiser *Aoba* was severely damaged. The United States lost a destroyer, *Duncan*, and a light cruiser, *Boise*, was badly damaged.

After this battle, Admiral Nimitz gave a dark estimate of the situation. "It now appears that we are unable to control the sea in the Guadalcanal area. Thus our supply of the positions will only be done at great expense to us. The situation is not hopeless, but it is certainly critical." Feeling the need for "a more aggressive commander," Nimitz relieved Admiral Ghormley, replacing him with Admiral Halsey, recovered from his case of shingles. Halsey took over from Ghormley at Noumea, he said later, with feelings of "astonishment, apprehension, and regret."

Halsey had no sooner assumed command than he was faced with a major sea battle, later known as the Battle of Santa Cruz. Admiral Yamamoto, with headquarters at Truk, was determined, once and for all, to blast the U.S. Navy out of the Solomons. For this purpose he had assembled the largest Japanese naval force since the Battle of

Midway. It consisted of four carriers (*Shokaku, Zuikaku, Zuiho,* and *Junyo*), five battleships, fourteen cruisers, and forty-four destroyers. To oppose the force, Halsey had *Enterprise* (back in action, but still not completely repaired) and *Hornet*, plus one battleship, six cruisers, and fourteen destroyers.

The battle, fought on October 26–27, was yet another devastating defeat for the U.S. Navy. The only remaining undamaged carrier, *Hornet*, was lost to air attack and the destroyer *Porter* to submarine attack. *Enterprise* was severely damaged, as was the battleship *South Dakota* and the cruiser *San Juan*. The loss of *Hornet* left the United States only two carriers in the Pacific—*Saratoga* and *Enterprise*, both damaged. The Japanese lost no ships. However, the carriers *Shokaku* and *Zuiho* were damaged, as were a cruiser and two destroyers.

Japanese submarines, prowling the Solomons in October, scored only minor successes compared with their September performance. On October 20, *I-176* believed she had torpedoed a battleship; her target turned out to be the cruiser *Chester*. *Chester* survived the attack, but she was put out of action for many months. After the battle of Santa Cruz, *I-21* found the brand new battleship *Washington* and attacked. One of her torpedoes was right on target but exploded prematurely 400 yards short. But for that, *Washington* might have gone to the bottom.

October, November, and December Patrols to Truk

After Halsey relieved Ghormley, he requested that, in addition to the submarine blockade of Truk, Nimitz send more fleet boats to operate from Brisbane, augmenting Squadron Two, moved around from Albany. Nimitz concurred. He ordered English to send the bulk of his modern submarines—most of Willard Downes's Squadron Eight and Gin Styer's Squadron Ten—to Brisbane along with the tenders *Fulton* and *Sperry*.

English complied with these orders as rapidly as possible. In October, four boats, *Tarpon, Plunger, Pollack,* and *Stingray*, maintained the Truk blockade, and English sent three boats—*Silversides, Growler,* and *Flying Fish*—to Brisbane by way of Truk. *Plunger*, damaged off Truk, made an unscheduled stop at Brisbane. *Grayling*, an exchange boat bound for Fremantle, patrolled off Truk on the way. The next month, November, English sent five boats to Brisbane by way of Truk: *Gato, Wahoo, Tuna, Grouper,* and *Albacore. Fulton* and *Sperry,* loaded with torpedoes and spare parts, sailed from Pearl Harbor in early November, reaching Brisbane in mid-month. In December, English sent another three boats, plus *Argonaut* and *Nautilus* for special missions.

Counting the boats bound for Brisbane and Fremantle, plus those returning to Pearl Harbor, English mounted a total of eighteen patrols off Truk, or to the south toward the Solomons, during the period October through December. They hunted more "wounded bears"—again the heavy carrier *Shokaku* and the light carrier *Zuiho*—from the battle of Santa Cruz and other engagements. They had little luck.

Dave White in *Plunger,* returning to combat after a second long period in overhaul, patrolled south of Truk toward the Solomons. He received an Ultra directing him to intercept a Japanese task force. A few hours later, while cruising on the surface at night, White picked up what he thought was an island on his new SJ radar. It turned out to be a *Natori*-class cruiser.

Exec David Hayward McClintock was standing watch on the bridge. In a snap decision, McClintock fired four torpedoes at the cruiser, believing he had scored for damage. Then White dived and went deep. At 130 feet, he hit bottom with a bone-jarring crash. The grounding badly damaged the hull and wiped off the sonar heads. When White radioed his plight, he was ordered into Brisbane for repairs, having been on station only five days.

In his endorsement, Christie went out of his way to congratulate McClintock for the snap firing but criticized White for precipitous diving after the attack, urging skippers to remain on the surface after a night attack and make repeated SJ radar attacks. In his endorsement, Admiral Halsey also congratulated McClintock.

Tarpon, returning to service after long overhaul with a new skipper, Thomas Lincoln Wogan, who had previously commanded *S-34* on an arduous Alaska patrol, patrolled the sea lanes south of Truk. One of the junior officers on *Tarpon* this trip was William Robert Anderson, class of 1943 (graduated, June 1942 on the accelerated wartime program) and fresh from sub school, which had now been telescoped to three months. (Many years later, Anderson would achieve fame as the skipper who guided the first nuclear-powered submarine, *Nautilus*, beneath the Arctic ice cap.)

"Wogan was extremely ambitious and very capable," Anderson said later. "But he had trouble putting it all together. We were almost run down by a tremendous convoy—ten ships, three destroyer escorts—going to the Solomons. It came right out of the blue, a complete surprise. Wogan shot some torpedoes but didn't hit a thing. The escorts held us down until the convoy was out of range. Wogan was plenty disappointed."

So were Bob English and the Pearl Harbor high command. The endorsements stated, "The fifth war patrol of *Tarpon* was most disappointing. The attack on November 7 was not pressed home. . . . [Wogan] failed to take advantage of a golden opportunity."

Raymond John Moore patrolled Truk in another old Asiatic boat returned from overhaul, *Stingray*. Moore, too, had trouble getting it all together. He made contact with twenty-one enemy vessels, including a light aircraft carrier which he attacked twice on November 13, firing two torpedoes on each attack. All missed. He was credited with damage to one freighter. The attack was conducted by Moore's exec, Paul Edward Summers, a youngster from the class of 1936.

Moore, relieved of command, said later, "It was at my own request." He spent most of the rest of the war at the General Motors engine factory in Cleveland.

Donc Donaho set off in *Flying Fish* for Truk and Brisbane with his new exec, John Walling, and a new face in the wardroom, Charles Wilkes Styer, Jr., son of Gin Styer, then en route to Brisbane in *Sperry*. After his fearless attack on the battleship at Truk, Donaho was held in new regard by his fellow skippers.

It was another frustrating patrol. On November 14, Donaho received an Ultra directing him to intercept an enemy task force. He found it—an awesome formation of four heavy cruisers and one light cruiser escorted by five destroyers—dived boldly beneath the destroyer screen, and fired six torpedoes at the second heavy cruiser in line from a range of 1,600 yards. All missed. On November 30, another Ultra moved him to intercept Japanese vessels off New Georgia. He found them, too, but was unable to gain a firing position. Admiral Halsey wrote in his endorsement, "This [patrol] shows how radio intelligence may be capitalized on. The fact that the contacts did not culminate in successful attacks does not detract from the utility of such procedure."

Chronically dissatisfied with his wardroom, Donaho asked that his new exec, John Walling, be relieved. Walling returned to the States and commanded school boats.

Pinky Kennedy's *Wahoo* also had a couple of new faces in the wardroom. One was Mush Morton, a PCO observer, whom Babe Brown had "saved" after his trouble on old *Dolphin*. The other was John Bradford Griggs III, son of English's chief of staff.

Below Truk, Kennedy found a southbound convoy of three ships, escorted by a destroyer. He first tried to attack the destroyer, on the theory that once it was out of the way he could pick off the three heavily laden freighters one at a time. However, he was unable to attain firing position on the destroyer, so he shot at the largest freighter, *Kamoi Maru*, 5,300 tons. It sank.

Immediately, the destroyer charged over *Wahoo* and dropped about forty depth charges, none close. Kennedy went deep and evaded, remaining submerged until sunset. When he came up for a periscope observation, he saw one freighter going off in the distance and the other stopped to pick up survivors from *Kamoi Maru*. The destroyer was zipping back and forth on patrol.

Mush Morton and Kennedy's exec, Dick O'Kane, urged him to mount a second attack. After dark, on the surface, using the new SJ radar, they argued, it would be easy to knock off the freighter. With luck, they might also get the destroyer. However, Kennedy had had enough. As George Grider wrote later, with a note of disappointment, "We left without a try at the other freighters."

When *Wahoo* arrived in Brisbane, the crew, Grider noted, was "more discouraged" than it had been at the end of the first patrol. "The *Wahoo* . . . was not making much of a record, and we knew it. We . . . had waited in the wrong places at the wrong time like unlucky fishermen; . . . we still felt thoroughly discouraged."

Pinky Kennedy lost his command—to Mush Morton. Later, Kennedy wrote that he was relieved because his superior believed that "a more aggressive conduct of the first two war patrols would have resulted in more enemy sinkings. In retrospect, I can see he was right, but I was not so philosophical about it at the time." Kennedy went on to command the destroyer *Guest*, on which he served with distinction, winning a second Silver Star.

* * *

Dick Lake in *Albacore,* making his second patrol, attacked several transports and destroyers, none successfully until December 18. On that day, while cruising off the north coast of New Guinea, Lake picked up what he thought to be one transport escorted by one destroyer. Closing to 2,000 yards, he fired three torpedoes at both. The "destroyer" blew up and exploded in a mass of flames. The freighter appeared to sink too. In Brisbane, Lake was credited with a destroyer and a freighter. Later it was realized that the "destroyer" was actually the light cruiser *Tenryu,* 3,300 tons. *Tenryu* was the second Japanese cruiser sunk by U.S. submarines in the war, after the heavy cruiser *Kako,* 8,800 tons, sunk by Dinty Moore in *S-44.*

The last wave going to Brisbane did better. These boats were skippered by old hands. Chester Bruton, having just completed a dazzling patrol in *Greenling* off the coast of Japan (four ships sunk, one light carrier damaged), sank four ships on the way to Brisbane, including an old 800-ton destroyer serving as an escort. C. C. Kirkpatrick, returning *Triton* from overhaul, was sent first to Wake Island to serve as a "beacon" for a U.S. carrier attack on that place; then, on the way to Brisbane, he sank two ships for 6,500 tons. (One was an Ultra which showed up right on the dot, with *Triton* in perfect position.) Burt Klakring in *Guardfish,* who bravely attempted to penetrate the harbor at Kavieng, sank three ships, including the fleet destroyer *Hakaze.* Bill Brockman in *Nautilus,* en route to a special assignment to evacuate twenty-nine Catholic missionaries from Bougainville, sank a small freighter, damaged a tanker and a freighter, and fired two torpedoes down the throat at an attacking destroyer.

When two of the old hands arrived in Brisbane, they had new orders. C. C. Kirkpatrick, who had been credited with ten ships sunk for 44,600 tons in three patrols, went to Washington for the exalted job of aide to Admiral King. Chester Bruton, then considered the leading scorer in the submarine force with eleven ships sunk for 82,600 tons and two damaged for 31,000 in four patrols, was promoted to command a division in Willard Downes's Squadron Eight.

November and December Patrols to Empire and East China Sea Waters

The transfer of Squadrons Eight and Ten to Brisbane, plus the decision to retire *Cachalot, Cuttlefish, Dolphin, Nautilus,* and *Narwhal* from regular patrol, drastically reduced Bob English's submarine force and virtually brought the war against Japanese shipping in Empire waters to a halt. In November and December, English mounted only ten Empire and East China Sea patrols. Because so many torpedoes had been sent to Brisbane, most boats departed with less than a full load. Three were assigned to lay minefields. Three were antiques: *Pike, Porpoise,* and *Pollack.* All ten ran into foul winter weather.

The three boats assigned to lay mines were *Drum, Trigger,* and a new boat, *Sunfish. Drum* had a new skipper, Barney McMahon. His exec was Manning Kimmel, climbing the wardroom ladder. On the way to his area, McMahon stumbled blindly on a major target: the light aircraft carrier *Ryuho,* with destroyer escorts, bound for Truk on her maiden voyage. (A hard-luck ship, she had been hit while being worked on in Tokyo Bay during the Doolittle raid and capsized.)

McMahon set up quickly and fired four bow tubes at the carrier.* One hit. Before he could bring his stern tubes to bear, the destroyers drove him deep. One of the main motors went out, and in the ensuing moments McMahon lost depth control, plunging toward the deep ocean floor. By the time McMahon regained control of the vessel and brought her to the surface, Japanese planes overhead drove him back down. He was unable to get another shot at the carrier, but his one hit forced her to return to a navy yard in Japan for lengthy repairs.

McMahon went on to lay his minefield and make two more attacks. He sank no ships, but his aggressive attack on *Ryuho* earned him a Silver Star and a reputation for boldness.

Sunfish, commanded by Richard Ward Peterson, who had never made a war patrol, and *Trigger,* now commanded by Roy Benson, who had been Brockman's exec on *Nautilus* at the Battle of Midway, were the second and third minelayers. No known sinkings resulted from *Sunfish*'s mines. However, Benson laid his off Inubo Zaki, a

---
* The other two forward tubes were filled with mines.

few miles north of Tokyo Bay, and then watched as a freighter with an escort steamed right into the field and blew herself up. Benson believed the escort had sunk too, but there was no Japanese record of it. The ship sunk was *Teifuku Maru*, 5,198 tons. This was probably the only ship sunk by any of the Pearl Harbor minelaying missions in 1942.

A few nights later, Christmas Eve, *Trigger* nosed quietly into Sagami Nada, just outside Tokyo Bay. One of the enlisted men proposed that the ship's record player be hooked to the PA system so the crew could hear Christmas carols. When this was done, the familiar music chorused throughout the boat—and also from the two speakers on the bridge. As the sound drifted across the dark waters toward Tokyo Bay, Ned Beach, standing watch on the bridge, felt a lump in his throat "the size of a watermelon." He wrote, "For the few minutes that those magic, so-well-remembered strains filled the air we were transported away from the battle, and the danger, and the lurking terror." There is no record that the Japanese heard the carols, but for many on *Trigger* the episode was an act of defiance, reflecting the bold spirit she now displayed under Roy Benson.

During this aggressive patrol, Benson attacked a freighter outside Tokyo Bay, a second freighter loaded with aircraft a little farther offshore, and the destroyer *Okikase*. In all, he was credited with sinking four ships for 24,000 tons, but JANAC reduced his score to the one freighter sunk in the minefield plus the destroyer *Okikase*.

The three antiques, *Pollack*, *Porpoise*, and *Pike*, all made difficult and dangerous voyages.

Pollack, commanded by Robie Ellis Palmer, was hit by bad weather and left station early—with 44,000 gallons of fuel, enough for ten more days. The Pearl Harbor command was not happy about this. *Porpoise*, commanded by John McKnight, was caught in the same typhoon. McKnight did mount several attacks and managed to sink one ship for 5,000 tons, but he also left station early without telling anybody.

Billy New, returning *Pike* from long overhaul, had the worst of it. Following an unsuccessful approach on a Japanese vessel, he was trapped by a destroyer which delivered what Pearl Harbor judged to be the worst depth-charging of the war up to then—a total of seventy-one charges. *Pike* was forced to 365 feet and suffered near-fatal damage. Everything leaked.

Luckily, few Japanese depth-charge attacks were persistently conducted. The Japanese apparently assumed their depth charges were finding the mark and that in most cases an attack resulted in a sinking. Few waited around for confirmation, such as debris bubbling to the surface, and many were apparently fooled by oil slicks which came from leaks, not fatal ruptures. *Pike*'s attacker left before the job was finished, and *Pike* returned to the navy yard for extensive repairs. Billy New, an unlucky skipper who had made six patrols (counting his eleven-day sortie at the Battle of Midway) without ever having sunk or damaged a ship, left submarines for good.

Three of the newer boats, all fighting the foul weather, sank six ships. Philip Harold Ross in *Halibut*, who had made two zero patrols in Alaskan waters, sank three for 12,500 tons. Vernon Long ("Rebel") Lowrance, making his second patrol in *Kingfish*, sank two for 10,000 tons. Art Taylor in *Haddock*, making his third and last patrol, sank one for 4,000 tons. Jesse Hull in *Finback* got caught in storms and flooded his conning tower. On this, also his third and last patrol, he fired no torpedoes.

During the second half of 1942, following the Battle of Midway and the foray to Alaska, Bob English had mounted a total of sixty-one war patrols from Pearl Harbor. Twenty-nine of these had been at Truk or to the waters south of Truk, twenty-seven had been to Empire or East China Sea waters, three were in Alaskan waters, and two were the special missions of *Argonaut* and *Nautilus* to Makin Island.

In all, only thirty-four of the sixty-one patrols resulted in sinkings —57 percent. Counting the two missions to Makin Island, there had been twenty-seven barren patrols. No ships were sunk by the three fleet boat patrols in Alaskan waters. The twenty-seven patrols in Empire waters had accounted for forty-seven ships. The twenty-nine patrols to Truk and vicinity had accounted for twenty-four ships, including three men-of-war: Dick Lake's light cruiser, *Tenryu*; Burt Klakring's fleet destroyer, *Hakaze*; and an "old destroyer" sunk by Chester Bruton. In addition, Red Ramage had inflicted positive damage on the light carrier *Taiyo* (*Otaka*), Barney McMahon had damaged the light carrier *Ryuho*, and Donc Donaho had probably damaged a battleship. The rate of sinkings in Empire waters remained twice that of boats patrolling to Truk.

13

Brisbane, October through December 1942

The Battle of Guadalcanal

Admiral Yamamoto was determined to retake Guadalcanal, no matter what the price in human life and suffering. After the Battle of Santa Cruz, where *Shokaku* and *Zuiho* were damaged, he withdrew his carriers and prepared his battleships and cruisers for the most furious and decisive battle of all. The plan was to annihilate Admiral Halsey's forces with battleships and heavy cruisers, supported by land-based aircraft, and then embark about 12,000 troops in a dozen first-rate transports for a new assault on Guadalcanal.

The engagement—known as the Battle of Guadalcanal—raged over three days, November 12–15. Before and during the battle, the codebreakers provided detailed radio intelligence to Admiral Halsey which enabled him to anticipate Japanese movements and attack accordingly, and as a result the U.S. Navy achieved a substantial victory in thwarting the Japanese plan. Losses were heavy on both sides. One Japanese battleship, *Hiei*, was sunk; another, *Kirishima*, was so badly damaged she had to be scuttled. In addition, the Japanese lost the heavy cruiser *Kinugasa*, two destroyers, and six—perhaps more—of the twelve big transports lifting the troops to Guadalcanal. The United States lost two light cruisers, *Atlanta* and *Juneau* (sunk by a Japanese submarine, *I-26*), and seven destroyers. In a subsequent last-gasp battle known as Tassafaronga, the Japanese lost another destroyer; the United States lost the heavy cruiser *Northampton*, and there was major damage to the heavy cruisers *New Orleans* (commanded by Stoney Roper, who received a Navy Cross for heroism), *Minneapolis*, and *Pensacola*.

After these battles, Yamamoto gave up all further efforts to recapture Guadalcanal. Most of the surviving Japanese naval units were withdrawn to Rabaul and then to Truk and the homeland for battle-damage repairs and upkeep, becoming the nucleus of a second-generation Japanese navy coming off the launching ways. Guadalcanal marked the end of the Japanese offensive action in the South Pacific and also of their threat to the New Hebrides, New Caledonia, and Australia. From November 1942 onward, the Japanese went on the defensive, trying to hold what had been gained during the drive that began on December 7, 1941.

During this period, the many fleet boats of Squadrons Two, Eight, and Ten, plus the tenders *Holland*, *Fulton*, and *Sperry*, arrived at New Farm Wharf in Brisbane. What had once been a small base, built around Christie's tender *Griffin* and his force of ten surviving S-boats, suddenly became an enormous enterprise, the largest concentration of U.S. submarine power in the Pacific. Although Christie was still merely a captain, MacArthur's naval boss, Chips Carpender, left him in charge, steadfastly beating off repeated requests from Rear Admiral Lockwood in Fremantle for the job.

Christie reorganized his command, which was named Task Force 42, to accommodate the influx of brass. Unofficially, he abolished the squadron echelon. Jimmy Fife, nominally commander of Squadron Two, had gone to Port Moresby as Carpender's special representative, leaving Marmaduke O'Leary in temporary command of the squadron. Although Gin Styer retained the title of Commander Submarine Squadron Ten, he became Christie's operations officer. Willard Downes, who likewise retained his title, Commander Submarine Squadron Eight, was appointed Christie's matériel officer. John Murphy (ex-*Tambor*), Carl Tiedeman (ex-*Snapper*), and Styer's brother-in-law, Adrian Hurst (ex-*Permit*), served as Styer's assistant operations officers. Mort Mumma (ex-*Sailfish*) was appointed Christie's liaison officer to Army Air Corps forces basing in Townsville. Jack Lewis (ex-*Trigger*) served as Christie's secretary.

There was a struggle on the higher levels for control of the boats.

General MacArthur wanted them to support his coming campaign in New Guinea; Halsey wanted them to support his campaign in the Solomons. In this tug-of-war, Ralph Christie proved to be a diplomat of considerable skill, serving both commanders but retaining operational control of the boats himself. "The setup of a task force operating under two different commands was unique," the official submarine historian observed, "but proved extremely satisfactory in that [Christie] was able to shift his units to support both the Solomons and the New Guinea campaigns and comply with the wishes of both his superiors."

The problem was, however, that the large concentration of submarines at Brisbane was still being employed *tactically* and *reactively* against Japanese fleet movements. In most cases, they were shunted here and there on Ultra contacts, often into the teeth of massive destroyer screens or against well-defended harbors at places where the Japanese had clear superiority in the air. It was Java all over again, and no one appeared to have learned the lesson.

Every Japanese ship in the southwest Pacific was dependent on oil to keep its engines running. The oil came from Borneo, Sumatra, and Java to the Palaus or Truk and then to Rabaul and other bases. A well-conceived strategic submarine offensive against Japanese tankers coming from these oil ports would almost certainly have done far more to immobillize Japanese naval units in the Solomons than all the futile chasing about. None of the tanker convoys was as heavily escorted as the Japanese fleet units in the Solomons. By utilizing radar they could have been attacked on the high seas north of New Guinea at night with relative ease and with far more rewarding results.

Submarine Patrols

From October through December 1942, while the final battles for Guadalcanal were being played out, Christie mounted twenty-four war patrols from Brisbane. Nineteen of these were conducted by fleet boats new to the command, the other five by the last of the S-boats. Nine of the twenty-four patrols were carried out by Squadron Two boats returning to Pearl Harbor for overhaul. Of the twenty-four patrols, most in areas infested with Japanese destroyers and aircraft, only three achieved anything. Although there were many Ultras, especially on Japanese submarines operating to and from Truk and Rabaul, and many ships and convoys were sighted, only six Japanese ships—two of them submarines—were sunk. These six were sunk by three fleet boats.

Tex Mewhinney, who had done much to lift spirits on *Saury*, patrolled off Rabaul with a new exec, Doug Rhymes. There he received many Ultras on Japanese forces preparing for the Battle of Guadalcanal. One bright moonlit night he intercepted a task force of several big ships, including a light carrier which, as the third officer, Bill Hazzard, recalled, was *Hosho*. Mewhinney maneuvered to attack the force while submerged, choosing *Hosho* as his target. He fired four torpedoes, but according to Hazzard a premature explosion gave away the game and *Saury* was driven off by destroyers.

After that, *Saury* headed for Pearl Harbor for overhaul. En route Mewhinney decided (without orders) to reconnoiter Nauru and the Ocean Islands, which lie between the Solomons and the Gilberts. There he found a sitting duck, but another premature spoiled the attack.

When he arrived in Pearl Harbor, Mewhinney was criticized by Bob English in his endorsement for poor torpedo shooting (thirteen fired, one possible hit). Later, Mewhinney said, "In my post-patrol interview with Admiral English, I told him that some of our torpedoes were exploding prematurely or not exploding at all. He replied that SubPac [Submarines Pacific] had never had a premature explosion."

When the boat went to overhaul, Mewhinney (who spoke Spanish) went to serve with the Naval Mission in Peru, replacing Tex McLean's brother-in-law, Murray Jones Tichenor, who headed for Fremantle for staff duty with McLean.

Snapper, with two skippers in four patrols, sailed on her fifth with yet another, Augustus Robert St. Angelo. "The Saint," as he was called, had been exec of *Bass* and then skipper of *S-25*, which was loaned to Britain and reloaned to Polish Free Forces. St. Angelo had trained the Polish crew before the boat was turned over to British command.

The Saint did no better than his predecessors, Ham Stone and Harold Baker. He was shunted to likely areas to intercept Japanese forces aimed at recapturing Guadalcanal, but *Snapper* saw nothing of consequence and mounted no attacks. The Brisbane high command was not happy. One endorsement stated, "The scarcity of contacts is noted. However, it is known that a major 12-ship transport convoy [the main Guadalcanal invasion force] with heavy escort passed through *Snapper*'s area three times between 12 and 14 November without being detected by the submarine."

Grampus, commanded by a new skipper, John Rich Craig, landed four coast-watchers on an island before conducting her regular patrol. In contrast to *Snapper*, *Grampus* must have seen almost every Japanese ship in the area—twice. Craig's official log listed twenty contacts with major Japanese forces, comprising forty-four cruisers and seventy-nine destroyers. Craig launched six torpedo attacks. He was credited with sinking one destroyer and damaging another, but postwar records failed to substantiate the sinking. In his endorsement, Admiral Halsey wrote that he was sorry that Craig had not sunk more ships, but the patrol was distinguished by the fact that the "Commanding Officer was thinking all the time, clearly and correctly."

On his second patrol, in December, Craig, assisted by his exec, a flamboyant and wild character named Wayne Rucker Merrill, again sighted an astounding number of Japanese ships: forty-one. In seven attacks, Craig fired at six of these vessels, including two freighters, two transports, a small destroyer, and a submarine. He was credited with sinking three ships for 24,000 tons and damage to one for 1,500, but postwar records failed to credit the sinkings. On return the exec, Merrill, went to the States for new construction.

Grayback, commanded by a new skipper, Edward Clark Stephan, patrolled in the same area. Stephan made eight attacks, firing all twenty-four torpedoes. Five of the eight attacks failed. Christie credited him with sinking two ships.

When Stephan returned to port, Christie was ready to relieve him, but Chips Carpender stood in the way. Christie wrote Lockwood:

> Grayback *had many opportunities and fired twenty-four torpedoes. The results were, to say the least, disappointing. My frank opinion is that Stephan is not well suited for the responsible job of Commanding Officer. You may well ask, then, why not take steps to relieve him. The answer to that is a pusillanimous one. My diplomacy is unequal to the task. I frankly told Admiral Carpender . . . before the patrol that Stephan was not in my opinion suited for the job but that I had*

previously so stated officially and had been overruled. . . . Now . . . there is no change.

Lockwood, ever eager to go to the mat with Carpender, replied:

I . . . agree that twenty-four torpedoes is a terrific number to accomplish the sinking of one ship . . . a second patrol after some intensive training [may] result better. If it doesn't then certainly he should be relieved. . . . I will certainly back your judgment in this or other cases if you desire to draw me into the argument.

Postwar records failed to credit Stephan with the two ships Christie credited, but he retained command.

On his second patrol, in December, Stephan did not improve his aim by much. In six attacks, he fired twenty torpedoes, sinking one ship, the Japanese submarine *I-18*, 2,000 tons. During the patrol, terminated after forty-seven days by a matériel failure, Stephan's pharmacist's mate, Harry B. Roby, removed an inflamed appendix from a crewman, W. R. Jones, in a replay of the appendectomy on Pete Ferrall's *Seadragon*.

Chet Smith reassumed command of *Swordfish* from Acey Burrows after the latter's one unfortunate patrol. Smith had recovered from his cold, but he found the crew of *Swordfish* still suffering from what he believed to be bad drinking water. On this patrol, *Swordfish*'s sixth, all hands were troubled by queasy stomachs, Smith reported. About one third of the crew vomited for days. Smith made two attacks, claiming one ship damaged, one sunk. However, postwar records failed to bear out the sinking.

When Smith returned from this, his fifth war patrol, he was the high scorer for Asiatic submarines with what was then believed to be eleven ships sunk for 68,000 tons, four damaged for 27,000 tons. He was promoted to command a division in Al McCann's Squadron Six in Fremantle.

Gudgeon, commanded by Shirley Stovall, had another fiercely active patrol, making contact with four separate convoys. One escaped in a rainsquall, but Stovall, assisted by his exec, Dusty Dornin, attacked three, hitting perhaps five or six ships. Christie credited Stovall with sinking three ships for 22,000 tons and damage to another, but postwar records denied any sinkings. In two patrols, Stovall's credited score was seven ships for 57,000 tons, only one of which was later confirmed. Again, Dornin blamed poor torpedo performance. In his glowing endorsement to the patrol, Admiral Halsey singled out Dusty Dornin for special praise.

Red Ramage in *Trout*, bound for Fremantle when his periscopes were damaged at Truk, made a brief unscheduled patrol out of Brisbane to the Solomons and got into the thick of the Battle of Guadalcanal, November 12–15. On November 12, Christie sent him an Ultra to intercept an important Japanese combatant force. The following morning at 7:39, the battleship *Kirishima*, escorted by a ring of destroyers, came along right on schedule. Ramage submerged and closed from 6 miles to 3, but when he was ready to fire, *Kirishima* zigged away. Later in the afternoon, Ramage found the battleship again, fending off a U.S. air attack. Ramage closed to 1,800 yards and fired five torpedoes—only the fourth time in the war (after *Nautilus*, *Flying Fish*, and *Amberjack*) that a U.S. submarine had attacked a Japanese battleship. None of the five torpedoes hit, and a destroyer drove *Trout* deep. After twenty-eight days, Ramage returned to Brisbane. *Trout* was ordered to Fremantle for refit and more patrols.

Pieczentkowski in *Sturgeon* and his exec, young Chester Nimitz, patrolled from Brisbane to Pearl Harbor by way of Truk. Pi made nine contacts, comprising thirteen enemy vessels. He attacked three, firing nine torpedoes and obtaining one hit for damage. When he arrived in Pearl Harbor, Bob English was furious. "This and many other patrol reports," English fumed, "show that too many targets are getting by at close range without well-aimed shots being fired at them before the situation is hopeless."

While the boat was in Pearl Harbor preparatory to returning to the States for overhaul, Admiral Nimitz took pride in pinning a Silver Star on his son's chest. Back at Mare Island, Pi retained command of *Sturgeon*, but young Nimitz went to the Electric Boat Company to become exec of a new boat.

Pete Ferrall in *Seadragon*, who had left his exec, Bub Ward, behind in the PCO pool at Brisbane, patrolled near Rabaul on the way to Pearl Harbor. He was loaded with old Mark X torpedoes left over from the S-boats because Christie wanted to keep all the available Mark XIVs for the Brisbane boats. Along the way, Ferrall fired nineteen torpedoes at a multiplicity of targets including two destroyers, a submarine, and a freighter. The Mark Xs were a nightmare. Ferrall had prematures, erratic running, and other problems. During a failed attack against a Japanese sub off Rabaul, the enemy fired a torpedo at *Seadragon*.

In Pearl Harbor, Ferrall was credited with sinking a freighter and one submarine, but postwar records credited only the submarine, *I-4*, 2,000 tons. The powers that be carped at Ferrall's shooting—four hits out of nineteen torpedoes—and for missing several other opportunities to attack. On return to the navy yard for overhaul, Ferrall was sent to the Bureau of Ships.

Lockwood—and others—were not happy at Ferrall's new assignment. All too many good skippers were being yanked out of the submarine force and sent to other duty. Lockwood believed that these older men, who had made many patrols, should be retained as instructors for the younger ones. Later, Ferrall did return to the force (as force matériel officer and division commander), but all too many, encouraged by the Bureau of Personnel to diversify their careers and experiences, did not.

Lucius Chappell in *Sculpin* patrolled home by way of Truk. Alerted by an Ultra, he made contact with a light aircraft carrier on the night of December 17 and closed from 12 miles to 9. At that point, two destroyer escorts turned toward *Sculpin*. One pinned her with a searchlight; both opened fire. Chappell dived to evade, sweating out a depth-charge attack. The following night, he attacked a tanker, achieving damage.

Dave White in *Plunger*, who had put into Brisbane to repair damage after grounding on the bottom, patrolled back to Pearl Harbor. Along the way, he sighted two submarines and four groups of destroyers. He attacked the destroyers, receiving credit for sinking one and damaging one; however, the sinking was not credited in postwar Japanese records. At Pearl Harbor, both White and his exec, Dave McClintock, were detached and returned to the States to fit out and commission a new boat.

The last five S-boats patrolling from Brisbane achieved little. Two made one attack each, resulting in damage to two ships. After these patrols, the boats returned to the States for extensive overhaul and reassignment to Alaska or to training duties. The S-boat tender *Griffin* left Brisbane November 11, returning to San Diego for conversion to a fleet boat tender.

Silversides, commanded by Creed Burlingame, was the last boat to leave Brisbane in 1942. She was assigned to patrol Truk and then return to Pearl Harbor. When she pulled away from New Farm Wharf, many of the officers and men were wearing strictly nonregulation "Digger" hats, obtained from Australian soldiers. The exec, Roy Davenport, broke out his trombone and played a miserable version of "Waltzing Matilda." Later, the teetotaler Davenport said, "The men on the tender looked at us kind of funny. I guess they were saying, 'Oh, well, they'll sober up in a few days.'"

This fourth patrol put Burlingame and his raffish, combat-hardened crew to the test in more ways than one. Off Rabaul, one of the crewmen, George Platter, complained of a serious stomachache. "We had left port nearly a week ago," Burlingame later wrote, "so upset stomachs resulting from hangovers were a thing of the past." Platter had acute appendicitis. For the third time a submarine pharmacist's mate, here Thomas Moore, twenty-two, performed an appendectomy. Roy Davenport quoted scripture. Platter survived.

A few hours after the operation, Burlingame brought *Silversides* to the surface. The bridge watch spotted what was believed to be a Japanese submarine. Burlingame went to battle stations, fired two stern torpedoes, and dived. One of the torpedoes, perhaps disturbed by *Silversides*' wake, exploded prematurely. "This blew our stern out of the water," Burlingame said later, "and us out of our wits." The target—in reality a Japanese destroyer—kept *Silversides* down until dawn, when Burlingame surfaced and poked up his periscope.

At that moment, *Silversides* was rocked by a thunderous explosion. An aircraft from Rabaul, perhaps called in by the destroyer—still unharmed and patrolling warily—dropped three bombs directly on top of the boat. "In a year of being depth-charged," Burlingame wrote later, exaggerating his time in combat, "we had never had one so close. . . . I thought the conning tower was being wrenched loose from the pressure hull." The men—including Platter, still anesthetized—were thrown violently from their bunks. Light bulbs shattered. *Silversides*, bow planes frozen on hard dive, plunged toward the bottom with a frightening down-angle. "Just short of collapse depth," Burlingame wrote, "we managed to get things under control and leveled off as deep as we could." For the remainder of the day—

SUBMARINE PATROLS

Christmas Eve—the destroyer passed overhead, dropping depth charges. When he finally went away, Burlingame broke out the medicinal whiskey. "We added it to powdered eggs and canned milk," Burlingame wrote later, "and with a lot of imagination, it tasted almost like eggnog."

After this, Burlingame moved north to Truk to patrol his assigned area. He found numerous targets. The first was an I-class Japanese submarine, which he believed he sank but which was not confirmed in postwar records. The second was a huge tanker which blew up in spectacular fashion. It was confirmed at 10,000 tons by JANAC.

In late January, while submerged, Burlingame picked up a convoy at twilight: four fat freighters, guarded by two escorts. He fired five torpedoes at three of the overlapping freighters (the sixth wouldn't fire), heard five hits, then went deep to avoid the escorts. During the evasion, the crew heard breaking-up noises from the direction of the targets but were unable to observe any ships sinking.

When Burlingame shook the escorts, his crew discovered an astonishing—and nerve-chilling—fact: the sixth torpedo had stuck half out of its tube. Had it armed? No one could be sure. It might blow up at any moment, taking Burlingame, Davenport, and the crew down forever. There was only one way to get it out: refire it. Burlingame gave the fateful order, with additional orders that the buddha's belly be rubbed. He backed *Silversides* emergency, to get as far from the torpedo as possible. It sizzled out of the tube and bore away.

Postwar analysis would show that Burlingame's attack on the convoy was one of the most perfectly executed of the war. His five torpedoes hit the three freighters, sinking them all. Counting the big tanker, Burlingame had actually sunk four ships for 27,798 tons—the best patrol of the war by tonnage to date—according to Japanese records. However, lacking positive verification of the convoy sinkings, Pearl Harbor credited only the tanker, plus damage.

Following this patrol, *Silversides* required a navy yard overhaul, and Roy Davenport was detached, with orders to command his own boat. Burlingame and Davenport parted company without shedding tears. Burlingame was happy to have no more of Davenport's religion, while for his part Davenport was delighted to leave the hard-drinking wardroom of *Silversides* for his own command.

Changes in Personnel

In late November, Ralph Christie, reveling in his job of commanding the largest congregation of submarines in the Pacific, received despairing news. Back in the States, torpedo production—and development—had turned into a fiasco. There was a hopeless logjam at Newport. The bureaucracy there seemed unable to gear itself for war. As a consequence, the United States was running out of torpedoes for submarines, destroyers, and aircraft. The electric torpedo, which held so much promise, was not moving forward. BuOrd's chief, Spike Blandy, had requested that Ralph Christie return to the States at once as Inspector of Ordnance in Charge, Newport, to clear up the mess.

Both Christie and Carpender put up a mighty effort to get the orders killed. Carpender cabled the Bureau of Personnel that Christie was "performing extremely important duty" in Brisbane and advised against his detachment. Christie fired off personal letters to Spike Blandy and Admiral Edwards, pleading his case. None of this helped. From the Washington viewpoint, the torpedo problem was acute. Christie was needed.

Who would succeed Christie in Brisbane? Lockwood was the logical man, but there is no evidence that Carpender even considered him. The Bureau of Personnel suggested John Wilkes. Christie endorsed Wilkes, with Jimmy Fife and Gin Styer as second and third choices. Carpender picked Fife. The decision was approved by MacArthur.

As the days dragged by before the relieving ceremony, Christie hoped for some miracle that would rescue him. Fife returned from Port Moresby. The official ceremony took place on December 22. Christie, to whom Carpender awarded a Legion of Merit for his work in Brisbane, returned to the States by air and after spending a few days with his family arrived at Newport in early January.

14

Fremantle, September through December 1942

In Fremantle, Rear Admiral Lockwood was an unhappy warrior. The decision to transfer Squadron Two from Albany to Brisbane and return the boats to Pearl Harbor for overhaul temporarily reduced his force from twenty submarines to eight. He faced a critical shortage of torpedoes; the boats on patrol shot about seventy-five a month and Lockwood received about eighteen. When Lockwood complained to Washington, Admiral Edwards replied, "We will give you new tools to work with some day, but at present, the tool shed is empty. . . . If there is anything that you want done from this end please let me know and I will probably send you my deepest sympathy in return."

One item arriving in Fremantle made him happy: a shipment of 5-inch submarine deck guns stripped from *Barracuda*, *Bass*, and *Bonita*. For well over fifteen years, Lockwood had urged larger deck guns on submarines for defensive purposes—notably in the 1938 General Board showdown with Admiral Hart—but he had always been turned down. Now, with a war on, they had been shipped to him as an experiment. He ordered the first two guns placed on *Gar* and *Thresher* and—somewhat imprudently—encouraged the skippers to use them *offensively* against suitable Japanese shipping.

During the four-month period September through December, while the great sea battles in the Solomons were taking place, Lockwood mounted seventeen war patrols from Fremantle. Five of the seventeen were conducted by Squadron Two boats that returned directly to Pearl Harbor without stopping for duty in Brisbane. Because of the torpedo shortage, five were the hated—and usually unproductive—minelaying missions.

Gar, commanded by Don McGregor, set off with her new 5-inch deck gun and a load of thirty-two mines and torpedoes. After laying the mines in shallow waters near the edge of the Gulf of Siam, McGregor conducted a lackluster patrol off Indochina. He did not use his new 5-inch gun. He found few contacts. When *Gar* returned to Fremantle, both the exec, John Fitzgerald, and the third officer, Maurice William ("Mike") Shea, asked for transfers.

The endorsements on McGregor's patrol report were blistering. Al McCann wrote, "It is difficult to understand how a submarine could spend thirty-nine days [off Indochina] and make only two contacts"; he speculated that McGregor had either patrolled too far off the coast or spent too much time submerged. Lockwood wrote, "The track of the ship during the last patrol indicates that the assigned areas in known traffic lanes were not sufficiently exploited," and relieved McGregor, Fitzgerald, and Shea in one fell swoop.

In contrast to *Gar*, Moke Millican in *Thresher* (also with new 5-inch deck gun and mines) turned in a sizzling patrol. After planting his mines near the edge of the Gulf of Siam, he found many targets. He made four torpedo attacks, firing off eight torpedoes, all he had on board. None hit. Then, off the south end of Makassar Strait, he boldly attacked a 3,000-ton freighter with his 5-inch gun and drove her into shallow water, where she probably sank (Japanese records provided no specific information on her loss). This was the largest—and one of the few—Japanese vessels sunk solely by deck gun. Lockwood was immensely pleased.

On his next patrol, Millican was ordered to reconnoiter Christmas Island (the tiny dot in the Indian Ocean where Freddy Warder had attacked three cruisers in late March) and Sunda Strait. The codebreakers had picked up word that the Japanese intended to try to mount salvage operations on the cruiser *Houston*, sunk in shallow water during the Battle of Java Sea, and were concerned that the Japanese might recover U.S. Navy codebooks and machines or discover from documents on *Houston* that the U.S. Navy was reading Japanese codes. One of *Thresher*'s missions was to torpedo any Japanese salvage vessels found at the scene of *Houston*'s grave.

On this patrol, Millican had a new exec, Bill Post, who had been

Steve Barchet's exec on the first patrol of *Argonaut* off Midway. Barchet had "surfaced" Post, but Al McCann had given him a second chance. Post made one patrol as exec of Kenneth Hurd's *Seal*. After that, McCann assigned him to *Thresher*.

Post was impressed by Moke Millican's aggressive spirit. "I learned everything I knew from him," Post said later. "He had a TDC in his head. He was a scrapper—he'd been a bantamweight fighter at the Academy. He was not too articulate, but he knew what he was doing."

Off Christmas Island, Millican had a near catastrophe. While "routining" the torpedoes, Number One tube was accidentally fired with the outer door closed. The torpedo made a "hot run" (the motor ran, the propellers turned furiously), and then it pushed halfway out the outer door. After dark, Millican surfaced and removed the torpedo. However, the outer door was jammed full open and wouldn't close. Millican returned to Fremantle to have it fixed.

Thresher returned to Christmas Island and then swung north through Sunda Strait. There was no sign of salvage vessels at *Houston*, so Millican went around to the Java Sea. On Christmas Day off Surabaya, he found a five-ship convoy and attacked, believing he sank one 7,000-ton freighter despite some torpedo failures. On the following day in the same area, alerted by an Ultra, Millican sighted a heavy cruiser and a "first-class" carrier, probably *Shokaku* or *Zuikaku*, returned from the Solomons. He closed to 6,000 yards, but before he could set up and fire, a destroyer drove him off.

A few nights later, near Lombok Strait, *Thresher* picked up a large freighter sailing alone. Millican, a Gun Clubber who had a master's degree in ordnance engineering, was by now convinced that the magnetic exploder was defective. He tried an experiment with the freighter, closing to 800 yards and firing one torpedo. No explosion. Millican again ordered his crew to man the 5-inch deck gun. Using binoculars strapped to the gun for a sight, the crew fired off eighty-five rounds. When the freighter failed to sink, Millican fired four more torpedoes at her. Down went *Hachian Maru*, 2,733 tons.

Lockwood, who gave Millican glowing endorsements, wrote Carpender, "He is really a remarkable type, and I wish I had a couple dozen more like him."

Grenadier, *Tambor*, and *Tautog* planted minefields along the coast of Indochina—two off Haiphong—and then made undistinguished regular patrols.

After laying his mines, Bruce Carr, with eight torpedoes on *Grenadier* for his second patrol, made seventeen contacts. He fired three torpedoes at the same ship; all missed. An Ultra from Lockwood directed him to intercept two Japanese cruiser divisions coming up from Singapore to Manila; Carr couldn't find them. On return to Fremantle, Lockwood was critical of Carr and relieved him of command. Later Carr wrote, "Having been awarded the Silver Star for *Grenadier*'s second patrol [under Pilly Lent], the Commendation Medal for her third, and having, on her fourth, successfully completed her primary mission, the laying of an effective minefield off Haiphong, I feel that my contribution to the war effort was fully positive."

Stephen Ambruster on *Tambor* laid his minefield and then patrolled aggressively, making four torpedo attacks, during which he sank one confirmed ship. However, on his next patrol in Sunda Strait (to drive any salvage vessels from the site of the *Houston* sinking), Ambruster apparently let down, for when he returned Lockwood wrote, "The results of this patrol are disappointing not only because of lack of results but also because the area was not thoroughly exploited."

Joe Willingham in *Tautog* planted his minefield and then made one gun and six torpedo attacks, the last of which brought on a severe depth-charging. Most of the torpedo attacks failed. On one, Willingham even heard the torpedo hit the side of the ship's hull, but it did not explode. McCann wrote, "There have been numerous reports of torpedoes failing to explode when passing under the target but this is the first report of a failure to function on actual impact. Every effort is being exerted to insure the proper function of exploders."

Willingham was relieved for new construction, and Lockwood gave command of *Tautog* to Barney Sieglaff, one of McCann's division engineers, who—by coincidence—had been relief crew commander of *Tautog* during the Pearl Harbor attack and helped shoot down a Japanese plane. Norman Dwight Gage, who had commissioned *Tautog* and moved up the ladder, served as Sieglaff's exec.

Sieglaff, who had never made a war patrol, turned in a splendid first effort. Taking advantage of Ultra reports—which he said later he did not fully trust—he intercepted two light cruisers in separate engagements. Finding the first off Ambon Island, he stopped it with one quick shot and then fired two more for hits. The damaged cruiser opened up on *Tautog*'s periscope with 5-inch guns before limping into Ambon. The second cruiser was in Salajar Strait on the south coast of Celebes. Sieglaff fired four bow tubes in heavy weather from an unfavorable position, but all missed, and a destroyer escort pinned *Tautog* down until the cruiser got away. In addition to these attacks, Sieglaff intercepted several convoys and sank two confirmed ships, earning a reputation for extreme aggressiveness.

Jim Coe in *Skipjack* returned to Pearl Harbor by way of Ambon, Halmahera, and the Marshall Islands. He carried twelve Mark XIV torpedoes and four antique Mark IXs, predecessors to the old Mark X, which had not been test-fired for twenty-three years. Along the way, 75 percent of the crew came down with nausea and loss of appetite, probably caused by bad drinking water. Even so, Coe managed several attacks, including one on a tanker, firing twelve torpedoes, three of them Mark IXs. Only two hit. Bob English commended Coe's aggressiveness but criticized his shooting. Upon return to Mare Island for overhaul, Coe was ordered to new construction.

Freddy Warder in *Seawolf* returned to Pearl Harbor by way of Davao Gulf and the Palaus, an island group no submarine had yet investigated and where the codebreakers reported carrier activity. Warder, making his seventh and last patrol of the war, might have chosen to take it easy. But Warder was Warder, and his final patrol was one of the most aggressive and productive of all.

Warder headed for Davao by way of Makassar Strait. Off Makassar City, he attacked a freighter but missed. Off Balikpapan, he found a tanker but was unable to get into firing position in time. He boldly poked *Seawolf*'s bow into Davao Gulf and within a few hours had sunk *Gigu Maru*, 3,000 tons. In nearby Talomo Bay, he sank a large transport, *Sagami Maru*, 7,000 tons. After evading subchasers and aircraft, he sank *Keiko Maru*, 3,000 tons, off Davao Gulf. When one of his torpedoes made a circular run, Warder coolly evaded it by going deep.

Seawolf moved east to the Palaus, arriving November 11. No sooner had she got there than two destroyers came charging out. Warder began an approach. While swinging the periscope around, he spotted a big aircraft carrier—*Shokaku* or *Zuikaku*?—coming out of the rain and twilight. Unfortunately, Warder could not attain a favorable attack position, but after dark he surfaced and pursued the carrier at full speed, trying to raise Pearl Harbor to report. The carrier got away. Eventually Pearl Harbor received the report.

At Pearl Harbor, Bob English gave Warder a "well done" and sent

Seawolf to Mare Island for overhaul and modernization. Warder was promoted to command a division of new boats being commissioned on the East Coast.

Kenneth Hurd in *Seal*, returning to Pearl Harbor, followed Warder to the Palaus. As he was nearby when Warder got off his contact report on the carrier, Dick Voge ordered Hurd to close and try to find it.

Hurd promptly ran into a large convoy and attacked from close range, shooting at a large freighter. A few seconds after firing, *Seal* was shaken to her keel by a terrifying explosion or other noise—no one was sure what had happened—and she broached, then plunged deep. A destroyer came over, dropping depth charges, holding *Seal* down until the convoy had proceeded beyond range. When Hurd surfaced that night, he found one periscope bent over at right angles and the other frozen in its mount. There was red bottom paint on the bent periscope. The destroyer had collided with *Seal*, smashing the periscope.

Because *Seal* was now blind, Hurd received permission to cut his patrol short. When he arrived at Pearl Harbor he met a cool reception. He claimed to have sunk one ship, but Voge decided the evidence was too slim. However, postwar records revealed that Hurd was right. In the wild melee that almost destroyed *Seal*, his torpedoes had found *Boston Maru*, 5,500 tons, and he was later credited with sinking her. Hurd relinquished command of *Seal* and reported to the Pearl Harbor staff.

Red Ramage in *Trout* set off for patrol in Indochina waters near Camranh Bay. Along the way, he received an Ultra ordering him to intercept a huge tanker, *Kyokuyo Maru*, 17,000 tons, loading oil at Miri, on the west coast of Borneo. Ramage found the ship at anchor. After dark, he fearlessly slipped into the channel on the surface, closed to about 3,000 yards, and fired four torpedoes. Two hit amidship, causing a tremendous explosion and brilliant flames. One torpedo prematured; one, Ramage claimed, was a dud.

Believing the ship had sunk, Ramage proceeded on to Camranh Bay, sinking two schooners with gunfire and a 3,000-ton freighter with two torpedoes. Then he attacked a destroyer from the point-blank range of 900 yards, firing three torpedoes. He watched them run hot, straight and normal toward the target, but they were, as Ramage reported, "DUDS!"

After that, Ramage received another Ultra, directing him to the Singapore—Manila sea lanes to eastward. While there, he saw three large tankers but was unable to make an attack. He commented in his report, "Sad day. With two cents' worth of luck we could have had a picnic. But here is the race track and the field is fast."

Ramage received yet another Ultra, directing him to return to Miri, where another huge tanker, *Nisshin Maru*, 17,000 tons, was expected. He found her at anchor. Believing the Japanese would now have defenses against night attacks, this time Ramage went in submerged in daylight. He fired two torpedoes, set on low speed, from a range of 5,000 yards. Then, on second thought, Ramage surfaced to man his deck gun, but *Nisshin Maru* opened fire with her own guns, driving Ramage under again. Exiting to sea, Ramage heard two explosions and saw smoke rising from the ship's stern.

Ramage swung north and rounded Borneo, then went south through Makassar Strait. There he received two Ultras, one informing him to take position north of Lombok Strait for expected enemy traffic, the second canceling the first, ordering him back near Balikpapan to intercept traffic. Right on schedule, Ramage found a 2,000-ton freighter off Balikpapan and fired two torpedoes from 700 yards. The first hit, blowing off the bow of the ship; the second was another "DUD!" as Ramage noted in his report.

Ramage battled-surfaced and closed the wildly maneuvering ship. It fired back with accurate machine guns, spraying the deck. Seven of Ramage's gun crew were struck during the fusillade. He hauled off, got the wounded below, submerged, and went in for a second torpedo attack, firing one torpedo from 700 yards. It hit and the ship sank.

When Ramage reached Fremantle, he was furious. Of the fourteen torpedoes he had fired, one had prematured and five were duds. This, he estimated, was about a 43-percent failure rate. Al McCann was concerned but not sure that all the failures could be blamed on the exploder; "control errors or firing at too close range might have accounted for them." However, the disparaging torpedo reports from Moke Millican and Red Ramage convinced both McCann and Lockwood that there might be something amiss in the exploder.

Information from the codebreakers corroborated Ramage's claim that he had hit both *Nisshin Maru* and *Kyokuyo Maru*. However, they reported, *Kyokuyo* had been salvaged. Ramage received credit for damage to both ships for 35,000 tons, plus credit for sinking two other ships for 10,000 tons and the two schooners. Postwar records confirmed the two sinkings but trimmed the tonnage to 4,900 tons.

One Fremantle boat, Shirley Stovall's *Gudgeon*, refitted at Brisbane after her fifth patrol from that port and then proceeded to Lockwood's area for her sixth. Stovall was ordered to the Philippines, where he was to land a guerrilla party of six, commanded by a Filipino war hero, a Major Villamor.

The patrol seemed jinxed from the beginning. Leaving Brisbane, *Gudgeon* had a crankcase explosion in one of her Fairbanks-Morse engines, forcing a return to port. After repairs she set off again, landing her guerrillas on Negros Island. Then she traveled farther north into the Philippines to have a look at Manila Bay and Lingayen Gulf. Although the area was teeming with Japanese shipping, Stovall found nothing to shoot at. Dornin, relentlessly aggressive, believed that *Gudgeon* should penetrate Lingayen Gulf, but Stovall refused.

Moving southward, *Gudgeon* received an Ultra that a big Japanese tanker would put into Davao Gulf on January 19, so Stovall set a course to intercept, taking station off the entrance to the gulf. Either the tanker failed to show up or Stovall didn't see it; he remained in the area a few days, patrolling carefully, but found nothing.

After this fruitless running about, *Gudgeon* was ordered off Ambon Island. There she was spotted by a small subchaser with an exceptionally capable and aggressive skipper. In a near-perfect sonar approach, the subchaser attacked *Gudgeon*, dropping eight depth charges, all terrifyingly close. *Gudgeon* was severely damaged. One charge dished in the hull in the after torpedo room, putting the torpedo tubes out of commission. Most of the gauges and lights were smashed. The concussion knocked men off their feet. Many were cut by flying glass. There were countless leaks.

Fortunately for *Gudgeon*, a heavy rainstorm fell during the attack, and the drumming of rain on the surface of the sea interfered with the subchaser's sonar. During the storm, Stovall evaded and ran for safety. In Dornin's opinion, the storm "may have saved the boat." After withdrawing to open ocean, Stovall's crew spent three days repairing the damage.

Stovall next received orders to carry out a second special mission: sneak to a designated point on the coast of Timor and evacuate a party of guerrillas who had been fighting on the islands for seven and a half months. The guerrillas—twenty-one Australians, one Portuguese, one Britisher, and five natives, many with malaria and other jungle diseases—were picked up successfully by rubber boats, and Stovall delivered them to Australia.

When *Gudgeon* returned to Fremantle, Stovall and Dornin were at swords' points. Said Dornin later, "Stovall had won a couple of Navy Crosses and wanted to go home. I put him on report for not being aggressive enough. Al McCann felt he should have penetrated Davao Gulf like Freddy Warder had done. So did I. We had not shot a single torpedo on this patrol and we'd gotten hell knocked out of us. The upshot was, they relieved us both."

Stovall returned to the States to commission a new fleet boat. Dornin was on the way back to the States to take command of an O- or S-boat, but Babe Brown stopped him at Pearl Harbor. There, under Brown's supervision, Dornin—still considered the best TDC operator in the force—established a TDC school.

Little had been achieved. In their seventeen war patrols, Lockwood's forces sank only sixteen ships, including one (Millican's) by deck gun and none—so far as Japanese records revealed—by minelaying. All too many skippers had been found wanting.

Although Lockwood's operations were hampered by the extreme shortage of torpedoes and the small number of submarines available, he had been in the best position to mount a strategic offensive against the flow of oil to the Japanese fleet units in the Solomons. Red Ramage in *Trout* had made a good contribution in this direction at Miri. But why hadn't Lockwood concentrated *all* available submarines off known oil ports? These ports could have been mined, perhaps causing havoc—or at least considerable confusion. Why bother with Indochina and Manila? "The answer," a submarine skipper said, years later, "was simple. There was too much concentration on the numbers racket. Lockwood wanted 'bags.' Tonnage sunk. The more the better. He didn't care what kind or where it was found. He assumed, I suppose, that his boats would find better bags off Indochina and Manila."

Too much time was expended on special missions—for example, *Gudgeon*'s patrol. These missions, primarily supporting guerrilla activity in the Philippines, were pet projects of General MacArthur and his intelligence officers, who were, perhaps, bedazzled by the glamour and secrecy surrounding them. In theory, the missions helped sustain "unrest" in the occupied territories. This may have been true, to a point. But at this stage of the war, a few tanker sinkings off Borneo would have been far more valuable to the overall war effort than support of a handful of brave but jungle-bound operatives on Luzon. However, MacArthur was Lockwood's boss—one step removed—and, considering Lockwood's unfriendly relationship with Chips Carpender, he was not in the best position to deny MacArthur the submarine support he requested for these missions. There is strong evidence, too, that Lockwood was also mesmerized by the glamour of spying and guerrilla activities and enthusiastically joined in the game.

15
Summary, 1942

So ended the first year of the submarine war against Japan.

During 1942, Pacific-based submarines had made a total of about 350 war patrols. They had been employed for costal defense (Lingayen Gulf, Java, Midway), for blockading (Truk-Solomons), for intercepting Japanese capital ships via Ultra, for interdicting merchant shipping, for commando raids (Makin), for delivering and retrieving guerrillas and spies in Japanese-held territory (mostly the Philippines), for minelaying, for reconnaissance (primarily in the Marshalls), for delivering supplies and evacuating personnel (Corregidor), for shifting staff around in the Asiatic theater, and for "beacons" and weather forecasting in support of a few carrier strikes (Doolittle raid, bombing of Wake Island).

In pursuit of these missions, seven submarines had been lost in the Pacific: three S-boats by grounding (*S-27*, *S-36*, and *S-39*), one fleet boat (*Sealion*) in the Cavite Navy Yard, and three most likely by enemy countermeasures (*Perch*, scuttled after being trapped in shallow water; *Shark* and *Grunion* to unknown causes, probably depth-charge attack).

Only one of these kinds of missions did real harm to the Japanese (and the harm was, on the whole, slight); this was interdiction of Japanese shipping. During the 350 patrols, the three submarine commands (Pearl Harbor, Fremantle, Brisbane) claimed they had sunk

274 Japanese ships for 1.6 million tons. According to postwar Japanese records (incomplete in some cases), the figures were 180 ships sunk for 725,000 tons. This figure was about equal to what thirty-eight operating German U-boats in the Atlantic sank during the two months of February and March 1942.

This effort had not seriously interfered with Japanese imports and exports. Imports of bulk commodities—coal, iron ore, bauxite, rice, lead, tin, zinc, and so on—for 1942 remained about the same as for 1941, about 20 million tons. While U.S. submarines were sinking ships, more were being built. Japan began the war with 5.4 million tons of merchant marine shipping, excluding tankers. By the end of December 1942, the figure stood at 5.2 million tons, excluding tankers, a net loss of only 200,000 tons. As for tankers, Japan began the war with 575,000 tons, built more during the year, and by the end of December 1942 the figure stood at 686,000 tons—an *increase* of about 111,000 tons. Combining the figures for merchant ships and tankers, the Japanese suffered a net loss in shipping of about 89,000 tons, a figure so slight as to be meaningless.

The considerable effort—there is no way of figuring the precise number of patrol days involved—expended in chasing Japanese capital ships from glamorous Ultra reports was likewise largely unproductive. Including the Battle of Midway and the Truk blockade, these reports (plus lucky finds) resulted in about twenty-three individual sight contacts on major Japanese units—five on battleships and eighteen on aircraft carriers. Four of the five battleship contacts * were developed into attacks, resulting in slight damage to one—Donaho's at Truk. Ten of the eighteen carrier contacts † were developed into attacks, resulting in slight damage to three, those by Red Ramage at Truk and Chester Bruton and Barney McMahon in Empire waters. Only two major Japanese naval vessels were sunk in all of 1942: Dinty Moore's (*S-44*) heavy cruiser *Kako* and Dick Lake's (*Albacore*) light cruiser *Tenryu*.

By contrast, Japanese submarine effort against U.S. surface forces

---

* *Flying Fish* (Donaho), *Amberjack* (Bole), *Trout* (Ramage), *Nautilus* (Brockman), and *Gudgeon* (Lyon) at Midway. *Gudgeon* did not fire torpedoes.

† *Skipjack* (Freeman), *Narwhal* (Wilkins), *Pollack* (Moseley), *Nautilus* (Brockman), *Trout* (Ramage), *Saury* (Mewhinney), *Gato* (Myers), *Greenling* (Bruton—at Truk and Empire), *Stingray* (Moore), *Drum* (McMahon), *Grayling* (Olsen), *Grouper* (Duke—at Midway), *Triton* (Kirkpatrick), *Wahoo* (Kennedy), *Albacore* (Lake), *Thresher* (Millican), and *Seawolf* (Warder). *Skipjack, Narwhal, Pollack, Trout, Saury, Gato, Greenling, Stingray,* and *Drum* actually fired torpedoes at carriers.

was rewarding—for the Japanese. Japanese submarines sank the damaged carrier *Yorktown* at Midway and the carrier *Wasp* and the light cruiser *Juneau* in the Solomons. The carrier *Saratoga* was twice torpedoed and put out of action for most of the year. In addition, Japanese submarines inflicted heavy damage on the brand-new battleship *North Carolina* and the older heavy cruiser *Chester*. Thanks in part to Ultra, Japanese submarine losses in 1942 were heavy: twenty-three. Six of these were sunk by U.S. submarines: *Gudgeon, Tautog* (two), *Triton, Grayback,* and *Seadragon*.

By far the most successful U.S. submarine effort of 1942 was the fifty-four fleet boat war patrols mounted from Pearl Harbor to Empire, East China Sea, and Formosan waters. These fifty-four, amounting to about 15 percent of all war patrols, accounted for eighty-one confirmed ships, about 45 percent of all sinkings. Had all the fleet boats been concentrated at Pearl Harbor at the beginning of the war and sent to these same waters—and Luzon Strait—to prey on merchant shipping (as Doenitz was doing in the Atlantic), they could probably have carried out an additional two-hundred-odd patrols accounting for an additional three hundred ships, a truly meaningful inroad in Japanese shipping services. The concentration of submarines in the Philippines, Java, Fremantle, Midway, Alaska, Truk, Brisbane, and Solomons achieved little compared to Empire patrols.

Much of the submarine failure in 1942 could be laid to poor skipper performance and poor torpedo performance. During 1942, the three commands relieved about 40 skippers out of 135—almost 30 percent—because of poor health, battle fatigue, or nonproductivity, mostly the last. Many younger officers from the class of 1931 and three from 1932 became skippers, but the three commanders chose these younger men all too slowly and cautiously, still obsessed by the peacetime emphasis on seniority. During 1942, Lockwood made a substantial contribution by confirming the deep-running fault of the Mark XIV torpedo—and getting BuOrd to admit it officially—but all three commands were derelict in follow-up investigations of the magnetic and contact exploders. At the end of December 1942, a full year into the war, no live controlled tests of the exploders had been conducted, in spite of the almost universal belief in the submarine force that something was wrong with both magnetic and contact types.

The major reason for the submarine failure of 1942 was not mechanical, physical, or psychological. It was, to put it simply, a failure of imagination on the highest levels by King, Edwards, Nimitz, Hart,

Wilkes, Withers, English, Lockwood, Christie, and Fife. All these men failed to set up a broad, unified strategy for Pacific submarines aimed at a single specific goal: interdicting Japanese shipping services in the most efficient and telling manner. The lessons of the German U-boat campaigns against Britain in World Wars I and II—the latter in progress almost on Washington's doorstep—had apparently not yet sunk home. The military and maritime theories of Clausewicz and Mahan were ignored. The U.S. submarine force was divided and shunted about willy-nilly on missions for which it was not suited, while the bulk of Japanese shipping sailed unmolested in Empire waters and through the bottleneck in Luzon Strait.

Part IV

16
Submarine Command, January 1943

Shortly after New Year's Day 1943, Bob English began to plan a trip to the United States to visit the submarine support facilities at Mare Island near San Francisco and, if time permitted, at Dutch Harbor and Panama. In addition, English and those accompanying him might have an opportunity to visit their families.

The plans were firmed up in mid-January, and a Pan Am clipper on loan to the navy and manned by a civilian crew took off on January 20 for San Francisco. In addition to English and his three senior staff officers,* there were six other navy passengers, one of them a nurse, plus nine crewmen including the chief pilot, Robert Elsey.

After a routine flight, the plane ran into a bad storm approaching San Francisco, with high winds, driving rain, and fog. It lost radio contact with San Francisco. When next heard from, it was far off course, over Bell Valley, between Boonville and Ukiah, California, about 115 miles north of San Francisco, not far from the ocean. It flew low over the home of Mrs. Charles Wallach, who was an aircraft spotter in her spare time, part of the Civilian Defense network formed to search the skies for enemy planes.

"There was a terrific storm at the time," Mrs. Wallach reported.

---

* John Jarvis Crane, the Pacific Submarine Force engineering officer; William Girard Myers, ex-*Gato*, who was in the process of relieving Crane as force engineering officer; and John Owen Reilly Coll, the force gunnery officer. In addition, Robert Holmes Smith, commanding officer of the tender *Sperry*, was on board.

"The wind was blowing so hard it blew over trees and disconnected our telephone service when the wires were blown down. The plane was flying very low. It had its lights on and came right over my house and disappeared in the storm to the north."

It was a mountainous area, rugged and empty country, with peaks of 2,000 and 3,000 feet. The plane smashed head on into the side of a cliff, only 150 feet below the crest. The plane evidently exploded in a fireball. English and the other eighteen people on board were probably killed instantly.

Because of the poor communications in the area, it took Mrs. Wallach two days to get word of the plane sighting to authorities. "No one believed me," she said later. Another eight days passed before the wreckage was positively located. The area was cordoned off by soldiers, who had orders to shoot to kill anyone who came into the area; it was assumed that English carried highly classified documents relating to submarine operations and codebreaking. On January 31, the bodies were found in a ravine near the wreckage, which was totally destroyed by fire.

The disaster sent a shock wave through the entire submarine force. In Pearl Harbor, Babe Brown assumed temporary command of Submarines Pacific until Admiral King selected a replacement.

In Perth, Lockwood learned the news of the missing plane from the newspapers. He immediately got off a letter to Jimmy Fife in Brisbane.

That is very bad news in the papers this morning about the probable loss of Bob English and nine other important officers. I can't think who they would be but certainly hope they are not submariners of whom we are badly in need. I expect that they will now make Babe Brown commander [of Pearl Harbor submarines] as he is on the spot and knows the job, although they might pull someone from the mainland about class of 1911 to take the job. "Reef" Snyder, Rood, Read and Bode are all possibilities but several of them would not be my choice.

Two days later, Lockwood wrote Admiral Edwards, "Am terribly sorry to hear about Bob English. . . . If it is true, I hope no one will think of the possibility of sending me to Pearl Harbor. By all means let someone else have Pearl Harbor." Lockwood, buried in Perth with only eight submarines, continuously insulted or denigrated by

Chips Carpender, wanted nothing more than the Pearl Harbor command.

Ralph Christie had just assumed command of the Newport Torpedo Station when word of English's death reached him. A few weeks before, a Navy Selection Board had promoted Christie to rear admiral. Like Lockwood, Christie believed himself qualified to replace English and hoped for the job.

It was not to be. Admiral King ordered Louis Emil Denfeld, then second in command of the Bureau of Personnel, to name Lockwood to replace English. When the word reached Lockwood, he wrote his classmate Denfeld, "I can see your fine Italian hand and that of Admiral Edwards in getting me this job. Actually I expected to be left alone where I was, but naturally I am much flattered and very glad to get this bigger job." Admiral Edwards wrote Lockwood, "You were selected on the platform that the officer best qualified to determine the submarine policy throughout the Pacific should be at Pearl Harbor."

After the Pearl Harbor commander was decided upon, Denfeld picked Christie to replace Lockwood in Perth-Fremantle. Christie, having done nothing to clear up the torpedo logjam, was immediately relieved by his exec at Newport, Frank George Fahrion, and went back to Pearl Harbor, arriving only a few days after Lockwood. Christie called on Nimitz—suffering from malaria caught on Guadalcanal—and then Lockwood. About that time, Christie's appointment to rear admiral came through. At a festive dinner, Lockwood pinned on Christie's shoulder boards.

From Pearl Harbor, Christie flew on to Brisbane, where he conferred with Chips Carpender and Jimmy Fife. Like Lockwood, Christie told Carpender that his proper place was Brisbane, commanding the larger concentration of submarines. Fife, Christie suggested, should go to Perth-Fremantle. Carpender did not agree. "He pinned Christie's ears back," an officer said later. Fife remained in Brisbane, commanding Task Force 42; Christie went to Perth. From then on, Christie tried to absorb Fife into *his* command, but Carpender would have none of it.

In all this shifting about, Chips Carpender managed one more slap at Lockwood. When Lockwood left Australia, he requested that Carpender transfer his chief of staff, Sunshine Murray, with him. Carpender disapproved the request, forcing Lockwood to go over Carpender's head with a direct appeal to Louie Denfeld. In a letter to Denfeld, Lockwood explained the impasse, adding, "I asked [Carpender] what were his reasons, and he said that I didn't rate it or words to that effect."

In a short while, Denfeld honored Lockwood's request. Sunshine Murray moved to Pearl Harbor, replacing John Griggs as chief of staff, and Griggs returned to the States to become commander of Squadron Twelve, the twelve submarines delayed with H.O.R. engine problems. Babe Brown remained as Commander, Squadron Four. One of Lockwood's old pals, Swede Momsen, took over Squadron Two, in the process of rotating from Australia.

In Fremantle, Al McCann remained as commander of Squadron Six in *Pelias*. Tex McLean moved up to replace Sunshine Murray as Christie's chief of staff. McLean's brother-in-law, Murray Tichenor, soon arrived from Peru to replace McLean as operations officer.

17

Brisbane, January through May 1943

The Death of Admiral Yamamoto

During the naval conflict in the Solomons in the fall of 1942, both the United States and Japan had suffered heavy losses. After the Battle of Tassafaronga, November 30, both Nimitz and Yamamoto withdrew many major naval units to the United States and Japan for extensive battle-damage repairs and replenishment. In the ensuing two months, the Japanese evacuated most of their soldiers from Guadalcanal, many by submarine. By February 8, 1943, all organized resistance on the island ceased. Then there was a lull.

That was far from the end of the story in the Solomons, however. Admiral Yamamoto seemed unwilling to give up another square foot of real estate. During the winter and spring of 1943, he sent a steady stream of reinforcements into the Solomons, New Georgia, Bougainville, New Britain, and New Ireland. The bastion of Rabaul was beefed up with additional aircraft. The war bogged down into a series of air attacks and counterattacks,* with an occasional meeting of small surface forces.

During the early weeks of the year 1943 as the lull set in, the

---

* The carrier *Enterprise*, repaired at Noumea, continued in combat service, mostly in the Solomons; *Saratoga*, having been repaired at Pearl Harbor, reached Noumea in December 1942, and she too operated in the Solomons.

Allied forces enjoyed a steady flow of intelligence from a variety of sources. One of these was a new Fleet Intelligence Center created by Arthur McCollum, formerly chief of ONI's Far Eastern Division, a close friend and ally of Joe Rochefort and Laurence Safford. McCollum came out to work for Carpender after the codebreaking shake-up in Washington. He patterned his organization—based in Brisbane—on the joint intelligence center at Pearl Harbor. Its primary source of information was Fabian's FRUMEL codebreaking unit, which remained in Melbourne, transmitting information to McCollum by means of a secure land line.

At about this time the codebreakers suffered a setback. On January 29, the New Zealand corvettes *Kiwi* and *Moa*, operating in Guadalcanal waters, intercepted a Japanese submarine, *I-1*, which was loaded with new Japanese codebooks. *Kiwi* and *Moa* cornered *I-1*, rammed her, and drove her aground in sinking condition. Some of the Japanese jumped ashore and buried some of the codebooks, but many were left behind on the hulk.

Unfortunately for the codebreakers, some of the personnel on *I-1* escaped and made their way back to Rabaul. When they reported the loss of the codebooks and their probable capture by Allied forces, the Japanese declared a cryptographic emergency. A submarine and then a plane were sent to destroy *I-1*. Neither could find the hulk. Assuming that many codes had been compromised, the Japanese issued new codebooks and altered their encoding procedures, which led to a temporary blackout of information from U.S. codebreakers. (For example, the Japanese carrier forces, mostly in the homeland, were temporarily lost track of.)

By early April, however, the codebreakers were back in business and soon provided information that led to one of the most spectacular coups of all: they picked up and decoded a message giving the precise itinerary of an inspection trip Admiral Yamamoto planned for Rabaul and Bougainville. Forewarned, Admiral Halsey sent long-range air force P-38s from Guadalcanal on April 18. The pilots intercepted Yamamoto's plane in mid-flight and shot it down, killing the admiral. Admiral Mineichi Koga succeeded Yamamoto as commander in chief. The Japanese did not discover until after the war that Yamamoto had died as a result of codebreaking.

"Playing Checkers" with Submarines

When Jimmy Fife relieved Christie of command of submarines basing in Brisbane, the port was growing into a sizable submarine facility. The tenders *Fulton* (Squadron Eight), *Sperry* (Squadron Ten), and *Holland* (Squadron Two) were moored at New Farm Wharf. The barracks for the relief crew personnel had been expanded to accommodate 550 enlisted men. There were overhaul shops for batteries, torpedoes, and periscopes. As a staff visitor from Fremantle observed somewhat jealously in a memo, "The base they're building is going to make Sub Base Pearl look like a farmer's garage."

Submariners returning from war patrol crowded the hotels, bars, and streets of Brisbane. Unwinding from combat tensions, they drank and played hard, as they did in Pearl Harbor, Perth, and Midway. Inasmuch as Brisbane was now filling up with other military personnel—American marines and soldiers, Australians returning from North Africa—there were frequent street brawls and, on occasion, serious riots.

This free-swinging horseplay worried Chips Carpender and Jimmy Fife. From the moment the fleet boats began arriving from Pearl Harbor and Fremantle, Carpender had believed the solution was to get the submariners out of town into remote rest camps, and when Fife took command he began construction of two major submarine rest and recuperation centers, based around resort hotels. One was at Coolangatta, on the seashore about 75 miles south of Brisbane; the other was at Toowoomba, in the mountains about 75 miles northwest of Brisbane. These bases, which cost about 85,000 Australian pounds, were paid for out of "reverse lend-lease" funds. In addition, Fife rented houses in Brisbane for commanding officers, members of the staff, and visiting firemen.

In keeping with his character, Fife's own quarters were austere. He set up his home in a Quonset hut on New Farm Wharf. "He literally lived and breathed his job," said Chester Bruton, who had become a division commander serving under Fife. "You could find him in the hut day and night. Surrounded by hard-drinking submariners fresh from combat, he was a strange, solitary, almost lonely figure. He didn't drink or fraternize. He never seemed concerned about *people*. When a submarine came in from patrol, he wanted to know about the condition of the battery or the engines or the periscopes or electrical equipment."

Not everyone in Brisbane was overjoyed by Fife's promotion. One who was not was Reuben Whitaker, ex-exec of Bull Wright's *Sturgeon*, who had commanded S-44 for one patrol. "Fife was ruthless," said Whitaker. "The S-44 which I commanded was scheduled to go back to the States for overhaul. Before he left, Christie called me in and said, 'Do you want to take her back? If not, I'll pull you off with the understanding that you get the first fleet boat command that opens up.' I said I'd wait in the PCO pool. When Fife took over, Christie called me in again and—in front of Fife—repeated the commitment, so as to inform Fife. Fife said, 'I'd be delighted to have Whitaker as a commanding officer of a fleet boat.' Well, two weeks later, after Christie had gone, I had orders to the *Flying Fish* as exec."

Soon after Fife took command, the naval war in the Solomons began winding down. Admiral King ordered that Gin Styer's Squadron Ten in *Sperry* and the remnants of Squadron Two, including the old tender *Holland*, return to Pearl Harbor—*Holland* to proceed from there to Mare Island for overhaul. This order, in effect, left Fife with only one squadron, Eight, basing in the tender *Fulton*.

Fife believed the generally poor showing of U.S. submarines basing in Brisbane up to then was due to overcaution. When he had his feet firmly planted beneath his desk, he abandoned caution. Each of his skippers would give a good account of himself or else he would be summarily relieved.

Up to then, most of the skippers had been assigned an area to patrol and left pretty much on their own. Before the Japanese changed the codes in February, there was a steady flow of information from the codebreakers about Japanese maritime forces reinforcing the Solomons from Palau and Truk. Fife believed the submarine force could better capitalize on this information if the boats were more tightly controlled from Brisbane and shifted about frequently as targets became known. He believed he should take a direct—and firm—hand in the shifting—or as he told his staff, "playing checkers" with submarines. In many respects, his new policy resembled that of Doenitz in the Atlantic. It led to many disasters and near disasters.

When Fife took command, the ancient and clumsy *Argonaut*, commanded by Jack Pierce, was en route from Pearl Harbor to Brisbane to help carry out the many special missions General MacArthur demanded of submarines. She had landed troops on Makin, but she had never made a real war patrol, firing torpedoes at Japanese ships.

Fife, believing *Argonaut* capable of combat, ordered her to patrol against Japanese shipping in the hazardous area between New Britain and Bougainville, south of St. George's Channel. On January 10, Fife directed Pierce to attack a convoy of five freighters with destroyer escorts. By happenstance, a U.S. Army aircraft, out of bombs, was flying overhead and witnessed the battle, *Argonaut's* first and last. Pierce apparently attacked the destroyers first, hitting at least one for damage. The destroyers counterattacked, churning the water with depth charges. The crew of the aircraft saw *Argonaut's* huge bow suddenly break water at a steep angle, hanging. One of the depth charges had obviously inflicted severe damage. The Japanese destroyers circled like sharks, pumping shells into *Argonaut's* hull. She slipped below the waves, never to be heard from again. One hundred and five officers and men went down with her.

Jack Pierce had a younger brother serving in the navy, George Ellis Pierce. In peacetime, George had also been a submariner, but he transferred to lighter-than-air craft (dirigibles). When Jack was lost on *Argonaut*, George was serving in Georgia. Upon receiving word of his brother's death, George immediately volunteered for submarines. Later he said he thought the decision to order *Argonaut* to attack was justified. "I do not blame Jimmy Fife."

Argonaut's loss, a sad event in its own right, caused further problems for the Australian submarine command. She had been sent there to carry out special missions—for MacArthur and his intelligence operations. Her loss meant that regular fleet boats would continue to be diverted from normal patrol for many of these time-consuming (and hazardous) chores, meaning fewer torpedo tubes on the firing line.

In the same month Howard Gilmore in *Growler*, "born under an unlucky star," as his buddy, Chuck Triebel, had put it, left Brisbane for his fourth patrol. Fife, manning his radio nightly, chivied *Growler* around, trying to put Gilmore in the path of known convoys or other targets. On January 16, Gilmore got a big one: the 6,000-ton passenger-cargo ship, *Chifuku Maru*, his sixth confirmed sinking. On the last day of the month, he attacked a 2,500-ton converted gunboat with a single torpedo that ran under the target without exploding.

A few nights later, Fife put Gilmore on the trail of a small convoy, but escorts, and mechanical failures on *Growler*, prevented an attack.

On the night of February 7, while charging batteries, Gilmore saw what he believed to be the converted gunboat he had unsuccessfully attacked the week before. Actually, it was *Hayasaki*, a 900-ton provision ship. Manning the bridge, Gilmore went to battle stations and began closing, but *Hayasaki* spotted *Growler* from a mile away and charged in to ram. *Growler*'s crew was slow to detect the target's change in course.

Gilmore's unlucky star now shone brightly. The small ship suddenly loomed out of the darkness. On the bridge, Gilmore sounded the collision alarm and then shouted, "Left full rudder!" His intent was probably to avoid both ramming and being rammed. However, the swing left put *Growler* on a collision course and *Growler*, making 17 knots, hit *Hayasaki* amidships.

The impact was massive. *Growler* heeled 50 degrees, throwing everyone belowdecks off his feet. The crew of the damaged *Hayasaki* manned machine guns, directing a withering fire at *Growler*'s bridge. The assistant officer of the deck, young Ensign William Wadsworth Williams, and a lookout, Fireman W. F. Kelley, were killed instantly. Howard Gilmore, wounded, clung to a bridge frame. Above the roar of machine gun fire, he shouted, "Clear the bridge!"

The officer of the deck, the quartermaster, and two wounded lookouts hurried down the hatch into the conning tower. Arnold Frederic Schade, the exec, stood at the foot of the ladder, waiting for Gilmore. Then came another shout from Gilmore—one that would become submarine legend:

"*Take her down.*"

Schade hesitated for thirty seconds. Save the ship or save the captain? Schade decided to follow his captain's last order and save the ship. He gave orders to dive. *Growler* went down, leaving Howard Gilmore, along with the bodies of Williams and Kelley, topside. No one knows how long Gilmore lived in the water. The Japanese on *Hayasaki* apparently made no effort to capture him. He probably drifted away in the darkness, borne along by the winds and current. For sacrificing his life to save his ship, Gilmore was posthumously awarded the Medal of Honor, the first man of the submarine force to be so decorated.

Beneath the waves, Schade, dazed and bruised from a fall from the conning tower to the control room, had his hands full. The impact of the collision had bent 18 feet of *Growler*'s bow at right angles to the submarine, rendering her forward torpedo tubes useless. Salt water poured through bullet holes in the conning tower. Schade gave orders to battle-surface and sink *Hayasaki*, but when *Growler* came up the seas were empty. Schade believed the ramming had sunk her, but she was only damaged and lived to fight on.

So did *Growler*. Schade got the leaks repaired and limped slowly back to Brisbane. On the endorsement to this patrol report, Fife wrote, "The performance of the officers and crew in effecting repairs and bringing the ship safely back to base is one of the outstanding submarine feats of the war to date. . . . *Growler* will be repaired and will fight again."

The next disasters befell three of the five boats leaving Brisbane for patrol in February. These were John Bole's *Amberjack*, out for blood, according to Fife; John Craig's *Grampus*; and *Triton*, now commanded by George Kenneth Mackenzie, Jr. The three boats were manned by battle-wise crews.

Fife controlled these boats strictly, repeatedly moving them around on his checkerboard. *Amberjack*, for example, was first moved from west of New Guinea to west of Shortlands, then to west of Buka. She was next ordered west of Vella Lavella. En route, she was ordered west of Ganongga Island. A few days later she was ordered north to cover traffic to the Shortlands. Then she was ordered farther north, and subsequently to the area between New Ireland and Bougainville. She was then shifted north of New Ireland, then ordered to a position west of New Hanover. Her last station was west of Cape Lambert.

In the course of all this jumping about, the three boats achieved little. Bole reported sinking a 5,000-ton freighter, but postwar records failed to substantiate it. MacKenzie attacked a convoy and sank one freighter, confirmed in postwar records at 3,000 tons, and damaged another of 7,000 tons. Craig in *Grampus* may have damaged one large vessel but sank none.

None of the three boats returned from patrol. All were declared "overdue, presumed lost," taking down Bole, Craig, MacKenzie, and 214 other officers and men. After the war, U.S. naval authorities made an intensive hunt in Japanese records to determine the causes for each loss. There were clues, giving rise to various speculations, but nothing positive was ever learned about any of them.

A sixth boat, *Gato*, commanded by Robert Joseph Foley, was very nearly lost. Fife had assigned Bub Ward to be Foley's exec. On their first patrol together, Foley and Ward had made eight attacks, claiming four ships sunk for 27,600 tons, a performance that led Halsey in his endorsement to compare Foley with the best of the submarine commanders. Postwar Japanese records credited Foley with three and a half ships for 11,500 tons, the half credit shared with naval aircraft.

On the second Foley-Ward patrol from Brisbane, *Gato* was first diverted to a special mission: twenty-seven children, nine mothers, three nuns, and a dozen commandos were delivered from Bougainville to a ship waiting off Tulagi. After that, Foley went on regular patrol, a piece on Fife's checkerboard.

On April 4, Fife directed Foley to intercept a freighter escorted by a destroyer. While making the approach, the destroyer detected *Gato* and turned to attack. Foley ordered deep depth, but before *Gato* responded the destroyer came over, dropping depth charges that fell close—and *beneath*—the boat. The blast was violent. *Gato* rocked and plunged out of control toward the bottom. Ward, helping the diving officer, caught the boat at 380 feet. The charges knocked out all propulsion and caused hot runs in the torpedo tubes and bad leaks. Said Ward later, "We almost came to the end of the road."

Foley terminated the patrol and limped into Brisbane. After a drydock inspection, it was determined that all of *Gato*'s stern torpedo tubes would have to be replaced. Foley was ordered to return to Pearl Harbor for the work. Bub Ward got off *Gato* and went into Fife's PCO pool.

Fife's reaction to the loss of four fleet boats with all hands was cold-blooded. "Tough luck," he wrote Lockwood, "but they can't get Japs without taking chances . . . don't think the time has arrived to inject caution into the system because it is too difficult to overcome again."

In peacetime, the loss of four submarines in so short a time would ordinarily prompt an exhaustive investigation to determine blame: heads would roll. In wartime, an investigation might produce more valuable results: information about how to avoid such losses in the future for all three submarine commands. From Fremantle, Christie proposed such an investigation to Carpender, asking permission to go to Brisbane to conduct it.

Christie was amazed and angered by Carpender's reaction and wrote Lockwood, "He [Carpender] told me it was none of my business, and forbade me to come east for that purpose. . . . It *is* my business and I shall act as I think I should—if possible, diplomatically."

In place of Christie, Carpender sent for Al McCann, who was senior to Fife by one year and presumably impartial, giving him orders to carry out a quiet one-man investigation. Christie wrote Sunshine Murray in Pearl Harbor:

His Nibs sent for Allan to investigate . . . hush-hush, one copy to be delivered by hand and locked in His Nibs's personal file and Allan not to discuss with me. Someone might think someone had something to hide by such maneuvers. I am tempted to ask, officially, for a copy, but a shot at me is a shot at submarines. . . . MacArthur appears to be running Subs, SouthWesPac with Jimmy [Fife] as his satellite. Expect him [Fife] to emerge as a general any day. Don't know if we can afford him. I urged moving [submarines] to other equally productive areas until the concentrated anti [submarine] effort cools off, but no soap. A good halfback tries to find the hole in the line.

Lockwood's reply to Christie:

Naturally I am surprised at the method selected for handling the investigation of Jimmy's losses. Certainly a thorough investigation should be made and certainly it would appear that you should be a party. . . . As you know I have always felt that we should operate the major force in that area [Australia] from the west coast and now that Jimmy's boats are getting such poor bags the need for a reshuffle should be entirely apparent. . . . I hope that you and Jimmy will not let any friction grow up between you. I realize you are not pals but I trust that you will not let that interfere with cooperation. God knows there are enough personnel problems in the Southwest Pacific without letting them creep into the submarine service.

In Brisbane, McCann carried forward his unusual investigation. He talked "informally" with Fife and members of Fife's staff, including Chester Bruton, Operations Officer John Murphy, and many others. He evidently followed Carpender's purported instructions about filing the report; neither Christie nor Lockwood ever saw it. Years later, McCann said, "I exonerated Fife completely. The losses were in no way his fault. The boats may have been sunk by our own aircraft. There was no way to tell."

Christie was not satisfied. He launched his own private investigation, studying the radio dispatches to the missing submarines. His conclusion was that Fife, like Doenitz, had been talking too much to his boats and requiring them to talk back too much and shifting them around too much. In a tough letter to Fife (probably meant also for Carpender) which severely strained the thin "cooperation" existing between the two commands, Christie said in part:

The probability that the enemy is able to derive information of value from a large number of submarine operational dispatches must be reckoned with. A study of the operations of patrols of the Grampus *and* Amberjack *focuses attention on one method of operation which may conceivably have contributed to the loss of these vessels. Radio dispatches concerning* Grampus *and* Amberjack *totalled 106. Forty-six of these were reports of positions of submarines for higher command. Many of these dispatches gave specific names, locations and times. . . . We have in numerous instances intercepted enemy transmissions revealing the positions of our submarines and ordering counter measures. Submarine transmissions have been repeatedly and expertly DF-ed. The obvious solution is rigid adherence to the fundamentals of radio security, particularly the elimination of all but essential traffic. The amount of traffic put on the air should be a minimum for reasons of external security. The number of addresses should be a minimum for reasons of internal security.*

In the wake of the three losses Fife offered to resign. Admiral Carpender refused him. Carpender, MacArthur, and Halsey stood staunchly behind Fife, and Fife remained in place—secure from further investigations by Ralph Christie. Fife thereafter was unshakably pro-MacArthur, a loyal and devoted member of "MacArthur's Navy," but the checker playing diminished markedly.

Fife's patrol report endorsements were long, detailed, professorial—and often harsh. Two skippers who felt the lash were Dick Lake in *Albacore* and Rob Roy McGregor in *Grouper*.

Lake, who had missed a carrier on his first patrol from Pearl Harbor but sunk the light cruiser *Tenryu* on the way down to Brisbane, became another piece on the checkerboard on his third patrol from Brisbane. Off the north coast of New Guinea, Lake found eleven targets in eleven days. The first group consisted of a destroyer and a frigate escorting a minelayer. Lake attacked, firing ten torpedoes, believing he had sunk the minelayer and damaged the destroyer with three hits. In subsequent days, he attacked a tanker, several freighters, and another destroyer, firing another eight torpedoes. All torpedoes missed.

Fife gave Lake credit for an aggressive patrol but severely criticized his torpedo shooting—three hits out of eighteen shots. He wrote, "In her three patrols to date, *Albacore* has fired forty-six torpedoes and obtained nine hits. This percentage is below average and unsatisfactory, not so much from the point of view of torpedo expenditure as from the number of valuable targets that got away. Overhaul of the fire-control party and thorough training are indicated."

Rob Roy McGregor had taken command of *Grouper* from Claren Duke following Duke's first patrol in the East China Sea. On McGregor's first and second patrols he had sunk a total of three ships for 15,000 tons. On his third patrol, from Brisbane, McGregor joined the checkerboard forces. Fife's endorsement:

[Grouper] was put in the channel between New Georgia and Santa Isabel in hopes she would stop enemy ships coming down to evacuate forces from Guadalcanal. She found herself between two columns of ten destroyers each (about twenty to twenty-five destroyers) about to be attacked by our own air forces and probably paying little attention to submarines. The situation called for a quick decision in firing all ten tubes. Instead the Commanding Officer chose to close the last destroyer of an additional group of four which was coming up astern of the main formation . . . and this attack was frustrated by a turn away during the ensuing bombing attack by our own forces. A golden opportunity for a coordinated submarine torpedo and air attack—which might have easily been disastrous to the enemy and discouraged further attempts to evacuate Guadalcanal—was lost.

After this patrol, McGregor was relieved of command. (He served on the staffs of Squadrons Eight and Six, then went to new construction.) To replace him, Fife chose Spike Hottel, whom English had relieved of command of *Cuttlefish* after the Battle of Midway and who was then serving as Fife's force gunnery officer. He was the first relieved skipper to get a second chance. Fife felt Hottel had not had a fair chance on ancient *Cuttlefish* to show his ability and deserved another crack at the Japanese. In addition, Fife had a critical shortage of qualified skippers.

Hottel conducted an aggressive first patrol, according to Fife's endorsement, but targets were scarce and he fired no torpedoes.

Wahoo's January Patrol

The transfer of Squadron Ten and the remnants of Squadron Two to Pearl Harbor set in motion a backward trek for the submarines that had come down to Brisbane. During the spring, seven (including two Squadron Two boats) returned: *Flying Fish, Wahoo, Gato, Grayback, Snapper, Swordfish,* and *Nautilus. Nautilus* went direct, without conducting a war patrol. The other six patrolled home, along the equator, in the Marianas, and elsewhere. With the exception of *Wahoo,* the patrols produced nothing spectacular.

Donc Donaho on *Flying Fish* had a new exec, his third in four war patrols, Reuben Whitaker. Whitaker said later, "*Flying Fish* was the most miserable boat I ever saw. . . . Donaho had cut off all the water to the enlisted men's showers. If a man made a simple mistake, he would fly into a rage and say he never wanted to see him again. After I had been on board a few days and met the officers in the wardroom, I said to Donaho, 'What the hell are you talking about? You've got a really fine bunch of officers.' Donaho just didn't know how to handle people."

Donaho's *Flying Fish* and St. Angelo's *Snapper* patrolled back to Pearl Harbor by way of the Marianas. Donaho, relentlessly aggressive, poked *Flying Fish*'s nose right into the harbors at Guam and Tinian and fired off ten torpedoes. The Saint torpedoed and sank one ship that Donaho had damaged in the Guam harbor, *Tokai Maru,* 8,350 tons, so both skippers shared credit for her. In addition, Donaho sank the 1,000-ton freighter, *Hyuga Maru. Snapper* seemed unable to shake the dark spell that had dogged her since the beginning of the war. On return to Pearl Harbor, St. Angelo was criticized for remaining submerged too much on the patrol, and when *Snapper* went in for overhaul, St. Angelo was relieved of command and sent to the staff of John Griggs's Squadron Twelve. Reuben Whitaker left *Flying Fish* for new construction.

Chet Smith's *Swordfish* was turned over to Jack Lewis, who had made the first luckless patrols of *Trigger* at Midway and in Alaska. Like Hottel, Lewis was being given a second chance because of the skipper shortage. Off Bougainville, he conducted a well-executed attack on a convoy, sinking a 4,000-ton freighter, but a few days later *Swordfish* was strafed by a U.S. B-17 which inflicted enough damage to require Lewis to terminate the patrol early. At Mare Island, Lewis went to new construction.

Before *Wahoo* left Brisbane on her first patrol under Mush Morton, the new skipper called the crew to quarters on deck and gave them a flaming pep talk. "*Wahoo* is expendable," Morton said, according to her yeoman, Forest J. Sterling. "We will take every reasonable precaution, but our mission is to sink enemy shipping. . . . Now, if anyone doesn't want to go along under these conditions, just see the yeoman. I am giving him verbal authority now to transfer anyone who is not a volunteer. . . . Nothing will ever be said about your remaining in Brisbane."

Nobody asked for a transfer. After the speech, Sterling reported, he became aware of

a different Wahoo. . . . *I could feel the stirring of a strong spirit growing in her. The officers acted differently. The men felt differently. There was more of a feeling of freedom and of being trusted to get our jobs done. A high degree of confidence in the capabilities and luck of our ship grew on us and we became a little bit cocky. It was a feeling that* Wahoo *was not only the best damn submarine in the Submarine Force but that she was capable of performing miracles.*

Wrote George Grider, a junior officer:

Mush . . . was built like a bear, and as playful as a cub. . . . The crew loved him. . . . Whether he was in the control room, swapping tall tales . . . or wandering restlessly about in his skivvies, talking to the men in the torpedo and engine rooms, he was as relaxed as a baby . . . constantly joking, laughing, or planning outrageous exploits against the enemy.

All this must have required considerable effort, for Mush Morton was not a well man; he suffered from prostate trouble. Young John Griggs recalled, "During our periods in port he would be hospitalized and on patrol he had to have semiweekly prostate massages. Yet he did not let this deter him from his goal, sinking Japs."

The wardroom—Grider, Roger Warde Paine, Jr., young John Griggs—considered Mush "magnificent" but still had reservations about the exec, Dick O'Kane. Grider wrote:

He talked a great deal—reckless, aggressive talk—and it was natural to wonder how much of it was no more than talk. During the second patrol Dick had grown harder to live with, friendly one minute and pulling his rank on his junior officers the next. One day he would be a martinet, and the next he would display an overlenient, what-the-hell attitude that was far from reassuring. With Mush and Dick in the saddle, how would the Wahoo *fare?*

Fife gave Morton orders to reconnoiter Wewak, a Japanese supply base on the north coast of New Guinea. Morton kept *Wahoo* on the surface. "It was a strange and unfamiliar experience," Grider wrote, "to see enemy land lying black and sinister on the port hand, to feel the enemy planes always near us, and yet it was invigorating."

There was one large problem about reconnoitering Wewak: *Wahoo* had no charts of the harbor. However, it turned out that one of the motor machinists, D. C. ("Bird-Dog") Keeter, had bought a cheap school atlas while he was in Australia. It had a map of New Guinea with a small indentation labeled "Wewak." With that as a reference, Morton located the unmarked area on a larger navy chart, and George Grider, an amateur photographer, made a blowup of the navy chart with an ingenious device composed of camera and signal lights. "It might have made a cartographer shudder," Grider wrote, "but it was a long way ahead of no chart at all."

Morton found Wewak. Then, to everyone's amazement, he announced that his interpretation of "reconnoiter" meant penetrate the harbor and sink whatever ships could be found. "Now it was clear," Grider wrote, "that our captain had advanced from mere rashness to outright foolhardiness."

Among the many innovations Morton had put in effect on *Wahoo* was one suggested by Fife: the exec, not the captain, manned the periscope. According to Grider:

This, he explained, left the skipper in a better position to interpret all factors involved, do a better conning job, and make decisions more dispassionately. There is no doubt it is an excellent theory, and it worked beautifully for him, but few captains other than Mush ever had such serene faith in a subordinate that they could resist grabbing the scope in moments of crisis.

The trip into the harbor was long and perilous. Throughout, Morton remained almost irrationally casual. "The atmosphere . . . would have been more appropriate to a fraternity raiding party than so deadly a reconnaissance," Grider wrote. "Mush was in his element.

He was in danger, and he was hot on the trail of the enemy, so he was happy. . . . Mush even kept up his joking when we almost ran aground."

Wahoo moved ahead, silently, boldly, dodging patrol craft. Nine miles inside the harbor, O'Kane saw a destroyer he believed to be at anchor, with several small Japanese submarines nested alongside. While O'Kane made periscope observations, Morton sent the crew to battle stations and prepared to attack this sitting duck. Grider wrote:

I found . . . myself marveling at the change that had come over Dick O'Kane. . . . It was as if, during all the talkative, boastful months before, he had been lost, seeking his true element, and now it was found. He was calm, terse, and utterly cool. My opinion of him underwent a permanent change. It was not the first time I had observed that the conduct of men under fire cannot be predicted accurately from their everyday actions, but it was the most dramatic example I was ever to see of a man transformed under pressure from what seemed almost adolescent petulance to a prime fighting machine.

As Morton prepared to shoot, O'Kane reported the duck no longer sitting. The destroyer was getting under way. Morton shifted his plan, firing three torpedoes at the moving target. All missed. The destroyer headed directly for *Wahoo*, its superstructure crowded with a hundred or more men on lookout duty. Morton, keeping the periscope up to lure the destroyer, prepared for a down-the-throat shot. When the destroyer closed to 1,200 yards, he fired another torpedo. It too missed. *Wahoo*'s crew was frozen in terror, expecting final disaster. Wrote Forest Sterling, "I had an almost uncontrollable urge to urinate." Morton fired a sixth torpedo at a range of 800 yards. It hit, with a massive explosion. Morton was certain the destroyer sank. He withdrew from the harbor, navigating by sonar.

That night after passing out a ration of brandy to the crew, Morton put *Wahoo* on a northwest course, following the convoy route from Wewak to Palau. The next day, slightly north of the equator, he found a four-ship convoy: two freighters, a huge transport, and a tanker. Morton fired two torpedoes at each of the freighters and three at the transport, achieving hits on all three ships. One freighter, with an unusually aggressive skipper, turned toward *Wahoo* to ram. At the last minute, Morton let her have two more torpedoes down the throat. Then he went deep to avoid being run down.

When *Wahoo* surfaced again, one freighter had sunk, the second was limping away slowly, and the transport was stopped dead in the water. Morton closed to 1,000 yards and fired another torpedo at the transport. It failed to explode. Morton fired another. The transport blew "higher than a kite," Morton wrote, and the thousands of soldiers aboard her "commenced jumping over the side like ants off a hot plate."

Meanwhile, the other freighter had pulled away beyond range, joining up with the tanker. Morton pursued, submerged, but could not overtake. "Mush cursed philosophically," Grider wrote, "swung the *Wahoo* around, and brought her to the surface to resume the chase afloat at a higher speed while we charged our batteries."

When *Wahoo* surfaced, Morton ordered all deck guns manned. He found himself in a "sea of Japanese." The survivors of the transport were hanging on the flotsam and jetsam or huddling in about twenty boats, ranging from scows to little rowboats. Grider wrote:

The water was so thick with enemy soldiers that it was literally impossible to cruise through them without pushing them aside like driftwood. These were troops we knew had been bound for New Guinea, to fight and kill our own men, and Mush, whose overwhelming biological hatred of the enemy we were only now beginning to sense, looked about him with exultation at the carnage.

Yeoman Sterling, who was topside, remembered the scene this way:

The water was filled with heads sticking up from floating kapok life jackets. They were scattered roughly within a circle a hundred yards wide. Scattered among them were several lifeboats, a motor launch with an awning, a number of rafts loaded with sitting and standing Japanese fighting men, and groups of men floating in the water where they had drifted together. Others were hanging onto planks or other items of floating wreckage. A few isolated individuals were paddling back and forth toward the center in search of some human solidarity.

Sterling remembered, roughly, an exchange between Roger Paine and Mush Morton:

"There must be close to ten thousand of them in the water," said Roger Paine's voice.

"I figure about nine thousand five hundred of the sons-a-bitches," Morton calculated.

Whatever the number, Morton was determined to kill every single one. He ordered the deck guns to open fire. Some of the Japanese,

Morton said later, returned the fire with pistol shots. To Morton, this signaled "fair game." What followed, Grider wrote, were "nightmarish minutes." Later, Morton reported tersely, "After about an hour of this, we destroyed all the boats and most of the troops."

Leaving the carnage, Morton now took up the pursuit of the remaining two ships. He caught up at dusk, submerged, and fired three torpedoes at the tanker, obtaining, he thought, at least one hit. After dark, Morton surfaced and started after the obstinate freighter. He then observed that the tanker was still going. He shifted targets and fired two of his four remaining torpedoes at the tanker. The torpedoes hit and Morton believed the tanker sank. After another hour of pursuit, Morton hastily fired his last two torpedoes at the freighter, which was firing shells at *Wahoo*.

In the conning tower, Grider said to Roger Paine, "If either one of those torpedoes hits, I will kiss your royal ass." Both hit. The freighter sank instantly. Wrote Grider, "Exulting on the bridge at his final victory . . . Mush missed the most unusual ceremony ever performed in the conning tower of the mighty *Wahoo*."

That night, Morton drafted a triumphant report for Pearl Harbor: IN TEN HOUR RUNNING GUN AND TORPEDO BATTLE DESTROYED ENTIRE CONVOY OF TWO FREIGHTERS ONE TRANSPORT ONE TANKER. . . . ALL TORPEDOES EXPENDED. "Let's head for the barn, boys," he said.

On the way to Pearl Harbor, Morton found yet another convoy and tried to attack one small lagging freighter with his deck gun, but a destroyer counterattacked *Wahoo*, forcing her down. That night, Morton got off another report to Pearl Harbor: ANOTHER RUNNING GUN BATTLE TODAY. DESTROYER GUNNING, WAHOO RUNNING.

Wahoo nosed into the Pearl Harbor sub base on February 7, twenty-three days after leaving Brisbane. Topside, she had embellishments to celebrate her victory. There was a straw broom lashed to her periscope shears to indicate a clean sweep. From the signal halyard fluttered eight tiny Japanese flags, one for each Japanese ship believed to have been sunk in all three of *Wahoo*'s patrols.[*] "She had left Brisbane a comparative nonentity," Sterling wrote, "and returned to Pearl Harbor a celebrity."

Sudden fame came to Mush Morton too. The story of his exploits was released almost at once to the press. By the time the crew reached the Royal Hawaiian Hotel, Sterling recalled, the Honolulu

---

[*] Merchant ship flags were white with a red ball in the center; Japanese man-of-war flags had red stripes radiating fanlike from a red, rising sun.

newspapers had headlines proclaiming *Wahoo*'s deeds. Lockwood nicknamed Morton "The One-Boat Wolf Pack" and gave him a Navy Cross. From Port Moresby, General MacArthur sent an Army Distinguished Service Cross. This patrol, one of the most celebrated of the war, gave the whole submarine force a shot in the arm—or a kick in the pants. "More than any other man," Ned Beach later wrote, "Morton—and his *Wahoo*—showed the way to the brethren of the Silent Service."

After analyzing the attacks, Pearl Harbor credited Morton with all he claimed: the destroyer at Wewak, the transport, the two freighters, and the tanker, a grand total of five ships for 32,000 tons. In the postwar analysis, however, this total was sharply reduced. The destroyer did not sink—it was beached and repaired—nor did the tanker. In the final tally, Morton received credit for the transport, *Buyo Maru*, 5,300 tons; a freighter, *Fukuei Maru*, 2,000 tons; and an "unknown maru," 4,000 tons. Total: three ships, 11,300 tons.

In his patrol report, Morton described the killing of the hundreds (or thousands) of survivors of the transport. To some submariners, this was cold-blooded murder and repugnant. However, no question was raised about it in the glowing patrol report endorsements, where policy was usually set forth. Many submariners interpreted this—and the honors and publicity showered on Morton and *Wahoo*—as tacit approval from the submarine high command. In fact, neither Lockwood nor Christie nor Fife ever issued a policy statement on the subject. Whether other skippers should follow Morton's example was left up to the individual. Few did.

The Palau–Rabaul Convoy Route

By spring 1943, when the Japanese codes were fully recovered, Fife had developed important information on the Japanese convoy routes reinforcing the New Guinea-Solomons area. The main route was from the Palaus, southeastward to the equator, to about longitude 150 degrees east, thence south to Kavieng, on the northern tip of New Ireland, then farther south to the stronghold, Rabaul. In addition, convoys came due south to Kavieng from Truk. Fife established that along the equator line the escorts from the Palaus and Truk turned back, handing the convoys over to the escorts from Kavieng or Rabaul. Sometimes the convoys milled around as they awaited the new escorts, presenting good targets.

Fife's strategy was to position as many of his boats as possible in the general area of the intersection of longitude 150 E and the equator. In some instances, he coordinated attacks with the boats in pairs. This was the crude beginning of wolf-packing by the Pacific Submarine Force. Between March and June it was not overwhelmingly successful. *Tuna* and *Guardfish* got one confirmed ship for 5,000 tons; the team of *Albacore* and *Grayback* sank two freighters for a total of 12,200 tons; *Growler* and *Greenling* sank just one ship, 5,000 tons, out of a large convoy.

At least part of the reason for this indifferent record was the Japanese antisubmarine measures, intensified after Mush Morton's attack on the convoy along the equator in January. Fife had good information from codebreakers and other intelligence sources, and would send several submarines to intercept convoys. But the Japanese convoy commander for the Palau–Kavieng run resorted to all kinds of defenses, such as changing course 180 degrees or utilizing weather fronts for cover.

But there were deficiencies in Fife's strategy as well. He had not devised tactics for a two-boat attack on a convoy; he had merely brought two boats to bear on the same set of targets. In none of these instances did the skippers of the submarines communicate with one another; each maintained strict radio silence, receiving information on the other from Fife. The skippers, generally, were not enthusiastic. Radio talk from Fife requiring response could bring on DF-ing and possible attack. There was also the danger that one submarine might torpedo the other.

During the first five months of 1943, Fife mounted twenty-five war patrols from Brisbane, including the six boats returning to Pearl Harbor. These patrols accounted for eighteen and a half confirmed Japanese ships—all but six sunk in January and February before the Japanese changed the codes. Four fleet boats were lost with all hands, one more than was lost by all three commands during the whole of 1942.

By May, the targets were few and far between, hardly worth the effort. The boats assigned to Brisbane—reduced to about eight—could have been far more profitably employed at Pearl Harbor on Empire patrols. However, Brisbane had been converted to a substantial submarine base, and military logic apparently dictated that it continue as such. MacArthur wanted submarines for special missions in the Solomons and New Guinea; Halsey and Carpender wanted them for their harassment value. And their presence was a morale builder for the Australian populace, many of whom still believed the Japanese might invade their country. The Brisbane submarines stayed.

18
Fremantle, January through July 1943

Experiment at Exmouth Gulf

In Perth, Christie moved into Lockwood's luxurious quarters at "Bend of the Road." Shortly after his arrival, *Otus*, which had been at Mare Island since August 1942 undergoing conversion to a full submarine tender, returned to Fremantle. Her arrival made possible the old idea of establishing an advance base at Exmouth Gulf—known as Potshot.

Ever since Lockwood had first proposed the scheme in June 1942, plans had slowly moved ahead. By the time Christie and *Otus* arrived, there was a small contingent of submariners at Potshot, about five officers and fifty men. They and the Australian military had built two landing strips, quarters for relief crews, antiaircraft emplacements, an infirmary, radio shack, power plant, and water distillers. The plan was to send *Pelias* to Potshot and retain *Otus* in Perth-Fremantle.

When Christie was briefed on this plan, he joined Al McCann, Tex McLean, Chet Smith, and others in opposing it. To him it seemed an act of madness to banish returning submarine crews requiring recuperation to a wilderness of mud and flies. But Admiral Carpender (ironically, in agreement with Lockwood for once) favored removing the rowdy submariners from Perth as he had removed them from Brisbane. He ordered that *Pelias* move north.

Conforming to Carpender's orders, in early May *Pelias* up-anchored and sailed to Exmouth Gulf, with McCann, Smith, and Dutch Will embarked. She remained there only one month. The deployment was an utter fiasco. Although it was supposedly the time of good weather, strong winds whipped the gulf, and, Christie reported, there was hardly a day when submarines could nest alongside *Pelias* uninterruptedly.

Somehow, the Japanese sniffed out the movement. "They were probably tipped off by McCann or the people on *Pelias*," Tex McLean later said, facetiously. On the night of May 20, when the moon was full, a Japanese reconnaissance plane, probably based in Timor, came over. Although McCann gave orders not to fire at it, to keep from revealing his fortifications, the ack-ack crews failed to get the word and pumped tracers into the sky. On the following night, Christie reported that a dozen or more Japanese planes came over and dropped ten to twelve 150-pound bombs "quite close to the ack-ack battery."

That was the end of Exmouth Gulf as an advance submarine base. Christie—with Carpender's concurrence—withdrew *Pelias* to Fremantle, abandoning Potshot except for a fuel barge to top off the tanks of the boats going to and from patrol. Christie wrote Lockwood, "Potshot is definitely of no value as a submarine advance base," and Lockwood, finally, had to agree.

With the return of *Pelias*, *Otus* became surplus. When Lockwood heard this, he informed Jimmy Fife that he would like to have her in the Central Pacific or Alaska. However, when Fife showed Admiral Carpender Lockwood's letter, Carpender, Christie reported later, "flew into a towering rage." He refused to release *Otus* to Lockwood and kept her in Australia for many more months, servicing miscellaneous craft of his 7th Fleet, including Amphibious Forces. *Otus* never did achieve status as a full-blown submarine tender.

Patrols and Losses

During January through July of 1943, the boats under Christie's command mounted twenty-two war patrols in Southeast Asia, an average of three per month. The patrols produced twenty-three confirmed sinkings, an average of slightly more than one vessel per patrol, one of the best averages for any command to date. However, nine of the patrols—41 percent—produced no confirmed sinkings. Two boats were lost.

Moke Millican in *Thresher* returned to Christmas Island and Sunda Strait. Because of the shortage, he carried only twenty torpedoes instead of twenty-four. Millican conducted five aggressive attacks, sinking a big freighter and a tanker near Balikpapan. He shot—and hit—a Japanese submarine, but the torpedo, Millican asserted, was a dud.

On return to Fremantle, Millican for the second time criticized torpedo performance, stating that on the submarine attack he had "clinked 'em with a clunk." This time Al McCann sided with Millican. In his endorsement, he denigrated torpedo design and made some suggestions of his own. Upon reading McCann's endorsement, Christie went down to *Pelias*. There was to be no "wrangling in print" about torpedoes. The torpedoes, Christie said, were fine. Millican was ordered back to the States for rest and new construction.

Red Ramage on *Trout*, who had also complained bitterly about torpedo performance, visited Christie just before leaving on his fourth patrol. *Trout* had been selected to lay mines off Borneo, a long-overdue effort to stop the flow of oil to the Solomons.

"What's your armament?" Christie asked Ramage.

"Sixteen torpedoes and twenty-three mines," Ramage replied.

"I want you to sink sixteen ships with those torpedoes," Christie replied lightheartedly.

This remark enraged Ramage. He said icily, "If I get 25 percent reliable performance on your torpedoes, I'll be lucky, and you will bless me."

Now it was Christie's turn for anger. He railed against those who were creating distrust and suspicion about the torpedoes.

"It got a little bit rough," Ramage recalled. "Tex McLean grabbed me by the neck and pulled me out of there, saying, 'It's time to leave.' When we got outside Christie's office, McLean said, 'You're goddamned lucky to be going to sea.' I said, 'It's the other way around, Tex. With these torpedoes you're giving us, I'll be goddamned lucky to get back. If you think I'm so lucky, how about packing your bag and coming along with me?' That cooled him."

Ramage laid his mines off Miri, Borneo. Afterward, his patrol was unlucky. He made four attacks for zero results, firing fifteen of his sixteen torpedoes. One torpedo hit a freighter, but Ramage reported it to be a dud. Later he fired three torpedoes each at three different ships—all misses.

Back in Fremantle, Ramage again complained about poor torpedo performance, but Christie blamed his failure on shooting errors and wildly maneuvering targets, noting in his diary, "Red had a miss last patrol—many chances and many failures. He is due for a relief and will be sent back to the U.S. for a new boat and rest at the same time."

Barney Sieglaff in *Tautog* conducted two patrols, each no less aggressive than his first. In February he carried a mixed load of mines and torpedoes. He laid his minefield off Balikpapan, in Makassar Strait. No ships struck the minefield immediately, but according to Jasper Holmes the Japanese destroyer *Amagiri* was sunk by one of these mines in April 1944. (*Amagiri* was the destroyer that rammed and sank *PT-109*, commanded by John F. Kennedy.)

Tautog had been fitted with the third 5-inch gun from the old V-class boats, and during this patrol Sieglaff made four battle surfaces to test it out. The first, a night attack on a ship, failed when the flash of the gun blinded both crew and skipper. On the second and third, Sieglaff sank small trawlers. On the fourth, he tried to sink a ship at anchor inside a harbor, but the gun jammed and he had to break off the attack.

In addition, Sieglaff conducted three torpedo attacks. In the first, he fired a single torpedo at a beached ship, to make certain she wasn't salvaged. Next, he fired three torpedoes at a freighter. All missed. For his third attack, he plowed into a small convoy, firing nine torpedoes and sinking two confirmed ships, a 5,000-ton freighter and a 2,000-ton destroyer, *Isonami*.

Sieglaff's second patrol took him back to Pearl Harbor, dropping off two agents en route. Though it included three gun attacks and six torpedo attacks, he sank only two freighters for 5,500 tons.

Bill Post, commanding *Gudgeon*, did the most to account for the respectable score made by the Fremantle boats during the first half of 1943. He and his exec, Mike Shea, were both post-Midway "rejects": Post had been surfaced from *Argonaut*, and Shea had been relieved on *Gar*. Although *Gudgeon* carried only sixteen torpedoes, Shea and Post were determined to make each one count.

They found plenty of targets. Off Surabaya, they attacked a seven-ship convoy with two escorts. Post fired two torpedoes each and believed he sank two and probably all three.

A few days later, while on the surface, Post saw a small vessel and ordered battle surface, gun action. As *Gudgeon* closed in, Post realized the vessel was a small destroyer; it turned to attack. Post kept charging, with deck gun manned and four bow tubes ready. At 1,800 yards he fired the bow tubes. The destroyer maneuvered to avoid. All the while, the deck gun crew pumped shells at the weaving target, scoring at least four good hits. However, Post elected to break off the attack and clear the area.

Later, Post attacked another convoy, firing five torpedoes at one tanker and two at another. He obtained good hits, leading him to believe he had sunk both. With only two torpedoes remaining, Post set course for Fremantle, arriving home after a twenty-four-day patrol. He had nothing but praise for the Mark XIV torpedo and its magnetic exploder. Christie was ecstatic. He credited Post with four ships for 29,600 tons (reduced postwar to two ships for 15,000 tons), by far the best score of any Fremantle skipper that year.

Post got a Navy Cross and went out again in April to earn another. This time *Gudgeon*, with a new exec, Frank Lloyd Barrows from *Gar*, returned to Pearl Harbor. Along the way, Post also was to conduct a special mission, putting ashore a party of four guerrillas and their three tons of equipment on Panay Island. Going north through Makassar Strait on the night of April 25, Post picked up a contact. In two separate attacks, he fired six torpedoes at the target, obtaining, he believed, several hits. But further attempts to close and attack were thwarted by an escort.

Shortly before reaching Panay, while running on the surface at night, Post spotted an enormous ship all alone. In the darkness, it looked like a battleship but turned out to be an ocean liner, zigzagging at 17½ knots on a southerly course. From the size and silhouette, Post correctly identified the ship as *Kamakura Maru*, 17,500 tons, which had often visited Hawaii prior to the war.

Post bent on flank speed, trying to gain a position ahead for firing, but the liner was too fast. She was pulling away. The best Post could do was come directly in from astern and fire the opposite of a down-the-throat shot—what he later named an "up-the-kilt" shot. He let go four torpedoes and dived. Going under, he heard three hits.

Coming to periscope depth, Post closed the range, maneuvering to bring his stern tubes to bear. But in his first periscope observation he saw that the target was stopped. On the next, he was astonished to see her bow rising high. *Kamakura Maru* went down stern first, like a rock.

Gudgeon surfaced. The waters were strewn with flotsam, lifeboats, and shouting survivors, military government personnel en route to Surabaya. The Japanese disclosed the loss of the liner in their newspapers, including photographs, as Jasper Holmes put it, of "government typists [rescued by Japanese vessels] looking very sexy in their wet dresses." *Kamakura Maru* was the largest ship sunk by U.S. submarines up to that time.

Post's patrol was not yet over. He landed his guerrillas and looked for more enemy ships. On May 4, he battle-surfaced on a small trawler and sank it. During the action, one of his officers was knocked overboard by a cartridge case ejected from the deck gun—a freak accident and a fatal one, since the officer was lost despite Post's two-hour search.

The following day, Post battle-surfaced on a freighter, scoring some hits. Later he saw what he believed to be a tanker and swung in, deck gun manned. The "tanker" turned out to be an armed ship that attacked *Gudgeon*. Post dived and went deep. The ship pummeled *Gudgeon* with close depth charges, which caused extensive minor damage.

Three days later, while on the surface, Post tangled with another trawler. With no time to man the deck gun, he fired off one quick torpedo; when it missed, he swung ship and fired a second from the stern tube; when this, too, missed, he dived and went deep. The trawler unleashed eleven depth charges, none close.

On May 10, reduced to only one or two torpedoes, Post spotted a fat freighter. He closed and fired. Down went *Sumatra Maru*, 5,800 tons. After that triumph, Post set a course for Pearl Harbor.

Lockwood credited Post with sinking three ships for 19,600 tons, with damage to another 9,000 tons of shipping. In fact, Post had sent two ships down for 23,000 tons. With a second Navy Cross in his possession, he took *Gudgeon* to Mare Island for overhaul. In two patrols on *Gudgeon*, Post had sunk 39,000 tons of confirmed shipping, twice as much as his predecessors, Grenfell and Stovall, on five patrols.

Grenadier, like *Snapper*, was a boat seemingly unable to shake the dark cloud that had dogged her since the beginning of the war. In four patrols, she had had three skippers: Allen Joyce, Pilly Lent, and

Bruce Carr. Setting off on her fifth patrol from Fremantle, she had a fourth, John Fitzgerald, who had been transferred from Don McGregor's *Gar*. Fitzgerald proved to be aggressive and fearless. Patrolling the Java Sea, he made six attacks, receiving credit for sinking one ship and damaging another.

On his second patrol in *Grenadier*, Fitzgerald was sent to an area no U.S. submarine had ever patrolled—Malacca Strait, the body of water lying between Malay and Sumatra—to interdict the flow of Japanese shipping between Rangoon and Singapore. Ordinarily this piece of geography fell under British control, but the British had asked for a U.S. fleet boat to explore the area. Tex McLean was opposed; the waters were confined and shallow. But he was overruled.

The area proved a disappointment. Although Fitzgerald patrolled aggressively off Rangoon, remaining on the surface a great deal of the time, he found no targets and moved southward. On the morning of April 21, he closed the port of Penang on the west coast of Malay. While only a few miles from shore, lookouts sighted a two-ship convoy. Remaining on the surface within sight of the Malay coast, Fitzgerald gave chase. At eight o'clock in broad daylight, a lookout suddenly shouted, "Aircraft on port quarter!"

Fitzgerald cleared the bridge and dived. At 130 feet, Fitzgerald's exec, George Harris Whiting (ex-*Triton*), relaxed and said, "We ought to be safe enough now." His statement was followed by a violent explosion that rocked *Grenadier* and pushed her to the bottom at 270 feet. A bomb had exploded over the maneuvering room. It twisted *Grenadier*'s stern out of shape and set off a fire in the electrical section. The main induction and some after hatches and sea valves were unseated and warped, causing leaks.

"Steady, men," Fitzgerald said over the PA system. "Everything is under control." He sent men wearing fire-fighting gear into the maneuvering room to extinguish the flames. He set up a bucket brigade and pumps to carry off the flooding water. Inspecting the boat, Fitzgerald found conditions worse than he had imagined. The hull was bashed in four inches, the shafts and after torpedo tubes bent out of line. Throughout the day, work parties, suffering heat prostration and exhaustion, worked to make repairs.

That night, Fitzgerald brought *Grenadier* to the surface. He tried to get off a radio dispatch to Christie, reporting the damage, but couldn't get through. Meanwhile, the engineering officer tried to make the bent and misaligned shafts turn. He couldn't. When Fitzgerald received this news, he put his men to work making a canvas sail, intending to sail *Grenadier* close to the shore and then blow her up. With luck, the crew might slip into the Malay jungle and obtain help from guerrillas or sympathetic natives.

At dawn, Fitzgerald was dismayed to find there was not a breath of air, no hope that *Grenadier* could come close to the shore. They would have to swim. He gave orders to prepare to abandon ship. While lookouts kept a sharp watch for planes and men manned the deck guns, others below destroyed the radio, radar, sound and TDC gear, and decoding machines, tossing the codebooks over the side.

While this work was in progress, a Japanese aircraft appeared on the horizon, making a beeline for *Grenadier*. Fitzgerald withheld fire until the last minute. When the gunners let go, the plane veered up and away, damaged. Coming in for a second run, the pilot dropped his bomb. It fell harmlessly into the water, 200 yards away. (Later Fitzgerald learned that this futile attack cost the Japanese pilot his life. Wounded, he crashed on returning to base and died.)

Preparing to abandon ship, Fitzgerald lined his men on deck in life jackets. Meanwhile, a Japanese merchant ship and small escort came into sight, headed for *Grenadier*. Fitzgerald gave orders to scuttle. The vents were opened and *Grenadier* sank by the stern. The men jumped or floated off into the water, while the Japanese ships circled, taking pictures. When the last man from below reached the deck, he and Fitzgerald went into the water together.

The men on the Japanese merchant ship rescued *Grenadier*'s men and took them to Penang. For many weeks thereafter, Fitzgerald and his men were treated brutally by Japanese interrogators, who tried to elicit technical information. Fitzgerald was tied to a bench with his head hanging over the end. The Japanese elevated his feet and then poured water into his nostrils, holding his mouth shut so he was forced to swallow the water. When they judged him sufficiently full of water, they clubbed him repeatedly and denied him food for a week.

In spite of all this, Fitzgerald maintained his sanity and composure. He left encouraging messages for his crew on the walls of the toilet room: "Don't tell them anything. . . . Keep your chins up." One of his men said later, "I think as much of Commander Fitzgerald, our skipper, as I do my father. He went through hell for us. They beat him, jumped on his stomach, and tortured him by burning splints under his nails. He never talked."

The *Grenadier* crew was removed to the prison camp in Ofuna,

Japan, where they underwent further relentless interrogation. After the war, for "extraordinary heroism" and "unflinchingly withstanding the cruelties of his captors," Fitzgerald was awarded the Navy Cross. Four enlisted crewmen died in the POW camp, but Fitzgerald, Whiting, and seventy others were released.

Grayling was also lost during this period. After Eliot Olsen, John Elwood Lee had taken command, patrolling to Fremantle by way of the Gilberts and the Marshalls. Lee sank one confirmed ship on that patrol. On his next three patrols out of Fremantle, he was credited with sinking seven ships for 34,600 tons, reduced in postwar accounting to two ships for 4,750 tons. Lee had then returned to the States for new construction, and Christie gave command of *Grayling* to a youngster, Robert Marion Brinker, class of 1934.

Brinker took *Grayling* by way of the Philippines, to conduct special missions and sink whatever ships he could find. On July 31, he delivered supplies to guerrillas on Panay. On August 19, he reported damaging a 6,000-ton freighter near Balikpapan. The following day he sank a small tanker with the deck gun and took a prisoner. On August 23, he delivered further supplies at Panay and proceeded to the Manila area. Four days later, Brinker sank the 5,500-ton passenger-cargo ship *Meizan Maru* off Mindoro. It is possible that a few days later he attacked another passenger-cargo vessel, *Hokuan Maru*.

Nothing was ever heard from *Grayling* again. She disappeared without trace. After the war, Japanese records indicated that a U.S. submarine was seen on the surface in Lingayen Gulf on September 9. This was probably *Grayling*. She was lost with all hands, either in Lingayen Gulf or along the approaches to Manila.

19

Pearl Harbor, January through March 1943

The Casablanca Conference

Early in 1943 the war in Europe had slowly turned in favor of the Allies. The Nazis had been stopped in Africa at the Battle of El Alamein, in Russia at the Battle of Stalingrad. Losses to the U-boat were still high, but radio intelligence, radar, and hundreds of new antisubmarine surface vessels and aircraft, plus the convoy system, promised an end to the carnage.

In January, Roosevelt and Churchill had met in Casablanca for a strategy conference. During these talks, the defeat of the Axis in Europe had remained the number-one goal, but there were discussions on Pacific strategy, anticipating the time when there would be sufficient military power to go on full offensive there.

Everybody seemed to have a different idea about how to defeat Japan. Admiral King believed there should be a two-pronged effort of equal weight: MacArthur to push up through the Solomons and New Guinea to the Philippines; Admiral Nimitz to advance through the mid-Pacific in an island-hopping campaign from Hawaii to the Gilberts (Tarawa-Makin), to the Marshalls (Kwajalein), and then to the Marianas (Guam-Saipan). General MacArthur—who had sworn publicly to return to the Philippines—did not like this plan. He believed the greater weight should be given his campaign, with the mid-

THE CASABLANCA CONFERENCE 399

Pacific drive only a diversionary action. Many naval planners thought the Philippines, Gilberts, Marshalls, and Marianas should be bypassed, with the main drive at Truk and Iwo Jima. The British wanted to push through Burma, recapture Singapore and Hong Kong, and then bomb Japan into submission from bases in China. Roosevelt favored the last scheme as a supplement to King's two-pronged strategy.

The submarine force had not played a very large role in these discussions. Submarines, the strategy papers stated, would merely continue to maintain pressure on Japanese lines of communication. No serious consideration was given the idea of a massive submarine blockade of Japan such as Germany had mounted against Britain in World Wars I and II. Most of the emphasis—and priority—was placed on air power (land and carriers), amphibious forces, and ground troops.

The decisions on Pacific strategy that had come from the Casablanca Conference were, in fact, rather vague. MacArthur would continue pressure on the Japanese in the Solomons and New Guinea, driving to Rabaul. What came next was left up in the air. Nimitz would continue pressure on the Japanese in the Alaskan area, with the aim of dislodging them from Attu and Kiska, meanwhile planning for a move westward toward the Gilberts, the Marshalls, Truk, and the Marianas.

The plans Nimitz conceived for a mid-Pacific drive were influenced by one overriding factor: the shortage of aircraft carriers. During 1942, Nimitz had lost four first-line carriers: *Lexington, Yorktown, Wasp,* and *Hornet.** By January 1943 only two remained in service, *Enterprise* and *Saratoga,* both committed to the struggle in the Solomons.

The Arsenal of Democracy was turning out more aircraft carriers. Seven new first-line carriers,† authorized by the 1940 Two-Ocean Navy bill, had been launched and were fitting out. In addition, nine light cruisers were being converted to light aircraft carriers.‡ Finally, the navy was in the process of converting about three dozen merchant ships to jeep carriers, designed specifically to support amphibious landings. However, few of these ships would be ready for combat before summer or fall of 1943. No mid-Pacific drive could be launched until this naval power arrived.

* The Japanese lost six carriers in 1942: *Kaga, Akagi, Soryu, Hiryu, Ryujo,* and *Shoho.*
† *Essex, Intrepid,* and *Bunker Hill,* and new *Lexington, Yorktown, Wasp,* and *Hornet.*
‡ *Independence, Princeton, Belleau Wood, Cowpens, Monterey, Langley, Cabot, Bataan,* and *San Jacinto.*

Submarine Command Credits and Debits

When Charles Lockwood returned to Pearl Harbor in January, he found it, as he noted, "vastly different." Everywhere there were new buildings, Quonset huts, supplies, aircraft, and new ships. The gloom that had hung over the base when he passed through on his way to Australia in April 1942 had disappeared. He felt a "spirit of confidence," positive thinking, a determination to get on with the war—and win it.

The navy housing development on Makalapa Hill, overlooking the sub base, was completed. One house had been taken over by Bob English and his senior staff for bachelor quarters. Lockwood moved in, sharing the well-staffed house with his temporary chief of staff, John Griggs, and big, genial Babe Brown.

After his bags were unpacked, Lockwood "went into a huddle" with Griggs and Brown "which lasted practically twenty-four hours" as they hashed over all the credits and debits of the Pearl Harbor submarine ledger.

The major asset was intelligence. The Joint Intelligence Center, commanded by Roscoe Hillenkoetter, was now a booming operation, with its own two-story quarters "on the hill" at Pearl Harbor. Hundreds of people worked there behind tight security guard. Hundreds more were on the way. The center's most valuable core, FRUPAC, commanded by communications expert Bill Goggins, was well organized and operating with exceptional efficiency.

There had been an important addition at FRUPAC, a new unit designated specifically to concentrate on Japanese merchant marine codes, which had been neglected during the crisis period of 1942. The man named to command this unit was a coast guard officer, Henry M. Anthony.

Anthony had begun his military career in 1920 as a navy enlisted man, serving on the submarines *R-3* and *S-3*. After switching to the coast guard, he specialized in breaking rumrunner codes. Beginning in 1935, Anthony had formed a close association with Pacific Fleet intelligence officers in Hawaii and had devoted much time to breaking simple Japanese "tuna clipper" codes, meanwhile teaching himself Japanese. He had boarded all Japanese merchant vessels calling at Hawaii, on the pretext of searching for smuggled narcotics but in reality to check their routings and other sailing data. Over the years, Anthony had become an authority on the Japanese merchant marine.

Anthony's merchant marine decoding section grew quickly to a large unit of seventy-five people. Helped by the regular personnel of FRUPAC—Tom Dyer, Ham Wright, and others—it produced a steady stream of valuable information decoded from instructions to Japanese merchant vessels, including destinations of vessels, departure and arrival dates, "noon positions" that the ships or convoys were to adhere to each day during their voyage, and locations of Japanese minefields.

Jasper Holmes relayed this information to Dick Voge via the hot line. Lockwood, who now got his first inside view of this machinery, later wrote:

It is impossible to assign too much credit to Captain Holmes and to the organization he represented for the part they played in the success of the submarine war. . . . Messages came in at all hours from Holmes, and Dick [Voge] relayed them to the boats on patrol. These enemy messages gave the noon positions of convoys for several days in advance. This, of course, was to inform their own forces, but we used it very effectively . . . sometimes our skippers would complain that "the convoy was an hour late reaching its noon position."

On the debit side of the ledger there were several items, none small. The first and most critical was the extreme shortage of submarines. This had been caused by three principal factors: the diversion of fleet boats to Brisbane, the failure of the H.O.R. engines in Squadron Twelve, and the diversion of four non-H.O.R. fleet boats to Scotland for Atlantic service. With so few submarines available, Voge could not take full advantage of the information from FRUPAC. The second and no less critical debit concerned torpedoes. It was a three-headed problem.

First, the shortage. In spite of all efforts on the part of the Bureau of Ordnance, submarine torpedo production had not yet caught up with expenditures. During all of 1942, the three submarine commands had fired 1,442 torpedoes. During that same period, the Bureau of Ordnance had manufactured about 2,000 submarine torpedoes, many of which had not yet even reached the submarine bases. If the shortage continued, it was clear that submariners would be forced to resort again to unpopular—and ineffective—minelaying missions.

Second, exploders. The magnetic exploder was now more controversial than ever. Many submarine skippers in Pearl Harbor favored deactivating the magnetic feature and trying for direct contact hits. However, Lockwood was still loath to do this. On his famous first patrol from Brisbane, Mush Morton had fired all twenty-four of his torpedoes with the magnetic exploder in operation. It was believed that all his torpedoes exploded magnetically, as designed, and that at least two had saved *Wahoo* in Wewak Harbor from certain loss to the Japanese destroyer. Morton was an outspoken advocate of the magnetic feature. His views no doubt strongly influenced Lockwood.

Third, the Mark XVIII electric torpedo. It had been promised to the submarine force by summer of 1942 but had not yet arrived. What was going on? After the dazzling beginning by Westinghouse, was it now going the way of all torpedo development?

To submariners back in the States who had an opportunity to look into the problem, it seemed that way. Among them were the senior officers on *Lapon*, one of the Squadron Twelve boats with H.O.R. engines. *Lapon* had been sent to Newport to assist in the test firing of the Mark XVIII electric torpedo. Her skipper was Oliver Kirk, who had commanded S-42 for two patrols from Brisbane.

"What we found at Newport," *Lapon*'s exec, Eli Thomas Reich, said later, "was simply sickening. The Mark XVIII was an extremely promising weapon. But the Newport guys—the steam torpedo guys—had a big NIH—Not Invented Here—attitude toward the Westinghouse torpedo. Maybe sabotage is too strong a word, but they weren't helping one bit."

Lapon remained at Newport for six weeks, with Kirk and Reich doing their best to overcome the inertia and push along the Mark XVIII. At the conclusion of this tour, they sat down and composed a damning memorandum, covering the development and testing program for the Mark XVIII. The memo, signed by Kirk, said that

basically, it's the Bureau's fault. They sent a boy to do a man's job. An Ensign. . . . What this set-up needs is a "Pushing Officer" with lots of enthusiasm and the backing of the Bureau, and (very important) some rank. What latent enthusiasm there was here has now petered out and it won't rise again until they know their efforts are amounting to something. . . . I suggest for a "Pushing Officer" a submarine skipper, Commander or Lieutenant Commander, with combat experience, preferably one who has fired a few duds, and had occasion to swear at a few expeditors and bureaus as the depth charges were raining down. *This officer should be familiarized with the devious workings of this queer place, then, with the authority and backing of the Bureau, he can do wonders.*

Eli Reich wrote in exasperated tones to Dick Voge, under whom he had served in peacetime on *Sealion*, "I'll do what fighting I can for the thing which I feel will do the submarines the most good in a military sense. I'll tell you frankly, though, I'd much prefer to be on patrol. . . . I don't think these people are war-minded."

The Kirk-Reich memorandum, duly forwarded through official channels, eventually wound up on the desks of Admirals Edwards and King. King called in the navy's Gestapo, the Inspector General, to make an investigation. He reported:

The delays encountered were largely the result of the manner in which the project was prosecuted and followed up. These difficulties indicate that the liaison officers of the Bureau of Ordnance failed to follow up and to properly advise the Westinghouse Company and the Exide Company during the development of the Mark XVIII torpedo. . . . The Torpedo Station had its own electric torpedo, the Mark II, and the personnel assigned to it appear to have competed and not cooperated with the development of the Mark XVIII.

Soon after Lockwood arrived in Pearl Harbor, he decided to make the inspection trip that had cost Bob English his life. As he went through Washington, he unloaded his concern about torpedo performance both on Edwards and King and at a meeting of the Submarine Officers' Conference, telling that large assemblage, "If the Bureau of Ordnance can't provide us with torpedoes that will hit and explode . . . then for God's sake, get the Bureau of Ships to design a boat hook with which we can rip the plates off a target's side."

Later that day, Lockwood went to see his old friend Spike Blandy, Chief of the Bureau of Ordnance. He found Blandy "boiling mad." "I don't know whether it's part of your mission to discredit the Bureau of Ordnance," Blandy said acidly, "but you seem to be doing a pretty good job of it."

"Well, Spike," Lockwood rejoined, "if anything I have said will get the Bureau off its duff and get some action, I will feel that my trip has not been wasted."

In this talk and later by mail, when Lockwood forwarded a copy of the Kirk-Reich memo on the delays in the Mark XVIII electric torpedo program, Lockwood and Blandy began closing the gap between the submarine force and the Bureau of Ordnance. In his covering letter, Lockwood wrote:

When you first read this memo I know that you will feel resentment . . . but when you think it over I believe you will realize that these lads are in dead earnest, that they are fired up by enthusiasm for the torpedo and that they are bitterly discouraged by the apparent lack of concern on the part of the Bureau and the Torpedo Station about the development of this torpedo for which the submarine service has been waiting so long and on which we have pinned so many hopes. You will possibly recall that in our younger days, you and I felt just as bitterly about the delays, red tape and sheer ignorance of the people with whom we had to deal in various Bureaus and Navy Yards. I read in this memo the same thoughts and protests which we have so often voiced and I know that you, with your great sense of fair mindedness, will give the memorandum at least a second reading . . . and if a purge is necessary somewhere, then for God's sake, purge.

Blandy replied:

Far from resenting the memorandum . . . I was damn glad to get it. . . . This bureau is not a closed corporation. I wish the submariners . . . would send their own people in here to look out for their own interests and get their work done. . . . We sadly lack submarine officers in the bureau and you won't get the best results from your torpedoes until you let me have some. . . . As you know yourself, every time I try to get some submarine officers who also know torpedoes, I am usually offered somebody who hasn't made good in the boats themselves, and my efforts to get a good man are usually met with the objection that he is too valuable as a commanding officer. . . . Send me a damn good officer who knows torpedoes as well as submarines and you will get results.

Departing Patrols

Because of the shortage of submarines and the need to overhaul many that had been diverted to Brisbane, Pearl Harbor mounted only twenty-eight patrols during the first three months of 1943. One of these was made by *Drum*, going to Brisbane to help fill the gap caused by Fife's heavy losses. The majority of these patrols—sixteen—were conducted at Truk, Palau, and the Marianas, from which the Japanese were reinforcing their possessions in the Solomons. Only twelve boats went to Empire and East China Sea waters to interdict Japanese commerce and oil shipments. All suffered from the shortage of Ultras brought on by the Japanese switchover in codes.

Off Kyushu, Eugene Thomas Sands, commanding the new boat *Sawfish*, sank two ships he wished he hadn't. Russia and Japan were still at peace. By mutual agreement, Soviet shipping from Vladivostok usually left the Sea of Japan through La Pérouse Strait, the body of water lying between Hokkaido and Sakhalin. But now, February, La Pérouse was frozen over. Unknown to either Sands or Dick Voge, Soviet shipping from Vladivostok had been routed to the south, leaving the Sea of Japan through Tsushima Strait and then moving to the open sea via the south end of Kyushu.

Early on the morning of February 17, the watch on *Sawfish* saw a light. Closing the range, Sands found two ships in company, both lighted. Somewhat mystified, and suspecting a trap, Sands pulled ahead, dived, and waited. About sunrise, he saw the outlines of a freighter and fired. About noon, another ship came along. She had Russian markings. Sands let her go by, very reluctantly, not convinced it was not a Japanese trick. That same night, Sands found another freighter with lights and sank her. During the remainder of the patrol, he approached four more ships with Soviet markings and let them all pass safely. Later he believed he sank a third Japanese freighter, but it was not confirmed in postwar records.

On return to Pearl Harbor, Sands received a glowing endorsement to his patrol report. Lockwood congratulated him for a "highly successful" patrol, during which the officers and crew "carried out their mission like seasoned veterans," and gave him credit for sinking three Japanese freighters. However, the two lighted ships turned out to be Russian, *Ilmen* and *Kola*. The Soviets lodged a strong protest. Sands was hauled on the carpet, but owing to the unusual circumstances of the sinkings, he escaped a reprimand and retained command of his boat. After this episode, the Soviets improved recognition markings and furnished more and better information on general traffic routing and individual ship movements.

Thomas Wogan, commanding the hard-luck *Tarpon* which had never yet sunk a ship, left Pearl Harbor under a cloud for the abysmal performance on his first patrol, south of Truk. This time he was determined to do better. En route to patrol station in Empire waters, Wogan kept his communications officer, William Anderson, working like a slave. Said Anderson, "Wogan insisted that *Tarpon* break *all* the traffic from Voge, every message for every boat. I stood eight hours on watch, then four hours in the yeoman's shack, locked up, decoding Ultras."

For a while it looked as though *Tarpon* would turn in another zero patrol; off Tokyo, she was caught up in a severe gale, with huge seas, and Wogan kept *Tarpon* at 120 feet to maintain depth control. However, after the storm subsided, Wogan picked up a contact on SJ radar. He closed and submerged, keeping the radar antennas above water. In two separate attacks, he fired six torpedoes, sending the 10,935-ton *Fushimi Maru* to the bottom. A week later, in a similar attack, Wogan sank the huge 16,975-ton passenger liner *Tatsuta Maru*, en route to Truk loaded with soldiers. In these two attacks, Wogan catapulted his own score—and *Tarpon*'s—from zero to 27,910 confirmed tons. In terms of tonnage, it was 110 more than Burlingame's fourth patrol off Truk and therefore the best of any submarine in the war so far.

Rebel Lowrance and his exec, Eric Lloyd Barr, Jr., taking *Kingfish* on her third patrol off Formosa, very nearly failed to return. Lowrance made five attacks—many ruined, he believed, by poor torpedo performance. An Ultra put him on the trail of a big troop transport, the 8,000-ton *Takachiho Maru*, taking reinforcements to the Philippines. She was escorted by what Lockwood would later describe as the "Dean Emeritus of the Tokyo Sound School."

Lowrance sank the troopship (which managed to get only one lifeboat away), but the Dean got on *Kingfish*'s track and delivered one of the severest depth-chargings of the war. When Lowrance went deep to evade, a squealing propeller shaft gave his position away, and the escort unleashed a heavy barrage of depth charges that forced *Kingfish* to the bottom at 300 feet. While Lowrance lay still, one salvo smashed and flooded the main induction lines. Another bashed in the pressure hull. During the attacks, which kept the boat pinned down sixteen hours, Lowrance vowed that if he got out of this scrape alive he would personally lead the entire crew to church to thank God for deliverance.

Lowrance got away, finally, and limped to Pearl Harbor. "That

DEPARTING PATROLS

Kingfish came back at all is miraculous," Lockwood wrote later. Lowrance and the crew went to church and then took *Kingfish* to Mare Island for overhaul.

After laying mines on his first patrol, Dick Peterson on *Sunfish* turned in such an inept performance that two of his officers, the exec, Carter Bennett, and William Philip ("Bud") Gruner, Jr., asked for transfers. The squadron commander allowed Gruner to leave but talked Bennett into staying. On his second patrol, Peterson went to the East China Sea, where he did better, hitting the liner *Asama Maru* for damage and sinking a freighter. (When *Sunfish* returned to port, Bennett went to the PCO pool, qualified for his own command.)

Donc Donaho in *Flying Fish*, on his fifth patrol and with his fourth exec, Walter Lowry Small, conducted six daylight periscope attacks, firing twenty-four torpedoes and achieving eleven hits. Lockwood credited Donaho with four freighters for 28,000 tons, but postwar analysis reduced this to three ships for 7,500 tons.

Pompano, commanded by Willis Thomas making his third patrol, found the best targets of all: two big aircraft carriers in Japanese home waters. When he got within 4,000 yards of one carrier—identified as *Shokaku*—Thomas fired six torpedoes. Three prematured on the way, probably because of heavy wave action, but Thomas believed he heard two distinct explosions at proper intervals. Although the evidence was thin and the range excessive, Lockwood credited Thomas with damage to *Shokaku* for 28,900 tons (later denied by JANAC). Privately, however, he worried about the prematures. Was there indeed something wrong with the magnetic exploder?

Mush Morton's second patrol as skipper of *Wahoo* was another bellringer. This time *Wahoo* sailed without George Grider, who had gone to *Pollack* as exec. O'Kane still served on *Wahoo*.

For this patrol, Dick Voge assigned Morton an area never before penetrated by U.S. submarines: the extreme northern reaches of the Yellow Sea, in the vicinity of the Yalu river and Dairen. One reason no submarines had been sent there before was that the water is extremely shallow, averaging 120 feet. But the "wading pond" barely fazed Morton. He welcomed the virgin territory.

En route from Pearl Harbor to the Yellow Sea, Morton kept *Wahoo* on the surface, except for routine morning dives. He wandered through the boat restlessly, talking to the enlisted men, telling them that this time *Wahoo* would make a killing.

Off Kyushu, the watch picked up a ship that was going around in circles and giving off dense smoke. Morton went to battle stations warily. He thought the ship must be a decoy, a Q-ship. Almost reluctantly, he fired a single torpedo. It missed. O'Kane, manning the periscope, urged Morton to fire again. Morton said no, he suspected a trap. When O'Kane pressed, Morton grew suddenly angry and, as the yeoman, Sterling, remembers, said approximately, "Goddamit, when you get to be a captain in your own sub you can shoot all the torpedoes you want, at whatever you want. . . . Break off the attack." Sterling added, "It was the first time I had seen Morton angry."

Entering the Yellow Sea, Morton found the area dense with sampans and junks—and unsuspecting targets. On March 19, he attacked two ships, believing that he sank one and the other got away. In the next four days he sank four more. On the twenty-fifth, when two torpedoes fired at a freighter prematured, Morton surfaced and sank it with the deck gun. While he was at it, he sank another freighter with the deck gun and then attacked a trawler, sampans, and junks. Leaving the area, he fired his last two torpedoes at a freighter, which sank.

When Morton reported his results to Pearl Harbor, Lockwood replied: CONGRATULATIONS ON A JOB WELL DONE. JAPANESE THINK A SUBMARINE WOLF PACK OPERATING IN YELLOW SEA. ALL SHIPPING TIED UP.

Returning to Midway for refit, Morton claimed eight ships for 36,700 tons, plus damage to the ship he believed got away. In fact, however, as postwar analysis would reveal, the damaged ship did not get away. It sank too, giving Morton a confirmed total of nine ships sunk on this single patrol, for about 20,000 confirmed tons. In terms of numbers of ships sunk, no skipper had ever come close to this record.

Augustus Howard Alston, Jr., took *Pickerel* to northeast Honshu, where Klakring on *Guardfish* had earned fame. In an aggressive series of attacks, Alston fired all his torpedoes. However, most missed and Alston received credit for only one sinking. Lockwood described the patrol as "disappointing" but was willing to give Alston a second chance.

On his second patrol, Alston asked for the same area. He topped

DEPARTING PATROLS 409

off *Pickerel*'s fuel tanks at Midway on March 22—and was never heard from again.

Postwar analysis of Japanese records helped piece together part of *Pickerel*'s last days. On April 3, Alston sank a small subchaser off the extreme northeast tip of Honshu. Four days later, he sank a 1,000-ton freighter. Several Japanese antisubmarine attacks were conducted in the area during that period. Although no specific proof of her loss was ever found, Dick Voge and Jasper Holmes believed that *Pickerel* was lost to depth charges during one of these attacks. Not counting *Grunion*, lost in Alaskan waters, *Pickerel* was the first fleet boat Pearl Harbor had lost in sixteen months of combat.

One of the sixteen boats sent to the Truk-Palau blockade was a new one, *Runner*, commanded by a savvy old hand, Mike Fenno, ex-*Trout*. Fenno made the first regular Pearl Harbor patrol to the Palaus, still considered somewhat of a mystery.

Fenno, ever aggressive, almost failed to return from this patrol. A land-based antisubmarine plane dropped a bomb close to *Runner* whose explosion knocked most of the crewmen off their feet. The bomb also wrecked both periscopes, forcing Fenno to cut the patrol short. Lockwood credited Fenno with sinking three ships for 19,800 tons, but postwar records failed to verify any.

Whale, commanded by John Azer, with Fritz Harlfinger as exec, patrolled the Marshalls. Off Kwajalein, Azer found a huge transport, evidently bringing in troop reinforcements; through the periscope he could see hundreds of soldiers crowding the decks. In a series of attacks, Azer fired nine torpedoes at the ship for an estimated seven or eight direct hits. Yet the target sank slowly. When it finally went under, *Whale* cruised submerged among eight lifeboats.

"One boat was passed close aboard," Azer reported, "and survivors made ready to hit the periscope with their oars." The ship was *Heiyou Maru*, 10,000 tons. Azer and Harlfinger subsequently got two more confirmed ships, totaling 9,000 tons.

All during this patrol, Azer had been feeling miserable; his ankle and wrist joints were swollen and painful. When he returned to Pearl Harbor, he checked in at the hospital. "The diagnosis," he said later, "was arthritis."

It thus became necessary to relieve Azer from command. Casting about for a qualified skipper, the staff lit on Acey Burrows, the lawyer who had fouled up his first patrol on *Swordfish* while Chet Smith was out with a cold.

Before Burrows set off for his second chance, Lockwood took him aside for a private chat, saying he must perform this time—or else. As Lockwood wrote Fife, "If no wishbones, curtains for Acey." Fife returned, "Hope [he] kicks through this time . . . will cheer loud if he does with *Whale* what he failed to do with *Swordfish*."

Burrows and Harlfinger patrolled the Marianas, making nine attacks, firing off all but one torpedo. This time, Burrows received glowing endorsements and was credited with sinking four ships for 33,500 tons, making him one of the high scorers in the Pearl Harbor command. However, postwar records confirmed only one ship for 6,500 tons on this patrol.

Two antiques—*Porpoise*, commanded by John McKnight, and *Pike*, with a new skipper, Sandy McGregor (formerly torpedo officer on *Canopus*)—patrolled Truk.

McKnight turned in a luckless patrol. Old *Porpoise* was feeling her age. He had got as far as Wake Island, which he intended to reconnoiter, when oil leaks and other matériel failures forced him back to Pearl Harbor for repairs. Twenty days later, he restarted the patrol, this time going to Truk by way of the Marshalls. McKnight found plenty of good targets, twenty-three in all, including a seaplane tender and a tanker. However, he failed to capitalize on his opportunities. When he returned, Lockwood criticized him for missing the seaplane tender and "regretted" that McKnight had not attacked more targets. McKnight left submarines for good, going to communications duty.

Sandy McGregor in *Pike* also found many targets and tried to sink them all. However, he had a run of bad luck. On his first attack against a small convoy off Truk, all torpedoes missed. McGregor wrote, "All hands feel terrible. First chance we get, we drop the ball." McGregor also bungled another attack against a small convoy, again missing with all torpedoes. *Pike* received a terrific depth-charging, her second in a row. But although he had failed to sink anything, Lockwood praised McGregor for a "well-conducted patrol."

When Roy Davenport took command of his own boat, he told the crew about his devout Christian Scientist faith and said he believed God would place a protective shield between *Haddock* and her ene-

DEPARTING PATROLS

mies that would save them from fatal counterattaks. On Sundays, Davenport conducted religious services in the forward torpedo room. "The first Sunday," he said later, "eighteen men showed up. Thereafter, the attendance rose to an average of about twenty-five, about half of the men not on watch."

Davenport took *Haddock* to Palau, by way of Truk. Off Truk, he found many targets, including two heavy cruisers. However, he was unable to get into position to fire. Davenport bucked up his crew, telling them God meant it to be that way and that perhaps He was saving *Haddock* for something bigger and better.

Moving to the Palaus, Davenport sank a large passenger-cargo vessel, *Arima Maru*, and a smaller freighter, *Toyo Maru*. Following the attack on *Arima Maru*, an escort counterattacked, forcing *Haddock* far below her test depth. At about 415 feet, Davenport saw a hair-raising sight: the chart desk in the conning tower moved inward! Believing that the conning tower was on the verge of imploding, Davenport immediately ordered it evacuated. He tried to close the lower hatch into the control room, but it was warped out of shape; Davenport bashed it shut with a sledgehammer. The conning tower held and *Haddock* escaped. Davenport set a course for Pearl Harbor.

Davenport told his crew that he now understood why God had not enabled them to attack the two heavy cruisers at Truk. If they had, *Haddock* would most certainly have received a punishing depth-charging from the escorting destroyers which would surely have collapsed the conning tower and sunk the boat.

While Davenport was on the way back to Pearl Harbor, the code-breakers re-established contact with Japanese carrier movements. They learned that the new Japanese Carrier Division Two, composed of two new first-line carriers, *Hiyo* and *Junyo* (converted from big merchant ships), were en route to Truk by way of the Marianas, bringing aircraft for the Solomons. Voge directed Davenport—despite the infirm conning tower—to close Saipan and look. At 9 A.M. on April 7, while submerged in a flat calm sea, Davenport picked up the targets: one large carrier, one auxiliary carrier, range 12,000 yards, moving fast. They zigged toward him, then away. By 9:43 the range was 20,000 yards. Said Davenport later, "With the calm sea, a long-range slow-speed shot would never have been successful."

After returning to Pearl Harbor, *Haddock* went into a long period of overhaul. There it was determined that the Portsmouth shipbuilders had made an error in the design and construction of the conning tower, undetected until this patrol. Davenport was credited with sinking *Arima Maru*, but *Toyo Maru* was denied until postwar records confirmed her sinking.

Even though Davenport had failed to attack two heavy cruisers at Truk and two aircraft carriers at Saipan, the patrol was judged successful. Davenport was awarded a Silver Star (his second, having received one on *Silversides*) and a Letter of Commendation. These awards were the first of many that would make Davenport one of the most highly decorated—and thus controversial—skippers in the submarine force.

Suspected torpedo failure continued to plague the patrols and still sparked plenty of controversy within the service. Rebel Lowrance had reported two prematures, one observed dud, and a probable dud in seventeen torpedoes fired on *Kingfish*. Willis Thomas, on old *Pompano*, had fired six torpedoes at a carrier, and three of them had prematured.

John Addison Scott, on the new boat *Tunny*, had been convinced on his first patrol that poor performance of the magnetic exploder had robbed him of some sinkings, and his distrust of it led him to change the settings when he went out again. Off Wake Island he managed to damage a 10,000-ton transport * and later sank two large cargo ships. But bigger game lay ahead.

On the night of April 8, Dick Voge sent Scott an Ultra, reporting the two carriers, *Hiyo* and *Junyo*, that Davenport had seen at Saipan. Ably assisted by his exec, Roger Myers Keithly, Scott moved to intercept. The force appeared at night on schedule. As Scott saw it, there was one large aircraft carrier, one escort carrier, and another "large ship" which was probably the auxiliary carrier *Taiyo (Otaka)*, guarded by two destroyers. Scott and Keithly boldly remained on the surface, working the radar and TDC, and maneuvered *Tunny* into the midst of the formation in position for a triple-header: they planned to fire the bow tubes at the escort carrier and "large ship" and the stern tubes at the largest carrier. Still distrusting the magnetic exploder, Scott set his torpedoes to run at a depth of 10 feet. If the magnetic exploder failed, the torpedoes would explode on contact.

Coolly watching his three magnificent targets approach, Scott got ready to shoot. But at the last moment, three smaller escorts, possibly

---

* This transport was later destroyed by John Augustine Tyree, another youngster from the class of 1933, commanding *Finback*.

DEPARTING PATROLS 413

torpedo boats, appeared dead ahead. This forced Scott to change the attack plan and settle for two out of three. Within the next few minutes, he fired ten torpedoes at two of the carriers from an average range of 800 yards. Going deep to evade, Scott believed he heard at least seven hits. The crew cheered wildly, believing *Tunny*'s unparalleled attack had sunk at least one and possibly two Japanese capital ships.

When Scott returned to Pearl Harbor, the endorsements on his patrol report were ecstatic, and the attack on the carriers became the classic of the war. "The efficiency and aggressiveness with which this attack was carried out reflects the outstanding ability of the entire *Tunny* organization," Lockwood wrote. "The audacity combined with superb judgment of the Commanding Officer on remaining on the surface is an illustrious example of professional competence and military aggressiveness."

Then Jasper Holmes brought in disappointing news from the codebreakers. The auxiliary carrier *Taiyo* (*Otaka*) had been damaged slightly but, according to the Japanese account, all four torpedoes aimed at the other carrier exploded prematurely some 50 meters away. *Hiyo* and *Junyo* had escaped unharmed. Evidently this time the torpedoes had worked as designed. "The shallow setting," Scott said later, "thus caused the torpedo to reach the activating flux density of the exploder some fifty meters from the target. The settings I had used worked well on lighter, less dense targets but backfired on these heavier men-of-war."

Lockwood was angered and puzzled by all these reported torpedo failures. Had the Japanese perfected some secret device for touching off the magnetic exploders at a safe distance from the ships?

Shortly after *Tunny* returned from patrol, Lockwood received a letter from Ralph Christie, who had just paid a visit to Brisbane to see Fife and Carpender.

Torpedo performance here is steadily improving [Christie wrote] and we are definitely not in accord with the opinions expressed in various patrol report endorsements such as—I quote Kingfish *third patrol—"two prematures, one observed dud and a probable dud in seventeen torpedoes fired do not tend to improve waning confidence in the weapon." What conceivable good such a remark can do is beyond me. . . . Difficulties with torpedoes should be put up squarely to the Bureau of Ordnance with all possible definite evidence. . . . I have read remarks where the Commanding Officer has stated that the torpedo was seen to hit and misfire under conditions where it was impossible that he could see it. . . .*

My visit to Brisbane was most successful except with respect to Fife. I cannot rid myself of the definite conviction that the sooner he goes to other duty the better for the Task Force and Submarines, Seventh Fleet. Incidentally, if you have anything to say to me—address it to me directly.

Christie's letter, arriving at a time when Lockwood was besieged on all sides by torpedo complaints, further strained relations between the two men. Lockwood responded:

Thank you for your letter. . . . From the amount of belly-aching it contains, I assume that the breakfast coffee was scorched or perhaps it was a bad egg. . . . In any case I am sorry to see you registering lack of accord with Jimmy or vice versa. . . . I'm not a "Gun Club" man and you boys may figure the problem out to suit your favorite theories but the facts remain that we have now lost six valuable targets due to prematures so close that the skippers thought they were hits. . . . sorry to note that you believe the operating personnel is usually wrong about what they see, or think they see. Your Bureau training has not been wasted. . . . Now as to my double-headed messages to you and James, they were sent to save time and paper work because they concerned both of you as Task Force Commanders of submarines. Sorry your dignity . . . was disturbed. When and if I find it necessary in the future to repeat this practice, I suggest you either read them or stuff them.

After receiving this letter, Christie, the junior admiral, retreated.

I have reread my letter . . . and cannot find what offended you. I assure you that it was written in the best of humor and very seriously. My remarks regarding Jimmy are not personal although I was wrong in making them to you. You may recall that . . . you suggested that we, as submarine Force Commanders, should discuss submarine matters directly. When you write to me through Jimmy, you write to me through Admiral Carpender . . . as you know he is not your strongest admirer. The shortcomings of the submarine torpedo can be laid to me very properly for, for 2½ years I had charge of the design of the XIV and for three tours at Naval Torpedo Station was concerned

DEPARTING PATROLS

directly with the magnetic exploder. I meant to emphasize the harm done in anything which lessens the confidence of the submariners in their weapon....

Lockwood concluded the exchange:

Perhaps I was a little touchy ... but it did seem to me a very snotty letter written in a very petulant mood. I am glad to wash the slate clean and start over again with the continued understanding that we will correspond directly and discuss anything we may see fit.

The two commanders continued to exchange correspondence, but they would never be friends again.

With the exception of Mush Morton's patrol, accounting for nine ships, the twenty-eight patrols leaving Pearl Harbor during the first three months of 1943 produced a disappointing bag. Less Morton's remarkable results, twenty-seven patrols accounted for only twenty-five ships. The eleven other Empire patrols accounted for ten ships (for a grand total of nineteen ships in Empire waters), the twelve patrols to Truk-Palaus produced fifteen sinkings. Clearly, there was now sufficient evidence to conclude that something was definitely wrong with torpedo exploders. The matter could have been resolved with a simple series of live tests at Pearl Harbor. Yet nothing was done. Lockwood was still hoping that Spike Blandy would produce a miracle that would fix the magnetic exploder's apparent defects.

20
Alaska, 1943

The U.S. Invasions of Attu and Kiska

All this while, the curious, rugged little war in Alaskan waters was in progress. During 1942, the United States had made an offensive move in occupying the island of Adak, which had been scratched from the Japanese invasion list. In January 1943, U.S. forces moved closer to the Japanese entrenched on Attu and Kiska, invading and securing Amchitka. At the Casablanca Conference, it had been decided that one of the 1943 objectives of the Pacific war was to throw the Japanese out of the Aleutians.

The Japanese zealously clung to the barren little islands of Kiska and Attu. Some Japanese strategists believed the Allies might attempt to use them as a staging base to invade the Japanese homeland from the north: the United States could join forces with the Russians, jump from Kiska and Attu to Russian-held Kamchatka, go down the Kurile Islands to Sakhalin, and move on to Hokkaido, the least populous and most vulnerable of the Empire islands. The idea was not farfetched; the Combined Chiefs of Staff drew up an invasion plan almost precisely along those lines, but it was never seriously considered.

Fearing this invasion, the Japanese made great efforts to reinforce Attu and Kiska and moved many aircraft to Hokkaido and the Kuriles. In the early months of 1943, the Japanese navy assigned its Fifth Fleet (heavy cruisers *Maya* and *Nachi*, light cruisers *Abukuma* and *Tama*, and six destroyers) to escort duty, guarding the ships taking reinforcements to the Aleutians. The Fifth Fleet escorted its first convoy to the islands on March 10.

The United States sent a small surface fleet to intercept these reinforcements, not suspecting the Japanese had brought up two heavy cruisers for escort. The U.S. force (the heavy cruiser *Salt Lake City*, the light cruiser *Richmond*, plus destroyers) met the strong Japanese force near the Komandorski Islands in late March. When the U.S. ships saw the heavy cruisers, they turned tail. The Japanese chased. During the battle, *Salt Lake City* and a destroyer were heavily damaged, but the other U.S. ships fought a delaying action—waiting for land-based aircraft to help out—and forced the Japanese to withdraw and return to Paramushiro. That was the last convoy the Fifth Fleet tried to escort to Alaskan waters.

On May 12, a strong U.S. naval force commanded by Rear Admiral Thomas Cassin Kinkaid, brother-in-law of Husband Kimmel, invaded Attu. The Japanese garrison put up a fanatical defense. When word of the invasion reached Tokyo, the Japanese considered it a grave matter, again raising the possibility of an invasion of Hokkaido. They immediately organized for a major counterattack which would employ the bulk of the Japanese navy. The force was ordered to assemble in Tokyo Bay. The major units at Truk—the carriers *Hiyo* and *Junyo*, three battleships, and two heavy cruisers—hurried home to join with the carriers *Shokaku* and *Unyo*, one other battleship, three heavy cruisers, and two light cruisers. Before this force sailed from Tokyo Bay, Attu fell.

During the invasion of Attu, two Pearl Harbor submarines, Bill Brockman's *Nautilus* and Frank Latta's *Narwhal*, played a minor role. Again converted to troop transports, the two submarines put ashore a total of 215 officers and men of the army's 7th Infantry Scout Company in advance of the general landing on Attu.

For the army troops, it was a miserable voyage. Cramped inside the submarine hulls, many were seasick and most were uneasy. Creeping into the dangerous, fog-shrouded Alaskan waters bristling with Japanese submarines, both boats remained submerged for as long as eighteen hours a day. The air became foul and oxygen had to be bled into the boat from storage bottles. Toward the end of each day, there was not enough oxygen in the air to keep a cigarette going. "The 7th Scouts went ashore with a will," said the *Nautilus* historian. "All they wanted by that time was fresh air, plenty of it, at whatever the cost."

After the fall of Attu, and still fearing an invasion of Hokkaido from the north, the Japanese decided to withdraw from Kiska and greatly strengthen northern Hokkaido and the Kuriles. Not wishing to expose their surface ships to attack from U.S. planes on Attu, the Japanese planned to evacuate the 5,000 troops on Kiska by submarine, as they had tried at Guadalcanal.

The codebreakers got wind of this plan, and as a result the Japanese lost three of the I-class submarines asigned to the evacuation. *I-9* was rammed and sunk by a U.S. patrol craft. *I-31* (or *I-24*, the records are not clear) was sunk by depth charges from a U.S. destroyer. When the conning tower of *I-7*, shelled by another U.S. destroyer off Kiska, was holed, the crew tried to scuttle her and then surrendered.

The scuttling attempt was not a success; the front half sank in very deep water, but the after half of *I-7* remained intact at 100 feet. Later, the navy sent the submarine rescue vessel *Florikan* to the scene. Seven divers entered the hulk and recovered "important documents" and "personal papers of value in intelligence work."

After the submarine evacuation failed, two Japanese light cruisers and ten destroyers sneaked in unharmed under cover of fog and took off the troops. On August 16, the United States landed 34,000 men on Kiska. They took the deserted island without a casualty.

Patrols from Dutch Harbor

Meanwhile, the little S-boat fleet based at Dutch Harbor had continued its miserable, ineffectual patrolling. There had been some changes. Ozzie Colclough was relieved by Franklin Oliver ("Fuel Oil") Johnson, a colorful character who had been the first peacetime skipper of *Snapper*. Johnson disdained office work. One of the S-boat skippers later wrote, "Johnson was so negligent with the paperwork that I never obtained a fitness report for the period until after the war. . . . Many of the patrol reports were never endorsed and presumably died in [his] incoming basket."

During the spring of 1943, the force was augmented; seven of the "40" boats that had been withdrawn from Brisbane and overhauled in

RECAPTURE of ATTU and KISKA
MAY–AUGUST 1943

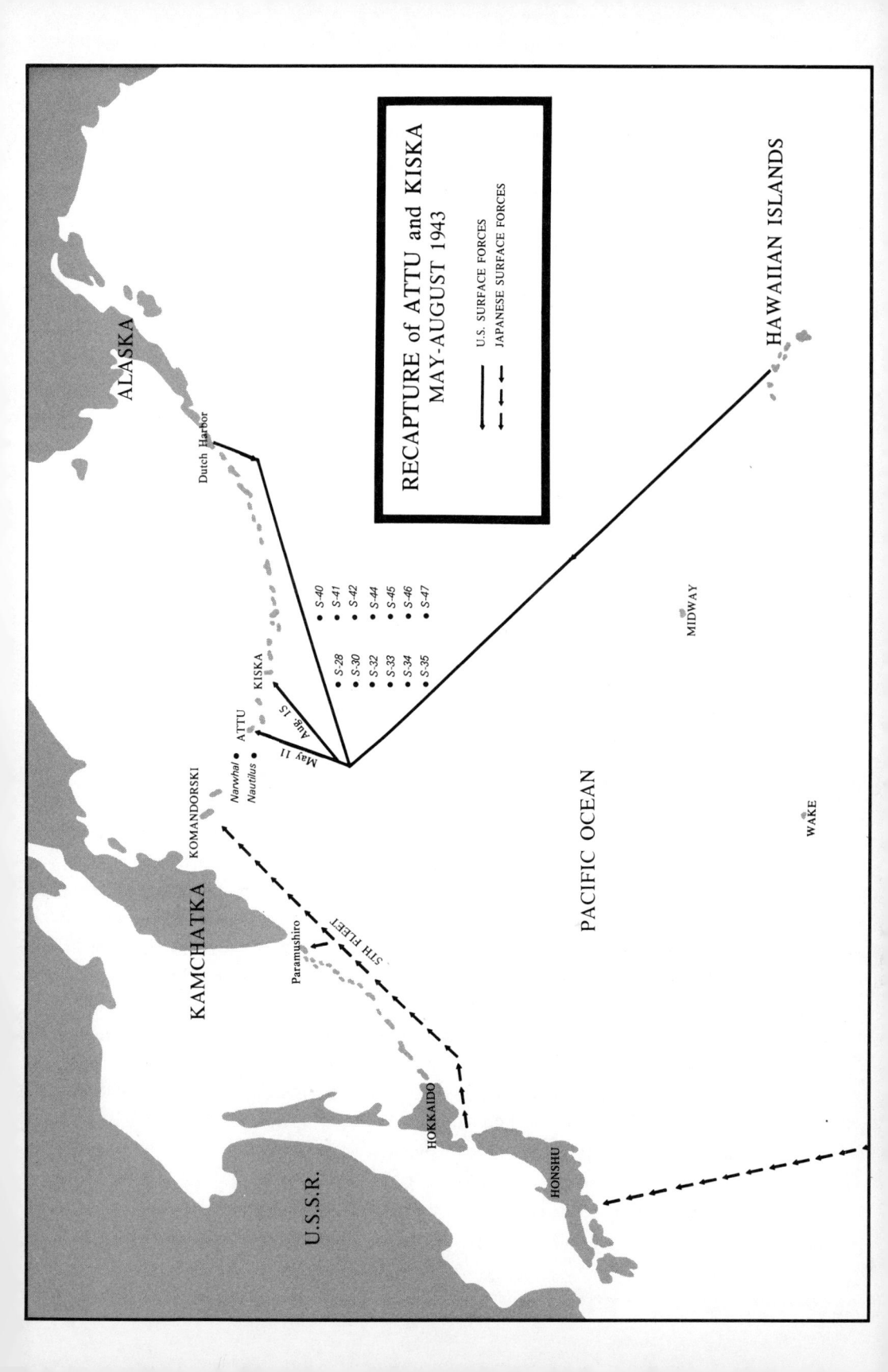

the States reported for duty.* Crews who had barely survived the debilitating heat of the tropics now struggled against the freezing cold of the Arctic. Like all Alaskan S-boat patrols, the main effort was put into physical survival rather than striking at the Japanese.

The results were thin. In the twenty war patrols mounted from January to July, when the Japanese evacuated Kiska, the S-boats sank three confirmed ships. William Alfred Stevenson in S-30 sank the 5,228-ton freighter *Jinbu Maru*, Henry Monroe in S-35 sank the 5,430-ton *Banshu Maru VII*, and Irvin Hartman in S-41 sank the 1,000-ton *Seiki Maru*.

After the recapture of Kiska, the S-boats went on patrolling, completing another thirteen arduous cruises by the end of the year. One of these patrols resulted in another confirmed sinking: Vincent Ambrose Sisler, Jr., in S-28 sank the 1,400-ton ex-gunboat *Katsura Maru II* near the Japanese base of Paramushiro in the Kuriles.

Another S-boat was lost, the famous old S-44 in which Dinty Moore had sunk the heavy cruiser *Kako*, still the largest enemy man-of-war U.S. submarines had sent to the bottom. S-44 was commanded by Francis Brown, who had lost S-39 by grounding in Australia.

Brown left Attu for patrol off Paramushiro on September 26. On October 7, he picked up a radar contact. Believing it to be a very small merchant vessel, he ordered battle surface. The target turned out to be a destroyer, which promptly opened up with all guns. Brown tried to get under, but Japanese shells holed S-44 below the waterline in the control room and after battery. With the boat flooding, Brown ordered abandon ship. One of the crewmen opened the forward torpedo room hatch and waved a white pillowcase in an effort to surrender, but the Japanese evidently did not see it or refused to honor it. They went on pumping shells and S-44 sank.

About eight men got into the water. Only two were picked up by the destroyer, Ernest A. Duva and William F. Whitmore. They were taken first to Paramushiro, then to the prison camp at Ofuna, and then to the copper mines at Ashio, where they worked throughout the war.

The submarine force did not have to wait until after the war to learn of S-44's tragedy. The codebreakers gave Lockwood her story.

Francis Brown, who died in the battle, was the only submarine skipper to lose two submarines. S-44 was the fifth S-boat to be lost since the beginning of the war.

* S-40, S-41, S-42, S-44, S-45, S-46, and S-47.

At the end of 1943, S-boat operations at Dutch Harbor were terminated. The surviving "40" boats were sent to training duty—as targets for U.S. antisubmarine forces. S-45 (which had a serious battery explosion) returned to the States for overhaul and then went to the Southwest Pacific. S-42 and S-47 went direct from Alaska to the Southwest Pacific. S-46 went to Pearl Harbor.

In the total seventy S-boat war patrols conducted from Dutch Harbor in 1942 and 1943, five confirmed ships had been sunk. Counting war patrols mounted from Panama, Manila, and Australia, the S-boats had conducted a total of about 190 war patrols, accounting for a total of fourteen Japanese ships. To mount this unrewarding effort had required the services of well over 1,000 qualified submarine officers and men, plus tenders, bases, and technical personnel. Clearly, all these experienced people would have served the war effort better manning fleet boats, which, ironically, were shorthanded.

21
Pearl Harbor, April through August 1943

Additions to the Pacific Fleet

While the invasion of Attu was in progress, the Combined Chiefs of Staff held another series of meetings on Pacific strategy, culminating in yet another conference, Trident. These conferences attempted to resolve the conflicts between the MacArthur view and the King-Nimitz view about how to defeat Japan and to determine what the first offensive steps would be. Again, the conclusions were limited and controversial. However, one positive agreement was reached for the Pearl Harbor forces: Nimitz should proceed with plans to invade the Gilberts (Tarawa-Makin) on or about November 1943.

The Pacific Fleet aircraft carrier inventory—crucial to the proposed invasion—was steadily swelling. In May, the battle-worn *Enterprise* was released from the Solomons for stateside overhaul and then reassignment to Nimitz (the *Saratoga* remained in the Solomons). That same month the first of the big new carriers, *Essex*, arrived in Pearl Harbor. She was followed by four new sister ships: *Lexington*, *Hornet*, *Yorktown*, and *Bunker Hill*. In addition, two light carriers, *Independence* and *Belleau Wood*, reported at Pearl Harbor, followed soon by three new sister ships: *Princeton*, *Cowpens*, and *Monterey*.

These additions boosted the Pacific carrier force to twelve, seven

ADDITIONS TO THE PACIFIC FLEET

heavy and five light. Most (including *Enterprise* and *Saratoga*) were earmarked for the Gilberts invasion.

In April 1943 fleet boats produced on an assembly-line basis at Electric Boat, Portsmouth, Mare Island, and Manitowoc began arriving at Pearl Harbor in significant numbers. The remainder of John Longstaff's Squadron Fourteen boats reported in, followed almost immediately by the long-delayed H.O.R.-powered boats of John Griggs's Squadron Twelve. In addition, week by week the older boats of Swede Momsen's Squadron Two returned from overhaul, modernized with SJ radar, new sonar gear, new engines, and trimmed-down silhouettes.

Counting all the new arrivals, and the older boats of Babe Brown's Squadron Four, Lockwood soon had about fifty fleet boats under his command. A few of these were sent temporarily or permanently to Australia to maintain that submarine force at twenty boats, but the majority based from Pearl Harbor. During the four-month period April to August 1943, Lockwood mounted ninety-one war patrols with these boats—an average of almost twenty-two per month, twice the average for a similar period in 1942.

The target priority for Pearl Harbor submarines remained fixed: Japanese carriers and battleships, followed by lesser ships. With Admiral Koga basing at Truk with his major fleet units, and with carriers and other vessels bringing in aircraft and supplies for the campaign in the Solomons, Truk remained an important patrol area for Pacific submarines. In addition, Lockwood continued to send submarines to the Marshalls, the Marianas, and the Palaus, also engaged in resupplying the Solomons. However, for the first time in the war, more submarines went to Empire and East China Sea waters than to the islands, fifty-three versus thirty-eight (including six boats patrolling to Australia).

The "bags" (as Lockwood called them) produced by these patrols maintained the usual trend: more for Empire boats, less for boats going to Truk and Palau. The fifty-three Empire–East China Sea patrols produced sixty-four confirmed sinkings, the thirty-eight patrols to the islands only twenty-one. Based on past statistical averages, the Empire boats should have produced even more sinkings. However, this group of boats was hobbled by a variety of problems, including the continuing shortage of torpedoes, torpedo failures, inexperienced fire-control parties, breakdowns of H.O.R. engines, inept or nonproductive skippers, and a flood of Ultras on major Japanese fleet units that brought on time-consuming—and usually futile—interceptions and chases.

Even so, the U.S. submarine force was beginning to inflict serious damage on the Japanese shipping services. In the spring of 1943, the seventy-odd fleet boats patrolling from Pearl Harbor, Fremantle, and Brisbane reached a confirmed sinking level of 100,000 tons per month. For the first time, the Japanese began to worry about this steady attrition. Merchant ship captains who had heretofore preferred to sail alone rather than in convoys showed interest in convoying, despite its disadvantages. The Imperial Naval Staff requested 360 frigates for convoy escort (the high command authorized only 40) and laid plans for a central convoy escort command.

A serious breach of security may have helped the Japanese antisubmarine forces. In June 1943, Congressman Andrew Jackson May, a sixty-eight-year-old member of the House Military Affairs Committee returning from a war zone junket, gave a press interview during which he said, in effect, Don't worry about our submariners; the Japanese are setting their depth charges too shallow. Incredibly, the press associations sent this story over their wires, and many newspapers, including one in Honolulu, thoughtlessly published it.

Lockwood and his staff were appalled—and furious—at this stupid revelation. Lockwood wrote Admiral Edwards in acid words, "I hear . . . Congressman May . . . said the Jap depth charges . . . are not set deep enough. . . . He would be pleased to know the Japs set 'em deeper now." And after the war, Lockwood wrote, "I consider that indiscretion cost us ten submarines and 800 officers and men."

Edwards and Lockwood took further steps to tighten submarine security. Edwards delayed publication of several books (including one by Robert Trumbull on Burlingame and *Silversides*) and braked the press releases on submarine sinkings and losses until long after the events. This pleased Lockwood, who wrote Edwards, "We are doing better now . . . the reports from Washington are long delayed and the actual attacks would be hard for the Japanese to identify. We can't even identify them ourselves. Everyone likes to see his name in print but . . . our people here . . . would rather miss that thrill than to increase the chance of seeing said name carved on a bit of white marble."

Ultra-directed Patrols

Meanwhile, the boats were being directed in great measure by Ultra information. In April and May, when the United States mounted its offensive against Attu and Admiral Koga returned his major units from Truk to Tokyo Bay for the sortie to Alaska, the codebreakers listened with more than casual interest. They tracked the recalled fleet to Japan and then, after the sortie to Alaska was canceled, its return to Truk. Following this, they tracked the many major fleet units—and tankers—engaged in running supplies from Japan to the Marianas, Palau, and Truk. Lockwood diverted many submarines from normal patrol duty to make interceptions on these movements.

Forewarned by the codebreakers that the Japanese intended to counter the Attu invasion by a major sortie of the fleet, Lockwood sent his top skipper to the Kuriles to intercept it: Mush Morton in *Wahoo*.

The *Wahoo* crew found this far-north area stark and bitterly cold. Yeoman Sterling wrote:

Each day, like a Chinaman, I added another piece of clothing to go up on lookout.... I came off ... shivering, teeth chattering, and my nose and ears so cold I was afraid to touch them for fear they would shatter into crystallized fragments. It had begun to sleet and snow, and I stood helplessly trying to peer into a darkness that was not penetrable with the human eye.

Later, when the weather cleared, he wrote:

There was no ocean to be seen but instead a vast thin ice plain. Jagged rock islands pierced this ice at irregular intervals.... Wahoo's nose was clearing a pathway through the six or eight inches of ice so smoothly that the surface seemed to part at her approach. It gave the illusion that Wahoo *was standing still and the ice was moving.*

While U.S. troops stormed ashore on Attu, Morton took station near Etorofu Island in the Kuriles, waiting for the Japanese fleet. When the sortie was canceled, Morton was released for general patrol, helped along by the codebreakers, who were tracking Japanese ships bringing reinforcements to the Kuriles and Paramushiro. On May 4, they positioned him to intercept a seaplane tender, *Kamikawa Maru*.

While Dick O'Kane manned the periscope, Morton closed to 1,300 yards and fired three torpedoes. One passed ahead, the second hit amidships, but the third failed and the tender got away. Morton wrote, "It must have been erratic or a dud. It is inconceivable that any normal dispersion could allow this last torpedo to miss a 510-foot target at this range."

Another Ultra directed Morton to Banten Zaki. On May 7, Morton intercepted two big northbound ships, one freighter and one large escort, right on schedule. He closed to 900 yards and fired six torpedoes, two at the freighter, four at the escort. The freighter, *Toman Maru*, 5,260 tons, went down, but the escort avoided the four torpedoes and escaped harm.

The following day, Morton shifted south to Kobe Zaki for another interception. On the afternoon of May 8 he picked up a three-ship convoy, two escorts and a large naval auxiliary. Morton closed to 2,500 yards and fired three torpedoes at the auxiliary. The first torpedo prematured after fifty-one seconds, halfway to the target. This evidently deflected the second torpedo, or else it failed to explode. The third hit at the point of aim but failed to explode. This ship, too, got away and Morton was forced deep by escorts. Later he wrote, "Both sound operators reported the thud of the dud at the same time that a column of water about ten feet high was observed at the target's side abreast of her foremast as the air flasks exploded."

That evening Morton surfaced, received new information from the codebreakers, and then reversed course northward to Kone Zaki. Early on the morning of May 9, he picked up two ships on radar. Closing to the point-blank range of 1,200 yards, Morton identified them as a tanker and freighter. He fired six torpedoes, three at each ship. The torpedoes hit, and down went *Takao Maru*, 3,200 tons, and *Jinmu Maru*, 1,200 tons.

Three days later Morton found two more freighters and attacked, firing four torpedoes from 1,200 yards. The two aimed at one ship missed. Of the two aimed at the other ship, one hit amidships and the other was not heard from. Morton wrote, "The second torpedo, fired at his stack amidships, is believed to have been erratic or a dud. The target course and speed had been most accurately determined and it is inconceivable that any normal dispersion could cause it to miss."

Morton surfaced to pursue the ship he damaged. He closed to 1,800 yards and fired his last remaining bow tube. "Nothing was seen of

ULTRA-DIRECTED PATROLS

the bow torpedo or its wake," he wrote, "and the enemy apparently did not know he had again been fired upon." Morton turned and fired his last stern tube. "It hit under the bridge with a dull thud much louder than the duds we have heard only on sound, but lacking the 'whacking' which accompanies a whole-hearted explosion. It is considered that this torpedo had a low-order detonation."

Having shot off all his torpedoes, Morton manned his deck gun, planning to polish off the damaged freighter by gunfire. However, the other freighter charged *Wahoo*, firing heavy guns and forcing Morton to break off the attack. He terminated the patrol and returned to Pearl Harbor after twenty-six days.

This patrol of *Wahoo*, Morton's third, was one of the most important of the war—not for what it achieved but for what it didn't achieve. Morton stormed into Lockwood's office on May 21 in a towering rage. He denounced the Mark XIV torpedo in salty language, detailing his prematures, duds, and erratics. Mush Morton was Lockwood's star; he had conducted a brilliantly aggressive patrol. *Wahoo* had one of the best fire-control parties in the submarine force. Had the torpedoes not failed, *Wahoo* would have sunk not three but six ships.

This patrol—following hard on the heels of the problems experienced by Rebel Lowrance in *Kingfish*, John Scott in *Tunny*, and Willis Thomas in *Pompano*—finally destroyed Lockwood's faith in the magnetic exploder. Now, after eighteen months of war, he decided it should be deactivated—but still he delayed a little longer, hoping his pressure on Spike Blandy might produce a quick fix that would save it.

On inspection, *Wahoo* was found to need a navy yard overhaul. Morton himself appeared tired and not in the best of health; in fact, he was still suffering from prostate problems. Lockwood ordered *Wahoo* to Mare Island. There, Dick O'Kane was detached to new construction and Roger Paine moved up to be Morton's exec.

Much farther to the south, the boats patrolling off Honshu in May, also alerted by Ultra dispatches, attempted to intercept and sink Admiral Koga and his fleet returning from Truk to Tokyo Bay for the sortie to Alaska. Eugene Sands in *Sawfish*, at the tail end of his second patrol south of Tokyo, was first to sight the force. He found it on radar at about 12,000 yards, speed 18 knots, on the night of May 20. It consisted, he believed, of three battleships, a large aircraft carrier, two destroyers, and two other ships. The weather was foul, and Sands was unable to get a clear picture of the formation or produce a fast firing solution. When he finally figured it all out, he reported later, "the chance of shooting had passed."

Lying in wait on the projected track off Tokyo, Roy Benson, making his fourth patrol in *Trigger*, picked up the task force on the morning of May 22. As Benson ticked off the targets—an aircraft carrier, three battleships, numerous cruisers and destroyers—his exec, Stephen Stafford Mann, Jr., and Ned Beach, serving as diving officer, could hardly believe their ears. It was, Beach later wrote, "an appreciable segment of the main Japanese battle fleet."

Benson was cool and soft-spoken at the periscope. He let a cruiser go by, waiting for the carriers and battleships. But at the last minute, these prizes zigzagged out of range. Benson, Beach reported, "watched helplessly." Short of a suicidal surface attack, there was nothing Benson or anyone else in *Trigger* could do. It was a bitter disappointment for all hands.

Two weeks later, the boats off Japan received another Ultra: several aircraft carriers were leaving Tokyo Bay, southbound. There were three boats nearby, *Trigger*, *Salmon*, and *Sculpin*, the last two being Squadron Two boats returned from long overhaul.

Roy Benson in *Trigger* was first to find the force, picking it up during the night of June 8 on radar, range 12 miles. He went to full power on all main engines, trying to reach firing position, but one engine was in bad shape and refused to put out maximum power. Benson was still 6 miles away. He could see the two carriers from the bridge but was not able to close the gap. Once more the *Trigger* crew missed a golden opportunity.

Nicholas John Nicholas, formerly exec of *Drum*, lay to the south of *Trigger* in *Salmon*. While waiting for the oncoming prizes, a convoy of three freighters and a destroyer passed by. Unable to resist this temptation, Nicholas chased the convoy, hitting two ships for damage. While *Salmon* was thus involved, the carrier force appeared on schedule, but Nicholas was too far away and couldn't catch up. Later, Lockwood wrote that it was "unfortunate" Nicholas went after the convoy instead of waiting for the carriers.

Farther south, Lucius Chappell on his seventh war patrol in *Sculpin* waited near Sofu Gan (Lot's Wife), a rocklike island in the ocean used by many navigators as a landfall for approaching and departing

Japan. Chappell picked up the force on June 9 around midnight, range 6 miles. He identified the targets as two carriers escorted by a cruiser. Ringing up flank speed, Chappell tried to close, but the task force pulled away. In desperation, Chappell fired four torpedoes from a range of 7,000 yards. One prematured, advertising his presence. He tried to bring his stern tubes to bear but it was too late. It was the second time in two consecutive patrols that Chappell had fired at—and missed—an aircraft carrier. Chappell was promoted to Babe Brown's training staff at Pearl Harbor.

Roy Benson in *Trigger*, alerted by yet another Ultra, remained on station off the mouth of Tokyo Bay. On the afternoon of June 10, his last day on station, a junior officer standing periscope watch suddenly shouted and sounded the battle alarm. He had picked up Koga's flagship, the carrier *Hiyo*, standing down the bay at 21 knots, with a destroyer on port and starboard bows.

Benson ducked under the destroyer screen and fired six bow tubes at *Hiyo* from 1,200 yards. Immediately after shooting, he went deep to avoid the destroyer escorts. On the way down, Benson counted four solid explosions and, as Ned Beach wrote, "we jubilantly credited ourselves with a sure sinking." A destroyer immediately counterattacked.

On board *Hiyo*, there was surprise, confusion—and error. One of the Japanese staff officers wrote Beach after the war:

At that time, just two minutes before sunset, the duty officer on the bridge saw the big white bubbles of torpedoes in the middle of the calm cobaltic seas and on the right at about 1,500 yards from the ship. He cried: "Torpedoes! This direction." We looked at it, six white tracers were coming at us. The Commanding Officer ordered the destroyers by the flag signal "Attack the enemy submarine." The Captain ordered "Port side helm. Full rudder." These events occurred instantaneously . . . the skipper should have ordered "starboard helm" in this case. But I did not suggest it because it would add to the confusion.

The third fish exploded itself after running about 1,000 feet and a big water column rose. The right side destroyer turned to the site of the bubbles and began a depth charge attack. Our ship turned to the left to avoid your torpedoes. But I thought it would be in vain; some of them would surely hit for you had a very favorable position to fire and the skipper failed to turn in the right direction. The first and second torpedoes passed before the bow. The fourth hit under the right hawse hole and splashed water higher than the bridge. The ship trembled terribly. The fifth one hit at the middle part between the bow and the bridge, but when it hit the torpedo's head dropped from the body and it flew along the side. . . . The last one hit just under the bridge for an instant. . . . All the crew on the bridge were staggered by the shock. The first hit did not do much damage; it only broke the chain locker. But the last hit damaged us vitally. It broke the first boiler room and the bulkhead of the second boiler room. . . . These rooms all took in water at once. The third boiler room leaked by and by. All fire was put out and all steam went out the ship stopped.

In summary, of the six torpedoes Benson fired, two missed ahead and one prematured. Three hit *Hiyo*, but one was a dud and only two exploded, one forward in the chain locker doing slight damage, one in the boiler rooms doing major damage.

Benson's attack on *Hiyo*—well outside Tokyo Bay—gave rise to another submarine myth: that a U.S. submarine stole quietly into Tokyo Bay, lay on the bottom for a month watching workers in a shipyard putting the finishing touches on a brand-new aircraft carrier, and then, when the carrier was launched, came to periscope depth and sank it as it was coming off the ways.

Trigger reached Pearl Harbor on June 22. Benson reported four hits and a probable carrier sinking, but Lockwood knew from the codebreakers that *Hiyo* had not gone down. Furthermore, he knew from the same source that only one of *Trigger*'s torpedoes had caused any real damage.

This failure to sink an important target was the final straw. After talking with Benson, Lockwood decided to deactivate the Mark VI magnetic exploder. The order went out—under Nimitz's name—on June 24, two days after Benson reached Pearl Harbor.

The Bureau of Ordnance and Ralph Christie immediately queried Nimitz on his reasons for giving this order. Nimitz replied it had been done "because of probable enemy counter-measures, because of the ineffectiveness of the exploder under certain conditions, and because of the impracticability of selecting the proper conditions under which to fire."

In Fremantle, Christie held a conference with his staff and after much discussion decided *not* to deactivate the magnetic exploder. (He was able to take this divergent course because he reported to Chips Carpender, not Nimitz.) Christie's reasoning: (a) the Mark VI magnetic exploder got *some* hits; (b) it was the only defense against very shallow draft antisubmarine vessels; and (c) if it were discarded, it was "gone forever" and any attempt to locate its possible defects would be terminated.

This split decision on the magnetic exploder further widened the gap between Lockwood and Christie. Christie wrote in his diary, "Conference on Mark VI. . . . Decided to keep it activated. . . . This is at variance with Charles Lockwood . . . who is 'agin' the magnetic exploder. He is 'agin' the torpedo but brags about the tonnage sunk. What sunk them, spuds?"

The split caused a complication for submarine skippers: while they worked for Lockwood, they set the torpedoes one way; while working for Christie, another. A boat going from Pearl Harbor to Australia on the exchange program departed with the magnetic feature deactivated. On the way down, when the boat fell under the operational control of Fife or Christie, the skippers had to reactivate the magnetic feature. Boats returning from Australia followed the opposite procedure, starting out with the magnetic feature activated, then deactivating it after falling under Lockwood's operational control.

Trigger, like *Wahoo*, went to a navy yard overhaul. Roy Benson and the exec, Steve Mann, departed, Benson to the New London Submarine School, Mann to new construction. Ned Beach, who had stood second in the class of 1939 (and first in his submarine school class), fleeted up to be *Trigger*'s exec.

The flow of Ultras continued unabated. The codebreakers discovered that the Japanese used an area southwest of Lot's Wife as a rendezvous for major fleet units forming up for the trip south to Truk or the Palaus. A few days after Benson's attack on *Hiyo*, *Flying Fish*, en route to the East China Sea, was directed there to intercept yet another Japanese task force.

Lockwood had decided that after a skipper had made five consecutive war patrols he should return to the States for a rest, so *Flying Fish* had a new—though temporary—skipper. Division commander Frank Thomas Watkins had asked Lockwood for permission to make a war patrol as skipper. Lockwood, who had been refused permission by Nimitz to make a war patrol himself, agreed to give his senior men combat experience, and when Donc Donaho finished his fifth patrol, Watkins was assigned to make the next. He was the first division commander to take a boat to sea, and—at forty-five—the oldest skipper.

Moving to intercept the task force, Watkins made contact on the night of June 17, range 6 miles, and raced along at flank speed, trying to get into position. Like many of his division skippers, however, he was not able to gain a favorable firing position, and the force—making 20 knots—escaped untouched. Watkins proceeded to patrol off Formosa. He made two attacks and was credited with sinking one ship for 8,700 tons (later trimmed to 2,820 tons by JANAC) and damaging another. On the way home, he spent two days chasing a fast convoy but had to break off because he was running low on fuel. He received a Bronze Star for the patrol. On balance, it had not been one of *Flying Fish*'s better efforts.

After Watkins reported his failure to attack the task force near Lot's Wife, Voge alerted *Spearfish*, patrolling near Truk with a skipper new to fleet boats, George Arthur Sharp. Sharp consulted his exec, Richard Albert Waugh, and decided to attack by periscope, at night, fearing that use of SJ radar might give him away.

The Japanese appeared right on schedule, June 21. It was a massive force: three carriers, three heavy cruisers, three light cruisers, several destroyers—in all, fourteen men-of-war. Remaining submerged, Sharp set up first on a cruiser but then shifted to a carrier, confusing his fire-control party. He fired four torpedoes at the carrier, but he had evidently underestimated the speed and fired too late; all torpedoes missed. He maneuvered to fire stern tubes at another carrier but, as he was getting set to fire, thought he saw a destroyer charging and went deep. When Sharp returned to Pearl Harbor, Lockwood summarily relieved him of command.

Edward Seabury Carmick in *Sargo*, patrolling in June off Woleai, a small but important Japanese base lying between Truk and Palau, also failed to profit by Ultra information. He was directed to intercept two important targets—*Tonan Maru III*, a huge, 19,000-ton converted whale factory carrying oil from Borneo to fleet units based at Truk, and an auxiliary carrier—but scored no hits.

The Japanese continued to shuttle carriers back and forth to Truk. In the early days of July, the codebreakers reported a small task force, composed of the auxiliary carrier *Unyo*, a light cruiser, and other vessels, en route from Japan. Lockwood and Voge directed three submarines to intercept near Truk: *Halibut*, *Steelhead*, and *Pogy*, operating not as a pack but independently. All three boats had deactivated their magnetic exploders.

Pogy, a Manitowoc boat on her second patrol commanded by George Herrick Wales, was too far off the track to shoot, but *Halibut* and *Steelhead* both scored. Philip Ross, making his fifth patrol in *Halibut*, attacked first, firing at *Unyo* and obtaining three hits. David Lee Whelchel in *Steelhead*, preparing to attack *Unyo* also, saw a bright orange flash as Ross's torpedoes struck. (Whelchel was on his second patrol. On his first he had not attacked any ships but he had lobbed forty-nine shells at a steel mill on Hokkaido, the first shore bombardment of the Japanese homeland by a naval vessel.) Boldly staying on the surface, Whelchel closed to within 2,000 yards of *Unyo* and fired five torpedoes, believing he also obtained three hits.

These were the first torpedo attacks against a major Japanese man-of-war after the deactivation of the magnetic exploder. Both—apparently—were successful. Hearing the reports of these attacks, Lockwood was pleased.

Hiram Cassedy in *Searaven* and Pi Pieczentkowski in *Sturgeon* were the next skippers to go off on an Ultra wild goose chase. Notified of another task force rendezvous in the staging area southwest of Lot's Wife, they converged there on July 11.

Pi Pieczentkowski made contact first; he saw *Chitose*, a seaplane tender he had tried to attack on his previous patrol from Brisbane to Pearl Harbor. Again the attack on *Chitose* failed. "He has a charmed life," Pi wrote. "This is the second time on two successive patrols I've tried to get him—with the same results." An hour later, Pi picked up two aircraft carriers and six light cruisers zigzagging at 20 knots. He closed to 8,500 yards, but the task force outran him. (He stayed in the area and was unable to attack a second large task force on July 23.)

Nearby, Hi Cassedy in *Searaven* found the same group of ships and identified them as two *Shokaku*-class carriers, *Chitose*, one heavy cruiser, and many destroyers. Unable to attack, he tracked them on a southbound course, speed 15 knots, and got off a contact report to Lockwood and Voge.

Pogy, *Steelhead*, and *Halibut*, still at Truk, had been joined by another boat, *Tinosa*, commanded by Lawrence Randall ("Dan") Daspit, making his second patrol. Only *Tinosa* and *Pogy* made contact with the oncoming task force. Daspit picked it up first on the morning of July 15, at 6:53—by sonar. He remained submerged, sighting first a destroyer, then a heavy cruiser leading two carriers, then a light cruiser, probably *Yubari*, leading *Chitose*, and an auxiliary carrier with more destroyer escorts. Daspit set up on the last ship in the column, the auxiliary carrier, but it zigged away, opening the range. In desperation, Daspit fired four deactivated torpedoes from a range of 3,800 yards. The target saw the torpedoes and turned away.

George Wales in *Pogy* also made contact, but by the time he found the task force, it was flying along at 25 knots. For the second time, Wales was unable to reach firing position. The task force entered Truk unharmed.

There were a few bright spots. In early August, the codebreakers provided intercepts on two important Japanese ships serving as aircraft ferries on the Japan–Truk supply run. On August 1, Wales in *Pogy* sank Truk-bound *Magamigawa Maru*; a week later, Acey Burrows in *Whale*, patrolling the Marianas, was directed northward to the Bonins, where he outfoxed a destroyer escort and sank the 7,149-ton *Naruto Maru*.

Dave Whelchel, patrolling off Truk in *Steelhead*, was alerted by Ultra to the departure of yet another big task force. Early in the evening of August 4, he made radar contact, range 9,500 yards. The force appeared to consist of three battleships, an auxiliary carrier, and five destroyers in screen. Whelchel tracked for six hours, maneuvering for a favorable firing position.

At about 2 A.M. August 5 he fired ten torpedoes, six at the auxiliary carrier and four at a battleship. He believed he heard two explosions on the carrier, but the evidence was thin. Immediately, *Steelhead* was rocked by violent explosions which may have been her own torpedoes making a circular run. In the darkness Whelchel picked up a cruiser or destroyer and tried to make an approach, but the ship pulled off at 24 knots. Whelchel was the fifth skipper (after Brockman, Donaho, Bole, and Ramage) to attack a Japanese battleship.

Another new boat, *Tullibee*, commanded by Charles Frederick Brindupke, also was directed to intercept the task force. Brindupke's first contact was a destroyer, range 1,480 yards; he dived immediately and went deep, staying down thirty-three minutes. While he was submerged, the task force sped by.

The task force proceeded northward from Truk. Sandy McGregor in old *Pike* was patrolling off Saipan, where he had sunk a small tanker. On the day after Whelchel's attack, McGregor spotted an auxiliary carrier off Saipan that either had split off from the task force or arrived independently. McGregor attacked, firing six torpedoes. He heard two distinct torpedo explosions and was later credited with damage to the carrier *Taiyo* (*Otaka*) for 22,500 tons. The carrier fired its guns at *Pike*'s periscope. Then a destroyer gave *Pike* such a stiff working over that McGregor on his return to Pearl Harbor, recommended that she be withdrawn from combat and consigned to training duty.

To sum up, the flow of Ultra during the Attu invasion and in the weeks following enabled eighteen submarines to make nineteen contacts with major groups of Japanese men-of-war, not counting the two aircraft ferries. Seven of the eighteen submarines managed to make eight attacks—*Sculpin, Trigger, Spearfish,* Steelhead (2), *Tinosa, Halibut,* and *Pike*—which resulted in confirmed damage to three ships: *Trigger*'s 27,500-ton carrier *Hiyo* (major damage), *Steelhead*'s and *Halibut*'s 18,000-ton auxiliary carrier *Unyo* (slight damage), and *Pike*'s 25,000-ton carrier *Taiyo* (*Otaka*) (heavy damage?). *Trigger*'s damage—a lucky hit in a vital spot—was inflicted before the magnetic exploder was deactivated, the other three afterward. The two aircraft ferries were sunk by *Pogy* and *Whale* after deactivation.

Final Isolation of the Mark XIV Torpedo Defects

Dan Daspit in *Tinosa* remained on station off Truk with orders to intercept the fleet tanker traffic plying between Palau and Truk. On July 20, the codebreakers put him on the track of a whale factory, *Nippon Maru*. Daspit found it and fired four torpedoes. All missed. Daspit later wrote, "Target had been carefully tracked and with spread used torpedoes could not have run properly and missed."

Daspit surfaced after dark and ran ahead. This time he found two targets on radar. One turned out to be a destroyer. Before Daspit could attack the target, the destroyer picked up *Tinosa* and opened fire with guns, driving her under. The tanker got away. Daspit spent the following day submerged, resting his crew and routining the torpedoes.

"All torpedoes were checked during this and next day," he reported. "Exploder mechanisms were not touched."

The codebreakers gave Daspit another juicy target: *Tonan Maru III*, the 19,000-ton whale factory Carmick had missed off Woleai in June. She was on an easterly course from Palau to Truk. Daspit found her on the morning of July 24. He made an end around and submerged ahead. When he got a good look at her through the periscope, he saw she was heavily loaded, making about 13 knots.

Daspit attacked, firing four torpedoes. He believed that two hit; he saw large splashes of water forward. However, the ship did not appear to be damaged. She turned away, leaving Daspit in a poor firing position. However, he fired two more torpedoes. Both hit, one aft, causing smoke. The target stopped with a port list, settling by the stern, but showed no signs of sinking.

Daspit studied his prey carefully. He could see her deck guns. Men were running around, dropping small depth charges over the side to intimidate him. There was still no sign of an escort, surface or air.

Daspit recorded what happened next in his patrol report:

1009. *Having observed target carefully and found no evidence of a sinking, approached and fired one torpedo at starboard side. Hit, heard by sound to stop at same time I observed large splash. No apparent effect. Target had corrected list and was firing at periscope and at torpedo wakes with machine guns and one inch [gun].*

1011. *Fired eighth torpedo. Hit. No apparent effect.*

1014. *Fired ninth torpedo. Hit. No apparent effect. Target firing at periscope, when exposed, and at wake when torpedoes were running.*

1039. *Fired tenth torpedo. Hit. No apparent effect.*

1048. *Fired eleventh torpedo. Hit. No effect. This torpedo hit well aft on the port side, made splash at the side of the ship and was then observed to have taken a right turn and to jump clear of the water about one hundred feet from the stern of the tanker. I find it hard to convince myself that I saw this.*

1050. *Fired twelfth torpedo. Hit. No effect.*

1100. *Fired thirteenth torpedo. Hit. No effect. Circled again to fire at other side.*

1122. *Picked up high-speed screws.*

FINAL ISOLATION OF MARK XIV TORPEDO DEFECTS

1125. *Sighted destroyer approaching from east.* ...
1131. *Fired fourteenth torpedo. Hit. No effect.*
1132½. *Fired fifteenth torpedo. Started deep. Destroyer range 1,000 yards. Torpedo heard to hit tanker and stop running by sound. Periscope had gone under by this time. No explosion. Had already decided to retain one torpedo for examination by base.*

In all, eleven of Daspit's torpedoes, fired under almost perfect conditions, had been duds. When he returned to Pearl Harbor, the normally cool and unflappable skipper was in a rage. "I expected a torrent of cusswords, damning me, the Bureau of Ordnance, the Newport Torpedo Station and the Base Torpedo Shop," Lockwood wrote, "and I couldn't have blamed him—19,000-ton targets don't grow on bushes. I think Dan was so furious as to be practically speechless. His tale was almost unbelievable, but the evidence was undeniable."

Daspit's attack on *Tonan Maru III* had been the nearest possible thing to a laboratory test. It was clear to him, to Lockwood, and to everyone else on the Pearl Harbor staff that the Mark XIV torpedo had yet another defect: something was wrong with the *contact* exploder. That defect had been obscured by dependence on the magnetic exploder, now deactivated. Lockwood ordered his force gunnery and torpedo officer, Art Taylor (ex-*Haddock*), to find out what was wrong. Everybody got in the act: Babe Brown, Swede Momsen, and Pi Pieczentkowski, who had been relieved of command of *Sturgeon* after his luckless patrol in the staging area southwest of Lot's Wife and was on his way to duty in the Bureau of Ordnance.

Swede Momsen, who, Lockwood wrote, "was always full of practical ideas," came up with a simple scheme. He proposed that they fire a load of torpedoes at the vertical cliffs on the little island of Kahoolawe. At the first dud, they could stop firing, recover the torpedo, dissect it in the torpedo shop, and find out what was wrong. This was, Lockwood wrote, "a thoroughly practical idea, but I suspected we would find ourselves shaking hands with St. Peter when we tried to examine a dud warhead loaded with 685 pounds of TNT."

Lockwood got approval from Nimitz and put Swede Momsen in charge of the tests. Momsen chose one of the new H.O.R. boats, *Muskallunge*, commanded by Willard Saunders (ex-*Grayback*), for the test bed. On August 31, three weeks after Daspit returned from patrol, Saunders set up and began firing torpedoes at the cliffs, including the one Daspit had brought back. The first and second torpedoes exploded. The third was a dud.

Saunders relayed word to Lockwood back at Pearl Harbor. The next day, Lockwood, Swede Momsen, and Pi boarded the submarine rescue vessel *Widgeon* and steamed to Kahoolawe to help recover the dud. Everybody jumped in the water wearing goggles. A boatswain's mate, John Kelly, found it. Then he free-dived to 55 feet and shackled a line to the tail of the torpedo. Crewmen on *Widgeon* gingerly hauled the torpedo on board.

All hands conducted an examination on the spot. Lockwood reported, "The warhead was crushed in at the forward end and, when we got the exploder mechanism out of it, we found the firing pin had actually traveled up its badly bent guide lines and hit the fulminate caps, but not hard enough to set them off."

While experts in the torpedo shops on the sub base and *Holland* studied the exploder firing pin and guide lines, Lockwood ordered further tests on dry land. With the help of an ordnance expert, a reserve officer named E. A. Johnson, Lockwood and Momsen worked out another testing scheme. They dropped dummy warheads, fitted with exploders, from a cherry picker (a traveling crane) onto a steel plate from a height of 90 feet. These tests—conducted by Art Taylor—showed that when the warhead hit the plate at a 90-degree angle, a perfect shot, the exploder mechanism was crushed before it struck the caps. When the warhead struck the plate at 45 degrees, a bad shot, only about half were duds.

These tests—and follow-up ones—proved beyond doubt that the exploder was improperly designed and had been inadequately tested. The torpedo experts at Pearl Harbor immediately began devising new firing pin designs that would work. The reservist ordnance expert, Johnson, worked on an electrical device; the base and *Holland* torpedo shops concentrated on making a stronger, lighter, mechanical pin. Some of the latter were fashioned from a tough metal obtained from Japanese aircraft propellers found on the island. Bill Hazzard, exec of *Saury*, who lunched one day with a lieutenant who was working with the Japanese propellers, was struck by the irony. "We gave them scrap metal to build their ships," he said later. "Now they were providing us with scrap metal which would be used to sink those same ships."

In further dry-land tests, the new firing-pin mechanisms devised by Lockwood's torpedo experts worked fine. After these tests, Lockwood ordered all Mark XIV torpedoes equipped with the new exploder innards, meanwhile telling the boats already at sea to try for "glancing blows" to help the performance of the defective exploders they carried. When all this was done, he informed Spike Blandy at BuOrd. The Newport Torpedo Station conducted further tests against submerged steel plates and then ordered a redesign of the contact exploder.

After twenty-one months of war, the three major defects of the Mark XIV torpedo had at last been isolated. First came the deep running, then the magnetic influence feature, then the contact exploder itself. Each defect had been discovered and fixed in the field—always over the stubborn opposition of the Bureau of Ordnance.

The H.O.R. Boats

The long-awaited boats of Squadron Twelve—with H.O.R. engines—had arrived in May with their tender, *Griffin*. Every boat of the squadron had experienced engine problems, but they were sent into combat anyway. The result was one of the great fiascoes of the submarine war.

Hoe, commanded by Victor B. McCrea, was first to go on patrol—at Palau. During most of the patrol, McCrea suffered from engine problems, and before the patrol was out he lost Number 4 engine altogether. He made one attack on a 9,500-ton transport and received a Bronze Star medal for it. The citation praised his performance "despite the unreliability of the ship's main engines." Lockwood wrote, "The efficiency of this patrol was handicapped a great deal by the unreliability of the main engines."

In August, McCrea took *Hoe* to Truk. On September 1, assisted by an Ultra dispatch, he found an auxiliary carrier northeast of Truk, escorted by destroyers. He picked it up at 8½ miles but was not able to close. On return to Pearl Harbor, Lockwood wrote, "Faulty engine performance was a detriment to the performance and efficiency of this patrol."

Junior McCain in *Gunnel*, whose father was now head of the powerful Bureau of Aeronautics in Washington, patrolled in June. He had made one Atlantic patrol—during the North African landings when all four H.O.R. engines broke down. The area of his second patrol was the northern reaches of the East China Sea and the Yellow Sea, the "wading pond" where Mush Morton had pioneered. McCain conducted a fearlessly aggressive patrol, making three attacks which resulted in two large confirmed ships sunk: *Koyo Maru*, 6,400 tons, and *Tokiwa Maru*, 7,000 tons.

During the whole patrol McCain was plagued with engine breakdowns. After a mere eleven days on station, he radioed Lockwood that he must terminate his patrol early and return to base. Lockwood was furious. He wrote Washington:

Gunnel is returning from patrol with two of her H.O.R. engines out of commission due to idler gear failures. McCain also says that the idler gears on the other two engines are badly worn. His breakdown occurred in the Yellow Sea, which is a damned bad place for a lousy set of engines to demonstrate their unreliability. I note from the papers that Congress has appropriated seventy-one billion dollars for the war. I suggest you set aside some of that with which to buy new and different engines for the H.O.R. boats.

H.O.R. engine flaws existed in Herb Andrews's *Gurnard* too, but the skipper's particular doggedness and skill with machinery partly overcame them. Andrews was small—five foot four—and, as he said later, he had an inferiority complex. "When I was a little kid, I was considered a sissy. I was the only boy in a house with three older sisters. My mother dressed me in velvet pants and Buster Brown collars. Faced with going into combat, I felt a very strong drive to prove myself—to carry my own weight."

Gurnard was sent to the Palaus, where Andrews patrolled close to the harbor entrances. Although he conserved his engines and treated them with loving care, the Number 2 main engine broke all its gear teeth and had to be put out of commission for the duration of the patrol. Andrews, however, remained on station.

One day a convoy steamed out, just beyond reach. After that, Andrews patrolled even closer, almost bumping up against the reefs. When destroyers came out, he played cat and mouse, going deep, slipping beneath them, coming up, then going down. "I worked up a little contempt for them," Andrews said later.

One morning during a cat-and-mouse game, *Gurnard*, submerged at 90 feet, was hit by two bombs. "It was a hell of a blast," Andrews said later. "They went off *under* us, blowing us upward with a terrific up-angle." Andrews and his exec, Bob Ward, reached the control room about the same instant. Ward shouted, "Flood everything. Flood! Get her *down*." The bow planes had jammed. The electricity had been blown out. "For a while," Andrews said, "I was certain we were going right to the surface and that destroyer would ram us."

The engineering officer, Robert Carlisle Giffen, Jr., son of Rear Admiral Giffen, had been in the head when the bombs went off. The force of the explosion jammed the door. Giffen was big: six foot two, 225 pounds. He broke down the door and ran to the control room, arriving to see the diving plane wheels spinning wildly. He lunged for the spinning bow-plane wheel; it flung him across the control room, where he fell in a heap, knocked out.

To help bring the bow down, Andrews sent every available man rushing to the forward torpedo room. "About fifty men ran up there," Ward said later. "That's about eight thousand pounds. That did it. We started down like a rock."

Gurnard plunged uncontrollably downward at a steep angle. "We passed by three hundred feet," Andrews said later. "I knew we were going too fast. I backed emergency and yelled at Ward to get all the men aft to try to get the down angle off." The fifty men in the forward torpedo room tore through the boat to the after torpedo room. By the time they got there, the depth gauge in the control room registered 495 feet.

With all that weight in the stern, *Gurnard* now took a steep up-angle. With the control room showing 495 feet, Andrews calculated that the after torpedo room was probably 520 or 530 feet deep, far below test depth—ready to cave in. About this time one of the electricians, Chief W. F. Fritsch, had an inspiration; he laid a toothbrush between two electrical connections. This restored power to the diving plane wheels, enabling Andrews and Ward to get the boat under control.

During the postbattle damage inspection, Ward, who was thin and wiry, volunteered to inspect the main induction piping. He got a flashlight, peeled down to his skivvies, and squirmed into the narrow pipe with a flashlight, inching his way from the engine room toward the control room. Returning, Ward got stuck near the engine room opening.

"I couldn't get out," he said later. "It was a very tight squeeze. This bothered me considerably. I hollered down and asked for a cigarette. They passed it up and I smoked and calmed down. Then

I maneuvered my body into the same position I'd used to get in the pipe and wriggled out."

All in all, the damage to *Gurnard* was severe. "It was a miracle she wasn't lost," said Ward later. "I've never seen a better man than Herb Andrews under pressure. The whole time, he was cool and precise about what to do. Everybody did the right thing—Andrews, Giffen, Fritsch." Said Andrews, "Following this patrol, I recommended [Ward] for his own command."

Later, leery of going below 70 feet, Andrews got off several spectacular shots at the enemy. A convoy came out, heavily escorted. Andrews maneuvered in, firing at the freighters and a destroyer that got in the way. He hit the destroyer and two of the freighters, sinking all three, he thought. Afterward, *Gurnard* got another working over with depth charges.

A short time later, Andrews poked up the periscope again. There, to his astonishment, he saw an aircraft carrier standing out. "I was surprised," he said later, "because the Japs knew we were sitting right out there." Andrews set up and fired three bow tubes—all that were ready—from 1,800 yards. One torpedo prematured after twenty-four seconds. Andrews fired a stern tube. He thought he got two solid hits in the carrier. He returned to periscope depth and saw her motionless in the water, listed over and smoking. Escorts charged in and prevented another look—or another shot.

When Andrews returned to Pearl Harbor, all torpedoes expended, he received ecstatic patrol report endorsements. Calling it "one of the finest, most aggressive first patrols on record," his division commander wrote, "The customary expression that the area was well covered does not fit this case, as the *Gurnard* stuck her head in the bottleneck and stopped traffic at its source. This patrol offers an excellent example of what can be accomplished by taking the fight into the enemy's back yard."

Andrews received credit for sinking three ships, including a destroyer, for 15,583 tons and for damage to five, including the carrier (estimated at 17,000 tons), for 43,482 tons. When the awards were passed out, Andrews (who got a Navy Cross) saw that electrician Fritsch got a Silver Star for his toothbrush fix. Postwar analysis cut Andrews's sinkings to one freighter for 2,000 tons. However, after this patrol nobody would ever again think of calling Herb Andrews a sissy.

* * *

Jack, another boat with H.O.R. engines, was commanded by Thomas Michael Dykers, a tall aristocratic man from New Orleans. His exec was John Paul ("Beetle") Roach, who came from shore duty in Washington. Neither he nor Dykers had ever made a war patrol.

Dykers, assigned to patrol off Honshu, found the area dense with convoys. On June 19 one went by, but Dykers was caught flatfooted and he soon realized it "had given us the slip." The next day, a 1,500-ton trawler came out of the mist. More alert this time, Dykers fired three torpedoes from 1,000 yards. The first torpedo—Dykers's first shot of the war—prematured after thirty seconds. The other two missed.

A little angry at himself (and more so at the torpedoes), Dykers moved *Jack* to within 3 miles of the Japanese coastline. On June 26 a five-ship convoy, apparently unescorted, came into view about dawn. Dykers maneuvered into position and dived. He came in close, firing bow and stern tubes and getting good hits which led him to believe he had sunk three of the five ships and damaged one. The fifth ship ran around in circles, with "all hands dropping small depth charges."

To Dykers, all this had seemed a breeze. While his torpedomen were reloading, he watched through the periscope. He wrote later:

One boat load of survivors passed within twenty yards of the periscope. Some hid behind the gunwale when they saw it. There was a sprinkling of soldiers amongst those men. I then left the periscope up to let some of the officers and men look at the sinking ship and this prevented my getting Number 5 in column and almost cost us our lives.

It seems this last ship was an auxiliary and had been looking for us all the time. Just after we passed the lifeboat, I swung the periscope around and saw No. 5 belching smoke from his stack and swinging toward us—range 1,500 yards. We had two torpedoes ready forward so we swung towards him to shoot down his throat. The set-up had just been cranked into the TDC and I opened my mouth to say fire when all hell broke loose. . . .

Evidently there had been a plane escort that we hadn't heard from. The charge landed very close aboard on our port quarter (it must have landed practically on the lifeboat) and blew our stern out of water. Bow and stern planes went out. She nosed over about 25 degrees. By blowing . . . we caught her at 380 feet. I don't know what became of No. 5 ship. The depth charge or the lifeboat made him change course. Whatever it was definitely saved us from being rammed when we broached. . . . If I hadn't been so eager to gloat I could have gotten the No. 5 and saved this vessel the damage which may yet require early termination of this patrol.

Dykers returned to Pearl Harbor with one engine out of commission. He was credited with sinking three ships for 24,000 tons. Postwar records confirmed the sinking of three ships on this patrol but reduced the tonnage to 16,500 tons.

Another H.O.R. boat, *Harder*, was commanded by Samuel David Dealey. Dealey came from a famous Texas family; his Uncle George was a founder and publisher of the *Dallas Morning News*. Up to then Dealey had had a lackluster naval career: he was "bilged" from the Naval Academy for low grades, got reinstated, graduated with the class of 1930, and then went on to a series of routine peacetime duties, during which he demonstrated little interest in the navy as a career, often stating he might return to civilian life. In the spring of 1941, he finally got a command: *S-20*, an old noncombatant tub at New London detailed to various experimental tasks. When war brought on a pressing need for qualified skippers, Dealey was ordered to commission *Harder*.

Dealey, who was soft-spoken, clean-living, and family-oriented, had the good luck to wind up with an exceptional wardroom. His exec was John Howard Maurer, who had been exec to Lew Wallace on *Tarpon* during the first part of the war. The third officer, Frank Curtis Lynch, Jr., a football star from the class of 1938, was also extraordinarily able. Lynch was huge (and therefore called "Tiny"), bright, and had a gift for organization and technical innovation.

On the way from New London to Pearl Harbor, *Harder* suffered the fate of all too many submarines. In the Caribbean, headed for Panama, she was attacked by a friendly aircraft—a navy patrol bomber. Although the men on *Harder*'s bridge flashed a recognition signal, the plane roared in, machine guns winking. As the bullets whined into the water alongside *Harder*, Dealey dived. The plane then dropped two bombs, one close, one distant. That night Dealey wrote in his log, "The aviator's poor approach was exceeded only by his poor marksmanship . . . but whose side are these crazy aviators on?"

Lockwood sent *Harder* to an area off Honshu. On the night of June 21, Dealey made his first attack, firing four torpedoes at a two-ship convoy, with Maurer serving in the conning tower as assistant approach officer, Tiny Lynch in the control room as diving officer. The first torpedo prematured—"a bit disconcerting," Dealey noted in his diary. He believed the others hit. An escort counterattacked and Dealey went deep—too deep. The fathometer showed 300 feet of water, but Lynch let *Harder* overshoot. The boat crashed into the muddy bottom, throwing men, dishes, and other loose gear forward.

Much later, Dealey would joke, "That night *Harder* made her first landing on the shores of Japan." At the time, however, it was far from a joke. *Harder* was stuck fast, with a steep down-angle, her stern bobbing up and down as the escort worked her over, dropping thirteen depth charges. After the ship went away, it took Lynch forty-five tense minutes to work *Harder* out of the mud.

Two nights later, June 23, radar reported a huge pip. Dealey went to battle stations. As he closed on the surface, the big ship spotted *Harder* and opened fire with her guns. Dealey fired four torpedoes, but only one appeared to hit. However, it was a mortal blow. Down went the ex-seaplane tender *Sagara Maru*, 7,000 tons.

In the next four days, Dealey attacked three separate convoys, adroitly firing first bow and then stern tubes, twisting and turning *Harder* as though he had been doing it all his life. "He had the vision and mind of an artist," Tiny Lynch said later. "His imagination pictured situations so vividly and scenes photographed themselves so clearly on the retina of his mind that he really did not need a TDC solution."

In all, Dealey made seven attacks. When he returned to Pearl Harbor, with one H.O.R. engine completely broken down, Lockwood credited him with sinking three ships for 15,000 tons and damaging four others for 27,000 tons, more than sufficient for a Navy Cross. Postwar accounting confirmed only the sinking of *Sagara Maru*.

The engineers patched up the H.O.R.s, and by August *Harder* was ready for her second patrol—loaded with spare engine parts. Dealey returned to the area off Honshu and turned in a second splendid patrol. In fourteen days he made nine attacks, claiming four ships sunk for 25,000 tons. Postwar accounting readjusted this to five ships for 15,000 tons, making it, in terms of ships sunk, one of the best patrols of the war. Throughout the patrol *Harder* still had engine problems, and at Pearl Harbor the engineers again set to work. John Maurer was transferred back to the States to new construction, and Tiny Lynch fleeted up to exec.

* * *

As these H.O.R. boats returned from patrol, it soon became clear that they would have to have new engines before they could become adequate fighting machines. Admiral King ordered this done, and one by one the Squadron Twelve boats returned to Mare Island for Winton engines.

From Brisbane, Jimmy Fife wrote Lockwood, "The history of the H.O.R. engine in Squadron Twelve seems to be rather smelly. I suppose no one will be blamed for the long period of immobility which has resulted for those twelve boats and that no one will ever get a court-martial for the fiasco." No one did.

Years later, Tommy Dykers of *Jack* said, "The H.O.R. engines saved the Japanese thirty or forty ships."

Some Good Patrols, and Some Bad Ones

With all the new boats arriving at Pearl Harbor, Lockwood faced an acute shortage of men qualified for command, a shortage that would continue for the duration. The Bureau of Personnel continued to transfer good men away from his command for career-broadening purposes; Lockwood himself sent his skippers for a rest after five consecutive patrols. To help fill the gap, Lockwood had dipped down to the class of 1933 for new skippers (John Tyree, Roy Davenport), but he was reluctant to go farther out of fear that less experienced (and in many cases brashly aggressive) young officers would cause his losses to increase. Pearl Harbor was still proud of its few casualties.

Lockwood's concern to save lives was commendably humane, but there was a war going on, and the sooner the Japanese merchant marine was cut to shreds, the sooner the war would be over and the losses stopped for good. Looking back years later, many officers (especially those from the class of 1935 and upward) believed that Lockwood's concern to hold down losses by keeping more senior men in command was a grave error. It meant that he had to make do with too many mediocre commanders (many without combat experience and including some alcoholics or near alcoholics) while qualified men with five, six, or seven war patrols under their belts chafed as execs or fretted in shore billets on squadron and division staffs.

Lockwood tried to head off the inevitable mediocrity and lack of experience by instituting a rigorous prepatrol training program, operated by Babe Brown. Brown had never made a war patrol, but by mid-1943 he had some excellent ex-skippers working for him. They took charge of the newly arriving boats and put them through a tough indoctrination at Pearl Harbor: practice approaches on friendly vessels, fast diving procedures, and so on.

All the while Brown and his men attempted to size up the skippers before they left for patrol, eliminating those who were obviously not fit. This was still a nebulous guessing game. No one had figured out a way to tell in advance who would perform well in combat. The result was an inevitable unevenness: excellent war patrols by some unlikely skippers and poor war patrols by others.

Among the new skippers bringing new fleet boats to Pearl Harbor was Chuck Triebel in *Snook* and his excellent wardroom: Sam Colby Loomis, Jr., son of a navy captain and onetime Naval Academy athlete, as exec, and reservist Vard Albert Stockton, a former All-American football player at the University of California at Berkeley, as third. To some, Triebel was an unlikely bet. Like his Medal-of-Honor-winning friend, Howard Gilmore, he still bore a scar from the time in Panama on *Shark*'s shakedown cruise when he got his throat cut by hoodlums. Triebel's capers ashore became legendary in the submarine force. At sea, however, he was a wholly different man: dedicated, shrewd, extraordinarily competent.

Between April and August, Triebel made three war patrols, mostly to the East China Sea. Each exemplified skill and aggressiveness, and each had good results.

On the first, Triebel began by laying a minefield off Shanghai. He had a difficult time getting rid of *Snook*'s twenty-four "eggs." The Yangtse River mouth was shallow and infested with sampans and junks. Approaching in daylight submerged, Triebel got stuck in the mud at 60 feet. He broke loose, bumping along the bottom until he found a hole 75 feet deep, where he lay until dark. Coming up that night, Triebel almost holed the bottom of a junk with his periscope. He laid his small minefield in two hours.

Following this, Triebel, who had only fourteen torpedoes, patrolled the Yellow Sea. In four aggressive attacks, he sank three freighters. In addition, he sank two sampans with his deck gun.

On the second patrol, Triebel carried a full load of Mark XIV torpedoes. On June 24, he attacked a convoy of six ships, escorted by two destroyers. He fired four torpedoes, damaging a tanker, but was driven under by the destroyers. On July 4, on a black, rainy night, he found a convoy of eight ships. In an epic three-hour night surface battle, Triebel got into the middle of the convoy and fired a total of nineteen torpedoes. Deciding that one of the ships was an aircraft carrier, he fired six torpedoes at it and saw hits. He believed it sank. When the codebreakers picked up reports of this attack, they identified the target not as a carrier but a big whale-factory tanker, *Nissen Maru*, 17,600 tons. It didn't sink, but two others did, *Koki Maru*, 5,200 tons, and *Liverpool Maru*, 5,800 tons.

On the third patrol, Vard Stockton replaced Sam Loomis as exec. *Snook* was now fitted with a brand new gadget for the radar known as the plan position indicator (PPI). This device, commonly used today in weather telecasts, translated information obtained from radar pulses to a "picture" with *Snook* at the center. It helped the skipper "see" the enemy formation relative to the position of the submarine.

Triebel experienced poor torpedo performance on this patrol. On September 12, alerted by the codebreakers, he intercepted an eight-ship convoy and fired six torpedoes at two ships. All missed. The following night, the codebreakers put him on another eight-ship convoy, and he again fired six torpedoes at two ships. One spread missed, but the other hit and sank *Yamato Maru*.

Later, on the night of September 22, he picked up a couple of singles. He fired four torpedoes at the first, sinking *Katsurahama Maru*. In the second attack, he began with four torpedoes, all of which missed. In another attack on this same ship, Triebel fired another four. The first and fourth missed ahead and astern; the second ran erratically to the left; the wake of the third was never seen.

Having expended all his torpedoes, Triebel set course for Pearl Harbor. On the way home, he battle-surfaced on a trawler. During this battle, the trawler fired back, wounding four of Triebel's men.

In three patrols, Triebel was credited with sinking six ships for 42,000 tons and damaging four for 31,800 tons. Postwar records showed that he actually sank seven. Triebel was on his way toward becoming one of the leading skippers of the war. Lockwood forgave his excesses on the beach.

Freddy Warder's famous old *Seawolf* returned from overhaul commanded by Royce Lawrence Gross. Gross had inherited Warder's exec, William Deragon, who had been on *Seawolf* for her seven previous times out. In addition, he was assigned a prospective exec,

Robert Dunlap Risser, who had been in graduate school for two years and had never made a war patrol.

Both Gross and Risser felt a strong duty to uphold *Seawolf*'s reputation. Between April 3 and September 15, Gross completed three war patrols in the East China Sea near Formosa, a turnaround record for the Pearl Harbor command.

Outbound on his first patrol, Gross received an Ultra reporting a freighter near Guam, so he submerged on the assigned position. The following day the ship, *Kaihei Maru*, escorted by a trawler, came along on schedule. Gross fired four torpedoes. The first—his first shot of the war—prematured at fourteen seconds, a performance that left him "amazed." This premature alerted the freighter, which dodged the other three. After dark, Gross surfaced and tracked the ship, firing three more torpedoes. He saw two explosions and believed he obtained two hits. He then turned on the escort, firing another two torpedoes. Both missed. He fired another two at the freighter, saw a big explosion, and went deep.

Some hours later, Gross returned to the surface. His radar still showed two pips. He was exasperated: he had now fired eleven torpedoes without sinking either of the ships. However, on closer inspection he saw that he had blown the bow off the freighter. He was tempted to battle-surface to polish it off, but Japanese aircraft appeared on the radar. Gross left the disabled freighter, which later sank.

Gross continued on to patrol area with only half a load of torpedoes. On April 19, he found a small tanker and fired two more. One hit and Gross saw the ship sink, bow down. He surfaced amid the debris and a lifeboat containing about thirty survivors, machine guns ready. He picked up three life rings, a briefcase, and charts and tried to find codebooks or other valuable intelligence without success. Somehow this ship must have remained afloat; there was no record of its loss in postwar Japanese accounts.

Three days later, Gross came upon another fine target, a big damaged ship escorted by a small old destroyer and a tugboat. Gross—running low on torpedoes—decided to sink the destroyer and then attack the damaged vessel with his deck gun. He fired three torpedoes at the destroyer. One hit amidships; the other two missed. He fired a fourth; it also missed. Again exasperated, Gross fired a fifth and a sixth. Both missed, but the destroyer (*Patrol Boat No. 39*, 750 tons) sank from the damage inflicted on the first salvo.

Gross now turned on the freighter and fired his last torpedo. When it failed to explode, he ordered his gun crew to prepare for action. However, about that time a fleet destroyer came on the scene and Gross decided discretion was the better part of valor. He turned east and headed for Pearl Harbor, arriving after a mere thirty days at sea. Lockwood, who blamed most of Gross's bad luck on defective torpedoes, heaped praise on this new skipper who seemed bent on outdoing Fearless Freddy Warder.

After only two weeks in port, Gross was on his way again. On this trip, Risser had replaced the exec, Deragon, who went to new construction. Gross returned to Formosa, circling around the north side into Formosa Strait. In a period of two weeks, *Seawolf* encountered five convoys composed of about thirty-seven ships. In five separate attacks, Gross fired sixteen torpedoes, but only two or three of these hit, sinking one confirmed ship, *Shojin Maru*, 4,739 tons.

Back in port, Bob Risser left the ship for new construction, replaced by Douglas Neil ("Red") Syverson, a youngster from the class of 1939. Returning to the East China Sea for a third patrol, on August 29 Gross found a fat convoy northeast of Formosa: five big freighters and escorts. In a dogged forty-eight-hour running battle—the most tenacious on record—Gross fired all his torpedoes for contact explosion, sinking two ships and damaging another which he finished off with his deck gun. He returned to port after thirty-two days. In his patrol report, Gross blamed himself for having missed with twelve of his torpedoes. His endorsers believed Gross had been a bit too severe on himself, taking pains to point out that many of his targets might have maneuvered out of the way.

In three patrols, Gross had fired about fifty-six torpedoes, sinking six ships. Like Triebel, Roy Gross was on his way to becoming one of the high scorers of the war.

Anthony Henry Dropp in *Saury* was an unlikely skipper. He came from command of the old *Bass*. During his command, *Bass* had suffered a battery fire off Panama which cost twenty-five lives. Many wondered if that disaster had cooled Dropp off and made him cautious.

Lockwood sent Dropp to the East China Sea to watch the approaches to Nagasaki. He had inherited Bill Hazzard for his exec. Dropp's courage amazed Hazzard. "He was cold and calculating," Hazzard said later. "We stumbled on a convoy. I was all for going after the first ship. Dropp said coolly, 'Let's wait. She looks a little seedy.' It was. Pretty soon something much better came along. It was *Kagi Maru*, 2,350 tons. Dropp sank it."

A few days later, while running on the surface (with Hazzard perched in the periscope shears serving as an extra lookout), *Saury* picked up smoke. It turned out to be a "beautiful" 10,216-ton tanker, *Akatsuki Maru*, steaming alone. Dropp fired four torpedoes. One hit aft, disabling the ship. Then he fired five more, sending her to the bottom.

In the days following, Dropp found three more convoys and sank two more ships, *Takimasau Maru* and *Shoko Maru*. Returning to Pearl Harbor, all torpedoes expended, Dropp was credited with three ships for 24,900 tons. Postwar accounting adjusted this to four ships for 20,000 tons, making this one of the best patrols of the war to date and the best by far for *Saury*.

On his next patrol, Dropp almost lost the ship. On the night of July 30, en route to patrol station in the East China Sea, Dropp picked up a northbound convoy halfway between Iwo Jima and Okinawa. Instead of attacking by radar, Dropp made a submerged approach, relying on sonar bearings and information from Hazzard, who manned the periscope. During the approach everything went wrong: sonar lost the bearings; the periscope fogged and leaked. In the confusion, Hazzard lost track of the escort. When he found it again, it was charging at *Saury* on a collision course.

Dropp shouted, "Take her down!" but it was too late; the destroyer struck the periscope shears with a thunderous crash. *Saury* reeled to starboard, righted herself, then reeled to port. Finally *Saury* started down, Dropp and Hazzard waiting for the click-swish-blam of depth charges. However, none came. The destroyer had apparently run over *Saury* without knowing it.

Later, when the convoy was out of sight, Dropp surfaced to assess damages. The shears and periscopes were wrecked. He was forced to end the patrol and return to Pearl Harbor after thirty days at sea. Admiral Nimitz was waiting on the dock to meet him. "We came home with our tails between our legs," Hazzard recalled. "It was really one of life's embarrassing moments."

Creed Burlingame took *Silversides* back to Brisbane on his fifth patrol. He was the same old jaunty, cocksure Burlingame and, like Triebel, legendary on shore leave. An entry in his patrol report for May 28 reads: "Proceeded on surface toward assigned position . . . a frigate bird made a high level bombing attack, scoring direct hit on the bare head and beard of the OOD. . . . No indication by radar prior to attack." Burlingame had a new exec, Robert Kemble Worthington, who stood 4 out of 438 in the class of 1938.

Silversides had two missions. The first was to lay a small minefield in Steffen Strait, between New Hanover and New Ireland. The second was to sink ships. Burlingame laid the field on the night of June 4 and hauled clear, reporting to Jimmy Fife in Brisbane. Fife ordered him northward to the intersection of the equator and longitude 150 degrees east, lying athwart the lane from Truk to Rabaul.

After Burlingame got into position, Fife sent an Ultra on a northbound convoy. While waiting for it to show up, Burlingame picked up what he believed to be a southbound convoy unreported by Fife. "In the belief that a southbound convoy was more valuable than the northbound one we were expecting," Burlingame wrote, "decided to surface and end around. . . . It then became evident that this group was northbound, whether the same convoy I do not know." He made his end around, taking advantage of generally poor weather, and waited on the surface. Shortly after midnight, the convoy reappeared. Burlingame fired four torpedoes at one of the largest ships in the formation. As he wrote later:

First hit looked to be a magnetic explosion. Ship seemed to jump out of the water and streak of flame twice ship's length on water line. Second hit under bridge, large column of water and smoke. Third hit and felt throughout ship but not observed . . . fourth missed . . . an explosion occurred on target, evidently gasoline as a bright flame shot up 200 feet in the air and completely enveloped ship. Also lit us up like a church.

An escort charged at *Silversides*. Burlingame let the ship close to 1,700 yards, fired a stern torpedo down the throat, and submerged. The torpedo forced the escort to turn away, which, Burlingame reported, "probably saved our necks." The escorts returned, pasting *Silversides* with several salvos of close depth charges that shook the boat violently but did no serious damage. Later, Burlingame surfaced and slipped away.

The ship Burlingame destroyed was *Hide Maru*, 5,200 tons, an important vessel probably being used as a destroyer or submarine tender. The codebreakers had followed her progress north and her final demise. Later, Burlingame learned there had been a Japanese admiral on board who was killed in the sinking, but Burlingame never discovered his name.

In Brisbane, Burlingame relinquished command of *Silversides* and was promoted to command a division of new boats in Squadron Eighteen then under construction. In his five patrols he had sunk eight confirmed ships, ranking him high on the list of top scorers.

On *Haddock*, Burlingame's old exec, Roy Davenport, returned to the Palaus for his second patrol. *Haddock*'s weak conning tower had been repaired. More and more of the crew were attending Davenport's religious services.

No sooner had Davenport taken station than a four-ship convoy came along. In a daylight periscope attack, Davenport ducked beneath the destroyer screen and fired eight torpedoes at all four transports, half from a range of 3,000 yards. He achieved many hits. One of the four transports, *Saipan Maru*, 5,533 tons, went down, but the troops on board her were probably saved.

A few days after this attack, Davenport received an Ultra ordering him south to the Palau-Wewak convoy line where Mush Morton had achieved fame on his first patrol in *Wahoo*. On July 26, two big modern tankers came into view heading for the Palaus. Davenport ran ahead and submerged for a daylight periscope attack. The tankers, Davenport reported, zigged, forcing him to fire from the extreme range of 4,250 yards. He shot four torpedoes, two at each tanker. He believed he hit one. After dark, Davenport surfaced for a second attack, firing four more torpedoes from 3,000 yards. All missed. Moving closer, he fired two more from 2,000 yards. Both missed. Pulling away, he fired four more from 3,370 yards and one more from 4,000 yards. All missed. Of fifteen torpedoes fired, two had hit, Davenport reported gloomily. He believed they were running deep.

With only one torpedo remaining, Davenport headed for home. The endorsement on his patrol report stated that the patrol was "superbly conducted" and a "model for aggressiveness and tenacity." He was credited with one ship sunk for 10,000 tons and four damaged for 35,000 tons. For this patrol, Davenport received his first Navy Cross.

Davenport's classmate, John Augustine Tyree, Jr., took *Finback* on a round trip to Fremantle, a spectacular voyage in every respect. On the way down, he patrolled the Palaus, where he made eight relentlessly aggressive attacks which resulted in the sinking of three confirmed ships for 13,000 tons. When he reached Fremantle, Christie, who had served with Tyree on the aircraft carrier *Ranger,* was unstinting in his praise, noting in his diary, "Good boy!"

Tyree remained in Fremantle only briefly. After refit, Christie ordered him to return to Pearl Harbor via the Java Sea and have a look at Surabaya.

On July 30 Tyree found plenty of targets. The first contact was a pair of light cruisers, escorted by destroyers which Tyree picked up fourteen miles north of Surabaya in shallow water—140 feet. These ships passed *Finback* at 5,000 yards, too far to shoot. An hour later, Tyree spotted a "huge" freighter and fired three torpedoes: one prematured, one missed, one hit. Down went *Ryuzan Maru,* 4,700 tons.

In subsequent days, Tyree sank a large freighter and a small submarine chaser and inflicted damage on other ships. On most of these attacks, Tyree experienced erratic torpedo performance. Upon reaching Pearl Harbor, he claimed he had had five prematures. Lockwood was pleased by Tyree's aggressiveness but angered that Christie still insisted that the magnetic exploder remain activated.

In his round trip to Fremantle, John Tyree had sunk six confirmed ships for 24,000 tons.

Bafford Edward Lewellen relieved Robie Palmer on the old *Pollack.* *Pollack* had a fine crew, and morale was high in spite of slight success under Palmer, a popular officer. In deference to her age, the exec, George Grider, later wrote, *Pollack* was sent to the Marshalls, which was now supposed to be a "quiet" area. Lewellen and Grider found it anything but quiet. The Japanese were using the Marshalls as a staging base to reinforce the Gilberts—Tarawa and Makin. Lewellen inspired *Pollack* with a new and aggressive fighting spirit.

Patrolling close off Wotje, Lewellen saw a freighter inside the harbor. He waited patiently for three days. When she came out, Lewellen attacked. Down went *Terushima Maru,* 3,000 tons. The next day, Lewellen shifted to Jaluit, arriving May 20, just in time to spot the 5,350-ton passenger-cargo ship, *Bangkok Maru,* converted from a light cruiser, standing in. With George Grider at the periscope, Lewellen promptly sank her. The escorts delivered a punishing depth-charge attack.

Unknown to the navy at that time, *Bangkok Maru* was hauling

1,200 troops and thousands of tons of supplies to Tarawa. Jasper Holmes reported later that the troops were rescued and sent to Jaluit, where they served out the war, never reaching their objective. The supplies went down with the ship. This single sinking probably saved the lives of untold numbers of U.S. Marines at Tarawa.

On his next patrol, Lewellen took *Pollack* to the east coast of Honshu. On the night of August 6 he attacked a convoy of freighters. Shortly after firing, a tremendous explosion shook *Pollack*, literally lifting her out of the water. Lewellen and Grider saw a great glow of light all around the hull as if they had wound up in Dante's Inferno. The force of the blow knocked men off their feet, and the ship came to a dead stop. Grider speculated that one of *Pollack*'s torpedoes had malfunctioned on firing, dropped straight down, and then exploded beneath the boat.

Later, *Pollack* was nearly lost again. During a nighttime attack on a convoy, an unseen destroyer charged out of the darkness and caught *Pollack* in a searchlight beam. Lewellen fired two down-the-throat shots at the destroyer and then dived at full speed. Going down, the bow planes failed to rig out; *Pollack* nosed down with what Grider described as a "positively incredible" angle, later estimated to be 53 degrees.

Grider wrote that

No one could stand anywhere aboard the Pollack *without support. Men were hanging on to hatches, tables, controls. Some could not even keep their feet swinging wildly in the air. The noise was terrific. A submarine's equipment is stored for a reasonable down angle, but this angle was utterly beyond the bounds of reason. All over the boat a roar like summer thunder sounded as equipment fell or dropped or poured out of its storage spaces.*

Lewellen backed emergency and blew all ballast tanks at 450 feet—200 feet below test depth. The fatal downward plunge stopped and *Pollack* shot back to the surface, coming up almost directly beneath the destroyer. Lewellen got the boat under control and managed to elude. On return to port, *Pollack* returned to Mare Island for a long overhaul, and George Grider left the ship for new construction.

One of the likeliest skippers, the tall, articulate, and handsome Dick Peterson on *Sunfish*, had yet to turn his boat into a smooth fighting machine. After Carter Bennett left the boat with ill feelings, one of the junior officers, Warren Collamore Hall, Jr., fleeted up to exec. On the third patrol, Peterson patrolled to Truk. During the entire fifty-seven-day patrol, Peterson made no attacks. Three days after he returned, June 27, Lockwood wrote Gin Styer at Midway, "*Sunfish* arrived two days ago with unsatisfactory results. I am still considering desirability of a change in command. What do you think?"

No change was made, but on the fourth patrol, Fred Connaway came aboard for a PCO run. Later, Hall wrote, "Our first patrol was unsuccessful; the second was successful; the third was unsuccessful; the fourth was successful. The one element which was notably present on the fourth patrol was Fred Connaway. . . . Both Peterson and Fred planned the next day's work in *Sunfish* with enthusiasm and obvious good results."

Peterson took *Sunfish* to Formosa for that patrol. On August 13, they attacked a convoy, torpedoing a large tanker and an escort, a converted gunboat of 1,300 tons. Peterson and Connaway believed the tanker sank, but postwar records failed to confirm it. The gunboat sank. On September 3, Peterson attacked a ten-ship convoy, sinking a 4,180-ton freighter, *Kozan Maru*. *Kozan* blew up with such force that *Sunfish*, Peterson wrote, was "literally picked up, moved a few yards and set down again." On the way home, Peterson attacked a pair of freighters in the Bonins, believing he sank one. Escorts attacked *Sunfish*, dropping depth charges so close Peterson thought they would "rip off the conning tower."

When *Sunfish* returned, Lockwood cited Peterson's aggressiveness and credited him with sinking three ships for 29,100 tons and damaging two others for 13,000 tons. (JANAC confirmed only one sinking for 2,000 tons.) Fred Connaway left the ship for his own command; Peterson retained command of *Sunfish*. On the next patrol in the Bonins, he made no attacks at all. After that he left *Sunfish*, returning to the States for new construction.

Peterson's old exec, Carter Bennett, who had gone to the PCO pool, relieved John McKnight on ancient *Porpoise*, the oldest boat left in combat after the departure of Sandy McGregor's *Pike*. Bennett and his exec, Morton Haynes Lytle, took *Porpoise* to the "quiet" Marshalls. Like Lewellen and Grider, Bennett and Lytle found them anything but quiet. Bennett made three attacks, damaging two freighters and sinking a 2,718-ton transport, *Mikage Maru No. 20,* all engaged in reinforcing Tarawa.

During the early part of this patrol, *Porpoise* received a stiff depth-charging. Like *Pike,* she leaked oil badly. "We took a shellacking," Bennett recalled, "and then we began to trail oil like a macadam road." Bennett cut the patrol short, returning after thirty-six days. When he reached Pearl Harbor, Lockwood decided *Porpoise,* too, must be withdrawn from combat. She returned to New London to serve as a school boat. Bennett, who had made one patrol in *Cuttlefish,* two in *Sunfish,* and one in *Porpoise,* returned to the PCO pool.

Despite the shortage, skippers were still being relieved. Among them were Edward Carmick, Howard Fletcher Stoner (Admiral Withers's son-in-law), Don McGregor (again), and William Naylor Wylie.

Edward Carmick in *Sargo* patrolled between Truk and the Marianas. Having missed *Tonan Maru III* and the auxiliary carrier off Woleai on his preceding patrol, he needed a good score this time out, but he didn't get it. During forty-six days, he made one attack for zero results. Moreover, he upset his bosses by leaving station four days early through "an unfortunate miscalculation" of fuel remaining. Carmick was relieved of command and sent to the repair unit in Australia. Years later, he said, "I do not consider that I was a most aggressive commanding officer."

Howard Stoner, relieving Jim Coe on *Skipjack,* also made two nonproductive patrols. He had just set out for the Marshalls on his first when he ran aground and bent his port propeller blade; only one of his subsequent contacts developed into an attack, and it failed. On his second patrol in Empire waters, he again made only one attack—which failed. Stoner was relieved and went to a staff job.

Don McGregor, whom Lockwood had previously relieved from command of *Gar* at Fremantle, patrolled off the Palaus in a new boat, *Seahorse.* Her exec was Slade Cutter, returning to the war zone after a long absence. While convoys left the harbor, McGregor watched from a distance. Cutter wrote later:

I cannot say anything commendable about D. McGregor as a skipper on patrol. As a skipper during training, he was really great. He organized Seahorse *like the very experienced naval officer he was. I feel that his background must be taken into consideration. First, he was too old [forty] to be in command of a submarine on patrol. Fur-*

ther, he was a communications and sonar expert. . . . He firmly believed it was suicidal to attack a convoy protected by a screen of destroyers with supersonic sonar gear. . . . When I said we had done it in Pompano *under both Lew Parks and Thomas, he wouldn't believe it and would say to the enlisted men that I was nuts and that the* Pompano *was in the Hooligan Navy.*

Seahorse remained off the Palaus many days. During that time Cutter, frustrated and angry, counted thirty-three ships go by. McGregor made only two attacks; he was credited with damage to one freighter. On the way back to Pearl Harbor, Cutter and McGregor fell into dispute. McGregor relieved Cutter of all his duties and drafted an unsatisfactory fitness report; Cutter drafted an official letter placing McGregor on report for lacking aggressiveness—but he didn't forward it.

All this had been a terrible strain on Slade Cutter. He was a loyal, dedicated naval officer with a long career ahead of him. A junior officer did not casually accuse his superior of failing in his duty—that is, of failing to fight the war as Cutter would have fought it. In peacetime, no doubt, Cutter would have destroyed himself professionally by such a move. But this was wartime, and Cutter, an open, honest young man, wholly lacking in guile, had called the shots as he saw them. He was not the first junior officer to follow such a course, nor would he be the last.

Lockwood and his staff officers investigated thoroughly. Upshot: McGregor was relieved. And in an extraordinary vote of confidence in Cutter, Lockwood gave him command of *Seahorse*.

Skipper William Wylie, commanding another new boat, *Scorpion*, gave every promise of success. Wylie was—like Howard Gilmore—a former enlisted man who graduated from Annapolis. His exec was the brilliant and much revered Reginald Marbury Raymond, who had graduated 15 in a class of 431. Raymond had served in peacetime on *Saury*, then under Lockwood in London, and had made a war patrol on a British submarine. The third officer was Paul Richard Schratz, who had served on *Mackerel*. Schratz was an expert on the TDC.

Scorpion had a new and simple device, a bathothermograph, that was to prove helpful to U.S. submarines in evading Japanese antisubmarine vessels. It roughly measured the temperature of the water outside the submarine, enabling a skipper to find thermoclines, colder layers of water which would deflect or distort enemy pinging. When time permitted, a shrewd skipper would go deep before an attack, measuring water temperature to 300 feet (a moving pen on the bathothermograph gave a continuous visual reading of outside temperatures), so that he would know where to find the thermoclines.

On her first patrol, *Scorpion* laid a minefield off Honshu. The next day, Wylie torpedoed a 2,000-ton converted gunboat and then battle-surfaced on a sampan. A couple of days later, he attacked two freighters for damage but was driven off by a destroyer. Several days later, Wylie attacked a four-ship convoy, sinking *Yuzan Maru*, 6,380 tons. Again, he battle-surfaced and sank a small patrol craft. With only one torpedo left, Wylie headed for the barn.

On the way home, tragedy struck *Scorpion*. North of Marcus Island, Wylie found a large (600-ton) patrol craft and rashly ordered another battle surface. The patrol craft fought back fiercely, spraying *Scorpion* with machine-gun fire. "We didn't do too well with our gun," Schratz said later. "Our aim was poor and we had a bad lot of ammo." Reggie Raymond, manning a Browning automatic rifle on the bridge, was killed by enemy gunfire and Schratz and three of the gunners were wounded. In the midst of the action, radar picked up an aircraft contact. Wylie was forced to dive and leave Raymond's body topside. As soon as the plane left, Wylie sank the patrol craft with his one remaining torpedo.

Raymond's death caused profound shock on *Scorpion*. To replace him, Lockwood picked Harry Clark Maynard, a torpedo expert from *Holland*. Maynard had served in peacetime on S-boats (*S-18* and *S-28*) but never on a fleet boat. From 1939 to 1942 he was in postgraduate school, where he obtained an M.S. degree from M.I.T.

Scorpion made her second patrol in the shallow waters of the Yellow Sea. On July 3, Wylie picked up an escorted convoy. Said Schratz later, "Wylie made the most perfect attack ever made. The torpedoes were dedicated to Reggie Raymond and nobody wanted to miss." Wylie fired all six bow tubes at three overlapping targets, obtaining, he believed, hits on all three targets, sinking two and damaging one. When the escorts counterattacked, Wylie went "deep"— to 90 feet, which was all the water he could find. *Scorpion* struck bottom, wiping off her sonar heads. "We got a pasting," Schratz said, "but it wasn't too bad."

After that attack, perfectly executed, something seemed to go wrong with Wylie. As Schratz remembers, "Wylie was having problems . . .

maybe brooding over Reggie's death . . . maybe he never forgave himself . . . he was reluctant to go farther north into the Yellow Sea to chase other ships . . . we turned around and went back to the southern part of the area where the water was deep."

Wylie decided to terminate the patrol early and returned *Scorpion* to Midway after forty-eight days. Gin Styer was not overwhelmed by his performance. He disallowed the two sinkings dedicated to the memory of Reggie Raymond, only giving Wylie credit for two ships damaged. He criticized Wylie for failing to give the area good coverage and did not consider the damage to *Scorpion* sufficient to justify terminating the patrol early. Ironically, postwar Japanese records confirmed the sinking of both vessels, at which time Wylie received a Bronze Star and Maynard a Letter of Commendation.

After refit, during trials, Wylie ran *Scorpion* aground on a reef at Midway. "We sat there for five hours trying to get off," Schratz said later. "Eventually it took four days for us to get back in—with the sound heads knocked off again. There was an investigation. Wylie was recommended for disciplinary action—a court-martial."

In a letter to Weary Wilkins at BuPers, Lockwood commented, "*Scorpion* went aground, inexcusably it seems to me, so we may have another spare skipper very soon." Lockwood relieved both Wylie and Maynard. Wylie left submarines for good, going to command the destroyer *Stormes*. Maynard was assigned to command the destroyer *Litchfield* and then returned to the Bureau of Ordnance, where he worked on torpedo design and testing.

The events on *Scorpion*'s first patrol had a direct impact on Mike Fenno's new boat, *Runner*. After damaging her periscopes at Palau on the first patrol, Fenno had laid a minefield off the China coast on the second. Afterward, he attacked one ship for damage and returned to base.

Reggie Raymond was to have replaced Fenno as *Runner*'s skipper, with Paul Schratz as exec. After Raymond's death, *Runner* was given to John Hunt Bourland, who had commissioned the boat and made the first patrol but not the second. The third on *Runner*, Jud Francis Yoho, Jr., fleeted up to exec, as Schratz had been kept on *Scorpion* for her second patrol to backstop the inexperienced Maynard.

Lockwood assigned Bourland to the polar circuit, the area Mush Morton had pioneered in *Wahoo*. *Runner* got under way a week after Morton returned—and was never heard from again.

SOME GOOD PATROLS, AND SOME BAD ONES

After *Runner* was lost, Jasper Holmes acquired many Japanese "Notices to Mariners" which listed in great detail the position and composition of Japanese minefields. Holmes noted that, just prior to *Runner*'s loss, the Japanese had planted a new minefield off northeast Honshu. He believed that *Runner* had probably struck one of these mines and went down with all hands. However, nothing positive is known of her loss.

Willis Thomas and his exec, Thomas Patrick McGrath, in *Pompano* had a frustrating and fruitless patrol off Honshu. On July 4 Thomas fired two torpedoes at a freighter run aground by Sam Dealey in *Harder*. On July 5 he attacked a small convoy, firing four torpedoes, all misses. On July 7 he came across two destroyers. Although destroyers were then low-priority targets, Thomas shot three torpedoes at both, missing again. On July 9 he picked up a three-ship convoy on radar. Unable to close, he fired from extreme range—another miss. The next night he chased a fat tanker, firing two torpedoes, both of which ran erratically and missed. On July 20 Thomas shot his last two torpedoes at a freighter from extreme range, missing again.

Thomas and McGrath set out again in August for northeast Honshu where *Runner* had been lost. *Pompano* was never heard from again either. Jasper Holmes believed that *Pompano*, like *Runner*, hit one of the mines in the new field and sank with the loss of all hands. Postwar records revealed that before she was lost *Pompano* got two good ships in the area, *Akama Maru*, 5,600 tons, and *Taiko Maru*, 3,000 tons.

Pompano was the third submarine lost by Lockwood between the months of April and August. All three were lost in the same area, northeast Honshu. Following the loss of *Pompano*, Lockwood decided to give the area a rest.

That spring and summer, some "30" boats returned from overhaul in the States to train antisubmarine warfare forces in the South Pacific under Jimmy Fife. Two of these, *S-31* and *S-38*, came by way of Pearl Harbor and, on the way to Fife's command, made war patrols in the Marshalls—considered a remarkable feat in that stage of the submarine war.

One of these was S-38, commanded by Doug Rhymes, ex-*Sargo*. Off Kwajalein, Rhymes found a fat freighter escorted by a subchaser.

He set up and fired four bow tubes. Immediately following the firing, Rhymes lost depth control and broached dead ahead of the subchaser. He managed to claw his way down to 50 feet before the first seven depth charges fell, jolting S-38 severely. By the time the second pattern fell, Rhymes had gone to maximum test depth, 200 feet. With S-38 leaking, he eased back to 120 feet, where he managed to survive two more seven-charge patterns.

On the way south, Rhymes picked up a radio report from Lockwood indicating possible enemy traffic off the island of Nauru. More or less on his own, he decided to divert for a look. Finding two small freighters anchored offshore, protected by three small vessels patrolling to seaward, he crept between the patrol craft and the beach, closing to 3,000 yards of the freighters. Wishing to come closer still, he edged to within 500 feet of the beach in water that was "like glass." As he came up for a firing observation, two aircraft bombs exploded overhead, again severely jolting S-38. Rhymes broke off the attack and slipped away, using the noise of the sea breaking on the reef as a sonar shield.

When Rhymes reported to Fife's command, he was royally dressed down for his aggressiveness and initiative. Later he wrote, "Admiral Fife put a scathing endorsement on my patrol report, scolded me for not following my orders, and branded me as unskilled and imprudent. He made it clear that there was small prospect, if any, of my getting command of a fleet submarine. Many submariners can verify that if one fell from favor with Jimmy Fife, there was little likelihood of recovery."

Another S-boat was *S-31,* commanded by Robert Frederick Sellars (from *S-34*), who after his one patrol in the Aleutians had returned the boat to the States for overhaul and transfer to Fife's force. Sellars followed Rhymes to Kwajalein, then (with orders) to Nauru, and then on to Noumea—a much less taxing patrol that earned Sellars a "well done." After taking *S-31* on another war patrol, which included a special mission and the firing of three torpedoes at an I-class submarine (all misses), Sellars retired *S-31* to training and got in line to command a fleet boat.

After Dick Voge left *Sailfish* (ex-*Squalus*) in Australia, the boat had again fallen on unlucky times. Her skipper, Dinty Moore, had been a sensation on *S-44*, but his two patrols in *Sailfish* were less than successful. He had yet to sink a confirmed ship.

SOME GOOD PATROLS, AND SOME BAD ONES

In May 1943, having returned *Sailfish* from a long overhaul and rest in the States, Moore set off on a third patrol off the east coast of Honshu. On June 15, he attacked a two-ship convoy escorted by three subchasers, firing three stern tubes. He believed he hit and sank one ship, but escorts drove him down with depth charges before he could positively confirm the results of the attack.

Ten days later, Moore picked up another convoy, three ships plus an aircraft and subchaser escort. Moore again fired three stern tubes at the leading freighter. The aircraft and the subchaser, plus three more escorts that appeared from nowhere, pinned Moore down for ten hours, dropping ninety-eight depth charges. When he shook loose from this bunch, Moore set a course for Midway.

The patrol report endorsements were cool. The division commander, Karl Goldsmith Hensel, a tough buzzard just arrived from the Submarine School in New London, reckoned that Moore had sighted about thirty-one ships, exclusive of escorts, and had fired at only two, obtaining one hit for damage in each. Moore and his exec for this one patrol, Joseph Robbins Tucker, left the boat, Moore to serve in Pearl Harbor as Lockwood's engineer and maintenance officer. As in the case of *Scorpion*, postwar records showed that Hensel had been niggardly in his assessment of the results. Both ships Moore hit sank.

Now *Sailfish* got yet another set of leaders. Command went to William Robert Lefavour, who came from Freeland Daubin's staff in the Atlantic and had made just one war patrol—as PCO on Gene Sands's *Sawfish*. Benjamin Campbell Jarvis, who had made two patrols under Dinty Moore, fleeted up to exec. Jarvis was a comer, another from the class of 1939. He had been a football and wrestling star at the Naval Academy, where he commanded the celebrated Color Company, and had stood first in his submarine class.

After brief training at Midway, Lefavour got under way for patrol in the East China Sea near Okinawa and the north end of the Formosa Strait. During twenty-nine days on patrol, he made only two contacts with the enemy. One was a steamer of about 2,500 tons standing into Naha, Okinawa; the other a small unidentified vessel, possibly a junk. Lefavour and Jarvis attempted to intercept the steamer, but it slipped into Naha before they could gain firing position.

During this luckless—and lackluster—patrol, morale on *Sailfish* plunged to rock bottom. Some of the crew resented Lefavour. They complained of his caution and *Sailfish*'s nonproductivity. When the boat returned to Pearl Harbor the division commander, Freddy

Warder, was harshly critical. "Good area coverage was not obtained. Focal points and harbors were not played sufficiently close. There was excessive submerged operations."

The exec, Ben Jarvis, went to see his former skipper, Dinty Moore, gave him a vivid account of the miserable state of morale on *Sailfish*, and said that another patrol under Lefavour would probably produce nothing better and would reduce the state of morale to a critical low. Subsequently, another division commander, Leon Nelson ("Chief") Blair, was appointed to conduct an unofficial investigation of the state of affairs on *Sailfish*. He took anguished testimony from Lefavour, Jarvis, and several others. "It was a real mess," Blair said later. The upshot was that both Lefavour and Jarvis were transferred from *Sailfish*. Lefavour went to surface craft, where he served with distinction, earning a Bronze Star for valor. Jarvis went to *Nautilus*, where he too served with distinction.

First Forays into the Sea of Japan

The climax of Lockwood's submarine offensive in the summer of 1943 was a daring penetration of the Sea of Japan, the body of water lying between Japan and the Asian mainland.

Lockwood and Voge had been eying the Sea of Japan all spring, logically assuming that it was crowded with shipping. The problem was how to get at it. The Sea of Japan is virtually landlocked. It has three narrow entrances: Tsushima Strait in the south, Tsugaru Strait in the middle, and La Pérouse Strait in the far north. Each of those shallow, narrow passages was believed to be mined and heavily patrolled by surface ships and aircraft. In winter months, La Pérouse was frozen solid.

After studying the problem with his usual thoroughness, Dick Voge concluded that in summer months submarines might penetrate the Sea of Japan by the northernmost passage, La Pérouse. Lying between Japan and Russian-held Sakhalin, it was used by Russian ships from Vladivostok. If Russian ships could get through, Voge reasoned, U.S. submarines might do the same, either by clandestinely following a Russian ship or by choosing the most likely route a Russian ship would follow. It was risky, but not unreasonably so.

The real problem—on paper—was getting out. If U.S. submarines suddenly appeared in the Sea of Japan, the Japanese were certain to

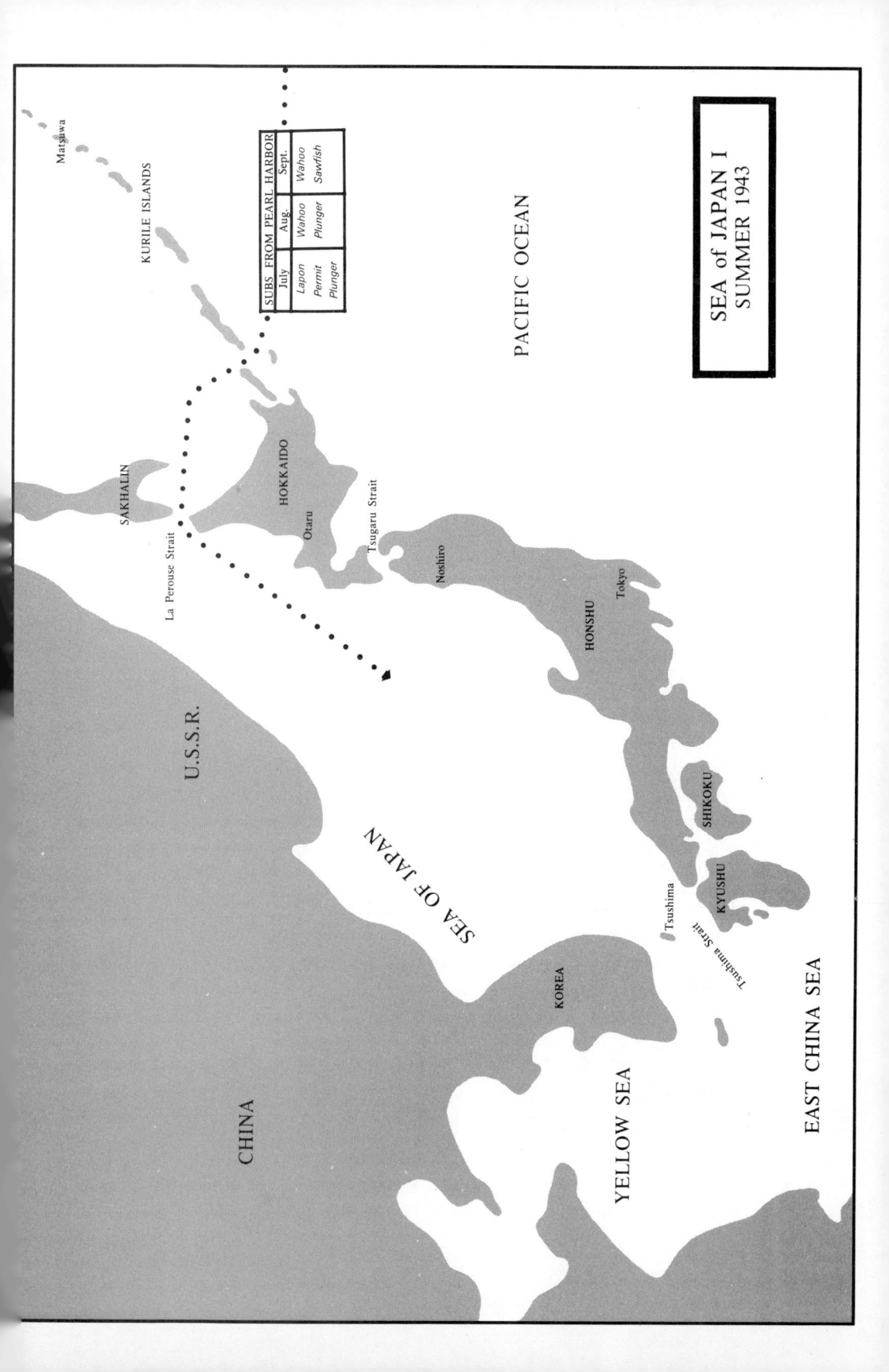

SUBS FROM PEARL HARBOR		
July	Aug.	Sept.
Lapon	Wahoo	Wahoo
Permit	Plunger	Sawfish
Plunger		

SEA of JAPAN I
SUMMER 1943

take vigorous measures to block the three passages and seal the submarines inside, where they could be systematically hunted down until they ran out of food and fuel. To minimize this possibility, Voge proposed that the first boats make a four-day hit-and-run assault. In addition, Frank Latta's *Narwhal* would be assigned to bombard Matsuwa To in the Kurile Islands, a diversion that might draw antisubmarine vessels away from La Pérouse.

For this unprecedented foray, Lockwood picked three submarines, old *Plunger* and *Permit* and the new H.O.R. boat *Lapon*, commanded by the torpedo critic, Oliver Kirk, supported by his exec, Eli Reich. *Lapon* had never made a war patrol.

Dave White on *Plunger* had been replaced by a remarkable young officer, Raymond Henry ("Benny") Bass, a fiercely competitive, coolheaded gymnast from the class of 1931. (In 1932, he had won an Olympic Gold Medal for rope climbing, the last year that sport was counted as a single event.) He had served in peacetime on *Porpoise* and *Snapper*, commanded O-2, and then made a PCO cruise on *Porpoise* under McKnight.

Bass had taken *Plunger* on two patrols in the "quiet" Marshalls, each memorable. On the first, he sank a small freighter and damaged a large tanker. On the second, he picked up a convoy of five big freighters, escorted by two subchasers, and in an epic chase that dragged over two days and nights had chipped away at it until he believed he had sunk three of the five ships for 24,000 tons. Postwar analysis reduced his claim to two ships for 15,000 tons, but the persistence and bravery of the battle had earned Benny Bass high praise.

Permit was still commanded by the indefatigable Moon Chapple, who had led her on five patrols since taking command from Adrian Hurst in Surabaya in February 1942. After returning from Australia, *Permit* had had a long overhaul, but she was still cranky and somewhat infirm. On two patrols from Pearl Harbor, one to Empire and one to Truk, Chapple had had both bad luck and faulty torpedo performance. Most of his bad luck was his own fault. Chapple had undeniable courage—his penetration of Lingayen Gulf in old S-38 proved that—but he was not an expert torpedo shooter.

Babe Brown, who had been aching to make a war patrol, was given tactical command of the operation. He flew his flag in Latta's *Narwhal*, which Brown had put in commission in 1930. At age fifty-one, Brown, class of 1914, was the oldest and most senior officer to make a patrol during the war.

FIRST FORAYS INTO THE SEA OF JAPAN

The four boats proceeded on the mission separately—*Narwhal* to the Kuriles to create the diversion; *Plunger, Permit,* and *Lapon* to La Pérouse Strait. On the night of July 4, *Plunger, Permit,* and *Lapon* went through the strait on the surface; it was crowded with lighted ships, presumably Russian. Benny Bass and Moon Chapple each made contact with what was believed to be an antisubmarine vessel and dived—Bass into what were believed to be mined waters, Chapple into uncharted shallow water. Chapple hit bottom and damaged his sonar head. Otherwise the boats were unharmed. Inside the Sea of Japan, Bass and Chapple remained concealed in their assigned areas, waiting for Kirk to reach his position, which was the southernmost.

While waiting, about half of Chapple's men came down with an "epidemic of food poisoning or water contamination," Chapple reported. "Symptoms are nausea and vomiting, which in most cases lasted from 5 to 10 minutes." The epidemic broke out again a week later. No explanation for it was ever discovered.

As the midnight firing time approached, Chapple and his exec, Frederick Leonard Taeusch, who had already let a dozen fat targets go by, grew impatient. They jumped the gun by an hour and a half and torpedoed a freighter. Shortly after midnight, they picked up a two-ship convoy. Chapple sank one and hit the other. Then he decided to surface.

Coming up, *Permit* was "pooped"—swept by a huge wave. Tons of seawater flooded the conning tower hatch and went down into the pump room, beneath the control room. For a while, many of the men on *Permit* believed she was lost. However, Chapple ordered emergency procedures to stop the flooding and managed to save the ship. But the conning tower was half full of water, and the SJ radar, located there, was put out of commission for the key ninety-six-hour period in the Sea of Japan. Chapple made four more night surface attacks, but with the radar out of commission he could only guess at the ranges. All torpedoes missed.

A few hours before he was due to leave his area and retreat through La Pérouse, Chapple sighted a small craft he believed to be a Japanese patrol vessel and ordered battle surface. After *Permit* fired a few well-placed shots, the men on the small vessel raised a large white flag. Coming alongside, Chapple discovered she was a Russian fishing trawler, manned by a crew that included women. One man had been killed and another mortally wounded and several of the women had been hit by shrapnel. The trawler was sinking. What to do?

Moon ordered the survivors, seven men and five women, to come on board *Permit* and then withdrew through La Pérouse to the Sea of Okhotsk, where he radioed Lockwood news of the unfortunate incident and requested permission to land the survivors on Russian soil. Lockwood was stunned, both by the news and by Chapple's suggestion. The Russians, he felt, might intern *Permit* or retaliate, so he ordered Chapple to take his survivors to Dutch Harbor.

On the way, the survivors were treated royally. The crew made quarters for them in the forward torpedo room. The women took their meals in the wardroom; the men in the crew's mess. After a week Chapple had so charmed the woman that they didn't want to get off *Permit* in Dutch Harbor. "They were crying when they left," Chapple said later. "We gave them all a U.S. Navy insignia, fifteen dollars apiece, shoes, and a little bag containing some clothes."

Moon got a chewing out for this attack. Everyone was sure it would lead to another international incident with the Russians, like the one Eugene Sands on *Sawfish* had caused. Conceivably, it might expose the secret of the penetration of the Sea of Japan. However, the Russian trawler captain rose to the occasion. Chapple said later, "In his official report, he stated that he had first been attacked by a Japanese submarine and that we came along and chased off the Jap sub and rescued them."

Like Chapple, Benny Bass on *Plunger* had seen many targets while awaiting "firing time." When it came, the seas were empty. About noon the following day, a small freighter came out of the fog. Bass attacked with torpedoes. When he saw men climbing down ropes into the lifeboats, he battle-surfaced to finish off the ship. However, the freighter fired back and radioed a distress call. Aircraft soon appeared, driving Bass under. Before the ninety-six hours expired, however, Bass found and sank a small freighter.

Oliver Kirk on *Lapon* cruised far to the south off Korea. The whole time *Lapon* was enveloped by an impenetrable fog and bedeviled by problems with the SJ radar. On the night of July 8, he fired four torpedoes by radar at an unknown target but missed. He withdrew through La Pérouse without having sunk anything.

Since Kirk had plenty of fuel and provisions remaining, Lockwood ordered him to patrol down the coast of Japan to the approaches to Tokyo on the way home. On July 23, while off Tokyo Bay, Kirk received an Ultra and picked up a magnificent sight in his periscope:

a large aircraft carrier, and two destroyers, range 4 miles. Kirk went to battle stations, but, before he could fire, an attack by an aircraft and the two destroyers drove him deep. When he was able to come up again, the carrier was gone. After that, he set course for Midway, noting in his patrol report, "Disappointed on fruitlessness of patrol."

Narwhal, also plagued by fog, was not able to close Matsuwa To in time to provide the diversion for the three boats withdrawing through La Pérouse. However, when she finally got there, Babe Brown and Frank Latta decided to carry out the mission anyway. Latta battle-surfaced at 14,000 yards and got off a few shots with *Narwhal*'s 6-inch guns, aiming at the Japanese airfield and hangars. However, the Japanese returned fire with salvos so accurate that Latta broke off and submerged. After some fruitless days of hunting ships in the Kuriles, *Narwhal* returned to Midway.

On return to port, both Moon Chapple and Oliver Kirk stepped down from command. Kirk's division commander wrote, "Results were disappointing." Lockwood said, "It is believed that more contacts would have been made had a patrol closer to the beach been conducted." Moon Chapple wrote in his patrol report, "In spite of the fact that the time submerged was negligible the health of the crew as a whole was poor. Several of the crew that have served aboard since the war began and have made nine successive war patrols show signs of needing a prolonged rest." Chapple himself had made eight war patrols, two on S-38 and six on *Permit*. He returned to new construction. Oliver Kirk, who returned from patrol in ill health, was sent to the Bureau of Ordnance to work on torpedoes, specifically as officer in charge of testing the Mark XVIII electric at Newport. Kirk's exec, Eli Reich, went to new construction.

Although the results of this foray had been disappointing in the extreme—three small freighters sunk for 5,000 tons—Lockwood and Voge planned a second penetration. The first man to volunteer was Benny Bass on *Plunger*. The second was Mush Morton. *Wahoo* had just returned from a long overhaul at Mare Island, and Mush himself was back from shore treatment for the chronic prostate problem that needed medical attention between every patrol.

There had been important personnel changes on *Wahoo*. The exec, Dick O'Kane, transferred to new construction, had been replaced by young Roger Paine, the third. However, when *Wahoo* reached Hawaii, Paine came down with appendicitis and had to be hospitalized. He was replaced by Verne Leslie Skjonsby, who stood seventh in the class of 1934. Skjonsby had come from a long tour of duty in the Bureau of Ordnance; he had never made a war patrol.

Morton did not tell Lockwood, but he had privately developed a new firing scheme for his trip into the Sea of Japan. He would shoot only one torpedo at each ship he attacked. If his marksmanship was as good as it had been in the past, Morton reasoned, he would probably sink fifteen or twenty ships, a record no one had ever achieved. He would do this in spite of the fact that he no longer had O'Kane on the periscope and Roger Paine on the TDC.

Bass and Morton were programmed to go through La Pérouse Strait together on the night of August 14. However, *Plunger* developed engine and motor trouble on the way. Morton went through La Pérouse as scheduled, at night, on the surface, full speed; Bass went through submerged during daylight, two days later.

Mush Morton found a convoy almost immediately and put into effect his single-torpedo concept. Each shot was fired for contact. A log of his attacks:

15 August. *Fired one torpedo at a freighter. Miss.*
Fired one torpedo at a freighter. Dud.
Fired two torpedoes at freighter. Both missed.
Fired one torpedo at same freighter. Miss.
17 August. *Fired one torpedo at a freighter. Miss.*
Fired one torpedo at a freighter. Miss.
18 August. *Fired one torpedo at a freighter. Miss.*
Fired one torpedo at a freighter. Miss.
Fired one torpedo at same freighter. Broach.

Blaming all his bad luck on torpedo performance, Morton noted in his patrol report, "Damn the torpedoes." He radioed Lockwood for permission to return to base for a torpedo reload, again damning the torpedoes. Lockwood gave his approval and on August 19, after four days in the Sea of Japan, Morton withdrew through La Pérouse Strait.

Benny Bass had only slightly better luck. His log:

17 August. *Fired four torpedoes at freighter. Miss.*
18 August. *Fired two torpedoes at freighter. Miss.*
20 August. *Fired two torpedoes at freighter. One hit.*
Crew abandoned, but ship didn't sink. Fired one more torpedo. No explosion. Fired another. Ditto. Fired another. Still no explosion. Fired one more. Hit. Ship sank.

> 22 August. *Fired two torpedoes at freighter. One hit, one dud. Second hit, blew off rudder. Fired a third. Hit. Ship sank.*

Bass withdrew from the Sea of Japan behind Mush Morton, returning to Pearl Harbor. Lockwood credited him with two ships for 9,000 tons and added a glowing endorsement to his patrol report which concluded, "More ships would have been sunk had the torpedo performance been better." Postwar analysis readjusted the credit upward to three ships. Bass took *Plunger* back to Mare Island for overhaul.

This time, the endorsements to Morton's patrol reports were not so glowing. For the first time, he had turned in a zero run. Although Morton blamed it on poor torpedo performance, Babe Brown blamed it on Morton's decision to only fire one torpedo at each ship. Brown wrote, "The decision of the commanding officer to fire single torpedoes, while understandable, is not concurred in. A minimum of two, preferably three, torpedoes, using a spread, should be fired at any target worthy of torpedo expenditure, taking into consideration the poor performance of the Mark XIV torpedo, the many unknowns in torpedo firing." Lockwood added, "Failure to use torpedo spreads during most of the attacks undoubtedly contributed materially to the lack of success. Torpedo spreads must be used to cover possible errors in data or possibility of duds."

The two forays into the Sea of Japan, from which so much was expected, produced very little. The six patrols involved (including *Narwhal*, on her diversionary raid) accounted for a total of five confirmed ships sunk for 13,500 tons, with Benny Bass doing most of the damage: three ships for 10,500 tons. It seemed hardly worth the risk.

22

Brisbane, June through December 1943

Surface-Force Engagements in the Solomons

In June 1943, Allied forces in the southwest Pacific—following the strategic plan agreed upon at the Trident conference—went on the offensive against the Japanese. The drive was a two-pronged, mutually supporting effort. Admiral Halsey's forces moved northward on an island-hopping campaign in the Solomons; General MacArthur's forces launched the reconquest of New Guinea. Halsey's forces landed on New Georgia June 30 and then advanced to Bougainville; MacArthur, after capturing some outlying islands on his right flank, landed north of Buna, New Guinea, June 30, and at Lae in September. To support these campaigns, Allied aircraft made repeated attacks on the Japanese bases at Rabaul, Kavieng, and Wewak.

Each forward step brought on a Japanese reaction. Admiral Koga sent a steady stream of reinforcements and aircraft from Truk and Palau and attempted to break up the Allied landings with surface forces composed of heavy and light cruisers and destroyers. After Halsey landed on New Georgia, Japanese naval units counterattacked in two battles known as Kula Gulf and Kolombangara, July 6 and July 12. In these two engagements, the U.S. Navy came off second best, losing the cruiser *Helena* and two destroyers, *Gwin* and *Strong*. The cruisers *St. Louis* and *Honolulu* were damaged. The Japanese lost the cruiser *Jintsu* and two destroyers, *Nagatsuki* and *Niizuki*.

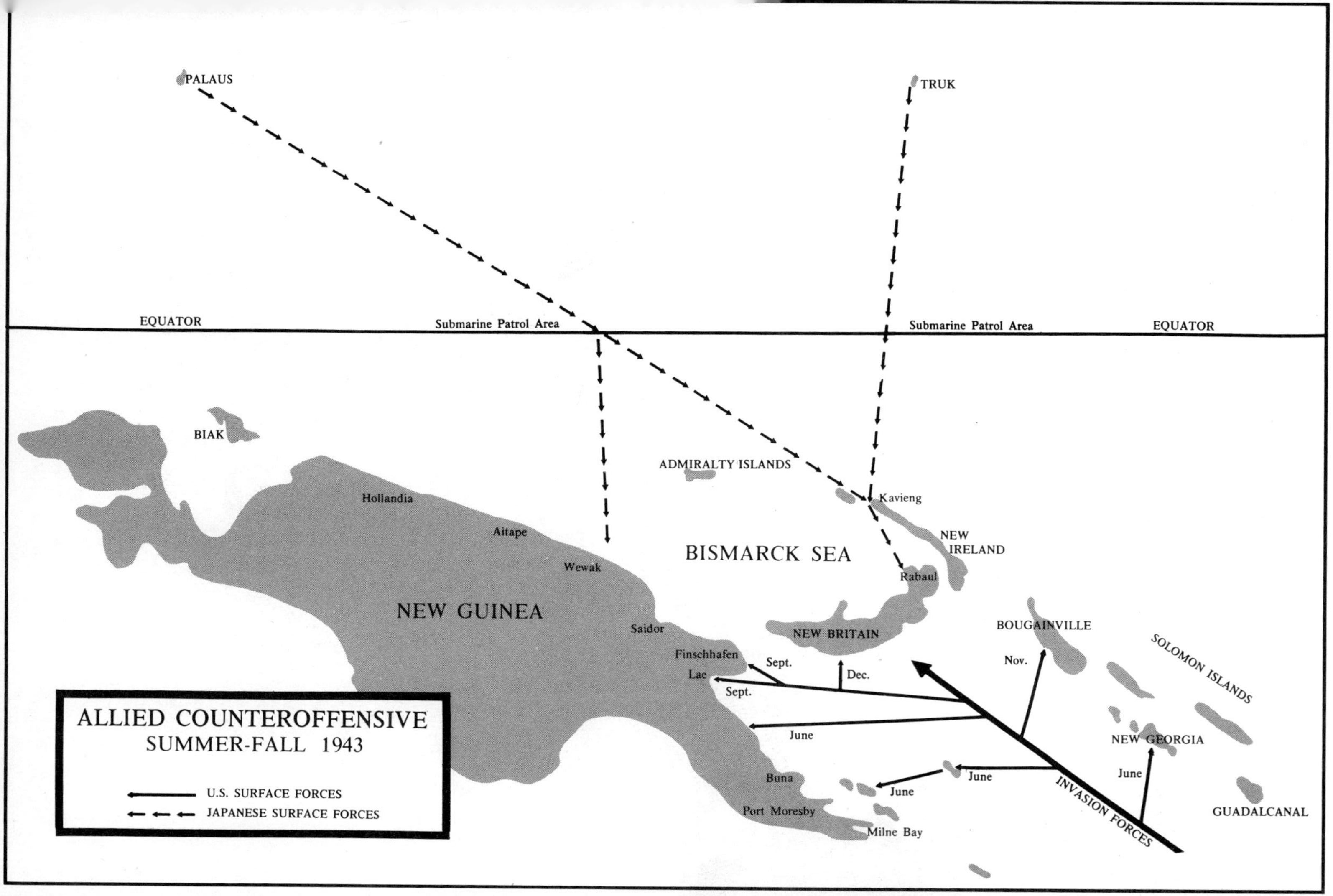
ALLIED COUNTEROFFENSIVE
SUMMER-FALL 1943
U.S. SURFACE FORCES
JAPANESE SURFACE FORCES
PALAUS
TRUK
EQUATOR
Submarine Patrol Area
Submarine Patrol Area
EQUATOR
BIAK
ADMIRALTY ISLANDS
Kavieng
NEW IRELAND
Hollandia
Aitape
Wewak
BISMARCK SEA
Rabaul
NEW GUINEA
Saidor
NEW BRITAIN
BOUGAINVILLE
SOLOMON ISLANDS
Finschhafen
Lae
Sept.
Sept.
Dec.
Nov.
June
NEW GEORGIA
June
June
June
Buna
Port Moresby
Milne Bay
INVASION FORCES
GUADALCANAL

As Halsey moved north from his bases in New Georgia, there were four more noteworthy surface force engagements: Vella Gulf, Vella Lavella, Empress Augusta Bay, and Cape St. George. The U.S. Navy won them all except Vella Lavella. In the battles, the Japanese lost the light cruiser *Sendai* and eight destroyers; the U.S. lost one destroyer, *Chevalier*. In addition, several Japanese cruisers and destroyers were badly damaged during the air strikes on Rabaul.

More Boats for Australia

All the while, Jimmy Fife in Brisbane pressed the submarine offensive against the flow of Japanese reinforcements from Truk and Palau. During the second half of 1943, his force consisted mainly of Squadron Eight, basing from the tender *Fulton* at New Farm Wharf. Counting the replacements for the losses he had incurred in the spring, this amounted to about twelve submarines, plus an occasional visitor from Pearl Harbor. Fife was able to send out an average of five boats per month.

Most of the submarine war patrols concentrated at the equator along the Truk-Rabaul and Palau-Rabaul resupply lines. Many boats operated in this confined area in cooperative attacks. The returns were generally poor, as they had always been for Brisbane submarines. The convoys from Truk and Palau were still heavily—and effectively—escorted. Admiral Carpender (at Christie's urging) would not permit deactivation of the magnetic exploder. Many Brisbane boats continued to experience prematures and erratic torpedo performance. At MacArthur's insistence, many war patrols were interrupted for special missions—landing and picking up commandos, spies, and coast watchers. As the Allies advanced in New Guinea and the Solomons and came closer to Fife's operating area along the equator, there was a greater danger of accidental bombing attacks by friendly planes, hence a greater need for caution. Three of Fife's boats—*Grouper*, *Stingray*, and *Albacore*—were bombed by Allied aircraft, *Albacore* twice within a week. As in all commands, there were continuing skipper problems.

By edict of Admiral King, the total submarine force basing in Australia had been fixed at twenty boats. Since Fife had twelve, Ralph Christie was forced to make do with eight. Christie believed the numerical distribution should be reversed: twelve boats for Fremantle, eight for Brisbane. He traveled to Brisbane and Noumea to press that idea on General MacArthur and Admirals Carpender and Halsey, taking along charts to prove that Fremantle boats got better results.

Initially, Christie was turned down. However, after the landings on Bougainville, Carpender and Halsey agreed to transfer some boats to Fremantle. On top of this good news, Christie received more: Admiral King decided to increase the number of Australian-based submarines to thirty, making a total of twenty-two for Christie at Fremantle and eight for Brisbane. McCann's Squadron Six would be rotated back to the States for navy yard overhaul. Fremantle would get two new squadrons: John Griggs's Twelve, after the boats had received new engines replacing the H.O.R.s, and Squadron Sixteen, a new outfit commanded by John Haines. The tender *Pelias* would remain in Fremantle; the new tender *Bushnell* would be sent to Fremantle to service Squadron Twelve.

Christie was ecstatic. He noted in his diary, "This is the culmination of a long battle against entangled command relationships. . . . I feel a source of pride in this acknowledgment that I have been correct in assessing the situation and am supported by the Commander-in-Chief."

The new boats of Squadron Sixteen began arriving in late summer. Most came directly to Australia from Panama. They stopped first in Brisbane for voyage repairs and combat indoctrination—a long professorial lecture from Jimmy Fife. From Brisbane they proceeded to Darwin for refueling, then went on patrol in Christie's area, afterward returning to Fremantle. With all this coming and going, Brisbane was once again a busy submarine base.

Fife helped offset his reduction to eight permanently assigned boats by establishing an advance base in Milne Bay, New Guinea, 1,200 miles closer to the operating areas along the equator. The tender *Fulton* was moved there in late October. With refueling facilities at Tulagi and Milne Bay, some boats made "double-barreled" war patrols, leaving from Brisbane, refueling at Tulagi or Milne Bay, and returning to Brisbane or Milne Bay for refit.

Single Patrols

Walter Gale Ebert, commanding one of the replacement boats, *Scamp*, had a busy and productive series of patrols. During the first, off Honshu, bedeviled by prematures and erratic torpedo performance, he had damaged one big freighter but sunk no confirmed ships. On the second, going to Brisbane, he sank a valuable target, the converted seaplane tender *Kamikawa Maru*, 6,800 tons.

Leaving Brisbane, Ebert was directed to intercept an I-class submarine engaged in resupplying Japanese infantry. Ebert found her on July 27 but, before he could attack, the submarine fired at *Scamp*. Ebert ducked to 220 feet to let the torpedo pass overhead, then returned cautiously to periscope depth, where he found the Japanese submarine still on the surface. Ebert set up quickly and fired four torpedoes. Several hit. *I-24* blew up and sank with a "tremendous explosion."

On his next patrol from Brisbane, Ebert conducted several tenacious attacks against Japanese convoys. During one, he sank the 8,600-ton transport *Kansai Maru*, loaded with Japanese troops. Following this attack, Japanese destroyers pounced on *Scamp*, delivering a persistent and vicious depth-charge attack. One of the charges caused leaks in the forward torpedo room. Before they could be plugged, *Scamp* took on three and a half tons of water, and for a while Ebert thought the boat might be lost.

During Ebert's November patrol, Allied aircraft conducted several big raids on Rabaul. On November 5 and 11, some of these aircraft hit the light cruiser *Agano*, inflicting severe damage. On November 12, the light cruiser *Nashiro* took *Agano* in tow, bound for the safer waters of Truk. Fife alerted Ebert, and *Scamp* moved to intercept. Ebert fired six torpedoes at *Agano* from 1,875 yards. One hit *Agano* amidships, stopping her cold, but *Nashiro,* helped by a flock of destroyers, drove *Scamp* away and got *Agano* to Truk.

Oscar Emil Hagberg, a Naval Academy football star from the class of 1931 who replaced Dick Lake on *Albacore*, was not so lucky. One reason was that Fife had transferred Lake and his exec at the same time, forcing Hagberg to find a new exec. He was William Ralph De Loach, Jr., class of 1939.

On his first patrol from Brisbane, Hagberg sighted four separate convoys. He attacked two, firing nine torpeodes into the first and five into the second. Only one of the fourteen torpedoes hit for damage. Fife was furious when he wrote the endorsement. "*Albacore* had the best attack opportunities of any submarine in this area for the last several months. She should have inflicted real damage on the enemy. Many deficiencies existed in the conduct of this patrol."

In subsequent patrols, *Albacore* was twice bombed by friendly aircraft. On November 8, while she was chasing a convoy, a Fifth Air Force bomber came on the scene and for inexplicable reasons ignored the Japanese convoy and attacked *Albacore*, fortunately causing slight damage. Four nights later—in bright moonlight—another Fifth Air Force bomber attacked *Albacore*. Hagberg dived. When he was passing 60 feet, the bombs landed near the bow, violently shaking the boat and flooding the main induction. Before the dive could be checked, *Albacore* plunged to 450 feet. For two hours Hagberg and his men battled to bring *Albacore* under control and save their own lives.

Following this episode, Hagberg received orders to close and attack the light cruiser *Agano*, which Ebert in *Scamp* had hit. Hagberg found *Agano* and tried to attack, but destroyers held *Albacore* down with a four-hour depth-charging. On return to port, Hagberg was relieved of command. He left submarines for good, going to Admiral Carpender's staff and then back to the Naval Academy as head football coach.

Stingray, commanded by Otis John Earle, had sunk only one ship in three patrols and arrived in Brisbane from Pearl Harbor with a severe morale problem. Fife sent *Stingray* back to Pearl Harbor. Leaving Australia, the boat was bombed by a friendly aircraft. It was, Earle reported, "one perfect straddle of four bombs, two on port side and two on the starboard side." The damage was considerable. When Earle reported the attack, Fife investigated and radioed Earle that it had been carried out by "a friendly plane." Earle noted in his report, "No friend of ours."

After Earle had made temporary repairs, Fife shunted him around on a series of Ultra intercepts: six changes of area in a period of ten days. He found no targets, proceeded on to Pearl Harbor, and from there to Mare Island for overhaul. Earle was relieved of command.

Spike Hottel, the torpedo expert who relieved Rob Roy McGregor on luckless *Grouper*, made two war patrols from Brisbane with no better luck. Returning from the second patrol, *Grouper* also was bombed by a friendly plane. Off Guadalcanal the plane dropped four depth charges, two of which exploded while *Grouper* was passing 50 feet. The blast jolted *Grouper* and tore away part of her bridge structure. The pilot gleefully claimed a sinking, but *Grouper* survived and reached Brisbane, where Hottel met the pilot and took him to sea for a brief indoctrination on submarines.

Fife was perplexed by Hottel's failure to sink targets. He wrote, "The present Commanding Officer had conducted the last two patrols in a thoroughly aggressive manner. In his last patrol he was especially energetic and persistent. . . . *Grouper* will be given special training prior to next patrol."

Hottel was next assigned to land commandos on New Britain and then return to Pearl Harbor for overhaul. Hottel was convinced that the magnetic exploder was less than useless. He begged Fife to let him deactivate, but Fife had to follow Carpender's orders. Later Hottel wrote:

Pleas and entreaties bringing no results, I decided that a demonstration might have some effect so before [leaving Brisbane] I got my torpedo crew together and we in-activated all of our exploders. Somebody squealed on us, however, and Fife held us over for a day with orders to re-activate and leave them strictly alone. [Later] we were patrolling south of Truk when a nice fat unescorted armed auxiliary came zigzagging down our way. A wide zig put him in a nice position for our four stern tube shots. The first one prematured and he turned away but not enough to avoid all the other three and one hit him aft. It slowed him down and he settled. . . . While we were maneuvering for another attack what comes down the line but a nice fat tanker with two escorts. The escorts were kind enough to leave the tanker and go to the rescue of our first target. The tanker came barging across our bow at about 1,500 yards away on a straight course and apparently too engrossed in the other ship to worry about us. I fired a spread of six torpedoes from our bow tubes. The sea was calm and the tracks ran hot, straight and true. He never even changed course. I presume because they were watching the other ship. The tracks wrapped him up like a blanket. Since they were magnetic exploders, they were set to run under him. Nothing happened. He went merrily on his way while the escorts convoyed the first victim to Rabaul. Trying to figure out how we missed him turned out not to be so difficult after all. The Torpedo Officer shamefully admitted that when they re-activated [the magnetic exploders] they had omitted the torpedoes in the bow tubes and he had completely forgotten to tell me. C'est la guerre!

When Hottel arrived in Pearl Harbor, having survived this incident, a circular run, and numerous prematures, he roundly condemned the Mark VI exploder in writing. "It would appear far better to sink the enemy vessels encountered—when targets in certain areas are so hard to find and attack—than to continue spoiling good chances just to prove that a really useless mechanism can be made to function a fair proportion of the time."

After stopping at Pearl Harbor, Hottel took *Grouper* back to Mare Island for an extensive overhaul. There he was relieved of command and ordered to help bring the Mark XVIII electric torpedo into service, the assignment for which he had been slated before Fife sent him to *Grouper*.

Another of Fife's replacements was *Balao,* a new boat commanded by Richard Henry Crane. *Balao,* built at Portsmouth, had a new superthick pressure hull. Her test depth was 400 feet; *in extremis,* she might survive at 800 feet. The engineer of *Balao* was Thomas Kimmel, son of the admiral, who had made five war patrols on S-40.

When Fife inspected *Balao,* he was disappointed and angry with Crane and wrote Lockwood:

All the boats coming from Manitowoc and the East Coast have been coming out here in good shape with exception of Balao. *At least I hope she is the exceptional case. She is full of S-boat sailors and arrived here dirty and poorly trained. The golden opportunity for working up an organization on the long trip across the Pacific was absolutely wasted. I was almost in the mood to relieve Crane and not let him take her out on first patrol.*

During this first patrol, Crane did nothing to redeem himself. On August 7 he picked up a three-ship convoy but was forced to break off the attack, he reported, in order to take up a new position ordered by Fife. On August 10 he found another three-ship convoy, but it got away from him. On August 11, another fat ship got away unharmed. Meanwhile, *Balao* had suffered a dangerous crankcase explosion because a crewman left a rag in an oil strainer, which shut off the flow of oil. When *Balao* returned to port, Fife gave Crane a chilly endorsement, but he retained command. Young Kimmel left the boat for new construction.

Crane did no better on his second patrol and was relieved of command. He returned to the States to commission another boat.

To replace Crane, Fife chose Cyrus Churchill Cole, another young officer from the class of 1935. Cole was the son of an admiral, Cyrus Williard Cole, who had commanded the submarine force in peacetime and presided over the rescue and salvage operations of *Squalus*. During the first two years of the war, young Cole had been in postgraduate school at the Naval Academy. Then he had made a PCO cruise on *Silversides*. His exec was a classmate, Jack Murray Seymour. Although this was a potentially awkward situation, Cole and Seymour worked in harmony. As Seymour said later, "Being friends (Cy was the coxswain of the Naval Academy crew in which I rowed), the relationship was even smoother."

However, *Balao* turned in another disappointing patrol. Cole encountered two *Mogami*-class heavy cruisers, hesitated, then fired four torpedoes at one. All missed. Again Fife was angry. He wrote, "It is unfortunate that the two cruiser contacts were not made by a more experienced commanding officer. Undue conjecture over enemy countermeasures permitted these valuable targets to escape. Two golden opportunities were missed."

Fife gave Burlingame's *Silversides* to John Starr Coye, Jr., a cool blue-eyed officer who had been working for Fife's operations officer, John Murphy. "Burlingame was a hard act to follow," Coye recalled later.

When Coye and the exec, Robert Worthington, took *Silversides* to sea, they carried a load of torpedoes whose exploders had been hair-triggered, one of the many (unofficial) experimental lots turned out by the Brisbane Torpedo Shop, which in its own way had been trying to find a solution to torpedo exploder problems.

While on station, Fife sent Coye and Worthington an Ultra on a valuable target, a big seaplane tender. Coye intercepted and attacked. The first four torpedoes prematured and the tender got away. (When he returned to port, Coye read an Ultra intercept, reporting his attack, which indicated, he said later, that he had "scared hell out of them.") Coye made two other attacks, expending fourteen torpedoes in all without a single hit. Many were prematures caused, Coye reported later, by the hair-trigger exploders, which were just too sensitive.

But the exploders worked well some of the time. On his second patrol from Brisbane, Coye returned *Silversides* to Pearl Harbor. He patrolled the equator along the Palaus-Rabaul convoy line, close to the area where Mush Morton had nearly wiped out a convoy. Coye found two convoys and attacked boldly and relentlessly. From the first, which he chased for sixty-four hours, he sank a 2,000-ton freighter. From the second, which he chased for eighty-five hours, he sank three ships for about 13,000 tons. He crippled the last ship with torpedoes, tried to sink it with his deck gun, then went back to torpedoes. Arriving at Pearl Harbor after thirty-six days, all torpedoes expended, Coye was credited with four ships for 22,000 tons (later reduced to 15,000), earning high praise from Lockwood. With this achievement, Coye believed he filled Burlingame's shoes.

Another replacement boat was *Blackfish*, commanded by John Frederick Davidson. Her exec was William Kinsella, who had served in peacetime in Warder's *Seawolf* and then went to the demothballed O-8 as exec, joining *Blackfish* when she returned to New London from five patrols in Scotland.

On her first Pacific sortie, *Blackfish* patrolled between Truk and Rabaul and north of New Guinea along the equator. For the first time, Davidson and Kinsella learned of the extensive use of Ultra. Said Kinsella later, "Johnny Davidson would read the Ultras and give me the positions we were concerned with so we could get into position to intercept. The information was extremely accurate. In virtually every case we made contact with the convoy or units reported. Sometimes due to navigational errors—on their part or ours—we couldn't do anything except look at them when they went by too far out of range."

In two attacks, for which Davidson claimed one sinking for 4,500 tons, disallowed by postwar analysis, he and Kinsella were plagued with torpedo problems. As Kinsella remembered:

We were instructed to use the Mark VI magnetic exploder. As it turned out, for some reason half the exploders had been in-activated—by the tender before they issued them to us, we believe. On several attacks, we had prematures, bringing on a counterattack, which was not appreciated. Then we had what we believed was a successful attack, sinking a ship. We were perplexed as to why we had had prematures in one case and not in the other. When we came back to Brisbane and turned in our remaining torpedoes, we found that they were in-activated. We suspect that the ones that performed right were some of the in-activated ones and some that prematured were activated.

Cooperative Efforts

In November, Fife received an Ultra on an important convoy en route from Palau to Rabaul. It was loaded with infantry, ammunition, and gasoline for the embattled Japanese garrisons. Fife then had four boats in the primary operating area: Bob Foley's *Gato*, *Peto*, and two brand-new boats, *Raton* and *Ray*. Although they did not operate as a formal wolf pack, the effectiveness of their combined firepower pointed the way to more cooperative efforts.

Raton, built at Manitowoc, was commanded by James White Davis. Less than one week after entering combat, Davis and his exec, Manning Kimmel, had found a convoy and sunk a big 6,700-ton freighter out of it. On November 28, Davis met the convoy coming from Palau. In a series of bold and skillful attacks, fouled by erratic torpedo performance, Davis sank two big freighters, one of 5,400 tons and the other of 6,800 tons. Running low on torpedoes, he radioed the results of his attack to Fife, then trailed.

Brooks Jared Harral, in another new boat, *Ray*, received orders to attack the same convoy. He rendezvoused with Bob Foley in *Gato* at sea, and the two skippers—conversing by megaphone—planned a joint attack.

Both boats submerged along the projected track of the convoy. Bob Foley attacked first, sinking a large transport, *Columbia Maru*, 5,600 tons. The escorts pounced on *Gato*, delivering a severe depth-charge attack. *Raton*, still trailing the convoy, drew the escorts from *Gato* by surfacing in broad daylight and offering herself as a target.

Foley's attack caused the remnants of the convoy to change course radically, and for that reason Harral in *Ray* could not shoot. However, later that night Harral surfaced and chased, firing his deck gun at the escorts in an effort to draw them away so he could get in to attack. The tactic failed, but Harral got an A-plus for effort. William Thackeray Nelson, commanding *Peto*, patrolled farther south along the projected track. He found the convoy, fired six torpedoes, and sank a freighter of 2,500 tons.

This action had not been a formal wolf-pack attack. No one skipper had been in charge. There had been no radio exchanges between the boats. It was, strictly speaking, a concentration of available firepower against a single convoy; the four boats sank four out of the five ships.

Foley in *Gato* turned his voyage into a double-barreled patrol. He put into Tulagi, took on fuel and torpedoes, and then returned to the area for more combat. On December 20, along the equator, Foley picked up a two-ship convoy with two escorts. He attacked and sank one of the freighters. The escorts attacked *Gato*, delivering nineteen close charges, the worst working over *Gato* had ever received. Wrote Foley, "Practically all the charges seemed right on top of us, and the ship was shaken violently with each."

Two hours later, when Foley found a rainsquall and surfaced inside it, the men on the bridge were greeted with a heart-stopping sight: an unexploded Japanese depth charge was lying on the afterdeck. Leaving it where it lay, Foley turned his attention to the remaining freighter and the two escorts. He set a course for the three ships, making flank speed through the murk. At 1,500 yards, one of the escorts appeared. Foley swung around; the escort fired. Foley continued on a course calculated to intercept the freighter. He wrote:

> *Situation resembled a five-ring circus. Gato was simultaneously: (a) outrunning two escorts, (b) trying to overtake the freighter, (c) reloading the forward tubes, (d) making some necessary minor repairs, and (e) trying to dispose of one unexploded depth charge without blowing off our rudder.*

While chasing the freighter and being chased himself, Foley sent a party aft on the deck to dispose of the depth charge. An officer copied down all the Japanese writing on the charge, then set it in a holed rubber raft and cast it adrift in the path of the escorts. Foley hoped it would sink and explode beneath one of the ships, but it didn't. With all this going on, Foley was unable to get into position to attack the second freighter, which got away.

Nine days later, December 29, Fife put Foley onto another convoy. As he was about to fire, a floatplane sighted *Gato* and warned the ships in the convoy. They turned to ram *Gato*, fouling up Foley's attack. Later Foley surfaced and chased the convoy, trying an end around. The seaplane returned. Having missed the submarine and a chance at the convoy, Foley was fighting mad and decided to remain on the surface and battle it out with the plane—contrary to doctrine and good sense. The plane dived for a bombing run. Foley's gunners sent up a storm of small-arms fire. Foley wrote, "Well before his release point he pulled up in a steep climb with surprise written all over both floats. In all, the plane came in five times but on each approach he was met with a hail of rapid fire, and each time thought better of it. He then commenced circling out of gun range."

The plane had not got *Gato*, but it had done its job; the convoy got away. Foley turned *Gato* northward for Truk, where he fell under Lockwood's jurisdiction. Admiral King let it be known in no uncertain terms that he took a poor view of Foley's battle with the plane, and Ralph Christie hastened to notify all submarines basing in Australia that "gun actions with airplanes are not approved."

That December three other boats carried out a similar cooperative attack on a convoy, this one composed of two destroyers and three tankers en route from Borneo to Truk with fuel for Admiral Koga's fleet units. The three boats were *Guardfish*, commanded by Bub Ward, the first officer from the class of 1935 to command a fleet boat, Wally Ebert's *Scamp*, and *Albacore*, with a new older skipper, James William Blanchard.* Bub Ward (who had been on special missions his last two patrols) sighted the convoy first. He set up on one of the destroyers but was unable to shoot; the destroyers headed for *Albacore* at high speed. Blanchard made repeated hurried setups, then fired four stern tubes. The destroyer *Sazanami* blew up and sank. Ward was close enough to take a periscope picture.

Following this attack, the second destroyer pinned *Albacore*, dropping fifty-nine depth charges, many close. While the destroyer was thus occupied, Ward in *Guardfish* and Ebert in *Scamp* moved to attack the three tankers. Ebert fired first, sinking *Nippon Maru*, 10,000 tons, with two torpedoes. Ward followed up with an attack on a sister ship, *Kenyo Maru*. The third tanker passed just beyond range of *Guardfish*. Escorted by the surviving destroyer, it reached Truk safely.

Again, this had been no formal wolf pack. However, the combined firepower of *Guardfish*, *Scamp*, and *Albacore*, brought to bear in a cooperative attack, had destroyed two out of three tankers and one out of two destroyers.

* * *

* Blanchard, class of 1927, had been stuck at the Submarine School since before the war, a job that gave him ulcers. Setting off on his first patrol, he had received two Ultras: the first, a Japanese submarine, failed to show up: the second, *Choko Maru*, taking munitions to New Guinea, appeared on schedule at night in a squall. About sunset the next day, although the first four torpedoes prematured after short runs, three others hit the target and "blew the whole side of the ship out," Blanchard reported. The sinking was confirmed in postwar records.

COOPERATIVE EFFORTS

In all, Fife mounted thirty-three patrols during the period June through December 1943. These patrols accounted for twenty-nine confirmed ships sunk. The single best scores were turned in by John Coye on *Silversides* (4 ships for 15,000 tons) and James Davis on *Raton* (3 ships, 18,000 tons). The most significant action was the *Gato-Peto-Ray-Raton* cooperative attack on the convoy in late November, when the four boats sank four ships out of a five-ship convoy. No serious harm had come to any of the boats. None had accidentally shot at the others. Boldness on the part of one skipper had tended to encourage the others. One boat had offered itself as a target to draw off and befuddle the screen. By comparison to other patrols, the results had been rewarding. And yet neither Fife nor Christie followed up the experiment vigorously. In Australia, at least, the submarine commanders were not yet ready for formal wolf-packing. Many more months would pass before they were.

23
Fremantle, August through December 1943

Tankers as Targets

In Fremantle, Ralph Christie, busy rotating the Squadron Six boats to Pearl Harbor and preparing for John Haines's Squadron Sixteen, received orders outlining a new target priority for his submarines: concentrate on Japanese tankers carrying oil from Borneo and Sumatra to Admiral Koga's fleet at Truk. The codebreakers made a special effort to identify and locate tankers and passed along valuable information on sailing dates, predicted noon positions, and other data. Why this order was not put out months earlier remains a mystery.

This presented Christie with a problem. As Dan Daspit and Dave Whelchel (among others) had found, tankers (like armor-plated battleships and carriers) were difficult to sink. They were well compartmented, able to close off areas hit by torpedoes and (if empty) flood compensating compartments to keep from capsizing. Some well-built tankers could absorb five, six, seven, or even ten direct torpedo hits without sinking.

One reason for this was the small size of the Mark XIV torpedo warhead. A warhead of 1,000 pounds (such as the Japanese had on their second-generation oxygen torpedo) would have made the task of sinking a tanker infinitely easier and would have required far fewer torpedoes. If the magnetic exploder could be made reliable, this deficiency could be overcome; one torpedo exploding underneath would break the keel of a tanker and send it to the bottom. This was one reason Ralph Christie steadfastly held to the magnetic exploder and kept on trying to fix it.

Unknown to Christie, there was an element working in his favor. The oil fields at Tarakan and Balikpapan produced oil pure enough to be used without processing. In many instances, the Japanese loaded it directly from the fields into tankers. However, the oil contained some elements which made it highly volatile—not as flammable as gasoline but easier to set on fire than processed oil. A lucky torpedo hit could start a raging, uncontrollable fire on a tanker, forcing the crew to abandon ship and leave it to its fate. That was as good as a sinking.

More Cooperative Efforts

The first two Squadron Sixteen boats to arrive were *Bowfin* and *Billfish*. *Bowfin* was commanded by one of the fine performers of 1942, Joe Willingham, who had won two Navy Crosses for his four patrols on *Tautog*. *Billfish* was commanded by Frederic Colby Lucas, Jr., a peacetime submariner who had been on the staff of Commander, Submarines Atlantic Fleet during the early months of the war and had never made a war patrol. His exec was Frank Gordon Selby, who had made the first two war patrols on Creed Burlingame's *Silversides*.

On their first patrol, *Bowfin* and *Billfish* conducted what might be described as an "extemporized" cooperative unit off Indochina, similar to Fife's experimental cooperative efforts with the Brisbane boats. There the two boats found a six-ship convoy.

Later, Willingham's exec, William Calhoun Thompson, Jr., wrote, "Willingham was a perfectionist. . . . We sank three ships, firing bow and stern tubes simultaneously—bow with the TDC but stern with his infallible eye and judgment. To the best of my knowledge this was an 'only feat' during the war." Postwar analysis trimmed these three ships to one, a transport, *Kirishima Maru*, 8,120 tons. Lucas in *Billfish* was credited with damage to two ships for 11,900 tons. His endorsement stated, "It is unfortunate that the attacks . . . were not productive of more visible results."

When Willingham returned *Bowfin* to Fremantle, Christie labeled his patrol "brilliant" and promoted him off the boat to command a division in Brisbane. Willingham recommended his exec, Thompson, for command, but Christie picked Walter Thomas Griffith, who had been exec on *Gar* and was a year senior to Thompson. Lucas retained command of *Billfish*, but his exec, Gordon Selby, went into the PCO pool.

Walt Griffith was, in Christie's words, a "studious-looking, red-haired, trim young man with blood pressure too high and a slight hand quiver." To his exec, Thompson, he was "absolutely fearless—maybe too much so" and a "reasonable and wonderful skipper and shipmate." Wrote Thompson, "I shared his cabin with him, at his suggestion, and one of us was 'always awake on feet' throughout the boat at all times. . . . Walt, at sea, was a fearless fighter; in port, a mild, kindly, even poetic type."

Going off on their second patrols, *Bowfin* and *Billfish* again operated as an extemporaneous unit off Indochina. On the way over, Griffith found a group of five two-masted schooners, steaming in company. He charged the formation at full speed, sending the crew to gun stations. Within one hour, three of the schooners were riddled and sinking. Each had been manned by about thirty people—men and women—and there were children aboard. All the schooners, Griffith reported later, were "heavily laden . . . each vessel sank like a stone after two good hits . . . no clue as to cargo." During the battle, a plane came over and dropped a small bomb, forcing Griffith to let the last two schooners go. However, later that night he found another, and after two hits it too "sank like a stone."

During this engagement, many women and children had been killed or drowned. Those who knew Griffith well said that in later years he regretted the attacks against these defenseless targets and brooded about it. Said Thompson, "I would not have sunk some of the sampans."

A few nights later, November 11, while going through Sibutu Passage, Griffith found two small unescorted tankers. Again he ordered battle surface. Within half an hour, he had holed both and set them afire. Wrote Griffith, "Nice fireworks for Armistice Day."

On November 20, Griffith joined up with Lucas in *Billfish* and began the wolf-pack operations, cruising toward the coast of Indochina near Camranh Bay. The weather turned foul. During the storm, *Bowfin* and *Billfish* separated and temporarily lost contact.

Early on the morning of November 26, Griffith, feeling his way through pitch blackness and solid sheets of rain, suddenly found pips on the radar ranging from 1,000 to 4,000 yards. At first he thought he had run right up on the beach. Then he realized he had steamed into the middle of a Japanese tanker convoy. He backed emergency to avoid colliding with one "enormous" ship.

A wild melee followed. Reversing to get range to shoot, Griffith made ready his torpedo tubes. He fired nine torpedoes (one tube door would not open) at two or three ships. (In the dark and confusion it was difficult to tell how many.) His magnetic exploders were activated. As Griffith maneuvered through the convoy, his torpedoes started exploding. Within the next few hours, three confirmed ships went down: a tanker of 5,000 tons and two freighters, one 5,400 tons and one smaller.

Two days later, Griffith made contact with Lucas in *Billfish*, who had been patrolling to seaward. Lucas picked up a convoy and helped put *Bowfin* on the track. A second furious close-in action ensued. Griffith sank two more big ships, including a tanker of 9,900 tons and a transport of 5,400 tons. One ship of the convoy fired back with a deck gun, piercing *Bowfin*'s main induction, and seawater flooded the engine room. Undaunted, Griffith set up and fired his last two torpedoes at another ship. One prematured after thirteen seconds, deflecting the second. Now out of torpedoes, Griffith withdrew from the convoy to repair the damages.

Lucas in *Billfish* was ready and waiting on the convoy track, but Griffith's attack had scattered it and alerted the escorts. Where Griffith had had the advantage of a dark land mass behind him, Lucas had open sea for backdrop. He trailed and got off one attack from long range, reporting damage to a 6,000-ton vessel.

On the way home, Griffith found another schooner, which he described as a "two-masted yacht, with jib, flying jib, foresail, mainsail and two topsails." He battle-surfaced and sank it, adding, "Did not observe crew closely but vessel was not a native craft. Looked like it might have been some planter's yacht taken over by the Japs."

Griffith arrived back in Fremantle after thirty-nine days at sea. When Christie heard the news of this patrol, he was awestruck, calling it in his diary the "classic of all submarine patrols."

It was. After carefully going over the accounts of the attacks, Christie credited Griffith with sinking a total of fourteen vessels—nine ships and five schooners—for 71,000 tons. This was 20,000 more tons than Klakring had been credited with on the first patrol of *Guardfish*, the largest single claimed score by any submarine up to then. Overnight the "poetic" Walt Griffith became a submarine superstar. Christie awarded him a Navy Cross and wined and dined the wardroom in spectacular fashion at "Bend of the Road." He gave the exec, William Thompson, a Silver Star and pronounced him qualified for command of his own boat. And when his cocker spaniel had a puppy, Christie named it Bowfin.

In all his torpedo attacks, Griffith had kept the Mark VI magnetic exploder activated as instructed. Christie noted triumphantly in the patrol report endorsement, "The torpedo performance on this patrol was excellent. Nineteen hits were obtained from the twenty-four torpedoes fired." It seemed to Christie proof that the magnetic exploder —in the proper hands—was still a marvelous weapon.

In the postwar accounting, Walt Griffith's confirmed score for this patrol—like almost everybody else's—was trimmed. There was no doubt about the five schooners, but the bigger ships sunk were reduced from nine to five, for a total of 26,958 tons. In terms of confirmed tonnage sunk, this made his patrol the third best of the war to date, after Creed Burlingame's fourth in *Silversides* and Tom Wogan's second in *Tarpon*.

When Lucas in *Billfish* returned to Fremantle thirteen days later, he had a painfully candid talk with Christie. He explained that he had never been comfortable in submarines and he now believed that over the period of a war patrol this mild phobia adversely affected his performance. He therefore felt that he was not doing justice to this fine submarine and crew, and recommended that the command be given to one of several war-experienced officers then in Fremantle awaiting their chance at command.

Christie noted with regret in his diary, "I am obliged to detach Lucas from command of *Billfish* on his own request. He is convinced that he is temperamentally unsuited for submarine command. I have been quite well satisfied with him although he has had two unproductive patrols [and] I would not have removed him." Lucas went to Brisbane to serve on the staff of Squadron Eight.

Bluefish, commanded by George Egbert Porter, Jr., who had made three patrols on *Greenling* as exec to Chester Bruton, left on her first patrol from Darwin. Porter's exec was young Chester Nimitz, who began the war on *Sturgeon*. Porter and Nimitz conducted six attacks and were credited with sinking four ships for 16,200 tons and damage to one for 7,000 tons. It was one of the shortest war patrols on record: twenty-five days port to port.

On the second patrol, Porter patrolled near Indochina in company with another new boat, *Cod*, commanded by Jim Dempsey, ex-*Spearfish*. On November 8, Porter picked up a big convoy near Dangerous Ground off Palawan in the South China Sea. Swinging in on the surface at night, Porter fired all ten tubes. The fifth torpedo to leave the tubes prematured right in the path of *Bluefish*. The others continued on, for what Porter believed were "eight or nine hits" in various ships.

After reloading, Porter swung around for another attack on a motionless ship that loomed large on radar. It turned out to be a big tanker, already disabled. Porter delivered three more attacks against the tanker, which finally blew up, sending a vast column of flame skyward. "This is the most beautiful sight I have ever seen," Porter exclaimed, watching his handiwork through the periscope. "This is beautiful." The ship was *Kyokuei Maru*, 10,570 tons. Porter retrieved a magnetic compass from a lifeboat and later presented it to Christie.

Dempsey in *Cod* was close enough to this battle to hear Porter's torpedo explosions, but he was unable to make an attack.

Ten days later, in the Celebes Sea, Porter and Nimitz found another tanker escorted by a destroyer. With only six torpedoes left, Porter cooked up an ingenious plan. He fired three torpedoes at the destroyer and one at the tanker, with the intent of sinking the former and damaging the latter, slowing it down. The destroyer blew up with an enormous explosion; the tanker, hit with one torpedo, slowed down as planned. Porter swung around and fired his last two torpedoes at the tanker, but he forgot to allow for the diminished speed, and both missed. He started to attack with his deck gun but broke off when the tanker fired back.

On the way home, Porter battle-surfaced on a small fishing sampan engaged in collecting turtles. Most of the crew dived overboard, but one old fisherman was badly burned in the flames that engulfed the craft. Porter brought him on board. One of *Bluefish*'s officers, James De Roche, reported later, "There was considerable division of opinion on the submarine as to whether we should bring this prisoner back or not. Some of the men who had been at Pearl Harbor and who had lost many shipmates from Japanese bombings and attacks felt that we should take no Japanese alive. One . . . felt that we should kill this man outright." The prisoner was not executed, however; he died of burns.

When Porter and Nimitz returned to Fremantle after thirty-two days, there was "much discussion" about what *Bluefish* had or had not sunk. Porter and Nimitz believed that they had sunk seven ships—a record performance—but Christie had Ultra information indicating otherwise. He credited Porter with sinking three ships for 22,800 tons and damage to five for 43,800 tons. Postwar records credited Porter with sinking only the tanker and the destroyer, which turned out to be an old 800-tonner.

After this patrol, Christie pulled Chester Nimitz from *Bluefish* for a rest. He went to the PCO pool, qualified for his own command.

Rasher was commanded by thirty-nine-year-old Ed Hutchinson, whom Lockwood had relieved of command of *Grampus* the year before for lacking aggressiveness. His exec was Stephen Henry Gimber, ex-*Trigger*. Patrolling in the Celebes Sea, Hutchinson, perhaps smarting from his previous relief, conducted an outstandingly aggressive patrol: eight attacks and four ships sunk, a claim sustained in postwar records. On the way home, *Rasher* was attacked by a friendly navy patrol bomber. Hutchinson dived. The bombs exploded when he was passing 47 feet, fortunately doing no serious damage. In Fremantle, Hutchinson stepped down as commanding officer and was promoted to command a division.

Command of *Rasher* went to Willard Ross Laughon, who came from the Atlantic and command of *R-1*, on which he made ten war patrols. Retaining Steve Gimber as exec, Laughon joined George Porter in *Bluefish* for a joint patrol in the South China Sea, along the approaches to the Gulf of Siam. Both boats would lay minefields and then conduct regular patrols. On the way to lay his field, Porter found a tanker in Karimata Strait and sank it.

On the night of January 3, after both Porter and Laughon had laid their minefields, Christie vectored them to intercept a convoy of three tankers. After making contact, Porter and Laughon talked by blinker tube. Porter, the senior skipper, generously offered Laughon the first attack. Laughon accepted.

Moving into position for a night surface attack, Laughon fired four torpedoes at one tanker. The first torpedo—Laughon's first shot of the war—prematured 400 yards out of the tube, alerting the convoy. The tankers began shooting at *Rasher*. But Laughon had got one hit and his target slowed down. Meanwhile Porter had attacked another tanker, which burst into flames. Laughon fired again—six torpedoes.

Two prematured but one hit. Laughon reloaded and attacked again with four torpedoes. One prematured but others hit, and the tanker exploded in a mass of flames. Wrote Laughon, "Three attacks—five prematures. Were we unhappy!"

The combined attack had netted two of the three tankers: *Hakko Maru*, 6,046 tons, for Porter; *Kiyo Maru*, 7,251 tons, for Laughon. After sinking his tanker, Laughon patrolled off Camranh Bay, where he made two more attacks, one marred by a premature and the other by a TDC error. On the way home, he found a "beautiful" 10,000-ton transport which he chased for fifteen hours before firing his last torpedo at extreme range. It missed.

When Porter returned to Fremantle, Christie was waiting with sad personal news: one of his two daughters had drowned. Porter returned to the States for new construction, to be with his wife and other daughter for a while.

Crevalle's First Two Patrols

Crevalle was commanded by Hank Munson, who had commanded S-38 for six patrols from Manila, Surabaya, and Brisbane. His exec was Frank Walker, who had made six patrols as exec of *Searaven*. Munson's third was Lucien Berry McDonald, and his torpedo officer was Bill Ruhe, who had served on S-37 in the early days of the war and was, according to Munson, "one of the best TDC operators in the Southwest Pacific." Munson—at Fife's suggestion—had adopted the Mush Morton-Dick O'Kane technique for fire control: Frank Walker manned the periscope, leaving Munson free for overall direction.

Crevalle touched at Darwin and then went on patrol near Manila. On November 10, Munson attacked a three-ship convoy, firing ten torpedoes before an escort drove them down. Although a hit was observed, no claims were made. The next night, Munson battle-surfaced and sank a 750-ton freighter. On November 15, a huge passenger-cargo vessel came out of the mist. Munson set up and prepared to shoot. The target zigged, placing it only 900 yards away. Munson fired four torpedoes down the throat. The ship disintegrated.

Two nights later, while Munson was patrolling off the west coast of Luzon, radar picked up a high-speed formation, with one large pip. Munson closed to attack, trying to figure out what he had. He was never certain. It looked like an escort carrier, or a cross between an escort carrier and a large amphibious tender, escorted by a destroyer. Munson closed to point-blank range and fired six torpedoes, set to run at 6 feet. One torpedo prematured off the bow; several others hit.

Munson said later, "The outcome was never known, for about that time I got a damn sight more interested in saving my neck than collecting historical evidence. We came under violent and intense gunfire (five-inch stuff) from both the target and the escorting destroyer as we passed down beneath them, about five hundred yards abaft. We can only hope they scored some hits on each other. A hunk of shrapnel went through the bow buoyancy tank, but we didn't know it . . . we pulled the plug and reached test depth in considerably under contract specification time."

A week later, Munson picked up another ship, a 4,000-ton unescorted freighter, and attacked her with his last four torpedoes. He believed he got two hits and claimed she sank.

During the course of this patrol, Munson stopped a fishing boat to interrogate the Filipino crew about Japanese shipping traffic. The fishermen were terrified, Bill Ruhe recalled in a brief account of the incident, and thrust peace offerings—baskets of fruit, bunches of bananas, struggling livestock—at Munson. When the Filipinos insisted that Munson take something, he "apologetically accepted one little dirty-gray emaciated chicken." Looking over the pathetic little bird, Munson decided no one could get any meat from it, so he pronounced it *Crevalle*'s mascot.

The chicken wound up in care of the gang in the forward torpedo room. As Ruhe told it, the torpedo gang, dreaming of fresh eggs, began feeding the chicken bread crumbs and cornmeal. The chicken ate ravenously, Ruhe reported, "and then decided to be grateful for the good treatment and produce an egg." The gang drew straws to see who would get it. The chief torpedoman, Howard, won. When the chicken announced with a loud cackle that she meant business, Howard put his hand underneath to catch the egg. Out came not an egg but a revolting shell-less ooze—all in Howard's hand.

Another torpedoman, Crowley, who was to get the next egg, pondered this situation. Why had there been no shell? Not enough calcium, he concluded. He went forward to the crew's mess and got some shells from the ship's supply of frozen eggs, ground them up, and fed them to the chicken. Reported Ruhe, "A day later her cackle held a note of triumph as out came an egg covered with a nice hard white shell."

When Munson returned to Fremantle, Christie was much pleased with the patrol. He noted in his diary, "Munson in *Crevalle* in today and a fine story he has to tell. Result: 1 auxiliary carrier, 18,000; 1 large, 1 medium and 1 small freighter . . . brought back a chicken mascot." In all, Munson claimed four ships for 29,800 tons, for which Christie gave him a Navy Cross. However, postwar analysis wiped out the escort carrier and two other ships, leaving him only the freighter *Kyokko Maru*, 6,783 tons, sunk on November 15.

Munson's second patrol was a frustrating one. At dawn on January 7, while crossing the Java Sea, *Crevalle* came across a submarine. Munson thought it must be Dutch or English, so he flashed the current recognition signal. In return, Munson recalled, he received the correct reply. Yet there was something strange about the boat. When the sky became lighter, Munson realized belatedly that the sub was a Jap, a small RO-class. Munson set up and fired two stern tubes just as the submarine dived. Both torpedoes, set for 6 feet, prematured. After that Munson—on his own—deactivated the magnetic exploder on all his torpedoes.

Munson continued to patrol off Indochina. Near Camranh Bay he laid a small minefield. A week later, he picked up a cargo vessel with one escort. He fired four torpedoes and sank *Busho Maru*, 2,500 tons. On the way home, transiting Alice Channel between the Sulu and Celebes seas, Munson battle-surfaced on a small subchaser and sank it.

During this action, Munson received an important Ultra from Christie. A large convoy was leaving the island of Halmahera, east of Makassar Passage, northbound, and Munson was directed to take station south of Talaud Island to intercept. He waited around for two days with no sign of the convoy. On the morning of February 15, as he was telling Frank Walker to set a course for Fremantle, the periscope watch reported a contact. It turned out to be the expected convoy: seven ships.

Munson tracked it during the day, watching two more ships join up. After dark, he surfaced and attacked. In his first salvo, Munson fired nine torpedoes at several of the ships. He saw hits in at least three ships, but escorts firing big shells drove him under. He reloaded the bow tubes with his last six torpedoes and fired them all at a single big target. The fire-control party misjudged the ship's speed, however, and only one of the five hit. Having expended all his torpedoes, Munson cleared the area and set course for Fremantle.

Upon completing this patrol, for which he received high praise and a second Navy Cross, Munson stepped down as skipper and went to the Squadron Sixteen staff. His exec, Frank Walker, moved up to take command.

Mixed Bags and Special Missions

For Ralph Christie, *Bonefish* was a very special boat. She had been sponsored at launching by Mrs. Freeland Daubin at Electric Boat about the time his own wife christened another boat, *Corvina*. Christie chose *Bonefish* for his new "flagship." She was commanded by Thomas Wesley Hogan, who had made three war patrols on *Nautilus* under Bill Brockman. The exec was Guy Edward O'Neil, Jr., who had made five patrols on *Salmon* under Gene McKinney.

Jumping off from Darwin, Hogan patrolled off the Indochina coast. Helped by numerous Ultra reports, he found no end of targets. In eight dogged attacks, Hogan fired off all his torpedoes, returning to Fremantle after forty-five days. Christie had followed Hogan's progress by Ultra intercepts and, when he returned to port, credited him with sinking six ships for 40,000 tons. Postwar accounting cut this total to three ships for 24,000 tons, but it was still one of the best patrols of the war; two of the ships were large and important troop transports: *Kashima Maru*, 10,000 tons, and *Teibi Maru*, 10,000 tons.

Christie surprised Hogan, on his arrival in Fremantle, by visiting the boat at seven thirty in the morning to give him a Navy Cross, and he wrote ecstatically in his diary, "This morning, Hogan's *Bonefish* arrived—my flag—with 40,000 tons.... His patrol was exceptional in all respects . . . ship arrived clean and fit."

Rebel Lowrance, making his fifth and last patrol on *Kingfish*, carried out two special missions before going commerce raiding. On October 2, he laid a small minefield at the south end of Celebes. Four days later, he landed a party of six agents with two and a half tons of gear on the northeast coast of Borneo. After that he moved over to Indochina, where he sank one confirmed freighter. He was credited with a large tanker also, but postwar accounting did not bear out the claim.

MIXED BAGS AND SPECIAL MISSIONS

Following this patrol Lowrance returned to the States for new construction, and command of *Kingfish* went to Herbert Jukes, who had lost *S-27* in the Aleutians. Jukes and his exec, Barney Flenniken, who had been exec to Dinty Moore on *S-44*, turned in a splendid first patrol off Indochina. On the night of January 3, Christie sent Jukes an Ultra on another tanker convoy a little to the north of the convoy that Porter and Laughon hit. In a brilliant and dogged attack, Jukes sank two tankers from the convoy. Four nights later, off northwest Borneo, Jukes sank a third tanker. After that he took *Kingfish* to Pearl Harbor for overhaul.

Both *Raton* and *Ray* reported to Ralph Christie in December. On *Raton*, James Davis and Manning Kimmel conducted another aggressive patrol near Halmahera. On Christmas Eve, Davis attacked a large convoy, sinking one ship and damaging another. In subsequent days, he attacked a tanker convoy, believing he had sunk one, but it was not confirmed in postwar records. On arrival in Fremantle, Manning Kimmel joined Chester Nimitz in the PCO pool.

Brooks Harral in *Ray* patrolled near Ambon. Two days after Christmas, Harral sank a 5,792-ton tanker, *Kyoko Maru*. On New Year's Day, he sank a 2,904-ton freighter. In the days following, he attacked several other ships without success and then returned to Fremantle.

On Frank Latta's first special mission to the Philippines in *Narwhal*, he unloaded all torpedoes except those in her tubes and took on board ten commandos and ninety-two tons of ammunition, food, and medical supplies to be delivered to Mindanao.

William Anderson (ex-*Tarpon*), engineer on *Narwhal*, wrote:

Frank Latta was a terrific skipper . . . a very versatile person . . . a real leader who was extremely popular with the crew . . . he slept in a cot in the conning tower and kept a motorcycle, dismantled, on board for his use when we got into ports. . . . When we entered the Philippines, with all that cargo and the commandos, we spotted a big tanker escorted by three destroyers. Typically, Latta attacked. The torpedoes missed and the three destroyers came after us . . . they dropped a few depth charges then, we thought, went away. . . .

Latta surfaced to make a run for it. The destroyers came charging, firing guns and trying to illuminate us with star shells. Latta ordered full speed, but the destroyers were keeping up. Our engines—christened Matthew, Mark, Luke and John—were roaring as they never had before. An hour passed. The enemy was still in pursuit, firing wildly. The Chief Engineer, below and not realizing fully the situation that the boat was in, called up to the skipper on the bridge: "Captain, if we don't slow down pretty soon we're not going to have any engines left back there." Latta replied immediately over the voice tube: "If we slow down we won't need those damn engines."

After that, the chief engineer squeezed out a few more turns. *Narwhal* cut through the water at the astonishing speed of 19.2 knots.

Latta evaded the destroyers. In the ensuing days, he delivered his cargo to various guerrilla units and then evacuated thirty-two people, including eight women, two small children, and an infant, who had been hiding from the Japanese for almost two years.

After a quick turn-around, Latta returned to the Philippines with guerrillas and another ninety tons of supplies. He evacuated other guerrillas and refugees, including three women and four children. On the way home, he battle-surfaced and sank an unescorted freighter, *Himeno Maru*, 834 tons.

Ike Holtz in *Tuna*, reassigned from Brisbane to Fremantle, left for patrol along the north coast of New Guinea. On the night of July 29, while running on the surface, *Tuna* was attacked by friendly aircraft which dropped first a flare and then four big lethal depth charges. Holtz dived. When he was passing 110 feet, the depth charges went off, badly damaging the ship. Holtz reurned to Brisbane for repairs, remaining seventeen days. Then he went to Darwin, refueled, and patrolled off Borneo. On return to Fremantle, Holtz was relieved and returned to the States for new construction.

The new skipper of *Tuna* was James Thomas Hardin from the class of 1929, who came from command of *R-4*. Hardin received orders to return *Tuna* to Pearl Harbor for overhaul. He patrolled home by way of Ambon and Molucca Passage with a distinguished passenger, his division commander, Dutch Will. Hardin attacked convoys on November 27 and December 12. Will was critical of both attacks. He credited Hardin with only damage to two ships for 12,000 tons. The postwar records gave Hardin credit for sinking *Tosei Maru*, 5,484 tons, during the December 12 attack.

Earle Clifford Hawk, who had commanded *S-26* when she was rammed and sunk off Panama, brought out a new boat, *Pompon*. On his first patrol from Brisbane, Hawk was aggressive, sinking a big freighter, *Thames Maru*, 5,871 tons.

On his second patrol, Hawk shifted to Christie's command, touching at Darwin to refuel. He made two attacks for zero results. On the first attack, he had three prematures out of four shots. After that—on his own—he deactivated the magnetic exploder. When he returned to Fremantle, Christie was not pleased and informed all his skippers that the magnetic exploder must be used. On his next patrol, Hawk laid a minefield off Indochina before going on to regular patrol. He battle-surfaced on two sampans, sinking both, but found no targets worthy of a torpedo and returned to Fremantle with only 750 gallons of fuel remaining. Christie relieved him of command, writing Lockwood that Hawk was "nonproductive." Hawk went to the Squadron Sixteen staff and later commanded a division.

Puffer's First Patrol

Marvin John Jensen, who had been exec on Anderson's *Thresher* for the first three war patrols in the early months of the war, including the severe depth-charging off Japan just prior to the Doolittle raid, arrived with a new boat, *Puffer*. After refueling at Darwin, he went to patrol in Makassar Strait. On the morning of October 9, he found a big tanker, *Hayatomo*, escorted by a 500-ton *Chidori*-class torpedo boat. On his first shots of the war, Jensen hit the tanker with two torpedoes. She didn't sink. He maneuvered for a second salvo. However, the escort got in the way, dropping depth charges. Jensen remained at periscope depth, trying to get off another shot at the tanker. While he was thus preoccupied, the escort came in for another run. This time it dropped six charges, in close. *Puffer* was not badly damaged. There were a few leaks, jammed planes, the usual electrical disconnects, and some flooding in the maneuvering room which required a bucket brigade. Jensen went deep—to 400 feet—planning to wait the torpedo boat out. If past experience was any guide, she would soon go away.

Not this time. The Japanese captain turned out to be one of the most persistent and determined submarine killers anyone had ever encountered. He evidently had excellent sonar operators, and sound conditions were favorable—for him. He remained overhead, pinging and dropping an occasional depth charge. Every time Jensen tried to maneuver, the torpedo boat picked him up again as though the sea were transparent. In desperation, Jensen dropped down to 500 feet. To reduce noise levels, he ordered the air conditioning shut down. The temperature in the boat climbed to an ovenlike 125 degrees. Hours dragged by. The men began wilting from heat and fatigue. That evening, while *Puffer* lay low, a second *Chidori*-type boat joined the first.

During the night, after being submerged some eighteen or twenty hours, Jensen and his exec, Franklin Grant Hess, lost control of discipline on *Puffer*. The strain and the heat rendered the normal leadership inoperative. "The worriers and the hurriers," the official submarine historian reported, "had all crapped out, leaving the plodders to bring home the ship." Both officers and men, the historian relates, were

mad at everything and anything. They were particularly mad at themselves for allowing themselves to be caught in such a situation. They cursed themselves for being such fools as to serve in submarines. They cursed the enemy for their persistence. They spent much time daydreaming about what they could do to the [torpedo boat] above them—discussing such fantastic schemes and ideas as discharging acid around the ship to eat holes in the hull.

Jensen and Hess tried to keep the crew together by broadcasting a play-by-play on the PA system, but the men resented this, believing the noise would help the enemy. In time, a good many were in a state of mental collapse. "From the stupor in which they sank," the historian related, "it became impossible to arouse them to go on watch. Toward the end, stations were manned by volunteers, and by men who had the stamina and will to move and think. Many of the others were past the stage of caring what happened."

During the late afternoon, Jensen considered the possibility of surfacing in daylight and fighting it out with his 3-inch deck gun. However, some of his officers and men believed this would be suicidal. Jensen polled the crew, an informal vote. Most said no, they would rather sweat it out. "In this connection," the historian relates, "one of the enlisted men [later reported] that he was asked by somebody to vote for or against an immediate rise to the surface. He reported that he was willing to go along either way but he refused to accept the responsibility of committing himself." Such was the disintegrating state of mind on *Puffer*.

All that night and the next day, they remained submerged at 500

LOSS OF CAPELIN AND CISCO

feet. After dark on the second day, Jensen and Hess had no choice left: it was surface or suffocate. He blew ballast and surfaced directly from deep submergence. *Puffer* had been down a record thirty-seven hours and forty-five minutes. One torpedo boat was picked up on radar, but Jensen outran him and escaped, returning directly to Fremantle.

When *Puffer* came into port, Christie had nothing but praise for the ship and her captain. He wrote in his diary that "strength of character . . . skill and experience and knowledge, the excellent state of training, saved the ship. . . . A brilliant job carried through by guts, determination and the inspired example of the Commanding Officer."

Christie's staff, meanwhile, conducted a thorough investigation of the episode. Those taking testimony then discovered the extent to which Jensen had lost control of the crew. In view of this and other factors, one *Puffer* officer suggested that the wardroom and crew be scattered to other boats. This was done, in part; Jensen was relieved of command, becoming an assistant to Murray Tichenor, but Hess remained as exec. Command of *Puffer* fell to Gordon Selby, who had been exec on the first patrol of *Billfish*.

For Selby, *Puffer* was a big challenge. Later he wrote, "I didn't have time to think about much of anything but *training* since I had at least a 50 percent turnover in officers and crew. And it was not only 'training' but 'retraining' since I felt it necessary to change attack procedures and various other things for psychological reasons."

Patrolling near Manila and in the Sulu Sea, Selby trained his crew and took on the enemy, firing at a destroyer and several freighters. When he returned to Fremantle, Christie credited the destroyer—an old one of 820 tons—and damage to four ships for 31,000 tons. In the postwar accounting, it was discovered that one of the damaged ships, the big 6,707-ton *Ryuyo Maru*, sank and Selby was so credited.

Loss of *Capelin* and *Cisco*

Christie, like Lockwood, was anxious to make a "brief" submarine war patrol. In October, a situation arose that seemed made to order. An air force B-24 crew went down on Celebes, where the men hid out, awaiting rescue. MacArthur ordered a submarine sent there to pick up the crew, leaving from and returning to Darwin.

Christie proposed to Carpender—by telephone—that he make this brief patrol. He believed he could fly to Darwin, join the submarine for the rescue mission, patrol Ambon, return to Darwin, and fly back to Fremantle, all in about twelve days. Carpender denied this request as he had others. Christie sent instead one of the new Squadron Sixteen division commanders, Philip Gardner ("P.G.") Nichols.

The submarine selected for this special mission was a new Squadron Sixteen boat, *Capelin*, commanded by Steam Marshall, who had made an Empire patrol on ancient *Cuttlefish*. His exec was Edward Dunbar Robertson.

P. G. Nichols joined *Capelin* in Darwin. She got under way on October 30. En route, the special mission to pick up the downed aviators was canceled. Marshall patrolled in Molucca Sea, around Ceram. On November 11, Armistice Day, Christie sent Marshall an Ultra reporting an important convoy off Ceram, escorted by two destroyers. "It was fifteen minutes late," Nichols recalled.

While Nichols watched, feeling rather like a fifth wheel, Marshall attacked the convoy. His first two torpedoes prematured, one on one side of his target, the other on the other. "After that we disconnected the Mark VI magnetic exploder," Nichols recalled, "and shot again for contact. He was running for the beach at Ceram, but we blew him up." Marshall claimed a second ship, but postwar analysis confirmed only one for 3,000 tons.

In the wake of the attack, the two destroyers attacked *Capelin* with depth charges. "We had a noisy bow plane," Nichols recalled, "and a defective conning tower hatch and radar tube." Nichols believed it would be prudent for Marshall to return to Darwin for repairs before continuing the patrol. After seventeen days, *Capelin* put into Darwin.

While there, Nichols telephoned Christie to report on the results of this first leg of the patrol, asking permission to make the second leg. Christie refused permission, informing Nichols that during his absence Christie's chief of staff, Tex McLean, had been ordered back to the States to command a new squadron of boats and that Nichols had been selected as McLean's replacement.

Nichols was somewhat astonished by all this, and a little disappointed. He was not one of Christie's admirers. He got off *Capelin* and returned to Fremantle to his new job.

Steam Marshall took *Capelin* to Makassar Strait. On December 1 *Capelin* encountered Tom Hogan in *Bonefish*, who was slashing away at a convoy, and Walt Griffith in *Bowfin*, returning from his famous first patrol off Indochina. Hogan had sunk two ships. Griffith was

LOSS OF CAPELIN AND CISCO

out of torpedoes and, having sighted both *Capelin* and *Bonefish*, continued on to Fremantle.

Later Hogan wrote:

On December 2, we sighted Capelin . . . *heading west about 10 miles off the coast. He was about 5 miles away and dove right away. By sonar I told him who I was, about the convoy, and named him by his nickname: "Steam." I told him that since he was in the area I was going to leave what was left of the convoy to him and would continue on to my patrol area. He receipted for the message by sonar. I left and did not see him again.*

Nor did anyone else. *Capelin* disappeared without a trace with all hands.

Another new Squadron Sixteen boat met much the same fate. It was *Cisco*, under the much-loved and much-respected Jim Coe, who had commanded *S-39* and *Skipjack* during the first year of the war.

After touching at Brisbane, *Cisco* topped off her fuel tanks in Darwin. Coe and his exec, August Frederick Weinel (who stood first in the class of 1936) left Darwin on September 18. That same evening, *Cisco* returned with a faulty main hydraulic system. After repairs, Coe sailed again the following day. According to his orders, on September 28 Coe should have been in the middle of the Sulu Sea, but nothing was ever heard from him.

In postwar Japanese records it was learned that on that date and at that place the Japanese discovered a U.S. submarine and delivered a well-coordinated air and sea attack. One Japanese pilot reported, "Found a sub trailing oil. Bombing. Ships cooperated with us. The oil continued to gush out, even on the 10th of October."

All things considered—submarine losses, the great number of torpedo failures—Christie's offensive against the Japanese tankers produced good results. Of forty-three ships sunk in the fall, twelve were tankers. Others had been damaged. The loss or delay in arrival of this oil was beginning to be felt at Truk and also in Japan itself. The pity was that the offensive had not been launched sooner. After the war the Strategic Bombing Survey reported, "Had submarines concentrated more effectively in the areas where tankers were in predominant use after mid-1942, oil imports probably could have been reduced sooner and the collapse of the fleet, the air arm, merchant shipping and all other activities dependent upon fuel oil hastened."

Christie, like Fife, had begun to experiment with cooperative patrolling. While the results thus far were less conclusive than the experiments by Fife, several of the Fremantle boats had clearly benefited from joint searching and exchange of information. Even so, Christie was not ready for formalized wolf packs.

Final Deactivation of the Mark VI Exploder

For Ralph Christie, the year 1943 ended with good news and bad news.

The good news was that Chips Carpender was relieved as MacArthur's naval chief—or Commander, 7th Fleet, as the unit was called. He was replaced by Husband Kimmel's brother-in-law, Thomas Kinkaid, an officer who had fought well and wisely in the Battle of the Coral Sea, the Solomons, and the Aleutians. Christie traveled cross-country to Brisbane to pay his respects to his new boss and then noted jubilantly in his diary, "This is a happy day for 7th Fleet! A new, fresh, good-natured attitude has come over the staff."

The bad news for Christie was that Admiral Kinkaid—under pressure from Lockwood and Nimitz—ordered him to deactivate the Mark VI magnetic exploder. As his diary noted, rather sadly, "Today, the long hard battle on the Mark VI magnetic feature ends—with defeat. I am forced to inactivate all magnetic exploders. We are licked." The war had been in progress almost two years when Christie received this order.

24

Pearl Harbor, September through December 1943

The U.S. Invasion of the Gilbert Islands

In September Admiral Nimitz was ready to proceed with the pioneering first step in his mid-Pacific island-hopping road to Japan, the invasion of the Gilbert Islands (Tarawa and Makin). Eleven fast aircraft carriers (including the old *Enterprise* and *Saratoga*) had reported to his command, plus new battleships, cruisers, destroyers, tankers, and eight of the new jeep carriers designed to provide close air support for infantry storming beachheads.

As a preliminary to the invasion, code-named Galvanic, the fast carriers, organized into small task forces, conducted three hit-and-run raids on the Gilberts and other islands. On August 31, they struck Marcus. On September 18, they hit Tarawa and Makin, joined by land-based bombers staging from Funafuti and Canton Islands. On October 5, they hit Wake. These raids provided both good photographic reconnaissance and invaluable combat experience for the green pilots on the new carriers. In addition, they destroyed many Japanese aircraft.

By this time, Admiral Koga had gathered the main units of his combined fleet at Truk. He was occupied primarily with the war in the south, the defense of the Solomons and the Bismarcks. However, following the strike on Wake, Koga mistakenly assumed the U.S. objective was an invasion there. On about October 18, he moved major units of his fleet from Truk to Eniwetok in the Marshalls in order to be in position to attack the U.S. invasion fleet. After about a week, he decided it was a false alarm and on October 24 returned his forces to Truk.

A week after that, Admiral Halsey's forces landed on Bougainville in the Solomons. Admiral Koga sent a force of cruisers south to Rabaul to prepare a counterattack. The codebreakers alerted Nimitz to this movement, and he sent one of the U.S. carrier task forces designated for Galvanic (*Saratoga* and *Princeton*) south to attack the cruisers in Rabaul. The task force badly mauled many of the cruisers, including *Agano*, which *Scamp* had intercepted and torpedoed while it was being towed back to Truk.

On November 20, the amphibious forces landed on Tarawa and Makin. The battle for Tarawa—heavily reinforced after the abortive *Nautilus-Argonaut* commando raid in August 1942—proved bloody. U.S. forces made many errors during—and after—the landings. About 1,000 marines and sailors died on Tarawa, and another 2,000 were wounded before a handful of Japanese troops (and Korean workers) finally surrendered.

When the landings took place, Admiral Koga's fleet at Truk was in no shape to do battle. All the carriers, including *Zuikaku*, had been stripped of aircraft to send to Rabaul. The large carrier *Zuiho* and two escort carriers, *Chuyo* and *Unyo*, arrived in Truk the day after the Tarawa invasion, November 21, with deckloads of planes, but these were not sufficient to mount a major counterattack. The cruiser force was badly damaged. *Atago, Mogami, Takao,* and *Tone* returned to Japan for repairs. The only ready forces were the giant battleship *Yamato* and her sister ship *Musashi,* four older battleships (*Nagato, Fuso, Kongo,* and *Haruna*), four heavy cruisers, and five light cruisers—not strong enough to send against carriers.

Unable to mount a naval attack, Admiral Koga attempted to reinforce the Gilberts with troops. On November 21, the light cruisers *Isuzu* and *Naka*, escorted by two destroyers, left Truk and picked up troops on Ponape to lift them to Tarawa. By the time these forces reached Kwajalein in the Marshalls, Tarawa had fallen, so the troops were debarked at Mili, to reinforce the Marshalls. The cruiser *Nagara* brought more troops to Kwajalein, followed by the heavy cruisers *Kumano, Chokai,* and *Chikuma* and the light cruiser *Noshiro*.

The only Japanese counterattacks on U.S. forces at Tarawa and

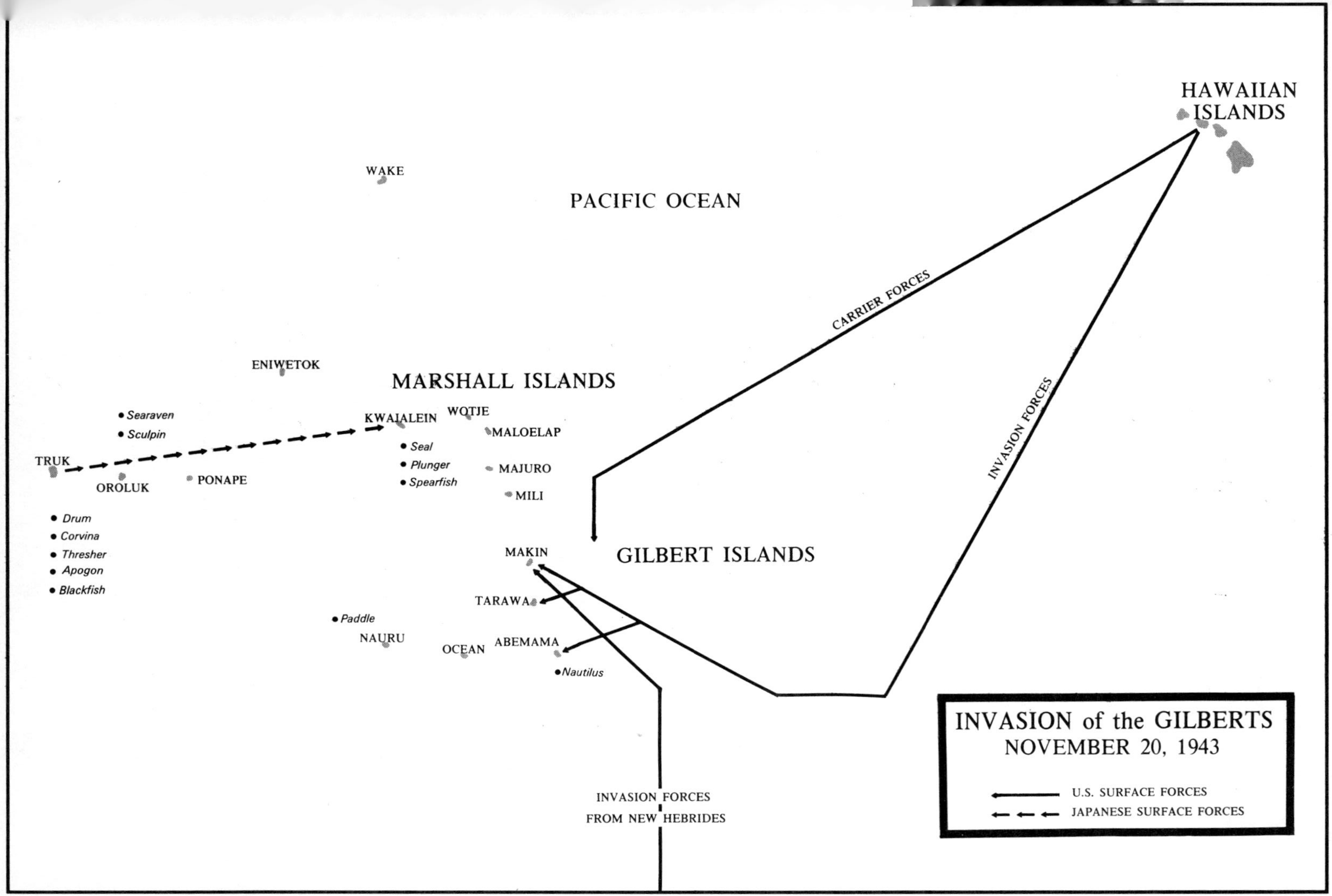
INVASION of the GILBERTS
NOVEMBER 20, 1943
U.S. SURFACE FORCES
JAPANESE SURFACE FORCES
HAWAIIAN ISLANDS
PACIFIC OCEAN
WAKE
CARRIER FORCES
INVASION FORCES
MARSHALL ISLANDS
GILBERT ISLANDS
ENIWETOK
KWAJALEIN
WOTJE
MALOELAP
MAJURO
MILI
TRUK
OROLUK
PONAPE
Searaven
Sculpin
Seal
Plunger
Spearfish
Drum
Corvina
Thresher
Apogon
Blackfish
MAKIN
TARAWA
ABEMAMA
OCEAN
NAURU
Paddle
Nautilus
INVASION FORCES
FROM NEW HEBRIDES

Makin were carried out by land-based aircraft, staging primarily from the Marshalls, and submarines. Most of the Japanese planes were shot down or beaten off, but one put a torpedo in the new light carrier *Independence*, causing damage that forced her to retire to Funafuti. Nine Japanese submarines (eight I-class, one RO-class) were sent. The codebreakers tracked these submarines with great precision, and U.S. forces destroyed all but three of them. One, *I-175*, attacked one of the eight jeep carriers, *Liscome Bay*. The little carrier blew up and sank with the loss of 644 men. *I-175* was slightly damaged in a depth-charge attack, but she was one of the three to survive.

Within about a week, the Gilberts were declared "secure." Some (notably U.S. Marine Corps General Holland M. Smith) would argue that the invasion had been an ill-conceived plan, that too much blood had been spilled for a worthless few acres of coral. Others (notably naval historian Samuel Eliot Morison) would argue that the Gilberts were a necessary stepping-stone for the capture of the Marshalls, next on Nimitz's agenda, and that the U.S. Navy and Marine Corps had learned invaluable lessons in amphibious warfare that would pay off in later campaigns.

Improvements in Submarine Weapons and Strategies

Meanwhile, Lockwood's Pearl Harbor submarine force, growing steadily in size every month, pressed the sea war against Japan. About a dozen boats were assigned directly in support of Galvanic, conducting photographic reconnaissance, landing commandos, broadcasting weather reports, and blockading Truk in hopes of sinking some of Admiral Koga's capital ships. Others preyed along the Japan-Truk shipping lanes, directed to targets by Ultra intercepts. A few were assigned to a new mission, "lifeguarding"—that is, standing off enemy islands during carrier air strikes to pick up U.S. pilots forced to ditch. Most continued regular war patrols in Empire and East China Sea waters, the Palaus, the Marianas, and the polar circuit. There were, as always, good patrols and bad.

By early September, Lockwood believed he had fixed the defects in the contact exploder. Four boats went to sea that month with new exploders hand-built by the Pearl Harbor torpedo shops. There was no spectacular upturn in results. As in the past, sinkings depended

IMPROVEMENTS IN WEAPONS AND STRATEGIES

on many factors: frequency of contacts, weather, position vis-à-vis the enemy, fire-control savvy, coolness under fire, torpedo maintenance, courage, and luck. What *was* important was that Lockwood's skippers put to sea for the first time in the war with growing confidence in the Mark XIV torpedo.

About the time this milestone was passed, another torpedo problem arose. The long-awaited electrics—the Mark XVIIIs—began to arrive in Pearl Harbor in a thin trickle. These mass-produced torpedoes were also full of bugs. Somewhat reluctantly, Lockwood sent some boats to sea with a mixed load of Mark XIVs and Mark XVIIIs, but at the same time he launched an intense debugging and test-firing program, carried to completion by Spike Hottel.* In addition, he set up training programs for fire-control parties so they could become used to firing the electrics, which were 10 to 15 knots slower than the steam torpedoes and whose speed was directly affected by the temperature of the seawater and the time elapsed since the last battery charge. Many more months would go by before the Mark XVIII would be accepted—and trusted—by the skippers.

During this same period, Lockwood had an abrupt change of heart about wolf-packing. Babe Brown, Swede Momsen, and others persuaded him to try packs. Japanese convoys were becoming larger and better organized with stronger escorting forces, including, in some cases, small carriers. Experience had proved that the submarine force needed more firepower to break up a big convoy. Brown and Momsen argued—logically—that several boats operating against a convoy not only brought more firepower to bear but also tended to be mutually supporting defensively: one boat could draw away escorts holding down and pounding another.

There was another major consideration. Pearl Harbor and Midway were now swelling with senior submariners with not much to do. Many had been appointed division commanders with important training jobs, but while the boats were gone there were many idle hands which were—in many cases—lifting too many glasses during too many leisure hours. Admiral King observed this concentration of brass during an inspection trip to Pearl Harbor and ordered Lockwood to trim it down drastically. Some of these men could be assigned to command wolf packs.

One of the most important innovations—or additions—to submarine strategy in the fall of 1943 was the belated realization that the bottleneck Luzon Strait, where so many convoy routes converged, was potentially a lucrative patrol area. A few skippers had tested the strait during preceding months of the year, notably Roy Gross in *Seawolf*. Almost all who had patrolled aggressively had had a superabundance of contacts which, because of torpedo problems and other factors, had not always been profitable. Now that story would change.

In another important innovation, Lockwood, following Jimmy Fife's lead, began to assign officers from the class of 1935 to command fleet boats. These men were about thirty years old, ten years younger than the skippers who began the war.* Most had made five or six war patrols as junior officers and execs and took considerable expertise into battle. Many wanted to prove that younger men could do better and that the class of 1935, in particular, would win the submarine war.

During the last four months of 1943, Lockwood mounted eighty-nine war patrols from Pearl Harbor and Midway, eleven of them by boats making first war patrols with green crews. This averaged about twenty-two boats per month. There were thirty-nine zero runs, or about 42 percent, some of them special missions in connection with Galvanic. The others accounted for ninety-nine confirmed ships sunk, slightly better than one ship per war patrol.

There were three losses—one of them especially painful to the force.

Wahoo's Last Patrol

Mush Morton in *Wahoo*, smarting from his luckless fourth patrol in the Sea of Japan in August, asked to return there. Lockwood gave his permission, assigning Eugene Sands in *Sawfish* to go with him. Although the Mark XVIII electric torpedo had not yet been debugged, Lockwood suggested that Morton and Sands take along a mixed load of these and Mark XIVs.

Sawfish and *Wahoo* got under way about September 10, going by different routes to La Pérouse Strait. Morton went into the Japan Sea first, with Sands following by a few days. Nothing further was ever heard from Morton.

On October 5, the Japanese news agency Domei announced to the world that a "steamer" was sunk by an American submarine off the

---

* More youthful skippers also meant more youthful wardrooms and crews, since officers had to be less senior than the skipper. (When two men were from the same class, the one with the higher class rank was senior.) In addition, by mid-1943, many of the older and "extremely cautious" chief petty officers had been sent to shore duty, replaced by younger regular navy men who fleeted up or by the many reserve enlisted men who entered the submarine service following the outbreak of war.

west coast of Honshu near Tsushima Strait, with the loss of 544 lives. This was the 8,000-ton *Konron Maru*. In addition, JANAC showed that Morton sank three other ships for 5,300 tons, making the total for this last patrol four ships for about 13,000 tons.

Japanese records also reported that on October 11, the date *Wahoo* was due to exit through La Pérouse, an antisubmarine aircraft found a submarine and attacked, dropping three depth charges. After Lockwood examined these records, he concluded that this attack fatally holed *Wahoo* and that she plunged to the bottom in the strait, taking down "Mush the Magnificent" and all hands.

Meanwhile, Sands in *Sawfish* experienced enough torpedo problems to drive an ordinary man berserk. During his eighteen days in or near the Sea of Japan, he made contact with an estimated eighteen ships. He made seven attacks, three against one freighter. Three electrics fishtailed while leaving the tubes, struck the shutters, and "were not heard to run thereafter." One electric plunged straight to the bottom. Seven electrics ran astern of the intended targets. The first Mark XIV broached and ran erratically. In a spread of three Mark XIVs, two hit the targets but were duds.

In his seven attacks, Sands had inflicted no damage on the enemy. When he returned to port, his patrol was declared unsuccessful. In his endorsement to the patrol report, Gin Styer wrote, "The fourth war patrol of the *Sawfish* is one of the first in which the Mark XVIII torpedoes were extensively employed. The results were disappointing, and indications are that considerable testing and proof firing will be necessary before the Mark XVIII is satisfactory for service use."

The loss of Morton and *Wahoo* caused profound shock in the submarine force. Lockwood and Voge ceased all further forays into the Sea of Japan. Morton was posthumously awarded a fourth Navy Cross. When he died, his claimed sinkings exceeded those of any other submarine skipper: seventeen ships for 100,000 tons. In the postwar accounting, this was readjusted to nineteen ships for about 55,000 tons, leaving Morton, in terms of individual ships sunk, one of the top three skippers of the war.

Ultra-directed Patrols

The codebreakers continued to supply the submarines with Ultra information resulting in attacks on major Japanese fleet units.

A new Squadron Sixteen boat, *Cabrilla*, patrolled from Pearl Harbor to Fremantle. Her skipper, Douglas Thompson Hammond, came from the Atlantic S-boats. On September 24, an Ultra put him on the track of two escort carriers en route from Truk to Japan. Hammond made contact north of the Bonins. He planned to fire his bow tubes at one carrier and his stern tubes at another, but one of the destroyer escorts came too close, so he settled for firing six bow tubes from a sharp angle at one carrier, range 1,000 yards. After he fired, Hammond went deep.

Returning to periscope depth, Hammond found the carrier motionless in the water and down by the stern. The undamaged carrier took the damaged one in tow and proceeded northward at a speed of 5 knots. Wary of the destroyer escort, Hammond did not make a second attack but surfaced and trailed, getting off a contact report. Then he lost the carriers in a rainsquall.

Farther north, Tommy Dykers in *Jack* patrolled off Honshu, still bedeviled by H.O.R. engine problems. When he received word of Hammond's attack on the two carriers, he plotted an intercept course and waited. On September 28 the force came limping along as predicted. Dykers set up and fired at one of the destroyer escorts, but he had chosen an unfavorable position, range 3,200 yards, and the destroyer charged. *Jack* was pinned down for five hours while the carriers went on by without harm.

When Dykers got back to Pearl Harbor, his division commander, Freddy Warder, wrote a severely critical endorsement. Dykers returned *Jack* to Mare Island as scheduled for new engines.

Hammond on *Cabrilla* continued to Fremantle by way of the Philippines and went on one more patrol in the South China Sea, where he planted a minefield and sank a 2,700-ton ship. After that, Christie somewhat reluctantly relieved Hammond, noting in his diary, "I had to take his command from him—a swell officer but not aggressive enough." Hammond returned to Washington for duty in the antisubmarine warfare section.

On October 16, Ralph Clinton ("Red") Lynch, Jr., making his second patrol in the H.O.R. boat *Mingo*, patrolled off Guam. *Mingo*, Lynch said later, "had the worst engines of the lot . . . an extreme danger to the ship and crew during the first two patrols." Lynch was directed to a large aircraft carrier on a northerly course, making 19 knots. He chased for forty-five minutes, trying to gain a favorable firing position, but was unsuccessful. In desperation he fired six torpedoes set on low speed, range 6,500 yards. Seven minutes later (it seemed like a week to Lynch), he heard and saw two "low order" hits on the carrier's port bow, and she swung left, stopped, and showed a distinct list to port. Then the carrier got under way again, trimmed down by the bow.

When Lynch returned to Pearl Harbor, he was given credit for damage to a 17,500-ton carrier and ordered to take *Mingo* back to Mare Island to have her engines replaced. During the long refit, Lynch left the boat and went to Fife's staff in Brisbane as operations officer.

Nearby, on October 18, the indefatigable Donc Donaho was directed by an Ultra to another aircraft carrier. Donaho, taking *Flying Fish* to the Palaus on his sixth war patrol (*Flying Fish*'s seventh), picked the carrier up by radar north of Saipan early in the morning. He tracked by radar, closing to 9,000 yards and then submerging.

Donaho had his six bow tubes loaded with new electric torpedoes, some of the first to arrive at Pearl Harbor. He fired six. At the moment of firing, the carrier zigged away. Donaho's sonarman reported at least three of the electrics ran erratically. Inside the hull, the crew could plainly hear the whine of torpedo propellers. Donaho had to go deep to avoid his own torpedoes, hearing as he did so one "unmistakable" hit in the carrier. He returned to periscope depth, but before he could raise the periscope, *Flying Fish* was rocked by a tremendous explosion. Donaho was certain that one of his own torpedoes had exploded nearby. Luckily, it did no damage.

Going on to the Palaus, Donaho conducted another aggressive patrol, firing the rest of his torpedoes. On return to Pearl Harbor, he was credited with sinking one ship, confirmed in postwar records, and with damage to the carrier and two freighters. He was promoted to command a new division of submarines.

Tom Wogan in *Tarpon*, patrolling off Honshu, also received an Ultra intercept on a carrier, probably the same one Donaho shot at. He made contact on October 20 and fired all four bow tubes. All missed. It was the second time in as many patrols that Wogan had encountered carriers off Honshu with zero results.

About this same time, Wogan sank a ship that was a mystery for many years. He found it at night: large, unescorted, fast-moving. Wogan fired four torpedoes, obtaining two hits. The damaged ship then turned toward *Tarpon* to ram, forcing *Tarpon* deep. After a while, Wogan came back to periscope depth and fired two separate up-the-kilt shots. Both missed. The ship then opened fire on *Tarpon*'s periscope with 6-inch guns. Wogan fired another single shot, obtaining a hit on the stern. When this appeared to stop the gunfire, Wogan circled the target and let go another torpedo, which hit and sank the ship.

Although the codebreakers had no record of this ship and noted no distress calls, Lockwood nonetheless credited Wogan with sinking one 10,000-ton Japanese "naval auxiliary." In the postwar analysis, it was discovered that the ship was not Japanese but German. She was the heavily armed *Michel*, the last of the merchant raiders, come around via the Indian Ocean to bring high-priority cargo to Japan. She was the first—and one of the few—German ships sunk by U.S. submarines in World War II, all in the Pacific.

Bill Post in *Gudgeon*, en route to the East China Sea, received an Ultra on a "damaged" enemy carrier proceeding northward to Japan—probably the one Donaho hit earlier. Post found it in the northern Bonins on November 9, range 12 miles, surrounded by many escorts. Despite a great—and bold—try on Post's part, *Gudgeon* was not able to penetrate the screen and attack. Post surfaced in broad daylight to chase, but a trawler forced him to dive and he lost contact. He got off a contact report and then went on to another aggressive patrol.

Halibut patrolled off Bungo Suido with a new skipper, Ignatius Joseph ("Pete") Galantin, who had made one patrol with Lucius Chappell on *Sculpin*. Early on the morning of November 5, Galantin received an Ultra on a Japanese task force coming up from the south. It consisted of a large carrier and several battleships, cruisers, and destroyers. Later Galantin wrote:

The contact was made shortly before dawn, giving little time for surface tracking. . . . We dived dead ahead of the formation, passed close down the port hand of the cruiser and headed for the carrier. We did not do well on that attack. Unknown to us then, the few radar ranges we had obtained were not on the carrier but on the lofty, massive battleship on the same bearing beyond the carrier. Fired six torpedoes from the bow tubes, but only one hit, far aft on the starboard side. Had only two torpedoes left in the stern tubes but swung rapidly around and fired them, apparently for hits on the carrier or other heavy ships in the melee. As soon as our sole remaining torpedo was reloaded forward, had the carrier broadside to, only 2,000 yards away, only to have a hot run in the tube! As I recall it, when I got back to Pearl I was told the Japs succeeded in getting the carrier in, drawing about 40 feet [of water] aft.

Dace, another new boat and a happy ship, was commanded by Joseph Francis Enright. As a morale-booster, Enright had obtained a slot machine. Everywhere *Dace* stopped—Panama, Pearl Harbor, Midway—the crew put the slot machine on deck for the amusement of local relief crews. It generated enormous illegal sums—up to $150 a day—which went into a slush fund for luxuries such as exotic canned seafood, cigarettes and cigars, and all the beer and liquor the crew could possibly drink ashore.

Off Honshu, Enright received an Ultra on November 15, reporting an enemy carrier movement. Enright found the carrier, escorted by several destroyers. He believed it was *Shokaku*. He made a halfhearted attempt to close, but with morning light coming on, he dived and the carrier got away. (A carrier he believed to be *Shokaku* also escaped Merrill Kinsell Clementson, who had relieved St. Angelo on *Snapper* and who made contact on the same day; she zigged out of range before he could attack.)

On November 19, when Enright picked up a tanker and made an approach, four escorts pinned *Dace* down and delivered a punishing depth-charge attack. Enright escaped into a huge, noisy school of shrimp and shook his attackers, but the experience (as he said years later) shattered his self-confidence, and on his return he asked to be relieved of command. The request was granted, and Enright went to a staff job.

Davenport, Dornin, and Cutter

Discrepancies between skippers' reports of what they had sunk and postwar Japanese confirmations were routine—but no case was more striking than Roy Davenport's on his two patrols off Truk in *Haddock* in the fall of 1943, before the invasion of Tarawa. Both lasted twenty-seven days. Both were eminently successful, according to Davenport's reports. They earned him two Navy Crosses and high praise and, together with his past patrols, they established him as one of Pearl Harbor's leading aces. However, postwar records denied all his claims.

During the first patrol, Davenport reported, he sighted an escorted ship on September 15, and fired four torpedoes from 3,000 yards, obtaining two hits. Fire appeared to break out, and the ship turned to ram. Davenport fired two more torpedoes down the throat from 1,700 yards and then went deep. On September 20 he attacked a very large tanker, described as *Tonan Maru II*, 19,000 tons, firing six torpedoes, range 3,700 yards. Davenport reported:

At least three certain hits were seen and heard, and the confusion of internal explosions did not permit us to note if another torpedo had hit or not.... Target burst into flames that enveloped the entire ship for several seconds, and then fires broke out all over the vessel. There were many internal explosions. Radar immediately reported target sinking, and from the bridge it was observed to sink bow first about four minutes after it was hit.

The following night, Davenport attacked a two-ship convoy with two escorts. He fired four torpedoes, range 3,000 yards, all misses. Next day he attacked again, firing four bow torpedoes from 3,000 yards and then four stern torpedoes from 1,500 yards.

Three torpedoes were seen to hit from the first batch. Four hits were seen from stern shot. This target was observed to sink both by sight and radar within a minute. Four torpedoes must have ripped her to pieces. The Number One target [the bow shot] started to go down immediately but it wasn't until about five minutes after it was first hit that it was observed to sink by sight and radar.

With all torpedoes expended, he returned to Midway.

Davenport returned to Truk for a second patrol there. On the night of November 1, Davenport reported, he picked up a two-ship convoy: a freighter and troopship, possibly escorted. He made a night surface attack, firing five torpedoes from 3,100 yards at the troopship and a single torpedo from a range of 4,150 yards at the freighter. "The freighter sank immediately," Davenport wrote, "as witnessed by sight and radar. The troopship began immediately to sink and was badly on fire. It was observed to sink by sight and radar within fifteen minutes... many survivors [were] in the water."

The following night, Davenport reported, three destroyers came to the area where he had sunk the two ships. Davenport thought it was a "killer group" out looking for *Haddock*. The destroyers sighted *Haddock* and charged. Davenport fired four torpedoes at one of the destroyers from a range of 2,000 yards. "The first torpedo hit the target in the middle," he wrote, "and he was observed to sink by sight and radar within thirty seconds."

On the night of November 5, Davenport stated, he found a convoy of two tankers, one escort. Davenport ordered a three-ship setup: Three bow torpedoes for each of the tankers, four stern tubes for the escort. The bow tubes were fired from a range of 3,000 yards, the stern tubes from 4,000 yards. Davenport reported he missed the escort but got hits on each of the tankers. After reloading his last four torpedoes, he fired two more at each of the tankers from a range of about 3,000 yards. "The [near] target was observed to sink by sight and radar within a minute. The [far] target was observed to sink by sight and radar within about eight minutes."

With all torpedoes again expended, Davenport returned to Pearl Harbor. In these two patrols, Davenport was credited with sinking a total of eight ships for 71,000 tons, including the destroyer, plus damage to one other vessel for 4,000 tons.

When postwar Japanese records failed to confirm any of these eight ships, Davenport said, "We were fortunate on these two patrols . . . to be on the surface during attacks. We saw by sight and radar that the ships sank. In connection with the tankers . . . there was an apparent attempt by the Japanese to continue to use ship calls of these two vessels to lead U.S. forces to think they were still in service." Davenport's two execs backed his judgment.

By now, Davenport had made eight consecutive war patrols, four as Burlingame's exec, four as commanding officer of *Haddock*. At his own request, he returned to the States for a rest and new construction.

After Roy Benson left *Trigger*, Lockwood gave the boat to Dusty Dornin, who had made six war patrols on *Gudgeon* before starting the TDC school at Pearl Harbor. He was the first officer from the class of 1935 to command a Pearl Harbor boat. Ned Beach, now a veteran of six war patrols, remained on *Trigger* as exec. In the fall of 1943 Dornin made two really spectacular patrols, both in the East China Sea.

On the evening of September 17, Dornin found an unescorted two-ship convoy and attacked. Using the Morton-O'Kane technique of exec on periscope or on the bridge, Dornin fired four torpedoes—his first of the war as skipper—at one ship. He got two hits, but both were duds. The ship turned to ram, firing deck guns, and Dornin submerged, ordering tubes reloaded. Shortly after midnight, he swung in for a second attack by periscope, firing four torpedoes. Two hit. "The target sank in two minutes," Dornin reported. "All hands in the conning tower got a look. . . . Have heard of targets sinking fast, but this is the first time this ship or this Commanding Officer has ever experienced such a thing. It seems very unreal."

For the next few days, *Trigger* was buffeted and held down by heavy weather, the fringes of a typhoon passing to eastward. However, on September 21 *Trigger* picked up another convoy: six ships with air escort. It was composed of one very large tanker, two smaller tankers, and three old freighters. Dornin moved *Trigger* in for a night surface attack, firing the rest of his torpedoes in a period of three and a half hours. Three confirmed ships went down, two tankers and a freighter. Total for the patrol: four ships for 27,095 tons. In terms of confirmed tonnage sunk, it was the third best war patrol thus far—after Wogan on *Tarpon's* sixth patrol (27,910 tons) and Burlingame on *Silverside's* fourth (27,798).

Dornin returned *Trigger* to Midway on September 30. On that very day, his classmate and football buddy, Slade Cutter, assumed command of *Seahorse* from Donald McGregor. Both men had much to celebrate, and they did so with gusto.

Trigger and *Seahorse* set off for patrol two days apart, *Seahorse* on October 20, *Trigger* on October 22. Dornin retained Beach for his exec; Cutter's exec was John Patterson ("Speed") Currie. Cutter said later, "I trained my *Seahorse* crew the same way I did my battleship *Idaho* football team years before. On each training period we would start with the individual and the fundamentals, then on to department training, then molding all departments into a team for surface gunfire and another team for battle stations, torpedo. The important thing was to develop in each man self-confidence and confidence in his team."

On the way to station, while still several hundred miles off the coast of Japan, Cutter sighted an unarmed fishing trawler. He was hesitant about attacking this puny target, but his young officers were hungry for battle so he ordered battle surface. The trawler went down, leaving nine fishermen in the water. Later, the gun crew sank another from the same little fleet.

His officers, Cutter recalled later, "loved gun action." When another trawler came into sight, they made ready for battle again. However, Cutter had been sickened by the slaughter and decided not to attack. Later he said, "One of my officers came to me with our operation order, which said something like 'You shall sink all vessels encountered, by torpedoes or gunfire.' He argued that these boats were feeding the Japanese and might be serving as aircraft and submarine warning patrols. So I said, 'Oh, hell,' or something like that and ordered battle stations surface. Another trawler went down. No survivors." All this was too bloodthirsty for Cutter. He never authorized another gun attack.

While Dornin and Cutter were proceeding westward, Pete Galantin in *Halibut*, patrolling off Bungo Suido, got on the trail of a large well-escorted convoy. He made a daylight attack, but the convoy veered away, leaving *Halibut* out in left field. Galantin fired a long-range low-speed shot which may have hit a freighter. Escorts pinned him down, but after dark he surfaced, continued trailing, and got off a contact report to Lockwood.

On the night of November 1-2, both Dornin and Cutter (unaware of the other's presence) stumbled into this convoy and attacked. Dornin shot first, sinking a large transport and a freighter, damaging others. Cutter, somewhat mystified by Dornin's initial torpedo explosion, shot next, sinking a large freighter and transport, damaging others. Pete Galantin in *Halibut* finally caught up and also attacked, sinking one freighter. Total: five ships, 26,400 tons.

Because of a rare lapse in Dick Voge's efficient staff organization, there was an amusing aftermath to this engagement which gave rise to another submarine legend that died hard. After receiving word from both Dornin and Cutter on their attacks, a junior officer on Voge's staff wondered if they might not be claiming the same ships sunk, so without Voge's knowledge he naïvely—and stupidly—sent each skipper a dispatch raising the question. This was the first indication to both Cutter and Dornin that they had attacked the same convoy. Dornin reacted calmly, but Cutter, who could be a bull in a china shop on occasion, was indignant that Pearl Harbor had questioned his veracity. He responded with a furious message. The following night, Lockwood, having upbraided the junior officer who caused the flap, sent an apology to Dornin and Cutter. All submarines on patrol copied these messages, and many skippers had a good laugh. But the episode gave rise to a myth that Dornin and Cutter delighted in poaching on one another's areas.

Following this, Dornin and Cutter went on to adjacent areas in the East China Sea, while Galantin returned to Bungo Suido. Dornin sank two additional ships and Cutter three, including a big tanker. Dornin's total confirmed score: four ships for 15,114 tons; Cutter's: five ships, 27,579 tons, one of the best patrols of the war. In terms of confirmed tonnage, Cutter's patrol now ranked third—after Wogan's and Burlingame's.

Special Missions

Two boats, *Nautilus* and *Skate*, carried out special missions before Operation Galvanic, the invasion of the Gilberts; *Nautilus* and nine others also had special assignments during the invasion.

In preparation for the landing on Tarawa, Lockwood assigned *Nautilus* to make detailed reconnaissance photographs of the beaches. Some submarine skippers in the past—notably Lew Parks in *Pompano*—had made periscope pictures of enemy-held beaches, but it was still a primitive art. Nobody had ever before obtained really good pictures.

The new skipper of *Nautilus*, William Davis Irvin, and his exec, Richard Barr ("Ozzie") Lynch, prepared for this mission with great care. Irvin, then one of the oldest submarine skippers at Pearl Harbor (class of 1927), was a stickler for detail. Lynch, fortunately, was an enthusiastic amateur shutterbug. He supervised the installation of camera mounts on the periscope and the creation of a darkroom in the lower sonar room.

Off the beaches at Tarawa, Lynch and a navy photographer assigned to the mission set to work with navy-issue cameras. Lynch found to his dismay that none of the three navy-issue cameras would work. He tried his own camera, a German-made Primaflex. It proved ideal. Irvin and Lynch returned with excellent detailed photographs of the beaches at Tarawa and the outlying islands which proved most of the charts to be grossly in error.

Lockwood and Voge recommended that the navy adopt the Primaflex for submarine photography, but no new cameras could be found. By advertising in various photographic trade journals for used Primaflexes, however, ten cameras were obtained that were used on all future submarine photo missions. "Thus a camera made in [Nazi] Germany," the submarine historian wrote, "contributed to the downfall of Japan." The contribution was slight.

* * *

Skate, a brand-new boat commanded by an old hand, Eugene McKinney, who began the war at Manila in *Salmon*, lifeguarded at Wake Island October 5 during the carrier strike. While the planes thundered overhead, bombing and strafing Wake, McKinney waited submerged, directly off the beach. Two or three U.S. Navy pilots bailed out. When McKinney believed the navy "had control of the air," he surfaced and approached one pilot, who was lying in a rubber raft. About that time, a Japanese Zero came out of the clouds, strafing. McKinney resubmerged in a hurry. Going down, he discovered that one of his junior officers, Willis Edward Maxson III, had been hit in the back by a Japanese bullet.

During the day, while Maxson received medical aid from the pharmacist's mate, McKinney tried to carry out his mission. Again and again enemy planes drove him under. That night, he surfaced and reported Maxson's wounds. Lockwood made arrangements for *Skate* to rendezvous with a destroyer to transfer Maxson following the attack on the second day. If the rendezvous failed to come off, McKinney was to return to Midway at full speed.

The next day, while the planes again thundered overhead, McKinney changed his tactics. He came to the surface "flooded down," with only the bridge and bow out of the water. A three-man rescue party clung to the bow; McKinney alone manned the bridge. That day, McKinney picked up two naval aviators, Lieutenant H. J. Kicker and Ensign M. H. Tyler. An attempt to rescue a third aviator was thwarted by another Japanese plane, which forced McKinney under and dropped two bombs.

That night Maxson, who insisted that McKinney stay at Wake, took a turn for the worse. McKinney decided to retire to Midway at full speed. However, about that same time, the carrier force reported to Lockwood that nine more aviators were down off Wake. Lockwood had a difficult decision to make: rescue the aviators or let *Skate* continue on to Midway, where Maxson could receive medical attention. He decided that *Skate* should continue her mission. Not many hours after McKinney received this tough news, Maxson died. *Skate* would not have reached Midway in time to save his life.

During the next few days McKinney committed Maxson's body to the deep and rescued four more aviators. One of these was Lieutenant Commander Mark Alfred Grant, and Air Group Commander from *Lexington*. In gratitude, the carrier's skipper, Captain Felix Budwell Stump, sent McKinney a message: ANYTHING ON LEXINGTON IS YOURS

FOR THE ASKING. IF IT IS TOO BIG TO CARRY AWAY WE WILL CUT IT UP IN SMALL PARTS.

McKinney transferred his aviators and went on to patrol off Truk.

The first of the ten Pearl Harbor submarines assigned special tasks during the invasion of the Gilberts was William Irvin's *Nautilus*. Again converted to a troop transport, she played a direct role, taking aboard seventy-eight men of the Marine Amphibious Reconnaissance Company, commanded by Captain J. L. Jones, whose mission was to reconnoiter the outlying island of Abemama. She went by way of Tarawa, performing lifeguard duty during the carrier strikes on the two days preceding the invasion.

On the night before the invasion, as *Nautilus* was making her way through a designated safety lane toward Abemama, she suddenly came nose to nose with two friendly ships in the vanguard of the main invasion force, the cruiser *Santa Fe* and destroyer *Ringgold*. *Ringgold* knew of the *Nautilus* mission but had been incorrectly informed that she was off someplace else rescuing a downed aviator. Believing *Nautilus* to be a Japanese patrol boat, *Ringgold* opened fire with her 5-inch guns.

Irvin reacted quickly. Although he was in shallow water and close to a reef, he fired off a green recognition signal and dived. Before he got under, one shell hit *Nautilus*. Fortunately it was a dud, later found and put on display at the Pearl Harbor Submarine Base. However, the salvo had distracted Irvin's crew. On the way down, *Nautilus* partially flooded the conning tower and the main induction. A second salvo ruptured a waterline and started leaks in the bilges. While the damage control party made repairs, Irvin fought to keep *Nautilus* from sinking forever.

This unexpected salute from friendly forces frightened the troops on board. As Captain Jones later understated it, "The seventy-eight Marines we had on board were stoic but they were unanimous in the attitude that they would much prefer a rubber boat on a very hostile beach to their present predicament. We managed to assure them they would get their boat ride and it was certain none of them would be hesitant about leaving the ship when the landing came."

When he got *Nautilus* under control, Irvin evaded the friendly surface craft and worked his way toward his objective. He reached Abemama the following afternoon, hours behind schedule, and the marines landed. *Nautilus* remained on station. On the following day,

SPECIAL MISSIONS

at Captain Jones's request, Irvin accurately bombarded the Japanese defenses with his two 6-inch guns, killing and wounding fourteen men. Afterward, he picked up two wounded marines and returned to Pearl Harbor.

The other nine boats supporting the invasion took station at various islands to the north and northwest of Tarawa to interdict the expected Japanese reinforcements or a thrust against the invasion force by a Japanese fleet. Three boats, Harry Hull's *Thresher*, just returned from a long overhaul, and two brand-new boats, *Apogon* and *Corvina* (sponsored by Ralph Christie's wife), were assigned to the waters off Truk. (*Apogon* was commanded by Walter Paul Schoeni, who had commanded S-33; *Corvina* was commanded by Roderick Shanahan Rooney, who had served on Bill Brockman's *Nautilus*.) They were augmented by two of Fife's Brisbane boats, John Davidson's *Blackfish* and *Drum*, now commanded by Delbert Fred Williamson. Hull in *Thresher* sank a 4,800-ton freighter off Truk; Schoeni in *Apogon* sank a 3,000-ton freighter north of Ponape.

Corvina was lost south of Truk. William Kinsella, exec on *Blackfish*, recalled:

We were south of Truk with Drum *and* Corvina *when we got an Ultra stating that a Japanese submarine was coming through the area. We were supposed to rendezvous with* Drum *and* Corvina. *Just after sunset we got into position where this Japanese submarine was supposed to pop up and sure enough, just at sunset, while we were submerged, it surfaced just to the south of us, not more than 5,000 yards away. It was starting to get dark, and we really could not see through the periscope well enough to ascertain that it was a Japanese submarine. Remembering that* Drum *and* Corvina *were in the vicinity we elected not to shoot. . . . As it turned out, we later established contact with* Drum *and determined it was not him. It was Japanese. We never did see* Corvina *again. . . . The Jap sub got her.*

The Japanese submarine was *I-176*. It reported, according to postwar Japanese records, that on November 16 it found a U.S. submarine on the surface and fired three torpedoes that hit, "causing a great explosion sound." *Corvina* was the only U.S. submarine positively known to be lost to a Japanese submarine in the war. Ironically, she was lost to the sub she had been sent to sink.

* * *

Drum was almost lost. A day or so after *Corvina* was sunk, Williamson attacked a convoy off Truk, sinking the huge supply ship *Hie Maru*, 11,621 tons. Destroyers counterattacked, delivering a depth-charging that blasted the paint off *Drum*'s interior bulkheads. Two days after the invasion, *Drum* attacked another convoy. Four subchasers boxed her in and delivered four massive depth charges. They exploded with such fury that the conning tower was almost crushed. Williamson got away, made temporary repairs, and limped into Pearl Harbor, where Lockwood sent *Drum* to Mare Island for a new conning tower.

Lockwood placed two submarines, *Searaven* and *Sculpin*, directly east of Truk, near the islands of Oroluk and Ponape. Both boats were commanded by new skippers. Fred Connaway, who had made a PCO run with Dick Peterson in *Sunfish*, commanded *Sculpin*. Melvin Hulquist Dry, who had been Junior McCain's exec on *Gunnel*, commanded *Searaven*. Dry sank a 10,000-ton tanker off Ponape. Connaway was not so lucky.

Embarked on Connaway's *Sculpin* was a senior officer, John Philip Cromwell, then commanding Division 43. Lockwood had sent Cromwell on *Sculpin* in case he wanted to form a wolf pack of *Sculpin* and *Searaven* or possibly *Sculpin* and *Apogon*. Cromwell had been fully briefed on all the plans for Galvanic and knew much more about Ultra than the ordinary submarine skipper.

On the night of November 18, two days after *Corvina* had been sunk by *I-176*, Connaway picked up a convoy en route from Truk to the Marshalls. He bent on full power to make an end around and get into position for a submerged attack at dawn. As he was preparing to attack, the convoy saw *Sculpin*'s periscope and turned toward the submarine as if to ram. Connaway went deep. When the convoy had passed over, he surfaced to make another end around in broad daylight.

The convoy commander was a clever fighter. He had left a "sleeper" behind, the destroyer *Yamagumo*. It spotted *Sculpin* and attacked, forcing Connaway to make a quick dive. *Yamagumo* dropped a barrage of depth charges, causing some damage. Connaway went deep to avoid, remaining submerged for several hours.

About noon, Connaway decided to come up again and have a look around. As he was rising, the depth gauge stuck at 125 feet. Not realizing this, the temporary diving officer, Ensign W. M. Fielder, a reservist, kept pumping water overboard and planing up. So deceived, Fielder broached the boat, and *Yamagumo*, which was still lurking nearby, charged immediately.

As Connaway hurriedly took *Sculpin* back down, eighteen depth charges exploded all around the boat, inflicting severe damage. There were serious leaks, and the planes and steering gear went out of commission. Connaway decided his best course was to surface and try to brazen it out with his deck gun. He passed the order and brought *Sculpin* back to the surface.

It was a one-sided engagement, with *Sculpin* the loser. One of *Yamagumo*'s first salvos hit the bridge, killing Connaway, his exec, Nelson John Allen, and the gunnery officer, Joseph Rollie DeFrees, Jr., son of a rear admiral. Command of *Sculpin* passed to the senior officer, Lieutenant G. E. Brown, Jr., another reservist. He decided to scuttle and passed the word: "Abandon ship." The crew struggled into life jackets, and the chief of the boat opened the vents.

Division Commander John Cromwell, only thirteen days at sea on his first war patrol, was in a predicament. If he abandoned ship and was taken prisoner, the Japanese might torture him and obtain not only the secrets of Operation Galvanic but also the secrets of Ultra. He told Brown that he "knew too much" and elected to go down with *Sculpin*. Ensign Fielder, perhaps feeling responsible for the disaster, made the same decision. These two and ten others—some dead, some probably fearing capture—rode the ship down for the last time.

In all, half of *Sculpin*'s total crew of eighty-four officers and men were rescued by the Japanese: Brown and two other officers and thirty-nine enlisted men. Of these, one crewman, badly wounded, was thrown over the side. Another, also wounded, managed to escape this fate by wrenching free and hiding among the other crewmen of *Sculpin*. The surviving forty-one were taken into Truk, where for ten days they were interrogated by Japanese intelligence officers. After this grilling, they were divided into two groups for transport to Japan on two of the carriers that had ferried aircraft to Truk: twenty-one on *Chuyo*, twenty on *Unyo*.

Later, when Lockwood learned what had happened on *Sculpin*, he recommended John Cromwell for the Medal of Honor. It was approved and awarded to his widow after the war.

Three of the ten boats assigned to support Galvanic were stationed in the Marshalls. These were Benny Bass's *Plunger*; *Spearfish*, commanded by Joseph Warford Williams, Jr.; and *Seal*, commanded by

Harry Benjamin Dodge. *Plunger* covered the island of Mili, *Spearfish* Jaluit, and *Seal* Kwajalein. Twice Dodge in *Seal* encountered the cruisers Admiral Koga sent from Truk with reinforcements, but neither time was he able to gain a favorable attack position. Off Mili, Benny Bass in *Plunger* rescued a downed aviator and suffered a casualty similar to McKinney's at Wake; a Japanese plane strafed *Plunger*, wounding six men, including Bass's exec, George William Brown, who was hit in the "stern." * Bass delivered the aviator—and his wounded men—to Pearl Harbor. The wounded recovered and returned to duty. Both *Seal* and *Spearfish* made photographic reconnaissances of the beaches which would later prove useful in the Marshalls invasion.

The tenth boat was *Paddle*, commanded by Bob Rice. He stood off the island of Nauru broadcasting weather reports prior to the invasion. After the invasion, he moved up to Eniwetok. On November 28, Rice picked up a formation of four heavy cruisers and two destroyers entering the lagoon. He closed the range to 9,000 yards, but heavy swells made periscope visibility poor; he was unable to attack. On return to Pearl Harbor, *Paddle* was sent back to Mare Island to have her H.O.R. engines replaced. Bob Rice stepped down as skipper, going to the Bureau of Personnel to replace Weary Wilkins, who went on to command a new division.

More Ultra Information

On November 30, ten days after the invasion of Tarawa, three aircraft carriers left Truk for Japan. These were *Zuiho* and the two escort carriers *Chuyo* and *Unyo* with the survivors of *Sculpin* on board.

The codebreakers picked up this movement and alerted Gene McKinney in *Skate*, who had just arrived at Truk for his second patrol in the new boat. McKinney found the three carriers on the morning of November 30. He closed to 9,000 yards and submerged on the track, preparing for a bow shot at *Zuiho* and one of the escort carriers. As he got ready to shoot, the formation zigged, forcing him

---

* "Weegee" Brown, class of 1938, was noted for his "stern," said by some to be the biggest in the navy. When he received his Purple Heart, a wag in the submarine force quipped, "It figures. How could the Japs have missed?"

to fire the stern tubes, one of which was not ready. At a range of 1,500 yards, with the carriers overlapping, McKinney fired three torpedoes at *Zuiho*. He saw a "large geyser" of water arise just forward of the center of *Zuiho*, and the big ship heeled to port. McKinney heard an explosion but saw no smoke.

To the north, off Iwo Jima, Junior McCain in *Gunnel*, the first Pearl Harbor H.O.R. boat to receive new engines and return to combat, received word of the oncoming formation. He picked them up on December 2 at about 10:30 P.M. The three carriers were zigzagging at high speed. McCain closed to 6,000 yards, then submerged ahead on the track, setting up on *Zuiho*. As he was getting set to shoot, *Zuiho* zigged directly at *Gunnel*, forcing her deep to avoid a collision and fouling the attack. In the confusion that followed, McCain fired four bow tubes. All missed. Immediately thereafter, McCain heard four explosions which he assumed were depth charges. Although it was night, he went to 300 feet and made no follow-up attack.

Farther north, off Japan, lay *Sailfish*, making her tenth war patrol. Following the unfortunate ninth, under Lefavour, command of the boat had been given to Bob Ward, class of 1935, who had been exec to Herb Andrews on *Gurnard* during his famous rugged first patrol off the Palaus. In the wake of the investigation on *Sailfish*, all the senior officers except the engineer, Stanley Joseph Cowin, Jr., had left. For his exec, Ward had picked George Floyd Richardson. Walter Patrick Murphy, Jr., was the new torpedo officer.

Ward, Richardson, and Murphy had worked hard to restore morale and fighting spirit to the demoralized crew. "I used every gimmick you could think of," Ward said. "For example, I asked a young officer to get a whole list of things—silly things—like an ice cream machine and a new piece of carpeting for my cabin. After a lot of digging around he came up with an old-fashioned ice cream machine, you know, the kind you turn the handle? So after the boys rigged a motor to it, we could have ice cream in the middle of a depth-charge attack. He had a little more trouble with the rug, but he finally discovered that the Admiral on the tender had a lovely rug and he went and asked him for a piece for my cabin. The Admiral told him if I'd come and ask him personally, he'd give me a piece of it. I did, and we got a big laugh over it. Now that showed real resourcefulness."

Ward had also resorted to brainwashing. "*Sailfish* was a thin-skinned boat," he said later. "By then, the thicker-skinned boats were coming out. They could dive deeper and withstand closer depth-charging. Well, some of the crew were complaining about our thin skin. So I told them that actually I thought a thin-skinned boat was better than a thick-skinned boat. The hull was more flexible. It could take more pounding. I told them I didn't want one of those stiff thick-skinned boats. And, you know, I think I got the crew believing that thin-skinned boats were superior."

On the way to Honshu, it seemed for a time the old *Sailfish* jinx was taking over again. While routining the torpedoes, the one in number eight tube had a hot run and partially ejected. Murphy went over the side in very rough seas to inspect the shutter doors. The torpedo was ejected safely, but the tube remained out of commission for the rest of the patrol.

Ward received Dick Voge's Ultra on the three carriers and moved *Sailfish* into intercept position, fighting mountainous seas generated by a winter typhoon. Nearing Japan, the Japanese carrier force went on submarine alert, but when it entered the full fury of the typhoon the task force commander rescinded the alert and stopped zigzagging, believing the ships safe in such foul weather.

On the evening of December 3, after a long day submerged, Ward came to the surface. The typhoon raged. The seas were "tremendous"; winds blew at 50 knots. Near midnight, Ward picked up the carrier force on radar, range 9,000 yards. Owing to the weather, Ward abandoned any idea of a methodical approach. He submerged to radar depth and, at twelve minutes after midnight, fired four bow tubes at one of the largest radar pips, range 2,100 yards. He heard two distinct and solid hits.

A destroyer charged out of the howling darkness, forcing Ward deep. It dropped twenty-one depth charges, two close, nineteen distant. During this interlude, Ward reloaded his torpedo tubes, and at about 2 A.M. he returned to the surface to see what was going on. His radar showed pips all around, including one moving very slowly. Ward tracked, working in heavy seas to attain firing position, still not sure what he had hit or what the slow-moving target might be.

With morning light coming on, Ward hurried to shoot again. He fired three more bow torpedoes, range 3,200 yards. He heard and observed two torpedo hits, including a puff of fire. The target replied with a barrage of bullets, fired first willy-nilly, then directly at *Sailfish*. Ward submerged to reload and make another attack.

At 7:58 A.M., Ward finally got a glimpse of his wounded target. It was an aircraft carrier, unmoving, with a small list to port and slightly down by the stern. There were "enough people on deck aft to populate a fair size village." To Ward, it seemed they were preparing to abandon ship. To hurry them on, he fired three more torpedoes at the carrier, range 1,700 yards. The sonarman reported "tremendous" breaking-up noises, but high waves prevented Ward from obtaining visual confirmation of hits.

Passing down the side of the carrier, Ward suddenly saw another big ship: a heavy cruiser. The cruiser apparently saw *Sailfish*'s periscope. It charged dead on and Ward, fearing *Sailfish* might broach in the heavy seas, ordered 90 feet. He obtained sonar data on the cruiser, but by the time he could set up to fire she was astern and disappearing in the mountainous seas. Ward chastised himself, stating in his report that he "threw away the chance of a lifetime."

After reloading, Ward crept back to look for the wounded carrier but could find no sign of it: *Chuyo*, 20,000 tons, had gone down with all hands, taking with her the survivors of *Sculpin* she was carrying. She was the first Japanese aircraft carrier sunk by a U.S. submarine. When submariners learned later of the Americans aboard, they would remark on the irony. In 1939, *Sculpin* had found and stood by *Squalus* when she sank. Now *Squalus*, renamed *Sailfish*, had killed half the survivors of *Sculpin*.*

Happily ignorant of this fact, Ward continued to his patrol station. On December 7, while cruising on the surface, he was caught by a Japanese plane and badly bombed and strafed. On December 13, he picked up a two-ship convoy with two escorts. He sank one, *Totai Maru*, 3,000 tons, and damaged the other. On December 21, he found another convoy: six big transports, escorted by three destroyers. He fired three stern tubes into the formation and sank the freighter *Uyo Maru*, 6,400 tons. During the attack, the diving officer lost control of the boat and broached. Ward sent all off-duty men to the forward torpedo room, and *Sailfish* went down like a rock to 327 feet before Ward could check her. The destroyers attacked, dropping thirty-one depth charges, some very close.

When Ward returned to Pearl Harbor, he was greeted by Lockwood, standing on the pier with a broad smile. Later, after presenting Ward his first Navy Cross, Lockwood wrote, "This patrol can be considered one of the most outstanding patrols of the war." Ward was credited with three ships for 35,729 tons and damage to one for 7,000 tons. Postwar analysis showed that his sinking claims were nearly

---

* But none of the original crew that found *Squalus* was among them. By that time—four and a half years later—all the old hands had rotated to other duty.

accurate: three ships, 29,571 tons. In terms of confirmed tonnage, it was the best patrol of the war to date.

When George Wales returned *Pogy* from the Palaus, where his third patrol had resulted in damage to some ships and the sinking of a big transport, *Maebashi Maru*, 7,000 tons, he was transferred to staff and Lockwood gave *Pogy* to her former exec, Ralph Marion Metcalf, another from 1935.

Metcalf returned *Pogy* to the Palaus. On the way, he received an important Ultra on a big navy auxiliary and a submarine tender, *Soyo Maru*. Metcalf skillfully intercepted the ships east of the Marianas on the night of December 7, fired at both ships simultaneously, and obtained hits for damage. After dark, he surfaced and tracked *Soyo Maru*, attacking again after moonset while a destroyer circled nearby. She blew up and sank. Six days later, off the Palaus, Metcalf found a three-ship convoy standing out with escorts. Metcalf fired, sinking one 4,000-ton freighter. The escorts counterattacked, disabling *Pogy's* fire-control system. Metcalf was forced to break off the patrol and return to Midway for repairs. Total time at sea: twenty-nine days. Total confirmed damage to the enemy: two ships sunk for 10,000 tons.

John Coye, making his third patrol in *Silversides*, replaced Metcalf at Palau. On the night of December 29, Coye (who had sunk four ships on his previous patrol) picked up a convoy and methodically sank three freighters. On January 2, a Japanese submarine found *Silversides* and fired three torpedoes. The officer of the deck, who saw the periscope, turned *Silversides* to comb the track—run parallel with the torpedoes to reduce the target area and thus the chance of being hit. One torpedo passed down the starboard side, range 50 yards; another came down the port side, range 75 yards.

Eugene McKinney in *Skate* was still patrolling off the north end of Truk. On December 21, he sank a 6,400-ton freighter. He recalled:

Lockwood sent me an Ultra. The super-battleship Yamato *was en route from Japan to Truk. . . . I was the last guy on the line . . . the last to get a crack at her. She was due in my area Christmas Day. He said, "Give the American people a Christmas present." They had decoded her exact course and turning points. . . . Lockwood warned me that the escorting destroyers had excellent radar and not to get within 30,000 yards of* Yamato *on the surface.*

McKinney maneuvered *Skate* into position. Just before dawn on

MORE ULTRA INFORMATION

December 25, he picked *Yamato* up at 27,000 yards. He closed and dived, making ready six torpedoes forward. For a while it seemed hopeless; *Yamato* was too far away. But suddenly she turned toward *Skate*. "I put up the periscope and saw this huge mound," McKinney recalled. "It looked as big as Alcatraz Island. She'd changed course." McKinney passed down her starboard beam and made a right turn, bringing stern tubes to bear. "I shot four torpedoes," he said. "Two hit. They did damage."

That night, McKinney sent off a message to Lockwood stating simply that he had scored two hits on "a ship." Lockwood was annoyed. "When I got back to Pearl Harbor, Dick Voge and Lockwood raised holy hell with me," McKinney said later. "I hadn't mentioned *Yamato* in my message. Lockwood had been all set to put out a Christmas press release stating that a U.S. submarine had damaged *Yamato*, but since I hadn't said *Yamato* in my message, he couldn't claim it." *

After this patrol, McKinney was promoted to an important job in the training section at Pearl Harbor.

Between September and late January, Roy Gross in *Seawolf* completed two patrols to the Hong Kong area—his specialty. On the first he sank two ships. On the second, on January 10, he picked up a seven-ship convoy and engaged in one of the most dogged submarine attacks of the war.

For his first attack on the convoy, Gross got in close and fired seven torpedoes. With this salvo he sank two big freighters and damaged others. The convoy scattered, the ships firing deck guns willy-nilly. A destroyer found *Seawolf* and dropped nine close depth charges.

Gross was held down the rest of the afternoon by the destroyer escorts and aircraft circling overhead. After dark he surfaced in bright moonlight. Finding one crippled ship being towed by another, he set up on the towing ship and fired three torpedoes, obtaining a hit. Then he fired all four stern tubes at both the crippled ship and the now-damaged towing ship, again obtaining hits. Soon the towing ship disappeared. Dodging destroyers and lifeboats filled with survivors, Gross moved in to fire three torpedoes at the cripple. All three hit, and the ship went down. With destroyers pursuing and firing, Gross hauled clear and submerged, leaving the scene of attack.

---

* Reason: if the Japanese were reading U.S. codes—always a possibility Voge had to consider—they would know from the Lockwood release that the United States was reading theirs.

Two days later, January 14, Gross received an Ultra from Dick Voge to intercept another convoy and left his regular patrol area in pursuit. On the way, he stumbled across another convoy, four freighters and two escorts. "Although assigned mission was important," Gross wrote, "decided to proceed on the bird-in-the-hand theory." Later he noted, "It is my recollection that very many Ultras were false alarms, whether from errors in decoding, uncooperative convoy commanders who changed their mind (and course) after the decoding, or maybe we on the boats made our own errors in copying the . . . schedules and/or in also decoding."

Gross made a night surface attack, firing his last four bow torpedoes. Two hits which started fires led Gross to believe the ship —a big freighter—was loaded with aviation gasoline. It sank. Wrote Gross, "This may keep some of the Rabaul fliers grounded for a while."

Having fired all his torpedoes, Gross sent off a contact report to Dick Voge. Voge alerted Acey Burrows, patrolling nearby in *Whale*, and Burrows hurried to close the convoy.

While trailing the convoy and waiting for Burrows, Gross decided to make a gun attack on one ship he believed to be a tanker full of aviation gasoline. He reasoned that one hit with his 3-inch gun might blow her up. He battle-surfaced and fired off six inaccurate rounds. When he heard shells "whistling close" Gross broke off the gun attack, dropped back out of range, and continued trailing.

In time, Burrows showed up. In his first attack, he sank *Denmark Maru*, a freighter of 5,870 tons. Standing off to one side, Gross watched and listened to the explosions with satisfaction. The convoy scattered. One ship, apparently intent on going on alone, came toward Gross.

Gross reasoned that a few rounds from his deck gun might turn the ship back toward *Whale*, so for the second time he sent his gun crews to battle station surface. His men fired off about thirty rounds. The ship returned the fire with big guns. However, Gross's gambit worked; the ship turned back toward *Whale*. Gross alerted Burrows, who attacked and sank the ship, *Tarushima Maru*, 4,800 tons.

When Gross returned to port, Lockwood was pleased. In a private note to Gross, he said, "Excellent, aggressive, and long headed patrol." Postwar records credited Gross with what he claimed: four ships, 23,361 tons. In addition, Lockwood gave Gross half credit with Burrows for the last ship sunk. This gave Gross a total of four and a half confirmed ships for 25,793 tons, one of the best patrols of the war. Burrows received credit for one and a half ships for 8,322 tons, both due to Gross's contact report.

After this, Gross returned *Seawolf* for overhaul and modernization at Mare Island and went to new construction.

Command of old *Swordfish* was given to another rising star from the class of 1935, Frank Barrows, who began the war on Don McGregor's *Gar* and then served ably as exec to Bill Post on *Gudgeon*. His exec was John Borden Hess.

Swordfish was feeling her age and the stress of eight war patrols. She had a nicked propeller that made too much noise and a rudder that chattered, making her presence easy to detect. When the stern planes jammed because of a bad gear, Barrows returned to Midway five or six days ahead of schedule. Wrote Hess:

Frank worried over whether or not we had done the right thing. His self-confidence was apparently shaken and he decided that he had not met the challenge properly. This being his conclusion, he decided he was not the man to take Swordfish *back to sea and asked to be relieved. I strongly disagreed with his personal decision since I felt that he had done a very fine job under very adverse circumstances and was an excellent commanding officer.*

Evidently, others agreed with Hess; Barrows went back for new construction.

All this time, tough old Karl Hensel, commanding Division 101 in Styer's Squadron Ten, had been aching to get command of a boat. "I had been telling students for so long how it should be done," Hensel said later, "that for my own self I wanted at least one chance to see if I could deliver a creditable patrol." Lockwood gave him *Swordfish*.

When Hess learned that Karl Hensel—then a captain who had just celebrated his forty-second birthday—would command the boat, he was apprehensive. "Hensel had been our training officer before the Barrows first patrol and had been a very demanding taskmaster. . . . My concern was that he might be reckless and ignore the odds in his desire to obtain maximum results." Said Hensel, "Morale was naturally low after such a patrol and when I came aboard the crew suspected I'd been sent to straighten things out, whether true or not."

Hensel oversaw repairs at Midway; then, when he believed the boat satisfactory, got under way to patrol off Tokyo. Plowing into the heavy December weather off Japan, old *Swordfish* suffered many more matériel casualties. Valves stuck. The radar was not dependable. The steering mechanism was noisy. There were electrical fires. Hensel, undaunted, pushed on, determined to prove *Swordfish*—and himself—combat-worthy.

On the evening of January 13, while cruising about 100 miles south of Tokyo, Hensel found a convoy. He charged in, sinking the freighter *Yamakuni Maru*, 6,921 tons. The escorts counterattacked, unleashing heavy—and close—depth charges. Hensel went deep, steering by his screws to avoid using the chattering rudder. At 320 feet, he leveled off and sneaked away.

The next day at dawn, when Hensel submerged, *Swordfish* almost went down for the last time. Unknown until then, her electrical controls had been knocked askew by the depth-charging. When Hensel attempted to shift to electric motors, he lost all power and control of the dive and fires broke out in two separate areas. Going down at a steep angle, Hensel blew everything, and *Swordfish* came up just as steeply as she had gone down. Then she lay helpless on the surface with no power. A Japanese patrol boat showed up, coming her way. Just in time, Hensel managed to get power on one screw, dive, and evade.

That night, Hensel came up again. By that time *Swordfish* had been patched up with "baling wire and glue," and Hensel was ready to go on the offensive again. About ten o'clock, he heard distant pinging, then picked up a contact on radar at 7 miles. Hensel got ready to attack.

Unknown to Hensel, the ship he was about to shoot at was *Delhi Maru*, a Q-ship designed especially to lure submarines to attack. Many skippers had reported contact with Q-ships. However, up to now all these contacts had been figments of uneasy imaginations. *Delhi Maru* was, in fact, the first Japanese Q-ship to put to sea. She was a converted 2,182-ton merchant ship with sonar, extra watertight compartments, depth-charge-launching gear, and concealed guns. She was on her maiden voyage, with two PT boat escorts.

Since it was a bright moonlit night, Hensel decided to attack submerged. About midnight he dived and closed, firing three bow tubes to hit. All did. The first blew the Q-ship's skipper off the bridge. The next two demolished the ship, touching off her heavy store of explosives and ammunition. Going deep to evade, Hensel believed he had hit a munitions ship. The PT boats held him down for three hours with depth charges, but he eluded them and cleared the area.

On the night of January 17, Lockwood sent Hensel an important Ultra: the aircraft carrier *Shokaku* and four destroyers were coming his way. *Shokaku* was now equipped with radar. Hensel moved into position and picked up the force at about 16,000 yards on his radar. The sky was black with heavy rain clouds, and Hensel could see nothing from the bridge. Radar tracked the force at 27 knots. Hensel submerged ahead to radar depth in order to minimize his own radar silhouette.

Hess later recalled what happened next:

We still had our shears sticking out when the range to the lead destroyer had closed to 2,000 yards and we were directly in front of him. The carrier was 2,000 to 2,500 yards behind the lead destroyer. To say I was scared to death at this point is a pretty fair statement. As the range on the lead destroyer rapidly dropped below 2,000 yards he would be on top of us in less than two minutes. If he sighted our exposed shears he would certainly ram us, and we were so close to his projected track that there was a fair chance he would hit us by accident even if he never saw us.

Hess urged Hensel to drop down to periscope depth. Hensel complied reluctantly, but when he found he couldn't see anything through the periscope he ordered *Swordfish* back to radar depth. Coming up, the radar was a mass of pips; *Shokaku* was probably no more than 400 yards away and had zigged right. Making the best of a bad situation, Hensel fired four stern tubes. All missed. *Shokaku* got away.

Later Hensel wrote, "We felt pretty low about this attack." Hess said, "The chance of getting a hit under such conditions [so close] was extremely remote. . . . I do not see how anyone could possibly have done more."

Barney Sieglaff in *Tautog* had received the same Ultra and was close by. He had sunk two freighters and had only one torpedo left forward. That same night, he picked up *Shokaku* at 16,000 yards and rapidly closed to 6,000. As Sieglaff swung to fire his stern tubes, the carrier zigged and opened the range. Sieglaff fired three torpedoes anyway. "This was an almost impossible shot," he wrote later, "but it was that or nothing." All missed.

Hensel remained on station. On January 27, he sank a third ship, *Kasagi Maru*, a converted salvage vessel of 3,140 tons. When he returned to port, the endorsements to his reports were glowing. The "old man" had sunk three confirmed ships for 12,243 tons and damaged another for an estimated 7,500 tons. For this he received a Navy Cross. Said Hess, "He was a very human individual and extremely solicitous of the welfare of each officer and man on the ship . . . he drove the *Swordfish* with skill and daring and made the most of each opportunity."

Patrols Good and Not So Good

A large Japanese tanker, *Kazahaya*, 10,000 tons, was the target for two boats patrolling the waters north of Truk in early October. Between them, Dave Whelchel in *Steelhead* and Dan Daspit in *Tinosa* fired twenty torpedoes at her. Whelchel obtained two or three hits before he was driven under, and Daspit finished the tanker off the next day, firing sixteen torpedoes in a near repeat of his previous patrol, when he'd spent fifteen on *Tonan Maru III*. The tanker, which Daspit nicknamed "obstinate maru," returned fire and dropped depth charges so close that men were knocked off their feet. Whelchel and Daspit shared the credit for her sinking.

After only nine days' rest and a torpedo reload at Midway, Daspit was off again, bound for Fremantle via Palau. Again it was a busy and fruitful patrol.

On the morning of November 22 Daspit found a convoy standing out of the harbor at Palau, zigzagging radically. It consisted of two freighters and two escorts. Daspit fired three torpedoes at one freighter, obtaining three hits. The freighter rolled over and settled on her side. Coolly dodging the escorts, Daspit fired another three torpedoes at the second freighter. It went down by the stern. The escorts attacked, dropping four close depth charges. The force of the explosion knocked out the diving planes and other gear, and *Tinosa*—in an almost exact repeat of Herb Andrews's experience on *Gurnard* at the same spot—plunged to 380 feet before Daspit got her under control.

Daspit waited for more targets to appear. On November 26, he attacked two, sinking one and damaging the other. As the escorts bore down, Daspit realized one of the torpedoes had not fired but was stuck in the tube. Daspit went deep, eluding the escorts. When he surfaced, the exec, C. Edwin Bell, and a junior officer, K. R. Van

PATROLS GOOD AND NOT SO GOOD

Gordgen, fixed the arming mechanism of the jammed torpedo so it would not fire. Then Daspit backed full (as Burlingame had done to eject a stuck torpedo on *Silversides*). The torpedo left the tube and sank.

Having survived this unnerving experience, Daspit again set a watch for the enemy. On December 3, a big tanker with a destroyer escort came out of the mist, en route from the Philippines to Palau. Daspit made a two-ship approach, but it was spoiled by a zig. He shot three torpedoes up the kilt at the tanker, obtaining at least one hit that set her afire and slowed her down. He came in on the surface for another shot, but the target opened fire with machine guns and two large deck guns. Daspit submerged, dodged the escort, closed to point-blank range, and fired three more torpedoes. The tanker blew up and sank.

When Daspit reached Fremantle, he was credited with four ships for 18,500 tons. After this, Daspit—ordered to the Bureau of Ships for duty in the Submarine Section of the Shipbuilding Division—turned the ship over to PCO Donald Frederick Weiss, who had been aboard *Tinosa* on this patrol. Later in the war, Daspit commanded a submarine division.

Two of the Squadron Twelve boats with new engines—*Hake* and *Haddo*—patrolled down to Fremantle. Both boats had gone from Scotland to Mare Island, where they were re-engined, and then to Pearl Harbor. *Hake* was commanded by John Cozine Broach, class of 1927, one of the oldest skippers still in command. *Haddo* was commanded by John Corbus. Neither man had yet made a Pacific war patrol.

Broach took *Hake* down the east coast of Luzon. His exec was Dixie Farrell, who had made three war patrols on *Gudgeon*. West of the Bonins, Broach and Farrell sank a magnificent target, the 9,500-ton transport *Nigitsu Maru*. Off Halmahera, they got into a convoy and sank two more ships, a 5,700-ton transport and a 4,000-ton freighter. Total: three ships for 19,384 tons.

John Corbus in *Haddo* took his boat to Fremantle by way of the west coast of Luzon, passing Lingayen Gulf and Manila. Although the area was dense with Japanese shipping, Corbus made no attacks and failed to link up with another Fremantle submarine chasing an important target. Both John Haines and Christie were critical of his performance but blamed it on the conditions under which Corbus had made his two previous patrols in the Bay of Biscay, where it was believed then that Corbus might have sunk a U-boat. Christie relieved him of command, placing him on the staff temporarily yet ready to give him a second chance.

A new skipper took *Thresher* on her eleventh patrol. He was Duncan Calvin MacMillan, class of 1926, the oldest regular skipper to command a fleet boat in December 1943. MacMillan, exec of *Argonaut* in 1939–40, was an engine specialist with a master's degree. For two years he had been stuck at the Fairbanks-Morse Company in Beloit, Wisconsin, supervising the manufacture of diesel engines. Later he had served in Styer's Squadron Ten as an engineering maintenance specialist.

MacMillan left from Midway to patrol the north end of Luzon Strait. On the way in, he destroyed a fishing trawler with his deck gun. On January 15, in foul weather, he picked up a large convoy which may have been escorted by an aircraft carrier. MacMillan turned to attack. As he was going in, two destroyers found *Thresher* and drove her under, dropping ten to fifteen depth charges. After dark MacMillan surfaced, made an end around, and re-established contact. Attacking in poor visibility, using only radar, he nevertheless sank two ships, freighters of 7,000 and 4,000 tons before the alert destroyers drove him under again and delivered a severe depth-charging.

A few days later, MacMillan found another convoy and attacked. In a furious fight, he sank two more medium freighters, one of 1,300 tons and one of 2,200 tons. During this melee, *Thresher* was jarred by a massive explosion that stopped clocks, broke lights, and made cork fly. By the time MacMillan could make repairs, the convoy had scattered out of sight. "Old Man" MacMillan returned to Midway, having sunk four credited ships for 14,523 tons.

Later MacMillan said, "The question of the best ages for a submarine skipper is moot; it depends largely on the characteristics of the officer. Obviously a balance has to be had between the daring of youth and caution of old age. The British experience, I am told, indicated that age thirty-five was the cut-off point. I doubt it. However, this would be an easy policy to administer and satisfactory if the supply of available skippers exceeds the demand. It should be realized that by so doing much good submarine experience is being wasted. Another view was that the older skippers did not have the resiliency to bounce back after a few patrols and would sustain psychological damage. I doubt if there is any evidence to sustain this point of view."

A new boat, *Batfish*, commanded by Wayne Merrill (formerly exec on *Grampus*), patrolled off Honshu in the foul December-January weather. His exec was Peter Gabriel Molteni, Jr.; the third was an able young officer from the class of 1939, James Monroe Hingson, who came from two war patrols on *Tuna*. Merrill was a strange and unstable character.

On January 14, in extremely bad weather, Merrill's radar operator picked up a galvanizing sight: a big pip that had to be a battleship. Jim Hingson later described what happened:

It was after dark and we had surfaced to charge batteries heading into seas fifteen to twenty feet plus strong winds. We went to an approach course, continuing the charge . . . we were pounding. It was raining and although we had not gone to battle stations I was kept below on station to take over the dive. . . . Radio information decoded [indicated contact] was Yamato. Merrill and Molteni were on the bridge but couldn't see anything because of green seas coming over the bow. . . . Merrill told Molteni he planned to dive when range closed to the battleship's 10-inch shell range. Molteni was begging Merrill to stay on the surface or it would be a TGB [target-got-by] situation. Merrill told Molteni that if we could pick up a battleship on radar, the battleship could pick us up because of the stable platform he had to scan from. Molteni came down disgusted: ordered the crew to General Quarters and asked me to go to the bridge and talk the Captain out of diving. I went up and told Merrill I had been a battleship turret officer and that it would be utterly impossible for a pointer and trainer of a fire-control party to stay on us the way we were bouncing around. . . . Merrill was still concerned over being "blown out of the water" by a 16 inch shell. . . . I was told to lay below and stand by to dive. We did. . . . I don't recall any range below 18,000 yards ever being reached and TGB. . . . Our chances of fame and glory had faded and Molteni made up his mind to get off Batfish *next time in at any cost.*

Aspro, another new boat reporting to Lockwood, was commanded by a remarkable officer, Harry Clinton Stevenson, class of 1930. He had a younger brother, William Alfred, class of 1934, who was also in submarines. In 1940, both brothers had come down with crippling diseases. Harry developed an inflammation of the optic nerve and the retina known as neuroretinitis and was hospitalized for eight months. William suffered a mild attack of polio, spent a year in the hospital, and was discharged with a withered left leg. Harry was limited to staff duty only, William to large surface ships only. However, after the attack on Pearl Harbor, both brothers managed to wangle their way back into submarines. Harry had commanded *Cachalot* on a luckless patrol to the Aleutians in 1942; William had served on *Marlin* and then commanded *S-30* in Alaska for four patrols, sinking one of the few Japanese vessels in those waters.

After *Cachalot*, Harry commissioned *Aspro* and took her to Formosa. On the way he battle-surfaced with his 5-inch gun on what he believed to be a fishing boat near Wake Island. The "fishing boat" fired back with a 3-inch gun. "We left the vicinity in a hurry," Stevenson wrote later.

Off Formosa, Stevenson found two good convoys. The first was a tanker and two freighters escorted by two destroyers. Stevenson fired three torpedoes at the tanker from an unfavorable position, obtaining one hit. The second convoy was a huge fifteen-ship affair, well-escorted. Stevenson attacked at night on the surface from very close range, firing ten torpedoes, achieving numerous hits, and scattering the convoy. He made an end around, submerged, and attacked a second time, firing another ten torpedoes. With only one torpedo remaining, Stevenson returned to Midway after a mere thirty-nine days.

Lockwood credited Stevenson with sinking three ships for 25,600 tons and damage to four for 31,400 tons, making this one of the better patrols of the war. However, postwar analysis confirmed none of the sinkings.

On the way home, Stevenson began to worry about his eyesight, particularly his night vision, which was very bad. "I felt that my vision was not good enough to perform my duties as commanding officer effectively and with safety," he wrote later. "It did not seem fair to needlessly hazard the officers, crew, and good ship *Aspro*." Stevenson confided in his exec, James Gold Andrews. Andrews, in turn, suggested they might adopt the Mush Morton-Dick O'Kane system of putting the exec on the periscope. Stevenson later said, "I do not have the type of personality for such a procedure and declined with a 'thank you' for his loyalty."

On reaching Midway, Stevenson flew to Pearl Harbor for an eye checkup. The result was: "disqualified for sea duty."

While in Pearl Harbor, Harry ran into his brother, William, who had just returned from the Aleutians. William was by then considered qualified for fleet boat command. Harry suggested to Lockwood that brother William be given *Aspro*. "I could think of no one better qualified or more to my liking," Harry said. Lockwood approved the idea, probably the first time in naval history that one brother relieved another in command of a man-of-war in wartime.

Young William moved into a difficult situation. "The crew and officers," he said later, "had been together through a construction and refit period in Portsmouth, a long training period and trip to Pearl, and then the first war patrol. The wives knew each other in Portsmouth. It was a happy family.... I am sure that there must have been a feeling on board that 'little brother' must be second best." When William took *Aspro* to the waters between Truk and the Marianas early in 1944, however, he proved to be no less aggressive than his older brother.

The First Three Wolf Packs

The first formal Pearl Harbor wolf pack was commanded by Swede Momsen, in charge of Squadron Two. His group consisted of three boats: *Shad*, recently arrived from her long tour in Scotland, commanded by Edgar John MacGregor III; a brand-new boat, *Cero*, in charge of the old hand, Dave White, helped by his exec, Dave McClintock, who had been with White on *Plunger*; and *Grayback*, returned from overhaul at Mare Island with a new skipper, John Anderson Moore.

Although Johnny Moore lacked experience in fleet boats, he was obviously headed for outstanding performance. An athlete at the Naval Academy (boxing and soccer), he had made a fine record in R and S boats. His classmate Hank Munson said later, "Professionally, Johnny was tops and we placed him second to nobody in the class"; MacGregor in *Shad* recalled that Moore was a "go-getter" with a "vivacious personality." During refit, *Grayback* had been fitted with a 5-inch gun, one of the first boats in the Pearl Harbor command to receive one. MacGregor recalled that Moore was very excited about the big gun and talked enthusiastically about how he planned to use it.

Momsen, who had never made a war patrol, chose to fly his flag with the most experienced skipper, Dave White. Before setting off, the three skippers and their execs game-boarded tactics with Momsen on the black and white tile dance floor of the sub base officers' club. Momsen also took the boats to sea, practicing against friendly convoys operating between California and Pearl Harbor. The three boats communicated with one another in code by means of a short-range radio known as the TBS (talk between ships).

In evolving wolf-pack tactics, caution was the watchword. The skippers were told not to use the radio often, lest Japanese antisubmarine warfare forces home in on the transmissions. The three boats would not attack a convoy simultaneously, lest they hit each other. One boat would attack first, then drop behind the convoy to reload and serve as a "trailer" to pick up damaged ships. The other two boats would take station on the starboard and port flanks of the convoy, attacking alternately in the hope that one attack would turn the convoy toward the other.

Momsen took his pack to the East China Sea near Okinawa to interdict the flow of traffic between Honshu and Formosa Strait. Although he received a steady—and useful—flow of Ultras, the pack was never able to solve communications and navigational problems sufficiently to make a well-coordinated attack. In effect, the pack was a "joint search" unit rather than a "joint attack" unit.

On October 12, Dave White in *Cero* attacked a three-ship convoy escorted by destroyers, damaging one freighter. The following day, Moore in *Grayback* picked up a convoy escorted by two light cruisers. He couldn't get into position on the cruisers, but that night he sank a 7,000-ton transport. About two days later, MacGregor in *Shad*, acting on an Ultra dispatch, intercepted an enemy task force composed of three or four heavy cruisers and possibly an escort carrier. MacGregor fired five torpedoes at the cruisers and counted three hits. A second attack was fouled when destroyers hove around and delivered a severe depth-charging. After dark, MacGregor surfaced and got off a contact report, but by then the pack was scattered, chasing other contacts. The next day, Moore in *Grayback* sank another 7,000-ton transport.

Five days later, the pack received word of an escorted four-ship troop convoy. In a nearer approximation of a wolf-pack attack, Moore in *Grayback* and MacGregor in *Shad* both attacked the same set of ships. Each put torpedoes into a big transport, *Fuji Maru*, 9,138 tons, and later were given one-half credit each for sinking her.

When the boats returned to Pearl Harbor, Lockwood called this pioneering wolf pack a complete success and awarded Swede Momsen a Navy Cross. The citation credited the pack with sinking five ships for 38,000 tons and damage to eight ships for 63,000 tons. In fact, only three ships had been sunk for 23,500 tons, two and a half for 19,000 tons by Moore in *Grayback* and one half for 4,500 tons by MacGregor in *Shad*.

The officers involved in the first pack had mixed feelings. Momsen believed the pack would be more effective if controlled from shore, à la Doenitz. MacGregor thought the whole thing a waste of time and effort and believed boats would do better operating alone. Everybody criticized the poor communications, which had, in effect, rendered the pack inoperable as a coordinated attack unit. On return to port, *Shad* was sent back for overhaul that would keep her out of combat for the next eight months. MacGregor, who had made a total of five patrols, went to the Submarine School as an instructor.

Later, Johnny Moore conducted a brilliant second patrol in the East China Sea. On the night of December 18, he picked up a four-ship convoy with three escorts. Sinking one of the freighters by periscope attack, he surfaced to chase the others. One of the escorts, *Numakaze*, a 1,300-ton destroyer, had lagged behind to trap *Grayback*. When Moore surfaced, the destroyer attacked, charging in from the stern. Moore dived and let go four stern tubes. *Numakaze* sank so quickly she was unable to get off a radio report. Two nights later, Moore picked up another convoy of six ships. He fired a spread of nine torpedoes into the formation, sinking one freighter and damaging others. Escorts drove *Grayback* under, but three hours later Moore surfaced and sank another ship. The following night, he made an attack that failed.

Having exhausted all his torpedoes in five days, Moore returned to port after a round trip of thirty-three days. On the way, he sank a trawler with his 5-inch deck gun. Total confirmed score: four ships, including the destroyer, for 10,000 tons. In two patrols, Moore achieved a confirmed score of six and one-half ships for almost 30,000 tons.

In October Lockwood organized a second wolf pack under Freddy Warder and sent it to the Marianas, to help shut off the flow of Japanese shipping during the invasion of Tarawa. The three boats were Sam Dealey's *Harder*, Chuck Triebel's *Snook*, and *Pargo*, commanded by Ian Crawford Eddy.

The codebreakers supplied Warder (who rode Eddy's *Pargo*) with good information on Japanese convoy movements, but communications between the submarines of the pack was poor and the "joint attacks" were not carried out as conceived on paper. On November 12, Sam Dealey picked up a freighter with two small escorts. He made a day periscope attack, firing three torpedoes; the freighter disintegrated. About the same time, Eddy on *Pargo*, making an approach on the same target from a different angle, was surprised to see it blow up in his face. Later that night, Dealey surfaced and sank one of the small escorts with gunfire. On *Snook*, Triebel noted in his log, "Surprised by *Harder*'s message that they had sunk two ships."

For the next week, the pack had no contacts. On November 19, Sam Dealey picked up another convoy: three big freighters with three escorts. He radioed a contact report to Triebel and Eddy. Triebel acknowledged, but there was no word from Eddy. Triebel wrote, "Received enemy's true bearing from *Harder* which was worthless as we did not know *Harder*'s movement during last three hours."

While Triebel flailed around trying to find the convoy, Dealey moved in to attack, with his exec, John Maurer, manning the periscope. Dealey fired ten torpedoes at the three ships, obtaining seven hits. One ship sank, one was badly damaged, and the third ran off. Triebel could hear the shooting and wrote, "Heard depth charges or torpedoes all morning. This was the most frustrated I have ever felt. On the surface at full speed, hearing explosions, and we couldn't make contact."

After firing his ten torpedoes, Sam Dealey was attacked by the three escorts. They drove him deep and dropped sixty-four depth charges. He waited them out until dark and then surfaced to chase the undamaged freighter. Finding it at ten o'clock, he fired four more torpedoes. All missed. He fired three more for two hits. The ship appeared to be sinking.

Dealey closed to 600 yards to give his crew a look through the periscope. What they saw were Japanese working frantically to save their ship, so Dealey set up and fired another torpedo. It ran erratically. He fired another, and it, too, was erratic, as was a third. The fourth, also erratic, circled back toward *Harder*, forcing the boat to go deep. Dealey battle-surfaced to polish off the ship, but return fire drove him off. Later, he wrote, "It was a bitter disappointment not to finish this ship off, but he was a worthy opponent. He won our grudging admiration for his fight, efficiency and unwillingness to give up." Later, when bad weather came up, Dealey decided neither of the damaged ships could survive.

Triebel wrote, "Received *Harder*'s message of torpedo expenditure.

Charles Herbert Andrews

Raymond Henry Bass

Edward Latimer Beach

Roy Stanley Benson    Carter Lowe Bennett

James William Blanchard

William Herman Brockman

Creed Cardwell Burlingame

Admiral Carpender presenting award to Greenling wardroom; Henry Chester Bruton and James Dorr Grant are first and second from left

Bernard Ambrose Clarey

Wreford Goss Chapple

Slade Deville Cutter
(foreground) in torpedo room

John Starr Coye, Jr.

Roy Milton Davenport

Samuel David Dealey

Admiral Nimitz and Glynn Robert Donaho

Thomas Michael Dykers

Robert Edson Dornin

Frank Wesley Fenno

Joseph Francis Enright

William Joseph Germershausen (left) and R. M. Wright on Spadefish

Howard Walter Gilmore

Eugene Bennett Fluckey

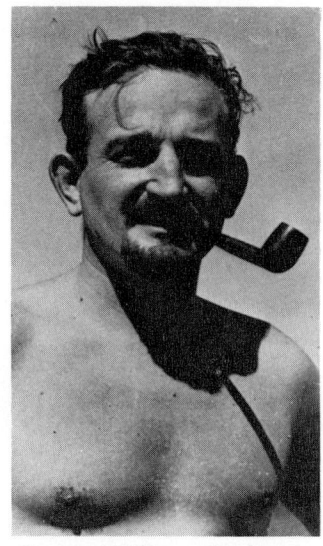

George William Grider

Walter Thomas Griffith

Thomas Wesley Hogan

William Thomas Kinsella (left) and Brooks Jared Harral

Herman Joseph Kossler

Charles Elliott Loughlin

Jack Hayden Lewis (left) and Thomas Burton Klakring

Eugene Bradley McKinney    *John Howard Maurer*

Admiral John Sidney McCain (left) and his son, John Sidney McCain, Jr., in Tokyo Bay

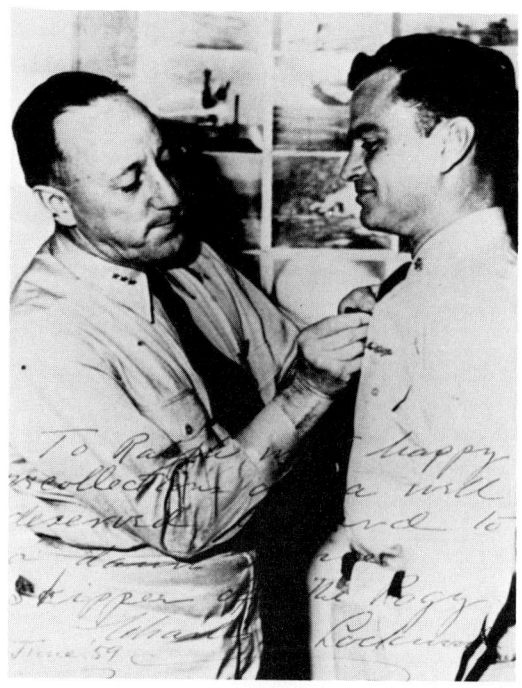

Admiral Lockwood and Ralph Marion Metcalf    Dudley Walker Morton on the bridge of Wahoo

Stanley Page Moseley, Lewis Smith Parks, Elton Watters Grenfell, and David Charles White (left to right)

Admiral Nimitz pins silver star on his son, Chester William Nimitz, Jr.

Henry Glass Munson

Richard Hetherington O'Kane

Admiral Nimitz and William Schuyler Post, Jr.

George Egbert Porter, Jr.    Lawson Paterson Ramage

Robert Henry Rice (center) and officers of Drum, Manning Kimmel at far right

Frank Gordon Selby

Harry Clinton Stevenson (left) and William Alfred Stevenson

Edward Dean Spruance (left) and his father, Admiral Raymond Ames Spruance, on board a captured Japanese submarine in Tokyo Bay

George Levick Street III

Gordon Waite Underwood

Charles Otto Triebel

John Augustine Tyree, Jr.

Frederick Burdett Warder

Reuben Thornton Whitaker (left) and Murray Jones Tichenor

Merrill Comstock (left) and Charles Warren Wilkins

Had no idea from it who he had shot or where or when. We had evidently missed the convoy if the *Harder* hadn't sunk it. . . . Sighted *Pargo* and closed for visual rendezvous. Found out a little of what had been going on."

Sam Dealey, out of torpedoes, left the pack. When he returned to port, he claimed five ships sunk (including the small trawler) for 24,800 tons. Postwar records denied Dealey the small freighter he claimed sinking on November 12, but confirmed all three ships of the convoy he attacked on November 19 and 20—for 15,273 tons.

Early in the patrol, the *Harder*'s number four (main) engine, an H.O.R., had broken down completely. Dealey kept the other three in commission by babying them and cannibalizing spare parts from the fourth. When he reached Pearl Harbor, where Lockwood awarded him his third Navy Cross, he was ordered back to Mare Island to re-engine *Harder*. There, Jack Maurer got off to go to his own command and Tiny Lynch moved up to exec.

After Dealey had shoved off, Freddy Warder in *Pargo* was left with only two submarines. They patrolled in company (about 20 to 30 miles apart, searching) for a week without sighting anything worthwhile. Then, on the night of November 28, Eddy and Warder picked up another convoy. Eddy flashed word to Triebel, who was about 40 miles away. Triebel homed in on *Pargo*'s radar emissions. "I believed they knew where the convoy was and [I] didn't want to get left chasing my own shadow 10 miles on a flank again," Triebel wrote.

Without conferring by radio or other means, both submarines maneuvered to attack the four big freighters. Just as Triebel was about to fire his bow tubes, he saw an explosion on the freighter at which he was aiming. He let go six torpedoes. One hit the ship Eddy had already hit, another hit a second ship. At about this same moment, *Pargo*'s radar emission disappeared. For a while, Triebel believed that one of his torpedoes might have hit *Pargo*. But he went on firing—four stern tubes, six more bow tubes, two stern tubes at an escort, four more at a freighter, more stern tubes—until he ran out of torpedoes. Meanwhile, *Pargo*'s radar emissions reappeared, and Triebel breathed easier.

Having shot all his torpedoes, Triebel broke off and returned to port, Warder and Eddy following close behind. Triebel was credited with sinking two ships and damaging two. Eddy was credited with sinking two ships and damaging two. In addition, they both shared one-half credit for damaging the ship both hit. Postwar analysis gave

Triebel credit for sinking two ships for 8,500 tons, Eddy two ships for 7,900 tons.

In all, Lockwood credited this second wolf pack with sinking nine ships for 58,000 tons. This was reduced in postwar analysis to seven ships for 31,500 tons. However, the experience soured Dealey, Triebel, and others on the wolf-pack concept. It was obvious that better communications would have to be devised before wolf packs could be effective. Warder suggested, if there were to be future wolf packs, that the pack commander was superfluous and command should be given to the senior skipper.

Following this patrol, Eddy's *Pargo*, another H.O.R. boat, followed *Harder* to Mare Island for new engines.

A third wolf pack set off in December. It was composed of Pete Galantin's *Halibut*; *Haddock*, commanded by Beetle Roach, who had relieved Roy Davenport; and Charles Brindupke's *Tullibee*. Following Freddy Warder's suggestion that wolf packs be commanded not by a division commander but by the senior skipper of the group, Brindupke took tactical command of the unit. The pack was assigned to the Marianas to intercept men-of-war running between Truk and Japan.

First contact with the enemy was made on January 2 by Brindupke in *Tullibee*, who sighted an I-class submarine off Guam in dawn light. Although there was a floatplane flying nearby, Brindupke remained on the surface, firing four torpedoes from 3,000 yards. The Jap sub evidently saw the torpedoes and evaded. Brindupke dived and went deep. The floatplane attacked *Tullibee*, dropping six bombs.

Having obtained word of an approaching enemy task force, Brindupke ordered his pack to form a scouting line. On January 7 Galantin in *Halibut* saw a heavy cruiser escorted by two destroyers but he was unable to gain attack position. Four days later Galantin saw the tops of one or several battleships, sent off a contact report to the other boats, and chased but couldn't overtake. Neither of the other boats could close. On January 14 Galantin spotted a destroyer, closed, and fired four torpedoes at shallow depth settings. Two, or possibly three, prematured.

After a couple of weeks of this, the three boats rendezvoused one night to plan tactics. Galantin and Roach left *Halibut* and *Haddock* in rubber boats and went on board *Tullibee*, the first time any submarine skipper had ever left his boat at sea. In *Tullibee*'s wardroom, they worked over charts and search plans and exchanged ideas. *Hali-*

THE FIRST THREE WOLF PACKS 547

but, which was running low on fuel, tried to refuel from *Tullibee* with a makeshift hose, but the experiment was a failure.

Once again, the boats deployed. On January 19, running on the surface, Beetle Roach in *Haddock* picked up an enemy task force through the high periscope (a periscope watch while on the surface), range 20,000 yards. Roach had no time to get off a contact report. He stayed up for several moments, then dived on the track, watching through the periscope. The force turned out to be a large carrier (identified as *Shokaku*) and a small carrier, escorted by a cruiser leading the formation and several destroyers on the flanks.

The Japanese ships came on swiftly. Roach set up on the large carrier. When the range had closed to 2,100 yards, he fired six torpedoes set for shallow depth; then he took *Haddock* deep. He heard two explosions, then more, followed by "tremendous milling around" of the destroyers. Roach remained deep and made no second attack.

Roach had hit not *Shokaku* but the smaller carrier *Unyo*, which had been hit by Dave Whelchel in *Steelhead* and Philip Ross in *Halibut* earlier in the year. *Unyo*, badly damaged, limped into Saipan. Following this, all three boats set up watch outside the harbor at Saipan. On January 23, Galantin (who could see *Unyo* clearly through his periscope) tried to get into position at the harbor entrance for a shot, but *Halibut* was driven off by a destroyer. On January 26, Brindupke, standing watch, reported *Unyo* still in the harbor. Two days later he took another look and *Unyo* was gone; evidently she had slipped away during the night.

After that, the wolf pack broke up and returned to base, Brindupke sinking a 500-ton net tender, the only bag for the three boats.

Unyo was towed on to Japan, escorted by three destroyers. Bill Post in *Gudgeon*, en route to patrol in the East China Sea, and Tony Dropp in *Saury*, returning from that area, intercepted *Unyo* off Lot's Wife on the afternoon of February 2. She was making about 10 knots under tow.

This was the second time in as many patrols that Post had been directed to intercept and sink a damaged carrier. The first time, he had been driven off by destroyers. This time, he was determined to succeed. *Gudgeon* was immediately picked up by a destroyer which charged. Post let him get to 900 yards, then fired four torpedoes down the throat; he was so close, he could see depth charges being thrown off the destroyer's stern. Post's torpedoes missed. He went deep, while thirty-five depth charges fell around *Gudgeon.*

A little later, Post raised his periscope and saw *Saury*. He fired a recognition smoke bomb and then surfaced. Post held a megaphone conference with Dropp, planning a joint submerged attack. Post would end-around to the east, Dropp to the west.

As Post closed the slow-moving formation again, he saw a plane rising from *Unyo*'s deck and another destroyer charging. For the second time that day, Post decided to fire down the throat. He let the range close to 800 yards and then shot four torpedoes. All missed and again depth charges rained down on *Gudgeon*.

Post wrote, "Had often wondered what would happen when one missed on a down-the-throat shot at a destroyer. Today we found out twice. Glad to report that it's not much worse than a routine working over."

About the same time, Dropp in *Saury* tried to get in from the opposite quarter. Another destroyer charged. Dropp went deep and stayed there, losing contact with the formation.

After dark, Post again tried to make an approach on the carrier. When another destroyer picked him up and opened fire with guns, Post submerged and prepared to fire at the destroyer, but one of his torpedoes slipped in the tube and had to be hand-held to prevent a hot run. Following this casualty, Post broke off the attack.

Unyo reached Japan. Post went on to another successful patrol in the East China Sea. Tony Dropp returned *Saury* to Midway. On the way home, the boat was pooped badly, taking tons of water down the conning tower hatch and main induction. She lay helpless on the surface for almost twenty-four hours, while her crew repaired flooded-out machinery, but fortunately was not discovered by the enemy.

Changes in Command

Toward the end of 1943, a great game of musical chairs in the Pearl Harbor submarine command involved many of the senior hands.

Lockwood's chief of staff, Sunshine Murray, who had been working in staff jobs without a rest since the outbreak of the war, first in Manila, then in Fremantle, and then in Pearl Harbor, was due for routine rotation back to the States for a new job. Lockwood recommended that Murray, like his predecessors, Gin Styer and John Griggs, be ordered to command a new submarine squadron under construction, but Louis Denfield, in the Bureau of Personnel, had other plans. He ordered Murray to Annapolis as Commandant of Midshipmen.

CHANGES IN COMMAND 549

Murray was crushed. Lockwood appealed to Denfeld.

I do not believe that a good seagoing officer and a top-notch submarine officer such as Murray should go to that particular job. As you will remember, we Midshipmen never knew anything about the seagoing record of our Commandant. He was merely the so-and-so that assigned demerits, and I believe that situation will always exist. In other words, an officer with a fine record is not so much needed as a good disciplinarian, preferably with a good personality. I know it will break Sunshine's heart to lose his new squadron and go ashore.

Lockwood lost; Sunshine Murray was sent to the Naval Academy. He was replaced by an old hand—and friend of Lockwood's—Merrill Comstock, class of 1917, who had commissioned *Cachalot* in 1933. When the war broke out, Comstock was serving with Atlantic Fleet submarines. In June 1942 he took the "submarine desk" in the Navy Department. Al McCann, who came up from Fremantle with his Squadron Six boats being rotated for overhaul, replaced Comstock on the submarine desk.* McCann was replaced as Commander, Squadron Six, by Shorty Edmunds, who had been commanding the sub base at Pearl Harbor.

During the shuffle, Lockwood tried to find a way to promote Babe Brown (Commander, Squadron Four) to a more responsible job. Except for Lockwood, Brown—class of 1914—was senior to everybody in the Pacific submarine force, including Jimmy Fife and Ralph Christie. However, the selection board had passed over Brown and denied him a good job.

In his efforts to boost Brown, Lockwood even proposed that Brown replace Christie. He wrote Denfeld:

I would like to get Babe Brown's name on your list for a top submarine command some day. As you know he has had a great deal of experience ... actually more than Christie.... I feel that he is my best assistant here and ... his personality, physique and all that sort of thing make him an excellent leader. He is actually senior to Ralph Christie.... I just wanted to mention it in case some opportunity turns up for his advancement.

In other letters to Denfeld, Lockwood said, "I am disappointed that he [Brown] has been overlooked so long and as you know I would be

---

* But not for long. He became ill and was relieved by Frank Watkins. Later in 1944, McCann returned to sea as commanding officer of the battleship *Iowa*.

delighted to have him in a top submarine job," and noted, "The place where I really need Babe is in the Southwest Pacific."

Still, no good. Babe Brown remained where he was in Pearl Harbor, serving as Lockwood's chief training officer. His Squadron Four was merged with Swede Momsen's Squadron Two, Momsen retaining title as Commander, Squadron Four.

Gin Styer, commanding Squadron Ten at Midway, then preparing to train and command a wolf pack, also got a jolt: Denfeld ordered him back to the States to command the sub base at New London. Again Lockwood's appeal failed. He was replaced in Squadron Ten by Charles Frederick Erck, an unpopular old hand in submarines who had been serving under Freeland Daubin in the Atlantic.

On a lower level, there were many comings and goings—mostly goings, as per Admiral King's edict to trim the excess of senior officers. Turkey Neck Crawford, commanding Division 43, and Leon Joseph ("Savvy") Huffman, commanding Division 42, literally tossed a coin to see who would go back to the Atlantic to serve as Freeland Daubin's chief of staff. Crawford "lost" and went to the Atlantic. Joe Grenfell, who had been serving as Dick Voge's assistant, was formally appointed strategic planning officer for Lockwood.

Lockwood himself received a nice surprise. On the recommendation of Admiral Nimitz, he was promoted to three stars—vice admiral. He found out about it in spectacular fashion. Returning from Midway to Pearl Harbor on Chuck Triebel's *Snook*, which was returning from patrol, he found a band on the pier and his staff—Babe Brown, Sunshine Murray, Swede Momsen, Dick Voge, and many others—"all grinning and offering congratulations." Lockwood believed at first that they were pulling his leg. When he found out it was really true, he was elated. "There was no real need for a Vice Admiral in submarines," he later wrote. "[It was] unnecessary, perhaps, but damned pleasant to take."

25
Summary, 1943

The second year of the submarine war against Japan was a far better year in every respect than 1942. The three commanders, Lockwood, Christie, and Fife, deployed their submarines more imaginatively. Where in 1942 Pearl Harbor sent only 15 percent of its boats to Empire and East China Sea waters, in 1943 Lockwood sent 50 percent to those waters and for the first time began to exploit the bottleneck in Luzon Strait. Christie and Fife gave up the unrewarding "port watching" and deployed most of their boats seaward, along known shipping lanes. Radar, better Ultra reports, improved Mark XIV torpedo performance, more experienced skippers and crews—all helped.

Twenty months into the war, the force commanders had at last commenced experiments with wolf-packing. However, the three wolf packs sent from Pearl Harbor in the fall of 1943 were more "search" than "attack" units, and it was clear that if wolf-packing was to produce any significant increase in sinkings, much improvement of tactics and gear was needed. Generally, the skippers objected to wolf-packing, especially to having a senior division commander on board making the decisions and trying to coordinate the tactics. All lived in dread that wolf-packing might sooner or later result in the sinking of one friendly submarine by another. But it had begun.

During the year, the three commands conducted about 350 war patrols in the Pacific, about the same number as 1941–42.* The three

---
* Many new boats were added to the fleet in 1943, but these additions were offset by losses, the gradual retirement of the S-boats and *Cachalot, Cuttlefish, Dolphin,*

commands claimed and were credited with sinking 443 Japanese men-of-war and merchant ships for 2.9 million tons. According to postwar records, a closer figure would be about 335 ships for 1.5 million tons, still an increase in tonnage of over 100 percent over 1941–42, when 180 ships for 725,000 tons were sunk.

The 1943 sinkings seriously impeded Japanese shipping services. Imports of bulk commodities for 1943 showed a sharp drop, from 19.4 million tons in 1942 to 16.4 million tons in 1943. Japanese shipbuilding—in all categories except tankers—could no longer keep pace with the losses. At the beginning of 1943, Japan had 5.2 million tons of shipping, excluding tankers. At the end of 1943, the figure stood at 4.1 million, a net loss of about 1.1 million tons of non-tanker shipping.

In terms of tankers alone, the picture was different. Japan began the year with 686,000 tons. During the year, she built more or converted regular ships to tankers. In spite of losing 150,000 tons in tankers to submarines in 1943, she ended the year with a net *increase* in tanker tonnage of 177,000 tons—to 863,000.

During 1943, as the submarine offensive became more effective, Japanese countermeasures grew tougher. The United States lost more than twice as many boats in the Pacific as in 1942: fifteen. Fife lost four, Christie four, and Lockwood seven.* Only three—*Grenadier*, *S-44*, and *Sculpin*—had survivors (the majority of them sent to work in the mines at Ashio).

As in 1942, enormous effort went into the pursuit of Japanese capital ships with the help of glamorous Ultra reports. These reports (plus lucky finds) resulted in about sixty major ship contacts (compared to only twenty-three in 1942), about ten contacts on battleships and forty-five on aircraft carriers. Two of the battleship contacts were developed into attacks—by Dave Whelchel in *Steelhead* and Gene McKinney in *Skate*. Whelchel missed; McKinney probably slightly damaged *Yamato*.

Pike, and *Porpoise,* the shifting of *Narwhal* and *Nautilus* to special missions, the need to re-engine the dozen H.O.R. boats of Squadron Twelve, and the need to overhaul and modernize the older boats.

* Fife lost *Argonaut, Amberjack, Grampus,* and *Triton.* Christie lost *Grenadier, Grayling, Cisco,* and *Capelin.* Lockwood lost *S-44* in Alaska; *Pickerel, Runner,* and *Pompano* off northeast Honshu; *Wahoo* in La Pérouse Strait; and *Corvina* and *Sculpin* during Operation Galvanic.

In addition, two boats were lost in Atlantic waters in 1943. *Dorado,* commanded by Earle Caffrey Schneider, was probably sunk by friendly air forces. *R-12,* commanded by Edward Ellis Shelby, sank during a training exercise off Key West; Shelby and twenty-one others survived.

The approximately forty-five carrier contacts were developed into about thirty attacks. Fourteen of these attacks resulted in possible (but credited) damage to the carrier attacked, notably Roy Benson's attack on *Hiyo* off Tokyo Bay, Beetle Roach's attack on *Unyo* off Saipan, Pete Galantin's attack on a carrier off Bungo Suido, and Herb Andrews's attack on a carrier off Palau. The great majority of the attacks produced nothing but frayed nerves. One small carrier, *Chuyo*, was sunk by Bob Ward in *Sailfish*. *Chuyo* was the only major Japanese man-of-war sunk in 1943 by U.S. submarines.

The Japanese submarine war against Allied forces, which had cost the United States the aircraft carriers *Yorktown* and *Wasp* plus severe damage to *Saratoga* and the battleship *North Carolina* in 1942, took a curious—even inexplicable—turn in 1943. For the most part, Japanese submarines were withdrawn from offensive patrolling and assigned to resupply (or evacuation) missions for forces left behind in the Japanese retreat. In 1943, Japanese submarines sank only three worthwhile U.S. Navy vessels: the jeep carrier *Liscome Bay*, the submarine *Corvina*, and a destroyer, *Henley*. Again in 1943, thanks in large part to Ultra, the Japanese submarine losses were heavy: twenty-two in 1943 compared to twenty-three in 1942. Two of these were sunk by U.S. submarines: *I-24* by Albert Clark, returning *Trout* from Fremantle to Pearl Harbor, and *I-182* by Wally Ebert in *Scamp*.

The "skipper problem" continued unabated all through the year 1943. Too many were still turning in zero patrols because they lacked aggressiveness. But mainly because of the acute shortage, fewer skippers were relieved for nonproductivity: about 25 out of 178, or 14 percent, compared to 30 percent in 1942. To help fill the gap, Lockwood had dipped first to the classes of 1933 and 1934, then to 1935. He was reluctant to dip further, or to appoint experienced and highly qualified reservists to command, for fear of increasing his loss rate.

The Mark XIV torpedo was declared "fixed" in September 1943; the Mark VI magnetic exploder was deactivated by Lockwood in June and by Christie later in the year. As yet it was too early to judge improved results from a statistical standpoint. In fact, the statistics were muddy. In 1942, Pacific submarines on about 350 war patrols had fired 1,442 torpedoes to sink 180 confirmed ships—an average of 8 torpedoes per sinking. In 1943 on about the same number of patrols, Pacific submarines fired 3,937 torpedoes to sink 335 ships—an average of 11.7 torpedoes per sinking (3.7 *more* torpedoes to sink a ship in

1943 than 1942). One factor that distorted the statistics was that in 1943, Pacific submarines were firing many more torpedoes at *larger* targets (carriers, tankers), and though JANAC did not try to confirm damage figures, the three commands claimed much higher damage figures in 1943, probably with ample justification. In any case, the three commands reported a higher percentage of *hits* from experienced skippers using the Mark XIV torpedo.

In general, then, the year 1943 was the year the submarine force, after much trial and error, learned how to fight a submarine war and got the equipment to do it. The top men in command—Lockwood, Christie, Fife—had now gained much experience on the job and knew what could and could not be done. Dick Voge had brought his superlative analytical talents to bear on operational problems and devised new strategies and tactics, including—at last—the wolf pack. The younger skippers moving up to command were, for the most part, experienced in combat. The flow of Ultras on Japanese convoys (as well as on fleet units) was much improved and used to better advantage by the skippers. By the end of the year, the torpedo shortage had at last been overcome, and the boats put to sea with a full load of armament (Mark XIV and XVIII) that on the whole worked as it was supposed to. Week by week the number of now-radar-equipped submarines operating from the three commands increased significantly, and the crews of most of the boats going on patrol were well trained. The morale in all three commands was superlative; Mush Morton, Slade Cutter, Dusty Dornin, Benny Bass, Sam Dealey, and others had seen to that. Submarines believed, with some justification, that they were beginning to make a substantial contribution to the defeat of Japan.

In one sense it could be said that the U.S. submarine war against Japan did not truly begin until the opening days of 1944. What had come before had been a learning period, a time of testing, of weeding out, of fixing defects in weapons, strategy, and tactics, of waiting for sufficient numbers of submarines and workable torpedoes. Now that all was set, the contribution of the submarine force would be more than substantial: it would be decisive.

Part V

26

Pearl Harbor, January through April 1944

The U.S. Invasion of the Marshall Islands

After the bloody invasion of Tarawa, General MacArthur reasserted his view that there should be but one road to Tokyo: his own. He argued that all the resources of Nimitz's command—in particular the aircraft carriers—should support his drive up New Guinea to the Philippines, thence to Okinawa and the Japanese home islands.

In Washington, the Combined Chiefs of Staff weighed MacArthur's arguments but held to the "two road" concept. Nimitz would advance across the mid-Pacific to the Marshalls, Truk, the Marianas, the Palaus. MacArthur would push up through New Guinea to Halmahera, then penetrate the soft underbelly of the Philippines by landing on Mindanao and capturing Davao Gulf. The Nimitz and MacArthur forces would meet in the Philippines. British forces staging from India would recapture Burma, Singapore, and Hong Kong. Afterward, the combined Allied forces would drive north from the Philippines to Formosa, Okinawa, and Japan.

Once the "final" strategy had been settled, Nimitz continued with his plans for the jump from the Gilberts to the Marshalls, code-named Operation Flintlock. The overriding question in Pearl Harbor was, "*Which* Marshalls?" The original plan envisioned simultaneous landings on Maloelap, Wotje, and the main Japanese bastion, Kwajalein. After Tarawa, however, the amphibious experts urged Nimitz to capture the Marshalls in "two bites": first the easternmost islands of Maloelap and Wotje, second Kwajalein.

Nimitz weighed the alternatives. The codebreakers provided valuable intelligence and guidance. The first was that Admiral Koga had written off the Marshalls (and possibly Truk). The new defensive line—to be held at all cost—ran through the Marianas and Palaus to western New Guinea. Admiral Koga's combined fleet was in no shape to do battle. It would not challenge Nimitz in the Marshalls. It would probably withdraw westward to the Palaus or the Philippines and challenge Nimitz in the Marianas, where Koga could obtain land-based air support from Guam, Saipan, and Tinian.

The codebreakers also told Nimitz much about the defenses of the various Marshall islands. Admiral Koga, who believed Nimitz would probably follow the "two bite" concept, had reinforced the easternmost islands: Maloelap, Wotje, and Mili. There were, for example, about 5,000 well-trained troops on Mili. To beef up the eastern islands, Koga had stripped Kwajalein, leaving only about 2,200 trained soldiers on that island, plus about 7,000 laborers, administrative personnel, marooned merchant marine sailors, and others. The island of Majuro, which had a large well-protected anchorage suitable for conversion to a fleet anchorage and support base, was virtually unoccupied. Based on this information and other intelligence, Nimitz made his decision: U.S. forces would bypass the heavily defended eastern islands (Maloelap, Wotje, Mili) in favor of lightly defended Kwajalein and undefended Majuro.

Accordingly, prior to the landings, carrier and land-based planes from the Gilberts attacked Wotje, Maloelap, Mili, Kwajalein, Majuro, and other islands where Admiral Koga had based planes. With little difficulty, Nimitz achieved total air superiority over the Marshalls.

The amphibious forces landed on Kwajalein and Majuro January 31, as scheduled. Majuro fell without a single U.S. casualty. The fighting on Kwajalein was tougher—it cost the United States 372 dead and 1,582 wounded—but compared to Tarawa these figures were modest. Only 265 prisoners were taken on Kwajalein, 100 Japanese and 165 Korean laborers. Within one week, the island was secure and the Seabees had begun an airstrip.

As the codebreakers had predicted, Admiral Koga did not come out to fight; his counterattack was limited to a few aircraft sorties and sub-

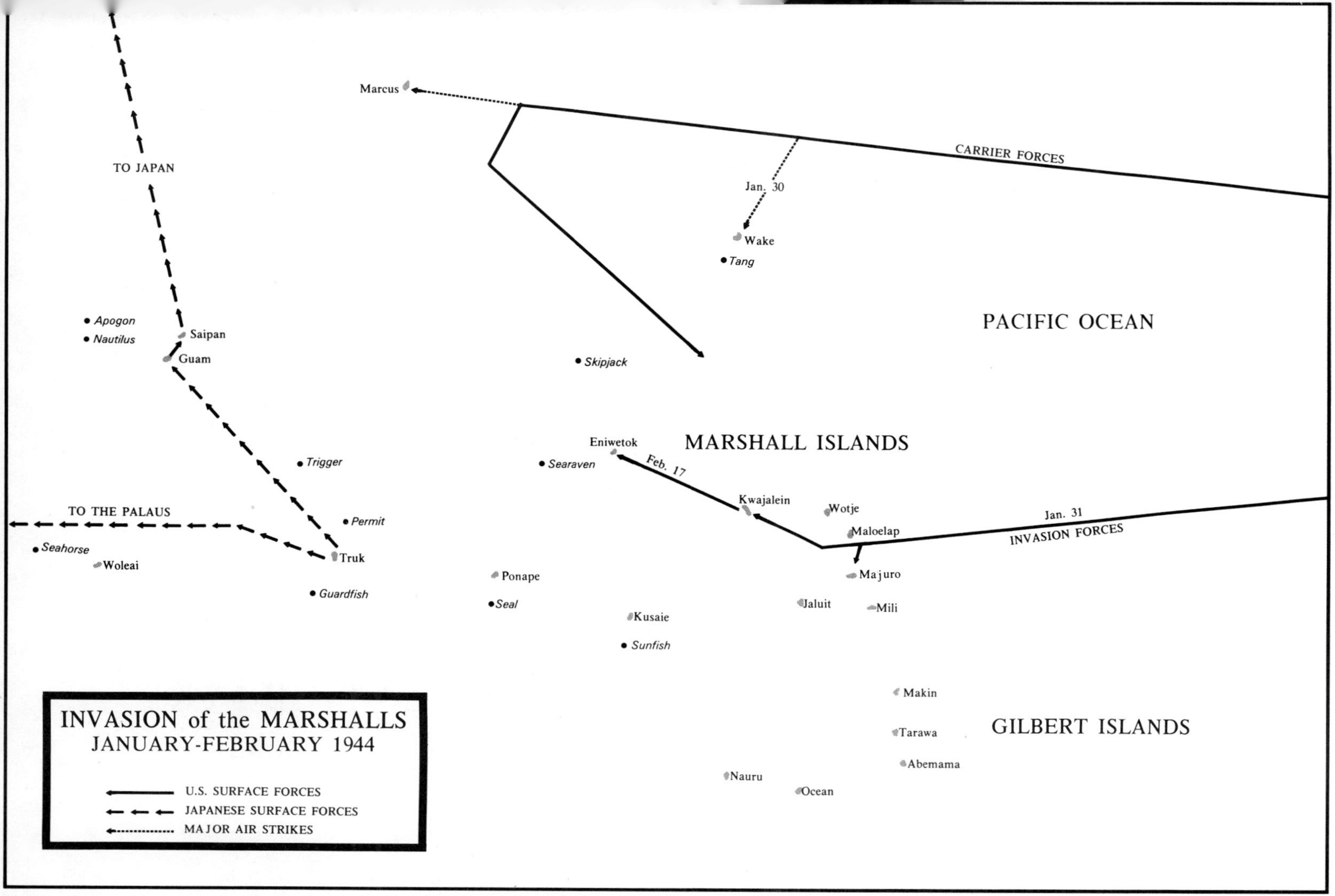
INVASION of the MARSHALLS
JANUARY-FEBRUARY 1944
U.S. SURFACE FORCES
JAPANESE SURFACE FORCES
MAJOR AIR STRIKES
TO JAPAN
Marcus
CARRIER FORCES
Jan. 30
Wake
Tang
PACIFIC OCEAN
Apogon
Nautilus
Saipan
Guam
Skipjack
Eniwetok
MARSHALL ISLANDS
Feb. 17
Searaven
Trigger
Kwajalein
Wotje
Jan. 31
Maloelap
INVASION FORCES
TO THE PALAUS
Permit
Seahorse
Woleai
Truk
Ponape
Majuro
Guardfish
Seal
Jaluit
Mili
Kusaie
Sunfish
Makin
Tarawa
GILBERT ISLANDS
Abemama
Nauru
Ocean

marine patrols. The aircraft did no serious damage. The four submarines had no opportunity to fire a torpedo; thanks in part to the codebreakers, all four were lost to U.S. forces. (One of these was *I-175*, which had sunk the jeep carrier *Liscome Bay* two months earlier in the Gilberts.) Later, two more Japanese submarines were sunk trying to take supplies to bypassed Mili.

Immediately following the invasion of Kwajalein and Majuro, Admiral Koga ordered the major elements of his combined fleet basing at Truk to retreat westward. On February 3, the giant battleship *Yamato* and several other battleships and cruisers left for Palau. The four carriers and Admiral Koga in his flagship, the super-battleship *Musashi*, returned to Japan for a conference. While some of the carriers remained in home waters, Admiral Koga on *Musashi* later joined his other ships at Palau.

The victory in the Marshalls had been achieved with consummate ease. Informed by the codebreakers that Admiral Koga's fleet had abandoned Truk, Nimitz ordered his amphibious forces to seize the westernmost of the Marshall Islands, Eniwetok, scheduled for invasion in May. Eniwetok was 1,000 miles from Saipan and 670 miles from Truk. It could serve as a base for aircraft to help soften up the Marianas.

In support of the Eniwetok invasion, Nimitz ordered a carrier strike on Truk, Operation Hailstone. This strike, carried out over two days, February 16–17, turned out to be one of the most devastating of the war. Achieving complete surprise, the carrier planes sank many fleet support ships that had not yet left: two light cruisers, four destroyers, three auxiliary cruisers, two submarine tenders, twenty-four merchant ships (including five tankers)—in all, about 200,000 tons of Japanese shipping. In addition, about 250 to 275 Japanese planes were destroyed. After that raid, Truk was scratched from the invasion agenda and added to the islands to be bypassed.

The invasion of Eniwetok—Operation Catchpole—took place on February 17, while the Truk strike was in progress. Nimitz believed that Eniwetok, like Majuro, was practically deserted. However, an amphibious brigade (about 2,200 men) of the Japanese army had landed there undetected on January 4. They put up a stiff fight. Before the island was secure, the United States suffered 195 killed and 521 wounded. The Japanese lost about 2,700 men. Only 64 surrendered.

Following the strike on Truk, Nimitz ordered an air strike on the

Marianas February 22. While approaching the islands, the carriers were detected by a Japanese search plane. The Japanese sent out aircraft to attack the carriers, but no ship was hit. On the morning of February 23, U.S. planes struck Saipan, Guam, and Tinian. These raids cost the Japanese about 150 aircraft, including torpedo bombers that had just been sent from Japan to augment Admiral Koga's fleet for the "showdown" battle. The pilots found few ships in the harbor.

Majuro was immediately turned into a major fleet anchorage and support facility. On February 9, a few days after Kwajalein was secure, Lockwood flew there to set up an advance submarine base, picking out a small paradisical island, Enimonetto, renamed Myrna, for a rest camp. When he returned to Pearl Harbor, he ordered Charles Erck, commanding Squadron Ten in *Sperry*, to move from Midway to Majuro. Erck arrived on April 12. Shortly afterward the new tender *Bushnell* joined *Sperry*. *Kingfish*, returning from her seventh patrol on April 7, was the first submarine to receive a refit at Majuro. This new base moved Lockwood's submarines 2,000 miles closer to Japan.

After a brief rest, the carrier forces staging from Majuro once more ranged to the west. They struck again at Truk, then proceeded farther west, launching a massive attack on the Palaus March 31 and April 1, known as Operation Desecrate. The major elements of the Japanese fleet retreated still farther west, to Davao, Tawi Tawi, Surabaya, and Singapore. U.S. planes sank two old destroyers, four small escorts, and twenty naval auxiliaries and merchant ships—in all, about 104,000 tons of Japanese shipping. In addition they destroyed 150 aircraft, most of the planes based on the Palaus. On the return to Majuro, the carriers sideswiped Yap, Ulithi, and Woleai.

During the strike on the Palaus, Admiral Koga decided to shift his headquarters to Davao. On the way there, his plane disappeared. It was the second time within a year that a Japanese commander in chief had died in a plane crash near the front lines. Some U.S. Navy officers believed Koga, like Yamamoto, had been shot down with the help of the codebreakers. It was not so. His plane encountered a fierce storm and was thrown into the sea. Admiral Koga was succeeded by Admiral Soemu Toyoda.

Interceptions in the Marshalls and Other Missions

By January 1, 1944, when Nimitz launched his big push against the Marshalls, Lockwood, Christie, and Fife had a combined force of almost one hundred modern fleet submarines. This was enough to maintain the cyclic war patrols against Japanese merchant shipping and to provide support to U.S. fleet operations. From January onward, enemy-controlled seas were thick with U.S. submarines, on station, going to and from station, or standing by enemy-held islands for fleet support. The Luzon Strait bottleneck became a regular patrol area. More and more wolf packs were sent there and to the usual areas.

During the invasion of the Marshall Islands and the carrier strikes on Truk, the Marianas, and the Palaus, submarines were assigned many missions: (1) interception of Admiral Koga's major fleet units withdrawing from Truk to Palau and Japan; (2) interception of vessels attempting to support the Marshalls; (3) interception of vessels fleeing Truk, Saipan, and Palau during the air strikes: (4) photographic and other reconnaissance; and (5) lifeguarding.

George Garvie Molumphy relieved Howard Stoner, Tommy Withers's son-in-law, on *Skipjack*. Molumphy had commanded *Dolphin* while she was a Pearl Harbor training vessel and then made a PCO cruise on *Finback*. Prior to the invasion, he made his first patrol in the Marshalls. He was criticized for not spending more time close by important harbors.

On his second patrol, during the invasion of the Marshalls, *Skipjack* patrolled off Eniwetok. On the night of January 26, acting on an Ultra, Molumphy intercepted a convoy that included *Okitsu Maru*, a converted seaplane tender of 6,666 tons, escorted by the destroyer *Suzukaze*, bringing more reinforcements to Eniwetok. Molumphy made a submerged approach at radar depth and fired four torpedoes at the destroyer. *Suzukaze* blew up and sank. Shifting targets, Molumphy fired his stern tubes at the seaplane tender but missed it: one hit a merchant ship; others prematured.

During this last attack, one of *Skipjack*'s torpedo tube valves stuck open. A torrent of seawater flooded the after torpedo room. Before the torpedomen could close emergency valves, *Skipjack* took on fourteen tons of water—and a large angle. By fine seamanship, Molumphy overcame the casualty, caught up with the convoy, and attacked the seaplane tender again, sinking it. Thanks to *Skipjack*, the invasion of Eniwetok was easier. After that, Molumphy went over to Truk to intercept Admiral Koga's fleet units leaving the island.

Permit lay off Truk. She, too, had a new skipper, Carter Bennett, who had replaced Moon Chapple. "Relieving Moon," Bennett said later, "was one of the damndest experiences I had in the war. It took me three days to find him. When I finally got him on board for the ceremony, Moon said to his exec, Fred Taeusch, 'Aw, shucks, Fred. You read my orders for me.'"

On his first patrol in *Permit*, Bennett, like Molumphy, went to the Marshalls. He had a busy time off Kwajalein. He damaged a seaplane tender and then attacked a convoy of three "big juicy ships," one of them a tanker bound for Truk. He believed he got hits on the tanker and two freighters. Dodging escorts, Bennett attacked the wounded targets again and again, plus a cruiser that came to the rescue. *Permit* was repeatedly depth-charged, bombed, and almost torpedoed by a Japanese PT boat, but Bennett persisted until he ran out of torpedoes. After this, Bennett took *Permit* back to Mare Island for a long overhaul and then returned to patrol Truk.

After the invasion of the Marshalls, when Admiral Koga ordered his fleet from Truk, Bennett was again a very busy skipper. On February 1, he spotted two battleships, escorted by destroyers, leaving the island at ten o'clock in the morning. Bennett tried to attack but could get no closer than 24,000 yards, so he surfaced within sight of the island, in broad daylight, and got off a contact report stating the battleships were westbound—toward the Palaus. A plane drove him down during the transmission, but he resurfaced and broadcast the message again. One of the battleships was probably *Yamato*.

A week later, February 10, Bennett picked up more big ships coming out of Truk. This time it was night and Bennett closed quickly, preparing to attack. When he got to 4,000 yards, he saw they were two *Mogami*-class heavy cruisers. Bennett submerged ahead, penetrating the destroyer screen. He fired four torpedoes and believed he hit one of the cruisers. Before he could make another attack, however, destroyers pounced on *Permit*, throwing depth charges. Later, Bennett surfaced and got off another valuable contact report.

During the early hours of the following morning, Bennett picked up another contact. He closed to 15,000 yards and saw his contact was an aircraft carrier coming *into* Truk. Bennett moved in to 9,000 yards but could get no closer. In desperation, he fired four torpedoes from this very long range.* All missed. Destroyers tracked *Permit* down and dropped more depth charges. Later, Bennett got off yet another contact report.

The next day, February 12–13, Bennett tangled with two separate convoys. After a long chase, he was preparing to attack when he was picked up by a destroyer. He went deep, hugging a reef to take advantage of "reef noise," but the Japanese destroyer skipper was not fooled. He pinned Bennett down—forcing him to 320 feet—and dropped thirty-five depth charges, many close. Bennett escaped and said later, "With just a modicum of persistence, that destroyer would have had our hide nailed to the barn for sure. It was the roughest time I had during the war."

By this time, *Permit* was low on fuel. Voge inquired if Bennett would like to obtain fuel from *Nautilus*, then entering the Marianas on a regular patrol, but Bennett declined. Instead, he went south to Milne Bay. He hoped to be sent on to Brisbane for a refit, but after his tanks had been filled Fife ordered him to return to Pearl Harbor by way of Palau. He sank no ships on this long and frustrating patrol.

Dusty Dornin and Ned Beach, returning *Trigger* from overhaul at Pearl Harbor, patrolled in the waters between Truk and the Marianas. For the first time, Dusty Dornin found poor hunting. Three weeks dragged by before he made his first contact, and then he botched the attack. The target, discovered on the morning of January 27, was a small RO-class Japanese submarine cruising the surface en route from Guam to Truk. Dornin submerged and moved in close, planning to shoot from 800 yards. However, when Beach raised the periscope for the final look, he found to his consternation that the target had discovered *Trigger* and had zigged directly toward him! The Japanese sub crossed *Trigger*'s bow, then swung stern tubes to bear. Dornin went deep, holding his breath and waiting for the impact of Japanese torpedoes. Inexplicably, the sub did not fire. Later Dornin surfaced to chase, but the sub got away.

Four days later, January 31, business picked up. *Trigger* found a convoy, and Dornin swung in for a night surface attack. Radar showed

---

* This shot tied Roland Pryce's on *Spearfish*, December 20, 1941, for the longest shot of the war. (Pryce missed also.)

three big ships and three escorts. Beach remained on the bridge, feeding bearings through the TBT *; Dornin was in the conning tower, overseeing the attack, checking the TDC and radar plan position indicator (PPI) scope. As the attack developed, *Trigger* would have to fire across the bows of an escorting destroyer at extremely close range. Dornin decided to shoot six torpedoes, three by radar at the biggest ship and three by TBT at the destroyer, now broadside to at 700 yards' range, in a single salvo. On the bridge, Beach saw the three fired at the destroyer spin off erratically just as she finally saw the surfaced submarine and turned to attack. Beach called for flank speed and full rudder, steadied with *Trigger*'s stern on the swinging destroyer, and fired four stern tubes. The destroyer, believing *Trigger* had submerged and possibly confused by the cloud of sudden exhaust smoke from her straining diesels, paused to drop depth charges, and the submarine hauled clear from a near thing.

All torpedoes fired from the stern tubes missed, but one of the initial salvo of three passed through the entire formation and hit one of the other escorts, *Nasami*, a small minelayer, which blew up and sank in minutes. Dornin then ordered a fast end around on the convoy. In a second attack, he again fired at the biggest ship. The ship blew up and went down. Dawn came before Dornin could mount a third attack.

Dornin and Beach returned from this patrol crestfallen. For the first time in many months, *Trigger* returned with torpedoes in her tubes and racks. However, when they reached Pearl Harbor, they received a tremendous welcome from Lockwood. The codebreakers had discovered from Japanese battle-damage reports that the big ship Dornin had sunk in the convoy was a real prize, the 12,000-ton submarine tender *Yasukuni Maru*. Recently overhauled, she was en route to Truk to replace the light cruiser *Katori*, then serving as submarine tender and needed elsewhere. The incoming tender had been loaded with valuable submarine stores and spare parts and the cream of the Japanese navy sub repairmen. There were only forty-three survivors. (Lockwood also believed that his counterpart, Vice Admiral Takeo Takagi, commanding the main Japanese submarine force, known as the Sixth Fleet, was on board, but he was mistaken. Takagi was in Truk, flying his flag on a sister ship of *Yasukuni Maru*, *Heian Maru*).

Dornin found another surprise waiting, a promotion of sorts. He

* Target Bearing Transmitter, a pair of binoculars in a swinging mount designed especially for night surface attacks.

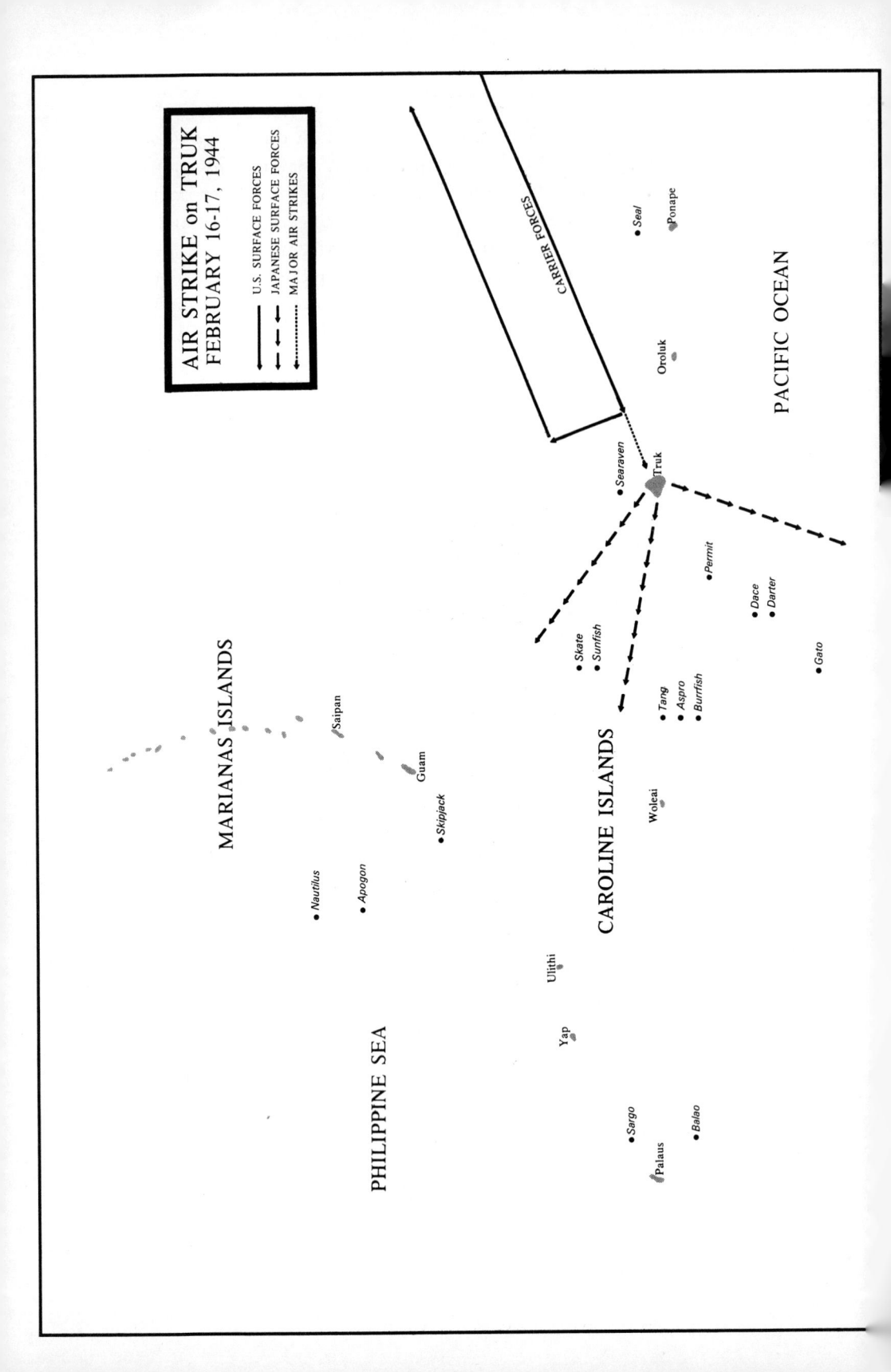

AIR STRIKE on TRUK
FEBRUARY 16-17, 1944

→ U.S. SURFACE FORCES
⇢ JAPANESE SURFACE FORCES
⋯▸ MAJOR AIR STRIKES

CARRIER FORCES

PACIFIC OCEAN

- Seal
- Ponape
- Oroluk
- Searaven
- Truk
- Skate
- Sunfish
- Permit
- Tang
- Aspro
- Burrfish
- Dace
- Darter
- Gato
- Woleai

CAROLINE ISLANDS

MARIANAS ISLANDS

- Saipan
- Guam
- Skipjack
- Apogon
- Nautilus
- Ulithi
- Yap
- Sargo
- Palaus
- Balao

PHILIPPINE SEA

was ordered to relieve C. C. Kirkpatrick in Washington, as aide to Admiral King. Lockwood was happy for Dornin's sake but generally angry at the Bureau of Personnel, and Bob Rice in particular; another first-rate submarine skipper had been removed from his command.

Bub Ward in *Guardfish*, enroute from Australia, patrolled south of Truk. On February 1, he picked up a two-ship convoy and began his approach. Just after Ward fired, the destroyer *Umikaze* crossed the torpedo track. One of the torpedoes hit the destroyer, blowing off her stern. She upended and sank. After that, Ward returned *Guardfish* to Pearl Harbor, then on to Mare Island for a long overhaul and modernization.

Skate, with Bud Gruner as her new skipper, patrolled off Truk during the February 16 air strike, Hailstone.

The day before the strike, Gruner found the new light cruiser *Agano*—which Wally Ebert in *Scamp* had damaged off Rabaul in November—coming out of North Pass escorted by two destroyers. In a workmanlike attack, he fired four torpedoes from 2,400 yards. Three hit. Unlucky *Agano* exploded, caught fire, and sank. Her two destroyer escorts picked up 523 survivors and started back to Truk. (One of these was *Oite*, sunk the following day during the air strikes. She went down with her own crew and some *Agano* survivors.)

After that, Gruner took *Skate* westward toward the Palaus. On February 25, off Ulithi, he picked up a Japanese aircraft carrier. Believing the carrier to be coming into Ulithi, he plotted a course to intercept, but it went hurrying off to the north, and Gruner could get no closer than 10 miles.

A new boat joined those patrolling off Truk. This was *Tang*, commanded by Dick O'Kane. His exec was Murray Bennett Frazee, Jr., another from the class of 1939. O'Kane and Morton had been quite a team. How would O'Kane do alone?

Tang came to her area by way of Wake, lifeguarding the air strikes on January 30 and February 5. On the morning of February 17, following the air strike on Truk, O'Kane picked up a fleeing convoy. During the approach, he was driven down but evaded, reapproached, and fired four stern tubes—his first of the war—sinking the big freighter *Gyoten Maru*, 6,800 tons. He trailed the convoy but was not able to get off another shot. After that, *Tang* moved up to Saipan to stand by for the February 22 air strike.

The convoy O'Kane attacked continued westward. Another new boat, *Burrfish*, commanded by William Beckwith Perkins, Jr., patrolled along the path. His exec was Talbot Edward Harper, who had made five war patrols on *Grayback*. Perkins and Harper made contact, but the fire-control party as a whole did not function efficiently and the ships got away. Later, *Burrfish* missed other opportunities. When she returned to port, Shorty Edmunds's endorsement described the patrol as "disappointing" and stated, "The fire-control party needs extensive training."

Melvin Dry in *Searaven* began his patrol off Eniwetok, where he made a photographic reconnaissance; then he shifted to Truk to lifeguard the air strike. The U.S. carrier force approaching Truk went right over *Searaven*. During the operations, Dry received a call for help from the carrier *Yorktown*. A torpedo bomber was down in Northeast Pass. With air cover provided by a carrier fighter, Dry took *Searaven* to the rescue. He picked up three men, the only naval aviators rescued by submarine during the Truk air strike. After that, he moved up to Saipan for the February 22 strike.

After Joe Enright asked to be relieved on *Dace*, following his unlucky first patrol, the ship went to Bladen Dulany Claggett, another member of the class of 1935, who began the war on Klakring's *Guardfish* and later served as exec to Ian Eddy on *Pargo*.

Dace took station south of Truk where, on January 26, she made contact with a tanker with two escorts. Claggett, assisted by his exec, Bill Holman, penetrated the screen and fired at the tanker, but the escorts foiled the attack. After refueling at Tulagi, Claggett returned to Truk for the air strike. On February 11, he made contact with a five-ship convoy but was unable to attack. Claggett concluded the patrol in Milne Bay, where it was declared unsuccessful.

Dace's sister ship, *Darter*, set off on her first patrol in January commanded by an old hand, Shirley Stovall, the ex-codebreaker who had made three war patrols on *Gudgeon* with Dusty Dornin for his exec. Stovall patrolled off Eniwetok and Ponape and then Truk. On January 26, he picked up a tanker with two escorts—probably the one Claggett had fired at—but could not get into attack position. Like *Dace*, *Darter* dropped down to Tulagi to refuel and then returned to Truk to lifeguard the air strike.

INTERCEPTIONS AND OTHER MISSIONS

On the way up to Truk, Stovall picked up a ship with four escorts. He fired all six bow tubes. All missed. He swung around and fired his stern tubes. Stovall believed some of these hit and the ship sank, but the evidence was considered too slim and it was denied. Off Truk, after the air strike, he intercepted a big ship under tow but was not able to get around the many escorts for a shot. Stovall returned to Milne Bay for refit.

Slade Cutter, making his second war patrol in command of *Seahorse*, patrolled off the Palaus. His exec was still Speed Currie, but on this trip Cutter took pains to develop the talents of his bright young TDC operator, William Alexander Budding, Jr., then twenty-two.

On the way to the Palaus, while passing near the area where Dornin and Beach were patrolling north of Truk, Cutter picked up a contact—one ship with four escorts. With Budding on the TDC doing "an excellent job," Cutter closed on the surface at night. He maneuvered around the escorts and delivered four electric torpedoes. Two hit, and the freighter went down.*

Continuing onward, Cutter took station on the Palaus-Wewak route. On January 20, he received an Ultra on a convoy and on the afternoon of January 21 picked it up by periscope: two fat freighters "heavily loaded, their decks piled with cargo," and three escorts. After dark, Cutter got into position and attacked. He set up on one freighter and fired three torpedoes from a range of 2,800 yards, obtaining hits in *both* vessels. One sank; one settled low in the water. "The Japs were no more surprised than we," Cutter wrote, "as we entertained no hope whatever of hitting second ship with first salvo. Both targets stopped and commenced firing their deck guns in every direction."

Cutter decided to reattack the settling ship and fired two more torpedoes from a range of 3,120 yards. No hits. Perplexed, Cutter huddled with Budding, then fired two more at 2,600 yards. Again no hits. Another huddle with the fire-control party. The guess was that the TBT on the bridge was either out altogether or putting out erroneous information. They were right and fixed it. "Regretting the waste of precious torpedoes," Cutter turned his stern to the target and fired two more from 2,250 yards. Later, he wrote:

At exactly the correct time (to the second) the first torpedo struck just abaft the stack. The target blew up and burst into flame. With the

* Lending further credence to the untrue submarine legend that Cutter and Dornin constantly poached on one another's area for the fun of it.

target brilliantly illuminated, the second torpedo hit forward of the bridge and the ship immediately sank. After she went down explosions were seen on the surface of the water, obviously gasoline drums exploding. During our retirement and for over an hour, the surface of the water where the target had sunk was a mass of burning gasoline. All hands were given an opportunity to witness the spectacular show and enjoy the unique experience of "below-decks-men" actually seeing the results of their work.

After sinking these two ships, Cutter moved *Seahorse* to Palau. On January 28 he spotted three freighters coming out, closely escorted. Cutter tracked this convoy for thirty-two hours before the escorts grew lax and gave him an opening. He fired three torpedoes at one of the freighters, obtaining three hits. The first two set the ship on fire; the third blew her stern off. It sank stern first, vertically.

Harassed by escorts and aircraft, Cutter continued to pursue this convoy for the next forty-eight hours.* Shortly after midnight on February 1, he got into position and fired four stern tubes at a second freighter. All missed. He came around and fired two bow tubes. No hits. With only two torpedoes remaining in his stern tubes, Cutter fired them both in a quick setup from an unfavorable position. He thought he missed and went deep to avoid a charging escort. While depth charges exploded around *Seahorse*, Cutter heard his torpedoes hit the target, followed by many light explosions. "They sounded like strings of Chinese firecrackers," Cutter wrote, "and indicated either ammunition or gasoline drums going off." Later he surfaced and observed, "Scene of sinking a mass of gasoline flames with drums still exploding on the surface." In all, the convoy chase had lasted eighty hours, one of the longest and most tenacious on record.

Postwar records credited Cutter with sinking five ships on this patrol. Total score for two patrols: ten confirmed ships sunk.

Philip Weaver Garnett, commanding old *Sargo*, followed Cutter to Palau. Garnett was there when Admiral Koga's ships retreated from

* During the chase Cutter paused briefly and had his men paint the periscope and shears pink, an idea originated by Sam Dealey, who had painted *Harder*'s periscopes pink on the theory that pink reflected the color of the medium it was in—that is, if the water was blue, the periscopes tended to take on a blue hue; if the sky was overcast and the water a muddy gray, the periscopes tended to take on a muddy-gray hue. Cutter intended to remain on the surface hull down, and hoped the periscopes would take on the prevailing color and be hard to detect. Later, when he returned to patrol off Palau, he repainted them black. (By that time, the hulls of most boats—after much experimentation—were painted grayish black.)

INTERCEPTIONS AND OTHER MISSIONS

Truk, but he failed to intercept them. Later he said, "I was alerted to a task force heading for Palau. I was in position for its daylight position off the south end of Palau, but I was probably detected by their radar. The force passed well outside and around us and entered Palau. The only warship tentatively identified was a *Chitose*-class seaplane tender."

Garnett missed the big targets, but he found plenty of action during his patrol. He made four attacks, firing all his torpedoes. On February 17 he sank the 6,500-ton transport *Nichiro Maru* and on February 29 the 5,300-ton transport *Uchide Maru*.

The Brisbane-based boat *Balao*, commanded by young Cy Cole, en route to Pearl Harbor and refit, patrolled south of the Palaus. Cole sailed under a shadow cast by his previous patrol, during which he botched an attack on two heavy cruisers. On February 23, south of the Palaus, Cole sank his (and *Balao*'s) first confirmed ship, *Nikki Maru*, a 5,900-ton transport. On February 28 he sank two more, a 2,700-ton freighter and a 6,800-ton transport. The latter two were probably from the same convoy from which Garnett sank two ships on the same day, a little farther south.

Cutter, Garnett, and Cole in total sank nine ships off Palau in the space of five weeks.

By his performance on this patrol, for which he earned a well-deserved Navy Cross, Cy Cole more than made up for missing the heavy cruisers. But he was unlucky. When *Balao* put into Pearl Harbor for extensive refit, Cole was hospitalized for minor surgery and the boat went to another skipper. When he was ready for duty, Cole had to settle for the only command then available, old *Spearfish*.

By the time U.S. carrier planes struck Saipan on February 22, Dick O'Kane in *Tang* was standing to the westward of the island to intercept fleeing ships.

On the night of February 22, O'Kane found a west-bound five-ship convoy: three freighters and two escorts. Going in and out of rainsqualls which made the targets hard to distinguish on radar, O'Kane eased in on the surface to 1,500 yards. With *Tang* "dead in the water, and holding her breath," he fired four torpedoes at a freighter. The ship, 3,600-ton *Fukuyama Maru*, blew up and sank instantly. O'Kane turned back for a second attack on the convoy. Setting up again at close range, he found another target and fired four torpedoes.

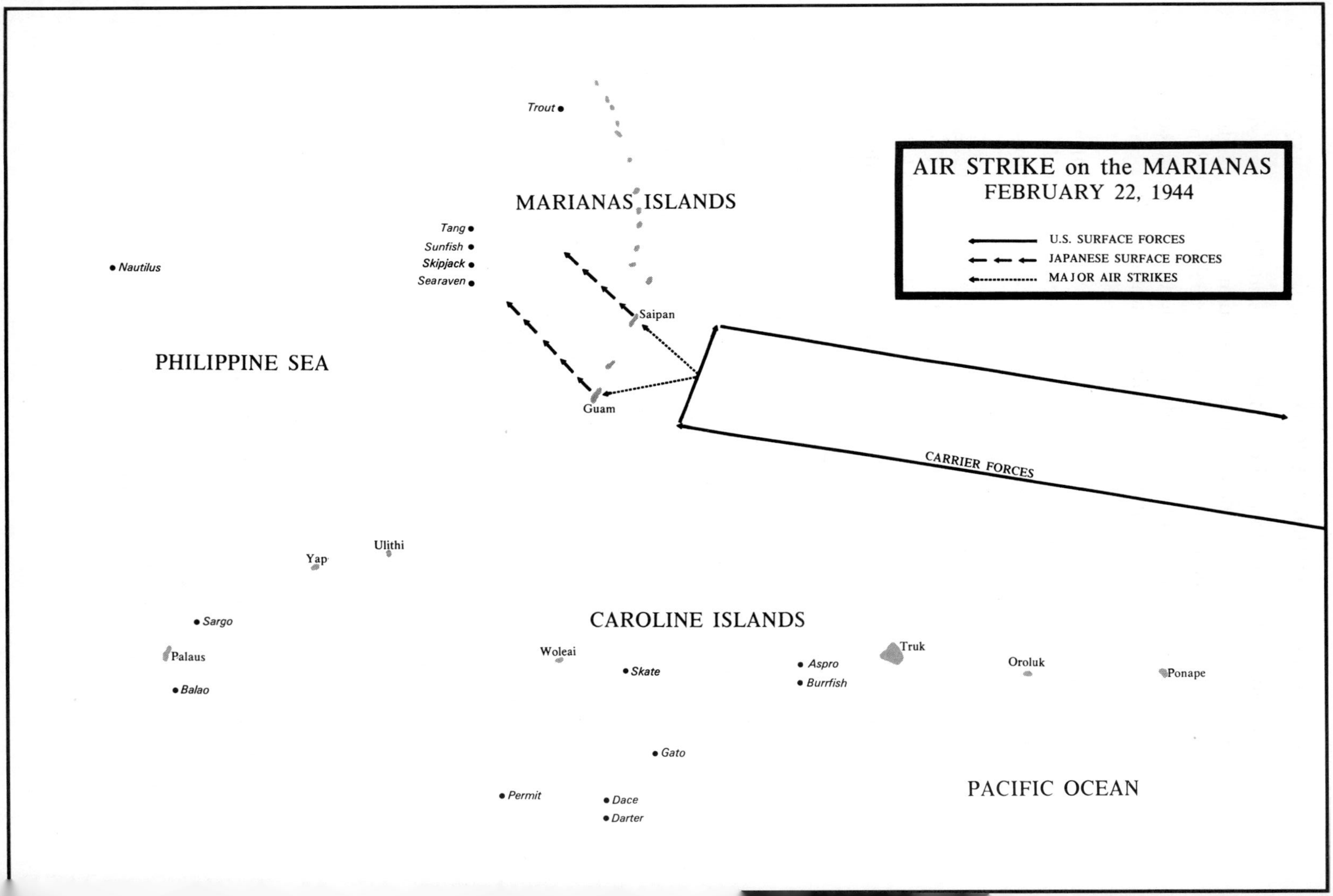

AIR STRIKE on the MARIANAS
FEBRUARY 22, 1944
U.S. SURFACE FORCES
JAPANESE SURFACE FORCES
MAJOR AIR STRIKES
Trout
MARIANAS ISLANDS
Tang
Sunfish
Skipjack
Searaven
Nautilus
Saipan
PHILIPPINE SEA
Guam
CARRIER FORCES
Ulithi
Yap
Sargo
CAROLINE ISLANDS
Palaus
Balao
Woleai
Skate
Aspro
Burrfish
Truk
Oroluk
Ponape
Gato
Permit
Dace
Darter
PACIFIC OCEAN

INTERCEPTIONS AND OTHER MISSIONS

The first two were beautiful hits in her stern and just aft of the stack [he wrote], but the detonation of the third torpedo hit forward of his bridge was terrific. The enemy ship was twisted, lifted from the water as you would flip a spoon on end and then commenced belching flame as she sank. The Tang *was shaken far worse than by any depth charge we could remember, but a quick check, as our jaws came off our chests, showed no damage.*

The ship was *Yamashimo Maru*, 6,800 tons.

Two days later, O'Kane picked up another westbound convoy: freighter, tanker, and destroyer. He tracked it during the day, running in and out of rainsqualls, and then moved in to attack after dark, firing four torpedoes at the freighter. "The ship went to pieces," O'Kane wrote, "and amidst beautiful fireworks sank before we had completed our turn to evade. The tanker opened fire fore and aft immediately, while the destroyer . . . closed the scene rapidly, spraying shells in every direction."

While the destroyer nuzzled close to the tanker, O'Kane tracked and got into position for a dawn periscope attack. He looked at both ships from close range, noting every detail, including an estimated 150 lookouts on one side of the tanker. Then, from the point-blank range of 500 yards, he fired four torpedoes at the tanker. "The first three hit as aimed," he wrote, "directly under the stack, at the forward end of his after superstructure and under his bridge. The explosions were wonderful, throwing Japs and other debris above the belching smoke. He sank by the stern in four minutes." This ship was identified in postwar Japanese records not as a tanker but as a freighter, *Echizen Maru*, 2,500 tons.

The next day O'Kane found a third convoy and tracked it, waiting for darkness. Then he surfaced and picked his target carefully, firing his last four torpedoes. He believed he had missed. However, postwar records credited him with sinking *Choko Maru* on that day, a freighter of 1,794 tons. With all torpedoes expended, O'Kane returned to Pearl Harbor.

Following this first sensational patrol, there was no longer any question about how Dick O'Kane would do on his own. He had sunk five ships for 21,400 tons.

Sunfish, now commanded by Edward Ellis Shelby, who had survived the accidental sinking of *R-12* at Key West (and was not blamed for her loss), patrolled near *Tang* during the strike. Shelby began his patrol with a photographic reconnaissance of the island of Kusaie and then shifted to the Marianas. On the night of February 23, fighting the same foul weather as *Tang,* Shelby found a target. At first he believed it might be the light carrier *Unyo,* which had left Saipan under tow several weeks before. Shelby fired six bow tubes from 2,300 yards. Moments later, the target blew up with an explosion so forceful it snapped the heads of personnel on *Sunfish's* bridge and "jerked the boat in the water." It was not a carrier (for which Shelby was credited) but a freighter, *Shinyubari Maru,* 5,354 tons.

A few hours later, Shelby broke out of the rain and found a weird, unmoving sight ahead. He believed it to be the carrier's bow, standing vertically in the water, but someone else said, no, it was a freighter, bows on. Whatever it was, Shelby set up fast and fired three torpedoes down the throat. The target blew up and sank. It was another freighter, 4,000 tons.

Action During the Palaus Air Strike

During the carrier air strike on the Palaus, March 30–31, there were a dozen submarines in the area, seven from Pearl Harbor and from Bisbane (or the advance base, Milne Bay). *Tullibee, Tang, Archerfish, Tunny, Gar, Blackfish,* and *Bashaw* lay offshore to intercept Japanese fleet units fleeing and merchant shipping. *Dace, Darter,* and *Scamp* patrolled near Davao Gulf to catch ships retreating to that place. *Pampanito* and *Harder* lifeguarded off Yap and Woleai.

John Scott returned *Tunny* from overhaul in advance of the strike. On March 22, he found a convoy and attacked, damaging a freighter. The following night, Scott picked up a Japanese submarine, *I-42,* en route from Palau to Rabaul with supplies. Scott fired four torpedoes from a range of 1,500 yards, then dived to avoid possible counterattack. As *Tunny* went under, Scott and his men heard and felt a violent explosion that lighted the interior of the conning tower. For a brief moment, Scott, fearing the sub had fired at *Tunny,* was not sure "who hit who." He went deep; his sonarman reported breaking-up noises. For Scott, this was the most nerve-racking attack on any of his five patrols to date. He remained submerged all the next day and passed out a ration of whiskey for the crew.

ACTION DURING THE PALAUS AIR STRIKE

While the U.S. carriers approached the Palaus, Scott took up station near the main pass leading from the islands. At noon on March 29, the day before the carrier planes were scheduled to attack, Scott saw a group of "motley" freighters leaving the Palaus. He violated Lockwood's bird-in-hand policy and let them go by, hoping for bigger game: Koga's *Musashi*, for example.

Scott's gamble paid off. That same night he saw a curious-looking vessel coming out of the pass with destroyer escorts. At first Scott thought the mass was a floating drydock; then, on closer inspection, a *Kongo*-class battleship. In fact, it was Koga's flagship (less Koga), the 63,000-ton *Musashi*. Scott, who had made the classic attack on three aircraft carriers at Truk in April 1943, made a second one: he outwitted the destroyers, closed to 2,000 yards, and fired a salvo of six torpedoes.

One of the destroyer escorts spotted the torpedoes and flashed a warning. While Scott went deep, *Musashi* turned to avoid. One of the torpedoes hit anyway, blowing off part of the bow and killing seven men, but the damage was not serious. By the time the carrier planes hit the Palaus the following day, *Musashi* was gone.

While *Tunny* was standing by on the surface 30 miles off the Palaus, a U.S. torpedo bomber attacked her, dropping a 2,000-pound bomb a few yards off the forward engine room that inflicted serious damage. Scott submerged to make emergency repairs, then surfaced to get off an angry report of the incident to Lockwood. Returning to lifeguard station, Scott found two Japanese aviators floating in the water. One came on board; the other refused. With the remaining torpedoes in the after torpedo room damaged by the U.S. Navy bomb, Scott left station, going to Brisbane by way of Milne Bay for refit.

In squally weather, Charles Brindupke in *Tullibee* made contact with one group of fleeing ships—a convoy consisting of a large troop transport and cargo ship, two medium-sized freighters, two escorts, and a large destroyer. Brindupke set up on the large transport, making several approaches through the rain.

The escorts picked him up and dropped fifteen to twenty depth charges to scare him off, but Brindupke did not scare easily. He maneuvered through the escorts, closed to 3,000 yards, and fired two bow tubes. A couple of minutes later, a violent explosion rocked *Tullibee*. Gunner's mate C. W. Kuykendall, who was on the bridge when the explosion occurred, was thrown into the water, along with some other men. *Tullibee* was nowhere to be seen. Following the explosion she sank immediately, a victim, Kuykendall believed, of a circular run of one of the torpedoes whose contact exploder, unfortunately, worked as designed.

For about ten minutes, Kuykendall heard voices in the water, then nothing. All night long he swam in the ocean. At ten o'clock the next morning a Japanese escort vessel found him. After firing at him briefly with a machine gun, the crew of the escort picked him up. Kuykendall was told that the transport Brindupke fired at was hit by the other torpedo.

Kuykendall suffered the fate of the survivors of Fitzgerald's *Grenadier* and Connaway's *Sculpin*: he was interrogated, beaten, taken to the Naval Interrogation Camp in Ofuna, Japan, and then put to work in the Ashio copper mines. He was the only survivor of *Tullibee*.

Gar, commanded by George William Lautrup, Jr., performed yeoman service as a lifeguard. Popping to the surface within a stone's throw of enemy gun emplacements on the Palau beaches, Lautrup carried out six separate missions, rescuing eight naval airmen.

Six hundred miles to eastward of the Palaus, Sam Dealey and his exec, Tiny Lynch, patrolled off Woleai in *Harder*, returning with new engines. On April 1, the withdrawing U.S. task force hit Woleai but found few good targets. During the strike, an aviator went down near the tiny island west of Woleai. Sam Dealey moved *Harder* in for a rescue.

By the time *Harder* got to the reported position, the aviator, Ensign John R. Galvin, was already stranded high and dry on the beach. Dealey lay to alongside a reef. His third officer, Samuel Moore Logan, and two volunteers jumped in the water with a rubber raft, secured to *Harder* by a line. They fought their way through the surf and coral to the island and picked up Ensign Galvin. As they were attempting to get back to *Harder*, a navy floatplane landed to help. It ran over the line and parted it. Another *Harder* volunteer jumped in the water and swam another line through the surf and coral to the beach. While navy planes circled overhead, providing protection, and Japanese snipers fired away from the foliage, *Harder*'s men pulled the raft and the five men aboard. This rescue was later hailed as one of the boldest on record.

Dealey lay off Woleai for two weeks more. On April 13, a patrol plane spotted *Harder*, forcing her under. Not long afterward, a destroyer that had arrived after the carrier strike nosed out, looking for *Harder*. Dealey decided to attack and closed to 3,200 yards. The destroyer picked up *Harder* on sonar and charged. Dealey let her get within 900 yards and then fired four torpedoes. Later, Dealey noted in his report, "Expended four torpedoes and one Jap destroyer." The ship was *Ikazuchi*, 2,000 tons. She sank within four minutes. Her armed depth charges exploded among her survivors.

Three days later, Dealey spotted a freighter with two destroyer escorts coming out of Woleai. Aircraft circled overhead. Dealey tracked, waiting for dark. Then he surfaced and attacked the formation, sinking his eleventh confirmed ship in four patrols, the freighter *Matsue Maru*, 7,000 tons. Returning to the island, Dealey bombarded it with his new 4-inch gun and then set off for Fremantle to join the other boats of Squadron Twelve.

Pampanito, a new boat, lifeguarded off Yap. She had been commissioned by Charles B. Jackson, Jr. (ex-*Spearfish*), but after an extensive shakedown cruise Jackson arrived in Pearl Harbor in a state of exhaustion and was relieved during training exercises. The exec, Paul Summers, fleeted up to command. After making seven war patrols on *Stingray*, he was one of the first from the class of 1936 to command a fleet boat.

Summers had no opportunity to provide a lifeguard rescue. However, after the air strike he patrolled in the Marianas, where he attacked a destroyer for damage.* In the melee, *Pampanito* was badly depth-charged and incurred damage to her hull. Summers sank no ships, but his superiors labeled this patrol "excellent."

The Brisbane boats lying in wait off Davao Gulf for the major fleet units fleeing Palau had many good opportunities to inflict severe damage on the enemy, but all attacks failed.

A new boat, *Bashaw*, commanded by Richard Eugene Nichols, formerly exec of *Grayback*, found an escort carrier guarded by two destroyers on April 5 near Davao Gulf. Nichols picked it up in the early afternoon while he was submerged, range 17,000 yards. He was able to close to 10,000 yards but no closer. The carrier had an air

---

* Admiral King, wishing to deplete the Japanese fleet in advance of confrontation with U.S. forces, had raised the priority of Japanese destroyers and encouraged Lockwood and Christie to sink them.

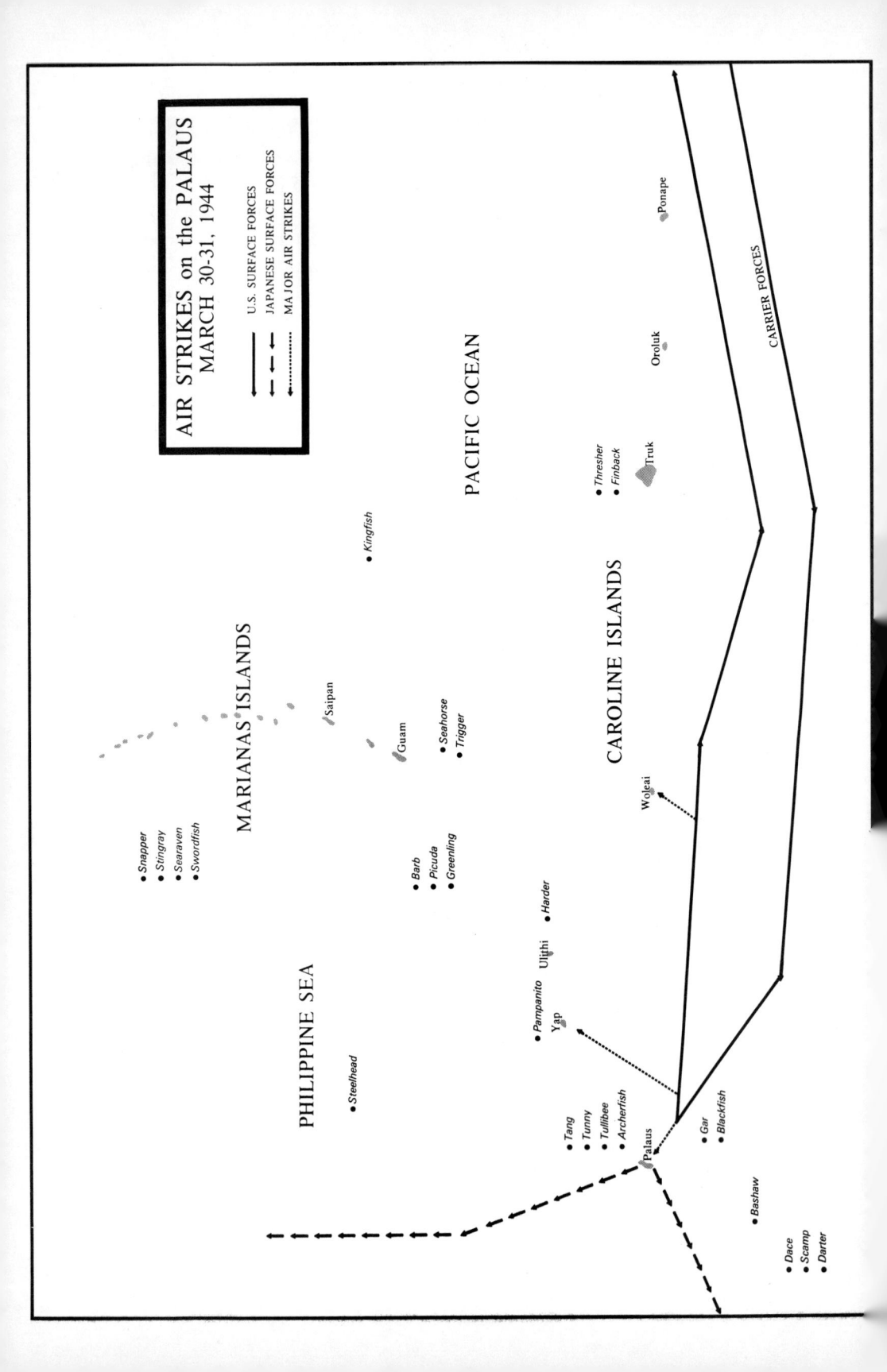

AIR STRIKES on the PALAUS
MARCH 30-31, 1944

U.S. SURFACE FORCES →
JAPANESE SURFACE FORCES ⇢
MAJOR AIR STRIKES ⋯⋯▶

PHILIPPINE SEA

PACIFIC OCEAN

MARIANAS ISLANDS

CAROLINE ISLANDS

CARRIER FORCES

- Snapper
- Stingray
- Searaven
- Swordfish
- Saipan
- Kingfish
- Guam
- Seahorse
- Trigger
- Barb
- Picuda
- Greenling
- Steelhead
- Harder
- Pampanito
- Ulithi
- Yap
- Wolwai
- Thresher
- Finback
- Truk
- Oroluk
- Ponape
- Tang
- Tunny
- Tullibee
- Archerfish
- Palaus
- Gar
- Blackfish
- Bashaw
- Dace
- Scamp
- Darter

ACTION DURING THE PALAUS AIR STRIKE

escort as well (probably land-based planes from Davao), so he refrained from chasing on the surface. On the way back to Brisbane, *Bashaw* was bombed by a U.S. B-24.

The sister ships *Dace* and *Darter* patrolled near Davao Gulf. On April 4, Bladen Claggett in *Dace* saw an aircraft carrier leaving the gulf but was unable to close for an attack. Early in the morning of April 6, *Dace* and *Darter* picked up a grand sight: three heavy cruisers and four destroyers. Claggett went in, firing two torpedoes at one cruiser, two at another, and one at the third. All missed, and he was unable to make another attack. Later he wrote, "Made a mistake, I guess, shooting at three different targets but what a jackpot if we'd collected!"

Shirley Stovall in *Darter* picked up the same set of targets, but by that time they were making 22 knots and Stovall could not overtake.

Another Brisbane boat, *Scamp*, got on the scent. *Scamp* had a new skipper, John Hollingsworth, the officer who had left *Triton* in a huff when his classmate, C. C. Kirkpatrick, was named to command. Since that unfortunate episode, Hollingsworth had been buried at San Francisco in a service unit. He got back into submarine duty and made his way to Brisbane just about the time Wally Ebert returned from his sixth and last patrol, and Jimmy Fife gave Hollingsworth a second chance.

Scamp was nearby when Claggett and Stovall picked up the enemy cruisers. Hollingsworth chased to no avail. The next day, while submerged off the mouth of Davao, Hollingsworth picked up a force of six cruisers standing out of the bay and dived for an approach. The sea was glassy calm. While running in, *Scamp* was detected and the destroyer escorts dropped twenty-two depth charges. Hollingsworth remained deep until early afternoon. Then, finding the horizon clear, he surfaced to get off a contact report. While he was so engaged, a Japanese floatplane came directly out of the sun. Hollingsworth dived. Then all hell broke loose inside *Scamp*.

When *Scamp* was passing 40 feet, a bomb landed near her port side. "Terrific explosion jarred boat," Hollingsworth wrote later. She assumed a steep up-angle yet slipped backward to 320 feet. From every compartment of the boat, Hollingsworth received grim news of fire, smoke, damage. To take the up-angle off, Hollingsworth ordered every available man to the forward torpedo room.

For a time *Scamp* bobbed up and down like a yo-yo. Finally, Hollingsworth got her under control. He lay quiet the rest of the day, surfacing after dark to send a distress call to John Haines. Haines ordered Claggett in *Dace* to provide assistance. Claggett escorted *Scamp* back to Milne Bay. From there, Hollingsworth took the boat back to Mare Island for a major overhaul.

After receiving a report, Christie noted in his diary, "A marvelous performance of duty saved the ship from: (1) diving to crushing depth, (2) surfacing under the guns of the enemy. I am sure, as in the case of *Puffer*, that the enemy was certain he had made a kill. Hats off to Hollingsworth and his stout crew."

A new boat, *Flounder*, operated near Halmahera, commanded by Carl Arthur Johnson, who came from *R-12* in the Atlantic. On this, his first Pacific war patrol, Johnson made two attacks against enemy convoys. On the first, he fired his torpedoes from 6,600 yards (over 3 miles) and on the second 7,250 yards (over 3½ miles). When Johnson returned to port, he was dressed down for these attacks and for failing to spend enough time training his crew during the patrol. He was relieved of command and sent to be exec of a new tender, *Apollo*.

Transfers to Fremantle

Early in 1944, Lockwood sent about eighteen boats from Pearl Harbor to Ralph Christie's command in Fremantle. Most were the re-engined H.O.R. boats of Squadron Twelve, replacing the boats of Squadron Six. Others were new boats, to bring Christie's total strength to thirty boats—the figure set by Admiral King.

Angler, a new boat, was commanded by Robert Irving Olsen,* who had been exec to Art Taylor on *Haddock* in 1942. On the way to Australia, Olsen tangled with a convoy north of the Marianas. He was credited with sinking one ship and damaging two, but postwar records confirmed only one of the escorts, an 890-ton net tender. *Angler* developed "structural noises" that made silent running impossible, and Olsen returned to Midway for repairs.

Setting off a second time, Olsen went to Fremantle by way of the west coast of Luzon. While he was there, General MacArthur learned

---

* No kin to Eliot Olsen, ex-*Grayling*, Robert was one of five sons of retired lieutenant Hjalmar E. Olsen. All five graduated from the Naval Academy.

the Japanese had launched a bloodbath on Panay, killing all civilians they could find hiding in the jungles. He requested that a submarine put in at Panay to rescue "about twenty" civilians. Christie gave the assignment to *Angler*.

When Olsen arrived at the rendezvous, he found not twenty but fifty-eight men, women, and children awaiting rescue. After two years in the jungles, most of these people were sick and undernourished, filthy, and full of lice. One woman was pregnant. Olsen took them all, berthing them in the forward and after torpedo rooms. To stretch his limited supply of food, he cut meals to two a day. Toward the end of the patrol, many of the passengers and crew became nauseous—possibly from contamination of the water supply. Altogether, the trip to Australia, through heavily patrolled and shallow waters, was a long and arduous one.

Flasher, a new boat commanded by Reuben Whitaker (who began the war on Bull Wright's *Sturgeon*, commanded S-44 from Brisbane, then made one patrol as exec of *Flying Fish*), went to Fremantle by way of Manila. Whitaker's exec was Raymond Dubois, who had served on the luckless *Snapper* for the first year of the war. Freddy Warder declared *Flasher* the best-trained fleet submarine he had ever seen.

On the way to Manila, Whitaker found his first target, a 3,000-ton ex-gunboat, near Marcus Island and sank it with his first torpedoes. Off the Philippines, he sank three more ships, believed to be tankers but confirmed in postwar records as freighters. Total for *Flasher*'s first patrol: four ships for 10,528 tons.

Victor McCrea, commanding the H.O.R. boat *Hoe*, re-engined at Mare Island, patrolled down the east coast of Luzon to Davao Gulf. On February 25 he found two big tankers, *Nissho Maru* and *Kyokuto Maru*. In an aggressive and well-conducted attack, McCrea sank the first ship, 10,526 tons, and damaged the second.

Another new boat, *Robalo*, was commanded by Stephen Ambruster, who had commanded *Tambor* on four patrols in 1942-43. His exec was a reservist, Charles Woodford Fell, who had graduated with the class of 1934, resigned, and then maintained active reserve status. On the way to Fremantle, Ambruster attacked one ship, firing four torpedoes from 3,100 yards. Christie was disappointed. He wrote

Lockwood, "Ambruster is not, in my opinion, of suitable temperament for a commanding officer. On his last patrol he spent thirty-six days submerged in area. He has had one good patrol . . . and three duds. If you have a spot for Ambruster, I think it would be advisable that he leave this area."

Ambruster went to Midway to serve as chief of staff to the base commander. Later, he said, "Ralph Christie and I were not members of the same mutual admiration society. This started long before World War II. . . . I was not the first nor the last submarine skipper to be put on the shelf. . . . My only regret is that I was not given the opportunity to defend my position when it happened."

Junior McCain in *Gunnel*, making his third Pacific patrol, went to Fremantle by way of Manila. On March 18, near Tawi Tawi, McCain picked up an escort carrier and two destroyers, range 9,000 yards. McCain tried to attack, but destroyers found him and forced him off, dropping sixteen depth charges. McCain lay in wait and, four days later, found the same carrier again. He closed to 11,000 yards but could get no closer. It was the second time in as many patrols that McCain had found a Japanese carrier but failed to inflict damage.

Mingo, another ex-H.O.R. boat, had a new skipper, Joseph Jarlathe Staley, who had been one of Herb Andrews's execs on *Gurnard*. Staley took *Mingo* by way of Luzon Strait, where he made several attacks but no hits. During the patrol, *Mingo* suffered a major motor casualty (unrelated to her previous engine problems). Staley requested emergency repairs and took *Mingo* to Milne Bay, the closest repair point, and then to Brisbane. The accident kept *Mingo* out of action for many more weeks.

Lapon, another ex-H.O.R. boat, commanded by Lowell Thornton Stone, patrolled off Hong Kong. On March 8-9, he found a convoy and sank two large freighters. A day or so later, in rough seas, Stone picked up a Japanese task force consisting of two battleships, an aircraft carrier, a heavy cruiser, and several destroyers. It was daytime and Stone was submerged. He set up, but at the last minute the force zigged away. "Thus was lost a submarine officer's dream," Stone wrote later. "The situation could have been avoided had I made a periscope observation at 1210, but the state of the sea, in which a lot of periscope had to be shown, made it imperative to hold exposures to a minimum.

With this opportunity irretrievably lost, gloom settled on *Lapon* after our very fine start."

A week later, Stone found the large transport *Hokuroku*, 8,359 tons. He attacked and sank her. His total for the patrol was three ships for 19,500 tons, an excellent performance.

Tommy Dykers in *Jack*, another ex-H.O.R. boat, went to Fremantle by way of Manila. This trip he had a new exec, Miles Permenter Refo III, son of a retired captain. *Jack* was caught by a Japanese plane which dropped three bombs, two of them close. In mid-February, when he reached the South China Sea on a line between Camranh Bay and Manila, Dykers received an Ultra on a convoy of tankers loaded with aviation gasoline. At three o'clock in the morning on February 19, he made contact with this convoy: five large tankers and three escorts in two columns.

Dykers proceeded to conduct one of the most brilliant—and effective—attacks of the war. First he fired three torpedoes at one tanker. Two hit. Dykers wrote, "In about two seconds she exploded with gasoline because flames shot hundreds of feet in the air and the whole area of the sea around the ship was instantly a seething mass of white hot flame."

With daylight coming on, Dykers made an end around and submerged twenty-one miles ahead of the convoy. The ships reached him about dusk, and he fired four torpedoes at two tankers. "Both of them exploded immediately and were completely enveloped in flames."

After dark, Dykers surfaced and fired three torpedoes at another target. All missed. The target fired back with a 5-inch gun, and one shell hit close, shaking *Jack*. Dykers reloaded, swung around, and fired four more torpedoes for three hits on one target that also "exploded and was completely enveloped in tremendous flames instantly." With fourteen torpedoes, four out of the five tankers had been sunk.

For the next ten days Dykers cruised about but could find no other targets. On February 28 he received another Ultra, reporting a *Nachi*-class cruiser coming his way. Dykers picked it up—as it traveled alone at 25 knots—the next day, shortly after lunch. Either *Jack* or the cruiser was slightly off course; Dykers was unable to get closer than 9,000 yards. "This one was a tough one to lose," he wrote.

Next night, Dykers made contact with another convoy, a tanker and three freighters with two escorts. Dykers had only seven torpedoes, four aft and three forward. Assisted by his exec, Miles Refo, he decided to fire the aft tubes first. That plan didn't work out, so he fired the three bow tubes at a freighter. Dykers saw two hits, and the target "exploded violently." Then he fired his last four at another freighter, observing two hits. An escort counterattacked, driving Dykers off, but he believed he had sunk two ships.

All torpedoes expended, Dykers set course for Fremantle. On the way, he sighted another convoy—a freighter and tanker with two escorts—which ran right over him, forcing Dykers to go deep to avoid detection. He wrote, "We sit on station for days with twenty-four torpedoes and see nothing and as soon as we expend them we run into one we can't get out of the way of."

When Dykers reached Fremantle, Christie was prepared. "As soon as the lines went over," Dykers recalled, "he came aboard and gave me a Navy Cross." In a glowing endorsement to Dykers's report, Christie credited him with sinking seven ships—five tankers and two freighters—for 53,486 tons. Postwar analysis reduced this to four ships —all tankers sunk during the February 19 attack—for 20,441 tons.

Later, at headquarters, Christie showed Dykers the text of an Ultra intercept reporting the effect of his attack on Tokyo. The paraphrased text, which Dykers copied, read:

While returning to Japan, a convoy of six tankers was attacked by enemy submarine on February 20th in the waters northwest of the Philippines and five tankers were sunk. Compared to our past losses, the losses sustained by our tankers since the beginning of the year have almost doubled. The present situation is such that the majority of tankers returning to Japan are being lost.

The dockside presentation of the Navy Cross to Dykers annoyed Admiral Kinkaid—and Charles Lockwood. For one thing, it was customary in the navy to go through a series of boards before a medal was finally awarded. In handing out a medal at dockside, Christie seemed to be adopting the technique of General MacArthur, who often gave out medals on the spur of the moment, bypassing army award boards. For another, some believed it might compromise the codebreakers. In meeting Dykers with a Navy Cross, Christie had obviously already confirmed his sinkings through Ultra.

In fact, the medal problem in the Southwest Pacific was even more complicated. Earlier, MacArthur (who had given army medals to Mike Fenno on *Trout* and Mush Morton on *Wahoo*, among others) had told Christie he was anxious to give army medals to other submariners. After Walt Griffith's famous first patrol commanding *Bowfin*, Christie had recommended Griffith (who received a Navy Cross) to MacArthur for further award, perhaps thinking of a Medal of Honor. Kinkaid had taken a dim view of this recommendation and may have taken steps with MacArthur's staff to prevent it. In any case, Christie had not heard from MacArthur about it.

Kinkaid gave Christie orders to stop the dockside presentations. In addition, he forbade Christie and other naval officers to recommend the award of army medals to naval personnel by MacArthur. This order would lead to further serious conflict between Kinkaid and Christie.

John Coye, who had made three fine patrols in *Silversides*, took the boat to Fremantle on his fourth. He patrolled through the Marianas and on to Palau and the area near Halmahera. On March 2 he picked up two heavy cruisers with destroyer escorts, moving at high speed. Coye withheld fire, believing the ships were moving too fast. They passed him at 2,800 yards. (Later, John Haines criticized Coye's decision.) On March 16 Coye sank a 1,900-ton freighter and later fired four torpedoes at a damaged ship under tow. Angry escorts prevented a second attack, and the ship got away.

Paddle, another ex-H.O.R. boat, was commanded by Byron Horne Nowell, who went to Fremantle by way of the Celebes Sea and Ambon. On the night of April 16, Nowell attacked a three-ship convoy with four escorts, sinking two freighters and damaging a tanker that later joined the formation. Nowell was credited with sinking a destroyer, but it was not confirmed in postwar records.

Ian Eddy in *Paddle*'s sister ship, *Pargo*, patrolled by way of Davao Gulf, where he sank a small net tender. On April 26, Eddy picked up two cruisers—one heavy, one light—off the entrance to the gulf. He closed to 1,400 yards, but a plane spotted him and dropped a bomb, alerting the formation. The cruisers turned toward *Pargo* and dropped eight depth charges, forcing Eddy to go deep and lose contact. "Certainly hated to let them get away with this," Eddy wrote later. He was sorely tempted to follow them right into the gulf but decided discretion was the better part of valor.

Empire and East China Sea Patrols

Other Pearl Harbor boats patrolled the usual stations in Empire, East China Sea, and Kurile waters. During January and February, the weather was foul everywhere; typhoons and near-typhoons in many cases interfered with attacks. Lockwood placed high priority on interdicting convoys en route to reinforce the Marianas.

Batfish, commanded by the unstable Wayne Merrill, underwent a trauma. The exec, Molteni, who refused to return to sea with Merrill after the abortive attempt to attack *Yamato* on the first patrol, made good his promise and got off the boat, and Jim Hingson fleeted up to exec. Merrill took *Batfish* to Empire waters for the second patrol but spent most of the time fighting heavy seas rather than Japanese. He made no attacks.

Batfish refitted in Midway and then set off on a third patrol. En route to the area, Hingson determined that Merrill was emotionally unfit and in a kind of Caine Mutiny procedure relieved him of command, reporting the fact to headquarters. *Batfish* was ordered to return to Midway, where Merrill was relieved of command and ordered out of submarines for good. "He was relieved at the same time they pinned a Silver Star on him for the first patrol," Hingson said later. "The same officer tore his dolphins from his chest." *

Chuck Triebel in *Snook*, making his fifth patrol, returned to the East China Sea, still with reservist Vard Stockton as his exec. On this trip Triebel decided to give Stockton more responsibility.

On the way to station, south of Honshu, while running on the surface at night, Triebel picked up a target. It was a dark, rainy night, visibility zero. Triebel fired six torpedoes into the void. Two hit, and the ship went down. "There were three more violent explosions aboard before he sank," Triebel reported. It was *Magane Maru*, 3,120 tons.

Arriving on station, Triebel found another convoy on February 8. After a long chase, *Snook* caught up. Triebel gave the attack to Stockton and took over as diving officer. Stockton fired four torpedoes

---

* In postwar years, Merrill got into serious difficulties; Hingson, a Pentagon staff officer, saved him from a general court-martial by seeing that he was "surveyed out" of the navy.

at two ships. One, *Lima Maru*, 6,989 tons, went down. Escorts charged and *Snook* went deep to evade.

On February 10 Triebel fired four torpedoes at a passing destroyer. All missed. Four days later he found a freighter, *Nittoku Maru*, sailing alone, not zigzagging. Triebel fired three torpedoes. The ship went down. The following morning he sank his fourth ship, *Hoshi Maru II*, 875 tons.

On February 19 Triebel received an Ultra from Lockwood on an aircraft carrier. Triebel moved in to intercept. About noon, February 20, he sighted the carrier and two destroyer escorts making 19 knots. However, *Snook* was 9,000 yards off the track and going the wrong way. Triebel bent on flank speed but could get no closer than 7,000 yards. A plane from the carrier came back to circle *Snook*. When it left, Triebel surfaced and got off a report to Lockwood. Just as the message cleared, another plane came over, driving him down. Later that evening Triebel set course for Midway.

En route, Triebel was directed to intercept a convoy headed south from Tokyo toward the Marianas. Benny Bass, who was making his sixth fine patrol as skipper of old *Plunger* in the same area, also received an Ultra from Lockwood on the convoy. Bass had sunk two freighters and, running low on fuel, was making his way back to Pearl Harbor. He had only one torpedo remaining on board.

Triebel, Bass, and the convoy all converged in mid-ocean early on the morning of February 23. Bass, unaware that Triebel was in the vicinity, headed southward on the surface to the point where he figured he would intercept the convoy. Triebel, who had submerged, watched *Plunger* go by close aboard. Then—partly as a joke—Triebel popped to the surface about 1,000 yards off *Plunger*'s port quarter.

"He scared me to death," said Bass later. "I was surprised, shocked. . . . I didn't know what to do. Some joke!"

Triebel maneuvered close to *Plunger* and talked to Bass by megaphone. "I just wanted to let him know I was there," Triebel said later with a straight face.

As the two skippers were exchanging information, radar picked up the convoy. Moments later, one of Bass's men saw smoke through the high periscope. Bass went north; Triebel went south.

It was a large convoy, six ships with many small escorts and one old coal-burning destroyer. Bass moved in with his one stern torpedo, picked out the biggest ship he could find, and fired. In one of the best shots of the war, he sank the cargo ship *Kimishima Maru*, 5,200 tons. The escorts jumped on *Plunger* and held her down for hours.

Watching from a distance, Triebel later wrote, "Observed one hit on ship in enemy convoy. . . . Later heard numerous explosions and observed two large distinctively separated smoke columns indicating two ships were hit."

Triebel was not able to reach firing position during the day. After dark, however, he surfaced and chased. He caught up and fired five torpedoes at two ships. He wrote, "Observed two good hits two minutes later. Eight minutes after firing felt a terrific explosion which shook the boat . . . target radar pip had just disappeared . . . evaded to the north for an hour and then set course for Midway." It was *Koyo Maru*, 5,471 tons.

On return to Pearl Harbor, both Triebel and Bass received high praise for these patrols. Triebel had sunk five confirmed ships for 21,046 tons; Bass three for 9,600 tons. Both men stepped down from command. In his six patrols on *Plunger*, Bass had sunk nine ships for about 38,000 tons, a remarkable achievement considering *Plunger*'s age and infirmities. He returned to Portsmouth to fit out and command a new boat.

When Triebel, who had sunk a total of fourteen ships, left, his division commander wrote, "It is with regret that . . . Triebel is being detached. It is hoped this valuable submarine skipper will not be lost to the submarine service." He was. Like Oliver Kirk and Eli Reich, Triebel had earlier written an official letter complaining about poor torpedo performance. "I practically accused the Bureau of Ordnance of sabotage," he said later. Lockwood had stopped the letter at his desk but later used it to advantage in private showings. Now he sent Triebel to the Bureau of Ordnance. Thus Triebel became the first truly outstanding submarine skipper to go to the Gun Club. He remained there for the rest of the war.

Before leaving *Snook*, Triebel did his best to help his exec, reservist Vard Stockton, move up to command and declared him qualified. Triebel's division commander agreed, writing of Stockton in the endorsement to Triebel's last patrol, "This officer has been previously observed during the training period and the Division Commander concurs with the C.O. that this officer be recommended for command of his own at an early date." Nothing came of it. At Lockwood's insistence, all fleet boats remained in the hands of Naval Academy graduates for the first three years of the war. He reasoned that reservists, by now composing about 50 percent of all wardrooms, were not nearly so experienced as Academy graduates. Few reservists had held down responsible jobs in the boats, such as exec, and Lockwood believed it was unfair to give command to a reservist when able men then serving as execs—from the class of 1939, for example—with five, six, or seven war patrols under their belts (plus two years in peacetime surface forces) were still being denied.

When the Gilberts and Marshalls were captured, thousands of classified Japanese documents had fallen into the hands of the U.S. Navy. Among these were some secret red-bordered "Notices to Mariners" showing the exact locations of Japanese minefields—vital information to U.S. submarines. The red borders made the documents easy to find. Jasper Holmes set up a special unit under a reserve officer, Edward McCormick Blair, to hunt out these valuable papers and get them translated. The results were then issued to submarine skippers in booklet form.

Holmes and Blair discovered from the red-bordered notices that the Japanese had laid new and extensive minefields in the East China Sea. One boat—*Scorpion*, commanded by Maximilian Gmelich Schmidt, making his second patrol—presumably hit one of these new mines and sank with all hands.

Grayback was lost about the same time. Her commander, the aggressive Johnny Moore, had been ordered to begin his patrol in the Formosa Strait. On February 19, he found a convoy and attacked, sinking two ships for 6,600 confirmed tons and damaging others. Moving north along the east coast of Formosa five days later, he sank a large tanker, *Nampo Maru*, 10,000 tons. After this attack, Moore radioed Lockwood that he had sunk or damaged 44,000 tons of Japanese shipping and had only six torpedoes left, five aft and one forward. The next day, February 25, Moore reported firing four torpedoes and damaging two more ships, leaving him with only two torpedoes. Upon receipt of this message, Lockwood ordered Moore to return to Pearl Harbor. Nothing further was ever heard from him.

Japanese records state that on February 26 a carrier plane near Okinawa discovered a submarine on the surface about 300 miles east of *Grayback*'s last reported position. According to the Japanese records, the plane "gave a direct hit at the sub, which exploded and sank immediately." If Moore received the message from Lockwood and headed home immediately, he would have been in the approximate position reported in the Japanese attack.

John MacGregor on *Shad*, Moore's wolf-pack mate in the fall of 1943, was inclined to believe that Moore, low on torpedoes, may have lost the boat by using his 5-inch gun on some targets. He said later, "I did feel that John was in a frame of mind to use that five-inch gun in cases where the risk to the submarine and crew did not warrant it."

In three patrols, Moore had sunk nine confirmed ships.*

Following his aggressive patrol to the Palaus, Ralph Metcalf in *Pogy* went to Luzon Strait and then up the east coast of Formosa and on to the Okinawa area. On February 10, he found a convoy and attacked, sinking *Malta Maru*, 5,500 tons, and one of the escorts, the destroyer *Minekaze*, 1,300 tons. Ten days later, off the east coast of Formosa, he penetrated another convoy, sinking two more ships: *Taijin Maru*, 5,154 tons, and *Nanyo Maru*, 3,610 tons. Three days later, he sank *Horei Maru*, 5,588 tons. His total for the patrol: five ships for 21,150 tons.

On his third patrol, Metcalf took *Pogy* to Empire waters with a new exec, Richard Thomas Fahy. On the night of April 28 off Bungo Suido, Metcalf and Fahy picked up the Japanese submarine *I-183*. After a tedious three-hour end around, Metcalf got into a favorable position and fired. One torpedo hit, and *I-183* went down for the last time. When Metcalf steamed through the area where she sank, he could smell gasoline and assumed she was a supply boat, taking gasoline to the Marianas or elsewhere.

Shortly afterward, Metcalf received an Ultra from Dick Voge stating, in effect, INDICATIONS ARE THAT JAPANESE SUBMARINES ARE LEAVING VIA BUNGO SUIDO EVERY NIGHT ON RESUPPLY MISSIONS. Metcalf responded, YES, YOU'RE RIGHT. I GOT ONE.

That was not all. On the night of May 5 he sank a 2,800-ton cargo vessel and on May 13 another freighter for 4,600 tons. One of the freighters was being used as a coastal tanker. It "burned like a Roman candle," Metcalf said later. Returning from this patrol, Metcalf took *Pogy* to San Francisco for overhaul and stepped down as skipper. In three patrols, he had sunk ten confirmed ships for about 40,000 tons, making him one of Lockwood's high scorers.

The Imperial Japanese Army ordered that Saipan and Guam be reinforced by the crack 29th Division, then based in Manchuria. It

---

* JANAC credited Moore with sinking yet another ship, *Ceylon Maru*, 5,000 tons. According to JANAC, it sank about 300 miles to the north of *Grayback*'s last reported position, however, so it could not have been sunk by Moore. This is merely one of many errors that have cropped up in JANAC.

was lifted in four big transports escorted by what Jasper Holmes later described as three of Japan's "best" destroyers: *Kishinami, Okinami,* and *Asashimo*.

As this important convoy approached the Marianas, Lockwood sent several boats to intercept. One was *Rock*, commanded by John Jay Flachsenhar, who had made eight war patrols on *Permit*. *Rock*, en route to Formosa, was redeployed along the convoy's path. On February 29 *Rock* picked it up, and Flachsenhar prepared to attack. One of the escorts spotted *Rock* and fired a 5-inch gun. A shell hit the port-side shears, shattering both periscope prisms and causing other damage. Flachsenhar got off a contact report and turned back to Midway.

On the same day, *Trout*, now commanded by Albert Clark, returning from long overhaul, also intercepted the convoy. Clark sank one of the big transports, *Sakito Maru*, 7,100 tons, and damaged another, 11,400-ton *Aki Maru*. On *Sakito Maru*, 2,300 of 4,000 troops were drowned and all the equipment was lost. Then the three skilled Japanese destroyers counterattacked. They claimed a kill, probably correctly. The famous *Trout* was never heard from again.

Nautilus, reconverted for regular duty, patrolled nearby, commanded by Bill Irvin. While other boats searched for the convoy without success, he intercepted it on March 1. Setting up, he fired six torpedoes, damaging two of the ships.

A few days later, Irvin received an Ultra on a convoy leaving Saipan. He found it on March 6 in the northernmost Marianas: three ships in "irregular column." Irvin fired four torpedoes at two of the ships. All four hit. The first ship was damaged; the second ship, which Irvin identified as *America Maru*, had its stern blown off. "Don't see how she can stay afloat," Irvin noted in his report. Irvin had no chance to watch her sink because escorts quickly moved in, dropping thirty depth charges that were, Irvin reported, deep, heavy, and close. Irvin escaped by taking big old *Nautilus* to 280 feet.

After the war, Japanese reports confirmed that *America Maru* was indeed sunk by *Nautilus* at this time and place. She had left Saipan three days earlier, loaded with 1,700 old people, women, and children —families of construction workers on Saipan—who had been ordered back to Japan. How many perished is not known.

* * *

One Pearl Harbor boat that did not make it on patrol was a new one, *Flier*, commanded by John Daniel Crowley, who came from five patrols on S-28 in the Aleutians. *Flier* was commissioned at Electric Boat Company in October 1943. After trials, she had a naval baptism by fire on the way to Panama and the Pacific; a friendly merchant ship saw her and fired thirteen shells before Crowley evaded in a rainsquall. She got under way from Pearl Harbor on January 12 for her maiden war patrol, planning to top off at Midway. She arrived at the island during a bad storm on January 16 and, while attempting to get inside, ran aground on a reef.

Crowley gave the alarm. Out came the submarine rescue vessel *Macaw* to pull *Flier* off. However, the storm winds and currents also drove *Macaw* on the reef. Both ships remained stuck fast, with heavy seas breaking over them, until the storm abated six days later. A floating derrick engaged in construction work at Midway finally pulled *Flier* to safety.

Macaw was not so fortunate. Every effort to get her off the reef failed, and she remained stuck until the night of February 12–13. That night, she broached and slid into deep water. During this disaster, her commanding officer, Paul Willits Burton, and four crew members were killed.

Lockwood sent another submarine rescue vessel from Pearl Harbor. This was *Florikan*, commanded by George Sharp (ex-*Spearfish*), whose divers had salvaged valuable documents from the Japanese submarine *I-7* in Kiska in the fall. Sharp had orders to tow *Flier* back to Pearl Harbor for drydocking. On the way, he encountered heavy seas. The tow line parted, and for five hours *Flier* drifted helplessly. Finally the tow line was remade and Sharp got *Flier* back to Pearl Harbor, where it was found that her screws and bottom were badly damaged. The workers fixed up the starboard shaft and *Flier* limped to San Francisco for extensive repairs.

In San Francisco, yet another problem developed. Crowley and his exec, Benjamin Ernest Adams, Jr., fell into an irreconcilable dispute. "It became a very bad situation," the senior officer in San Francisco reported. He considered sending Adams to surface forces because Adams, he said, was not willing to work. The situation was resolved by transferring Adams to Jim Blanchard's *Albacore*, then in San Francisco for overhaul. Blanchard's exec, Ralph De Loach, was due for new construction. Adams was replaced in *Flier* by James Liddell, the former All-American football player from Northwestern who began the war on *Snapper*. Many months would drag by before *Flier* was again ready for combat.

As a reward for the fine job he had done in bringing *Flier* safely through the storm, George Sharp got a second chance at submarine command. He was named to replace Irvin on *Nautilus*. His exec was Ben Jarvis, who had become involved in the dispute on Lefavour's luckless patrol in *Sailfish*. *Nautilus* was shifted to Darwin to help her sister ship, *Narwhal*, with special missions to the Philippines.

John Tyree, making his fifth patrol in *Finback*, patrolled the East China Sea in foul weather with his usual aggressiveness. In spite of hard hunting, he found only a few targets worth torpedoes. In four attacks he damaged three ships (and sank a trawler by gunfire) but sent nothing big to the bottom.

When Tyree returned from patrol, Lockwood (in keeping with his policy of rotating skippers to the States for rest after five war patrols) sent him to new construction. Tyree reported to Portsmouth to fit out and commission the new boat *Tigrone*. About that time, President Roosevelt's naval aide, Admiral Wilson Brown, requested the Bureau of Personnel to assign a man with a good combat record to the White House. Bob Rice picked Tyree.

Lockwood exploded. Here again another fine, aggressive submarine skipper had been yanked from the force to serve in what Lockwood considered a "coat holder's" job. First C. C. Kirkpatrick, then Dusty Dornin, then John Tyree (among many others). Lockwood wrote blistering letters to Bob Rice and Louis Denfeld, protesting Tyree's reassignment, but it did no good. BuPers, then as now, had immense power over the destiny of the professional naval officer, and it was not about to yield to Lockwood. In spite of all objections, the bureau continued to siphon off aggressive (as well as not-so-aggressive) skippers. Lockwood complained to Christie, "Possibly after we get the entire navy manned by submarine personnel we will be allowed to retain a few of our good men."

The Polar Circuit

A new boat, *Sandlance*, commanded by Malcolm Everett Garrison, made the polar circuit. Garrison had helped fit out and commission *Trout*. In May 1943 he had reported to Portsmouth to put *Sandlance* in commission. Caught up in the backwaters of Portsmouth, Garrison had never made a real war patrol.

Garrison traveled far north to Kamchatka. The weather was bitterly cold, and the seas were full of floating ice. Garrison struck an ice floe with his periscope and it jammed in the fully elevated position, a serious handicap. Later he wiped off a sonar head in shallow water while attempting to look in a harbor.

Garrison picked up a ship which, he said later, "I positively identified as the *Florida Maru*." He fired and the ship sank while Garrison took photographs through the periscope. It was not *Florida Maru* but *Bella Russa*, a Soviet ship. It had no markings and was "not within the safe conduct lane" given the Russians. With that, Garrison joined the exclusive club of Russian-ship sinkers, founded by Eugene Sands in *Sawfish* and Moon Chapple in *Permit*.

During the days following, Garrison found many targets. He sank two freighters in the far north: *Kaiko Maru*, 3,548 tons, and *Akashisan Maru*, 4,541 tons. In addition, he wasted five torpedoes on what he concluded later was a shallow-draft decoy vessel. With only six torpedoes remaining, Garrison dropped southward to patrol off Honshu.

On March 12, Voge notified Garrison of a big convoy that had left Tokyo crammed with men and supplies to reinforce the Marianas. Garrison found the convoy in moonlight on the night of March 13, right on schedule. It consisted of five big freighters and several smaller ships, escorted by several destroyers and the 3,300-ton light cruiser *Tatsuta*. Regretting the wastage of five torpedoes against the decoy, Garrison prepared to attack with his remaining six.

Coming in submerged with the jammed periscope, Garrison chose the cruiser and one big freighter, planning to fire two stern torpedoes at each and then swing around and fire his last two bow torpedoes at another freighter. He executed his plan with cool precision. Two torpedoes hit *Tatsuta*, which sank immediately. The other two hit *Kokuyo Maru*, a 4,667-ton cargo vessel. The two bow torpedoes hit another freighter for damage.

In the confusion, the escorts could not at first find *Sandlance*. Garrison remained at periscope depth for a while, surveying his work with satisfaction. Then two escorts charged, and Garrison took *Sandlance*, a thick-skinned boat, to 550 feet. For the next eighteen hours, the destroyers zipped back and forth, dropping a total of 105 depth charges. But the charges were set to go off for 250 feet, 300 feet above *Sandlance*, and no damage was done. With all torpedoes expended,

THE POLAR CIRCUIT 595

Garrison returned to Pearl Harbor from his first patrol. He had sunk a light cruiser, three Japanese freighters, and one Russian ship. Damage to the Japanese: four confirmed ships for 16,000 tons.

On his next patrol, Garrison went to Fremantle by way of the Marianas. Between May 3 and May 11, he sank three confirmed ships: *Kenan Maru*, 3,129 tons; *Mitakesan Maru*, 4,441 tons; and *Koho Maru*, 4,291 tons. On May 17 he joined forces to attack a convoy with John Scott in *Tunny*, coming up from Milne Bay. Garrison sank two more ships, one for 3,834 and one for 2,633 tons. John Scott sank one for 5,000 tons.

At about this time *Gudgeon* was lost. Scott in *Tunny* and Garrison in *Sandlance* were looking for a convoy near Saipan, and *Gudgeon* was in the area, presumably looking for the same convoy. Scott and Garrison may have heard the fatal attack on *Gudgeon*; Garrison reported "about forty depth charges eight to ten miles away." Since no other submarine reported being under attack at that time and place, Lockwood and Voge presumed the attack Garrison heard was on *Gudgeon*. Nothing was ever heard from her again. She was skippered by Robert Alexander Bonin, class of 1936, making his first patrol in her without benefit of a PCO cruise. (Bonin had formerly been exec on *Grayling*.) *Gudgeon*'s young exec was Donald Raymond Midgley, class of 1941.

Scott remained in the Marianas. Garrison, who had shot off all his torpedoes, proceeded to Fremantle, arriving thirty-five days after leaving port. Total for the patrol: five ships for 18,328 tons. In two brief patrols, Garrison had sunk nine ships—and he submitted two of the briefest patrol reports on record (five or six pages), describing the action.

Tautog, commanded by Barney Sieglaff going on his sixth patrol, followed *Sandlance* on the polar circuit. On board for a PCO run was Tom Baskett, who had made two patrols in *S-44* as exec to Dinty Moore and then commanded *S-37* for one patrol. Baskett had been trapped in San Diego for a long time, trying to get cranky old *S-37* in working order. Now he was making his first patrol in a fleet boat.

On the way to station, Sieglaff paused at sea to make some topside repairs. During the pause, a new sailor on *Tautog*, R. A. Laramee, a motor machinist mate, was swept over the side. Sieglaff spent a futile half hour circling the vicinity, but nothing was ever seen of Laramee—a needless death, it seemed to Sieglaff, and it cast a pall over the crew.

Tautog spent a week in northwestern waters before finding a target worthy of a torpedo. It was cold. "At times," Sieglaff wrote, "*Tautog* was completely surrounded by a solid mass of floating ice about two inches thick." Snow fell from time to time.

On March 13, Sieglaff found two ships. He closed to 1,500 yards and fired three torpedoes. Two hit one of the targets, and the Japanese began to abandon ship. Observing that the ship had not yet sunk, Sieglaff put another four torpedoes into her, one at a time. Still the ship would not sink. (Sieglaff later called it a "rubber ship.") He then battle-surfaced with his 5-inch deck gun.

While he was busy, the other ship came up to rescue survivors of the first. Sieglaff submerged, approached, and fired three torpedoes at her. She "sank in short order." In time, the first ship also sank.

Following this action, Sieglaff dropped south to patrol the northeast coast of Honshu. On March 16, he found a seven-ship convoy. He set up and fired four torpedoes at one freighter, another spread of three at a second, then another of four at a third. With explosions going off and escorts charging, Sieglaff was not positive of what he hit; postwar records revealed that he sank a freighter and one of the escorts, the destroyer *Shirakumo*. His total for the patrol was four ships for about 11,000 tons.

Following this patrol, Sieglaff stepped down as skipper of *Tautog* and returned to new construction. In six patrols, he had sunk thirteen confirmed ships, including two destroyers.

Replacing Sieglaff as skipper, Tom Baskett returned to the polar circuit for *Tautog*'s eleventh patrol. On May 2, Baskett found a big ship at anchor near Matsuwa and fired six torpedoes. Down went *Ryoyo Maru*, 6,000 tons.

The next day at dawn Baskett stumbled across a large unescorted freighter in the fog near Matsuwa. He remained on the surface, using the fog for protection, and fired four torpedoes. Two hit, and *Fushimi Maru*, a 5,000-ton transport, sank.

Following this, Baskett dropped down to the northeast coast of Honshu, reaching the area May 8. He found swarms of ships. He set up on one 4,000-ton freighter, fired five torpedoes, and watched it sink. The next day at dawn he fired two torpedoes at a small freighter but missed. On May 12, he fired his last three torpedoes at a small freighter of 1,100 tons. It sank. Baskett returned *Tautog* to Pearl Harbor. The total for his first patrol: four confirmed ships for 16,100 tons.

Wolf Packs Four and Five

In March and April Lockwood organized two more wolf packs. The first consisted of *Parche*, *Bang*, and *Tinosa*. *Parche*, commanded by Red Ramage from *Trout*, was a new boat. *Bang*, also new, was commanded by a new skipper, Anton Renki Gallaher, who came from command of *R-13* in the Atlantic but had never served in a fleet boat. *Tinosa* had been brought back from Fremantle by Don Weiss, who —in a brilliantly daring action—had sunk four confirmed ships for 15,600 tons on the way.

The pack was led by George Edmund Peterson, 1924, commanding SubDiv 141. Peterson had spent most of the war in the Atlantic, serving with the boats operating out of Scotland, and had never made a Pacific war patrol. Before setting off, the pack developed new and simplified techniques to facilitate communications.

The three boats took up station in Luzon Strait in mid-April, and for the next two weeks they milled about without any contacts. Red Ramage was so bored he filled his patrol report with humorous entries, such as the one on April 18: "Picked up sky lookout—bird—which took station on Number One Periscope going round and round and up and down, hanging on with dogged determination over four hours. Genus: unknown. Sex: undetermined. Habits: not altogether proper."

In the late afternoon of April 29, J. W. Champ, a keen-eyed quartermaster on *Bang*, alternating periscope watch with the officer of the deck, picked up smoke on the horizon. The smoke developed into a huge southbound convoy: fifteen to twenty ships and numerous destroyer escorts. Gallaher surfaced and got off contact reports—repeated every hour—to *Parche* and *Tinosa*, some 60 to 70 miles northwest of the convoy. *Tinosa* receipted after one hour, *Parche* after three hours.

Gallaher submerged again for a night periscope attack, selecting a tanker and two freighters for his initial ten-torpedo salvo. He was all set to fire when one of the destroyers, looking as big as a heavy cruiser to Gallaher, got in the way. In a change of tactics, Gallaher fired four torpedoes at the destroyer and two at the tanker. He missed the destroyer, which turned out of the way, but one or two torpedoes hit a freighter behind it. Another destroyer charged *Bang*, and Gallaher went deep to evade.

An hour or so later, after the escort broke off, Gallaher surfaced to chase. He caught up with the convoy in an hour, threaded through the escorts, and set up on a big freighter, firing six torpedoes. All missed. He swung around and fired his four stern tubes. There was confusion in the fire-control party; all four stern tubes also missed. Gallaher began reloading his tubes and making an end around.

Shortly after five o'clock in the morning, April 30, he caught up again and fired his four remaining bow tubes at a big freighter. Gallaher wrote, "The first explosion caused a tremendous flash.... The concussion was so great on the bridge that it felt as if there had been a bodily push away from the target. The second hit caused a ripple of flame.... Target sank amid a cloud of dense smoke." The escorts charged again and drove *Bang* down for eleven hours.

In these attacks, Gallaher had fired twenty torpedoes. He sank two confirmed ships.

All the while, *Tinosa* and *Parche* were hurrying down from the northwest at full speed, trying to find the convoy. At 4:20 A.M., Ramage saw flames on the horizon, the result of Gallaher's earlier attacks. About the time Gallaher made his dawn attack, Ramage picked up the convoy on radar. He counted ten large ships. Ramage and Weiss ran around the convoy to get ahead for a day periscope attack; Gallaher, with only four torpedoes left, was ordered to trail and sink any stragglers.

Ramage and Weiss dived in front of the convoy and waited. At about nine o'clock in the morning, it came into Weiss's range. He saw a "dream setup": five overlapping ships. He fired all six bow tubes, hearing and feeling four hits. With destroyers charging, Weiss went deep and remained there, losing contact. An hour later, Ramage set up and fired four torpedoes—two each at two freighters. All missed. Aircraft and destroyers charged *Parche*, and Ramage went deep for the rest of the day, also losing contact. The convoy ran into Lingayen Gulf, and none of the three boats could make another attack on it. Neither Weiss nor Ramage received credit in postwar records for a sinking on this day.

Three days passed. About daylight on May 3, Weiss in *Tinosa* picked up another convoy and flashed the word. It consisted of twelve ships. The pack tracked it submerged during the day and surfaced after dark to chase. The boats caught up about midnight. Weiss attacked first, firing six torpedoes at a tanker and freighter. He saw two hits on the tanker and hits on the freighter, but destroyers drove him under before he could make a follow-up attack. Ramage attacked next, firing six bow tubes—four at one freighter and two at another. He saw three hits in the first ship, which "appeared to blow up" and sink immediately, and two hits on the second, which began settling in the water. He swung around and fired his four stern tubes at another freighter, observing two hits.

Gallaher on *Bang*, meanwhile, set up on another target with his last four stern torpedoes. When he fired, he believed he obtained two hits on a freighter and one hit on a destroyer. Both, he reported, "sank."

Weiss in *Tinosa* surfaced and prepared to attack again. He fired six torpedoes at a big freighter, obtaining three hits which seemed to disintegrate the target, and then fired four more for misses. He submerged for a daylight attack on another ship, firing his last four torpedoes—all misses. During the day the remnants of the convoy eluded *Parche*, the only boat of the three with any torpedoes left. In this combined attack the three boats sank five ships, almost half the convoy.

After *Tinosa* and *Bang* reported all torpedoes expended, the pack commander, Peterson, ordered them to return to base. Ramage hung around a few more days but found no further opportunity to shoot. In total, Pack Number Four sank seven confirmed ships for about 35,300 tons. Gallaher was credited with three freighters for 10,700 tons, Ramage two for 11,700 tons, and Weiss two for 12,900 tons.

Wolf Pack Number Five set off in April for Luzon Strait. It consisted of Albert Raborn commanding *Picuda*, Paul Van Leunen, Jr., on *Peto* (both making their second patrols), and a brand-new boat, *Perch II*,* commanded by Blish Charles Hills, who had been Dick Lake's exec on *Albacore* for the first four patrols. The pack, known as "Fenno's Ferrets," was commanded by Mike Fenno (making his eighth patrol of the war) in *Picuda*.

Fenno's Ferrets had bad luck. On May 22, Raborn in *Picuda* picked up a convoy and sank the 1,200-ton river gunboat *Hashidate* and damaged a freighter with the same salvo. On May 24, Hills in *Perch* attacked a convoy, firing four torpedoes at a medium-sized tanker. In the counterattack, *Perch* was almost lost. She flooded her pump room, putting the air compressors out of commission, and was forced to return early. On June 2, Raborn found a twelve-ship convoy. He damaged one tanker but was not able to sink anything. Van

---

* Named for Dave Hurt's boat, lost in the retreat from Manila.

Leunen in *Peto* saw six ships but delivered no attacks. Net results: one boat almost lost, one 1,200-ton river gunboat sunk.

During the course of this luckless patrol, a fourth boat joined the pack briefly. It was a new one, *Guitarro*, on the way to Fremantle, commanded by Enrique Haskins, who had commissioned *Flying Fish* and served as Donaho's first exec. On May 30 Haskins sank a 2,000-ton freighter and on June 2 the frigate *Awaji*. Then he went on to Darwin and Fremantle.

On return to port, Paul Van Leunen in *Peto* received harsh endorsements on his patrol report, being criticized for not pressing attacks home and for failing to intercept a *Picuda* contact report. He was relieved of command and went to serve on Lockwood's staff. Al Raborn—who was praised for his aggressiveness—stepped down voluntarily, going to a shore job on the West Coast.

Patrols to the Marianas

Slade Cutter took *Seahorse* to the Marianas for his third patrol. This trip he had a new exec, Elbert Crawford ("Spud") Lindon, replacing Speed Currie. Young William Budding manned the TDC. *Seahorse*'s mission was to stop the Japanese from reinforcing Guam and Saipan.

On March 31, Cutter rendezvoused with *Stingray* in the northern Marianas. *Stingray*, returning from overhaul, was now commanded by Sam Loomis, who had been exec to Chuck Triebel in *Snook*. Loomis had got on the trail of a convoy and sunk a 4,000-ton freighter the previous day. The two classmates (they had been to the same secondary schools and roomed together at the Naval Academy) exchanged information; then Cutter headed south, in pursuit of a convoy thought to be headed for Saipan. He took station at the normal channel, but the convoy gave him the slip and went into Saipan by a new route.

Another convoy soon came along. Cutter found it on April 8 and attacked, firing three torpedoes each at two freighters. He sank two ships: *Aratama Maru*, a 6,784-ton converted submarine tender, and *Kizugawa Maru*, a 1,915-ton freighter. Both were loaded with troops and supplies for the defense of the Marianas.

Meanwhile, *Trigger*, with a new skipper, Fritz Harlfinger, set off for patrol at Palau. His exec was the seemingly indefatigable Ned Beach, who had made all eight of *Trigger*'s patrols under Jack Lewis,

Roy Benson, and Dusty Dornin. Lockwood detoured *Trigger* to the Marianas to lend Cutter a hand.

On April 8, while Cutter was sinking his two ships, Harlfinger found one of the largest convoys anyone in the submarine force had ever seen. Manning the periscope, Ned Beach counted four columns of ships—tankers, freighters, transports, and auxiliaries—with about five ships in each column surrounded by ten or more escorts. *Trigger's* fire-control party set up to fire a ten-torpedo salvo at a tanker and two other targets.

After Harlfinger had fired four torpedoes, a destroyer charged in, firing machine guns at the periscope. It was so close that it blanked out Beach's vision. Harlfinger ordered a deep dive, but nobody in the conning tower believed *Trigger* would make it in time; the destroyer was too close. Beach thought, "How long does it take a depth charge to sink fifty feet?"

Apparently it had all happened too fast for the depth-charge team on the destroyer. The first explosion the men in *Trigger's* conning tower heard were "four solid torpedo hits" which were, Beach believed, two in the tanker and two in a freighter. By then *Trigger* had reached 300 feet.

A nightmare followed. The destroyer dropped twenty-five depth charges. They were, Beach wrote, "absolute beauties.... How *Trigger* managed to hold together we'll never know." Lights went out. Cork insulation flew. Switches came undone. Valves leaked. The hull buckled in and out.

Then, as Beach remembered later, six of the escorts formed a ring around *Trigger*, keeping the submarine at the center. Every half hour or so, one charged in to pummel *Trigger* with a new series of charges. The attack went on for eighteen hours. Water leaked up to the level of the floor plates in the forward torpedo room. The temperature in the boat rose to 135 degrees. It was, Beach reported, a "long and horrible day," the worst beating *Trigger* had ever received, and one of the worst on record.

During the late afternoon, Harlfinger and Beach decided to surface and fight their way clear. They would make ready all torpedoes and man the deck gun. However, around sunset the escorts became lax, and *Trigger* slipped out of the deadly circle. That night, Harlfinger surfaced and set a course for the Palaus.

On the following day, April 9, Slade Cutter intercepted this same large convoy as it neared Saipan. It was, Cutter estimated, a fifteen-to-twenty ship convoy, the "largest we have ever seen." Cutter set up and fired four torpedoes from a range of 1,800 yards. "There were four ships overlapping in the field of the periscope with no open water between them," Cutter reported. However, just as Cutter fired, the targets zigged and all four torpedoes missed. One of the four made a circular run and, Cutter reported, "passed close aboard several times." Cutter fired two more at a freighter and obtained two hits. He lost depth control and went deep, just as two destroyers swung over dropping depth charges. Cutter went deeper.

Later that night, when Cutter came up, he found the freighter he hit still afloat, guarded by two destroyers. "Most discouraging," Cutter wrote. He moved in for another attack, but planes drove him under. Postwar records showed that the ship, *Bisaku Maru*, a 4,467-ton freighter, sank anyway.

On April 20, while Cutter was patrolling submerged off Saipan, he suddenly sighted a small RO-class Japanese submarine. Setting up fast, he fired two torpedoes from 1,800 yards. Again he lost depth control and went unavoidably deep. He reported one very loud explosion, "the loudest we have ever heard or felt." Cutter believed, "It must have been helped by an explosion in the target." The submarine was *RO-45*.

A week later, April 27, Cutter picked up yet another convoy about forty-five miles west of Saipan. It consisted of four freighters, a destroyer, and three smaller escorts. He attacked, firing four torpedoes at a freighter. Three hit, and down went 5,244-ton *Akigawa Maru*. Cutter's score: five ships (including *RO-45*) for 19,500 tons. In three patrols, Cutter had sunk fifteen ships—five on each time out.

Arriving at Palau on April 14, *Trigger* rendezvoused with Dick O'Kane in *Tang*. Following the air strike on the Palaus, Operation Desecrate, O'Kane had had a discouraging two weeks. The seas were empty of targets. He gave *Trigger* some spare parts to repair her damage and headed eastward toward Truk.

Patrolling off the Palaus, Harlfinger and Beach picked up a six-ship convoy on the night of April 26. Harlfinger attacked, firing six torpedoes at overlapping targets and obtaining four hits. He believed he had sunk two freighters and an escort. He chased the remaining three, attacking again, believing he sank two more and damaged the other. Harlfinger received credit for sinking five ships for 33,200 tons, but JANAC reduced that to one ship sunk off the Palaus, the large 11,700-ton transport *Miike Maru*.

When *Trigger* returned from patrol, she was found to be so weakened by her encounter with the escorts off the Marianas that she required a lengthy overhaul. During that period, Ned Beach went to new construction.

Herbert Jukes, who had sunk three tankers on his first patrol on *Kingfish*, en route from Fremantle to Pearl Harbor, took the boat to the Marianas. The patrol was unsuccessful. The endorsements pointed out that "opportunities to attack were missed on three occasions." One of these was a convoy. The endorsement stated, "The Commanding Officer apparently became confused and went deep, losing an opportunity to attack. The convoy passed over *Kingfish* fifteen minutes later."

Jukes—who had lost S-27 in Alaska—retained command for one more patrol, also unsuccessful. Then he was relieved of command and ordered to commission a new boat, *Cutlass*.

Patrols to Okinawa

When Donc Donaho finally left *Flying Fish*, Lockwood gave the boat to an officer far different in character and turn of mind. This was Robert Risser, who had made two patrols as exec to Roy Gross in *Seawolf*. Risser, who had a master's degree in ordnance, had graduated in the top 10 percent of the class of 1934; Donaho had graduated in the bottom 10 percent of the class of 1927. Where Donaho had been indifferent to personal relationships and the welfare of his men, Risser was thoughtful, easygoing, self-effacing. He inherited one of the best-trained crews in the submarine force. Walt Small, class of 1938, remained as exec.

On his first patrol, Risser had taken the boat to Formosa Strait and sunk two ships, a large tanker, 10,171 tons, and a large transport, 8,613 tons. On his second patrol, he went to the area near Okinawa. On the way out, he sank a ship near Iwo Jima. Off Okinawa, he dodged torpedoes from a Japanese submarine and attacked a convoy, sinking a 5,439-ton transport. Returning home, he found a freighter at anchor off Daito Jima, a tiny island east of Okinawa, sank it, and then returned to Majuro for refit. In two skillful patrols, Risser had sunk five ships for 28,712 tons.

Beetle Roach in *Haddock*, going on his second patrol, became involved in one of the most unusual Ultra episodes of the submarine war. On board for this patrol for a PCO cruise was William Joseph Germershausen, who had served in peacetime on *Nautilus* and then demothballed and commanded *O-6*. Since the outbreak of the war, Germershausen, like Jim Blanchard on *Albacore*, had been stuck at the Submarine School "hollering like hell to get out." He reached Pearl Harbor in January 1944 and was assigned to *Haddock*.

The patrol, also conducted in the Okinawa area, was long and dull. Roach made two attacks on small vessels, claiming to have sunk one escort for 1,000 tons, but there had been nothing big or challenging.

On the way home, Roach received an Ultra. As Germershausen remembered it, the message ordered *Haddock* to intercept a small supply boat which was taking food and "many classified documents" to Wake Island; the documents might have included new codebooks for the Japanese garrison stationed there. The Ultra gave specific times and positions for the ship. On the way to the intercept, Roach and Germershausen planned to capture the ship intact and sail it back to Pearl Harbor, like privateers. They argued over who would take command of the captured vessel.

Unknown to Roach and Germershausen, Lockwood had also alerted another boat to intercept this important little ship. This was *Tuna*, commanded by James Hardin, who had just returned from long overhaul and was setting off on his second patrol. Hardin made contact first and attacked with his 5-inch deck gun.

Germershausen recalled:

We reached the intercept point and suddenly Roach, who was at the periscope, saw the little ship—and shells hitting it. It burst into flames. We surfaced immediately and joined in the fun. She was already on her way down. We put a rubber boat in the water. An officer and an enlisted man from Haddock *went in the rubber boat to pick up classified documents which were floating out of the sinking ship all over the water.*

I was then the Officer of the Deck. I asked Roach if I could join the fellows in the water. He said, "Yes, go ahead." I took off my clothes and jumped over the side and grabbed some of the papers. Books and things. Meanwhile, people from the Tuna *were doing the same thing. We were all in the water together, the Japanese, ourselves, the floating documents and the sinking ship.*

When I got back to the boat, we watched the officer and the en-

listed man in the raft from Haddock. *They had found two Japanese whom they wanted to take as prisoners. The Japanese didn't want to come on board. So the officer whacked them across the head with a paddle and then they came aboard.*

During the efforts to salvage the ship's papers, Hardin lost one of his men. The chief of the boat, John Kirkman Huff, apparently a nonswimmer, fell over the side and disappeared.

Tuna and *Haddock* recovered only about thirty documents apiece. Roach took these—and the two prisoners—and turned them all over to the intelligence center at Pearl Harbor. Germershausen was disappointed that Hardin had attacked and sunk the vessel. Had *Haddock* captured it, he believed, they could have gotten much more classified material. The little trawler—*Takima Maru*—would have been a fine trophy for Admiral Lockwood.

Hardin took *Tuna* on to patrol near the Palaus but made no attacks. After his third patrol—again, with no attacks—his division commander, Dutch Will (who had come up from Australia on *Tuna*), wrote Lockwood, "I again wish to state that I do not recommend Hardin for another patrol nor do I recommend him for new construction." Hardin was relieved after these three patrols on *Tuna* and went to be exec of the tender *Bushnell*. Hardin said later, "It is true that we had poor results on the three patrols when I had command."

27

Australia, January through March 1944

Codebreaking and the New Guinea Campaign

In the Southwest Pacific, General MacArthur continued his portion of the "two roads" to Tokyo strategy, the reconquest of New Guinea. There had been one important revision in his plan: Rabaul and Kavieng would be bypassed. He concentrated on north New Guinea.

On the eve of this push, the general became the beneficiary of a valuable intelligence legacy from the Japanese. In January 1944, following a landing on the northeast coast of New Guinea, one of MacArthur's army units found a trunkful of Japanese army codebooks, buried in the sand along the beach. The covers had been carefully removed and perhaps sent to Tokyo as "proof of destruction," but the books were intact. They were rushed to MacArthur's intelligence center in Brisbane and turned over to MacArthur's Navy Intelligence Chief and Japanese linguist, Arthur McCollum.

McCollum discovered to his delight that the books were still current. To help with the translations, he put in a call to the codebreaking unit, FRUMEL, to ask for the loan of two linguists.

There had been changes in the unit at FRUMEL. In September 1943 the Naval Communicators in Washington sent out Ernest Sidney Goodwin to relieve Rudolph Fabian as commander of the unit. In January 1944, following the turnover, Fabian was transferred to serve with the Commander in Chief, British Eastern Fleet in India, to coordinate the codebreaking functions of the United States and the Allies. Swede Carlson returned to duty in Washington.

On the lower levels there had also been changes. Rufus Taylor had returned to Washington for duty. Forrest Rosecrans ("Tex") Biard moved down from FRUPAC to FRUMEL to help Tom Mackie with the heavy hauling. Gill Richardson and John Lietwiler were still the leading codebreakers for the unit. They were now assisted by many of the former enlisted men on Corregidor who had been field-promoted to officer rank.

In response to McCollum's call, Goodwin picked his two best linguists, Tom Mackie and Tex Biard. Mackie and Biard traveled to Brisbane and reported to McCollum, who turned over the books and sent the two men to work with army intelligence officers. "The books were beautiful," Mackie recalled. "I guess the Japanese general who had charge of them couldn't bear to see them destroyed."

For the next twelve days Mackie and Biard, using the codebooks, eavesdropped on conversations between the Japanese generals in charge of defending New Guinea. "They were arguing back and forth," Mackie recalled, "about which places should be heavily defended and which places they ought to ignore." When the Japanese generals finally resolved the debate, MacArthur knew not only the places marked for defense concentrations but how many soldiers and aircraft would be assigned to each. His staff then laid plans to move up the New Guinea coast by invading the lightly defended areas and bypassing those that were heavily defended.

The outcome was one of the most remarkable chapters in the history of the Pacific War. Having slogged painfully up through the Solomons for seventeen long months, the Allies conquered much of the northern coast of New Guinea in a few weeks with almost no casualties.

Bypassing Japanese strongholds at Wewak and Hansa Bay, MacArthur's troops prepared to strike the Hollandia area on April 22, landing at three points: Aitape, Humboldt Bay, and Tanahmerah. As a preliminary to these landings, Admiral Nimitz sent fast carrier task forces (a total of twelve carriers) from Majuro for an air strike. On the way back, April 30, the carriers hit Truk again, wiping out the last of the Japanese aircraft based there and sinking most everything left afloat in the harbor.

During this raid, there were several Pearl Harbor boats lying off

RECONQUEST of NEW GUINEA
JANUARY-APRIL 1944

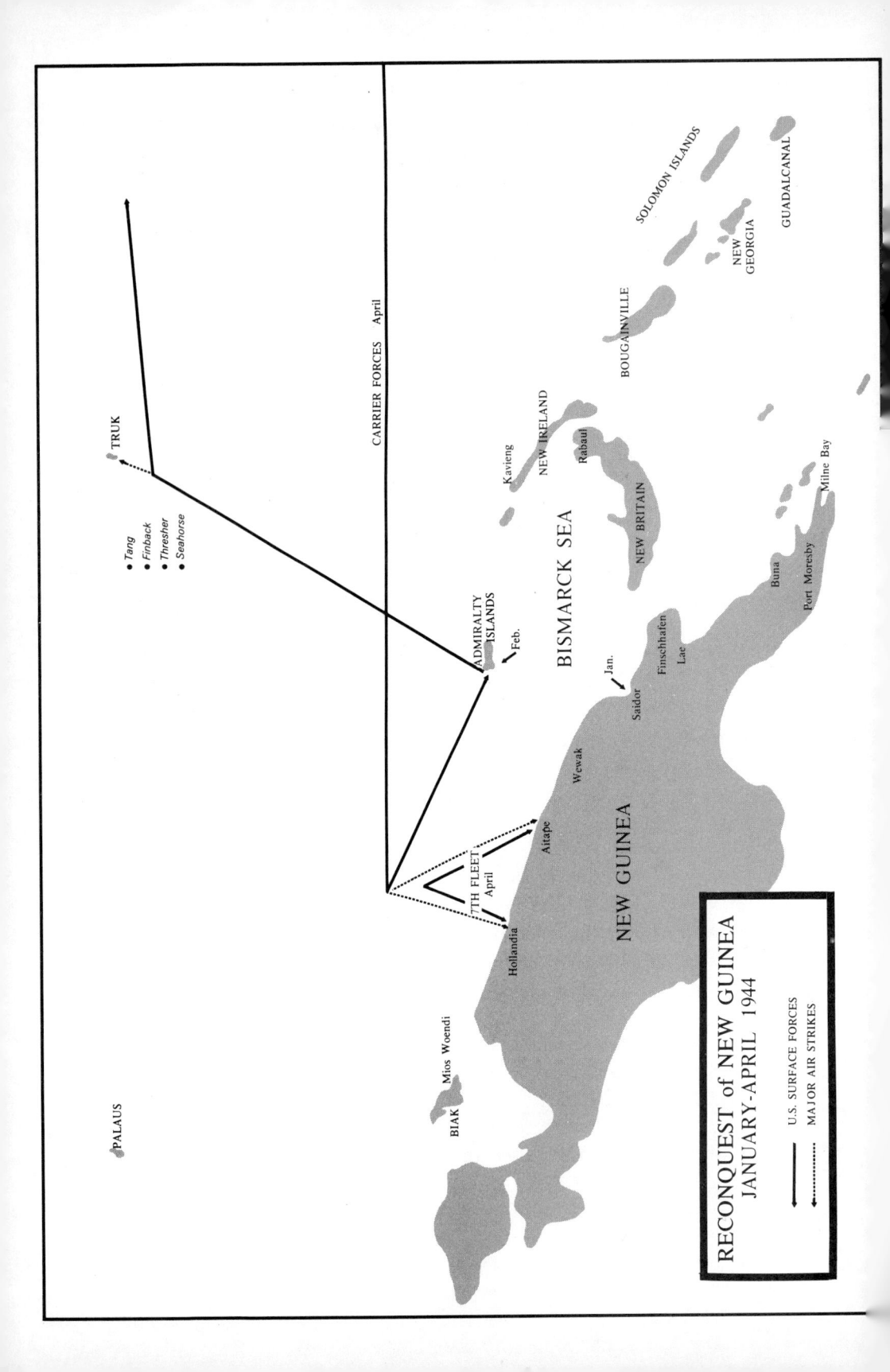

→ U.S. SURFACE FORCES
⇢ MAJOR AIR STRIKES

Truk lifeguarding: Dick O'Kane's *Tang*, returning from his long luckless patrol off the Palaus; Slade Cutter in *Seahorse*, returning from his spectacular patrol in the Marianas; John Tyree in *Finback*; Duncan MacMillan in *Thresher*; and *Permit*, now commanded by Donald Arthur Scherer, who had served on *Pike* and *Lapon*. Slade Cutter was accidentally bombed by U.S. forces (slight damage); Dick O'Kane in a daring series of rescues picked up twenty-two naval airmen.

Following this, MacArthur's forces landed at Hollandia. Enemy forces were slight. At Aitape, U.S. casualties were two killed and thirteen wounded; at Humboldt Bay, six killed, sixteen wounded. After the landings, Japanese troops marched overland from Wewak, but they were thrown back and defeated.

Patrols from Fremantle

As MacArthur's troops advanced up the coast of New Guinea, the areas formerly covered by U.S. submarines basing from Brisbane or Milne Bay became empty of targets or fell into friendly hands. During the early spring, most of the boats transferred to Pearl Harbor or Fremantle. The few that were left operated as lifeguards during the carrier strikes on Truk and Palau and patrolled farther to westward—around Davao Gulf. The Brisbane base was all but closed down. A new tender, *Eurayle*, replaced the workhorse *Fulton* at Milne Bay; *Fulton* returned to the States for overhaul.* After MacArthur captured the Admiralty Islands, *Eurayle* moved forward from Milne Bay to Manus Harbor in the Admiralties.

With the reduction in Brisbane operations, Jimmy Fife (an acting commodore) had little to do and not sufficient forces to justify his rank and seniority. He was transferred back to shore duty in Washington as a war planner for Admiral King, working under Rear Admiral Donald Bradley Duncan. All the while, he kept in close contact with Lockwood by mail and helped push along some of Lockwood's pet technical projects. In Fremantle, Ralph Christie's force was building toward thirty submarines. In addition to the tender *Pelias*, a new one, *Orion*, arrived on January 5. Another, *Griffin*, the tender for the re-engined H.O.R. boats of Squadron Twelve, came later in the spring.

Fife's departure created some changes in Christie's command. John

---

* Administratively, Squadron Eighteen, commanded by Eliot Hinman ("Swede") Bryant, replaced Squadron Eight.

Haines, commanding Squadron Sixteen in *Pelias*, was named to succeed Fife as overall boss of submarine operations at Brisbane–Milne Bay–Manus Harbor. Upon Haines's departure, Tex McLean, Christie's waterfront boss, assumed additional duties as commander of Squadron Sixteen. The other key men, P. G. Nichols (chief of staff) and Murray Tichenor (operations), remained in place. Frederick Kent Loomis filled the post vacated by Dutch Will as chief maintenance officer.

During the early months of 1944, Christie continued the war on Japanese shipping—with priority on tankers—in much the same manner as in the late months of 1943. With refueling facilities available in Darwin, many boats made double-barreled patrols. Many edged up into Luzon Strait, where skippers exchanged information on convoys with Pearl Harbor boats operating in the same area. In February, when Admiral Koga ordered his major fleet units to abandon Truk and withdraw to the west, many of these went to Davao, Tawi Tawi, Surabaya, and Singapore—all ports in Christie's area. As the spring progressed, Christie's boats spent much time lying in wait for these units, helped by information from the codebreakers. He also continued the many special missions requested by General MacArthur. Most were carried forward by *Narwhal* (joined at Darwin by *Nautilus* in April), but many fleet boats were also diverted for this purpose.

Although Christie had ordered his submarines to deactivate the magnetic exploder on January 20, he was not yet ready to let go entirely. He set two officers in the PCO pool to work on a study of the exploder: young Chester Nimitz and James Lowell Page McCallum, who had a master's degree in ordnance. After an exhaustive technical study, Nimitz and McCallum evolved some new ideas for improving the reliability of the exploder. Christie ordered the torpedo shops to modify some exploders along the lines they suggested and then sent them to sea, but many of them exploded prematurely, and they proved as unreliable as any of the earlier versions.

A new boat, *Redfin*, commanded by Robert Donovan King,* reported from the States in January. His exec was Mike Shea, who had served on *Gar* and *Gudgeon*. *Redfin* went on patrol from Darwin. On January 9, King found a convoy and fired a salvo of three torpedoes,

---

* No kin to Chief of Naval Operations Admiral King.

his first war shots. All three exploded prematurely. After surfacing, King found pieces of his own torpedoes scattered along his deck.

A week later King found a destroyer, *Amatsukaze*. He fired four torpedoes down the throat from a range of 2,900 yards. King believed he got four hits and that the destroyer sank. However, *Amatsukaze* survived the encounter and limped into the nearest port with eighty of her crew dead from the explosions. The ship was out of action for a full year.

On return to Fremantle, King complained of eye trouble. He had a blind spot on his retina, perhaps caused by not using a sun shade on the periscope while looking into the sun. Christie relieved King of command and sent him to a hospital for treatment. Later the spot diminished, and King took command of the submarine repair unit in Brisbane.

Tom Hogan in Christie's flagship, *Bonefish*, conducted a third aggressive patrol off Indochina. On the way out, he received an Ultra from Christie cautioning him that Balabac Strait had just been mined. Hogan went through anyway, taking care to remain in deep water. All the boats that followed him did likewise.

While south of Camranh Bay, Hogan received another Ultra, reporting the movement of an important tanker convoy. "It was coming down the coast and going into harbors to anchor for the night," Hogan said later. Actually, the convoy turned out to be two days late. When Hogan found it, he set up on a huge whale-factory tanker. "The area between the bridge and the after superstructure had been decked over," Hogan recalled. "I counted twenty aircraft as cargo."

Hogan penetrated the screen and fired three torpedoes at the tanker. A destroyer charged, forcing *Bonefish* to the bottom, where Hogan wiped off a sonar head. Hogan heard three hits in the tanker, but she did not sink. After dark, Hogan surfaced and tried to find the convoy again, but it was gone.

Jim Dempsey in *Cod* patrolled the same area. On the way out, he sank two ships, including a 7,350-ton tanker. After that, most of the crew came down with poisoning from tetrachloride or food. Christie sent Dempsey an Ultra on an important tanker convoy, but Dempsey and the crew were so ill they were not able to carry off an attack. "The commanding officer accepts full responsibility for this fiasco," Dempsey wrote later. "The officers and crew, nearly all of whom are still suffering from the effects [of the] poisoning, did the best they could. Nothing seemed to click and each unsuccessful attempt to gain attack position made the next try more difficult."

Walt Griffith in *Bowfin* made a double-barreled patrol. On the first half, he patrolled the South China Sea. In a furious few days of action, Griffith fired off most of his torpedoes, sinking one confirmed freighter for 4,408 tons and damaging several other ships.

After a mere fourteen days, Griffith was back in Darwin to obtain a load of torpedoes and more fuel. In addition, he received some mines and orders to plant them off the coast of Borneo. Ralph Christie, still eager to make a brief submarine war patrol, decided to go with Griffith on this second leg. Not wanting to risk another turn-down, he did not ask permission of his new boss, Admiral Kinkaid.

Leaving P. G. Nichols and Murray Tichenor in charge, Christie flew to Darwin on January 29 and joined *Bowfin*. The mines had been loaded on board. In addition, Griffith carried sixteen torpedoes. The boat got under way immediately. Christie established his quarters in the wardroom, sleeping in a pull-down bunk over the wardroom table. He was quite pleased with himself. "If I came back," he wrote later, "I would be congratulated. If I did not, well..."

On the evening of the second night out, Griffith found a 4,300-ton merchant ship en route from Ambon to Timor, bringing food and supplies to the Japanese garrison. While Christie stood on the bridge looking on from a "box seat," Griffith swung and fired two torpedoes. Both hit, Christie reported later, and "sank the enemy ship in less than one minute." There was, he reported, "no applause—just silence—and everybody went about his own business." Postwar records failed to credit Griffith with sinking a ship on this day and at this place.

On the way to Borneo to lay the minefield, Griffith received an important Ultra from P. G. Nichols. A Japanese seaplane tender, the 17,000-ton *Kamoi*,[*] was en route to Makassar City. Griffith found her in the shallow waters of Salajar Strait the next night and trailed. She had three small escorts and air cover. Griffith could not achieve a firing position that night. He tracked her all the following day on the surface, diving eight times to avoid detection by Japanese aircraft. During the afternoon, Rear Admiral Christie stood watch as officer of the deck so the officers could rest up for the long night ahead.

That night about eleven o'clock, Griffith maneuvered around the

---

[*] Converted from a 20-knot tanker orginally built in the United States.

escorts and attacked, firing six bow tubes. Owing to a fire-control error, all missed. The torpedoes alerted the escorts. They thrashed about, dropping depth charges at random to scare Griffith away. *Kamoi* began twisting and turning with radical zigs and zags to complicate Griffith's problem.

Griffith remained on the surface, maneuvering slowly for a second attack. Christie, who was on the bridge watching, became uneasy. "We were very close to him," Christie wrote. "Too close, within machine gun range. I thought we would dive, but [Griffith] chose to hold the initiative by remaining on the surface. . . . I thought surely he must see us. . . . I was most uncomfortable. . . . The enemy could easily have sunk us with gunfire or at least swept our bridge with machinegun fire."

Griffith swung around and fired two stern tubes from a range of about 1,000 yards. Christie heard the first torpedo leave the tube. He wrote, "I could see the luminous wake and WHAM! an enormous detonation which shook us up as though our own ship had been hit. We got two hits smack under his bridge this time. Debris was thrown skyward in a background of fire and smoke. I was slammed against the bridge railing by the force of the explosion and broke my binocular strap and lost my cap."

About then, the target responded with searchlights and gunfire. To Christie, the light seemed like a "million flashbulbs." After it came whizzing shells: 4-inch, 40-mm., and 20-mm. Griffith raced away from the target and then cleared the bridge of all personnel except himself. Admiral Christie lunged for the hatch like any lookout. "I don't think I hit a rung of the ladder to the conning tower."

There was one torpedo remaining aft. Griffith was determined to put it in *Kamoi*. He outran the guns, then swung around in the darkness, avoiding the searchlights. He set up and fired. Christie, taking station in the forward torpedo room, believed he heard a hit, but it was drowned out by the diving alarm. Griffith took *Bowfin* to 442 feet to evade. No depth charges followed. For that, Christie was grateful.

Kamoi did not sink. Christie learned from Ultra reports that, following the attack, the Japanese beached her. Later, they towed her into Surabaya for temporary repairs. Months later, according to Christie, she was towed to Singapore for major repairs.

Following this action, Griffith took *Bowfin* to the approaches to Balikpapan, where he planted the small minefield. On the way home, he shot up two sampans "loaded with cement." Then he dropped Christie at Exmouth Gulf, where a plane was waiting to fly him back to Fremantle. Christie arrived back at his office nine days after departing, the second oldest officer * and first force commander—and admiral—in the history of the U.S. Navy to make a submarine war patrol. In this two-part patrol, Griffith had fired a total of thirty-five torpedoes, achieving sixteen hits.

After a brief refit, Griffith went out again for his third patrol, another double-barrel. This time he carried a special load of the "modified" exploders recommended by young Nimitz and McCallum. They did not work very well. During his thirty-three days at sea, Griffith attacked seven ships, firing forty-one torpedoes. Of these, *eight* of the first twenty-four prematured; fourteen hit, sinking three big freighters for 15,000 tons; others caused damage to two ships. During the patrol, Griffith took *Bowfin* into narrow, shallow, and restricted waters, received six close depth-charge attacks and three close bombs from aircraft, and was twice shot at by shore guns.

When Griffith came in from this patrol, Christie decided he should return to the States for new construction and rest. To replace him, Christie picked Frederick Williams Laing, who came from command of *S-30* in Alaska. However, Laing was found to be suffering from gout, so the boat went to John Corbus, whom Christie had relieved in *Haddo* but believed deserved a second chance.

Gordon Selby, taking *Puffer* out for his second patrol, hunted north of Singapore. Shortly after sunset on the night of February 20, Selby found a ten-ship convoy made up of large ships, southbound. "Three of the first four ships sighted," he wrote later, "were very large, their superstructures having the triangular appearance of battleships and cruisers. . . . The night was too dark and the horizon too hazy to make out any definite type characteristics on the larger ships but the overall silhouettes were those of men-of-war and not freighters, tankers or transports."

Unaware at first that he had intercepted fast-moving combatant ships, Selby underestimated the convoy's speed. He gave chase, but the formation soon pulled out of range. These ships were probably units of the Japanese main fleet, en route to Singapore from Truk or Japan to be closer to the oil supply.

In midafternoon on February 22, Selby picked up another convoy.

* After Babe Brown in *Narwhal,* supporting the 1943 Sea of Japan foray.

PATROLS FROM FREMANTLE

This one was northbound and consisted of several medium or small freighters. Selby began chasing, looking for deeper water to make his attack. Meanwhile, high-periscope lookouts reported two more ships; Selby moved his periscope around and saw what appeared to be a large camouflaged transport with one escort, zigzagging.

Turning to attack, Selby fired two torpedoes at the transport and two at the escort. One torpedo hit the transport, throwing up a column of smoke and debris. Closing in, Selby saw lifeboats being lowered into the water. Selby fired two more torpedoes into the transport. Both hit. As the ship began to sink slowly by the stern, Selby took periscope pictures.

The ship, which soon slid beneath the waves, was later identified from Selby's excellent photographs as an ocean liner, *Teiko Maru*, 15,100 tons—which, as the French liner *D'Artagnan*, had been captured in the early days of the war. She was the third largest Japanese merchant ship sunk to that time, after Post's 17,526-ton liner *Kamakura Maru* and Tom Wogan's 16,975-ton liner *Tatsuta Maru*.

The rest of this patrol was frustrating. Selby found two more convoys, one of which he attempted to attack on three separate occasions but failed for one reason or another. "Except for *Teiko*, I was not too happy with our third patrol," Selby said later. "I should have had a big haul—too cautious I guess." When he returned to Fremantle, Selby received a "rude shock." After three days of "letting off steam," he went down to the docks and saw what appeared to be *Teiko* moored in a slip. It turned out to be her sister ship, *Porthos*, still in Allied hands.

Willard Laughon, making his second patrol as skipper of *Rasher*, got under way from Fremantle February 19, a day after James Davis left for his third patrol in *Raton*. Just north of Lombok Strait, Laughon received an Ultra on a convoy going from Surabaya to Ambon. Davis received the same report and joined with Laughon in a coordinated search. On February 25 the two boats rendezvoused and agreed on a battle plan. One and a half hours later, they found the convoy: two freighters with two escorts.

Laughon attacked first, just after dark, firing four torpedoes at one freighter from 1,000 yards and another four torpedoes at the second from 1,300 yards. He obtained three hits in each target, and both sank. They were *Tango Maru*, 6,200 tons, and *Ryusei Maru*, 4,800 tons. Laughon then noted in his report, "Told *Raton* that there were no more targets and that we were clearing the area and apologized for hogging the show."

Laughon took *Rasher* north through Molucca Passage to the Celebes Sea. On March 3, he picked up a big convoy: six freighters, three escorts. After a hard chase, during which his SJ radar went out of commission, he attacked at night, firing three torpedoes at one ship, three at another. Escorts drove him under, preventing another attack. One of the freighters, *Nittai Maru*, 6,400 tons, went down.

On the night of March 4, Laughon chased and attacked another convoy, firing two torpedoes at one ship and four at another. All missed or ran under. He swung, maneuvered, and fired his last four at another ship. It was a bad setup; all missed. Laughon returned to Darwin to take on another load of torpedoes and resume the patrol.

Davis in *Raton* went on to Indochina, where he joined in a loosely coordinated search with Brooks Harral in *Ray* (who had laid a minefield off Saigon), *Bluefish* (now commanded by Charles Mitchell Henderson, who had served on *Sculpin* and *Cabrilla*), and Selby in *Puffer*. On March 3, Christie sent all four boats an Ultra on a tanker convoy. Henderson in *Bluefish* sank one tanker for 10,500 tons, but the other three boats did not fare so well. Neither Davis nor Harral sank a confirmed ship on their patrols.

Haddo, brought down from Pearl Harbor by John Corbus, went to young Chester Nimitz, the first from the class of 1936 in Fremantle to get a command. Like Griffith, Nimitz carried a load of torpedoes with the modified magnetic exploders he and McCallum had designed. Nimitz went up through Lombok Strait in early March.

While Nimitz was en route, Ralph Christie received "evidence of a movement" (as he noted in his diary) of many Japanese men-of-war from Singapore to Surabaya, possibly a carrier, two battleships, three heavy cruisers, and many destroyers. The information—obtained from the codebreakers—led Christie to believe that the Japanese might be planning a hit-and-run attack against Fremantle, so he alerted Nimitz to patrol the north end of Lombok Strait and watch for a possible sortie south.

Early on the morning of March 12, while *Haddo* was slowly cruising 12 miles east of Bali, Nimitz noted in his log, "We are relying on our SJ radar to prevent somebody from running our blockade." That same morning, radar produced several large pips at ranges of 6,700 to

16,000 yards. Nimitz bent on full power, turning toward the bearings of the pips. They disappeared mysteriously.

Nimitz was torn: report these pips or not? He wrote later, "Finally decided to send message reporting possibility of enemy ships passing through Lombok. 'Remember Pearl Harbor' was the message that kept sticking in my mind."

In Fremantle, the Nimitz message touched off a monumental flap. Christie was now certain the Japanese were headed his way. He noted in his diary, "We are busy making 'Estimates of the Situation' and studying our defenses against a probable air raid by carrier planes." He ordered all submarines in refit except *Crevalle*, revamping her conning tower and lacking periscopes and radar, to stop work and get into "fully ready" status. *Flasher, Hoe, Robalo, Hake,* and *Redfin* got under way and stood out to sea to attack the incoming Japanese. Many aircraft were concentrated at Fremantle. The tenders there—*Pelias* and *Orion*—were sent to Albany. At sea, Laughon in *Rasher*, having just taken on board a new load of torpedoes at Darwin, was ordered to take position in Lombok Strait. William Thompson (who had been Griffith's exec on *Bowfin*), starting off on his first patrol in *Cabrilla*, was ordered to guard Sunda Strait and later to reconnoiter Christmas Island. Other boats were ordered to likely points of intercept, to catch the Japanese task force on the way back.

Tom Hogan in *Bonefish*, returning from Indochina, still had thirteen torpedoes on board but little fuel and food. He put into Exmouth Gulf, picking up fuel and ten sheep and fifteen lambs. Returning to sea, to stand watch off the approaches to Fremantle, *Bonefish* ran into a tremendous hurricane with winds as high as 120 knots. The storm lasted three days. Hogan's men got seasick. The cook prepared lamb and mutton sandwiches, all that he could put out in those mountainous seas. "It was the worst thing you can imagine," Hogan wrote later. "And when we got into Fremantle and got to the hotel, the first meal they served us was lamb stew!"

MacArthur did not send as many aircraft as Christie would have liked. On March 10 he noted in his diary, "So we face zero hour—dawn Saturday, March 11—without much help from Mr. Kenney [General George C. Kenney]'s famed 5th Air Force. Despite the tremendous development of aircraft, they are not yet that independent of the weather to the extent that ships are. Twenty-three aircraft arrived out of 82 ordered."

Zero hour passed without an attack. Christie delayed zero hour another day, thinking perhaps the Japanese task force had been slowed by the storm. On Sunday, March 12, he noted, "No Japs this morning as expected."

The Japs never did appear; it had all been a false alarm. Christie wrote Lockwood, "The 'threat to Fremantle' was a lot of fun and of value to the area. The highlight, in my opinion, was the remarkable performance of the tenders in getting out seven boats under refit to sea fully ready for offensive operations within twelve hours."

Laughon in *Rasher* spent eighteen terrible days on station in Lombok Strait to intercept the expected forces, constantly harassed by Japanese patrol boats. After being released from this hazardous assignment, he went on to sink another ship for 2,700 tons. In all, his total for this double-barreled patrol was four ships for 20,100 tons.

Unaware of the commotion he had stirred up, Nimitz continued his patrol. On March 8, two nights after his encounter with the mysterious pips in Lombok Strait, he came upon a submarine tender and escort. Nimitz set up and fired three torpedoes with his modified magnetic exploders. Two of the three prematured after twenty-three seconds, and the third missed aft when the tender, alerted by the premature explosions, veered away. After that, Nimitz deactivated the experimental magnetic exploders. Later he said, "I told Christie that night by [radio] dispatch that I was inactivating all of my remaining exploders and suggested that somebody get back to the drawing board."

On March 12, Christie noted in his diary, "We have reached the positive end of the long trail with the magnetic exploder.... From now on BuOrd can do the experimenting.... Finis!"

Nimitz went up Makassar Strait. On the night of March 14, off Balikpapan, he found a tanker escorted by a destroyer and fired three torpedoes at each, but missed. Off Indochina on March 29, he attacked a seven-ship convoy, damaging at least one large freighter but achieving no sinkings. On April 1 he fired at a shallow-draft coastal steamer, but the torpedoes ran under. On April 5 he found another tanker but was driven off by accurate gunfire. On the way home, he was ordered to pick up a group of guerrillas on the northeast coast of Borneo, but the rendezvous misfired and he could not find them.

In addition, Nimitz was alerted to yet another special mission. Rumors came down from the Philippines that Admiral Koga had not been killed in the plane crash after the U.S. raid on the Palaus but was in fact being held prisoner by MacArthur's guerrilla chief on Cebu, Lieutenant James Cushing. MacArthur requested a submarine to pick up Admiral Koga. Christie, thinking what a fine story it would make if young Nimitz "delivered" Admiral Koga to Australia, ordered Nimitz to stand by in the Sulu Sea. As it turned out, Cushing had captured not Koga (who was definitely dead) but Koga's chief of staff, Admiral Shigeru Fukudome. However, Fukudome escaped and the Nimitz mission was cancelled.

John Broach in *Hake* and Marshall Harlan ("Cy") Austin, new skipper of *Redfin*, both found important Japanese men-of-war.

On April 3, Broach in *Hake*, patrolling off the west coast of Borneo on the Singapore-Manila traffic lanes, picked up a *Shokaku*-class aircraft carrier escorted by two destroyers. The force was making 22 knots, and Broach was unable to gain a favorable attack position. Later that morning he found two light cruisers and fired four stern tubes at one, believing he obtained a hit. On April 8 he picked up four cruisers and five destroyers but was unable to close.

Cy Austin, patrolling on the other side of Borneo in the Celebes Sea, also sighted several cruisers. He picked up the first, a light cruiser, on April 1 and closed to 8,000 yards, but the ship got away. On April 8, he sighted two cruisers, one heavy and one light. He closed to 10,000 yards, but again the men-of-war slipped out of range. On April 12, he sighted yet another light cruiser escorted by destroyers. Austin went in, closing the range to 2,800 yards. During the approach, the TDC went out of commission, fouling the attack, but Austin fired four stern tubes anyway. All missed.

Both Broach and Austin got bags of a different kind. Off Borneo, Broach sank a tanker, *Yamamizu Maru*, 5,174 tons, and damaged others. Austin sank two medium-sized freighters and the destroyer *Akigumo* for 10,300 confirmed tons. On the way home, Austin was ordered to pick up the guerrillas on northeast Borneo that Nimitz had missed. His small boat was ambushed by the Japanese, who very nearly killed four of his men. He had to leave the guerrillas behind.

28
Australia, April through June 1944

Showdown in the Marianas

In May 1944 the Allied juggernaut in the Pacific—reinforced by more carriers, amphibious craft, soldiers, marines, and airmen—rolled swiftly down the twin roads to Tokyo. At Pearl Harbor, Admiral Nimitz laid final plans for the invasion of the Marianas. As a preliminary, the carrier task forces prepared to make air strikes. In western New Guinea, MacArthur's forces, supported by Admiral Kinkaid's growing naval force, leaped from Hollandia to Wakde and Sarmi (May 18) and then to the island of Biak (May 27). During these operations, a British-U.S. task force conducted an air strike on Surabaya (May 17).

Admiral Toyoda, who had replaced Admiral Koga as commander in chief of the Japanese combined fleet, was determined to make a stand in the Marianas and the Palaus, to blunt any further westward movement of Allied forces. His battle plan, issued on May 4, was known as A-Go. It called for the Japanese army and navy to reinforce the Marianas, Palau, and the Philippines with troops and aircraft. All Japanese forces would fight to the death. Toyoda (like Koga before him) hoped to draw the U.S. Pacific Fleet into a decisive battle near the Palaus which he would win with the help of land-based aircraft supplementing his inferior carrier forces. In addition, he estab-

SHOWDOWN IN THE MARIANAS

lished a line of submarines between Truk and New Guinea to intercept the fleet.

Toyoda ordered the major units of the Japanese fleet to assemble at Tawi Tawi, the big anchorage off the northeast coast of Borneo. Carriers, battleships, and cruisers steamed down from Japan and over from the anchorage at Lingga Roads near Singapore. With them came a steady stream of fleet tankers and auxiliaries. While the fleet was staging at Tawi Tawi, the tankers shunted back and forth between Tawi Tawi and Borneo, hauling oil. The codebreakers followed these movements, predicting courses, speeds, and rendezvous points with a high degree of accuracy.

Both submarine forces—Christie's in Australia, Lockwood's in Pearl Harbor—geared for the coming showdown. Their primary missions: (1) to intercept, report, and attack Japanese fleet units, troop convoys, and tankers based on Ultra information; (2) to report movements of major Japanese fleet units and other vessels discovered without the help of Ultra information, and then attack; and (3) to provide advance reconnaissance on islands to be struck or invaded and lifeguard support during preliminary raids.

Christie's submarines carried out all three missions with much success.

Eric Lloyd Barr, Jr., son of a noted World War I submariner who had commanded *E-1*, arrived at Milne Bay in a new boat, *Bluegill*. Barr, who had served as exec to Rebel Lowrance on *Kingfish*, was notoriously aggressive and determined to uphold the family's fine name in submarines.

Barr patrolled near Halmahera. On about April 26 he received an Ultra: the light cruiser *Yubari* and destroyer escorts were en route from Davao with 900 troop reinforcements for the tiny island of Sonsorol, lying between Halmahera and Palau. Another boat, *Blackfish*, commanded by Robert Sellars, was also directed to the scene. Early on the morning of April 27, *Bluegill* and *Blackfish* met off Sonsorol.

At about 4:20 A.M., Barr's radar operator reported two high-speed pips on radar headed for Sonsorol. Barr moved to intercept. At 7:07, he spotted the tops of ships coming out of a rainsquall, range 13 miles. Barr dived, but the ships eluded him and reached the island, where they unloaded troops. Later in the morning, Barr saw a destroyer lying to off the island. He was preparing to attack it when suddenly

Yubari appeared. Undeterred by two depth charges from Japanese aircraft, Barr set up quickly and fired six torpedoes at the cruiser, range 2,600 yards. Three hit and *Yubari*, 3,300 tons, often shot at by U.S. submarines, went down.

The destroyer, *Samidare*, charged at *Bluegill*. Barr swung his stern tubes to bear and fired four torpedoes down the throat. All missed. *Samidare* unleashed a persistent depth-charge attack, driving *Bluegill* deep. Later, three other destroyers joined *Samidare*, and Barr, believing in discretion, eased away.

Eric Barr was the third skipper within a period of a few weeks to sink a light cruiser on his first war patrol. The others were Bud Gruner in *Skate* (*Agano*, February 16) and Malcolm Garrison in *Sandlance* (*Tatsuta*, March 13).

The Japanese organized a convoy at Shanghai for the purpose of lifting two divisions of reinforcements to New Guinea. The convoy, commanded by Rear Admiral Sadamichi Kajioka, who had captured Wake and led the Port Moresby invasion forces during the Battle of the Coral Sea, headed for Manila. Kajioka's flagship was a coal-burning minelayer, *Shirataka*, which gave off heavy smoke. The convoy left Shanghai on April 17, its progress followed closely by the codebreakers.

Two of Christie's boats were patrolling near Manila as the convoy approached: Tommy Dyker's *Jack* and Jim Dempsey's *Cod*. On the morning of April 26, *Jack* intercepted the convoy off the northwest coast of Luzon. As Dykers was taking up position, he spotted a Japanese submarine and evaded at high speed. A few minutes later, a plane came over and dropped a bomb. Dykers was certain the Japanese would route the convoy around him, but they didn't; at noon, Dykers picked up the heavy smoke of the flagship *Shirataka* again and trailed. An hour before sunset he surfaced to make an end around, but a plane came over and drove him down.

After dark, Dykers again surfaced and tracked the convoy, waiting for moonset. When it came, he moved in to attack. The escorts were more alert than usual, and Dykers, trying one side and then the other, couldn't find a hole. Finally he decided to shoot spreads of low-speed torpedoes under the escorts at the mass of overlapping targets in the convoy. In three separate attacks, he fired off nineteen torpedoes. They appeared to hit, and Dykers believed he had sunk one or more, but Christie only credited Dykers with damage to five ships.

In the postwar accounting, however, it was discovered that Dykers had hit and sunk a very valuable target, the 5,425-ton freighter *Yoshida Maru I*, packed with an army regiment of 3,000 men. She sank quickly, and all the troops, including the regimental commander, drowned. After that disaster, the convoy put into Manila, where it received more escorts before setting off again.

Jim Dempsey in *Cod* was unable to attack this convoy, but he made his presence felt later; on May 10, he attacked a convoy off the west coast of Luzon, sinking an old 820-ton destroyer and a big 7,200-ton freighter and damaging two other ships. Upon return to Fremantle, Dempsey stepped down as commander of *Cod*, going to serve as operations officer on Freeland Daubin's staff. Jim Dempsey had made a record ten Pacific war patrols as commanding officer, three on *S-37*, four on *Spearfish*, and three on *Cod*.

Herb Andrews in *Gurnard*, one of the last of the re-engined H.O.R. boats to shift from Pearl Harbor to Fremantle, went by way of Manila. Andrews had yet another new exec, his fourth in four patrols, George Stuart Simmons III. By then, Admiral Kajioka's convoy was under way from Manila, bound for New Guinea, now reinforced by more destroyers. Christie put Andrews on the track.

Andrews intercepted on May 6 in the Celebes Sea. He submerged and began a slow, cautious approach to avoid detection by aircraft. Four hours later, the convoy bore down on him: eight transports in three columns with many escorts.

Andrews let a destroyer escort go by, then fired a salvo of six bow tubes at two of the transports in the near column. One torpedo of his first salvo hit his first target, but the second salvo missed the second target and traveled on to the far column, hitting another transport. Andrews swung around and fired his stern tubes, which hit the second target. An escort charged up, and Andrews went deep as about a hundred depth charges rained down, none close. Two hours later, Andrews came up cautiously, raising the periscope to find three sinking ships and a massive rescue operation in progress. He cruised around for a while, taking photographs through the periscope, and later that night he fired at one of the cripples which was still afloat.

In all, Andrews had sunk three big ships crammed with soldiers and equipment, the transports *Aden Maru*, 5,824 tons, and *Taijima Maru*, 6,995 tons, and a cargo ship, *Tenshinzan Maru*, 6,886 tons. (Andrews was told later that about 6,000 Japanese troops drowned that day. It is possible but not probable. Jasper Holmes reported after the war that the rescue operations had been unusually efficient, with the Japanese even lashing field guns to floating rafts.)

Since leaving Shanghai, the convoy had lost four valuable ships: one to Tommy Dykers on *Jack* and now three to Herb Andrews on *Gurnard*. What remained of the force went not to New Guinea, as planned, but to Halmahera, where efforts were made to transship them to New Guinea by barge. These efforts either failed or came too late. Between them, Dykers and Andrews stopped the better part of two army divisions from reaching New Guinea.

Frank Walker, exec to Hank Munson on *Crevalle*, moved up to command when Munson stepped down. On his first time out as skipper, Walker patrolled off the west coast of Borneo. On April 25 he sank a small 1,000-ton freighter, but the next two weeks were a time of utter frustration. On April 26 he tried to attack an eight-ship convoy, but a destroyer beat him off. On May 3 he picked up two ships with one escort, tracked them in driving rain, and attacked after dark, firing eight torpedoes. (Walker believed he sank one ship, but postwar records failed to confirm it.) On May 4 he found a six-ship convoy, but it went into shallow water before he could attack.

On May 6—the day Herb Andrews sank three ships from the troop convoy—Walker's luck changed. He picked up an eleven-ship convoy with several destroyer escorts. With these ships was *Nisshin Maru*, 16,801 tons, a huge tanker (once a whale factory) similar to *Tonnan Maru III*, which Dan Daspit had tried to sink off Truk. Maneuvering in shallow water, less than 200 feet, Walker expertly outguessed swarms of escorts and circling planes and fired three torpedoes at *Nisshin Maru*. Two hit, and the great ship blew up and sank. It was the third largest Japanese merchant ship sunk to date.

The escorts counterattacked violently, dropping sixty-one close depth charges and aerial bombs. Walker took *Crevalle* to the bottom —only 174 feet—and lay still. A little later, there was a terrifying scraping sound along the outer hull. The Japanese, Walker believed, were trying to snare *Crevalle* with grappling hooks. This was more than anybody could stand. Walker got off the bottom and cleared the area safely.

After that, Walker was ordered to a special mission: proceed northward to Negros Island to evacuate refugees. He took aboard a total of forty-one, including thirty-five women and children. Four of the men were survivors of the Bataan Death March who had escaped into the Philippine jungles. On the way home with his passengers, Walker picked up a six-ship convoy with five escorts. He went to battle stations to attack, but before he could get off any torpedoes a destroyer attacked *Crevalle*, dropping eight depth charges right on top of the boat. It was the worst working over *Crevalle* had ever received and a near thing. The damage was heavy and the passengers were terrified. Afterward, Walker set course for Darwin.

When the Japanese fleet left Singapore to shift to the anchorage at Tawi Tawi, Christie, thanks to the codebreakers, could deploy his submarines to intercept and confirm its movements.

The first to make contact was Lowell Stone in *Lapon*, lying off the west coast of Borneo. At eight on the morning on May 13, Stone saw at least three aircraft carriers, five cruisers, and several destroyers, range 6 miles. He submerged, hoping for a shot, but got no closer than 5,000 yards and didn't shoot. That night he sent out a contact report. He then shifted to Indochina for a regular patrol.

Tom Hogan in Christie's flagship, *Bonefish*, patrolled in the Sulu Sea, where he had attacked several convoys, shooting off all his torpedoes but six. He had been bombed by a Japanese plane that damaged his periscope and radar. Christie ordered Hogan to look into Tawi Tawi to see if the fleet had arrived, and Hogan went south at full speed. At about 2 A.M. on May 14, Hogan picked up a convoy of three big tankers and three destroyers, apparently headed for Tawi Tawi. Hogan closed and fired five of his six torpedoes, range 1,300 yards. He got two hits—one in a tanker and one in the destroyer *Inazuma*, which blew up and sank. The other destroyers worked over *Bonefish*, but Hogan slipped away submerged.

The following morning at about eleven, while Hogan was submerged about 40 miles northwest of Tawi Tawi, he saw through his periscope the Japanese fleet reported by Stone in *Lapon*: a large carrier, two battleships, many heavy or light cruisers, and about ten destroyers. That night, Hogan withdrew into the Sulu Sea and sent off a contact report.

After sending his message, Hogan returned to Tawi Tawi during the night. The next morning, lying off the coast, he raised his periscope and saw a grand sight inside the anchorage: "six carriers, four or five battleships, eight heavy cruisers, light cruisers, and many destroyers." That night, Hogan moved south a little and sent off another contact report. The report was evidently DF-ed because two destroyers charged out to attack. Hogan, who had no torpedoes (the one left was defective), eluded and waited for Christie to send a relief submarine.

Brooks Harral in *Ray* patrolled off Davao Gulf. On May 14, he picked up a task force heading into the gulf: a big aircraft carrier, a heavy cruiser, and a light cruiser, escorted by many destroyers. Harral could get no closer than 9,000 yards. That night he withdrew to sea and got off a contact report. Two days later, May 16, he saw the same force standing out of Davao Gulf at high speed but could get no closer than 6,500 yards. He did not shoot. "It was a sad disappointment," he wrote, "to see a plum like this go by just out of reach." He remained on station. These ships also went to Tawi Tawi.

After Christie had relieved Ambruster on *Robalo*, he gave command of the boat to Manning Kimmel, a son of the admiral. The exec, Charles Fell, remained. Christie sent Kimmel to the South China Sea to interdict Japanese tankers resupplying the fleet at Tawi Tawi.

Kimmel conducted a wildly aggressive patrol. In four attacks, he fired twenty torpedoes. He was credited with sinking a tanker, but it was not confirmed in postwar records. During one attack, Kimmel was caught by a Japanese plane. On diving, the main induction flooded "due to personnel error" and *Robalo* plunged toward the bottom, out of control. Kimmel caught the boat at 350 feet. The bombs badly damaged *Robalo*'s periscopes, shattering and flooding number one and ruining the low-power adjustment on number two. "High power is usable but not clear," Kimmel noted. In addition, the bombs sprung the conning tower hatch and knocked out the SJ radar. In spite of all this, Kimmel remained on station.

When he finally returned to Fremantle, Tex McLean was upset. Later he said, "Anybody else would have come home long before. I worried that Kimmel was a little too anxious to put the name of Kimmel high in Navy annals." Christie and McLean thought maybe they should replace Kimmel, to save his neck, but since Kimmel was Admiral Kinkaid's nephew it might prove awkward.

Herb Andrews in *Gurnard*, still in the Celebes Sea, was ordered up near Davao Gulf. On May 18, about eight o'clock in the morning, Andrews intercepted a battleship escorted by destroyers. The enemy force was clocked at 23 knots. Andrews set up and fired six torpedoes, range 2,300 yards. Destroyers charged at *Gurnard* and Andrews went deep. He heard two solid hits. Later, he was credited with damage to the battleship for 32,700 tons. Andrews was only the fourth submarine skipper to have hit and damaged a battleship, after Donaho on *Flying Fish*, Gene McKinney on *Skate*, and John Scott on *Tunny*.

Victor McCrea in *Hoe* patrolled off Indochina and Luzon. On May 8, while off the northwest coast of Luzon, he made contact with a convoy en route from Formosa to Manila with troop reinforcements. The convoy was escorted by a light carrier. McCrea could not get position on the carrier, but he attacked a tanker and a freighter, causing damage. He got off a contact report (Dempsey in *Cod* was still near Manila) and trailed. Off Lingayen Gulf and Manila, McCrea found several more convoys to attack. He was credited with sinking one ship and damaging four, but postwar records failed to credit the sinking.

Reuben Whitaker in *Flasher* patrolled off Indochina. On April 29, he found a convoy and sank two ships, a 644-ton gunboat and a 1,000-ton freighter. After several more actions, Whitaker set course for Fremantle. On May 3, in the Sulu Sea, he sank a 6,709-ton freighter, *Teisen Maru*. Three days later, Whitaker expended the last of his torpedoes against another freighter for damage.

The Joint Strike on Surabaya

In early May, the U.S. carrier *Saratoga*, detached from Nimitz's force and assigned to Kinkaid, arrived in southwest Australia. After intelligence had confirmed the relocation of major Japanese fleet units to Tawi Tawi, Christie conceived a mission for *Saratoga*: a strike on the antisubmarine shore batteries at Lombok Strait and the Wanikroma Oil Refineries, the navy yard and the Bratte Engineering Works in Surabaya. The strike would be launched from Indian Ocean waters.

Christie believed that, with radio silence, *Saratoga* could carry out this mission with complete surprise and then withdraw to Fremantle. He drew up an operational order and passed it up to Kinkaid.

Although Kinkaid had authority to conduct such a strike on his

STRIKE on SURABAYA
MAY 17, 1944

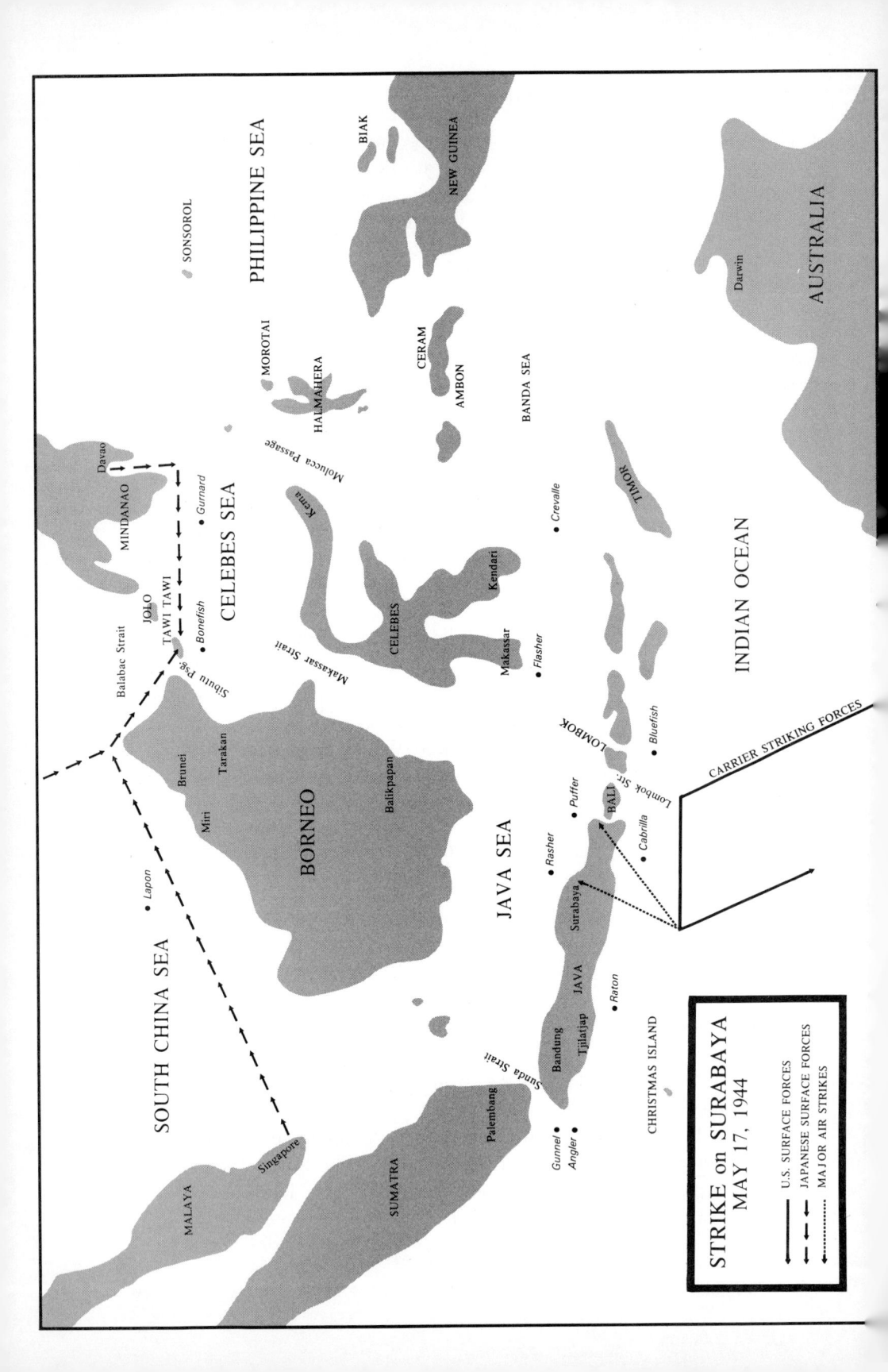

→ U.S. SURFACE FORCES
--→ JAPANESE SURFACE FORCES
······→ MAJOR AIR STRIKES

own, he passed the proposal along to Admiral King for approval. In Washington, the proposal was discussed with the Combined Chiefs of Staff. During these discussions, the British offered the services of the Eastern Fleet, basing in India. "The whole thing got out of hand," Christie said later. "So instead of a nice neat operation, it became almost a major effort."

The main units of the British Eastern Fleet made available for the strike were commanded by Admiral Sir James Somerville. They were: the World War I battleship *Queen Elizabeth* (flag); the battle cruiser *Renown*; the Free French battleship *Richelieu*, recently overhauled in the United States; the carrier *Illustrious*, also recently refurbished in the United States; the cruisers *Valiant, London,* and *Suffolk*; plus destroyers and tankers. This force, together with *Saratoga*, gathered at Exmouth Gulf for the proposed strike. Admiral Kinkaid flew over from Brisbane for last-minute strategy talks, stopping with Christie at "Bend of the Road." The two men then went up to Exmouth Gulf to inspect the combined force.

Christie ordered eight of his submarines to support the Surabaya strike—as lifeguards, to sink fleeing ships, and to guard the major entrances from the Java Sea to the Indian Ocean (Sunda and Lombok straits) in case Japanese submarines or men-of-war attempted to move into the Indian Ocean to attack the strike force. The eight submarines were *Rasher, Puffer, Gunnel, Angler, Bluefish, Cabrilla, Raton,* and Reuben Whitaker's *Flasher*, returning from Indochina. (Whitaker put into Darwin May 13, picked up twelve torpedoes, and reversed course for the Java Sea.)

The raid took place, as scheduled, on May 17. The aircraft from *Saratoga* and *Illustrious*, Christie reported in his diary, achieved complete surprise, met no opposition, and demolished the refineries and the engineering works "for the duration." However, they missed five Japanese submarines in the Surabaya dockyards. Christie believed that if a second strike had been mounted those too could have been destroyed, but Admiral Somerville, the senior officer, declined.

None of the eight submarines diverted for this sideshow accomplished anything—no rescues, no ships sunk fleeing the raid. Many valuable patrol days were lost. The submarines probably would have accomplished far more had they been stationed off Tawi Tawi while the Japanese fleet was gathering.

* * *

Junior McCain in *Gunnel* and Robert Olsen in *Angler* stood guard in Sunda Strait. During *Angler*'s refit, Olsen had asked that special attention be given his fresh-water tanks; the water had tasted strange and many people (including those rescued from Panay) had become sick on his last patrol. "When I got back from the hotel," Olsen said later, "I found out they hadn't had time to do anything about the water tanks. I went up to see my division commander to tell him they were dangerous—too much chlorine had been added to the water originally in Pearl Harbor and I thought some of it might have settled in the concrete lining of the tanks. The division commander said it looked O.K. and that if I didn't want to take the boat on patrol he'd find somebody else."

While lying in Sunda Strait, Olsen found a freighter and attacked, sinking it. Afterward, escorts gave *Angler* a bad pounding. On the following day, everybody on *Angler* once again became nauseous. "I figured the depth charges shook up the chlorine in the concrete," Olsen said later. He reported the calamity to Christie, who ordered *Angler* to return to Fremantle at once.

On the way home, the situation worsened. On May 22, Olsen noted in his log, "Physical condition of officers and crew is so bad that it is difficult to maintain watch, either surface or submerged. Put crew on fruit juice alone, no water. Held thorough field day in case boat is contaminated. Exercised special supervision in cooking, dishwashing." On May 23 he wrote, "Decided to run submerged as we did not have enough able-bodied people to maintain proper surface watch."

Christie ordered *Flasher,* returning to Fremantle, to intercept *Angler* and lend assistance. In addition he sent U.S.S. *Childs,* an ancient destroyer converted to patrol plane tender. Frank Walker in *Crevalle,* who had just unloaded his forty-one refugees from Negros at Darwin and embarked a doctor for passage from Darwin to Fremantle, also went to intercept *Angler.* On May 24, *Flasher, Crevalle, Childs,* and *Angler* met at sea. The doctor on *Crevalle* went on board *Angler* to help the busy (and ill) pharmacist's mate, L. M. Neidlinger, with the sick officers and crew. *Flasher, Crevalle,* and *Childs* gave *Angler* fresh water. *Angler* continued to Fremantle, arriving after a patrol of twenty-seven days.

Debarking at Fremantle to make his report to Christie, Olsen noted that the gangway put over was old and rickety. He told the officer of the deck to get a new one, "before someone falls and breaks their neck." About an hour later Olsen returned to the boat, and as he boarded the gangway gave way. Olsen fell, fracturing his skull, and—the final irony—was sent to a hospital in Sydney for three months, losing command of *Angler*.

While he was gone, Christie's men conducted an investigation into the illness. During the taking of testimony, it was determined that one of the electricians had brought a can of carbon tetrachloride on board as a cleaning agent—strictly prohibited. The illness was laid to that. "But that was a lot of bunk," Olsen said later. "A cover-up That can was *never* opened. The cause was the same cause as the illness on the previous patrol: bad water. They blamed it on the carbon tet to cover up the fact they hadn't cleaned the fresh-water tanks."

For Junior McCain too this patrol was a frustrating one. *Gunnel* left Sunda Strait after the raid and went up to patrol off Indochina. On June 8, McCain picked up a convoy. It was guarded by a small escort carrier, perhaps the same McCrea in *Hoe* had seen the previous month near Manila. McCain commenced tracking on the surface from 15 miles. In the middle of the chase, the officer of the deck "inadvertently dived on an aircraft contact at 24 miles." McCain lost contact and was not able to regain it. It was the third time in as many patrols that McCain had seen an aircraft carrier and failed to damage it. When he returned to Fremantle, he was sent to new construction, having achieved little on *Gunnel* in five patrols.

At the time of the Surabaya strike, James Davis in *Raton* lifeguarded at a station south of Java. Afterward, he went to patrol off Indochina near *Gunnel* and Lowell Stone's *Lapon*, which had gone there after making the initial contact with the Japanese fleet, May 13. On the way up, Davis sank an 800-ton frigate.

Stone in *Lapon* found good hunting off Indochina. On May 23–24 he got into a convoy, sinking two large freighters confirmed in postwar records at about 6,500 and 4,600 tons. Three days later, Stone found what he believed to be an I-class Japanese submarine. (In fact, it was James Davis in *Raton*.) He went to battle stations, turning away to fire all four stern tubes. At 5:13, Stone fired two torpedoes at *Raton*, range 1,400 yards. He was on the point of firing two more when he suddenly had doubts and checked firing. Was his target a U.S. submarine? Stone went to 200 feet and heard two explosions that sounded like torpedoes reaching the end of their run.

On *Raton*, meanwhile, Davis felt two violent explosions which shook the ship "considerably." He was puzzled, believing at first that he might have run aground, and changed course radically, moving ahead full speed and clearing the area.

After this episode, Stone in *Lapon* returned to Fremantle. Davis remained in Indochina waters for another two weeks, sinking a second small frigate before returning to Fremantle. Later, when the two skippers compared notes—and patrol reports—they discovered Stone had fired at Davis. It was the only confirmed instance of one U.S. submarine firing at another during the war.

On the way to lifeguard station north of Surabaya, Willard Laughon in *Rasher* made contact with a five-ship convoy near Ambon on the afternoon of May 11. For the next eighteen hours, Laughon attacked repeatedly, firing off all twenty-four of his torpedoes. Many torpeodes ran under targets without exploding or otherwise malfunctioned. Although many of the ships were damaged, Laughon received credit for sinking only one.

After that—all torpedoes expended—Laughon took station north of Surabaya for the strike. When it was done, he returned to Darwin, took on eighteen more torpedoes, and went north near Halmahera for further action.

Patrols to Tawi Tawi and Davao

While standing watch off Surabaya during the air strike, Gordon Selby in *Puffer* had sunk a 3,000-ton freighter that happened along. Following this, he was ordered up Makassar Strait to Tawi Tawi with Henderson's *Bluefish*.

In the north end of Makassar Strait on May 22, approaching Tawi Tawi, Selby picked up a portion of the Japanese main body conducting maneuvers to train the many green pilots in the air wings. Selby found the force at 9:12 A.M. while submerged, range 7,000 yards. It consisted of two aircraft carriers and three destroyers, all "milling around." (*Bluefish* was nearby but did not see the carriers.) While Selby was concentrating on one carrier, the other passed five hundred yards astern! "The general effect," Selby wrote later, "was similar to the dazzling speed with which the participants in a Walt Disney cartoon sizzle past and disappear in a cloud of vapor."

Having missed several opportunities, Selby "settled down" and prepared to make another approach at 10:24. He closed to 1,400 yards and fired six torpedoes. Only one hit, but Selby was later credited with damage to a 26,900-ton aircraft carrier. The destroyer escorts counterattacked *Puffer*, dropping many depth charges, but Selby evaded and slipped away. Postwar Japanese records did not confirm damage to a carrier that day; however, the destroyer *Yukikaze* was damaged by a submarine at that time and place. Later Selby concluded that he had "used the wrong ranges."

Puffer and *Bluefish* arrived at Tawi Tawi, joining Tom Hogan in *Bonefish*. Both Selby and Henderson observed the many men-of-war in the anchorage. With their arrival, Hogan left Tawi Tawi to proceed to Fremantle. On May 25, his radioman picked up a puzzling plain-language message, addressed to all naval vessels: WHAT HAS GOD WROUGHT? Hogan examined the message for codes. He then decided it could have meant one of the following (as he noted in his log): (1) a national calamity had occurred; (2) Hitler was dead; (3) prohibition was back in effect. "Decided no action required this vessel," Hogan wrote. An hour later, another message clarified the first; it had been sent in commemoration of the centennial of the telegraph. "Entire crew vastly relieved," Hogan wrote.

Other boats converging on or guarding at Tawi Tawi, or off Davao or in the Celebes Sea, found targets. William Thompson in *Cabrilla* sank the ex-seaplane tender *Sanyo Maru*. On June 5, Gordon Selby in *Puffer* sank two tankers in the north end of Sibutu Passage: *Ashizuki*, 2,100 tons, and *Takasaki*, 2,500 tons. Eric Barr in *Bluegill* sank an 8,800-ton freighter off Davao and another off Halmahera. Edward Farwell Dissette in *Cero* sank one off Halmahera and damaged two others. And Willard Laughon in *Rasher*, on the second half of a double-barreled patrol, sank a 2,600-ton converted gunboat near Halmahera.

Brooks Harral in *Ray* and Herb Andrews in *Gurnard* patrolled off Davao. On the afternoon of May 21, Harral in *Ray* sighted a nine-ship convoy with surface and air escorts. In a furiously aggressive series of attacks, Harral believed he sank six of the nine. Something must have gone drastically wrong with his torpedoes; postwar records confirmed only one sinking, a freighter of 6,000 tons. Undoubtedly many other ships were damaged. Harral was driven off by land-based aircraft.

Shortly after this, Herb Andrews in *Gurnard* picked up a tanker convoy and attacked, sinking one of the fleet tankers, *Tatekawa Maru*, 10,000 tons.

Thompson in *Cabrilla*, taking station south of Tawi Tawi in the same area Selby had found the carriers in training, found another training operation in progress. This force consisted of three battleships and three carriers. Thompson closed, setting up on a battleship. He made one long (forty-five-second) observation, which he later called an "error," dipped the periscope, then went back for a final look. A Japanese plane dived at *Cabrilla*, dropping a "close and violent" depth charge which shook the ship badly. A second close string drove *Cabrilla* off, and the battleships and carriers veered out of range. Thompson evaded but later that night he surfaced, chased, and got off a contact report. The Japanese ships—out for a day's training—slipped back into Tawi Tawi.

The Japanese Reinforcement of Biak

Meanwhile, Admiral Jisaburo Ozawa, who had been named to command the Japanese naval forces in battle, waited in Tawi Tawi to execute Plan A-Go, hoping for a decisive battle with the Pacific Fleet off the Palaus. The plan was thrown into jeopardy when MacArthur's forces landed on Biak on May 27. An airfield on Biak in Allied hands would place U.S. land-based bombers within 500 miles of the Palaus and the seas where Ozawa hoped to meet the Nimitz forces. Ozawa was determined to reinforce Biak and throw out the invaders.

The Japanese reaction to Biak, known as Plan Kon, was spliced into the middle of Plan A-Go. It called for men-of-war to deliver about 2,500 troops to Biak. The first effort was a task force consisting of the battleship *Fuso*, four cruisers, and eight destroyers. They would embark troops at Zamboanga in western Mindanao and deliver them to Biak, going by way of Davao.

On the night of May 30, some ships of this force left Tawi Tawi for assigned missions. William Thompson in *Cabrilla* and Charles Henderson in *Bluefish* spotted them leaving the anchorage.

Henderson in *Bluefish* saw a battleship (*Fuso*), four heavy cruisers, and three of the eight destroyers. He went to battle stations but could get no closer than 6,000 yards. "Everybody was ready," he wrote

INVASION of BIAK
MAY 27–JUNE 10, 1944

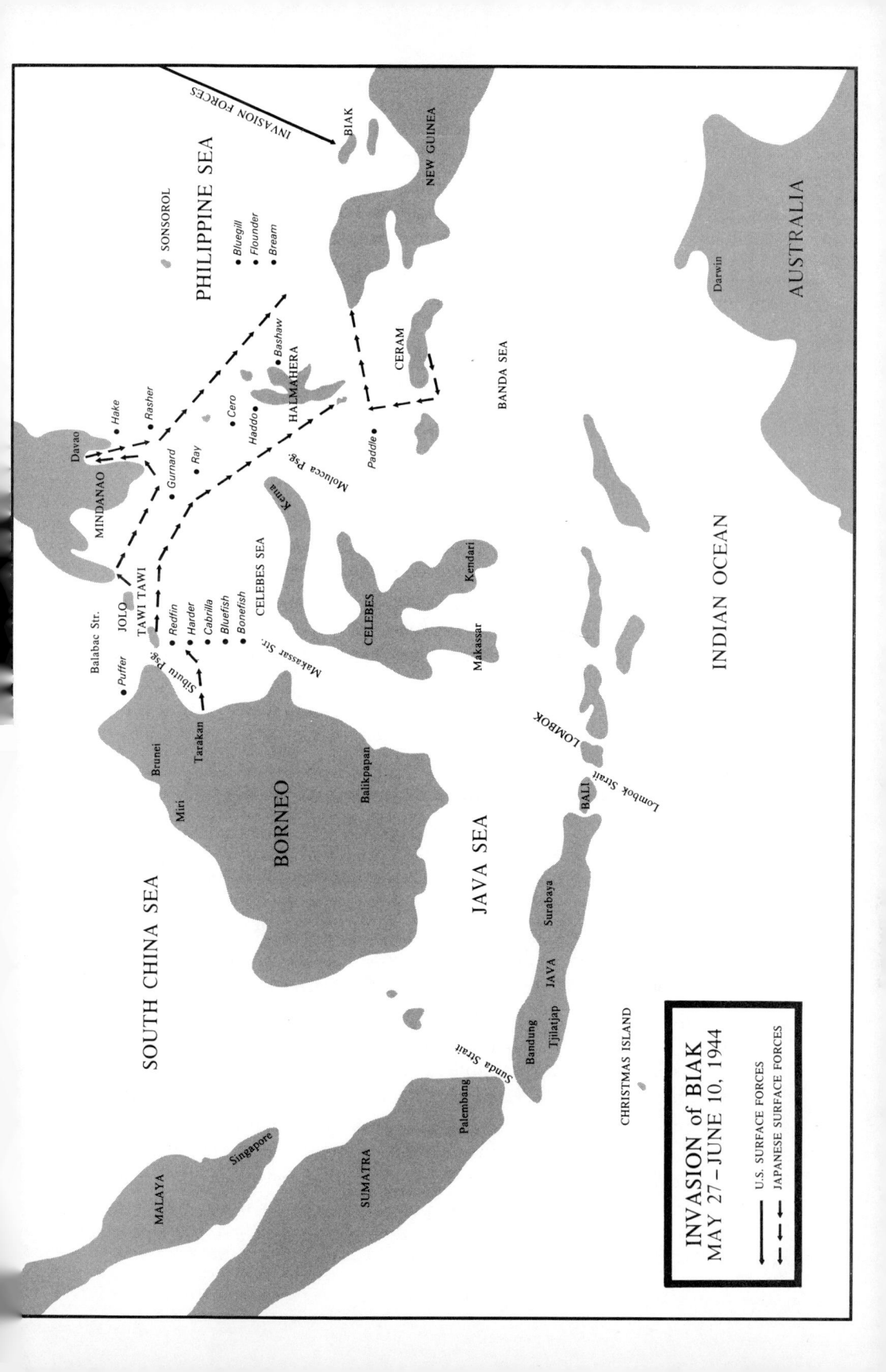

U.S. SURFACE FORCES
JAPANESE SURFACE FORCES

later, "but could only watch helplessly as they went by out of range." That night, Henderson got off a contact report.

The Kon force for the relief of Biak continued toward Mindanao to pick up troops. Herb Andrews in *Gurnard* and Brooks Harral in *Ray* moved to intercept. They made contact at 8:57 on the morning of May 31, south of Mindanao. Andrews thought it was three battleships and five other vessels. They were on an easterly course (toward Davao Gulf), making 18 knots. Andrews tried to maneuver into firing position but could get no closer than 5 miles. He wrote, "To have in sight the targets all submariners dream of yet be unable to close in to firing range remains a bitter disappointment." After this encounter, Andrews got off a contact report and headed for Fremantle. Altogether, Andrews had sunk four ships for 29,795 tons, making this —in terms of confirmed tonnage—the best patrol of the war to date.

Harral in *Ray* believed the force to be one battleship, one heavy and one light cruiser, and three destroyers. The cruisers passed him at 8,000 yards, but Harral was not able to close. He picked up the battleship at 16 miles and got within 7 miles—but no closer. Harral tracked the force toward Davao Gulf on June 1, sending off a contact report. Then he headed for Fremantle, pausing near Talaud Island, where Laughon in *Rasher* was patrolling.

The Kon force stopped at Davao as planned, then got under way for Biak in two separate units. On the morning of June 3, Willard Laughon in *Rasher* picked up part of the force, what he believed to be two heavy cruisers, a light cruiser, and several destroyers. He could not gain firing position, but he got off a contact report which the Japanese heard. The Japanese, distressed that they had been spotted so soon and so far from their destination, called off Kon and drew up another plan. *Fuso* and two cruisers went back to Davao. Two cruisers proceeded to disembark troops on New Guinea. Two other cruisers went directly from Davao to Batjan with troops.

Laughon in *Rasher* moved up to Davao Gulf, replacing *Gurnard* and *Ray*. On June 4 he spotted the retiring Japanese cruisers returning to Davao but was unable to attack. A little later, a destroyer picked up *Rasher* and closed to 100 yards. Laughon went deep, while the destroyer—soon joined by another—dropped depth charges. After dark, Laughon surfaced and got off a contact report on the cruisers.

After that, Laughon withdrew to seaward to patrol the traffic lanes. On June 7 he found two merging convoys but was unable to gain attack position. The following day he found another convoy and fired six of his eighteen torpedoes at the 4,000-ton tanker *Shioya*. It caught fire and sank.

Laughon was replaced at Davao by John Broach in *Hake* and by young Chester Nimitz in *Haddo*, who had been patrolling off Halmahera. On the night of June 8, Broach picked up a task force—part of the retiring Kon force—of two cruisers and several destroyers. He attacked one of the destroyers, *Kazegumo*, and sank it. Later, he saw another cruiser and several destroyers inside Davao Gulf. He penetrated the gulf but could get no closer than 6,000 yards to the ships.

Nimitz had no major contacts. He was shifted from the Davao area to Tawi Tawi.

Sam Dealey in *Harder*, going on his fifth patrol, was ordered to Tawi Tawi. Christie's operations officer, Murray Tichenor, who had never made a war patrol, went along for the ride. In addition to a regular patrol, Dealey was asked to try to pick up the guerrillas on northeast Borneo that both Chester Nimitz in *Haddo* and Cy Austin in *Redfin* had missed. Dealey agreed to the special mission—reluctantly.

On the night of June 6, while going into Sibutu Passage just south of Tawi Tawi on his way to pick up the guerrillas, Dealey ran into a convoy of three empty tankers and two destroyers headed for Tarakan for a refill. One of the destroyers picked up *Harder* and charged. Dealey let it get within 1,100 yards, then fired three torpedoes. *Minatsuki* blew up and sank immediately.

Dealey chased the convoy, making an end around. He submerged to radar depth and prepared to attack. A second destroyer peeled off and charged at *Harder*. Dealey let it get within 1,200 yards before firing six bow tubes. All missed. Dealey went to 300 feet to evade. One of his diving plane operators, a new man misread his instruments and took *Harder* to 400 feet by mistake. As a result, Dealey lost another opportunity to attack the convoy.

Dealey turned back for Sibutu Passage, submerging for the transit shortly after 8 A.M. on June 7. At 11:43, he sighted another destroyer. Dealey let it get within the point-blank range of 650 yards and then fired three torpedoes at five-second intervals. All three torpedoes hit *Hayanami*.

Dealey went ahead full with hard right rudder to get out of the path of the destroyer. He later wrote, "At a range of 300 yards we were racked by a terrific explosion believed to have been the destroyer's magazine. Less than one minute after the first hit and nine minutes after it was sighted, the destroyer sank tail first."

A sister ship of the *Hayanami* came over and dropped seventeen depth charges in the next two hours. Shortly after 3 p.m., Dealey returned to periscope depth and found two more destroyers. They went away, but he found another, about 5:30, and then a line of eight. Feeling he had worn out his welcome, Dealey withdrew to pick up the guerrillas.

On the night of June 8, Dealey nosed *Harder* near the appointed rendezvous and sent two small boats ashore into the gloom. The boats picked up the guerrilla force and returned to *Harder*. Dealey cleared the area and went through Sibutu Passage to see what he could turn up at Tawi Tawi.

The following night he found two more destroyers. He submerged for an approach, firing four torpedoes at overlapping targets. Two of the four hit *Tanikaze*, which blew up and sank. Dealey thought one of his other torpedoes hit the other destroyer, but he must have been mistaken. There is no record of a second Japanese destroyer being lost on June 9 off Tawi Tawi.

During this time, the Japanese mounted a second Kon effort to reinforce their besieged troops on Biak. Two cruisers and six destroyers embarked troops from Sorong, on the northwestern tip of New Guinea, with the intent of landing them on Biak. Allied aircraft discovered this force, sank the destroyer *Harusame*, and damaged three others, one seriously. The air attack was followed up by cruisers and destroyers of Kinkaid's Seventh Fleet supporting the Biak landings. Kinkaid's surface forces—in a minor engagement known as the Battle of Biak—drove the remaining Japanese forces back into ports.

Following this the Japanese made a third Kon attempt, this time with a major force consisting of the huge battleships *Yamato* and *Musashi*, five cruisers, seven destroyers, and other miscellaneous craft. The plan was to send this force to Batjan, south of Halmahera, embark troops, and then fight into Biak. *Yamato* and *Musashi* got underway at Tawi Tawi on the evening of June 10.

Sam Dealey in *Harder* was patrolling off Tawi Tawi that evening. At about 5 p.m., he sighted *Yamato* and *Musashi* coming out of the anchorage. While Dealey maneuvered *Harder* for an approach, a Japanese pilot spotted his periscope and dropped a smoke bomb and a destroyer peeled off and headed for *Harder*. Dealey let him close to 1,200 yards, fired three torpedoes down the throat, and then went deep.

Going down, Dealey was positive that at least two of the torpedoes hit; he heard explosions far louder than depth charges. Passing 80 feet, he later wrote that "all hell broke loose. It was not from his depth charges—for if they had been dropped, this report would not have been completed—but a deafening series of progressive rumblings that seemed to almost blend with each other. Either his boilers or his magazine, or both, had exploded and it's a lucky thing that ship explosions are vented upward and not down."

Dealey took *Harder* to 400 feet to evade. The escorts—and land-based aircraft—delivered a violent counterattack that kept him down until after dark. Dealey wrote in his log, "It is considered amazing that [*Harder*] could have gone through such a terriffic pounding and jolting around with such minor damage. Our fervent thanks go out to the workmen and designers at the Electric Boat Company for building such a fine ship." In the postwar records, there was no evidence that a Japanese destroyer was lost this day off Tawi Tawi. The noise Dealey heard might well have been close aerial bombs or depth charges.

After dark, Dealey surfaced and got off a contact report on the departure of *Yamato* and *Musashi*, which continued on to Batjan without further interference from U.S. submarines.

Dealey remained off Tawi Tawi for another day, watching the anchorage and reporting the ships he saw. On the evening of June 12, Christie ordered him to patrol northward along the Sulu Archipelago. Going north, Dealey rendezvoused with Chester Nimitz in *Haddo*, who was having another frustrating patrol. So far, Nimitz had found nothing to shoot at except a couple of mangy sampans, sunk by deck gun. Dealey continued on to Zamboanga, then to Davao, then back south through Molucca Passage to Darwin.

When Dealey reached Darwin, Christie was ecstatic. He credited him with sinking five destroyers, and the endorsements called the patrol "epoch-making" and "magnificent." Since Dealey had sunk a destroyer on his previous patrol off Woleai, his total was thought to be six. For this reason, he was nicknamed "The Destroyer Killer."

John Crowley finally got *Flier*—the boat that had gone aground at Midway in January—ready for his first patrol. With his exec, Jim

Liddell, the onetime All-American from Northwestern, he patrolled from Pearl Harbor to Fremantle by way of Lingayen Gulf. They were anxious to make up for the five months they had lost because of the grounding. Crowley offered a prize to the lookout who spotted the most ships—$15 and a bottle of Old Taylor bourbon.

On June 4, while west of the Bonins, Crowley picked up a convoy en route from the Marianas to Japan. After dark, he closed to attack, misjudged the enemy course, and dived in the wrong place. He surfaced and chased, making an end around, and then dived for a dawn attack. Crowley got between the columns in the convoys and fired all bow tubes, three each at two ships. He was about to fire stern tubes at the other column when he saw one of the freighters boring in to ram. He went deep and the convoy got away. Postwar records credited him with a fine sinking, *Hakusam Maru*, a 10,400-ton transport.

Crowley took up station on the west coast of Luzon near Subic Bay about June 12. There was another submarine in the vicinity, *Jack*, now commanded by a new skipper, Arthur Elmer Krapf. Both Crowley and Krapf had orders to report any movement of Japanese fleet units they detected and then attack. They were also free to attack convoys.

On June 13 Crowley spotted a large convoy, eleven ships and six escorts. The sea was flat calm, the sun bright. Yet Crowley and Liddell slipped inside the escorts and attacked, firing stern tubes at a medium-sized tanker. When Crowley got ready to fire his bow tubes, he found he was too close. Escorts charged in and blasted *Flier* with over a hundred "moderately well placed depth charges." After dark, Crowley attempted an end around, but the convoy got into Subic Bay before he could attack again.

Next, Crowley was ordered to drop down to Tawi Tawi. Going through Mindoro Strait he picked up another convoy "quite by accident." He let the convoy pass and then surfaced after dark, caught up, and fired all six bow tubes at two ships, obtaining two hits in each. After reloading, Crowley fired his remaining four bow torpedoes at a freighter, obtaining three hits. With only four stern torpedoes remaining, Crowley closed in on a cripple, but before he could fire, he reported later, the ship "obligingly sank."

When Crowley reported this encounter to Fremantle, Christie ordered him to head for the barn. On his arrival, Crowley was credited with sinking four ships for 20,000 tons and damaging two for 13,000 tons, but postwar records credited only the transport sunk west of the Bonins on June 4.

All these activities by Christie's submarines cost Admiral Ozawa and his A-Go plan for annihilating the U.S. Pacific Fleet dearly. Almost every movement of his fleet units—from Singapore to Tawi Tawi, maneuvers outside Tawi Tawi, plan Kon for Biak—had been spotted and reported by submarines. Submarine activity off Tawi Tawi forced the Japanese to curtail valuable training for new air wings. Two major men-of-war, a carrier and a battleship, had been attacked by torpedoes, the carrier by Selby, the battleship by Andrews. Seven men-of-war had been sunk: the light cruiser *Yubari* (Barr), five fleet destroyers (three by Dealey, one by Hogan, one by Broach), and an old destroyer (Dempsey). In addition, twenty-four important merchant ships had been sent to the bottom: six tankers (two by Selby and one each by Andrews, Laughon, Walker, and Cy Austin in *Redfin*), four troopships (three by Andrews, one by Dykers), and fourteen freighters. Dozens of other merchant ships had been damaged; convoys had been thrown into confusion and, in some cases, forced to return to port.

In addition, Admiral Ozawa's submarine line, stretching from Truk to New Guinea, was devastated, thanks to marvelous information furnished by the codebreakers. Having been given the precise location of the line, U.S. destroyer hunter-killer groups (equipped with forward-throwing depth charges) sank nine out of about a dozen Japanese submarines. In the most remarkable antisubmarine operation of the war, one destroyer, *England*, was directly responsible for sinking six of the nine. This feat led Admiral King to say, "There'll always be an *England* in the United States Navy." *

* The pledge was not completely kept. *England* was decommissioned in 1945 and sold in 1946. There was no *England* in the navy until 1960, when the guided missile frigate *DLG-22* was christened *England*.

29

Pearl Harbor, May and June 1944

Patrols to the Marianas

In Pearl Harbor Admiral Nimitz gave the final green light for Operation Forager, the invasion of the Marianas, with the sequence of landings to be Saipan, then Guam, then Tinian.

Nimitz had no illusions about the Marianas. He knew it would be a tough fight all the way, perhaps as tough as Tarawa. But victory would be worth the price. The Marianas were decisive to the control of the western Pacific. Saipan and Guam would provide a staging base for another leap in any direction: the Palaus, the Philippines, Formosa, Okinawa, or the Bonins. In addition, the air force wanted the Marianas as a base for a new bomber, the B-29 Superfortress, which could reach the Japanese mainland. Finally, the Marianas would provide Lockwood with an advance submarine base—3,300 miles beyond Pearl Harbor and only 1,500 miles from Luzon Strait.

Before the invasion, Nimitz merged the forces under his command with those of Admiral Bull Halsey, who had been basing in Noumea. In effect, he combined the Fifth Fleet under Raymond Spruance with Halsey's Third Fleet. Thereafter, Spruance and Halsey alternated in command. The main striking force—known as the Fast Carrier Force—was commanded by Marc Andrew Mitscher. When Halsey had overall command, the Fast Carrier Force was called Task Force 38; when Spruance had overall command, Task Force 58.

PATROLS TO THE MARIANAS

Nimitz named Spruance to lead the invasion of the Marianas. He commanded a huge armada: 535 ships and auxiliaries that would land 128,000 troops, two thirds marines and one third army. The Fast Carrier Force—Task Force 58—now numbered fifteen heavy and light carriers. It would soften up the islands and stand by for battle, should Admiral Ozawa elect to sortie from Tawi Tawi and oppose the landings.

While this armada was assembling for the voyage west, Lockwood sent a last wave of submarines into the Marianas to interdict Japanese attempts to reinforce the islands.

John Coye in *Silversides*, coming up from Fremantle, entered the Marianas shortly after Malcolm Garrison in *Sandlance* departed. Coye performed like a one-boat wolf pack. On May 10 he intercepted a convoy and sank three ships: the freighter *Okinawa Maru*, 2,254 tons; the transport *Mikage Maru No. 18*, 4,310 tons; and the converted gunboat *Choan Maru II*, 2,631 tons. On May 20, while attacking a freighter off Guam, Coye missed the freighter but hit one of the escorts, the converted gunboat *Shosei Maru*, 998 tons. On May 29 he found another convoy bringing aviation gasoline into Saipan and sank two ships from it: *Shoken Maru*, 1,949 tons, and *Horaizan Maru*, 1,999 tons. With only two torpedoes remaining, Coye looked for other targets, along with John Scott in *Tunny*.

In addition, Lockwood sent a three-boat wolf pack to the Marianas. All three boats were new, all commanded by new skippers who were classmates from 1934: *Pilotfish*, commanded by Robert Hamilton ("Boney") Close, who had been Spike Hottel's exec on *Grouper*; *Pintado*, commanded by Chick Clarey, who began the war as exec of *Dolphin* and then made two patrols on Bole's *Amberjack* and a PCO run; and *Shark II*, commanded by Edward Noe Blakely, who had made seven patrols on *Tuna* under Johnny DeTar and Ike Holtz. The pack was commanded by Leon Blair, Commander, Submarine Division 44, making his first war patrol. Blair rode with Clarey in *Pintado*. The pack was dubbed "Blair's Blasters."

When the pack reached the Marianas on May 31, John Coye in *Silversides* was trailing—and giving contact reports on—an outbound convoy. Blair's Blasters were ordered to close Coye's convoy and take over.

When the pack made contact, they found three freighters and two escorts. Blakely in *Shark* and Coye in *Silversides* wound up on one side of the convoy. Blakely held back so that Coye could go in and fire his last two torpedoes. Both missed. By allowing Coye to go in, Blakely deprived himself of a chance to attack. On the other side of the convoy, Clarey in *Pintado* tried to get in but was chased off by gunfire from one of the escorts. He trailed and then mounted a second attempt near daybreak, firing six torpedoes. All six hit *Toho Maru*, 4,700 tons. The ship, Clarey wrote, "disintegrated before my eyes and sank immediately."

Meanwhile, Coye, having sunk six ships, set off for Pearl Harbor and found a second convoy—inbound—of five ships and several escorts. Boney Close in *Pilotfish* gave up trying to attack Convoy Number One in favor of Convoy Number Two. In the late afternoon of June 1, Close reported he had the convoy in sight. Blair, knowing an outbound convoy to be less valuable than an inbound one with reinforcements, ordered all boats to break off from the first and concentrate on the second. Boney Close trailed but was not able to get in an attack. Nor were the other boats. Convoy Number Two, which was carrying half of the Japanese 43rd Division, reached Saipan without damage.

In the meantime Close found yet another convoy, Number Three. It was outbound. On the evening of June 2, Blakely in *Shark* also made contact with this convoy. He set up and fired four torpedoes at a freighter, and all four hit. Down went *Chiyo Maru*, 4,700 tons. Clarey in *Pintado* tried to get in from the other side but was driven down by an escort and received a stiff depth-charging. Close was also unable to attack.

During the early hours of June 3, while chasing Convoy Number Three for another attack, Blakely found a fourth convoy, also inbound. It consisted of about seven big freighters and four or five escorts. Again, knowing that an inbound convoy was a more significant target than an outbound one, Blair ordered his three boats to close Convoy Number Four.

It took the boats twenty-four hours to get into shooting position. Late on the afternoon of June 4, *Shark* made the first attack. Blakely took the boat submerged into the middle of the convoy, watched an escort pass about 180 yards down his side, then set up on a freighter at 1,500 yards. "In the few brief looks taken on this target," Blakely reported, "it was noted that the topside, forecastle in particular, was heaped high with military packs and what appeared to be landing force equipment, the topside was jammed with personnel, apparently troops." As he learned later, Convoy Number Four was carrying the other half of the 43rd Division.

Blakely fired four torpedoes. All hit. During the attack, he lost depth control and went deep. An escort charged over, dropping four depth charges very close. *Shark* remained deep while the escorts unleashed another forty-nine charges in the next two hours, none close. After dark, Blakely surfaced to chase. Neither Clarey in *Pintado* nor Close in *Pilotfish* was able to get in an attack. After dark, they too surfaced to chase.

Next day, it was Blakely who again got in the lucky position. Late in the afternoon of June 5, he made a submerged attack, firing six torpedoes at two freighters. Three torpedoes hit each target. Blakely paused a moment to swing the periscope on an escort, then back to the first freighter. "There was nothing left except his masts in a swirl of water sticking out," Blakely wrote. "It was unbelievable to me that a ship could sink so fast." Blakely had sunk two ships in this attack: *Tamahime Maru*, 3,000 tons, and *Takaika Maru*, 7,000 tons. He then went deep and received another drubbing, one which damaged his port shaft.

That night, all three submarines again surfaced to chase. Shortly after midnight, Clarey got into position and fired four torpedoes at overlapping targets. All four slammed into *Kashimasan Maru*, 2,800 tons, which was loaded with gasoline and burned far into the night before sinking. The escorts drove Clarey down before he could confirm that she sank or mount a second attack. He came up shortly and began an end around to get ahead of the convoy for a daylight periscope attack.

The opportunity came just before noon. Clarey got inside the escorts and fired six torpedoes at two overlapping targets. He heard six hits and then looked through the periscope. He wrote:

What was left of the near ship was burning furiously; she had broken in two and her bow and stern both projected up in the air as she sank. The second target was partially obscured by fire from the first ship. I could see that her stern was all under water and she had listed over to port about 40 degrees. She was enveloped in the most tremendous fire I have ever seen.

Five escorts closed on Clarey and drove him under, dropping fifty depth charges. Postwar assessment gave him only one of the ships, *Harve Maru*, 5,600 tons.

After this attack, Blair ordered the boats to break off and regroup. When the score was tallied up in the postwar Japanese records, it was found that, in the four convoys, Clarey and Blakely had sunk a total of seven ships for about 35,000 tons: one each out of outbound convoys One and Three and Blakely three and Clarey two out of the important inbound Convoy Four. In all this action, Boney Close in *Pilotfish* had not shot a single torpedo. His patrol was declared "nonsuccessful."

The virtual destruction of the inbound Convoy Four—five out of seven ships sunk—made the invasion of Saipan and Guam an easier task for the U.S. Navy. Most of the Japanese troops were rescued, but their equipment had been lost and the troops did not arrive in time to be integrated into the defense plan.

With the invasion forces bearing down on the Marianas, Lockwood ordered Blair's Blasters out of the area. Blakely in *Shark* went back to base for battle-damage repairs; John Scott in *Tunny*, still in the area, joined Clarey and Close; and Blair took the pack west toward Luzon Strait to watch for major Japanese fleet units.

After Blair's Blasters cleared out of the Marianas, Lockwood sent four boats there for lifeguard duty during the reconnaissance and air strikes preceding the invasion. These were: *Growler*, commanded by a new skipper, Thomas Benjamin Oakley, Jr., who had served on Daspit's *Tinosa* and commanded *Tarpon* for one patrol; a new boat, *Pipefish*, commanded by William Deragon, who had made seven patrols as exec of *Seawolf*; Sam Loomis's *Stingray*; and *Finback*, commanded by a new skipper, James Langford Jordan, who had made eight war patrols on *Greenling*.

Planes of Task Force 58 struck the Marianas on June 11 and every day thereafter, destroying dozens upon dozens of aircraft. During the strikes on Guam and Saipan, only Sam Loomis in *Stingray*, maneuvering boldly and close to shore, made any rescues; he picked up five airmen. In one case he employed a novel technique: he approached Ensign Donald Carol Brandt's raft submerged, ran up the periscope, and had Brandt tie his life raft to the periscope with a line. Loomis then moved out to sea beyond range of Japanese shore-based guns, surfaced, and took Brandt below.

After the air strikes, Lockwood ordered the four boats away from the Marianas. Oakley in *Growler* moved west to Surigao Strait to keep watch for enemy fleet units; *Pipefish*, *Finback*, and *Stingray*

PATROLS TO THE MARIANAS 647

took positions on a scouting line west of the Marianas, joined by two other boats, Jim Blanchard's *Albacore*, returning from overhaul, and Anton Gallaher in *Bang*. *Finback*, *Albacore*, *Bang*, and *Stingray* were positioned in a "square" 60 miles on a side, while *Pipefish* roved to the south.

Other Pearl Harbor submarines took stations at various islands. *Gato*, commanded by a new skipper, Dixie Farrell, lifeguarded off Truk, along with *Snapper*, commanded by William Warren Walker. Michael Peter Russillo, returning the last H.O.R. boat to get new engines, *Muskallunge*, patrolled near Ulithi. *Seawolf*, back from long overhaul with a new skipper, Ozzie Lynch, went to Peleliu, an island in the Palaus, to make photos of the beaches. James Hardin in *Tuna* lifeguarded at Woleai.

Flying Fish, commanded by Robert Risser, went to the Palaus, where John Corbus in *Bowfin*, coming up from Fremantle, and William Stevenson in *Aspro*, going to Fremantle, had been patrolling. After sinking a Japanese submarine, *I-43*, the first confirmed ship sunk by *Aspro*, Stevenson had gotten a freighter of 6,440 tons. When Risser arrived, Stevenson and Corbus were making a joint attack on a convoy which resulted in the sinking of another freighter of 4,500 tons, for which they shared equal credit. Corbus, chasing the convoy to the northwest, inflicted further damage but no more sinkings. Risser heard the explosions and the ensuing counterattack by the escorts.

On May 24 Risser picked up a southbound convoy, two freighters and two escorts. He closed for a night surface attack, firing four torpedoes at one of the freighters. At the moment of firing, the Japanese saw *Flying Fish* and maneuvered wildly to avoid being hit. One minute and twenty seconds after firing, Risser felt "the biggest explosion I have felt to date." He believed it was a circular run of one of his own torpedoes which blew up close aboard. The escorts turned toward *Flying Fish* and opened fire, driving the boat under.

During the night, Risser made an end around and dived for a daylight attack. The convoy came directly at him. When the range closed to 3,300 yards, Risser fired four more torpedoes at one of the freighters. Three torpedoes hit the main target, and one hit the other freighter. Both sank. They were two transports taking supplies and troops to reinforce the Palaus: *Taito Maru*, 4,500 tons, and *Osake Maru*, 3,700 tons. The escorts delivered a vicious counterattack. When he finally got back to the surface, Risser sent off a contact re-

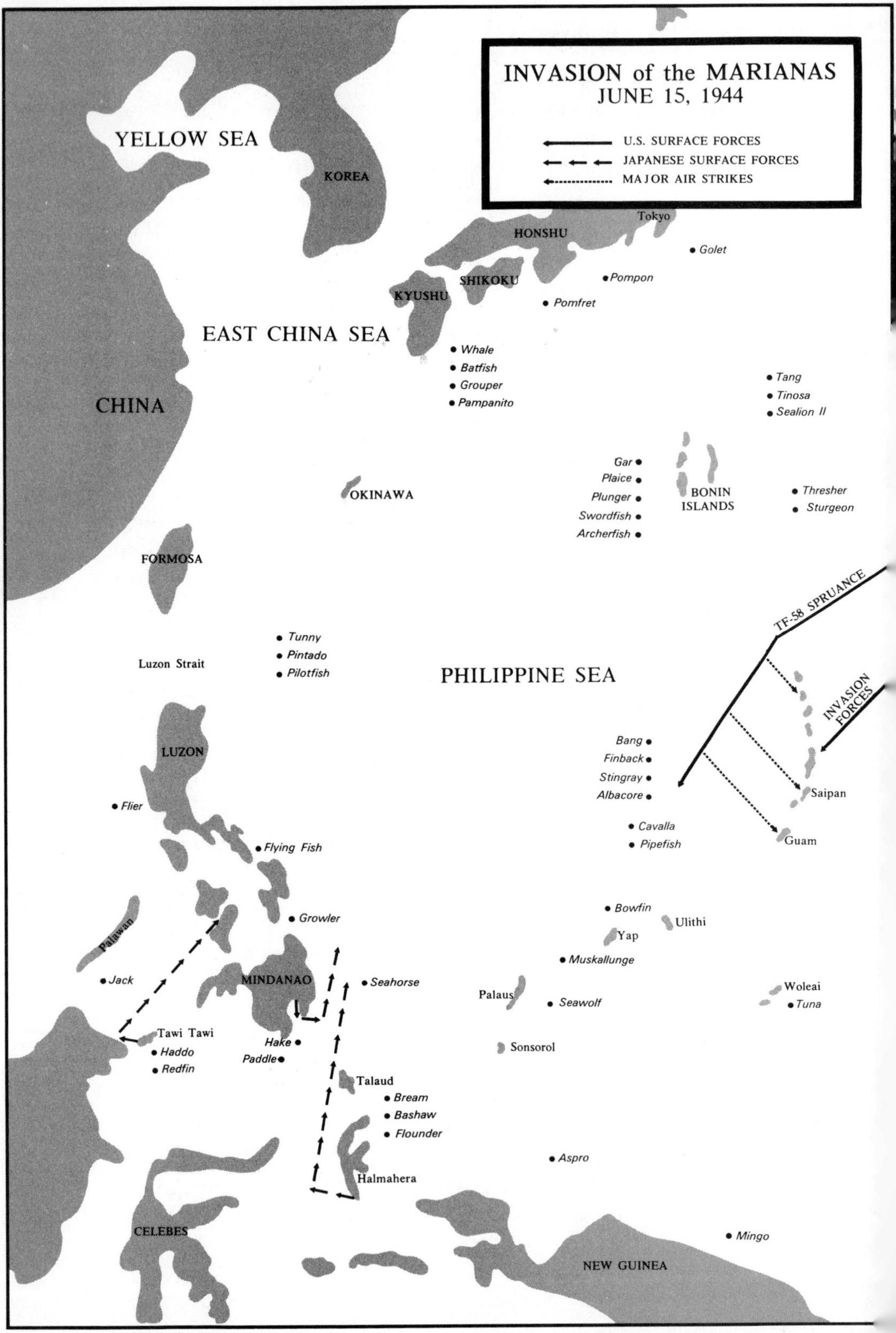

INVASION of the MARIANAS
JUNE 15, 1944
U.S. SURFACE FORCES
JAPANESE SURFACE FORCES
MAJOR AIR STRIKES
YELLOW SEA
KOREA
Tokyo
HONSHU
SHIKOKU
KYUSHU
EAST CHINA SEA
CHINA
Golet
Pompon
Pomfret
Whale
Batfish
Grouper
Pampanito
Tang
Tinosa
Sealion II
Gar
Plaice
Plunger
Swordfish
Archerfish
BONIN ISLANDS
Thresher
Sturgeon
OKINAWA
FORMOSA
TF-58 SPRUANCE
Tunny
Pintado
Pilotfish
Luzon Strait
PHILIPPINE SEA
INVASION FORCES
LUZON
Bang
Finback
Stingray
Albacore
Saipan
Flier
Cavalla
Pipefish
Guam
Flying Fish
Bowfin
Ulithi
Growler
Yap
Palawan
Muskallunge
Jack
MINDANAO
Seahorse
Woleai
Palaus
Seawolf
Tuna
Tawi Tawi
Haddo
Redfin
Hake
Paddle
Sonsorol
Talaud
Bream
Bashaw
Flounder
Aspro
Halmahera
CELEBES
Mingo
NEW GUINEA

port in hopes that Corbus and Stevenson might profit from it, but nothing was left except the escorts.

After that, Risser circled from Yap to Ulithi, to Peleliu, and then back north. On June 9 he dropped down to Sonsorol, where Eric Barr had sunk *Yubari*. He thought he saw a Japanese submarine cruising alone on the surface, but by that time Lockwood had ordered him to San Bernardino Strait to watch for Ozawa's fleet. He arrived on station—the west entrance of San Bernardino Strait—on June 12. Ozzie Lynch in *Seawolf*, having completed his photo reconnaissance of Peleliu, replaced Risser.

Six Pearl Harbor submarines took position in the Bonins to guard the northern approaches to the Marianas. These were: *Archerfish*, commanded by a new skipper, the first from the class of 1937 to get command, William Harry Wright, who had been exec of *Pompon*; George Lautrup's *Gar*; *Plunger*, commanded by a new skipper, Edward Joseph Fahy; Edmund Keats Montross's *Swordfish*; *Plaice*, commanded by Clyde Benjamin Stevens, Jr., another new boat with a new skipper; and Bafford Lewellen's *Pollack*.

Three of the six boats in the Bonins sank seven ships. On May 22 Lewellen in *Pollack* attacked a ten-ship convoy, sinking the destroyer *Asanagai*. The counterattack was vicious, forcing Lewellen to return from patrol after thirty-two days. Montross in *Swordfish*, on June 9, attacked a convoy, sinking the destroyer *Matsukake*. A week later he sank a 4,800-ton freighter. On June 28 Wright in *Archerfish* sank an 800-ton frigate. Stevens in *Plaice*, conducting a remarkable first patrol, sank three confirmed escorts and thought he sank two freighters and a transport, but they were not confirmed in postwar records.

During the patrol, *Plaice* suffered a misfortune similar to that which befell Olsen in *Angler*; many of the crew came down with an illness. However, most recovered quickly and Stevens continued the patrol.

The Battle of the Philippine Sea

When Admiral Ozawa at Tawi Tawi heard about the massive air strikes on the Marianas, he realized he had been outwitted. The U.S. Navy was aiming not for the Palaus, where Ozawa had hoped to lure it, but Guam and Saipan. Ozawa "temporarily" postponed Plan Kon, the reinforcement of Biak, and ordered the execution of Plan A-Go, the annihilation of the U.S. Pacific Fleet "with one blow." From naval headquarters in Japan came this exhortation: "This operation has immense bearing on the fate of the Empire. It is hoped that the forces will exert their utmost and achieve as magnificent results as in the Battle of Tsushima." *

Ozawa was confident of victory. He had fewer carriers—nine to fifteen for the United States—but he was counting on the support of not less than 500 land-based aircraft from Guam, Rota, Yap, and other bases. His carrier planes could also use these bases for refueling and rearming, shuttling between the bases and the carriers. The United States would have no land-based planes. Japanese carrier-based aircraft had longer ranges, giving Ozawa a slight edge in searching out his foes. The wind (important for launching and recovering carrier aircraft) was in Ozawa's favor.

At ten on the morning of June 13, the Japanese fleet steamed out of Tawi Tawi, with destroyers and two heavy cruisers in the van. Cy Austin in *Redfin* saw them come out. He went to battle stations, but the cruisers commenced zigzagging radically; he tried to follow and attack but could not close the range. Two hours later, Austin saw most of the main body of the fleet come out: at least six carriers, four battleships, five heavy cruisers, one light cruiser, and destroyers. He tried to attack a battleship, but the earlier chase of the cruisers had pulled him out of position and again he was not able to close the range. That night at eight, however, he got off a vital radio report announcing that the Japanese fleet was on the move.

Austin trailed the fleet, but it soon outran him, so he turned northeast to take station in the western end of Surigao Strait, hoping to catch cripples returning to Tawi Tawi from the battle.

Admiral Ozawa took his fleet through Sibutu Passage, northward into the Sulu Sea. He stopped at Guimaras on June 14 to refuel. At 8 A.M. on June 15, he got under way again, crossed the small Visayan Sea, then headed for San Bernardino Strait, lying between the southern tip of Luzon and Samar. Meanwhile, a supply force set out from Davao, and the last Kon elements—*Musashi* and *Yamato* plus supporting vessels—left from Batjan. Both the latter sailed to the east of Mindanao, directly into the Philippine Sea. The plan was that all three forces would rendezvous in the middle of the Philippine Sea on June 16.

* The 1905 battle of the Russo-Japanese War in which the Japanese navy virtually destroyed the Russian fleet.

THE BATTLE OF THE PHILIPPINE SEA

At 4:22 on the afternoon of June 15, while patrolling submerged in San Bernardino Strait, Robert Risser in *Flying Fish* picked up Ozawa's fleet, hugging the coastline 11 miles away. Risser could see three carriers, three battleships, and several cruiser and destroyers. It was a beautiful group of targets, but Risser had orders to report first, then attack. He watched the ships go by; then, after dark—at 7:25 P.M.—he surfaced and commenced transmitting and trailing. Risser's valuable report was received, although he didn't know it. After this, Risser, low on fuel, was ordered to Brisbane for refit.

Slade Cutter, who had taken *Seahorse* to Brisbane following his tough third patrol in the Marianas, got under way on June 3. He topped off his fuel tanks in the Admiralties and proceeded northwestward toward Surigao Strait to join Ben Oakley in *Growler*, who had moved to that station after his lifeguard duty in the Marianas. These boats were to guard the east entrance of the strait in case Ozawa's fleet—or parts of it—came out that way.

At 6:45 P.M. on June 15, the same day and almost the same hour that Risser picked up the Ozawa force in San Bernardino Strait, Cutter saw smoke on the horizon about 200 miles due east of Surigao Strait. At first it appeared to be coming from "four large unidentified men-of-war."

Cutter immediately commenced tracking at maximum speed, setting up to attack, and obtaining the enemy course, speed, and zigzag plan. He had closed to 19,000 yards when one of his main motors began sparking badly, forcing him to reduce speed to 14½ knots. *Seahorse* gradually fell behind the formation. At 3 A.M. the following day, he got off a vital contact report to Lockwood.

AT 1330 ZEBRA [Japanese] TASK FORCE IN POSITION 10–11 NORTH, 129–35 EAST. BASE COURSE 045, SPEED OF ADVANCE 16.5. SIGHT CONTACT AT DUSK DISCLOSED PLENTY OF BATTLESHIPS. SEAHORSE WAS ASTERN AND COULD NOT RUN AROUND DUE TO SPEED RESTRICTIONS CAUSED BY MAIN MOTOR BRUSHES. RADAR INDICATES SIX SHIPS RANGES 28,000 TO 39,000 YARDS. CRUISERS AND DESTROYERS PROBABLY COULD NOT BE DETECTED AT THESE RANGES WITH OUR RADAR. POSSIBLE CARRIER PLANE FORCED US DOWN THIS MORNING. SEAHORSE TRAILING.

The unit Cutter found was the last Kon force, built around the super-battleships *Musashi* and *Yamato*. The force soon outdistanced Cutter. He got off a final contact report which stated in part:

SEAHORSE LOST CONTACT 15 HOURS ZEBRA FIFTEEN [3 P.M. June 15, local time] DUE TO MOTOR FAILURE. REGRET UNABLE TO CLOSE TO AMPLIFY PREVIOUS REPORT. SIGHTED TOPS OF FOUR UNIDENTIFIED LARGE MEN-OF-WAR AND SIX OTHER SOURCES OF SMOKE AT DUSK FIFTEENTH.

By the time these reports from Risser and Cutter were received, U.S. troops were storming ashore against heavy opposition at Saipan. The invasion of Guam was set for June 18. However, it was now clear to Admiral Spruance that Admiral Ozawa was on the way to fight with all he had. Spruance postponed the invasion of Guam and redeployed Task Force 58 to meet the oncoming threat from the west.

A brand-new Pearl Harbor submarine, *Cavalla*, with a new skipper, Herman Kossler, who had been exec to Burt Klakring for *Guardfish*'s first five patrols, left Midway on June 4 to relieve Risser at San Bernardino Strait. On the way to station June 9, *Cavalla*, under way on the surface, collided with a whale, which broached in a pool of blood. Kossler was concerned that the collision might have bent one of his shafts or a screw. However, he felt no vibrations or other defects and continued on his way. On June 11 he passed Corbus in *Bowfin*, who had left Palau and was headed for Majuro for refit.

On June 15, after Lockwood received the contact reports from Risser and Cutter, he shifted *Cavalla* and Deragon's *Pipefish* to advance scout stations along the probable track of the main body. The two boats rendezvoused about 8 A.M. June 16, directly on the "estimated track" and about 360 miles due east of San Bernardino Strait. According to the arrangement made between them, Kossler would patrol 5 miles north of the estimated track and Deragon 5 miles south. The two boats searched all day without finding anything. At about 8 P.M., Kossler got off a negative search report and informed Lockwood that he was proceeding to San Bernardino Strait to relieve Risser.

Three hours later, at 11:03 P.M., Kossler picked up a contact on radar. It was four ships. This was not the main body—which had veered southeastward off the estimated track—but a supply force which had continued due east from San Bernardino. Kossler made an end around and dived about 3:40 A.M. He went in to attack, setting up stern tubes on one of the tankers. As he was about to fire, one of the destroyers charged at *Cavalla*, forcing Kossler to break off the attack and go deep to avoid a collision. Kossler later estimated that the

THE BATTLE OF THE PHILIPPINE SEA 653

destroyer came over *Cavalla*'s engine room as he was passing 75 feet.

When he came up again about 5 A.M. Kossler could not see the convoy. He decided not to chase, reasoning that his relief of Risser took priority. He had already expended much fuel and a full day looking for Ozawa; to chase the tanker convoy would take at least another day and more fuel. Kossler radioed Lockwood his decision.

When Lockwood received the message, he was of a different mind. Risser had already reported the fleet coming out; his relief was not urgent. Obviously these tankers had come to the area to refuel Ozawa's fleet. If Kossler trailed the tankers, they might lead him to the carriers and battleships. If they were sunk, Ozawa's fleet could not refuel and would be left sitting ducks. At 7:04 A.M. on June 17, Lockwood radioed Kossler: "CAVALLA IS [TO TAKE] ACTION. COMSUBPAC ALSO SENDS TO MUSKALLUNGE, SEAHORSE AND PIPEFISH FOR INFO. . . . DESTRUCTION THESE TANKERS OF GREAT IMPORTANCE. TRAIL, ATTACK, REPORT."

Kossler spent thirteen seemingly fruitless hours running down the track of the tankers. However, at about eight that night, June 17, he ran into a Japanese task force. At about 20,000 yards, his radar showed seven good-sized pips, which Kossler presumed to be a carrier, battleships, and cruisers. He submerged and ran in.

Believing it more important first to report this force, then attack if possible, for the next hour or so Kossler remained submerged, letting the task force pass by. At 10:45 P.M. he surfaced and got off a contact report—"fifteen or more large combatant ships"—to Lockwood and attempted to trail. Upon receiving this information, Lockwood told Kossler—and all other submarines—to shoot first and report later. To Kossler he said: HANG ON AND TRAIL AS LONG AS POSSIBLE REGARDLESS OF FUEL EXPENDITURE. . . . THEY MAY SLOW TO FUEL FROM YOUR PREVIOUSLY REPORTED TANKERS AND YOU MAY HAVE A CHANCE TO GET IN AN ATTACK. But by then Kossler had lost track of the force.

The contact report from Kossler puzzled Admiral Spruance. From the time of Risser's report to the time of Kossler's report, Admiral Ozawa had advanced only 500 miles for a very low average speed of about 8.8 knots. Moreover, Kossler had only reported "fifteen or more" large ships, and Spruance believed Ozawa capable of sending over forty. Spruance was suspicious. The idea took root that Ozawa had split his force and would attempt to flank Task Force 58 and break up the landing on the beaches at Saipan. But Ozawa had not split his forces. He was killing time. Admiral Toyoda had got him under way a day too early. He was waiting for land-based aircraft to congregate in the Marianas to help him attack.

Based on Kossler's several reports, it appeared to Lockwood that the four submarines—*Albacore, Bang, Finback,* and *Stingray*—in the "square" scouting line west of the Marianas were too far north. At eight on the morning of June 18, he ordered all four to shift position 100 miles southward. During the morning hours, the four boats carried out these orders.

All day on June 18 the two carrier forces lay back, trying to find one another with search aircraft. None of the U.S. planes found the Japanese forces. Ozawa's planes found Spruance's forces, about 250 miles southwest of the Marianas, and he decided that the next day— June 19—he would launch the "decisive" battle.

Spruance was still concerned that Ozawa might have split his forces to make an end run against the amphibious forces at Saipan. Another submarine report seemed to lend credence to that theory. At about eight on the night of June 18, Sam Loomis in *Stingray*, one of the "square" submarines, tried to get off a routine report on a minor fire in his radio antenna. The Japanese jammed his transmission, making it unreadable. Spruance thought Loomis might have found the Japanese and his radio transmission was a contact report. If so, it put the Japanese much farther *east* than anyone had guessed, possibly making the end run Spruance feared. Accordingly, Spruance took up an easterly course—back toward Saipan and away from Ozawa—during the night.

Shortly after Spruance gave these orders, Ozawa broke radio silence. He called headquarters on Guam to make arrangements for land-based air support for the morrow's attack and to tell Guam to be prepared to service carrier planes that might land there to refuel and rearm after hitting the enemy. Spruance's radio intelligence specialists DF-ed these transmissions, obtaining an accurate fix. The fix placed Ozawa's forces much farther *west* of *Stingray*'s position. But Spruance did not trust DF-ing and preferred to be guided by *Stingray*'s unreadable message.

About this time James Jordan in *Finback*, patrolling the northwest corner of the square, saw two searchlight beams on the southern horizon. Jordan charged south toward the beams at full speed but could not get close enough to pick up whatever it was on his SJ radar. Six hours later—11 p.m.—Jordan reported what he had seen to Lockwood. Another three hours went by before the message reached Spruance.

Jordan had probably detected the main body, but his six-hour delay in getting off the report and the further three-hour delay in relaying the message to Spruance—a total lapse of nine hours—had rendered the contact meaningless.

When dawn broke on the morning of June 19, Ozawa had 430 aircraft on his nine carriers. He launched these against Task Force 58 in four major raids, all the while expecting massive raids from his land-based aircraft on Guam. Unknown to Ozawa, none of the four raids went well. His planes were pounced upon by U.S. carrier aircraft or chewed to pieces by barrages of antiaircraft fire. On that day, which would become famous as "The Great Marianas Turkey Shoot," Ozawa lost about 330 planes without sinking a single U.S. ship. Nor did he receive much support from land-based aircraft, most of which had already been destroyed by U.S. carrier raids.

At about eight on the morning of June 19, as Ozawa was preparing Raid One, Jim Blanchard in *Albacore*, working the southwest corner of the square, raised his periscope. Thanks to Lockwood's decision the day before to shift the square 100 miles south, Blanchard found himself right in the midst of Ozawa's main carrier group.

Blanchard let one carrier go by and selected a second one for his target. The initial range was 9,000 yards. A destroyer loomed in his crosshairs. Blanchard coolly changed course to allow the destroyer to pass ahead. The range to the carrier closed to 5,300 yards. As Blanchard went in, he took another periscope look. It was immediately apparent that something had gone wrong with the TDC. Cussing his luck, Blanchard fired six bow tubes by "seaman's eye."

At least three destroyers immediately charged *Albacore*. Blanchard went deep. Going down he heard—and felt—one solid torpedo explosion which timed perfectly for the run of his number-six torpedo. About that time, twenty-five depth charges rained down, many so close that cork flew off the overhead. Then Blanchard heard "a distant and persistent explosion of great force." Then another.

One of Blanchard's torpedoes had hit the carrier. It was Ozawa's flagship, *Taiho*, 31,000 tons, newest and largest in the Japanese fleet. The explosion jammed the forward aircraft elevator; its pit filled with gasoline, water, and fuel. However, no fire erupted and the flight deck was unharmed. Blanchard believed that he had got a second hit as well, but he was mistaken. A Japanese pilot, Sakio Komatsu, who had just taken off from *Taiho* for Raid Two, launched at 8:56, hero-

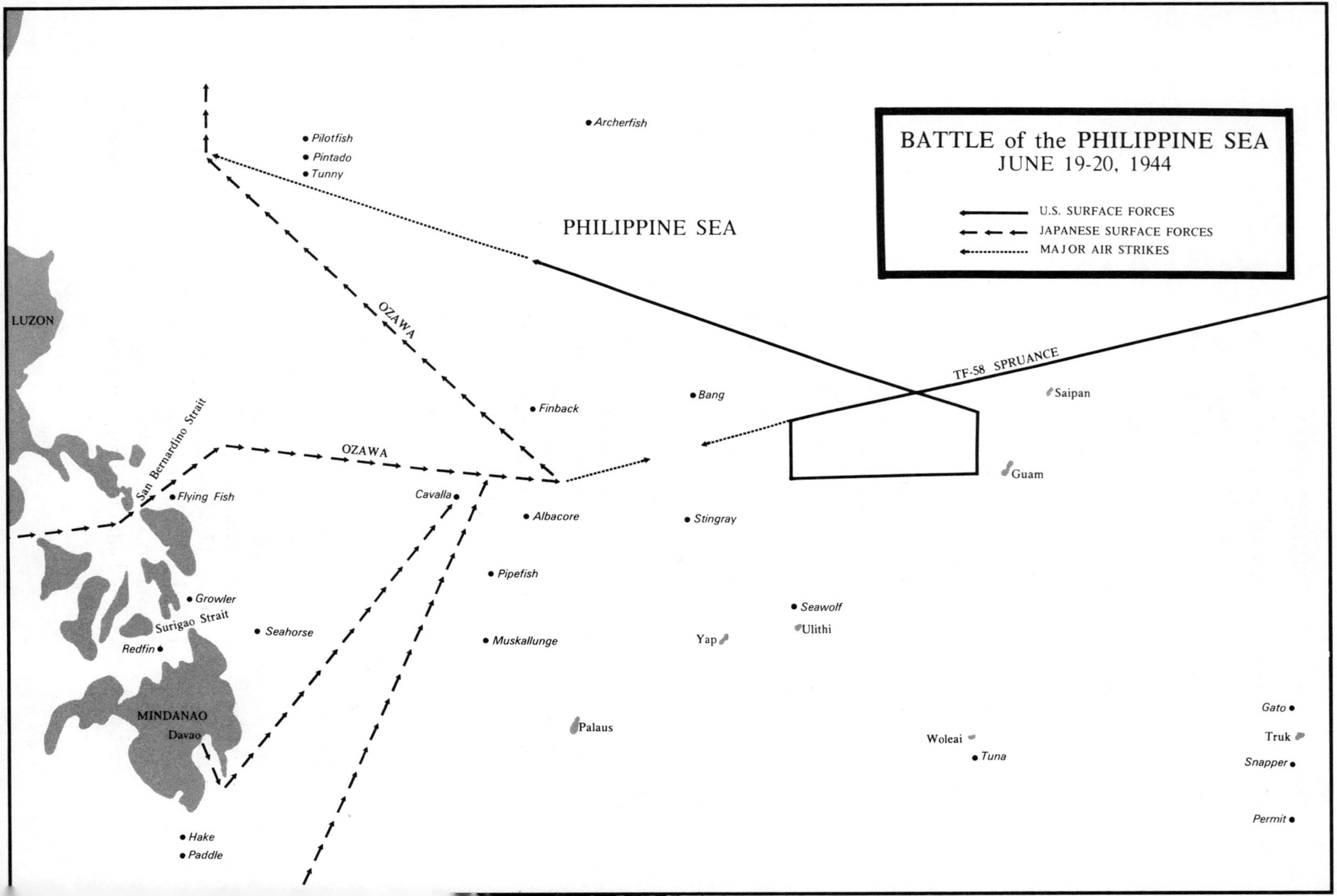
BATTLE of the PHILIPPINE SEA
JUNE 19-20, 1944
U.S. SURFACE FORCES
JAPANESE SURFACE FORCES
MAJOR AIR STRIKES
PHILIPPINE SEA
TF-58 SPRUANCE
OZAWA
OZAWA
LUZON
MINDANAO
Davao
San Bernardino Strait
Surigao Strait
Saipan
Guam
Yap
Ulithi
Palaus
Woleai
Truk
Archerfish
Pilotfish
Pintado
Tunny
Finback
Bang
Flying Fish
Cavalla
Albacore
Stingray
Pipefish
Growler
Seahorse
Redfin
Muskallunge
Seawolf
Hake
Paddle
Tuna
Gato
Snapper
Permit

THE BATTLE OF THE PHILIPPINE SEA 657

ically dived his plane at one of Blanchard's torpedoes, exploding it—and himself—100 yards short of the carrier.

The one torpedo hit on *Taiho* caused little concern on board. Ozawa still "radiated confidence and satisfaction" and by 11:30 had launched raids Three and Four. Meanwhile, a novice took over the damage-control work. He thought the best way to handle the gasoline fumes was to open up the ship's ventilation system and let them disperse. When he did, the fumes spread all through the ship. Unknown to anybody on board, *Taiho* became a floating time bomb.

About 3:30 that afternoon, *Taiho* was jolted by a severe explosion. A senior staff officer on the bridge saw the flight deck heave up. The sides blew out. *Taiho* dropped out of formation and began to settle in the water, clearly doomed. Though Admiral Ozawa wanted to go down with the ship, his staff prevailed on him to survive and to shift his quarters to the cruiser *Haguro*. Taking the Emperor's portrait, Ozawa transferred to *Haguro* by destroyer. After he left, *Taiho* was torn by a second thunderous explosion and sank stern first, carrying down 1,650 officers and men.

Less than three hours after Blanchard shot at *Taiho*, Herman Kossler in *Cavalla*, who had been chasing one Japanese group or another for about sixty hours, raised his periscope. "The picture was too good to be true," he later wrote. There was the heavy carrier *Shokaku*, veteran of Pearl Harbor, the Battle of the Coral Sea, and many other engagements, with a "bedspring" radar antenna on her foremast and a large Japanese ensign. The carrier was launching and recovering aircraft.

Kossler closed and fired six torpedoes, range 1,200 yards. Then he went deep. He heard three solid hits and figured the other three missed. Eight depth charges fell near *Cavalla*. During the next three hours, over a hundred more were dropped, fifty-six of them "fairly close." Kossler went very deep and evaded.

In fact, four of Kossler's torpedoes hit *Shokaku*, setting off unmanageable internal explosions and flames. *Shokaku* fell out of formation. Her bow settled. Water flooded into the hangar space through an elevator. Shortly after three o'clock in the afternoon, she turned over and plunged beneath the waves.

After sinking *Shokaku*, Kossler took *Cavalla* to her original destination, San Bernardino Strait, to relieve Risser in *Flying Fish*. On June 26 he picked up an eight-ship convoy but bungled the attack.

He tried to recover with an end around but lost the convoy and was not able to find it again.

Kossler returned a hero from this, his first war patrol. Lockwood knew from the codebreakers that *Shokaku* had sunk.

Neither Jim Blanchard nor anyone else on *Albacore*—and not even Lockwood—believed *Taiho* had sunk. Rather, Blanchard was angry at himself for "missing a golden opportunity." After the action, he was sent on to lifeguard for follow-up carrier strikes on Yap and Ulithi. During a raid on June 29, *Albacore* was strafed by a Japanese plane, which left several holes in the superstructure but did no major damage. On July 2, Blanchard shifted over to intercept traffic between Yap and Palau.

Shortly after eight the following morning, Blanchard picked up a ship and dived to attack. On closing, he saw it was a "wooden interisland steamer, approximately 900 tons." It was not worth torpedoes, Blanchard decided, so he surfaced for a gun attack. He set the ship on fire, ensuring its destruction, but was driven down by Japanese aircraft.

After the plane went away, Blanchard surfaced and picked up five wounded survivors, clinging to wreckage. When their wounds had been attended to by the pharmacist's mate, Blanchard had them locked up in the empty 4-inch ammo magazine locker, a tiny cell beneath the crew's mess. Later, he found a half-submerged lifeboat. He wrote, "When close aboard saw two women clinging to side of boat and a child four to five years old lying on the forward thwart." Blanchard—shaken by the sight—ordered a rubber raft put over the side alongside the lifeboat. It contained food, water, and fruit juices.

As Blanchard recalled the sorry episode years later, the interisland freighter he sank, *Taimei Maru*, was loaded with "lots of civilians . . . construction workers and their families . . . who were returning to the mainland." The survivors who reached Japan claimed that Blanchard had treated them ruthlessly. Emperor Hirohito, Blanchard recalled, lodged an official protest with the United States, one of the rare cases a Japanese ship sinking was officially protested.

After that, Blanchard put into the Admiralty Islands, unloaded his prisoners, refueled, and returned to Majuro for refit, arriving July 15. He was praised for an aggressive patrol and received credit for damaging a "*Shokaku*-class" carrier. For this, he was awarded only a Commendation Ribbon. Between "missing" *Taiho* and sinking a ship that drew a protest from the Emperor, Blanchard was less than pleased with this patrol.

As Blanchard recalled, the codebreakers lost track of *Taiho* after this battle. They were puzzled but did not think she had been sunk. "Months and months went by," Blanchard recalled. "Then they picked up a POW someplace who said *Taiho* went down in the Battle of the Philippine Sea. Even then, intelligence was doubtful. So I said, 'Keep him alive until he convinces them.'"

When the confirmation finally was obtained, Lockwood substituted a Navy Cross for Blanchard's Commendation Ribbon.

During the night of June 19, Admiral Ozawa on *Haguro* retired his forces and regrouped for refueling on the following day and then shifted his flag to *Zuikaku*. Even though he had lost two carriers to U.S. submarines, most of his planes had failed to return, and he had had no help from land-based aircraft, he was not dispirited. He believed that many of the aircraft which failed to return had gone on to bases in the Marianas and would be ready for battle again soon. Ozawa prepared for a second strike on June 21 which would truly annihilate the U.S. Pacific Fleet.

That night at 9:21, James Jordan in *Finback*, patrolling the northwest corner of the square, again sighted searchlights on the horizon. These must have come from Ozawa's force, which passed close to *Finback*'s area. Again Jordan charged in, and this time he made radar contact. He had closed to 14,000 yards when four destroyers came up astern, seemingly attacking *Finback*. Jordan submerged. Later he said, "The destroyers passed over us without attacking, followed closely by the major ships, which numbered more than twenty-five."

Three hours later, Jordan surfaced with all these ships still in sight. He trailed and tried to get off a contact report, but the radio transmitter was out of commission. Jordan said later, "We continued to track on the surface, hoping the transmitter could be quickly repaired, but were again forced down by one or more high-speed ships. The pattern continued all night. Each time we surfaced we were forced to dive by returning aircraft or surface ship, although none stayed to attack us."

Jordan's radio transmitter remained out of commission for several days. Later, when *Finback* returned from patrol, Jordan's squadron commander wrote in despair, "*Finback*'s inability to transmit information on contact with enemy force on June 19 was one of the costly misfortunes of the war." The episode left Jordan in a deep depression, and he requested immediate relief.

I was despondent and morose after making nine patrols in less than three years [he wrote later]. I felt my next one would be my last. . . . I now believe I had a simple case of combat fatigue and should have turned myself in for treatment. Instead I represented to my superior that I felt unfit and unsafe to command the boat any longer and feared for the safety of the ship and its crew. My boss was most understanding and urged me to take two weeks to reconsider my decision since the consequences of such an act can be disastrous to an officer's career. I understood this but stuck with my decision. It caught up with me about fifteen years later when I failed of selection [i.e., was not promoted].

That same night, Admiral Spruance made a move that was strangely reminiscent of his move in the Battle of Midway: he again let the surviving and badly mauled Japanese fleet slip away. At Midway he may have been lucky; this time it was, beyond doubt, a tactical error. He lost contact with Ozawa's forces, now maintaining strict radio silence. Nobody sent out night search planes to find it. While Ozawa retired to the northwest to rendezvous with his tankers, Spruance steamed east. Hour by hour the distance between the two forces grew greater.

Had Spruance followed up more aggressively and obtained a position report on Ozawa, U.S. submarines might have inflicted even more damage on the Japanese. Lockwood had three boats to the north of the battle scene ideally positioned to intercept: the wolf pack Blair's Blasters, composed of *Pilotfish, Pintado,* and *Tunny.* If Spruance had determined earlier that Ozawa was retiring northwestward toward Okinawa, these three boats could have intercepted. Having no positive information on Ozawa's movements, Lockwood kept the pack in place to the north, hoping Ozawa would head for Japan, passing through the pack's area. In addition, he moved *Archerfish* west from the Bonins to cover a northward retreat to Japan.

On June 20, Spruance belatedly headed west, launching the hunt for Ozawa. That afternoon, at about four, a search plane from *Enterprise* found Ozawa 275 miles away. It was the first time in the whole battle that a U.S. carrier plane had even *seen* the Japanese surface

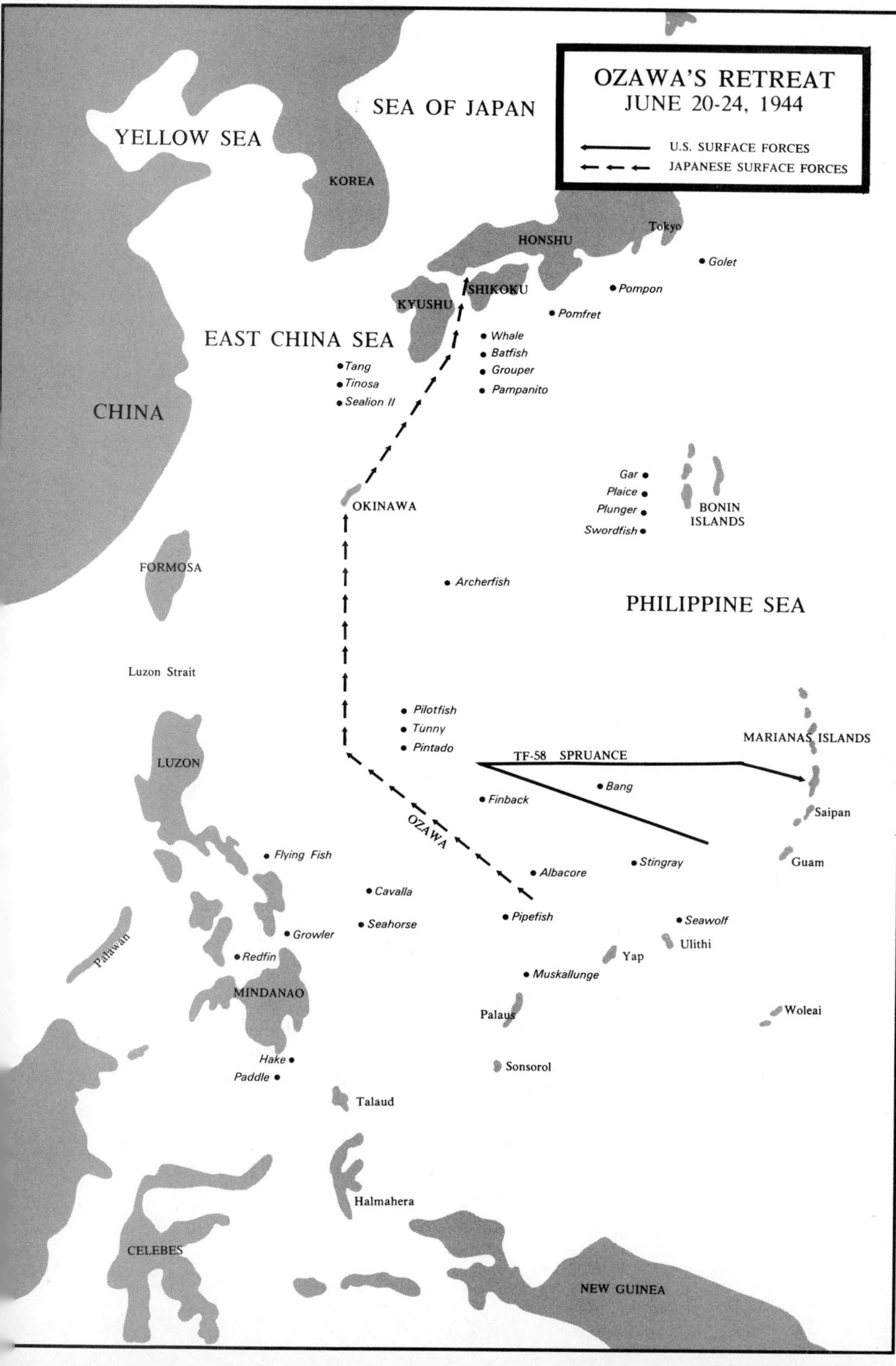
OZAWA'S RETREAT
JUNE 20-24, 1944
U.S. SURFACE FORCES
JAPANESE SURFACE FORCES
YELLOW SEA
SEA OF JAPAN
KOREA
HONSHU
Tokyo
Golet
Pompon
SHIKOKU
KYUSHU
Pomfret
EAST CHINA SEA
Whale
Batfish
Grouper
Pampanito
Tang
Tinosa
Sealion II
CHINA
Gar
Plaice
Plunger
Swordfish
BONIN ISLANDS
OKINAWA
FORMOSA
Archerfish
PHILIPPINE SEA
Luzon Strait
Pilotfish
Tunny
Pintado
MARIANAS ISLANDS
LUZON
TF-58 SPRUANCE
Bang
Finback
Saipan
OZAWA
Flying Fish
Stingray
Guam
Albacore
Cavalla
Seahorse
Pipefish
Seawolf
Growler
Ulithi
Palawan
Redfin
Yap
Muskallunge
MINDANAO
Palaus
Woleai
Hake
Paddle
Sonsorol
Talaud
Halmahera
CELEBES
NEW GUINEA

forces. Although it was late in the day and the Japanese lay almost at the extreme range of U.S. aircraft, Spruance gave the go-ahead for an all-out attack.

The planes reached the Japanese shortly before sunset. In a confused but lucky fight, they sank the carrier *Hiyo* (which Roy Benson had damaged off Tokyo Bay in June 1943) and two fleet tankers, *Genyo* and *Seiyo Maru*. They inflicted heavy damage on the battleship *Haruna* and the cruiser *Maya* and light damage on Ozawa's new flagship *Zuikaku* and the carriers *Junyo*, *Ryuho*, and *Chiyoda*. In addition, they shot down another twenty-two Japanese planes, leaving Ozawa with only about thirty-five operational aircraft.

The U.S. carrier planes involved in this long-range sunset action had a rough time getting home. One hundred of the 216 that took off for battle failed to make a safe return. Twenty were shot down or unaccounted for. The other eighty ran out of fuel and had to ditch or make crash landings on the carriers. To help them find the way home, Marc Mitscher ordered his carrier captains to turn on their lights. But for that bold action, many more might have been lost.

Following this attack, Ozawa realized he was in no position to make a second strike against Spruance. He retired to Okinawa at best speed, and offered his resignation, which was not accepted. Spruance ordered up a stern chase, but Ozawa, who had a good head start, outran him.

After stopping at Okinawa to refuel, Ozawa returned his fleet to the Inland Sea. Lockwood had four submarines patrolling off southern Honshu near the entrances to the Inland Sea: *Batfish*, *Grouper*, *Whale*, and *Pampanito*. None made contact with Ozawa's forces. In this greatest carrier air battle in history, later to be known officially as the Battle of the Philippine Sea, Ozawa had lost three of his nine carriers: *Shokaku*, *Taiho*, and *Hiyo*—two to submarines.

While Ozawa was beating his retreat, Admiral Toyoda ordered the Japanese submarine commander, Admiral Takagi, to throw every submarine he could lay his hands on into a close-in defense of the Marianas, an order reminiscent of Bob English's abortive plan to save Midway from Japanese invaders in 1942. With the help of codebreakers, DF experts, radar, and sonar, U.S. forces sank a dozen RO- and I-class boats in June and July, mostly in the waters of the Marianas. After the battle, Admiral Takagi himself was missing, perhaps lost escaping from Saipan in one of his boats. Other Japanese

THE BATTLE OF THE PHILIPPINE SEA

submarines trying to bring supplies to Saipan and Guam were driven off and were unable to complete their missions.

Thus far in the year 1944, Japan had lost about forty submarines from all causes. Counting the forty-five boats lost in 1942 and 1943, the total was about eighty-five. The force had been, in truth, cut in half. In Japan's increasingly desperate shipbuilding program, submarine replacement held a relatively low priority. The Japanese submarine force never recovered from the June–July holocaust. From that point forward, submarine construction was aimed in a different direction: the production of scores of midget submarines to be used in Japanese home waters against an anticipated Allied invasion force and the equipping of the remaining (and replacement) I-class with suicidal man-guided torpedoes called *kaitens*.

30
Pearl Harbor and Australia, June to July 1944

The Fight for Saipan

Saipan was invaded June 15, and the fighting there was indeed bloody. For once, the codebreakers and other intelligence forces failed Nimitz. There were 32,000 Japanese on the island, twice as many as intelligence had estimated. The resistance was suicidal. The island was not "secure" until July 9. After that, the invasion forces landed on Guam and Tinian, where the Japanese also put up fanatical resistance. By August 10, all three islands were in U.S. hands, but to capture them the United States lost about 5,000 killed and 20,000 wounded.

The invasion of the Marianas turned out to be even more decisive than Nimitz had foreseen. The battle not only cost Toyoda three aircraft carriers but also most of his carrier air wings, a blow from which the Japanese naval air arm never really recovered. The remaining carriers were relegated to the role of divisionary forces for the future, and Japan began training pilots for its kamikaze corps: flying bombs, piloted by humans who would achieve everlasting fame by diving their craft into U.S. warships.

In Tokyo, the loss of the Marianas brought shock on an unprecedented scale. "Saipan was really understood to be a matter of life and death," said Vice Admiral Paul H. Wenneker, German naval attaché to Tokyo. Said Marine General Holland M. Smith, "Its loss caused a greater dismay than all her previous defeats put together." And Admiral King noted, "Saipan was the decisive battle of the war."

On July 18, the day the loss of Saipan was announced to the Japanese people, Prime Minister Tojo and his entire cabinet resigned. General Kuniaki Koiso formed a new cabinet. "And, although Koiso took office with a promise to prosecute the war vigorously and issued a defiant statement," Samuel Eliot Morison later wrote, "everybody who understood Japanese double-talk knew that a change in ministry meant an admission of defeat and a desire for peace. Yet nobody in Japanese military or political circles would accept the onus of proposing peace, so the Pacific war dragged on for another twelve months."

Patrols from Pearl Harbor

While the big battle in the Philippine Sea was in progress—and in the days and weeks following—Lockwood and Christie sent other boats on patrol to the usual areas. Most of these were single boats, operating alone, but both commanders organized more wolf packs.

A Lockwood pack went on the polar circuit. It was a twosome made up of *Herring*, commanded by another Naval Academy football star, David Zabriskie, Jr., and *Barb*, now commanded by Eugene Bennett Fluckey.

Fluckey had been caught up in backwater assignments since the beginning of the war. After making five patrols out of Panama on the ancient *Bonita*, he had returned to the States for a postgraduate course in naval engineering. During *Barb*'s seventh war patrol (the second in the Pacific), Fluckey had made a PCO cruise.

While Fluckey was preparing to get under way from Midway, Lockwood flew out for an inspection. Fluckey said later, "I had never known the man but I did know he was a tough one and he wanted good skippers and good producers. I liked his methods. . . . If you produced, he supported you and gave you everything he could possibly give you. If you failed, he would give you another opportunity, but if you came back the second time with an empty bag, you usually were forced out of command."

For a brief moment, Fluckey feared he might be forced out of command before he set sail. "As he walked down the dock with my crew at quarters," Fluckey said later, "I had my heart in my throat for fear that he was coming aboard to tell me he didn't think I had enough experience and that he was going to remove me from command until I had proven myself. On his arrival on board, after saying hello, I immediately took an aggressive attitude and said, 'Admiral Lockwood, how many ships would you like us to bring back in our bag this time?' He looked at me with a smile and replied, 'How many do you think you can sink?' and I said, 'Would five be enough?' Lockwood said, 'I think five would be enough.' Then I said, 'What types do you want?' Lockwood said, 'Forget the types, you just get five. Now get out there and give 'em hell.' "

The two boats proceeded north. On the way, Lockwood sent them an Ultra about a three-ship convoy departing Matsuwa To in the Kuriles. Fluckey, the senior skipper, laid out the intercept plan: *Herring* close in, *Barb* to seaward. The convoy came out right on schedule. Zabriskie set up and sank an escort, then a 2,000-ton freighter. The remaining ships scattered and ran—directly toward Fluckey in *Barb*. Fluckey moved fast and fired three torpedoes; a freighter blew up and sank while he took pictures. It was *Koto Maru*, 1,000 tons.

After that, Fluckey surfaced to chase. He caught up with *Madras Maru*, 3,800 tons, and fired three stern tubes. This ship also blew up and sank. Fluckey then returned to the scene of his first sinking to capture a survivor for intelligence purposes.

He wrote, "It was a gruesome picture . . . an unholy sight . . . it was getting dark, the atmosphere was much like one you'd expect from Frankenstein. The people were screaming and groaning in the water. There were several survivors on rafts. The water at that time was very cold, about 27 degrees. These people were gradually freezing and dying. We took the most lively looking specimen aboard."

Meanwhile Dave Zabriskie closed in on Matsuwa and found and sank two ships at anchor in the harbor, *Iwaki Maru*, 3,100 tons, and *Hiburi Maru*, a transport of 4,400 tons.

Immediately after his torpedoes exploded, the shore batteries on Matsuwa * opened fire on *Herring*. The Japanese evidently scored two direct hits on *Herring*'s conning tower, destroying the boat.

---

* The same batteries that had shot at Frank Latta and Babe Brown in *Narwhal*, July 1943, when they were assigned to create a diversion so that *Lapon, Plunger,* and *Permit* could leave the Sea of Japan.

The Japanese reported "bubbles covered an area about 5 meters wide and heavy oil covered an area of approximately 15 miles." Nothing further was ever heard from Zabriskie.

On his first patrol, Zabriskie had not sunk a confirmed ship and had been roasted for inadequacies in the fire-control party. On this, his second, he sank four confirmed ships for almost 10,000 tons within a two-day span and gave Fluckey an opportunity to sink two other ships fleeing his attack.

Fluckey wrote later that his POW turned out to be a "traitor to his country." Using sign language, he poured out valuable intelligence on Japanese ships and minefields. Fluckey radioed some of this—information on minefields off Hokkaido and northeast Honshu—to Lockwood.

Lockwood relayed it to Fluckey's classmate, James Seerley Clark, who was making his first patrol as skipper of *Golet* to the south. *Golet*, a new Manitowoc boat, had arrived in the Pacific earlier in the year, commanded by James Markland Clement. After an inspection cruise, Lew Parks decided the wardroom was ill-trained and ill-led and that it should be scattered. Mike Fenno, who also went to sea on her, thought they might get by with relieving the skipper. In the end, it was decided to relieve Clement and his exec and make do with the others.

Phil Ross was drafted from his job in operations at the Training Command to take *Golet* on her first war patrol and bring her up to snuff. His new exec—and prospective commanding officer—was James Clark, who had served on Chet Smith's *Swordfish* and then made one patrol on *Archerfish*. When *Golet* returned to port, Ross was still not satisfied with her wardroom and crew. Clark passed with flying colors, but Ross recommended that four other officers and two senior chiefs (from the original group) be sent to shore duty. His recommendation was not followed.

Despite the information on minefields, Clark ran into trouble. On June 14, two weeks after *Herring* had sunk, the Japanese attacked and sank a submarine off northeast Honshu—evidently *Golet*. The Japanese report stated, "On the spot of fighting, we later discovered corks, raft, etc., and a heavy oil pool." Clark was never heard from again.

Now alone, Fluckey shifted northwest to the Sea of Okhotsk, cutting among icebergs, bedeviled by mirages. He found some trawlers out sealing and sank them with his deck gun. On the night of June

11, he picked up two more ships and sank both with torpedoes; they were *Toten Maru*, 3,800 tons, and *Chihaya Maru*, 1,100 tons. Two nights later, Fluckey found another ship with a small escort. He fired two torpedoes and sank the large transport *Takashima Maru*, 5,600 tons. After that Fluckey returned to Matsuwa, poking *Barb*'s nose into the anchorage there and at other islands, threading through dozens of sampans. Twice Fluckey got caught in Japanese fishing nets. The first time he backed down submerged and got out. The second time, *Barb* was hooked solidly and Fluckey had to surface to cut himself loose.

When Fluckey returned to base, he was showered with congratulations. Later he said, "Admiral Lockwood reminded me that, by God, I was the only skipper during the war that told him exactly how many ships I was going to sink and then went out and did it."

Pomfret, a new boat, was commissioned by Frank Clements Acker, who came from *S-15*. Acker had always prided himself on keeping physically fit, but shortly after the commissioning ceremony he experienced a severe backache. It was diagnosed as an extended disc pressing on a nerve. Acker spent ten days in the hospital and then returned to his ship, as he said later, "back to normal nicely."

After reporting at Pearl Harbor, Acker went off on his first Pacific war patrol to Bungo Suido. One day, the watch spotted two freighters coming out of the channel. Acker plotted an intercept course, but the two ships went behind a minefield and anchored. Acker ordered *Pomfret* to close the minefield. His exec, Fredric B. Clarke, who had come from *Sawfish*, asked Acker what in the world he was doing. Acker replied that they had been sent out to sink Jap ships and that was what he intended to do.

Later, Clarke wrote, "Now I think that I am as brave a guy as many, but my stomach flipped over. Any submariner in the world is afraid of minefields—if you strike one while submerged, death is instantaneous. There is no chance of survival."

Clarke prevailed on Acker to stop the headlong pursuit into the minefield and wait to see what the ships would do next. After dark, they got under way, hugging the dark coast. Acker tracked, skirting the minefield, and then fired six torpedoes—three at a freighter, three at an escort. All missed, probably running under.

Early on the morning of June 14, while the moon was bright, radar reported a big contact at 23,000 yards. It was zigzagging, heading for

Bungo Suido. Acker put on full power to intercept. At 14,000 yards, there was no longer any doubt about the target. It was a battleship, looking "big as the Empire State Building," escorted by a cruiser and some destroyers.

By good luck and good seamanship, Acker got position 2,000 yards off the target's projected track, with a fair chance at a shot. Acker thought they should dive and wait, while Clarke suggested holding on for ten more minutes. The officer of the deck swore at the brilliance of the moon. Two or three minutes after Acker agreed to remain on the surface, the battleship, which had probably picked *Pomfret* up on its own radar, beamed a searchlight on the bridge of *Pomfret*. Clarke wrote later, "It gave me the most naked feeling I have ever had."

Acker dived, while everybody waited for the splash of big shells from the battleship, the cruiser, or the destroyer escorts. None came, so Acker poked up the periscope. The formation had zigged and then turned back toward *Pomfret*. Acker set up and fired six torpedoes at the battleship at extremely long range. All missed.

Acker continued the patrol—aggressively. On the last night on station, he closed to 3,000 yards of the Japanese coast to bombard a small town with his deck gun. *Pomfret* ran aground and stuck fast in the mud. After several spine-tingling hours Acker got her loose and made flank speed for deep water. During this patrol, he experienced no further difficulty with his back.

Search for the Nickel Ship

After the Battle of the Philippine Sea, and while the fight for Saipan was in progress, Ralph Christie decided to make a second war patrol. Looking at the schedules, he saw that Enrique Haskins in *Guitarro* would be arriving in Darwin about June 19 from Pearl Harbor. Christie decided that Haskins could refuel and get a new load of torpedoes at Darwin and take him out for a "three-week patrol."

On June 21, Christie flew up to Darwin. Upon arrival, however, he discovered that *Guitarro* had engine problems that required immediate repairs in Fremantle. What to do? There was one possible answer. That same day, Sam Dealey in *Harder* arrived in Darwin from his epic destroyer-killing patrol off Tawi Tawi. His crew was worn out from this arduous cruise. Yet when Christie asked, Dealey agreed to make a brief extension. Thereafter, the forepart of the patrol would be known unofficially as 5A and the extension as 5B.

According to some accounts, the extension did not sit well with the crew. Lockwood later wrote that the news caused "bitter disappointment," and he quoted one of *Harder*'s radio technicians: "After blowing up the last destroyer on June 10, everyone was overjoyed, figuring on a short patrol and then back to Rest Camp in Perth. Unfortunately we pulled into Darwin and Admiral Christie wanted to go out with us. The crew was pretty sore."

In effect, Christie changed places with his operations officer, Murray Tichenor, who had gone along for the ride on 5A. Dealey got under way that same day, June 21. Christie wrote later, "The primary purpose of this short patrol was to intercept and sink what we called the 'Nickel Ship,' which left from Pomalaa in the Gulf of Boni, Celebes, about once a month. This was the sole source of nickel for the Japanese. We generally knew when it was leaving."

On the way to the Gulf of Boni, *Harder* received an Ultra. A damaged Japanese cruiser with two escorts, returning from the Battle of the Philippine Sea en route to Surabaya or Singapore, would pass their way, probably through Salajar Strait, south of Celebes. Dealey took up station 5 miles east of the strait.

On the morning of June 27, Dealey, expecting the cruiser any moment, dived at dawn. Christie, who was standing junior-officer-of-the-deck watch, manned the periscope. At 7:30 A.M., Christie sighted the cruiser and two destroyer escorts, right on schedule. However, as happened so many times with Ultra intercepts, *Harder*—or the cruiser—was slightly off course. The range was 9,000 yards. Dealey rang up flank speed, but he could get no closer than 5,600 yards.

After the cruiser and destroyers disappeared over the horizon, Christie turned to Dealey and said only half jokingly, "Why didn't you expose your conning tower and lure the destroyers in and sink them?"

Later, in private, Dealey asked Christie, "Admiral, were you serious about luring them in?"

Christie, who had unbounded faith in Dealey, replied, smiling, "Well, Sam, you're the Destroyer Killer." He explained later, "I was neither criticizing nor directing . . . the way we felt about Sam and *Harder*, the risk was not great."

Christie and Dealey then turned their attention to the Nickel Ship, going north into the Gulf of Boni to patrol off Pomalaa. Christie said later, "We could see the Nickel Ship being loaded under lights at night. However, we couldn't do anything then because there was a breakwater between *Harder* and the target. The only thing to do was withdraw to Salajar Strait and wait for it to come out."

On June 30, *Harder* submerged at the east entrance of Salajar Strait, waiting. About 7:15 that morning, the periscope watch picked up a ship coming eastward through the strait. Dealey and Christie had a look. The ship was close to shore, merging with the backdrop, making it difficult to identify. Both men agreed it was small, a tugboat, fishing trawler, or small freighter.

Dealey thought whatever it was might be worth attacking, either by torpedo or deck gun. Christie agreed. Dealey ordered the gun crew to stand by below, then surfaced and ran in at 17 knots. On the way in, a lookout spotted an aircraft. Dealey dived for twenty-four minutes. Seeing no further sign of the aircraft, he surfaced to resume the chase.

When they came to within 5 miles of the target, Christie and Dealey received a jolt. There were now two ships: the small one they had been chasing and the Nickel Ship. Both were westbound, the smaller ship trailing. Belatedly, it dawned on Christie and Dealey that the "trawler" was in fact a small escort vessel which had come to meet the Nickel Ship. Moreover, there were two aircraft circling overhead. They banked and headed for *Harder*.

Dealey dived. The planes dropped three small bombs, none close. Afterward, the men in the after section of the ship reported they could hear something rolling around on the deck topside. An unexploded bomb? Dealey put the rudder hard over and rang up full speed. The rolling noise stopped. "Whether the sound was caused by an imagination or by a dud," Dealey wrote, "it now ceased."

The escort churned over to help the aircraft. For the next two and a half hours, depth charges fell at a distance. This was not a real attack, Dealey thought, but rather a harassing action to keep them from getting at the Nickel Ship. The tactic worked. The escort and the planes kept Dealey down all day, and the ship got away.

Christie and Dealey were chagrined. They had been faked out. Had Dealey ignored the escort, he might easily have maneuvered around it to sink the Nickel Ship. It was, Christie wrote later, "one of the very rare instances in which Sam was fooled." Dealey wrote, "We had been maneuvered into trying to stop the ball carrier on an end run while he made an off-tackle play."

Having missed both these Ultra contacts, Dealey set course for

Darwin. On the night of July 1, while passing close to Timor Island on the surface, the sky around *Harder* was suddenly illuminated "bright as day." The officer of the deck, scared out of his wits, dived *Harder* instantly. A Royal Australian Air Force Catalina patrol plane pilot had picked them up on radar and dropped a magnesium flare to see what he had found. Fortunately he dropped no bombs. An angry Sam Dealey kept *Harder* submerged four hours. Then he continued on to Darwin without incident, arriving July 3.

On the way to Darwin, Christie and Dealey had a long discussion about what to do with Sam Dealey and *Harder*. Dealey had made his five patrols. It was time for him to step aside. As Christie saw it, Sam's exec, Tiny Lynch, should take command of *Harder*; Sam should return to the States for thirty days' leave, after which he could go to new construction or back to Christie's staff to serve as Tichenor's assistant, or possibly to command a division if BuPers was ready to give the class of 1930 that responsibility.

Sam had other ideas. He agreed that Lynch should take command of *Harder* but thought that Lynch, who had also made five patrols, ought to have shore leave before taking on the heavy responsibilities of command. There were eighteen or twenty men scheduled to leave *Harder* after the fifth patrol; it was not fair to have Lynch assume command and train a new crew all at once. Dealey wanted to take *Harder* on one more patrol, shape up the new men, and then turn over the boat to Lynch.

Christie replied, "Sam, let's don't try to decide all this now. When you get to Fremantle, I want you to be my guest at Bend of the Road, if you want. It will be quiet and you can think it all out."

Dealey agreed.

While Christie was at sea on *Harder* his staff was preparing for a momentous political event in the submarine war, a summit conference between Admirals Lockwood and Christie. The two men had not talked face to face for sixteen months. The last time had been in February 1943 at Pearl Harbor, after Lockwood had come up from Fremantle to replace Bob English and Christie was en route to Fremantle to replace Lockwood.

The idea for the meeting had originated with Admiral Nimitz, who believed that as the "two roads" to Tokyo began to merge, Lockwood and Christie should integrate submarine activities more closely. In a letter to Christie May 29, Lockwood passed along the Nimitz idea, proposing that they meet at Pearl Harbor since it was "inconvenient" for him to come to Australia.

But Lockwood's own staff disagreed with this proposal. Without exception, every man who would attend the conference—Merrill Comstock, Dick Voge, Joe Grenfell, Art Taylor, Pete Ferrall, Bill Irvin— voted to meet in Perth. This vote, Lockwood wrote Christie, "shows what a lure your city has." A compromise was worked out. All hands would meet in Brisbane, July 5.

Immediately after leaving *Harder*, Christie boarded Admiral Kinkaid's plane at Darwin and flew to Brisbane for the conference, arriving in a driving rain on July 4. Lockwood flew in the following day. The two submarine force commanders instantly locked horns. Christie later noted in his diary, "Charlie as insufferably smart aleck as ever. . . . Almost impossible to discuss anything with him without his witless jokes and personal remarks. That bird has gotten away with 'moider.' "

After Christie got back to Fremantle, he wrote Lockwood, "I am extremely sorry that we had a personal spat of words at the outset. I felt I was being subjected to ridicule and lost my temper. It would be most unfortunate if such a thing could react on our official relations, in which we are substantially in accord. I regret it and do apologize." Lockwood replied, "As to your flare-up the other night, maybe my sense of humor is a bit unhumorous at times. Almost had a fight with Gnu Mayer [Andrew DeGraff Mayer, class of 1916] in almost the same way. Your apology is accepted."

The conference dealt with many technical matters, among them exchange of areas, rotation of boats for overhaul, radio frequencies, combat awards, spare parts, and officer and enlisted personnel. In the evenings, there were cocktail parties and formal dinners for all the visitors.

The most important matter was the creation of advance submarine bases. Lockwood had obtained permission from Admirals King and Nimitz to put a base on Saipan as soon as it was feasible. The old *Holland* would provide the first refit and refueling services beginning later in the month. In September, Christie would move *Orion* forward from Fremantle to Mios Woendi, a small island on the eastern end of Biak. Mios Woendi and Saipan were only 1,000 miles apart. With the creation of these advance bases, the submarines of both commands could shift back and forth with little difficulty.

Throughout the conference, Lockwood and Christie remained more or less at arm's length. One factor that may have helped open the distance was Christie's recent ride on *Harder*. Some in the Lockwood camp believed it had been a "stunt," an unnecessary strain on Dealey and the *Harder* crew. Lockwood may have been jealous. Christie had now made two brief patrols, where he had made none.

After Lockwood had departed, Christie, through no real fault of his own, got into hot water with his boss, Admiral Kinkaid. Christie paid his customary call on General MacArthur, during which he briefed the general on Sam Dealey's patrol 5A at Tawi Tawi and the sinking of what was then believed to be five destroyers. This reminded MacArthur that Christie had not yet accepted his offer to give army awards to submarine skippers. Christie corrected MacArthur politely, reminding him that he had already put forward such a recommendation for Walt Griffith in *Bowfin*. The recommendation, MacArthur replied, had never reached his desk.

It was now clear to Christie that his proposal for Griffith had been killed by Admiral Kinkaid. Christie later wrote, "Then to my embarrassment, surprise, astonishment, etc., he said he was going to give me a Distinguished Service Cross and Sam Dealey a Silver Star regardless of [Kinkaid's] policy of no Army awards to Navy personnel. . . . This turn of events put me rather on the spot because I had run counter to Admiral Kinkaid on the recommendation for an Army award to Commander Griffith. So I at once reported the whole affair to Kinkaid in his quarters where he was confined for a day with a severe cold."

What was said in this meeting has not been revealed. However, MacArthur was determined to present both Dealey and Christie an army medal. In the end, he quite properly reversed the order, presenting Dealey the higher award, the Army Distinguished Service Cross, and Christie the Army Silver Star. Kinkaid was not pleased.

Wolf Packs in Luzon Strait

Immediately following the Battle of the Philippine Sea, Lockwood improvised a wolf pack for Luzon Strait composed of boats that had been deployed for the battle. These were Slade Cutter's *Seahorse*, Anton Gallaher's *Bang*, and Ben Oakley's *Growler*. The three boats met in the strait on June 25. Gallaher was senior, so he took command. Cutter and Oakley went on board *Bang* to plan tactics.

Shortly after midnight on June 27, Cutter picked up a ten-ship convoy: five big ships, five escorts. In keeping with pack policy, he prepared a contact alert but deferred sending it in the belief that both *Growler* and *Bang* were too far away to help. Cutter dived for a submerged attack, firing six torpedoes at a tanker and two freighters. He believed he got five out of six hits—three in the tanker, one each in two freighters. He wrote, "First hit in tanker at point of aim, forward of bridge. It was a beautiful hit, producing a huge sheet of flame and setting the ship on fire." Cutter was positive that the tanker and a freighter sank, but postwar records credited him only with the tanker, *Medan Maru*, 5,000 tons.

Gallaher in *Bang* was not as far away as Cutter thought. He saw the tanker burning on the horizon and closed in. But he was too late. The following night, Cutter and Gallaher rendezvoused again. Later, Cutter wrote, "*Bang* told us that they had seen the fire from our tanker last night and believed that they could have gotten in had we notified them early enough. If that is so, we made a grave error in judgment, and deeply regret the decision to maintain radio silence. We apologize to *Bang* for what they may consider a lack of cooperation on the part of *Seahorse*."

The next day, *Growler*, by now seriously low on fuel, departed for Midway, leaving Cutter and Gallaher as a two-boat pack. Oakley's fuel problem was so acute he was forced to proceed on only one engine. Nevertheless, on the day he left he found a cargo ship with four escorts and managed to track and attack. He sank *Katori Maru*, 2,000 tons, early on the morning of June 29. The ship was evidently carrying gasoline. It blew up with an awesome explosion, "like a 4th of July flowerpot."

Cutter and Gallaher went on patrolling the strait. Near dawn on June 29, Gallaher picked up another convoy. He made a long end around in daylight, getting off a contact report to Cutter. But *Seahorse* did not receive the report. About 3 P.M. Gallaher attacked the convoy submerged, firing ten torpedoes at three ships. Gallaher believed he had sunk one or two of the ships, but postwar records failed to confirm his estimate.

That night, Cutter noted in his report, "Received the rebroadcast of *Bang*'s dispatch reporting her brilliant attack this afternoon. Our radio had been manned continuously, but the contact reports the

Bang sent out were not received. Cannot understand this as we were hearing Jap stations clearly on the assigned frequency. We were particularly happy to hear of *Bang*'s good fortune in view of what happened the night before last."

On the night of July 3, Cutter picked up another convoy and flashed an alert to Gallaher. Then he closed in and fired at two freighters loaded with troops and equipment. He hit both. They each gave off many secondary explosions, probably caused by exploding gasoline drums. An escort charged in, forcing *Seahorse* deep. Forty minutes later, Cutter returned to periscope depth to find one ship sunk and the other severely damaged and lying to.

Meanwhile, Gallaher in *Bang*, receiving the contact report from Cutter, moved in to attack. He tried to torpedo the cripple, but a destroyer got in the way. Gallaher fired three torpedoes down the throat at the destroyer and went deep. At the last minute, the destroyer turned and avoided. Then it attacked *Bang*, dropping twenty depth charges.

After daylight, both Cutter and Gallaher made end arounds, gaining position ahead of the convoy. About noon, Cutter, who had ignored aircraft flying over him all morning, submerged ahead of the convoy to attack. He let the ships come close, so close that one passed directly over *Seahorse*. Cutter came up to periscope depth for a look at her stern. He wrote, "Troops were packed tight on the fantail and sitting up on the canvas-covered deck cargo. Every bit of deck space appeared to be utilized.... It was a fascinating picture."

Cutter fired at two of the freighters; he hit one and missed the other. Gallaher, harassed by aircraft and escorts, was not able to make an attack. Later he was commended for drawing off some of the escorts, enabling Cutter to make his attacks without excessive interference.

Following this attack, Cutter departed for Pearl Harbor, leaving Gallaher alone. Cutter had sunk four ships for about 11,000 tons. His total score in four patrols: nineteen ships. In his endorsement to Cutter's patrol report, Lockwood stated, "This was the fourth successive brilliantly conducted war patrol for *Seahorse*." He presented Cutter with his fourth Navy Cross.

When Cutter returned to Midway for refit, he was exhausted and asked for two weeks' leave to return to the States to see his wife and young daughter. Babe Brown gave him thirty days, turning *Seahorse* over to Weary Wilkins, who had come from BuPers and was anxious to make one more war patrol in a "modern boat." "Weary was wonderful," Cutter said later, "and said *Seahorse* was my boat and he was only borrowing it for one run. He said he would change nothing and didn't—including taking along young Budding, whom I had promised to be exec."

After Cutter had been home for a while, he received unexpected orders to new construction—*Requin*, which his wife was to sponsor at commissioning. "By this time," Cutter said later, "I had accepted the new situation and was perfectly willing to remain with my family."

Like the late Mush Morton, Slade Cutter had been an inspiration to the submarine force, a skipper's skipper and Lockwood's pride and joy. Like Burlingame and Triebel, Cutter was sometimes a terror while unwinding on the beach. But at sea he was awesomely cool and able, and possessed of an uncanny ability to find Japanese ships. (Lockwood wrote, in jest, that he believed that, if asked, Cutter could even find Japanese ships in Pearl Harbor.) In the postwar accounting, his nineteen confirmed ships sunk put him in a tie for second place with Mush Morton for the greatest number of ships sunk by a U.S. skipper. For years afterward, whenever submariners gathered to recount the war and spin yarns, the name of Slade Deville Cutter —football star, heavyweight boxer, and submariner extraordinary— would soon surface.

Three other wolf packs patrolled Luzon Strait during this period. Between them they sank twelve ships, by postwar accounting.

One of them began as a four-boat pack: *Apogon*, commanded by Walter Schoeni; a new boat, *Piranha*, commanded by Harold Eustace Ruble; *Thresher*, commanded by Duncan MacMillan; and *Guardfish*, back from a long overhaul and still commanded by Bub Ward. The commander was William Vincent ("Mickey") O'Regan, who called his pack the "Mickey Finns." O'Regan, who commanded Submarine Division 42, rode in *Guardfish*.

Late in the evening of July 11, the Mickey Finns moved in on a convoy. Harold Ruble in *Piranha* sank one ship for 6,500 tons, but Schoeni's boat, making a submerged attack, was rammed: the leading freighter in the center column hit *Apogon* on the starboard side, bending the periscopes and shears 45 degrees, tearing off the number-one periscope, and flooding the conning tower. Seven depth charges rained down. Schoeni managed to hold everything together, and *Apogon* escaped to go to overhaul. Schoeni, congratulated for saving his boat, went to shore duty.

Now short one boat, O'Regan received an Ultra on July 15 on an important southbound convoy. The pack changed course to intercept —all but *Piranha*, which didn't receive the message. Ironically it was *Piranha*, off course, that found the convoy at 4 A.M. and flashed the word. While *Guardfish* and *Thresher* were coming up, Ruble sank another ship.

That night—July 16—Ward in *Guardfish* closed the convoy for a night surface attack. He counted ten ships and several escorts. He fired six torpedoes at five overlapping ships, including a tanker. As he later described it, "The tanker was loaded with gas and blew up immediately, sending flames thousands of feet high. The large freighter was also loaded with combustibles, commencing to burn aft, and later blew up. The third ship in line, a freighter, broke in two in the middle and sank, and the fourth ship in line went down bow first. The scene was lit up as bright as day by the explosions and burning ships."

Ward then maneuvered around for a stern shot, firing three torpedoes at a freighter. One torpedo missed, two hit. Ward wrote, "Target leaned over on its starboard side and disappeared from sight and SJ [radar] screen." Finding another target, Ward "became impatient" and fired two torpedoes which missed. He turned around and fired two more at the same target. Both hit. Ward believed the ship sank, but he claimed only damage. He hauled clear to reload and rest, noting, "Everyone in the control party was beginning to show fatigue after six hours at battle stations under constant tensions. . . . Commanding Officer had had no rest for over fifty hours."

In action no less furious, MacMillan in *Thresher* attacked the convoy from another quarter, firing off twenty-three torpedoes. He believed he had sunk four ships and two destroyers, but postwar records credited him with only two ships: *Sainei Maru*, 5,000 tons, and *Shozan Maru*, 2,800 tons. Ward believed he had sunk five ships during his series of attacks, but postwar analysis gave him credit for three: *Jinzan Maru*, 5,200 tons; *Mantai Maru*, 5,900 tons; and *Hiyama Maru*, 2,800 tons. There was no record of a tanker sunk on this night at this place.

When Ward came back up at 6 P.M. on July 18, having rested himself and his crew, he found that a gale had kicked up huge seas. But he had surfaced in the middle of a massive convoy: two aircraft carriers (type unknown), two large tankers, one transport, one seaplane tender, and a naval auxiliary—all southbound. Ward fired three bow tubes at the naval auxiliary, range 1,370 yards. He swung to set up on a tanker, but it was coming in to ram, so Ward had to go deep to avoid and lost contact.

At dawn the following morning, July 19, he found yet another convoy. He submerged and fired four torpedoes at a target. One of them made a circular run around *Guardfish*; two hit. "Target broke in half immediately," he reported later. In these two attacks, according to postwar records, Ward sank only one ship, *Teiryu Maru*, 6,500 tons.

Following Bub Ward's attack, the Mickey Finns, out of torpedoes, left the area and returned to Midway. In all, the pack had sunk eight confirmed ships for about 40,000 tons, making it the best wolf-pack performance to date. Bub Ward, who had fired twenty torpedoes in the space of fifty-six hours, sank half: four ships for 20,400 tons.

A second pack operating in the strait arrived to attack Ward's convoy of the nineteenth. It consisted of three boats: John Flachsenhar's *Rock*, Alan Boyd Banister's *Sawfish*, and Roger Keithly's *Tilefish*. (Gallaher in *Bang* had come down from Formosa to join the pack for about nine days and had returned to base independently.) The pack, "Wilkin's Wildcats," was commanded by Warren Dudley Wilkin, head of Division 142, in *Tilefish*. All three boats closed and inflicted damage, but postwar records credited no ships sunk.

More significant action came a week later, when they were alerted by Ultra to an important contact. A Japanese submarine, *I-29*, was returning from a sea voyage to Germany, bringing a "precious cargo" (as Jasper Holmes later put it) of "German technical material." *Tilefish*, *Rock*, and *Sawfish* formed an ambush. The prize fell to Banister in *Sawfish*. When a submarine came along, right on schedule, Banister fired four torpedoes, three of which hit. Keithly in *Tilefish* was beginning an approach when he saw the explosion.

There was no immediate rejoicing in Pearl Harbor when Banister reported sinking what he assumed to be *I-29*. Nothing had been heard from Ruble's *Piranha* since the Mickey Finns had cleared the area, and Lockwood and Voge were convinced that, by a tragic error, Banister had actually sunk *Piranha*. It wasn't till a few days later that Ruble spoke up with a radio dispatch and Lockwood breathed easier.

The third wolf pack in the Luzon Strait in July was commanded by Lew Parks, riding Red Ramage's *Parche*. Besides *Parche*, the pack was made up of Dave Whelchel's *Steelhead* and a new boat, *Ham-*

merhead, commanded by John Croysdale Martin.* "Parks' Pirates," as the pack was called, had spent much of its patrol in frustration since leaving Midway on June 17. En route, Red Ramage had bagged just one small patrol craft with *Parche*'s deck gun. In the strait on July 5, when Ramage was moving in to attack what appeared to be two cruisers and a destroyer, he had to take his boat deep when one of the cruisers opened fire and he lost contact. After many days of bad weather and no targets, Parks received a report from Ward, on the Mickey Finns' boat *Guardfish*, of the massive convoy Ward had discovered on July 18, when he'd surfaced in its midst. Parks' Pirates never made contact with it. On the way to intercept, Parks and Ramage came upon an unescorted aircraft carrier—"the perfect dream come true"—only to have this vulnerable target zig and escape them.

It was only after eleven empty days that Parks' Pirates made their next convoy contact, and again bad luck plagued them. In the early hours of July 30, Martin in *Hammerhead* picked up a big convoy—twelve to fifteen freighters and tankers and many escorts—and flashed the alert. While Martin trailed, Red Ramage and Dave Whelchel moved in. With daylight fast approaching, Martin attacked, firing ten torpedoes at two big ships. He believed he sank one and damaged another, but postwar records showed no sinking at this time and place. Martin then attempted to trail the convoy submerged, but it got away. That night, running low on fuel, he surfaced and set course for Fremantle.

The contact reports that Martin flashed to Parks and Ramage were confused, erroneous, and niggardly. While Martin attacked, both Ramage and Whelchel thrashed around the dark seas, unable to make contact. They were somewhat puzzled, then angry. Ramage wrote bitterly, "As the sun came up, it finally dawned on us that we were the victims of another snipe hunt. That was bad enough but we never expected to be left holding the well known burlap bag by one of our own teammates."†

During the day, July 30, Whelchel and Ramage kept up the hunt, both harassed by planes. At 10:30 A.M., Whelchel spotted smoke and sent off a contact report. At about noon, Ramage saw the smoke, trailed, then lost it. After dark, Whelchel, who was still in contact,

---

* Martin himself was called "Hammerhead," a nickname he got after he became the first skipper of that submarine.

† Ramage learned later that partly as a result of these faulty contact reports, Martin's communications officer, who had coded and transmitted them, was removed at Martin's request from further sea duty in submarines.

vectored Ramage into position. At 2:40 A.M. on the morning of July 31, Ramage made radar contact and went to battle stations.

Meanwhile, Whelchel attacked. At 3:32 A.M. he fired ten torpedoes at a tanker and two freighters. He observed a hit in the first freighter and black smoke near the waterline of the tanker. He missed the second freighter. He pulled off and began reloading his torpedo tubes.

The next forty-eight minutes were among the wildest of the submarine war. Ramage cleared the bridge of all personnel except himself and steamed right into the convoy on the surface, maneuvering among the ships and firing nineteen torpedoes. Japanese ships fired back with deck guns and tried to ram. With consummate seamanship and coolness under fire, Ramage dodged and twisted, returning torpedo fire for gunfire.

After Ramage hauled clear, Whelchel came in again. At 4:49, he fired four stern tubes at a freighter. He heard two explosions and saw a flash under the stacks. At 5:16, he fired four bow tubes at another freighter, observing two hits amidships. Escorts charged, forcing Whelchel under. He received a bone-jarring depth-charging.

Both boats remained submerged the following day, and that night Parks gave orders to leave the area. When the pack returned to Pearl Harbor, Lockwood credited Ramage with sinking five ships for 34,000 tons, Whelchel two ships for 14,000 tons. In the postwar reckoning, Ramage received confirmation for sinking two ships for 14,700 tons, Whelchel two for 15,400. In addition, each skipper received half credit for sinking the 9,000-ton transport *Yoshino Maru*. Total for both: five ships, 39,000 tons.

The attack mounted on the convoy by Red Ramage was the talk of the submarine force. In terms of close-in, furious torpedo shooting, there had never been anything like it. Although the score was no record, Lockwood's staff believed Ramage deserved more than a Navy Cross. Accordingly, the recommendation went forward that Ramage be awarded the Medal of Honor. The recommendation was subsequently approved and Ramage became the third—and at the time the only living—submariner, after Howard Gilmore and John Cromwell, to receive this recognition.

Patrols in the East and South China Seas

Three boats went to the East China Sea. They were not a formal wolf pack, since they operated in separate—but adjacent—areas, but they mapped out a semicoordinated attack plan. The boats were Dick O'Kane's *Tang*, Donald Weiss's *Tinosa*, and a new boat, *Sealion II*, commanded by Eli Reich.

Weiss in *Tinosa* went to the area by way of the Bonins. On the night of June 15 he sighted a five-ship convoy: two tankers, a small transport, and two destroyer escorts. He tracked and dived for a daylight attack, firing six torpedoes at the two tankers. All missed and the destroyers charged in, forcing Weiss deep. He was not able to make another attack.

On the night of June 18, Weiss battle-surfaced on a fishing sampan, riddling the craft with small-arms fire and getting an occasional hit with the deck gun. When the sampan stubbornly refused to sink, Weiss decided on more drastic action. Later he wrote, "Tommy guns, hand grenades, rags and fuel oil were mustered topside. Moving close aboard the sailer, rag firebrands and about a half a dozen buckets of fuel oil were tossed on board. . . . The target quickly became a raging mass of flame."

On the night of June 24, the three boats rendezvoused about 120 miles southwest of Nagasaki. Since Donald Weiss was the senior skipper, O'Kane and Reich sent their execs, Murray Frazee and Henry Conrad Lauerman, to *Tinosa* for a strategy meeting.

The next night O'Kane picked up a large convoy heading into Nagasaki. He flashed the word to *Tinosa* and *Sealion*, but neither boat was able to close, so O'Kane had this one all to himself. It consisted of six large ships with an enormous number of escorts, probably sixteen. O'Kane came in on the surface, firing six torpedoes at a freighter and tanker. Later, he wrote, "Observed two beautiful hits in the stern and amidships of the freighter. . . . The explosions appeared to blow the ship's sides out and he commenced sinking rapidly. . . . Our fourth and fifth torpedoes hit under the stack and just forward of the superstructure of the tanker. His whole after end blazed up until extinguished as he went down by the stern." Escorts drove *Tang* under.

O'Kane claimed two sinkings for that night and Lockwood so credited him, but O'Kane's torpedoes evidently did far more damage than he thought. Postwar Japanese records revealed that four ships of the convoy went down: two transports and two freighters, totaling 16,000 tons. If the records are accurate, it means that O'Kane sank four ships with six torpedoes, making this the single best attack of the war. If his report that he saw two torpedo hits in both the freighter and tanker is correct, then the other two torpedoes got one ship each.

After that, the three boats moved northward, taking station off the southwest coast of Korea in the shallow waters of the Yellow Sea. On June 26, O'Kane picked up a lone freighter and fired four torpedoes. All missed. On June 28, Eli Reich in *Sealion* sank a 2,400-ton ship near the minefields in Korea Strait. The next day, O'Kane picked up another single, fired two torpedoes, and missed again. He attacked this ship a second time, firing a single torpedo. Down went *Nikkin Maru*, a 5,700-ton freighter. On July 1, O'Kane sank a small freighter and a small tanker.

Two days later, O'Kane and Reich rendezvoused again to compare notes. (Weiss in *Tinosa* had moved south.) Reich decided to have a look near Shanghai; O'Kane would stay off the coast of Korea. The following day, July 4, O'Kane sank two large freighters: 6,886-ton *Asukazan Maru* and 7,000-ton *Yamaika Maru*, from which he took a prisoner. On July 6, he fired his last torpedoes at a 1,500-ton freighter. It sank immediately.

While O'Kane and Reich were conferring on July 3, Weiss found a convoy and sank two ships: *Kosan Maru*, 2,700 tons, and *Kamo Maru*, 8,000 tons. Reich also found other ships. On July 6, off Shanghai, he sank a 2,000-ton freighter; moving up into the shallows of the Yellow Sea on July 11, he sank two more ships, one for 2,400 tons and one for 1,000 tons.

One by one the three boats left the area and returned to base. When *Tang* reached Midway, Lockwood credited O'Kane with sinking eight ships for 56,000 tons. In the postwar accounting, the number of sinkings was readjusted upward to ten and the tonnage cut to 39,100. In terms of confirmed ships sunk, this was the best war patrol by any submarine in the war. For it, O'Kane received his third Navy Cross.

Eli Reich in *Sealion II* turned in an excellent maiden patrol; he had sunk four confirmed ships for 7,800 tons. Weiss sank two confirmed ships. After this patrol, he took *Tinosa* back for an overhaul and then moved up to command a division. In three patrols on *Tinosa*, Weiss had sunk eight confirmed ships for 40,000 tons.

Altogether, the three-boat foray into the East China Sea cost the Japanese sixteen confirmed ships for 58,000 tons.

Ralph Christie's first formal wolf pack put to sea in June shortly after the Battle of the Philippine Sea. It consisted of three boats: Reuben Whitaker's *Flasher*, Frank Walker's *Crevalle*, and *Angler*, now commanded by Franklin Hess, who had been Jensen's exec on the disastrous first patrol of *Puffer*. Whitaker, the senior skipper, commanded the pack. To avoid a concentration in Lombok Strait, the boats left for patrol in the South China Sea independently.

Whitaker went up through Lombok Strait into the Java Sea. He traveled along the southern coast of Borneo, going through Karimata Strait, until he reached the equator, directly on the Surabaya–Singapore traffic lanes. Shortly after sunset on June 28, he picked up a thirteen-ship convoy bound for Singapore. Because the water was shallow and pitted with uncharted shoals and reefs, Whitaker elected to attack on the surface. He fired six torpedoes at two freighters, obtaining hits in both. "The first target," he later wrote, "with three hits, was seen to break in two and sink almost immediately." It was *Nippo Maru*, a 6,000-ton freighter. Whitaker believed the second also went down, but postwar records failed to bear him out.

While waiting for the other members of his pack to arrive, Whitaker took up station north of Camranh Bay. On the night of July 7, he saw a freighter with one escort. He sank the freighter, *Koto Maru*, 3,500 tons, with four stern tubes. The escorts zipped back and forth menacingly but never did find *Flasher*.

On July 13, *Angler* and *Crevalle* arrived and the pack was officially formed up. For five days, the boats rotated between the middle of the South China Sea and the Indochina coast, finding nothing. Whitaker, somewhat discouraged, got off a message to Christie stating that in view of the lack of traffic he doubted the need for three submarines to patrol the area; then he ordered a routine surface patrol on July 19 in the middle of the South China Sea.

At 10:46 that morning, Whitaker's officer of the deck saw a ship approaching through the haze and dived immediately. When Whitaker got a look through the periscope, his heart skipped a beat; the target he saw was a Japanese light cruiser escorted by a single destroyer, approaching at 18 knots. Whitaker set up quickly. Twenty-four minutes after diving, he fired four stern tubes at the cruiser. The destroyer was a mere 500 yards distant, headed dead on. "Don't think he saw us," Whitaker recorded, "but he sure looks mean."

Whitaker went deep, hearing two torpedoes hit. The destroyer dropped fifteen depth charges, but Whitaker outwitted him and eased away. An hour and twenty minutes after shooting, Whitaker came to periscope depth for a look. He saw the cruiser stopped dead in the water, down by the stern with a port list. At 1:26 P.M., Whitaker moved in for another attack, firing four bow tubes. The destroyer charged again, forcing Whitaker deep. Something went wrong with the attack. "I didn't see how we could miss," Whitaker wrote, "but we did." Whitaker took *Flasher* deep. The destroyer dropped thirteen more charges, none close.

While down, Whitaker was forced to reload, a time-consuming process, since it had to be carried out with absolute silence. When he came up again at 4:08, the destroyer was there but the cruiser was gone. Whitaker did not know whether the cruiser had sunk or had crept off toward Saigon. Assuming the latter, Whitaker surfaced after dark and alerted *Angler* and *Crevalle* to watch for a damaged cruiser heading for Saigon. For the next twenty-four hours, Whitaker jockeyed the boats around, looking for the cruiser. It was all wasted effort. Whitaker's first salvo had been successful, and the light cruiser *Oi*, 5,700 tons, had gone down while he was reloading.

Christie next ordered the pack to move up the South China Sea to a position off the west coast of Luzon, north of Manila. About dawn on July 25, Hess in *Angler* picked up a large northbound convoy and flashed the word. An hour later, Whitaker found it and got off a contact report but was driven down by an airplane. An hour and a half later, the entire convoy passed directly over Whitaker. He raised his periscope to find one escort passing over his after torpedo room, 100 feet away from the periscope. In his look, Whitaker counted fourteen large ships plus half a dozen escorts.

At that time, Whitaker had only six torpedoes. Since both *Crevalle* and *Angler* had a full load, Whitaker believed it would be better if Walker and Hess attacked first; then he could pick off what was left. He let the convoy go by and trailed. At 12:22, Walker in *Crevalle* submerged in a driving downpour, made a snap setup, and fired four stern tubes at one of the largest freighters. At the moment of firing, Walker sighted an escort carrier which was evidently providing the convoy air protection. After the torpedoes left the tubes, he lost depth control, almost broached, then went deep. Escorts found him and dropped fifty-two depth charges.

After dark, Whitaker surfaced, regained contact with the convoy, and flashed a report to his packmates. At 2:11 on the following morning, July 26, he attacked, firing his last six torpedoes at two ships, obtaining two hits in one freighter and one in another. He was feeling pretty good about that, he reported later, but then "our feeling of security" came to an abrupt end. One of his torpedoes had run through the near formation and hit a tanker beyond. Whitaker wrote that

the whole scene was lighted up as bright as daylight by the explosion of a tanker in the center column. One of our torpedoes which had missed the second target hit this large tanker about amidships. The ocean appeared full of ships and we were in an uncomfortable position. We cleared the bridge immediately and started down. By the time we hit fifty feet we could hear shells landing all around where we had been. We felt that we must have been seen and went to three hundred feet, turning at high speed and expecting an immediate depth charge attack. Although many high speed screws passed over us, and although escorts were pinging in our vicinity for a long time, it appears that they still thought we were on the surface as they dropped no depth charges. We were giving out a tremendous cloud of smoke when we submerged, and I believe that they were firing at our smoke thinking that we were still on the surface. We took a southerly course to clear the vicinity in order to surface and trail.

The tanker, which blew up and sank, was *Otoriyama Maru*, 5,280 tons.

After Whitaker withdrew, Frank Walker moved in for a second attack, firing nine torpedoes at two freighters just before dawn. He believed he hit and sank both targets, but postwar records failed to credit him. Escorts drove *Crevalle* deep. When Walker came up again, he saw a ship Whitaker had damaged. He fired four torpedoes, obtaining four hits. The ship, *Tosan Maru*, an 8,700-ton transport, sank quickly, while Walker snapped pictures of it through the periscope. Escorts again drove Walker deep, delivering many depth charges.

That night, when all the boats surfaced, Whitaker reported he was out of torpedoes and returning to Fremantle. The next-senior skipper, Frank Walker, took command of the pack. Two days later, Walker and Hess picked up another convoy: eight ships, four escorts. Walker fired his last six torpedoes, sinking the 6,600-ton transport *Hakubasan Maru*. Hess made two attacks but failed to achieve any sinkings.

This first formal Fremantle pack had done well. Whitaker had sunk four and a half confirmed ships for almost 25,000 tons (sharing credit with Walker for *Tosan Maru*); Walker had sunk one and a half ships for almost 11,000 tons. (Hess had sunk no confirmed ships.) The pack as a whole got six ships for about 36,000 tons.

Manning Kimmel in *Robalo* was sent to Indochina via Balabac Strait, a maze of waterways and islands. By that time, the codebreakers had given Christie at least four intercepted messages regarding Japanese minefields in Balabac Strait, containing specific details on which waters were mined—or likely to be mined. Kimmel's Operations Order contained specific information on how to transit the strait and what to avoid. Since the Japanese mined the strait in March 1943, it had been used about forty times by U.S. submarines. In 1944 *Crevalle*, *Tinosa*, *Puffer*, *Ray*, *Bluefish*, and *Lapon* (among others) had passed through safely. Kimmel himself in *Robalo* had passed through it in April, westbound to Indochina on his first patrol.

On July 3 Kimmel again made the transit, passing into the South China Sea. That same night, he received an Ultra and intercepted a *Fuso*-class battleship. He got off a contact report but did not state whether or not he had attacked it—probably not. It was the last message received from Kimmel. He then apparently patrolled his assigned area off Indochina without success. On July 26 he set course for Australia, returning via Balabac Strait. That night, while traveling on the surface, Kimmel evidently strayed into shallow waters. *Robalo* struck a mine, blew up, and sank swiftly.

Kimmel and perhaps half a dozen men—probably flung from the bridge into the water—may have survived the explosion. They made their way through the jungle up the east coast of Palawan, looking for friendly guerrillas. Instead, the Japanese found them and put them in jail at the Puerto Princesa prison camp, on the island. A few days later one of the *Robalo* prisoners managed to drop a note from a window to a U.S. Army prisoner who was on a work detail outside. The note described the loss of *Robalo* (by mine) and named four survivors held in that part of the prison. The army POW turned the note over to a U.S. Navy POW, who later made contact with the wife of a guerrilla leader. Her husband, a Dr. Mendosa, in turn relayed word that ultimately reached Christie.

None of *Robalo*'s survivors—the exact number has never been determined—survived the war. Many, perhaps all, were murdered by the Japanese on Palawan.

There were two versions of Manning Kimmel's death. During the war, Christie's command put out the word (and told his family) that he went down with the boat. After the war, Christie gave a grimmer version. He said that he received word from intelligence (probably from the guerrillas on Palawan) that when some Allied aircraft attacked Palawan, the Japanese became enraged, "went into a frenzy, pushed Kimmel and some other POWs in a ditch, then poured gasoline into the ditch and set it on fire." According to this version, Manning Kimmel died in the blaze.

Manning's brother Thomas, who had just returned to Christie's command as exec of a new boat, was summoned to Christie's office after one patrol. Christie informed Thomas that he was being relieved and sent to shore duty and that he could not and would not change the orders. Later Thomas recalled, "Dusty Dornin told me that Admiral King had directed I be ordered home when he found out about my brother being lost." This was a great disappointment to Thomas, who had hoped to move up to command before the war ended. (In the final days, he was ordered to command *Bergall*—too late to make a war patrol.) *

All this submarine activity had a devastating impact on Japan. Now that wolf-packing had been formalized and perfected and the torpedoes fixed, Japan was losing an average fifty merchant ships a month for about 200,000 tons. There was no way the shipbuilding yards could keep pace. Imports—especially oil imports—fell off drastically. There was a critical shortage of escorts for the convoys, and mounting chaos in the ranks of Japanese merchant seamen. Many hundreds were shipwrecked and marooned in southern waters, unable to get home. Others feared to leave Japanese home waters and sail off into the crosshairs of a hundred U.S. periscopes, almost certain of attack and perhaps a terrifying death at sea.

---

* Years later, Thomas held the opinion that *Robalo* had not strayed off course but that the Japanese had probably changed the position of the minefield. He doubted Christie's wisdom in continuing to use Balabac Strait this late in the war. Wrote Thomas, "The Japanese were obviously in retreat and the urgency for transiting a dangerous strait with known minefields was certainly greatly reduced if not nonexistent."

31
Washington, Summer 1944

In Washington, the breaking of Japanese and German codes had become a huge enterprise and a massive bureaucracy. By mid-1944 there were well over 5,000 people engaged directly or indirectly in the task. The navy had established a Japanese language school; it had recruited hundreds of reserves to help with codebreaking—including people such as the famous bridge expert Oswald Jacoby. Thanks to a combination of codebreaking and direction finding, U-boats in the Atlantic were being hounded and sunk by the dozens.

That summer, two episodes shook the bureaucracy to its foundations and threatened to blow the whole operation.

The first was an unknowing blunder by a navy captain, Daniel Vincent Gallery. Gallery commanded a navy hunter-killer group in the Atlantic whose mission was to sink U-boats. In the spring of 1944, Gallery conceived a plan to capture one of these U-boats intact. With this in mind, he trained a special boarding team that would rush inside a U-boat, close the sea cocks, and prevent scuttling.

On May 31, 1944, Gallery was put on the trail of *U-505*, which was returning to base in Brest, France, from war patrol. On the morning of June 4, one of Gallery's vessels found it off Cape Blanco, French West Africa, and forced it to the surface with depth charges. The Nazi captain abandoned ship. One of Gallery's destroyers, *Pills-*

bury, quickly lowered a whaleboat carrying the boarding team, led by Lieutenant (j.g.) Albert L. David. David and his men performed brilliantly, shutting off sea cocks and dismantling demolition charges. *U-505* was seized intact, the first enemy man-of-war captured by the U.S. Navy since the War of 1812. David later received a Medal of Honor, his teammates the Navy Cross.

Although Gallery's accomplishment has survived in navy annals as one of the more brilliant feats of World War II, Admiral King and the codebreakers viewed it otherwise. When they learned of the capture of *U-505* they were thunderstruck—and furious.

If word got back to Admiral Doenitz that one of his U-boats had been captured intact, he would assume that the codebooks had fallen into U.S. hands (as they had) and would undoubtedly completely change the U-boat codes, requiring another massive (and perhaps unsuccessful) attempt to break them.* According to Al McCann, who was then commanding the 10th Fleet (the paperwork fleet charged with wiping out the U-boats), King was angry enough to want to court-martial Gallery.

Gallery had planned to tow the U-boat into a U.S. base in North Africa. Admiral King immediately sent orders to tow it to Norfolk and to swear the whole hunter-killer group to strictest secrecy. This was a monumental task, since there were about 3,000 men in the group, but Gallery managed to do it and his career was saved. No word leaked out. Doenitz never knew *U-505* had been captured; he assumed it was sunk. †

The second episode was political.

The Republican Party, led by Governor Thomas E. Dewey of New York, the presidential candidate in 1944, sought a powerful issue with which to unseat the entrenched Roosevelt, then running for a fourth term. The many secret investigations into the Pearl Harbor attack conducted up to that time had led to the impression in some circles that Roosevelt had had, through codebreaking, ample warning of the Japanese attack and had been derelict in preventing it. Admiral Kim-

---

* In 1943, operatives of the Office of Strategic Services (OSS) broke into the Japanese Embassy in Portugal without first informing Marshall, King, or the codebreakers. As a result, the Japanese had changed the entire military attaché code. It had not yet been broken again, and the United States had lost an important source of information, particularly regarding the European situation.

† After the war, *U-505* was towed to Chicago and wound up as a display outside the Museum of Science and Industry.

mel and his anti-Roosevelt backers (which included the *Chicago Tribune*) were eager to foster that impression, which Kimmel sincerely believed to be fact. Some extremist Republican isolationists (and a few extremist naval officers) even professed to believe that Roosevelt had deliberately invited the Japanese attack in order to involve the United States in the war.

To many Republicans, all this seemed a heaven-sent issue. Some hinted at it publicly: for example, Congressman Forest A. Harness of Indiana, who said on the House floor that "the government had learned very confidentially that instructions were sent out from the Japanese government to all Japanese emissaries in this hemisphere to destroy the codes."

Would Dewey go all the way and break the secret? Admiral King and General Marshall feared he might. General Marshall, with King concurring, took it upon himself to warn Dewey that any disclosure about codebreaking at that point in the war would be a grave disservice to the country and the war effort. He wrote a three-page single-spaced letter to Dewey, which stated that none of the codebreaking information obtained prior to the Pearl Harbor attack disclosed Japanese intentions on Hawaii. Marshall went on to say:

> *Now the point to the present dilemma is that we have gone ahead with this business of deciphering their codes until we possess other codes, German as well as Japanese, but our main basis of information regarding Hitler's intentions in Europe is obtained from Baron Oshima's messages from Berlin reporting his interviews with Hitler and other officials to the Japanese government. These are still in the codes involved in the Pearl Harbor events.*
>
> *To explain further the critical nature of this set-up which would be wiped out almost in an instant if the least suspicion were aroused regarding it, the battle of the Coral Sea was based on deciphered messages and therefore our few ships were in the right place at the right time. Further, we were able to concentrate our limited forces to meet their naval advance on Midway when otherwise we almost certainly would have been some 3,000 miles out of place. We had full information of the strength of their forces in that advance and also of the smaller force directed against the Aleutians which finally landed troops on Attu and Kiska.*
>
> *Operations in the Pacific are largely guided by information we obtain of Japanese deployments. We know their strength in various*

garrisons, the rations and other stores continuing available to them, and what is of vast importance, we check their fleet movements and movements of their convoys. The heavy losses reported from time to time which they sustain by reason of our submarine action largely result from the fact that we know the sailing dates and routes of their convoys and can notify our submarines to lie in wait at the proper points....

The conduct of General Eisenhower's campaign and of all operations in the Pacific are closely related in conception and timing to the information we secretly obtain through these intercepted codes. They contribute greatly to the victory and tremendously to the saving in American lives, both in the conduct of the current operations and in looking towards an early termination of the war.

I am presenting this matter to you in the hope that you will see your way clear to avoid the tragic results with which we are now threatened in the present political campaign.

After reading this letter, Dewey decided against making the Pearl Harbor attack a political issue. The codebreakers breathed easier.

32

Pearl Harbor and Australia, July and August 1944

Debate over Pacific Strategy

After the Marianas were secure, the next steps on the dual road to Tokyo were for MacArthur's forces to invade Morotai, an island off the northeast tip of Halmahera, and for Nimitz's forces to invade the Palaus. After that, the two roads would merge into one for an assault on the Philippines: Mindanao, then Luzon. Once the Philippines had been recaptured, fulfilling MacArthur's promise to return, the merged forces would push northward to Formosa and the Japanese homeland, securing the western flank by capturing bastions along the coast of China.

In Washington, Admiral King and his war planners (who now included Jimmy Fife) began to have second thoughts. King objected to the idea of "battering our way through the Philippines." He proposed that the Philippines be bypassed altogether and that Allied forces move directly against Formosa. With Formosa in Allied hands, the navy could "put a cork in the bottle" of Japanese sea communications, choking off shipping between Japan and the southern possessions. King believed Japan could be strangled by submarine blockade while U.S. carrier units and B-29s basing from the Marianas pounded her warmaking potentional to rubble.

This was a bold and imaginative idea. While it is doubtful that air strikes on the Japanese homeland would have inflicted sufficiently severe damage (as time would prove), a submarine blockade could have been decisive. Between them, Lockwood and Christie now had almost 140 fleet boats (roughly 100 at Pearl Harbor and 40 in Australia) manned by combat-wise officers and crews. The torpedo problems had finally been licked: both the Mark XIV steam and Mark XVIII electric were completely debugged and the production bottleneck had been overcome.* The codebreakers were tracking most major Japanese ship and convoy movements. They knew the precise location and composition of Japanese minefields. Japanese antisubmarine warfare tactics had been proven relatively ineffective. After a fumbling, inept, and much-belated beginning, Lockwood had worked out the search, communications, and attack problems of wolf-packing. The Marianas were merely a three-day voyage from Tokyo and the gateway to the East China Sea.

With Formosa in Allied hands and a submarine blockade imposed on the homeland, the flow of oil and other strategic materials to Japan could have been shut off completely. Under conditions of total sea blockade, Japan would soon have used up her remaining oil reserves, immobilizing ships, aircraft, automobiles, electrical plants and production lines. Conceivably, Japan could have been "starved out" and demoralized to the point of surrender within a matter of two or three months. "In every phase of the war," the U.S. Strategic Bombing Survey reported, "oil determined Japan's strategy and governed the tactical operations of its Navy and Air Forces."

When MacArthur heard about this new idea, he was outraged. For one thing, it was clear that if the new strategy were adopted General MacArthur would play only a minor role. For another, MacArthur had promised to return to the Philippines, and now that promise might not be carried out. Some sixteen million Filipinos, MacArthur complained, would be left to "wither on the vine" until Japan was defeated. He argued that if the new strategy were adopted the Filipinos would continue to suffer unspeakable hardship for an indefinite period, and all Asia would lose faith in American honor. Admiral King rejoined that he was reluctant to slow up the war and shed American blood for mere sentimental reasons.

The debate was dumped into President Roosevelt's lap. On a trip to Honolulu, he met with Nimitz and MacArthur, who flew up from

---

* Beginning in July 1944, boats going on patrol carried 75 percent electrics, 25 percent steam. The speed of the electric had been increased to about 40 knots, depending on water temperature.

Brisbane. During these meetings, MacArthur eloquently presented his case. Nimitz, who was not wholly in favor of the direct thrust at Formosa, did not strongly oppose MacArthur, and years later he said he thought MacArthur was correct. Roosevelt made no hard and fast decision in Honolulu. In the weeks following, the Joint Chiefs of Staff, vastly overrating Japan's ability to continue the war of production and strongly influenced by General Marshall, who finally backed MacArthur's concept, decided the original plan for liberating the Philippines should be adhered to. The dual roads would merge at the Palaus and Morotai on September 15, as scheduled, and then point toward Mindanao, Leyte, and Luzon.

In the final analysis, Pacific strategy was dictated by political expediency and the considerable ego of General MacArthur. In giving way to his arguments, the Joint Chiefs committed the United States to tens of thousands of unnecessary casualties. Even though Britain had twice been brought to the point of collapse by German submarines in two wars, they overlooked the tremendous potential of the existing submarine force. Not only that; from this decision onward, the submarine force was called upon more and more to provide support for Allied invasion forces—guerrilla activity in the Philippines, photographic reconnaissance, lifeguard duty, scouting for enemy fleet units—all of which reduced the number of submarines on anticommerce patrol and needlessly prolonged the war.

Patrols from Pearl Harbor

In the lull between the invasion of the Marianas and the invasion of the Palaus and Morotai during July and August 1944, Lockwood and Christie mounted over ninety war patrols. Many were special missions in the Philippines or in support of fleet operations; many others were wolf packs; one boat, William Perkins's *Burrfish*, took a team of eleven frogmen to explore the beaches at Peleliu and Yap. A few of Lockwood's boats used the facilities at Saipan provided by *Holland*; Christie's Brisbane-based boats left from the new base at Manus Island in the Admiralties and resupplied at the new base in Mios Woendi. Many boats went to Luzon Strait to shut off the flow of reinforcements from Japan to the Philippines and the flow of oil from the south to Japan. In order to give Lockwood's submarines more legroom in the strait, the boundary separating the two commands was moved 90 miles south. In some cases, Lockwood's submarines and

Christie's submarines attacked the same convoys, passing along information.

A new boat, *Hardhead*, commanded by a colorful character, Fitzhugh McMaster, set off from Pearl Harbor for Fremantle. Along the way McMaster was assigned to patrol San Bernardino Strait. Shortly after midnight on August 18, he picked up two large pips on his radar. About an hour and a half later, he could see the targets through binoculars at 8,000 yards. He—and others on *Hardhead*—believed them to be one battleship and one light cruiser. *Hardhead* maneuvered to intercept.

At 2:37 A.M., from 2,800 yards, McMaster fired at the "battleship"—five bow torpedoes and then four stern tubes. The bow tubes missed, but one or two of the stern-tube shots hit, causing an explosion and flame. In the glow, McMaster believed he had hit and sunk a battleship. He then chased the "cruiser," achieving attack position just before dawn and firing six more torpedoes. He believed that some of these hit and the "cruiser" went down too.

In all, McMaster had fired fifteen torpedoes, claiming ten hits which sank a battleship and a cruiser. He got off a triumphant contact report which mystified everybody. According to the codebreakers, all the battleships were still in Singapore or Empire waters.

The mystery was cleared up two weeks later by Sam Loomis in *Stingray*, who was taking his boat to Australia for special missions. About 600 miles due east of Surigao Strait, Loomis came upon a rubber raft painted with red and white stripes. In it were four Japanese, one naval officer and three ratings. All were seriously ill from exposure and lack of food.

When questioned, the four men reported they were survivors of the Japanese light cruiser *Natori*, 5,700 tons, torpedoed off Surigao Strait on the morning of August 18. They reported that *Natori* had received one hit from McMaster's first attack, that they had tried to retreat to eastward, but that heavy seas caused flooding. The other vessel in the formation had been a 1,000-ton transport, similar in appearance to a destroyer. It was undamaged and fled the scene.

Meanwhile, McMaster, replaced at Surigao by *Gar*, took *Hardhead* into Fremantle, where he staged a legendary party to celebrate his victory. He was, he believed, the first U.S. submarine skipper in the war to sink a battleship. Christie was not much impressed with McMaster or his celebration. He wrote in his diary, "He appeared at lunch Saturday in such condition [that the] Chief of Staff had him sent away before I arrived. This young man didn't get a battleship and may lose a submarine."

McMaster said later, "I did have a run-in with Captain Nichols who was Admiral Christie's Chief of Staff. . . . Anyhow, with the firewater in me talking, I told Nichols that if the Admiral didn't believe that we had sunk a battleship, he could get a new 'boy' for the *Hardhead* and to stick both the Navy Cross (for which I had been recommended) and the *Hardhead*. . . . He got a new boy!" (In about 1950, McMaster was awarded a Bronze Star for sinking *Natori*.)

Pollack, *Tambor*, and *Pompon* were among the boats leaving Pearl Harbor in July. Old temperamental *Pollack*, commanded by a new skipper, Everett Hartwell Steinmetz, lifeguarded off the Palaus and Yap during some air strikes and then refueled at Manus and continued to Pearl Harbor. On August 27 *Pollack* was strafed by a friendly B-24, causing Steinmetz to note wryly in his report, "I now have positive proof that four men can go through the conning tower hatch simultaneously." This was the last war patrol for *Pollack*. She was sent to serve as a training vessel for U.S. antisubmarine forces.

Tambor, commanded by William Germershausen (a star boxer at the Naval Academy), and *Pompon*, commanded by Steve Gimber, ex-*Trigger*, made the polar circuit, each sinking one ship. Germershausen also attacked a tanker and another ship, probably Russian. "I knew she was Russian but she didn't have proper markings," he said later. "I thought it sank but I must have missed."

Leaving in August were *Batfish*, *Bang*, *Plaice*, *Scabbardfish*, and *Bowfin*, among others. *Batfish*, now commanded by John Kerr ("Jake") Fyfe (who retained Jim Hingson as his exec), having made one extremely aggressive patrol off Honshu, where Fyfe sank one confirmed ship, patrolled the Palaus during some preliminary air strikes. Fyfe put six torpedoes into the destroyer *Samidare*, damaged by the air strike, leaving her "sinking fast and smoking heavily" and blowing off her stern. He was credited with half the destroyer, plus a 500-ton minesweeper which was assisting in the salvage operations.

In a patrol Lockwood called "brilliant," Anton Gallaher in *Bang* picked up three convoys off the north end of Formosa, sinking three ships for 4,200 tons and damaging others.

Plaice, patrolling off the south coast of Kyushu under Clyde Stevens, picked up a set of targets one morning that brought her skipper's heart into his throat: two *Fuso*-class battleships escorted by four destroyers "coming out of the mist": range 7½ miles, speed 15 knots, course south. Stevens set up on the lead battleship, let it close until it "filled three fourths of the periscope," and fired six torpedoes. On the way down to avoid being hit, he heard explosions, four of which he judged to be torpedo hits and one an "internal explosion" on the target; he later received credit for damage to a battleship of 30,000 tons, but postwar records did not verify it.

Frederick Arthur Gunn in a new boat, *Scabbardfish*, was patrolling to the south of *Plaice*. That evening, when Stevens got off a contact report, Gunn tried to plot an intercept course but failed to make contact. Both battleships were en route to Singapore, to be closer to the oil supply. They made it without further submarine attack.

In a brilliant attack on July 22, John Corbus in *Bowfin*, patrolling to the south near Okinawa, zipped in and out of a seven-ship convoy and shotgunned eighteen torpedoes left and right. When it was all done, Corbus believed he had wiped out the whole convoy: five big ships, two destroyers. However, postwar records gave him credit for only one ship, a 6,754-ton transport, *Tsushima Maru*.

Later in that same patrol, approaching Minami Daito, a small island east of Okinawa, Corbus daringly put *Bowfin*'s nose in the mouth of the harbor and fired six torpedoes at two freighters, one anchored, one at the wharf. All torpedoes appeared to hit, blowing up both ships and the wharf, including a bus which was embarking a liberty party, but none was confirmed in postwar accounting.

Chick Clarey in *Pintado* and the old hand John Lee (ex-*Grayling*) in a new boat, *Croaker*, were sent to the East China Sea as a loosely coordinated twosome, and together they sank five ships for 38,500 tons.

On the way to station, Lockwood sent them an Ultra on a convoy southbound from Japan to the Bonins. Clarey and Lee made the intercept near Lot's Wife, but neither was able to achieve attack position, so after trailing and sending off contact reports to the boats in the Bonins, they took station along the approaches to Nagasaki.

On August 4 Clarey saw a light cruiser that appeared to be going in and out of Nagasaki on training cruises. He lay in wait, hoping it would come out the following day or the next, while Lee in *Croaker* patrolled nearby.

On August 6 Clarey picked up a large southbound convoy. He attacked, firing six torpedoes—three each at two ships—and thought both sank, but postwar records credited only one, a 5,400-ton freighter. Shortly after this attack, *Pintado* suffered a freak accident: while reloading a torpedo, the forward torpedo room gang accidentally tripped the starting switch, flooding the compartment with steam and gas.

This was a grave matter. Clarey ordered all air lines and doors to the compartment shut. In order to get the men out, he was forced to surface in broad daylight, immediately following his attack on the convoy, within sight of the Japanese mainland. Clarey's exec ran forward on the deck and battered open the forward torpedo room hatch with a maul. In this manner, the compartment was evacuated. Meanwhile, Clarey ordered the main induction and conning tower hatch shut and "took a suction" through the boat to get rid of the gases. "Papers, dust, curtains and loose rags sailed towards the engine rooms in the hurricane winds," he reported later.

The next day at about eleven o'clock in the morning, John Lee in *Croaker* spotted the light cruiser coming out of Nagasaki for another training cruise. It was zigzagging. Lee let it close to 1,300 yards and then fired four stern tubes. Some hit and, Lee reported, "flames and water rose to the mast top." Soon the ship began to settle by the stern. While Lee took color movies through the periscope eyepiece, he heard a "tremendous explosion," followed by breaking-up noises. *Nagara*, 5,700 tons, went to the bottom. In the next week, Lee sank two more ships for 8,200 tons.

On August 21, Clarey received an Ultra reporting a convoy in the middle of the East China Sea. It showed up right on schedule: a whale-ship tanker, half a dozen other tankers and freighters, and many escorts. Clarey picked the whale factory for his main target and fired ten torpedoes. Several hit the target, and several went on to hit another tanker. The whale factory blew up and caught fire, an "incredible sight," Clarey reported. She was *Tonan Maru II*, 19,262 tons, the largest merchant ship sunk thus far by U.S. submarines. By a curious coincidence, Clarey had helped "sink" this ship once before; when he was exec of Bole's *Amberjack* they had caught *Tonan Maru II* in Kavieng Harbor, October 10, 1942, but she had been salvaged to fight on.

Patrol scores in Empire waters had been declining during the summer of 1944. Dick O'Kane suspected the reason might be that Japanese merchant ships were running very close to the beach in shoal water. He postulated that this might be an advantage for the submarine; running close to the beach cramped zigzagging, forcing ships to steer a more or less straight course.

When he took *Tang* to Empire waters, therefore, he patrolled only a mile and a half (3,000 yards) off the shore of Nagoya, in less than 250 feet of water. He proved his point.

On August 10 he found an old tanker, hugging the beach. He fired three torpedoes. All missed. Seeing aircraft, O'Kane turned away to evade, bouncing off an uncharted upturn on the bottom. The following day, O'Kane picked up two freighters, escorted by a gunboat. He crept into position 1,800 yards away and fired six torpedoes, three at each freighter. One freighter, *Roko Maru*, 3,328 tons, "disintegrated with the explosion." The other was damaged. The gunboat jumped on *Tang*, dropping twenty-two close depth charges, trying to force O'Kane toward the beach. O'Kane evaded to seaward and deep water.

A week went by with no targets in sight. Then on August 20 O'Kane found a freighter coming out of the mist with two small escorts. He closed to 900 yards and fired two torpedoes. The first missed astern and exploded on the beach. The second "left the tube with a clonk but did not run," O'Kane reported later. The next day, O'Kane found another freighter "unbelievably close to the beach" with two small escorts. O'Kane eased into 200 feet of water and fired three electrics. All missed and exploded on the beach.

The next night, O'Kane found one of the escorts anchored in a cove. O'Kane stuck *Tang*'s nose in the cove and fired one electric torpedo. The torpedo ran erratically and sank, hitting bottom, where it blew up "with a loud rumble." O'Kane fired two more electrics, one at a time. The first evidently ran under; the second missed astern. O'Kane—now whispering orders from the bridge—closed to 900 yards and fired another electric. Forty seconds later the escort blew up. "The explosion," O'Kane reported later, "was the most spectacular we've ever seen, topped by a pillar of fire and more explosions about five hundred feet in the air. There was absolutely nothing left of the gunboat." O'Kane estimated her at 1,500 tons, but she must have been under 500 because the sinking was not listed in postwar Japanese records.

The next day, hugging the beach, O'Kane found two more freighters. He couldn't get into position to attack them, but a few hours later he found a ship, well escorted by surface ships and aircraft, standing out to sea. "The decks on his long superstructure," O'Kane reported, "were lined with men in white uniforms, as was his upper bridge." This indicated a navy auxiliary. He closed to point-blank range of 800 yards and fired three torpedoes. "The first and third torpedoes hit beautifully in his short well deck forward and the after part of his long superstructure, giving him a 20 degree down-angle which he maintained as he went under with naval ensign flying." It was a navy transport, *Tsukushi Maru*, 8,135 tons.

In the following days, O'Kane (with three torpedoes left) kept close to the beach, searching. On August 25 he closed to 600 yards of the beach and fired his three torpedoes at a tanker, heavily escorted. O'Kane believed that two hit the tanker and sank it and one "blew hell out of the leading escort," but neither ship was listed in postwar accounts.

O'Kane returned to Pearl Harbor after a mere thirty-four days at sea. He was credited with six ships sunk for 31,000 tons, a total trimmed by postwar records to two ships for 11,500 tons. Squadron Commander Charles Erck commented, "As the wide open sea areas diminish by reason of further U.S. Naval conquest, it is incumbent upon all submariners to develop the tactic of attack and evasion in shoal water. The tactics used in this patrol point the way."

Not many would follow. Many believed O'Kane was simply nuts.

Four Wolf Packs in Luzon Strait

Lockwood sent Stan Moseley to command a three-boat wolf pack in Luzon Strait: Vernon Clark Turner's *Billfish;* Bob Ward's *Sailfish,* returning from a long overhaul and modernization; and *Greenling,* with a new skipper, Jack Gerwick, who had made a patrol on *Cuttlefish* with Steam Marshall and on *Gurnard* as exec to Herb Andrews. The pack was known as "Moseley's Maulers."

The Maulers had bad luck. August storms with gale-force winds lashed the strait, making patrol difficult. On August 7 Bob Ward picked up a convoy and attacked in cooperation with Gerwick in *Greenling.* Ward fired three torpedoes at a medium-sized tanker; he believed it sank, but postwar records did not credit it. Gerwick also believed he had got a ship, but neither Lockwood nor postwar records credited it.

On August 18, shortly after midnight, Ward picked up another contact on radar: one very large pip and three small ones. Ward flashed the word to his packmates and began maneuvering at maximum speed to attack. The target group turned out to be a battleship with three escorts moving at high speed. By 1:35 A.M. August

19, Ward had got as close as he could: 3,500 yards. It was a long shot but worth a try. He fired all four bow tubes. One of the escorts crossed his path and caught two of the torpedoes. The others missed. Ward went deep, expecting a terrible pasting, but no depth charges fell. He resurfaced to chase, but the battleship quickly outpaced him. Ward was credited with sinking the escort, but postwar records showed no sinking for that night at that place.

Six days later, August 24, Ward picked up another convoy during the early morning hours. He flashed the word and moved to attack, firing four torpedoes at a freighter. He saw two hits and was certain the ship sank. He dived and attacked a second ship, firing another four torpedoes. He saw and heard hits, but postwar records credited only the first, *Toan Maru*, 2,100 tons. Neither *Greenling* nor *Billfish* was credited with a sinking.

A new Lockwood pack under Donc Donaho (who took temporary command of *Picuda* from Al Raborn), patrolled Luzon Strait also and turned in a smashing success. This was Donaho's seventh war patrol. The other boats were new ones: *Spadefish*, commanded by Gordon Waite Underwood, who had made two patrols in Scott's *Tunny* as PCO and exec, and *Redfish*, commanded by Sandy McGregor, who had commanded *Pike* on her last two patrols.

The pack, known as "Donc's Devils," departed Pearl Harbor on July 23, reaching station August 11 in stormy seas. Sandy McGregor thought it was a typhoon. He estimated the winds at 100 knots. The heavy seas jarred loose many plates in the superstructure of *Redfish*.

On the evening of August 17, when the seas had abated, McGregor picked up a very large southbound convoy. He did not know it, but this was a special convoy, HI-71, consisting of about a dozen big tankers and freighters, escorted by the small carrier *Taiyo (Otaka)* often shot at by U.S. submarines.* McGregor passed the word to his packmates and attacked.

By about 5:00 A.M. on the morning of August 18, McGregor was in position. He fired four torpedoes at a big unidentified ship; then he saw *Taiyo (Otaka)*. He shifted targets quickly—perhaps too quickly—and prepared to fire two torpedoes at the carrier. He got the first one off, but then the solution light on the TDC went out, forcing him to withhold fire. With daylight fast approaching, McGregor submerged. Four hours later, he saw a tanker riding high. He sur-

* Not to be confused with the large carrier *Taiho*, sunk by Blanchard in *Albacore* June 19 during the Battle of the Philippine Sea.

faced and chased it in a driving rain, firing two torpedoes that missed. Then he lost the target and hauled clear.

"Decided it was time to think things over," he wrote later, "and find out where we went wrong. Already muffed the ball twice."

Meanwhile, all submarines in the vicinity were converging on HI-71 to capitalize on McGregor's contact report. Hank Munson, who relieved Willard Laughon in *Rasher*—south of the boundary—picked up the alert and in turn alerted his packmate Charles Henderson in *Bluefish*, plus Mike Shea commanding *Raton* in the adjacent area. Because he had not been able to obtain a good navigational fix for several days, McGregor's position report was inaccurate. Donaho in *Picuda* and Underwood in *Spadefish* tore around for many hours, unable to make contact.

Munson in *Rasher* moved northward in a blinding rain. At 8 P.M. on August 18, Munson ran right into the southbound HI-71. He counted about twenty ships and fifteen escorts. The dark, rainy night was "absolutely ideal for night attack," he wrote.

At 9:22 P.M., Munson commenced firing four torpedoes. After two had left the tubes, he ordered cease fire, thinking that the gyros were not matching properly. He drew off and ran along the starboard flank of the convoy to make another attack. As he was steadying down, he saw that both torpedoes had hit the target. It was apparently a tanker. It blew up with "an appalling explosion" that sent a column of flame 1,000 feet into the sky. Later Munson wrote:

The entire sky was a bright red momentarily and the target and the whole convoy was seen for an instant. Part of the ship blew off and landed about 500 yards from the remainder of the tanker and both parts burned fiercely for about twenty minutes and then disappeared from sight in one grand final explosion. The near escort decided something was wrong, he fired his guns at all points of the compass, reversed course and fiercely depth charged something or other two miles astern of us. Pandemonium reigned in the convoy, lights flashed on and off, side lights turned on, depth charges fell in every direction, gun fire broke out all over and some badly aimed 40mm tracer passed astern of us about 100 yards wrong in deflection and way over. Two ships appeared to indulge in a spirited gun duel for a few moments. We proceeded up the starboard side of the convoy about 4000 yards off reloading and enjoying the spectacle.

The ship Munson hit was not a tanker but the escort carrier *Taiyo* (*Otaka*). While she was sinking, Munson went in for a second attack, firing ten torpedoes at two big freighters. He saw and heard three hits in the bow tube target. He believed one of the bow torpedoes ran on and hit another ship in the far column. Two of the stern tubes slammed into the other target. Munson believed one of the stern torpedoes also ran on and hit a ship in the far column. He then hauled clear to reload, broadcasting for help.

Following the reload (he had only six torpedoes left, four forward, two aft), Munson came in for another attack. He fired all six torpedoes at two targets and believed he hit both.

After Munson finished this attack and was out of torpedoes, he received orders to go on to Pearl Harbor. When he arrived there, he was credited with sinking four ships that rainy night, plus one sunk earlier, on August 6, for a total of five for 45,700 tons. In addition, he was credited with damaging four ships for 22,000 tons. Later, when it was discovered that he had sunk not a tanker but *Taiyo* (*Otaka*), the tonnage figure was revised upward to 55,700 tons. Postwar Japanese records credited five ships for 52,600 tons, making this patrol, in terms of confirmed tonnage sunk, the best of the war to date.

All the while, two other submarines were nibbling at the convoy. Henderson in *Bluefish*, who came up too late to make a coordinated attack with Munson, found two tankers. He attacked, believing he sank both, but postwar records credited him with only one, *Hayasui*, 6,500 tons.

Shortly after midnight on August 19, Gordon Underwood in *Spadefish*, who was stern-chasing the convoy, found several large ships, evidently some that had reversed course and fled northward after Munson attacked. Underwood fired four torpedoes—his first as commanding officer—from a range of 3,000 yards. All missed. He went deep, then came up again, to receive a report of Munson's attack on the convoy. "This explained the mystery," Underwood later wrote, "of unescorted ships running all around the ocean."

At 3:33, Underwood picked another target and fired six bow tubes. He reported, "Loud explosion from target. Radar pip died down and disappeared. No doubt about this fellow." He surfaced and ran through the place where the ship had been, reporting "wreckage and oil slick of our target." The ship Underwood had sunk was the large transport *Tamatsu Maru*, 9,500 tons.

Munson, Henderson, and Underwood had riddled convoy HI-71.

Munson sank three big freighters plus *Taiyo* (*Otaka*); Henderson sank one tanker; Underwood sank one 9,500-ton troopship. Total: six ships. There are no existing records about what went down with these ships. Whatever it was—troops, ammunition, supplies, guns, gasoline—it would not be in the Philippines to face MacArthur's armies when he landed.

Donc's Devils continued on patrol. On August 22 Underwood picked up another convoy, two large empty tankers with escorts. Underwood fired three torpedoes at each, sinking *Hakko Maru II*, 10,000 tons. The second tanker, severely damaged, ran into Pasaleng Bay on the coast of Luzon, where a destroyer was patrolling. Underwood coolly took *Spadefish* into the glassy waters at the entrance of the bay, intent on sinking the destroyer and firing again at the beached tanker. For three uneasy hours he played cat and mouse with the destroyer, trying to get into position to fire electrics from his stern tubes. Finally, at 10:15 A.M., he shot four. All missed. Later in the afternoon, Underwood again tried to penetrate the bay submerged, but the destroyer began dropping depth charges and Underwood prudently hauled clear. Donaho called for a rendezvous of his three boats and ordered Underwood to put into Saipan, get a new load of torpedoes from *Holland*, and then return to station.

On August 25, Donaho in *Picuda* picked up a ten-ship convoy hugging the coast of Luzon. He slipped past five escorts, got in close, and sank the 2,000-ton transport *Kotoku Maru*. A destroyer charged. Donaho turned and fired down the throat, sinking 1,200-ton *Yunagi*. Hearing all this racket, Sandy McGregor in *Redfish* picked up the convoy, maneuvered between it and the beach—some 3,000 yards distant—and fired four torpedoes at a freighter. This time, McGregor did not muff the ball; as he went deep he heard three hits, then breaking-up noises. The ship he sank was the 6,000-ton *Batopaha Maru*. Escorts delivered forty-three depth charges, none close.

After this attack, Donaho and McGregor followed Underwood into Saipan to refuel and get a fresh load of torpedoes. By September 5, they were en route back to the area.

Slightly ahead of his packmates, Underwood arrived back at Luzon Strait on September 5. Three days later, he picked up another convoy: eight big ships, three escorts. In a flawless series of attacks, Underwood fired twenty torpedoes and sank four ships for 12,000 tons. He followed the rest of the convoy to a harbor and then sent a call for help to Donaho and McGregor, who were coming back into the area. After Donaho and McGregor arrived on station, Underwood was ordered back to Pearl Harbor.

Donaho and McGregor went back to work. On September 12 McGregor picked up a small ship and fired three torpedoes, but they all ran under. On September 16 Donaho found an eight-ship convoy from which he sank one ship, the 6,000-ton *Tokushima Maru*. Part of the convoy came McGregor's way. He sank *Ogura Maru II*, a 7,300-ton tanker. On September 21, Donaho and McGregor attacked another convoy. Donaho sank a 2,000-ton freighter, McGregor an 8,500-ton transport.

Donc's Devils turned out to be one of the most successful double-barrel packs of the war. In the two forays, Donaho, McGregor, and Underwood sank thirteen confirmed ships for almost 65,000 tons. Underwood got six for 31,500 tons, Donaho four for 11,270 (including the destroyer *Yunagi*), McGregor three for 21,800. The advance base at Saipan, which enabled all three boats to refuel and reload, had already paid for itself.

In August, Lockwood sent two more packs to Luzon Strait. The first was commanded by his flag secretary, Edwin Robinson Swinburne, class of 1925, who had never made a war patrol. Known as "Ed's Eradicators," it consisted of Gene Fluckey's *Barb* (flag); a new boat with a new skipper, *Queenfish*, commanded by Charles Elliott Loughlin, an All-American basketball player who had been stuck in Panama commanding the old *S-14*; and an old boat with a new skipper, *Tunny*, commanded by George Pierce (brother of Jack Pierce, lost on *Argonaut*), who had made a PCO run in *Steelhead*.

Ed's Eradicators went to Luzon Strait by way of the Bonins. On August 18 they encountered Gordon Selby in *Puffer*, returning to Pearl Harbor. At first Fluckey thought he was a Japanese submarine, and the pack evaded at high speed. Three days later the pack passed Hank Munson in *Rasher*, also returning to Pearl Harbor. On August 24, the pack arrived on station.

The second pack departed Midway on August 17. It consisted of three boats: Ben Oakley's *Growler*, Paul Summers's *Pampanito*, and Eli Reich's *Sealion*. Ben Oakley, the senior skipper, named his pack "Ben's Busters." They reached Luzon Strait on August 29.

A day later, both packs received an Ultra on a southbound convoy, and all six boats rushed to intercept. Elliott Loughlin in *Queenfish*, who had never fired a torpedo in anger, made the first attack at 2:23

A.M., shooting three torpedoes at a freighter and three at a tanker. The tanker blew up and sank. Eli Reich in *Sealion*, who was watching, wrote that it "burned with an immense flame and heavy black smoke—silhouettes of ships could be seen against the backdrop of the burning ship." It was *Chiyoda Maru*, 4,700 tons.

With that, the convoy scattered in all directions. Ben Oakley in *Growler* fired his stern tubes at a destroyer for damage. Eli Reich in *Sealion* fired ten torpedoes at a tanker and a freighter for damage. Then Reich fired three at a freighter and three at what he believed to be a destroyer. He hit both, sinking the minelayer *Shirataka*, 1,300 tons. Later he fired three more torpedoes at a patrol craft. All missed. Gene Fluckey in *Barb* fired three stern tubes at a freighter and tanker, sinking the freighter, *Okuni Maru*, 5,600 tons. (He believed he sank another freighter with three torpedoes, but it was not confirmed in postwar records.) All that night and the next day, depth charges and aerial bombs rained down on the submarines.

The convoy turned around and headed back to Formosa. Whatever it was carrying never reached the Philippines. In the confusion of this six-boat attack against a multiplicity of scattering targets, the postwar accounting may not have been accurate; it credited three ships: Reich's minelayer, one of Fluckey's freighters, and Loughlin's tanker. Afterward, the two packs regrouped and went to separate areas.

Ed's Eradicators—*Barb*, *Tunny*, and *Queenfish*—patrolled the strait near the northwest coast of Luzon. Radar-equipped antisubmarine aircraft attacked the group relentlessly. Shortly after dark on the evening of September 1, the planes caught *Tunny* and delivered a devastating bombing attack. Fluckey in *Barb* submerged about 4 miles away and watched. The bombs dished in *Tunny*'s hull. Pierce was granted permission to withdraw and go home for repairs.

About noon on September 8, Loughlin in *Queenfish* picked up a convoy and trailed. After dark, he surfaced and flashed word to Swinburne and Fluckey in *Barb* and then made an end around, submerging in bright moonlight. At about 2 A.M. September 9, the convoy came right over Loughlin. He fired ten torpedoes at four targets, sinking the 7,000-ton transport *Toyooka Maru* and the 3,000-ton transport *Manshu Maru*. Fluckey in *Barb* fired three torpedoes at what he believed to be a destroyer. One made a circular run over *Barb*; the other two missed. Aircraft, dropping close bombs, prevented Fluckey from firing any more torpedoes.

* * *

The other pack, Ben's Busters—*Growler*, *Pampanito*, and *Sealion* (after a quick dash to Saipan for more torpedoes)—moved 300 miles to the west and lay in wait along the Singapore-Formosa convoy routes. On September 6, an important convoy consisting of six ships and five escorts had departed Singapore for the Empire. There were 1,350 British and Australian POWs crammed in the hold of one ship, *Rakuyo Maru*, and 750 in another. These POWs, survivors of a large group of slave laborers who had built a railroad for the Japanese in Malaya, were being shipped to Japan to work in the factories and mines. Three ships from Manila joined the convoy, making a total of twelve big ships plus escorts.

Dick Voge had information on this convoy from the codebreakers, but not on the POWs aboard. He gave Oakley the position reports. On the night of September 11-12, the Busters made contact. Oakley opened the attack by sinking the lead escort, a frigate, *Hirado*, 860 tons. He then pulled around and sank the destroyer *Shikinami*, 2,000 tons. Eli Reich in *Sealion* followed up, firing six torpedoes at a big transport and a tanker. The transport was *Rakuyo Maru*, 9,400 tons. His torpedoes hit her and the tanker and another transport, *Nankai Maru*, 8,400 tons. Both transports sank. Although many Japanese were rescued from the two transports, the POWs on *Rakuyo Maru* were left to fend for themselves. They went into the water; some found small life rafts.

The convoy turned west to flee toward Hainan, 200 miles away. The three boats followed. Oakley in *Growler* fired off all his torpedoes and then broke off to go down to Fremantle. Reich, the next-senior officer, took charge of the pack. Summers in *Pampanito*, who had not yet been able to attack, trailed the convoy westward. Reich, driven down by escorts, lost contact. When he surfaced, he wrongly assumed the convoy would continue its general route toward Formosa and planned an interception course to the north.

Summers trailed the convoy to the coast of Hainan and then attacked, firing nine torpedoes at three targets after dark and sinking a 5,000-ton tanker and a big transport, *Kachidoki Maru*, 10,500 tons. The remnants of the convoy evidently rounded the north coast of Hainan and scurried into Hainan Strait.

All the next day, September 13, Reich headed westerly in an effort to correct his mistake. Near midnight he found Summers's tanker, which was still on fire. He continued north to parallel the east entrance of Hainan Strait, where he patrolled all the following day. The convoy did not come out. Early on the morning of September 15, Reich rendezvoused with Summers and laid out a search plan that would take them east, back to Luzon Strait.

That afternoon about four o'clock, Summers, who was patrolling to the south of Reich, re-entered the area where the pack had first attacked the convoy. For miles the water was filled with debris and dead bodies held afloat by oily life jackets. Then Summers began finding live survivors—the British and Australians left behind by the Japanese. They had now been in the water four days and three nights. Those still alive, Summers reported later, were "a pitiful sight none of us would ever forget." He sent a call for help to Reich, who came barreling south at full speed.

Summers maneuvered *Pampanito* from raft to raft, gingerly taking on board survivors. He picked up seventy-three men. When Reich came on the scene, he rescued another fifty-four. By ten that night, no more could be safely taken aboard either submarine. Reich got off a report to Lockwood, then ordered both boats to head for Saipan. "It was heartbreaking to leave so many dying men behind," Reich wrote. On the way, four of his passengers died and were buried at sea.

Upon receiving Reich's report, Lockwood ordered the two boats remaining in Ed's Eradicators—Fluckey's *Barb* and Loughlin's *Queenfish*—to head immediately to the scene and rescue as many survivors as they could find. The scene was 450 miles away. The two boats rang up flank speed and proceeded southward at 19 knots. At midday they passed Reich in *Sealion* heading north. The seas were rising, the barometer falling.

At about 9:40 P.M. September 16, when they were within 150 miles of the scene, Loughlin in *Queenfish* picked up a northbound convoy. A few moments later, Fluckey found it too. The pack commander, Ed Swinburne, ordered an attack; the POW survivors would have to wait. Loughlin shot first, firing his last four torpedoes for damage. Twenty minutes later, Fluckey moved in, maneuvering through escorts at very close range. He could see "several large, deeply laden tankers." Then he saw something else in the darkness, the target of a lifetime:

> *Ye Gods, a flat top! This was the large pip about 300 yds to port and just ahead of the very large after tanker in the starboard column. Range 4900 yards. Went ahead standard to close for a good shot.*
>
> 2328 *Working for an overlap. This is undoubtedly the prettiest target I've ever seen.*
>
> 2331 *At 2000 yds slowed to 10 kts. We have a perfect overlap of*

	the tanker and just beyond, the flat top. About 1000 feet of target.
2332	Commenced firing all bow tubes, point of aim bow of tanker, range 1820 yards. First torpedo broached badly. Other torpedoes normal. As soon as all fish fired went ahead emergency with full right rudder to put the stern tubes into the carrier. Can't make it without being rammed by escort.
2333	Dived. Rigged for depth charge, going deep.
2334–16	First hit in tanker.
2334–24	Second hit in tanker.
2334–53	First hit in carrier.
2335–01	Second hit in carrier.
2335–10	Third hit in carrier.
2337	Breaking up noises, very heavy underwater explosions, whistlings, cracklings. One ship sunk. Random depth charges started.

In retrospect, Fluckey was critical of his attack. He said, "Being so excited, I fired a continuous salvo with my point of aim on the bow of the tanker, so that three torpedoes were to hit the tanker and three [were] to hit the carrier . . . if I had been in my normal senses . . . I would have fired all six at the carrier. That is what I should have done."

The carrier Fluckey hit was *Unyo*, 20,000 tons, an escort type that had often been a target for U.S. submarines. This time she blew up and sank. At the same time, the tanker went down. It was *Azusa*, 11,000 tons. In one famous salvo—nobody had ever sunk two huge ships with one shot—Fluckey had sunk two ships for 31,000 tons.

Fluckey had three torpedoes left and was sorely tempted to try to sink another ship, but he broke off and continued on the rescue mission. He and Loughlin reached the scene about dawn the following morning. By then the survivors had been in the water six days and five nights. The seas were steadily rising. Fluckey and Loughlin searched all that day and the next. In all, Fluckey picked up fourteen men, Loughlin eighteen. On the evening of September 18, with a typhoon coming on, they gave up the search and headed for Saipan.

Both these packs were extremely successful, demonstrating what aggressive, well-coordinated packs in Luzon Strait could do. Ed's Eradicators—*Barb, Queenfish, Tunny*—had sunk six ships for 51,600 tons: Fluckey three for 36,800, including *Unyo*, and Loughlin three for 14,800 tons. Ben's Busters—*Growler, Pampanito, Sealion*—had sunk seven ships for 37,500 tons: Reich three for 19,100 tons, Summers two for 15,600 tons, and Oakley two for 2,800 tons, including the destroyer. Total for both packs: thirteen ships for 89,100 tons.

Patrols from Australia

Christie's boats, staging from Fremantle, Mios Woendi, and Manus, also chipped away at the shrinking target list, concentrating on the convoys trying to reach Manila and Indochina.

Gordon Selby in *Puffer* turned in another aggressive patrol en route to Pearl Harbor for refit. On August 1, north of Sibutu Passage, he attacked and believed he sank a ship, but postwar records did not credit it. On August 12 he attacked a convoy, sinking the 5,000-ton tanker *Teikon Maru* and severely damaging another tanker, *Shimpo Maru*, 5,000 tons. The captain of *Shimpo* beached his ship. Selby, who had run out of torpedoes, could not follow up. He reported this to Christie, who sent Charles Henderson in *Bluefish* to finish the job.

Selby took *Puffer* on to Pearl Harbor and Mare Island for overhaul and then stepped down as skipper, going to work for Dick Voge as an assistant operations officer. On four patrols in *Puffer*, Selby had not only restored the fighting spirit of the boat but also sunk seven and a half ships for about 38,000 tons.

James Alvin ("Caddy") Adkins, who had been Freddy Warder's exec in peacetime on *Seawolf*, replaced Jim Dempsey on *Cod*. Adkins, disqualified from submarines after an unfortunate patrol in the Atlantic on *S-21*, had arrived in Australia in the latter part of 1943 as a navigator on the cruiser *San Diego*. When Warder found him in that job, he put him back into submarines, sending him with John Broach in *Hake* for a PCO cruise.

On his first patrol, Adkins (an "oldster" from 1930) patrolled near Surabaya and Makassar Strait. In a series of aggressive attacks, he fired off most of his torpedoes and returned to Darwin for a reload. There, John Griggs, commanding Squadron Twelve, joined the boat for the second leg. During this double-barreled patrol, Adkins was credited with sinking four ships and damaging one. Postwar accounting reduced the sinkings to two, but Warder was proud at having found this "lost sheep."

Enrique Haskins in *Guitarro* took station near Manila. On August 7 he picked up a large convoy and attacked. After missing his main target, he fired three torpedoes at an escort, the frigate *Kusakaki*, blowing off her bow, after which she sank with a "spectacular explosion." The other escorts drove Haskins deep and the convoy got away.

Three days later off Lingayen Gulf, Haskins, joining forces with Mike Shea in *Raton*, found another convoy. It was an impressive sight: a light cruiser and several destroyers leading tankers and freighters. Haskins fired four stern tubes at the cruiser and saw two hits. Shea in *Raton* later reported the cruiser "burning furiously"—but she did not sink. Haskins then fired four torpedoes and sank a freighter, *Shienei Maru*, 5,000 tons. Escorts attacked, dropping charges that smashed part of *Guitarro*'s superstructure but did no internal damage. Shea was not able to fire.

Malcolm Garrison, who had brought *Sandlance* to Fremantle following two sensational patrols for Lockwood, was nearly lost. On July 3, he left to patrol the Celebes Sea. On the way, he sank a 3,000-ton freighter south of Celebes. It was his tenth and last ship.

In the Celebes, Garrison found a convoy and tried to attack. A Japanese plane spotted him. Later, Garrison wrote:

When at 70 feet, I heard something I don't care to have repeated. Everyone in the conning tower distinctly heard the splash of a bomb about three seconds before the explosion. Two bombs went off directly under the stern and blew the whole ship about three feet in the air. I started down and as we passed 300 feet, the escorts started depth charging. The port reduction gear sounded like a cement mixer. So that shaft was secured. The starboard controls were jammed by a broken washer. At 430 feet, we discovered that No. 8 torpedo was running hot in the tube and was so hot it couldn't be touched by naked hand. It couldn't be fired that deep. So, in spite of the escorts, we had to come up to 150 feet. Torpedo was jammed. Couldn't be fired. At 100 feet, it was fired and the torpedo prematured 8 seconds after firing, which did not help our already battered stern. After dark we surfaced and cleared the area.

Sandlance was so badly smashed up she had to return to port. After looking her over, Christie's engineering chief, Kent Loomis, recommended a complete navy yard overhaul. Eight months would go by before *Sandlance* returned to combat. When it did, one of the junior officers was the reservist R. Sargent Shriver, who later married Eunice Kennedy, served as ambassador to France, and was the Democratic Vice-Presidential candidate in 1972.

Eric Barr in *Bluegill* patrolled off Davao Gulf. On July 20, close to shore, Barr picked up a *Natori*-class light cruiser boiling along at 26 knots. Barr, who had sunk the light cruiser *Yubari* on his first patrol, was eager to sink another on his second. He rang up flank speed but was unable to gain a favorable firing position. Later he wrote, "Oh boy! . . . Damnation. . . . Radical zig. Twenty-six knots. She's not coming any closer." Barr fired six torpedoes anyway. All missed.

Farther along on this aggressive patrol Barr sank three confirmed ships, two freighters and a subchaser, raising his total in two patrols to six ships, including *Yubari*. During the patrol, Barr (like Walt Griffith and many other Australia-based skippers) battle-surfaced on a native sailing craft and sank it. This prompted Christie to change policy. He wrote, "The destruction of a small sailing vessel is regretted. We are not at war with inhabitants of the Netherlands East Indies and Philippine Islands. The destruction of their craft does the enemy little or no harm and is forbidden."

Carl Tiedeman in *Guavina*, patrolling along the west coast of Mindanao, found what he believed to be a light cruiser anchored in a cove and "swarming with men," so he eased his boat to the mouth of the cove, closed to 2,000 yards, and fired four torpedoes. The first missed astern and smashed against the beach, blowing up. The excited Japanese "started shooting at it," Tiedeman wrote. The second and third hit the "cruiser" on the stern; the fourth missed ahead, also striking the beach.

There was, Tiedeman reported, a "tremendous explosion" that evoked "huge flames and black clouds." Tiedeman set up and fired two more torpedoes. Both hit, sending up more smoke and flame. Tiedeman eased out of the mouth of the cove, opening the range to 2,500 yards. From there, he fired electrics. Some missed, some hit, causing further damage. One blew the bow off the ship. In all, twelve torpedoes, eight hits. When Tiedeman left the scene, the "wreckage left above water was a jumbled twisted mass."

When Tiedeman returned to port with photographs, his target was something of a mystery. Headquarters did not think it was a cruiser but rather a minelayer that resembled a cruiser. However, postwar records showed that it was a new type of landing craft, estimated at a mere 1,500 tons.

John Crowley in *Flier*, the unlucky boat that had grounded at Midway, got under way at Fremantle for his second patrol in company with Michael Russillo's *Muskallunge*. Crowley and Russillo were to go up through Lombok and Makassar straits, Sibutu Passage, and Balabac Strait into the South China Sea, conducting patrols off the coast of Indochina.

On about August 12, while Crowley was still in the Sulu Sea preparing to go through Balabac, Christie sent him an Ultra on a convoy in the South China Sea. In order to make the intercept, Crowley had to put on more speed. The weather had been bad and Crowley did not have a precise navigational fix. In his eagerness to get at the Ultra targets, he ran through Balabac at 15 knots and strayed off the usual safe course into shallow water—40 fathoms. *Flier* struck a mine and, like Manning Kimmel's *Robalo*, blew up with a thunderous explosion.

Crowley was on the bridge when the disaster occurred. "The force of the explosion dazed me," he said later. "It injured several of the personnel on the bridge and caused the vessel to start down with astounding rapidity, sinking in 20 or 30 seconds. . . . When I came to I was on the after part of the bridge holding on to the rail. I immediately ran forward to sound the collision alarm. . . . There was a very strong smell of fuel oil, terrific venting off of air through the conning tower hatch, the sounds of flooding and the screams of men from below. Personnel were pouring out of the conning tower hatch as fast as they could . . . At that point the water came over the bridge deck with a force that was positively amazing. . . . It swept me out of the after section of the bridge, and thereafter I did not see nor feel any part of the *Flier* again."

Crowley's exec, Jim Liddell, was one of those in the conning tower when *Flier* blew up. Liddell heard a muffled explosion and started to go up to the bridge to ask Crowley what was going on. "The air started running through the conning tower with tremendous pressure," he said later, "and lifted me bodily to the bridge, tearing my shirt off. I walked aft to the cigarette deck and when I got there the water was waist deep and the next thing I knew I was swimming."

There were about fifteen men in the water: Crowley, Liddell, lieutenants W. L. Reynolds, J. E. Casey, and P. Knapp, ensigns A. E.

Jacobson, Jr., and P. S. Mayer, and about eight enlisted men. They banded together to swim to the coral reefs lying to the northwest. "It was extremely difficult to keep going in the proper direction," Liddell said later. "I think we swam back and forth through the oil slick several times. . . . After moonrise we were able to orient ourselves and head for land. At dawn we were able to see an island ahead, and at this time the seas and wind began to pick up and the party began to disperse—all of them could see the island closely."

During the night, some of the injured and weak swimmers drifted off, never to be heard from again. Among these were four of the five junior officers, Reynolds, Casey, Knapp, and Mayer. During the forenoon, Liddell saw what he believed to be a native boat and swam toward it. The boat turned out to be a floating palm tree. When Liddell reached it, he found three survivors, including the other officer, Ensign Jacobson. Crowley, a notoriously poor swimmer at the Naval Academy, came to the tree about half an hour later. The five men pushed the tree along toward the island, reaching it about 3 P.M. after seventeen hours in the water. They found three more enlisted men already there.

For the next few days, *Flier*'s eight survivors lived on land—it was Manatangule Island—as castaways, building lean-tos of palm fronds and foraging for seafood among the coral reefs. Then they built a raft of driftwood and set off for Palawan, working from island to island. On August 19, they made contact with some friendly natives who took them to a group of commandos who had been landed some weeks before by Cy Austin in *Redfin*. The commandos notified Australia, and arrangements were made for *Redfin* to evacuate the *Flier* survivors. (While being cared for by these underground agents, Crowley heard the news about *Robalo* and was told that Kimmel was a POW.)

The rendezvous was set up for the night of August 30. Crowley and his men put out to sea in small boats, quietly skirting a Japanese ship anchored near the rendezvous point. Early on the morning of August 31, Austin's men hauled them aboard *Redfin* and set course for Darwin, where they arrived about a week later.

Since there were survivors of *Flier*, by navy regulation there had to be an official investigation into the loss. It was broadened to include *Robalo*, lost in the same area and apparently by the same cause. Inasmuch as *Robalo* and *Flier* were following operational orders from Christie, Christie named himself an "interested party," in order that he might get on the record his own version of events. He then asked Admiral Kinkaid to name a submarine officer senior to himself to conduct the investigation. There was no submariner in Kinkaid's command senior to Christie. Kinkaid asked Admiral King to name a man. King chose Freeland Daubin, Commander, Submarines Atlantic.

Daubin arrived in Fremantle about September 12. Christie got him rooms at the Weld Club, a private hostelry in Perth. Daubin found this place extremely uncomfortable. "There was nobody in the Weld Club under age 80," Christie said later. "Daubin wanted out so bad I believe he would have stayed in a hall closet in Bend of the Road." At Christie's invitation, Daubin took over P. G. Nichols's room there.

The investigation took on the aspect of a formal legal proceeding. John Crowley, who was technically a defendant, retained Herb Andrews as his counsel. P. G. Nichols, Murray Tichenor, and Tex McLean (who had prepared the operational orders for *Robalo* and *Flier* while Murray Tichenor was at sea on *Harder*'s Patrol 5A) all testified.

As the investigation went along, Herb Andrews, no admirer of Daubin's, gained the impression that Daubin was "using" the proceedings. He said later, "I felt pretty certain that Daubin had in mind trying to get Christie's job. He tried to develop a case that Christie had been careless, or negligent in operating his boats, that he had not paid enough attention to his job. Later on, I saw Dusty Dornin, Admiral King's aide. He said King was annoyed at the way Daubin handled the thing, saying, 'Goddammit, I sent Daubin out there to get facts, not to get in a pissing contest with Christie. I ought to relieve them both.'"

Officially, at any rate, Daubin found no fault with Christie or his staff. "We got a clean bill of health," P. G. Nichols recalled later. "Daubin had nothing but praise for the way we conducted our operations," Christie said. However, after the investigation Christie declared Balabac Strait off limits and routed his boats into the South China Sea by way of Karimata Strait.

The Loss of *Harder*

After a two-week vacation at "Bend of the Road" following his extended patrol with Christie aboard, Sam Dealey had decided he was sufficiently rested to make another patrol in *Harder*, while Tiny Lynch, who was to assume command of *Harder* on the next patrol, stayed for a longer rest. Samuel Moore Logan, the third officer, who had graduated first in the class of 1942 and had made all five patrols on *Harder*, would move up to be exec.

This decision did not sit well with Lynch, who believed that Sam Dealey was mentally exhausted and that Lynch, not Dealey, should take the boat out. "Sam was showing unmistakable signs of strain," Lynch said later. "He was becoming quite casual about Japanese antisubmarine measures. Once, on the previous patrol, I found Sam in a sort of state of mild shock, unable to make a decision." Dealey's former roommate at the Academy later reported receiving a letter from Dealey written from "Bend of the Road" that, he believed, showed signs of extreme fatigue; the letter was incoherent and the penmanship almost unreadable.

Christie himself was not fully convinced that Dealey should go out again. He said, "Sam, I give great weight to whatever you say, but I want you to know that I stand ready to send you to the States for thirty days' leave. Whatever job you want, I'll try to get it for you." Christie remembers that Dealey said, "I've got to make this patrol."

Christie's operations officer, Murray Tichenor, later wrote, "I believe that when he came in from his fifth patrol, Sam was quite tired and Admiral Christie seriously considered taking him off. However, Dealey had marvelous recuperative powers and bounced back to real health and fighting spirit in a very few days."

Dealey was to command a three-boat pack. In addition to *Harder* there would be Chester Nimitz's *Haddo*, and *Hake*, commanded by a new skipper, Frank Edward Haylor. Dealey and Haylor got under way on August 5; Nimitz departed three days later. The boats were to rendezvous near Subic Bay and concentrate on the traffic south of Luzon Strait.

Just before they left Fremantle, Bill Kinsella, a new skipper on *Ray*, patrolling off southwest Borneo, had received an Ultra on an important northbound convoy and had moved in to intercept. Kinsella already had had a busy patrol; he had fired twenty-two torpedoes at a single tanker (*Janbi Maru*, 5,250 tons) before she finally sank. After sinking three ships of this convoy—a troop transport, a freighter, and a tanker—he had only four torpedoes left of his second load, so he sent out a call for help. By that time he had tracked the convoy up the western coast of Borneo, past the entrance to Balabac Strait, and north to Mindoro, where he watched it go into Paluan Bay.

Sam Dealey and Chester Nimitz answered the call first, arriving alongside *Ray* about eight on the night of August 20. In addition, Enrique Haskins in *Guitarro* and Mike Shea in *Raton*, patrolling off Manila, came southward to join the group. There were now five submarines lying in wait for the convoy holed up inside the harbor: *Harder*, *Haddo*, *Ray*, *Guitarro*, and *Raton*. Sam Dealey, the senior skipper, deployed the boats for action.

The convoy came out at 5:45 the following morning. Kinsella was in the most favorable position to attack. He fired his last four torpedoes at a 7,000-ton transport, *Taketoyo Maru*, which sank immediately. Kinsella went deep, withdrew, and returned *Ray* to Fremantle, having sunk five confirmed ships on his double-barreled first patrol.

Kinsella's attack evoked a tremendous counterattack by the escorts. Chester Nimitz wrote, "Depth-charging was started on all sides and it kept up, almost without interruption, until 0616. I have never heard such a din, nor would I have believed it possible for the whole Jap fleet to unload so many charges so rapidly. . . . I had to shout to make myself heard in *Haddo*'s conning tower."

When Kinsella sank his ship, others in the column veered off, presenting a perfect target for Nimitz. He fired six bow tubes at two targets, sinking his first ships, two large transports: *Kinryo Maru*, 4,400 tons, and *Norfolk Maru*, 6,600 tons. Haskins in *Guitarro* sank the 4,400-ton transport *Naniwa Maru*. Neither Dealey nor Shea could get into position to attack, but in one morning the five submarines had sunk four more ships from the convoy for 22,400 tons. After this action, Haskins and Shea separated from the Dealey pack and went south to the Sulu Sea.

Dealey and Nimitz moved northward to the mouth of Manila Bay, arriving the same evening, August 21. Shortly after midnight, they picked up three small pips on radar heading into the bay. Nimitz sent Dealey a message stating the targets were too small to bother with. Dealey responded succinctly: NOT CONVINCED.

The three vessels were small 900-ton frigates, escorts from the battered convoy HI-71. Dealey directed an attack. About 4 A.M. he fired a bow salvo at two, stopping *Matsuwa* and *Hiburi*. Nimitz stopped the third, *Sado*. At dawn's first light, Dealey fired again at *Matsuwa*, sinking it. Nimitz attacked the two remaining frigates, sinking *Sado* but missing *Hiburi*. Dealey fired again and sank *Hiburi*.

The two boats moved northward along the west coast of Luzon with plans to rendezvous with the third boat of the pack, Haylor's *Hake*, which had come a roundabout way and had missed all the action so

THE LOSS OF HARDER

far. That night, August 22, Nimitz picked up a destroyer and attacked. The destroyer saw *Haddo* and turned to counterattack, forcing Nimitz to fire four down-the-throat shots which missed. Near daybreak the following day, Nimitz picked up a tanker escorted by another destroyer. He fired four torpedoes at the destroyer, blowing off her bow. He fired another but missed. Two trawlers and another destroyer came out to tow the crippled ship into Dasol Bay, south of Lingayen on the gulf. But unknown to Nimitz the destroyer (*Asakaze*, 1,500 tons) slid beneath the sea before they could help. Having shot off all his torpedoes, Nimitz set course for the new advance base at Mios Woendi to refuel and reload.

Dealey in *Harder* and Frank Haylor in *Hake*, meanwhile, rendezvoused off Dasol Bay. Believing *Asakaze* had been towed inside and that the Japanese might tow her down to Manila the following day, Dealey decided he and Haylor should lie in wait. Dealey graciously offered Haylor first crack.

At 5:54 the following morning, August 24, Haylor picked up propeller screws on sonar. Two ships were emerging from Dasol Bay, a destroyer and a minesweeper. The destroyer was an old tub, *Phra Ruang*, which belonged to the Thailand navy. Haylor maneuvered to attack, but the Thai destroyer turned off and went back inside the bay. The minesweeper continued on, pinging. Haylor did not like the setup, so he broke off the attack and began evading. At 6:47, he saw *Harder*'s periscope.

Later he wrote, "I believe that at 0710, the minesweeper actually had two targets, Sam and myself, and was probably somewhat confused. But at any rate, at 0728, we heard a string of fifteen depth charge explosions. . . . We remained in the vicinity the rest of the day. . . . We surfaced at 2010 and attempted to contact *Harder*, as previously arranged, with no success."

For the next two weeks, Haylor continued to try to contact Dealey. There was no reply. Gradually, Haylor let himself think the unthinkable: Sam Dealey, destroyer killer, had been killed by the minesweeper attack on the morning of August 24.

On September 10, Chester Nimitz returned for rendezvous. Haylor still hoped that Dealey had been forced to return to base and that Nimitz had word of him, but after talking it over by megaphone Nimitz concluded that Dealey had been lost. He sent a shattering message to Christie: I MUST HAVE TO THINK HE IS GONE.

When Christie received Nimitz's radio dispatch reporting the certain loss of Sam Dealey and *Harder*, he noted in his diary, "The most ghastly, tragic news we could possibly receive. . . . We can't bear this one." In just over five patrols in *Harder*, Dealey—her only skipper—had sunk sixteen ships for 54,000 tons, including four destroyers and two frigates.

The loss of the revered and seemingly indestructible Sam Dealey caused profound shock and grief all through the submarine force. It also contributed to the growing gulf between Lockwood and Christie. Lockwood and his staff took the view that Christie had pushed Dealey too hard with the luckless Patrol Number 5B and had made an error in judgment in permitting him to take *Harder* on Patrol Number 6. Thirty years and more after the event, submariners still argued as to whether Dealey was overly fatigued, Frank Lynch, for example, insisting that he was, Ralph Christie that he wasn't.

The death of Dealey also indirectly intensified the dispute about awards and worsened relations between Christie and Admiral Kinkaid. By the time the bad news came, General MacArthur had approved the Army Distinguished Service Cross for Dealey for his fifth patrol. Upon learning of his loss, Christie decided that Dealey should receive a posthumous Medal of Honor. Accordingly, he drew up the recommendation and forwarded it to Admiral Kinkaid for approval. Kinkaid turned it down, stating that since Dealey had already received an Army Distinguished Service Cross for that patrol he should not get a navy award.

Christie was furious. He wrote angrily in his diary that Kinkaid's decision was

a bad blow to submarines. Admiral Kinkaid personally assured me before General MacArthur made the award that he offered no objection. This is a result of a personal difference of opinion between the General and the Vice Admiral [with] our very most distinguished submariner in between. . . . If Sam Dealey doesn't rate the Medal of Honor, no one ever did. I feel like turning in my suit.

Instead of that, Christie undertook a frontal assault on Kinkaid. He wrote Admiral Edwards asking his help. Then he wrote General MacArthur, outlining the problem, requesting that MacArthur consider withdrawing the Distinguished Service Cross so that the Medal of Honor might be substituted. MacArthur replied, "I most heartily recommend approval of the award of the Naval Medal of Honor to this gallant officer. If he is not entitled to it, no man ever was. I do not believe the award of the Army Distinguished Service Cross conflicts with Naval recognition. If necessary, however, I will withdraw the lesser decoration."

Then Christie sent Kinkaid a radio dispatch in a low-order code which almost everybody in the theater could read:

YOUR ENDORSEMENT THAT NO NAVY AWARD BE GIVEN DEALEY IS A VERY SERIOUS BLOW TO THE SUBMARINE SERVICE PARTICULARLY IN VIEW OF HARDER'S LOSS. IT WAS MY UNDERSTANDING THAT YOU APPROVED THE ARMY AWARD AND THAT IT WOULD NOT RESTRICT NAVY ACTION. EARNESTLY REQUEST RECONSIDERATION.

To many who still recalled the episode years later, Christie's message to Kinkaid was so public as to amount to insubordination. Kinkaid evidently saw it in that light. He responded angrily, I CONSIDER YOUR [dispatch] INAPPROPRIATE AND UNNECESSARY. Upon receiving this, Christie wrote in his diary, "Submarines . . . have received a double blow from one who should give them all his support."

In time, thanks largely to Christie's push, Sam Dealey was awarded the Medal of Honor, the fourth submariner so honored. But those on Christie's staff who were privy to his feud with Kinkaid were uneasy. It seemed to them that Christie, in his grief and frustration over Dealey's loss and the loss of *Robalo* and *Flier*, was pushing Kinkaid too hard.

The most noteworthy activity in the summer of 1944 between the Marianas operation and Palau-Morotai operations was the unqualified success of the wolf packs operating in Luzon Strait. In all, Lockwood sent eight packs to the area, composed of about twenty-five submarines. The eight packs sank fifty-six ships for 250,000 tons, not including contributions from Christie's submarines (notably Munson in *Rasher*) operating near the boundary. The bag included two escort carriers assigned to protect the convoys. In spite of fierce antisubmarine activity—particularly from land-based aircraft—no Pearl Harbor submarine had been lost. To be sure, the advance bases at Majuro and Saipan had helped furnish these high scores (enabling some boats to make double-barreled patrols), but it was clear that submarines operating in Luzon Strait in number—and in packs—in the early years of the war, and with a reliable torpedo, could have shut off the flow of oil and strategic materials to Japan much earlier.

33

Pearl Harbor and Australia, September to October 1944

The U.S. Invasions of the Palaus and Morotai

In September 1944, Nimitz's forces prepared to invade the Palaus; MacArthur made ready to invade Morotai. Admiral Bull Halsey, commanding the Third Fleet (and the fast carrier Task Force 38, now composed of sixteen carriers), supported both operations, which were only 500 miles apart.

As a preliminary, Halsey took Task Force 38 to the Palaus for pre-invasion softening up. After that, he swept toward the coast of Mindanao, launching air strikes there and then against the central Philippines and Manila. To Halsey's amazement, his carrier planes met little or no resistance. He concluded that the central Philippines were a "hollow shell with weak defenses and skimpy facilities." Halsey's pilots claimed to have destroyed 1,000 Japanese aircraft (mostly on the ground) and sunk about 150 ships.

The weakness of the opposition led Halsey to a bold idea. On September 13, following the strike in the central Philippines, he sent off a dispatch to Nimitz urging the Joint Chiefs to change the whole battle plan. He proposed that Allied forces skip the invasions of the Palaus, Morotai, and Mindanao and leap directly at Leyte in the heart of the Philippines.

Nimitz and MacArthur agreed—in part. It was almost too late to cancel the landings on the Palaus and Morotai; moreover, Nimitz was not keen on skipping the Palaus, just why has never been made clear. MacArthur held to invading Morotai but readily agreed to skipping Mindanao and reported that if this were done he could advance the timetable for invading Leyte by two months, from December 20 to October 20.

When Halsey sent off his proposal, President Roosevelt, Prime Minister Churchill, and the Combined Chiefs of Staff were meeting in Quebec at the Octogon conference.* Within ninety minutes, those assembled agreed to a wholly new plan. The invasions of the Palaus and Morotai would continue as scheduled, but Mindanao would be skipped and the timetable for Leyte moved ahead to October 20.

On September 15 MacArthur's forces, supported by his naval forces under Admiral Kinkaid, landed virtually unopposed on Morotai. The island was captured with little difficulty and few casualties. In subsequent mopping up, thirteen Americans were killed and eighty-five wounded. The biggest hurdles were rain and mud; because of mud, construction of the airfields was delayed.

The Palau Islands—Operation Stalemate II—were a different story. The Palaus are made up of three major islands: Peleliu, Angaur, and Babelthuap, the largest. Nimitz knew from codebreaking and other intelligence sources (including aerial reconnaissance) that Babelthuap was the most heavily defended (25,000 troops), Peleliu next (10,000 Japanese, 5,000 of them troops), and Angaur least (about 1,600 troops). Accordingly, Nimitz bypassed Babelthuap and landed on Peleliu and Angaur.

From the outset, Peleliu was a disaster. The Japanese had prepared strong defenses, including pillboxes and an interlocking labyrinth of caves. The marines were pinned down on the beach; some landing parties became lost and didn't know where to go. In spite of all the prelanding intelligence, the invaders found the terrain tough and forbidding.

Angaur was much easier. It was captured in a matter of a few days after the 1,600-man Japanese garrison had been wiped out. (There were only 45 prisoners.) The troops committed to Angaur were pulled out and shifted to Peleliu to make up for the massive casualties. Other troops went about 300 miles northeast and took Ulithi, which was undefended.

After a bloody week, the major objectives on Peleliu were attained.

* Jimmy Fife was at the Quebec conference as a war planner.

For weeks thereafter, however, the marines were busy rooting suicidal Japanese out of caves; they were still at it when Allied forces leapfrogged to Leyte. The whole operation cost the United States 10,000 casualties—2,000 killed and 8,000 wounded. Later, Admiral Morison wrote, "It would take more arguments than this writer can muster to prove that Operation STALEMATE II was necessary, or that the advantages were worth the cost. Admiral Halsey had the right idea: they should have been by-passed."

Pearl Harbor Support of the Landings

While these operations were in progress, the codebreakers kept close watch on the remaining units of the Japanese fleet. Most of the cruisers and battleships, including *Musashi* and *Yamato*, moved from Japan to Singapore to be closer to the oil sources and to discourage British attempts to recapture that place. The six remaining aircraft carriers and their supporting units remained in home waters training new air wings.

Although the disposition of Japanese fleet units was well known to both Nimitz and Halsey, no one could be sure of the Japanese intentions. Conceivably, Admiral Toyoda might order Admiral Ozawa to sail under radio silence and make a suicidal thrust at the forces landing in the Palaus. For this reason and others, Halsey requested that Lockwood and Christie lend heavy submarine support to the operation. Lockwood protested, wishing to intensify the blockade in Luzon Strait and tighten the pressure on the home islands, but Nimitz overruled him.

In all, Lockwood diverted over a dozen fleet boats to support Operation Stalemate II. A new boat, *Barbero*, commanded by Irvin Hartman (ex-*S-41*), took station in the east end of San Bernardino Strait, watching for Japanese fleet units that might come out. During the softening-up air strikes, *Gar*, with a new skipper, Maurice Ferrara (the first from the class of 1937 to command a fleet boat), lifeguarded off Yap, and *Grouper*, commanded by Frederick Henry Wahlig, lifeguarded off Peleliu. Ferrara picked up no airmen, but Wahlig rescued seven.

In addition to the boats initially deployed, Halsey requested that Lockwood provide a sizable force of submarines to form a scouting line between the Palaus and the Philippines. According to Halsey's plan, these boats were dispersed in two parallel lines, 100 miles apart, the submarines on each line 50 miles apart.

This unhappy flotilla consisted of nine submarines, organized into three wolf packs, all commanded by Weary Wilkins in *Seahorse*. The other two boats in his pack, known as Wilkins' Bears, were James Bizzell Grady's *Whale* and a new boat, *Segundo*, commanded by James Douglas Fulp, Jr. The second pack, Benson's Dogs, commanded by Roy Benson (ex-*Trigger*), returning with a new boat, *Razorback*,* and joined by Herm Kossler's *Cavalla* and Harold Ruble's *Piranha*. The third pack was commanded by Ike Holtz, ex-*Tuna*, returning with a new boat, *Baya*. The other two boats in his pack, known as Holtz's Cats, were also new: *Becuna*, commanded by Henry Dixon Sturr, and *Hawkbill*, commanded by Francis Worth Scanland, Jr.

These nine boats, known collectively as "Zoo," got under way from Pearl Harbor and other bases in late August. They deployed on station (joined by *Grouper* after her lifeguard duty) during the invasion of the Palaus. Since the Japanese fleet units did not oppose the landings, Wilkins' Zoo had nothing to report or shoot at. For days, they patrolled the area between Mindanao and the Palaus, killing time.

After the September 22 strike on Manila, Halsey released the Zoo submarines for normal patrol, and all three packs entered Luzon Strait to resume the assault on Japanese convoys. However, the air strikes on Manila had apparently caused a temporary cessation of convoys. The three Zoo packs found only a few targets during the last week in September and the first few days of October. One boat, Holtz's *Baya*, was pooped on September 25 and three men washed overboard. The crew caught the boat at 45 feet, resurfaced to rescue the three men, and remained on station.

On October 6 Wilkins' Bears—*Seahorse*, *Whale*, and *Segundo*—found a convey in Luzon Strait. Wilkins in *Seahorse* sank an 800-ton frigate which was serving as escort. Grady in *Whale* sank a 1,200-ton tanker. The pack then returned to Pearl Harbor and other bases. Wilkins stepped down as skipper of *Seahorse* after this one patrol, to relieve John Griggs, in command of Squadron Twelve in Fremantle.

* *Razorback* had been commissioned by Albert Marion Bontier, who served on *Spearfish*, *Sculpin*, and *Snapper*. His exec was John Lyman Haines. While coming into New London, they ran *Razorback* aground and were relieved because of the error. Benson, beginning a tour at the New London PCO school, asked for and was given *Razorback*. Bontier later wound up commanding the old *Seawolf*, consigned to special missions from Australia.

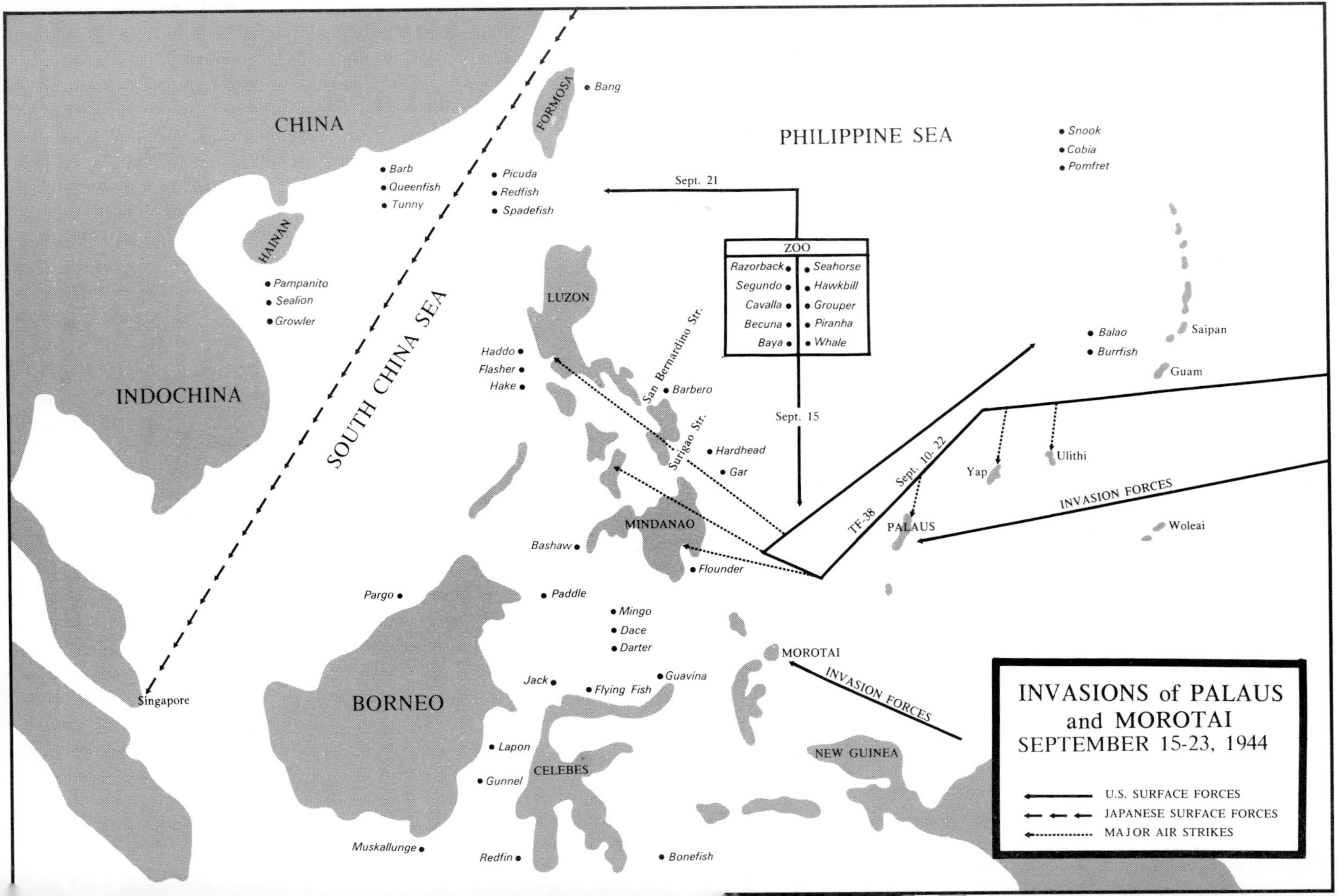
INVASIONS of PALAUS
and MOROTAI
SEPTEMBER 15-23, 1944
U.S. SURFACE FORCES
JAPANESE SURFACE FORCES
MAJOR AIR STRIKES
CHINA
INDOCHINA
HAINAN
FORMOSA
LUZON
MINDANAO
BORNEO
CELEBES
NEW GUINEA
MOROTAI
PALAUS
PHILIPPINE SEA
SOUTH CHINA SEA
Singapore
Bang
Barb
Queenfish
Tunny
Picuda
Redfish
Spadefish
Pampanito
Sealion
Growler
Sept. 21
ZOO
Razorback
Segundo
Cavalla
Becuna
Baya
Seahorse
Hawkbill
Grouper
Piranha
Whale
Sept. 15
Snook
Cobia
Pomfret
Balao
Burrfish
Saipan
Guam
Yap
Ulithi
Woleai
Sept. 10-22
TF-38
INVASION FORCES
INVASION FORCES
San Bernardino Str.
Surigao Str.
Haddo
Flasher
Hake
Barbero
Hardhead
Gar
Bashaw
Flounder
Pargo
Paddle
Mingo
Dace
Darter
Jack
Flying Fish
Guavina
Lapon
Gunnel
Muskallunge
Redfin
Bonefish

Roy Benson's Dogs—*Razorback, Cavalla,* and *Piranha*—harassed by Japanese aircraft in Luzon Strait, also found poor hunting. On October 9 the pack attacked a large convoy, but none of the boats was able to make a confirmed sinking. The Dogs returned to port without having sunk a ship—the first wolf pack to fail completely. Roy Benson stepped aside as skipper of *Razorback* and went on to command a division.

Holtz's Cats did better. After patrolling in Luzon Strait, the pack went on to Fremantle by way of the South China Sea. On the night of October 7, they intercepted an important convoy escorted by two carriers about 250 miles west of Manila in the middle of the South China Sea. All three boats attacked. Scanland in *Hawkbill*, assisted by his exec, George Grider, set up on a large freighter and fired six torpedoes. All missed. He dodged an escort, then fired three more which hit. Grider wrote:

I was standing on the bridge . . . when . . . a mighty concussion shook my insides. A wave of heat enveloped me, and at the same moment came the sound of a tremendous explosion. We held on to keep from falling and watched the sight before us with awestruck eyes.

We had hit an ammunition ship, touching off fireworks that made the combined displays of a dozen Fourth of Julys look like a pair of tired lightning bugs by comparison. The entire area was bathed in light. White and yellow flames rose in a vast mushroom hundreds of feet into the air. Rockets and tracer ammunition blazed weird diagrams across the sky as flaming bits of wreckage flew up and fell smoking back into the ocean. We were witnessing the utter destruction of a large and heavily loaded ship. . . . Worth Scanland was filled with a delight reminiscent of Mush Morton's fierce glee.

The ship was the 8,400-ton *Kinugasa Maru*. Holtz in *Baya* had also fired torpedoes at her. When the attack was analyzed, each skipper received half credit for the sinking.

A few hours later, Scanland picked up one of the carriers escorting the convoy. She was accompanied by two destroyers. While Scanland was maneuvering to attack, one of the destroyers peeled off and drove him under. He remained submerged until well after daylight. When he came up, he saw a carrier and dived for a daylight periscope attack. Scanland spent eight hours trying to maneuver into position, but it was all wasted effort.

On the afternoon of October 9, near Mindoro Strait, Hank Sturr in *Becuna* picked up a convoy and flashed an alert to the other boats. As Sturr surface-attacked, Grider reported that "hell broke loose in the convoy," for at the same time Scanland in *Hawkbill* attacked submerged, firing four torpedoes at one freighter and two at another. Then an escort dropped a close depth charge on *Hawkbill*, knocking people off their feet, and Scanland went deep. Although both skippers claimed sinkings, in the postwar accounting only one ship was reported sunk: *Tokuwa Maru*, 2,000 tons. Since the attack analysis indicated it had been torpedoed by both submarines, each skipper received half credit.

At about the same time that Ike Holtz in *Baya*, patrolling to the south of *Hawkbill* and *Becuna*, received Sturr's contact report, he suffered an engine breakdown so severe he thought he might have to scuttle the boat and ordered the coding machines destroyed. But his enginemen repaired the engines and *Baya* continued on to Fremantle without further mishap.

Wolf Packs from Pearl Harbor

Following the Zoo boats, Lockwood flooded Luzon Strait and the Formosa area with wolf packs to impede the flow of reinforcements to the Philippines. Most of them were lashed by typhoons that swept the strait in early October, greatly hampering combat operations.

The first pack was a threesome, led by Frank Acker in *Pomfret*, the other two boats being *Snook*, commanded by George Henry Browne, and *Cobia*, commanded by Albert Lilly Becker. The pack departed Pearl Harbor in early September, arriving in Luzon Strait shortly after the Palau-Morotai invasions.

Acker's back, which had given trouble in Portsmouth, seemed fine—for a while. Then one day the watch reported a contact (false, as it turned out). Acker jumped up to run to the bridge but was brought to his knees by overwhelming pain. His exec, Fredric Clarke, found him sitting at the wardroom table, face buried in his arms, and carried him to his cabin. He was paralyzed from the waist down.

The next day, while running submerged, the periscope watch picked up the masts of *two* battleships, range 15 miles. Clarke (acting for Acker) went within 8 miles but could get no closer. Not seeing any aircraft cover, he surfaced *Pomfret* in broad daylight to chase, tried unsuccessfully to get off a contact report (nobody answered), and continued the chase, regaining contact at 20 miles. Both *Pomfret* and the battleships were making 20 knots. Since the battleships were zigzagging, Clarke figured *Pomfret* might overtake during the night on a straight course.

That plan was soon upended by a chilling sight: a Japanese periscope close on the port bow, an ideal firing position for the Japanese. The officer of the deck dived *Pomfret* instantly (the standard procedure) and went deep, all hands holding their breath. No torpedoes came. Was it friendly? Clarke tried to exchange recognition signals by sonar. No response. The battleships got away.

As the days passed, Acker's illness became worse. Clarke recalled, "He ate absolutely nothing and each day he seemed more gray and lined with pain . . . if something didn't change he was going to die."

On the morning of September 30, Acker called Clarke to his cabin. Clarke said later, "He told me he felt that he had taken so much medication that his judgment was temporarily impaired and he considered that he couldn't morally retain command. I relieved him of command and so informed the ship's company." That night, Clarke reported the situation to Lockwood, adding that if Lockwood did not order *Pomfret* home so Acker could get medical attention, he, Clarke, would come home anyway. Just before dawn came a message from Lockwood to return *Pomfret* to Saipan.

On the night of October 2, while on the way to Saipan, *Pomfret* made contact with a convoy: five freighters and five escorts. Clarke ordered an end around and dived ahead. The problem was "developing beautifully" when Clarke heard a noise on the conning tower ladder. He looked down and there was Acker, pulling himself up hand over hand from the control room, legs dangling in space.

"This is probably going to be my last chance to make an attack on a Japanese ship," Acker said, "and I would like to take command back from you for a while."

Clarke readily gave way. Later he said, "Frank's legs couldn't support his weight so he would support himself by his elbows hooked over the periscope handles; I would train the periscope for him while he took the bearings. When the periscope was lowered through the well in the deck, Frank would just lie on the deck until the periscope was raised for the next observation. He would grab hold of the periscope handles as the scope was being raised and let it haul him to an upright position for the next observation."

When the ships came close, Acker fired two salvos of three torpedoes at two ships. The first salvo hit the target with a resounding explosion. The ship broke in the middle and sank. It was a big transport, *Tsuyama Maru*, 6,962 tons. Some torpedoes in the second salvo hit the second target, but she didn't sink. Escorts charged and *Pomfret* went deep. Said Clarke, "Frank was so exhausted after the attack that he lay on the conning tower deck for an hour or so until he regained strength enough to haul himself below."

Clarke reassumed command and brought *Pomfret* into Saipan through the typhoon. Acker took a turn for the better, but when he reached Saipan he was relieved of command and flown to Pearl Harbor for medical treatment. The doctors thought it might have been a polio attack or a recurrence of the old disc problem. They kept Acker on light duty for a week or so; then he went to staff duty. Later he received a Bronze Star for the patrol. Clarke thought it should have been more.

Four other wolf packs followed Acker's into Luzon Strait. Alan Banister in *Sawfish* led *Icefish*, a new boat commanded by Dick Peterson, and *Drum*, commanded by Maurice Herbert Rindskopf (the first from the class of 1938 to command a fleet boat); Edward Blakely took *Shark II*, with *Blackfish*, commanded by Robert Sellars, and *Seadragon*, back from overhaul, commanded by James Henry Ashley, Jr.; Beetle Roach in *Haddock* directed *Tuna*, under a new skipper, Edward Frank Steffanides, Jr., and Pete Galantin in *Halibut*; and Chick Clarey in *Pintado*, going on his third patrol, led John Maurer (who had been exec to Sam Dealey on his early patrols in *Harder*), now commanding the new *Atule*, and another new skipper, Joseph Bryan Icenhower, commanding another new boat, *Jallao*. Tom Wogan (ex-*Tarpon*), in a new boat, *Besugo*, led Karl Raymond Wheland's *Gabilan* and Henry Stone Monroe's *Ronquil* to Bungo Suido. Three older boats returning from overhaul went to the north end of Formosa Strait, led by John Coye in *Silversides*: *Trigger*, still commanded by Fritz Harlfinger, and the aging *Salmon*, commanded by Harley Kent Nauman.

Dick O'Kane in *Tang*, going out on his fifth patrol, was given a choice of joining this pack or patrolling alone. He chose to patrol alone in the south end of Formosa Strait. On this trip O'Kane had a new exec, F. H. Springer, a reservist who replaced Murray Frazee.

O'Kane got under way in a hurry on September 24, topped off his fuel tanks in Midway, and proceeded onward.

On October 6, while nearing Formosa, O'Kane ran into a typhoon. Hoping to sight an enemy ship, he remained on the surface, buttoned up, running on his battery. The sea, O'Kane wrote later, "was a sight such as none of us had witnessed before." The storm put *Tang* 60 miles off course.

On October 10 O'Kane rounded the northern tip of Formosa and turned south into Formosa Strait. That night he picked up a freighter steaming alone. He fired three electrics and sank *Joshu Maru*, 1,700 tons, loaded with supplies for the Philippines. The next day O'Kane sank another small freighter, *Oita Maru*, 700 tons, with a single torpedo. Afterward he returned to the northern coast of Formosa and patrolled off Kirun, adjacent to the area being patrolled by John Coye's pack.

In addition to all these boats, Lockwood sent a pack to the East China Sea led by the aggressive Moke Millican, ex-*Thresher*, bringing out a new boat, *Escolar*,* with Blish Hills in *Perch II* and John Lee in *Croaker* as packmates. The pack got under way in late September. On September 30, passing through the Bonins, Millican attacked a small gunboat with his deck gun. On October 9 Lee in *Croaker* sank a 2,200-ton freighter, *Shinki Maru*, in the East China Sea. On October 17 Millican reported to Hills in *Perch* that he was proceeding to the mouth of Tsushima Strait. Nothing was ever heard from Millican again. Although the location of the minefields in Tsushima Strait was known to Millican, Lockwood and Voge presumed that *Escolar* hit a mine and sank instantly.

Single Patrols from Pearl Harbor

Apart from all these packs, Lockwood sent many individual boats on patrol. *Scamp*, *Pogy*, *Pilotfish*, *Sargo*, *Kingfish*, and *Snapper* patrolled the Bonins. *Sterlet*, *Barbel*, *Burrfish*, *Sea Dog*, *Skate*, *Saury*,

---

* *Escolar* was the first product of the Cramp Shipbuilding Company in Philadelphia. The Cramp experiment did not turn out well. The company was saddled with poor management; there were continuous labor difficulties. Cramp only finished seven submarines during the war (another four on order had to be finished by other shipyards), and those boats that were finished, including *Escolar*, were not well built and had a poor reputation in the submarine force.

Billfish, and *Sea Fox* patrolled the area between Formosa and Okinawa. *Trepang*, *Tambor*, and *Greenling* patrolled off Tokyo Bay. Others made the polar circuit. Two of these boats, *Sterlet* and *Trepang*, had unhappy wardrooms.

Sterlet, going on her second patrol, was commanded by Orme Campbell ("Butch") Robbins. Paul Schratz, class of 1939, who had made the two miserable patrols on *Scorpion* when Reggie Raymond was killed, was Robbins's exec.

On the first patrol from Pearl Harbor in July, Robbins and Schratz had a falling out. It was the usual problem: a young, eager exec believing the boat should do more; Robbins, the senior man, having his own way. On that patrol, Robbins made five attacks and was credited with sinking four ships for 14,200 tons, but none was confirmed in the postwar accounting. When *Sterlet* returned to Midway, Schratz began looking for a way off the boat.

The other unhappy exec was on *Trepang*, a new boat commanded by Roy Davenport. The exec was reservist Dick Garvey, who began the war on *Trigger*. Garvey, a close friend of Dusty Dornin and the hard-playing "*Trigger* crowd," did not cotton to Davenport. "I put him down as a glory seeker," Garvey said later. "He kept telling us that God would protect *Trepang*; that He had a protective shield around the boat."

Garvey was not so sure about that shield. During shakedown, *Trepang* had had two close calls. On the first trip to sea, she collided with a ferryboat near San Francisco. The Court of Inquiry exonerated—indeed, commended—Davenport, but Garvey thought that *Trepang* had not been handled well in the incident. Later, during training, three men were left topside during a dive and the conning tower was partly flooded. "This episode went unreported," Garvey said later.

Off Honshu, Davenport reported, on the night of September 30, he picked up a convoy consisting of two large tankers and one large freighter, with one escort, and fired six torpedoes, one at the escort, five at the two tankers which were "overlapping." The torpedo missed the escort, Davenport reported, but hit a tanker. "He immediately started smoking badly and I later saw him go down," Davenport wrote. "We were very happy on our first attack to have sunk one large tanker." Postwar records showed no tanker sinking at this time and place but gave Davenport credit for sinking the 750-ton freighter *Takunan Maru*.

After weathering the typhoon, Davenport reported picking up a second convoy on the night of October 10, consisting of two tankers with one escort. Davenport fired four stern tubes, reported three hits, and claimed credit for another tanker sinking. "We did not actually see it go down but heard it break up on the sound gear," Davenport said later. The Japanese records did not confirm this sinking either.

On the following day, October 11, the periscope watch picked up a Japanese landing craft. Davenport set up and fired four torpedoes. He believed all four missed, but postwar records credited him with sinking *Transport No. 5* on this day, estimated to be 1,000 tons.

The next day, October 12, Davenport took up station twelve miles southwest of Iro Zaki, a point southwest of the entrance to Tokyo Bay. That night, after he surfaced, Davenport made radar contact "on two very large ships and two escorts" moving at very high speed: 23 knots. Davenport tentatively identified the big pips as two aircraft carriers and two destroyers. He discussed the situation with a PCO on board, William Bismarck Thomas. They agreed, according to Davenport, that a night surface attack would be hopeless. The water was extremely phosphorescent; they would be blown out of the water before they could fire torpedoes. Davenport reported later:

I returned to the bridge and while watching the scene develop something came over me to tell me what to do and how to do it. If I hadn't already been a religious man I soon would have been as I saw the events of this attack take place. With the aid of a power far beyond our own we started in for the attack. I passed the word over the loudspeaker system, "We're going in on the surface, gang," and ordered left 15 degrees rudder. Only by Divine Guidance and protection could his attack be successful and the submarine escape undamaged.

Davenport rang up flank speed and started in. As he came closer, he decided the targets were not carriers but two battleships escorted by two destroyers. Davenport closed in to point-blank range and fired six bow tubes at the "battleship."

One torpedo hit in the bow of the far destroyer and the second torpedo hit in the middle of the leading battleship. Radar reported that the destroyer sank immediately and the explosion from the torpedo hit in the battleship sent flame far out over the water and this was followed by several explosions during the next ten minutes. One explosion sent flames high above the foremast. It appeared like the torpedo had hit at their number three turret.

Davenport then swung around, he reported, and fired his last torpedoes—four stern tubes—at the second "battleship." It zigged and these four missed.

The second battleship about this time turned on a seachlight, directing it forward, apparently looking for the destroyer that had been sunk to see what was happening ahead of him and then made a sweep with his light in our direction and came within 30 or 40 degrees of our position. At this time I cleared the bridge of all but the Officer personnel and made ready to dive if we actually were illuminated. They turned the searchlight off, turned it on again in a few seconds and this time turned it directly on the damaged battleship and we were able to make out clearly the pagoda-type foremast and could see again his stack midway between his fore and mainmast and were certain of our identification that it was a battleship. He turned the light out again and we could detect no countermeasures.

Davenport opened out at flank speed. When he received no gunfire, he turned back again to close the target for a look-see. The ships were now tracked at only 16 knots. Said Davenport, "It was evident that we may have gotten one of his fire rooms, he had lost some of his boiler power, he undoubtedly was drawing more water."

When Davenport returned to Majuro, he was credited with sinking three ships for 22,300 tons and damaging a battleship for 29,300 tons. The endorsements congratulated Davenport for a "splendid" attack on a *"Yamashiro*-class battleship," stating, "This will keep this formidable ship out of the enemy battle line for some time to come." Davenport received another Navy Cross, his fourth. Postwar records credited only the 750-ton freighter plus the 1,000-ton landing craft which Davenport did not claim. Total: two ships for 1,750 tons.

The exec, Dick Garvey, said later he doubted that Davenport had seen battleships.

Australian Support of the Landings

Ralph Christie diverted many submarines from regular patrol to support the Palau-Morotai invasions. *Flounder* lifeguarded in Davao Gulf during Halsey's air strikes on Mindanao. *Mingo, Dace, Darter, Guavina, Flying Fish, Jack, Paddle,* and *Bashaw* formed a scouting line in the Celebes south of Mindanao, to intercept Japanese fleet

AUSTRALIAN SUPPORT OF THE LANDINGS

units should they sortie from Singapore. *Pargo* patrolled off northwest Borneo with the same mission. *Haddo* and *Flasher* lifeguarded off Manila during the air strike.

Crevalle, commanded by Frank Walker, was scheduled to join this formation, but she never made it. On the morning of September 11, just after passing through Lombok Strait northbound, Walker ordered a routine early morning dive. All went well. Walker then ordered the boat to the surface.

The officer of the deck, reservist Howard J. Blind, rushed to the bridge, followed by his lookouts. Someone in the control room evidently forgot to close the main ballast tank vents. After *Crevalle* surfaced normally, the air rushed out of the tanks through the open vents and *Crevalle* suddenly went down again, making standard speed. The upper and lower conning tower hatches were still open. *Crevalle* plunged like a stone with a tremendous down-angle, 42 degrees, with Blind and his lookouts still on the bridge. Tons of seawater flooded through the open conning tower hatches and down into the conning tower, control room, and pump room, until the lower hatch was shut.

The men in the conning tower could not get through the torrent of water to close the upper conning tower hatch. At 150 feet, when the water in the conning tower had reached armpit level, the hatch closed of its own accord. Evidently Howard Blind had freed it while *Crevalle* was going under.

All the while, *Crevalle* was plunging toward the bottom with the fatal down-angle. One of her crew, Robert Yeager, noticed that *Crevalle* was still making standard speed. He telephoned the maneuvering room on his own and ordered, "All back full." On his orders, the props were reversed and turned up full power. At 190 feet, *Crevalle* stopped plunging downward. The men in the control room blew main ballast, and the boat returned to the surface, backing full.

Crevalle lay on the surface in broad daylight, disabled. All the gear in the conning tower, control room, and pump room was flooded out, including the radio transmitters. Frank Walker hurried to the bridge, ordering machine guns manned. They found one of Blind's lookouts—gunner's mate W. L. Fritchen—and hauled him on board. They saw Blind's head momentarily, but then he disappeared from sight.

Luckily for Walker, there were no Japanese planes in the vicinity. The crew patched up *Crevalle* and the boat limped back to Darwin, arriving September 15. For freeing the conning tower hatch, Howard Blind was awarded a posthumous Navy Cross, given to the Australian girl he had married just before sailing. Robert Yeager, whose orders had undoubtedly saved the boat, was awarded a Silver Star. Walker, who was not blamed for the accident, returned *Crevalle* to Mare Island for complete overhaul and then stepped down as skipper, going to new construction.

During the invasion of Morotai, there was a partial breakdown in communications between the U.S. surface forces involved in the invasion and Christie's submarines. The breakdown caused the loss of one submarine and nearly a second.

The Japanese sent five RO-class submarines to attack the Morotai invasion forces. On October 3, one of these, *RO-41*, fired torpedoes at the jeep carrier *Midway* (later renamed *St. Lo*). The torpedoes missed *Midway* but hit a destroyer escort, *Shelton*, which later capsized under tow. A companion destroyer, *Richard M. Rowell*, drove off the Japanese submarine with a few depth charges and took off *Shelton*'s crew. Aircraft from *Midway*, meanwhile, hunted Japanese submarines with a vengeance.

Later that morning Sam Loomis in *Stingray*, returning to the Admiralties submerged in the submarine safety lane from a special mission off Samar, arrived on the scene and was immediately attacked by two torpedo bombers from *Midway*, who believed *Stingray* to be the submarine that fired at *Midway* and sank *Shelton*. One of the planes dropped a bomb; the other accidentally crashed into the sea while making a run on *Stingray*. Fortunately, the bomb missed.

That same morning, *Seawolf* was en route from the Admiralties to Samar with seventeen U.S. Army agents and about ten tons of supplies. She was commanded by Al Bontier, who had been relieved on *Razorback* after he put her aground off New London. *Seawolf* also passed close to the scene. She had been bucking heavy seas and had fallen a day behind in her schedule, but she was also in a safety lane. At eleven, a navy airplane spotted *Seawolf*. Wrongly assuming *Seawolf* to be the Japanese submarine that torpedoed *Shelton*, the pilot dropped two bombs and a dye marker. *Seawolf* dived. The U.S. destroyer *Rowell* hurried over. At 1:10 P.M. *Rowell*'s skipper, Harry Allan Barnard, Jr., picked up a submarine on his sonar gear.

Barnard knew that he was in a submarine safety lane, but all his information indicated there was no U.S. submarine within 70 miles.

Seawolf had reported her one-day delay in schedule to Christie, who relayed it to Kinkaid's headquarters, but the word never got to Barnard. He attacked with depth charges. The sub made no effort to evade and sent signals on her sonar—long dashes and dots. However, Barnard later reported, "the stuttering transmission bore no resemblance to the proper recognition signal." Believing the Japanese sub skipper was trying to jam his sonar, Barnard attacked again. Although the evidence was circumstantial, and Barnard stoutly insisted his target was a Jap, Jasper Holmes and other submarine authorities concluded "with little doubt" that this attack sank *Seawolf*. A large bubble came to the surface, then debris. *Seawolf* went down with all hands, plus the agents Bontier had intended to land on Samar.

That night in Fremantle, Christie made repeated attempts to call *Seawolf*. There was no answer. The famous old boat that had carried Fearless Freddy Warder, Roy Gross, and many others into battle was the first—and only—U.S. submarine lost to Allied forces in the Pacific. After *Robalo*, *Flier*, and *Harder*, *Seawolf* was the fourth submarine Christie had lost in slightly over two months.

While patrolling a lifeguard station on the southwest tip of Mindoro, Byron Nowell in *Paddle* found a small convoy. He sank one confirmed ship, *Shiniyo Maru*, 2,500 tons. By happenstance, *Shiniyo* was transporting hundreds of Allied POWs being evacuated from Mindanao to Manila or the Empire. They had been herded into the holds and told by prison guards that if an American submarine attacked the ship they would kill them all. When Nowell's torpedoes struck home and the ship started down, the guards opened fire on the POWs with tommy guns. However, a hundred or more fought up through the hatches with clubs and improvised weapons and jumped over the side. About fifteen or twenty were picked up by Japanese boats engaged in rescuing *Shiniyo* survivors and were immediately shot. Eighty-one reached shore on Mindanao and made contact with friendly guerrillas, who sent word for a submarine to evacuate them.

Christie ordered *Narwhal*, now commanded by Jack Clarence Titus, to rescue the POWs; he picked them up on the night of September 29 and proceeded toward the Admiralties. They were in pitiful condition and grateful for their escape. However, they were almost shipwrecked a second time. The very next day, *Narwhal* was caught on the surface by a Japanese plane. During the hasty dive *Narwhal's* stern planes jammed on hard dive, and before Titus could catch the boat she plunged at a terrifying angle. Titus backed emergency and blew all ballast tanks, catching the boat at 170 feet. *Narwhal* broached—stern first—with the Japanese plane showing on her radar. Titus dived again immediately, this time without a problem. The plane dropped no bombs.

On the way to port *Narwhal* passed through the scene of the *Shelton* sinking early on the morning of October 3 (exchanging signals with *Seawolf*) but was spared an attack by *Midway*'s eager-beaver pilots.

Big Ian Eddy, commanding *Pargo*, had made four long, aggressive patrols that had resulted in a credited total of nine ships sunk (four confirmed by JANAC). He was scheduled to make one more, but when he came off the fourth, he was in bad physical shape and feeling depressed because he thought he hadn't done enough! Deciding he needed a good long rest, Christie relieved him and sent him back to the Atlantic. *Pargo* went to David Bonar Bell, the second man in the class of 1937 to get command of a fleet boat. Bell had commissioned *Pargo* with Eddy and made all her patrols, gradually moving up the ladder to command.

Christie assigned Bell to lay a minefield off Brunei Bay, northwest Borneo, an oil port where important ships, including Japanese fleet units, frequently called and might call again in the future. Bell carried out this mission with skill and courage and afterward made repeated attacks on Japanese vessels going and coming through his area. He sank two ships, both small, a minelayer of 1,600 tons and a former net tender of 600 tons. In addition, he inflicted damage on several freighters and an escort carrier, at which he fired eight torpedoes for three hits.

Bell was relieved in that area by Hammerhead Martin in *Hammerhead*. Martin had no sooner arrived than he ran into a large convoy on October 1. In a brilliant series of attacks, Martin sank three big ships, each over 5,000 tons. On October 20 he found another convoy and in a no less brilliant attack sank two big transports. His total for the patrol: five confirmed ships for 25,200 tons. Having shot all his torpedoes, Martin was ordered to Fremantle, where he received high praise for this—one of the best patrols on record.

Martin was relieved on station by *Gurnard*, now commanded by Norman Dwight Gage, who began the war on *Tautog* and later com-

AUSTRALIAN SUPPORT OF THE LANDINGS

manded *R-1* in the Atlantic. Gage also carried a load of mines. Shortly after arriving in the area, Gage picked up a large convoy (fifteen ships, two large tankers) headed for Singapore to join Japanese fleet units. Gage, with two stern tubes filled with mines, attacked, firing six bow torpedoes, but he was unable to sink any ships. He took position off Brunei Bay, keeping a sharp lookout for Japanese fleet units.

Both Reuben Whitaker and his exec, Ray DuBois, returned from *Flasher*'s third patrol physically and mentally drained. There had been a serious question in Whitaker's mind about making another patrol. He had reached the point, he said later, where he hated to make contact with the enemy. However, while DuBois stayed in port for a "blow," replaced by one of the junior officers, Philip Thompson Glennon, Whitaker took *Flasher* out for a fourth time. "DuBois goofed," Whitaker said later. "That rest cost him command. Instead of getting *Flasher*, he was sent back to New London to command a little school boat."

Whitaker led a pack consisting of *Flasher*, *Lapon*, and *Bonefish*. *Lapon* was commanded by a new skipper, Donald G. Baer. *Bonefish* was commanded by Lawrence Lott Edge, making his second patrol.

Flasher departed Fremantle first and went up through Lombok and Mindoro straits to the Manila area. On September 18, Whitaker arrived on station and almost immediately picked up a big transport, loaded with troops, heading into Manila with four destroyers for escorts. He maneuvered in for a daylight periscope attack and fired five torpedoes, sinking *Saigon Maru*, 5,350 tons, formerly a light cruiser. The destroyers delivered a severe depth charge-attack, which drove Whitaker deep and knocked out the SJ radar.

During the next several days, Whitaker was assigned to lifeguard duties during Halsey's air strikes on Manila. Donald Baer in *Lapon* arrived off Manila on September 19. On the afternoon of September 21, Halsey's planes attacked a nearby convoy. Baer pursued the remnants of the convoy that night and sank one ship, *Shun Yuan*, 1,600 tons, but because of his lifeguard assignment Whitaker was not able to join in the attack.

Early on the morning of September 27, Whitaker sighted two battleships. He bent on four engines to make an end around and notified Baer in *Lapon*, but neither boat was able to get into position to attack. However, at about daylight, Whitaker picked up a convoy and alerted Baer. Both attacked. Baer sank a tanker, *Hokki Maru*, 5,600 tons; Whitaker sank another big transport, *Ural Maru*, 6,400 tons. The other ships of the convoy fled into Lingayen Gulf.

Meanwhile, the third boat of the pack, Edge's *Bonefish*, was on the way, pausing on September 28 near Mindoro to sink *Anjo Maru*, a 2,000-ton tanker. She joined up with the pack on September 30 off Lingayen Gulf. On October 4 Whitaker found another convoy and sank one ship, *Taihin Maru*, 6,900 tons. *Bonefish* intercepted and attacked the convoy later that night, but her torpedoes missed. On October 10 Baer in *Lapon* sank another ship, *Ejiri Maru*, 7,000 tons. On October 14 Edge in *Bonefish* sank a 2,500-ton freighter.

Whitaker, who had arrived first, departed first, going home by the usual route. Baer and Edge remained on station. On return to Fremantle, Whitaker stepped down as skipper of *Flasher*, going to the Submarine School as an instructor. In his five patrols as skipper—one on *S-44*, four on *Flasher*—he had sunk a total of fourteen confirmed ships for 56,513 tons, making him one of the leading scorers of the war.

Bluegill, commanded by Eric Barr, made up a pack with *Angler*, commanded by Frank Hess. On October 12 the relentlessly aggressive Barr battle-surfaced on some barges, for which he was later criticized by Christie; one fired back, wounding five of Barr's men. On October 14, in the Sulu Sea, Hess sank a 2,400-ton freighter. In the early morning hours four days later, Barr tore into a large southbound convoy off Manila and sank three ships for 19,630 tons. These included two big transports, *Arabia Maru*, 9,500 tons, and *Hakushika Maru*, 8,000 tons. After this attack, escorts delivered forty-seven punishing depth charges that fell so close men in the forward torpedo room reported seeing fire at the edge of the torpedo loading hatch. Barr returned to Mios Woendi to reload and refuel, leaving *Angler* on station.

Mike Shea in *Raton*, making his second patrol, was slightly to the south of these boats. Picking up Barr's contact report on the convoy, he moved to intercept, making contact in a torrential downpour about five o'clock in the afternoon on October 18. Shea tracked and attacked in the blinding rain, obtaining position in the middle of the convoy. He fired ten torpedoes and sank two ships, a 4,700-ton freighter and a 3,800-ton transport. With seas rising and winds blowing at 40 knots, Shea bored in for a second attack, firing ten more torpedoes. Eight of them missed, probably thrown into erratic runs

AUSTRALIAN SUPPORT OF THE LANDINGS

by the heavy seas; the other two hit for damage. Believing any further attacks would be futile, Shea hauled clear and returned to Mios Woendi to reload torpedoes and refuel.

The sister ships *Dace*, commanded by Bladen Claggett, and *Darter*, commanded by Dave McClintock, left Mios Woendi as a wolf pack off Palawan. On October 12 McClintock picked up a seven-ship southbound convoy, escorted by two destroyers. He attacked, firing four torpedoes, believing he obtained two hits but no sinkings. He flashed word to Claggett in *Dace*, patrolling to the south. Shortly after midnight on October 14, Claggett made contact and fired a ten-torpedo salvo at overlapping targets. One bow torpedo made a circular run, forcing Claggett to maneuver wildly to avoid; the other torpedoes hit hard and sank two big freighters: *Nittetsu Maru*, 6,000 tons, and *Eikyo Maru*, 7,000 tons. Claggett tried to attack again, but the convoy eluded him.

McClintock and Claggett picked up Eric Barr's convoy contact on October 18 and moved to intercept. They did not find the convoy but ran into two northbound destroyers. Both McClintock and Claggett fired four torpedoes each at the destroyers. All missed. They remained on station at the south end of Palawan Passage.

Aspro, *Cabrilla*, and *Hoe* patrolled as a pack near Manila. William Thompson in *Cabrilla* turned in a fine performance. On the night of October 1–2, he teamed with William Stevenson in *Aspro* to attack a large convoy. Thompson sank two tankers, *Zuiyo Maru*, 7,400 tons, and *Kyokuho Maru*, 10,000 tons; Stevenson sank a 6,900-ton freighter. Five nights later the two boats again teamed to attack a convoy. Thompson sank two freighters, one for 5,000 tons, one for 2,000 tons; Stevenson sank a 4,000-ton transport. During these attacks, Victor McCrea in *Hoe* sank one confirmed ship for 2,500 tons and damaged others.

Upon completion of these attacks, Thompson and Stevenson returned *Cabrilla* and *Aspro* to Pearl Harbor. McCrea returned *Hoe* to Fremantle. In this fine patrol, Thompson had sunk four ships for over 24,000 tons.

Cod, commanded by Caddy Adkins making his second patrol, and *Ray*, commanded by Bill Kinsella, patrolled as a pack near Manila.

For Kinsella, who had sunk five ships on his first patrol, the second was a frustrating experience. On October 3, he saw what he believed to be a light cruiser but was unable to gain attack position. He had four battery explosions in his electric torpedoes, which ruined the warheads on three and forced him to eject one. On October 5, after rendezvousing with Adkins in *Cod*, a convoy slipped by Kinsella in a rainsquall. Adkins attacked and sank a 7,000-ton freighter, but *Ray* was too far away to join in. On October 6 Kinsella attacked a big tanker escorted by two destroyers. He fired six torpedoes and missed. Escorts drove him down, but later he resurfaced and fired six more, achieving, he believed, only damage. He wrote, "All in all, it was a very discouraging night."

His luck changed—momentarily—on October 12. During the afternoon he found a transport escorted by two destroyers. He fired four torpedoes and sank *Toko Maru*, 4,100 tons.

Two days later, October 14, the bad luck returned. While diving from a Japanese plane, *Ray* suffered a near-fatal accident: the upper conning tower hatch jammed, and a "terrific" rush of water flooded the conning tower. Kinsella, who had dropped to the control room, ordered the lower conning tower hatch shut. He then resurfaced, plane or no plane, to save the men in the conning tower. By the time *Ray* got back to the surface, the conning tower was two thirds flooded, but no one drowned.

After this, Kinsella returned to Mios Woendi for repairs. Adkins in *Cod* remained on station.

About this time, Christie's force was augmented by a squadron of ten British and Dutch submarines, some released from combat duty in Europe where they were no longer needed. They were smaller boats, comparable to the older S-boats. The squadron was commanded by Captain L. M. Shadwell, R.N. The first boat of this squadron to arrive was H.M.S. *Clyde*. Christie noted in his diary, "*Clyde*, the dirtiest submarine that ever made a dive, now in port after several false starts. I hope this isn't a sample of what we are to experience with the Limeys." And later, "*Clyde* now must remove battery for repair. Looks as if she'd have to be generally refitted and then *blasted* out of port. H.M.S. *Porpoise* in today. She too arrives unready for her job." On September 2 he noted, "The submarines of the Royal Navy arriving here are in the most horrible condition. Looks as though we'll have to rebuild [them] before they are able to do any work in enemy areas—if they have that in mind."

Christie deployed these short-legged boats to the Java Sea for patrol near Surabaya and Singapore. One of the boats turned in a good patrol. It was a British-built submarine, *Zwaardvisch* (*Swordfish*) manned by a Dutch crew commanded by H. A. W. Goossens, R.N.N. When Christie asked him where he wanted to patrol, he replied Surabaya. The Japanese had interned some relatives of his, and he wanted revenge.

While Goossens was patrolling off Surabaya, Christie received important information from the codebreakers. A German submarine, *U-168*, was en route from Germany to Japan with important technical information on radar and plans for a new submarine. The boat had put into Surabaya and was scheduled to leave on the morning of October 6.

Christie alerted Goossens, who moved into position to intercept. "The German sub was five minutes late," Christie said later. As the boat approached on the surface, Goossens fired four torpedoes. *U-168* blew up and went to the bottom in 120 feet of water. Twenty men, including the sub skipper, Commander Pich, the doctor, and eighteen ratings made it to the surface. Goossens kept Pich and the doctor and two technicians and put the other sixteen on a native boat.

Goossens was not yet finished. On October 17, he found and torpedoed the Japanese minelayer *Itsutshima*. Christie and the British squadron commander, Shadwell, met Goossens on his return to Fremantle. Christie was struck by the international flavor of the event. He later wrote, "A Dutch sailor in a British submarine under American task force command returning to an Australian port after sinking a German submarine in waters the Japanese thought were theirs. Canada was represented, too, when I presented Goossens a bottle of Canadian Club."

34

Pearl Harbor and Australia, October to November 1944

Air Strikes on Formosa and the Philippines

Admiral Bull Halsey, commanding the Third Fleet (and Task Force 38), joined forces with General MacArthur and made preparations for the invasion of Leyte. The operation was code-named King Two. On the opposite side of the fence, Admiral Toyoda drew up a counterattack, known as Sho 1. Although the Japanese fleet had been severely mauled in the Battle of the Philippine Sea, Toyoda intended to make an all-out last-ditch fight. His plan was simple. After U.S. troops landed in the Philippines (Mindanao? Leyte?), Admiral Ozawa would steam down from Japan with his four remaining "fast" aircraft carriers (*Zuikaku*, *Zuiho*, *Chitose*, and *Chiyoda*) and three jeep carriers (*Junyo*, *Ryuho*, and *Jinyo*, also known as *Shinyo*) and lure Admiral Halsey's Task Force 38 away from the landing area. After this had been achieved, the more powerful battleship force from Singapore would steam up and annihilate the U.S. landing force. Japanese land-based aircraft in the Philippines, Formosa, and Okinawa would support these attacks, helping to make up for Ozawa's overwhelming disparity in aircraft carriers. This time, Japanese kamikaze pilots would lend extra punch to the Japanese counterattack. Conceivably, great damage could be inflicted on Halsey's force and the invasion of the Philippines could be thwarted.

AIR STRIKES ON FORMOSA AND THE PHILIPPINES

As a preliminary to the Leyte landings, Admiral Halsey employed Task Force 38 in a series of strikes aimed at softening up the area and reducing Japanese air power in the Philippines, Formosa, and Okinawa. On October 6 this force steamed out of the newly acquired Ulithi anchorage right into a typhoon. On October 8, Halsey refueled his ships at sea in heavy weather. On October 10, he struck Okinawa and the Ryukyus.

Many of Lockwood's submarines lifeguarded these air strikes. One was *Sterlet*, commanded by Butch Robbins, off Okinawa. When some naval aviators went into the water, *Sterlet* picked up six. *Saury*, commanded by Richard Albert Waugh, picked up one.

The October 10 strikes alerted Admiral Toyoda, then on Formosa, to the fact that something important was in the wind. He sent out a general warning for all bases to gear for more attacks. In addition, he ordered the carrier force in the Inland Sea to transfer its operational aircraft to land bases. This was a controversial order that would have considerable bearing on operations in the near future.

Halsey again refueled and then considered where to strike next, Luzon or Formosa. The plan called for a strike at Aparri on northeast Luzon. Following the plan, Halsey carried out that strike on October 11. It accomplished nothing worthwhile and Halsey later said, "I should have struck Formosa first." The strike on Aparri gave Toyoda an additional day to prepare his defenses and gather more planes at Formosa.

On Columbus Day, October 12, Halsey wheeled north and hit Formosa. Toyoda sent about 600 planes in counterattack. This first great fight between land- and carrier-based aircraft stretched over three brutal days—October 12, 13, and 14—with catastrophic consequences for the Japanese. Halsey destroyed most of Toyoda's aircraft, while losing only about 76. The Japanese claimed a smashing victory, stating that Japanese planes had eliminated eleven carriers, two battleships, and three cruisers and damaged eight carriers, two battleships, and four cruisers. In fact, Japanese planes had sunk no ships and seriously damaged only two, the cruisers *Canberra* and *Houston*, which were towed home.

During the strike on Formosa, Bob Ward in *Sailfish*, Fritz Harlfinger in *Trigger*, and George Browne in *Snook* were on lifeguard duty. On the first day of the strike, October 12, Ward remained on the surface in full view of Japanese air- and shore-based units and penetrated minefields to rescue twelve navy airmen. During one rescue, a Japanese patrol boat tried to get at the aviator on his raft, but Ward sank the Japanese with his deck gun. Not far away, Fritz Harlfinger in *Trigger* picked up one aviator. On October 16 Banister in *Sawfish* picked up a navy pilot who had been in the water four and a half days.

After Ward had rescued the airmen, his radio transmitter went out of commission. Red Ramage, who was nearby in *Parche,* following a couple of weeks of barren patrolling off San Bernardino Strait, moved in and escorted *Sailfish* back to Saipan. After the transmitter had been fixed, Ward and Ramage, joined by John Hess in *Pomfret,* returned to Luzon Strait as a newly created wolf pack. Hess had good luck on his maiden patrol, sinking three ships for 14,000 tons.

During the Formosa strike, October 12, Lockwood alerted all his packs and individual submarines patrolling from Luzon Strait to Tokyo Bay to be on the alert for major Japanese fleet movements. In subsequent days, his packs were disposed as follows: two in Luzon Strait (*Sawfish, Icefish,* and *Drum,* plus *Snook,* which joined them; and *Shark, Blackfish,* and *Seadragon*); one moving north toward southern Kyushu (*Silversides, Trigger, Salmon,* and *Sterlet,* which joined them); one guarding Bungo Suido, the southern outlet from the Inland Sea (*Besugo, Gabilan,* and *Ronquil*); and one in the East China Sea near Nagasaki (*Perch* and *Croaker,* less *Escolar,* which had been lost). In addition, there were many individual boats disposed along probable routes to the south: *Sea Dog, Skate, Saury, Barbel, Burrfish, Sea Fox,* and *Billfish*; and Dick O'Kane in *Tang,* patrolling inside the Formosa Strait.

The heaviest responsibility fell on the shoulders of Tom Wogan in *Besugo,* leading the pack guarding Bungo Suido. If Admiral Toyoda ordered Admiral Ozawa to sortie his depleted carrier force, Wogan's pack would be first to sight it and give the alarm. His orders were to maintain a close, observant patrol and, if he saw anything, report first and then attack.

Admiral Toyoda, meanwhile, evidently believed his pilots' reports to the effect that they caused tremendous damage to Admiral Halsey's force during the strike on Formosa. On October 15, he ordered a force of two heavy cruisers, *Nachi* and *Ashigara,* and one light cruiser, *Abukuma,* plus supporting destroyers, to leave the Inland Sea and pursue the "crippled" U.S. carriers. This force, commanded by Vice

Admiral Kiyohide Shima, passed through Bungo Suido between 8 and 9 A.M., range 7,500 yards. Tom Wogan in *Besugo* saw it and reported to Lockwood. The next night, Wogan saw what he believed to be more cruisers coming out and fired six torpedoes at one. It turned out to be the destroyer *Suzutzuki*. Wogan had blown off her bow, but she made it back to Kobe.*

When Wogan flashed the initial alert, Ozzie Lynch in *Skate*, patrolling the northern Ryukyus, moved to intercept Shima's force. He found it at 10:24 that evening and attacked one cruiser, firing three electric torpedoes. He thought he got one hit, but according to Japanese records no cruiser was hit. The Shima force continued south toward Okinawa, refueled, and then retired when it received a message that "more than six carriers" were still operating east of Formosa.

By that time, Admiral Halsey was pounding the Philippines. It was now clear to Toyoda that Leyte was the invasion target. He ordered his forces to execute Sho 1. Shima was to proceed south in Formosa Strait to the Pescadores Islands (in the middle of Formosa Strait) and then cross Luzon Strait and join with the battleship forces coming from Singapore.

At about 10:30 on the morning of October 18, Butch Robbins in *Sterlet*, patrolling west of Okinawa, picked up the Shima force shortly after it left Okinawa. He reported two heavy cruisers, one light cruiser, and six destroyers, which was a near-accurate picture of the formation. The range was 15 miles. Robbins closed to 4 miles, but because it was daylight he could not overtake and gain position ahead for a submerged attack. He got off a contact report.

Farther south, John Coye's wolf pack (*Silversides*, *Salmon*, and *Trigger*) moved to intercept. Fritz Harlfinger in *Trigger* picked up the force, range 9 miles. He closed to 5 miles, preparing to make a night surface attack, but a Japanese aircraft and submarine (which fired a torpedo at *Trigger*) drove him off. Coye in *Silversides* did not make contact. Harley Nauman in *Salmon* was temporarily absent; one of his officers, Lieutenant J. M. McNeal, had come down with an illness—diagnosed as gallstones—and Nauman was rendezvousing with Saipan-bound *Barbel* to transfer McNeal to that boat.

Farther south still, in Formosa Strait, Dick O'Kane on *Tang* was alerted and, at 4 A.M. on October 20, made contact with the Shima force. By this time, the force was zigzagging "erratically" at 19 knots.

* On January 16, 1944, Charlton Lewis Murphy, Jr., in *Sturgeon*, had blown off *Suzutzuki*'s bow in almost the same location.

O'Kane, who had no steam torpedoes left forward, made five attempts to guess the zigzag pattern, but each time he "guessed wrong." He trailed—or tried—until dawn, but was not able to get off a shot.

After a one-night stop in the Pescadores, the Shima force got under way again to cross Luzon Strait and join the force from Singapore. A few hours after leaving port, Shima encountered the wolf pack commanded by Edward Blakely, consisting of his *Shark*, James Ashley's *Seadragon*, and Robert Sellars's *Blackfish*. Ashley picked the force up first, incorrectly identifying it as a carrier, two cruisers, and six destroyers. He notified Blakely in *Shark* and Sellars in *Blackfish* and then maneuvered in on the surface from 30,000 yards to 3,000 yards. He fired four stern tubes at the "carrier" and a cruiser which were overlapping, then went deep. He claimed hits in both ships, but the Japanese had no record of it. Blakely and Sellars made contact but were unable to get close enough to shoot.

Shima next ran into the pack commanded by Alan Banister, consisting of his *Sawfish*, Mike Rindskopf's *Drum*, and Dick Peterson's *Icefish*. At 8 A.M. the morning of October 22, while submerged, Peterson got a good look at the force and more accurately described it as two heavy cruisers and destroyer escorts. Peterson was unable to gain attack position, so two hours later he surfaced in heavy seas to get off a contact report, but Japanese planes forced him under before he could deliver the message. That night, Peterson finally managed to raise a station in Australia which took the message.

While Shima had been going south, Admiral Ozawa had been feverishly preparing his carrier force, designed to lure Halsey from the Philippines. His worst problem was trying to find aircraft. Admiral Toyoda had stripped the carriers to help defend Formosa; all Ozawa could get together were about 110 planes. For this reason, he left the jeep carriers *Junyo, Ryuho,* and *Jinyo (Shinyo)* behind. Instead of them, he had two curiosities: *Ise* and *Hyuga,* old battleships that had been fitted with a small hangar and flight deck on the after portion of the hull, making each vessel half aircraft carrier, half battleship, accommodating about twenty-four planes. However, there were not enough planes for *Ise* and *Hyuga,* and they had to go as quasi-battleships. In addition to *Ise* and *Hyuga,* Ozawa had three light cruisers, *Isuzu, Oyodo* and *Tama,* plus about eight destroyers.

All this time Tom Wogan in *Besugo*, lying outside Bungo Suido, had been growing restless. It seemed to him that the carriers were not going to come out. On the evening of October 18, he asked if he could attack first and then report. Lockwood granted permission. Wogan deployed *Besugo* and Henry Monroe's *Ronquil* in the westward exit of Bungo Suido and ordered Karl Wheland in *Gabilan* to watch the eastern exit.

Meanwhile, Lockwood was worried about the northern exit from the Inland Sea, Kii Suido. He reasoned that since Wogan had attacked the destroyer on the night of October 16, Admiral Ozawa knew submarines guarded Bungo Suido and might attempt to avoid them by going out Kii Suido. On October 19, Lockwood ordered Wheland in *Gabilan* to detach from the pack and shift to Kii Suido. Since Wogan kept both *Besugo* and *Ronquil* at the western exit, Lockwood's order left the eastern exit of Bungo Suido unguarded.

On the night of October 20, Ozawa gathered his force together and steamed through the eastern exit. Since Wogan and Wheland were busy looking the wrong way, Ozawa was not detected. In one sense, this was a disappointment for Ozawa because, as a decoy, he *wanted* to be seen. On the other hand, Wogan's impatience and failure to shift Monroe in *Ronquil* to guard the east exit, together with Lockwood's decision to move Wheland in *Gabilan* to Kii Suido, cost Pearl Harbor submarines a chance to deliver attacks on Ozawa's four carriers prior to the battle.

The U.S. Invasion of Leyte

Far to the south, the main Japanese surface force at Singapore executed Sho 1. Admiral Toyoda divided this force into three units. The First Force was commanded by Vice Admiral Takao Kurita. It consisted of *Yamato, Musashi*, and other newer battleships and support units. It would go through San Bernardino Strait, circle south, and attack the landing ships at Leyte. The Second Force, commanded by Vice Admiral Shoji Nishimura, was composed of older, slower battleships and support units. It would go through Surigao Strait and attack the landing ships at Leyte from the south. The Third Force consisted of the heavy cruiser *Aoba*, the light cruiser *Kinu*, a destroyer, and five troop carriers, similar to destroyer transports. The purpose of this last group was to pick up troops from the north coast of Mindanao and shuttle them over to the west coast of Leyte.

The Singapore force departed Lingga shortly after midnight, Octo-

INVASION of LEYTE
OCTOBER 20, 1944

→ U.S. SURFACE FORCES
⇢ JAPANESE SURFACE FORCES
⋯ MAJOR AIR STRIKES

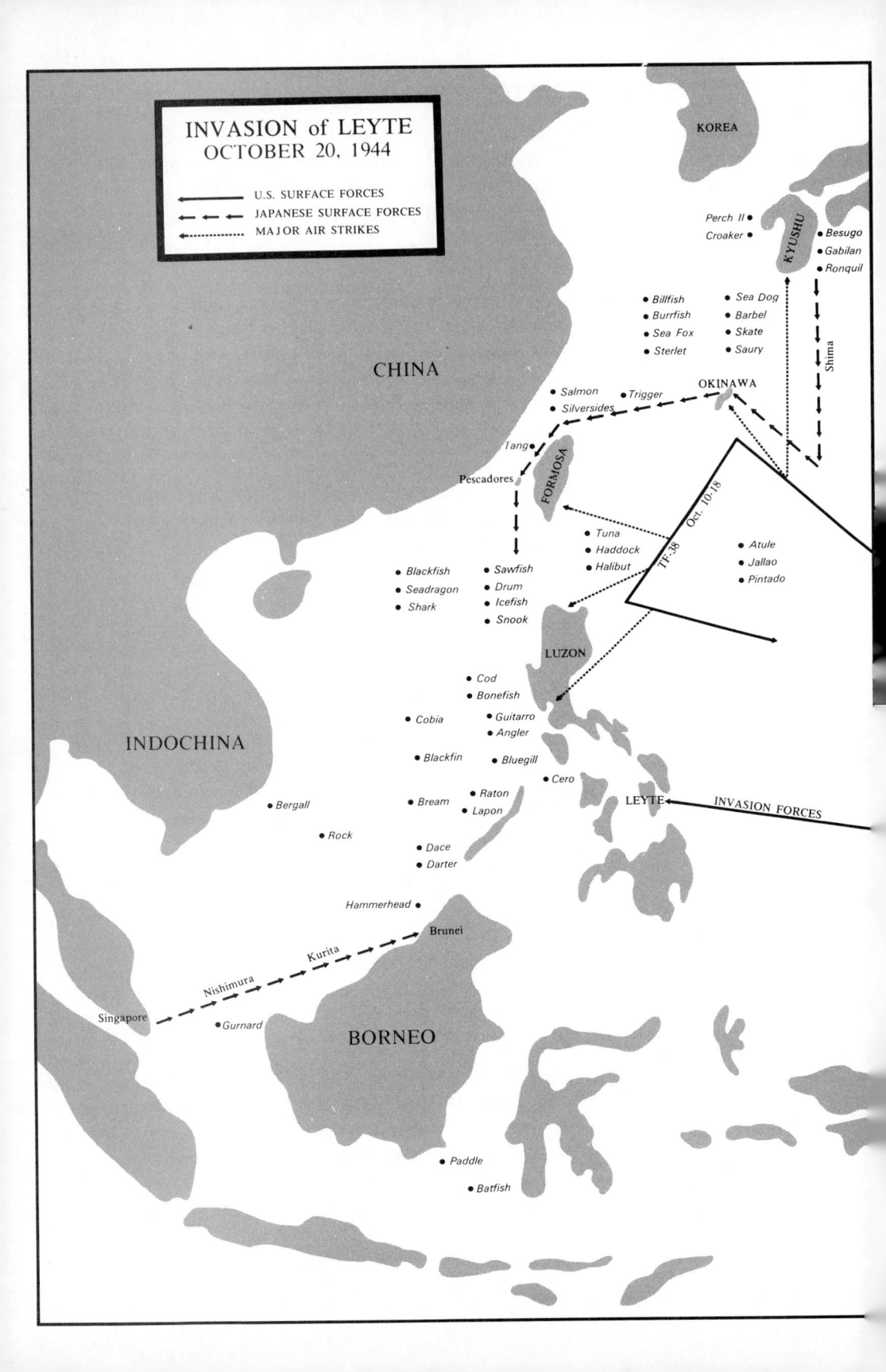

ber 18. It proceeded northeast about 700 miles to Brunei Bay, on northwest Borneo, to refuel, arriving at noon, October 20. *Gurnard,* headed to Brunei Bay to lay mines and relieve the departing *Hammerhead,* had paused to attack a convoy. For that reason, the Japanese fleet got into Brunei Bay unseen by Christie's submarines. However, the codebreakers followed its movements and kept Christie informed.

Christie deployed a dozen submarines to intercept and report on Japanese fleet movements. Claggett's *Darter* and McClintock's *Dace* took station at the south end of Palawan Passage and the west entrance of Balabac Strait. Flachsenhar's *Rock* and a new boat, *Blackfin,* commanded by a new skipper, George Hays Laird, Jr., en route from Pearl Harbor to Fremantle, took stations to the west of *Darter* and *Dace,* forming a line across the South China Sea. Another new boat, *Bergall,* en route from Pearl Harbor to Fremantle under skipper John Milton Hyde, who had been Chet Smith's exec on *Swordfish* and who had been patrolling off Indochina (where he sank a 4,200-ton ship on October 13), joined *Blackfin* and *Rock.* Moon Chapple in *Bream,* Enrique Haskins in *Guitarro,* Frank Hess in *Angler,* Lawrence Edge in *Bonefish,* and Caddy Adkins in *Cod* patrolled the area extending from the north end of Palawan Passage to Manila. Albert Becker's *Cobia,* en route from Pearl Harbor to Fremantle, patrolled Sibutu Passage. Jake Fyfe in *Batfish,* en route from Fremantle to Pearl Harbor, patrolled Makassar Strait, along with Joseph Paul Fitz-Patrick in *Paddle.*

For security reasons, none of these skippers had been forewarned about the Leyte invasion. Late on the night of October 20, after the first U.S. troops started going ashore, they heard about it from news broadcasts on the ships' radios. After that, all skippers understood the reason for their deployment and went on the alert for movements of the Japanese fleet toward Leyte.

McClintock in *Darter* was first to make contact. On the night of October 20, the Japanese Third Force—the troop ferry unit led by the heavy cruiser *Aoba* and light cruiser *Kinu*—got under way from Brunei Bay for Manila, where it would join forces with the transport destroyers to carry out the mission of lifting troops from Mindanao to Leyte. It came up to the west of Palawan Passage, making 23 knots. Shortly before midnight, McClintock intercepted. He chased at flank speed, sending off contact reports to Christie and to Claggett in *Dace,* trying to coach Claggett into intercept position. Neither *Dace* nor *Darter* could get close enough to attack, but the boats up the line near

Mindoro picked up the contact report, or received it by relay from Christie, and set a sharp watch.

The Japanese force was lucky—for a while. It got by Hess in *Angler* near the north end of Palawan Passage and Haskins in *Guitarro* in the southern region of Mindoro Strait. However, at 2:40 A.M. on the morning of October 23, Moon Chapple, who was slightly north of Haskins, picked it up on radar. Chapple chased the force for forty minutes, identifying it as two cruisers, "very large." At 3:24, he commenced firing six torpedoes at one of the cruisers. The escorts charged and Chapple went deep. Chapple hit *Aoba* * with two torpedoes. She did not sink, but she was so badly damaged she had to be towed into Manila.

Early that same morning, Claggett and McClintock picked up the main Japanese fleet coming north through Palawan Passage. It was moving slowly, seemingly oblivious to submarines, the destroyers not even pinging. McClintock in *Darter*, the pack commander, sent off a contact report to Christie. Claggett kept radio silence. McClintock maneuvered the two boats into a favorable attack position. At 5:09, McClintock in *Darter* submerged. Seven minutes later, Claggett in *Dace* submerged. By the dawn light, both skippers examined this awesome sight, preparing to fire.

McClintock let the ships come within 1,000 yards. The tension in *Darter*'s conning tower was almost unbearable. The TDC operator, Eugene ("Dennis") Wilkinson, a reservist, who would later be the first skipper of the nuclear-powered submarine, *Nautilus*, kept shouting, "Give me a range! Give me a range! I want you to shoot. You can't shoot without a range!"

Each time McClintock shifted his cross hairs from ship to ship, his exec, Ernest Louis ("Ernie") Schwab, Jr., 1939, would ask, "What's there?" McClintock replied calmly, "Battleship. . . . Cruiser. . . . Battleships. . . . Cruisers."

At 5:32 A.M., McClintock fired six torpedoes at one of the cruisers. Then he swung around and fired all four stern tubes at another cruiser. While he was firing his stern tubes, the bow tubes hit the first cruiser. Later, McClintock wrote:

Whipped periscope back to the first target to see the sight of a

---

* Admiral Samuel Eliot Morison, *History of United States Naval Operations in World War II*, volume XII, page 164, in a small oversight in an otherwise magnificent account of the battle, incorrectly states that *Aoba* and *Kinu* "split off" from Shima's force, coming down from the Inland Sea.

lifetime: (Cruiser was so close that all of her could not be seen at once with periscope in high power). She was a mass of billowing black smoke from number one turret to the stern. No superstructure could be seen. Bright orange flames shot out from the side along the main deck from the bow to the after turret. Cruiser was already going down by the bow, which was dipping under. #1 turret was at water level. She was definitely finished. Five hits had her sinking and in flames. It is estimated that there were few if any survivors.

A few minutes later McClintock heard four hits in his second target. Then he went deep. He could hear breaking-up noises and depth charges and many ships roaring overhead. Curiously, the destroyers dropped no depth charges. Over on *Dace*, Claggett, awaiting his chance, wrote:

0532 *Heard five torpedo explosions.* DARTER *must be getting in.*
0534 *Four more torpedo hits.* DARTER *is really having a field day. Can see great pall of smoke completely enveloping spot where ship was at last look. Do not know whether he has sunk but it looks good. Ship to left is also smoking badly. Looks like a great day for the* DARTER. *Can see two destroyers making smoke headed for scene. There is much signalling, shooting of Very stars, etc. It is a great show. The big ships seem to be milling around; I hope they don't scatter too far for me to get in. Light is still pretty bad but I have counted eight large ships, battleships or cruisers, plus two destroyers. Two of these large ships have been hit so far.*

Claggett was low on torpedoes. He had none aft. As the fleet bore down on him, he picked his targets carefully. The tension in his conning tower was no less than McClintock's. His exec, Rafael Celestino ("Ralph") Benitez, 1939, read off the ranges and bearings. Two heavy cruisers came into his crosshairs, but Claggett saw something bigger behind them, probably a battleship. Later he wrote, "Famous statement: 'Will let them go by—they're only heavy cruisers.'" Then:

0552 *The two cruisers passed ahead at about 1,500 yards. They were overlapping; appeared to be running screen for my target, presenting a beautiful target—a submarine should have 24 torpedo tubes. Had a beautiful view of them and identified them positively as* ATAGO *or* NACHI *class. My target can be seen better* now, and appears to be a KONGO *class battleship. He looks larger than the two cruisers that have just passed ahead—he has two stacks, and superstructure appears much heavier. Have not checked the identification as well as I should as I have been busy getting complete composition of force which I consider essential for contact report. Sound also reports target screws as heavier and slower than those of cruisers.*

Two minutes later, Claggett fired all six bow tubes at his "battleship." He heard four solid hits. Then:

0601 *Heard two tremendous explosions both on sound and through the hull. These explosions were apparently magazines as I have never heard anything like it. The soundmen reported that it sounded as if the bottom of the ocean was blowing up. They were obviously shallow as there was neither any shaking of the boat nor water swishing through the superstructure. Nothing could cause this much noise except magazines exploding.*

0603 *Heard tremendous breaking up noises. This was the most gruesome sound I have ever heard. I was at first convinced that it was being furnished by the* DACE, *and called for a check of all compartments and was much relieved to receive reports that everything was all right. Noise was coming from northeast—the direction of the target, and it sounded as if she was coming down on top of us. I have never heard anything like it. Comment from Diving officer: 'We better get the hell out of here.' After about five minutes of these tremendous breaking up noises, continued to have smaller ones and much crackling noises for next twenty minutes. These noises could be heard on sound and throughout boat. I am convinced that this ship sank; nothing else can explain these noises.*

Since both boats remained submerged for several hours, neither skipper was certain what damage he had inflicted on the Japanese force. Postwar records cleared it up. In his ten-torpedo salvo, McClintock had hit and sunk Vice Admiral Kurita's flagship, the heavy cruiser *Atago*, and severely damaged a second cruiser, *Takao*. Claggett had not hit a battleship but rather the heavy cruiser *Maya*. *Atago* sank in nineteen minutes, *Maya* in four.

The loss of the flagship *Atago* caused much confusion in the Japanese high command. The destroyer *Kishinami* came close aboard to take off Kurita, but the admiral had to jump in the water and swim for his life. While he was being rescued and dried out, Rear Admiral Matome Ugaki in *Yamato* took tactical command. Three hundred and sixty officers and men were lost on *Atago*.

Counting Chapple's *Aoba*, U.S. submarines had sunk or knocked out four heavy Japanese cruisers, all within the space of about two and a half hours.

A couple of hours later, McClintock returned to periscope depth and saw the damaged cruiser *Takao* lying motionless in the water. For most of the day, McClintock tried to get in for another shot, but Japanese destroyers hovered close by, blocking him, and aircraft circled over the cruiser. Claggett found *Takao* at about three o'clock that afternoon but decided his chances of getting in were "slim." McClintock decided to wait until nightfall and then coordinate with Claggett in a night surface attack. Meanwhile, *Takao* got her damage under control and set off for Brunei Bay, making 6 to 10 knots.

Later, Kinkaid's chief of staff, Rear Admiral Clifford Evans Van Hook, was critical of McClintock and Claggett for failing to exploit this opportunity. In part of the endorsement to the patrol report of *Dace*, Van Hook wrote, "It is regrettable that with two submarines in the vicinity, the damaged cruiser remained helpless for over twelve hours and finally escaped at creeping speed." This comment in an otherwise glowing endorsement made Christie furious—his submarines had knocked four heavy cruisers out of action in one morning—and led to the widening of the already large gap between himself and Kinkaid.*

After dark, McClintock rendezvoused with Claggett and laid out a plan of attack on *Takao*. It would take McClintock near an area of water filled with rocks and shoals, appropriately named Dangerous Ground. McClintock had not been able to get an accurate navigational fix for about twenty-four hours and during that day had been pushed along by uncertain currents in Palawan Passage. However, his mind was more intent on getting *Takao* than precise navigational fixes. He gave Claggett his orders and both boats commenced an end around at 17 knots.

The main force, meanwhile, was steaming north. Hess in *Angler*, Haskins in *Guitarro*, and Moon Chapple in *Bream* were in position to intercept. Chapple somehow failed to get the word, but Hess and

---

* Van Hook was an old friend of Lockwood's. They served together in the Naval Mission to Brazil in 1930.

Haskins picked up the main force about 8:30 P.M. Hess was closer. He bent on all possible speed and got off contact reports to Christie and Haskins. During the stern chase, Hess ran across a convoy and was tempted to break off and attack it. However, he wisely decided it was more important to trail the main body of the Japanese fleet and see exactly where it was going. By this time, Haskins in *Guitarro* was on the trail, too. Both boats tracked the fleet as it turned eastward toward Leyte. The Japanese jammed Hess's radio, but Haskins got off an accurate report to an Australian radio station, which rebroadcast it to Halsey and Kinkaid in the early morning hours of October 24. Unable to overtake and attack, Hess and Haskins returned to patrol stations off Mindoro and the northern end of Palawan Passage. U.S. carrier planes picked up the trail of the fleet the following morning.

Back at the south end of Palawan Passage, meanwhile, McClintock and Claggett were wolf-packing the damaged *Takao*. At five minutes past midnight, October 25, *Darter* ran aground with such a crash that for a moment McClintock, who was on the bridge, believed he had been torpedoed.

The exec, Ernie Schwab, who was navigating in the conning tower, rushed to the bridge. "What was that?" he said.

"We're aground," McClintock said grimly.

Schwab disappeared back in the conning tower to consult a chart. He returned to the bridge a moment later and said, "Captain, we can't be aground. The nearest land is nineteen miles away."

Darter stayed aground while McClintock tried every way possible to get his ship off the reef. He ordered all excess weight jettisoned: ammunition, food, fuel oil, fresh water. Then at high tide, 1:40 A.M., he backed the engines full and sallied ship—had the crew run back and forth to set up a rocking motion. Nothing worked. *Darter* was stuck high and dry.

When he saw it was hopeless, McClintock reluctantly radioed Claggett in *Dace*. He was reluctant, he said later, because he knew Claggett would give up trying to sink *Takao* and come to his rescue. After that, McClintock gave orders for his crew to destroy the sonar and TDC and begin destruction of classified papers and other gear.

One of the Japanese destroyers escorting *Takao*, apparently having heard *Darter* crunch aground, came close but then turned away. Belowdecks, as crewmen fed the mountain of confidential papers on the fires, *Darter* filled with smoke, causing much gagging and temporary discomfort.

Hearing the news of *Dace*'s sister ship, Claggett immediately broke off his attack on *Takao* to rescue the crew of *Darter*. Kinkaid's deputy, Van Hook, may not have believed this decision to be the wisest either. Claggett still had four torpedoes. He could have shot them at *Takao* and then rescued the *Darter* crew later in the night. But Christie approved of Claggett's decision. Had Claggett attacked *Takao*, he might have been held down by the destroyers until daylight. McClintock and his crew would have been picked up by the Japanese and probably executed for the damage they had inflicted on the fleet.

McClintock continued destroying papers and machinery and then transferred his crew to *Dace* by rubber boat, a slow, tricky operation that went on for two and a half hours. He then set demolition charges and left the ship, carrying a wardroom ashtray for a souvenir. Claggett hauled clear at full speed. The charges exploded. But in place of a deafening explosion, there was only a dull pop. Something had gone wrong.

What to do? McClintock and Claggett decided there was only one answer: torpedo *Darter*. During the next hour or so, Claggett fired four torpedoes, one at a time. All hit the reef on which *Darter* had grounded and blew up without inflicting any damage on *Darter*. The two skippers then decided to destroy *Darter* with *Dace*'s deck gun. The crew pumped twenty-one shells into *Darter*, doing some damage but not destroying her; then a Japanese plane came over and forced Claggett to break off this effort. Fortunately, the Japanese plane attempted to bomb *Darter*, not *Dace*, though unsuccessfully.

During the day, Claggett hung around, intending to put another demolition party on board *Darter* that night. A Japanese destroyer came alongside *Darter* and probably sent a boarding party on her. That night, when Claggett got within 2,000 yards of *Darter*, his sonarman picked up echo ranging. Since there was nothing on radar, Claggett and McClintock assumed the ranging to be a Japanese submarine and hauled clear again, this time setting course for Fremantle. It took eleven days to get there. With eighty-five officers and men from *Darter* on board, plus her own eighty, *Dace* soon ran low on food. By the time the boat reached Fremantle, the men were subsisting on nothing but mushroom soup and peanut butter sandwiches.

Christie made two more efforts to destroy *Darter*. He ordered John Flachsenhar in *Rock* to try torpedoes again. Flachsenhar came down and fired ten torpedoes at *Darter*, but these too apparently blew up on the reef without inflicting serious damage. Finally, Christie called in

George Sharp in *Nautilus*, then in the Philippines on another special mission. With her big six-inch guns, *Nautilus* pumped fifty-five shells into *Darter*. She didn't blow up as hoped, but she was so badly holed that she was not worth trying to salvage and remained on that reef for years afterward. Her crew was transferred as a unit to new construction: *Menhaden*, in Manitowoc.

Takao limped into Brunei Bay. From there she made Singapore, where she remained for the rest of the war, unable to find parts to repair a smashed engine.

The Battle of Leyte Gulf

The main Japanese fleet, as planned, split into two groups. Kurita's First Force steamed eastward from Mindoro for San Bernardino Strait; Nishimura's Second Force steamed through Balabac Strait eastward for Surigao Strait. Meanwhile, Admiral Ozawa was approaching Luzon from the northeast with his carrier force to "lure" Halsey away from the landing beaches. Admiral Shima's small cruiser force had been lost in the vast shuffle of Japanese forces. More or less on his own, he decided to follow Admiral Nishimura through Surigao Strait.

What took place over the next forty-eight hours—to be known as the Battle of Leyte Gulf—was the greatest naval engagement in the history of the world. In the first exchange, October 24, U.S. aircraft hit both Kurita's First Force and Nishimura's Second Force while Japanese land-based planes struck at the conglomeration of ships near the Leyte beaches. The United States sank the super-battleship *Musashi*, damaged two battleships and two cruisers from Kurita's force, and damaged a battleship and destroyer from Nishimura's force. The badly mauled Kurita First Force reversed course, requesting land-based air support, then came about and charged again for San Bernardino Strait. Nishimura's Second Force continued on, reducing speed to allow for Kurita's double turnabout. Admiral Shima's cruiser force, not yet integrated into the battle plan, followed behind Nishimura's force.

Meanwhile, Admiral Ozawa was approaching from the north. On the afternoon of October 24, about the time Kurita was doubling back, planes from Halsey's carrier force found Ozawa. Halsey then made a decision that would keep naval strategists busy arguing for decades. Concluding that Kurita and Nishimura had been decisively attacked

THE BATTLE OF LEYTE GULF

and presented no real threat to the landing forces, Halsey turned his carrier force north to attack Ozawa. He took the bait, just as the Japanese had hoped. San Bernardino Strait was unguarded; there was not even a submarine there.

Left by Halsey to his own resources, Admiral Kinkaid deployed his forces to stop the pincers aimed at him. To oppose Nishimura's Second Force, followed by Shima's cruiser force, Kinkaid deployed PT boats, six old battleships (some of which had been raised from the Pearl Harbor mud), six cruisers, and thirty-odd destroyers. These met and annihilated Nishimura's force, sinking everything except one destroyer, *Shigure*. Shima came up after this battle, wondering what was going on. His light cruiser, *Abukuma*, was damaged by torpedo boats and later abandoned. His heavy cruiser, *Nachi*, collided with one of Nishimura's crippled heavy cruisers, *Mogami*.* Shima then withdrew with all he had left.

Kurita's First Force, meanwhile, pushed eastward through San Bernardino Strait. To oppose this mighty fleet, Kinkaid had little more than his dozen jeep carriers, which were slow and thin-skinned. These naval forces met on the morning of October 25. The jeep carrier pilots fought gallantly, sinking three heavy cruisers, all the while sending urgent calls for help to Halsey. Kurita badly damaged the light carrier *Princeton* (later abandoned and sunk by U.S. forces), and sank the jeep carrier *Gambier Bay*, two destroyers, and a destroyer escort. With victory almost in his grasp, Kurita made a decision as controversial as Halsey's: he ordered his fleet to withdraw. This decision, he explained later, was based on misinformation and an incomplete grasp of the situation. Kurita believed that Halsey was coming up with a powerful carrier force, that land-based U.S. aircraft were gathering to assault his fleet, and that even if he did proceed to the landing beaches the landing ships would have fled by the time he got there. He retired through San Bernardino Strait, where he was further hounded by U.S. planes, which damaged *Yamato* and other vessels. He returned to Brunei Bay, evading submarines in Palawan Passage by going to the west of Dangerous Ground.

That same morning, October 25, Halsey's massive fast carrier force engaged Ozawa's decoy force and devastated it, sinking all four carriers—*Zuikaku*, *Zuiho*, *Chitose*, and *Chiyoda*—and three destroyers. The hybrid carrier-battleships, *Ise* and *Hyuga*, three light cruisers (in-

---

* Poetic justice, perhaps. *Mogami* had rammed *Mikuma* in the withdrawal from the Battle of Midway after sighting *Tambor*.

BATTLE for LEYTE GULF
OCTOBER 23-25, 1944

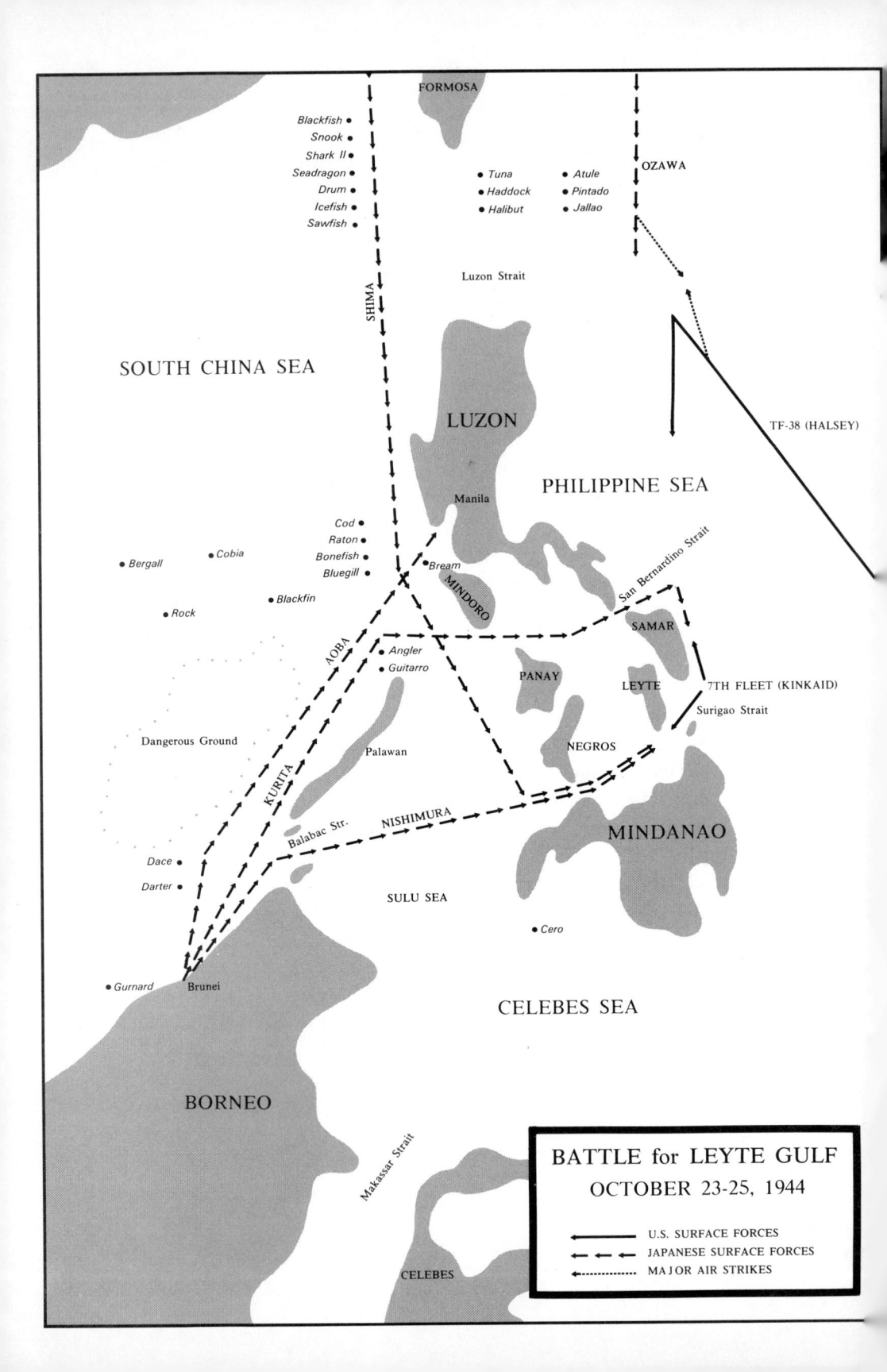

— U.S. SURFACE FORCES
⇠ ⇢ JAPANESE SURFACE FORCES
··· MAJOR AIR STRIKES

THE BATTLE OF LEYTE GULF

cluding *Tama*, badly damaged), and five destroyers escaped and retreated northward. Halsey might well have annihilated this force, too, but he turned back to support Leyte, unaware that Kurita had already retreated through San Bernardino Strait.

While this battle was in progress, two packs arrived in Luzon Strait, one commanded by Chick Clarey in *Pintado* (*Pintado*, *Jallao*, and *Atule*) and one commanded by Beetle Roach in *Haddock* (*Haddock*, *Halibut*, and *Tuna*). Lockwood directed them to form a scouting line to intercept retiring Japanese cripples from the battle between Ozawa and Halsey.

By chance, Pete Galantin in *Halibut* was closest to the scene. At five o'clock on the evening of October 25, he heard U.S. carrier pilots on radio directing the follow-up (and unsuccessful) attacks on the carrier-battleships *Ise* and *Hyuga* and their escorts, including the cruiser *Oyodo*. Then he saw smoke and antiaircraft fire on the horizon.

At 5:42, Galantin saw something else: pagoda masts of a battleship coming his way. This was probably *Ise*. Galantin got off a contact report to his packmates and then submerged to attack. At 6:43 he fired six bow tubes at *Ise* from very long range, 3,400 yards. There was a destroyer coming right at him so he elected not to fire his stern tubes—a decision he later regretted—and went deep. He heard what he believed were hits in *Ise* and believed he sank her. Actually, however, he hit not *Ise* but the destroyer *Akitsuki*, 2,000 tons, one of the escorts which wandered into the torpedo track. *Akitsuki* sank.

At about 8 P.M., Galantin surfaced. To the northward, he saw signal lights, which he believed to be the escorts of the "late" battleship. To the southward he could see gunfire flashes on the horizon. He took off northward after the "escorts" (actually his original target, *Ise*). While pursuing, he received a contact report from a packmate, Edward Steffanides in *Tuna*. Thinking *Tuna*'s targets better than the "escorts" he was chasing, Galantin broke off the chase and headed for *Tuna*'s position.

Actually *Tuna* had probably sighted *Ise* and *Hyuga*; Beetle Roach in *Haddock* also picked them up and chased. At about 11 P.M., Galantin found them again. The Japanese force was making 19 knots. There was no way any of the three boats could overtake and gain a firing position, so they flashed word to Clarey's pack, which had taken position farther north.

Clarey was then busy with another target. At about 8 P.M., one of his boats, *Jallao*, commanded by Joseph Icenhower making his maiden patrol as skipper, had picked up the damaged light cruiser *Tama* and flashed word to Clarey. Clarey directed his own boat, *Pintado*, and the third boat of the pack, John Maurer's *Atule*, into intercept position and gave the honors to Icenhower. Shortly after eleven o'clock, Icenhower fired seven torpedoes at *Tama*, obtaining three hits. *Tama* sank almost instantly, while Clarey, who was 15,000 yards away, watched on his bridge. When Icenhower surfaced, he learned that on his first shots of the war he had sunk a light cruiser.

During this time, John Coye's pack (*Silversides*, *Trigger*, and *Salmon*) had been moving down to backstop the scouting line. On the morning of October 26, Harlfinger in *Trigger* intercepted *Ise*, *Hyuga*, and escorts. He was slightly out of position to attack, blaming this on Galantin's contact report, which had not, Harlfinger noted, contained *Halibut*'s position. Coye in *Silversides* chased on the surface in broad daylight, with land in sight 15 miles away. Nauman in *Salmon* joined the chase, but he sighted a Japanese periscope and turned away. Lockwood ordered all three boats of this pack to pursue the force northward at high speed.

Rebel Lowrance in *Sea Dog* lay along the track. On the evening of October 28, at about 9:20, he picked up the force at 10 miles. He submerged ahead to radar depth and fired six electrics at *Ise*, but at the last minute the ship zigzagged and all the torpedoes missed. By that time, the Japanese force was making 22 knots. There was no way Lowrance could end-around. He chased—making a contact report—but lost the force at 15 miles. "It was a heartbreaker," he said.

Butch Robbins in *Sterlet* lay to the north of *Sea Dog*. Robbins had sunk a big 10,000-ton tanker on the day of the battle and then joined forces with John Lee in *Croaker*, returning from the East China Sea. Robbins received Lowrance's contact report, then "went to full power to intercept." Wogan in *Besugo* and *Ronquil* dropped down from Bungo and Kii Suido to intercept. The three boats—*Sterlet*, *Besugo*, and *Ronquil*—formed an informal pack, Wogan leading.

At 4:15 on the morning of October 29, Robbins made contact with the two ships and destroyer escorts, range 12 miles. Robbins reported later he went to "full emergency power," meanwhile alerting the other boats. He closed to 6 miles but then, as dawn began to break, gave

OZAWA'S RETREAT
OCTOBER 25-29, 1944

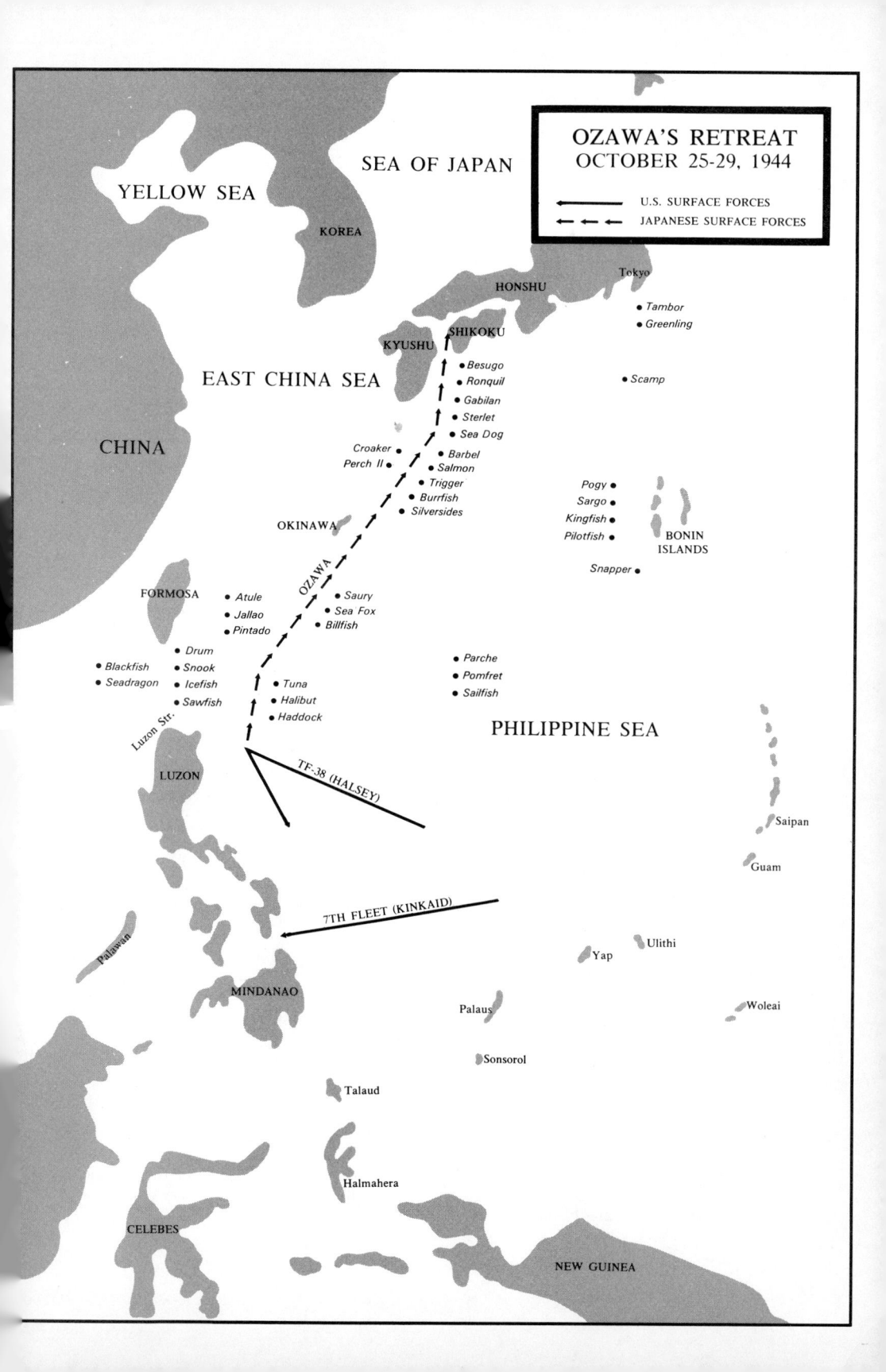

← U.S. SURFACE FORCES
←-←-← JAPANESE SURFACE FORCES

YELLOW SEA
SEA OF JAPAN
KOREA
HONSHU
Tokyo
KYUSHU
SHIKOKU
EAST CHINA SEA
CHINA
• Besugo
• Ronquil
• Gabilan
• Sterlet
• Sea Dog
Croaker • Barbel
Perch II • Salmon
• Trigger
• Burrfish
• Silversides
OKINAWA
OZAWA
• Tambor
• Greenling
• Scamp
Pogy •
Sargo •
Kingfish •
Pilotfish •
BONIN ISLANDS
Snapper •
FORMOSA
• Atule
• Jallao
• Pintado
• Saury
• Sea Fox
• Billfish
• Drum
• Blackfish • Snook
• Seadragon • Icefish
• Sawfish
• Tuna
• Halibut
• Haddock
• Parche
• Pomfret
• Sailfish
Luzon Str.
LUZON
TF-38 (HALSEY)
PHILIPPINE SEA
Saipan
Guam
7TH FLEET (KINKAID)
Palawan
MINDANAO
Yap
Ulithi
Palaus
Woleai
Sonsorol
Talaud
Halmahera
CELEBES
NEW GUINEA

up the chase.* *Besugo* and *Ronquil* also made radar and visual contact with the force, but they were not able to gain firing position either.

The chase after *Ise* and *Hyuga* had taken Coye's pack northward toward Empire waters. On October 30, Fritz Harlfinger in *Trigger* picked up a large tanker with four escorts and attacked. One torpedo broached, alerting the tanker, which turned to avoid the others. Harlfinger fired again. This time his torpedoes hit, blowing off the tanker's stern. Escorts forced *Trigger* deep. Later, Harlfinger surfaced and notified his packmates, who hurried over. Harley Nauman, commanding *Salmon*, was next on the scene. That night he found the tanker, unmoving and guarded by the four alert escorts. Nauman set up, fired four torpedoes, and got two hits. The escorts charged angrily. Nauman went to 300 feet and received a severe depth-charging that drove the old thin-skinned boat to 500 feet. *Salmon* was badly damaged and leaking heavily. Nauman and his exec, Richard Boyer Laning, decided the only hope lay in returning to the surface and fighting it out with their deck guns.

Salmon came up and lay on the surface, almost helpless. The near escort was only 7,000 yards away, but he appeared to be waiting for his cohorts to join him before he attacked. This gave Nauman a few precious minutes to correct a 15-degree list, get his engines on the line, and plug some leaks. Finally, the escort charged, apparently intent on ramming. Nauman, believing the best defense to be a good offense, charged at the escort, firing everything he had, and the two vessels passed each other only 50 yards apart, like two frigates of old. As *Salmon* raked the escort from stem to stern, she apparently killed all the Japanese who were topside. The escort stopped dead in the water.

Nauman could scarcely believe his good luck. Emboldened, he fought off a charge by a second escort and ducked into a rainsquall to hide and call his packmates for help. *Silversides* and *Trigger* answered the call at flank speed, as did *Sterlet*, *Besugo*, *Ronquil* and *Burrfish*. *Salmon* dived again to await their arrival.

The next night, the boats congregated near *Salmon*. Robbins in *Sterlet* took time out to polish off the tanker, *Korei Maru*, 10,000 tons

---

*This incident led to further friction on *Sterlet*. While the eager Schratz would probably have chased the ships right into the Inland Sea, Robbins felt he had done all that was reasonably possible.

THE BATTLE OF LEYTE GULF

(for which *Trigger*, *Salmon*, and *Sterlet* split credit, one third each); then he helped Coye and Harlfinger with *Salmon*. *Sterlet* escorted *Salmon* back to Saipan, arriving on November 3. When the engineers got a look at *Salmon*, they decided she was so badly damaged and so old there was no point in trying to fix her up again for combat. She went back to Portsmouth, where she was repaired and became a training vessel for the Atlantic Fleet. Nauman and her crew were transferred intact to a new boat, *Stickleback*, under construction at Mare Island.

The unhappiness on *Sterlet* was resolved by transferring both the skipper and the exec. Robbins went to a job in operations in Squadron 10; Schratz went into the exec pool and wound up on Maurer's *Atule*. Command of *Sterlet* went to Hugh Howard Lewis, formerly exec of *Seal*, who became the first reservist to command a fleet boat.*

Allied troops continued to storm the beaches on Leyte. For a while it looked easy. On the first day, in a carefully staged ceremony, General MacArthur waded ashore from a landing craft in knee-deep water and said, "People of the Philippines, *I have returned*." After that, the fighting—and the weather—grew worse. In spite of repeated carrier strikes against the Visayas and Luzon, the Japanese managed to reinforce the 22,000 troops on Leyte with another 45,000. The land fighting dragged on for weeks. Before it was done, 68,000 Japanese were killed. The U.S. sustained 15,500 casualties, about 3,500 killed.

The Japanese sent submarines and kamikaze pilots to attack the invasion ships and carrier forces. Five RO-class and eight I-class were moved into position. The ROs found no targets and returned to port unharmed. The I-class torpedoed the jeep carrier *Santee* and the light cruiser *Reno* for damage and sank a destroyer escort, *Eversole*. U.S. forces sank six of the eight I-class boats—and sank others later.

The pioneering kamikaze pilots hit the fast carriers *Franklin*, *Belleau Wood*, *Intrepid*, *Cabot*, *Essex*, *Lexington*, and *Hancock*; the jeep carriers *Kalinin Bay*, *Kitkun Bay*, and *St. Lo* (formerly *Midway*); plus many other U.S. ships. *St. Lo* sank. Many were severely damaged and sustained high casualties.

During the invasion of Leyte, the Japanese launched their first *kaiten* (human torpedo) attacks. Four I-class submarines were as-

---

* Lewis was actually a Naval Academy man who graduated second from the bottom in the class of 1934, resigned from the navy, but maintained a standing in the reserves and was called to duty when war came.

signed to the mission: *I-36*, *I-37*, *I-38*, and *I-47*. *I-36*, *I-37*, and *I-47* were each fitted with four human torpedoes; *I-38* was to provide advance reconnaissance information. The targets were the U.S. fleet anchorage at Ulithi and Kossol Pass in the Palaus. On the way to station, both *I-37* and *I-38* were sunk with help from codebreakers. *I-36* and *I-47* reached Ulithi as planned. *I-36* fired one *kaiten*; the other three were defective and had to be thrown away. *I-47* fired four. At least one *kaiten* hit a fully loaded fleet tanker, *Mississinewa*. It blew up in spectacular fashion, caught fire, and sank, killing about sixty men as the salvage vessel *Extractor*, recently arrived from the States, lent assistance. The Japanese, who believed they had sunk an aircraft carrier at Ulithi, celebrated this first success and planned other forays. But the *kaiten* project was hobbled by a shortage of everything except volunteer operators: submarines for conversion to mother ships, torpedo experts (lost on Japanese submarines), and torpedoes (whose production had all but stopped because of the shortage of steel and fuel).

From a naval standpoint, the real significance of Leyte was not the land fighting and what was gained there but the four sea battles fought in support of the landings. The U.S. Navy had demolished much of the remaining striking seapower of the Japanese: the super-battleship *Musashi*, four aircraft carriers (*Zuikaku*, *Zuiho*, *Chitose*, and *Chiyoda*), and numerous other vessels. U.S. submarines had made a substantial contribution during the fight, sinking two heavy cruisers (*Atago* and *Maya*), one previously damaged light cruiser (*Tama*), and a destroyer (*Akitsuki*) and inflicting serious damage to the heavy cruisers *Aoba* and *Takao*.

After Leyte, the Japanese navy was reduced to a few major units that never again fought as an integrated force: the super-battleship *Yamato*, several other battleships and heavy cruisers—many damaged —including *Ise* and *Hyuga*, and the jeep carriers *Junyo*, *Ryuho*, and *Jinyo* (*Shinyo*), which were pressed into service escorting convoys. In Japan, two other Japanese carriers were nearing completion: *Unryu* and the gigantic 60,000-ton *Shinano*, sister ship of *Musashi* and *Yamato*, converted to a carrier.

Patrols from Pearl Harbor

While the fighting was in progress on Leyte, the majority of U.S. submarines on patrol—or going on patrol—were assigned to shut off the flow of Japanese military reinforcements to the Philippines. Lockwood's boats attacked from the north—in the East China Sea, Formosa Strait, and Luzon Strait. Christie's boats attacked from the south, concentrating in the South China Sea near the approaches to Manila. Some boats operated alone, but most were organized into wolf packs.

After missing Shima's southbound cruiser force in the north end of Formosa Strait, Dick O'Kane in *Tang* shifted his effort to merchant shipping. In the early hours of October 23 he found a ten-ship convoy near the China coast, five freighters and five escorts. O'Kane maneuvered inside the escorts and joined the convoy, firing nine torpedoes from point-blank range at what he believed to be three small overlapping tankers. The convoy scattered in confusion, one freighter ramming a transport. Postwar records credit O'Kane with sinking three small freighters that night: *Toun Maru*, 2,000 tons; *Wakatake Maru*, 2,000 tons; and *Tatsuju Maru*, 2,000 tons. It is possible—even probable—that all three ships were carrying aviation gasoline for Japanese aircraft in the Philippines and that in the resulting explosions and confusion O'Kane mistook them for tankers. Counting the two ships O'Kane had sunk on October 10 and October 11, his score for the patrol now stood at five ships.

The following evening, October 24–25, as Kurita and Nishimura were charging through San Bernardino and Surigao straits, O'Kane found another convoy. He again maneuvered *Tang* inside the escorts to point-blank range and fired ten torpedoes, sinking two big, heavily laden freighters, *Kogen Maru*, 6,600 tons, and *Matsumoto Maru*, 7,000 tons, and damaging at least one other. With only two torpedoes remaining, O'Kane hauled out to catch his breath and check the torpedoes. Then he bored in again to polish off the cripple.

O'Kane set up and fired these last two torpedoes. The first ran true; the second broached and began a circular run, turning back toward *Tang*. Later, O'Kane wrote:

Rang up emergency speed. Completed part of a fishtail maneuver in a futile attempt to clear the turning circle of this erratic circular run. The torpedo was observed through about 180° of its turn due to the phosphorescence of its wake. It struck abreast the after torpedo room with a violent explosion about 20 seconds after firing. The tops were blown off the only regular ballast tanks aft and the after three compartments flooded instantly. The TANG *sank by the stern much as you would drop a pendulum suspended in a horizontal position. There was insufficient time even to carry out the last order to close the hatch.*

O'Kane and eight other men on the bridge were hurled into the water. One other officer in the conning tower escaped to join them. During the night these ten men tried to hang together, but one by one they slipped away and drowned. By dawn, only O'Kane and three others were left.

Belowdecks, *Tang* was a shambles. Thirty men survived the blast, many with serious injuries. Some in the control room flooded the forward ballast tanks, bringing *Tang* to rest, more or less level, at 180 feet. The thirty survivors gathered in the forward torpedo room with the intent of getting out through the escape trunk. An attempt was made to burn the confidential papers, but the smoke drove the men forward. Fire broke out in the forward battery compartment, further complicating the problem.

Commencing at about 6 A.M., four parties, comprising a total of about thirteen men, began the escape procedure they had learned in sub school, using the escape trunk and Momsen Lungs—the only known case in the war where the Momsen Lung provided escape.*
Only five men survived the ascent or subsequent exposure in the water. In all, eight men, including O'Kane, his chief boatswain, W. R. Leibold, two officers, H. J. Flanagan and L. Savadkin, and three other enlisted men survived. They were picked up by a Japanese patrol boat and severely beaten. O'Kane said later, "When we realized that our clubbings and kickings were being administered by the burned, mutilated survivors of our own handiwork, we found we

---

* Actually, all the emphasis on the Momsen Lung, including training ascents in the sub school's 100-foot water tower, was an unfortunate error, born of ignorance. It made submariners think that a Momsen Lung was necessary for escape. After the war, experiments carried out by submariner Walter Frederick Schlech, Jr., and others demonstrated that trapped submariners could safely ascend from a sunken submarine without a lung or any other breathing device from depths up to 300 feet. Had this been known during the war, many more submariners might have saved themselves. Thus, in one sense, the Momsen Lung concept may have killed far more submariners than it rescued.

could take it with less prejudice." O'Kane and the other seven served out the remainder of the war in a POW camp.

After the war, when O'Kane submitted a patrol report from memory, Lockwood credited him with sinking thirteen ships for 107,324 tons: five tankers, four transports, three freighters, and one destroyer. According to these figures, this was by far the best war patrol of the war, and for it O'Kane was awarded a Medal of Honor. Japanese records reduced the total to seven ships for 21,772 tons.

In just over four war patrols, Dick O'Kane sank twenty-four confirmed ships for 93,824 tons, which made him the leading skipper of the submarine war in terms of ships sunk. (Slade Cutter and Mush Morton tied for second place with nineteen ships each.) In addition to the Medal of Honor, O'Kane received three Navy Crosses and three Silver Stars and a Legion of Merit.

The Blakely (*Shark*) and Banister (*Sawfish*) wolf packs patrolled due south of *Tang* in Formosa Strait. The seven boats in these two units (*Shark II, Icefish, Drum, Snook, Sawfish, Blackfish,* and *Seadragon*) picked up several Manila-bound convoys during the period October 23–26. Some of these ships were northbound, some southbound. Some may have been the same ships attacked by O'Kane.

During the nights of October 23 and 24, the two packs sank a total of ten confirmed ships. Banister in *Sawfish* got the first, *Kimikawa Maru*, a 6,900-ton converted seaplane tender. Browne in *Snook* got the next, a 5,900-ton transport. Before the day was over, Browne sank two more, a 3,900-ton tanker and a 6,900-ton freighter. Rindskopf in *Drum* got a 4,700-ton freighter. Ashley in old *Seadragon* got three: a 6,500-ton transport, a 7,400-ton transport, and a 1,900-ton freighter.

Unknown to any skipper in either pack, one of the ships in the vicinity of the combined attack that day was an old freighter transporting 1,800 U.S. POWs from Manila to Japan. It is believed that Ed Blakely in *Shark* made contact with this vessel and then attacked. The ship was torpedoed, and all but five of the POWs were lost. These five somehow got to China and made contact with friendly forces, reporting the tragedy. Counting the work of *Paddle* on September 7 and *Sealion, Growler,* and *Pampanito* on September 12, this new loss meant that U.S. submarines had accidentally killed or drowned well over 4,000 Allied POWs within a period of six weeks. Perhaps more went unrecorded.

Blakely reported to Ashley in *Seadragon* that he was making this attack. That was the last word ever heard from Blakely. Japanese records revealed that on October 24 a submarine was attacked in Blakely's vicinity and that "bubbles, and heavy oil, clothes, cork, etc." came to the surface. Lockwood and Voge believed this was *Shark*. Since Lockwood's boats had been ordered to search for POWs after sinking an Empire-bound ship, Blakely may have been engaged in a rescue mission when he was attacked.*

One officer who was particularly shocked by the loss of *Shark II* was young John Griggs, who had left the boat just before she sailed. (Griggs had also left *Wahoo* just before she sailed to her tragic end.) When Griggs reported to *Picuda* for duty, her new skipper, Evan Tyler ("Ty") Shepard, told him, "You are not leaving this boat before I do."

Two days after *Shark* was lost, Banister's pack got into another convoy. Rindskopf in *Drum* sank two ships, both large freighters of 6,900 tons. Dick Peterson in *Icefish* sank a freighter of 4,200 tons. After that, the Banister pack withdrew from the strait and returned to port.

In the seventy-two-hour period from October 23 to October 26, O'Kane and the Blakely-Banister wolf packs sank a total of seventeen Japanese ships. Many of these had been transporting reinforcements to the Philippines.

The packs led by Chick Clarey (*Pintado*, *Jallao*, and *Atule*) and Beetle Roach (*Haddock*, *Halibut*, and *Tuna*) picked up where the Blakely-Banister packs left off. On November 1, Icenhower in *Jallao* got a contact and flashed word to his packmate, Clarey. Clarey and Icenhower chased hard but were unable to gain attack position. That same night, Jack Maurer in *Atule* found a large northbound freighter with three escorts. Poor visibility helped the attack—his first of the war—and he fired off a salvo of torpedoes, claiming two hits had sunk a 10,000-ton ship. In fact, Maurer had hit and sunk the huge ex-ocean liner *Asama Maru*, 16,975 tons.

On November 2, Lockwood sent Clarey and Roach an important Ultra: a task force consisting of a carrier, battleship or cruiser, and three destroyers was southbound in Formosa Strait. Clarey's three boats and Roach's three boats formed a scouting line to intercept. At

---

* October 24 was a black-letter day for the submarine force; *Darter*, *Shark II*, and *Tang* were all lost. Including *Seawolf* and *Escolar*, five boats were lost in October in both commands.

8 P.M., just after moonrise, Clarey in *Pintado* made contact. He flashed word to Maurer in *Atule* and Icenhower in *Jallao*, then dived ahead to attack. According to Clarey's log:

As the horizon cleared with moonrise, sighted the largest enemy ship any of us have ever seen. . . . The moon was quite bright—about one and one half hours high in the east. The carrier was plainly visible as were the masts of two ships on either side of the carrier. . . . Identified the carrier as a large one with a small island forward of amidships similar to SHOKAKU *class, with one destroyer ahead, one on either beam and a light cruiser astern. The port DD was identified as a single stack modern streamlined ship.*

Clarey planned to fire six torpedoes at the carrier and four at the nearest destroyer. He fired the six bow tubes. Immediately after firing, one of the destroyers cruised into the line of fire. Four of the torpedoes smashed into *Akikaze*, 1,300 tons. She blew up and sank in four minutes. Clarey believed that at least one of his torpedoes hit the carrier (the new one, *Unryu?*), but postwar records did not bear him out. Neither Maurer nor Icenhower was able to gain attack position. The carrier—whatever it was—got away.

Ten days later, Clarey received another important Ultra: a Japanese battleship, probably *Yamato* with a heavy cruiser escort, was coming up from the south. Clarey ordered his boats into intercept position, but Icenhower in *Jallao* stumbled across a carrier, a cruiser, and four destroyer escorts, northbound, probably the same carrier Clarey had fired at on November 3. Icenhower gained attack position and got off six torpedoes, with no results. None of the boats found *Yamato*.

On November 14, Pete Galantin in *Halibut*, one of Roach's pack, picked up a four-ship convoy with three escorts. He fired four torpedoes at the largest ship from 3,100 yards, which was as close as he could get. He may have got two hits, but he couldn't stick around to find out because several aircraft pounced on *Halibut* and delivered one of the most devastating depth-charge attacks of the war. *Halibut* was almost destroyed.

Chick Clarey, close by in *Pintado*, had made an unsuccessful effort to close this same convoy and came over to lend Galantin a hand. When Lockwood was informed of the extent of *Halibut*'s damage, he ordered Clarey to escort her to Saipan. Clarey left Maurer in charge of the pack. At Saipan and later in Pearl Harbor, the engineers who examined *Halibut* decided that, like *Salmon*, she was so badly wrecked she was not worth repairing. Lockwood wrote, "The stellar performance of duty by the officers and men of the *Halibut* undoubtedly saved this ship from destruction."

The other four boats—*Haddock, Tuna, Atule,* and *Jallao*—remained in the strait for two more weeks, but only Jack Maurer in *Atule* sank more ships: a 630-ton minesweeper, an 820-ton escort (classed as an old destroyer), and a 7,300-ton freighter. Total score for Maurer: four confirmed ships for almost 26,000 tons, one of the best maiden patrols on record.

When the packs returned to Saipan, Beetle Roach was severely injured in a jeep accident and spent the next six months in various navy hospitals. Command of *Haddock* was assumed by Roach's division commander, Bill Brockman, ex-*Nautilus*.

Two Lockwood packs patrolled the shallow waters of the Yellow Sea. The first was commanded by Gordon Underwood in *Spadefish*, leading Ed Shelby in *Sunfish* and a new skipper, Robert Hugh Caldwell, Jr., in *Peto*. The second was commanded by Elliott Loughlin in *Queenfish*, leading Gene Fluckey in *Barb* and Ty Shepard in *Picuda*. These two packs, operating mostly between Shanghai and southwest Korea, exchanged information and attacked the same convoys.

First contact was made by Elliott Loughlin in *Queenfish* on the night of November 8: two ships, three escorts. Loughlin fired six torpedoes at the two ships—freighters of 1,000 and 2,000 tons—and sank both. In the early hours of the morning, he found another three-ship convoy and fired another six torpedoes at a tanker and freighter, sinking the freighter, 2,100 tons, following which he was forced down by escorts.

While this was going on, his packmate Gene Fluckey in *Barb* happened on a large unescorted ship and attacked, firing three torpedoes and obtaining two hits. The ship did not sink. Fluckey came in for another attack, firing a single torpedo which broached and "ran off into the night." He fired another; it, too, missed. Fluckey then submerged and closed to point-blank range of 500 yards and fired one more. This torpedo hit. *Gokoku Maru*, a fine ship of 10,400 tons, rolled over and sank stern first.

On Armistice Day, November 11, Loughlin picked up a large convoy of a dozen freighters with six escorts. He fired four torpedoes from an unfavorable position, obtaining one hit on one freighter before escorts drove him deep and delivered an expert working-over with fifty depth charges. Later, Loughlin surfaced and flashed news of the convoy to his packmates. Fluckey in *Barb* got the word and shortly after midnight, in heavy seas, fired eight torpedoes at four ships. Some of these hit, but many of the torpedoes were thrown off course. Fluckey's crew conducted a difficult reload; then he attacked submerged, firing three torpedoes at a freighter from about 500 yards. He hit *Naruo Maru*, 4,800 tons. Later, Fluckey wrote, "First torpedo hit in forward hold and target blew up in my face, literally disintegrating. This explosion was terrific. . . . Parts of the target commenced falling on top of us, drumming on the superstructure."

Underwood's pack, patrolling to the east of the convoy, picked up Loughlin's original contact. Underwood was at that moment engaged in a lifeguard mission, but he directed Caldwell in *Peto* to intercept the convoy. Caldwell saw Fluckey's target blow up and then he attacked, firing ten torpedoes at three targets. He heard hits in all three ships, but postwar records credited only one sunk, *Tatsuaki Maru*, 2,700 tons.

About the same time, an important convoy left Manchuria, transporting the Japanese 23rd Infantry Division to the Philippines; it was the jeep carrier *Jinyo* (*Shinyo*), carrying a load of aircraft to Manila, plus freighters and tankers, all heavily escorted by about six destroyers. Lockwood received word of this convoy from the codebreakers and flashed Ultras to his two packs. All six submarines went on sharp alert for this prize.

Loughlin in *Queenfish* made the first contact on November 15. The convoy was swarming with aircraft and escorts. Submerged, Loughlin closed what he believed to be the carrier to 1,500 yards and fired four stern tubes. As destroyers drove him deep, he believed he heard two hits in the carrier, but what Loughlin had hit—and sunk—was an aircraft ferry, *Akitsu Maru*, 9,200 tons.

That night, 30 miles away, Fluckey in Barb found *Jinyo* (*Shinyo*) and her destroyer escorts. She looked huge to Fluckey, who identified her as a *Shokaku*-class carrier. He got as close as he could on the surface—3,500 yards—and fired five torpedoes. He believed he got one hit but there was no record of it. Fluckey chased but could not catch up. He found a freighter, fired his last two torpedoes, and then headed for home.

The other two boats of the pack, Loughlin's *Queenfish* and Shepard's *Picuda*, pursued the convoy, edging down into Underwood's territory, where the two packs merged. On the evening of November 17, Shepard attacked, sinking a troop transport, *Mayasan Maru*, 9,400 tons, and damaging a tanker. That same night, one of Underwood's boats, Shelby's *Sunfish*, found *Jinyo (Shinyo)* and chased, giving contact reports. Shelby could not get into position to fire, and he broke off to go after the freighters. That evening and the next morning, he sank a 7,000-ton freighter and the 5,400-ton troop transport *Seisho Maru*. Another of Underwood's boats, Caldwell's *Peto*, attacked the convoy and sank two freighters, one 7,000 tons and one 2,800 tons.

The big prize fell to Gordon Underwood in *Spadefish*, who on November 14 had sunk a 5,400-ton freighter independently of all this. Hearing Shelby's contact report on the night of November 17, Underwood moved into the probable course of *Jinyo (Shinyo)*. He picked her up about 9 P.M., went in, and fired six torpedoes at her and four at a tanker. Later he wrote:

The carrier burst into flames and started settling by the stern. The fire could be seen spreading the length of the ship below the flight deck. . . . The carrier was loaded with planes that could be seen rolling off the deck as the ship settled aft and took a starboard list. When last seen, the bow was sticking up in the air, still burning. The stern was on the bottom in 23 fathoms of water.

Underwood had evidently missed the tanker. After reloading, he came in for a second attack. His helmsman misinterpreted an order and slowed *Spadefish* to 8 knots. An escort 1,000 yards away turned toward *Spadefish*, firing 20- and 40-mm. guns. Underwood avoided these shells, lined up on another escort, and fired four torpedoes, sinking a subchaser.

In all, these two packs sank eight ships of this convoy, including Underwood's *Jinyo (Shinyo)*; Loughlin's aircraft ferry, *Akitsu Maru*; and Shepard's large troop transport, *Mayasan Maru*. There are no precise records as to how many Japanese troops of the 23rd Division were drowned or knocked out of action, but the figure must have been high. In addition, ammunition, supplies, field guns, and other equipment, including many airplanes, failed to reach the Philippines. All this made MacArthur's job in the coming weeks easier.

The packs sank four more ships. On November 23, Shepard in *Picuda* got a 7,000-ton freighter and a 5,300-ton transport. On

November 29, Underwood sank a 4,000-ton freighter. The next day, Shelby in *Sunfish* sank a 3,700-ton transport. All boats except *Sunfish* then returned to port.

In terms of confirmed sinkings these two packs, Underwood's and Loughlin's, were among the most successful of the war. Their grand total: nineteen ships for about 110,000 tons.

Four Pearl Harbor boats patrolled the southern waters of the East China Sea. These were a three-boat pack commanded by Sandy McGregor in *Redfish*, leading Anton Gallaher in *Bang* and Lawrence Virginius Julihn in *Shad*, and a fourth boat patrolling alone, *Sealion II*, commanded by Eli Reich.

Reich entered the East China Sea via Tokara Strait and proceeded more or less toward Shanghai. On November 15 he picked up Loughlin's report of the Shanghai-bound convoy but decided that *Sealion* was "out in left field" and broke off the chase. Off Shanghai, Reich had two torpedo malfunctions. First, during a drill, his men accidentally fired one tube with the outer door closed; the torpedo smashed through, breaking the outer door and putting the tube out of commission. A day or so later, he had a battery explosion in another tube and was forced to surface in a fleet of junks in order to back down at flank speed and eject the damaged torpedo. After that, Reich left the Shanghai area and went south toward Formosa Strait.

On November 21, Reich was at the northern mouth of Formosa Strait. Shortly after midnight he picked up three huge pips at a range of 20 miles. It was a dark moonless night, with bad visibility. Closing at flank speed, Reich saw that he had two battleships escorted by two destroyers, one ahead of the battleships, one astern. The battleships were *Kongo* and *Haruna*, en route from Brunei Bay to Japan. (*Kongo* had supported the carrier attack on Pearl Harbor and then fought in many Pacific engagements, most recently as a part of Kurita's fleet at Leyte.) Reich decided to attack on the surface. He got off a contact report and then bent on flank speed to overtake.

Three hours went by before Reich could turn in to attack. From the long range of 3,000 yards, he fired six slow electric torpedoes at the first battleship, then three stern tubes at the second. Reich saw and heard three hits on the first battleship; his stern tubes were intercepted by one of the destroyer escorts, *Urakaze*, which blew up and sank. When Reich realized what had happened, he was "chagrined," he reported.

The battleships continued on at 16 knots. Reich again bent on flank speed, trying to catch up and turn in. During the long tedious chase, the torpedomen reloaded the nine usable tubes. Green water crashed over *Sealion*'s bridge as Reich ordered maximum power and more. Then, luck! One battleship with two destroyers began dropping astern, making only 11 knots. This was *Kongo*, badly damaged by Reich's first salvo. Reich easily overtook this group and got ready to attack *Kongo* again. But before he could fire another shot, as he wrote in his report:

0524 *Tremendous explosion dead ahead—sky brilliantly illuminated, it looked like a sunset at midnight. Radar reports battleship pip getting smaller—that it has disappeared—leaving only the two smaller pips of the destroyers. Destroyers seen to be milling around vicinity of target. Battleship sunk—the sun set.*
0525 *Total darkness again.*

Reich was stunned. He had done what no other submarine skipper had done, sunk a battleship—and he had done it with three electric torpedoes, fired from extreme range.

Reich tried to chase the other battleship, *Haruna*, but the seas were too heavy. He sent out another contact report and then turned off, returning to the scene of his battle for evidence of the kill or a prisoner. He found a large oil slick and circling planes.

McGregor's pack—*Redfish, Bang,* and *Shad*—had entered the East China Sea near northern Formosa and spent the next two weeks coping with a series of problems: a huge storm that battered the boats for five days, appendicitis attacks on two of the boats (though no surgery was improvised this time), and zero rewards in their efforts to find worthwhile targets. Finally, on the day after Reich—only 150 miles away—had sunk the battleship *Kongo*, the pack found a seven-ship convoy. McGregor ordered his three boats to attack.

In a furious three-hour battle, Gallaher in *Bang* fired off all twenty-four of his torpedoes. He believed he sank four ships for 18,000 tons, but postwar analysis gave him credit for sinking only two, one freighter of 2,800 tons and one of 2,400 tons. McGregor in *Redfish* fired twenty torpedoes. Thirteen missed. Seven hit, sinking, he believed, two ships; however, postwar records credited him with only one, a 2,300-ton freighter. Julihn in *Shad* fouled up his attack, firing many torpedoes (some by accident) but sinking nothing.

After this battle, McGregor ordered his pack to Saipan to reload torpedoes and conduct a second leg of the patrol. Leaving the area, Gallaher found a small fishing sampan. Later he wrote:

Surfaced. Thought perhaps sampan had picked up some survivors from the previous night's attack. Set sampan on fire with 20 mm. and a .30 cal. Crew consisted of three men, two boys and a woman. All but the woman jumped overboard. Picked up two of the men and a boy. All seemed to be unintelligent fishermen so brought them back close aboard their burning sampan, and let them go back aboard to put the fire out if they could. Continued search for convoy survivors on the surface.

The evening after the McGregor pack left station, November 23, Lockwood sent Reich an important Ultra: another Japanese battleship force was coming down Formosa Strait en route from Japan. It was probably *Ise* and *Hyuga* taking reinforcements to the Paracel Islands for transshipment to the Philippines. Reich maneuvered *Sealion* to the probable course and waited seventy-two hours. On November 26, at about 8 P.M., his radar picked up the force at the phenomenal range of 35 miles. At first, Reich believed his pip must be land, but it was a battleship (*Ise?*) and four destroyers.

Reich began maneuvering to attack. For a while, he doubted that he could gain a favorable position. However, the formation turned toward him, and he dived and set up to fire. Rechecking, Reich realized that the formation would pass at extreme range, 4,500 yards. That was the limit of the electric torpedo, but he fired six anyhow. All missed. Escorts drove him to the bottom in 270 feet of water and dropped two close charges. Then the formation went off.

Shortly after midnight, November 27, Reich came to the surface again. His radar picked up another Japanese task force, range 35 miles: another battleship (*Hyuga?*). However, *Ise* evidently warned *Hyuga*. The ships detoured around Reich, and he was not able to make an attack. After he sent off contact reports on both formations, Lockwood ordered Reich to Guam.

On November 24 and 27, over a hundred B-29 Superfortresses based at the newly completed airfield in the Marianas made their first two bombing runs over the Japanese mainland. Patrolling off Tokyo Bay, Frederick Gunn, commanding *Scabbardfish*, and Joseph Enright, commanding *Archerfish*, were ordered to lifeguard for these attacks.

As it turned out, neither was called upon for rescues, and both boats were subsequently released to conduct regular antishipping patrols in the immediate area off Tokyo Bay. Gunn on *Scabbardfish* sank a Japanese submarine, *I-365*, 1,500 tons, almost immediately. For Enright there was bigger game.

It was Enright who had made the first patrol on *Dace* and then asked to be relieved because he had no confidence in himself. He had come to *Archerfish* after nearly a year of shore duty. Now, on the night of November 28, Enright made contact with *Shinano*, brand new sister ship of *Yamato* and *Musashi*, which had been converted to an aircraft carrier while still being built. Her conversion being almost finished, she had been hurriedly commissioned on November 18, with Captain Toshio Abe in command, and was getting her finishing touches in Tokyo Bay when the B-29 raids began. Though these initial raids did relatively little damage, they made the Japanese uneasy. On November 28 *Shinano* got under way under orders from Imperial Naval Headquarters that she be moved out of the bay to the relatively safer waters of the Inland Sea. Four destroyers escorted her.

Structurally, *Shinano* was finished, but many details, such as fire pumps, were not yet complete. There were 1,900 people on board, some of them crew, others yard workers who would finish the ship, which at 60,000 tons would be the largest warship in the world (slightly larger than *Yamato*). Many of the crew were green; they had never been to sea. There had been no training.

That night, Joe Enright in *Archerfish* patrolled the outer entrances to Tokyo Bay. At 8:48, his radar operator reported a pip at 24,700 yards. Fifty-two minutes later, Enright knew he had an aircraft carrier, headed south, speed 20 knots. He laid a course to intercept and called for flank speed. "From here on," Enright wrote later, "it was a mad race for a possible firing position. His speed was about one knot in excess of our best, but his zig plan allowed us to pull ahead very slowly."

Enright thought he was losing the race and sent off two contact reports to Lockwood, so that he could alert submarines to the south. But then at 3 A.M.—about six hours after the chase began—the carrier changed course and headed right for *Archerfish*. Enright submerged ahead. The huge ship came onward while Enright's crew made everything ready.

At 3:16, Enright began firing his bow tubes from a range of about 1,500 yards. Sigmund Albert ("Bobo") Bobczynski, his exec, was watching the TDC, holding his breath. After four torpedoes had left the tubes, he shouted, "Check fire! New setup. Switch to stern tubes." Then Enright fired two stern tubes.

Forty-seven seconds after the first torpedo was fired, Enright, manning the periscope, saw and heard a hit in the carrier's stern. "Large ball of fire climbed his side," Enright noted. Ten seconds later, he saw a second hit, 50 yards forward of the first.

There was a destroyer only 500 yards on *Archerfish*'s quarter. Enright went deep. On the way down, he said later, he heard four more properly timed hits, indicating all six of his torpedoes had hit *Shinano*. Sonar reported breaking-up noises. The escorts dropped fourteen depth charges, the nearest, Enright reported, 300 yards distant. When that noise died away, the sonarman reported more breaking-up noises. The heavy screw noise of the carrier could not be heard.

At 6:10, Enright returned to the surface for a look through the periscope. "Nothing in sight," he reported. He was certain that the carrier went down on the spot.

After the war, the records revealed that *Shinano* took four hits. Captain Abe was not overly concerned; the sister ship, *Musashi*, had taken nineteen torpedoes and many bombs before sinking at Leyte. He continued on his course at 18 knots. His inexperienced damage-control parties tried to stop the flow of water, but they fought a losing battle. It was discovered that *Shinano* did not have all her watertight doors, and some that were in place leaked. Captain Abe could have grounded *Shinano* in shallow water and saved her, but he continued on. By dawn, it was evident to all that she was sinking. At 10:18, Abe ordered abandon ship. Half an hour later, the world's largest warship slid beneath the waves, taking down Abe and 500 men.

Enright remained on station another two weeks, lifeguarding B-29 raids. He received two calls for help but could never find the downed pilots. On December 9, another off day, he fired four torpedoes at two small patrol boats and missed. He returned *Archerfish* to Guam December 15, claiming to have sunk a *Hayatake*-class carrier of 28,-000 tons.

Some people were naturally skeptical. The codebreakers believed they had identified all the remaining Japanese carriers and knew where they were. But Enright's division commander, Burt Klakring, submitted a drawing of the carrier composed by Enright, and Babe Brown, acting in Lockwood's absence, credited him with sinking a

28,000-ton carrier. It was not until after the war that the whole story of *Shinano*, converted in secret and unknown to the codebreakers, came out. Then the tonnage was upped to 71,000 and Enright received a Navy Cross.

The unlikely Joe Enright, a cautious and uncertain skipper, had by the luck of the draw sunk the largest warship in history and the largest ship ever sunk by a submarine. Although in the postwar accounting the tonnage was reduced to 59,000, from a tonnage standpoint Enright's first patrol on *Archerfish* was still the best of the war.

During this period, Lockwood lost two boats. Hugh Raynor Rimmer, who had served on *Rock* during her fitting out and commissioning and on *Tautog* for a year, relieved Jim Blanchard in command of *Albacore*. On this, his first patrol in command, he was ordered to patrol off northeast Honshu, the dangerously mined area where *Pickerel*, *Runner*, *Pompano*, and *Golet* had been lost. He had strict orders to beware of mines and stay outside waters less than 100 fathoms deep.

Albacore left Pearl Harbor on October 24, topped off her fuel tanks at Midway October 28, and was never heard from again. According to Japanese records recovered after the war, she struck a mine very close to shore off northeast Hokkaido on November 7. The Japanese witness was a patrol boat. Her crew testified that the submarine was submerged and that after the explosion much heavy oil, cork, bedding, and food supplies rose to the surface.

A week later, John Hollingsworth, who had nearly lost *Scamp* to a Japanese plane on his first patrol the previous April, was ordered to patrol off Tokyo Bay. Nothing more was ever heard from *Scamp* or from Hollingsworth either. On November 29 Lockwood received information that the area in which *Scamp* had been ordered to take station, Inubo Zaki, had been mined. He and Voge believed *Scamp* might have struck one of these mines and gone down with all hands, but nothing positive is known about her loss.

Patrols from Australia

After the battle of Leyte Gulf, Christie's skippers found the hunting poor. The first boat to sink a Japanese ship was *Rock*, which torpedoed an 800-ton tanker in Palawan Passage on October 26, not far from the stranded *Darter*, at which skipper John Flachsenhar had fired ten torpedoes. The following day, October 27, John Hyde in

Bergall, slightly to the west of Palawan Passage in Dangerous Ground, sank another tanker, the 10,528-ton *Nippo Maru,* giving him a total of two ships for 14,700 tons for this patrol, which he was forced to terminate because of low fuel and torpedoes.

Off Manila, Moon Chapple in *Bream* and Enrique Haskins in *Guitarro,* coached into position by contact reports from Caddy Adkins in *Cod,* got on the trail of a convoy October 30. Chapple fired six torpedoes and probably got a hit in one transport. Haskins fired eight torpedoes and sank two freighters, 2,900 tons and 5,800 tons. One of these was a loaded ammunition ship. It blew up with a thunderous explosion that drove *Guitarro* down 50 feet. As Haskins noted in his report, "The Commanding Officer never wishes to hit an ammunition ship any closer than that one."

The next boat was *Blackfin,* commanded by the new skipper George Laird. On the morning of November 1, south of Mindoro, he found a five-ship convoy with three or four escorts and he sank a 2,700-ton freighter. Unknown to Laird, Bill Kinsella in *Ray* (who had reloaded and refueled at Mios Woendi) was approaching from the south. Kinsella saw Laird's target blow up with a "terrific explosion." As the convoy scattered, four small tankers headed Kinsella's way. He fired three torpedoes at two tankers and was certain he sank both, but postwar records credited him with only one ship, an 865-ton freighter. Escorts drove Kinsella deep and dropped depth charges.

That night Kinsella took time off for a special mission. He landed men and supplies on Mindoro and picked up two downed naval aviators and three refugees, two American POWs who had escaped from the Japanese on Corregidor and Maximo Kalaw, former Dean of Liberal Arts at the University of the Philippines, who was a guerrilla leader with a high price on his head.

On November 3, Kinsella joined Chapple in *Bream,* Haskins in *Guitarro,* and Shea in *Raton* to form a temporary four-boat wolf pack near Lingayen Gulf. On the afternoon of November 4, Shea found a convoy standing out of Manila. He fired six torpedoes at a large transport but they all missed, and Shea went deep as aircraft and escorts worked over the boat. The transport headed toward Moon Chapple; he fired four torpedoes and got a hit. Next, Haskins in *Guitarro* fired, obtaining four hits. After dark, Kinsella in *Ray* found the burning ship and fired two torpedoes, blowing off the bow and finally sinking her. Chapple, Haskins, and Kinsella were each awarded one third credit for *Kagu Maru,* 6,800 tons.

On the morning of November 6, the pack picked up a convoy

escorted by the heavy cruiser *Kumano*, which had been damaged by Halsey's planes off Samar and, until then, undergoing repairs in Manila Bay. Halsey's fighters had struck Manila again on November 5 and driven these ships out. All four boats—*Bream, Guitarro, Ray,* and *Raton*—closed in to fire at *Kumano*. Haskins in *Guitarro* shot nine torpedoes and observed three hits. Chapple in *Bream* fired four more, claiming two hits. Shea in *Raton* fired six, at least two of which passed immediately over Kinsella in *Ray*, who was making an approach; Shea claimed four hits, but they were not credited. Kinsella fired four torpedoes and then went deep. Later he wrote, "Bombs dropped close aboard, observed splashes ahead of us. . . . It is impossible to describe the pandemonium that was taking place during these last six minutes. Bombs, torpedoes and depth charges were exploding constantly." In all, the four boats had fired twenty-three torpedoes at *Kumano*. Her bow was blown off, but she was still afloat.

Kinsella was in the best position for a second attack. He went deep, intending to get between the cruiser and the beach, but at 370 feet he struck an uncharted ledge and wiped off his sonar head, causing a bad leak. In order to stop the leak, he had to come up to periscope depth. Later, he wrote, "This is the most heartbreaking experience I have ever had or hope to have in my naval career. We are in perfect position for a kill on the cruiser and the tanker, but not being able to go deep it would be suicide to fire with the escorts only 800 yards away."

Kinsella plugged the hole and crept away. Later he saw the tanker take *Kumano* in tow; the Japanese beached her nearby. Still later, Halsey's planes found her and finished the destruction. Chapple and Haskins, having shot off all their torpedoes, returned to Fremantle.

Kinsella and Shea joined up with Jake Fyfe in *Batfish* to form another wolf pack with Kinsella, the senior man, in charge. On November 14, the pack picked up a convoy off Lingayen Gulf. After dark, Kinsella fired the first torpedoes—six at a big ship. He hit it with four, and it blew up with "terrific explosions." He also believed that one of his torpedoes hit an escort. Postwar records credited Kinsella with sinking only one ship that night, an 800-ton escort. Kinsella believed that the records were in error and that he had been short-changed. Shea in *Raton* sank two ships from this convoy, both freighters, one of 2,800 tons and one of 1,000 tons. Jake Fyfe believed he had sunk the last two ships of the convoy and was so credited, but postwar records did not confirm his claim.

After that, Kinsella fired two torpedoes at a beached freighter, both of which missed. Then all three boats—*Ray*, *Raton*, and *Batfish*—proceeded on to Pearl Harbor and the States, where *Ray* received an overhaul. If Kinsella's claims are credited, as they are not in postwar Japanese records, he sank five and one third ships for about 17,000 tons. Mike Shea sank four confirmed ships for 12,300 tons.

Ben Oakley in *Growler* led a pack consisting of Francis Albert Greenup's *Hardhead* and Frank Haylor's *Hake* in the area south of Mindoro. On the way to station, Greenup found a navy aviator in a life raft, Commander Fred Edward Bakutis, a friend then commanding Fighter Group 20 on the carrier *Enterprise*. Bakutis had been adrift for seven days. Greenup transferred Bakutis to *Angler*, which was returning to Fremantle.

On November 7 Oakley notified Christie that he was having problems with his radar and urgently needed spare parts. Christie ordered Moon Chapple in *Bream*, heading home, to rendezvous with *Growler* and transfer the spare parts. Early on the morning of November 8, Oakley (whose radar was evidently working at least part of the time) made contact with a small convoy and directed Greenup and Haylor to join him in the attack. About an hour later, Greenup heard what he believed to be one of Oakley's torpedoes exploding, followed by depth charges. Greenup set up and sank a 5,300-ton tanker. He was charged by escorts and badly worked over. Haylor in *Hake* saw the tanker sink, but before he could mount an attack he was attacked by escorts and pinned down for sixteen "harrowing" hours, during which time he counted 150 depth charges, many close.

That night, Greenup and Haylor attempted to contact Oakley without success. Nothing more was ever heard from him. The famous *Growler*, which had taken Medal-of-Honor winner Howard Gilmore into combat, was gone. For Haylor, who had been with Sam Dealey when he was lost, it was the second patrol in a row in which his pack commander disappeared. Oakley's friend, Moon Chapple, arrived at the rendezvous point on the afternoon of November 10. He circled the point for twenty-four hours, waiting—until Christie told him to come on home.

Hardhead and *Hake* now became a two-boat pack, commanded by the senior man, Francis Greenup. On November 5 Greenup picked up a light cruiser off Manila but was not able to shoot. On November 18, in the same area, he found two light cruisers but, again, was unable to get close enough to shoot. On November 19 he found another light cruiser, closed, and fired six torpedoes. He sank a small frigate off Manila November 25. On November 30 he found a carrier escorted by three destroyers off Manila, but again he was unable to close.

Haylor went into Panay on a special mission and took off twenty-nine aviators who had been shot down during raids in the Philippines. The two boats returned to Australia.

Mingo, commanded by John Robert Madison, lifeguarded in Makassar Strait. In a spectacular series of rescues, Madison picked up six aviators from rubber rafts and another ten from the beaches of southern Celebes, once being bombed by a U.S. Air Force plane. Madison delivered his human cargo to Fremantle and received high praise from Christie.

The codebreakers were now the happy recipients of another windfall. An army paratroop commando team surprised and captured a small Japanese patrol boat off the north coast of Mindoro, obtaining many Japanese codebooks and ciphers, all current. The commando team notified MacArthur's staff, which in turn asked Christie to dispatch a submarine to rendezvous with the commandos and get the codebooks.

Christie alerted Laird in *Blackfin*, who attempted to rendezvous with the commandos on the north coast of Mindoro, failed, but made contact the following day, November 18. He received three bags of codebooks labeled top secret. Some of *Blackfin*'s crew overheard the commandos telling Laird what the bags contained. "The Commanding Officer," Laird later wrote in third person, "subsequently lectured the entire crew on the utmost secrecy of the information and enjoined them to forget they ever heard about it."

Laird withdrew from enemy territory and proceeded south to Morotai Island. There, off Point Anna, he transferred his valuable cargo to the Australian man-of-war *Kiama* and then proceeded to Fremantle. Christie's endorsement stated, "A special mission of great importance to Allied war strategy was accomplished. . . . This special mission was of tremendous importance to the United States and the skill and courage attendant to its conclusion are very gratifying."

During refit Laird became ill and lost command of *Blackfin*.

Irvin Hartman in *Barbero* led a three-boat pack composed of Cy Austin's *Redfin* and *Haddo*. When young Nimitz stepped down from command of *Haddo*, Christie gave the boat to Tiny Lynch, formerly exec to Sam Dealey on *Harder*. Although targets were scarce, the threesome patrolled aggressively, especially Lynch, whose endorsements called his attacks "brilliant."

On November 2, off Makassar City, Hartman sank a 2,000-ton freighter. On November 8–9, not far from the place *Growler* was lost, the pack attacked a convoy, Hartman sinking a 2,900-ton tanker, Lynch an 860-ton freighter, and Austin a 5,300-ton tanker. Lynch took *Haddo* on to Pearl Harbor and the States for overhaul. Hartman in *Barbero* and Austin in *Redfin* refueled and reloaded at Mios Woendi and took their boats to Indochina.

Guy O'Neil in *Gunnel* led a two-boat pack consisting of himself and Leonce Arnold Lajaunie, Jr., in *Muskallunge*. South of Mindoro on November 8, O'Neil sank a ship; then he and Lajaunie moved west to the South China Sea, where Albert Schorr Fuhrman in *Jack* was patrolling.

On the night of November 12, O'Neil found a heart-stopping sight: the super-battleship *Yamato* and a heavy cruiser northbound to Japan. O'Neil picked up these targets at 15 miles but was not able to get close enough for an attack. He got off a contact report and the Lockwood wolf packs in Luzon Strait went on alert, but none ever found the ships and they reached Japan safely.

Continuing on patrol, the pack found more action. On the night of November 14–15, Fuhrman got into a convoy and sank two big freighters, one of 5,400 tons and another of 6,800 tons. Two days later, O'Neil in *Gunnel* sank a 5,600-ton transport and an escort of 600 tons. On November 20, O'Neil found a light cruiser but could not get close enough to attack. Upon concluding these patrols, *Gunnel*, *Jack* (which had had severe engine problems the whole time), and *Muskallunge* (which suffered a major casualty in a generator) returned to Pearl Harbor and the States for overhaul. Lajaunie in *Muskallunge* was relieved of command after the boat completed its overhaul, going to new construction.

James Edward Stevens in *Flounder* led a pack consisting of Richard Nichols in *Bashaw* and Carl Tiedeman in *Guavina*. On the way to patrol area, Christie sent an Ultra message that a German submarine, *U-537*, basing from Surabaya, was en route for operations off Perth. Christie positioned this pack to trap the German north of Lombok Strait. Stevens in *Flounder* got on the precise track and, on November 10, fired four torpedoes. Stevens saw one hit, then smoke and flame. *U-537* went down for the last time.*

Continuing northward, on November 21, when the pack found a convoy west of Palawan Passage in Dangerous Ground, Tiedeman sank a 2,000-ton freighter and he and Stevens shared credit for sinking the 5,700-ton freighter *Gyosan Maru*.

---

* She was the second German U-boat sunk in the same area—after *U-168*, sunk by Goossens in the Dutch submarine *Zwaardvisch*. *U-537* was part of a small force of U-boats sent to help Japan. The force operated mostly in the Indian Ocean, achieving little, inasmuch as the codebreakers kept a close eye on it and routed shipping away from the U-boats.

35
Pearl Harbor and Australia, November and December 1944

New Inventions for U.S. Boats

In the fall of 1944, scientists and technicians in the States, working hand in glove with submariners, developed several secret new devices for the fleet submarine designed to enhance its effectiveness in combat. These were: (1) a "noisemaker," a decoy device fired from a submarine undergoing depth-charge attack, to fool enemy sonar; (2) a "night" periscope (one that admitted much more light in darkness), also fitted with a radar known as the ST; (3) a new and extremely short-range sonar, QLA (but called FM because frequency modulated); and (4) a small electric acoustical torpedo, called a "Cutie," which would home on the noise of an enemy ship. Lockwood, forever fascinated by new gadgets that might improve sinkings or provide greater protection for his boats, took a deep and personal interest in each of these devices.

The most promising in many ways were the Cuties, which Spike Hottel and Harry Hull (ex-*Thresher*), Lockwood's force gunnery and torpedo officer, began receiving in the summer of 1944. They were based on a German design and manufactured by Westinghouse. Like all new torpedoes produced by the Bureau of Ordnance, they were imperfect. In tests, they repeatedly malfunctioned, and the first models were useless against a target going more than 8½ knots—a severe limitation.

In the fall, when the Cutie had been improved somewhat, Carter Bennett arrived in Pearl Harbor in a new boat, *Sea Owl*. Since Bennett had a master's degree in torpedo ordnance and much combat experience, Lockwood selected him to make the first combat test of the Cutie. Bennett led a wolf pack consisting of *Sea Owl*, *Piranha*, commanded by Harold Ruble, and *Sea Poacher*, commanded by Francis Michael Gambacorta, to the East China and Yellow seas. Bennett carried several Cuties in his racks.

The pack, often diverted to lifeguard B-29 raids (staged from bases in China), had little opportunity to conduct coordinated attacks, but Bennett made three opportunities to test the Cutie. The first was in the shallow waters of the Yellow Sea. Bennett picked up a small patrol craft, then took position ahead and dived to 150 feet, the depth considered safe to fire a Cutie (anything less and the Cutie might turn and home on the launching submarine). The Cutie performed as designed, presumably, homing on the propeller noise of the patrol craft. Hearing an explosion, Bennett surfaced to investigate. He found the patrol craft in "sinking condition" and left, judging this first combat employment of the secret weapon an unqualified success.

The next two opportunities were not so conclusive. On the second, Bennett found what he believed to be a destroyer off Nagasaki. Employing the same tactics, Bennett fired a Cutie, heard an explosion, and surfaced. The target (not a destroyer but a patrol craft) appeared to be damaged but not severely. Bennett approached from dead ahead of the target and fired a Mark XVIII electric from 1,000 yards. The electric hit solidly and the patrol craft disintegrated; Bennett ran through the debris to make certain.

Not long afterward, Bennett saw what he believed to be a destroyer coming out of Nagasaki, presumably to aid the ship Bennett had just sunk. Bennett submerged (it was almost dawn by then), took position on the enemy track, and fired a couple of more Cuties. This time, no luck, either because the target was going much too fast or because it spotted the torpedoes and evaded. "The last time we saw him," Bennett said later, "he was going over the hill for Nagasaki."

When Bennett returned from patrol, Lockwood was pleased. Although the test had been "spotty" (as Lockwood described it), it seemed to him that the Cutie had merit, especially as a weapon to use against shallow-draft antisubmarine vessels. Even if the Cutie didn't sink them, it might damage the propellers and force them to stop, as had been the case in Bennett's first two attacks. Then, once they had been stopped, a submarine might actually sink them with another Cutie or with a regular electric set to run at shallow depth from short range, as Bennett had done in his second attack. However, follow-up combat tests of the Cutie were not so successful. Hull, Hottel, and others went on trying to debug it and waited for later models that could hit faster targets.

The other gadget that held promise was the FM sonar. This supersensitive device was conceived to detect mines, to prevent the tragedy that befell *Robalo* and *Flier* and probably three or four other boats off northeast Honshu. In tests conducted off the coast of California, the FM picked up dummy mines at a range of 450 yards—about a quarter of a mile. When a mine was detected on the machine, it gave off a peculiar and chilling gonging, which the submarine crews appropriately called "Hell's Bells."

One of the first FMs was mounted on *Tinosa* while she was undergoing refit in San Francisco. During that time, Richard Clark Latham, who had made one war patrol on *Perch* as a PCO, relieved Don Weiss as skipper. Latham found his crew hostile to the FM gear. It could have only one purpose, searching out enemy minefields, and few men were anxious to engage in that risky task.

Latham said later, "*Tinosa* had made seven consecutive successful war patrols under Dan Daspit and Don Weiss. The original crew was still intact . . . [reunited] with their families and loved ones again after a long time facing death. They had been promised—or had dreamed—that when *Tinosa* got back to the States, they would be transferred to refrigeration school or you-name-it, after which they would get new construction and spend a year building a sub—maybe they wouldn't have to go to war again if they were lucky."

After the refit, Latham took *Tinosa* to San Diego for more FM training with dummy minefields. The crew was less and less enthusiastic. The FM did not always perform, and many became convinced that this new inexperienced skipper would take them into a Japanese minefield and blow them all to hell. Many asked for transfers, but Latham denied these requests—at least until *Tinosa* reported to Pearl Harbor for duty. On the way out, Latham interviewed each man, learning that not less than half wanted off the boat. He sent a message to Pearl Harbor, reporting that he had never seen morale as low on any ship in the navy as *Tinosa*, and requested a rate-for-rate exchange for these men, which included some chiefs. At Pearl Harbor, Latham recalled, they didn't know whether to transfer Latham off or the men, but in the showdown Latham stood pat. Thirty-five of *Tinosa*'s crew went to other duty (many to *Shark*, on which, ironically, they were lost); thirty-five new men (many from *Shark*) reported on board.

Latham took *Tinosa* on her first patrol to the vicinity of Okinawa in December. He did not have specific orders to investigate minefields but kept the gear operating to see what he could find. One day the crew was galvanized by Hell's Bells gonging from the FM receiver. Later Latham said, "We had no doubt but that it was a minefield. . . . *Tinosa* reported the event. . . . Lockwood was elated by the news of the first minefield detection by his pet development."

Upon receiving the news, Lockwood ordered Latham to make a complete FM survey of Okinawa. Latham closed to two miles of the beach and began this arduous and nerve-racking chore. "I don't know anyone who liked it," Latham said later. "I had a St. Christopher's medal blessed by a priest which hung on a chain in my cabin—until somebody swiped chain, medal and all. I used to go in my cabin and hold the medal and bow and pray fervently and then figure that if I kept my wits and used my brain and did the best that I possibly could under whatever circumstances I found myself, I'd done all that could be done and the rest was in the hands of fate. Talk about alert! I could feel, see, hear, smell, and taste better than an Indian or a wolf. . . . I remember thinking that if I got through the war, I would never again worry about life's little travails." Latham received a Navy Cross and high praise from Lockwood for this first FM mission.

Burt's Brooms

After the Leyte invasion, Admiral Halsey planned to take Task Force 38 on a strike against the Japanese mainland, the first carrier attack since the Doolittle raid in April 1942. Halsey hoped to catch the remaining ships of the Japanese fleet in their anchorages and to damage portions of the aviation industry. The raid was code-named Operation Hotfoot.

Lockwood planned to support Operation Hotfoot. Seven submarines would steam ahead of Task Force 38, sweeping out Japanese picket boats between the Bonins and Japan which might warn Japanese authorities of the approaching fleet. Burt Klakring, commanding

Submarine Division 101, was selected to head this group, and it was named in his honor: Burt's Brooms.

The Brooms staged from the Marianas, now growing into a full-scale submarine base. The tender *Fulton* had joined old *Holland* at Saipan. *Sperry* had arrived in Apra Harbor, Guam, October 20, with the headquarters of Squadron Ten, commanded by George Lucius Russell, who had relieved Charles Erck. Russell's men built a rest and recuperation camp on Guam and named it Camp Dealey, in honor of the Destroyer Killer.

As it turned out, because of the stiff fighting on Leyte, Halsey was forced to cancel Operation Hotfoot. Nevertheless, Lockwood ordered Burt's Brooms to conduct the sweep more or less as practice. The seven boats—*Ronquil*, *Burrfish*, *Sterlet*, *Silversides*, *Trigger*, *Tambor*, and *Saury*—left Saipan on November 10. Klakring flew his flag in *Silversides*, commanded by John Coye.

Through no fault of Klakring's, who in fact was later presented with a Silver Star for his "conspicuous gallantry and intrepidity" as commander, Burt's Brooms was a complete disaster. The weather was foul and the seas rough, making the use of deck guns perilous. Richard Waugh in *Saury* unsuccessfully attacked an armed trawler on November 18. Later, he fired eight torpedoes at a small tanker, achieving one hit. (On return to port, old *Saury* was retired from combat.) William Germershausen in *Tambor* fired six torpedoes at a patrol vessel, missing with all. Next day he battle-surfaced and sank the craft, which fired back and seriously wounded one of his men. (When he returned *Tambor* to port, she too was retired.) Butch Robbins in *Sterlet* sank a small subchaser with torpedoes. Henry Monroe in *Ronquil* and William Perkins in *Burrfish* teamed up to make a gun attack on a couple of trawlers. They sank these small craft—but at high cost; two men were wounded on *Burrfish*, and Monroe in *Ronquil* blew two holes in his own pressure hull. (His exec, Lincoln Marcy, 1939, led a repair crew that fixed *Ronquil* so she could dive again and for that risky job received a Navy Cross.)

The Brooms returned to the Marianas about November 25. In all, the seven boats had sunk two or three trawlers. Later Jasper Holmes wrote, "The Japanese responded to the raid by rushing additional patrol craft and air search planes into the area and there were probably more pickets in the area after the sweep than there were when it started."

The U.S. Invasions of Mindoro and Luzon

When Leyte was finally secure, MacArthur's invasion forces leaped 300 miles northwestward to the island of Mindoro. These forces were detected by the Japanese and assaulted by kamikaze pilots, one of whom hit the cruiser *Nashville*, killing 133 and wounding 190. Later, kamikazes demolished two LSTs. In spite of being detected, however, the soldiers went ashore without opposition.

During the landings, Bull Halsey's Task Force 38 provided air support. His planes ranged over Luzon, destroying many Japanese aircraft, including kamikazes. On December 17, while refueling, Task Force 38 ran into a typhoon. Three destroyers, *Hull*, *Monaghan*, and *Spence*, which had failed to take on salt-water ballast, capsized and sank. Seven other ships were badly damaged. About 186 aircraft were blown overboard or jettisoned. In all, 800 officers and men were lost.

The Japanese made a futile effort to counterattack the landing craft on Mindoro. On December 24–25, Admiral Masanori Kimura left Camranh Bay with a force of two cruisers (heavy cruiser *Ashigara* and light cruiser *Oyodo*) and six destroyers (part of Admiral Shima's original group) and proceeded across the South China Sea toward Mindoro, protected by foul weather generated by the typhoon. Kimura was spotted 200 miles west of Mindoro by an army plane. Nevertheless, he approached the beaches of Mindoro on the night of December 26–27 and conducted a brief—and ineffectual—bombardment; U.S. aircraft forced him to return hurriedly to Camranh Bay, and a PT boat sank one of his destroyers.

After Mindoro was secure, MacArthur's forces made another leap, the biggest and grandest of all. On January 9 they landed on Luzon, going ashore in Lingayen Gulf, where the Japanese had landed three years before. Kamikaze pilots mounted a furious assault on navy ships, sinking the jeep carrier *Ommaney Bay* and severely damaged the jeep carrier *Manila Bay*, the cruisers *Louisville* and *Australia*, a destroyer, and other ships in the initial attacks and hitting sixteen ships, badly damaging ten, on January 6.

But the Allied ground troops landed virtually unopposed, and in the following days and weeks other troops landed at Subic Bay, Manila Bay, and elsewhere. The Japanese were disorganized and dispirited and completely lacking in air power. General MacArthur reconquered

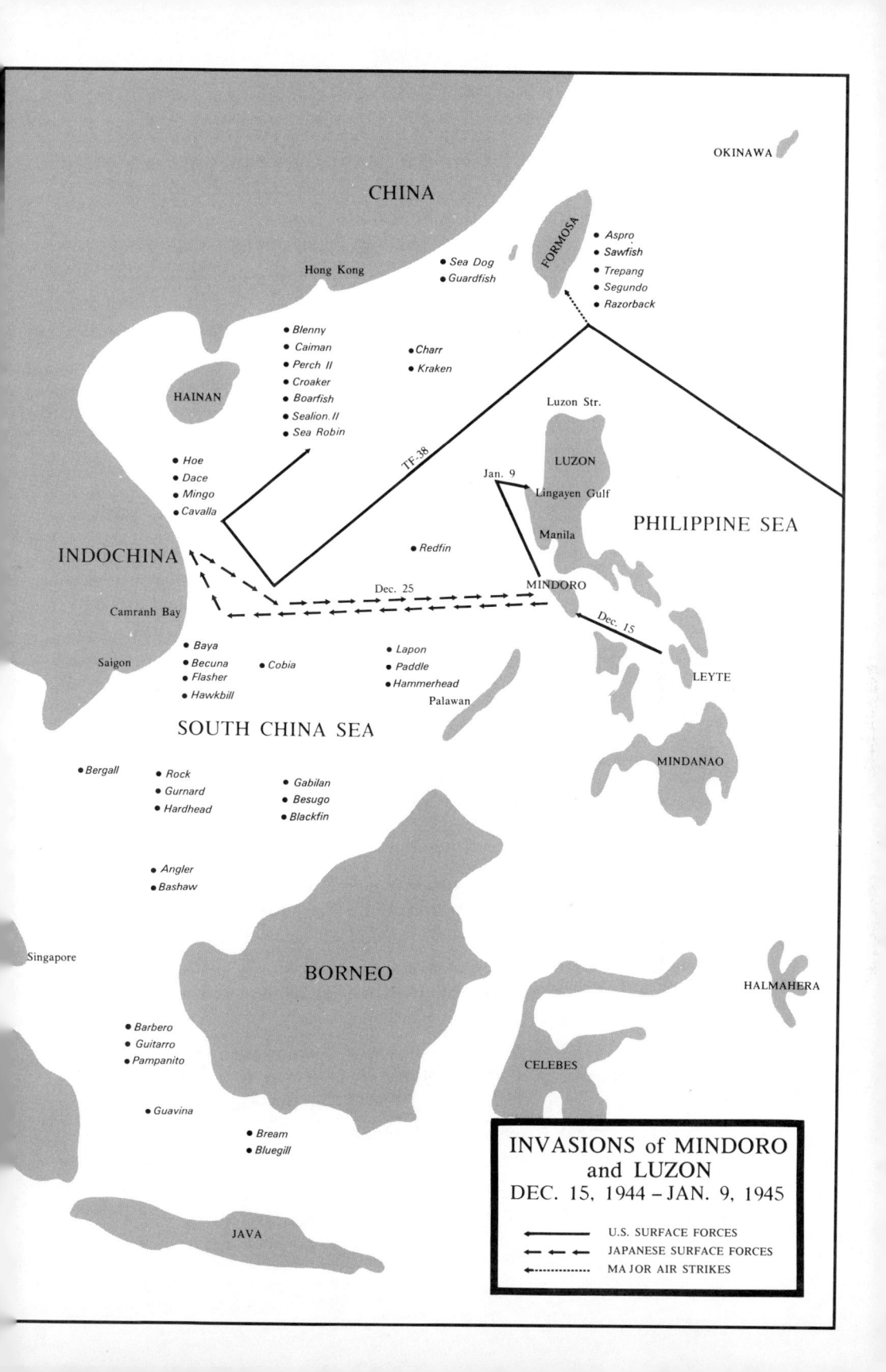

INVASIONS of MINDORO and LUZON
DEC. 15, 1944 – JAN. 9, 1945

U.S. SURFACE FORCES
JAPANESE SURFACE FORCES
MAJOR AIR STRIKES

Luzon at his leisure and with light casualties. By February 4, Manila was his. In subsequent months his troops (aided by the 100,000 guerrillas MacArthur had supplied all these years of the occupation) recaptured the rest of the Philippine Islands.

During the landings on Luzon, Halsey, having repaired his battered Task Force 38, supported the ground troops with air strikes. On the night of January 9–10, while the troops were consolidating positions in Lingayen Gulf, Halsey steamed boldly through Luzon Strait into the South China Sea. Believing the carrier-battleships *Ise* and *Hyuga* to be in Camranh Bay, he swung south and launched air strikes there on January 12. *Ise* and *Hyuga* were not in the bay—they were in Singapore loading drums of oil for shipment to Japan—but Halsey's planes sank forty-seven ships off Indochina, including seven large tankers. Withdrawing through Luzon Strait, Halsey's planes hit Formosa on January 15 and Hong Kong on January 16. On January 17 Halsey slipped back through Luzon Strait, hit Formosa again, and then conducted a photo-reconnaissance of Okinawa. During the last days of this foray, the Japanese bombed the new carrier *Langley*; kamikazes hit the carrier *Ticonderoga* and destroyer *Maddox*. On January 25 Halsey arrived back in Ulithi, where he turned the task force over to Admiral Spruance.

Patrols from Australia

During these operations, Ralph Christie's submarines—joined by half a dozen or more Pearl Harbor boats en route to Australia—were plying the South China Sea and other waters, lifeguarding, attacking enemy shipping, and watching for enemy fleet units. After the landings on Mindoro, the boats were excluded from Philippine waters. They concentrated in the areas near Singapore, Borneo, and Indochina. High priority was given to remaining enemy men-of-war and, as always nowadays, tankers.

Herman Kossler in *Cavalla*, going on his third patrol, took up station off Singapore with *Baya* and *Hoe*. On the night of November 25, Kossler came across what he thought was a cruiser or two; he set up on one and fired four torpedoes. It was a destroyer, *Shimotsuki*, 2,300 tons, which blew up and sank instantly. The other destroyer tried to find *Cavalla*, but Kossler evaded at high speed on the surface.

A week later, December 2, Kossler picked up a "task force" on radar. It was a battleship—perhaps *Ise* or *Hyuga*—escorted by three destroyers. Kossler made an end around and submerged to attack the battleship, but just as he was ready to fire, an escort came right down his track, forcing him to go deep to avoid being rammed. On the way down, Kossler fired six torpedoes at the battleship anyway. All missed.

Swede Bryant, Commander, Squadron Eighteen, led a wolf pack using Worth Scanland's *Hawkbill* for his flagship. The pack consisted of *Hawkbill*; Reuben Whitaker's famous *Flasher*, now commanded by George Grider, moving up from serving as exec in *Hawkbill*; and Hank Sturr's *Becuna*. The pack patrolled west of Mindoro during the invasion to stop the approach of Japanese fleet units, should they elect to sortie from Singapore.

On December 4, Scanland picked up a westbound convoy about 200 miles west of Mindoro. Grider in *Flasher* was 15 miles off his proper position and, by chance, right on the track of the convoy. When it came in sight, Grider was apprehensive. Later he wrote, "I stood in the quiet conning tower, feeling the rush of blood to my skin, knowing the test I had dreamed and wondered and worried about since my earliest days at the Naval Academy was upon me at last. My day of command in combat had arrived. What would I do with it?"

Assisted by his exec, Philip Glennon, who had been Whitaker's last exec on *Flasher*, Grider prepared to attack, submerging and maneuvering for favorable position. Then it began to rain. Grider felt heartsick. Glennon reported high-speed screws coming close, obviously an escort. Grider swung the periscope, searching, worrying that he would bungle his first attack. Then he saw the destroyer.

Grider fired four torpedoes and felt two hits. Later he wrote that "as I swung the scope to look, a feeling of exaltation like nothing I had ever experienced before swept over me. By heaven, I had paid my way as a skipper now, no matter what happened." The destroyer began to smoke heavily. Its screws stopped; the ship fell off to the left, settling aft and listing.

Through the mist, Grider saw a large tanker. Setting up quickly, he fired two torpedoes, then checked fire when he saw the tanker turning. He turned his attention back to the damaged destroyer. Then he saw another destroyer or patrol boat boiling in and he went deep.

As *Flasher* was going down, Grider heard two timed hits in the tanker. Phil Glennon said, almost in disbelief, "My God. We hit him!" When *Flasher* reached 250 feet, the depth charges began to explode. In all, there were sixteen, mostly close.

About an hour and a half later, Grider returned to periscope depth. He found the tanker burning furiously and settling aft. In addition—unbelievably—he saw another destroyer motionless on the water. Grider was wary. Why was this destroyer making himself a perfect target? He fired four torpedoes: three at the stopped destroyer, one at the tanker just beyond. Three torpedoes hit the destroyer.

Grider went deep again to avoid depth charges from the other escorts. When he returned to the surface, he could see the tanker, still burning. Then he saw Sturr's *Becuna*. Grider surfaced. Both boats approached the burning tanker cautiously. It was abandoned. Sturr went on his way; Grider held back to deliver the coup de grace, one more stern torpedo. The tanker sank quickly.

In this, his first attack of the war, Grider claimed he sank two destroyers and one large tanker. Postwar records bore him out. With only eleven torpedoes he had sunk the destroyers *Kishinami* and *Iwanami*, both 2,100 tons, and *Hakko Maru*, 10,000 tons.

Bryant's pack remained on scouting line west of Mindoro during the invasion while, to the south, Hammerhead Martin in *Hammerhead* disposed another pack—*Hammerhead, Paddle, Lapon,* and *Mingo*—near Brunei Bay. On December 8, Martin in *Hammerhead* and Fitz-Patrick in *Paddle* sank a 2,800-ton tanker in a joint attack, but none of the boats on the scouting lines encountered any major units of the Japanese fleet. For the time being they were keeping to Singapore and Camranh Bay.

Bergall, under John Hyde, and *Dace*, commanded by a new skipper, Otis Robert Cole, Jr., both carried a load of mines aft to be laid off Indochina.

On the evening of December 13, while preparing to lay his mines, Hyde picked up masts on the horizon at 35,000 yards. On this patrol, he was assisted by PCO Ben Jarvis (ex-*Sailfish*), who had been serving in *Nautilus* as exec. The water was extremely shallow, about 80 feet average. Hyde and Jarvis decided to attack—and escape—on the surface.

Closing in, Hyde got radar contact at 26,000 yards. An hour later he identified the contact as two cruisers; in fact, it was the heavy cruiser *Myoko* and a destroyer escort en route from Singapore to Camranh Bay. Hyde closed to 3,300 yards and, with both targets overlapping, fired six bow tubes. Moments later he saw an awesome explosion. Flames billowed up to 750 feet. To Hyde, the cruiser seemed to break in two. However, *Myoko* was only badly damaged. She limped back to Singapore, where she stayed until the end of the war.

Hyde hauled clear to reload. The other "cruiser" did not pursue, leading Hyde and Jarvis to conclude she too had been hit. Hyde came back in for a second attack, but when he had closed to 9,000 yards the destroyer opened fire. One shell landed behind *Bergall*, the other directly on her forward torpedo loading hatch, smashing a large opening in the pressure hull. Hyde retreated at full speed.

After a thorough inspection, Hyde found himself in a serious predicament. There was no way to patch the pressure hull. *Bergall* could not dive. The ship was 2,000 miles from the closest Allied base—Exmouth Gulf—and 1,200 miles of that was controlled by the enemy. What to do?

Hyde got off a report to Christie. Christie consulted his operations board and found that *Angler*, commanded by a new skipper, H. Bissell, Jr.,[*] was patrolling in the Java Sea with *Bashaw*. Christie ordered *Angler*, *Bashaw*, and *Paddle* to rendezvous, remove the crew of *Bergall*, and then destroy *Bergall*. *Angler* found *Bergall* on the night of December 15. Neither *Bashaw* nor *Paddle* could find her.

Hyde was reluctant to sink his own ship and decided to disobey Christie's orders. Later he wrote:

> *I was convinced that, if no other boat was contacted, I could get through Karimata, the Java Sea and Lombok on the surface with a good chance of success. This was based on two previous trips over the same route in which no plane contacts were made. By adjusting speed to pass through and well clear of Karimata during darkness; to cross the Surabaya-Balikpapen route at night and to stay well north of Lombok until dark, I felt sure of avoiding aircraft. Therefore I decided to head on down towards Karimata.*

Splitting his crew, Hyde sent one officer and fifty-four men to *Angler* and kept eight officers and twenty-one men on *Bergall*. Then he destroyed confidential gear, set demolition charges by his torpedoes and mines, and got under way for Exmouth Gulf. *Angler* trailed be-

---

[*] Bissell was the second reserve officer, after Hugh Lewis, to command a fleet boat. The third was James L. Hunnicutt (ex-*Tinosa*), who put the new boat *Carp* in commission.

hind, ready to take *Bergall*'s men on board if the Japanese threatened.

Hyde got away with it, traveling 1,200 miles of enemy-controlled waters without being seen by an aircraft or surface ship. On December 20 *Bergall* and *Angler* arrived at Exmouth Gulf. *Angler* then returned to patrol. Christie said later that he was pleased that Hyde had elected to disobey his orders.

Bashaw and *Guavina*, operating as a two-boat wolf pack, patrolled south of Camranh Bay. On the morning of December 14, Nichols in *Bashaw* found what he believed to be "two *Nagato*-class battleships," a light cruiser, and several destroyers heading north. Believing a report more important than attack, Nichols waited, withheld fire, then surfaced and got off a report. Carl Tiedeman in *Guavina* saw the same ships, identifying them as two *Fuso*- or *Nagato*-class battleships. He too got off a contact report and chased, but he could not catch up. These ships might have been *Ise and Hyuga*, bound for Camranh Bay.

John Madison in *Mingo* replaced *Bergall* off Indochina. Otis Cole in *Dace* had arrived in the area and, on December 16, laid his minefield off Palau Gambir. The next morning, in typhoon weather, Madison saw many ships standing out of Camranh Bay, including what he reported as "two *Ise*-class battleships," one or two heavy cruisers, and several destroyers. Madison reduced the range from 6 miles to 4 miles but could get no closer. Later he sent off a contact report.

After receiving Madison's report, the staff at Fremantle ordered half a dozen submarines to converge on Camranh Bay, among them *Dace*, *Hoe*, *Paddle*, and two boats from Swede Bryant's pack, *Flasher* and *Becuna*. The seas were mountainous; George Grider reported "forty-foot waves."

On December 19, Cole in *Dace* picked up a five-ship convoy with three escorts coming out of Camranh Bay, headed north. He made a submerged approach in the heavy seas, but the weather defeated him. A Japanese plane or escort detected *Dace* and dropped bombs or depth charges, forcing Cole to break off the attack. In her evasion, *Dace* hit bottom, and the strong current carried her bumping, scraping, and clanking along the seabed. (During this busy patrol for *Dace*, Cole later picked up a large convoy escorted by a jeep carrier and fired three torpedoes at the carrier, but they all missed.)

Grider picked up Cole's contact report and tried to move north to intercept. "It was impossible to make over seven knots into the sea," Grider reported, "and the current was setting south at four knots." Making northward progress of only 3 knots, *Flasher* gave up the chase after half an hour. That night, she exchanged places with *Dace*, guarding the Camranh Bay entrance.

On December 21 the weather moderated slightly. Shortly after 9 A.M., Grider spotted a convoy: five fat tankers, three small escorts, and a destroyer bringing up the rear. The destroyer passed by at 2,000 yards but Grider withheld fire, believing that his torpedoes would broach in the heavy seas. After the convoy passed by, Grider surfaced and headed north in pursuit. The best speed Grider could make in the heavy seas was 12½ knots. He was fighting a 3-knot southerly current, so his true speed was 9½ knots. The convoy was making 8½ knots. Grider's speed advantage: 1 knot.

Grider chased north all day and into the night. The convoy pulled out of reach, Grider reported; "Our spirits began to droop." But he decided to go on another three hours, hoping he would regain contact; the seas had calmed down and he could make better speed. At 1 A.M. on December 22, as Grider was preparing to break off and return to Camranh Bay, Phil Glennon saw the convoy on radar.

In one of the most daring attacks of the war, Grider eased *Flasher* into shallow water between the convoy and shore. He fired three bow tubes that hit two tankers. One blew up and "illuminated the area like a night football game." Grider swung and fired four stern tubes at a third tanker. All hit and the tanker blew up. "The flames from the second and third targets flowed together," Grider wrote in his report, "and made a really impressive fire." Moments later the first target blew up and "added his light to the flames. The entire sea aft was covered with billowing red fire which burned for about forty minutes." None of the escorts attacked *Flasher*. The tankers sunk by Grider in this brilliant attack were *Omurosan Maru*, 9,200 tons; *Otowasan Maru*, 9,200 tons; and *Arita Maru*, 10,238 tons.

When Grider reported the results to Christie, the latter replied: WONDERFUL CHRISTMAS PRESENT GRIDER. CONGRATULATIONS TO YOU ALL. COME ON HOME. REUBEN IS GOING TO BE PROUD OF HIS OLD SHIP.

There was every reason to be. On this, Grider's first patrol, he had sunk a total of six ships, two destroyers and four large tankers. He was credited with six ships for 41,700 tons, upped postwar to 42,800 tons. In terms of confirmed tonnage sunk, it was the third best patrol of the war, after Enright in *Archerfish*'s fifth patrol and Hank Munson in *Rasher's* fifth. In terms of tanker tonnage, it was the best of the war.

After *Flasher* left, Christie directed Norman Gage in *Gurnard* to take his place. On Christmas Eve, then, there were many submarines lying in wait off Camranh Bay, including *Gurnard*, *Guitarro* *Hoe*, *Dace*, *Paddle*, and *Becuna*. Others, including *Hawkbill*, *Baya*, *Cavalla*, *Redfin*, *Hammerhead*, and *Lapon*, lay to the eastward between Camranh Bay and Mindoro.

On December 22, Joseph Fitz-Patrick in *Paddle*, making his seventeenth patrol of the war—a record—reported "two very large ships." These, undoubtedly, were Admiral Kimura's heavy cruiser *Ashigara* and the light cruiser *Oyodo*, preparing for the dash to bombard the beaches of Mindoro. The next day, Hank Sturr in *Becuna* saw the force go into Camranh Bay. (Sturr mistakenly identified *Ashigara* as a "*Yamato*-class battleship.") But when Admiral Kimura left Camranh Bay on Christmas Eve, none of the boats off Camranh Bay saw him; nor did any of the boats lying to the east toward Mindoro.

On Kimura's return trip to Camranh Bay, Thomas Bullard Dabney in *Guitarro* and Gage in *Gurnard* saw the force barreling in at 25 knots. It passed within 5,000 yards of *Guitarro*, but so fast that Dabney had no chance to set up and shoot. Neither did Gage in *Gurnard*. In all, going and coming, Admiral Kimura had eluded about a dozen submarines.

In the days following, the boats off Camranh Bay made other contacts, but heavy antisubmarine measures drove them off and prevented many attacks. Irvin Hartman in *Barbero*, returning to Fremantle by way of Karimata Strait, was nearly lost. While attacking a Japanese vessel on December 27, Hartman was caught by a Japanese aircraft whose bombs hit *Barbero*. Going deep to evade and assess damage, Hartman found the boat to be badly wrecked. He surfaced and limped back to Fremantle, where, after a close inspection, *Barbero* was ordered back to the States for a navy yard overhaul. She did not make another war patrol.

Patrols from Pearl Harbor

After the Burt's Brooms fiasco, Lockwood resumed his normal patrol cycles, sending boats in packs or singly to Luzon Strait, the East China Sea, and elsewhere.

On December 2 Ralph Emerson Styles in *Sea Devil* found a seven-ship convoy off southwest Kyushu. Maneuvering around four escorts, Styles sank two large ships: a 6,900-ton freighter, *Akigawa Maru*, and a 9,500-ton transport, *Hawaii Maru*.

About December 7 Lockwood received word from the codebreakers that an important task force would arrive in the Nagasaki area. By then Carter Bennett had tested his Cuties, so Lockwood concentrated Bennett's pack—*Sea Owl*, *Piranha*, and *Sea Poacher*—plus Sandy McGregor in *Redfish*, Shelby in *Sunfish*, Clyde Stevens in *Plaice*, and Styles in *Sea Devil*, near the island of Danjo Gunto.

On the night of December 8, Sandy McGregor made contact with the enemy force on radar at 15 miles. It consisted of the light carrier *Junyo* and several destroyers. He sent off a contact report to all submarines and began tracking.

About 9:30 that night, Styles in *Sea Devil* made contact with the task force, range 8 miles. Styles approached submerged to radar depth and fired four torpedoes at the largest target—*Junyo*, range 4,300 yards. He was lucky. Two torpedoes hit the carrier. He raised his radio antenna and got off a contact report.

Clyde Stevens in *Plaice* picked up the task force shortly after midnight, range 12 miles. As he was closing to attack, he heard torpedo explosions—*Sea Devil's* attack. Stevens picked the closest target, a destroyer, and fired three torpedoes. Then "the big boy" popped out of the mist. Stevens had no chance to fire at the carrier, but he shot another three torpedoes at another destroyer. He heard hits in the first destroyer and believed it sank, but postwar records did not bear out the claim.

On the other side of the formation, Sandy McGregor in *Redfish* moved in close to the carrier and fired six steam torpedoes at a range of 2,900 yards. One made an erratic circular run, forcing McGregor to maneuver wildly to avoid it, but the other five ran true. McGregor "heard and saw one terrific hit in carrier." He reloaded his forward tubes, came in for another attack, and fired six more torpedoes. One prematured, but others hit. *Junyo* limped into Nagasaki so badly damaged she was out of the war for the duration.

McGregor in *Redfish* rendezvoused with Lawrence Julihn in *Shad* about December 12, and the two boats snooped around Shanghai and then dropped down toward the mouth of Formosa Strait. On about December 16, McGregor received an Ultra from Lockwood stating that "an important enemy task force" was proceeding south.

McGregor took up position "along track that Jap task forces use between Empire and Formosa and/or Philippines." He was not altogether confident of his location; the weather had been bad for several days. A day passed, and then another, with no sign of the Japanese task force. (Later McGregor said, "They were late because they had trouble getting out of the shipyard.")

At 4:27 on the afternoon of December 19, while submerged, McGregor picked up the enemy force. It was a brand-new carrier, *Unryu*, with three destroyer escorts, one ahead and one on either beam. McGregor closed to point-blank range (1,470 yards) and fired four torpedoes. One hit, causing *Unryu* to stop. She took a strong starboard list and McGregor saw a fire break out aft. When *Unryu* trained her guns on *Redfish*'s periscope and commenced firing, McGregor responded by firing his four stern tubes, which missed.

While his torpedo crews reloaded one torpedo aft, McGregor fearlessly kept his periscope eye on the damaged carrier. The destroyers zipped about wildly, dropping depth charges. When the torpedo was in in the tube, McGregor closed to 1,100 yards and fired. As he wrote later, "Torpedo hit carrier at point of aim. The sharp crack of the torpedo explosion was followed instantly by thundering explosions apparently from magazine or gasoline stowage, probably the latter. Huge clouds of smoke, flame, and debris burst into the air completely enveloping the carrier. . . . He has sunk!" The escorts came after *Redfish* in a fury, and McGregor hastily ordered 200 feet. As he recorded the results of their attack:

On passing 150 feet all Hell broke loose when seven well placed depth charges exploded alongside starboard bow. The closest one of these charges is believed to have exploded a little above keel depth and gave the sensation of pushing the bow sideways to port. At this time the following casualties were reported: Steering gear jammed on hard left and hydraulic leak in after room manifold, bow planes jammed on 20 degrees rise, and hydraulic oil leak in pump room and loss of all hydraulic power, all sound gear out of commission, pressure hull cracked in forward torpedo room with gear out of commission, pressure hull cracked in forward torpedo room with water leaking through #1 M.B.T. riser [main ballast tank pipe] and #1 Sanitary Tank discharge valve numerous air leaks throughout boat and a torpedo making a hot run in #8 torpedo tube. One man was injured when a W.T. [watertight] door jolted loose and hit him in the head practically severing one ear.

McGregor crept away from the scene of the battle as quietly as he could. Then he limped to Midway, where he received full credit for dispatching *Unryu* and relinquished command of the battered boat to his exec, Robert Lakin Gurnee, going on to command a division. In his four war patrols—two on *Pike*, two on *Redfish*—he had fired at three aircraft carriers, severely damaging two and sinking one.

Gurnee returned *Redfish* to Portsmouth Navy Yard, where she had been built. Later he described his arrival:

A large crowd waited on the dock for the ship to tie up. This crowd was composed mainly of the same yard workmen who had helped build the Redfish. *They swarmed aboard and sped immediately to the areas on the ship that they had built to see if their portion had held together. I overheard more than one as he left the ship telling his buddy proudly, "Yes, sir, my welds held together even though the steel hull was dimpled and the whole bow knocked off center." Needless to say, many of us who had been aboard during the depth charging were emotionally moved by this incident and more than one of the brave* Redfish *sailors dried damp eyes.*

Roy Davenport in *Trepang* led a pack to Luzon Strait, the other boats being James Fulp's *Segundo* and *Razorback*, with a new skipper, Charles Donald Brown, 1938. On December 6, bedeviled by heavy seas, the pack picked up a seven-ship convoy with three escorts. Davenport fired twenty-two torpedoes, claiming four ships sunk for 35,000 tons, postwar records credited three ships for about 13,000 tons. Brown on *Razorback* and Fulp on *Segundo* shared credit for sinking a 7,000-ton freighter from the convoy. Davenport, who had only two torpedoes remaining, left the strait, returning to Pearl Harbor three days before Christmas. *Segundo* and *Razorback* remained on station during the month of December. Brown in *Razorback* sank an old destroyer, *Kuretake*, December 30. Total for the pack: five confirmed ships for about 21,000 tons.

After this patrol, Davenport, who felt that he no longer had "quite the punch" that he used to have, asked for shore duty and returned to the Naval Academy as an instructor in marine engineering. In all, he had made ten war patrols, four on Burlingame's *Silversides*, four as skipper of *Haddock*, and two as skipper of *Trepang*. In his six patrols as commanding officer, Davenport had been credited with sinking seventeen ships for 151,900 tons, ranking him third behind Dick O'Kane (227,800 tons) and Gene Fluckey (179,000 tons) in tonnage. Postwar accounting reduced Davenport's claims to eight ships for only about 30,000 tons.

Davenport had earned five Navy Crosses during his six patrols in command of *Haddock* and *Trepang*, more than any other skipper. Except for the men who won Medals of Honor, he was the most-decorated submariner of the war.

Another pack followed Davenport into Luzon Strait, remaining there during the invasion of Luzon. It was commanded by Rebel Lowrance in *Sea Dog*. The other two boats were *Sea Robin*, commanded by Paul Cecil Stimson, and the famous *Guardfish*, now commanded by Douglas Hammond, whom Christie had relieved from command of *Cabrilla* after two luckless patrols but to whom Lockwood had decided to give a second chance.

By the time this pack reached Luzon Strait, the area was barren of shipping. It was raked by Halsey in early January when Task Force 38 entered the South China Sea to strike Camranh Bay. Lowrance went far west—toward Hainan. Stimson in *Sea Robin* was lucky to find a small convoy and sink a tanker off Hainan January 6. That same day, Hammond fired three torpedoes from long range at what he believed to be a decoy or Q-ship but may have been Stimson's convoy. Hammond, conducting an extremely cautious patrol, did not follow up the attack.

On January 23, when *Guardfish* was returning to Guam, Hammond picked up a radar contact in the middle of the Philippine Sea. Believing this might be a Japanese I-class submarine, he began tracking by radar and sent off two messages to Lowrance and Lockwood, reporting the contact and asking if any U.S. submarines or surface ships might be in the area. Lockwood replied that there were no U.S. submarines in the area and stated that if it turned out to be a surface ship it was probably friendly. Lockwood reminded Hammond that he was in a "joint area," where friendly surface ships might be operating, and that positive evidence that the ship was enemy had to be obtained before firing.

The ship was indeed friendly. She was the salvage vessel *Extractor*, commanded by H. M. Babcock, which had helped the stricken tanker *Mississinewa* at Ulithi. *Extractor* was en route from Guam to the Philippines, unescorted. The day before, she had been sent a message ordering her back to Guam, but the message arrived "badly garbled." Later, Babcock reported, "Numerous attempts were made to decipher the message using all available effective codes with no results. I did not consider it advisable to break radio silence to request a repeat." The people at Guam who kept track of U.S. vessels assumed *Extractor* had received this message and was on her way back.

Hammond continued tracking. At 5:42, he submerged ahead to inspect his target through the periscope. It was almost sunrise. The sky was overcast. There were passing light rainsqualls. Hammond and his exec made six separate observations, ranges 6,800 yards to 1,800 yards. These looks convinced them absolutely that *Extractor* was an I-class Japanese submarine, running on the surface. At 6:20, Hammond fired four electric torpedoes from his bow tubes, range 1,200 yards.

Two torpedoes hit and *Extractor* blew up and sank. Four men in the bow were killed instantly; two others drowned. But seventy-three, including Babcock, survived. Twenty minutes after the firing, Hammond surfaced to run through the wreckage. Later, he wrote, "Upon drawing close aboard the first life raft realized the full extent of our mistake. The survivors were American."

With a heavy heart, Hammond picked up the seventy-three men in the water and sent them below—to an awkward confrontation with *Guardfish*'s crew. Hammond spent three hours futilely looking for the missing six men. Then he sent a dispatch to Lockwood reporting the tragic mistake and set course for Guam. Forty-eight hours later, he rendezvoused with the destroyer escort *George*, which took off the *Extractor* crew.

Once-proud *Guardfish* moored alongside *Sperry* in Apra Harbor, Guam, and her crew went to the rest area, Camp Dealey. Ironically, it fell to Burt Klakring, the man who made *Guardfish* famous, to write the patrol report endorsement. During the refit, a Court of Inquiry was conducted. Hammond and Babcock more or less shared blame for the incident, Babcock for not requesting a rebroadcast of the message that would have removed him from danger, Hammond for mistakenly identifying *Extractor*. Babcock and the *Extractor* crew returned to the States for survivor's leave. Hammond retained command of *Guardfish* and her fine—but hangdog—crew.

Extractor was the only U.S. ship sunk by U.S. submarines in the war.

Dragonet, the second Cramp Shipyard boat to reach combat (after *Escolar*), went on the polar circuit. She was commanded by Jack Lewis, who commanded *Trigger* on her first patrol and *Swordfish* on her seventh. Lewis had so much trouble getting *Dragonet* mechanically ready for patrol that wags dubbed the boat "The Reluctant Dragonet."

Off Matsuwa To on December 15, Lewis submerged for routine patrol. At 7:17 A.M., while at 70 feet, Lewis felt a jar he thought might have been a Japanese bomb. In fact, he had run aground. In the mishap, the whole forward torpedo room flooded, giving *Dragonet* a terrific down-angle. The men in the torpedo room escaped aft and slammed the watertight doors. Lewis put "salvage air" into the forward room, and *Dragonet* settled on the bottom—making ominous noises.

In a fine piece of seamanship, Lewis finally emptied the forward torpedo room of water, but *Dragonet* was badly damaged. Lewis surfaced in sight of Matsuwa, later writing, "Exchanged feel of temporary relief for one of shameful nakedness." He put all four engines on the line and ran out to sea.

Lewis headed for Midway. On the way, he ran into a bad storm; one time, *Dragonet* rolled 63 degrees to port—and hung there. She finally arrived at Midway on December 20 with a heavy port list and was sent back to the States for a navy yard overhaul. *Dragonet* was the only submarine in the war to completely flood her forward torpedo room and survive.

Spearfish, commanded by Cy Cole, made a photographic reconnaissance of Iwo Jima and then lifeguarded during a B-29 strike against Japan. On December 19 a B-29 ditched and Cole rescued seven members of the crew, the first of many B-29 crews rescued by U.S. submarines.

During the course of this patrol (as Cole later officially reported), he was caught on the surface by a friendly bomber. Cole had his radio tuned to the aircraft circuit and heard the following exchange:

"Looks like a sub."

"May be a ship."

"Let's bomb the bastard anyway."

Cole dived quickly. His officer of the deck saw bombs hit close aboard and heard bullets whine. Cole radioed Lockwood, LIBERATOR FAILED TO SCORE. . . . DAMAGE TO PRIDE AND TEMPER ONLY.

On return to port, Cole was praised for his patrol, but old *Spearfish* was retired from combat, and Cole went to a staff job at Pearl Harbor.

Jack Gerwick, commanding *Greenling* for a third time out, patrolled to the north of Okinawa. On January 25 he found a well-escorted convoy and attacked. The escorts counterattacked with awesome speed and persistence, four of them boxing *Greenling* at 300 feet and dropping about a hundred depth charges. "Those boys were experts," Gerwick reported later. *Greenling* was knocked down 60 feet—to 360 feet—by one of the charges, which started five hot runs in the tubes. Finally, *Greenling* shook loose and limped into Saipan. She was considered to be so badly damaged she was retired from combat and sent to New London.

The famous old *Swordfish*, commanded by Keats Montross, went to Okinawa to conduct a photographic reconnaissance. Two other boats were in the same area: a new one, *Kete*, commanded by Royal Rutter, and *Puffer*, commanded by Carl Redmond Dwyer. Dwyer sank a small ship on January 10.

Early on the morning of January 12, *Swordfish* and *Kete* exchanged calls. Four hours later, Rutter heard heavy depth-charging. After that, nothing further was heard from Montross. *Swordfish* was lost either by this depth-charging or by striking a new minefield that had been planted at Okinawa. John Briscoe Pye, son of the admiral, perished with her.

Tautog, commanded by Tom Baskett, made her final combat patrol of the war in the East China Sea as half of a two-boat wolf pack. Her packmate *Silversides*, now commanded by John Culver Nichols (the only *Squalus* officer to command a boat during the war), had little luck, but Baskett made five attacks and sank two confirmed ships—a 1,500 ton transport and a PT-boat tender of 1,800 tons. Nichols in *Silversides* wound up the patrol by finally sinking a freighter, and the two boats then returned to base. *Tautog*, which had made thirteen war patrols, was also retired from combat, and Baskett went to the PCO pool.

When all the Japanese records had been compiled and studied, it was discovered that *Tautog* sank more confirmed ships than any other submarine: twenty-six. Joe Willingham had gotten five ships (including two submarines); Barney Sieglaff thirteen ships (including two destroyers but not including a third destroyer, *Amagiri*, sunk by a minefield laid by Sieglaff); and Baskett, eight ships.

Two new boats patrolled from Pearl Harbor to Australia. These were *Boarfish*, commanded by Roy Gross (ex-*Seawolf*), and *Blenny*, commanded by William Hazzard. Both patrols were among the most aggressive on record; Gross and Hazzard made eight attacks each, firing most of their torpedoes into convoys. The confirmed results, however, were thin. Hazzard was credited with an 800-ton frigate and a 4,000-ton freighter, Gross with sinking one 7,000-ton freighter plus half credit for a 6,900-ton ship shared with land-based army aircraft.

Gene Fluckey in *Barb*, Elliott Loughlin in *Queenfish*, and Ty Shepard in *Picuda* teamed up again to make a three-boat pack. They were assigned to Formosa Strait with the mission of stopping any reinforcements the Japanese might send to the Philippines.

The pack left from Guam, sweeping northward toward the Bonins before turning west. On January 1, Shepard and Loughlin came across a patrol craft and attacked with their deck guns. Then Fluckey came up behind and sent a boarding party on the riddled craft to pick up charts and codebooks. Unknown to Fluckey, there were some Japanese hiding belowdecks. After the boarding party returned to *Barb*, Fluckey ordered his gun crew to sink the boat. Later Fluckey wrote, "When the diesel tanks caught fire, the eight or nine Japs came running out . . . on deck. They stopped for a minute and our 4-inch crew, being very blood-thirsty at that time, landed a shot right in their midst which blew them all apart."

The pack took station in Formosa Strait in shallow water, close to the spot where Dick O'Kane in *Tang* had gone down. Early on the morning of January 7, Fluckey picked up a seven-ship convoy and broadcast a contact report. Then he made an end around in broad daylight, submerging ahead of the convoy. When the convoy came along an hour later, visibility was bad and Fluckey had a hard time getting set on a target. He picked a big tanker, but it zigged away just as he got ready to fire. A destroyer came by but Fluckey withheld his fire, writing later, "I have now developed enough self-control to resist the temptation to let three torpedoes fly at an escort unless conditions are right. The latter the result of twelve torpedoes I have wasted in the last three patrols."

The convoy got by Fluckey. At 9:41 A.M. he surfaced to make another end around. While this was in progress, Shepard in *Picuda*, who had received Fluckey's contact report and submerged in good position, fired four torpedoes at a 10,000-ton tanker, *Munakata Maru*. Some hit and the tanker was severely damaged, but the attack alerted the convoy, which scattered and scurried into Formosa before Fluckey or Loughlin in *Queenfish* (too far away) could attack. All in all, it was a less than satisfactory beginning. "Some consolation in *Picuda* making the grade," Fluckey wrote.

The pack regrouped close to the China coast. The next day, January 8, at about one in the afternoon, Fluckey picked up another big convoy and flashed the word. Again he made an end around on the surface, submerging ahead of the convoy. It came along on track and Fluckey planned his attack to drive the ships away from the coast and toward his packmates. He began to fire, shooting three torpedoes at one freighter and three at another. While swinging around for a stern shot, there was an awesome explosion that forced *Barb* down sideways. Fluckey had hit an ammunition ship. Loughlin saw it blow up and "completely disintegrate in a sheet of fire, explosions and bursting shells." Fluckey went "deep" to 140 feet to reload. After dark, he surfaced.

About that time, Loughlin in *Queenfish* attacked, firing ten torpedoes: four at one ship, three each at two others. All torpedoes missed. "It seemed incredible," Loughlin wrote in his report, "but no explosions were seen or heard." Loughlin pulled off to reload.

Then it was Shepard's turn. Like Loughlin, he fired ten torpedoes in one great salvo: four at a tanker, three each at two freighters. Shepard got hits in at least two of his targets, maybe three. He pulled off to reload and Fluckey moved in for his second attack.

Fluckey fired six more torpedoes, three each at two targets. One blew up with another awesome explosion. Fluckey wrote later, "Three hits timed and observed followed by a stupendous earth-shaking eruption. This far surpassed Hollywood and is one of the biggest explosions of the war.... A high vacuum resulted in the boat. Personnel in the control room said they felt as if they were being sucked up the hatch." Loughlin saw this explosion, too.

Queenfish moved in for another attack. Loughlin picked out a tanker and fired four bow tubes. Two hit. A destroyer charged

Queenfish and *Loughlin* fired two stern torpedoes down the throat. Both missed, forcing him to make evasion maneuvers. Meanwhile, Shepard in *Picuda* conducted a second attack.

No one is really certain who sank what in these series of attacks, but in the postwar accounting Fluckey was credited with sinking three ships: *Shinyo Maru*, a 5,892-ton freighter; *Anyo Maru*, a 9,256-ton transport; and *Sanyo Maru*, a 2,854-ton tanker. In addition, he shared one third credit with Loughlin and Shepard for sinking *Hokishima Maru*, another 2,854-ton tanker. The pack also inflicted severe damage on two freighters, *Meiho Maru* and *Hisagawa Maru*, and a 6,516-ton tanker, *Manju Maru*. Whatever the convoy was carrying never reached the Philippines.

In subsequent days, the boats of the pack operated more or less independently. On January 18, Loughlin picked up a small convoy near the China coast and fired eight torpedoes at several ships, but all of them missed. He returned to Pearl Harbor. Shepard in *Picuda* attacked a small convoy on January 29, firing his last torpedoes at a transport and freighter. He hit both, and the transport *Clyde Maru*, 5,500 tons, sank.

Gene Fluckey still had twelve torpedoes left. Although he hunted relentlessly, he could find no targets. Based on information from coast watchers in China and the China Air Force, he reasoned that the convoys were hugging the coast very close and holing up in harbors at night. When he received word on a northbound convoy, Fluckey closed the coast, mingled with some fishing craft, and confirmed his belief: radar showed a mass of ships anchored in Namkwan Harbor.

Fluckey decided the best way to get at these ships was simply to proceed up the long, ill-charted, and perhaps mine-infested channel into the harbor and shoot. He put his exec on the bridge to conn the ship and took station in the conning tower at the radar set. On the long and scary trip in, the fathometer registered 36 feet of water, sometimes less.

Once inside the harbor, Fluckey decided he would fire eight torpedoes, leaving four in case he had to shoot his way out through the escorts. He fired four bow tubes, range to targets 3,200 yards, swung around, and fired four stern tubes, range 3,000 yards. Ordering flank speed, he took station on the bridge. All over the harbor, he saw ships blowing up and firing guns. He believed he had sunk at least four, but postwar records credited him only one, *Taikyo Maru*, 5,244 tons.

Threading her way through the junks and sampans to deep open water, *Barb* was not even scratched.

Fluckey fired his last four torpedoes at a freighter, but they all missed. After that he returned to Pearl Harbor, where he was received with a red carpet. His endorsements were ecstatic. One stated, "*Barb* is one of the finest fighting submarines this war has ever known." Fluckey was credited with sinking eight big ships for 60,000 tons and damaging four for 25,000 tons, making his total bag (sunk and damaged) 85,000 tons. The sinkings were reduced in postwar records to a total of four and one third for 24,197 tons.

For this outstanding performance, Gene Fluckey was awarded the Medal of Honor.

36

Submarine Command, December 1944

All during the fall of 1944, Lockwood was involved in a bitter feud with Louis Denfeld and Bob Rice in the Bureau of Personnel. Angry letters and radio dispatches flowed from Pearl Harbor almost daily. Lockwood objected strenuously to Admiral King's edict to trim his "overhead" of older men. He also accused Denfeld and Rice of raiding his staff of fine younger men to fill nonsubmarine jobs. He complained—repeatedly—about the shortage of qualified Naval Academy graduates available to command fleet boats. The shortage had forced him and Christie to reach down to the class of 1938 for skippers and even to appoint two reservists—Lewis (*Sterlet*) and Bissell (*Angler*) —to command. He accused Freeland Daubin of keeping too many qualified people in his outfit and complained that most submarine wardrooms were composed of "mere children."

In the end, Lockwood lost all these personnel battles. The skippers became younger and younger; more execs came from the reserve ranks. There was another game of musical chairs.

Gin Styer, commanding the Submarine School in New London, was slated to command a battleship. However, Freeland Daubin was relieved as Commander Submarines Atlantic, and sent to be commandant of the New York Navy Yard; Styer, promoted to rear admiral, took Daubin's job. Lockwood, still looking for a good job for Babe Brown (finally promoted to rear admiral), was disappointed, believing Brown should have had the Daubin job. As a consolation,

Brown was named "Deputy Commander," Submarines Pacific Fleet. Merrill Comstock, promoted to the honorary rank of commodore, remained as Lockwood's chief of staff. The "genius," Dick Voge, remained as Lockwood's operations officer. Tex McLean, commanding Squadron Sixteen, relieved Gin Styer in command of the sub school. McLean was relieved in Squadron Sixteen by Pilly Lent.

Swede Momsen, who had been relieved as commander of Squadron Four (and Two), worked briefly in the Navy Department's postal service and then was sent to command the battleship *South Dakota*. William Vincent O'Regan took over as commander of Squadron Four.

John Haines, who had been commanding the Brisbane submarines, was sent to command the battleship *New Mexico*.

Christie's chief of staff, P. G. Nichols, was relieved by Swede Bryant, commanding Squadron Eighteen. Dutch Will, who hoped to get Nichols's job, went back to the States to command a new squadron, Twenty-eight. Nichols, after making a war patrol on John Hyde's *Bergall*, went to be Deputy Chief of Staff (Personnel), 13th Naval District, Seattle, Washington. Swede Bryant was relieved as commander of Squadron Eighteen by Stan Moseley. Bull Wright replaced Murray Tichenor as operations officer.

John Griggs, commanding Squadron Twelve, was sent to command the cruiser *St. Louis,* and Weary Wilkins was appointed to command Squadron Twelve.

Willard Downes, commanding Squadron Eight, was sent to command the light cruiser *Boise*. He was relieved by George Edmund Peterson.

John Bailey Longstaff, commanding Squadron Fourteen, was sent to be chief of staff to the commandant of the 8th Naval District. He was replaced by Warren Dudley Wilkin.

Leo Leander Pace, commanding Squadron Twenty, left to relieve Swede Momsen in the navy's postal service. Lew Parks replaced Pace as commander of Squadron Twenty.

Charles Erck, commanding Squadron Ten, who was replaced by George Russell, was sent to command the navy's amphibious training base in Norfolk.

Shorty Edmunds, commanding Squadron Six, was sent to command the U.S. Naval Reserve Midshipman's School at Columbia University. His job was not filled. Squadron Six was more or less disbanded and moved to New London.

Joe Connolly, who began the war in Manila commanding a division, took command of a new squadron, Twenty-two. Turkey Neck Crawford, relieved as chief of staff to Commander Submarines Atlantic, took command of another new squadron, Twenty-four. Savvy Huffman got command of Squadron Twenty-six. Karl Hensel took command of Squadron Thirty and Kenneth Hurd (ex-*Seal*), Squadron Thirty-two. Freddy Warder became officer in charge of the Submarine School.

The biggest job change—and biggest shock—came to Ralph Christie: Admiral Kinkaid asked that Christie be relieved. Kinkaid gave no reasons for this decision. However, Christie and those close to him believed Kinkaid was upset with Christie because of his push for Sam Dealey's Medal of Honor and for his habit of presenting medals to some skippers at dockside. Kinkaid may also have been upset over the loss of his nephew, Manning Kimmel, on *Robalo* (and other Christie losses).

The dispatch pronouncing this change arrived in late November. It named Jimmy Fife, recently promoted to rear admiral, as Christie's relief. Christie noted in his diary, "Received about the same news I got two years ago and I don't like it any better: detachment and same relief, Fife. It disturbed my sleep."

As he had two years before in Brisbane, Christie took immediate steps to have the orders revoked. He flew up to Hollandia to see Kinkaid and Van Hook. Both men were away. Christie took the matter up with Kinkaid's staff. There was then a plan afoot to shift the Brisbane submarine unit to Subic Bay, Luzon, after that place had been recaptured. Christie suggested that he stay on until this shift had been made—perhaps another six months.

It was no use. Jimmy Fife, who had been in Washington close to Admirals King and Edwards, was on his way to Perth, via Pearl Harbor, and was determined to get the job. He arrived in Pearl Harbor December 13, where he found Nimitz and Lockwood preparing to move their headquarters forward to Guam. Lockwood was disappointed that Babe Brown had not been selected to replace Christie, but he wrote Fife that he was "delighted" at Fife's appointment. The two men conferred for two days, planning future operations and discussing Fife's move forward to Subic Bay. Fife left for Australia on December 15.

While Fife was en route to his new post, Kinkaid sent a message to the Secretary of the Navy which seemed to Lockwood to imply that

Kinkaid might want to delay the change of command, as Christie had proposed. Lockwood radioed Fife in the Admiralties to detour via Leyte, where Kinkaid and Van Hook were then basing, to clear the matter up.

Fife found Kinkaid in his flagship, *Wasatch*. When Fife inquired what was going on—whether Christie would stay—Kinkaid said Christie had "given him the impression Daubin was coming out" to relieve Christie. Fife later wrote Lockwood, "Admiral Kinkaid said had he known I was lined up he would not have agreed to sending any messages . . . he seemed to me genuinely pleased that I was out here and was familiar with the geography."

Fife went on to Perth, where he arrived Christmas Eve. Kinkaid had told him to take over in a "day or two," but Christie dragged his heels. The official relieving ceremony did not take place until December 30. After it, Christie stayed on for a few days of leave and recreation and then returned to the States, having been informed by Kinkaid that he would be recommended for a Distinguished Service Medal.

Christie went to Washington to confer with the navy high command. His next job was to be commandant of the Puget Sound Navy Yard, Bremerton, Washington. This assignment, Christie noted in his diary, "doesn't thrill me." He asked Admiral Edwards why he had been relieved and sent to this shore job. Later Christie said, "Admiral Edwards evaded my question . . . saying only that I had done a very super job and since our submarine war was about over, he was mighty glad to have me to help with a very bad situation in Bremerton."

While in Washington, Christie ran into the chairman of the U.S. Navy's Board of Awards and Decorations. Before Christie could even say hello, the chairman said, "Christie, every member of my board wanted to give Dealey the Medal of Honor but we couldn't because of Kinkaid's endorsement. Why don't you put in a request for reconsideration now that you are out from under Kinkaid? The routing now will go through MacArthur first, then Kinkaid."

After Christie arrived at Bremerton, he followed the chairman's advice. MacArthur promptly approved the award and, as Christie later said, "Kinkaid hardly had the nerve to stand in the way." The Medal of Honor was awarded posthumously to Dealey's widow—a tardy consolation for Edwina Dealey and at best a Pyrrhic victory for Ralph Christie.

37
Summary, 1944

The third year of the submarine war against Japan was devastatingly effective. During the year, and allowing for losses, the force level increased another thirty-three boats. These additions, plus the use of advance bases in Milne Bay, Manus, Mios Woendi, Majuro, Saipan, and Guam, enabled the three commanders to mount a total of 520 war patrols (some double-barreled), compared to about 350 in 1941–42 and 1943. The commands claimed sinking 849½ men-of-war and merchant ships for about 5.1 million tons. The postwar records credited 603 ships for about 2.7 million tons. This was more shipping and tonnage than in 1941, 1942, and 1943 combined (515 ships for 2.2 million tons).

The 1944 sinkings drastically impeded Japanese shipping services. Imports of bulk commodities fell from 16.4 million tons in 1943 to a disastrous 10 million tons. At the beginning of 1944 the Japanese had 4.1 million tons of merchant shipping afloat, excluding tankers. At the end of 1944 this figure had declined to about 2 million tons, excluding tankers. As for tanker tonnage, the Japanese began the year with 863,000 tons, built 204 tankers for 624,000 tons, and ended the year with 869,000 tons. Including tankers and merchant ships, the net loss in 1944 was over 2 million tons.

The flow of oil from the southern regions to Japan was almost completely stopped after the invasion of Mindoro. In September 1944 (in spite of all the losses), about 700,000 tons of Japanese tanker tonnage was engaged in transporting oil from the south to the home islands. By the end of the year this figure had been reduced to about 200,000 tons. Reserve stocks were so low that Japanese leaders launched experiments in making oil from potatoes.

U.S. submarines took a heavy toll of Japanese men-of-war. During the year there were about one hundred contacts on major Japanese fleet units. These developed roughly into ten attacks against battleships, twenty-five attacks against aircraft carriers, fifteen attacks against heavy cruisers, and twenty attacks against light cruisers. U.S. submarines sank one battleship, seven aircraft carriers, two heavy cruisers, seven light cruisers, about thirty destroyers, and seven submarines. In addition, they severely damaged the carrier *Junyo* and four heavy cruisers: *Myoko, Aoba, Takao,* and *Kumano.*

The major sinkings were:

Carriers and Battleships

Shokaku (30,000 tons)	June 19	*Cavalla* (Kossler)
Taiho (31,000 tons)	June 19	*Albacore* (Blanchard)
Taiyo (*Otaka*) (20,000 tons)	August 18	*Rasher* (Munson)
Unyo (20,000 tons)	September 16	*Barb* (Fluckey)
Jinyo (*Shinyo*) (21,000 tons)	November 17	*Spadefish* (Underwood)
Kongo (31,000 tons)	November 21	*Sealion II* (Reich)
Shinano (59,000 tons)	November 29	*Archerfish* (Enright)
Unryu (18,500 tons)	December 19	*Redfish* (McGregor)

Cruisers

Agano (7,000 tons)	February 16	*Skate* (Gruner)
Tatsuta (3,300 tons)	March 13	*Sandlance* (Garrison)
Yubari (3,500 tons)	April 27	*Bluegill* (Barr)
Oi (5,700 tons)	July 19	*Flasher* (Whitaker)
Nagara (5,700 tons)	August 7	*Croaker* (Lee)
Natori (5,700 tons)	August 18	*Hardhead* (McMaster)
Maya (12,200 tons)	October 23	*Dace* (Claggett)
Atago (12,000 tons)	October 23	*Darter* (McClintock)
Tama (5,200 tons) *	October 25	*Jallao* (Icenhower)

U.S. submarine losses continued to mount. Lockwood lost thirteen fleet boats † and Christie lost six,‡ for a total of nineteen, compared to seven in 1942 (excluding *S-26,* lost in the Gulf of Panama) and fifteen in 1943 (excluding *Dorado* and *R-12,* lost in the Atlantic). In

---

* Previously damaged by naval aircraft.
† *Scorpion, Grayback, Trout, Tullibee, Gudgeon, Herring, Golet, Shark II, Tang, Escolar, Albacore, Scamp,* and *Swordfish.*
‡ *Robalo, Flier, Harder, Seawolf, Darter,* and *Growler.*

addition, S-28, commanded by a reservist, J. G. Campbell, was lost in a training accident at Pearl Harbor. Forty-nine men died on S-28.

During 1944 lifeguarding became big business for the submarine force; Pacific submarines rescued 117 navy and air corps airmen. Dick O'Kane in *Tang* was the leading rescuer, having picked up 22 airmen in his daring cruise off Truk.

During the year, twenty-three older submarines were retired from combat or readied for retirement * and three (*Barbero, Halibut,* and *Redfish*) were retired because of battle damage. Most of the famous old boats went to training duties.

Japanese submarines, many detailed to resupply missions, continued to be ineffective and to suffer heavy losses. Japanese submarines deployed to stop the invasions of the Marshalls, Marianas, Palaus, and Philippines achieved almost nothing. During the year, the Japanese submarine force lost fifty-six boats—seven to U.S. submarines.

The "skipper problem" in the U.S. submarine force remained constant. There was always a shortage and always nonproductivity. During the year, perhaps 35 of about 250 skippers were relieved for nonproductivity. This was 14 percent, compared to 30 percent in 1942 and about 14 percent in 1943. Both Lockwood and Christie were forced to dip down to the class of 1938 for new skippers and even to use a few reserve officers, who had been steadfastly denied command during three years of war. The impetus came from Admiral Nimitz: foreseeing a large postwar navy which would have to be manned for the most part by reservists, Nimitz encouraged Lockwood (and others) to give them credit and command. After Lewis (*Sterlet*), Bissell (*Angler*), and Hunnicutt (*Carp*), four more reservists were named in 1945, making a total of seven reserve officers who commanded fleet boats on war patrol in World War II.

During the 520 war patrols in 1944, Pacific submarines fired a total of 6,092 torpedoes. This was more than all the boats had fired in 1942 and 1943 put together (5,379). In spite of improved torpedo performance on both the Mark XIV steam and Mark XVIII electric, statistically it took an average 10 torpedoes to sink a ship—compared to 8 in 1942 and 11.7 in 1943. One reason was that many skippers, no longer under orders to conserve torpedoes, fired full salvos. Another was that submarines, generally, encountered many more big tar-

---

* *Gar, Greenling, Narwhal, Nautilus, Permit, Plunger, Pollack, Sailfish, Salmon, Sargo, Saury, Seadragon, Seal, Searaven, Skipjack, Snapper, Spearfish, Stingray, Sturgeon, Tambor, Tarpon, Tautog,* and *Tuna*.

gets (and convoys) deserving of full salvos. Again, skippers reported many more hits for damage. Had the torpedo warheads been larger—as large as Japanese submarine torpedo warheads—many more ships would have gone to the bottom.

For all practical purposes, the U.S. submarine war against Japanese shipping ended in December 1944. The enemy ships that were left were forced to operate in the confined waters of the Sea of Japan or the Yellow Sea, running very close to shore and holing up in harbors at night, making it almost impossible for submarines to get at them.

Part VI

38

Pearl Harbor and Guam, January through March 1945

The U.S. Invasions of Iwo Jima and Okinawa

By January 1945 the war that had involved most of the world since 1939 was drawing to a close. In Europe, General Eisenhower's troops were poised to drive for the Rhine River. The Russian army crossed the Vistula and swept toward Germany from the east. In four months Hitler would be crushed, Germany defeated.

In the Pacific, Japan was almost beaten. Her navy had been reduced to a few remaining units, notably the carrier-battleships *Ise* and *Hyuga* in Singapore and the super-battleship *Yamato* in the Inland Sea. The merchant marine had been riddled by U.S. submarines and carrier aviation. In the homeland, there was almost no oil for the fleet or aviation gasoline for the aircraft. Production of new weapons had fallen off drastically for want of raw materials and electricity.

President Roosevelt and Prime Minister Churchill had agreed—and let it be known—that Japan would not be permitted to surrender except unconditionally. There would be no deals. Japan must lay down all her arms, give up all conquered territory, and face total occupation by Allied troops. Her leaders (except perhaps the Emperor) would be tried for war crimes.

Few militarists believed Japanese leaders would accept these terms. Almost everywhere that Allied troops had met Japanese troops, they

823

had encountered fanatical, suicidal resistance. Kamikazes (and their submarine counterparts, the *kaitens*) were still being trained by the hundreds. Nimitz and MacArthur concluded that Japan could only finally and totally be brought to her knees by an invasion of the homeland, an immense enterprise that would probably cost many hundreds of thousands of Allied casualties.

Most of the military planning was now dominated by this objective. The initial plan, Operation Olympic, called for an invasion of Kyushu, the southernmost Japanese home island, on November 1. To support it, Allied navies, armies, and air forces from all over the world would converge in the Pacific. The troops would stage from the Marianas, the Philippines, and Okinawa, scheduled to be seized in April.

Part of the overall plan for crushing Japan was to subject the homeland to massive bomber attack by B-29 Superfortresses basing from the Marianas. During late 1944, the U.S. Air Force built airstrips and supply depots on Saipan, Guam, and Tinian. The strikes, begun in November, continued regularly thereafter. The bombers did not do as well as expected. It was a 3,000-mile round trip from the Marianas to Tokyo. In order to make it, the bombers had to reduce their pay load from ten to three tons of bombs. Since fighter planes had nowhere near that range, the bombers had to fly unescorted. To protect themselves, they flew—and bombed—from high altitude (28,000 feet) where precision was impossible. Going and coming to Japan, they were attacked by Japanese fighters based in the Volcano and Bonin islands.

The logical solution to the bomber problem was to seize a way station in the Bonins: Iwo Jima. With Iwo Jima in Allied hands, Japanese interdiction would cease. U.S. fighters basing on Iwo Jima could escort the bombers to and from Tokyo. Iwo Jima could also provide a base for air rescue teams to hunt for downed pilots and an emergency strip for damaged B-29s returning from Japan.

This plan—code-named Operation Detachment—was approved and the job handed to Admiral Nimitz, who designated Admiral Spruance overall naval commander. Halsey stepped down to plan the follow-on invasion of Okinawa. In accordance with custom, the Fleet designation was changed from Third to Fifth and the Fast Carrier Task Force from 38 to 58. The invasion date was set for February 19.

As a preliminary to the invasion, Spruance decided to conduct a carrier strike on Tokyo on February 16–17. The main objective of this strike was to find and destroy Japanese air and sea power that might be thrown against the Iwo Jima invasion forces—in short, to "isolate" Iwo Jima. Spruance knew that *Yamato* and some other old battleships, heavy cruisers, and one or two new carriers were basing in Japanese waters. Perhaps he hoped they might make a suicidal dash at his mighty fleet and be destroyed.

In a reincarnation of Burt's Brooms, Lockwood provided eight submarines to conduct an antipicket sweep for Task Force 58. This time the plan was more sophisticated. Three of the boats were ordered to conduct a noisy, blatant diversionary sweep aimed toward the Inland Sea. The other five were ordered to proceed ahead of Task Force 58, blasting pickets from the seas by making undetected attacks with the homing torpedoes, or Cuties. The hope was that a picket hit by a Cutie would blow up and sink before it could get off a radio warning.

The five submarines leading the real cleanup toward Honshu were *Sterlet*, *Pomfret*, *Piper*, *Trepang*, and *Bowfin*. This unit, known as "Mac's Mops," was commanded by Barney McMahon, skipper of the new boat *Piper*. Mac's Mops went to work about February 10. None of the boats found any pickets and thus had no chance to experiment further with the Cuties. Afterward, the five boats deployed off Tokyo as lifeguard submarines.

The three boats assigned to the diversionary sweep—toward Shikoku and access to the Inland Sea—were *Haddock*, *Lagarto*, and *Sennet*. This unit, known as "Latta's Lances," was commanded by Frank Latta (ex-*Narwhal*) in the new boat *Lagarto*. Bill Brockman, now a division commander, took command of *Haddock* for this one patrol, replacing Beetle Roach, who had been injured in a jeep accident on Saipan. The Lances carried out their job well, making a lot of noise and even turning on searchlights at night. The group destroyed three pickets. Afterward, Latta in *Lagarto* sank a small freighter and a submarine, *RO-49*, off Bungo Suido. George Porter, commanding *Sennet*, sank a small coastal minelayer.

Task Force 58, helped by foul overcast weather, reached launch position off Japan without being detected and Spruance sent his planes over Tokyo. Hampered by the same foul weather, they did little damage.

Pomfret, commanded by John Hess, made a spectacular rescue. A pilot from the carrier *Cabot* was forced to ditch in the outer waters of Tokyo Bay. Fighters circled over *Pomfret*, guiding Hess to the rubber life raft. Hess fearlessly took *Pomfret* into these restricted waters and

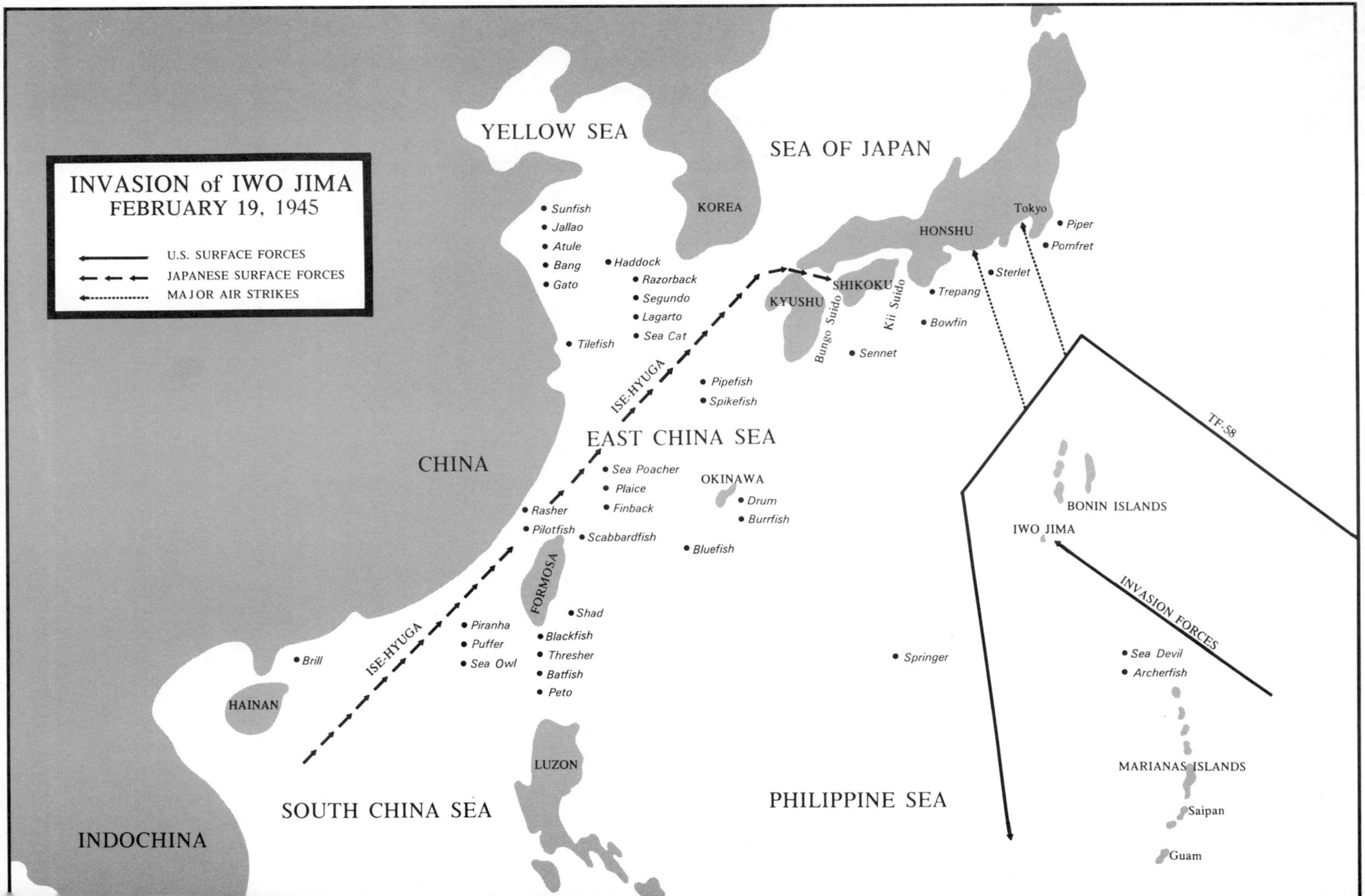
INVASION of IWO JIMA
FEBRUARY 19, 1945
U.S. SURFACE FORCES
JAPANESE SURFACE FORCES
MAJOR AIR STRIKES
YELLOW SEA
SEA OF JAPAN
KOREA
HONSHU
Tokyo
Piper
Pomfret
Sterlet
Trepang
Bowfin
SHIKOKU
KYUSHU
Bungo Suido
Kii Suido
Sennet
Sunfish
Jallao
Atule
Bang
Gato
Haddock
Razorback
Segundo
Lagarto
Sea Cat
Tilefish
ISE-HYUGA
Pipefish
Spikefish
EAST CHINA SEA
CHINA
Sea Poacher
Plaice
Finback
OKINAWA
Drum
Burrfish
Rasher
Pilotfish
Scabbardfish
Bluefish
FORMOSA
Shad
Piranha
Puffer
Sea Owl
Blackfish
Thresher
Batfish
Peto
Brill
ISE-HYUGA
HAINAN
LUZON
SOUTH CHINA SEA
INDOCHINA
PHILIPPINE SEA
Springer
TF-58
BONIN ISLANDS
IWO JIMA
INVASION FORCES
Sea Devil
Archerfish
MARIANAS ISLANDS
Saipan
Guam

rescued the pilot, Ensign R. L. Buchanan. During this same bold operation, Hess picked up another pilot, Lieutenant Joseph P. Farrell from *Hornet*, and a Japanese pilot. War correspondent Ernie Pyle devoted a column to the rescue entitled "Even If You Was Shot Down in Tokyo Harbor, the Navy Would Be In to Get You."

The Mops had other adventures. *Bowfin*'s skipper, Alexander Kelly Tyree, younger brother of John Tyree, rescued two more aviators and sank what was believed to be a destroyer but which postwar records identified as an 800-ton frigate. Reservist Hugh Lewis, in *Sterlet*, sank a 1,150-ton freighter. Allen Russell Faust, commanding *Trepang*, sank two small freighters for 2,261 tons.

After this swipe at Japan, Spruance took Task Force 58 southward to hit Iwo Jima. On February 19, the invasion forces went ashore as planned. They met fierce resistance, and the fighting went on for three bloody weeks. Kamikaze pilots hit the old carrier *Saratoga*, causing 300 casualties, and sank the jeep carrier *Bismarck Sea*, with the loss of 350 men. Before the island was secure, U.S. casualties totaled 17,000—7,000 dead. Soon after the island was secure, air force fighters moved there and began assisting the B-29s in raiding Japan.

After lending support to the Iwo Jima invasion, Task Force 58 wheeled around and hit Tokyo again, coordinating the assault with a massive B-29 raid. The 200 B-29s were carrying new incendiary bombs to test their efficiency against what were believed to be the highly inflammable residential districts of Tokyo. In this "test," the B-29s burned out 2 square miles of the city. The carrier planes, attacking military targets, destroyed about 150 Japanese planes. After that, Task Force 58 swung south to Ulithi to rest and replenish for the next mission: the invasion of Okinawa.

In early March, the air force launched an all-out B-29 fire raid against major Japanese cities. On the night of March 9–10, about 334 B-29s left bases in the Marianas and bombed Tokyo from low level. The bombs burned out 15 square miles of the city, destroying 267,000 buildings. About 84,000 people were killed and 40,000 wounded during that one night, and over a million were left homeless. In subsequent raids, the air force hit Nagoya, Kobe, Osaka, Yokohama, and Kawasaki, killing and wounding tens of thousands more. In all, these bombers destroyed 105 square miles of Japanese cities—including half of Tokyo. Still there was no sign that Japanese leaders were ready to surrender.

* * *

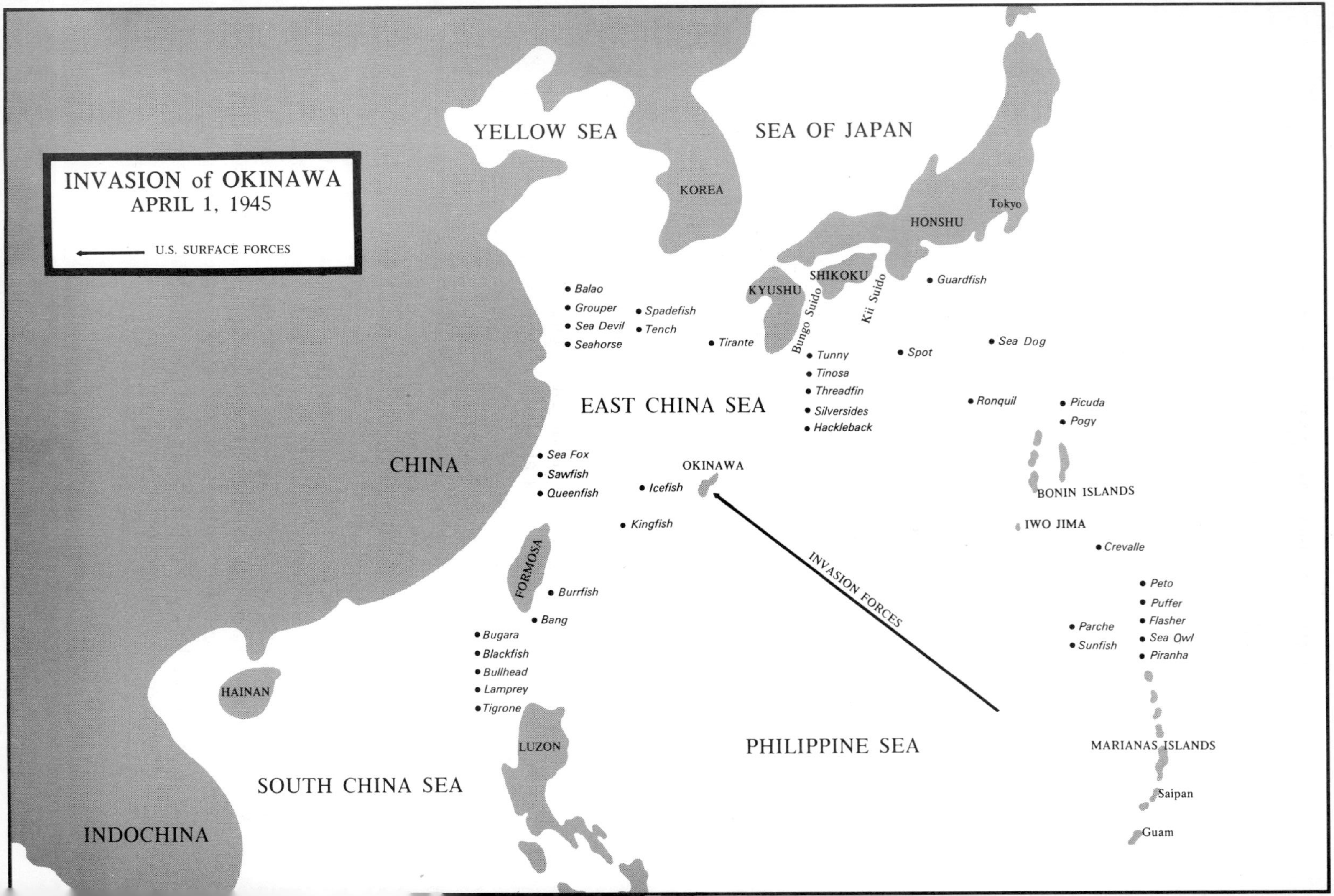

INVASION of OKINAWA
APRIL 1, 1945
U.S. SURFACE FORCES
YELLOW SEA
SEA OF JAPAN
KOREA
HONSHU
Tokyo
SHIKOKU
KYUSHU
Bungo Suido
Kii Suido
Guardfish
Balao
Grouper
Sea Devil
Seahorse
Spadefish
Tench
Tirante
Tunny
Tinosa
Threadfin
Silversides
Hackleback
Spot
Sea Dog
Ronquil
Picuda
Pogy
EAST CHINA SEA
CHINA
Sea Fox
Sawfish
Queenfish
OKINAWA
Icefish
Kingfish
BONIN ISLANDS
IWO JIMA
Crevalle
FORMOSA
Burrfish
Bang
Bugara
Blackfish
Bullhead
Lamprey
Tigrone
INVASION FORCES
Peto
Puffer
Flasher
Sea Owl
Piranha
Parche
Sunfish
HAINAN
LUZON
PHILIPPINE SEA
MARIANAS ISLANDS
Saipan
Guam
SOUTH CHINA SEA
INDOCHINA

THE U.S. INVASIONS OF IWO JIMA AND OKINAWA

The navy, meanwhile, continued plans for the invasion of Okinawa, code-named Operation Iceberg. Lockwood's submarines played a small role in the preliminaries. *Swordfish* had already been lost while conducting a reconnaissance mission there, photographing the beaches. Dick Latham had charted minefields with the new FM sonar. George Pierce in *Tunny*, using the FM gear (plus plenty of nerve), plotted the location of 222 mines, later swept up by U.S. forces. The information on mines proved useful to the amphibious forces.

As a preliminary to the invasion, Spruance again attacked the Japanese home islands with Task Force 58. This time the targets were Kyushu and the fleet unit in the Inland Sea. U.S. aircraft destroyed dozens of Japanese planes on the ground and in the air but inflicted only light damage on targets inside the Inland Sea. They missed several prizes: the super-battleship *Yamato* and two new carriers, *Amagi* and *Katsuragi*.

During this action, March 18–19, the Japanese counterattacked Task Force 58. Japanese planes bombed the carriers *Enterprise*, *Yorktown*, *Franklin*, and *Wasp*. *Franklin* was severely damaged, and more than 700 crewmen were killed, but the ship, racked by fire and exploding stores, was saved by a brave and efficient damage-control party. Later, she headed for the United States under her own steam, to finish out the war in a navy yard.

During the strikes on Kyushu, many of Lockwood's submarines served as lifeguards and lookouts, should *Yamato* steam out of the Inland Sea. Douglas Hammond in *Guardfish* joined two boats left over from Mac's Mops, *Sterlet* and *Bowfin*, to guard Kii Suido. *Guardfish* began one day by dodging a torpedo from a Japanese submarine and then surfacing in sight of land to pick up two airmen from the carrier *Hancock*. Alex Tyree in *Bowfin* picked up two more.

Two submarines in this concentration between Japan and Okinawa were lost. The first was *Kete*, making her second patrol under Edward Ackerman, one of the first officers from the class of 1939 to command a fleet boat. On March 10, Ackerman attacked a convoy, sinking three small freighters for 6,881 tons. On March 20, he broadcast a special report for Spruance. Nothing further was heard from *Kete*. Jasper Holmes thought she may have been sunk by a Japanese submarine en route to Okinawa, but he could never confirm his belief.

The second boat lost was the famous old *Trigger*, commanded by

David Rikart Connole. On March 18 and March 27, Connole sank two small ships for 2,500 tons. Nothing further was heard from him either.

Lockwood organized some of the boats into combinations of wolf packs. In late March, he ordered Earl Twining Hydeman to form a pack consisting of Hydeman's *Sea Dog*, *Trigger*, and *Threadfin*, commanded by John Joseph Foote. When the response from *Trigger* was only silence, Lockwood gave up forming that pack. He ordered *Sea Dog* to carry out an individual patrol and *Threadfin* to join a new pack consisting of John Nichols in *Silversides* and Frederick Emery Janney, commanding a new Cramp boat, *Hackleback*. This pack moved north to cover Bungo Suido.

A second pack moved up to take position south of Nichols's pack. The threesome, commanded by Arthur Chester Smith in a new boat, *Trutta*, included another new one, *Lionfish*, commanded by the son of Admiral Spruance, Edward Spruance, and *Parche*, commanded by Woodrow Wilson McCrory, Ramage's old exec. On leaving Saipan, *Trutta* struck a submerged cable and damaged a propeller, so while *Parche* and *Lionfish* proceeded on patrol, *Trutta* followed a few days behind. Another boat, *Crevalle*, commanded by Everett Hartwell Steinmetz, patrolled in the same area.

The landings on Okinawa, supported by Task Force 58, proceeded as scheduled on April 1. Within the first five days, Japanese kamikazes hit thirty-nine naval vessels, including Spruance's flagship *Indianapolis*, two old battleships, three cruisers, and a jeep carrier. On April 6, 355 kamikaze planes attacked Task Force 58 and the landing beaches, sinking two destroyers, *Bush* and *Calhoun*, and damaging many others.

On about April 5, Admiral Toyoda ordered the super-battleship *Yamato*, the light cruiser *Yahagi*, and eight destroyers to get under way for Okinawa, their mission to damage further the landing craft and support vessels he hoped were already badly smashed up by the kamikaze raids. The commander of this unit, Vice Admiral Seiichi Ito, could find no more than 2,500 barrels of oil, not enough for a round trip. Clearly it had to be a one-way suicidal voyage. Toyoda knew this but, as he said after the war, "We had to do everything to help our troops at Okinawa."

Many senior Japanese naval officers opposed the mission, but on the evening of April 6 Admiral Ito got under way and stood out of

YAMATO SORTIE
APRIL 6, 1945

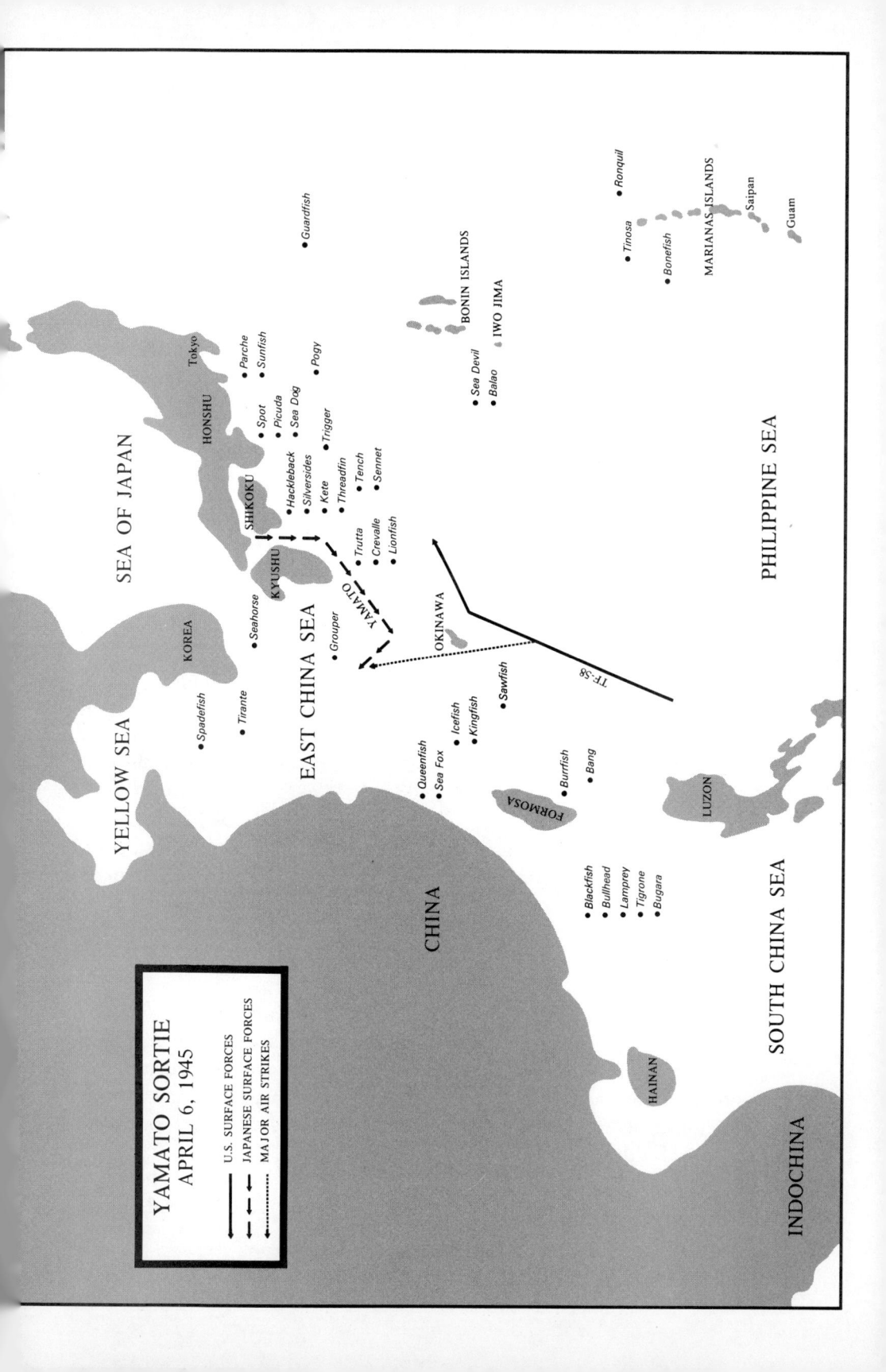

→→→ U.S. SURFACE FORCES
--→ JAPANESE SURFACE FORCES
······ MAJOR AIR STRIKES

Bungo Suido. At 7:44 P.M., John Foote in *Threadfin* picked up the force at 5 miles. He was not certain what it included: a carrier? *Yamato?* Some other battleship?

The tension in *Threadfin's* conning tower was high. Foote blew all ballast tanks dry and began a chase. His orders were to report first and then attack. He closed to 4 miles and reported the force by radio, giving approximate composition, course, and speed—22 knots. By the time this was accomplished, *Yamato* had opened to 10 miles and there was no hope *Threadfin* could catch up. Later, Foote wrote dejectedly, "*Threadfin's* chance for the Hall of Fame passed before contact report was cleared." He added, "Our remaining hope was that *Silversides* or *Hackleback* would [attack and] slow [the force] down somewhere near our speed." Later, Lockwood called this contact report "brilliant."

To the south, Frederick Janney in *Hackleback* picked up Foote's report and was lucky enough to make contact. He found the group at 25,000 yards and immediately began a steady series of contact reports. Janney brought *Hackleback* in close (13,000 yards) on three separate occasions, but the strong destroyer screen thwarted any hope of attack.

After Admiral Spruance had been told what was going on, Lockwood lifted the report-attack restriction, freeing all submarines to attack and then report. However, none of the other boats made contact. Young Spruance in *Lionfish* missed a golden opportunity to beat his father to the punch.

On April 7, the morning after the *Threadfin-Hackleback* contact report, aircraft from Task Force 58, which had moved northward from Okinawa to intercept *Yamato*, found the formation. At noon, Task Force 58 aircraft struck, sinking *Yamato*, *Yahagi*, and two of the destroyers; two other destroyers were so badly damaged the Japanese sank them before fleeing to the nearest friendly port.

During the days and weeks that followed, kamikaze pilots inflicted more damage on the landing forces and Task Force 58. The U.S. carriers *Bunker Hill*, *Hancock*, and *Enterprise* and four British carriers assigned to the U.S. fleet were hit and damaged, some severely. In all, a dozen destroyers were sunk, including *Mannert L. Abele*, named for the skipper of *Grunion*, lost on her first patrol.

The fighting on Okinawa dragged on for weeks. When the island was finally secure, the United States counted 13,000 dead, nearly

5,000 of them navy. Many B-29s had been diverted to support the U.S. Navy, carrying out strikes on airfields on the Ryukyus and elsewhere and planting mines in Japanese seaports. On May 11 they were released to resume their main objective of destroying Japanese cities, aircraft factories, shipyards, and other industrial targets. Day after day they flew over Japan by the score, dropping tens of thousands of tons of bombs, but Japan hung on stubbornly.

Patrols from Guam

Throughout this period, Lockwood, who had established his main headquarters in Guam on the tender *Holland*, continued to send submarines on patrol, singly or in wolf packs. A number of these were assigned to lifeguard duty and rescued many downed pilots. Others cruised Luzon Strait and the East China and Yellow seas. Lockwood was running out of sea room—and targets.

A wolf pack led by Joe Enright in *Archerfish* took station in Luzon Strait. The other boats were *Batfish*, commanded by Jake Fyfe, and *Blackfish*, commanded by Robert Sellars.

About the time this pack reached Luzon Strait, the codebreakers picked up information that the Japanese intended to evacuate some pilots from Luzon to Formosa by submarine. The four boats detailed to this mission were *RO-46*, *RO-112*, *RO-113*, and *RO-115*. The routes and sailing dates were relayed to Enright, who deployed his pack in a probable intercept position in the strait. The pack was joined by another made up of *Plaice*, *Scabbardfish*, and *Sea Poacher*.

The scouting line waited patiently. On the night of February 9, at about 10:15, Jake Fyfe in *Batfish* picked up radar emissions on a device known as the APR. A little later, he got radar contact at 6 miles. Believing this to be one of the Japanese submarines southbound from Formosa, he closed to 1,850 yards and fired three torpedoes. All missed. The Japanese skipper evidently did not see the torpedoes; he continued on course. When only 1,000 yards away, Fyfe fired three more torpedoes. One ran hot in the tube, but the second hit the sub, causing a "brilliant red explosion that lit up the whole sky." This was *RO-115*.

The following morning Fyfe intended to remain on the surface for a daylight search, but friendly aircraft (perhaps also looking for the

Japanese submarines) drove him under. At about 10 A.M., when Fyfe came up to have a look through his periscope, the friendly planes attacked *Batfish*, firing an aerial torpedo. Fyfe went deep in a hurry. The torpedo passed over *Batfish*. "A tender moment," Fyfe wrote later, "and a very unfriendly act."

Plaice, Scabbardfish, and *Sea Poacher* left the scouting line to patrol elsewhere. *Batfish, Archerfish,* and *Blackfish* remained in position. On the evening of February 11, shortly after surfacing to charge batteries, Fyfe again picked up radar emissions on his APR. Then he saw a Japanese submarine, range 1,200 yards. As Fyfe was setting up to fire, the submarine dived. Fyfe thought that was that, but the sub surfaced again half an hour later, giving off radar emissions. Fyfe made an end around and at about ten o'clock fired four torpedoes from the point-blank range of 880 yards. Fyfe later wrote, "The target literally blew apart and sank almost immediately." This was *RO-112*, southbound from Formosa.

The next night, shortly after midnight, Fyfe again picked up Japanese radar emissions on APR. At 2:15, he made contact on his own radar, range 5 miles. Fyfe moved in but the sub dived. An hour later, Fyfe picked the target up on radar again and attacked, firing three torpedoes from 1,500 yards. One hit, and the submarine blew up in a "large yellow ball of fire." This was *RO-113*, southbound from Formosa.

On the following evening, February 14, Joe Enright in *Archerfish* believed he picked up yet another Japanese submarine. Firing two salvos of four torpedoes, he saw a "large white flash" that illuminated the target and believed he sank a submarine. Lockwood credited him with the sinking, but postwar records did not bear it out. After this attack, the pack returned to Saipan and Guam.

Joe Willingham, on the first patrol of *Tautog*, had sunk two Japanese submarines and nearly sunk two or three more, but no other skipper had ever actually sunk three on one patrol, let alone three in three days. Lockwood, sparing no praise, called Fyfe's performance "brilliant." The Japanese gave up trying to evacuate the aviators by submarine. Counting *RO-49*, sunk by Frank Latta in *Lagarto* on February 24, the Japanese lost four boats to U.S. submarines in February.

In April the Japanese lost another. Carter Bennett, returning to Pearl Harbor in *Sea Owl* at the end of a long unrewarding wolf-pack patrol in Luzon Strait and the South China Sea, received an Ultra reporting a Japanese submarine en route from Japan to Wake Island on a resupply mission. "It was very specific information," Bennett said later. Bennett had a tough time finding the sub, but on the morning of April 16 he picked it up 7 miles northwest of the island. Taking his time to be sure of a kill, Bennett tracked the boat "playing hide and seek," but it slipped into the Wake anchorage before he could shoot. Seeing the sub anchored at the boat landing, Bennett crept into shallow water submerged and fired his torpedoes. *RO-56* blew up and sank.

The U.S. submarine *Snook*, commanded by John Walling, was lost in April. After patrolling in Luzon Strait with a pack led by Hiram Cassedy in *Tigrone*, Walling was assigned on April 12 to lifeguard east of Formosa for a British carrier strike. On April 20, the British officer commanding the force reported a plane down in *Snook*'s vicinity and requested Walling to rescue. Walling did not reply. Nothing more was ever heard from him. *Snook* disappeared with all hands. There was no clue in Japanese records as to her loss.

Bill Post, ex-*Gudgeon*, brought out a new boat, *Spot*. On his first patrol, he led a pack called "Post's Panzers" (*Spot*, *Icefish*, and *Balao*) to the coast of China, firing off all his torpedoes. He believed he had sunk four ships and was so credited, but postwar records failed to confirm any. During the patrol, Post emulated his feats on *Gudgeon* by conducting a gun attack on a fairly large auxiliary. After he had disabled it, he sent over a boarding party, which gathered intelligence data and got a prisoner. During the boarding, the ship sank. Four of Post's men jumped on *Spot*, but three others had to be fished from the water.

On his second patrol, commencing in March, Post led another threesome, "Post's Panzers II." The other boats were *Sea Fox*, commanded by Roy Craig Klinker, and *Queenfish*, commanded by Elliott Loughlin. *Sea Fox* had recently suffered a senseless tragedy. While the crew was resting at Camp Dealey on Guam, seven enlisted men persuaded a native Guamanian to take them on a strictly forbidden souvenir hunt in the jungles. A group of about thirty Japanese holdouts ambushed the sightseers; shooting them with carbines. Six, including the guide, died instantly. Two of *Sea Fox*'s crewmen, badly wounded, managed to crawl off and survive.

Post took the pack to northern Formosa Strait, patrolling close off the coast of China. He found action right away, again firing all his torpedoes. He sank *Nanking Maru*, a 3,000-ton freighter, and shared half credit with navy aircraft for sinking *Ikomasaw Maru*, a 3,173-ton transport. He again engaged in a running gun battle with a fairly large vessel, a minelayer which came within 100 yards of ramming *Spot*. After this, Post requested permission to return to Guam for more torpedoes.

On the way to Guam, Post had a harrowing experience. After sunset on the evening of March 31, *Spot* encountered a friendly destroyer of Task Force 58, supporting the Okinawa invasion, U.S.S. *Case*. *Case* was in a "safe" submarine zone and was prohibited from attacking any submarine unless it had been identified as enemy "beyond possibility of doubt." *Case* made some attempt at exchanging recognition signals but then opened fire with her guns from 3,000 to 4,000 yards. After *Case* had fired three shots, Post fired a red flare and dived. The skipper of *Case* then realized his error and ceased firing. Post made it into Guam without further incident. After this, he stepped down as skipper of *Spot* and was promoted to command a division.

With Post gone, command of the pack, now reduced to *Queenfish* and *Sea Fox*, devolved upon the senior man, Elliott Loughlin in *Queenfish*. While they were patrolling, a curious drama was coming to its climax which would directly involve Loughlin. It had begun in mid-1944. The U.S. government, concerned over the brutal treatment given U.S. prisoners of war in the southern territories, had asked Japan (through neutral Switzerland) if she would transport Red Cross packages provided by the United States from Japan to the southern regions. The Japanese were initially cold to the idea. But after the sea lanes to the south had been cut, they seized on the request as a way of surreptitiously shipping some ammunition and supplies to cut-off troops and returning hundreds of stranded sea captains and crewmen to Japan.

Accordingly, in February 1945, the U.S. request was granted. The Japanese picked huge *Awa Maru* and loaded her with tons upon tons of spare aircraft parts and ammunition, along with a mere 2,000 tons of relief supplies. The Japanese broadcast her routing: she would leave Meji, Japan, February 17, go to Singapore and Indonesian ports, return via Hong Kong and Takao, Formosa, and thence up the Formosa Strait to Japan. She would have special markings: a white cross on each side of her funnel and lighted white crosses at night. She would also run with navigation lights at night.

Lockwood and Fife were among those who were skeptical about this voyage. They (and other naval officers) had long been suspicious of the excessive number of Japanese hospital ships which plied the waters to and from Japan. However, they raised no protest. It was State Department business, and it would be futile—and seemingly cold-blooded—to question the matter. In early February, both men sent out plain-language dispatches notifying all submarines in detail of *Awa Maru*'s routing with instructions to let her pass. Lockwood sent his message three times each for three nights, nine times in all.

Awa Maru passed safely to the south and made her rounds, observed closely by submarines on patrol. While making these rounds, she loaded her holds with thousands upon thousands of bales of raw rubber and other critically needed strategic materials. In addition, she rounded up about 1,700 passengers, mostly stranded merchant ship captains, mates, engineers, and seamen, plus some government officials.

A further item in this bizarre drama that made Lockwood still more suspicious was the return route of *Awa Maru*, as provided by the Japanese. He and Dick Voge noticed that it would take her through a big minefield lying between the west coast of the Ryukyus and the China coast. Lockwood and Voge knew from intelligence sources that the field was there but wondered if the Japanese were trying to deceive the U.S. Navy into believing the area was clear, hoping to lure U.S. submarines into the field.

But before setting off on the return voyage, *Awa Maru* broadcast a corrected return route that would take her outside the minefield. In early March, Lockwood sent a message to "all submarines" concerning the return route of *Awa Maru*. Again, he sent the message in plain language, three times a night for three nights. On March 28, Lockwood sent an additional message, this one encoded, to "all submarines" which stated, in effect, LET PASS SAFELY THE AWA MARU CARRYING PRISONER OF WAR SUPPLIES. SHE WILL BE PASSING THROUGH YOUR AREAS BETWEEN MARCH 30 AND APRIL 4. SHE IS LIGHTED AT NIGHT AND PLASTERED WITH WHITE CROSSES.

Loughlin received this encoded message, but he had not previously been briefed on *Awa Maru*, nor had his communications officer bothered to show him any of the many plain-language broadcasts regarding her that had been received on *Queenfish*. When Loughlin saw Lockwood's decoded message of March 28, he thought it (as he recalled later) "the stupidest message" he'd ever seen. It was not directed to any specific submarine and gave no details of course, speed, or routing.

On April 1, Loughlin's packmate, Roy Klinker in *Sea Fox*, got into a small convoy and attacked, damaging a freighter. That night at 7:40, Klinker broadcast a contact report to Loughlin. Two hours and twenty minutes later, *Queenfish* made radar contact on a single ship, range 17,000 yards. Loughlin judged from the radar pip that it was a Japanese destroyer, hunting the submarine that had attacked the convoy.

A dense fog reduced visibility to 200 yards. Loughlin could see nothing from the bridge. Watching his radar, he closed to 1,200 yards, swung around, and fired four stern tubes set on 3 feet with a 300-foot spread. He heard and saw four hits, properly timed. The radar pip disappeared quickly. Loughlin must have privately marveled at his accuracy: four hits in a 300-foot destroyer!

Easing *Queenfish* to the scene of the sinking to pick up a survivor, Loughlin found a large oil slick and fifteen or twenty men clinging to wreckage. One agreed to come aboard. He was in bad shape and "no coherent information was immediately forthcoming," Loughlin wrote later. However, within a few hours Loughlin learned the dreadful truth: he had sunk *Awa Maru*.

Loughlin immediately reported his error to Lockwood. When the duty officer woke Lockwood with the news, the admiral was gravely concerned on at least three counts: (1) that the incident would cause an international furor (similar to *Lusitania*), embarrassing to the United States; (2) that the Japanese might "wreak barbarous reprisals" upon U.S. prisoners of war, especially submariners; and (3) that Loughlin, one of his best skippers, would be crucified. Lockwood notified Nimitz and Admiral King and then ordered Loughlin and Klinker to search the area for additional survivors.

When Admiral King received the news, his response was typically cold and curt. He radioed Lockwood: ORDER QUEENFISH INTO PORT IMMEDIATELY . . . DETACH LOUGHLIN FROM HIS COMMAND AND HAVE HIM TRIED BY A GENERAL COURT-MARTIAL.

At the scene of the sinking, neither Loughlin nor Klinker could find any more survivors. The crew and the 1,700 passengers had evidently drowned. As the two boats steamed around hunting through the debris, they saw an estimated four thousand bales of raw rubber floating on the sea. Loughlin recovered four of the bales and stored them below. Then, with heavy heart, he set course for Saipan.

Along the way, Loughlin received word that some airmen were down in his vicinity. Detouring to search, he found thirteen men—the crew of a big navy patrol plane—in rubber rafts. They had been in the water almost four days. He took them on board and proceeded to Guam, arriving on April 12, the day President Roosevelt died.

Once in Guam, Loughlin was somewhat startled—and relieved—to find his boss 100 percent on his side. Lockwood had already fired off half a dozen memos to Nimitz and others, partly blaming himself for the disaster because he had not been more specific in his March 29 encoded dispatch. He had lined up lawyer Chester Bruton and a marine assistant to defend Loughlin. When the court-martial convened, Lockwood, in absentia (he had returned briefly to the States for an FM sonar conference), submitted depositions in Loughlin's behalf.

At the court-martial, Chester Bruton and his assistant tried everything they could think of. The chief line of defense was that by carrying munitions and contraband *Awa Maru* had sacrificed her right to safe conduct. To prove this, Loughlin's lawyers produced the lone survivor rescued by Loughlin, Kantora Shimoda, a steward. However, the court * dismissed this as irrelevant on the grounds that Loughlin had no way of knowing what the ship carried, and even if he did he had no right to disregard the safe-conduct granted by the State Department.

Loughlin's lawyers then shifted to another defense, lack of intent. This was easily proved by the way Loughlin had attacked. Had he been trying to sink a big ship like *Awa Maru* instead of the destroyer he believed it to be, he would have set his torpedoes to run deeper and used a much broader spread. (As Dick Voge later pointed out, they might have raised another point in Loughlin's behalf: if he had deliberately sunk *Awa Maru*, why rescue and bring home a survivor who could convict him of the crime?)

The way Bruton handled the defense enabled him to introduce Loughlin's superior war record—not normally allowed in a court-martial. This impressed the court favorably. Another point in Loughlin's favor was the fact that he steadfastly refused to put any blame on

---

* The president of the board was Vice Admiral John Howard Hoover, known ironically as "Genial John"; the youngest and least senior member, representing the submarine force, was Lew Parks.

the communications officer or on others who had failed to bring all the messages regarding *Awa Maru* to his attention. This display of loyalty "down" also impressed the court.

After hearing the evidence, the court returned a murky verdict. It dismissed charges against Loughlin of culpable inefficiency in the performance of duty and disobeying the lawful order of a superior but found him guilty of negligence in obeying orders and sentenced him to receive a Letter of Admonition from the Secretary of the Navy. Nimitz, who believed the punishment should have been sterner, was furious. He gave the members of the court a Letter of Reprimand—a more serious punishment than the court gave Loughlin—but apparently did not put it in their records, at least not in that of Lew Parks.

But temporarily, at least, Loughlin was hurt professionally. "By edict of Admiral King," he said later, "I could not have another command." Lockwood transferred Loughlin to his staff and assigned him to the training command. Later, he became operations officer to Gin Styer in the Atlantic Fleet.

A similar tragedy was only narrowly avoided. *Razorback*, commanded by Charles Brown, picked up a solitary vessel in the East China Sea. Bedeviled by fogging periscopes, Brown believed it to be a transport, even though it was steering a steady course without escort. Brown closed to 3,200 yards and fired five steam torpedoes. After they left the tube, Brown saw a red cross on the side of the hull, indicating a hospital ship, which all submarines were to give free passage. Brown held his breath while the torpedoes streaked toward the hull. All missed; luckily, Brown had overestimated the range. An endorser, in one of the great understatements of the war, wrote, "It is fortunate the attack was not successful."

Boats that patrolled to the East China and Yellow seas also found that targets were increasingly scarce and hard to find. A pack led by Ben Adams (who had been fired from *Flier*), in the famous *Rasher*, with *Pilotfish* and *Finback*, made only two attacks for zero results, and Adams was relieved after this, his only patrol as skipper. Ed Shelby in *Sunfish*, Dixie Farrell in *Gato*, and Joseph Icenhower in *Jallao* all conducted extremely aggressive patrols as a pack, but the only confirmed sinkings were Farrell's: two small ships for 3,125 tons. The combination of Barney Sieglaff in the new *Tench*, Robert Worthington in *Balao*, Ralph Styles in *Sea Devil*, and Frederick Wahlig in *Grouper* was most successful; Worthington sank two confirmed ships for 11,293 tons and Styles three for about 10,000 tons. Afterward, old *Grouper* was retired and Sieglaff turned *Tench* over to Tom Baskett and went to work on Lockwood's staff.

Caddy Adkins, returning *Cod* from a long overhaul in the States, also patrolled the East China Sea, sinking a tugboat and a minesweeper. A day after *Cod* received "the most severe depth-charging of her career," fire broke out in the after torpedo room, caused by a short circuit in one of the electric torpedoes. The compartment instantly filled with smoke and had to be evacuated. A party of volunteers donned breathing apparatus to enter the compartment, load the burning torpedo into a tube, and fire it to sea. Quartermaster Lawrence E. Foley and another man, going aft topside to open the torpedo room deck hatch to help, were caught by a wave and knocked overboard. Foley had a life jacket; his helper did not. They drifted off into the darkness. Adkins launched a search that went on for eight hours. Near dawn—by what seemed to be a miracle—he found the two men and recovered them. All that time, Adkins reported later, Quartermaster Foley had kept his shipmate afloat.

Attacks from the Air

With the skies now black with Allied aircraft, the number of accidental bombings increased—in spite of all precautions. U.S. submariners came to fear the sight of any aircraft.

Bullhead, a new boat commanded by Walt Griffith (ex-*Bowfin*), patrolled the South China Sea en route to report to Jimmy Fife. She carried a unique passenger: Martin Sheridan, a reporter for the *Boston Globe,* the only war correspondent permitted to make a submarine war patrol in World War II. Nimitz had authorized his trip—without checking with Admiral King.

Griffith found few targets. On April 8, while *Bullhead* was cruising the surface, a B-24 Liberator, flying low, popped out of the clouds. The pilot set up on *Bullhead* and dropped three bombs. They fell about 75 yards astern of the boat.

Later, Sheridan reported, "Though the boat dove rapidly, it didn't seem half fast enough.... Men in the maneuvering and after torpedo rooms were shaken up a bit by the underwater blasts.... One serious case of constipation was known to be cured by the attack."

Griffith picked up three airmen and returned to base, stepping down to join Lockwood's staff after one more patrol. When King learned Sheridan had been on board *Bullhead*, he sent a dispatch to all submarine commands: WAR CORRESPONDENTS MAY NOT REPEAT NOT GO ON SUBMARINE WAR PATROLS.

Pogy, commanded by John Michael Bowers, was strafed by a U.S. Army Liberator while lifeguarding near Tokyo Bay, and a flight of navy aircraft attacked Gordon Underwood in *Spadefish* as he led *Pompon* (commanded by Stephen Gimber), *Bang* (commanded by Anton Gallaher), and *Atule* (commanded by John Maurer) to the Yellow Sea. The navy planes dropped two bombs before Underwood could dive, as Maurer in *Atule* witnessed this senseless performance. (Fortunately, the bombs did only slight damage.) When the planes flew over *Atule*, Maurer exchanged recognition signals in time and was spared a similar fate.

Maintaining his record—he had sunk ten confirmed ships, including the carrier *Jinyo (Shinyo)*—Underwood sank four ships for 13,-423 tons; Maurer sank one big freighter, *Taiman Maru I*, 6,888 tons; Gallaher in *Bang*, who had eight confirmed ships to his credit, was fiercely aggressive but had bad luck; and Gimber in *Pompon* had to leave station early, after a dive with the conning tower hatch open flooded the pump room and damaged the machinery there. (Gimber and Underwood asked for transfers, Gimber going to new construction and Underwood to the Bureau of Ships.)

Tirante's First Patrol

In March a new boat, *Tirante*, commanded by George Levick Street III, arrived at Saipan for her first war patrol. Street's exec was Ned Beach, who had made ten previous patrols on *Trigger*; Street had made nine previous war patrols on *Gar*. The two men got along famously, Street later describing Beach as "one of the outstanding young submariners of all times."

Lockwood sent *Tirante* to the East China Sea. Street began by patrolling the approaches of Nagasaki (in the area where John Lee in *Croaker* had sunk the light cruiser *Nagara*) and on March 25 sank a small tanker, *Fuji Maru*. Three days later, he sank a small freighter, *Nase Maru*. During the next few days, while U.S. troops went ashore at Okinawa, Street stood guard at the western exit of the Inland Sea in case major Japanese fleet units should come out.* During this time, he battle-surfaced and sank a lugger and missed an amphibious vessel with three electric torpedoes.

After being released from reconnaissance duty, Street moved north to patrol off the south coast of Korea. Soon after reaching these waters, Street battle-surfaced on a schooner. A boarding party captured three Koreans, one of whom escaped by diving over the side. On April 7 Street attacked a small single freighter, firing two electric torpedoes and observing the thunderous double explosion through the periscope. He surfaced immediately and surveyed the wreckage, saw two survivors clinging to debris, and by hand signals vectored a nearby native Korean craft to rescue them. This is another sinking that must have slipped through, for postwar records failed to confirm it.

Tirante had an extraordinarily powerful SJ radar, and her engineers had fixed the speed governors on her Fairbanks-Morse diesels so as to increase her maximum speed by about a knot. When Street learned from the *Threadfin* and *Hackleback* reports that *Yamato* had sortied from the Inland Sea, it seemed logical to him and Beach that she might round Kyushu, perhaps heading for the naval base at Sasebo, in *Tirante*'s area (since the only other way to get there, through Shimonoseki Strait, was now blocked by aircraft-laid mines). With her speed and radar both operating at maximum, *Tirante* ran a "retiring search curve" which completely blanketed all *Yamato*'s possible positions, had Sasebo been her destination. To Street and his eager crew, it seemed certain they would have a shot at her. They were of course disappointed, but there was other business coming their way.

Responding to an Ultra on April 9, *Tirante* attacked a small convoy. Street fired six electric torpedoes at two different ships. He missed one but the others hit *Nikko Maru*, a 5,500-ton transport which was jammed with troops and seamen returning from Shanghai. Escorts jumped *Tirante* and delivered a close attack. Street responded by firing one Cutie. It apparently hit the mark because there was a terrific overhead explosion and breaking-up noises. The escort either was too small for the records or did not sink.

On the night of April 12 or 13 (as Beach later recalled) *Tirante* received an Ultra reporting that an important transport had holed up

---

* It was during this period that Voge ordered *Trigger* to form up with *Sea Dog* and *Threadfin*. When *Trigger* wasn't heard from, Voge directed her to rendezvous with *Tirante*. Street and Beach waited three days. When Beach realized his old ship was gone forever, he was devastated. After the war he immortalized her in a book, *Submarine!*

for the night in a small harbor on Quelpart Island (Cheju Do) about 100 miles due south of the southwestern tip of Korea. Street proceeded there, arriving the night of April 13. *Tirante* went to battle stations and, proceeding boldly on the surface past an escort, crossed into 60 feet of water. Then Street nosed *Tirante*'s bow into the harbor—à la Gene Fluckey.

Beach, manning the TBT binoculars on the bridge, picked up three targets anchored in the murk: the transport and two small frigate escorts. While Beach aimed from the bridge, Street in the conning tower made ready torpedo tubes and fired three steam torpedoes at the transport. Moments later, it blew up with an awesome explosion. Street ordered *Tirante* to head for deep water, changed his mind, paused, and fired three torpedoes at the two frigates. Both blew up and sank while *Tirante* was making flank speed out of the harbor. Confirmed result: with six torpedoes, Street and Beach had sunk *Juzan Maru*, 4,000 tons, and two frigates of about 900 tons each.

With only one torpedo remaining, Street headed for the barn. On the way home, he found three Japanese airmen sitting on the overturned float of a seaplane. He captured two, but the third drowned himself. For all these exploits—including the sinking of six confirmed ships for 12,621 tons—George Street received the Medal of Honor and Ned Beach, one of a few execs so honored, a Navy Cross. Following this, Beach received orders to command his own boat.

Generally, targets were now scarce. Of the eighty-seven war patrols mounted from Pearl Harbor and Guam from January to March, sixty —almost 70 percent—were without sinkings. The other twenty-seven produced 51½ sinkings. The high scorer was George Street. Next was John Ward Reed in *Sunfish*, who was lucky to find—and sink— four ships for 5,461 tons off the east coast of Honshu.

39

Fremantle and Subic Bay, January through August 1945

The Move to Subic Bay

When Jimmy Fife relieved Ralph Christie in Fremantle, he found the staff busy with plans to move the Brisbane repair base forward to Subic Bay, Philippines—a monumental operation. After the Subic Bay area had been recaptured by MacArthur's troops, Fife flew there for an inspection, chose a site for the base, and set work crews in motion. The tender *Fulton* arrived in Subic Bay on February 11 with the advance contingent.

This move reminded many old hands on the staff of the abortive move to Exmouth Gulf in 1943. Subic Bay was a humid, unhealthy, desolate Siberia. "And," said Chester Smith, who moved there commanding Squadron Thirty, "it was too far from everything." Few (except Fife) wanted to move there, let alone build the big submarine base the plans called for.

Unmoved by these objections, Fife pushed ahead, believing that submarines would be based there after the war had been won. The Seabees who did the construction were in a race with time, hoping to finish the base before the heavy seasonal rains began in mid-May. They made one grave error: they built the staff headquarters and communications building before they built the roads. Everything fell behind schedule, and the rains came before the roads were finished.

The result was a vast quagmire of mud. The heavy equipment brought up from Brisbane on the Liberty ship *Ganymede* had to be stored on the beach, and much of it was damaged or lost.

By March, most of the staff had moved. Two other tenders joined *Fulton*, *Anthedon*, and *Gilmore*, arriving March 13. A rest camp—named for James Wiggins Coe, lost on *Cisco*—was hacked out of the jungle. But all this was primitive, a far cry from the pleasant climate, facilities, and girls of Australia.

Pursuit of *Ise* and *Hyuga*

Meanwhile, Fife directed his submarines against the shrinking list of Japanese vessels stationed in southern waters. The most important of these were basing in Singapore: the carrier-battleships *Ise* and *Hygua*, the heavy cruisers *Tone*, *Haguro*, and *Ashigara*, two damaged heavy cruisers, *Takao* (hit by *Darter*) and *Myoko* (by *Bergall*), the light cruiser *Isuzu*, several destroyers, and a number of tankers and freighters converted to tankers.

Fife's skippers performed remarkably well against the tankers and small men-of-war. The reservist H. S. Simpson, commanding *Bashaw*, sank the 10,000-ton tanker *Ryoei Maru*. Bill Hazzard, making a spectacular second patrol in *Blenny*, sank the 10,000-ton tanker *Amato Maru*, a smaller tanker, and two freighters. Ben Jarvis, commanding *Baya*, sank the 5,236-ton tanker *Palembang Maru*. Hank Sturr in *Becuna* sank a 2,000-ton tanker. Paul Stimson, making an aggressive second patrol in *Sea Robin*, sank four freighters. Ralph Huntington Lockwood (no kin to the admiral) in *Guavina* sank the 8,673-ton tanker *Eiyo Maru*. Eric Barr in *Bluegill* damaged and beached the 5,542-ton tanker *Honan Maru* and then sent a demolition party ashore to finish her off. Dave Bell in *Pargo* sank the destroyer *Nokaze*, and William Lawrence Kitch in *Blackfin* sank the destroyer *Shigure*. Other skippers picked off a freighter here and there.

The two targets that fascinated Fife most were *Ise* and *Hyuga*, arrived in Singapore to load drums of oil for the homeland. The codebreakers watched their movements closely. Fife was determined to do all in his power to prevent these ships—and the oil—from reaching Japan.

Ise and *Hyuga* left Singapore on February 11, with thousands of drums of oil aboard. On that day, one of Fife's British submarines,

Tantalus, was patrolling off Singapore. *Tantalus*, commanded by Rufus MacKenzie, saw the ships come out. MacKenzie tried to attack, but Japanese aircraft screening the force drove him away. He sent off a contact report. Fife had already laid an ambush of fourteen fleet boats along the projected route north.

The next day at about 1:45 P.M., *Charr*, commanded by Francis Dennis Boyle, patrolling down from Pearl Harbor to Fremantle, picked up the force on radar at 9 miles. *Flounder*, *Blackfin*, *Tuna*, *Pintado*, and *Pargo* were nearby. Boyle surfaced and got off a contact report. An hour later, Kitch in *Blackfin* picked up the force on radar at 15 miles. *Charr*, *Blackfin*, *Flounder*, *Pargo*, and *Tuna* chased after *Ise* and *Hyuga* for the next fourteen hours, trying to make an end around, but they never could do it. Said James Edward Stevens in *Flounder*, "It was heartbreaking, to say the least."

Three more boats lay to the north, waiting: *Hake*, commanded by Frank Haylor; *Pampanito*, commanded by Paul Summers; and Ralph Lockwood's *Guavina*. None of these three managed to attain firing position.

Three more lay north of these: *Bergall*, commanded by John Hyde; *Blower*, a new boat patrolling down from Pearl Harbor, commanded by James Harry ("Soupy") Campbell; and *Guitarro*, commanded by Thomas Dabney. On February 13 Hyde picked up the force at 12:13 P.M. Being submerged right on the track, he saw *Ise* and *Hyuga*, a heavy cruiser, and several destroyers. Hyde rang up full speed to get into position. He could not decrease the range below 4,800 yards, but he fired six torpedoes. Hyde heard one explosion and was later credited with a hit, but it was not confirmed in postwar records.

Campbell, on *Blower*, was in the best position. He closed for a daylight periscope attack and fired five torpedoes at one of the battleships and one at the heavy cruiser. Campbell claimed two hits on the battleship but Fife did not credit it, nor did postwar Japanese records. Campbell missed the cruiser, too. Fife was exasperated by this failure. After Campbell made one more war patrol he went to staff duty.

The last two of Fife's fifteen submarines deployed to sink *Ise* and *Hyuga* lay to the north. They were *Flasher*, commanded by George Grider, and *Bashaw*, commanded by H. S. Simpson. The task force came out of a rainsquall at 3:15. Before Simpson could set up, one of the battleships saw *Bashaw*, launched a plane, and opened fire with her big guns. One shell landed a mile off the starboard quarter "with

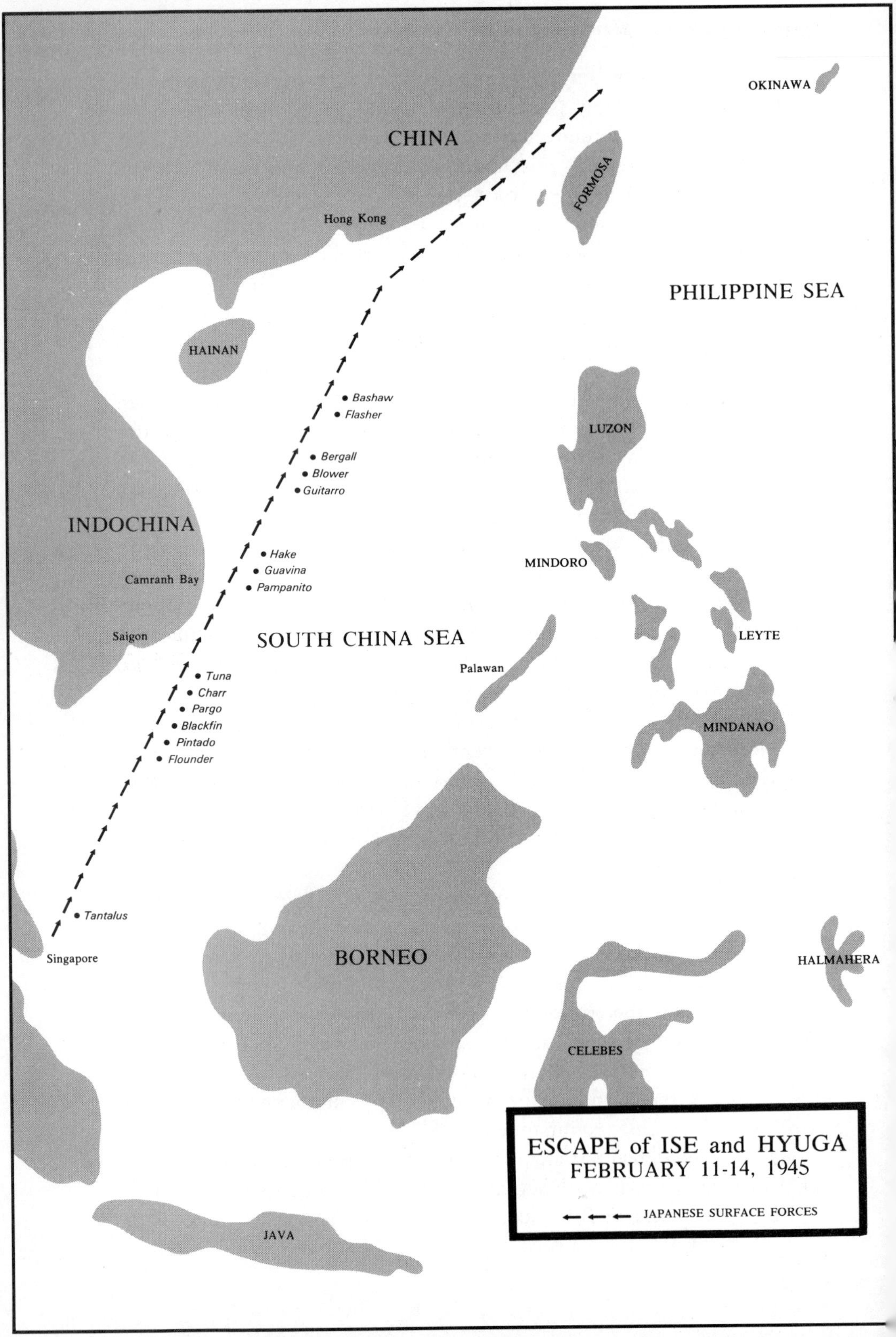
OKINAWA
CHINA
FORMOSA
Hong Kong
PHILIPPINE SEA
HAINAN
Bashaw
Flasher
LUZON
Bergall
Blower
Guitarro
INDOCHINA
Hake
Guavina
Pampanito
MINDORO
Camranh Bay
Saigon
SOUTH CHINA SEA
LEYTE
Palawan
Tuna
Charr
Pargo
Blackfin
Pintado
Flounder
MINDANAO
Tantalus
Singapore
BORNEO
HALMAHERA
CELEBES
ESCAPE of ISE and HYUGA
FEBRUARY 11-14, 1945
JAPANESE SURFACE FORCES
JAVA

a loud roar and tremendous flash." Simpson dived. After dark, he and Grider in *Flasher* joined in the mass chase. None could overtake.

Lockwood and Voge followed all this by radio and, after projecting the probable course of *Ise* and *Hyuga* from Luzon Strait to Japan, deployed eleven submarines to intercept. None made contact. On this, the final voyage of *Ise* and *Hyuga*, the ships eluded a total of twenty-six submarines.

Both Fife and Lockwood were nonplussed by this failure. Fife, blaming the failure on bad weather, the high speed of the task force, and a new ability on the part of the Japanese to detect radar, wrote Lockwood, "It was a bitter pill to take and I make no alibi." Lockwood blamed his failure on incorrect codebreaking information which led him to position his eleven boats too far to the west. He wrote Fife, "Our dope certainly went sour at the last moment. Perhaps I depended too much on it."

After his futile chase, George Grider in *Flasher* sank a small freighter, *Koho Maru*, 850 tons. He did not know it then, but that sinking gave *Flasher* the record for Japanese tonnage sunk by a single U.S. submarine: 100,231 tons. (Second place was *Rasher* with 99,-901 tons.) *Flasher*'s total was a result of Reuben Whitaker's 56,513 tons and George Grider's 43,718 tons.

One boat not available for the *Ise-Hyuga* chase was *Barbel*, commissioned by Conde LeRoy Raguet. Raguet, another youngster from the class of 1938, was the son of a navy captain, and had been exec of *Blackfin*.

On February 1, Edward Steffanides, commanding *Tuna*, told Raguet to patrol near the southern end of Palawan. On February 3, Raguet reported by radio to *Tuna* that he was patrolling the station but had been driven down by numerous aircraft contacts and had been attacked by aircraft and depth charges three times. Japanese records reported an air attack of a U.S. submarine on February 4 which scored one hit near the bridge. Jasper Holmes wrote, "It appears almost certain that this attack sank *Barbel*."

Raguet, thirty years old, was the youngest fleet boat skipper lost in the war.

One boat involved in the *Ise* chase was almost lost afterward. On the afternoon of February 23, James Stevens in *Flounder* was cruising submerged off Indochina. There was no traffic visible in the periscope and no enemy on sonar. At about 5 P.M., *Flounder* was suddenly shaken by a terrifying jolt and started down, out of control. Then came another jolt. The sonar operator reported screws and then the sound of a submarine blowing ballast tanks.

Stevens realized at once what had happened: *Flounder* had been hit by a submerged submarine. He believed it must be Japanese. He came back to periscope depth for a cautious look but saw nothing.

Later in the afternoon, Stevens saw a U.S. submarine through his periscope and realized it was the boat that had hit *Flounder*. It was *Hoe*, commanded by Miles Refo. When Stevens surfaced, he found that *Hoe*'s keel had sliced a 25-foot gash in *Flounder*'s superstructure on the starboard side. Stevens broke off his patrol and returned to Subic Bay for repairs.

This was the only submerged collision of two submarines in the war. Both Stevens and Refo were lucky that it was not more serious.

The Remaining Targets: *Isuzu, Haguro, Ashigara,* and *Takao*

After the *Ise-Hyuga* fiasco, Fife was ready to move his own bag and baggage from Fremantle to Subic Bay. He decided to return to the Philippines by the same means he had left there three years earlier: submarine. Along the way, the boat would conduct a regular patrol. Thus Fife, after Christie, became the second and last admiral to go on patrol.

Fife chose *Hardhead*, commanded by Francis Greenup, for his transportation. The boat departed March 20, going to Indochina by way of Lombok and Karimata straits. On April 2, Greenup laid a small minefield off Indochina and then conducted a regular war patrol in the Gulf of Siam, an area believed to be heavily mined and not hitherto exploited.

Hardhead had a busy time. On the night of April 5, Greenup picked up a small convoy consisting of a big tanker, a freighter, and a trawler. Greenup chose the tanker, which was empty, as his target. He made a night surface attack, firing six torpedoes. One hit forward of the bridge. The men in the tanker fired at *Hardhead* with a gun of "medium" caliber. Greenup responded by firing another three torpedoes. All missed. Greenup fired another two. Both missed.

Somewhat chagrined by all this missing with his boss on board, Greenup submerged to avoid the gunfire and made another approach at radar depth, closing to point-blank range of 400 yards. He fired another torpedo. It missed. Greenup surfaced and fired another two bow tubes. The first of these hit below the tanker's funnel amidships, the second hit below the bridge. Greenup saw "satisfactory explosions with flames." The ship, identified in postwar records as *Araosan Maru*, 6,886 tons, sank.

Having expended sixteen torpedoes in this effort, Greenup had none left for the freighter. He battle-surfaced on the trawler escort, firing about fourteen rounds. None hit. The trawler returned fire, so Greenup broke off the attack and lobbed four shells at the freighter from 3,000 yards. None of these hit either.

Following this, Greenup took *Hardhead* to Subic Bay, arriving on April 11 after a voyage of twenty-two days. Fife declared the patrol successful, so he received a submarine combat pin. He wrote Lockwood, "My jaunt in *Hardhead* was the best vacation I have had since the war started. . . . We have now covered the entire Gulf [of Siam] without getting trouble." He expressed the hope that one of the minefields in the Gulf of Siam would "legally catch a playmate of *Awa Maru*."

After this ice-breaking voyage, Fife sent many submarines into the Gulf of Siam. Generally, they found poor hunting, since Allied aircraft had sunk those ships the submarine force had not already eliminated. One boat, John Hyde's *Bergall*, ran into a minefield planted by the Allies, and one of the mines exploded. *Bergall* was lucky; she received only minor damage in her stern. She made it back to Subic Bay for temporary repairs and then returned to the States for permanent repairs.

Another boat, *Lagarto*, commanded by the immensely capable—and popular—Frank Latta, was lost in the Gulf of Siam. On May 2, Latta rendezvoused with Ben Jarvis in *Baya* to conduct a joint patrol. Later in the day, Jarvis found a small convoy and alerted Latta. They made a joint approach but were driven off by radar-equipped escorts. The two skippers met again and drew up a new plan for an attack the following day. This attack, too, was repulsed.

After this, when Jarvis tried to raise Latta, he got no answer. Japanese records showed that *Hatsutaka*, a minelayer (and believed to be one of the radar-equipped escorts) attacked a submarine at this time and place. Jasper Holmes believed *Hatsutaka* sank *Lagarto*. She went down with all hands.

Hatsutaka did not long celebrate her victory. About two weeks later—May 16—Worth Scanland in *Hawkbill* found her inside the gulf and torpedoed her. She blew up and sank immediately.

After Fife moved to Subic Bay, he became ill with a mild case of malaria. Even so, he kept on the job, determined to sink everything Japanese that floated in southern waters. One target that intrigued him was the light cruiser *Isuzu*, then engaged in shifting Japanese troops from base to base.

In early April, intelligence reported *Isuzu* was in Surabaya. A three-boat wolf pack, led by Francis Boyle in *Charr*, patrolled the Java Sea off Surabaya. The other boats were *Besugo*, commanded by Herman Edward Miller, and *Gabilan*, commanded by William Brownlee Parham. They lay in wait along the probable track of the cruiser.

On the morning of April 4, Herman Miller in *Besugo* made contact with *Isuzu* and an escort of four small vessels. Miller was too far off the track to shoot, so he surfaced to trail. About that time, William Parham in *Gabilan* picked up the force through his periscope at 10 miles. Parham saw *Besugo* trailing. After waiting for *Besugo* to pass, he surfaced to join the chase. Francis Boyle in *Charr* saw smoke at 13 miles. He too joined the chase. However, aircraft forced all three boats down and *Isuzu* got away.

Intelligence reported the next stop for *Isuzu* was Bima Bay on the north coast of the island of Soembawa. The pack took up station there on April 6, joined by one of Fife's British submarines, *Spark*.

On the morning of April 6, *Isuzu* showed up on schedule. All four boats, waiting submerged, saw her. Parham in *Gabilan* picked her up at 6,500 yards, running close to the beach. He prepared to attack, but *Isuzu* opened out to 7,500 yards—beyond reach. Miller in *Besugo* had a better chance. The cruiser, "loaded with troops," came close. Miller fired three stern tubes from 500 yards, then six bow tubes. All nine torpedoes missed the cruiser, but one or more hit one of the escorts, *Minesweeper No. 12*, 630 tons. It sank.

Isuzu went into Bima Bay unharmed, while the pack waited for her to come out again. The following morning at about 3 A.M., Boyle in *Charr* made radar contact at 7 miles and alerted Parham in *Gabilan*. Almost immediately, Parham got contact. He closed and fired six bow tubes. One tube failed to fire, but the other five torpedoes streaked

THE REMAINING TARGETS

toward *Isuzu* and at least one torpedo hit. The sonarman reported *Isuzu*'s screws had stopped. Escorts drove Parham under and dropped depth charges.

Boyle in *Charr* now closed in. At 5:20—when it was getting light—he submerged and prepared to attack. Parham, he saw, had done good work; *Isuzu* was down by the bow and listing, but she was still making 10 knots. At 1,200 yards, Boyle fired four torpedoes. Two hit. Boyle fired two more torpedoes. Another hit. Boyle's TDC operator jumped up and down excitedly, exclaiming, "Jeezie beezie! We hit him. We hit him!" Escorts charged *Charr* and Boyle went to 420 feet. Boyle heard "loud breaking-up noises."

All this time, the British submarine *Spark* stood off to one side, watching. The skipper saw the hits on *Isuzu*, then smoke and flame, then Japanese leaping over the side. That night when *Charr* and *Gabilan* surfaced, he reported that the cruiser had sunk. Parham and Boyle shared equal credit for her sinking.

Later, Miller in *Besugo*, who was too far off the track to see the final battle, sank another man-of-war. On April 23, off Surabaya, he picked up a submarine flying a Japanese flag. He closed and fired six torpedoes. At least one hit. The submarine sank instantly, leaving one man—the officer of the deck—in the water. Miller picked him up. He identified the submarine as the German *U-183*. She was the third U-boat sunk in the Pacific by Allied submarines (two of them by U.S. boats). In all, U.S. submarines sank four German vessels in the Pacific: the two U-boats, Herb Andrews's freighter, and Tom Wogan's merchant raider, *Michel*.

Once *Isuzu* went down there were only two important Japanese men-of-war left in Singapore, the heavy cruisers *Haguro* and *Ashigara*. Fife kept close watch on both.

In early May, *Haguro*, escorted by one destroyer, sortied from Singapore to carry supplies to the Japanese army in Burma. She swung northwest and went up Malacca Strait, where British submarines basing from India were patrolling. Two of these, *Statesman* and *Subtle*, sighted *Haguro* and were able to fire torpedoes at her. Both missed.

The two boats got off contact reports, alerting British surface forces operating in the Indian Ocean. None could get into position in time, but when *Haguro* got ready to return to Singapore, the ambush had been laid. On May 16, a British aircraft from a jeep carrier found *Haguro* and attacked, achieving damage. That same night, four British destroyers closed on her like a pack of wolves. The destroyers boldly attacked, firing guns and torpedoes. *Haguro* went down.

After that, there remained only *Ashigara*. On June 5, Merrill Clementson in *Blueback* and Doug Rhymes in *Chub*, alerted by an Ultra, picked her up coming into Djakarta, on the northwest tip of Java, but neither boat had an opportunity to shoot.

Fife's staff calculated that *Ashigara* would soon return to Singapore. *Blueback* and *Chub*—joined by other fleet boats—lay in wait off Djakarta. Meanwhile, Fife, believing that *Ashigara* would return to Singapore via the narrow mined waters of Bangka Strait, positioned two of his British submarines in the strait close to the minefields. These were *Trenchant,* commanded by Arthur Richard Hezlet, and *Stygian,* commanded by Commander Clarabut.

On June 7, Clementson picked up *Ashigara* leaving Djakarta. Neither Clementson nor Rhymes was able to reach attack position in time, but Clementson got off a contact report and Fife alerted Hezlet and Clarabut in Bangka Strait.

Ashigara was escorted by a destroyer—leading. Early on the morning of June 8, Hezlet in *Trenchant* picked up the destroyer in Bangka Strait, boldly remaining on the surface. Hezlet did not fire at the destroyer, not wishing to alert *Ashigara* to the ambush. The destroyer saw *Trenchant* and opened fire. Hezlet avoided this fire and submerged to await the oncoming *Ashigara*.

Later that morning, Hezlet's tactics paid off. While lying submerged in the strait, he saw *Ashigara* coming north, hugging the coast of Sumatra. He set up and fired his bow tubes at the extreme range of 4,700 yards. The Japanese on *Ashigara* saw the torpedoes coming and tried to avoid, but the ship was too close to shore for radical maneuvers. Five of Hezlet's torpedoes slammed into the ship, leaving it, according to Jasper Holmes, "a broken wreck." Hezlet swung around and fired his stern tubes—while *Ashigara* shot at his periscope. The stern tubes missed, but *Ashigara* was mortally holed nevertheless and sank later in the day.

The British proposed that some of their midget submarines be brought from Europe to make raids on the Japanese men-of-war in Singapore. Two of these little 35-ton craft had succeeded in damaging the German battleship *Tirpitz* on September 22, 1943, putting her out of action for about six months.

THE REMAINING TARGETS

Both Lockwood and Fife were opposed to this scheme. They doubted that the midgets could do the job, and the risks involved did not appear to justify the possible rewards. *Tirpitz*, Germany's largest battleship, had been a definite threat to Allied naval forces in European waters. But the Japanese had no comparable prize in Singapore after *Ise* and *Hyuga* left. However, the British persisted. Singapore had been a British base; they wanted to strike a blow.

In July the British tender *Bonaventure* arrived at Subic Bay with several midgets on board. By that time there were only two worthwhile targets left in Singapore, the heavy cruisers *Takao* and *Myoko*, both damaged by U.S. submarines. Allied reconnaissance showed them to be anchored in shallow water behind torpedo nets, safe from attack by conventional submarines.

In late July the British set off to get these ships. The midgets were towed to a launch point off Singapore by British submarines. *Spark*, towed *XE-1*, commanded by Lieutenant J. E. Smart, and *Stygian* towed *XE-3*, commanded by Lieutenant I. E. Fraser. On midnight, July 30, the midgets were launched off Horsburg Light.

The two little boats crept 25 miles up the channel toward Singapore in bright moonlight. About 10:30 A.M., *XE-3* went into Singapore Harbor. *XE-1* followed her through a little later. *XE-3* found *Takao*, attached limpet mines and saddle charges (with delayed fuses) to her, and withdrew. *XE-1*, unable to reach *Myoko*, shifted to *Takao* and added her explosives to *XE-3*'s. Both boats then withdrew to sea and rendezvoused with *Spark* and *Stygian* as planned.

The explosives detonated on schedule. They blew the bottom out of *Takao*, which settled in the mud and remained there for the duration. Lockwood and Fife were amazed—and relieved—when all this was finished.

Fife's boats finally ran out of targets. During the waning days of the war, they roved the seas on the surface like destroyers, blasting away with deck guns at trawlers, sampans, and other small craft, most of them manned by natives, not Japanese. When the boats ran out of ammunition, they boarded the craft and blew them up with grenades and demolition charges. On one patrol, Bill Hazzard in *Blenny* sank sixty-three such vessels. On another, Arnold Schade in a new boat, *Bugara*, sank fifty-seven. Edwin Monroe Westbrook, Jr., commanding *Cod*, temporarily lost one of his boarding parties when a Japanese plane drove him under and an escort came along. Later, Hazzard in *Blenny* found the party and took them aboard. Eric Barr in *Bluegill*, looking for something colorful to do, sent a commando party ashore on the deserted island of Pratas (160 miles southeast of Hong Kong) and "captured" it. Roy Gross in *Boarfish* landed a commando party on the coast of Indochina near Hue and set a demolition charge on a railroad track, receiving credit for "derailing and/or damaging" a train.

One skipper who missed this sport was Edward Rowell Holt, Jr., who had relieved Walt Griffith in *Bullhead*. Holt, the eighteenth—and last—officer from the class of 1939 to command a fleet boat in combat, was caught by a Japanese army plane in Lombok Strait. The pilot claimed two direct hits and said thereafter he saw a "great amount of gushing water and air bubbles rising in the water." *Bullhead* went down with all hands.

40
Pearl Harbor and Guam, April through August 1945

New Forays in the Sea of Japan

In their endless search to find targets, Lockwood and Voge once again cast covetous eyes on the Sea of Japan. It had not been exploited since September 1943, when Mush Morton was lost in *Wahoo* trying to exit through La Pérouse Strait. Now, Lockwood and Voge believed, the Sea of Japan must be thick with ships, forced there by U.S. submarines and carrier task forces.

The big problem still was how to get in and out. The east and west straits (separated by the island of Tsushima) were heavily mined. The narrow center exit, Tsugaru Strait, was also mined. The northern exit, La Pérouse, where Morton was lost, was believed to be heavily patrolled by aircraft and surface vessels. Lockwood doubted that a submarine could enter from La Pérouse (as the eight boats had done in the summer and fall of 1943) without being detected.

By now, Lockwood believed, the FM sonar gear was sensitive enough to pick up mines—as *Tinosa* and *Tunny* had demonstrated at Okinawa. If the sets proved reliable enough, if a group of operators could be trained to use them properly, they might serve to guide a submarine through the minefields of Tsushima Strait into the Sea of Japan, and the boats could get out by making a dash through La Pérouse.

This scheme dominated Lockwood's waking hours for weeks. He

appointed Barney Sieglaff to work on it full time; hence the plan was called Operation Barney. Lockwood himself worked on the FM sonar problems, urging the manufacturers who were hand-building the sets to hurry up and to make improvements. When boats arrived at Guam equipped with FM sonar, Lockwood took them to a dummy minefield and personally trained both operators and skippers in the use of the gear. He was an exacting taskmaster.

As a preliminary, Lockwood sent out two boats to probe minefields—that is, to check the FM against the real thing. The boats were *Tinosa*, commanded by Dick Latham, and *Spadefish*, now commanded by William Germershausen. Latham was ordered to minefields in the East China Sea, Germershausen to the field at Tsushima Strait.

On the way out, Lockwood sent the two boats an Ultra to intercept a convoy southbound from Japan. Germershausen found it and sank a 2,300-ton freighter. Latham, trying to intercept, was driven down by a Japanese plane. On the way down, the bow planes failed to rig out. Latham went to 180 feet and remained there, trying to fix them. During that time, *Tinosa* was swept along by strong currents and grounded lightly on an island, damaging one of the outer torpedo doors. With all this trouble, *Tinosa* missed an opportunity to attack the convoy.

Latham then proceeded to his minefield plotting mission, determined to do it on the surface if necessary. The FM gear was operating "beautifully" at first, and Latham was getting a good minefield plot. But in the middle of the operation, the FM broke down—with mines all around. *Tinosa* was then in about 100 fathoms of water. Latham decided the best thing he could do until the FM gear was repaired was anchor, so he began walking the anchor out. He had 120 fathoms of anchor chain. At 89 fathoms, the chain broke—from the weight of the anchor and chain. However, the FM gear was repaired and Latham slipped out to sea, finishing out the patrol with a cruise along the China coast.

Germershausen took *Spadefish* to the edge of the minefields at Tsushima Strait. His FM gear was not working properly either. He made three separate attempts to close—and chart mines—but all failed. Later, he wrote, "I must say mine-hunting was dull, unrewarding work that could not compare with the thrill of coming to grips with a big, fat enemy ship." Germershausen returned to regular patrol in the Yellow Sea, where he sank another freighter.

Next, Lockwood sent a pack of four FM-equipped boats to probe the minefields: *Bowfin*, commanded by Alexander Tyree; *Seahorse*, commanded by Harry Holt Greer, Jr.; *Bonefish,* commanded by Lawrence Edge; and *Crevalle,* commanded by Everett Steinmetz. (On the way to her job, *Seahorse* was bombed and strafed by a B-24 Liberator, which fortunately did little damage.) At the Tsushima minefields, these boats did good work. The FM gear was more reliable, and the operators obtained more information on mine locations.

After completing these special tasks, the boats went on to normal patrol. Tyree in *Bowfin* sank two ships off northeast Honshu, one a transport and one a freighter. Greer in *Seahorse* sank a junk. Later the boat was attacked by two patrol boats that delivered a punishing depth-charge attack. The boat survived, but, her historian reported, "*Seahorse* was a shambles of broken glass, smashed instruments, cork and dirt, with hydraulic oil spilled over everything," and she was returned to Pearl Harbor for a complete overhaul. Her FM gear (still intact) was shifted to *Sea Dog.*

By May, Lockwood felt he had enough information—and the FM gear worked well enough—to send a submarine task group into the Sea of Japan. He asked Nimitz's permission to lead the group in person—his sixth request to make a war patrol. Nimitz, of course, denied the request.

To lead the expedition, Lockwood picked Earl Hydeman, an older officer from the class of 1932 who had had relatively little combat experience. Hydeman had spent most of the war in New London and Washington. He had made his first war patrol as a PCO on *Pampanito,* October 1944, when that boat was commanded by Mike Fenno. After Fenno's OK, Hydeman was ordered to relieve Rebel Lowrance in *Sea Dog.* On his first patrol off Tokyo Bay, Hydeman had sunk a 6,850-ton freighter and rescued a fighter pilot from the carrier *Intrepid.*

In all, Lockwood assigned nine FM-equipped boats to make the foray. The group, code-named "Hell Cats," was divided into three wolf packs, as follows:

Hydeman's Hep Cats
Sea Dog (Earl T. Hydeman)
Crevalle (Everett H. Steinmetz)
Spadefish (William J. Germershausen)

Pierce's Pole Cats
Tunny (George E. Pierce)
Skate (Richard B. Lynch)
Bonefish (Lawrence L. Edge)

Risser's Bob Cats
Flying Fish (Robert D. Risser)
Bowfin (Alexander K. Tyree)
Tinosa (Richard C. Latham)

Before departure, each of the nine boats was equipped with external "clearing wires." These were steel cables strung from the bow to the tips of the bow planes and from the stern deck to the tips of the stern planes. The wires—in theory—would prevent a mine cable from hooking on bow or stern planes.

Hydeman and five other skippers left from Pearl Harbor on May 27 and May 29. *Tunny*, *Skate*, and *Bonefish* received last-minute additional FM training under Lockwood's supervision at Guam and then left from there on May 28.

On the way to the rendezvous at the south end of the strait, Dick Latham in *Tinosa* picked up ten airmen from a B-29. Later Jasper Holmes wrote, "When the aviators learned of *Tinosa*'s destination they were unanimous in their desire to be put safely back in their rubber boats." Lockwood arranged a rendezvous with *Scabbardfish*, returning from patrol, and Latham turned the pilots over to her.

South of Kyushu, the expedition commander, Earl Hydeman in *Sea Dog*, had a severe casualty: his radar went out of commission. He joined up with Steinmetz in *Crevalle* and Steinmetz provided "Seeing-Eye" services, leading *Sea Dog* toward the strait in bad weather by short-range radio.

The boats went through the field by packs. *Sea Dog*, *Crevalle*, and *Spadefish* went first on June 4. All stayed deep—below 150 feet—to avoid the mines. Some of the boats had the FM sound head mounted near the keel. These went through with a 6-degree up-angle, so the FM gear could "look" forward and pick up mines. Hydeman reported, "During this passage, no FM contacts were made which could possibly have been mines."

There were, however, many disquieting moments. A few hours after submerging, Hydeman heard "several distant explosions." An hour later he heard "nine distant explosions, heavy enough to shake us a bit," followed by six more. Germershausen in *Spadefish* and Steinmetz in *Crevalle* also heard these explosions. Germershausen later described them as "loud." He wrote, "From then on our spirits were considerably depressed. Had *Sea Dog* or *Crevalle* come to grief?" They had not. All three boats made it safely. The explosions remained a mystery.

After *Sea Dog* reached the Sea of Japan, as Hydeman wrote, "All hands breathed a little easier. The emotional strain, especially on the officers, was very heavy and its effects were now quite evident. Everybody was on their toes at all times however; officers and men performed their duties in a manner deserving of the highest praise."

The next day, June 5, Pierce took his pack through (*Tunny, Skate,* and *Bonefish*). Ozzie Lynch on *Skate* had a spine-chilling experience. At about 9 A.M., his FM operator picked up the unmistakable bell-like tone of a mine line 400 yards ahead. The mines were closely set. Lynch dropped to 175 feet and proceeded. Then every man on the boat heard a noise none ever forgot: a mine cable scraped down the entire length of the boat. Lynch and his crew held their collective breath, praying that the cable would not snag and drag the mine down to *Skate*. The clearing lines evidently worked.

After passing the second of four mine lines (that is, while in the middle of the field), Lynch, perhaps feeling *Skate* had developed some kind of mine immunity, decided to come up to periscope depth and get a fix on the location of the field. He rose slowly to 60 feet, poked up "the pole," and took bearings on landmarks on the shoreline. Then —having obtained this valuable information—Lynch went deep again and proceeded to underrun the last two lines.

The next day, June 6, Bob Risser led the Bob Cats (*Flying Fish, Bowfin,* and *Tinosa*) through the fields. *Tinosa,* too, had a close call. Latham ran right up on a mine, maneuvered to avoid it, and then stopped his screws. Later he wrote:

Tinosa stopped swinging right and started left again, but that mine was coming closer and closer abeam until it was too close any longer to show on the [FM] scope. Then there was a scraping, grinding noise as the mine cable slid down the starboard side. No one moved or spoke. Would it snag and drag the mine into us? We were at 120 feet keel depth and the mine was hopefully clear of us. God bless the fairing cables leading from the hull to the outboard forward edge of our stern planes! That mine cable slid on aft past the stern planes and our silent screw and off the end. How much it dragged down the mine or how close the mine came to us, we'll never know.

Tinosa went safely through two more lines of mines.

Once inside the sea, the nine boats deployed to patrol stations. (Like the boats on the first foray into the Sea of Japan in the summer of 1943, all had orders to withhold fire until sunset on the evening of June 9—to allow time for the boats going to the farthest point to get

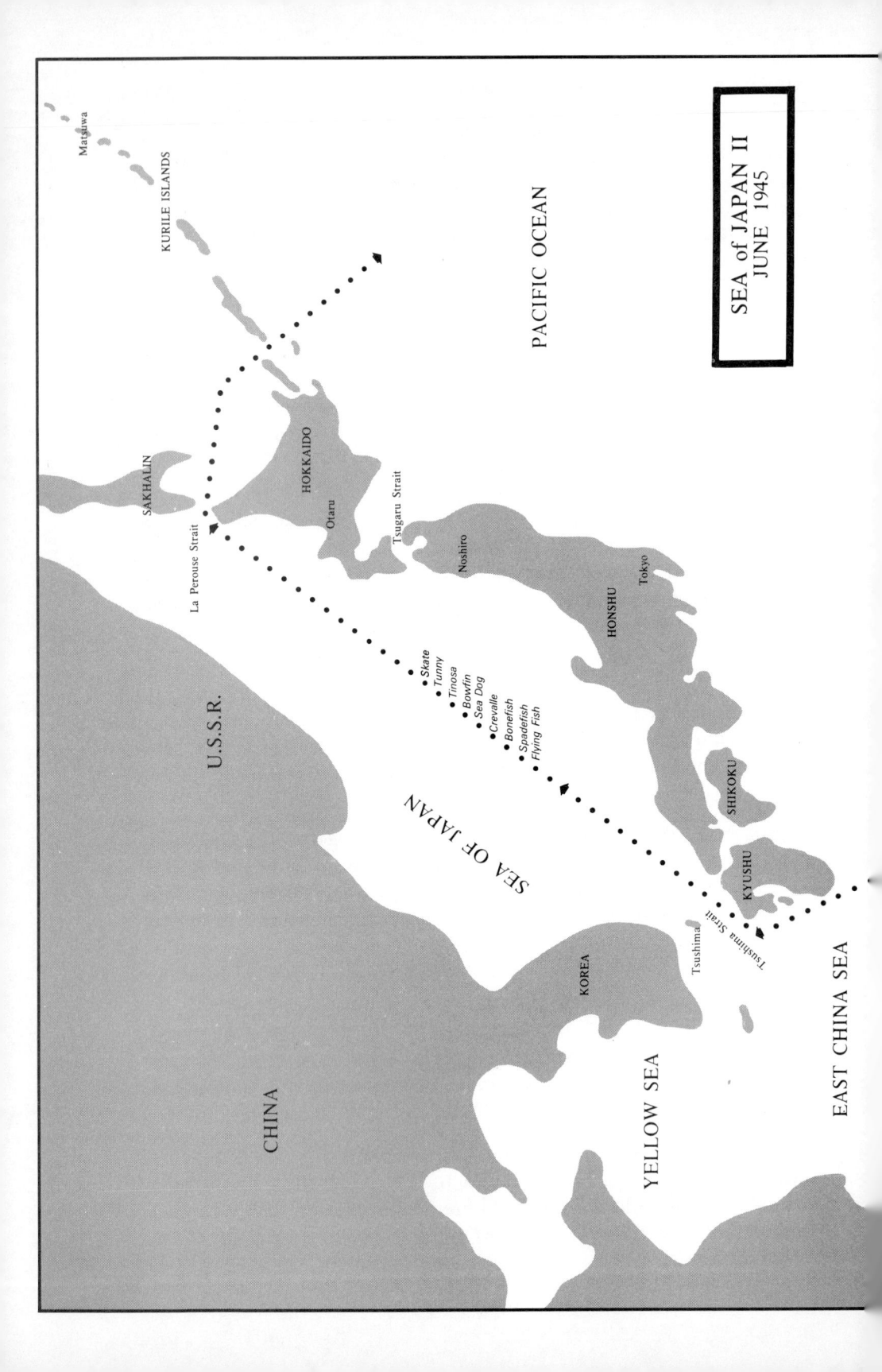

SEA of JAPAN II
JUNE 1945

Matsuwa
KURILE ISLANDS
SAKHALIN
PACIFIC OCEAN
HOKKAIDO
Otaru
Tsugaru Strait
La Perouse Strait
Noshiro
U.S.S.R.
Skate
Tunny
Tinosa
Bowfin
Sea Dog
Crevalle
Bonefish
Spadefish
Flying Fish
HONSHU
Tokyo
SEA OF JAPAN
SHIKOKU
KYUSHU
Tsushima
Tsushima Strait
KOREA
CHINA
YELLOW SEA
EAST CHINA SEA

into position.) Hydeman led the Hep Cats far to the northeast, to patrol the western coast of Hokkaido and Honshu. Pierce led the Pole Cats to station along central and southern Honshu. Risser led the Bob Cats to the east coast of Korea, where the pack encountered dense fog. While waiting for Germershausen in *Spadefish* to reach his far north position off Hokkaido, the other Hell Cats passed many ships. They were all sitting ducks—unescorted, not zigzagging, burning running lights. Most of the skippers had itchy trigger fingers and were tempted to shoot before the deadline. After sighting his fifth Japanese ship, Steinmetz in *Crevalle* wrote, "Of all contacts this was the toughest to throw back in the pond. Was strongly tempted to swing left, shoot and then use as an excuse 'I was just cleaning my torpedoes and . . . !'"

The Hell Cats turned out to be one of the most successful submarine operations of the war. Hydeman in *Sea Dog* sank six ships in ten days. Germershausen in *Spadefish* sank five ships. Lynch in *Skate* sank four, including a submarine, *I-122*. Latham in *Tinosa* also sank four. Steinmetz in *Crevalle* sank three. Edge in *Bonefish*, Risser in *Flying Fish*, and Tyree in *Bowfin* each got two. Total: twenty-eight ships for 54, 784 tons.

Only George Pierce in *Tunny* failed to sink a confirmed ship. It was not from lack of trying. Like the other skippers, Pierce practically put his boat's bow on the beaches of Japan, but he had bad luck; he saw only a few targets. He attacked two, firing seven torpedoes, but missed on both, and he had a "running gun battle" with two destroyers.

One boat was lost. After sinking one big ship, Lawrence Edge in *Bonefish* met with Pierce on June 18 and asked permission to penetrate Toyama Bay, a relatively shallow and confined body of water. As soon as he got in the bay, Edge sank another big ship, but he was spotted and pounced on by Japanese antisubmarine forces. They delivered a depth-charge attack which fatally holed the famous *Bonefish*. She was lost with all hands.

The pack made one serious error. On the night of June 13, Germershausen in *Spadefish*, patrolling to the northwest of La Pérouse Strait, picked up a freighter on radar. This was an area where Russian ships passed en route to and from Vladivostok, so Germershausen closed to 1,100 yards to look over his quarry. The ship had no lights burning and "was not following a designated Russian route." Germershausen fired two torpedoes and sank it. It was the Russian ship *Transbalt*, 11,000 tons.*

The Russians protested almost immediately. Lockwood radioed the Hell Cats, DID ANYBODY SHOOT NORTHWEST OF LA PEROUSE STRAIT? Germershausen, who by then suspected he had made a mistake, replied GUILTY.

Not wishing to disclose that U.S. submarines were again operating in the Sea of Japan, Nimitz or King blamed the incident on a Japanese submarine. But the Russians weren't fooled. Germershausen joked later, "They blamed it on a reactionary U.S. submarine skipper."

With this sinking (actually giving *Spadefish* a total of six ships sunk), Germershausen swelled the Russian-ship-sinking club membership to four, joining Eugene Sands (two Russian ships), Moon Chapple (one), and Malcolm Garrison (one).

After two weeks inside the Sea of Japan, the Hell Cats prepared to leave. This, they feared, would be the hardest part of all; surely the Japanese would be guarding the exits with everything they had. Hydeman decided the best way out was to exit through La Pérouse Strait at night on the surface, gun crews standing by. Should the group be attacked by Japanese destroyers, they could fight back with the combined firepower of nine 5-inch deck guns—a considerable array of armament.

In addition, Lockwood provided a diversionary act to trick the Japanese into believing the boats were going out through Tsushima Strait. Early on the morning of June 24, *Trutta*, now commanded by a reserve officer, Frank P. Hoskins, shelled the island of Hirado Shima on the east channel of Tsushima Strait in a "purposely conspicuous manner."

On the night of June 24, the boats rendezvoused just inside La Pérouse Strait—all but *Bonefish*. With eight submarines bunched together, Hydeman could not wait. He ordered the pack to enter the strait at 18 knots. Hydeman in *Sea Dog* led one column, but his radar failed again and *Crevalle* resumed her role as Seeing-Eye dog. A dense fog shrouded the boats as they barreled through the strait. There were two contacts—a lighted ship, probably Russian, and a Japanese minelayer that did not see them. By 5:20 A.M. on June 25, all eight boats had made it out without a shot being fired at them. No one could understand why it had been so easy.

Pierce in *Tunny* received permission from Hydeman to go into

---

* It was the second time Germershausen had shot at a Soviet ship. The first time—on *Tambor*—he missed.

the Sea of Okhotsk to wait for—and radio—*Bonefish*. On the night of June 25, Pierce sent two messages to *Bonefish*. When no reply was received, Pierce set course for Midway. He arrived on July 2, a day or two after the other boats. Then all went to Pearl Harbor for an epic party—and medals and praise from Lockwood.

Germershausen had some unfinished business regarding the Russian ship he sank. As he recalled it later, when he got into port, Lockwood said, "Go see Nimitz." Germershausen reported as ordered, expecting a royal chewing out or worse. "He asked what happened," Germershausen recalled. "I told him I didn't see any markings. All he said was, 'Glad you made it back safely, son.'"

After this "first wave," Lockwood sent seven other boats singly into the Sea of Japan: *Sennet, Piper, Pargo, Pogy, Jallao, Stickleback,* and *Torsk*. Charles Robert Clark, Jr., in *Sennet*, another young officer from the class of 1939, went first and sank the most ships: four for 13,105 tons, thereby establishing himself as the top skipper of that class. He returned via La Pérouse Strait with no difficulty.

Rescues and Targets

While this submarine spectacular was in progress, other Lockwood boats roamed familiar hunting grounds, picking up aviators and looking for ships to attack.

Gato—the boat that was famous for having fought it out with a Japanese plane on the surface in the Solomons—lifeguarded off Kyushu. Now commanded by Richard Holden, *Gato* rescued ten airmen from ditched B-29s, some very close to the coast. On April 29, about to make one of these rescues, *Gato* was again caught on the surface by a Japanese fighter. Holden, anxious to save the airman, manned his deck guns and fired back at the aircraft, emulating *Gato*'s former skipper, Bob Foley. The Japanese fighter dropped two bombs—fortunately near misses—and wheeled around for a strafing run. Holden submerged. Later, when the plane was gone, he surfaced and picked up the airman.

Hiram Cassedy, lifeguarding off Honshu in his new boat *Tigrone*, received a call for help on May 26; a navy bomber had two engines out and had to ditch. The pilot put the plane down near *Tigrone*. Cassedy's efficient rescue crew pulled five men on board.

Four days later, Cassedy got another call for help. An army seaplane which had landed to pick up the crew of a ditched B-29 had itself crashed on takeoff. Cassedy responded to the call and took off the B-29 crew and the seaplane crew, sixteen men in one swoop. One died, leaving *Tigrone*'s airman population at twenty.

In the days following, Cassedy picked up ten more airmen, bringing his total to thirty-one, a record for a single patrol.

Off northeast Honshu, Tom Baskett in *Tench* sank four confirmed ships in June—one of them just a half mile offshore. George Street, with six confirmed ships to his credit for his first patrol (plus a Medal of Honor), returned *Tirante* to Nagasaki for his second patrol and added two more.

Another Medal-of-Honor skipper waged a land as well as a sea campaign on his next patrol. Gene Fluckey, who had fourteen confirmed ships to his credit, took *Barb* to Hokkaido and the Kuriles. On this trip *Barb* was fitted with an experimental gadget, a 5-inch rocket launcher for shore bombardment.

Arriving June 21 on station off the northeast coast of Hokkaido, Fluckey saw two trawlers. He battle-surfaced and sank both with his deck gun, then was driven under by a Japanese plane. Fluckey surfaced after dark and shortly after midnight, June 22, fired twelve small rockets on shore. The next day, Fluckey sank another trawler, taking one prisoner.

Going northward, Fluckey found a small convoy and attacked. He expended many torpedoes but achieved no sinkings; the escorts drove him off. On July 2, he closed Kaiyo on the eastern extremity of the Karafuto Peninsula (the lower half of Sakhalin Island) and bombarded the town with his deck gun, setting fires, damaging a seal rookery, and destroying three sampans at dockside. The next day he launched a rocket attack on the town of Shikuka, and the day after, in another area, he sank a 2,800-ton freighter with torpedoes.

Shifting areas again, Fluckey battle-surfaced and sank a lugger and a sampan and then torpedoed a frigate with his last torpedoes.

While cruising off Otasamu, on the east coast of Karafuto, Fluckey noted a railroad running along the coast and sent a commando party ashore to set demolition charges on the tracks. As they were pulling away from shore in their rubber boats, a train came along and set off the charges. The engine blew up with a terrific explosion, and about twelve freight cars, two passenger cars, and a mail car rolled over the tracks. "Wreckage flew two hundred feet in the air . . . cars piled up and rolled off the tracks in a writhing, twisting mass of wreckage. Cheers!" Fluckey wrote. Later reports from a prisoner of war stated that 150 passengers—including women and children—had been killed in the wreckage.

Again shifting locations, Fluckey fired thirty-two 5-inch rockets into the town of Shiritori and twelve rockets into the town of Kashiho. Withdrawing, Fluckey bombarded Shibertoro and Chiri, destroying a lumberyard and a nest of sampans.

Returning to port, Fluckey was praised for his ingenuity and resourcefulness. He stepped down from command of *Barb*, having earned, in addition to his Medal of Honor, four Navy Crosses. Fluckey went to new construction and eventually wound up as aide to Admiral Nimitz.

Tiny Lynch, returning *Haddo* from a long overhaul, patrolled in the Yellow Sea. On July 1, off Inchon, Korea, in a dense fog, Lynch picked up a four-ship convoy with two escorts. Maneuvering in water only 65 feet deep, Lynch set up and fired eight torpedoes—two at each freighter in the convoy. Two of these blew up and sank.

At that point, the fog, which had afforded Lynch good protection, lifted and Lynch saw one of the escorts—a frigate—charging in. He sent his lookouts below and ordered flank speed. The frigate and *Haddo* passed on opposite courses, like *Salmon* and her attacker, the frigate firing all its guns. Lynch and the officer of the deck, J. H. M. Nason, crouched behind the shears, laughing hysterically—from fear.

When Lynch reached "deep water"—that is, 80 feet—he dived. The two escorts followed. At that point, Lynch fired two Cuties (which were not supposed to be fired from a depth less than 150 feet) and prayed. One hit one of the escorts, *Coast Defense Vessel No. 72*, an 800-ton frigate. It blew up and sank. The other escort broke off to go collect survivors.

In the space of fifteen minutes, Tiny Lynch had sunk two ships of a four-ship convoy, damaged two others, and sunk one of two escorts.

The Japanese Surrender

In early July, Admiral Halsey, commanding the Third Fleet, left from Leyte Gulf for another series of strikes on the Japanese homeland. Most of these were to be air strikes, but this time he planned to bring some of his battleships close to shore and conduct a bombardment. Lockwood provided submarines to conduct an antipicket sweep in front of the carriers and to lifeguard. Two FM-equipped boats, *Runner II*, commanded by Benny Bass, and *Redfin*, commanded by Charles Kilday Miller, conducted mine location probes along the coast where the bombardment was to be conducted.

Task Force 38, joined by twenty-eight British warships, reached Japanese home waters without incident. On July 10, Halsey's planes struck Tokyo. Four days later they raked Hokkaido, and the battleships blasted coastal cities, including the steel mills bombarded by Dave Whelchel in *Steelhead* in May 1943. Wheeling south, Halsey struck Tokyo again, then Kure and the ships in the Inland Sea. In the following days, he struck Hokkaido again and returned to Tokyo. In all, the air raids went on for well over a month.

The strikes against ships in the Inland Sea July 24 and July 28 destroyed what was left of the Japanese navy. The carrier-battleships *Ise* and *Hyuga*, the battleship *Hurana*, two new aircraft carriers, *Amagi* and *Katsurage*, and the cruisers *Tone*, *Aoba*, *Oyodo*, *Twatem*, *Izume*, and *Settsu* were ruined beyond repair. Only the carrier *Ryuho* (severely damaged in the March raids) survived afloat. She had been skillfully camouflaged and moored next to a secluded beach.

During these activities, Lockwood's submarines lifeguarded, picking up dozens of pilots. And, in spite of all precautions, on four occasions his boats were attacked by friendly air and surface forces.

Sea Robin, commanded by Paul Stimson and returned from Fife's command, patrolled on lifeguard station off Honshu. On June 26, a B-29 attacked her, dropping a "full load of bombs" through a heavy overcast. Fortunately for *Sea Robin*, the bombs all missed by half a mile. *Sea Robin* rescued one airman during her lifeguarding.

Gabilan, commanded by William Parham, picked up fifteen airmen in a remarkably bold series of rescues—three at the entrance of the bay. Then she was told on July 18 to vacate the area because U.S. surface forces were approaching for a strike. This word came a little late. Parham rang up flank speed and pushed northeastward through heavy seas.

Three hours later, Parham picked up the U.S. force on radar and turned on electronic identification signals. Two destroyers peeled out of the formation and began shooting. After they had fired six salvos at *Gabilan*, Parham fired a green star rocket—the proper recognition

THE JAPANESE SURRENDER

signal for that hour. This move brought a "rain" of shells from the U.S. task force. Parham dived and went to 300 feet, remembering the fate of *Seawolf*. He gave orders to rig for depth charge and ran silently, evading at deep depth. He outwitted the two U.S. destroyers and got away, writing in his log, "It is an act of God that we are still here."

Toro, a new boat commanded by James Dorr Grant (ex-*Greenling*), lifeguarding off Shikoku on July 24, had an encounter with a destroyer similar to the *Spot-Case* incident. After a mix-up in recognition signals, the destroyer *Colahan* opened fire on *Toro*, firing fifty-two rounds. Grant fired a flare and smoke bomb and dived and saved his ship.

Batfish, commanded by Walter Small (ex-*Flying Fish*), was caught south of Kyushu. On August 1, while *Batfish* cruised the surface lifeguarding, an army B-25 turned and challenged her with a signal light. Small replied with the correct recognition signal and called the plane on his radio. In spite of all this, the B-25 came in and dropped five bombs on *Batfish*'s port beam. All missed.

While the July carrier strikes were in progress, a group of nuclear physicists led by Dr. J. Robert Oppenheimer set off the first atomic bomb in the desert of Alamagordo, New Mexico. After this test, two atomic bombs were completed and shipped to a special Air Force B-29 unit on Tinian. Parts of the bombs were delivered by the cruiser *Indianapolis*, which continued on to the Philippines. On July 30, west of the Marianas, she was torpedoed and sunk either by regular torpedoes or by *kaitens* launched from *I-58*. Although the codebreakers picked up and decoded *I-58*'s report of the sinking, no search efforts were launched until a navy plane from the Palaus, on a routine mission, found some survivors. Of *Indianapolis*'s 1,199 men, 883 died.

The first atomic bomb was loaded on a B-29 named *Enola Gay*, piloted by Colonel Paul W. Tibbets, Jr. He took off from Tinian at 2:45 on the morning of August 6. At 8:15 Hiroshima time, he released the bomb over the city. It exploded at about 2,000 feet, destroying 4.7 square miles of Hiroshima and killing an estimated 72,000 men, women, and children. Another 68,000 were wounded, and thousands were inflicted with radiation sickness. Tibbets returned to Tinian, landing at 2:58 P.M. Sixteen hours after the bomb fell, President Harry Truman gave the news to the rest of the world.

Two days later, Russia, which had steadfastly maintained a neutral attitude toward Japan, declared war. Russian troops immediately invaded Manchuria and northern Korea.

On August 9, the second atomic bomb was loaded into a B-29 named *Bock's Car,* piloted by Major Charles W. Sweeney. Sweeney's drop was more difficult. His primary target was Kokura, but there he ran into cloudy weather and switched to the secondary target, Nagasaki. At 10:58 A.M. (Nagasaki time) he found an opening in the clouds. This bomb killed about 40,000 people and injured 60,000. Because he was low on fuel, Sweeney had to make a stop at Okinawa. Later that night, he returned to Tinian.

On the following day, while Task Force 38 roamed up and down the Japanese coast with impunity, Emperor Hirohito advised his cabinet to accept the unconditional surrender terms demanded by the Allies. Hirohito's advisers agreed to do this—provided the Allies would not dethrone or charge the Emperor with war crimes. The message was relayed through Swiss and Swedish channels. The Allies replied that these terms were acceptable, provided the Emperor submit to the authority of a Supreme Allied Commander and give the Japanese people the right to decide his ultimate status through free elections.

While these messages were going back and forth, Lockwood's submarines continued to fire away at Japanese shipping. On August 11, Joseph Icenhower in *Jallao,* patrolling the Sea of Japan, sank a big transport, *Teihoku Maru,* 5,795 tons. On August 13, Robert Raymond Managhan in *Spikefish* sank *I-373* off Okinawa. On that same day, Bafford Lewellen in *Torsk,* patrolling the Sea of Japan, sank a small freighter, *Kaiho Maru,* 873 tons. The following day, August 14, Lewellen sank two frigates, *Coast Defense Vessels Nos. 13 and 47,* each about 800 tons. These were the last torpedoes fired by any naval vessel in World War II and the last Japanese ships sunk.

Emperor Hirohito accepted the terms imposed by the Allies and notified them. At fifty-six minutes to midnight, August 14, Admiral Nimitz sent a message to all naval units:

CEASE OFFENSIVE OPERATIONS AGAINST JAPANESE FORCES. CONTINUE SEARCH AND PATROLS. MAINTAIN DEFENSIVE AND INTERNAL SECURITY MEASURES AT HIGHEST LEVEL AND BEWARE OF TREACHERY OR LAST MOMENT ATTACKS BY ENEMY FORCES OR INDIVIDUALS.

Lockwood relayed this message to his submarines. Privately, he was not happy with the surrender terms. Later he wrote, "Why we ever acceded to [the terms] I will never understand, for certainly in the

THE JAPANESE SURRENDER

opinion of everyone I talked to among the fighting forces, he [Hirohito] had earned a place right alongside Hitler and Mussolini."

When the cease-fire message was received on board U.S. submarines on war patrol, most skippers and men cheered wildly. Some did not. One was Ned Beach, commanding *Piper*, who had just penetrated the minefield into the Sea of Japan. After having helped Roy Benson, Dusty Dornin, Fritz Harlfinger, and George Street sink twenty-two confirmed ships for 88,000 tons, Beach wanted to sink at least one for himself. When the cease-fire came, Beach later wrote, "Instead of wild exultation, a fit of the deepest despondency descended upon me."

Herman Kossler in *Cavalla* was lifeguarding off the coast of Honshu near Tokyo Bay when he got the word. He remained on the surface in broad daylight 25 miles from land. It occurred to Kossler that he should celebrate by passing out a ration of medicinal brandy. He asked his exec to break it out, mix it with pineapple juice, and give every man one drink.

While the exec was attending to this, Kossler remained on the bridge, planning to run in and look at the coast close up. Two minutes after noon, August 15, Kossler's radar operator picked up an aircraft contact dead ahead. "He was coming right at us," Kossler said later. "So, just in case, I rang up full power."

The plane roared in. Kossler watched, half hypnotized. Then he saw a bomb falling toward *Cavalla* and swung ship to avoid; the bomb landed 100 yards off the starboard quarter. Seeing the plane climb for another run, Kossler cleared the bridge and dived.

When *Cavalla* was safely at deep depth, Kossler remembered the brandy ration and asked where it was. His exec replied, "Captain, I talked it over with the boys and they decided to wait until the treaty was signed."

Half an hour later, Kossler surfaced and reported the incident to Admiral Halsey in Task Force 38. Several hours later, Halsey sent a message to his fleet units. "He said," Kossler remembered, "that if you saw an enemy plane approaching you directly, shoot it down—but do it in a gentlemanly fashion."

Admiral Nimitz invited Lockwood to attend the surrender ceremonies which would take place September 2 on the deck of Halsey's flagship, the battleship *Missouri*, in Tokyo Bay. Lockwood received permission to have a dozen submarines and a tender, *Proteus*, present for the ceremony, and *Proteus*, with Lew Parks, commanding Squadron Twenty, got under way for Japan immediately.

Lockwood flew from Guam to Yokosuka Naval Base in a seaplane. Lew Parks, meanwhile, having arrived in Japan, moved boldly ashore, taking possession of the submarine base at Yokosuka. He found several old Japanese submarines moored there, as well as dozens of midget submarines and *kaitens* being assembled for use against U.S. invasion forces. Parks and two of his division commanders, Rob Roy McGregor and Barney McMahon, then slipped into Tokyo to visit the Emperor's palace—before General MacArthur arrived. Said Parks later, "We were the first U.S. military forces to set foot inside Tokyo."

The Japanese surrendered three submarines to U.S. forces at sea. These were amazing craft, huge I-class submarines with hangars capable of storing four planes. They had been built for a special mission: to bomb the Panama Canal.* Hi Cassedy and Barney Sieglaff were assigned to head prize crews for two of these submarines. Cassedy violated strict orders not to take souvenirs (he passed out some swords). When Halsey heard about it, he was furious and ordered Cassedy relieved of command. Cassedy thus had the distinction of being the only U.S. submarine skipper relieved of command of a Japanese submarine for cause.

Missouri steamed into Tokyo Bay early on the morning of August 29. Her skipper was Lockwood's old chief of staff, Sunshine Murray, and it fell to Murray to make all the incredibly complex arrangements for the ceremony.

The British, who wanted to contribute something to the surrender, sent over a table and chairs to be used for signing the papers. Murray said later, "It was a small thing. There wasn't room for one copy of the surrender documents on it, much less two." Murray rushed around, finally got a table and chairs from the crew's mess, and covered the stainless steel tabletop with a green felt cloth that had covered a table in the officers' wardroom.

On September 2 Murray's boatswain piped Nimitz and MacArthur on board at 8:05. After them came legions of Allied admirals and generals, including Lockwood, who, Murray recalled, "got a place in

---

* Why the Japanese had not bombed the Panama Canal long ago with earlier-model I-class submarines carrying aircraft remained a mystery to the U.S. Navy. Had they done so, they would have severely retarded movement of U.S. warships and supply vessels to the Pacific.

the front rank." The Japanese contingent, led by the new foreign minister, Mamoru Shigemitsu, and including Admiral Toyoda's operations officer, Rear Admiral Sadatoshi Tomioka, arrived at 8:55. The principals gathered at the mess table. After the last signature had been put to the papers, General MacArthur turned and addressed the huge assemblage on *Missouri*'s deck:

"Let us pray that peace be now restored to the world, and that God will preserve it always. These proceedings are closed."

Part VII

41
After the War

After the surrender ceremonies, most of the submarines in the Pacific returned almost immediately to the United States. They nested in seaports and were opened to the public. The skippers and crews were permitted—for the first time—to discuss their exploits freely with friends and newsmen. The books on submarine operations written during the war but held up by Admiral Edwards were released. But in the flood of postwar news, the submarine service failed to get its story across—it remained a silent victory.

Meanwhile, Lockwood and his staff tabulated the final results for all submarine commands and submitted the figures to the Navy Department. Lockwood claimed that U.S. submarines had sunk about 4,000 Japanese vessels for about 10 million tons. His figures included one battleship, eight heavy and light aircraft carriers, and twenty heavy and light cruisers. Fifty-two submarines had been lost from all causes (including training) during the war, including forty-five fleet boats. About 375 officers and 3,131 enlisted men had died out of about 16,000 who actually made war patrols. This was a casualty rate of almost 22 percent, the highest for any branch of the military.*

The Joint Army-Navy Assessment Committee (JANAC) drastically trimmed Lockwood's sinking figures. By the (imperfect) reckoning

---

* But small compared to other submarine forces. The Germans lost 781 U-boats (including two captured); of a total enlistment of 39,000 men, 28,000 were killed and 5,000 taken prisoner. The Japanese lost 130 submarines; the Italians 85.

of this group, the U.S. submarine force actually sank 1,314 enemy vessels for 5.3 million tons.* The figures included one battleship, eight heavy and light carriers, and three heavy and eight light cruisers. The tonnage figure, 5.3 million, represented 55 percent of all Japanese vessels lost. The other 45 percent were lost to army and navy aircraft, mines, and other causes. (In addition, JANAC gave submarines "probable" credit for another 78 vessels of 263,306 tons.)

The JANAC figures significantly altered the scores of many leading skippers. Medal-of-Honor winner Dick O'Kane, for example, had been credited with sinking thirty-one ships for 227,800 tons; JANAC reduced him to twenty-four ships for 93,824 but still left him the leading submarine ace of the war, in terms of ships sunk. By JANAC figures, Slade Cutter and Mush Morton tied for second place with nineteen confirmed ships each. Medal-of-Honor winner Gene Fluckey came in fourth with sixteen and a third ships for 95,360 tons. This was the highest tonnage sunk by any skipper. The most spectacular drop in standing was Roy Davenport's. Credited with seventeen ships sunk for 151,900 tons during the war, his score as confirmed by JANAC was only eight ships for 29,662 tons.†

This downward readjustment caused an awkward moment for the navy. Most of the medals awarded submarine skippers during the war had been given out on the basis of ships or tonnage scores. Should they now be withdrawn? There was no way, and nobody was inclined to do it. Roy Davenport, for example, kept his five Navy Crosses, just as many air force and naval aviators kept medals awarded for claims that were undoubtedly exaggerated or were disclaimed by postwar accounting. The only complaint raised about medals was that there should have been more Medals of Honor awarded. Only six skippers had received them; many more were deserving.

The loss of men in the Japanese merchant marine was heavy. Japan began the war with about 122,000 merchant marine personnel. About 116,000 of these became casualties: 27,000 killed, 89,000 wounded or "otherwise incapacitated." Of this total, the majority of the casualties—16,200 killed and about 53,400 wounded or "otherwise incapacitated"—were inflicted by submarine attack.

---

* In World War I, primitive German submarines sank 5,078 merchant ships for about 11 million tons and ten battleships and eighteen cruisers, losing 178 submarines and about 5,000 officers and men. In World War II, Nazi U-boats sank 2,882 Allied merchant vessels, for 14.4 million tons, plus 175 men-of-war.

† For a listing of most skippers and Medal-of-Honor winners, see Appendix G.

When confronted with the revised sinking figures according to JANAC, Lockwood laid most of the blame for the large discrepancy between claims and actuality on defective torpedoes. A total of 14,748 torpedoes had been fired. Had all these run, hit, and detonated as designed, the claims might well have been closer to the actuality, he maintained. Few could disagree. The torpedo scandal of the U.S. submarine force in World War II was one of the worst in the history of any kind of warfare.

Lockwood took pains to point out that the actual damage inflicted on the Japanese navy and merchant marine by U.S. submarines was, in reality, large compared with the effort expended. The U.S. submarine force, composed in total of about 50,000 officers and men (including back-up personnel and staffs), represented only about 1.6 percent of the total navy complement. In other words, a force representing less than 2 percent of the U.S. Navy accounted for 55 percent of Japan's maritime losses.

No matter how the figures were looked at, the damage inflicted by the U.S. submarine force on Japan was severe and contributed substantially to winning the war in the Pacific. As the report of the United States Strategic Bombing Survey stated, "The war against shipping was perhaps the most decisive single factor in the collapse of the Japanese economy and logistic support of Japanese military and naval power. Submarines accounted for the majority of vessel sinkings and the greater part of the reduction in tonnage."

After the cessation of hostilities, Lockwood looked forward to a peacetime in which the navy—and the submarine force—would remain large and strong. In the back of his mind he had created a job for himself: Deputy Chief of Naval Operations for Submarines, the "czar" concept that Daubin had proposed during the war and Lockwood strenuously opposed.

But none of this was to be. There was a strong national sentiment to "bring the boys home." President Truman ordered a general demobilization of the armed forces. Most of the fleet submarines in commission were mothballed and moored upriver from the New London Submarine Base and at other places. When Admiral Nimitz replaced Admiral King as Chief of Naval Operations in January 1946, he ordered Lockwood to become the Navy's Inspector General—in short, chief of what Lockwood called the "Gestapo." For Lockwood, who prized friendships and loyalty above all else, the job was reprehensible.

He worked at this job halfheartedly for a little over a year. One task assigned to him was to investigate the Green Bowl Society, a secret Naval Academy drinking club. It had been alleged in Congress that members of the Green Bowl had an inside track on promotions; that its members looked after one another on selection boards. Lockwood's best friend, Gin Styer, was a Green Bowler.

Seeking a way out of the "Gestapo," Lockwood proposed to Nimitz that he create a Deputy Chief of Naval Operations for Submarines. The Secretary of the Navy, James Forrestal, approved the idea, but Nimitz did not and would not create the job. When it became known that Lockwood's friend Louis Denfeld would succeed Nimitz as Chief of Naval Operations in the fall of 1947, Lockwood approached Denfeld with the idea. Denfeld didn't like it either and countered by offering Lockwood four stars and a fleet, Atlantic or Pacific. Lockwood declined the offer and asked for retirement. It was granted and took effect September 1, 1947.

Gin Styer, commanding Submarines Atlantic, soon followed in Lockwood's steps. He was replaced by John Wilkes and transferred to the Navy Department. There he got into a squabble with the new Secretary of the Navy, John Sullivan, about the extent of the Soviet submarine threat. Sullivan, not a popular Secretary of the Navy, told the press it was serious. Styer told the press the truth: it was not. On July 1, 1948, Styer voluntarily retired.

During the war, Lockwood and Styer had bought a ten-acre tract on a beautiful hillside in Los Gatos, California, south of San Francisco. After retirement, both men moved there. Styer went into the real estate business; Lockwood busied himself with civic affairs, hunting, and writing books about his peacetime years in submarines, submarine disasters, and the wartime submarine years.

When Wilkes was ready to retire, Ralph Christie, winding up two years at the Bremerton Navy Yard, sought the Atlantic submarine command. Denfeld gave it to Jimmy Fife, who was in the Navy Department working for the General Board and Joint Chiefs of Staff. Christie was sent to command U.S. naval forces in the Philippines; he retired after a year as of August 1, 1949, lived on the West Coast selling life insurance and dabbling in other ventures, and then gave it all up and moved to Hawaii, where in 1973, hale and hearty, he celebrated his eightieth birthday.

Dick Voge spent the last half year of the war and the following year writing a massive, classified operational and administrative history of the submarine war. After that was done, he decided to take a fling at the business world. Retiring from the navy in August 1946, he had a heart attack two years later and died.

Others who had served Lockwood in a staff capacity had long and distinguished careers. Sunshine Murray climbed the ranks to three stars and then retired. So did Swede Momsen, Dutch Will, Al McCann, Swede Bryant, and George Russell. Cliff Crawford, Savvy Huffman, Tex McLean, and others made two stars.*

After the war, the codebreakers stood temporarily, and uneasily, in the limelight; many were called to testify in the Pearl Harbor hearings conducted by Congress. They talked about their work up to and including the attack on Pearl Harbor but not about their work during the war itself. Generally, most supported the Roosevelt Administration thesis that the codebreaking information had not pinpointed a Japanese attack on Pearl Harbor. Admiral Kimmel and his supporters testified to the contrary.

After that, the codebreakers retired to obscurity, reluctant to talk further about their contribution to the war. They received small reward for their work. The Navy handed out only five important decorations—Distinguished Service Medals; these went to Thomas Dyer, Jasper Holmes, Joseph Wenger, Rosey Mason, and Howard T. Engstrom, who was in charge of breaking U-boat codes. Joe Rochefort, Tom Mackie, and others who decoded key messages during the war received no official recognition. Few involved in codebreaking made flag rank. One notable exception was linguist Rufus Taylor, who rose to vice admiral and to the post of deputy director of the Central Intelligence Agency.

All submariners, Lockwood included, were astonished when they finally had an opportunity to look over captured German and Japanese submarines and torpedoes. German submarine technology was superior in almost every respect to U.S. submarine technology. German submarines had better surface and submerged speed and superior sonar, optics, diesel engines, and batteries. They could dive deeper and faster. The Japanese submarine torpedo was far superior to anything the Bureau of Ordnance had turned out. Both the Germans and the Japanese had built submarines with snorkels—breathing pipes that

* A complete list of submarine skippers selected to flag rank appears in Appendix B.

enabled the submarine to run submerged on diesel engines, thereby obviating the need to surface at night to charge batteries.

During the postwar years, American submariners grafted some of the best features of the German boats—snorkels and streamlining—onto the U.S. fleet boat. These modified boats were called Guppies, an acronym for Greater Underwater Propulsion. In addition, the submarine force drew up plans for an improved fleet boat, designed from scratch, incorporating the best features of the German boats. These submarines, known as the *Tang* class (in honor of Dick O'Kane's famous old boat), were launched in 1951 and included *Tang, Trigger, Wahoo, Trout, Gudgeon,* and *Harder.* They were powered by a radically new "pancake" diesel engine, produced by General Motors. They were supposed to have a new homing torpedo based on the superior German acoustical torpedoes. The engines were a complete failure, reminiscent of the H.O.R.s. The torpedo fell years behind schedule.*

While these abortive projects were in progress, a senior captain in the Bureau of Ships named Hyman George Rickover became fascinated with the concept of adapting nuclear power to submarines.† He took a course in nuclear physics at the atomic energy facility at Oak Ridge, Tennessee and, after deft bureaucratic maneuvering, got plans approved for the first nuclear-powered submarine, *Nautilus.* It was contracted for in 1950 and launched in 1954.

Nautilus was crude but successful. With the publicity attendant on its launching, Rickover rose to be the new Mr. Submarine, displacing Lockwood and Fife and the other wartime submarine leaders. He not only turned out submarines, he also insisted on the right to pick the men to command and man them. Thus the new nuclear submarine navy bore Rickover's personal stamp, and the new age was his alone. Lockwood died in June 1967, holding bitter feelings toward Rickover.

Rickover worked diligently, if not fanatically, to improve the nuclear-powered submarine. The next models launched at Electric Boat (among them *Swordfish, Sargo, Seadragon,* and *Skate*) were significant improvements over the prototype *Nautilus.* In 1960, after the

---

* So did all the follow-on models. For example, the most recent torpedo, the Mark 48, is years behind schedule and cost hundreds of millions more than estimated.

† Rickover had served on S-48 (the worst of the S-boats), in the late 1920s and early 1930s, rising to exec. However, he was a man of difficult temperament and was judged not qualified for command. He left submarines and became an engineering specialist. During the war, he specialized in electrical machinery and held down a desk in the Bureau of Ships in Washington.

navy had perfected the solid-propellant, long-range ballistic missile Polaris, it was "married" to the nuclear-powered submarine to form the Polaris weapons system.* In the late 1960s, the Polaris boats were equipped with a new missile, Poseidon, with a longer range and more warheads. In 1970, the navy embarked on a super-Polaris system called Trident, whose missiles would have a range of 5,000 miles.

In the immediate postwar years, the younger submariners did not fare exceptionally well in the navy. There were only two flag-rank billets: Commander Submarines Atlantic and Commander Submarines Pacific.† To get ahead, most men had to branch out into other parts of the navy. Even so, they found it difficult. Herman Kossler (a rear admiral) maintained that aviators and destroyer men dominated the navy and were able to "divide up the flag rank vacancies as they saw fit," that there was a "general feeling, particularly by destroyer officers, that submariners were not qualified to man surface flag billets," and that there was "jealousy between destroyer men and submariners."

When Polaris came on the scene as a major weapons system, the situation changed. By 1970 the submarine force began to dominate the navy, spending 25 percent of the navy's entire budget on new weapons and personnel. The commanders of Atlantic and Pacific submarine forces were elevated to vice admirals, thereby opening up many more submarine flag billets. In addition, the navy finally adopted the Lockwood plan for a Deputy Chief of Naval Operations for Submarines.

There were 465 skippers who commanded submarines in combat in World War II. Almost all made it to the rank of captain. About sixty—13 percent—became rear admirals, some of the first being Lew Parks, C. C. Kirkpatrick, Freddy Warder, Gene McKinney, Chester Bruton, Chuck Triebel, Roy Benson, Mike Fenno, Pete Ferrall, Barney Sieglaff, Bill Post, Reuben Whitaker, and Weary Wilkins.

One of the younger skippers who later made rear admiral (in 1961) was Elliott Loughlin, who had received a general court-martial for sinking the safe-conduct ship *Awa Maru*. His selection astounded many fellow officers; he had been found guilty of negligence in obeying orders and that damning note had gone in his record, seemingly

---

* The Polaris boats, big 6,000-ton submarines, were named not for fish but historical figures such as *George Washington, Patrick Henry,* and *Robert E. Lee.*
† For a listing of men who held those commands, see Appendixes C and D.

denying him flag rank forever. However, after the dust of the war settled, Loughlin went on to a splendid professional career: command of a submarine division, director of athletics at the Naval Academy, command of the cruiser *Toledo*, and command of a cruiser-destroyer flotilla.

Said Roy Benson, "I think submariners fared very well indeed in the peacetime years; not because they were submariners, nor in spite of it. They simply did a good job in other assignments."

Twelve of the 465 skippers—those who branched out—went a notch farther, to vice admiral: Chick Clarey, Pete Galantin, Fritz Harlfinger, Junior McCain, Donc Donaho, Joe Grenfell, Rebel Lowrance, Red Ramage, Eli Reich, Arnold Schade, John Tyree, and Frank Watkins. Three of these—Junior McCain, Chick Clarey, and Pete Galantin—went all the way to full admiral. In terms of power and prestige, McCain held down the biggest job: Commander in Chief, Pacific. As such, he commanded all U.S. Navy, Air Force, and Army units in the Pacific Theater, including those who fought the Vietnam war. Chick Clarey was next; he became Commander in Chief, Pacific Fleet, working under McCain, and later Vice Chief of Naval Operations, the second highest job in the U.S. Navy. Pete Galantin rose to four stars commanding the navy's Matériel Command.

About 25 percent of all World War II submarine skippers retired from the Navy under the tombstone promotion law.* Most of them retired in 1957, 1958, and 1959, when the tombstone law was finally abolished. For this reason, there were many "rear admirals" among the retired submarine skippers.

Some outstanding skippers left the navy to follow other pursuits. George Grider retired in 1947, returned to college for a law degree, and ran successfully for Congress from Memphis. He served one term and was then unseated.† Chester Nimitz, Jr., retired in 1957 to take a job in industry, with the tombstone rank of rear admiral. Tommy Dykers took a tombstone retirement in 1949 and went on to produce a popular weekly television series, *The Silent Service*. Mur-

---

* In 1949, the Congress repealed that section of the law which gave added retirement pay. After that, the only additional benefit was the honorary increase in rank.

† Another submariner elected to Congress was William R. Anderson, who served on *Tarpon, Narwhal,* and *Trutta*. After the war, Anderson became the second skipper of the nuclear-powered *Nautilus*, took her on a famous voyage beneath the ice cap, later retired from the navy, and, like Grider, ran for Congress in Tennessee. He served four terms before being unseated in 1972.

ray Tichenor took a tombstone retirement to rear admiral to enter business.

By 1965, all but a few World War II skippers were retired. Only a small handful had died. (Three committed suicide.) The retirees clustered in groups near navy hospitals and base exchanges—San Francisco, Washington, D.C., San Diego, Norfolk, Charleston, South Carolina, Boston, New London—in fine houses, elegantly furnished. They were, as a whole, among the most affluent of the senior citizens. Almost every home had a single room in common, a den decorated with nautical gewgaws and photographs of Lockwood, Christie, Fife, submarines, Japanese ships sinking, and shipmates, living or dead.*

Over the years, some of the old shipmates slipped away, and there were funerals to attend. The most unusual farewell took place at the small submarine base in Key West, Florida, for Hiram Cassedy (*Searaven/Tigrone*). Friends and fellow submariners placed his ashes in a flare box covered by canvas and took them aboard a new, small experimental submarine, *Barracuda*. The submarine got under way and put to sea. When the appointed place had been reached, the crew gently placed Cassedy's remains in a forward torpedo tube. On command, the tube was fired, and Hi Cassedy joined Howard Gilmore, Mush Morton, Sam Dealey, and many others who had gone long before.

---

* Many had pictures, too, of sons who were Naval Academy graduates, carrying on the family tradition. Two skippers, Junior McCain and Chuck Triebel, had sons who were POWs in North Vietnam. Both returned in 1973.

Appendixes

Appendix A
World War II Submarine Squadron Commanders, Pacific

(Odd-numbered squadrons, far fewer in number, were stationed in the Atlantic)

Squadron Two
(merged with Four)
James Fife, class of 1918
Charles Bowers Momsen, 1919

Squadron Four
John Herbert Brown, 1914
William Vincent O'Regan, 1923
Edward S. Hutchinson, 1926

Squadron Six
(returned to New London)
Allan Rockwell McCann, 1917
Charles Dixon Edmunds, 1920

Squadron Eight
(merged with Ten)
Clifford Harris Roper, 1916
Willard Merrill Downes, 1920
George Edmund Peterson, 1924

Squadron Ten
Charles Wilkes Styer, 1917
Charles Frederick Erck, 1921
George Lucius Russell, 1921
George Edmund Peterson, 1924

Squadron Twelve
John Bradford Griggs, 1918
Charles Warren Wilkins, 1924

Squadron Fourteen
John Bailey Longstaff, 1920
Warren Dudley Wilkin, 1924

Squadron Sixteen
John Meade Haines, 1917
Willis Ashford Lent, 1925

Squadron Eighteen
Eliot Hinman Bryant, 1918
Stanley Page Moseley, 1925

Squadron Twenty
Leo Leander Pace, 1921
Lewis Smith Parks, 1925

Squadron Twenty-two
Joseph Anthony Connolly, 1921
Edward S. Hutchinson, 1926

Squadron Twenty-four
George Clifford Crawford, 1921
Frank Wesley Fenno, 1925

Squadron Twenty-six
Leon Joseph Huffman, 1922
Barton Elijah Bacon, Jr., 1925

Squadron Twenty-eight
John Mylin Will, 1923
Joseph Harris Willingham, 1926

Squadron Thirty
Karl Goldsmith Hensel, 1923
Chester Carl Smith, 1925

Squadron Thirty-two
Kenneth Charles Hurd, 1925

Squadron Thirty-four
Elton Watters Grenfell, 1926

Squadron Thirty-six
Jesse Lyle Hull, 1926

Appendix B
World War II Submarine Skippers Selected to Flag Rank

Admiral

Bernard Ambrose Clarey (*Pintado*)	1934
Ignatius Joseph Galantin (*Halibut*)	1933
John Sidney McCain, Jr. (*Gunnel, Dentuda*)	1931

Vice Admiral

Glynn Robert Donaho (*Flying Fish, Picuda*)	1927
Elton Watters Grenfell (*Gudgeon*)	1926
Frederick Joseph Harlfinger II (*S-32, Trigger*)	1935
Vernon Long Lowrance (*Kingfish, Sea Dog*)	1930
Lawson Paterson Ramage (*Trout, Parche*)	1931
Eli Thomas Reich (*Sea Lion II*)	1935
Arnold Frederic Schade (*Growler, Bugara*)	1933
John Augustine Tyree, Jr. (*Finback*)	1933
Frank Thomas Watkins (*Flying Fish*)	1922

Rear Admiral

Donald G. Baer (*Lapon*)	1937
David Bonar Bell (*Pargo*)	1937
Roy Stanley Benson (*Trigger, Razorback*)	1929
Francis Dennis Boyle (*Charr*)	1934
Henry Chester Bruton (*Greenling*)	1926
John Starr Coye, Jr. (*Silversides*)	1933
Earl Russell Crawford (*S-46*)	1936
Lawrence Randall Daspit (*Tinosa*)	1927
John Frederick Davidson (*Mackerel, Blackfish*)	1929
James White Davis (*S-47, Raton*)	1930
James Charles Dempsey (*S-37, Spearfish, Cod*)	1931

SUBMARINE SKIPPERS SELECTED TO FLAG RANK

Edward Joseph Fahy (*Plunger*)	1934
Frank Wesley Fenno (*Trout, Runner I, Pampanito*)	1925
William Edward Ferrall (*Seadragon*)	1927
Eugene Bennett Fluckey (*Barb*)	1935
Harry Hull (*Thresher*)	1932
William Davis Irvin (*Nautilus*)	1927
Donald Greer Irvine (*Piranha*)	1934
Frederick Emery Janney (*Hackleback*)	1937
Russell Kefauver (*Tambor, Springer*)	1933
Charles Cochran Kirkpatrick (*Triton*)	1931
Herman Joseph Kossler (*Cavalla*)	1934
Charles Elliott Loughlin (*S-14, Queenfish*)	1933
Richard Barr Lynch (*Seawolf, Skate*)	1935
John Howard Maurer (*Atule*)	1935
Woodrow Wilson McCrory (*Parche*)	1938
Lucien Berry McDonald (*Lamprey*)	1938
Eugene Bradley McKinney (*Salmon, Skate*)	1927
Henry Stone Monroe (*S-35, Ronquil*)	1933
Charles Derick Nace (*Rasher*)	1939
William Thackeray Nelson (*R-7, Peto, Lamprey*)	1930
Lewis Smith Parks (*Pompano*)	1925
William Schuyler Post, Jr. (*Gudgeon, Spot*)	1930
Robert Henry Rice (*Drum, Paddle*)	1927
Maurice Herbert Rindskopf (*Drum*)	1938
Walter Frederick Schlech, Jr. (*Tilefish*)	1936
William Bernard Sieglaff (*Tautog, Tench*)	1931
Walter Lowry Small (*Batfish*)	1938
Chester Carl Smith (*Swordfish*)	1925
Edward Clark Stephan (*Grayback, Devilfish*)	1929
Arthur Howard Taylor (*Haddock*)	1927
Charles Otto Triebel (*S-15, Snook*)	1929
George Herrick Wales (*S-22, Pogy*)	1929
Norvell Gardiner Ward (*Guardfish*)	1935
Robert Elwin McCramer Ward (*Sailfish*)	1935
Frederick Burdett Warder (*Seawolf*)	1925
Reuben Thornton Whitaker (*S-44, Flasher*)	1934
Charles Warren Wilkins (*Narwhal, Seahorse*)	1924
Joseph Warford Williams, Jr. (*Spearfish, Bumper*)	1933

Appendix C
Postwar Commanders of Submarines Atlantic Fleet

RAdm. John Wilkes	1946 to 1947
RAdm. James Fife	1947 to 1950
RAdm. Stuart S. Murray	1950 to 1952
RAdm. George C. Crawford	1952 to 1954
RAdm. Frank T. Watkins	1954 to 1957
RAdm. Charles W. Wilkins	March 1957 to September 1957
RAdm. Frederick B. Warder	September 1957 to 1960
RAdm. Lawrence R. Daspit	January 1960 to September 1960
VAdm. Elton W. Grenfell	September 1960 to 1964
VAdm. Vernon L. Lowrance	1964 to 1966
VAdm. Arnold F. Schade	1966 to 1970
VAdm. Eugene P. Wilkinson *	1970 to 1972
VAdm. Robert L. J. Long	1972 to ——

* Last World War II submariner to hold the command

Appendix D
Postwar Commanders of Submarines Pacific Fleet

RAdm. Allan R. McCann	1946 to 1948
RAdm. Oswald S. Colclough	1948 to 1949
RAdm. John H. Brown	1949 to 1951
RAdm. Charles B. Momsen	1951 to 1953
RAdm. George L. Russell	1953 to 1955
RAdm. Leon J. Huffman	1955 to 1956
RAdm. Elton W. Grenfell	1956 to 1959
RAdm. William E. Ferrall	1959 to 1960
RAdm. Roy S. Benson	1960 to 1962
RAdm. Bernard A. Clarey	1962 to 1964
RAdm. Eugene B. Fluckey	1964 to 1966
RAdm. John H. Maurer	1966 to 1968
RAdm. Walter L. Small	1968 to 1970
RAdm. Paul L. Lacy, Jr.*	1970 to 1972
RAdm. Frank D. McMullen	1972 to ——

* Last World War II submariner to hold the command

Appendix E
Submarine War Patrols, Atlantic

After the United States declared war on Nazi Germany, Admiral Doenitz decided to launch U-boats against the East Coast of the United States, choosing eleven ace skippers whose boats had been equipped with electric torpedoes. The results were gratifying—for Doenitz. From January to March 1942, while Withers's fifteen Pearl Harbor boats sank 15 ships in Japanese waters, Doenitz's eleven boats sank 204 ships in U.S. waters—over one million tons of shippping.

The U.S. Navy, which had put the bulk of its resources into building big ships, was utterly unprepared for the U-boat onslaught. Lacking other antisubmarine forces, it ordered every available submarine into the winter battle: about twenty S-boats Ralph Christie was preparing for the European submarine force, some demothballed R-class, the demothballed *Barracuda*, *Bass*, and *Bonita*, and the new experimental boats *Mackerel* and *Marlin*.

These boats stood out to sea from bases along the U.S. East Coast, Bermuda, and Panama. Several encountered U-boats. One was *R-1*, commanded by James Dorr Grant. On April 18, while 300 miles northeast of Bermuda, he made contact with a U-boat and fired four torpedoes. Grant believed the torpedoes had hit and the U-boat sank. His superiors gave him credit for the sinking—the only credited U-boat sinking by U.S. submarines in the Atlantic—and awarded Grant a Navy Cross. However, in postwar accounting the credit was reduced to damage.

Because the United States feared at first that the Japanese might bomb the Panama Canal, some submarines basing in Panama made limited patrols on the Pacific approaches to the canal. The Japanese mounted no such attack, so the submarines saw no action. One, *Bass*, suffered a battery fire which killed twenty-five men, but the boat was saved.

In all, these submarines conducted eighty-six patrols in 1942. *Mackerel* made two, *Marlin* two, *Barracuda* six, *Bass* four, *Bonita* seven, the R-boats six, and the S-boats fifty-nine. Confirmed sinkings: zero. Many boats were mistakenly bombed by U.S. aircraft. One, *S-26*, was rammed by its escort and sank with the loss of forty-six lives.

Afterward, *Mackerel*, *Marlin*, *Barracuda*, *Bass*, *Bonita*, and the Rs were sent to noncombatant duty. Said one S-boat skipper, "I think we probably made a lot of U-boat skippers nervous and caused them to lose sleep. The real miracle is that we didn't lose one of our own boats to friendly aircraft."

The anti-U-boat patrols and the Panama Canal pickets are lumped together on the following chart. The area is labeled simply "Atlantic," but some Panama Canal patrols were conducted in the Pacific.

SUBMARINE WAR PATROLS DEPARTING ATLANTIC AND PANAMANIAN BASES, 1942

Boat, Patrol Number	Skipper and Class	Days	Ships/Tonnage Wartime Credit	Postwar Credit	Area
Barracuda-1	James M. Hicks '25	16	zero	zero	Atlantic
Barracuda-2	James M. Hicks '25	15	zero	zero	Atlantic
Barracuda-3	?	16	zero	zero	Atlantic
Barracuda-4	?	20	zero	zero	Atlantic
Barracuda-5	Mason J. Hamilton '32	25	zero	zero	Atlantic
Barracuda-6	Mason J. Hamilton '32	19	zero	zero	Atlantic
Bass-1	Gordon Campbell '26	20	zero	zero	Atlantic
Bass-2	Gordon Campbell '26	?	zero	zero	Atlantic
Bass-3	Anthony H. Dropp '32	26	zero	zero	Atlantic
Bass-4	Anthony H. Dropp '32	23	zero	zero	Atlantic
Bonita-1	Stanley G. Nichols '26	22	zero	zero	Atlantic
Bonita-2	Stanley G. Nichols '26	15	zero	zero	Atlantic
Bonita-3	Stanley G. Nichols '26	?	zero	zero	Atlantic
Bonita-4	Stanley G. Nichols '26	?	zero	zero	Atlantic
Bonita-5	Stanley G. Nichols '26	12	zero	zero	Atlantic
Bonita-6	Stanley G. Nichols '26	25	zero	zero	Atlantic
Bonita-7	Charles F. Brindupke '32	20	zero	zero	Atlantic
Mackerel-1	John F. Davidson '29	?	zero	zero	Atlantic
Mackerel-2	John F. Davidson '29	?	zero	zero	Atlantic
Marlin-1	George A. Sharp '29	?	zero	zero	Atlantic
Marlin-2	Paul H. Grouleff '32	?	zero	zero	Atlantic

R-1-1	James D. Grant	'30	?	zero	Atlantic
R-1-2	James D. Grant	'30	12	zero *	Atlantic
R-5-1	Dudley W. Morton	'30	?	zero	Atlantic
R-7-1	William T. Nelson	'30	?	zero	Atlantic
R-7-2	William T. Nelson	'30	?	zero	Atlantic
R-7-3	William T. Nelson	'30	?	zero	Atlantic
S-11-1	William B. Perkins, Jr.	'32	20	zero	Atlantic
S-11-2	William B. Perkins, Jr.	'32	15	zero	Atlantic
S-11-3	William B. Perkins, Jr.	'32	17	zero	Atlantic
S-11-4	William B. Perkins, Jr.	'32	?	zero	Atlantic
S-11-5	William B. Perkins, Jr.	'32	19	zero	Atlantic
S-11-6	William B. Perkins, Jr.	'32	17	zero	Atlantic
S-12-1	John E. Lee	'30	?	zero	Atlantic
S-12-2	John E. Lee	'30	?	zero	Atlantic
S-12-3	John E. Lee	'30	?	zero	Atlantic
S-12-4	John E. Lee	'30	?	zero	Atlantic
S-12-5	Fitzhugh McMaster	'33	?	zero	Atlantic
S-12-6	Fitzhugh McMaster	'33	16	zero	Atlantic
S-13-1	David L. Whelchel	'30	20	zero	Atlantic
S-13-2	David L. Whelchel	'30	5	zero	Atlantic
S-13-3	David L. Whelchel	'30	25	zero	Atlantic
S-13-4	Karl R. Wheland	'31	17	zero	Atlantic

* Credited with damaging a U-boat for 700 tons

SUBMARINE WAR PATROLS DEPARTING ATLANTIC AND PANAMANIAN BASES, 1942 (Cont.)

Boat, Patrol Number	Skipper and Class		Days	Ships/Tonnage Wartime Credit	Ships/Tonnage Postwar Credit	Area
S-14-1	Charles E. Loughlin	'33	32	zero	zero	Atlantic
S-14-2	Charles E. Loughlin	'33	10	zero	zero	Atlantic
S-14-3	Charles E. Loughlin	'33	17	zero	zero	Atlantic
S-14-4	Charles E. Loughlin	'33	24	zero	zero	Atlantic
S-15-1	Charles O. Triebel	'29	?	zero	zero	Atlantic
S-15-2	Charles O. Triebel	'29	20	zero	zero	Atlantic
S-15-3	Charles O. Triebel	'29	6	zero	zero	Atlantic
S-16-1	Oscar E. Hagberg	'31	?	zero	zero	Atlantic
S-16-2	Oscar E. Hagberg	'31	8	zero	zero	Atlantic
S-16-3	Oscar E. Hagberg	'31	?	zero	zero	Atlantic
S-16-4	Oscar E. Hagberg	'31	20	zero	zero	Atlantic
S-16-5	Oscar E. Hagberg	'31	16	zero	zero	Atlantic
S-16-6	Oscar E. Hagberg	'31	5	zero	zero	Atlantic
S-17-1	Thomas B. Klakring	'27	?	zero	zero	Atlantic
S-17-2	Brooks J. Harral	'32	6	zero	zero	Atlantic
S-17-3	Brooks J. Harral	'32	?	zero	zero	Atlantic
S-17-4	Brooks J. Harral	'32	20	zero	zero	Atlantic
S-17-5	Brooks J. Harral	'32	11	zero	zero	Atlantic
S-17-6	Brooks J. Harral	'32	5	zero	zero	Atlantic
S-17-7	Brooks J. Harral	'32	5	zero	zero	Atlantic
S-18-1	William J. Millican	'28	?	zero	zero	Atlantic

S-21-1	John A. Bole, Jr.	'28	17	zero	Atlantic
S-21-2	John A. Bole, Jr.	'28	14	zero	Atlantic
S-21-3	John A. Bole, Jr.	'28	19	zero	Atlantic
S-22-1	George H. Wales	'29	16	zero	Atlantic
S-22-2	?		?	zero	Atlantic
S-22-3	?		20	zero	Atlantic
S-24-1	John Corbus	'30	16	zero	Atlantic
S-24-2	John Corbus	'30	?	zero	Atlantic
S-24-3	John Corbus	'30	20	zero	Atlantic
S-24-4	John Corbus	'30	21	zero	Atlantic
S-26-1	Earle C. Hawk	'28	17	zero	Atlantic
S-26-2	Earle C. Hawk	'28	lost	zero	Atlantic
S-29-1	Eugene T. Sands	'30	17	zero	Atlantic
S-29-2	Eugene T. Sands	'30	16	zero	Atlantic
S-29-3	Eugene T. Sands	'30	19	zero	Atlantic
S-30-1	Frederick W. Laing	'30	?	zero	Atlantic
S-30-2	Frederick W. Laing	'30	?	zero	Atlantic
S-30-3	Frederick W. Laing	'30	?	zero	Atlantic
S-31-1	Thomas F. Williamson	'32	?	zero	Atlantic
S-31-2	Thomas F. Williamson	'32	?	zero	Atlantic
S-32-1	Maximilian G. Schmidt	'32	?	zero	Atlantic
S-32-2	Maximilian G. Schmidt	'32	?	zero	Atlantic
S-33-1	Walter P. Schoeni	'31	?	zero	Atlantic

Later in the year 1942, the United States sent a small force of fleet boats to the British Isles, as described on page 263. The boats conducted twenty-seven war patrols in 1942–43, claiming the sinking of four Nazi ships or submarines for 8,100 tons. None of the four sinkings was confirmed in postwar German records.

The European patrols are shown on the following chart.

SUBMARINE WAR PATROLS DEPARTING EUROPEAN BASES, 1942–1943

Boat, Patrol Number	Skipper and Class	Days	Ships/Tonnage Wartime Credit	Postwar Credit	Area
OCTOBER 1942					
Barb-1	John R. Waterman '27	36	zero	zero	North Africa
Blackfish-1	John F. Davidson '29	37	zero	zero	North Africa
Gunnel-1	John S. McCain, Jr. '31	49	zero	zero	North Africa
Herring-1	Raymond W. Johnson '30	35	1/7,000	zero	North Africa
Shad-1	Edgar J. MacGregor III '30	35	zero	zero	North Africa
NOVEMBER					
Gurnard-1	Charles H. Andrews '30	30	zero	zero	Europe
DECEMBER					
Barb-2	John R. Waterman '27	31	zero	zero	Europe
Blackfish-2	John F. Davidson '29	29	zero	zero	Europe
Herring-2	Raymond W. Johnson '30	58	zero	zero	Europe
Shad-2	Edgar J. MacGregor III '30	44	2/600	zero	Europe

FEBRUARY 1943				
Barb-3	John R. Waterman	'27	37	zero	Europe
Blackfish-3	John F. Davidson	'29	22	zero	Europe
MARCH				
Herring-3	John Corbus	'30	37	1/500	Europe
Shad-3	Edgar J. MacGregor III	'30	37	zero	Europe
APRIL				
Barb-4	Nicholas Lucker, Jr.	'30	44	zero	Europe
Blackfish-4	John F. Davidson	'29	39	zero	Europe
Haddo-1	Willis A. Lent	'25	21	zero	Europe
Hake-1	John C. Broach	'27	23	zero	Europe
MAY				
Haddo-2	Willis A. Lent	'25	37	zero	Europe
Hake-2	John C. Broach	'27	51	zero	Europe
Herring-4	Raymond W. Johnson	'30	35	zero	Europe
Shad-4	Roland F. Pryce	'27	43	zero	Europe
JUNE				
Barb-5	John R. Waterman	'27	41	zero	Europe
Blackfish-5	Eliot Olsen	'27	48	zero	Europe
JULY				
Haddo-3	John Corbus	'30	19	zero	Europe
Herring-5	Raymond W. Johnson	'30	19	zero	Europe
Shad-5	Edgar J. MacGregor III	'30	19	zero	Europe
		TOTALS:		4/8,100

Appendix F
Submarine War Patrols, Pacific

In January 1943 the Chief of Staff, U.S. Army, and the Commander in Chief, U.S. Navy, ordered the formation of a committee to assess Japanese naval and merchant-ship losses to submarines, carrier-based aircraft, land-based aircraft, mines, and other causes. During and after the war the committee, known as the Joint Army-Navy Assessment Committee (JANAC), tried to determine just who had sunk what Japanese ship of more than 500 gross tons. It made use of many sources: codebreaking, POW reports, captured documents, photographic intelligence, action reports of submarines, aircraft, and surface vessels, and lists of losses prepared by the Japanese after hostilities ceased. In February 1947 the final reports were issued. Japanese shipping losses to submarines were itemized by the name of the submarine and included name of the Japanese ship, its approximate tonnage, date and position lost.

The JANAC task was not easy. Japanese records were not complete or precise. Some vessels, sailing alone, had disappeared without trace and there was no way to determine why. Sinkings attributed to certain submarines could not possibly have taken place. Other positive sinkings by submarines were denied because no record could be found. Most U.S. submarine skippers found fault with the JANAC list. Recently, many conveyed to the author specific examples of inconsistencies and inaccuracies.

In the belief that JANAC did the best possible job with the tools at hand, the author has not attempted to revise or correct the submarine sinkings as reported, except in one or two flagrant instances. To revise JANAC's list would require years of work in the United States and Japan, and even after that no one could be certain that the revised list was any better. Thus JANAC's figures should be viewed more or less as an approximation—a fairly reliable yardstick—rather than as a precise accounting.

According to JANAC, U.S. submarines sank 540,192 tons of Japanese naval vessels and 4,779,902 tons of merchant shipping. Taken together the figures—5,320,094 tons—represent 54.6 percent of all Japanese naval and shipping losses to all causes. The three submarine commands credited the skippers with sinking a total of 10,689,800 tons and damage to 5,785,500 tons. The sinking credits, from a tonnage standpoint, were overclaimed, according to JANAC, by almost precisely 100 percent.

In the following charts, compiled from patrol reports, command war diaries, ships' histories, interviews with skippers, reports of the Submarine Operations Group (SORG) at Pearl Harbor, biographies, and JANAC, the submarine war patrols are broken down by place of departure, skipper (and Naval Academy class), days at sea, area patrolled, credited results during wartime, and results according to JANAC. In some instances, both wartime credits and postwar credits are rounded off to the nearest 100 tons.

SUBMARINE WAR PATROLS DEPARTING PEARL HARBOR, DECEMBER 1941

Boat, Patrol Number	Skipper and Class		Days	Ships/Tonnage Wartime Credit	JANAC Credit	Area
Gudgeon-1	Elton W. Grenfell	'26	50	2/6,500	1/1,800	Empire
Pollack-1	Stanley P. Moseley	'25	39	2/16,000	2/7,600	Empire
Plunger-1	David C. White	'27	52	1/7,200	1/4,700	Empire
Pompano-1	Lewis S. Parks	'25	43	1/16,000	zero	Marshalls
Dolphin-1	Gordon B. Rainer	'25	42	zero	zero	Marshalls
Tautog-1	Joseph H. Willingham	'26	41	zero	zero	Marshalls
Thresher-2 *	William L. Anderson	'26	58	1/4,500	zero	Marshalls
On patrol at Midway						
Argonaut-1	Stephen G. Barchet	'24	59	zero	zero	
Trout-1	Frank W. Fenno	'25	22	zero	zero	
On patrol at Wake						
Tambor-1	John W. Murphy, Jr.	'25	35	zero	zero	
Triton-1	Willis A. Lent	'25	42	zero	zero	
			TOTALS:	8/50,200	4/14,100	

* Prewar patrol to Wake counted as #1

SUBMARINE WAR PATROLS DEPARTING MANILA, DECEMBER 1941

Boat, Patrol Number	Skipper and Class	Days	Ships/Tonnage Wartime Credit	Ships/Tonnage JANAC Credit	Area
First Patrol					
Seawolf-1	Frederick B. Warder '25	18	zero	zero	East Luzon[1]
Sculpin-1	Lucius H. Chappell '27	45	1/5,000	zero	East Luzon[2]
Skipjack-1	Charles L. Freeman '27	36	zero	zero	East Luzon[3]
S-39-1	James W. Coe '30	18	1/5,000	zero	East Luzon[1]
Tarpon-1	Lewis Wallace '25	33	zero	zero	East Luzon[3]
S-36-1	John R. McKnight '30	18	zero	zero	West Luzon[1]
Sailfish-1	Morton C. Mumma, Jr. '25	9	1/1,500	zero	West Luzon[1]
Saury-1	John L. Burnside, Jr. '26	53	zero	zero	West Luzon[2]
Perch-1	David A. Hurt '25	38	1/5,000	zero	Formosa[3]
Permit-1	Adrian M. Hurst '24	9	zero	zero	West Luzon[1]
Stingray-1	Raymond S. Lamb '26	13	zero	zero	West Luzon[1]
Seal-1	Kenneth C. Hurd '25	53	1/5,000	1/856	West Luzon[2]
Salmon-1	Eugene B. McKinney '27	55	1/1,500	zero	West Luzon[2]
Porpoise-1	Joseph A. Callaghan '24	39	zero	zero	West Luzon[2]
Shark-1	Louis Shane, Jr. '26	12	zero	zero	South Luzon[1]
S-37-1	James C. Dempsey '31	10	zero	zero	South Luzon[1]
S-38-1	Wreford G. Chapple '30	18	2/10,000	1/5,445	South Luzon[1]
S-40-1	Nicholas Lucker, Jr. '30	9	zero	zero	South Luzon[1]
S-41-1	George M. Holley, Jr. '30	31	zero	zero	South Luzon[2]
Sturgeon-1	William L. Wright '25	17	zero	zero	Formosa[1]
Searaven-1	Theodore C. Aylward '26	41	zero	zero	Formosa[3]
Pike-1	William A. New '25	21	zero	zero	Hong Kong[1]
Snapper-1	Hamilton L. Stone '25	53	zero	zero	Hong Kong[2]

Swordfish-1	Chester C. Smith	'25	19	4/31,700	1/8,662	Indochina [1]
Pickerel-1	Barton E. Bacon, Jr.	'25	21	zero	zero	Indochina [1]
Spearfish-1	Roland F. Pryce	'27	51	zero	zero	Indochina [2]
Sargo-1	Tyrrell D. Jacobs	'27	48	zero	zero	Indochina [2]
Seadragon-1	William E. Ferrall	'27	45	2/10,000	1/6,441	Indochina [2]

Second Patrol

Permit-2	Adrian M. Hurst	'24	6	zero	zero	Lingayen [1]
Pickerel-2	Barton E. Bacon, Jr.	'25	30	2/10,000	1/2,929	Celebes [2]
Pike-2	William A. New	'25	25	zero	zero	Celebes [3]
S-36-2	John R. McKnight	'30	lost	1/5,000	zero	Celebes
S-37-2	James C. Dempsey	'31	35	zero	zero	Celebes [2]
S-38-2	Wreford G. Chapple	'30	20	zero	zero	Celebes [2]
S-39-2	James W. Coe	'30	23	zero	zero	Celebes [2]
S-40-2	Nicholas Lucker, Jr.	'30	42	zero	zero	Celebes [2]
Sailfish-2	Richard G. Voge	'25	55	zero	zero	Formosa [2]
Seawolf-2	Frederick B. Warder	'25	10	zero	zero	special mission *
Stingray-2	Raymond J. Moore	'27	44	1/10,700	1/5,167	Indochina [2]
Sturgeon-2	William L. Wright	'25	46	3/20,000	zero	Celebes [2]
Shark	Louis Shane, Jr.	'26	7	zero	zero	special mission †
Swordfish	Chester C. Smith	'25	8	zero	zero	special mission ‡

Third Patrol

Permit-3	Adrian M. Hurst	'24	38	zero	zero	Celebes [2]

TOTALS: 21/120,400 6/29,500

* Transporting staff to Australia
† Transporting Admiral Hart to Surabaya
‡ Transporting Wilkes to Surabaya

[1] Returned to Manila
[2] Returned to Java
[3] Returned to Darwin

SUBMARINE WAR PATROLS DEPARTING JAVA AND AUSTRALIA, JANUARY 1942

Boat, Patrol Number	Skipper and Class	Days	Ships/Tonnage Wartime Credit	Ships/Tonnage JANAC Credit	Area
From Surabaya, Java					
S-38-3	Henry G. Munson '32	22	zero	zero	Barrier [1]
Sculpin-2	Lucius H. Chappell '27	29	1/1,500	zero	Barrier [2]
Swordfish-2 *	Chester C. Smith '25	52	4/20,000	1/4,124	Celebes [2]
Shark-2	Louis Shane, Jr. '26	lost			Celebes
From Darwin, Australia					
Searaven-2	Theodore C. Aylward '26	43	1/1,500	zero	Indochina [2]
Seawolf-3 †	Frederick B. Warder '25	22	zero	zero	special mission † [1]
Skipjack-2	Charles L. Freeman '27	40	zero	zero	Celebes [2]
Tarpon-2	Lewis Wallace '25	40	zero	zero	Barrier [2]
		TOTALS:	6/23,000	1/4,124	

* Evacuated Quezon and Sayre parties from Corregidor
† Took ammunition to Corregidor

[1] Returned to Java
[2] Returned to Australia

SUBMARINE WAR PATROLS DEPARTING JAVA AND AUSTRALIA, FEBRUARY 1942

Boat, Patrol Number	Skipper and Class	Days	Ships/Tonnage Wartime Credit	Ships/Tonnage JANAC Credit	Area
From Java					
Permit-4	Wreford G. Chapple '30	44	zero	zero	special misison † [1]
Pickerel-3	Barton E. Bacon, Jr. '25	41	zero	zero	Barrier [1]

Porpoise-2	John R. McKnight	'30	49	zero	Barrier [1]
S-37-3	James C. Dempsey	'31	18	zero	Barrier [2]
S-37-4	James R. Reynolds	'31	21	1/1,900	Barrier [1]
S-38-4	Henry G. Munson	'32	19	zero	Barrier [1]
S-39-3	James W. Coe	'30	32	zero	Barrier [1]
S-40-3	Nicholas Lucker, Jr.	'30	26	1/5,000	Barrier [1]
S-41-2	George M. Holley, Jr.	'30	34	1/6,500	Barrier [1]
Sailfish-3	Richard G. Voge	'25	28	zero	Barrier [1]
Salmon-2	Eugene B. McKinney	'27	31	1/6,440	Barrier [1]
Sargo-2	Tyrrell D. Jacobs	'27	25	zero	special mission *[2]
Saury-2	John L. Burnside, Jr.	'26	38	zero	Barrier [1]
Seal-2	Kenneth C. Hurd	'25	48	2/10,000	Barrier [1]
Spearfish-2	Roland F. Pryce	'27	27	zero	Barrier [2]
Seawolf-4	Frederick B. Warder	'25	51	3/14,000	Barrier [1]
From Australia					
Perch-2	David A. Hurt	'25	lost	zero	Barrier
Pike-3	William A. New	'25	51	zero	Barrier [1]
		TOTALS:		7/34,000	3/14,840

Note: The following submarines evacuated staff from Java to Australia:

Snapper — Hamilton L. Stone
Stingray — Raymond John Moore
Sargo — Tyrrell D. Jacobs
Spearfish — James C. Dempsey
Sturgeon — William L. Wright
Seadragon — William E. Ferrall

* Took ammunition to Mindanao
† Corregidor

[1] Returned to Australia
[2] Returned to Java

SUBMARINE WAR PATROLS DEPARTING FREMANTLE, MARCH 1942

Boat, Patrol Number	Skipper and Class	Days	Ships/Tonnage Wartime Credit	Ships/Tonnage JANAC Credit	Area
Sargo-3	Richard V. Gregory '32	52	zero	zero	Indochina
Sculpin-3	Lucius H. Chappell '27	45	zero	zero	Banda Sea
Seadragon-2	William E. Ferrall '27	39	zero	zero	special mission *
Snapper-2	Hamilton L. Stone '25	50	1/3,000	zero	special mission *
Spearfish-3	James C. Dempsey '31	54	2/10,000	2/10,995	special mission *
Stingray-3	Raymond J. Moore '27	48	zero	zero	Java Sea
Sturgeon-3	William L. Wright '25	53	2/6,500	2/1,592	Java Sea
Tarpon-3	Lewis Wallace '25	52	zero	zero	→Pearl Harbor [1]
	TOTALS:		5/19,500	4/12,587	

* Corregidor

[1] Returned to Pearl Harbor via Palau, Marianas, Truk

SUBMARINE WAR PATROLS DEPARTING PEARL HARBOR, JANUARY–MARCH 1942

Boat, Patrol Number	Skipper and Class	Days	Ships/Tonnage Wartime Credit	JANAC Credit	Area
January					
Cachalot-1	Waldeman N. Christensen '25	66	zero	zero	Carolines
Cuttlefish-1	Martin P. Hottel '27	54	zero	zero	Marshalls
Grayling-1	Eliot Olsen '27	61	zero	zero	Carolines
Triton-2	Willis A. Lent '25	52	2/12,000	2/5,982	East China Sea
Trout-2	Frank W. Fenno '25	50	1/5,200	1/2,719	special mission *
Tuna-1	John L. DeTar '27	54	1/6,000	1/4,000	Empire
February					
Gar-1	Donald McGregor '26	54	1/10,000	1/1,520	Empire
Grampus-1	Edward S. Hutchinson '26	48	2/20,000	1/8,636	Marshalls
Grayback-1	Willard A. Saunders '27	54	2/11,800	1/3,291	Marianas
Grenadier-1	Allen R. Joyce '26	48	zero	zero	Empire
Gudgeon-2	Elton W. Grenfell '26	52	2/15,000	2/8,000	East China Sea
Narwhal-1	Charles W. Wilkins '24	54	2/12,000	1/1,244	East China Sea
Pollack-2	Stanley P. Moseley '25	49	1/5,400	1/1,454	Formosa
March					
Grayling-2	Eliot Olsen '27	51	1/6,000	1/6,243	Empire
Tambor-2	John W. Murphy, Jr. '25	58	1/7,000	zero	Marshalls
Thresher-3	William L. Anderson '26	37	1/5,000	1/3,039	special mission †
Trout-3	Frank W. Fenno '25	54	5/31,000	2/7,133	Empire
		TOTALS:	22/146,400	15/53,261	

* Corregidor
† Supported Doolittle raid on Tokyo

SUBMARINE WAR PATROLS DEPARTING PEARL HARBOR, APRIL–JUNE 1942

Boat, Patrol Number	Skipper and Class	Days	Wartime Credit	JANAC Credit	Area
APRIL					
Cuttlefish-2	Martin P. Hottel	'27	56	zero	zero	Marianas *
Drum-1	Robert H. Rice	'27	56	4/24,000	4/20,000	Empire *
Gar-2	Donald McGregor	'26	50	1/4,000	zero	→Fremantle
Gato-1	William G. Myers	'26	51	zero	zero	Marshalls *
Grampus-2	Edward S. Hutchinson	'26	51	zero	zero	→Fremantle
Greenling-1	Henry C. Bruton	'26	57	1/5,800	1/3,300	Truk *
Grenadier-2	Willis A. Lent	'25	59	2/24,000	1/14,500	East China Sea *
Pompano-2	Lewis S. Parks	'25	58	2/16,400	2/8,900	East China Sea *
Silversides-1	Creed C. Burlingame	'27	52	4/25,600	1/4,000	Empire *
Tautog-2	Joseph H. Willingham	'26	47	6/19,500	3/7,500	→Fremantle
Triton-3	Charles C. Kirkpatrick	'31	52	5/24,200	5/15,843	East China Sea
Tuna-2	John L. DeTar	'27	60	1/8,000	1/800	East China Sea *
MAY					
Grayback-2	Willard A. Saunders	'27	50	zero	zero	→Fremantle
Pollack-3	Stanley P. Moseley	'25	45	1/900	zero	Empire *
Deployed for Battle of Midway					
Gudgeon-3	Hyland B. Lyon	'31	20	zero	zero	Midway
Grouper	Claren E. Duke	'27	15 [1]	zero	zero	Midway
Nautilus	William H. Brockman	'27	15 [1]	1/30,000 †	zero	Midway
Grayling	Eliot Olsen	'27	15 [1]	zero	zero	Midway
Trout-4	Frank W. Fenno	'25	26	zero	zero	Midway

Dolphin	Royal L. Rutter	'30	15[1]	zero	Midway
Tambor	John W. Murphy, Jr.	'25	15[1]	zero	Midway
Flying Fish	Glynn R. Donaho	'27	15[1]	zero	Midway
Cachalot	George A. Lewis	'27	15[1]	zero	Midway
Plunger	David C. White	'27	15[1]	zero	Midway
Narwhal-2	Charles W. Wilkins	'24	15	zero	Midway
Trigger	Jack H. Lewis	'27	15[1]	zero	Midway
Growler	Howard W. Gilmore	'26	15[1]	zero	Midway
Finback	Jesse L. Hull	'26	15[1]	zero	Midway
Tarpon-4	Lewis Wallace	'25	9	zero	Midway
Pike-5	William A. New	'25	11	zero	Midway
Porpoise-3 [2]	John R. McKnight, Jr.	'30	53	zero	Midway
JUNE					
Cachalot-2	George A. Lewis	'27	47	zero	Empire
Dolphin-2	Royal L. Rutter	'30	68	zero	Empire
Nautilus-1	William H. Brockman	'27	48	3/13,200	Empire
Flying Fish-1	Glynn R. Donaho	'27	51	zero	East China Sea
Grouper-1	Claren E. Duke	'27	56	zero	East China Sea
Plunger-2	David C. White	'27	36	2/19,000	East China Sea
Thresher-4	William J. Millican	'28	50	1/6,000	→Fremantle
		TOTALS:		34/220,600	22/87,600

* Participated in Battle of Midway en route home
† *Soryu*, later discredited

[1] Estimated
[2] En route from Australia

909

SUBMARINE WAR PATROLS DEPARTING FREMANTLE, APRIL–AUGUST 1942

Boat, Patrol Number	Skipper and Class	Days	Ships/Tonnage Wartime Credit	Ships/Tonnage JANAC Credit	Area
APRIL					
Pickerel-4	Barton E. Bacon, Jr. '25	52	zero	zero	Philippines [1]
Pike-4	William A. New '25	35	zero	zero	→Pearl Harbor
Porpoise-3	John R. McKnight, Jr. '30	53	zero	zero	→Pearl Harbor
Sailfish-4	Richard G. Voge '25	28	zero	zero	special mission *
Saury-3	John L. Burnside, Jr. '26	61	zero	zero	Davao
Searaven-3	Hiram Cassedy '31	23	zero	zero	special mission †
Skipjack-3	James W. Coe '30	50	4/28,300	3/12,800	Camranh Bay
Swordfish-3	Chester C. Smith '25	31	zero	zero	special mission *
MAY					
Permit-5	Wreford G. Chapple '30	38	zero	zero	Makassar Strait
Salmon-3	Eugene B. McKinney '27	52	2/9,800	2/15,800	Indochina
Saury-3	John L. Burnside, Jr. '26	61	zero	zero	Manila
Sculpin-4	Lucius H. Chappell '27	78	1/7,000	zero	South China Sea
Seal-3	Kenneth C. Hurd '25	53	1/5,000	1/2,000	Indochina
Seawolf-5	Frederick B. Warder '25	51	zero	1/1,200	Manila
Snapper-3	Harold E. Baker '32	49	zero	zero	Celebes
Stingray-4	Raymond J. Moore '27	50	zero	1/1,300	→Pearl Harbor
Swordfish-4	Chester C. Smith '25	50	2/11,900	2/6,500	South China Sea
JUNE					
Sailfish-5	Richard G. Voge '25	49	1/7,000	zero	Indochina
Sargo-4	Richard V. Gregory '32	56	zero	zero	South China Sea

910

Seadragon-3	William E. Ferrall	'27	52	3/18,100	3/15,900	Indochina
Searaven-4	Hiram Cassedy	'31	40	zero	zero	Kendari
Spearfish-4	James C. Dempsey	'31	52	1/12,000	zero	South China Sea
Sturgeon-4	William L. Wright	'25	47	1/10,000	1/7,300	Manila

JULY

Gar-3	Donald McGregor	'26	50	zero	zero	South China Sea
Grampus-3	Edward S. Hutchinson	'26	54	zero	zero	Manila
Grayback-3	Willard A. Saunders	'27	51	zero	zero	Indochina
Permit-6	Wreford G. Chapple	'30	50	zero	zero	→Pearl Harbor
Salmon-4	Eugene B. McKinney	'27	49	zero	zero	South China Sea
Saury-4	Leonard S. Mewhinney	'27	55	1/10,000	1/8,600	Manila
Seawolf-6	Frederick B. Warder	'25	52	2/8,100	2/4,462	Celebes
Skipjack-4	James W. Coe	'30	49	zero	zero	Java Sea
Swordfish-5	Albert C. Burrows	'28	55	zero	zero	Celebes
Tautog-3	Joseph H. Willingham	'26	57	1/7,000	1/5,900	Celebes

AUGUST

Sargo-5	Richard V. Gregory	'32	59	1/7,000	1/4,500	Celebes
Seadragon-4	William E. Ferrall	'27	55	2/12,500	1/2,500	Indochina
Seal-4	Kenneth C. Hurd	'25	53	zero	zero	Indochina
Snapper-4	Harold E. Baker	'32	79	zero	zero	South China Sea
			TOTALS:	23/153,000	20/88,762	

[1] Returned to Brisbane

* Corregidor
† Timor

911

SUBMARINE WAR PATROLS DEPARTING BRISBANE, APRIL–SEPTEMBER 1942

Boat, Patrol Number	Skipper and Class	Days	Ships/Tonnage Wartime Credit	Ships/Tonnage JANAC Credit	Area
APRIL					
S-38-5	Henry G. Munson '32	25	zero	zero	Solomons
S-42-1	Oliver G. Kirk '29	24	1/9,800	1/4,400	Solomons
S-44-1	John R. Moore '29	29	1/1,900	1/5,644	Solomons
S-47-1	James W. Davis '30	30	zero	zero	Solomons
MAY					
S-39-4	Francis E. Brown '33	27	zero	zero	Solomons
S-40-4	Nicholas Lucker, Jr. '30	30	zero	zero	Solomons
S-41-3	George M. Holley, Jr. '30	27	zero	zero	Solomons
S-43-1	Edward R. Hannon '29	28	zero	zero	Solomons
S-45-1	Ian C. Eddy '30	38	zero	zero	Solomons
S-46-1	Ralph C. Lynch, Jr. '29	35	zero	zero	Solomons
JUNE					
S-37-5	James R. Reynolds '31	29	zero	zero	Solomons
S-38-6	Henry G. Munson '32	13	zero	zero	Solomons
S-40-5	Nicholas Lucker, Jr. '30	27	zero	zero	Solomons
S-44-2	John R. Moore '29	28	1/1,100	1/2,626	Solomons
S-47-2	James W. Davis '30	25	zero	zero	Solomons
JULY					
Pickerel-5	Barton E. Bacon, Jr. '25	47	zero	zero	→Pearl Harbor
S-38-7	Henry G. Munson '32	25	1/8,000	1/5,628	Solomons*
S-39-5	Francis E. Brown '33	lost	zero	zero	Solomons
S-42-2	Oliver G. Kirk '29	25	zero	zero	Solomons
S-43-2	Edward R. Hannon '29	31	zero	zero	Solomons

912

S-44-3	John R. Moore	'29	30	1/7,100	1/8,800	Solomons
S-46-2	Ralph C. Lynch, Jr.	'29	26	zero	zero	Solomons
S-47-3	James W. Davis	'30	56	1/7,100	zero	Solomons
AUGUST						
S-37-6	Thomas S. Baskett	'35	27	zero	zero	Solomons
S-40-6	Francis M. Gambacorta	'35	28	zero	zero	Solomons
S-41-4	Irvin S. Hartman	'33	25	1/1,500	zero	Solomons *
S-42-3	Harley K. Nauman	'34	29	zero	zero	Solomons
S-45-2	Ian C. Eddy	'30	28	zero	zero	Solomons
Shifted from Fremantle						
Sailfish	Richard G. Voge					
Sculpin	Lucius H. Chappell					
Sturgeon	William L. Wright					
SEPTEMBER						
Sailfish-6	John R. Moore	'29	49	zero	zero	Solomons
Sculpin-5	Lucius H. Chappell	'27	54	3/24,100	2/6,652	Solomons
Sturgeon-5	Herman A. Pieczentkowski	'30	51	2/17,000	1/8,033	Solomons
S-38-8	Henry G. Munson	'32	30	zero	zero	→Pearl Harbor
S-41-5	Irvin S. Hartman	'33	42	zero	zero	→Pearl Harbor
S-43-3	Francis E. Brown	'33	35	zero	zero	Solomons *
S-44-4	Reuben T. Whitaker	'34	28	1/1,500	zero	Solomons *
S-46-3	Earl R. Crawford	'36	31	zero	zero	Solomons *
Shifted from Fremantle						
Grampus	Edward S. Hutchinson					
Grayback	Willard A. Saunders					
Gudgeon	William S. Stovall					
			TOTALS:	13/79,100	8/41,783	

* Then to the States

SUBMARINE WAR PATROLS DEPARTING ALASKA, 1942

Boat, Patrol Number	Skipper and Class	Days	Ships/Tonnage Wartime Credit	Ships/Tonnage JANAC Credit	Area
FEBRUARY					
S-18-2	William J. Millican '28	20	zero	zero	Alaska
S-23-1	John R. Pierce '28	10	zero	zero	Alaska
MARCH					
S-18-3	James H. Newsome '30	12	zero	zero	Alaska
APRIL					
S-34-1	Thomas L. Wogan '31	28	zero	zero	Alaska
S-35-1	James E. Stevens '30	19	zero	zero	Alaska
MAY					
S-18-4	James H. Newsome '30	51	zero	zero	Alaska
S-23-2	John R. Pierce '28	43	zero	zero	Alaska
S-27-1	Herbert L. Jukes '32	lost	zero	zero	Alaska
S-28-1	John D. Crowley '31	40	zero	zero	Alaska
S-34-2	Thomas L. Wogan '31	29	zero	zero	Alaska
S-35-2	James E. Stevens '30	35	zero	zero	Alaska
JUNE					
Growler-1*	Howard W. Gilmore '26	27	2/3,400	1/1,500	Alaska
Finback-1*	Jesse L. Hull '26	48	zero	zero	Alaska
Trigger-1*	Jack H. Lewis '27	51	zero	zero	Alaska
Triton-4*	Charles C. Kirkpatrick '31	60	2/3,100	1/1,600	Alaska
Grunion-1*	Mannert L. Abele '26	lost	3/4,500	2/600	Alaska

914

JULY						
S-18-5	James H. Newsome	'30	18	zero	zero	Alaska
S-23-3	Harold E. Duryea	'30	34	zero	zero	Alaska
S-28-2	John D. Crowley	'31	34	zero	zero	Alaska
S-31-3	Thomas F. Williamson	'32	34	zero	zero	Alaska
S-32-3	Maximilian G. Schmidt	'32	34	zero	zero	Alaska
S-33-2	Walter P. Schoeni	'31	36	zero	zero	Alaska
S-35-2	James E. Stevens	'30	29	zero	zero	Alaska
Gato-2 *	William G. Myers	'26	50	1/9,300	zero	Alaska
Tuna-3 *	Arnold H. Holtz	'31	42	zero	zero	Alaska
AUGUST						
S-30-4	Frederick W. Laing	'30	32	zero	zero	Alaska
S-31-4	Robert F. Sellars	'34	33	zero	zero	Alaska
S-32-5	Maximilian G. Schmidt	'32	19	zero	zero	Alaska
S-33-3	Walter P. Schoeni	'31	33	zero	zero	Alaska
Halibut-1 *	Philip H. Ross	'27	45	zero	zero	Alaska
SEPTEMBER						
S-28-3	John D. Crowley	'31	24	zero	zero	Alaska
S-30-5	Frederick W. Laing	'30	20	zero	zero	Alaska
S-34-3	Robert A. Keating, Jr.	'33	25	zero	zero	Alaska
Cachalot-3 *	Harry C. Stevenson	'30	46	zero	zero	Alaska
OCTOBER						
S-18-6	George H. Browne	'34	29	zero	zero	Alaska
S-31-5	Robert F. Sellars	'34	28	1/3,000	1/2,864	Alaska
S-32-5	Maximilian G. Schmidt	'32	19	zero	zero	Alaska

* From Pearl Harbor

SUBMARINE WAR PATROLS DEPARTING ALASKA, 1942 (Cont.)

Boat, Patrol Number	Skipper and Class	Days	Ships/Tonnage Wartime Credit	Ships/Tonnage JANAC Credit	Area
S-33-4	Walter P. Schoeni	'31	27	zero	zero	Alaska
S-34-4	Robert A. Keating, Jr.	'33	29	zero	zero	Alaska
S-35-4	Henry S. Monroe	'33	30	zero	zero	Alaska
Halibut-2	Philip H. Ross	'27	21	zero	zero	Alaska
Dolphin-3	Royal L. Rutter	'30	51	zero	zero	Alaska
NOVEMBER					
S-18-7	George H. Browne	'34	28	zero	zero	Alaska
S-33-5	Walter P. Schoeni	'31	16	zero	zero	Alaska
DECEMBER					
S-23-5	Harold E. Ruble	'33	20	zero	zero	Alaska
S-28-4	John D. Crowley	'31	27	zero	zero	Alaska
S-34-5	Robert A. Keating, Jr.	'33	24	zero	zero	Alaska
S-35-5	Henry S. Monroe	'33	18	zero	zero	Alaska
		TOTALS:	9/22,300	5/6,564	

SUBMARINE WAR PATROLS DEPARTING PEARL HARBOR, JULY–DECEMBER 1942

Boat, Patrol Number	Skipper and Class	Days	Ships/Tonnage Wartime Credit	JANAC Credit	Area
JULY					
Cuttlefish-3	Elliott E. Marshall '31	69	2/29,600	zero	Empire
Drum-2	Robert H. Rice '27	54	zero	zero	Truk
Grayling-3	Eliot Olsen '27	43	1/10,000	zero	Truk
Greenling-2	Henry C. Bruton '26	53	2/24,000	2/17,250	Truk
Grenadier-3	Bruce L. Carr '31	67	1/15,000	zero	→Fremantle *
Gudgeon-4	William S. Stovall '29	53	4/35,000	1/4,900	→Fremantle *
Haddock-1	Arthur H. Taylor '27	52	3/24,300	2/6,200	East China Sea
Narwhal-3	Charles W. Wilkins '24	49	4/14,500	3/7,000	Empire
Pompano-3	Willis M. Thomas '31	55	3/9,000	2/9,600	Empire
Silversides-2	Creed C. Burlingame '27	56	3/15,000	2/9,800	Empire
Tambor-3	Stephen H. Ambruster '28	57	2/12,000	2/5,800	→Fremantle *
AUGUST					
Albacore-1	Richard C. Lake '29	53	zero	zero	Truk
Argonaut-2	John R. Pierce '28	18	zero	zero	special mission †
Flying Fish-2	Glynn R. Donaho '27	31	1/400	zero	Truk
Grouper-2	Rob Roy McGregor '29	53	2/12,000	2/11,100	East China Sea
Growler-2	Howard W. Gilmore '26	49	4/26,000	4/15,000	East China Sea
Guardfish-1	Thomas B. Klakring '27	40	6/50,000	5/16,709	Empire
Nautilus-2	William H. Brockman '27	18	zero	zero	special mission †

* Via Truk
† Makin Island raid

SUBMARINE WAR PATROLS DEPARTING PEARL HARBOR, JULY–DECEMBER 1942 (Cont.)

Boat, Patrol Number	Skipper and Class	Days	Ships/Tonnage Wartime Credit	JANAC Credit	Area
Trout-5	Lawson P. Ramage '31	47	1/8,200	1/900	→Brisbane *
Wahoo-1	Marvin G. Kennedy '29	55	1/6,500	zero	Truk
SEPTEMBER					
Amberjack-1	John A. Bole, Jr. '28	57	3/28,500	2/5,200	→Brisbane *
Drum-3	Robert H. Rice '27	46	3/19,500	3/13,200	Empire
Finback-2	Jesse L. Hull '26	58	2/14,100	3/22,000	East China Sea
Greenling-3	Henry C. Bruton '26	41	4/32,100	4/20,400	Empire
Guardfish-2	Thomas B. Klakring '27	59	2/15,400	2/10,400	East China Sea
Kingfish-1	Vernon L. Lowrance '30	55	2/12,000	2/5,500	Empire
Nautilus-3	William H. Brockman '27	56	2/10,100	3/12,000	Empire
Trigger-2	Roy S. Benson '29	46	1/5,000	1/5,900	Empire
OCTOBER					
Flying Fish-3	Glynn R. Donaho '27	50	2/3,000	zero	→Brisbane *
Grayling-4	John E. Lee '30	55	1/5,300	1/4,000	→Fremantle *
Growler-3	Howard W. Gilmore '26	49	zero	zero	→Brisbane *
Haddock-2	Arthur H. Taylor '27	54	3/24,000	2/8,500	East China Sea
Plunger-3	David C. White '27	27	zero	zero	→Brisbane *
Pollack-4	Robie E. Palmer '27	49	zero	zero	Truk
Silversides-3	Creed C. Burlingame '27	54	2/10,800	2/5,500	→Brisbane *
Stingray-5	Raymond J. Moore '27	55	zero	zero	Truk
Tarpon-5	Thomas L. Wogan '30	42	zero	zero	Truk
Whale-1	John B. Azer '30	32	1/9,400	zero	Empire ‡

918

NOVEMBER					
Albacore-2	Richard C. Lake	'29	49	2/9,200	1/3,300	→Brisbane *
Drum-4	Bernard F. McMahon	'31	56	zero	zero	Empire ‡
Gato-3	Robert J. Foley	'27	48	zero	zero	→Brisbane *
Grouper-3	Rob Roy McGregor	'29	49	1/8,400	1/4,000	→Brisbane *
Halibut-3	Philip H. Ross	'27	54	4/30,300	3/12,400	Empire
Kingfish-2	Vernon L. Lowrance	'30	58	2/14,100	2/10,000	East China Sea
Porpoise-4	John R. McKnight, Jr.	'30	47	1/5,300	1/5,000	Empire
Sunfish-1	Richard W. Peterson	'31	53	zero	zero	Empire ‡
Tuna-4	Arnold H. Holtz	'31	48	zero	zero	→Brisbane *
Wahoo-2	Marvin G. Kennedy	'29	48	2/7,600	1/5,400	→Brisbane *
DECEMBER						
Argonaut-3	John R. Pierce	'28	lost	zero	zero	→Brisbane
Finback-3	Jesse L. Hull	'26	52	1/200	zero	Empire
Haddock-3	Arthur H. Taylor	'27	51	2/13,300	1/4,000	Empire
Greenling-4	Henry C. Bruton	'26	52	4/20,700	4/14,600	→Brisbane *
Guardfish-3	Thomas B. Klakring	'27	56	3/11,500	3/6,000	→Brisbane *
Nautilus-4	William H. Brockman	'27	55	1/1,000	1/1,500	→Brisbane *
Pike-6	William A. New	'25	48	zero	zero	Empire
Pollack-5	Robie E. Palmer	'27	41	zero	zero	Empire
Trigger-3	Roy S. Benson	'29	51	4/23,700	2/6,500	Empire ‡
Triton-5	Charles C. Kirkpatrick	'31	40	3/17,300	2/5,300	→Brisbane *
			TOTALS:	98/643,300	71/288,750	

* Via Truk
‡ Planted minefield

SUBMARINE WAR PATROLS DEPARTING BRISBANE, OCTOBER–DECEMBER 1942

Boat, Patrol Number	Skipper and Class	Days	Ships/Tonnage Wartime Credit	JANAC Credit	Area
OCTOBER					
Grampus-4	John R. Craig '30	58	1/1,400	zero	Solomons
Grayback-4	Edward C. Stephan '29	41	2/15,200	zero	Solomons
Gudgeon-5	William S. Stovall, Jr. '29	54	3/22,000	zero	Solomons
Saury-5	Leonard S. Mewhinney '27	51	zero	zero	→Pearl Harbor
Snapper-5	Augustus R. St. Angelo '29	64	zero	zero	Solomons
Swordfish-6	Charles C. Smith '25	50	1/4,400	zero	Solomons
Trout-6	Lawson P. Ramage '31	28	zero	zero	Solomons
S-37-7	Thomas S. Baskett '35	28	zero	zero	Solomons *
S-40-7	Francis M. Gambacorta '35	30	zero	zero	Solomons *
S-42-4	Harley K. Nauman '34	27	zero	zero	Solomons *
S-45-3	Robert H. Caldwell, Jr. '36	28	zero	zero	Solomons *
S-47-4	Frank E. Haylor '36	28	zero	zero	Solomons *
Shifted from Fremantle					
Swordfish	Chester C. Smith				
Saury	Leonard S. Mewhinney				
Snapper	Augustus R. St. Angelo				
Seadragon	William E. Ferrall				
Sargo	Richard V. Gregory				
Holland	Perley E. Pendleton				
NOVEMBER					
Amberjack-2	John A. Bole, Jr. '28	51	zero	zero	Solomons
Plunger-4	David C. White '27	53	1/1,300	zero	→Pearl Harbor
Sailfish-7	John R. Moore '29	53	zero	zero	→Pearl Harbor

Boat, Patrol Number	Skipper and Class	Days	Ships/Tonnage Wartime Credit	JANAC Credit	Area
Sargo-6	Edward S. Carmick '30	53	zero	zero	→Pearl Harbor
Sculpin-6	Lucius H. Chappell '27	52	zero	zero	→Pearl Harbor
Seadragon-5	William E. Ferrall '27	46	2/7,400	1/2,000	→Pearl Harbor
Sturgeon-6	Herman A. Pieczentkowski '30	51	zero	zero	→Pearl Harbor
DECEMBER					
Grampus-5	John R. Craig '30	37	3/24,000	zero	Solomons
Grayback-5	Edward C. Stephan '29	47	1/2,000	1/2,000	Solomons
Gudgeon-6	William S. Stovall, Jr. '29	53	zero	zero	Manila †
Silversides-4	Creed C. Burlingame '27	46	1/10,000	4/27,798	→Pearl Harbor
Spearfish-6	James C. Dempsey '31	55	zero	zero	→Pearl Harbor
		TOTALS:	15/87,700	6/31,800	

* Then to the States
† Returned to Fremantle

SUBMARINE WAR PATROLS DEPARTING FREMANTLE, SEPTEMBER–DECEMBER 1942

Boat, Patrol Number	Skipper and Class	Days	Ships/Tonnage Wartime Credit	JANAC Credit	Area
SEPTEMBER					
Gar-4	Donald McGregor '26	51	zero	zero	South China Sea*
Searaven-5	Hiram Cassedy '31	58	2/21,900	1/6,800	South China Sea
Skipjack-5	James W. Coe '30	60	1/7,000	zero	→Pearl Harbor
Spearfish-5	James C. Dempsey '31	64	1/3,000	zero	Manila †
Thresher-5	William J. Millican '28	61	1/3,000	1/3,000	South China Sea*

* Laid minefields
† Returned to Brisbane

921

SUBMARINE WAR PATROLS DEPARTING FREMANTLE, SEPTEMBER–DECEMBER 1942 (*Cont.*)

Boat, Patrol Number	Skipper and Class	Days	Wartime Credit	JANAC Credit	Area
OCTOBER					
Grenadier-4	Bruce L. Carr '31	58	zero	zero	Indochina *
Salmon-5	Eugene B. McKinney '27	58	1/6,100	1/5,900	→Pearl Harbor
Seal-5	Kenneth C. Hurd '25	37	1/5,500	1/5,500	→Pearl Harbor
Seawolf-7	Frederick B. Warder '25	55	3/16,800	3/13,000	→Pearl Harbor
Tambor-4	Stephan H. Ambruster '28	38	1/10,000	1/2,500	Indochina *
Tautog-4	Joseph H. Willingham '26	44	1/5,100	1/4,000	Indochina *
Shifted from Brisbane					
Trout	Lawson P. Ramage				
NOVEMBER					
Gar-5	Philip D. Quirk '32	53	zero	1/600	Manila
DECEMBER					
Searaven-6	Hiram Cassedy '31	55	1/5,900	1/5,700	→Pearl Harbor
Tambor-5	Stephan H. Ambruster '28	41	zero	zero	Sunda Strait
Tautog-5	William B. Sieglaff '31	46	2/6,900	2/2,900	Java Sea
Thresher-6	William J. Millican '28	25	2/17,000	1/2,700	Java Sea
Trout-7	Lawson P. Ramage '31	58	2/10,800	2/4,900	Indochina
		TOTALS:	19/118,200	16/57,500	

* Laid minefields
† Returned to Brisbane

SUBMARINE WAR PATROLS DEPARTING BRISBANE, JANUARY–MAY 1943

Boat, Patrol Number	Skipper and Class	Days	Ships/Tonnage Wartime Credit	JANAC Credit	Area
JANUARY					
Albacore-3	Richard C. Lake '29	50	1/1,300	2/2,500	Solomons
Flying Fish-4	Glynn R. Donaho '27	54	2/13,000	1½/5,000 *	→Pearl Harbor
Gato-4	Robert J. Foley '27	44	4/27,600	3½/11,500 †	Solomons
Grouper-4	Rob Roy McGregor '29	56	zero	zero	Solomons
Growler-4	Howard W. Gilmore '26	48	2/7,900	1/5,900	Solomons
Snapper-6	Augustus R. St. Angelo '29	46	zero	½/4,150 *	→Pearl Harbor
Swordfish-7	Jack H. Lewis '27	46	1/4,200	1/4,200	→Pearl Harbor
Tuna-5	Arnold H. Holtz '31	31	zero	zero	Solomons
Wahoo-3	Dudley W. Morton '30	23	5/31,900	3/11,300	→Pearl Harbor
Shifted to Pearl Harbor: *Holland, Sperry*					
FEBRUARY					
Amberjack-3	John A. Bole, Jr. '28	lost	1/4,000	zero	Solomons
Grampus-6	John R. Craig '30	lost	zero	zero	Solomons
Grayback-6	Edward C. Stephan '29	47	1/6,400	zero	Solomons
Greenling-5	James D. Grant '30	64	zero	zero	Solomons
Triton-6	George K. MacKenzie, Jr. '31	lost	2/8,000	1/3,000	Solomons
MARCH					
Gato-5	Robert J. Foley '27	72	zero	zero	→Pearl Harbor
Guardfish-4	Thomas B. Klakring '27	52	zero	zero	Solomons
Tuna-6	Arnold H. Holtz '31	47	1/8,500	1/5,000	Solomons

* *Flying Fish* and *Snapper* shared credit
† Shared credit with Navy Air

SUBMARINE WAR PATROLS DEPARTING BRISBANE, JANUARY–MAY 1943 (*Cont.*)

Boat, Patrol Number	Skipper and Class	Days	Ships/Tonnage Wartime Credit	Ships/Tonnage JANAC Credit	Area
Shifted to Pearl Harbor					
Nautilus	William H. Brockman				
APRIL					
Albacore-4	Richard C. Lake '29	50	zero	zero	Solomons
Grayback-7	Edward C. Stephan '29	36	zero	2/12,300	→Pearl Harbor
Grouper-5	Martin P. Hottel '27	47	zero	zero	Solomons
Peto-1	William T. Nelson '30	48	zero	zero	Solomons
MAY					
Greenling-6	James D. Grant '30	52	1/5,400	zero	Solomons
Growler-5	Arnold F. Schade '33	48	1/4,500	1/5,200	Solomons
Guardfish-5	Norvell G. Ward '35	70	1/4,000	1/900	Solomons
Tuna-7	Arnold H. Holtz '31	47	zero	zero	Solomons
		TOTALS:	23/126,700	18½/70,950	

SUBMARINE WAR PATROLS DEPARTING FREMANTLE, JANUARY–JULY 1943

Boat, Patrol Number	Skipper and Class	Days	Ships/Tonnage Wartime Credit	Ships/Tonnage JANAC Credit	Area
JANUARY					
Grayling-5	John E. Lee '30	49	3/14,400	1/750	Manila
Grenadier-5	John A. Fitzgerald '31	51	2/1,300	zero	Java Sea
Thresher-7	William J. Millican '28	45	2/14,000	2/11,000	Sunda Strait

924

FEBRUARY						
Gar-6	Philip D. Quirk	'32	53	zero	zero	South China Sea
Tambor-6	Stephen H. Ambruster	'28	55	zero	zero	Davao
Tautog-6	William B. Sieglaff	'31	53	2/6,800	2/7,000	Flores Sea *
MARCH						
Grayling-6	John E. Lee	'30	38	3/14,600	1/4,000	Manila
Grenadier-6	John A. Fitzgerald	'31	lost	zero	zero	Malacca Strait
Gudgeon-7	William S. Post, Jr.	'30	24	4/29,600	2/15,000	Java Sea
Trout-8	Lawson P. Ramage	'31	42	zero	zero	South China Sea *
APRIL						
Gar-7	Philip D. Quirk	'32	34	5/16,500	3/8,000	Manila
Gudgeon-8	William S. Post, Jr.	'30	41	3/19,600	2/23,000	→Pearl Harbor
Thresher-8	Harry Hull	'32	50	zero	zero	Java Sea
MAY						
Grayling-7	John E. Lee	'30	50	1/5,600	zero	South China Sea
Tambor-7	Russell Kefauver	'33	50	3/17,000	1/2,500	Indochina
Tautog-7	William B. Sieglaff	'31	53	2/14,300	2/5,300	→Pearl Harbor
Trout-9	Albert H. Clark	'33	59	3/17,200	2/5,800	Indochina
JUNE						
Gar-8	Philip D. Quirk	'32	34	zero	zero	Java Sea
Thresher-9	Harry Hull	'32	42	2/20,000	1/5,000	→Pearl Harbor
JULY						
Finback-6	John A. Tyree, Jr.	'33	56	3/17,100	3/11,000	→Pearl Harbor
Grayling-8	Robert M. Brinker	'34	lost	1/5,500	1/5,500	→Pearl Harbor
Tambor-8	Russell Kefauver	'33	55	1/4,400	zero	→Pearl Harbor
			TOTALS:	40/211,800	23/103,850	

* Laid minefields

SUBMARINE WAR PATROLS DEPARTING PEARL HARBOR, JANUARY–MARCH 1943

Boat, Patrol Number	Skipper and Class	Days	Ships/Tonnage Wartime Credit	JANAC Credit	Area
JANUARY					
Pickerel-6	Augustus H. Alston, Jr. '31	37	1/6,100	1/2,000	Empire
Pompano-4	Willis M. Thomas '31	44	zero	zero	Marshalls
Runner-1	Frank W. Fenno, Jr. '25	48	3/19,800	zero	Palau
Sawfish-1	Eugene T. Sands '30	53	3/13,300	zero	Empire
Stingray-6	Otis J. Earle '30	55	zero	zero	Truk
Tarpon-6	Thomas L. Wogan '30	47	2/21,000	2/27,910	Empire
Tunny-1	John A. Scott '28	43	2/16,700	1/5,300	East China Sea
Whale-2	John B. Azer '30	30	2/19,300	3/19,000	Truk
FEBRUARY					
Finback-4	John A. Tyree, Jr. '33	44	½/5,300	½/2,500*	Truk
Halibut-4	Philip H. Ross '27	50	2/15,100	2/10,711	Palau
Kingfish-3	Vernon L. Lowrance '30	52	2/13,000	1/8,000	East China Sea
Permit-7	Wreford G. Chapple '30	38	2/10,300	1/2,700	Empire
Plunger-5	Raymond H. Bass '31	29	1/9,000	1/1,800	Marshalls
Porpoise-5	John R. McKnight, Jr. '30	48	1/3,000	zero	Truk
Sunfish-2	Richard W. Peterson '31	58	2/12,200	1/3,200	East China Sea
Trigger-4	Roy S. Benson '29	56	zero	1/3,000	Palau
Wahoo-4	Dudley W. Morton '30	42	8/36,700	9/20,000	East China Sea
Whale-3	Albert C. Burrows '28	42	4/33,500	1/6,500	Marianas
MARCH					
Drum-5	Bernard F. McMahon '31	47	3/15,900	2/10,000	→Brisbane
Flying Fish-5	Glynn R. Donaho '27	48	4/28,000	3/7,500	Empire
Haddock-4	Roy M. Davenport '33	39	1/11,900	2/9,200	Palau

926

				Ships/Tonnage		
				Wartime Credit	JANAC Credit	
Pickerel-7	Augustus H. Alston, Jr.	'31	lost			Empire
Pike-7	Louis D. McGregor, Jr.	'30	40	zero	zero	Truk
Pollack-6	Robie E. Palmer	'27	44	zero	zero	Marshalls
Pompano-5	Willis M. Thomas	'31	52	zero	zero	Empire
Scamp-1	Walter G. Ebert	'30	26	zero	zero	Empire
Tarpon-7	Thomas L. Wogan	'30	47	zero	zero	Truk
Tunny-2	John A. Scott	'28	36	2½/18,700	2½/17,000 *	Truk
S-31-6	Robert F. Sellars	'34	28	zero	zero	→Brisbane
		TOTALS:		46/308,800	34/156,321	

* *Finback* and *Tunny* shared credit (Wake Island)

SUBMARINE WAR PATROLS DEPARTING ALASKA, 1943

Boat, Patrol Number	Skipper and Class		Days	Ships/Tonnage		Area
				Wartime Credit	JANAC Credit	
JANUARY						
S-18-8	George H. Browne	'34	23	zero	zero	Alaska
S-23-6	Harold E. Ruble	'33	28	zero	zero	Alaska
FEBRUARY						
S-28-5	John D. Crowley	'31	22	zero	zero	Alaska
S-32-6	Maximilian G. Schmidt	'32	23	3/4,300	zero	Alaska
MARCH						
S-23-7	Harold E. Ruble	'33	28	zero	zero	Alaska
S-32-7	Maximilian G. Schmidt	'32	22	1/9,000	zero	Alaska

SUBMARINE WAR PATROLS DEPARTING ALASKA, 1943 (*Cont.*)

Boat, Patrol Number	Skipper and Class	Days	Ships/Tonnage Wartime Credit	Ships/Tonnage JANAC Credit	Area
APRIL					
S-30-6	William A. Stevenson '34	28	zero	zero	Alaska
S-33-6	Clyde B. Stevens, Jr. '30	28	zero	zero	Alaska
S-34-6	Robert A. Keating, Jr. '33	28	1/3,000	zero	Alaska
Narwhal-4	Frank D. Latta '32	38	zero	zero	special mission *
Nautilus-5	William H. Brockman '27	36	zero	zero	special mission *
MAY					
S-30-7	William A. Stevenson '34	29	zero	1/5,228	Alaska
S-32-8	Frederick J. Harlfinger '35	19	zero	zero	Alaska
S-41-6	Irvin S. Hartman '33	31	2/6,200	1/1,036	Alaska
Shifted from States					
S-40					
S-41					
S-42					
S-44					
S-45					
S-46					
S-47					
JUNE					
S-33-7	Clyde B. Stevens, Jr. '30	27	zero	zero	Alaska
S-34-7	Robert A. Keating, Jr. '33	39	zero	zero	Alaska
S-35-6	Henry S. Monroe '33	38	1/8,200	1/5,430	Alaska
S-40-8	Francis M. Gambacorta '35	37	zero	zero	Alaska

S-41-7	Irvin S. Hartman	'33	36	zero	Alaska
JULY					
S-28-6	Vincent A. Sisler, Jr.	'35	33	zero	Alaska
S-30-8	William A. Stevenson	'34	34	zero	Alaska
S-33-8	Clyde B. Stevens, Jr.	'30	23	zero	Alaska
AUGUST					
S-30-9	William A. Stevenson	'34	28	zero	Alaska
S-35-7	Henry S. Monroe	'33	23	zero	Alaska
S-40-9	Francis M. Gambacorta	'35	30	zero	Alaska
S-41-8	Irvin S. Hartman	'33	39	zero	Alaska
SEPTEMBER					
S-28-7	Vincent A. Sisler, Jr.	'35	40	1/4,000	Alaska
S-42-5	Harley K. Nauman	'34	40	zero	Alaska
S-44-5	Francis E. Brown	'33	lost	zero	Alaska
S-46-4	Earl R. Crawford	'36	33	zero	Alaska
OCTOBER					
S-47-5	Frank E. Haylor	'36	28	zero	Alaska
NOVEMBER					
S-35-8	Robert B. Byrnes	'38	20	zero	Alaska
DECEMBER					
S-45-4	Robert H. Caldwell	'36	28	zero	Alaska
S-46-5	Gordon Campbell	'26	33	zero	Alaska
S-47-6	Frank E. Haylor	'36	26	zero	Alaska
			TOTALS:	9/34,700	4/13,062

* From Pearl Harbor to land commandos at Attu

SUBMARINE WAR PATROLS DEPARTING PEARL HARBOR, APRIL–AUGUST 1943

Boat, Patrol Number	Skipper and Class		Days	Ships/Tonnage Wartime Credit	Ships/Tonnage JANAC Credit	Area
APRIL						
Permit-8	Wreford G. Chapple	'30	49	2/15,000	zero	Truk
Plunger-6	Raymond H. Bass	'31	29	3/24,100	2/15,000	Marshalls
Pogy-1	George H. Wales	'29	51	2/9,100	2/3,300	Empire
Runner-2	Frank W. Fenno	'25	35	zero	zero	East China Sea
Salmon-6	Nicholas J. Nicholas	'32	51	zero	zero	Empire *
Sawfish-2	Eugene T. Sands	'30	53	zero	1/3,000	Empire
Scamp-2	Walter G. Ebert	'30	46	1/15,600	1/7,000	→Brisbane
Scorpion-1	William N. Wylie	'30	33	3/13,100	2/8,300	Empire *
Seal-6	Harry B. Dodge	'30	50	1/10,200	1/7,354	Palau
Seawolf-8	Royce L. Gross	'30	30	3/13,100	2/5,300	East China Sea
Skipjack-6	Howard F. Stoner	'32	45	zero	zero	Marshalls
Snook-1	Charles O. Triebel	'29	42	3/12,000	3/8,600	East China Sea *
Steelhead-1	David L. Whelchel	'30	49	zero	zero	Empire *
Stingray-7	Otis J. Earle	'30	46	1/7,500	1/8,156	East China Sea *
Sunfish-3	Richard W. Peterson	'31	57	zero	zero	Palau
Trigger-5	Roy S. Benson	'29	53	1/8,200	1/2,000	Empire
Wahoo-5	Dudley W. Morton	'30	26	3/24,700	3/10,500	Empire †
MAY						
Finback-5	John A. Tyree, Jr.	'33	44	4/23,200	3/13,000	→Fremantle
Hoe-1	Victor B. McCrea	'32	45	1/9,500	zero	Palau
Pollack-7	Bafford E. Lewellen	'31	46	2/9,300	2/8,400	Marshalls
Runner-3	Joseph H. Bourland	'33	lost	zero	zero	Empire †
Sailfish-8	John R. Moore	'29	49	zero	2/5,800	Empire

930

Sargo-7	Edward S. Carmick	'30	43	1/6,600	1/5,200	Truk
Saury-6	Anthony H. Dropp	'32	38	3/24,900	4/20,000	East China Sea
Scorpion-2	William N. Wylie	'30	48	zero	2/10,000	East China Sea
Sculpin-7	Lucius H. Chappell	'27	41	zero	zero	Empire
Seadragon-6	Royal L. Rutter	'30	43	zero	zero	Truk
Seawolf-9	Royce L. Gross	'30	56	1/4,300	1/4,700	East China Sea
Silversides-5	Creed C. Burlingame	'27	44	1/10,000	1/5,200	→Brisbane*
Tinosa-1	Lawrence R. Daspit	'27	47	zero	zero	Empire
Tunny-3	John A. Scott	'28	50	1/3,100	1/2,000	Marianas
Whale-4	Albert C. Burrows	'28	47	2/13,000	1/3,500	Empire

JUNE

Flying Fish-6	Frank T. Watkins	'22	55	1/8,700	1/2,820	East China Sea
Gunnel-2	John S. McCain, Jr.	'31	31	3/15,600	2/13,300	East China Sea
Gurnard-2	Charles H. Andrews	'30	43	3/15,600	1/2,000	Palau
Haddock-5	Roy M. Davenport	'33	41	1/10,900	1/5,500	Palau
Halibut-5	Philip H. Ross	'27	49	zero	zero	Truk
Harder-1	Samuel D. Dealey	'30	33	3/15,400	1/7,000	Empire
Jack-1	Thomas M. Dykers	'27	40	3/24,300	3/16,400	Empire
Lapon-1	Oliver G. Kirk	'29	41	zero	zero	Empire‡
Mingo-1	Ralph C. Lynch, Jr.	'29	57	zero	zero	Palau
Narwhal-5	Frank D. Latta	'32	42	zero	zero	Empire§
Permit-9	Wreford G. Chapple	'30	37	3/16,100	2/3,000	Empire‡‡
Plunger-7	Raymond H. Bass	'31	32	1/5,100	1/2,500	Empire‡‡
Pogy-2	George H. Wales	'29	53	1/15,600	1/7,500	Truk
Pompano-6	Willis M. Thomas	'31	52	zero	zero	Empire

* Laid mines
† Polar patrol—Kuriles and Hokkaido
‡ Sea of Japan
§ Supported Sea of Japan mission

SUBMARINE WAR PATROLS DEPARTING PEARL HARBOR, APRIL–AUGUST 1943 (*Cont.*)

Boat, Patrol Number	Skipper and Class		Days	Ships/Tonnage Wartime Credit	JANAC Credit	Area
Porpoise-6	Carter L. Bennett	'33	36	2/17,300	1/3,000	Marshalls
Sawfish-3	Eugene T. Sands	'30	41	3/25,600	1/720	East China Sea
Seal-7	Harry B. Dodge	'30	30	zero	zero	Empire
Searaven-7	Hiram Cassedy	'31	43	zero	zero	Marianas
Snook-2	Charles O. Triebel	'29	40	1/17,600	2/11,000	East China Sea
Spearfish-7	George A. Sharp	'29	57	zero	zero	Truk
Steelhead-2	David L. Whelchel	'30	47	1/4,800	zero	Truk
Stingray-8	Otis J. Earle	'30	50	zero	zero	→Brisbane
Sturgeon-7	Herman A. Pieczentkowski	'30	51	zero	zero	Empire
S-38-9	Cassius D. Rhymes	'35	30	zero	zero	→Brisbane
JULY						
Paddle-1	Robert H. Rice	'27	54	1/5,500	1/5,248	Empire
Pike-8	Louis D. McGregor, Jr.	'30	50	1/5,000	1/2,000	Marianas
Sailfish-9	William R. Lefavour	'31	51	zero	zero	East China Sea
Salmon-7	Nicholas J. Nicholas	'32	40	2/11,100	1/2,500	Empire †
Saury-7	Anthony H. Dropp	'30	30	zero	zero	Empire
Sculpin-8	Lucius H. Chappell	'27	54	1/4,500	1/3,183	East China Sea
Seadragon-7	Royal L. Rutter	'30	43	zero	zero	Marshalls
Skipjack-7	Howard F. Stoner	'32	49	zero	zero	Empire
Snapper-7	Merrill K. Clementson	'33	54	2/10,400	1/860	Truk
Sunfish-4	Richard W. Peterson	'31	60	3/29,100	1/2,000	East China Sea
Tarpon-8	Thomas L. Wogan	'30	40	1/1,000	zero	Empire
Tinosa-2	Lawrence R. Daspit	'27	27	zero	zero	Truk

932

Tullibee-1	Charles F. Brindupke	'32	50	1/7,000	1/4,000	Truk
Whale-5	Albert C. Burrows	'28	46	1/10,000	1/7,149	East China Sea
Swordfish-8	Frank M. Parker	'32	57	1/7,000	2/6,000	Palau
Pollack-8	Bafford E. Lewellen	'31	47	zero	2/7,000	Empire
Kingfish-4	Vernon L. Lowrance	'30	56	zero	zero	→Fremantle
AUGUST						
Halibut-6	Ignatius J. Galantin	'33	28	2/9,700	2/9,800	Empire
Harder-2	Samuel D. Dealey	'30	46	4/25,300	5/15,272	Empire
Hoe-2	Victor B. McCrea	'32	59	zero	zero	Truk
Narwhal-6	Frank D. Latta	'32	31	1/4,500	1/4,200	→Fremantle
Pargo-1	Ian C. Eddy	'30	49	4/27,600	zero	East China Sea
Permit-10	Carter L. Bennett	'33	32	3/27,700	zero	Marshalls
Plunger-8	Raymond H. Bass	'31	30	2/9,000	3/10,500	Empire ‡
Pompano-7	Willis M. Thomas	'31	lost	zero	2/8,500	Empire
Sargo-8	Edward S. Carmick	'30	46	zero	zero	Truk
Seahorse-1	Donald McGregor	'26	55	zero	zero	Palau
Seal-8	Harry B. Dodge	'30	50	zero	zero	Empire †
Searaven-8	Hiram Cassedy	'31	47	zero	zero	Empire
Seawolf-10	Royce L. Gross	'30	32	2/15,300	3/13,000	East China Sea
Snook-3	Charles O. Triebel	'29	52	2/12,400	2/10,000	East China Sea
Spearfish-8	Joseph W. Williams, Jr.	'33	47	2/12,600	zero	Empire
Sturgeon-8	Charlton L. Murphy, Jr.	'32	59	zero	zero	Empire
Tunny-4	John A. Scott	'28	34	zero	zero	Palau
Wahoo-6	Dudley W. Morton	'30	27	zero	zero	Empire ‡
			TOTALS:	101/683,000	86/348,264	

† Polar patrol—Kuriles and Hokkaido
‡ Sea of Japan

SUBMARINE WAR PATROLS DEPARTING BRISBANE, JUNE–DECEMBER 1943

Boat, Patrol Number	Skipper and Class	Days	Ships/Tonnage Wartime Credit	JANAC Credit	Area
JUNE					
Albacore-5	Oscar E. Hagberg '31	45	zero	zero	Bismarck
Drum-6	Bernard F. McMahon '31	49	1/8,700	1/5,000	Bismarck
Grouper-6	Martin P. Hottel '27	46	zero	zero	Bismarck
Peto-2	William T. Nelson '30	53	1/2,000	zero	Bismarck
Scamp-3	Walter G. Ebert '30	47	1/2,300	1/2,000	Bismarck
JULY					
Balao-1	Richard H. Crane '31	51	zero	zero	Bismarck
Growler-6	Arnold F. Schade '33	53	zero	zero	Bismarck
Pompon-1	Earle C. Hawk '28	43	1/6,600	1/5,871	Bismarck
Silversides-6	John S. Coye '33	53	zero	zero	Bismarck
Greenling-7	James D. Grant '30	51	zero	zero	→Pearl Harbor
S-31-7	Robert F. Sellars '34	21	zero	zero	Bismarck
AUGUST					
Albacore-6	Oscar E. Hagberg '31	26	1/4,200	1/2,600	Bismarck
Grouper-7	Martin P. Hottel '27	47	zero	zero	→Pearl Harbor
Guardfish-6	Norvell G. Ward '35	70	2/13,000	1/5,460	Bismarck
Drum-7	Bernard F. McMahon '31	51	3/12,900	1/1,334	Bismarck
Stingray-9	Otis J. Earle '30	50	zero	zero	→Pearl Harbor
S-31-8	Robert F. Sellars '34	27	zero	zero	Bismarck
SEPTEMBER					
Peto-3	William T. Nelson '30	51	2/10,500	2/10,000	Bismarck
Scamp-4	Walter G. Ebert '30	30	2/14,600	1/8,600	Bismarck

OCTOBER					
Albacore-7	Oscar E. Hagberg	'31	54	1/9,000	1/4,700	Bismarck
Balao-2	Richard H. Crane	'31	43	1/5,000	zero	Bismarck
Growler-7	Arnold F. Schade	'33	35	zero	zero	→Pearl Harbor
Scamp-5	Walter G. Ebert	'30	35	1/6,500	1/6,400	Bismarck
Silversides-7	John S. Coye	'33	36	4/22,100	4/15,000	→Pearl Harbor
Blackfish-6	John F. Davidson	'29	47	1/4,500	zero	Bismarck
NOVEMBER					
Gato-7	Robert J. Foley	'27	54	3/21,100	2/8,544	Bismarck
Peto-4	William T. Nelson	'30	54	1/8,200	1/2,345	Bismarck
Ray-1	Brooks J. Harral	'32	24	2/14,300	1/2,562	Bismarck
Raton-1	James W. Davis	'30	24	3/18,700	3/18,000	Bismarck
Drum-8	Delbert F. Williamson	'27	34	1/11,900	1/11,621	→Pearl Harbor
DECEMBER					
Albacore-8	James W. Blanchard	'27	59	2/6,800	2/4,500	→Pearl Harbor
Balao-3	Cyrus C. Cole	'35	38	zero	zero	Bismarck
Guardfish-7	Norvell G. Ward	'35	54	2/11,900	2/11,500	→Pearl Harbor
Scamp-6	Walter G. Ebert	'30	52	1/10,000	1/10,000	Bismarck
Blackfish-7	John F. Davidson	'29	50	1/6,000	1/2,000	Bismarck
TOTALS:				38/230,800	29/138,037	

SUBMARINE WAR PATROLS DEPARTING FREMANTLE, AUGUST–DECEMBER 1943

Boat, Patrol Number	Skipper and Class	Days	Ships/Tonnage Wartime Credit	Ships/Tonnage JANAC Credit	Area
AUGUST					
Billfish-1 *	Frederic C. Lucas Jr. '30	59	zero	zero	South China Sea
Bowfin-1 *	Joseph H. Willingham '26	57	3/23,900	1/8,120	South China Sea
Gar-9	George W. Lautrup, Jr. '34	37	1/4,000	1/1,000	Celebes
Puffer-1 *	Marvin J. Jensen '31	54	1/5,300	zero	Makassar Strait
Trout-10	Albert H. Clark '33	54	3/15,000	3/12,542	→Pearl Harbor
Tuna-8 *	Arnold H. Holtz '31	54	zero	zero	South China Sea
SEPTEMBER					
Bluefish-1 *	George E. Porter '32	25	4/16,200	2/3,822	South China Sea
Bonefish-1 *	Thomas W. Hogan '31	45	6/40,200	3/24,206	South China Sea
Cisco-1 *	James W. Coe '30	lost	zero	zero	South China Sea
Kingfish-5 †	Vernon L. Lowrance '30	52	2/19,100	1/3,365	South China Sea
Pompon-2 *	Earle C. Hawk '28	55	zero	zero	South China Sea
Rasher-1 *	Edward S. Hutchinson '26	61	4/21,300	4/8,894	Celebes
OCTOBER					
Bluefish-2	George E. Porter '32	32	3/22,800	2/11,390	South China Sea
Cod-1 *	James C. Dempsey '31	63	1/7,100	zero	South China Sea
Crevalle-1 *	Henry G. Munson '32	49	4/29,800	1/6,783	Manila
Narwhal-7	Frank D. Latta '32	31	zero	zero	special mission
Capelin-1 *	Elliott E. Marshall '31	lost	2/7,400	1/3,000	Makassar Strait
NOVEMBER					
Billfish-2	Frederic C. Lucas, Jr. '30	53	zero	zero	South China Sea

936

Bonefish-2	Thomas W. Hogan	'31	27	3/16,600	2/7,367	Celebes
Bowfin-2	Walter T. Griffith	'34	39	9/70,900	5/26,458	South China Sea
Narwhal-8	Frank D. Latta	'32	23	1/4,000	1/834	special mission
Pompon-3 †	Earle C. Hawk	'28	60	zero	zero	South China Sea
Puffer-2	Frank G. Selby	'33	49	1/1,500	2/7,527	South China Sea
Tuna-9	James T. Hardin	'29	56	zero	1/5,484	→Pearl Harbor
DECEMBER						
Bluefish-3 †	George E. Porter	'32	27	2/20,100	2/11,000	South China Sea
Cabrilla-2 †	Douglas T. Hammond	'31	52	1/4,100	1/2,700	South China Sea
Crevalle-2 †	Henry G. Munson	'32	60	3/19,900	1/2,552	South China Sea
Kingfish-6	Herbert L. Jukes	'32	42	3/22,300	3/14,571	→Pearl Harbor
Rasher-2 †	Willard R. Laughon	'33	36	1/7,200	1/7,251	South China Sea
Raton-2 *	James W. Davis	'30	45	2/18,000	1/5,578	Celebes
Ray-2 *	Brooks J. Harral	'32	24	2/14,300	2/8,696	Celebes
Gar-10	George W. Lautrup, Jr.	'34	55	3/21,500	2/9,000	→Pearl Harbor
			TOTALS:	65/432,500	43/192,140	

* From Brisbane via Darwin
† Laid minefield

SUBMARINE WAR PATROLS DEPARTING PEARL HARBOR, SEPTEMBER–DECEMBER 1943

Boat, Patrol Number	Skipper and Class	Days	Ships/Tonnage Wartime Credit	JANAC Credit	Area
SEPTEMBER					
Barb-6	John R. Waterman '27	53	1/8,000	zero	East China Sea
Cabrilla-1	Douglas T. Hammond '31	54	zero	zero	→Fremantle
Cero-1	David C. White '27	52	1/6,000	zero	East China Sea
Grayback-8 ‡	John A. Moore '32	45	2½/18,700	2½/19,000	East China Sea
Gudgeon-9	William S. Post, Jr. '30	37	2/15,000	1/3,158	Marianas
Gurnard-3	Charles H. Andrews '30	52	2/18,000	2/11,000	East China Sea
Gato-6	Robert J. Foley '27	50	zero	zero	→Brisbane
Haddock-6	Roy M. Davenport '33	27	3/39,200	zero	Truk
Jack-2	Thomas M. Dykers '27	30	zero	zero	Empire
Lapon-2	Lowell T. Stone '29	39	1/2,900	1/2,000	Empire
Mingo-2	Ralph C. Lynch, Jr. '29	53	zero	zero	Truk
Muskallunge-1	Willard A. Saunders '27	48	zero	zero	Palau
Nautilus-6 *	William D. Irvin '27	31	zero	zero	Gilberts
Pogy-3	George H. Wales '29	49	1/6,600	1/7,000	Palau
Salmon-8	Nicholas J. Nicholas '32	51	zero	zero	Empire
Sawfish-4	Eugene T. Sands '30	36	zero	zero	Empire [1]
Seadragon-8	Royal L. Rutter '30	42	1/8,200	zero	Marshalls
Shad-6 ‡	Edgar J. MacGregor '30	58	1½/13,400	½/4,500	East China Sea
Skate-1 *	Eugene B. McKinney '27	31	zero	zero	Wake
Skipjack-8 *	George G. Molumphy '31	43	zero	zero	Marshalls
Steelhead-3 ‡	David L. Whelchel '30	72	zero	½/4,000	Palau
Tinosa-3 ‡	Lawrence R. Daspit '27	23	1/10,500	½/4,000	Palau

938

Trigger-6	Robert E. Dornin	'35	29	5/40,000	4/27,095	East China Sea
Tullibee-2	Charles F. Brindupke	'32	52	1/6,000	1/5,866	East China Sea
Wahoo-7	Dudley W. Morton	'30	lost	1/7,100	4/13,000	Empire [1]

OCTOBER

Dace-1	Joseph F. Enright	'33	49	zero	zero	Empire
Flying Fish-7	Glynn R. Donaho	'27	34	1/7,000	1/6,500	Palau
Gudgeon-10	William S. Post, Jr.	'30	41	3/13,700	2/7,644	East China Sea
Haddock-7	Roy M. Davenport	'33	27	5/32,600	zero	Truk
Halibut-7	Ignatius J. Galantin	'33	37	1/3,500	1/4,653	Empire
Harder-3	Samuel D. Dealey	'30	31	5/24,800	3/15,273	Marianas
Paddle-2 †	Robert H. Rice	'27	58	zero	zero	Marshalls
Pargo-2	Ian C. Eddy	'30	40	2/17,700	2/7,810	Marianas
Sargo-9	Philip W. Garnett	'33	55	2/15,900	2/6,419	East China Sea
Saury-8	Anthony H. Dropp	'32	53	zero	zero	Truk
Scorpion-3	Maximilian G. Schmidt	'32	53	zero	zero	Marianas
Seahorse-2	Slade D. Cutter	'35	53	6/48,700	5/27,579	East China Sea
Seawolf-11	Royce L. Gross	'30	53	2/14,000	2/6,399	East China Sea
Snapper-8	Merrill K. Clementson	'33	56	3/20,300	1/4,575	Empire
Sunfish-5	Richard W. Peterson	'31	59	zero	zero	East China Sea
Snook-4	Charles O. Triebel	'29	38	2/14,500	2/8,440	Marianas
Swordfish-9	Frank L. Barrows	'35	42	zero	zero	Empire
Tarpon-9	Thomas L. Wogan	'30	34	1/10,000	1/German	Empire
Tautog-8	William B. Sieglaff	'31	41	1/3,800	1/100	Palau
Trigger-7	Robert E. Dornin	'35	49	6/44,700	4/15,114	East China Sea
Tinosa-4	Lawrence R. Daspit	'27	49	4/18,500	4/18,000	→Fremantle

* Special mission
† Galvanic
‡ Shared credit: *Grayback* and *Shad*, *Steelhead* and *Tinosa*

[1] Sea of Japan

SUBMARINE WAR PATROLS DEPARTING PEARL HARBOR, SEPTEMBER–DECEMBER 1943 (*Cont.*)

Boat, Patrol Number	Skipper and Class	Days	Ships/Tonnage Wartime Credit	Ships/Tonnage JANAC Credit	Area
NOVEMBER					
Apogon-1 †	Walter P. Schoeni '31	45	1/3,000	1/3,000	Truk
Aspro-1	Harry C. Stevenson '31	39	3/25,600	zero	East China Sea
Corvina-1 †	Roderick S. Rooney '29	lost	1/1,600	zero	Truk
Flying Fish-8	Robert D. Risser '34	59	2/15,800	2/18,784	East China Sea
Gunnel-3	John S. McCain, Jr. '31	51	1/9,500	1/4,086	Empire
Gurnard-4	Charles H. Andrews '30	40	2/11,000	3/14,000	Empire
Herring-6	Raymond W. Johnson '30	56	4/30,000	2/10,000	East China Sea
Muskallunge-2	Michael P. Russillo '27	56	1/8,200	zero	Palau
Nautilus-7 †	William D. Irvin '27	27	zero	zero	Gilberts
Plunger-9 †	Raymond H. Bass '31	42	zero	zero	Marshalls
Pogy-4	Ralph M. Metcalf '35	29	3/19,500	2/9,860	Palau
Sailfish-10	Robert E. M. Ward '35	49	3/35,700	3/29,571	Empire
Sawfish-5	Eugene T. Sands '30	48	1/6,000	1/3,267	Bonins
Sculpin-9 †	Fred Connaway '32	lost	zero	zero	Truk
Seal-9 †	Harry B. Dodge '30	42	zero	zero	Marshalls
Searaven-9 †	Melvin H. Dry '34	49	1/10,100	1/10,000	Truk
Skate-2	Eugene B. McKinney '27	54	1/6,400	1/6,429	Truk
Spearfish-9 †	Joseph W. Williams, Jr. '33	41	zero	zero	Marshalls
Thresher-10 †	Harry Hull '32	29	1/5,600	1/4,862	Truk
DECEMBER					
Archerfish-1	George W. Kehl '32	53	1/9,000	zero	East China Sea
Balfish-1	Wayne R. Merrill '34	50	2/15,700	1/5,486	Empire

940

Darter-1	William S. Stovall, Jr.	'29	66	zero	→Brisbane
Finback-7	John A. Tyree, Jr.	'33	58	1/10,200	1/10,000 East China Sea
Grayback-9	John A. Moore	'32	33	6/24,000	4/10,000 East China Sea
Greenling-8	James D. Grant	'30	39	1/1,900	1/2,000 Truk
Haddo-4	John Corbus	'31	53	zero	zero →Fremantle
Hake-3	John C. Broach	'27	55	3/16,500	3/19,384 →Fremantle
Halibut-8	Ignatius J. Galantin	'33	50	zero	zero Marianas
Salmon-9	Nicholas J. Nicholas	'32	59	zero	zero Empire
Saury-9	Anthony H. Dropp	'32	62	zero	zero East China Sea
Seadragon-9	Royal L. Rutter	'30	46	1/7,400	zero Truk
Seawolf-12 ‡	Royce L. Gross	'30	36	4/24,000	4½/25,793 East China Sea
Silversides-8	John S. Coye	'33	42	3/18,500	3/7,192 Palau
Steelhead-4	David L. Whelchel	'30	61	1/9,000	1/6,795 Empire
Sturgeon-9	Charlton L. Murphy, Jr.	'32	55	3/19,200	2/8,603 Empire
Swordfish-10	Karl G. Hensel	'23	40	2/15,200	3/12,543 Empire
Tarpon-10 *	Thomas B. Oakley, Jr.	'34	39	zero	zero Marshalls
Tautog-9	William B. Sieglaff	'31	49	2/9,700	2/6,000 Empire
Thresher-11	Duncan C. MacMillan	'26	54	4/26,300	4/14,523 East China Sea
Tullibee-3	Charles F. Brindupke	'32	58	1/2,500	1/549 Marianas
Whale-6 ‡	Albert C. Burrows	'28	44	2/14,000	1½/8,322 Bonins
Cero-2	Edward F. Dissette	'34	29	zero	zero →Brisbane
Haddock-8	John P. Roach	'32	53	zero	zero Marianas
			TOTALS:	130/900,400	99/475,981

* Special mission
† Galvanic
‡ *Seawolf* and *Whale* shared credit

941

SUBMARINE WAR PATROLS DEPARTING PEARL HARBOR, JANUARY–APRIL 1944

Boat, Patrol Number	Skipper and Class		Days	Ships/Tonnage Wartime Credit	JANAC Credit	Area
JANUARY						
Angler-1	Robert I. Olsen	'33	25	1/8,700	1/890	Marianas
Apogon-2	Walter P. Schoeni	'31	55	2/24,000	zero	Marianas
Dace-2	Bladen D. Claggett	'35	48	zero	zero	→Brisbane
Darter-1	William S. Stovall, Jr.	'29	66	zero	zero	→Brisbane
Flasher-1	Reuben T. Whitaker	'34	53	4/26,500	4/10,528	→Fremantle
Grayback-10	John A. Moore	'32	lost	4/20,800	3/16,689	East China Sea
Gudgeon-11	William S. Post, Jr.	'30	49	1/10,100	zero	East China Sea
Hoe-3	Victor B. McCrea	'32	38	4/29,500	1/10,526	→Fremantle
Jack-3	Thomas M. Dykers	'27	51	7/53,500	4/20,441	→Fremantle
Nautilus-8	William D. Irvin	'27	57	1/6,100	1/6,100	Marianas
Permit-11	Carter L. Bennett	'33	74	zero	zero	Truk
Plunger-10	Raymond H. Bass	'31	55	4/22,500	3/9,600	Empire
Pogy-5	Ralph M. Metcalf	'35	54	4/22,400	5/21,150	East China Sea
Robalo-1	Stephen H. Ambruster	'28	57	zero	zero	→Fremantle
Sargo-10	Philip W. Garnett	'33	46	1/7,000	2/11,800	Palau
Scorpion-4	Maximilian G. Schmidt	'32	lost	zero	zero	East China Sea
Seahorse-3	Slade D. Cutter	'35	41	5/30,900	5/20,900	Palau
Seal-10	Harry B. Dodge	'30	50	zero	zero	Truk
Searaven-10	Melvin H. Dry	'34	47	zero	zero	Truk
Skipjack-9	George G. Molumphy	'31	57	2/8,400	2/8,200	Marianas
Snook-5	Charles O. Triebel	'29	60	5/26,800	5/21,046	East China Sea
Spearfish-10	Joseph W. Williams, Jr.	'33	43	4/21,800	1/3,600	Luzon Strait
Sunfish-6	Edward E. Shelby	'33	53	2/30,400	2/9,400	Marianas
Tambor-9	Russell Kefauver	'33	60	4/30,100	4/18,400	East China Sea

942

Tang-1	Richard H. O'Kane	'34	41	5/42,000	5/21,400	Marianas
Trigger-8	Robert E. Dornin	'35	55	2/11,800	2/12,443	Truk
FEBRUARY						
Angler-2	Robert I. Olsen	'33	53	zero	zero	→Fremantle
Aspro-2	William A. Stevenson	'34	54	1/2,200	1/2,200	Truk
Batfish-2	Wayne R. Merrill	'34	53	zero	zero	Empire
Burrfish-1	William B. Perkins, Jr.	'32	50	zero	zero	Truk
Flying Fish-9	Robert D. Risser	'34	49	3/10,500	3/9,928	East China Sea
Growler-8	Arnold F. Schade	'33	55	zero	zero	East China Sea
Gunnel-4	John S. McCain, Jr.	'31	60	zero	zero	→Fremantle
Herring-7	David Zabriskie, Jr.	'36	54	zero	zero	Empire
Kingfish-7	Herbert L. Jukes	'32	49	zero	zero	Marianas
Lapon-3	Lowell T. Stone	'29	47	4/32,700	3/19,500	→Fremantle
Mingo-3	Joseph J. Staley	'34	73	zero	zero	→Brisbane
Picuda-1	Albert Raborn	'34	49	3/24,400	3/10,000	Truk
Pollack-9	Bafford E. Lewellen	'31	43	4/21,400	3/5,400	Empire
Rock-1	John J. Flachsenhar	'35	35	zero	zero	East China Sea
Sandlance-1	Malcolm E. Garrison	'32	44	5/28,300	4/16,056	Polar circuit
Silversides-9	John S. Coye	'33	52	2/7,500	1/1,900	→Fremantle
Skate-3	William P. Gruner	'35	42	1/7,000	1/7,000	Palau
Tautog-10	William B. Sieglaff	'31	28	5/17,700	4/11,277	Polar circuit
Trout-11	Albert H. Clark	'33	lost	1/9,200	1/7,100	East China Sea
Tunny-5	John A. Scott	'28	44	1/2,100	1/2,200	→Brisbane
MARCH						
Archerfish-2	George W. Kehl	'32	42	zero	zero	Palau
Bang-1	Anton R. Gallaher	'33	46	3/20,200	3/10,700	Luzon Strait
Barb-7	John R. Waterman	'27	55	1/2,200	1/2,200	Marianas
Finback-8	John A. Tyree, Jr.	'33	55	zero	zero	Truk
Gar-11	George W. Lautrup, Jr.	'34	49	zero	zero	Palau

SUBMARINE WAR PATROLS DEPARTING PEARL HARBOR, JANUARY–APRIL 1944 (*Cont.*)

Boat, Patrol Number	Skipper and Class		Days	Wartime Credit	JANAC Credit	Area
Golet-1	Philip H. Ross	'27	46	zero	zero	Polar circuit
Greenling-9	James D. Grant	'30	53	zero	zero	Marianas
Grouper-8	Frederick H. Wahlig	'33	59	zero	zero	Luzon Strait
Haddock-9	John P. Roach	'32	62	1/1,000	zero	Empire
Halibut-9	Ignatius J. Galantin	'33	58	2/4,800	3/5,550	Empire
Harder-4	Samuel D. Dealey	'30	47	2/5,300	2/9,000	→Fremantle
Paddle-3	Byron H. Nowell	'35	54	2/10,800	2/9,700	→Fremantle
Pampanito-1	Paul E. Summers	'36	54	zero	zero	Marianas
Parche-1	Lawson P. Ramage	'31	56	3/23,900	2/11,700	Luzon Strait
Pargo-3	Ian C. Eddy	'30	60	2/12,200	1/758	→Fremantle
Seahorse-4	Slade D. Cutter	'35	56	4/25,700	5/19,374	→Brisbane
Searaven-11	Melvin H. Dry	'34	45	2/6,500	zero	Bonins
Snapper-9	William W. Walker	'34	57	zero	zero	Bonins
Steelhead-5	David L. Whelchel	'30	62	zero	zero	East China Sea
Stingray-10	Sam C. Loomis, Jr.	'35	54	1/8,600	1/3,900	Marianas
Swordfish-11	Keats E. Montross	'35	46	zero	zero	Marianas
Tang-2	Richard H. O'Kane	'34	61	zero	zero	Palau
Thresher-12	Duncan C. MacMillan	'26	51	zero	zero	Truk
Tinosa-6	Donald F. Weiss	'29	46	4/31,200	2/12,900	Luzon Strait
Trigger-9	Frederick J. Harlfinger II	'35	58	5/33,200	1/11,700	Palau
Tullibee-4	Charles F. Brindupke	'32	lost	zero	zero	Palau
Whale-7	James B. Grady	'33	57	1/5,000	1/5,400	East China Sea
APRIL						
Apogon-3	Walter P. Schoeni	'31	49	zero	zero	Empire
Aspro-3 *	William A. Stevenson	'34	54	2/11,500	1½/8,650	→Fremantle

944

Balao-5	M. Ramirez DeArellano	'35	48	zero	Palau
Burrfish-2	William B. Perkins, Jr.	'32	52	1/5,000	Empire
Drum-9	Delbert F. Williamson	'27	50	zero	Bonins
Gabilan-1	Karl R. Wheland	'31	46	zero	Marianas
Gato-9	Richard M. Farrell	'35	48	zero	Truk
Guavina-1	Carl Tiedeman	'33	52	3/19,500	Bonins
Gudgeon-12	Robert A. Bonin	'36	lost	zero	Marianas
Gurnard-5	Charles H. Andrews	'30	56	4/26,900	→Fremantle
Muskallunge-3	Michael P. Russillo	'27	65	zero	→Fremantle
Perch II-1	Blish C. Hills	'33	35	zero	Luzon Strait
Permit-12	Donald A. Scherer	'34	42	1/2,200	Truk
Peto-6	Paul Van Leunen, Jr.	'34	52	zero	Luzon Strait
Pogy-6	Ralph M. Metcalf	'35	52	3/12,900	Empire
Rock-2	John J. Flachsenhar	'35	55	zero	Empire
Salmon-10	Harley K. Nauman	'34	51	zero	Palau
Sandlance-2	Malcolm E. Garrison	'32	35	4/22,300	→Fremantle
Sargo-11	Philip W. Garnett	'33	49	1/5,000	Empire
Sawfish-6	Alan B. Banister	'28	49	1/5,100	Empire
Seadragon-10	James H. Ashley, Jr.	'34	54	zero	Empire
Skate-4	William P. Gruner, Jr.	'35	50	zero	Bonins
Spearfish-11	Joseph W. Williams, Jr.	'33	58	2/14,900	East China Sea
Sturgeon-10	Charlton L. Murphy, Jr.	'32	50	3/15,400	Bonins
Tambor-10	Russell Kefauver	'33	54	1/6,700	Marianas
Tautog-11	Thomas S. Baskett	'35	35	4/20,500	Polar circuit
Tilefish-1	Roger M. Keithly	'35	54	zero	Empire
Tuna-10	James T. Hardin	'29	56	zero	Palau
Tunny-6	John A. Scott	'28	66	1/5,200	Marianas
Shifted to Australia					
Nautilus	George A. Sharp	'29	TOTALS:	156/960,000	124½/524,477

* Shared ½ credit with *Bowfin* coming from Fremantle

SUBMARINE WAR PATROLS DEPARTING AUSTRALIA, JANUARY–MARCH 1944

Boat, Patrol Number	Skipper and Class	Days	Ships/Tonnage Wartime Credit	JANAC Credit	Area
January—Fremantle					
Billfish-3	Vernon C. Turner '33	66	1/1,000	zero	Indochina
Bonefish-3	Thomas W. Hogan '31	60	2/21,300	zero	South China Sea
Bowfin-3 *	Walter T. Griffith '34	28	3/12,600	1/4,408	Makassar
Cod-2	James C. Dempsey '31	62	2/9,900	2/9,823	Halmahera
Narwhal-9	Frank D. Latta '32	29	zero	zero	special mission
Tinosa-5	Donald F. Weiss '29	55	3/16,900	4/15,600	→Pearl Harbor
Redfin-1 †	Robert D. King '31	45	1/1,700	zero	South China Sea
January—Brisbane					
None					
February—Fremantle					
Bluefish-4	Charles M. Henderson '34	58	1/7,500	1/10,500	South China Sea
Bowfin-4	Walter T. Griffith '34	33	3/21,000	3/15,000	Celebes
Cabrilla-3	William C. Thompson, Jr. '35	56	zero	zero	Sunda Strait
Haddo-5	Chester W. Nimitz, Jr. '36	54	zero	zero	Makassar
Narwhal-10	Frank D. Latta '32	33	zero	zero	special mission
Pompon-4	Stephen H. Gimber '35	50	zero	zero	→Pearl Harbor
Puffer-3	Frank G. Selby '33	61	1/15,100	1/15,100	South China Sea
Rasher-3	Willard R. Laughon '33	45	5/28,600	4/20,100	Celebes
Raton-3	James W. Davis '30	45	zero	zero	South China Sea
Ray-3 *	Brooks J. Harral '32	50	zero	zero	South China Sea
February—Brisbane					
Balao-4	Cyrus C. Cole '35	43	4/20,300	3/15,300	→Pearl Harbor
Cero-3	Edward F. Dissette '34	23	1/6,100	zero	Bismarck

946

Boat	Skipper and Class	Days	Ships/Tonnage Wartime Credit	JANAC Credit	Area
Gato-8	Robert J. Foley '27	60	3/17,300	2/6,070	→Pearl Harbor
Peto-5	Paul Van Leunen, Jr. '34	57	1/4,400	1/4,370	→Pearl Harbor
MARCH—FREMANTLE					
Hake-4	John C. Broach '27	42	2/20,400	1/5,174	South China Sea
Redfin-2	Marshall H. Austin '35	44	5/30,200	3/10,300	Celebes
MARCH—BRISBANE					
Bashaw-1	Richard E. Nichols '34	60	zero	zero	Davao
Blackfish-8	Robert F. Sellars '34	80	zero	zero	→Pearl Harbor
Dace-3	Bladen D. Claggett '35	55	zero	zero	Davao
Darter-2	William S. Stovall '29	63	1/6,800	1/2,800	Davao
Flounder-1	Carl A. Johnson '29	54	zero	zero	Halmahera
Scamp-7	John C. Hollingsworth '31	51	zero	zero	→Pearl Harbor
		TOTALS:	39/241,100	27/134,745	

* Laid minefield
† Via Darwin

SUBMARINE WAR PATROLS DEPARTING AUSTRALIA, APRIL–JUNE 1944

Boat, Patrol Number	Skipper and Class	Days	Ships/Tonnage Wartime Credit	JANAC Credit	Area
APRIL—FREMANTLE					
Bonefish-4	Thomas W. Hogan '31	48	4/27,400	2/2,756	Celebes
Bowfin-5 *	John Corbus '30	58	1/6,500	½/2,250	→Pearl Harbor
Billfish-4	Vernon C. Turner '33	57	1/8,500	zero	→Pearl Harbor
Cod-3	James C. Dempsey '31	56	2/10,100	2/8,076	Manila
Crevalle-3	Francis D. Walker '35	54	2/26,400	2/17,771	South China Sea

*Shared ½ credit with *Aspro*

SUBMARINE WAR PATROLS DEPARTING AUSTRALIA, APRIL–JUNE 1944 (Cont.)

Boat, Patrol Number	Skipper and Class	Days	Ships/Tonnage Wartime Credit	JANAC Credit	Area
Flasher-2 *	Reuben T. Whitaker '34	54	3/12,600	3/6,709	South China Sea
Hoe-4	Victor B. McCrea '32	59	1/4,000	zero	South China Sea
Jack-4	Thomas M. Dykers '27	35	zero	1/5,425	Manila
Lapon-4	Lowell T. Stone '29	42	2/15,000	2/11,253	South China Sea
Puffer-4 *	Frank G. Selby '33	52	3/24,300	3/7,600	Manila
Rasher-4 *	Willard R. Laughon '33	55	4/24,400	4/10,900	Celebes
Ray-4	Brooks J. Harral '32	53	6/42,500	1/6,000	Celebes
Robalo-2	Manning M. Kimmel '35	51	1/7,500	zero	Indochina
Silversides-10	John S. Coye '33	47	5/23,600	6/14,141	→Pearl Harbor
APRIL—BRISBANE					
Bluegill-1	Eric L. Barr, Jr. '34	67	3/13,600	3/14,100	Davao
Cero-4	Edward F. Dissette '34	60	zero	1/2,800	Davao
Tunny-6	John A. Scott '28	66	1/5,200	1/5,000	→Pearl Harbor
MAY—FREMANTLE					
Angler-3 *	Robert I. Olsen '33	27	1/5,700	1/2,100	Sunda Strait
Bluefish-5 *	Charles M. Henderson '34	53	2/7,000	2/4,700	Celebes
Cabrilla-4	William C. Thompson, Jr. '35	34	1/8,500	1/8,360	Celebes
Gunnel-5 *	John S. McCain, Jr. '31	63	zero	zero	South China Sea
Haddo-6	Chester W. Nimitz, Jr. '36	59	zero	zero	Celebes
Hake-5	John C. Broach '27	50	3/14,500	3/13,375	Celebes
Harder-5	Samuel D. Dealey '30	45	5/8,500	3/6,500	Celebes
Narwhal-11	Jack C. Titus '33	33	zero	zero	special mission
Nautilus-9	George A. Sharp '29	13	zero	zero	special mission
Raton-4 *	James W. Davis '30	46	5/7,200	2/1,660	South China Sea
Redfin-3	Marshall H. Auston '35	47	2/16,100	2/8,000	Celebes

MAY—BRISBANE					
Bashaw-2	Richard E. Nichols	'34	50	1/5,700	1/6,440	Halmahera
JUNE—FREMANTLE					
Angler-4	Franklin G. Hess	'35	54	zero	zero	South China Sea
Bonefish-5	Lawrence L. Edge	'35	49	2/12,800	1/10,000	Sulu Sea
Crevalle-4 †	Francis D. Walker, Jr.	'35	50	3½/28,000	1½/10,950	South China Sea
Flasher-3 †	Reuben T. Whitaker	'34	49	6½/47,900	4½/24,949	South China Sea
Hoe-5	Victor B. McCrea	'32	55	zero	zero	Manila
Jack-5	Arthur E. Krapf	'34	39	4/25,000	3/15,748	Manila
Lapon-5	Lowell T. Stone	'29	42	3/18,000	2/6,560	South China Sea
Narwhal-12	Jack C. Titus	'33	27	zero	zero	special mission
Nautilus-10	George A. Sharp	'29	15	zero	zero	special mission
Paddle-4	Byron H. Nowell	'35	54	1/1,200	1/1,300	Celebes
Pargo-4	Ian C. Eddy	'30	57	1/6,600	1/5,236	Celebes
Robalo-3	Manning M. Kimmel	'35	lost	zero	zero	South China Sea
JUNE—BRISBANE					
Bream-1	Wreford G. Chapple	'30	29	zero	1/5,700	Davao
Cero-5	Edward F. Dissette	'34	56	1/8,000	1/6,500	Davao
Dace-4	Bladen D. Claggett	'35	60	2/3,200	1/1,100	Davao
Darter-3	David H. McClintock	'35	48	1/4,400	1/4,400	Davao
Flounder-2	James E. Stevens	'30	39	1/4,000	1/2,680	Davao
Mingo-4	Joseph J. Staley	'34	46	1/1,700	1/2,100	Celebes
S-47-7	Lloyd V. Young	'41	29	zero	zero	special mission
Seahorse-5	Slade D. Cutter	'35	47	6/37,000	4/11,000	→Pearl Harbor
			TOTALS:	92/522,600	70½/274,139	

* Surabaya air strike, May 17
† *Crevalle* and *Flasher* shared credit

SUBMARINE WAR PATROLS DEPARTING PEARL HARBOR, MAY–JUNE 1944

Boat, Patrol Number	Skipper and Class		Days	Ships/Tonnage Wartime Credit	JANAC Credit	Area
MAY						
Albacore-9	James W. Blanchard	'27	48	2/30,800	2/32,000	Philippine Sea
Archerfish-3	William H. Wright	'36	48	1/1,400	1/800	Bonins
Barb-8	Eugene B. Fluckey	'35	49	5/37,500	5/15,472	Polar circuit
Batfish-3	John K. Fyfe	'36	43	4/9,500	1/1,000	Empire
Finback-9	James L. Jordan	'33	50	zero	zero	Philippine Sea
Flier-1	John D. Crowley	'31	44	4/19,500	1/10,400	→Fremantle
Flying Fish-10	Robert D. Risser	'34	61	1/4,000	2/8,200	→Brisbane
Gar-12	George W. Lautrup, Jr.	'34	47	1/900	zero	Bonins
Golet-2	James S. Clark	'35	lost			Polar circuit
Grouper-9	Frederick H. Wahlig	'33	50	1/3,500	1/2,800	Empire
Growler-9	Thomas B. Oakley, Jr.	'34	64	1/10,000	1/2,000	Philippine Sea
Guitarro-1	Enrique D. Haskins	'33	51	3/21,200	2/3,100	→Fremantle
Herring-8	David Zabriskie, Jr.	'36	lost	3/8,200	4/9,960	Polar circuit
Kingfish-8	Herbert L. Jukes	'32	50	zero	zero	Bonins
Picuda-2*	Albert Raborn	'34	54	3/13,000	1½/2,786	Luzon Strait
Pilotfish-1	Robert H. Close	'34	49	zero	zero	Marianas
Pintado-1	Bernard A. Clarey	'34	46	4/31,000	3/13,200	Marianas
Pipefish-1	William N. Deragon	'34	52	zero	zero	Philippine Sea
Plunger-11	Edward J. Fahy	'34	56	zero	zero	Bonins
Pollack-10	Bafford E. Lewellen	'31	32	1/1,500	1/1,300	Empire
Pompon-5	Stephen H. Gimber	'35	50	1/2,300	1/742	Empire
Shark II-1	Edward N. Blakely	'34	32	4/32,200	4/21,672	Marianas
Snapper-10	William W. Walker	'34	56	zero	zero	Truk

Stingray-11	Sam C. Loomis, Jr.	'35	45	zero	Marianas
Swordfish-12	Keats E. Montross	'35	49	2/7,000	Bonins
Whale-8	James B. Grady	'33	50	zero	Empire

JUNE

Apogon-4	Walter P. Schoeni	'31	37	zero	Luzon Strait
Bang-2	Anton R. Gallaher	'33	58	3/24,000	Philippine Sea
Cavalla-1	Herman J. Kossler	'34	64	1/29,900	Philippine Sea
Cobia-1	Albert L. Becker	'34	49	5/24,300	Bonins
Drum-10	Maurice H. Rindskopf	'38	51	zero	Palau
Gabilan-2	Karl R. Wheland	'31	49	1/1,700	Empire
Guardfish-8	Norvell G. Ward	'35	46	8/58,200	Luzon Strait
Guavina-2	Carl Tiedeman	'33	42	1/5,800	→Brisbane
Hammerhead-1	John C. Martin	'34	65	1/8,700	→Fremantle
Pampanito-2	Paul E. Summers	'36	50	zero	Empire
Parche-2 †	Lawson P. Ramage	'31	59	4/34,300	Luzon Strait
Perch II-2	Blish C. Hills	'33	59	zero	Philippine Sea
Permit-13	Donald A. Scherer	'34	45	1/800	→Brisbane
Piranha-1	Harold E. Ruble	'33	52	2/17,400	Luzon Strait
Plaice-1	Clyde B. Stevens, Jr.	'30	52	4/18,900	Bonins
Pomfret-1	Frank C. Acker	'32	54	zero	Empire
Rock-3	John J. Flachsenhar	'35	52	zero	→Fremantle
Saury-10	Anthony H. Dropp	'32	54	zero	Philippine Sea
Sawfish-7	Alan B. Banister	'28	55	1/1,900	Luzon Strait
Sealion II-1	Eli T. Reich	'35	42	4/19,700	East China Sea
Seawolf-13	Richard B. Lynch	'35	32	zero	Palau

				zero	
				2/5,100	
				zero	
				zero	
				zero	
				1/30,000	
				3/11,455	
				zero	
				1/492	
				4/20,400	
				1/3000	
				zero	
				zero	
				2½/19,200	
				zero	
				zero	
				2/12,300	
				3/2,150	
				zero	
				zero	
				1/2,200	
				4/7,800	
				zero	

* Shared ½ credit with land-based aircraft
† Shared ½ credit with *Steelhead*

SUBMARINE WAR PATROLS DEPARTING PEARL HARBOR, MAY–JUNE 1944 (*Cont.*)

Boat, Patrol Number	Skipper and Class		Days	Ships/Tonnage Wartime Credit	JANAC Credit	Area
Skate-5	William P. Gruner, Jr.	'35	45	3/13,300	3/4,500	Polar circuit
Snook-6	George H. Browne	'34	51	zero	zero	Empire
Steelhead-6 *	David L. Whelchel	'30	60	2/14,000	2½/20,000	Luzon Strait
Sturgeon-11	Charlton L. Murphy, Jr.	'32	55	2/18,600	2/14,000	Empire
Sunfish-7	Edward E. Shelby	'33	40	4/18,500	2/8,800	Polar circuit
Tang-3	Richard H. O'Kane	'34	36	8/56,000	10/39,100	East China Sea
Tarpon-11	Saverio Filippone	'37	41	zero	zero	Truk
Tautog-12	Thomas S. Baskett	'35	48	2/4,300	2/2,787	Empire
Thresher-13	Duncan C. MacMillan	'26	44	6/35,100	2/7,700	Luzon Strait
Tilefish-2	Roger M. Keithly	'35	55	1/1,700	zero	Luzon Strait
Tinosa-7	Donald F. Weiss	'29	54	2/19,000	2/10,700	East China Sea
			TOTALS:	107/659,600	80½/348,229	

* Shared ½ credit with *Parche*

SUBMARINE WAR PATROLS DEPARTING PEARL HARBOR, JULY–AUGUST 1944

Boat, Patrol Number	Skipper and Class	Days	Ships/Tonnage Wartime Credit	Ships/Tonnage JANAC Credit	Area
JULY					
Balao-6	Marion Ramirez DeArellano '35	48	zero	zero	Palau
Barbel-1	Robert A. Keating, Jr. '33	36	4/32,900	3/5,170	Empire
Billfish-5	Vernon C. Turner '33	65	zero	zero	Empire
Bowfin-6	John Corbus '30	59	9/26,700	1/6,754	Empire
Burrfish-3	William B. Perkins, Jr. '32	46	zero	zero	Palau
Croaker-1	John E. Lee '30	43	4/17,600	3/13,900	East China Sea
Gato-10	Richard M. Farrell '35	49	zero	zero	Bonins
Greenling-10	John D. Gerwick '35	63	zero	zero	Luzon Strait
Hardhead-1	Fitzhugh McMaster '33	60	1/5,200	1/5,700	→Fremantle
Picuda-3	Glynn R. Donaho '27	66	5/20,000	4/11,270	Luzon Strait
Pilotfish-2	Robert H. Close '34	49	zero	zero	Bonins
Pintado-2	Bernard A. Clarey '34	54	5/46,300	2/24,663	East China Sea
Plunger-12	Edward J. Fahy '34	51	1/5,000	zero	Truk
Pollack-11	Everett H. Steinmetz '35	60	zero	zero	→Brisbane
Pompon-6	Stephen H. Gimber '35	46	1/4,300	1/2,200	Polar circuit
Redfish-1	Louis D. McGregor, Jr. '30	65	5/33,500	3/21,800	Luzon Strait
Ronquil-1	Henry S. Monroe '33	39	1/7,100	2/10,600	Formosa
Sailfish-11	Robert E. M. Ward '35	58	4/13,200	1/2,100	Luzon Strait
Shark II-2	Edward N. Blakely '34	50	zero	zero	Bonins
Spadefish-1	Gordon W. Underwood '32	59	6/40,000	6/31,500	Luzon Strait
Sterlet-1	Orme C. Robbins '34	53	4/14,200	zero	Bonins
Tambor-11	William J. Germershausen '35	47	1/4,000	1/2,300	Polar circuit

953

SUBMARINE WAR PATROLS DEPARTING PEARL HARBOR, JULY–AUGUST 1944 (Cont.)

Boat, Patrol Number	Skipper and Class		Days	Ships/Tonnage Wartime Credit	JANAC Credit	Area
Tuna-11	James T. Hardin	'29	51	zero	zero	Empire
Shifted to Australia						
Seawolf	Albert M. Bontier	'35				
AUGUST						
Albacore-10	James W. Blanchard	'27	49	3/11,000	2/1,050	Empire
Archerfish-4	William H. Wright	'36	53	zero	zero	Empire
Bang-3	Anton R. Gallaher	'33	32	5/31,400	3/4,200	Empire
Barb-9	Eugene B. Fluckey	'35	59	4/42,100	3/36,800	Luzon Strait
Barbero-1	Irvin S. Hartman	'33	55	zero	zero	→Fremantle
Batfish-4 *	John K. Fyfe	'36	41	2/2,900	1½/1,500	→Fremantle
Cavalla-2	Herman J. Kossler	'34	52	zero	zero	→Fremantle
Finback-10	Robert R. Williams, Jr.	'34	50	2/1,900	1/1,390	Bonins
Gar-13	Maurice Ferrara	'37	54	zero	zero	→Brisbane
Grouper-10	Frederick H. Wahlig	'33	62	zero	zero	Palau
Growler-10	Thomas B. Oakley, Jr.	'34	45	5/22,800	2/2,800	→Fremantle
Guardfish-9	Norvell G. Ward	'35	62	1/3,100	1/873	East China Sea
Hawkbill-1 †	Francis W. Scanland, Jr.	'34	53	2/11,500	1/5,075	→Fremantle
Baya-1	Arnold H. Holtz	'31	57	1/7,500	½/4,204	→Fremantle
Becuna-1	Henry D. Sturr	'33	56	2/10,000	½/871	→Fremantle
Pampanito-3	Paul E. Summers	'36	42	3/23,600	2/15,600	Luzon Strait
Pipefish-2	William N. Deragon	'34	52	1/4,000	1/1,000	Empire
Piranha-2	Harold E. Ruble	'33	56	zero	zero	Philippine Sea

954

Plaice-2	Clyde B. Stevens, Jr.	'30	56	2/10,600	1/800	Empire
Queenfish-1	Charles E. Loughlin	'33	59	6/48,800	3/14,800	Luzon Strait
Razorback-1	Roy S. Benson	'29	55	zero	zero	Philippine Sea
Scabbardfish-1	Frederick A. Gunn	'34	56	zero	zero	Empire
Seahorse-6	Charles W. Wilkins	'24	71	1/1,700	1/800	Luzon Strait
Seal-11	John H. Turner	'36	41	3/7,700	2/6,330	Polar circuit
Sealion II-2	Eli T. Reich	'35	44	6/51,700	3/19,100	Luzon Strait
Searaven-12	Melvin H. Dry	'34	52	1/5,100	1/4,700	Polar circuit
Segundo-1	James D. Fulp, Jr.	'34	60	zero	zero	Philippine Sea
Shad-7	Lawrence V. Julihn	'37	50	3/6,900	1/900	Empire
Sunfish-8	Edward E. Shelby	'33	38	4/33,500	2/11,100	East China Sea
Tang-4	Richard H. O'Kane	'34	34	5/22,500	2/11,500	Empire
Tarpon-12	Saverio Filippone	'37	45	zero	zero	Truk
Thresher-14	John R. Middleton, Jr.	'35	50	3/20,600	3/9,170	East China Sea
Tunny-7	George E. Pierce	'32	44	zero	zero	South China Sea
Whale-9	James B. Grady	'33	68	1/10,000	1/10,200	Philippine Sea

Shifted to Australia

Stingray	Sam C. Loomis, Jr.					

TOTALS: 117/660,900   66½/302,517

---

* Shared ½ credit with carrier-based aircraft
† Shared ½ credit with *Baya* and ½ credit with *Becuna*

SUBMARINE WAR PATROLS DEPARTING AUSTRALIA, JULY–AUGUST 1944

Boat, Patrol Number	Skipper and Class	Days	Ships/Tonnage Wartime Credit	JANAC Credit	Area
JULY—FREMANTLE					
Aspro-4	William A. Stevenson '34	41	4/19,500	1/2,300	South China Sea
Bluefish-6 ‡	Charles M. Henderson '34	54	2½/34,500	1½/9,067	→Pearl Harbor
Cabrilla-5	William C. Thompson, Jr. '35	47	4/27,900	1/3,145	South China Sea
Cod-4	James A. Adkins '26	53	4/9,000	2/1,708	South China Sea
Guitarro-2	Enrique D. Haskins '33	48	5/11,800	4/11,200	Manila
Gunnel-6	Guy E. O'Neil, Jr. '37	54	zero	zero	Celebes
Gurnard-6	Charles H. Andrews '30	59	zero	zero	→Pearl Harbor
Rasher-5	Henry G. Munson '32	43	5/55,700	5/52,600	Manila
Raton-5	Maurice W. Shea '37	55	zero	zero	South China Sea
Ray-5	William T. Kinsella '34	52	4/36,400	5/26,000	→Pearl Harbor
Sandlance-3	Malcolm E. Garrison '32	45	1/7,500	1/3,000	→Pearl Harbor
Puffer-5 ‡	Frank G. Selby '33	48	4½/37,700	1½/7,680	→Pearl Harbor
Nautilus-11	George A. Sharp '29	27	zero	zero	special mission
JULY—BRISBANE					
Bluegill-2	Eric L. Barr, Jr. '34	49	3/8,600	3/6,950	Davao
Bream-2	Wreford G. Chapple '30	48	zero	zero	Davao
AUGUST—FREMANTLE					
Flier-2	John D. Crowley '31	lost	zero	zero	South China Sea
Haddo-7	Chester W. Nimitz, Jr. '36	52	5½/17,100	5/14,460	South China Sea
Hake-6	Frank E. Haylor '36	50	1/1,500	zero	South China Sea
Harder-6	Samuel D. Dealey '30	lost	1½/3,200	2/1,760	South China Sea

956

Jack-6	Arthur E. Krapf	'34	48	2/8,200	Celebes
Mingo-5	John R. Madison	'37	46	zero	Celebes
Muskallunge-4	Michael R. Russillo	'27	54	1/800	Indochina
Paddle-5 *	Byron H. Nowell	'35	34	1/5,000	Sulu Sea
Redfin-4 †	Marshall H. Austin	'35	57	1/5,100	Celebes
Narwhal-13	Jack C. Titus	'33	27	zero	special mission
Seawolf-14	Albert M. Bontier	'35	24	zero	→Brisbane
Stingray-12	Sam C. Loomis, Jr.	'35	35	zero	→Brisbane
AUGUST—BRISBANE					
Bashaw-3	Richard E. Nichols	'34	55	1/7,700	Davao
Flounder-3	James E. Stevens	'30	61	zero	Davao
Flying Fish-11	Robert D. Risser	'34	80	zero	→Pearl Harbor
Guavina-3	Carl Tiedeman	'33	44	3/3,000	Davao
S-42-6	Paul E. Glenn	'39	29	zero	special mission
			TOTALS:	54/300,200	

				2/6,287	
				zero	
				1½/5,000	
				zero	
				zero	
				zero	
				zero	
				1/2,800	
				zero	
				zero	
				1/1,500	
				zero	
				37½/155,457	

* Shared credit with carrier-based aircraft
† Laid minefield
‡ *Bluefish* and *Puffer* shared credit

SUBMARINE WAR PATROLS DEPARTING PEARL HARBOR, SEPTEMBER–OCTOBER 1944

Boat, Patrol Number	Skipper and Class	Days	Ships/Tonnage Wartime Credit	Ships/Tonnage JANAC Credit	Area
SEPTEMBER					
Apogon-5	Arthur C. House, Jr. '34	46	1/6,300	1/2,000	Polar circuit
Barbel-2	Robert A. Keating, Jr. '33	40	3/6,100	1/1,200	Empire
Bergall-1	John M. Hyde '34	60	3/21,500	2/14,700	→Fremantle
Besugo-1	Thomas L. Wogan '30	39	1/700	zero	Empire
Blackfin-1	George H. Laird, Jr. '33	60	1/4,000	2/2,700	→Fremantle
Blackfish-9	Robert F. Sellars '34	60	zero	zero	Luzon Strait
Burrfish-4	William B. Perkins, Jr. '32	69	1/7,600	zero	Empire
Cobia-2	Albert L. Becker '34	57	zero	zero	→Fremantle
Croaker-2	John E. Lee '30	48	4/16,600	3/5,800	East China Sea
Drum-11	Maurice H. Rindskopf '38	59	4/25,100	3/18,500	Luzon Strait
Escolar-1	William J. Millican '28	lost	zero	zero	East China Sea
Gabilan-3	Karl R. Wheland '31	46	1/2,200	1/100	Empire
Icefish-1	Richard W. Peterson '31	61	2/13,300	2/8,400	Luzon Strait
Parche-3	Lawson P. Ramage '31	77	zero	zero	Luzon Strait
Perch II-3	Blish C. Hills '33	48	zero	zero	East China Sea
Pomfret-2	Frank C. Acker '32	30	1/7,500	1/6,900	Luzon Strait
Rock-4	John J. Flachsenhar '35	61	zero	1/834	→Fremantle
Ronquil-2	Henry S. Monroe '33	57	zero	zero	Empire
Sailfish-12	Robert E. M. Ward '35	70	1/800	zero	Luzon Strait
Salmon-11 *	Harley K. Nauman '34	38	⅓/3,300	⅓/3,333	Empire
Saury-11	Richard A. Waugh '37	65	zero	zero	Empire
Sawfish-8	Alan B. Banister '28	58	2/17,900	2/13,400	Luzon Strait
Sea Devil-1	Ralph E. Styles '33	51	1/1,900	1/1,000	Empire

958

Sea Dog-1	Vernon L. Lowrance	'30	53	1/4,000	2/7,400	East China Sea
Seadragon-11	James H. Ashley, Jr.	'34	44	3/13,500	3/15,700	Luzon Strait
Shark II-3	Edward N. Blakely	'34	lost	zero	zero	Luzon Strait
Silversides-11	John S. Coye, Jr.	'33	60	zero	zero	Formosa
Skate-6	Richard B. Lynch	'35	54	1/4,000	1/3,700	Empire
Snapper-11	William W. Walker	'34	52	1/4,000	2/2,720	Bonins
Snook-7	George H. Browne	'34	63	3/22,500	3/16,600	Luzon Strait
Sterlet-2 *	Orme C. Robbins	'34	64	3⅓/21,900	1⅓/13,833	Empire
Tang-5	Richard H. O'Kane	'34	lost	13/107,324	7/21,772	Formosa
Tilefish-3	Roger M. Keithly	'35	44	4/8,100	zero	Polar circuit
Trepang-1	Roy M. Davenport	'33	36	3/22,300	2/1,750	Empire
Trigger-10 *	Frederick J. Harlfinger II	'35	49	⅓/3,300	⅓/3,333	Empire

OCTOBER

Albacore-10	Hugh R. Rimmer	'37	lost	zero	zero	Empire
Archerfish-5	Joseph F. Enright	'33	43	1/28,000	1/59,000	Empire
Atule-1	John H. Maurer	'35	60	5/26,700	4/25,691	Luzon Strait
Bang-4	Anton R. Gallaher	'33	40	4/18,400	2/5,200	Formosa
Barb-10	Eugene B. Fluckey	'35	30	5/28,900	2/15,200	East China Sea
Barbel-3	Robert A. Keating, Jr.	'33	38	2/9,400	2/8,800	→Fremantle
Billfish-6	Vernon C. Turner	'33	53	zero	zero	Empire
Greenling-11	John D. Gerwick	'35	48	3/9,900	3/2,695	Empire
Haddock-10	John P. Roach	'32	60	zero	zero	Luzon Strait
Halibut-10	Ignatius J. Galantin	'33	49	1/10,000	1/1,900	Luzon Strait
Jallao-1	Joseph B. Icenhower	'36	61	1/5,200	1/5,200 [1]	Luzon Strait
Kete-1	Royal L. Rutter	'30	60	zero	zero	Empire
Kingfish-9	Talbot E. Harper	'37	46	2/7,500	3/3,737	Bonins
Pampanito-4	Frank W. Fenno	'25	59	1/7,500	1/1,200	→Fremantle

* Salmon, Sterlet, and Trigger shared credit

[1] The light cruiser Tama, previously damaged by naval aircraft

959

SUBMARINE WAR PATROLS DEPARTING PEARL HARBOR, SEPTEMBER–OCTOBER 1944 (*Cont.*)

Boat, Patrol Number	Skipper and Class	Days	Ships/Tonnage Wartime Credit	Ships/Tonnage JANAC Credit	Area
Peto-7	Robert H. Caldwell, Jr.	'36	43	4/28,000	3/12,600	East China Sea
Picuda-4	Evan T. Shepard	'35	35	4/35,300	3/21,600	East China Sea
Pilotfish-3	Allan G. Schnable	'34	56	zero	zero	Bonins
Pintado-3	Bernard A. Clarey	'34	74	4/21,300	3/5,100	→Brisbane
Pipefish-3	William N. Deragon	'34	70	zero	1/800	Luzon Strait
Pogy-7	Peter G. Molteni, Jr.	'37	48	zero	zero	Bonins
Pomfret-3	John B. Hess	'37	45	2/2,600	3/14,000	Luzon Strait
Queenfish-2	Charles E. Loughlin	'33	35	4/38,500	4/14,300	East China Sea
Redfish-2	Louis D. McGregor, Jr.	'30	64	3/36,100	2/20,800	East China Sea
Sargo-12	Philip W. Garnett	'33	53	zero	zero	Bonins
Scamp-8	John C. Hollingsworth	'31	lost	zero	zero	Empire
Sea-Cat-1 *	Rob Roy McGregor	'29	58	1½/15,000	zero	Indochina
Sea Fox-1	Roy C. Klinker	'35	49	2/8,000	zero	Empire
Seal-12	John H. Turner	'36	50	2/10,000	1/5,700	Polar circuit
Skipjack-10	Richard S. Andrews	'31	49	zero	zero	Polar circuit
Spadefish-2	Gordon W. Underwood	'32	49	4/33,200	4/30,400	East China Sea
Sunfish-9	Edward E. Shelby	'33	56	4/23,800	3/16,200	East China Sea
Tambor-12	William J. Germershausen	'35	55	2/5,200	zero	Empire
Tuna-12	Edward F. Steffanides, Jr.	'31	52	zero	zero	→Brisbane
Sealion II-3	Eli T. Reich	'35	32	1/30,000	2/32,900	East China Sea
Shad-8	Lawrence V. Julihn	'37	63	zero	zero	East China Sea
			TOTALS:	121½/784,200	91/468,885	

* Shared credit with *Searaven*

SUBMARINE WAR PATROLS DEPARTING AUSTRALIA, SEPTEMBER–OCTOBER 1944

Boat, Patrol Number	Skipper and Class	Days	Wartime Credit	JANAC Credit	Area
SEPTEMBER—FREMANTLE					
Angler-5	Franklin G. Hess '35	50	1/4,000	1/2,400	Manila
Aspro-5	William A. Stevenson '34	46	4/25,500	2/10,900	→Pearl Harbor
Bluegill-3	Eric L. Barr, Jr. '34	64	5/23,300	3/19,630	Manila
Bonefish-6	Lawrence L. Edge '35	62	3/22,000	2/4,500	→Pearl Harbor
Cabrilla-6	William C. Thompson, Jr. '35	43	5/29,900	4/24,557	→Pearl Harbor
Cod-5	James A. Adkins '26	59	1/10,000	1/6,900	→Pearl Harbor
Crevalle-5	Francis D. Walker '35	20	zero	zero	Java Sea
Flasher-4	Reuben T. Whitaker '34	51	4/23,000	3/18,610	Manila
Hammerhead-2	John C. Martin '34	54	6/41,500	5/25,178	South China Sea
Hoe-6	Victor B. McCrea '32	37	2/15,000	1/2,500	South China Sea
Lapon-6	Donald G. Baer '37	56	4/25,600	3/14,170	South China Sea
Narwhal-14	Jack C. Titus '33	22	zero	zero	special mission
Nautilus-12	George A. Sharp '29	19	zero	zero	special mission
Pargo-5	Davis B. Bell '37	34	1/4,000	2/2,200	South China Sea [1]
Ray-6 *	William T. Kinsella '34	70	6½/35,100	5⅓/12,645	→Pearl Harbor
Stingray-13	Sam C. Loomis, Jr. '35	9	zero	zero	special mission
Stingray-14	Sam C. Loomis, Jr. '35	22	zero	zero	→Brisbane
SEPTEMBER—BRISBANE					
Cero-6	Edward F. Dissette '34	62	zero	zero	→Pearl Harbor
Dace-5	Bladen D. Claggett '35	60	3/30,000	3/25,141	South China Sea
Darter-4	David H. McClintock '35	lost	1/12,500	1/12,000	South China Sea
Permit-14	Donald A. Scherer '34	50	1/500	zero	→Pearl Harbor
Seawolf-15	Albert M. Bontier '35	lost	zero	zero	special mission

* Shared credit with *Bream* and *Guitarro*

[1] Laid minefield

961

SUBMARINE WAR PATROLS DEPARTING AUSTRALIA, SEPTEMBER–OCTOBER 1944 (Cont.)

Boat, Patrol Number	Skipper and Class		Days	Ships/Tonnage Wartime Credit	JANAC Credit	Area
OCTOBER—FREMANTLE						
Barbero-2	Irvin S. Hartman	'33	65	4/21,700	3/9,200	South China Sea
Bashaw-4	Richard E. Nichols	'34	63	zero	zero	South China Sea
Batfish-5	John K. Fyfe	'36	53	2/5,000	zero	→Pearl Harbor
Bream-3*	Wreford G. Chapple	'30	50	½/5,000	⅓/2,270	South China Sea
Growler-11	Thomas B. Oakley, Jr.	'34	lost	zero	zero	Celebes
Guavina-4†	Carl Tiedeman	'33	60	3½/24,800	2/6,117	South China Sea
Guitarro-3*	Enrique D. Haskins	'33	38	3½/28,200	2⅓/10,999	South China Sea
Gunnel-7	Guy E. O'Neil, Jr.	'37	65	3/14,600	3/6,795	→Pearl Harbor
Gurnard-7	Norman D. Gage	'35	38	1/5,000	1/6,900	South China Sea [1]
Haddo-8	Frank C. Lynch, Jr.	'38	60	3/9,000	1/860	→Pearl Harbor
Hake-7	Frank E. Haylor	'36	57	zero	zero	South China Sea
Hardhead-2	Francis A. Greenup	'36	45	2/9,800	2/6,100	South China Sea
Jack-7	Albert S. Fuhrman	'37	58	1/4,000	2/12,200	→Pearl Harbor
Muskallunge-5	Leonce A. Lajaunie, Jr.	'37	56	zero	zero	→Pearl Harbor
Narwhal-15	William G. Holman	'36	22	zero	zero	special mission
Nautilus-13	George A. Sharp	'29	41	zero	zero	special mission
Paddle-6	Joseph P. Fitz-Patrick	'38	29	2/1,100	zero	Celebes
Pargo-6	David B. Bell	'37	53	1/10,000	1/5,200	South China Sea
Raton-6	Maurice W. Shea	'37	55	8/57,200	4/12,300	→Pearl Harbor
Redfin-5	Marshall H. Austin	'35	68	1/10,000	1/5,300	→Pearl Harbor
OCTOBER—BRISBANE						
Flounder-4	James E. Stevens	'30	46	1/700	½/2,849	South China Sea
			TOTALS:	84/508,000	59½/268,495	

* *Bream*, *Guitarro*, and *Ray* shared credit
† Shared credit with carrier-based aircraft (½) and *Flounder* (½) and sank one ship independently

[1] Laid minefield

SUBMARINE WAR PATROLS DEPARTING PEARL HARBOR, NOVEMBER–DECEMBER 1944

Boat, Patrol Number	Skipper and Class		Days	Ships/Tonnage Wartime Credit	JANAC Credit	Area
NOVEMBER						
Apogon-6	Arthur C. House, Jr.	'34	46	zero	zero	Polar circuit
Besugo-2	Thomas L. Wogan	'30	23	2/8,000	1/1,000	→Fremantle
Blenny-1	William H. Hazzard	'35	62	2/11,100	2/4,950	→Fremantle
Caiman-1	Frederic C. Lucas, Jr.	'30	62	zero	zero	→Fremantle
Dragonet-1	Jack H. Lewis	'27	49	zero	zero	Polar circuit
Finback-11	Robert R. Williams, Jr.	'34	50	1/5,000	1/2,100	Bonins
Grouper-11	Frederick H. Wahlig	'33	54	zero	zero	Empire
Guardfish-10	Douglas T. Hammond	'31	60	zero	zero	Luzon Strait
Piranha-3	Harold E. Ruble	'33	52	zero	zero	East China Sea
Plaice-3	Clyde B. Stevens, Jr.	'30	39	zero	zero	East China Sea
Razorback-2 *	Charles D. Brown	'38	47	3½/20,800	1½/4,287	Luzon Strait
Scabbardfish-2	Frederick A. Gunn	'34	47	3/8,600	2/2,345	Empire
Sea Devil-2	Ralph E. Styles	'33	54	2/17,500	2/16,300	Empire
Sea Dog-2	Vernon L. Lowrance	'30	68	zero	zero	Luzon Strait
Sea Owl-1	Carter L. Bennett	'33	54	1/1,600	zero	East China Sea
Sea Poacher-1	Francis M. Gambacorta	'35	52	zero	zero	East China Sea
Segundo-2 †	James D. Fulp, Jr.	'34	49	2½/20,200	1/6,363	Luzon Strait
Searaven-13 ‡	Raymond Berthrong	'38	52	2½/25,800	zero	South China Sea

* Shared ½ credit with *Segundo*
† Shared ½ credit with land-based aircraft and ½ credit with *Razorback*
‡ Shared credit with *Sea Cat*

SUBMARINE WAR PATROLS DEPARTING PEARL HARBOR, NOVEMBER–DECEMBER 1944 (*Cont.*)

Boat, Patrol Number	Skipper and Class	Days	Ships/Tonnage Wartime Credit	Ships/Tonnage JANAC Credit	Area
Sea Robin-1	Paul C. Stimson '36	62	1/4,000	1/5,600	→Fremantle
Spearfish-12	Cyrus C. Cole '35	64	zero	zero	Empire
Spikefish-1	Nicholas J. Nicholas '32	47	zero	zero	Polar circuit
Tilefish-4	Roger M. Keithly '35	48	1/9,000	1/527	Polar circuit
Trepang-2	Roy M. Davenport '33	35	4/35,000	3/13,048	Luzon Strait
Whale-10	James B. Grady '33	54	zero	zero	Empire
"Burt's Brooms"	(Thomas Burton Klakring)				
Ronquil	Henry S. Monroe				
Saury	Richard A. Waugh				
Tambor	William J. Germershausen				
Sterlet	Orme C. Robbins				
Burrfish	William B. Perkins, Jr.				
Silversides	John S. Coye				
Trigger	Frederick J. Harlfinger II				
DECEMBER					
Aspro-6 *	William A. Stevenson '34	59	1/8,000	½/4,000	Luzon Strait
Balao-7	Marion Ramirez DeArellano '35	42	2/11,200	1/5,200	East China Sea
Barb-11 †	Eugene B. Fluckey '35	56	8/60,000	4⅓/24,197	East China Sea
Blueback-1	Merrill K. Clementson '33	61	zero	zero	→Fremantle
Boarfish-1 ‡	Royce L. Gross '30	52	1½/9,800	1½/10,445	→Fremantle
Charr-1	Francis D. Boyle '34	63	zero	zero	→Fremantle
Croaker-3	William B. Thomas '36	60	zero	zero	→Fremantle
Devilfish-1	Edward C. Stephan '29	41	zero	zero	Empire
Drum-12	Frank M. Eddy '37	42	zero	zero	Empire

Greenling-12	John D. Gerwick	'35	45	zero	Empire
Icefish-2	Richard W. Peterson	'31	42	zero	East China Sea
Kingfish-10	Talbot E. Harper	'37	40	2/15,500	Empire
Kraken-1	Thomas H. Henry	'35	64	zero	→Fremantle
Parche-4	Woodrow W. McCrory	'38	53	1/2,000	Empire
Perch II-4	Blish C. Hills	'33	59	zero	→Fremantle
Picuda-5	Evan T. Shepard	'35	48	3/22,500	East China Sea
Pogy-8	Peter G. Molteni, Jr.	'37	46	zero	Empire
Puffer-6	Carl R. Dwyer	'38	30	4/18,900	Empire
Queenfish-3	Charles E. Loughlin	'33	32	1/10,100	East China Sea
Sawfish-9	Douglas H. Pugh	'38	47	zero	Luzon Strait
Seadragon-12	James H. Ashley, Jr.	'34	60	zero	Bonins
Sea Fox-2	Roy C. Klinker	'35	46	zero	Empire
Sealion II-4	Charles F. Putman	'37	43	1/15,800	→Fremantle
Silversides-12	John C. Nichols	'34	50	zero	East China Sea
Snook-8	John F. Walling	'35	54	zero	Polar circuit
Spot-1	William S. Post, Jr.	'30	55	4/11,200	East China Sea
Swordfish-13	Keats E. Montross	'35	lost	zero	Empire
Tautog-13	Thomas S. Baskett	'35	42	3/8,500	East China Sea
Threadfin-1	John J. Foote	'35	54	1/2,000	Empire
Tinosa-8	Richard C. Latham	'34	56	zero	Empire
Trigger-11	Frederick J. Harlfinger II	'35	37	zero	Empire
Shifted to Australia					
Gabilan	William B. Parham	'36			
		TOTALS:		58/362,100	33½/129,961

* Shared credit with carrier-based aircraft
† Shared credit with *Picuda* and *Queenfish*
‡ Shared credit with land-based aircraft

SUBMARINE WAR PATROLS DEPARTING AUSTRALIA, NOVEMBER–DECEMBER 1944

Boat, Patrol Number	Skipper and Class	Days	Wartime Credit	JANAC Credit	Area
NOVEMBER—FREMANTLE					
Baya-2	Arnold H. Holtz '31	55	zero	zero	South China Sea
Becuna-2	Henry D. Sturr '33	53	1/1,100	zero	South China Sea
Flasher-5	George W. Grider '36	48	5/41,700	6/42,800	South China Sea
Hammerhead-3 †	John C. Martin '34	52	1/5,000	½/1,427	South China Sea
Hawkbill-2	Francis W. Scanland, Jr. '34	50	1/1,300	1/760	South China Sea
Hoe-7	Miles P. Refo III '38	50	zero	zero	South China Sea
Lapon-7	Donald G. Baer '37	56	zero	zero	→Pearl Harbor
Mingo-6	John R. Madison '37	52	1/10,000	1/9,500	South China Sea
Paddle-7 †	Joseph P. Fitz-Patrick '38	53	2/10,800	½/1,427	→Pearl Harbor
Cavalla-3	Herman J. Kossler '34	60	3/6,300	3/4,180	South China Sea
NOVEMBER—BRISBANE					
Gar-14	Maurice Ferrara '37	26	1/1,000	zero	special mission
DECEMBER—FREMANTLE					
Angler-6	H. Bissell, Jr. USNR	72	zero	zero	→Pearl Harbor
Bergall-2 *	John M. Hyde '34	21	1/12,500	zero	South China Sea
Besugo-3	Thomas L. Wogan '30	53	2/11,000	2/10,800	South China Sea
Bluegill-4	Eric L. Barr, Jr. '34	52	zero	zero	South China Sea
Bream-4	James L. P. McCallum '35	52	zero	zero	South China Sea
Cobia-3	Albert L. Becker '34	54	1/700	1/720	South China Sea
Dace-6 *	Otis R. Cole, Jr. '36	56	1/4,000	1/1,000	→Pearl Harbor
Guitarro-4	Thomas B. Dabney '36	83	zero	zero	South China Sea
Gurnard-8	Norman D. Gage '35	51	zero	zero	South China Sea
Hardhead-3	Francis R. Greenup '36	53	1/2,500	1/834	South China Sea
Rock-5	John J. Flachsenhar '35	63	zero	zero	South China Sea

DECEMBER—BRISBANE

Gabilan-4	William B. Parham	'36	48	zero	zero	South China Sea
Gar-15	Maurice Ferrara	'37	24	zero	zero	→Pearl Harbor
Stingray-15	Howard F. Stoner	'32	27	zero	zero	special mission
		TOTALS:		21/107,900	17/73,448

* Laid minefield
† *Hammerhead* and *Paddle* shared credit

SUBMARINE WAR PATROLS DEPARTING PEARL HARBOR, JANUARY–MARCH 1945

Boat, Patrol Number	Skipper and Class		Days	Ships/Tonnage Wartime Credit	JANAC Credit	Area
JANUARY						
Archerfish-6	Joseph F. Enright	'33	49	1/1,100	zero	South China Sea
Atule-2	John H. Maurer	'35	59	1/6,700	1/6,888	East China Sea
Bang-5	Anton R. Gallaher	'33	50	zero	zero	East China Sea
Batfish-6	John K. Fyfe	'36	61	3/4,500	3/3,262	South China Sea
Blackfish-10	Robert F. Sellars	'34	50	zero	zero	South China Sea
Blower-1	James H. Campbell	'33	60	zero	zero	→Fremantle
Bowfin-7	Alexander K. Tyree	'36	56	2/2,700	1/750	Empire
Brill-1	Harry B. Dodge	'30	62	zero	zero	→Fremantle
Burrfish-5	Morton H. Lytle	'37	48	zero	zero	Empire
Finback-12	Robert R. Williams, Jr.	'34	62	zero	zero	East China Sea
Gato-11	Richard M. Farrell	'35	45	2/4,700	2/3,125	East China Sea
Haddock-11	William H. Brockman, Jr.	'27	51	zero	zero	Empire
Jallao-2	Joseph B. Icenhower	'36	65	zero	zero	East China Sea
Lagarto-1	Frank D. Latta	'32	55	1/900	2/1,845	→Fremantle
Peto-8	Robert H. Caldwell, Jr.	'36	67	zero	zero	Luzon Strait

967

SUBMARINE WAR PATROLS DEPARTING PEARL HARBOR, JANUARY–MARCH 1945 (*Cont.*)

Boat, Patrol Number	Skipper and Class		Days	Ships/Tonnage Wartime Credit	Ships/Tonnage JANAC Credit	Area
Pilotfish-4	Allan G. Schnable	'34	64	zero	zero	East China Sea
Pipefish-4	William N. Deragon	'34	53	zero	zero	Empire
Piper-1	Bernard F. McMahon	'31	60	1/2,000	zero	Empire
Plaice-4	Clyde B. Stevens, Jr.	'30	58	zero	zero	Luzon Strait
Pomfret-4	John B. Hess	'37	62	zero	zero	Empire
Pompon-7	Stephen H. Gimber	'35	34	zero	zero	Yellow Sea
Rasher-6	Benjamin E. Adams, Jr.	'35	53	zero	zero	East China Sea
Ronquil-3	Robert B. Lander	'37	43	1/10,100	zero	Bonins
Scabbardfish-3	Frederick A. Gunn	'34	52	zero	zero	Luzon Strait
Sennet-1	George E. Porter, Jr.	'32	25	1/500	zero	Bonins
Shad-9	Lawrence V. Julihn	'37	57	zero	zero	South China Sea
Spadefish-3	Gordon W. Underwood	'32	38	4/16,400	4/13,423	East China Sea
Spikefish-2	Nicholas J. Nicholas	'32	51	zero	zero	Empire
Sterlet-3	H. H. Lewis	USNR	66	2/15,000	1/1,148	Empire
Sunfish-10	Edward E. Shelby	'33	37	zero	zero	East China Sea
Thresher-15	John R. Middleton, Jr.	'35	82	zero	zero	Luzon Strait
Tilefish-5	Walter F. Schlech, Jr.	'36	56	1/700	1/492	Empire
Trepang-3	Allen R. Faust	'36	57	1/6,100	2/2,261	Empire
FEBRUARY						
Balao-8	Robert K. Worthington	'38	40	3/20,300	2/11,293	East China Sea
Bluefish-7	Charles M. Henderson	'34	42	zero	zero	Empire
Bugara-1	Arnold F. Schade	'33	54	zero	zero	→Fremantle
Chub-1	Cassius D. Rhymes, Jr.	'35	64	zero	zero	→Fremantle
Drum-13	Frank M. Eddy	'37	51	zero	zero	Empire

968

Guardfish-11	Douglas T. Hammond	'31	44	zero	Empire
Icefish-3	Richard W. Peterson	'31	57	zero	East China Sea
Lamprey-1	William T. Nelson	'30	59	zero	→Fremantle
Piranha-4	Donald G. Irvine	'34	69	zero	Luzon Strait
Puffer-7	Carl R. Dwyer	'38	70	zero	→Fremantle
Queenfish-4	Charles E. Loughlin	'33	46	1/12,000	1/11,600 Formosa Strait
Razorback-3	Charles D. Brown	'38	53	zero	East China Sea
Sea Cat-2	Richard H. Bowers	'38	52	1/2,000	East China Sea
Sea Devil-3	Ralph E. Styles	'33	63	6/17,600	3/10,017 East China Sea
Sea Owl-2	Carter L. Bennett	'33	70	1/2,800	1/889 South China Sea
Sea Poacher-2	Francis M. Gambacorta	'35	48	zero	Formosa Strait
Segundo-3	James D. Fulp, Jr.	'34	54	1/4,000	1/3,087 East China Sea
Sennet-2	George E. Porter, Jr.	'32	30	1/2,000	1/720 Empire
Spot-2 *	William S. Post, Jr.	'30	61	2/11,700	1½/4,592 East China Sea
Springer-1	Russell Kefauver	'33	48	1/1,500	1/1,500 Empire
Tench-1	William B. Sieglaff	'31	55	1/4,300	zero Empire
Tunny-8	George E. Pierce	'32	52	zero	zero Empire
"Mac's Mops"	(Bernard F. McMahon)				
Bowfin	Alexander K. Tyree				
Piper (flag)					
Pomfret	John B. Hess				
Sterlet	H. H. Lewis				
Trepang	Allen R. Faust				
"Latta's Lances"	(Frank D. Latta)				
Haddock	William H. Brockman				
Lagarto (flag)					
Sennet	George E. Porter, Jr.				

* Shared credit with naval land-based aircraft

SUBMARINE WAR PATROLS DEPARTING PEARL HARBOR, JANUARY–MARCH 1945 (*Cont.*)

Boat, Patrol Number	Skipper and Class	Days	Ships/Tonnage Wartime Credit	Ships/Tonnage JANAC Credit	Area
MARCH					
Bang-6	Oliver W. Bagby '38	55	zero	zero	Luzon Strait
Blackfish-11	Robert F. Sellars '34	50	zero	zero	South China Sea
Bullhead-1	Walter T. Griffith '34	37	zero	zero	→Fremantle
Burrfish-6	Morton H. Lytle '37	49	zero	zero	Formosa Strait
Cabrilla-7	Henry C. Lauerman '38	48	zero	zero	→Fremantle
Cero-7	Raymond Berthrong '38	56	4/9,800	3/8,834	Empire
Cod-6	James A. Adkins '26	65	3/5,000	1/492	→Fremantle
Crevalle-6	Everett H. Steinmetz '35	46	1/1,300	zero	East China Sea
Devilfish-2	Stephen S. Mann, Jr. '38	21	zero	zero	Empire
Grouper-12	Frederick H. Wahlig '33	54	zero	zero	East China Sea
Hackleback-1	Frederick E. Janney '37	51	zero	zero	Empire
Kete-2	Edward Ackerman '39	lost	3/12,000	3/6,875	East China Sea
Kingfish-11	Talbot E. Harper '37	50	zero	zero	Empire
Parche-5	Woodrow W. McCrory '38	42	3/5,200	1/615	Empire
Picuda-6	Evan T. Shepard '35	63	zero	zero	Empire
Pogy-9	John M. Bowers '38	61	zero	zero	Empire
Pompon-8	John A. Bogley '38	52	zero	zero	East China Sea
Ronquil-4	Robert B. Lander '37	45	zero	zero	Bonins
Sawfish-10	Douglas H. Pugh '38	47	zero	zero	Formosa
Sea Dog-3	Earl T. Hydeman '32	47	1/6,700	1/6,850	Empire
Sea Fox-3	Roy C. Klinker '35	59	zero	zero	East China Sea
Seahorse-7	Harry H. Greer, Jr. '34	46	zero	zero	Empire
Silversides-13	John C. Nichols '34	50	1/2,000	zero	Empire
Snook-9	John F. Walling '35	lost	zero	zero	Luzon Strait

970

Boat	Skipper	Class	Days	Wartime Credit	JANAC Credit	Area
Spadefish-4	William J. Germershausen	'35	35	1/7,000	1/4,127	East China Sea
Sunfish-11	John W. Reed	'38	29	4/13,200	4/5,461	Empire
Threadfin-2	John J. Foote	'35	51	zero	1/900	Empire
Tigrone-1	Hiram Cassedy	'31	43	zero	zero	East China Sea
Tinosa-9	Richard C. Latham	'34	30	zero	zero	East China Sea
Tirante-1	George L. Street III	'37	52	8/28,300	6/12,621	East China Sea
Trigger-12	David R. Connole	'36	lost	1/4,000	2/2,576	Empire
Trutta-1	Arthur C. Smith	'34	42	zero	zero	East China Sea
			TOTALS:	68/244,100	51½/126,243	

SUBMARINE WAR PATROLS DEPARTING AUSTRALIA, JANUARY–AUGUST 1945

Boat, Patrol Number	Skipper and Class		Days	Wartime Credit	JANAC Credit	Area
JANUARY—FREMANTLE						
Bashaw-5	H. S. Simpson	USNR	47	1/10,700	1/10,016	South China Sea
Bergall-3	John M. Hyde	'34	28	1/900	2/974	South China Sea
Blackfin-2	William L. Kitch	'38	45	1/1,500	1/1,580	South China Sea
Flasher-6	George W. Grider	'36	75	1/2,100	1/850	South China Sea
Flounder-5	James E. Stevens	'30	42	zero	zero	South China Sea
Guavina-5	Ralph H. Lockwood	'38	42	2/20,000	2/15,565	South China Sea
Hake-8	Frank E. Haylor	'36	61	zero	zero	→Pearl Harbor
Nautilus-14	Willard D. Michael	'38	28	zero	zero	special mission
Pampanito-5	Paul E. Summers	'36	20	2/12,500	2/10,488	South China Sea
Stingray-16	Howard F. Stoner	'32	34	zero	zero	special mission
Pargo-7	David B. Bell	'37	54	3/14,800	1/1,300	→Pearl Harbor

971

SUBMARINE WAR PATROLS DEPARTING AUSTRALIA, JANUARY–AUGUST 1945 (Cont.)

Boat, Patrol Number	Skipper and Class		Days	Ships/Tonnage Wartime Credit	Ships/Tonnage JANAC Credit	Area
JANUARY—BRISBANE						
Pintado-4	Bernard A. Clarey	'34	51	zero	zero	→Pearl Harbor
Tuna-13	Edward F. Steffanides, Jr.	'31	64	zero	zero	special mission
FEBRUARY—FREMANTLE						
Barbel-4	Conde L. Raguet	'38	lost	zero	zero	South China Sea
Baya-3	Benjamin C. Jarvis	'39	46	3/13,500	2/5,760	South China Sea
Becuna-3	Henry D. Sturr	'33	46	1/7,500	1/1,945	South China Sea
Blenny-2	William H. Hazzard	'35	49	4/25,500	4/12,611	South China Sea
Caiman-2	William L. Fey, Jr.	'37	48	zero	zero	South China Sea
Cavalla-4	Herman J. Kossler	'34	46	zero	zero	South China Sea
Cobia-4	Albert L. Becker	'34	51	zero	zero	South China Sea
Hammerhead-4	George H. Laird, Jr.	'33	22	1/800	1/900	South China Sea
Hawkbill-3	Francis W. Scanland, Jr.	'34	58	2/12,800	3/5,596	South China Sea
Hoe-8	Miles P. Refo III	'38	46	1/2,300	1/900	→Pearl Harbor
Mingo-7	John R. Madison	'37	76	zero	zero	→Pearl Harbor
Pampanito-6	Paul E. Summers	'36	57	zero	zero	South China Sea
Sealion II-5	Charles F. Putman	'37	47	1/7,300	1/1,458	South China Sea
Sea Robin-2	Paul C. Stimson	'36	66	5/15,900	4/7,113	→Pearl Harbor
MARCH—FREMANTLE						
Bashaw-6	H. S. Simpson	USNR	33	zero	zero	South China Sea
Bergall-4	John M. Hyde	'34	43	zero	zero	South China Sea
Besugo-4	Herman E. Miller	'38	54	3/2,700	1/630 [1]	South China Sea
Blackfin-3	William L. Kitch	'38	36	zero	zero	South China Sea
Blueback-2	Merrill K. Clementson	'33	44	zero	zero	South China Sea
Bluegill-5	Eric L. Barr, Jr.	'34	37	1/5,700	1/5,542	South China Sea

972

Boarfish-2	Royce L. Gross	'30	42	zero	South China Sea
Bream-5	James L. McCallum	'35	16	1/2,600	Java Sea
Charr-2 * †	Francis D. Boyle	'34	51	2/5,700	South China Sea
Croaker-4	William B. Thomas	'36	42	zero	South China Sea
Flounder-6	James E. Stevens	'30	38	zero	South China Sea
Gabilan-5 †	William B. Parham	'36	60	3/6,800	→Pearl Harbor
Guavina-6	Ralph H. Lockwood	'38	48	zero	South China Sea
Gurnard-9	George S. Simmons III	'39	59	zero	→Pearl Harbor
Hammerhead-5	Frank M. Smith	'35	28	1/1,800	South China Sea
Hardhead-4 *	Francis A. Greenup	'36	56	1/10,300	Siam Gulf
Kraken-2	Thomas H. Henry	'35	43	zero	South China Sea
Perch II-5	Blish C. Hills	'33	10	zero	Java Sea
Rock-6	Robert A. Keating, Jr.	'33	58	1/600	→Pearl Harbor
APRIL—FREMANTLE					
Bergall-5	John M. Hyde	'34	37	zero	South China Sea
Blackfin-4	William L. Kitch	'38	31	zero	→Pearl Harbor
Blueback-3	Merrill K. Clementson	'33	62	1/1,100	Java Sea
Bluegill-6	Eric L. Barr, Jr.	'34	41	zero	South China Sea
Boarfish-3	Edward C. Blonts, Jr.	'39	23	zero	Java Sea
Bugara-2	Arnold F. Schade	'33	40	zero	South China Sea
Bullhead-2	Walter T. Griffith	'34	43	2/1,800	South China Sea
Chub-2	Cassius D. Rhymes, Jr.	'35	38	3/2,700	Java Sea
Cobia-5	Albert L. Becker	'34	40	2/15,100	South China Sea
Croaker-5	William B. Thomas	'36	22	2/5,800	Java Sea
Hawkbill-4	Francis W. Scanland, Jr.	'34	44	1/2,400	South China Sea
Kraken-3	Thomas H. Henry	'35	45	3/3,000	South China Sea
Lamprey-2	Lucien B. McDonald	'38	40	zero	South China Sea

* Laid minefields
† *Charr* and *Gabilan* shared credit

[1] Plus *U-183*

SUBMARINE WAR PATROLS DEPARTING AUSTRALIA, JANUARY–AUGUST 1945 (*Cont.*)

Boat, Patrol Number	Skipper and Class	Days	Ships/Tonnage Wartime Credit	JANAC Credit	Area
MAY—FREMANTLE					
Baya-4	Benjamin C. Jarvis '39	28	3/13,000	1/2,500	South China Sea
Becuna-4	Henry D. Sturr '33	39	zero	zero	South China Sea
Blenny-3	William H. Hazzard '35	55	1/800	1/524	South China Sea
Blower-2	James H. Campbell '33	40	zero	zero	South China Sea
Bream-6 *	James L. McCallum '35	54	1/10,000	1/1,230	→Pearl Harbor
Brill-2	Harry B. Dodge '30	41	zero	zero	South China Sea
Caiman-3	William L. Fey, Jr. '37	62	zero	zero	South China Sea
Cavalla-5	Herman J. Kossler '34	38	zero	zero	→Pearl Harbor
Guitarro-5 *	Thomas B. Dabney '36	61	zero	zero	South China Sea
Hammerhead-6	Frank M. Smith '35	25	2/8,500	2/6,823	South China Sea
Lagarto-2	Frank D. Latta '32	lost	zero	1/5,819	South China Sea
Perch II-6	Charles D. McCall '39	53	zero	zero	→Pearl Harbor
Sealion II-6	Charles F. Putman '37	62	zero	zero	South China Sea
JUNE—FREMANTLE					
Baya-5	Benjamin C. Jarvis '39	41	1/700	1/595	Java Sea
Becuna-5	William J. Bush '38	36	zero	zero	South China Sea
Besugo-5	Herman E. Miller '38	42	zero	zero	South China Sea
Blower-3	Nelson P. Watkins '37	35	zero	zero	South China Sea
Bluefish-9	George W. Forbes, Jr. '39	33	1/2,000	2/2,750	South China Sea
Hammerhead-7	Frank M. Smith '35	60	1/1,100	2/1,734	South China Sea
Hardhead-5	Francis A. Greenup '36	33	2/2,500	3/500	South China Sea
Lizardfish-2	Ovid M. Butler '36	39	zero	zero	South China Sea

974

Cod-7	Edwin M. Westbrook, Jr.	'38	47	zero	South China Sea
Charr-3	Francis D. Boyle	'34	42	zero	South China Sea

JULY—FREMANTLE

Blenny-4	William H. Hazzard	'35	40	1/5,700	South China Sea
Boarfish-4	Edward C. Blonts, Jr.	'39	36	zero	South China Sea
Brill-3	Harry B. Dodge	'30	37	zero	South China Sea
Bugara-3	Arnold F. Schade	'33	34	zero	South China Sea
Bullhead-3	Edward R. Holt, Jr.	'39	lost	zero	South China Sea
Bumper-2	Joseph W. Williams, Jr.	'33	34	2/2,500	South China Sea
Caiman-4	William L. Fey, Jr.	'37	28	zero	South China Sea
Chub-3	Cassius D. Rhymes, Jr.	'35	33	1/1,500	South China Sea
Cobia-6	Frederick N. Russell	'39	34	zero	South China Sea
Croaker-6	William B. Thomas	'36	47	zero	South China Sea
Hardhead-6	John L. Haines	'38	24	1/1,800	South China Sea
Hawkbill-5	Francis W. Scanland, Jr.	'34	31	1/700	South China Sea
Icefish-5	Richard W. Peterson	'31	24	zero	South China Sea
Kraken-4	Thomas H. Henry	'35	23	zero	Java Sea
Lamprey-3	Lucien B. McDonald	'38	25	zero	South China Sea

AUGUST—FREMANTLE

Capitaine-2	Ernest S. Friedrick	'37	14	zero	South China Sea
Carbonero-2	Charlton L. Murphy, Jr.	'32	15	zero	South China Sea
Loggerhead-2	Ralph M. Metcalf	'35	9	zero	South China Sea
Puffer-9	Carl R. Dwyer	'38	14	zero	South China Sea

	TOTALS:	74/267,000	54/128,407

* Laid minefields

SUBMARINE WAR PATROLS DEPARTING PEARL HARBOR, APRIL 1945

Boat, Patrol Number	Skipper and Class	Days	Ships/Tonnage Wartime Credit	Ships/Tonnage JANAC Credit	Area
Atule-3	John H. Maurer '35	59	zero	zero	Empire
Billfish-7	L. C. Farley, Jr. USNR	54	2/7,800	2/3,211	Empire
Bluefish-8	George W. Forbes, Jr. '39	38	zero	zero	→Fremantle
Bonefish-7	Lawrence L. Edge '35	31	zero	zero	East China Sea
Bowfin-8	Alexander K. Tyree '36	23	2/9,300	2/3,599	Empire
Bumper-1	Joseph W. Williams, Jr. '33	53	zero	zero	→Fremantle
Dragonet-2	Jack H. Lewis '27	50	zero	zero	East China Sea
Gato-12	Richard Holden '37	52	zero	zero	Empire
Haddock-12	Albert R. Strow '39	42	zero	zero	Empire
Jack-8	Albert S. Fuhrman '37	51	zero	zero	Empire
Jallao-3	Joseph B. Icenhower '36	55	zero	zero	East China Sea
Lionfish-1	Edward D. Spruance '37	51	zero	zero	→Fremantle
Lizardfish-1	Ovid M. Butler '36	52	zero	zero	Empire
Pipefish-5	William N. Deragon '34	47	zero	zero	Empire
Piper-2	Bernard F. McMahon '31	47	1/2,000	zero	Polar circuit
Plaice-5	Richard S. Andrews '31	47	zero	zero	Polar circuit
Pomfret-5	John B. Hess '37	42	zero	zero	Polar circuit
Rasher-7	Charles D. Nace '39	44	zero	zero	→Fremantle
Raton-7	Maurice W. Shea '37	47	3/14,500	3/5,758	→Fremantle
Ray-7	William T. Kinsella '34	49	zero	zero	→Fremantle
Sandlance-4	Malcolm E. Garrison '32	54	1/2,000	zero	Empire
Scabbardfish-4	Frederick A. Gunn '34	53	zero	zero	East China Sea
Sea Cat-3	Richard H. Bowers '38	57	zero	zero	East China Sea
Sea Poacher-3	Charles F. Leigh '39	24	1/700	zero	Polar circuit

Segundo-4	James D. Fulp, Jr.	'34	54	4/13,800	1/1,578	East China Sea
Sennet-3	George E. Porter, Jr.	'32	43	3/8,700	2/3,901	Empire
Spikefish-3	Robert R. Managhan	'38	52	zero	zero	Empire
Springer-2	Russell Kefauver	'33	28	3/4,300	3/2,440	East China Sea
Sterlet-4	H. H. Lewis	USNR	42	1/4,000	2/4,155	Polar circuit
Tinosa-10	Richard C. Latham	'34	19	zero	zero	Truk
Toro-1	James D. Grant	'31	54	zero	zero	Empire
Torsk-1	Bafford E. Lewellen	'31	63	zero	zero	Empire
Trepang-4	Allen R. Faust	'36	32	3/11,600	3/6,159	East China Sea
			TOTALS:	24/78,700	18/30,801	

SUBMARINE WAR PATROLS DEPARTING PEARL HARBOR, MAY 1945

Boat, Patrol Number	Skipper and Class		Days	Ships/Tonnage Wartime Credit	JANAC Credit	Area
Apogon-7	Arthur C. House	'34	48	4/12,700	1/2,614	Polar circuit
Balao-9	Robert K. Worthington	'38	35	zero	zero	Empire
Bonefish-8	Lawrence L. Edge	'35	lost	2/14,000	2/12,380	Japan Sea
Bowfin-9	Alexander K. Tyree	'36	37	2/6,300	2/2,785	Japan Sea
Cabezon-1	George W. Lautrup, Jr.	'34	46	1/4,000	1/2,631	Polar circuit
Capitaine-1	Ernest S. Friedrick	'37	62	zero	zero	→Fremantle
Carbonero-1	Charlton L. Murphy, Jr.	'32	42	zero	zero	→Fremantle
Crevalle-7	Everett H. Steinmetz	'35	38	4/8,500	3/6,643	Japan Sea
Dace-7	Otis R. Cole, Jr.	'36	46	1/4,400	1/1,391	Polar circuit
Dentuda-1	John S. McCain, Jr.	'31	58	1/4,000	zero	East China Sea
Devilfish-3	Stephen S. Mann, Jr.	'38	47	zero	zero	Empire

SUBMARINE WAR PATROLS DEPARTING PEARL HARBOR, MAY 1945 (*Cont.*)

Boat, Patrol Number	Skipper and Class		Days	Ships/Tonnage Wartime Credit	Ships/Tonnage JANAC Credit	Area
Flying Fish-12	Robert D. Risser	'34	36	2/3,200	2/4,113	Japan Sea
Guardfish-12	Douglas T. Hammond	'31	49	zero	zero	Empire
Hackleback-2	Frederick E. Janney	'37	49	zero	zero	Empire
Haddo-9	Frank C. Lynch, Jr.	'38	46	6/18,600	3/6,126	East China Sea
Icefish-4	Richard W. Peterson	'31	50	zero	zero	→Fremantle
Lapon-8	Donald G. Baer	'37	50	zero	zero	Empire
Loggerhead-1	Ralph M. Metcalf	'35	64	zero	zero	→Fremantle
Manta-1	Edward P. Madley	'37	46	zero	zero	Polar circuit
Muskallunge-6	William H. Lawrence	'34	52	zero	zero	East China Sea
Paddle-8	Joseph P. Fitz-Patrick	'38	60	zero	zero	East China Sea
Parche-6	Woodrow W. McCrory	'38	59	2/7,200	2/3,669	Empire
Peto-9	Robert H. Caldwell, Jr.	'36	44	zero	zero	Empire
Pilotfish-5	Allan G. Schnable	'34	51	zero	zero	Empire
Piranha-5	Donald G. Irvine	'34	49	3/9,800	zero	Empire
Puffer-8	Carl R. Dwyer	'38	53	zero	zero	→Fremantle
Queenfish-5	Frank N. Shamer	'37	69	zero	zero	East China Sea
Quillback-1	Richard P. Nicholson	'37	53	zero	zero	Empire
Razorback-4	Charles D. Brown	'38	50	zero	zero	Empire
Redfin-6	Charles K. Miller	'39	36	zero	zero	Empire
Ronquil-5	Robert B. Lander	'37	67	1/4,000	zero	East China Sea
Sea Devil-4	Charles F. McGivern	'38	54	1/2,500	1/2,211	East China Sea
Sea Dog-4	Earl T. Hydeman	'32	39	6/29,500	6/7,186	Japan Sea
Sea Owl-3	Warren C. Hall, Jr.	'37	67	1/2,600	1/800	Empire
Shad-10	Donald L. Mehlop	'37	45	3/13,500	2/5,309	East China Sea

Silversides-14	John C. Nichols	'34	59	zero	zero	Empire
Skate-7	Richard B. Lynch	'35	49	5/8,700	4/6,398	Japan Sea
Spadefish-5	William J. Germershausen	'35	39	6/26,100	5/8,578	Japan Sea
Steelhead-7	Robert B. Byrnes	'38	74	zero	zero	Empire
Tench-2	Thomas S. Baskett	'35	37	4/15,800	4/5,069	Empire
Tigrone-2	Hiram Cassedy	'31	44	zero	zero	Empire
Tinosa-11	Richard C. Latham	'34	37	4/12,100	4/6,701	Japan Sea
Tirante-2	George L. Street III	'37	57	3/7,400	2/3,265	East China Sea
Tunny-9	George E. Pierce	'32	49	zero	zero	Japan Sea
			TOTALS:	62/213,900	46/87,869	

SUBMARINE WAR PATROLS DEPARTING PEARL HARBOR, JUNE 1945

				Ships/Tonnage		
Boat, Patrol Number	Skipper and Class		Days	Wartime Credit	JANAC Credit	Area
Angler-7	H. Bissell	USNR	56	zero	zero	Empire
Argonaut II-1	John S. Schmidt	'37	52	zero	zero	East China Sea
Aspro-7	James H. Ashley, Jr.	'34	49	1/500	zero	Empire
Barb-12	Eugene B. Fluckey	'35	54	3/11,200	2/3,620	Empire
Batfish-7	Walter L. Small	'38	58	zero	zero	Empire
Blackfish-12	Robert C. Gillette	'39	57	zero	zero	East China Sea
Cabrilla-8	Henry C. Lauerman	'38	58	zero	zero	→Fremantle
Carp-1	J. L. Hunnicutt	USNR	54	5/9,800	zero	Empire
Cero-8	Raymond Berthrong	'38	33	zero	zero	Empire
Gabilan-6	William B. Parham	'36	56	zero	zero	Empire

SUBMARINE WAR PATROLS DEPARTING PEARL HARBOR, JUNE 1945 (*Cont.*)

Boat, Patrol Number	Skipper and Class	Days	Wartime Credit	JANAC Credit	Area
Gunnel-8	Guy E. O'Neil, Jr. '37	41	zero	zero	Empire
Haddock-13	Albert R. Strow '39	51	zero	zero	Empire
Kingfish-12	Thomas D. Keegan '39	55	zero	zero	Polar circuit
Lionfish-2	Bricker M. Ganyard '38	58	1/1,400	zero	Empire
Moray-1	Frank L. Barrows '35	52	1/600	zero	Empire
Pintado-5	Romondt Budd '35	41	zero	zero	Truk
Pompon-9	John A. Bogley '38	34	zero	zero	→Fremantle
Rasher-8	Charles D. Nace '39	53	zero	zero	→Fremantle
Raton-8	Guy F. Gugliotta '38	32	zero	zero	Empire
Runner II-1	Raymond H. Bass '31	30	1/600	1/630	Empire
Sea Fox-4	Roy C. Klinker '35	49	zero	zero	East China Sea
Sea Poacher-4	Charles F. Leigh '39	54	zero	zero	East China Sea
Sea Robin-3	Paul C. Stimson '36	65	4/5,600	1/1,224	Empire
Spot-3	Jack M. Seymour '35	58	zero	zero	Empire
Springer-3	John F. Bauer '38	40	zero	zero	Empire
Thornback-1	Ernest P. Abrahamson '32	52	1/5,200	1/630	East China Sea
Threadfin-3	John J. Foote '35	53	3/3,700	1/606	Empire
Trepang-5	Allen R. Faust '36	47	zero	zero	East China Sea
Trutta-2 *	F. P. Hoskins USNR	46	zero	zero	Empire
Whale-11	Freeland H. Carde, Jr. '38	68	zero	zero	Empire
	TOTALS:		20/38,600	6/6,710	

* Supported Japan Sea operations

SUBMARINE WAR PATROLS DEPARTING PEARL HARBOR, JULY 1945

Boat, Patrol Number	Skipper and Class	Days	Ships/Tonnage Wartime Credit	JANAC Credit	Area
Archerfish-7	Joseph F. Enright '33	59	zero	zero	Empire
Atule-4	John H. Maurer '35	51	1/800	1/800	Empire
Balao-10	Robert K. Worthington '38	47	zero	zero	Empire
Billfish-8	L. C. Farley, Jr. USNR	44	2/5,200	1/1,091	East China Sea
Catfish-1	William A. Overton '33	40	zero	zero	Empire
Blackfin-5	William L. Kitch '38	37	zero	zero	East China Sea
Dragonet-3	Gerald G. Hinman '38	50	zero	zero	Empire
Entemedor-1	William R. Smith, Jr. '37	30	zero	zero	Empire
Gato-13	Richard Holden '37	61	1/800	zero	Empire
Hake-9	Frank E. Haylor '36	49	zero	zero	Empire
Jack-9	Albert S. Fuhrman '37	48	zero	zero	Formosa
Jallao-4	Joseph B. Icenhower '36	51	1/4,000	1/5,795	Japan Sea
Macabi-1	Anthony H. Dropp '32	42	zero	zero	Truk
Muskallunge-7	William H. Lawrence '34	40	zero	zero	Polar circuit
Pargo-8	David B. Bell '37	41	2/7,200	1/5,454	Japan Sea
Perch II-7	Charles D. McCall '39	47	zero	zero	Empire
Peto-10	Robert H. Caldwell, Jr. '36	47	zero	zero	Empire
Pipefish-6	A. L. Redon USNR	42	zero	zero	Empire
Piper-3	Edward L. Beach '39	46	zero	zero	Japan Sea
Plaice-6	Richard S. Andrews '31	35	zero	zero	East China Sea
Pogy-10	John M. Bowers '38	47	2/12,500	2/4,668	Japan Sea
Pomfret-6	John B. Hess '37	59	zero	zero	East China Sea
Ray-8	William T. Kinsella '34	30	zero	zero	→Fremantle

981

SUBMARINE WAR PATROLS DEPARTING PEARL HARBOR, JULY 1945 (Cont.)

Boat, Patrol Number	Skipper and Class		Days	Ships/Tonnage Wartime Credit	JANAC Credit	Area
Razorback-5	Charles D. Brown	'38	39	zero	zero	Polar circuit
Redfin-7	Charles K. Miller	'39	34	zero	zero	South China Sea
Sandlance-5	James G. Glaes	'39	54	zero	zero	Empire
Scabbardfish-5	Frederick A. Gunn	'34	51	zero	zero	Empire
Seahorse-8	Harry H. Greer, Jr.	'34	38	zero	zero	Empire
Sennet-4	Charles R. Clark, Jr.	'39	34	4/24,500	4/13,105	Japan Sea
Shad-11	Donald L. Mehlop	'37	41	zero	zero	Marcus Island
Spikefish-4	Robert R. Managhan	'38	54	1/1,800	1/1,660	East China Sea
Sterlet-5	H. H. Lewis	USNR	48	zero	zero	Empire
Tench-3	Thomas S. Baskett	'35	49	zero	zero	Empire
Tigrone-3	Vincent E. Schumacher	'38	41	zero	zero	Empire
Toro-2	James D. Grant	'31	36	zero	zero	Empire
Torsk-2	Bafford E. Lewellen	'31	50	4/6,000	3/2,476	Japan Sea
			TOTALS:	18/62,600	14/35,049	

SUBMARINE WAR PATROLS DEPARTING PEARL HARBOR, AUGUST 1945

Boat, Patrol Number	Skipper and Class		Days	Ships/Tonnage Wartime Credit	JANAC Credit	Area
Apogon-8	Arthur C. House, Jr.	'34	26	zero	zero	Marcus Island
Cavalla-6	Herman J. Kossler	'34	36	zero	zero	Empire

Cutlass-1	Herbert L. Jukes	'32	22	zero	Polar circuit
Devilfish-4	Stephen S. Mann, Jr.	'38	20	zero	Empire
Haddo-10	Frank C. Lynch, Jr.	'38	31	zero	Empire
Pilotfish-6	Allan G. Schnable	'34	32	zero	Empire
Pintado-6	Romondt Budd	'35	19	zero	Empire
Runner II-2	Raymond H. Bass	'31	29	zero	Empire
Sea Cat-4	Richard H. Bowers	'38	27	zero	Polar circuit
Sea Devil-5	Charles F. McGivern	'38	25	zero	East China Sea
Segundo-5	Stephen L. Johnson	'39	30	zero	Polar circuit
Stickleback-1	Harley K. Nauman	'34	34	zero	Japan Sea
Tilefish-6	Walter F. Schlech, Jr.	'36	33	zero	Empire

PRESENT AT SURRENDER CEREMONY, TOKYO BAY, SEPTEMBER 2, 1945

Proteus   Lewis S. Parks, Commander, Squadron Twenty

Runner II	Raymond H. Bass
Archerfish	Joseph F. Enright
Haddo	Frank C. Lynch, Jr.
Gato	Richard Holden
Sea Cat	Richard H. Bowers
Muskallunge	William H. Lawrence
Tigrone	Vincent E. Schumacher
Razorback	Charles D. Brown
Pilotfish	Allan G. Schnable
Hake	Frank E. Haylor
Segundo	Stephen L. Johnson
Cavalla	Herman J. Kossler

Appendix G
Top Skippers of World War II
By Number of Confirmed Ships Sunk†

Asterisk indicates Medal-of-Honor winner

	NUMBER OF PATROLS	SHIPS/TONS CREDITED	SHIPS/TONS JANAC
1. Richard H. O'Kane, 1934 * *Tang*	5	31/227,800	24/93,824
2. Slade D. Cutter, 1935 *Seahorse*	4	21/142,300	19/72,000
3. Dudley W. Morton, 1930 *R-5, Wahoo*	6	17/100,500	19/55,000
4. Eugene B. Fluckey, 1935 * *Barb*	5	25/179,700	16⅓/95,360
5. Samuel D. Dealey, 1930 * *Harder*	6	20½/82,500	16/54,002
6. Reuben T. Whitaker, 1934 *S-44, Flasher*	5	18½/111,500	14½/60,846
7. Gordon W. Underwood, 1932 *Spadefish*	3	14/89,600	14/75,386
8. Royce L. Gross, 1930 *Seawolf, Boarfish*	7	13½/80,500	14/65,735
9. Charles O. Triebel, 1929 *S-15, Snook*	8	13/83,300	14/58,837
10. John S. Coye, Jr., 1933 *Silversides*	6	14/71,700	14/39,000
11. William B. Sieglaff, 1931 *Tautog, Tench*	7	15/63,500	13/32,886
12. Thomas S. Baskett, 1935 *S-37, Tautog, Tench*	7	13/50,700	12/27,273
13. Henry C. Bruton, 1926 *Greenling*	4	11/82,600	11/54,564
14. Bafford E. Lewellen, 1931 *Pollack, Torsk*	6	11/38,200	11/23,685
15. Charles H. Andrews, 1930 *Gurnard*	6	11/71,500	10/57,243 ‡
16. Robert E. Dornin, 1935 *Trigger*	3	13/96,500	10/54,595
17. Eric L. Barr, Jr., 1934 *Bluegill*	6	12/51,200	10/46,212

† Skippers who sank fewer than five ships are not listed.
‡ Including German ship, not listed in JANAC but officially credited.

TOP SKIPPERS OF WORLD WAR II

	Number of Patrols	Ships/Tons Credited	Ships/Tons JANAC
18. Ralph M. Metcalf, 1935 *Pogy, Loggerhead*	5	10/54,800	10/40,040
19. Raymond H. Bass, 1931 *Plunger, Runner II*	8	12/70,300	10/37,977
20. Malcolm E. Garrison, 1932 *Sandlance*	4	11/60,100	10/37,368
21. Thomas B. Klakring, 1927 *S-17, Guardfish*	5	11/76,900	10/33,122
22. John A. Moore, 1932 *Grayback*	3	12½/63,500	9½/45,757
23. Glynn R. Donaho, 1927 *Flying Fish, Picuda*	7	14/71,400	9½/29,870
24. Eli T. Reich, 1935 *Sealion II*	3	11/101,400	9/59,839
25. Walter T. Griffith, 1934 *Bowfin, Bullhead*	5	17/106,300	9/45,874
26. Edward E. Shelby, 1933 *Sunfish*	5	14/106,200	9/45,613
27. Robert D. Risser, 1934 *Flying Fish*	5	8/33,500	9/40,931
28. Norvell G. Ward, 1935 *Guardfish*	5	14/90,200	9/39,302
29. Willard R. Laughon, 1933 *Rasher*	3	10/60,200	9/38,340
30. George E. Porter, Jr., 1932 *Bluefish, Sennet*	6	14/70,300	9/30,940
31. John E. Lee, 1930 *S-12, Grayling, Croaker*	10	16/74,100	9/28,562
32. Russell Kefauver, 1933 *Tambor, Springer*	6	13/64,000	9/23,081
33. William J. Germershausen, 1935 *Tambor, Spadefish*	4	10/42,300	9/16,277
34. William S. Post, Jr., 1930 *Gudgeon, Spot*	7	19/110,900	8½/54,213
35. William T. Kinsella, 1934 *Ray*	4	10½/80,500	8½/34,101
36. Charles E. Loughlin, 1933 *S-14, Queenfish*	8	12/109,400	8⅓/41,718
37. Enrique D. Haskins, 1933 *Guitarro*	3	11½/61,200	8⅓/25,400
38. Henry G. Munson, 1932 *S-38, Crevalle, Rasher*	9	13/113,400	8/67,630

	Number of Patrols	Ships/Tons Credited	Ships/Tons JANAC
39. Creed C. Burlingame, 1927 *Silversides*	5	11/71,700	8/46,865
40. Bernard A. Clarey, 1934 *Pintado*	4	13/98,600	8/42,956
41. Thomas M. Dykers, 1927 *Jack*	4	10/77,900	8/42,417
42. Lowell T. Stone, 1929 *Lapon*	4	10/68,600	8/39,266
43. Robert H. Rice, 1927 *Drum, Paddle*	5	8/49,000	8/39,100
44. Donald F. Weiss, 1929 *Tinosa*	3	9/67,100	8/39,047
45. Vernon L. Lowrance, 1930 *Kingfish, Sea Dog*	7	9/62,200	8/34,199
46. Roy M. Davenport, 1933 *Haddock, Trepang*	6	17/151,900	8/29,662
47. Charles C. Kirkpatrick, 1931 *Triton*	3	10/44,600	8/22,749
48. Anton R. Gallaher, 1933 *Bang*	5	15/94,000	8/20,181
49. George L. Street III, 1937 * *Tirante*	2	11/35,700	8/15,886
50. John A. Tyree, Jr., 1933 *Finback*	5	8½/55,900	7½/39,371
51. Frank G. Selby, 1933 *Puffer*	4	9½/78,600	7½/38,159
52. Lawson P. Ramage, 1931 * *Trout, Parche*	7	10/77,600	7½/36,681
53. Robert J. Foley, 1927 *Gato*	6	10/66,000	7½/26,235
54. George W. Grider, 1936 *Flasher*	2	6/43,800	7/43,718
55. John C. Broach, 1927 *Hake*	5	8/51,400	7/37,923
56. Thomas W. Hogan, 1931 *Bonefish*	4	15/105,500	7/34,329
57. James C. Dempsey, 1931 *S-37, Spearfish, Cod*	10	9/52,100	7/30,794
58. William H. Hazzard, 1935 *Blenny*	4	8/43,100	7/18,087
59. Francis A. Greenup, 1936 *Hardhead*	4	6/25,100	7/14,246

TOP SKIPPERS OF WORLD WAR II

	Number of Patrols	Ships/Tons Credited	Ships/Tons JANAC
60. Earl T. Hydeman, 1932 *Sea Dog*	2	7/36,200	7/14,036
61. Thomas L. Wogan, 1930 *S-34, Tarpon, Besugo*	9	9/51,700	6/46,730 †
62. Louis D. McGregor, Jr., 1930 *Pike, Redfish*	4	9/74,600	6/44,637
63. William C. Thompson, Jr. 1935 *Cabrilla*	4	10/66,300	6/36,062
64. John H. Maurer, 1935 *Atule*	4	7/34,200	6/33,379
65. Joseph H. Willingham, 1926 *Tautog, Bowfin*	5	11/55,500	6/25,636
66. Howard W. Gilmore, 1926 * *Growler*	4	8/37,300	6/22,681
67. Duncan C. MacMillan, 1926 *Thresher*	3	10/61,400	6/22,277
68. Frederick B. Warder, 1925 *Seawolf*	7	8/38,900	6/18,719
69. William H. Brockman, 1927 *Nautilus, Haddock*	6	8/29,500	5½/23,829
70. Walter G. Ebert, 1930 *Scamp*	6	6/49,000	5/34,108
71. James W. Coe, 1930 *S-39, Skipjack, Cisco*	7	7/45,300	5/26,130
72. John R. Moore, 1929 *S-44, Sailfish*	6	3/10,100	5/23,978
73. Philip H. Ross, 1927 *Halibut, Golet*	6	6/45,400	5/23,226
74. William J. Millican, 1928 *S-18, Thresher, Escolar*	7	6/40,000	5/21,525
75. Roy S. Benson, 1929 *Trigger, Razorback*	5	6/36,900	5/17,652
76. Chester W. Nimitz, Jr., 1936 *Haddo*	3	5½/17,600	5/14,636

† Including the German raider *Michel*.

Appendix H

Best War Patrols by Number of Ships Sunk

Boat and Patrol No.	Skipper	Ships Sunk*	Tonnage
1. *Tang*-3	Richard H. O'Kane	10	39,100
2. *Wahoo*-4	Dudley W. Morton	9	20,000
3. *Tang*-5	Richard H. O'Kane	7	21,772
4. *Flasher*-5	George W. Grider	6	42,800
5. *Spadefish*-1	Gordon W. Underwood	6	31,500
6. *Silversides*-10	John S. Coye, Jr.	6	14,141
7. *Tirante*-1	George L. Street III	6	12,621
8. *Sea Dog*-4	Earl T. Hydeman	6	7,186
9. *Ray*-6	William T. Kinsella	5⅓	12,645
10. *Rasher*-5	Henry G. Munson	5	52,600
11. *Seahorse*-2	Slade D. Cutter	5	27,579
12. *Bowfin*-2	Walter T. Griffith	5	26,458
13. *Ray*-5	William T. Kinsella	5	26,000
14. *Hammerhead*-2	John C. Martin	5	25,178
15. *Tang*-1	Richard H. O'Kane	5	21,400
16. *Pogy*-5	Ralph M. Metcalf	5	21,150
17. *Snook*-5	Charles O. Triebel	5	21,046
18. *Seahorse*-3	Slade D. Cutter	5	20,900
19. *Seahorse*-4	Slade D. Cutter	5	19,374
20. *Sandlance*-2	Malcolm E. Garrison	5	18,328
21. *Guardfish*-1	Thomas B. Klakring	5	16,709
22. *Triton*-3	Charles C. Kirkpatrick	5	15,843
23. *Barb*-8	Eugene B. Fluckey	5	15,472
24. *Harder*-2	Samuel D. Dealey	5	15,272
25. *Haddo*-7	Chester W. Nimitz, Jr.	5	14,460
26. *Spadefish*-5	William J. Germershausen	5	8,578

* According to JANAC figures.

Appendix I

Best War Patrols by Tonnage of Ships Sunk

Boat and Patrol No.	Skipper	Ships Sunk*	Tonnage
1. *Archerfish*-5	Joseph F. Enright	1	59,000
2. *Rasher*-5	Henry G. Munson	5	52,600

* According to JANAC figures.

Boat and Patrol No.	Skipper	Ships Sunk *	Tonnage
3. *Flasher*-5	George W. Grider	6	42,800
4. *Tang*-3	Richard H. O'Kane	10	39,100
5. *Barb*-9	Eugene B. Fluckey	3	36,800
6. *Sealion II*-3	Eli T. Reich	2	32,900
7. *Albacore*-9	James W. Blanchard	2	32,000
8. *Spadefish*-1	Gordon W. Underwood	6	31,500
9. *Spadefish*-2	Gordon W. Underwood	4	30,400
10. *Cavalla*-1	Herman J. Kossler	1	30,000
11. *Gurnard*-5	Charles H. Andrews	4	29,700
12. *Sailfish*-10	Robert E. M. Ward	3	29,571
13. *Tarpon*-6	Thomas L. Wogan	2	27,910
14. *Silversides*-4	Creed C. Burlingame	4	27,798
15. *Seahorse*-2	Slade D. Cutter	5	27,579
16. *Trigger*-6	Robert E. Dornin	4	27,095
17. *Bowfin*-2	Walter T. Griffith	5	26,458
18. *Ray*-5	William T. Kinsella	5	26,000
19. *Seawolf*-12	Royce L. Gross	4½	25,793
20. *Atule*-1	John H. Maurer	4	25,691
21. *Hammerhead*-2	John C. Martin	5	25,178
22. *Dace*-5	Bladen D. Claggett	3	25,141
23. *Flasher*-3	Reuben T. Whitaker	4½	24,949
24. *Pintado*-2	Bernard A. Clarey	2	24,663
25. *Cabrilla*-6	William C. Thompson	4	24,557
26. *Bonefish*-1	Thomas W. Hogan	3	24,206
27. *Barb*-11	Eugene B. Fluckey	4⅓	24,197

* According to JANAC figures.

Appendix J
Top Submarines by Number of Ships Sunk

Boat	Skippers	Ships Sunk *
1. *Tautog*	Willingham, Sieglaff, Baskett	26
2. *Tang*	O'Kane	24
3. *Silversides*	Burlingame, Coye, J. C. Nichols	23
4. *Flasher*	Whitaker, Grider	21
5. *Spadefish*	Underwood, Germershausen	21
6. *Seahorse*	Cutter, Wilkins	20

* According to JANAC figures.

Boat	Skippers	Ships Sunk*
7. Wahoo	Kennedy, Morton	20
8. Guardfish	Klakring, N. G. Ward	19
9. Rasher	Hutchinson, Laughon, Munson	18
10. Seawolf	Warder, Gross	18
11. Trigger	Benson, Dornin, Harlfinger, Connole	18
12. Barb	Waterman, Fluckey	17
13. Snook	Triebel, Browne	17
14. Thresher	W. L. Anderson, Millican, H. Hull, MacMillan, Middleton	17
15. Bowfin	Willingham, Griffith, Corbus, A. K. Tyree	16
16. Harder	Dealey	16
17. Pogy	Wales, Metcalf, Bowers	16
18. Sunfish	R. W. Peterson, Shelby, Reed	16
19. Tinosa	Daspit, Weiss, Latham	16
20. Drum	Rice, McMahon, Williamson, Rindskopf	15
21. Flying Fish	Donaho, Watkins, Risser	15
22. Greenling	Bruton, Grant, Gerwick	15
23. Jack	Dykers, Krapf, Fuhrman	15
24. Grayback	Saunders, Stephan, J. A. Moore	14
25. Kingfish	Lowrance, Jukes, Harper	14

* According to JANAC figures.

Appendix K

Top Submarines by Tonnage of Ships Sunk

Boat	Skippers	Tonnage*
1. Flasher	Whitaker, Grider	100,231
2. Rasher	Hutchinson, Laughon, Munson	99,901
3. Barb	Waterman, Fluckey	96,628
4. Tang	O'Kane	93,824
5. Silversides	Burlingame, Coye, J. C. Nichols	90,080
6. Spadefish	Underwood, Germershausen	88,091
7. Trigger	Benson, Dornin, Harlfinger, Connole	86,552
8. Drum	Rice, McMahon, Williamson, Rindskopf	80,580
9. Jack	Dykers, Krapf, Fuhrman	76,687
10. Snook	Triebel, Browne	75,473
11. Tautog	Willingham, Sieglaff, Baskett	72,606
12. Seahorse	Cutter, Wilkins	72,529
13. Guardfish	Klakring, N. G. Ward	72,424

* According to JANAC figures.

Boat	Skippers	Tonnage *
14. Seawolf	Warder, Gross	71,609
15. Gudgeon	Grenfell, Stovall, Post	71,047
16. Sealion II	Reich, Putman	68,297
17. Bowfin	Willingham, Griffith, Corbus, A. K. Tyree	67,882
18. Thresher	W. L. Anderson, Millican, H. Hull, MacMillan, Middleton	66,172
19. Tinosa	Daspit, Weiss, Latham	64,655
20. Grayback	Saunders, Stephan, J. S. Moore	63,835
21. Pogy	Wales, Metcalf, Bowers	62,633
22. Bonefish	Hogan, Edge	61,345
23. Wahoo	Kennedy, Morton	60,038
24. Sunfish	R. W. Peterson, Shelby, Reed	59,815
25. Archerfish	Wright, Enright	59,800

* According to JANAC figures.

Appendix L
Submarine Losses in World War II
In Pacific Unless Otherwise Noted
SOURCE: *U.S. Submarine Losses in WW II*

Submarine	Skipper	Date	
1941			
1. Sealion	Richard G. Voge	12-10-41	
1942			
2. S-36	John R. McKnight, Jr.	1-20-42	
3. S-26	Earle C. Hawk	1-24-42	(Atlantic)
4. Shark	Louis Shane, Jr.*	2- 42	
5. Perch	David A. Hurt	3-3-42	
6. S-27	Herbert L. Jukes	6-19-42	
7. S-39	Francis E. Brown	8-14-42	
8. Grunion	Mannert L. Abele *	7/8 -42	
1943			
9. Argonaut	John R. Pierce *	1-10-43	
10. Amberjack	John A. Bole, Jr.*	2-16-43	
11. Grampus	John R. Craig *	3/5 -43	
12. Triton	George K. MacKenzie, Jr.*	3-15-43	
13. Pickerel	Augustus H. Alston, Jr.*	4-3-43	
14. Grenadier	John A. Fitzgerald	4-22-43	

* Killed in action.

Submarine	Skipper	Date	
15. *Runner*	Joseph H. Bourland *	5-28/7-4-43	
16. *R-12*	Edward E. Shelby	6-12-43	(Atlantic)
17. *Grayling*	Robert M. Brinker *	9-9/9-12-43	
18. *Pompano*	Willis M. Thomas *	8-29/9-27-43	
19. *Cisco*	James W. Coe *	9-28-43	
20. *S-44*	Francis E. Brown *	10-7-43	
21. *Dorado*	Earle C. Schneider *	10-12-43	(Atlantic)
22. *Wahoo*	Dudley W. Morton *	10-11-43	
23. *Corvina*	Roderick S. Rooney *	11-16-43	
24. *Sculpin*	Fred Connaway *	11-19-43	
25. *Capelin*	Elliott E. Marshall *	11-23/12-9-43	

1944

Submarine	Skipper	Date
26. *Scorpion*	Maximilian G. Schmidt *	1-5/2-24-44
27. *Grayback*	John A. Moore *	2-26-44
28. *Trout*	Albert H. Clark *	2-29-44
29. *Tullibee*	Charles F. Brindupke *	3-26/27-44
30. *Gudgeon*	Robert A. Bonin *	4-7/5-11-44
31. *Herring*	David Zabriskie, Jr.*	6-1-44
32. *Golet*	James S. Clark *	6-14-44
33. *S-28*	J. G. Campbell *	7-4-44
34. *Robalo*	Manning M. Kimmel *	7-26-44
35. *Flier*	John D. Crowley	8-13-44
36. *Harder*	Samuel D. Dealey *	8-24-44
37. *Seawolf*	Albert M. Bontier *	10-3-44
38. *Darter*	David H. McClintock	10-24-44
39. *Shark II*	Edward N. Blakely *	10-24-44
40. *Tang*	Richard H. O'Kane	10-24-44
41. *Escolar*	William J. Millican *	10-17/11-3-44
42. *Albacore*	Hugh R. Rimmer *	11-7-44
43. *Growler*	Thomas B. Oakley, Jr.*	11-8-44
44. *Scamp*	John C. Hollingsworth *	11-9/16-44

1945

Submarine	Skipper	Date
45. *Swordfish*	Keats E. Montross *	1-12-45
46. *Barbel*	Conde L. Raguet *	2-4-45
47. *Kete*	Edward Ackerman *	3-20/31-45
48. *Trigger*	David R. Connole *	3-26/28-45
49. *Snook*	John F. Walling *	4-8/20-45
50. *Lagarto*	Frank D. Latta *	5-3-45
51. *Bonefish*	Lawrence L. Edge *	6-18-45
52. *Bullhead*	Edward R. Holt, Jr.*	8-6-45

* Killed in action.

Sources

I. General Bibliography

The books and periodicals listed here deal with the history of submarines, torpedoes, diesel engines, World War I, the naval policy in the peacetime years 1918 to 1939, and general studies of World War II. All proved useful in writing this book. In particular, the author is indebted to Samuel Eliot Morison for his magnificent fifteen-volume naval history of World War II and to specialized articles in the quasi-official naval journal *United States Naval Institute Proceedings*, published at Annapolis, Maryland, and identified below as *U.S.N.I.P.*

Alden, Carroll Storrs. "American Submarine Operations in the War," *U.S.N.I.P.*, June 1920.

Barnes, Robert Hatfield. "Japan's First Submarines," *U.S.N.I.P.*, February 1943.

―――. *United States Submarines*. New Haven, Conn.: H. F. Morse Associates, 1946.

Braisted, William R. *United States Navy in the Pacific 1909–1922*. Austin, Tex.: University of Texas Press, 1971.

Cable, F. T. *The Birth and Development of the American Submarine*. New York: Harper & Brothers, 1924.

Churchill, Winston S. *The Second World War*. 6 vols. Boston: Houghton Mifflin Company, 1948–53.

Cohen, Jerome B. *Japan's Economy in War and Reconstruction* (Institute of Pacific Relations). Minneapolis, Minn.: University of Minnesota Press, 1949.

Corbett, Sir Julian. *Naval Operations*. 3 vols. London: Longmans, Green & Company, 1920–23.

Craven, Francis S. "The Painful Development of a Professional Navy," *U.S.N.I.P.*, May 1966.

Craven, Wesley F., and James L. Cate, eds. *Army Air Forces in World War II*. 7 vols. Chicago: University of Chicago Press, 1948–58.

Cross, Wilbur. *Challengers of the Deep.* New York: William Sloane Associates, 1959.

Davis, Vincent. *The Admiral's Lobby.* Chapel Hill, N.C.: University of North Carolina Press, 1967.

Dictionary of American Naval Fighting Ships, Vol. 1 (A-B), Vol. 2 (C-F), Vol. 3 (G-K), Vol. 4 (L-M), Vol. 5 (N-Q), Vol. 6 (R-S) not yet published, Vol. 7 (T-Z) not yet published. Washington, D.C.: U.S. Government Printing Office.

Doenitz, Karl. *Memoirs: Ten Years and Twenty Days.* New York: World Book Company, 1959.

Douglas, Lawrence Henry. "Submarine Disarmament 1919–36." Unpublished dissertation on file in Navy Library, Washington, D.C.

Frothingham, Thomas G. *The Naval History of the World War.* 3 vols. Cambridge, Mass.: Harvard University Press, 1927.

Fuchida, Mitsuo, and Okumiya Masatake. *Midway: The Battle That Doomed Japan.* Annapolis, Md.: U.S. Naval Institute, 1955.

Fukaya, Hajime. "Japan's Wartime Carrier Construction," *U.S.N.I.P.,* September 1955.

———. "The Shokakus—Pearl Harbor to Leyte Gulf," *U.S.N.I.P.,* June 1952.

———. "Three Japanese Submarine Developments," *U.S.N.I.P.,* August 1952.

General Board, U.S. Navy, Minutes, 1930–38. Unpublished, on file in the Classified Operational Archives, Building 210, Navy Yard, Washington, D.C. A priceless source on U.S. submarine development.

Gibson, R. H., and Maurice Prendergast. *The German Submarine War.* New York: R. R. Smith, 1931.

Hara, Tameichi, Fred Saito, and Roger Pineau. *Japanese Destroyer Captain.* New York: Ballantine Books, 1961.

Hashimoto, Mochitsura. *Sunk: The Story of the Japanese Submarine Fleet 1941–45.* New York: Henry Holt & Company, 1954.

Herzog, Bob, and Allison W. Saville. "Top Submarines in Two World Wars," *U.S.N.I.P.,* September 1961.

Hezlet, Arthur. *The Submarine and Sea Power.* New York: Stein and Day, 1967. A brilliant study of European submarine development.

Howard, Warren S. "The Dragon Puts to Sea," *U.S.N.I.P.,* August 1951.

———. "Japanese Destroyers in World War II," *U.S.N.I.P.,* January 1952.

———. "Japan's Heavy Cruisers in the War," *U.S.N.I.P.,* May 1950.

———. "The Kongos [Japanese battleships] in World War II," *U.S.N.I.P.,* November 1948.

———. "The Mogamis: Cheat Cruisers Extraordinary," *U.S.N.I.P.,* November 1949.

Interrogations of Japanese Officials. 2 vols. U.S. Strategic Bombing Survey (Pacific). Washington, D.C.: U.S. Government Printing Office.

Irwin, Mariette W., and Julie A. Joa, eds. *Dolphin Tales.* Norfolk, Va.: Teagle and Little, 1971.

Ito, Masanori, with Roger Pineau. *The End of the Imperial Japanese Navy.* New York: W. W. Norton & Company, 1956.

Jameson, William, K.B.E. *Most Formidable Thing.* London: Rupert-Hart-Davis, 1965.
Karig, Walter. *Battle Report.* 6 vols. New York: Rinehart & Company, 1944–52.
―――― with Russell Harris and Frank A. Manson. "Battleship Banzai," *U.S.N.I.P.,* October 1949. The *Yamato* sortie.
King, Ernest J., and Walter M. Whitehill. *Fleet Admiral King—A Naval Record.* New York: W. W. Norton & Company, 1952.
Kittredge, G. W. "Stalking the *Takao* in Singapore Harbor," *U.S.N.I.P.,* April 1957.
Kuenne, Robert E. *The Attack Submarine.* New Haven, Conn.: Yale University Press, 1965.
Lake, Simon. *The Submarine in War and Peace.* Philadelphia: J. B. Lippincott Company, 1918.
Lockwood, Charles A., and Hans C. Adamson. *Hell at 50 Fathoms.* Philadelphia: Chilton Books, 1962.
Long, E. John. "Japan's Underseas Carriers," *U.S.N.I.P.,* June 1950.
Lord, Walter. *Day of Infamy.* New York: Henry Holt & Company, 1957.
――――. *Incredible Victory.* New York: Harper & Row, 1967.
Lundeberg, Philip K. "American Anti-Submarine Operations in the Atlantic, May 1943–May 1945." Ph.D. thesis, Harvard University, 1953.
Maas, Peter. *The Rescuer.* New York: Harper & Row, 1967.
MacArthur, Douglas. *Reports of General MacArthur.* 4 vols. Washington, D.C.: U.S. Government Printing Office, 1966.
Magdeburger, E. C. "Diesel Engines in Submarines," *A.S.N.E.,* Vol. 37, 1925.
Masland, John W. "Japanese-German Naval Collaboration in World War II," *U.S.N.I.P.,* February 1949.
Matsumoto, Kitaro, and Chihaya Masataka. "Design and Construction of Yamato and Musashi," *U.S.N.I.P.,* October 1953.
Meigs, J. F. "Japanese Sea Power," *U.S.N.I.P.,* February 1944.
Moore, Lynn L. "Shinano: The Jinx Carrier," *U.S.N.I.P.,* February 1953.
Morison, Samuel Eliot. *History of United States Naval Operation in World War II.* 15 vols. Boston: Little, Brown and Company, 1947–62.
Morris, Richard K. *John P. Holland, 1841–1914.* Annapolis, Md.: U.S. Naval Institute Press, 1966.
Morton, Louis. *The Fall of the Philippines.* Washington, D.C.: Office of the Chief of Military History, Department of the Army, 1953.
――――. "The Japanese Decision for War," *U.S.N.I.P.,* December 1954.
Nakayama, Sadayoshi. "Japan's Phenomenal Shipbuilders," *U.S.N.I.P.,* August 1966.
Nimitz, Chester, and E. B. Potter. *The Great Sea War.* Englewood Cliffs, N.J.: Prentice-Hall, 1960.
Niven, John, Courtlandt Canby, and Vernon Welsh, eds. *Dynamic America: A History of the General Dynamics Corporation and Its Predecessor Companies.* Garden City, N.Y.: Doubleday & Company, 1958.

Ofstie, R. A. *The Campaigns of the Pacific War*. U.S. Strategic Bombing Survey (Pacific). Washington, D.C.: U.S. Government Printing Office.

Perry, Milton F. *Infernal Machines*. Baton Rouge, La.: Louisiana State University Press, 1965.

Possony, Stefan T. "Japanese Naval Strategy," *U.S.N.I.P.*, May 1944.

Potter, E. B. "The Navy's War Against Japan—A Strategic Analysis," *U.S.N.I.P.*, August 1950.

Powel, R. J. H., "Newport Torpedo Station." Unpublished monograph, U.S. Navy Library, Washington, D.C.

Prange, Gordon W. "Miracle at Midway," *Reader's Digest*, November 1972.

Reinertson, J. H. "The Bureau of Ships' Part in the Development of a Deisel Engine for the U.S. Navy," A.S.N.E. paper no. 58-OGP-9.

———, L. E. Alsager, and T. J. Morley. "The Submarine Propulsion Plant—Development and Prospects," *Naval Engineer Journal*, May 1963.

Robinson, Walton L. "Akagi—Famous Japanese Carrier," *U.S.N.I.P.*, May 1948.

Roskill, Stephen W. *Naval Policy Between the Wars*. London: William Collins Sons & Co., 1968.

———. *The War at Sea 1939–1945*. 3 vols. London: H.M. Stationery Office, 1954–61.

Rowland, Buford, and William B. Boyd. *U.S. Navy Bureau of Ordnance in World War II*. Washington, D.C.: U.S. Government Printing Office.

Saville, Allison W. "German Submarines in the Far East," *U.S.N.I.P.*, August 1961.

Sherrod, Robert. *History of Marine Corps Aviation in World War II*. Washington, D.C.: Combat Forces Press, 1952.

Ships' Data, U.S. Naval Vessels. Washington, D.C.: U.S. Government Printing Office, January 1, 1938.

Sims, W. S. *The Victory at Sea*. Garden City, N.Y.: Doubleday, Page, 1921.

Smith, S. E., ed. *The United States Navy in World War II*. New York: William Morrow & Company, 1966.

Sprout, Harold and Margaret. *The Rise of American Naval Power*. Princeton, N.J.: Princeton University Press, 1939.

Stafford, Edward P. *The Far and the Deep*. New York: G. P. Putnam's Sons, 1967.

Sternhell, Charles M., and Alan M. Thorndike. *ASW in World War II*. Washington, D.C.: Navy Department, 1946.

Tanabe, Yabachi. "I Sank the Yorktown at Midway," *U.S.N.I.P.*, May 1963.

Taylor, John C. *German Warships of World War I*. Garden City, N.Y.: Doubleday & Company, 1970.

Toland, John. *The Rising Sun*. New York: Random House, 1970.

Torisu, Kennosuke, and Chihaya Masataka. "Japanese Submarine Tactics," *U.S.N.I.P.*, February 1961.

"U.S. Naval Administration in World War II." Bureau of Ordnance. Unpublished manuscript on file in the Navy Library, Washington, D.C.

U.S. Submarine Data Book. Submarine Force Library and Museum, Naval Submarine Base, New London, Conn.

Von Tirpitz, Alfred P. *My Memoirs.* New York: AMS Press, 1919.

Von der Porten, Edward P. *The German Navy in World War II.* New York: Thomas Y. Crowell Company, 1969.

Wilkinson, J. Burke. "Sneak Craft Attack in the Pacific," *U.S.N.I.P.*, March 1947.

Yokoi, Toshiyuki. "Thoughts on Japan's Naval Defeat," *U.S.N.I.P.*, October 1960.

Yokota, Yutaka. *The Kaiten Weapon.* New York: Ballantine Books, 1962.

Yoshida, Mitsuru. "The End of Yamato," *U.S.N.I.P.*, February 1952.

II. Submarine Operations

1. *Patrol Reports, Ship's Histories, and Log Books*

Every submarine making a war patrol turned in an official patrol report. The bulk of the material for this book was drawn directly from the patrol reports. In all, there were 1,682 patrols. The reports, often one hundred pages or more, contain a daily log of noteworthy events, plus (in some cases) track charts, supplements on torpedo attacks, machinery failure, ship and aircraft sightings, weather and other technical data. Usually, a Special Mission or an Ultra contact produced a separate—more highly classified—supplement because it dealt with intelligence matters. In the preparation of this book, the author consulted all 1,682 patrol reports and the endorsements to these reports appended by the division, squadron, and force commanders.

The patrol reports may be consulted at two locations: the Classified Operational Archives at Building 210, the Navy Yard, Washington, D.C., and in the Submarine Force Library, U.S. Submarine Base, New London, Connecticut. All have been declassified. The Special Mission supplements have been—or may be—declassified under new declassification rules. They are on file in the Classified Operational Archives, but not in New London. The Ultra supplements have not been declassified.

Many of the patrol reports have been summarized in chronological order and produced as "Ship's Histories" in multilith form. Some of these histories are excellent and accurate; others are not and must be used with care. These may be obtained for a small fee from the Department of the Navy, Naval History Division, Washington Navy Yard, Washington, D.C. 20390.

The Ship's Histories are further summarized in the *Dictionary of American Naval Fighting Ships* already listed with the exception of volumes 6 and 7, which have not yet been published. Some of the errors in the multilith ship's histories have been carried forward to the *Dictionary*. The submarine histories summarized in volume 1 (A to B) are hopelessly brief. This same volume contains a valuable index listing submarine contracts and characteristics (size, armament, engines) from 1900 to 1953.

The Classified Operational Archives also has on file ship's deck logs kept by the quartermaster of the watch. These are highly detailed, hour-by-hour —sometimes minute-by-minute—records of events on each submarine at sea and in port. The logs provided much of the raw material for the patrol reports. In addition, there are on file "sailing lists," a list of all personnel sailing with the boat.

2. *Lockwood Papers*

Admiral Lockwood left his official papers, personal diaries, speeches, correspondence, and other items to the Library of Congress. In all, there are twelve lineal feet of papers, covering the years from about 1925 to 1945. The official correspondence (and personal diaries) for the war years is an indispensable source for anyone writing a history of the submarine war. There are hundreds of letters from Lockwood to Christie and Fife and vice versa. The author drew heavily on this material for this book.

3. *Christie Papers*

Admiral Christie, who was living in Hawaii at the time this book was completed, has not yet consigned his papers to a repository. However, he made available to the author considerable official correspondence on specific subjects and responded to many queries. He also made available his personal diary for the years 1943–44, a detailed day-by-day account of his activities, problems, and other matters.

4. *Biographies*

Fortunately for the researcher, the Navy Department has on file brief— but officially correct—biographies of all Naval Academy graduates, compilied from information supplied by each officer. These contain names of parents, birthplace, schooling, maiden name of wife, names of children, a detailed chronological summary of naval service, and promotions and awards with abbreviated citations. The author made use of over five hundred such biographies for this book, all kindly furnished by the navy. Biographies may be obtained by writing Biographies Branch, Department of the Navy, Office of Information, Washington, D.C. 20350.

In addition, the United States Naval Academy Alumni Association, Inc., annually publishes a highly useful document, *Register of Alumni*. This is a thoroughly indexed list of all Naval Academy graduates and nongraduates, living or deceased. Officers are listed by class in order of their standing at graduation, and the entries include the current address of each officer or widow, if any. The author has made use of this document in countless ways and through it was able to establish direct contact with scores of retired officers (see below). A copy may be obtained by writing The U.S. Naval Academy Alumni Association, Inc., Alumni House, Annapolis, Maryland.

Finally, the Naval Academy Yearbook *The Lucky Bag* proved useful in some cases. Issues are on file in Annapolis, the Library of Congress, and the Navy Library in Washington.

5. *Interviews, Letters, Special Reports*

During World War II, Admiral Lockwood assigned several men to conduct classified taped interviews with some staff officers and submarine skippers. These interviews, now declassified, transcribed, and filed in the Classified Operational Archives, proved useful as source material.

In addition, several key officers submitted special reports on certain phases of the war, notably Admiral Thomas C. Hart and his submarine commander, John Wilkes (whose report was actually written by James Fife). Both were indispensable in sorting out the complex retreat of the Asiatic Fleet (and submarines) from Manila to Australia. Their reports are on file in the Classified Operational Archives.

In 1971, 1972 and 1973, the author conducted numerous and exhaustive taped interviews with scores of staff officers and skippers or their widows. These interviews covered the peacetime years, the evolution of the submarine, diesel engines and torpedoes, and the Submarine School, as well as the war. In addition, he mailed extensive questionnaires to many skippers who were invited to respond on tape—in effect a taped self-interview. Finally, he corresponded by mail with scores of officers and widows on various points. These sources provided much material for this book. The tapes and letters will be turned over to officials at the Archive of Contemporary History, University of Wyoming, Laramie.

The men—or in some cases their widows—who contributed material in wartime reports and interviews and letters to the author are listed below.

Mrs. Mannert L. Abele
Frank C. Acker
Stephen H. Ambruster
William L. Anderson
William R. Anderson
Charles H. Andrews
Theodore C. Aylward

John B. Azer
Barton E. Bacon, Jr.
Eric L. Barr, Sr.
Thomas S. Baskett
Raymond H. Bass
Edward L. Beach
Rafael C. Benitez

Carter L. Bennett
Roy S. Benson
Leon N. Blair
James W. Blanchard
John H. Brady
William H. Brockman
Henry C. Bruton
Eliot H. Bryant
Creed C. Burlingame
Mrs. John L. Burnside, Jr.
Joseph A. Callaghan
Gordon Campbell
Edward S. Carmick
Bruce L. Carr
Wreford G. Chapple
Ralph W. Christie
Bladen D. Claggett
Frederic B. Clarke
Robert H. Close
Merrill Comstock
John S. Coye
Mrs. John R. Craig
George C. Crawford
John D. Crowley
Slade D. Cutter
Lawrence R. Daspit
Roy M. Davenport
James W. Davis
Samuel D. Dealey
Glynn R. Donaho
Robert E. Dornin
Willard M. Downes
Claren E. Duke
Thomas M. Dykers
Ian C. Eddy
William C. Eddy
Mrs. Robert H. English
Joseph F. Enright
William E. Ferrall
James Fife
John A. Fitzgerald
Clifton W. Flenniken, Jr.
Eugene B. Fluckey

Robert J. Foley
John J. Foote
Charles L. Freeman
John K. Fyfe
Ignatius J. Galantin
Philip W. Garnett
Malcolm E. Garrison
Richard S. Garvey
William J. Germershausen
James D. Grant
Louis P. Gray III
Richard V. Gregory
Elton W. Grenfell
George W. Grider
John B. Griggs, Jr.
John B. Griggs III
Royce L. Gross
William P. Gruner, Jr.
Mrs. Robert Lakin Gurnee
Oscar E. Hagberg
John L. Haines
John M. Haines
Warren C. Hall, Jr.
Edward R. Hannon
James T. Hardin
Frederick J. Harlfinger II
Brooks J. Harral
Thomas C. Hart
Earle C. Hawk
William H. Hazzard
Charles M. Henderson
Thomas H. Henry
Karl G. Hensel
Franklin G. Hess
John B. Hess
James M. Hingson
Thomas W. Hogan
George M. Holley
William G. Holman
Martin P. Hottel
Leon J. Huffman
Jesse L. Hull
Adrian M. Hurst

Tyrrell D. Jacobs
Benjamin C. Jarvis
Carl A. Johnson
James L. Jordan
Allen R. Joyce
Roger M. Keithly
Marvin G. Kennedy
Thomas K. Kimmel
Robert D. King
Oliver G. Kirk
William T. Kinsella
Charles C. Kirkpatrick
Thomas B. Klakring
Robert A. Knapp
Herman J. Kossler
H. J. Kuehn
Richard C. Latham
John E. Lee
William R. Lefavour
Bafford E. Lewellen
James W. Liddell
Mrs. Charles A. Lockwood
Frederick K. Loomis
Charles E. Loughlin
Vernon L. Lowrance
Frederic C. Lucas, Jr.
Nicholas Lucker, Jr.
Frank C. Lynch, Jr.
Ralph C. Lynch, Jr.
Hyland B. Lyon
Edgar J. MacGregor III
Duncan C. MacMillan
Harry C. Maynard
John S. McCain, Jr.
Allan R. McCann
David H. McClintock
Victor B. McCrea
Louis D. McGregor, Jr.
Eugene B. McKinney
Heber H. McLean
Bernard F. McMahon
Fitzhugh McMaster
Ralph M. Metcalf

Leonard S. Mewhinney
Peter G. Molteni
Keats E. Montross
John R. Moore
Raymond J. Moore
Dudley W. Morton
Henry G. Munson
John W. Murphy, Jr.
Walter P. Murphy, Jr.
Stuart S. Murray
William T. Nelson
John C. Nichols
Philip G. Nichols
Stanley G. Nichols
Chester W. Nimitz, Jr.
Richard H. O'Kane
Robert I. Olsen
Frank M. Parker
Lewis S. Parks
Richard W. Peterson
George E. Pierce
Mrs. John R. Pierce
William S. Post, Jr.
Roland F. Pryce
Lawson P. Ramage
Robert P. Ramsey
Eli T. Reich
James R. Reynolds
Cassius D. Rhymes, Jr.
Robert A. Rinehart
Robert D. Risser
Orme C. Robbins
Samuel M. Robinson
J. D. Roche
Francis W. Rockwell
Philip H. Ross
Royal L. Rutter
Mrs. Willard A. Saunders
Kenneth G. Schacht
Paul R. Schratz
John A. Scott
Frank G. Selby
Robert F. Sellars

Jack M. Seymour
Mrs. Louis Shane, Jr.
William B. Sieglaff
Arthur C. Smith
Chester C. Smith
Joseph J. Staley
Harry C. Stevenson
William A. Stevenson
Mrs. John J. Broderick
  (Mrs. Vard A. Stockton)
Augustus R. St. Angelo
William S. Stovall, Jr.
George L. Street III
Charles W. Styer
Paul E. Summers
Arthur H. Taylor
William C. Thompson, Jr.
Charles O. Triebel
John A. Tyree, Jr.
Gordon W. Underwood
George H. Wales
Edward K. Walker
Francis D. Walker, Jr.
Norvell G. Ward
Robert E. M. Ward
Frederick B. Warder
David L. Whelchel
Reuben T. Whitaker
Bruce E. Wiggin
John Wilkes
Charles W. Wilkins
Delbert F. Williamson
William H. Wright
Lloyd V. Young

6. *War Diaries, Operational Orders, Submarine Bulletins*

Each of the three submarine commands kept a War Diary. This was a day-by-day account of the command activities (mostly listings of submarines going on or arriving from patrol and the claimed results). These diaries—on file in the Classified Operational Archives—proved invaluable for compiling the sailing charts of war patrols (Appendix F). They were also useful in many other ways.

Every submarine going on patrol was issued an Operational Order, a lengthy document giving specific instructions about where and how to conduct the war patrol. These documents are also on file in the archives.

From time to time, the Pacific submarine force issued Submarine Bulletins. These documents—classified at the time—contain information on Japanese antisubmarine tactics, technical gear (sonar, radar), outstanding (or unusual) U.S. submarine war patrols, and so on. By 1945, the Bulletin had assumed the form of a classified magazine. Bulletins—now declassified—are on file in the Classified Operational Archives.

7. *Official Administrative and Operational History*

During the closing stages of the war, Lockwood detailed his operations officer, Richard Voge, to write an official administrative and operational history of the submarine war. Voge was assisted in this large undertaking by W. J. Holmes, W. H. Hazzard, D. S. Graham, and H. J. Kuehn.

The Administrative History forms a portion of the navy's unpublished series known as "United States Naval Administration in World War II." It is subtitled "Submarine Commands, Volumes I and 2." Copies are on file in the Navy Library, Washington, D.C., and at the Submarine Force Library and Museum, Submarine Base, New London. The Administrative History deals with personnel, bases, submarine construction, repair and refit, communications, and other matters. The author made extensive use of these volumes and is grateful to the Submarine Force Library for their long-term loan.

The Operational History produced by Voge et al. is a massive document of more than 1,500 pages dealing with every conceivable operational aspect of the submarine war. No one attempting a serious submarine history should begin without consulting it. Generally, it tells a positive story; the "skipper problem," for example, is not dealt with. However, the torpedo section contains a long and frank account of torpedo problems which the author has consulted extensively, along with other sources. Copies of the Operational History are on file in the Classified Operational Archives. It contains, among other valuable information, a complete copy of JANAC, with sinkings credited to each submarine.

8. Published Books and Articles

After the war, John M. Will, while attached to the Bureau of Personnel (Assistant Director of Training), hired a writer, Theodore Roscoe, to reduce the Operational History to publishable form. The result was *United States Submarine Operations in World War II*, published in 1949 by the U.S. Naval Institute, Annapolis, Maryland. It is in effect a truncated version of the Operational History (sometimes reproduced word for word). Since it was produced by the navy, it too is a positive story—the Operational History in more manageable form. This work was published in condensed form in paperback by Bantam Books, under the title *Pigboats*.

Wilfred Jay Holmes, who had worked on most of these projects and, in addition, compiled a book titled *U.S. Submarine Losses in World War II*, wrote his own version of the submarine war. Called *Undersea Victory*, it was published by Doubleday & Company in 1966. This is an excellent distillation of preceding official accounts and benefits from Holmes's intelligence, keen insight, and his knowledge of codebreaking—about which, however, he was regrettably denied permission to write. For anyone undertaking a history of the submarine war, Holmes is an indispensable source.

Finally, Lockwood himself published two books that are pertinent. The first, *Sink 'Em All* (New York: E. P. Dutton & Company, 1951) is a personal account of the submarine war, from his arrival in Australia in 1942 to war's end. The second, *Down to the Sea in Subs* (New York: W. W. Norton & Company, 1967) is an autobiography including a brief section on the war, drawn in part from *Sink 'Em All*. Both proved useful, although Lockwood deals with neither the "skipper problem" nor codebreaking nor many other controversial matters.

In addition to the foregoing, the author has consulted other published works on World War II submarine operations (some by submariners). These were:

Beach, Edward L. *Dust on the Sea* (a novel). New York: Holt, Rinehart & Winston, 1972.

———. *Run Silent, Run Deep* (a novel). New York: Henry Holt & Company, 1955.

———. *Submarine!* New York: Henry Holt and Company, 1952.

———. "Unlucky in June: *Hiyo* Meets *Trigger*," *U.S.N.I.P.*, April 1957.

Benitez, Ralph C. "Battle Stations Submerged," *U.S.N.I.P.*, January 1948.

Bowers, Richard H. "Servicing the Silent," *U.S.N.I.P.*, November 1943.

Carmer, Carl. *The Jesse James of the Java Sea*. New York: Rinehart, 1945.

Chambliss, William C. *The Silent Service*. New York: New American Library, 1959.

Cope, Harley F., and Walter Karig. *Battle Submerged—Submarine Fighters in World War II*. New York: W. W. Norton & Company, 1957.

Davis, H. F. D. "Building U.S. Submarines in World War II," *U.S.N.I.P.*, July 1946.

Frank, Gerald, and James D. Horan. *U.S.S. Seawolf*. New York: G. P. Putnam's Sons, 1945.

Grider, George, and Lytel Sims. *War Fish*. Boston: Little, Brown and Company, 1958.

Horie, Y. "The Failure of the Japanese Convoy Escort," *U.S.N.I.P.*, October 1956.

Lockwood, Charles A., and Hans C. Adamson. *Battles of the Philippine Sea*. New York: Thomas Y. Crowell Company, 1967.

——— and ———. *Hellcats of the Sea*. New York: Greenberg, Publisher, 1956.

——— and ———. *Through Hell and Deep Water*. New York: Greenberg, Publisher, 1956.

——— and ———. *Zoomies, Subs and Zeroes*. New York: Greenberg, Publisher, 1956.

Oi, Atsughi. "Why Japan's Anti-submarine Warfare Failed," *U.S.N.I.P.*, June 1952.

Oil in Japan's War. U.S. Strategic Bombing Survey. Washington, D.C.: U.S. Government Printing Office.

Pratt, Fletcher. "Two Little Ships," *U.S.N.I.P.*, July 1947. About *Harder* and destroyer *England*.

Sheridan, Martin. *Overdue and Presumed Lost: The Story of the U.S.S. Bullhead*. Francestown, N.H.: Marshall Jones Co., 1947.

Sterling, Forest J. *Wake of the Wahoo*. Philadelphia: Chilton Books, 1960.

Trumbull, Robert. *Silversides*. New York: Henry Holt & Company, 1945.

CODEBREAKING

Underbrink, Robert L. *Destination Corregidor*. Annapolis, Md.: U.S. Naval Institute, 1971.

U.S. Submarine Losses in World War II (prepared initially by W. J. Holmes). Washington, D.C.: U.S. Government Printing Office, 1946, 1963.

Voge, Richard G., "A Case of Too Much Accuracy," *U.S.N.I.P.*, March 1950. About *Queenfish* and *Awa Maru*.

War Against Japanese Transportation. U.S. Strategic Bombing Survey. Washington: U.S. Government Printing Office, 1947.

Withers, Thomas C. "Preparing SubPac for War," *U.S.N.I.P.*, April 1950.

Zimmerman, Sherwood R. "Operation Forager," *U.S.N.I.P.*, August 1964.

III. Codebreaking

Since the beginning of the enterprise, anything having to do with the breaking of Japanese codes has been classified. During the preparation of this book, the author requested the U.S. government to declassify certain documents and unit histories. After considering the request for eighteen months, the government declined.

1. *Interviews and Letters*

Most of the codebreaking information in this book was gathered through interviews or letters—with submarine skippers and submarine staff officers and with nine codebreakers willing to talk on a background or off-the-record basis. The codebreakers—who cannot be named—provided the author with information on the history of breaking the Japanese codes, on personnel, on the Japanese Language Program, on specific examples of codebreaking triumphs in World War II, on organization, and other matters. The author is grateful to the unnamed codebreakers who were willing to cooperate.

2. *Other Sources*

The author made use of two additional primary sources for Ultra information to submarines: the Pacific and Australian War Diaries for the first year of the war, which contain numerous summaries of Ultra dispatches, and the patrol reports in which some submarine skippers inadvertently included specific mention of Ultra dispatches (by number). The Pearl Harbor hearings conducted after the war contain many hundreds of pages of testimony on breaking the Japanese codes. And in published memoirs and books, some naval leaders have mentioned the contribution of codebreaking to the overall conduct of the war.

In addition, the author consulted the following books, manuscripts, and articles which deal in whole or in part with breaking Japanese codes:

Ardman, Harvey. "U.S. Code-Breakers vs. Japanese Code-Breakers in World War II," *American Legion Magazine*, May 1972.

Davis, Burke. *Get Yamamoto*. New York: Random House, 1969.

Dyer, George C. *The Amphibians Came to Conquer: The Story of Admiral Richmond Kelly Turner*. 2 vols. Washington, D.C.: U.S. Government Printing Office, 1972. (Contains detailed Ultra on Guadalcanal.)

Farago, Ladislas. *The Broken Seal*. New York: Random House, 1967.

Kahn, David. *The Codebreakers*. New York: The Macmillan Company, 1967.

Kimmel, Husband E. *Admiral Kimmel's Story*. Chicago: Henry Regnery Co., 1955.

"New Pearl Harbor Facts, Full Story: How U.S. Got Jap Secrets." *Chicago Tribune*, special supplement, December 7, 1966.

Operational History of Naval Communications (Japanese), prepared by Military History Section H.Q. Army Forces, Far East. Army Library, Washington, D.C. Manuscript.

Stark, Harold R. Unpublished manuscript, Classified Operational Archives.

Thorpe, Elliott R. *East Wind, Rain*. Boston: Gambit, Inc., 1969.

Tuchman, Barbara. *The Zimmermann Telegram*. New York: Viking Press, 1958.

Wohlstetter, Roberta. *Pearl Harbor Warning and Decision*. Stanford, Cal.: Stanford University Press, 1962.

Zacharias, Ellis M., and Ladislas Farago. *Secret Missions: The Story of an Intelligence Officer*. New York: G. P. Putnam's Sons, 1946.

Index

ABDA (American, British, Dutch, Australian) forces, 163
Abe, Capt. Toshio, of *Shinano,* 778, 779
Abele, Mannert Lincoln, in *Grunion,* lost, 271, 832
Abele (Mannert L. Abele), destroyer, 832
Abemama, 522–23
Aboukir, British cruiser, 37
ABSD No. 2, floating drydock, 263
Abukuma, Japanese cruiser, 416, 746, 759
Acker, Frank Clements: in *Pomfret,* patrols, 668–69, 728–30; paralyzed, 728–30
Ackerman, Edward, in *Kete,* lost, 829
Adak, 268, 270, 416
Adams, Benjamin Ernest, Jr.: in *Flier,* 592; in *Rasher,* 840
Adder (A-2), 30*n*, 66
Aden Maru, Japanese transport, 623
Adkins, James Alvin ("Caddy"), in *Cod,* patrols, 711–12, 741–42, 751, 781, 841
Admiral Graf Spee, German raider, 70
Admiral Scheer, German raider, 70
Admiralty Islands, 609, 651, 658, 695, 736, 737, 815
Aerial torpedoes, 238
Africa, *see* North Africa
Agano, Japanese cruiser, 476, 477, 506, 567, 622
Agattu, 270

Air conditioning on submarines, 65, 68
Aircraft: as danger to submarines, 66, 83–84, 156, 841–42; in preparation for World War II, 81
Aircraft carriers, 57, 64; first, 49*n*; new, in 1943, 399, 422; Japanese, lost in 1942, 399*n*
Aitape, 607, 609
Akagi, Japanese aircraft carrier, 175, 205, 209, 399*n*; in Battle of Midway, lost, 237, 238, 244
Akama Maru, Japanese ship, 461
Akashisan Maru, Japanese freighter, 594
Akatsuki Maru, Japanese tanker, 451
Aki Maru, Japanese transport, 591
Akigawa Maru, Japanese freighter, 602, 801
Akigumo, Japanese destroyer, 619
Akikaze, Japanese destroyer, 771
Akin, Spencer B., 304
Akitsu Maru, Japanese aircraft ferry, 773, 774
Akitsuki, Japanese destroyer, 761, 766
Alamogordo, N.M., 869
Alaska, 267–72, 337, 361, 416–21; Japanese forces sent to, 268–69; strategic plans for, 399
Albacore, 360, 360*n*, 387, 592, 599, 604; 1942 patrols, 316, 331, 334; 1943 patrols, 378–79, 476–77; bombed by Allied aircraft, 474, 477; in cooperative attack, 484;

1007

Albacore (cont.)
1944 patrols, 647, 654; in Battle of Philippine Sea, 655, 657, 658; lost, 780, 817*n*
Albany, Australia, 192, 197, 275, 277, 302–4, 330, 349, 617
Alden, Carroll Storrs, 38
Aleutian Islands: Yamamoto plans invasion, 219, 234; Japanese movements against, 235 (map), 268; patrols in, 321, 325, 592; recaptured, 416–18, 419 (map)
Alexandria, Va., torpedo factory, 41, 54, 69
Alice Channel, 495
Allen, Nelson John, 525
Alston, Augustus Howard, Jr., 408–9
Amagi, Japanese aircraft carrier, 868
Amagiri, Japanese destroyer, 392, 808
Amato Maru, Japanese tanker, 846
Amatsuke, Japanese destroyer, 611
Amberjack, 344, 360*n*, 643, 699; in Truk patrol, 316; last patrol, lost, 375, 552*n*
Ambon, 163, 165, 180, 196, 352, 353, 356, 497, 498, 585, 612, 615, 632
Ambruster, Stephen Henry, 312, 626; in *Tambor*, 352; in *Robalo*, 581–82
Amchitka, 268, 272, 416
America Maru, Japanese ship, 591
Anderson, William Lovett, 499; in Pearl Harbor attack, 101–2; in *Thresher*, patrol, 107, 116, 121, 122; supports Tokyo bombing raid, 214–15
Anderson, William Robert: in *Tarpon*, 331–32, 406; in *Narwhal*, describes mission to Philippines, 497–98; postwar career, 884*n*
Andrews, Charles Herbert, 527, 536, 553, 582, 701, 853; in *Gurnard*, Atlantic service, 265–66; 1943 patrol from Pearl Harbor, 440–42; 1944 patrols, 623–24, 626–27, 633–34, 636, 641; in investigation of loss of *Flier*, 716
Andrews, James Gold, 540

Angaur, 723
Angler, 580, 783, 812, 818; rescues civilians from Panay, 580–81; 1944 patrols, 629, 630, 649, 684, 685, 740, 797–98; support of Leyte invasion, 751, 752, 755
Anjo Maru, Japanese tanker, 740
Annapolis, *see* Naval Academy
Anthedon, submarine tender, 846
Anthony, Henry M., in FRUPAC, 400–401
Anyo Maru, Japanese transport, 810
ANZAC (Australia–New Zealand Area Command), 218
Aoba, Japanese cruiser, 329, 749, 751, 752, 755, 766, 817, 868
Aparri, 153, 164; submarine attacks near, 136, 137; air strike on, 745
Apogon, 523, 524, 677
Apollo, submarine tender, 580
Appendectomies at sea, 291–92, 343, 346
APR, radar detection device, 833–34
Arabia Maru, Japanese transport, 740
Arabic, passenger ship, 38
Araosan Maru, Japanese tanker, 851
Arare, Japanese destroyer, 270
Aratama Maru, Japanese submarine tender, 600
Archerfish, 574, 799; 1944 patrols, 649, 660, 777–80; 1945 wolf pack, 833–34
Archimedes, 23
Argentia, Newfoundland, 79, 80
Argonaut (*V-4*), 57, 59*n*, 83*n*, 84, 122, 123, 320, 351, 392, 538, 706; in Midway attack, 102, 104–5, 119–20; in Makin commando raid, 308, 309, 317, 318, 337, 506; sent to Brisbane, 311; lost, 372–73, 552*n*
Arima Maru, Japanese passenger freighter, 411, 412
Arita Maru, Japanese tanker, 799
Arizona, battleship, 99
Ark Royal, British aircraft carrier, 71
Arma Corporation, 65, 67*n*

INDEX

Arms limitation conferences: Washington, 1921–1922, 50–52, 58; London, 1930, 58–60, 62
Arno, 115
Asahi, Japanese repair ship, 289
Asakaze, Japanese destroyer, 719
Asama Maru, Japanese passenger freighter, 254, 407, 770
Asanagai, Japanese destroyer, 649
Asashimo, Japanese destroyer, 591
ASDIC, sonar, 49, 71
Ashigara, Japanese cruiser, 143n, 746, 792, 800, 846, 853; sunk, 854
Ashio, Japanese prison, 189, 420, 552, 576
Ashizuki, Japanese tanker, 633
Ashley, James Henry, Jr., in *Seadragon,* 730, 748, 769
Asiatic Fleet, 76–77, 79, 81, 85, 129, 201, 207
Aspro: Stevenson brothers in command, 539–41; patrols, 647, 741
Astoria, cruiser, 296
Asukazan Maru, Japanese freighter, 683
Atago, Japanese cruiser, 506, 754–55, 766
Atago class, Japanese cruisers, 753
Athenia, passenger ship, 71
Atlanta, cruiser, 338
Atlantic Fleet, 78–80
Atomic bombs, 18, 869–70; at Hiroshima, 869; at Nagasaki, 870
Atsuta Maru, Japanese transport, 226
Attu, 399; Japanese landing on, 268; recaptured, 416–18, 419 (map), 425
Atule, 765; patrols and wolf packs, 730, 770–72, 842; in Battle of Leyte Gulf, 761, 762
Augusta, cruiser, 264
Austin, Marshall Harlan ("Cy"), in *Redfin,* patrols and wolf packs, 619, 637, 641, 650, 715, 784–85
Australia, 81, 339, 423; in ABDA, 163; submarines retire to, 189, 191–92; personnel rescued from Timor, 196, 357; Admiral King's decision on submarines in, 201–3; command structure in, 218; Japan wants bases in, 294; POWs in Japanese ships, 708–10; *see also* Brisbane; Darwin; Fremantle; other localities
Australia, cruiser, 792
Australia–New Zealand Area Command, *see* ANZAC
Awa Maru, Japanese relief supply ship, 836–37, 851; Loughlin sinks, 837–39, 883; Loughlin's court-martial, 839–40
Awaji, Japanese frigate, 600
Aylward, Theodore Charles, 151, 155, 164, 165, 171, 176, 177, 183, 187; in *Searaven,* patrols, 138, 178, 189–90; and Mark XIV torpedo test, 275–76
Azer, John Behling, in *Whale,* 325, 409
Azores, 43, 44
Azusa, Japanese tanker, 710

B-17s (Flying Fortresses), 128, 129, 143n; in Battle of Midway, 237, 245
B-25s, in Tokyo raid, 205
B-29s (Superfortresses), 642, 693, 779, 788; bombing of Japan, 777, 778, 806, 824, 827, 833
Babcock, H. M., in *Extractor,* 805
Babelthuap, 723
Bacon, Barton Elijah, Jr., 151, 164–66, 171, 189; in *Pickerel,* patrols, 139, 180–81
Baer, Donald G., in *Lapon,* 739–40
Bagley, David Worth, 262
Baker, Harold Edward, 341; in *Snapper,* 285–86
Bakutis, Fred Edward, 783
Balabac Strait, 611, 687, 688n, 714, 716, 717, 751
Balao, patrols and wolf packs, 479–80, 571, 835–40
Bali, 163, 616; Japanese capture, 180, 181

Balikpapan, 166, 172, 175–78, 201, 290, 353, 355, 391, 392, 397, 487, 613, 618
Balikpapan, Battle of, 168–69
Banda Sea, 164, 165, 176
Bandung, 163, 175, 186
Bang, patrols and wolf packs, 597–99, 647, 654, 674–76, 679, 697, 775–77, 842
Bangka Strait, 854
Bangkok Maru, Japanese passenger freighter, 454–55
Banister, Alan Boyd, in *Sawfish*, patrols and wolf packs, 679, 730, 746, 748, 769–70
Banshu Maru VII, Japanese freighter, 420
Banten Zaki, 426
Barb, 264, 266; on polar circuit, 665–68; 1944 wolf packs, 706–7, 709–10, 772–73, 808–11; 1945 patrols, 866–67
Barbel: patrols, 731, 746, 747; lost, 849
Barbero, 818; patrols and wolf packs, 724, 784–85, 800
Barchet, Stephen George, 351; in Midway attack, 102, 104–5, 119–20
Barnard, Harry Allan, Jr., 736–37
Barr, Eric Lloyd, Jr., 406, 649; in *Bluegill*, 1944 patrols, 621–22, 633, 641, 713, 740, 741; 1945 patrols, 846, 855–56
Barracuda (F-2), 35
Barracuda (V-1), 56, 59n, 73, 80, 125, 349
Barracuda (new, experimental), 885
Barrows, Frank Lloyd, 393; in *Swordfish*, 533
Bashaw, 574; patrols and wolf packs, 577, 579, 734, 785, 797, 798, 846, 847, 849
Baskett, Thomas Slack, 298, 808; in *Tautog*, on polar circuit, 595–96; in *Tautog*'s last patrol before retirement, 807; in *Tench*, 841, 866

Bass, Raymond Henry ("Benny"), 554; in *Plunger*, 466–71; supports Gilbert Islands invasion, 525–26; 1944 patrol, 587–88; in *Runner II*, 868
Bass (V-2), 56, 59n, 73, 80, 125, 341, 349, 450
Bat, Marshall Islands, 116
Bataan, 46, 129, 160, 175, 192; U.S. forces withdrawn to, 153, 159, 163; submarines bring aid to, 172–73; fall of, 195; Death March survivors, 625
Bataan, aircraft carrier, 399n
Batfish: patrols and wolf packs, 539, 586, 662, 697, 751, 782–83, 833–34, 869; Merrill's command problems, 586
Bathothermograph, 458–59
Batjan, 636, 638, 639, 650
Batopaha Maru, Japanese freighter, 705
Batteries, storage, 26, 65
Bay of Biscay, 263, 265, 266, 537
Baya: 1944 patrols, 725, 727, 728, 794, 800; 1945 patrols, 846, 851
Beach, Edward Latimer: in *Trigger*, 247–48, 336, 386, 428, 431, 517, 518, 564–65, 569, 600–603; in *Tirante*, 842–44; *Submarine!* (book), 843n; and cease-fire message, 871
Beaver, submarine tender, 264
Becker, Albert Lilly, in *Cobia*, 728, 751
Becuna, 795; patrols and wolf packs, 725, 728, 796, 798, 800, 846
Bell, C. Edwin, in *Tinosa*, 536–37
Bell, David Bonar, in *Pargo*, 738, 846
Bell Valley, Cal., 365
Bella Russa, Russian ship, 594
Belleau Wood, aircraft carrier, 399n, 422, 765
Belote, James H., 100n
Belote, William M., 100n
Benitez, Rafael Celestino, in *Dace*, 753
Bennett, Carter Lowe, 251, 455; in *Cuttlefish*, 320–21; in *Sunfish*, 407;

INDEX

1011

in *Porpoise,* 456–57; in *Permit,* 563–64; in *Sea Owl,* test of Cutie torpedoes, 788–89, 801; patrol and wolf pack, 801, 834–35

Benson, Roy Stanley ("Ensign"), 244, 431, 517, 553, 601, 662, 871; in *Trigger,* patrols, 335–36, 428–30; torpedo failure, 430; in *Razorback,* 725, 727; postwar rank, 883, 884

Benson, William Shepherd, 49

Bergall, 688, 813, 846; 1944 patrols, 751, 780–81, 796–98; Hyde refuses to destroy, 797–98; 1945 patrols, 847, 851

Bermuda, 80

Besugo: patrols and wolf packs, 730, 746, 748–49, 852–53; in Battle of Leyte Gulf, 762, 764

Biak, 620; Allied invasion of, 634, 635 (map), 638; Japanese reinforcement of, 634, 636–41; submarine support of invasion, 634, 636–41

Biard, Forrest Rosecrans ("Tex"), codebreaker, 607

Bifuku Maru, Japanese freighter, 319

Bikini, 116

Billfish, 487; joint patrols with *Bowfin,* 487–90; 1944 patrols, 701, 732, 746

Bima Bay, 852

Bisaku Maru, Japanese freighter, 602

Bismarck Islands, 505

Bismarck Sea, jeep carrier, 827

Bissell, H., Jr., in *Angler,* 797, 812, 818

Bittern, minesweeper, 134

Black Chamber, codebreaking, 52

Blackfin, 849; patrols, 751, 781, 784, 846, 847

Blackfish, 264, 266, 574; 1943 patrols, 481, 523; 1944–1945 patrols and wolf packs, 621, 730, 746, 748, 769, 833–34

Blair, Edward McCormick, 589

Blair, Leon Nelson ("Chief"), 464; commands wolf pack, 643, 644, 646

Blakely, Edward Noe: in *Shark II,* wolf packs, 643–46, 730, 748, 769; lost, 770

Blanchard, James William, 484n, 592, 604, 780; in *Albacore,* cooperative attack, 484; 1944 patrol, 647; in Battle of Philippine Sea, 655, 657; sinks passenger ship, 658

Blandy, William Henry ("Spike"), 348, 415, 427; and Mark XIV torpedo tests, 277–78, 439; and Lockwood's criticism of Bureau of Ordnance, 403–4

Blenny, patrols, 808, 846, 855

Blind, Howard J., 735–36

Blower, 847

Blueback, 854

Bluefish, 687; 1943 patrols, 490–93; 1944 patrols, 611, 616, 629, 632–34, 703–4, 711

Bluegill: 1944 patrols, 621–22, 633, 713, 740; 1945 patrols, 846, 855–56

Boarfish, patrols, 808, 856

Bobczynski, Sigmund Albert ("Bobo"): in *Gudgeon,* 108; in *Archerfish,* 778–79

Bock's Car, B-29, 870

Bode, Howard, 296

Boise, cruiser, 329, 813

Bole, John Albert, Jr., 434, 643; in *Amberjack,* 316; last patrol, lost, 375

Boling Strait, 181

Bonefish, 502–3; 1943 patrol, 496; 1944 patrols and wolf packs, 611, 617, 625–26, 633, 739–40, 751; 1945 wolf pack, 859–61, 863; lost, 863–65

Bonin, Robert Alexander, 595

Bonin Islands, 207, 208, 434, 456, 512, 537, 640, 641, 649, 682, 698, 706, 731, 808; invasion of, *see* Iwo Jima

Bonita (C-4), 30n

Bonita (V-3), 56, 59n, 66, 73, 80, 125, 349, 665

Bontier, Albert Marion, 725n; in *Seawolf,* lost, 736, 737

Bora Bora, 218
Borneo, 128, 163, 183, 292, 340, 432, 484; Japanese invasion of, 166, 167 (map); patrols near, 285, 290, 354–55, 391, 497, 619, 624, 625, 717, 735, 794; tankers from, as targets, 486–87; personnel and supplies landed on, 496; rescuing guerrillas on, 618, 619, 637–38; oil from, 621
Boston Maru, Japanese freighter, 354
Bougainville, 297, 334, 369, 370, 380; civilians and commandos evacuated from, 376; Allied landings on, 472, 475, 506
Bourland, John Hunt, 460
Bowfin, 502, 585, 674, 841; in Fremantle, 487; joint patrols with *Billfish*, 487–90; Christie on patrol in, 612–14; 1944 patrols, 612–14, 647, 652, 697, 698; 1945 patrols and wolf pack, 825, 827, 829, 858–61, 863
Boyle, Francis Dennis, in *Charr*, 847, 852–53
Brady, John Huston, 249, 251, 307, 308
Brandt, Donald Carl, 646
Brayton, George, engine, 26
Brazil Maru, Japanese transport, 309–10
Bream, patrols and wolf packs, 751, 755, 781–83
Breckenbridge, Richard F., 320
Bremerton, Wash., Puget Sound Navy Yard, 815, 880
Brewer, Eugene, 324*n*
Bridgeport, Conn., Navy Yard, 40
Brindupke, Charles Frederick: in *Tullibee*, 434; wolf pack, 546–47; last patrol, lost, 575–76
Brinker, Robert Marion, 397
Brisbane, 367, 370, 401, 413, 493, 498, 582, 611, 651, 695; S-boats sent to, 217–18, 263, 268; U.S. officers in, 218, 294; 1942 patrols from, 296–306, 340–47, 359, 361; transfers of command and vessels to, 302–3; submarines sent to, by way of Truk, 330–34; New Farm Wharf, 339, 371, 474; Fife's reforms and discipline, 371–72; 1943 patrols from, 372–88, 424, 474–85; submarines exchanged with Pearl Harbor, 380, 451–53; Torpedo Shop, 480; cooperative attacks from, 482–85; submarines from, in support of air strike on Palaus, 574, 575, 577, 579; codebreaking at, 606, 607; base nearly closed, 609; Christie-Lockwood conference, 673; unit moved to Subic Bay, 814, 845–46
Britain: French plans for war with, in 19th century, 27–28; torpedoes, early, 30–31; submarines before World War I, 32–33, 36; in World War I, 36–39, 42–43, 45; proposes abolition of submarines, 49, 50, 52, 59; in Washington arms limitation conference, 50–52; in London arms limitation conference, 58–60; in World War II, 70–72, 78, 81, 135, 265; U.S. aid to, 72, 79, 319; U.S. codebreaking secrets shared with, 75–76; losses in Pacific area, 135; in ABDA, 163; S-boats loaned to, 217*n*, 341; in strategy for Pacific area, 557; operations in Pacific area, 620, 629; Eastern Fleet, 629; POWs in Japanese ships, 708–10; submarines at Fremantle, 742–43; aircraft carriers in U.S. fleet, 832, 835; submarines in action, 852–55; *Haguro* sunk by British units, 853–54; midget submarines, 854–55; contribution to surrender ceremonies, 872
Broach, John Cozine: in *Hake*, 537, 711; patrols, 619, 637, 641
Brockman, William Herman, Jr., 298, 334, 417, 434, 496, 523; in *Nautilus*, at Battle of Midway, 241, 243–45; refuses to bombard palace at Hayama, 252–53; sinks *Yamakaze*, 252–53; in Makin commando

raid, 317, 318; patrol near Japan, 321; in *Haddock,* 772, 825
Brown, Charles Donald, in *Razorback,* 803, 840
Brown, Francis Elwood: and loss of *S-39,* 300–301; in *S-43,* 301; in *S-44,* death, 420
Brown, G. E., Jr., 525
Brown, George William ("Weegee"), 526
Brown, John Herbert ("Babe"), 251, 328, 333, 357, 366, 400, 423, 429, 666n, 676, 779–80; commands Sea of Japan patrols, 466, 469, 471; commands Squadron Four, 223, 368; training program, 447; in torpedo tests, 437, 438; and wolf-packing, 509; Lockwood wants his promotion, 549–50, 812, 814; becomes rear admiral, 812–13
Brown, Wilson, 593
Browne, George Henry: in *Snook,* 728; patrols and wolf packs, 745, 769
Brunei Bay, 738, 739, 751, 755, 758, 759, 775, 796
Bruton, Henry Chester, 288, 325, 326, 337, 360, 377, 490, 883; in *Greenling,* first patrol criticized, 229; pursuit of *Shokaku,* 230–31, 233; second patrol to Truk, 309–10; sent to Brisbane, 334; promoted, 334; on Fife's character, 371–72; in Loughlin's court-martial, 839–40
Bryant, Eliot Hinman ("Swede"), 609n, 813, 881; leads wolf pack, 795–96, 798
Buchanan, R. L., 827
Budding, William Alexander, Jr., in *Seahorse,* 569, 600, 677
Bugara, 855
Bullhead: bombed by U.S. aircraft, 841–42; lost, 856
Buna, 472
Bungo Suido, 110, 215, 231, 251, 514, 519, 520, 553, 590, 668–69, 730, 746–49, 825, 830, 832

Bunker Hill, aircraft carrier, 399n, 422, 832
Bureau of Ordnance (BuOrd), 30, 41, 160, 185, 348, 401, 437, 460, 469, 470, 588, 787, 881; torpedo experiments, 53–56; and Mark XIV torpedo, 170, 361, 439; and Mark XIV tests, 275–78; oxygen and electric torpedo experiments, 279–81; Lockwood criticizes, 403–4
Bureau of Personnel (BuPers), 345, 348, 526, 548, 567; Lockwood protests to, 593; Lockwood's 1944 feud with, 812
Bureau of Ships, 345, 537, 842
Burlingame, Creed Cardwell, 480, 481, 487, 490, 517, 518, 520, 537, 677, 804; in *Silversides,* first patrol, 228–29; patrol from Brisbane, 346–47; book on, 424; patrol, Pearl Harbor to Brisbane, 451–53
Burma, 192, 399; strategy for recapture, 557
Burnside, John Lockwood, Jr., 151, 164, 168, 183, 198n; in *Saury,* 1943 patrols, 143, 147–50, 288–89
Burrfish: 1944 patrols, 568, 731, 746, 791; frogmen on, 695; in Battle of Leyte Gulf, 764
Burrows, Albert Collins ("Acey"), 343; in *Swordfish,* 288; in *Whale,* 409–10; patrols, 434, 532–33
Burton, Paul Willits, 592
"Burt's Brooms," 790–91, 825
Busch-Sulzer, engineering firm, 49, 56
Bush, destroyer, 830
Bushnell, David, *Turtle,* early submarine, 23, 24
Bushnell, Hart's flagship in World War I, 44n
Bushnell, submarine tender, 475, 561, 605
Busho Maru, Japanese freighter, 495
Buyo Maru, Japanese transport, 386

Cabot, aircraft carrier, 399n, 765, 825
Cabrilla, 616, 617, 804; 1943 patrol, 511–12; 1944 patrols and wolf

Cabrilla (cont.)
pack, 629, 633, 634, 741
Cachalot (K-2), 36
Cachalot (V-8), 60, 64, 65, 83n, 107, 205, 209, 224, 251, 540, 549; in Pearl Harbor attack, 99–100; in Battle of Midway, 236n, 241; withdrawn, 321, 335, 551n
Calcutta Maru, Japanese freighter, 225
Caldwell, Robert Hugh, Jr., in *Peto*, 772–74
Calhoun, destroyer, 830
California, battleship, 99
Callaghan, Joseph Anthony, 157, 166, 189; at Lingayen Gulf, 150–51; at Balikpapan, 168
Campbell, J. G., 818
Campbell, James Harry ("Soupy"), in *Blower*, 847
Camranh Bay, 176, 178, 201, 202, 611, 792, 794, 796–97, 804; patrols to, 138–41, 155n, 273, 274, 287, 354, 488, 493, 495, 684, 798–800; *Seadragon* attack on Japanese ships, 170–71
Canberra, cruiser, 296, 745
Canopus, submarine tender, 77, 78, 82, 130, 132, 134–35, 173, 195, 197, 410; and loss of Manila, 153, 154, 160
Canton Island, 505
Cape Blanco, 689
Cape St. George, 474
Capelin, lost, 501–3, 552n
Caribbean area, 72
Carlson, Evans F., in Makin raid, 316–18
Carlson, Spencer August, codebreaker, 89, 607
Carmick, Edward Seabury: in *Sargo*, 432, 457
Carnegie Institute, 55
Caroline Islands, 46, 70; Japanese bases in, 205; 1942 patrols to, 210, 216, 224, 229; *see also* Truk
Carp (F-1), 35
Carp, 797n, 818

Carpender, Arthur Schuyler ("Chips"), 285, 339, 342–43, 348, 351, 358, 370, 371, 388, 431, 477, 478, 501–2; Lockwood's friction with, 283–84, 303, 367–68; replaces Leary at Brisbane, 302–4; and investigation of Fife's loss of submarines, 376–78; and Exmouth Gulf base, 389–90; and submarines based in Australia, 474–75; detached as Commander of Seventh Fleet, 504
Carr, Bruce Lewis, 312, 395; in *Grenadier*, 352
Casablanca Conference, 398–99, 416
Case, destroyer, 836, 869
Casey, J. E., 714, 715
Cassedy, Hiram, 195; in *Sailfish*, 143; in *Searaven*, 190; *Searaven* on fire, 196; 1943 patrol, 433; in *Tigrone*, 835, 865–66; in surrender ceremonies, 872; funeral, 885
Cast codebreaking unit, *see* Codebreaking
Cavalla: in Battle of Philippine Sea, 652–53, 657–58; 1944 patrols, 725, 727, 794–95, 800; and cease-fire message, 871
Cavite, 74, 77, 130, 154; Japanese attack on, 132, 134–35, 160; codebreaking unit, *see* Codebreaking, Cast
Cebu, 194, 618
Celebes, 163, 496, 784; Japanese invasion of, 165–66, 167 (map); air force crew in, 501–2
Celebes Sea, 164, 173, 192, 201, 285, 492, 585, 616, 619, 623, 626, 712, 734
Ceram, 502
Cero, patrol and wolf pack, 541–42, 633
Ceylon Maru, Japanese ship, 590n
Champ, J. W., 597
Chappell, Lucius Henry, 169, 192, 303, 304, 514; in *Sculpin*, patrol from Manila, 137; in defense of Java, 177, 179; on failure of tor-

pedoes, 192; 1942–1943 patrols, 305, 306, 345, 428–29
Chapple, Wreford Goss ("Moon"), 155, 187, 285; in S-38, patrol from Manila, 138; in Lingayen Gulf, 147–48, 150, 466; in *Permit,* 165; evacuates personnel from Corregidor, 193–94; Wilkes criticizes, 194; 1942 patrols, 290; 1943 patrol in Sea of Japan, 466–69; sinks Russian trawler, rescues crew, 467–68, 594, 864; Bennett relieves, 563; in *Bream,* support of Leyte invasion, 751, 752, 755; 1944 patrols and wolf packs, 781–83
Charr, patrol and wolf pack, 847, 852–53
Chebia, 187
Chester, cruiser, 330, 361
Chiang Kai-shek, 70
Chicago, cruiser, 296
Chicago Tribune, 256, 260, 691; and security leak on Battle of Midway, 257–59
Chidori class, Japanese torpedo boats, 499, 500
Chifuku Maru, Japanese passenger freighter, 373
Chihaya Maru, Japanese ship, 668
Chikuma, Japanese cruiser, 123, 506
Childs, aircraft tender, 630
China, 191, 399; Japanese conquest of, 70; Doolittle and Tokyo raiders in, 215; in U.S. strategic plans, 693; POWs escape to, 769
China Air Force, 810
China Sea, *see* East China Sea; South China Sea
Chiri, 867
Chitose, Japanese carrier, 744, 759, 766
Chitose, Japanese seaplane tender, 86, 433–34
Chitose class, Japanese seaplane tenders, 571
Chiyo Maru, Japanese freighter, 644
Chiyoda, Japanese aircraft tender, 86, 270, 315

Chiyoda, Japanese carrier, 662, 744, 759, 766
Chiyoda Maru, Japanese tanker, 707
Choan Maru II, Japanese gunboat, 643
Chokai, Japanese cruiser, 506
Choko Maru, Japanese freighter, 484*n*, 573
Christensen, Waldeman Nichlous, 107, 209, 224
Christie, Ralph Waldo, 109, 218, 310, 316, 331, 362, 372, 386, 454, 485, 537, 549, 593, 694; torpedo research, 54–55, 61–62; and torpedo production, 69; commands Submarine Division 15, 76; with Atlantic Fleet, 79, 80; with S-boats sent to Brisbane, 217–18, 263, 268; in Battle of Coral Sea, 220, 222; oxygen torpedo experiments, 279; and patrols from Brisbane, 296–97, 299–306, 340, 342–44; and Mark XIV torpedo, 304–5; command at Brisbane, 339–40; becomes rear admiral, 367; replaces Lockwood at Fremantle, 367, 389; investigation of Fife's loss of submarines, 376–78; and Exmouth Gulf base, 389–90; and 1943 patrols from Fremantle, 390–93, 397, 495–97, 499, 501–3, 512, 551, 552, 554; in torpedo controversy, 391–92, 430–31; quarrel with Lockwood on torpedoes, 413–15; and deactivation of Mark VI, 430–31, 486–87, 499, 504, 553, 610, 618; submarine force at Fremantle increased, 474–75; disapproves of *Gato*'s battle with airplane, 484; tankers as targets, 486–87, 503; and cooperative submarine attacks, 487–93, 504; and 1944 patrols, 562, 577*n*, 580–82, 584, 610–14, 619, 639–41, 665, 684, 695–96, 711–16, 721, 724, 734–38, 740–43, 767, 780, 783–85, 794, 797–800, 804, 817, 818; disagreement with Kinkaid on medals, 584–85,

Christie, Ralph Waldo (cont.) 674, 720–21, 814, 815; command changes, 609–10; on *Bowfin* for patrol, 612–14; and false alarm of Japanese attack, 616–18; submarines in preparation for invasion of Marianas, 621–23, 625, 626; and Surabaya air strike, 627, 629–31; on *Harder* for patrol, 669–72, 674; Lockwood's conference with, 672–74; 1944 wolf pack, 684, 685; and death of Manning Kimmel, 687–88; forbids attacks on native vessels, 713; in investigation of loss of *Flier,* 715–16; and loss of Dealey in *Harder,* 717, 719–21; submarines in support of Palau and Morotai invasions, 734–36; and British submarines, 742–43; submarines in support of Leyte invasion, 751, 752, 755–58; orders destruction of *Bergall,* 797–98; and end-of-1944 command changes, 812, 813; relieved of command, dispute with Kinkaid, 814–15; postwar career, 880

Christie, Mrs. Ralph W., 496, 523

Christmas Island, 617; Warder and *Seawolf* at, 190–91, 301, 350; patrols to, 350, 351, 391

Chub, 854

Churchill, Winston, 72, 263; at Casablanca Conference, 398; at Quebec Conference, 723; wants unconditional surrender of Japan, 823

Chuwa Maru, Japanese freighter, 207

Chuyo, Japanese aircraft carrier, 506; *Sculpin* survivors on, 525, 526, 529; sunk, 528–29, 553

Cisco, lost, 503, 552*n*, 846

Civil War, submarines in, 24–25

Claggett, Bladen Dulany: in *Dace,* patrols, 568, 579–80, 741; support of Leyte invasion, 751–57

Clarabut, Commander, in *Stygian,* 854

Clarey, Bernard Ambrose ("Chick"), 316; in *Dolphin,* patrol, 116, 205; in *Pintado,* patrols and wolf packs, 643–46, 698–99, 730, 761, 770–71; in Battle of Leyte Gulf, 761–62; postwar rank, 884

Clark, Albert Hobbs, 206, 552; in *Trout,* lost, 591

Clark, Charles Robert, Jr., in *Sennet,* 865

Clark, Harry Lawrence, codebreaker, 74

Clark, James Seerley, in *Golet,* lost, 667

Clark Field, Manila, Japanese attack, 127–29, 131, 158, 160

Clarke, Fredric B.: in *Pomfret,* 668–69; commands *Pomfret* when Acker is paralyzed, 728–30

Clausewitz, Karl von, 362

Clement, James Markland, 667

Clementson, Merrill Kinsell: in *Snapper,* 515; in *Blueback,* 854

Clermont, Fulton's steamship, 24

Close, Robert Hamilton ("Boney"), in *Pilotfish,* 643–46

Clyde, British submarine, 742

Clyde Maru, Japanese transport, 810

Coast Defense Vessel No. 13, Japanese, 870

Coast Defense Vessel No. 47, Japanese, 870

Coast Defense Vessel No. 72, Japanese, 867

Cobia, 728, 751

Cod: joint patrol with *Bluefish,* 491; 1944 patrols, 611–12, 622–23, 627, 711–12, 741–42, 751, 781; 1945 patrols, 841, 855

Codebreaking, 18, 19; in World War I, 38, 44, 71; Japanese codes before World War II, 52–53, 62–63, 73–76, 87–92, 400; Red code, 53; Blue code, 63; Red machine, 63, 73, 75, 89; Purple code and machine, 73–76, 87–90; Black code, 74; Japanese Flag Officers' Code, 74, 88, 117; JN-25, 74–75, 87–89, 92, 117; Cast, 74–75, 87–89, 173, 175, 260, 262; Hypo,

INDEX

74–76, 87, 88, 90, 117–19, 123, 175, 219, 227, 234, 239, 248–49, 260–63; Negat, 74–75, 87–90, 175, 219, 260–62; Enigma machine, German, 75–76; Magic output, 87, 89; Ultra, definition of, 87, *see also* Ultra messages; after the Pearl Harbor attack, 117–19; evacuation of Cast unit from Corregidor, 173–74, 185, 193, 195, 218; and Japanese fleet movements, 175–78, 185, 191, 192, 205, 209–11, 213; Cast unit in Melbourne, 218–19, 222, 294; and Port Moresby attack, 220, 222; and *Shokaku* pursuit, 230, 231; and Battle of Midway, 234, 239, 248–49, 262; and security leak on Battle of Midway, 256, 258–60; changes in operation and staff, 260–63; FRUPAC (formerly Hypo), 263, 308, 400–401, 607; FRUMEL (formerly Cast), 294, 370, 606–7; in 1942 operations, 269, 294–95, 301, 302, 305, 338, 350, 353, 355; and death of Yamamoto, 370; Japanese code, new, 370; in 1943 operations, 372, 386, 411, 420, 425–26, 433–35, 448, 486, 506, 508, 526; in Marshall Islands invasion, 558, 560; Japanese documents from Gilberts and Marshalls, 589; in New Guinea campaign, 606–7; in 1944 operations, 610, 616, 621, 622, 625, 641, 664, 687, 694, 723, 724, 743, 784, 786n, 801; events in Washington, 689–92; Japanese code broken, 690n; Japanese codebooks from Mindoro, 784; in 1945 operations, 833, 849; codebreakers after war, 881

Coe, James Wiggins, 169, 177, 183, 191, 198n, 846; in *S-39*, in Battle of Java Sea, 186–87; in *Skipjack*, 189, 273; Mark XIV performance analyzed, 274–75; in Mark XIV tests, 276; patrol, 353; in *Cisco*, lost, 503

Colahan, destroyer, 869

Colclough, Oswald Symister, 268, 269, 271, 418

Cole, Cyrus Churchill: in *Balao*, 479–80; in *Spearfish*, 571, 806–7

Cole, Cyrus Willard, 480

Cole, Otis Robert, Jr., in *Dace*, 796, 798

Coll, John Owen Reilly, 365n

Columbia Maru, Japanese transport, 482

Columbia University, Naval Reserve Midshipmen's School, 813

Comstock, Merrill, 549, 673, 813

Connaway, Fred, 456, 576; in *Sculpin*, lost, 524–25

Connole, David Rikart, 319, 320; in *Trigger*, lost, 830

Connolly, Joseph Anthony, 82, 813–14

Conte Verde, Italian ship, 254

Cooke, Charles Maynard ("Savvy"), 126

Coolangatta, rest camp, 371

Coral Sea, 302

Coral Sea, Battle of, 218–20, 221 (map), 222, 230, 296, 622; security leak connected with, 256–60

Corbett, Sir Julian, 45

Corbus, John, 616; in *Haddo*, 537–38; in *Bowfin*, 614; patrols, 647, 649, 652, 698

Corregidor, 46, 89, 129, 130, 132, 134, 135, 160, 192, 607, 781; U.S. headquarters moved to, 153, 154, 159, 160, 163; Japanese attacks on, 154, 175; submarines bring aid to, 172–74, 193–95, 206–7; submarines evacuate personnel from, 173–75, 193–97, 218, 359; MacArthur leaves, 193; surrender of, 197; gold and silver removed from, 207–8; submarine missions to, 273

Corvina, 496; lost, 523, 552n, 553

Corwin, Stanley Joseph, Jr., 527

1018　INDEX

Courageous, British aircraft carrier, 71
Cowpens, aircraft carrier, 399n, 422
Coye, John Starr, Jr.: in *Silversides,* 1943 patrols, 480–81, 484, 530; 1944 patrols and wolf packs, 585, 643–44, 730, 731, 747, 791; in Battle of Leyte Gulf, 762, 764, 765
Craig, John Rich: in *Grampus,* 342; last patrol, lost, 375
Cramp Shipbuilding Company, Philadelphia, 731n, 806, 830
Crane, John Jarvis, 365n
Crane, Richard Henry, in *Balao,* 479
Crawford, George Clifford ("Turkey Neck"), 254, 278, 881; commands Division 43, 213; criticism of Mark VI, 213, 216; returns to Atlantic, 550; command change, 814
Cressy, British cruiser, 37
Crevalle, 617, 687; 1943 patrols, 493–96; 1944 patrols and wolf packs, 624–25, 630, 684–86, 735–36; 1945 patrols and wolf pack, 830, 859, 860, 863, 864
Croaker, patrols and wolf packs, 698, 699, 731, 746, 762, 842
Cromwell, John Philip: in *Sculpin,* lost, 524–25; Medal of Honor, 525, 681
Crowley, John Daniel: in *Flier,* 592; patrols, 639–41, 714; survives loss of *Flier,* 714–16
Crutchfield, Jack Randolph, 224
Currie, John Patterson ("Speed"), 518, 569, 600
Cutie, electric acoustical torpedo, 787–89, 825, 843, 867
Cutter, Slade Deville, 138, 189, 211, 225, 255, 319, 320, 554, 769; in *Pompano,* 114–15, 205; in *Seahorse,* 457–58, 518–20; and Dornin, supposed rivalry, 519, 569n; support of air strike on Palaus, 569–70; 1944 patrols and wolf pack, 600–602, 609, 674–76; report on Japanese fleet in Philippine Sea, 651–52; in *Requin,* 677; sinking records, final, 878
Cuttlefish (B-2), 30n
Cuttlefish (V-9), 60, 64, 83, 83n, 100, 205, 209, 224, 231, 250, 251, 327, 379, 502, 701; in Battle of Midway, 236n, 237, 241, 248; patrol near Japan, 320–21; withdrawn, 321, 335, 551n

Dabney, Thomas Bullard, in *Guitarro,* 800, 847
Dace, 515, 778; 1944 patrols and wolf packs, 568, 574, 579–80, 734, 741, 796, 798–800; support of Leyte invasion, 751–57
Dairen, 208, 407
Daito Jima, 603
Dakar, 265
Dangerous Ground, South China Sea, 491, 755, 759, 786
Danjo Gunto, 801
D'Artagnan, French liner, later *Teiko Maru,* 615
Darter, 846; support of air strike on Truk, 568–69; patrols, 574, 579–80, 734, 741; support of Leyte invasion, 751–56; aground, destroyed, 756–58, 770n, 780, 817n
Darwin, 165, 177, 191–93, 199, 284, 475, 493, 499, 502, 503, 600, 610, 616, 625, 629, 630, 639, 711, 715, 735; submarines withdrawn to, 155, 164; Japanese air raid, 180; 1943 patrols from, 490, 496, 498, 501–2; *Nautilus* and *Narwhal* at, 593, 610; 1944 patrols from, 610, 612, 670, 672
Dasol Bay, 719
Daspit, Lawrence Randall ("Dan"), 486, 624, 646, 789; in *Tinosa,* patrols, 433–34, 536–37; torpedo failure, 435–38
Daubin, Freeland Allan, 83, 106, 149, 263, 292n, 463, 550, 623, 879; in Pearl Harbor attack, 98; rear admiral, commands Submarines Atlantic, 213; investigation of

INDEX

loss of *Flier,* 716; command changes, 812, 815
Daubin, Mrs. Freeland A., 496
Davao Gulf, 163, 171, 192, 194, 201, 285, 288, 290, 353, 356, 634, 650; submarines ordered to, 164, 165; plans for recapture, 557; Japanese naval retreat to, 561, 577, 610; patrols near, 574, 577, 579, 581, 585, 609, 621, 626, 633, 636, 637, 734
Davenport, Roy Milton, 228–29, 446, 546; in *Silversides,* 346–47; in *Haddock,* patrols, 410–12, 453, 515–17; in *Trepang,* patrols and wolf pack, 732–34, 803–4; medals, 804; retired to shore duty, 804; sinking record revised, 878
David, Albert L., 690
Davidson, John Frederick, 523; in *Blackfish,* 481
Davis, James White: in *Raton,* 482, 484, 497; patrols, 615–16, 631–32
Dealey, Samuel David, 554, 570*n,* 730, 783, 785, 791; in *Harder,* 444–45, 461; 1943 wolf pack, 543–46; support of air strike on Woleai, 576–77; 1944 patrols, 637–39, 641, 669–72, 674; "Destroyer Killer," 639; Christie on patrol with, 669–72; Medal of Honor, 674, 720–21, 814, 815; last patrol, 716–19; death, 719–21
Dealey, Mrs. Samuel D., 815
DeBril Bank, 179, 183, 290
DeFrees, Joseph Rollie, Jr., 525
Delhi Maru, Japanese Q-ship, 534
De Loach, William Ralph, Jr., 476, 592
Dempsey, James Charles, 166, 187, 193, 198*n,* 711; in *S-37,* defense of Makassar City, 177–78, 186; in *Spearfish,* 184, 186; at Corregidor, evacuates personnel, 196–97; in *Cod,* joint patrol with *Bluefish,* 491; 1944 patrols, 611–12, 622–23, 627, 641
Denfeld, Louis Emil, in Bureau of Personnel, 367, 368, 548–50, 593; Lockwood's feud with, 812; postwar career, 880
Denmark Maru, Japanese freighter, 532
Dennison, Robert Lee, 165
Deragon, William Nolan: in *Seawolf,* 172, 173, 448, 450; in *Pipefish,* 646, 652
De Roche, James, 491
DeRuyter, Dutch cruiser, 186
De Tar, John Leslie, 249–50, 271, 643; in *Tuna,* first patrol, 208; East China Sea patrol, 224–25
Deutschland, German raider, 70
Deutschland, German submarines, 48
Dewey, George, 29
Dewey, Thomas E., 690–92
DF, *see* RDF
Diesel, Rudolf, 33, 35
Diesel-electric drive, 64–65
Diesel-powered submarines: first, 33–36; problems, 48, 60–61
Dissette, Edward Farwell, in *Cero,* 633
Djakarta, 854
Dodge, Harry Benjamin, in *Seal,* 526
Doenitz, Adm. Karl, German submarine commander, 70–72, 79, 80, 84, 280, 361, 372, 378, 543, 690
Dolphin (V-7), 58, 60, 83*n,* 84, 97, 98, 122, 143, 251–52, 333, 562, 643; in Pearl Harbor attack, 99; patrol to Marshalls, 107, 115–16, 121, 122, 205; in Battle of Midway, 236*n,* 245; patrol to Alaska, 321; withdrawn, 321, 335, 551*n*
Donaho, Glynn Robert ("Donc"), 253, 315, 326, 337, 360, 432, 434, 600, 627; in *Flying Fish,* 1943 patrols, 313–14, 332–33, 380, 407, 513; discipline problems, 380; leaves *Flying Fish,* 603; commands wolf pack, 702–6; postwar rank, 884
Doolittle, James, in Tokyo raid, 205, 214–15

Doorman, Karel, Dutch admiral, 186
Dorado, sunk in Atlantic, 552*n*, 817
Dornin, Robert Edson ("Dusty"), 114, 138, 189, 212, 255, 554, 568, 569, 593, 601, 688, 716, 732, 871; in *Gudgeon*, first patrol, 108, 111, 112, 118; in Battle of Midway, 242; 1943 patrols, 310, 312, 343–44, 356–57; TDC school, 357, 517; in *Trigger*, patrols, 517–20, 564–65; and Cutter, supposed rivalry, 519, 569*n*; aide to Admiral King, 567
Downes, Willard Merrill, 242, 329, 330, 334, 339, 813
Doyle, Walter Edward ("Red"), 155; Commander, Submarines Asiatic, 82, 131; and Japanese attack on Philippines, 132, 135
Dragonet, 806
Drew, George F., 271
Driscoll, Mrs. Agnes Meyer, codebreaker, 53, 63, 74
Dropp, Anthony Henry: in *Saury*, 450–51; attack on *Unyo*, 547–48
Drum, 227, 231, 254, 309, 326, 327, 360*n*, 404; in Battle of Midway, 236*n*, 248; minelaying patrol, 335; support of Gilbert Islands invasion, 523–24; 1944 patrols and wolf packs, 730, 746, 748, 769, 770
Dry, Melvin Hulquist, in *Searaven*, 524, 568
DuBois, Raymond Francis, in *Flasher*, 285, 581, 739
Duke, Claren Emmett, 253, 379; in *Grouper*, 241–42
Dunbar, Palmer Hall, Jr. ("Crow"), 273–74
Duncan, Donald Bradley, 609
Duncan, destroyer, 329
Dutch, see Netherlands
Dutch Harbor, 58, 63, 267–69, 321, 365, 468; submarines sent to, 267–68; Japanese bombardment, 268; patrols from, 269–72, 418, 420–21

Duva, Ernest A., 420
Dwyer, Carl Redmond, 807
Dyer, Thomas Harold, codebreaker, 63, 74, 88, 117, 401, 881
Dykers, Thomas Michael: in *Jack*, 443–44, 446, 512; patrols, 583–84, 622–24, 641; postwar career, 884

Eagle, Lord Howe's flagship, 23
Earhart, Amelia, 52
Earle, Otis John, in *Stingray*, 477
East China Sea: 1942–1943 patrols, *Eiyo Maru*, Japanese tanker, 846 208, 224–26, 251, 253, 321–22, 326, 361, 379, 405, 407, 423, 440, 447, 449–51, 463, 514, 517–20, 548, 551; 1942–1943 wolf packs, 542–43, 731, 746, 767, 775, 788, 807; 1944 patrols, 586, 593, 682–84, 698–99, 775, 801; Japanese minefields, 589; 1945 patrols, 833, 840–42, 858
Ebert, Walter Gale, 567, 579; in *Scamp*, 475–76, 484
Echizen Maru, Japanese freighter, 573
Eddy, Ian Crawford, 568; in *Pargo*, patrols and wolf pack, 543–46, 585, 738
Edge, Lawrence Lott: in *Bonefish*, patrols and wolf packs, 739–40, 751, 859, 863; lost, 863
Edmunds, Charles Dixon ("Shorty"), 83, 549, 568, 813; criticizes patrols, 287
Edwards, Richard Stanislaus, 348, 349, 361, 403, 720, 814, 815, 877; and *Tambor* submarines, 68; Commander, Submarines Atlantic Fleet, 79, 80, 125–26; Lockwood's correspondence with, 274, 366–67, 424; and Mark XIV torpedo tests, 274, 277; and submarine security, 424
Eichmann, John Holbrook, 224
Eikyo Maru, Japanese freighter, 741
Eisenhower, Dwight D., 692, 823

INDEX

Ejiri Maru, Japanese ship, 740
El Alamein, Battle of, 398
Electra, H.M.S., 186
Electric Boat Company, 28, 30, 32, 33-34*n*, 34, 40, 48; in World War II, 72, 344, 423, 496, 592, 639; nuclear-powered submarines, 882
Elsey, Robert, 365
Empire Celt, British ship, 213
Empress Augusta Bay, 474
England, *see* Britain
England, destroyer, 641
English, Robert Henry, 214, 216, 253, 254, 284, 290, 304, 362, 379, 400, 403; commands Squadron Four, 213; Commander, Submarines Pacific, 223; in Mark VI and Mark XIV controversy, 227, 304; criticizes Bruton, 229; and Battle of Midway, 234, 236–39, 241–43, 246, 248, 249, 662; staff and command changes, 249–52, 254–55; proposes bombardment of Hayama palace, 252–53; and Alaska patrols, 269, 271; and Mark XIV torpedo tests, 276–78; and Truk patrols, 307–10, 314–16; and July–December 1942 patrols from Pearl Harbor, 320–23, 335–37; press conference, 323–24; character, 326; in "subversive literature" incident, 327–29; submarines sent to Brisbane by way of Truk, 330–32; denies premature explosion of torpedoes, 341; criticizes patrols from Australia, 344, 353; killed in airplane accident, 365–66
Engstrom, Howard T., codebreaker, 881
Enigma machines, German, 75–76
Eniwetok, 229, 506, 526; U.S. invasion of, 560; submarine support of invasion, 562–63, 568
Enola Gay, B-29, 869
Enright, Joseph Francis: in *Dace,* 515, 568; in *Archerfish,* patrol, 777–80, 799; sinks *Shinano,* 778–80; wolf pack, 833–34
Enterprise, aircraft carrier, 64, 105, 123, 204, 234, 295, 399, 422, 423, 829, 832; bombers from, attack U.S. submarines, 114, 115, 211; in Tokyo bombing raid, 214, 215, 220; in Battle of Midway, 238, 247*n*; damaged, 301–2, 330; repaired, 369*n*; in Gilbert Islands invasion, 505; in Battle of Philippine Sea, 660, 662
Erck, Charles Frederick, 701, 791, 813; commands Squadron Ten, 550; at Majuro, 561
Ericsson, destroyer, 62
Erimu, Japanese tanker, 187
Escolar, lost, 731, 746, 770*n*, 806, 817*n*
Esperance, Battle of, 329
Espiritu Santo, 302
Essex, aircraft carrier, 399*n*, 422, 765
Etorofu, 319, 425
Eurayle, submarine tender, 609
Eversole, destroyer, 765
Exeter, British cruiser, 185
Exide Storage Battery, 65, 280
Exmouth Gulf, 614, 617, 629, 797, 798; proposed advance base (Potshot), 284–85, 389–90, 845
Extractor, salvage vessel, 766; sunk by *Guardfish,* 805–6

Fabian, Rudolph Joseph, codebreaker, 89, 91*n*, 173–74, 218, 606–7
Fahrion, Frank George, 367
Fahy, Edward Joseph, in *Plunger,* 649
Fahy, Richard Thomas, in *Pogy,* 590
Fairbanks-Morse engines, 61, 64, 68*n*, 79, 157, 198, 266, 356, 538, 843
Farragut, David G., 25
Farrell, Joseph P., 827
Farrell, Richard Marvin ("Dixie"): in *Gudgeon,* 108, 118; in *Hake,* 537; in *Gato,* 647, 840
Faust, Allen Russell, in *Trepang,* 827

Federal Bureau of Investigation (FBI), 52
Fell, Charles Woodford, in *Robalo,* 581, 626
Fenno, Frank Wesley ("Mike"), Jr., 208, 249, 584, 667, 859; in *Trout,* in Midway attack, 102, 104; at Corregidor, 205–7; gold and silver removed from Corregidor, 207–8; patrol, 213–14; in *Runner,* 409, 460; commands wolf pack, 599; postwar rank, 883
Ferrall, William Edward ("Pete"), 155n, 176, 185, 186, 193, 198n, 199, 343, 673; at Cavite in Japanese attack, 132, 134; in *Seadragon,* attack on ships at Camranh Bay, 170–71, 212; at Corregidor, evacuates personnel and delivers supplies, 173–74, 194–95; 1942 patrols, 291, 344–45; and removal of seaman's appendix, 291–92; assigned to Bureau of Ships, 345; postwar rank, 883
Ferrara, Maurice, in *Gar,* 724
Fielder, W. M., in *Sculpin,* 524–25
Fife, James, Jr., 82, 131, 135, 160, 164, 213, 274n, 302, 339, 362, 367, 390, 404, 410, 413, 431, 452, 493, 510, 513, 523, 549, 837, 841; and loss of Manila, 153, 155; in Australia, 186, 191, 192, 197; report to Admiral King, 197–201; and Mark XIV torpedo tests, 275–77; commands Squadron Two, 282; criticizes patrols, 286, 288, 290–92; at Port Moresby, 304; at Brisbane, replaces Christie, 348, 371; letter from Lockwood on English's death, 366; character, 371–72; reforms and discipline at Brisbane, 371–72; 1943 patrols sent from Brisbane, 372–80, 386–88, 474–80, 482, 485, 551, 552, 554; submarine operations directed, 372–79; reaction to loss of four submarines, 376; investigated for loss of submarines, 376–78; and January 1943 *Wahoo* patrol, 382, 386; Christie wants him removed from Brisbane, 414; on H.O.R. engines, 446; S-boats under his command, 461–62; and cooperative submarine attacks, 482–83, 485, 487, 504; and 1944 patrols, 562, 579; transferred to shore duty, 609; in strategic planning, 693, 723n; replaces Christie at Fremantle, 814–15, 845; Brisbane unit moved to Subic Bay, 845; pursuit of *Ise* and *Hyuga,* 846–47, 848 (map), 849–50; moves to Subic Bay, 850; patrol in *Hardhead,* 850–51; patrols sent from Subic Bay, 851–55; postwar career, 880, 882
Fifth Fleet, U.S., 642, 824
Fiji Islands, 219
Finback, 325–26, 337, 562; in Battle of Midway, 236n; Alaska patrols, 269–71; 1943 patrol, 453–54; 1944 patrols, 593, 609, 646–47, 654–55, 659–60
Fisher, Sir John, First Sea Lord, 32
Fitzgerald, John Allison, 230, 350, 576; in *Grenadier,* 395–96; prisoner of Japanese, 396–97
Fitz-Patrick, Joseph Paul, in *Paddle,* 751, 796, 800
Flachsenhar, John Jay: in *Rock,* 591; 1944 patrols, 679, 780; support of Leyte invasion, 751, 757
Flanagan, H. J., 768
Flasher, 617; first patrol, 581; 1944 patrols and wolf packs, 627, 684–87, 735, 738–39, 795–96, 798–99; support of air strike on Surabaya, 629, 630; pursuit of *Ise* and *Hyuga,* 847, 849; record for tonnage sunk, 849
Fleet Intelligence Center, 370
Flenniken, Clifton W., Jr. ("Barney"), 298, 299, 497
Fletcher, Frank Jack, 220, 234
Flier, 737, 789; first patrol, 592–93; 1944 patrols, 639–41, 714; lost,

INDEX

714–15, 721, 817n; investigation of loss, 715–16
Floating Drydock Training Center, Tiburn, Cal., 263
Flores Sea, 176, 177
Florida Maru, Japanese ship, 594
Florikan, submarine rescue vessel, 418, 592
Flounder, 580; 1944 patrols and wolf packs, 734, 785–86, 847; collision with *Hoe*, 849–50
Fluckey, Eugene Bennett, 804; in *Barb*, on polar circuit, 665–68; 1944 wolf packs, 706–7, 709–10, 772–73, 808–11; Medal of Honor, 811; 1945 patrols, 866–67; final sinking record, 878
Flying Fish, 227n, 251, 253, 344, 360n, 372, 380, 581, 600, 627, 869; in Battle of Midway, 236n, 241; Truk patrol, 313–14; sent to Brisbane by way of Truk, 330, 332–33; 1943 patrols, 407, 431–32, 513; Watkins's patrol in, 431–32; 1944 patrols, 603, 647, 649, 651, 657, 734; 1945 wolf pack, 860, 861, 863
FM sonar, 787, 789–90, 829, 857; in Sea of Japan, guidance, 857–61
Foley, Lawrence E., in *Cod*, 841
Foley, Robert Joseph, 865; in *Gato*, patrols, 376; cooperative attack, 482–83
Foote, John Joseph, in *Threadfin*, 830, 832
Forand, Aime J., Congressman, 69
Ford Instrument Company, 67n
Forel, German submarine sold to Russia, 33
Formosa, 128, 129, 135, 156, 158, 225, 707, 748; 1942–1943 patrols to, 138, 145, 322, 361, 449, 450, 456, 540; surrender, 164; strategy for recapture, 557, 693–95; 1944 patrols to, 590, 697; wolf packs near, 728, 730–31; air strikes on, 744–46, 794; submarine support of air strikes, 745–46

Formosa Strait, 206, 207, 210, 212, 322, 542, 747; 1944 patrols and wolf packs, 603, 730–31, 746, 767, 770, 775, 777, 802, 808
Forrestal, James V., Navy Secretary, 880
France: submarines, early interest in, 24, 27–28, 32, 36; in Washington arms limitation conference, 50–52; in London arms limitation conference, 58–59; in World War II, 70, 71; Vichy government, 76, 265
Franklin, aircraft carrier, 765, 829
Fraser, I. E., in *XE-3*, 855
Frazee, Murray Bennett, 567, 682, 730
Freeman, Charles Lawrence ("Larry"), 164; in *Skipjack*, patrol from Manila, 137; in defense of Java, 179
Fremantle, 195, 196, 199, 282–85, 303, 343, 344, 389, 502–3, 512, 595, 600, 708; submarine forces at, 191, 192, 197, 201–3, 218, 273–74, 577; submarines exchanged with Pearl Harbor, 223–24, 251, 285, 290, 310, 312, 486, 580–85; personnel changes, 282–83; 1942 patrols from, 285–93, 349–59, 361; 1943 patrols from, 390–97, 424, 486–504; 1943 patrols to, 453–54, 537–38; submarine forces increased, 474–75, 609; cooperative attacks from, 487–93, 504; 1944 patrols from, 609–19, 629–34, 636, 639–41, 643, 647, 695–96, 711–16, 734–43, 780–86, 794–800; command changes, 609–10; Japanese attack, false alarm, 616–18; wolf packs from, 684–87, 739–42, 781–86, 795–96, 798; British and Dutch submarines at, 742–43; submarines in support of Leyte invasion, 751–58; Fife replaces Christie, 814–15; headquarters moved to Subic Bay, 850

Friedell, Wilhelm Lee, 76, 83, 282
Friedman, William Frederick, codebreaker, 53, 73–74
Fritchen, W. L., 735
Fritsch, W. F., in *Gurnard,* 441, 442
FRUMEL (Fleet Radio Unit, Melbourne), 294, 370, 606–7
FRUPAC (Fleet Radio Unit, Pacific), 263, 308, 400–401, 607
Fubaki, Japanese destroyer, 329
Fuhrman, Albert Schorr, in *Jack,* 785
Fuji Maru, Japanese tanker, 842
Fuji Maru, Japanese transport, 542
Fukei Maru, Japanese freighter, 386
Fukudome, Adm. Shigeru, 619
Fukuyama Maru, Japanese freighter, 571
Fulp, James Douglas, Jr., in *Segundo,* 725, 803
Fulton, Robert: *Nautilus* submarine, 23–24; *Clermont,* 24
Fulton, submarine tender, 223, 250, 275, 307, 327, 372; in Battle of Midway, 237, 239; at Brisbane, 330–31, 339, 371, 474; at Milne Bay, 475, 609; at Saipan, 791; at Subic Bay, 845, 846
Funafuti, 505, 508
Furutaka, Japanese cruiser, 329
Fushimi Maru, Japanese freighter, 406, 596
Fuso, Japanese battleship, 506, 634, 636
Fuso class, Japanese battleships, 687, 697–98, 798
Fyfe, John Kerr ("Jake"), in *Batfish,* patrols and wolf packs, 697, 751, 782–83, 833–34

Gabilan, patrols and wolf packs, 730, 746, 749, 852–53, 868–69
Gage, Norman Dwight, 352; in *Gurnard,* 738–39, 800
Galantin, Ignatius Joseph ("Pete"): in *Halibut,* 514–15, 519, 520, 553; wolf packs, 546–47, 730,
761, 771; in Battle of Leyte Gulf, 761, 762; postwar rank, 884
Gallaher, Anton Renki, in *Bang,* patrols and wolf packs, 597–99, 647, 674–76, 679, 697, 775–77, 842
Gallery, Daniel Vincent, captures *U-505,* 689–90
Galvin, John R., 576
Gambacorta, Francis Michael, in *Sea Poacher,* 788
Gambier Bay, jeep carrier, 759
Ganges Maru, Japanese transport, 289
Ganymede, Liberty ship, 846
Gar, 83n, 211, 224, 229, 230, 285, 349, 392, 393, 395, 457, 533, 610, 818n, 842; in pursuit of *Shokaku,* 230–31; 1942 patrol, 350; lifeguarding near Palaus, 574, 576, 724; 1944 patrol, 649
Garfish (H-3), 35
Garnett, Philip Weaver, in *Sargo,* 570–71
Garrison, Malcolm Everett, 622, 864; in *Sandlance,* polar circuit, 593–95; 1944 patrols, 595, 643, 712–13
Garvey, Richard S.: in *Trigger,* 247–48; in *Trepang,* 732, 734
Gato, 224, 229–30, 360n, 380; in Battle of Midway, 236n, 245; Alaskan patrols, 269, 271; sent to Brisbane by way of Truk, 331; 1943 patrols, 376; in cooperative attack, 482–85; 1944 patrol, 647; 1945 wolf pack, 840; lifeguarding near Kyushu, 865
General Board, U.S. Navy, 39, 40, 48, 50, 51, 57, 60, 68, 349
General Electric Company, 61, 280
General Motors Corporation, 882
General Motors Winton, *see* Winton engine
Genyo, Japanese tanker, 622
George V, King, 50
George, destroyer, 805
Germany: submarines before World War I, 33–34, 36; submarines (U-boats) in World War I, 36–39, 41–45, 47–49, 362, 878n; mine-

INDEX

exploding device, magnetic pistol, 54; submarines (U-boats) in World War II, 70–72, 79, 80, 84, 120, 213, 263, 265, 266, 271, 280, 360–62, 398, 689–90; pact with Japan, 76; codebreaking operations against, 260; electric torpedoes, 280; *U-505* captured by U.S., 689–90; submarines in Pacific area, 743, 785–86, 853; defeated, 823; submarines, losses, 877n; submarine sinking records, World Wars I and II, 878n; submarine technology, 881–82

Germershausen, William Joseph: in *Haddock*, describes salvage of papers from Japanese ship, 604–5; in *Tambor*, 697, 791; in *Spadefish*, 858–60, 863–65; sinks Russian ship, 863–65

Gerwick, John Day, 320–21; in *Greenling*, 701–2, 807

Ghormley, Robert Lee, 257, 307, 308; and security leak on Battle of Midway, 257, 259–60, 304; defense of Guadalcanal and Tulagi, 295–96; holds Guadalcanal, 301–2; replaced by Halsey, 329

Gibraltar, 79

Giffen, Robert Carlisle, Jr., in *Gurnard*, 441, 442

Gigu Maru, Japanese freighter, 353

Gilbert Islands, 318, 397, 454, 560; in strategic plans, 398, 399, 422, 423; U.S. invasion of, 505–6, 507 (map), 508, 589; submarine support of invasion, 520–26, 552n

Gilmore, Howard Walter, 325, 458; in *Growler*, Alaskan patrols, 269–70; last patrol and death, 373–74; Medal of Honor, 374, 447, 681, 783

Gilmore, submarine tender, 846

Gimber, Stephen Henry, 492; in *Pompon*, 697, 842

Glennon, Philip Thompson, in *Flasher*, 739, 795, 796, 799

Goggins, William Bernard, 262–63, 400

Gokoku Maru, Japanese ship, 772

Golet, lost, 667, 780, 817n

Goodwin, Ernest Sidney, codebreaker, 606–7

Goossens, H. A. W., in *Zwaardvisch*, 743, 786n

Gould Battery Company, 65

Goyo Maru, Japanese ship, 231

Grady, James Bizzell, in *Whale,* 725

Graf Spee, German raider, 70

Grampus (A-3), 30n

Grampus, 83n, 212, 224, 229, 285, 539; in pursuit of *Shokaku*, 230–31; 1942 patrols, 287, 342; last patrol, lost, 375

Grant, James Dorr, 869

Grant, Mark Alfred, 521

Grayback, 83n, 212, 285, 361, 380, 568, 577; 1942 patrols, 287–88, 342–43; 1943 wolf pack, 541–43; lost, 589–90, 817n

Grayling (D-2), 30n

Grayling, 83n, 205, 209, 213, 215, 309, 360n, 387, 595, 698; in Battle of Midway, 236n, 245; sent to Fremantle by way of Truk, 330–31; lost, 397, 552n

Great Britain, *see* Britain

Greater Underwater Propulsion, *see* Guppy submarines

Green Bowl Society, 880

Greenling, 224, 227n, 229, 325, 360n, 387, 490, 869; in pursuit of *Shokaku*, 230–31, 233; in Battle of Midway, 236n, 248; second patrol to Truk, 309–10; sent to Brisbane, 334; 1944 patrols and wolf pack, 701–2, 732, 807; retired, 807, 818n

Greenup, Francis Albert: in *Hardhead*, wolf pack, 783–84; patrol with Fife, 850–51

Greer, Harry Holt, Jr., in *Seahorse*, 858–59

Greer, destroyer, 80

Gregory, Richard Victor, 181, 193n, 198n, 285; in *Sargo*, 185; patrol from Fremantle, 286–87

Grenadier, 83n, 211, 224, 231, 311,

1026 INDEX

Grenadier (cont.)
576; East China Sea patrol, 224–26; in Battle of Midway, 236n, 245; patrols from Fremantle, 351–52, 394–96; lost, 396, 552

Grenfell, Elton Watters ("Joe"), 107–8, 394, 673; in Pearl Harbor attack, 100, 101; in *Gudgeon,* patrol in Japanese waters, 107, 109–12, 120, 121; sinks *I-173,* 118; bombed by friendly aircraft, 210–11; injured in plane crash, 212; on staff at Pearl Harbor, 550; postwar rank, 884

Grew, Joseph C., 254

Grider, George William, 315, 333, 407, 456; *Wahoo* patrol described, 381–85; in *Pollack,* 454–55; in *Hawkbill,* 727, 728; in *Flasher,* wolf pack, 795–96, 798–800; in pursuit of *Ise* and *Hyuga,* 847, 849; postwar career, 884

Griffin, submarine tender, 80, 218, 302, 303, 339, 345–46, 439, 609

Griffith, Walter Thomas, 502–3, 585, 674, 713, 856; in *Bowfin,* joint patrol with *Billfish,* 488–90; 1944 patrols, 612–14; in *Bullhead,* bombed by U.S. aircraft, 841–42

Griggs, John Bradford, Jr., 249, 368, 400, 548, 711, 725; commands Squadron Twelve, 380, 423, 475; commands *St. Louis,* 813

Griggs, John Bradford, III, 333, 381; in *Picuda,* 770

Gripsholm, Swedish ship, 254n

Gross, Royce Lawrence, 603, 737; in *Seawolf,* 1943 patrols, 448–50, 510, 531–33; in *Boarfish,* 808, 856

Grouper, 251, 253, 360n, 643; in Battle of Midway, 236n, 241–42, 248; sent to Brisbane by way of Truk, 331; 1943 patrols, 378, 379, 477–78; bombed by Allied aircraft, 474, 477; 1944–1945 patrols, 662, 724, 725, 840; retired, 841

Growler, 325, 387, 785; in Battle of Midway, 236n; Alaskan patrols, 269–70; sent to Brisbane by way of Truk, 330; disastrous patrol, death of Gilmore, 373–75; 1944 patrols and wolf packs, 646, 651, 674–75, 706–8, 711, 769, 783; lost, 783, 817n

Gruner, William Philip, Jr. ("Bud"): leaves *Sunfish,* 407; in *Skate,* 567, 622

Grunion, 832; Alaskan patrols, 269, 271; lost, 271, 272, 409

Guadalcanal, 294–96, 299, 317, 318, 329, 477; Japanese landing on, 294–95; U.S. Navy and Marines capture, 295–96; August 1942 battle for, 301–2; Japanese forces leave, 369, 379

Guadalcanal, Battle of, 338–39, 341, 344

Guam, 17, 46, 116, 122, 398, 449, 558, 642, 646, 649, 650, 662; Japanese capture, 105; patrols near, 380, 512, 546, 643; air strikes on, 561, 646; Japanese reinforcements for, 590–91; U.S. invasion of, 652, 664; Japanese aircraft prepare for invasion, 654, 655; submarine base, 777, 779, 791, 804, 805, 808, 816, 858; Camp Dealey, 791, 805, 835; headquarters moved to, 814, 833; aircraft based on, 824; patrols and wolf packs from, 833–44, 860; Loughlin's court-martial, 839

Guantanamo Bay, 80

Guardfish, 334, 387, 408, 489, 568, 652; patrol near Japan, "racetrack" incident, 322–25; in cooperative attack, 484; 1944 patrols and wolf packs, 567, 677–80, 804–5; sinks *Extractor,* 805–6; 1945 patrol, 829

Guavina: 1944 patrols and wolf packs, 713, 734, 785, 798; 1945 patrols, 846, 847

Gudgeon, 83n, 107–9, 123, 210–12, 249, 360n, 361, 517, 533, 537, 568, 610, 835; in Pearl Harbor attack, 100, 101; patrol in Japanese waters, 107, 109–12, 120, 121; sinks *I-173,* 118; in Battle of Mid-

INDEX

way, 236n, 241–43; 1942 patrols, 310, 312, 343–44, 356–57; 1943 patrols, 392–94, 514; attack on *Unyo*, 547–48; lost, 595, 817n
Gudgeon (1951), 882
Guest, destroyer, 333
Guimaras, 650
Guitarro, 600, 669; 1944 patrols and wolf packs, 712, 718, 781–82, 800; support of Leyte invasion, 751, 752, 756; 1945 patrol, 847
Gulf of Boni, 670
Gulf of Panama, 265, 817
Gulf of Siam, 288, 350, 492, 851
Gunn, Frederick Arthur, in *Scabbardfish,* 698, 777–78
Gunnel: in North Africa landing, 264–66; 1943 patrols from Pearl Harbor, 439–40, 527; 1944 patrol and wolf pack, 582, 785; support of air strike on Surabaya, 629–31
Guppy submarines, 882
Gurnard, 536, 582, 701; in Atlantic, 264–66; 1943 patrols from Pearl Harbor, 440–42, 527; 1944 patrols, 623–24, 626–27, 633–34, 636, 738, 751, 800
Gurnee, Robert Lakin, in *Redfish,* 803
Gwin, destroyer, 472
Gyosan Maru, Japanese freighter, 786
Gyoten Maru, Japanese freighter, 567

Haaworth, Emerson J., 53
Hachian Maru, Japanese freighter, 351
Hackleback, 830, 832, 843
Haddo, 266, 614; H.O.R. engines replaced, 537; 1943 patrol, 537–38; Chester Nimitz, Jr., in command, 616–19; 1944–1945 patrols and wolf packs, 637, 639, 717–19, 735, 784–85, 867
Haddock (K-1), 35–36
Haddock, 326, 327, 337, 580, 804; first SJ radar patrol, 321–22; 1943 patrols and wolf pack, 410–12, 453, 515–17, 546–47; conning tower defects, 411–12; 1944 patrols and wolf packs, 603–5, 730, 761, 770, 772; in Battle of Leyte Gulf, 761; 1945 patrol, 825
Hagberg, Oscar Emil, in *Albacore,* 476–77
Haguro, Japanese cruiser, 657, 659, 846, 853; sunk, 854
Hainan, 128, 135, 151, 158, 164, 171, 708; patrols to, 138, 139, 155, 804
Hainan Strait, 708
Haines, John Lyman, 725n
Haines, John Meade, 251, 537, 580, 585; commands Division 42, 213; in Makin commando raid, 317, 318; commands Squadron Sixteen, 475, 486; replaces Fife at Brisbane, 609–10; commands *New Mexico,* 813
Haiphong, 351, 352
Hakaze, Japanese destroyer, 334, 337
Hake, 266, 617, 711; H.O.R. engines replaced, 537; 1943 patrol, 537; 1944–1945 patrols and wolf pack, 619, 637, 717–19, 783, 847
Hakko Maru, Japanese tanker, 493, 705, 796
Hakubasan Maru, Japanese transport, 686
Hakusam Maru, Japanese transport, 640
Hakushika Maru, Japanese transport, 740
Halibut, 337, 818; 1943 patrols, 433, 435, 514–15, 519; 1943–1944 wolf packs, 546–47, 730, 761, 770–72; in Battle of Leyte Gulf, 761, 762
Hall, Warren Collamore, Jr., 456
Halmahera, 165, 353, 495, 497, 537, 557, 580, 585, 621, 624, 632, 633, 637
Halsey, William Frederick ("Bull"), 234, 331–33, 338, 340, 370, 378, 388, 642, 734, 739, 746, 748, 804; in Tokyo bombing raid, 214–15, replaces Ghormley, 329–30; and Brisbane patrols, 342, 344, 376; 1943 counteroffensive, 472, 474; and submarines in Australia, 475; in Gil-

Halsey, William Frederick (cont.)
bert Islands invasion, 506; in Palau Islands invasion, 722, 724–25; proposes direct attack on Leyte, 722–24; preparations for Leyte invasion, 744–45, 747; in Battle of Leyte Gulf, 758–59, 761; air strikes after battle, 782; Operation Hotfoot, proposed carrier attack on Japanese mainland, 790–91; in invasion of Mindoro and Luzon, 792, 794; in Okinawa invasion, 824; July 1945 air strikes against Japan, 867–68; message after cease-fire, 871; in surrender ceremonies, 872

Hammann, destroyer, 239

Hammerhead, 1944 patrols and wolf packs, 679–80, 738, 751, 796, 800

Hammond, Douglas Thompson: in *Cabrilla,* 512; in *Guardfish,* 804–5; sinks *Extractor,* 805–6; 1945 patrol, 829

Hancock, aircraft carrier, 765, 829, 832

Hannon, Edward Robert ("Irish"), 299–301

Hansa Bay, 607

Harbin, Michael, 228

Harder, 444–45, 461, 570n, 730, 737, 785; in 1943 wolf pack, 543–46; H.O.R. engines replaced, 545; support of air strike on Woleai, 574, 576–77; 1944 patrols, 637–39, 669–72; Christie on patrol in, 669–72, 674; last patrol, 716–19; lost, 719–21, 817n

Harder (1951), 882

Hardhead: 1944 patrol and wolf pack, 696–97, 783; Fife on patrol in, 850–51

Hardin, James Thomas: in *Tuna,* 498, 604–5; 1944 patrol, 647

Harding, Warren G., 49, 50

Harlfinger, Frederick Joseph, II, 267, 325, 409, 410, 871; in *Trigger,* 1944 patrols, 600–602, 730, 745–47; in Battle of Leyte Gulf, 762, 764, 765; postwar rank, 884

Harness, Forest A., Congressman, 691

Harper, Talbot Edward, 568

Harral, Brooks Jared: in *Ray,* 482, 497, 616; 1944 patrols, 626, 633, 636

Hart, Thomas Charles, 49, 56, 80–82, 89, 91, 127, 128, 138, 144, 217, 349, 361; in World War I, 43; 44n; S-boat maneuvers, 47; opposes new submarines, 68, 198; commands Asiatic Fleet, 77–79; and Japanese attack on Philippines, 129–32, 135; Warder's dispute with, 136; leaves Philippines for Java, 153, 155; and loss of Philippines, 153, 158, 159; commands ABDA forces, 163–64; and submarines sent to Corregidor, 172, 173; request for relief, 175

Hartman, Irvin Swander, 149, 420; in *Barbero,* patrols and wolf packs, 724, 784–85, 800

Haruna, Japanese battleship, 143n, 159, 176, 506, 662, 775, 776

Harusame, Japanese destroyer, 638

Harve Maru, Japanese freighter, 645

Hashidate, Japanese gunboat, 599

Haskins, Enrique D'Hamel, 313, 314; in *Guitarro,* 600, 669; patrols and wolf packs, 712, 718, 781–82; support of Leyte invasion, 751, 752, 755–56

Hatsukata, Japanese minelayer, 851–52

Hawaii, 43, 48; see also Pearl Harbor

Hawaii Maru, Japanese transport, 801

Hawk, Earle Clifford, in *Pompon,* 498–99

Hawkbill, patrols and wolf packs, 725, 727–28, 795, 800, 852

Hayama, bombardment of palace proposed, 252–53

Hayanami, Japanese destroyer, 637–38

Hayasaki, Japanese provision ship, 374

Hayasui, Japanese tanker, 704

Hayatake class, Japanese aircraft carriers, 779

Hayatomo, Japanese tanker, 499

INDEX

Haylor, Frank Edward: in *Hake*, and last patrol of *Harder*, 717–19; patrols and wolf packs, 783–84, 847
Hayo Maru, Japanese transport, 148
Hazzard, William Hockett: in *S-37*, 177, 184; in *Saury*, 288–89, 341, 438, 450–51; in *Blenny*, 808, 846, 855
Heian Maru, Japanese submarine tender, 565
Heiyou Maru, Japanese transport, 409
Helena, cruiser, 213, 472
Helfrich, Conrad E. L., 175; and defense of Java, 176, 178, 180, 183, 185–86
Henderson, Charles Mitchell: in *Bluefish*, 616; patrols and wolf packs, 632–34, 636, 703–5, 711
Henley, destroyer, 553
Hensel, Karl Goldsmith, 463; in *Swordfish*, 533–36
Herring, 264, 266, 278; lost, 665–67, 817n
Hess, Franklin Grant: in *Puffer*, 500, 501; in *Angler*, patrols, 684–86, 740; support of Leyte invasion, 751, 752, 755–56
Hess, John Borden: in *Swordfish*, 533, 535, 536; in *Pomfret*, 746, 825, 827; lifeguarding in Tokyo Bay, 825, 827
Hezlet, Arthur R., 28; in *Trenchant*, 854
HI-71, Japanese convoy, 702–5, 718
Hiburi, Japanese frigate, 718
Hiburi Maru, Japanese transport, 666
Hide Maru, Japanese ship, 452
Hie Maru, Japanese supply ship, 524
Hiei, Japanese battleship, 338
Hillenkoetter, Roscoe Henry, 263
Hills, Blish Charles, in *Perch II*, 599, 731
Himeno Maru, Japanese freighter, 498 539, 586, 697
Hingson, James Monroe, in *Batfish*,
Hirado, Japanese frigate, 708
Hirado Shima, 864
Hirohito, Emperor, 252, 658, 659; accepts terms of surrender, 870–71
Hiroshima, atomic bomb, 869
Hiryu, Japanese aircraft carrier, 123, 176, 399n; in Battle of Midway, lost, 237, 238
Hisagawa Maru, Japanese freighter, 810
Hitler, Adolf, 64, 70, 71, 78, 823
Hiyama Maru, Japanese ship, 678
Hiyo, Japanese aircraft carrier, 411–13, 417, 429–30, 435, 553; sunk, 662
Hoe, 439, 617; H.O.R. engines replaced, 581; patrols and wolf packs, 627, 631, 741, 794, 798, 800; collision with *Flounder*, 850
Hogan, Thomas Wesley, 502–3; in *Bonefish*, 1943 patrols, 496; 1944 patrols, 611, 617, 625–26, 633, 641
Hogue, British cruiser, 37
Hokishima Maru, Japanese tanker, 810
Hokkaido, 416–18, 863, 866; bombardment by *Steelhead*, 433; minefields near, 667, 780; bombed, 868
Hokki Maru, Japanese freighter, 740
Hokuan Maru, Japanese passenger freighter, 397
Hokuroku, Japanese transport, 583
Holden, Richard, in *Gato*, 865
Holland, Elmer J., Congressman, 259
Holland, John Philip: submarines designed by, 26–30, 32, 40; Japan buys submarines from, 33–34n
Holland, submarine tender, 82, 127, 130–32, 157, 164, 176, 192, 224, 276, 438, 459; withdrawn from Philippines, 155; in Australia, 185, 191, 197, 302, 303, 339, 371; returned for overhaul, 372; in Saipan, 673, 695, 705, 791; in Guam, Lockwood's headquarters, 833
Holland VI (U.S.S. *Holland*), 29–30
Hollandia, 620, 814; Allied landing at, 607, 609
Holley, George Michael, Jr.: in *S-41*, 155, 157, 166, 177, 179, 183, 299
Hollingsworth, John Christie: in *Tri-*

Hollingsworth, John Christie (*cont.*) ton, 208, 224; in *Scamp*, 579–80; lost, 780
Holman, William Grizzard, 285, 568
Holmes, Wilfred Jay ("Jasper"), codebreaker, 88, 117–19, 123, 125, 227, 238, 308, 318, 392, 394, 409, 413, 455, 461, 589, 591, 624, 679, 737, 791, 829, 849, 852, 854, 860; Lockwood praises, 401; medal, 881
Holt, Edward Rowell, Jr., in *Bullhead*, lost, 856
Holtwick, Jack Sebastian, codebreaker, 63, 88
Holtz, Arnold Henry ("Ike"), 643; in *Tuna*, 271, 498; in *Baya*, 725, 727, 728
Honan Maru, Japanese tanker, 846
Hong Kong, 85, 128, 135, 164, 399; patrols near, 138–39, 531, 582; strategy for recapture, 557; air strike on, 794
Honolulu, cruiser, 472
Honshu, 542; 1943 patrols near, 319, 323, 408–9, 427, 443, 444, 455, 459, 461, 463, 475, 511, 513, 515, 539, 552*n*; minefields near, 461, 667, 780; 1944–1945 patrols near, 586, 594, 596, 662, 697, 732, 780, 789, 825, 859, 863, 865–66, 868
Hoover, John Howard, 839*n*
H.O.R. (Hoover-Owens-Rentschler) engines, 61, 64, 66, 157, 198, 402; problems and defects, 263–66, 368, 401; submarines with, 423, 437, 439–46, 475, 512–13, 552*n*; failure, 439–46; replaced, 580, 609
Horaizan Maru, Japanese tanker, 643
Horei Maru, Japanese ship, 590
Horne, Frederick Joseph, 261
Hornet, aircraft carrier, 234, 301*n*, 302, 399; in Tokyo bombing raid, 205, 214, 220; in Battle of Midway, 238, 247*n*; lost, 330
Hornet, aircraft carrier (new, 1943), 399*n*, 422, 827
Hoshi Maru, Japanese ship, 587

Hosho, Japanese aircraft carrier, 209–10, 215, 341
Hoskins, Frank P., in *Trutta*, 864
Hottel, Martin Perry ("Spike"), 209, 250, 327, 328, 380, 643; in *Cuttlefish*, at Battle of Midway, 237; in *Grouper*, patrols, 379, 477–79; protests on Mark VI exploder, 478–79; Mark XVIII torpedo tests, 509; and Cutie torpedoes, 787, 789
Housatonic, sloop in Civil War, 24
Houston, cruiser, 77, 185; lost, 186; Japanese salvage plans reported, 350–52
Houston, cruiser (second), 745
Howe, Adm. Richard, Lord, 23
Huckins, Thomas Averill, radio intelligence expert, 117–18
Hue, 856
Huff, John Kirkman, 605
Huffman, Leon Joseph ("Savvy"), 550, 814, 881
Hughes, Charles Evans, 50
Hull, Harry: in *Thresher*, 523; and Cutie torpedoes, 787, 789
Hull, Jesse Lyle, 325–26, 337; in *Finback*, Alaskan patrols, 270–71
Hull, destroyer, 792
Humboldt Bay, 607, 609
Hunley, H. L., Confederate submarine, 24–25
Hunley, Horace L., 24
Hunnicutt, James L., in *Carp*, 797*n*, 818
Hunter, Samuel Howard, Jr., 134
Hurana, Japanese battleship, 868
Hurd, Kenneth Charles, 288, 351, 814; in *Seal*, 1942 patrols, 144, 151, 155, 164; defense of Java, 183, 187, 198*n*; patrols from Fremantle, 290–91, 354
Hurst, Adrian Melvin, 285, 339, 466; in *Permit*, patrols, 145, 164, 165; in Lingayen Gulf, 147, 151
Hurt, David Albert, 179, 183, 320, 599*n*; in *Perch*, patrols, 145, 151, 164, 184–85; loses *Perch*, captured by Japanese, 188–89

INDEX

Hutchinson, Edward Shillingford, 212; in *Grampus,* 287; in *Rasher,* 492

Hyde, John Milton, 813; in *Bergall,* 1944 patrols, 751, 780–81, 796–98; refuses to destroy *Bergall,* 797–98; 1945 patrols, 847, 851

Hydeman, Earl Twining, in *Sea Dog,* patrol and wolf pack, 830, 859–61, 863, 864

Hydrophone, 38

Hypo codebreaking unit, *see* Codebreaking

Hyuga, Japanese battleship–aircraft carrier, 748, 759, 761, 762, 764, 766, 777, 794, 795, 798, 855; pursuit of, 846–47, 848 (map), 849–50; destroyed, 868

Hyuga Maru, Japanese freighter, 380

I class, Japanese submarines, 508, 662, 663, 765, 804, 805, 872; human torpedoes (*kaiten*) used, 766
  I-1, 370; *I-7,* 418, 592; *I-15,* 302; *I-18,* 343; *I-19,* 302; *I-21,* 330; *I-24,* 418, 476, 553; *I-25,* 271n; *I-26,* 338; *I-28,* 231, 233; *I-29,* 679; *I-31,* 418; *I-36,* 766; *I-37,* 766; *I-38,* 766; *I-42,* 574; *I-43,* 647; *I-47,* 766; *I-58,* 869; *I-64,* 233; *I-122,* 863; *I-168,* 239; *I-173,* 117–18; *I-175,* 508, 560; *I-176,* 330, 523; *I-182,* 533; *I-183,* 590; *I-365,* 778; *I-373,* 870

IBM punch cards, 63

Icefish, patrols and wolf packs, 730, 746, 748, 769, 770, 835

Icenhower, Joseph Bryan: in *Jallao,* 1944 patrols and wolf packs, 730, 770, 771; in Battle of Leyte Gulf, 762; 1945 patrol and wolf pack, 840, 870

ICPOA (Intelligence Center, Pacific Ocean Area), 263

Ikomasaw Maru, Japanese transport, 836

Illustrious, British aircraft carrier, 629

Ilmen, Russian freighter, 405

Inazuma, Japanese destroyer, 625

Inchon, 867

Independence, aircraft carrier, 399n, 422, 508

India: Japanese raid on, 192; British forces in, 557, 629

Indian Ocean, 213, 853; German submarines in, 786n

Indianapolis, cruiser, 61–62; Spruance's flagship, 830; sunk, 869

Indochina, 164, 192, 794; Japanese bases in, 76, 77, 128, 135, 163, 164, 181, 183; 1942–1943 patrols near, 285, 289–91, 350, 351, 354–55, 357, 487, 488, 491, 495–97, 499; 1944 patrols near, 611, 616, 618, 625, 627, 631, 632, 687, 714, 785, 794, 796; *see also* Camranh Bay

Inland Sea, 746, 749, 778, 825; Japanese forces in, 745; U.S. bombing of Japanese fleet, 829, 868

Innis, Walter Deane, 269

Internal combustion engine, 26, 29

Intrepid, aircraft carrier, 399, 765, 859

Inubo Zaki, 335–36, 780

Iowa, battleship, 549n

Ireland, 44

Iro Zaki, 733

Irvin, William Davis, 593, 673; in *Nautilus,* in Gilbert Islands invasion, 520, 522–23; 1944 patrol, 591

Isabel, former gunboat, 284

Ise, Japanese battleship–aircraft carrier, 748, 759, 761, 762, 764, 766, 777, 794, 795, 798, 855; pursuit of, 846–47, 848 (map), 849–50; destroyed, 868

Isonami, Japanese destroyer, 392

Isuzu, Japanese cruiser, 506, 748, 852–53

Italy: submarines before World War I, 33; in London arms limitation conference, 58–59; pact with Japan, 76; submarines lost in World War II, 877n

Ito, Vice Adm. Seiichi, 830

Itsushima, Japanese minelayer, 743
Ives, Norman Seton, 83, 121; in Pearl Harbor attack, 100–101; commands Squadron Fifty in Scotland, 263–64
Iwaki Maru, Japanese freighter, 666
Iwanami, Japanese destroyer, 796
Iwo Jima, 18, 399, 527, 603, 806; U.S. invasion of, 824–25, 826 (map), 827
Izume, Japanese cruiser, 868

Jack, 443–44, 446, 512; patrols, 583–84, 622–24, 640, 734, 785
Jackson, Charles B., Jr., 577
Jacobs, Tyrell Dwight, 171, 176, 185, 206, 275; in *Sargo*, 140, 151, 169; discovers failure of Mark VI and Mark XIV, 140–41, 160; controversy with Wilkes on Mark XIV, 169–70; delivers supplies to Mindanao, 174
Jacobson, A. E., Jr., 714–15
Jacoby, Oswald, codebreaker, 689
Jallao: 1944 patrols and wolf packs, 730, 770–72; in Battle of Leyte Gulf, 761, 762; 1945 patrols and wolf pack, 840, 865, 870
Jaluit, 115, 454, 455, 526
JANAC (Joint Army-Navy Assessment Committee), 121, 122, 168, 299, 312, 336, 347, 407, 456, 511, 554, 590*n*, 602, 738; revised sinking figures, total, 877–79
Janbi Maru, Japanese tanker, 717
Janney, Frederick Emery, in *Hackleback*, 830, 832
Japan: Russo-Japanese War, submarines in, 33–34*n*; possessions after World War I, 46; strategy plan against, *see* Plan Orange; in Washington arms limitation conference, 51, 52; in London arms limitation conference, 58–60; Manchuria invaded, 64, 70; military expansion, 69–70; China invaded, 70; pact with Germany and Italy, 76; plans for World War II, 85–86, 89–90, 128; plans for Pearl Harbor attack, 85–90; negotiations with U.S., 90–91; Pearl Harbor attack, 97–102, 103 (map), 106; patrols near, 224, 251, 319–20, 322–26, 443, 444, 468–69, 527, 534; submarine warfare against, summaries, 1942, 359–62, 1943, 551–54, 1944, 816–819; U.S. bombing of, 777, 778, 806, 824–25, 827, 829, 833, 867–68; in 1945, 823–24; surrender, 870–73; action in World War II, *see entries for specific actions*; codebreaking against, *see* Codebreaking
Japanese merchant ships: U.S. offensive against, 17–18, 359–60, 688, 816–17, 819, 823; personnel losses, 878
Japanese navy: strength, 85–86; report by Wilkes and Fife on, to Admiral King, 198; antisubmarine measures, 387, 424; retreats westward, 560, 561, 610; documents on minefields, 589; Battle of Philippine Sea, 649–55, 656 (map), 657–60, 661 (map), 662–63; Battle of Leyte Gulf, 758–59, 760 (map), 761–62, 763 (map), 764–66; 1944 losses, 816–17, 819; 1945 losses, 823
Japanese submarines, 117–19; types, 85–86; midget, 86, 118*n*, 663, 872; summary of operations, 1942, 360–61, 1943, 553; sunk in 1944, 641, 662–63, 818; surrendered, 872; losses, total, 877*n*; technology, 881–82
Japanese torpedoes: oxygen, 279–80*n*, 282*n*; electric, 281–82*n*; kaitens (man-guided), 663, 765–66, 824; technology, 881
Jarvis, Benjamin Campbell: in *Sailfish*, 463–64; in *Nautilus*, 593; in *Bergall*, 796, 797; in *Baya*, 846, 851
Jastrazab, former S-25, 217*n*
Java, 85, 128, 163, 195, 226, 324, 340, 359, 361; Hart's headquarters,

INDEX

163; Japanese drive toward, 166, 175–76, 178, 180, 181, 183; submarines in defense of, 175–91; Japanese invasion of, 182 (map), 183; U.S. forces leave, 186; submarine patrols near, 285, 290
Java, Dutch cruiser, 186
Java Sea, 193, 201, 395, 454, 495, 629, 684, 742–43, 852
Java Sea, Battle of, 185–86, 263
Jensen, Marvin John, in *Puffer,* 499–501
Jinbu Maru, Japanese freighter, 420
Jinmu Maru, Japanese ship, 426
Jintsu, Japanese cruiser, 301, 472
Jinyo (*Shinyo*), Japanese aircraft carrier, 744, 748, 766, 773; sunk, 774, 842
Jinzan Maru, Japanese ship, 678
Johnson, Carl Arthur, in *Flounder,* 580
Johnson, E. A., ordnance expert, 438
Johnson, Franklin Oliver ("Fuel Oil"), 418
Johnston, Stanley, war correspondent: in sinking of *Lexington,* 256–57; story of *Lexington* and security leak, 257–60
Johnston Island, 203
Joint Intelligence Center, 400
Jolo Island, 181, 183
Jones, J. L., Marine captain, 522–23
Jones, W. R., 343
Jordan, James Langford: in *Finback,* patrol, 646, 654–55; in Battle of Philippine Sea, 659–60
Joshu Maru, Japanese freighter, 731
Joyce, Allen Raymond, 211–12, 394
Jukes, Herbert Lollis: in *S-27,* 268–69; in *Kingfish,* 497, 603
Julihn, Lawrence Virginius, in *Shad,* 775, 776, 802
Juneau, cruiser, 338, 361
Junyo, Japanese aircraft carrier, 268, 330, 411–13, 417, 662, 744, 748, 766; damaged, 801–2, 817
Jupiter, first U.S. aircraft carrier, 49*n*
Juzan Maru, Japanese transport, 844

Kachidoki Maru, Japanese transport, 708
Kaga, Japanese aircraft carrier, 175, 187, 205, 209, 399*n*; in Battle of Midway, lost, 237, 238, 244–45
Kagi Maru, Japanese ship, 451
Kagu Maru, Japanese transport, 781
Kahoolawe, 437–38
Kaihei Maru, Japanese freighter, 449
Kaiho Maru, Japanese freighter, 870
Kaiko Maru, Japanese freighter, 594
Kaitens (Japanese man-guided torpedoes), 663, 765–66, 824, 869, 872
Kaiyo, 866
Kajioka, Rear Adm. Sadamichi, 622, 623
Kako, Japanese cruiser, 298–99, 334, 360, 420
Kalaw, Maximo, 781
Kalinin Bay, jeep carrier, 765
Kamakura Maru, Japanese ship, 393–94, 615
Kambala, Russian submarine, 33
Kamchatka, 416, 594
Kamikawa Maru, Japanese seaplane tender, 425–26, 476
Kamikaze pilots, 824; in Battle of Leyte Gulf, 765; in invasion of Mindoro and Luzon, 792, 794; at Iwo Jima and Okinawa, 827, 830, 832
Kamo Maru, Japanese freighter, 683
Kamogawa Maru, Japanese aircraft ferry, 187
Kamoi, Japanese seaplane tender, 612–13
Kamoi Maru, Japanese freighter, 333
Kansai Maru, Japanese transport, 476
Kanto Maru, Japanese aircraft ferry, 289
Karafuto, 867
Karas, Russian submarine, 33
Karimata Strait, 176, 177, 183, 492, 684, 716, 797, 800
Karp, Russian submarine, 33, 34
Kasagi Maru, Japanese salvage ship, 535

Kashima Maru, Japanese transport, 496
Kashimasan Maru, Japanese tanker, 645
Kasumi, Japanese destroyer, 270
Katoomba, Australian ship, 300–301
Katori, Japanese cruiser, 565
Katori Maru, Japanese freighter, 675
Katsura Maru II, Japanese former gunboat, 420
Katsurage, Japanese aircraft carrier, 868
Katsuragi Maru, Japanese aircraft ferry, 305
Katsurahama Maru, Japanese ship, 448
Kavieng, 297, 298, 306, 316, 334, 699; Japanese convoy routes, 386–87; U.S. attacks on, 472; bypassed in New Guinea campaign, 606
Kawasaki, U.S. bombing of, 827
Kazahaya, Japanese tanker, 536
Kazegumo, Japanese destroyer, 637
Keeter, D. C. ("Bird-Dog"), 382
Keijo Maru, Japanese gunboat, 298
Keiko Maru, Japanese freighter, 353
Keithly, Roger Myers, 412; in *Tilefish,* 679
Kelley, W. F., 374
Kelly, Colin, 143*n*
Kelly, John, 438
Kema, 165, 166, 172
Kenan Maru, Japanese ship, 595
Kendari, 165; Japanese base, 175–79, 183, 191, 192, 205, 211, 288
Kennedy, John F., 392
Kennedy, Marvin Granville ("Pinky"), in *Wahoo,* 315–16, 333
Kenney, George C., 617
Kenyo Maru, Japanese tanker, 484
Kete, 807; lost, 829
Key West, Fla., submarine base, 44, 885
Keyport, Wash., torpedo factory, 69
Kiama, Australian man-of-war, 784
Kicker, H. J., 521
Kii Suido, 113–14, 213, 231, 325, 749, 829

Kimikawa Maru, Japanese seaplane tender, 769
Kimishima Maru, Japanese freighter, 587–88
Kimmel, Husband Edward, 79, 87, 106–7, 125, 417; and warning of Pearl Harbor attack, 89–92, 881; in Pearl Harbor attack, 98–99, 101; scapegoat for Pearl Harbor, 123; opposes Roosevelt, 690–91
Kimmel, Manning Marius, 227, 335, 814; in *Raton,* 482, 497; commands *Robalo,* 626; last patrol and death, 687–88, 714, 715
Kimmel, Thomas Kinkaid, 227, 300; in *S-40,* 149–50; in *Balao,* 479; death of his brother, 688
Kimura, Adm. Masanori, 792, 800
King, Ernest Joseph, 79, 80, 173, 175, 176, 191, 234, 262, 268, 361, 372, 509, 550, 567, 609, 629, 673, 688, 691, 812, 814, 864, 879; Commander in Chief, United States Fleet, and Chief of Naval Operations, 125–26; report of Wilkes and Fife to, 197–201; decides to leave submarines in Australia, 201–3; sends S-boats to Pacific, 217; and security leak, 257–59; opposes sending submarines to Scotland, 263; and Mark XIV torpedo tests, 277; and experimental oxygen or electric torpedoes, 279–80; and Guadalcanal landing, 295, 296; target priorities, 306, 577*n*; command changes, 366, 367; strategy against Japan, 398, 399, 693, 694; and Mark XVIII torpedo report, 403; orders replacement of H.O.R. engines, 446; and submarines in Australia, 474, 475, 580; disapproves of *Gato*'s battle with airplane, 484; and destroyer *England,* 641; on invasion of Saipan, 665; and *U-505* capture, 690; and investigation of loss of *Flier,* 716; and Loughlin's court-martial, 838,

840; and war correspondents on submarines, 841, 842
King, Robert Donovan, in *Redfin,* 610–11
King Two (Leyte invasion), 744–45, 747
Kingfish, 337, 427, 561, 621; 1943 patrols, 406–7, 412, 496–97; 1944 patrols, 603, 731
Kinjosan Maru, Japanese ship, 229
Kinkaid, Thomas Cassin, 612, 620, 626, 673, 716, 723, 737, 755–57; invasion of Attu, 417; commands Seventh Fleet, 504; disagreement with Christie on medals, 584–85, 674, 720–21, 814, 815; and Surabaya air strike, 627, 629; and Biak invasion, 638; in Battle of Leyte Gulf, 759; Christie transferred from Fremantle, 814–15
Kinryu Maru, Japanese transport, 718
Kinsella, William Thomas: on training, 156; in *Blackfish,* 481; describes loss of *Corvina,* 523; in *Ray,* and last patrol of *Harder,* 717–18; 1944 patrols and wolf packs, 741–42, 781–83
Kinu, Japanese cruiser, 749, 751, 752n
Kinugasa, Japanese cruiser, 338
Kinugasa Maru, Japanese freighter, 727
Kirishima, Japanese battleship, 338, 344
Kirishima Maru, Japanese transport, 487
Kirk, Oliver Grafton, 222, 588; memorandum on Mark XVIII, 402–4; in *Lapon,* 466–69
Kirkpatrick, Charles Cochran, 255, 567, 579, 593, 883; in *Triton,* East China Sea patrol, 224–25, 254; Alaskan patrols, 270; in pursuit of *Shokaku,* 231, 233; sent to Brisbane, 334; aide to Admiral King, 334
Kirun, 731

Kishinami, Japanese destroyer, 591, 754–55, 796
Kiska, 270, 271, 399, 592; Japanese landing on, 268; U.S. forces recapture, 416–18, 419 (map); Japanese evacuation from, 418
Kitakata Maru, Japanese ship, 228
Kitch, William Lawrence, in *Blackfin,* 846, 847
Kitkun Bay, jeep carrier, 765
Kiwi, New Zealand corvette, 370
Kiyo Maru, Japanese tanker, 493
Kizugawa Maru, Japanese freighter, 600
Klakring, Thomas Burton, 337, 408, 489, 568, 652, 779, 805; in *Guardfish,* patrol near Japan, "racetrack" incident, 322–25; sent to Brisbane, 334; "Burt's Brooms," 790–91, 825
Klinker, Roy Craig, in *Sea Fox,* 835, 838
Knapp, P., 714, 715
Knox, Frank, Navy Secretary, 258
Kobe, U.S. bombing of, 827
Kobe Zaki, 426
Koga, Adm. Mineichi, 370, 423, 425, 427, 429, 484, 486, 508, 526, 574, 610, 620; and Allied counteroffensive, 472; in Gilbert Islands invasion, 505–6; in Marshall Islands invasion, 558, 560–63, 571; death, 561; false report of his capture, 618–19
Kogen Maru, Japanese freighter, 767
Kogosan Maru, Japanese freighter, 214
Koho Maru, Japanese ship, 595, 849
Koiso, Gen. Kuniaki, 665
Koki Maru, Japanese ship, 448
Kokura, 870
Kokuyo Maru, Japanese freighter, 594
Kola, Russian freighter, 405
Kolombangara, Battle of, 472
Komandorski Islands, 417
Komatsu, Sakio, aircraft pilot, 655, 657
Kone Zaki, 426

Kongo, Japanese battleship, 159, 176, 506, 775; sunk, 776
Kongo class, Japanese battleships, 313, 575, 754
Konron Maru, Japanese ship, 511
Korea, patrols near, 208, 468, 683, 772, 843, 844
Korei Maru, Japanese tanker, 764
Körting Brothers, engines made by, 33, 34, 36
Kosan Maru, Japanese freighter, 683
Kossler, Herman Joseph: in *Guardfish*, "racetrack" incident, 322, 324; in *Cavalla*, Battle of Philippine Sea, 652–54, 657–58; patrols, 725, 794–95; and cease-fire message, 871; postwar opinions, 883
Kossol Pass, 766
Koto Maru, Japanese freighter, 666, 684
Kotoku Maru, Japanese transport, 705
Koyo Maru, Japanese ship, 440, 588
Kozan Maru, Japanese freighter, 456
Krapf, Arthur Elmer, in *Jack*, 640
Krupp firm, submarines, 33, 34
Kula Gulf, Battle of, 472
Kumano, Japanese cruiser, 506, 782, 817
Kuretake, Japanese destroyer, 803
Kurile Islands, 86, 416, 418, 425, 466, 586, 866
Kurita, Vice Adm. Takao, 749, 754–55; in Battle of Leyte Gulf, 758–59, 761, 767, 775
Kusaie, 574
Kusakaki, Japanese frigate, 712
Kuykendall, C. W., in *Tullibee*, 575–76
Kwajalein, 115, 116, 118, 205, 229, 230, 398, 461, 462, 506, 526; U.S. invasion of, 558
Kyokko Maru, Japanese freighter, 495
Kyoko Maru, Japanese tanker, 497
Kyokuei Maru, Japanese tanker, 491
Kyokuho Maru, Japanese tanker, 741
Kyokuto Maru, Japanese freighter, 581

Kyokuyo Maru, Japanese tanker, 354, 355
Kyushu, 408, 697, 746, 801, 843, 869; invasion planned, 824; bombing of, 829

Lae, 472
Lagarto, 825; lost, 851–52
Laing, Frederick Williams, 614
Laird, George Hays, Jr., in *Blackfin*, 751, 781, 784
Lajaunie, Leonce Arnold, Jr., in *Muskallunge*, 785
Lake, Richard Cross, 476, 599; in *Albacore*, Truk patrol, 316, 337, 360; sent to Brisbane, 334; patrols from Brisbane, 378–79
Lake, Simon, submarines designed by, 34n, 35n, 40, 59n
Lamb, Raymond Starr, in *Stingray*, 145–47, 151, 155, 159, 165
Lamon Bay, Japanese landing in, 137, 153
Langley, aircraft carrier, 399n, 794
Laning, Richard Boyer, in *Salmon*, 764
La Pérouse Strait, 405, 464, 467–70, 510, 511, 552n, 857, 863–65
Lapon, 402, 609, 666n, 687; patrol in Sea of Japan, 466–69; 1944 patrols and wolf packs, 582–83, 625, 631–32, 739–40, 796, 800
Laramee, R. A., 595
Latham, Richard Clark: in *Tinosa*, FM sonar tests, 789–90, 829, 858; wolf pack, 860, 861, 863
Latta, Frank De Vere, 319, 417, 666n; in *Narwhal*, bombards Matsuwa To, 466, 469; mission to Philippines, 497–98; in *Lagarto*, 825; lost, 851–52
Lauerman, Henry Conrad, 682
Laughon, Willard Ross, 497, 703; in *Rasher*, joint patrol with *Bluefish*, 492; 1944 patrols, 615–18, 632, 633, 636–37, 641
Laurenti, submarine designer, 35n

INDEX

Lautrup, George William, Jr., in *Gar*, 576, 649
Layton, Edwin Thomas, 92
Leary, Herbert Fairfax, 218, 283, 285, 302
Lee, John Elwood, 397, 842; in *Croaker*, 1944 patrols, 698, 699, 731; in Battle of Leyte Gulf, 762
Lefavour, William Robert, in *Sailfish*, 463–64, 527, 593
Legaspi, 153
Leibold, W. R., 768
Lent, Willis Ashford ("Pilly"), 208, 231, 249, 312, 352, 394; in *Triton*, at Wake Island, 105–6, 120, 123; in *Grenadier*, 224; complains of torpedo performance, 226; patrol in East China Sea, 226, 230*n*; in Battle of Midway, 245; in *Haddo*, 266; commands Squadron Sixteen, 813
Lewellen, Bafford Edward, 456; in *Pollack*, 454–55, 649; in *Torsk*, 870
Lewis, Frank, 264
Lewis, George Alexander, 251
Lewis, Hugh Howard, 797*n*; in *Sterlet*, 765, 812, 818, 827
Lewis, Jack Hayden, 339, 600; in *Trigger*, in Battle of Midway, 247–48; Alaskan patrol, 271; in *Swordfish*, 380–81; in *Dragonet*, 806
Lexington, aircraft carrier, 57, 104, 123, 204, 399; in Battle of Coral Sea, lost, 220; Johnston's story on sinking of, 256–59
Lexington, aircraft carrier (new, 1943), 399*n*, 422, 521–22, 765
Leyte, 695, 791, 792, 815, 867; Halsey proposes direct attack on, 722–24; preparations for invasion (King Two), 744–45, 747; Japanese counteroffensive before invasion, 744, 747, 749, 751; U.S. invasion of, 749, 750 (map), 751, 765; submarine support of invasion, 751–58
Leyte Gulf, Battle of, 758–59, 760 (map), 761–62, 763 (map), 764–66, 775; submarine support, 761–62, 764–66
Liddell, James W., 285, 592–93, 639–40; survives loss of *Flier*, 714–15
Lietwiler, John Marion, codebreaker, 89, 195, 607
Life magazine, 253, 325
Lifeguarding, 508, 521, 522, 568, 609, 745–46; in Palau Islands action, 574, 576, 724; in Marianas invasion, 646; in Makassar Strait, 784; in B-29 raids, 806; 1944 summary, 818; in 1945 operations, 825, 827, 829, 865–66, 868–69; in Tokyo Bay, 825, 827, 842
Lima Maru, Japanese ship, 587
Lindbergh, Charles, 52
Lindon, Elbert Crawford ("Spud"), 600
Lindsay, Harry Meakin, Jr., 288
Lingayen Gulf, 128, 141, 144–45, 153, 173, 193, 196, 359, 397, 598, 740; "battle" of, 145–51, 152 (map); failure to defend, 158–59; patrols and wolf packs near, 287, 356, 466, 537, 627, 640, 712, 781, 782; U.S. landing in, 792, 794
Lionfish, 830, 832
Lipes, Wheeler, 291–92
Liscombe Bay, jeep carrier, 508, 553, 560
Litchfield, destroyer, 107, 460
Liverpool Maru, Japanese ship, 448
Lockwood, Charles Andrews, Jr., 76, 78, 79, 126, 303–4, 310, 312, 339, 342–43, 345, 348, 362, 386, 394, 420, 479, 499, 501, 609, 618, 642, 694, 755*n*, 855; commands Division 13, 66–67; and improved submarine design, 67–68; at Fremantle, replaces Wilkes, 274; Mark XIV torpedo tests, 275–78, 326; personnel changes, 282–83; Carpender's friction with, 283–84, 303, 367–68; proposal for advance

1038 INDEX

Lockwood, Charles Andrews, Jr. (*cont.*) base (Potshot), 284–85, 389, 390; and patrols from Fremantle, 285–93, 349–52, 355, 357–58; replaces English in Pearl Harbor command, 366–68, 400; and investigation of Fife's loss of submarines, 376–77; survey of submarine performance, 400–404; and Mark VI magnetic exploder, 402, 427, 430–31, 504; criticizes Bureau of Ordnance torpedo production, 403–4; and 1943 patrols, 407–10, 413, 423–25, 428, 431–33, 445, 446, 448, 450, 454, 456–64, 481, 508, 510, 511, 514, 519–21, 524, 525, 529–33, 539, 541, 551–54; in torpedo controversy, quarrel with Christie, 413–15; and submarine security, 424; Mark XIV defects identified, 437–39, 508–9; and H.O.R. engine failures, 440, 446; and patrols in Sea of Japan, 464, 468–71, 511; Mark XVIII torpedo tests, 509; and wolf-packing, 509, 542, 543, 545, 546, 694; command changes, end of 1943, 548–50; becomes vice admiral, 550; and Majuro advance base, 561; and 1944 patrols, 562, 565, 575, 577*n*, 580, 584, 586, 587, 589–91, 595, 597, 601, 603–5, 665–68, 670, 674, 677, 682, 683, 695–98, 712, 731, 767, 777, 778, 780, 790–91, 801, 802, 805, 806, 817; choice of commanding officers, 588–89, 818; objects to removal of officers from submarine service, 593; 1944 wolf packs, 597, 643–46, 674, 679, 681, 694, 701, 702, 706, 722, 728, 729, 731, 746, 761, 769–73, 785, 801, 804; submarines in preparation for invasion of Marianas, 621, 643, 646, 649; submarines in Battle of Philippine Sea, 651–55, 658–60; Christie's conference with, 672–74; blames Christie for loss of Dealey in *Harder*, 720; submarines in support of Palau Islands invasion, 724–25; submarines in preparation for Leyte invasion, 745, 746, 749; submarines in Battle of Leyte Gulf, 761, 762; and new devices for submarines, 787, 788, 790; command changes, disagreements on, 812–15; and Fife's replacement of Christie, 814–15; support of Iwo Jima and Okinawa landings, 825, 829, 830; 1945 wolf packs, 830, 832, 833, 858–61, 863–65; 1945 patrols from Pearl Harbor and Guam, 833, 834, 842, 848, 851, 857–60, 865, 868, 870; in *Awa Maru* incident, 837–40; FM sonar used in Sea of Japan, 857–60; cease-fire message, 870–71; in surrender ceremonies, 871–72; records of submarine performance, 877, 879; postwar career, 879–83

Lockwood, Ralph Huntington, in *Guavina*, 846, 847

Logan, Samuel Moore, 576, 717

Lombok Strait, 178, 180, 183, 186, 187, 189, 351, 355, 615–18, 627, 629, 684, 714, 735, 739, 785, 856

London, arms limitation conference, 1930, 58–60, 62

London, British cruiser, 629

Long, Willie, 248

Longstaff, John Bailey, 423, 813

Loomis, Frederick Kent, 610

Loomis, Sam Colby, Jr.: in *Snook*, 447, 448; in *Stingray*, 600; patrols, 646, 654, 736

Los Angeles, Japanese submarines fire at refinery near, 117

Lot's Wife (Sofu Gan), 428, 431–33, 437, 698

Loughlin, Charles Elliott: in *Queenfish*, wolf packs, 706–7, 709–11, 772–75, 808–10, 835–36; sinks *Awa Maru*, 837–39; court-martial, 839–40; postwar career, 883–84

Louisville, cruiser, 792

Low, Francis Stuart ("Frog"), 126, 205
Lowrance, Vernon Long ("Rebel"), 337, 427, 621, 859, 884; in *Kingfish*, 406, 412, 496-97; in *Sea Dog*, 762, 804
Lucas, Frederic Colby, Jr., in *Billfish*, joint patrols with *Bowfin*, 487-90
Lucker, Nicholas, Jr.: in *S-40*, 155, 168, 266; in Lingayen Gulf, 149-51
Luppis, Giovanni, torpedo design, 25
Lusitania, 38, 838
Luzon, 128, 130, 159, 164, 171; Japanese invasion of (map), 133; patrols near, 135-38, 141, 143-44, 207, 493, 580, 581, 622, 623, 627, 640, 685, 695, 746; plans for recapture, 693, 695; air strikes on, 745, 765; U.S. invasion of, 792, 793 (map), 794
Luzon Strait, 202-3, 216, 293, 361, 362, 538, 747, 748, 794; bottleneck, importance recognized, 509-10, 551, 562; 1944 patrols, 582, 590, 610, 646, 674-81, 725, 801; 1944 wolf packs, 597-600, 674-81, 701-11, 721, 727, 728, 731, 746, 761, 767, 785, 804; 1945 patrols and wolf packs, 833, 835
Lynch, Frank Curtis, Jr. ("Tiny"): in *Harder*, 444-45, 545, 576, 672, 716-17, 720; in *Haddo*, 785, 867
Lynch, Ralph Clinton, Jr. ("Red"), in *Mingo*, 512-13
Lynch, Richard Barr ("Ozzie"): in *Nautilus*, photography, 520; in *Seawolf*, 647, 649; in *Skate*, 747, 859, 861, 863
Lyon, Hyland Benton ("Hap"), in *Gudgeon*, 108, 118, 241-43, 249
Lytle, Morton Haynes, 456

MacArthur, Douglas, 89, 192, 294, 340, 348, 475, 609, 617, 744, 774, 845; adviser in Philippines, 77; defense plans, 81-82, 128-29; in Japanese attack on Philippines, 128-30, 143*n*; and loss of Philippines, 153-56, 159; at Corregidor, 172, 173, 175; leaves Corregidor, 193; Supreme Allied Commander, 203, 218; in Australia, 218, 222, 294; hostility to Navy, 295; strategy for counteroffensive, 295; forces defeat Japanese at Port Moresby, 302; Christie admires, 303; headquarters at Port Moresby, 303-4; submarines used for special missions, 357-58, 373, 388, 501, 610, 619; and Fife's management of submarines, 377, 378; honors Morton for *Wahoo* patrol, 386; Casablanca Conference decisions on strategy, 398-99; strategy plans, conflicts with Nimitz, 422, 557, 693-95; reconquest of New Guinea, 472, 474, 557, 606-7, 609, 620; orders rescue of civilians from Panay, 580-81; presentation of medals by, 584-85, 674, 720-21, 815; invasion of Biak, 634; invasion of Morotai, 722-23; returns to Leyte, 765; invasion of Mindoro and Luzon, 792, 793 (map), 794; invasion of Japan planned, 824; in surrender ceremonies, 872-73
Macaw, submarine rescue vessel, 592
McCain, John Sidney, 265, 439
McCain, John Sidney, Jr., 524, 885*n*; in *Gunnel*, North African landings, 265, 266; 1943 patrols, 439-40, 527; 1944 patrols, 582, 630-31; postwar rank, 884
McCallum, James Lowell Page, study of Mark VI exploder, 610, 614, 616
McCann, Allan Rockwell, 66, 83, 105, 106, 210, 216, 223-24, 343, 351, 690; in Pearl Harbor attack, 99; criticizes patrols, 120-21, 211-12, 216, 287, 350, 357; at Fremantle, 282, 368, 475; and torpedo failure, 352, 355, 391; investiga-

McCann, Allan Rockwell (cont.)
  tion of Fife's loss of submarines, 377; and Exmouth Gulf base, 389–90; in command change, 549; postwar career, 881
McCann Rescue Chamber, 65–67, 273
McClintock, David Hayward: in Plunger, 331, 345; in Cero, 541; in Darter, 741; support of Leyte invasion, 751–56; Darter aground, destroyed, 756–58
McCollum, Arthur Howard, 261; and Japanese codebooks, 606, 607; and Fleet Intelligence Center, 370
McCormick, Robert R., 258
McCrea, Victor B.: in Hoe, 439, 581; patrols, 627, 631, 741; in Parche, 830
McDonald, Lucien Berry, 493
McGrath, Thomas Patrick, 461
McGregor, Donald, 395, 518, 533; in Gar, 211, 230, 350, 457–58; in Seahorse, 457–58
MacGregor, Edgar John, III: in Shad, 541–43; comment on Moore's last patrol, 589–90
McGregor, Louis Darby ("Sandy"), Jr., 173, 174, 193, 207, 456; leaves Corregidor, 195; in Pike, patrols, 410, 434–35; in Redfish, patrols and wolf packs, 702–3, 705, 775–77, 801–3; sinks Unryu, 802–3
McGregor, Rob Roy, 477, 872; in Grouper, 378, 379
Mackenzie, George Kenneth, Jr., in Triton, lost, 375
Mackenzie, Rufus, in Tantalus, 847
Mackerel, 68, 80, 458
Mackie, Thomas Robert, codebreaker, 193, 222, 607, 881; and warning before Pearl Harbor, 90–91
McKinney, Eugene Bradley, 151, 155, 198n, 199, 201, 229, 288, 298, 496, 627, 883; in Salmon, in Lingayen Gulf, 149, 150; 1942 patrols, 164, 184, 187, 289–90;

in Skate, lifeguarding at Wake Island, 521; 1943 patrols, 521, 526–27, 530–31; 552; battle with Zuiho, 526–27
McKnight, John Roland, Jr., 456, 466; in S-36, 144–45; loss of S-36, 169; in Porpoise, 189, 336, 410
McLean, Heber Hampton ("Tex"), 282, 286, 341, 368, 391, 395, 502, 626, 716, 881; and Exmouth Gulf base, 389, 390; commands Squadron Sixteen, 610; command changes, 813
McMahon, Bernard Francis, 327, 360, 872; in Drum, 335; in Piper, 825
McMaster, Fitzhugh, in Hardhead, 696–97
MacMillan, Duncan Calvin, in Thresher, 538–39, 609, 677–78
McNeal, J. M., 747
Maddox, destroyer, 794
Madison, John Robert, in Mingo, 784, 798
Madras Maru, Japanese freighter, 666
Maebashi Maru, Japanese transport, 530
Magamigawa Maru, Japanese aircraft ferry, 434
Magane Maru, Japanese ship, 586
Magdeburger, Dr. E. C., 61
Magic output, see Codebreaking
Magnetic exploder for torpedoes, 54–56, 71; see also Mark VI
Magnetic pistol, 54
Mahan, Alfred Thayer, 85, 362; theory of sea power, 27, 42, 46
Majuro, 116, 607; U.S. invasion of, 558; submarine base, 561, 603, 658, 721, 734, 816
Makassar City, 180, 186, 187, 189, 353, 612, 785; Japanese capture, 177–78
Makassar Strait, 163, 164, 166, 169, 171, 176, 178, 179, 183, 289, 290, 350, 353, 355, 392, 393,

499, 502, 618, 632, 711, 714, 751, 784
Makin, 398, 422, 454; commando raid, 308, 309, 316–18, 321, 337, 359, 506; U.S. invasion of, 505, 506, 508
Malacca Strait, 395, 853
Malay Barrier, 81, 153, 172; Japanese drive to, 163–66, 175–76, 178, 180, 181, 183; submarine defense of, 164–66
Malay Peninsula, 85, 128, 135
Maloelap, 115; U.S. invasion of, 558
Maloney, J. Loy ("Pat"), 259
Malta Maru, Japanese ship, 590
M.A.N. (Maschinenfabrik-Augsburg-Nürnberg) submarine engines, 34, 48, 58, 60, 266
Managhan, Robert Raymond, in *Spikefish,* 870
Manchuria: Japan invades, 64, 70; Japanese convoy from, 773
Manila, 43, 47, 48, 66, 201, 202, 324, 493; before World War II, 77, 81, 82; Japanese attacks on, 127–32, 134–35; patrols from, 131, 135–41, 142 (map); 143–45; loss, 153–60; faults as sub base, 157–58; patrols near, 285, 287–90, 356, 357, 397, 493, 501, 537, 581, 582, 622, 623, 627, 712, 718, 735, 739–41, 783, 784; air strikes on, 782; U.S. forces recapture, 792, 794
Manila Bay, jeep carrier, 792
Manitowoc Shipbuilding Company, 73, 304, 423, 482, 667, 758
Manju Maru, Japanese freighter, 810
Mann, Stephen Stafford, Jr., 428, 431
Manshu Maru, Japanese transport, 707
Mantai Maru, Japanese ship, 678
Mantangule, 715
Manus, 609, 610; submarine base, 695, 697, 711, 816
Mao Tse-tung, 70
Marblehead, cruiser, 77, 185, 263

Marconi-Adcock direction finder, 75–76
Marcus Island, 210, 225, 459, 581; U.S. raids, 205, 505
Marcy, Lincoln, in *Ronquil,* 791
Mare Island Navy Yard, San Francisco, 40, 72, 83*n*, 100, 203, 205, 215, 224, 344, 365, 381, 389, 423, 765; submarines repaired at, 353, 354, 372, 394, 407, 427, 446, 455, 469, 471, 477, 479, 512, 513, 524, 526, 533, 537, 545, 546, 563, 567, 580, 581, 711, 736
Mariana Islands, 46, 70, 116, 411, 425, 694; 1942 patrols to, 212, 216, 224, 380; strategic plans on, 398, 399, 557, 558; 1943 patrols to 405, 410, 423, 434, 457; wolf packs near, 543, 546, 643–46; air strikes on, 560–61, 572 (map), 646; submarine support of air strikes, 562, 564, 574, 577; 1944 patrols to, 585, 595, 600–3, 642–47, 649; Japanese reinforcements for, 586, 587, 591, 594, 600, 620–21, 662; submarine preparations for invasion, 620–27, 642–47, 648 (map), 649; U.S. invasion of, 642–43, 652, 664–65, 818; aircraft based on, 693, 777, 824, 827; submarine base, 791; base for invasion of Japan, 824
Marinduque, 137, 193
Marines: on Guadalcanal and Tulagi, 295–96; in Makin commando raid, 316–18
Mariveles, 130, 132, 153, 154
Mark 1, Mark 2, and Mark 3 Torpedo Data Computers, *see* TDC
Mark II electric torpedo, 280–81, 403
Mark V dummy exploder, 62, 84
Mark VI magnetic exploder, 61–62, 71, 84, 97, 113, 130, 131, 292; unreliability, 141–42, 198, 206–9, 214, 216, 351, 352, 354–55, 361, 401–2, 407, 412–15, 427; controversy on, 213, 226–27, 304–5,

Mark VI magnetic exploder (*cont.*) 413–15, 430–31, 504; and Mark XIV tests, 278–79; deactivation, disagreement on, 430–31, 486–87, 490, 499; deactivated, 437, 504, 553, 610, 618; Hottel protests on, 478–79; deactivation creates problems, 478–79, 481; modifications recommended, 610, 614, 616, 618

Mark IX torpedo, 353

Mark X torpedo, 41, 160, 187, 218, 226, 253, 304, 344–45; electric model proposed, 280

Mark XIV torpedo, 61, 134, 218, 226, 344, 353, 393, 447, 471, 509–11, 551; unreliability, 141, 160, 171, 198, 206, 207, 216, 226, 292, 427; controversy on, 169–70, 226–27; Coe's analysis of, 273–74; tests, 275–79, 437–39; with hydrogen peroxide engine, 279; electric models proposed, 280; Christie's opinion of, 304–5; depth defect corrected, 326, 361; final isolation of defects, 435–39, 553; warhead size, 486; performance evaluated, 553–54, 694, 818

Mark XVI electric torpedo, 279

Mark XVII electric torpedo, 279

Mark XVIII electric torpedo, 281, 469, 479, 510, 513, 554, 788; Kirk-Reich memorandum on, 402–4; defects, 509, 511; performance evaluated, 694, 818

Mark 48 torpedo, 882*n*

Marlin, 68, 540

Marshall, Elliott Eugene ("Steam"), 701; in *Cuttlefish*, 320–21; in *Capelin*, lost, 502–3

Marshall, George Catlett, 75, 81–82, 87, 295; warns Dewey against disclosure of codebreaking, 691–92; in strategic planning, 695

Marshall Islands, 46, 70, 76, 106, 353, 359, 397, 410; Japanese bases in, 205, 508; first patrols to, 107, 114–16, 119–23; 1942 patrols to, 209, 210, 213, 216, 224, 229; strategic plans on, 398, 399, 508; 1943 patrols to, 409, 423, 454, 456, 461–62, 466, 525; Japanese reinforcements on, 506; U.S. invasion of, 557–58, 559 (map), 560–61, 589, 818; submarine support of invasion, 562–63

Martin, John Croysdale ("Hammerhead"), in *Hammerhead*, 680, 738, 796

Maryland, battleship, 99, 213

Maschinenfabrik-Augsburg-Nürnberg, *see* M.A.N.

Mason, Redfield ("Rosey"), codebreaker, 74, 89, 261, 881

Massachusetts Institute of Technology, 54, 55

Matsue Maru, Japanese freighter, 577

Matsumoto Maru, Japanese freighter, 767

Matsuwa, Japanese frigate, 718

Matsuwa To, 596, 666, 806; bombardment of, 466, 469, 471

Maumee, tanker, 35

Maurer, John Howard, 181, 765; in *Harder*, 444–45, 544, 545; in *Atule*, 730, 770–72, 842

Maxson, Willis Edward, III, 521

May, Andrew Jackson, Congressman, 424

Maya, Japanese cruiser, 416, 662, 754, 766

Mayasan Maru, Japanese transport, 774

Mayer, Andrew DeGraff ("Gnu"), 673

Mayer, P. S., 715

Maynard, Harry Clark, in *Scorpion*, 459, 460

Mayrant, destroyer, 249

Medals, 122*n*; disagreement of Christie and Kinkaid on, 584–85, 674, 720–21, 814, 815; retained after postwar recounting, 878

Medan Maru, Japanese tanker, 675

Meiho Maru, Japanese freighter, 810

Meiwa Maru, Japanese freighter, 319

Meiyo Maru, Japanese freighter, 299

INDEX

Meizan Maru, Japanese passenger freighter, 397
Melbourne, U.S. command headquarters, 218, 294
Mendosa, Dr., 687
Menhaden, 758
Merrill, Wayne Rucker, 342; in *Batfish,* 539, 586
Metcalf, Ralph Marion, in *Pogy,* 530, 590
Mewhinney, Leonard Sparks ("Tex"), in *Saury,* 289, 341
Michel, German merchant raider, 514, 853
Midget submarines: Japanese, 86, 118n, 663, 872; British, 854–55
Midgley, Donald Raymond, 595
Midway, 76, 84, 118, 203, 268, 324, 359, 361, 408, 460, 463, 521, 587; Japanese approaches to (maps), 92, 235; Japanese attacks on, 102, 103 (map), 104–5, 119–20; Yamamoto's plan for invasion, 219, 222, 234; submarine base, 250, 323, 509, 533, 536, 548, 550, 580, 582, 586, 679, 731, 780, 803, 806, 865; patrols from, 510, 680
Midway, Battle of, 234, 235 (map), 236–39, 240 (map), 241–49, 294, 360, 660, 662; submarines in, 236–37, 239, 241–49, 326; security leak, 256–60
Midway (St. Lo), jeep carrier, 736, 738, 765
Miike Maru, Japanese transport, 602
Mikage Maru No. 18, Japanese transport, 643
Mikage Maru No. 20, Japanese transport, 457
Mikuma, Japanese cruiser, 246–47, 759n
Mili, 506, 526; U.S. invasion of, 558
Miller, Charles Kilday, in *Redfin,* 868
Miller, Herman Edward, in *Besugo,* 852–53

Millican, William John ("Moke"), 267, 355, 357; in *Thresher,* 350–51, 391; in *Escolar,* lost, 731
Milne Bay, submarine base, 475, 564, 568, 569, 574, 575, 580, 582, 609, 610, 621, 816
Milwaukee, cruiser, 35
Minami Daito, 698
Minatsuki, Japanese destroyer, 637
Mindanao, 193, 636, 713, 722, 734; supplies delivered and personnel evacuated, 174; plans for recapture, 557, 693, 695, 722, 723; POWs evacuated, 737
Mindoro, 397, 740, 752, 756, 758; refugees rescued from, 781; Japanese codebooks recovered from, 784; U.S. invasion of, 792, 793 (map), 794, 816; patrols near, 795, 796, 800
Mindoro Strait, 640, 728, 739, 752
Minekaze, Japanese destroyer, 590
Mingo, 512–13; H.O.R. engines replaced, 582; patrol and wolf pack, 734, 796; lifeguarding, 784
Mios Woendi, submarine base, 673, 695, 711, 719, 740–42, 781, 816
Miri, 354, 355, 357, 391
Mississinewa, fleet tanker, 766, 805
Missouri, battleship, 871–73
Mitakesan Maru, Japanese ship, 595
Mitchell, William, U.S. general, 50, 52
Mitchell, William L., 258
Mitscher, Marc Andrew, 642, 662
Mizuho, Japanese seaplane carrier, 227
Moa, New Zealand corvette, 370
Moccasin (A-4), 30n
Mogami, Japanese cruiser, 246–47, 506, 759
Mogami class, Japanese cruisers, 480, 563
Molteni, Peter Gabriel, Jr., in *Batfish,* 539, 586
Molucca Passage, 163–65, 171, 173, 176, 179, 190, 498, 502, 616, 639

Molumphy, George Garvie, in *Skipjack*, 562–63
Momsen, Charles Bowers ("Swede"), 65, 368, 423, 550, 881; in torpedo tests, 437, 438; and wolfpacking, 509; commands wolf pack, 541–43; command changes, 813
Momsen Lungs, 65, 768
Monaghan, destroyer, 792
Monroe, Henry Stone: in *S-35*, 272, 420; in *Ronquil*, 730, 749, 791
Monterey, aircraft carrier, 399n, 422
Montross, Edmund Keats: in *Swordfish*, 649, 807; lost, 807
Moore, John Anderson: in *Grayback*, 541–43; lost, 589–90
Moore, John Raymond ("Dinty"), 360, 420, 464, 497, 595; in *S-44*, patrols, 297–99, sinks *Keijo Maru* and *Kako*, 298–99, 334; in *Sailfish*, 304, 305; leaves *Sailfish*, 462–63; in *Stingray*, 155, 166, 168, 171, 176, 185, 193, 332
Moore, Thomas, 346
Morison, Samuel Eliot, 296, 329, 508, 665, 752n
Morotai, 784; invasion planned, 693, 695; U.S. invasion of, 722–23, 726 (map), 734, 736
Morton, Dudley Walker ("Mush"), 251, 415, 440, 453, 460, 480, 493, 517, 540, 554, 566, 584, 677, 769, 857; in *Wahoo*, receives command, 333; character, 381; January 1943 patrol, Brisbane to Pearl Harbor, 381–86, 402; 1943 patrols from Pearl Harbor, 407–8, 425–27, 469–71; denounces torpedo failures, 427; patrol in Sea of Japan, 469–71; last patrol, lost, 510–11; sinking record, final, 878
Moseley, Stanley Page, 211, 212, 231, 249, 813; in *Pollack*, patrols in Japanese waters, 107, 112–13, 121, 233; commands wolf pack, 701
Mumma, Morton Claire, Jr., 149, 151, 155, 190, 339; in *Sailfish*, 143–44

Munakata Maru, Japanese tanker, 809
Munson, Henry Glass, 186, 187, 222, 541, 624, 799–800; in *S-38*, 298, 299; in *Crevalle*, 493–96; in *Rasher*, 703–6, 721
Murphy, Charlton Lewis, Jr., in *Sturgeon*, 747n
Murphy, John Williams, Jr., 250, 327, 328, 339, 377, 480; in *Tambor*, at Wake Island, 105, 123; in Battle of Midway, 246–47
Murphy, Walter Patrick, Jr., in *Sailfish*, 527, 528
Murray, Stuart Shadrick ("Sunshine"), 82, 274–75, 550; and Japanese attack on Philippines, 131, 135; and loss of Manila, 153, 155; at Fremantle, 282, 284; at Pearl Harbor on Lockwood's staff, 367–68; letter from Christie, 377; sent to Naval Academy, 548–49; in surrender ceremonies, 872; postwar career, 881
Musashi, Japanese battleship, 245–46n, 506, 560, 724, 778; damaged, 575; in Biak reinforcement, 638–39; in Battle of Philippine Sea, 650, 651; and Leyte invasion, 749; sunk, 758, 766, 779
Muskallunge: in torpedo test, 437; patrols and wolf pack, 647, 714, 785
Mussolini, Benito, 78
Myers, G. A., 100
Myers, William Girard, 365n; in *Gato*, 229–30, 271
Myoko, Japanese cruiser, 796–97, 817, 846, 855
Myrna (Enimonetto), rest camp, 561

Nachi, Japanese cruiser, 416, 746, 759
Nachi class, Japanese cruisers, 165, 583, 753
Nagara, Japanese cruiser, 506, 699, 842
Nagasaki, 208, 450, 682, 698, 699,

INDEX

746, 788, 801, 802, 842, 866; atomic bomb, 870
Nagato, Japanese battleship, 506
Nagato class, Japanese battleships, 798
Nagatsuki, Japanese destroyer, 472
Nagoya, 227, 700; bombing of, 827
Naha, 463
Naka, Japanese cruiser, 191, 506
Namkwan Harbor, 810
Nampo Maru, Japanese tanker, 589
Naniwa Maru, Japanese transport, 312, 718
Nankai Maru, Japanese transport, 708
Nanking Maru, Japanese freighter, 836
Nanyo Maru, Japanese ship, 590
Napoleon, and Fulton's *Nautilus,* 24
Naquin, Oliver Francis, in *Squalus,* 67
Naruo Maru, Japanese ship, 773
Naruto Maru, Japanese aircraft ferry, 434
Narwhal (D-1), 30n
Narwhal (V-5), 57, 59n, 60, 83n, 84 97–98, 107, 210–13, 315, 360n, 466, 552n, 593, 610, 666n, 825, 884n; in Pearl Harbor attack, 98, 99, 106; in Battle of Midway, 236n, 246; patrols, 319, 417; bombards Matsuwa To, 466, 469, 471; missions to Philippines, 497–98, 737–38; retired, 818n
Nasami, Japanese minelayer, 565
Nase Maru, Japanese freighter, 842
Nashiro, Japanese cruiser, 476
Nashville, cruiser, 792
Nason, J. H. M., 867
National Industrial Recovery Act, 64
Natori class, Japanese cruisers, 331, 713
Natushie, Japanese destroyer, 178
Nauman, Harley Kent; in *Salmon,* 730, 747; in Battle of Leyte Gulf, 762, 764, 765
Nauru, 341, 462, 526
Nautilus, Fulton's submarine, 23–24
Nautilus (H-2), 35
Nautilus (V-6), 57, 59n, 60, 82, 83n, 251, 252, 282, 344, 360n, 380, 464, 496, 523, 552n, 564, 604, 610, 772, 796; in Battle of Midway, 236n, 241, 243–45; in Makin commando raid, 308, 309, 317, 318, 337, 506; 1942 patrol, 321; sent to Brisbane for special missions, 331, 334, 335; in recapture of Attu, 417–18; in Gilbert Islands invasion, 520, 522–23; 1944 patrol, 591; shells *Darter,* 758; retired, 818n
Nautilus, nuclear-powered submarine, 332, 752, 882, 884n
Naval Academy, Annapolis, 548–49, 804, 884; "class year" as basis for command selection, 107n; graduates as submarine commanders, 588
Navol (G-49) oxygen torpedo, 279
Navy, U.S.: Washington conference on limitation of, 50–51; construction program before World War II, 64; preparations for World War II, 72–73, 78–85; strength compared with Japanese, 85; *see also* Asiatic Fleet; Atlantic Fleet; Pacific Fleet
Navy Cross, 122n; disagreement on presentation of, 584–85
Negat codebreaking unit, *see* Codebreaking
Negros Island, 356; refugees evacuated from, 624–65, 630
Neidlinger, L. M., 630
Nelson, William Thackeray, in *Peto,* 482
Nenohi, Japanese destroyer, 270
Neosho, tanker, 220
Netherlands: in World War II, 81; in ABDA, 163–64; submarines at Fremantle, 742–43
Nevada, battleship, 99
New, William Adolph: in *Pike,* patrols, 139, 151, 164, 165, 186, 190; in defense of Timor, 180–81; last patrol, 336–37
New Britain, 222, 295, 305, 369, 478
New Caledonia, 219, 295, 339
New Georgia, 229, 332, 369; Allied landings on, 472

New Guinea, 128, 334, 340, 378, 386, 388, 498, 621; U.S. raids on, 205; strategic plans on, 398, 399; reconquest of, 472, 474, 557, 606–7, 608 (map), 609, 620; Japanese reinforcements for, 622–24, 636

New Hebrides, 295, 339

New Ireland, 299, 305, 369

New London, Conn.: Submarine Base, 40, 43, 44, 125, 126, 266, 321, 550; Submarine School, 40, 43, 54, 66, 82, 213, 431, 457, 604, 740, 812, 814; submarines retired to, 879

New London Ship and Engine Company, 34

New Mexico, battleship, 813

New Orleans, cruiser, 329, 339

New York Navy Yard, 58, 812

New Zealand, 81

Newport, R.I.: Torpedo Station and factory, 31, 41, 54–56, 61–62, 69, 280–81, 348, 402–3, 469; Mark XIV torpedo tests, 277, 278, 439; electric torpedoes, 280–81, 402–3

Nichiro Maru, Japanese transport, 571

Nicholas, Nicholas John, in *Salmon,* 428

Nichols, John Culver, in *Silversides,* 807, 830

Nichols, Philip Gardner ("P.G."), 610, 612, 716; in *Capelin,* 502; command changes, 813

Nichols, Richard Eugene, in *Bashaw,* patrols and wolf packs, 577, 579, 785, 798

Nickel Ship, search for, 669–71

Night periscope, 787

Nigitsu Maru, Japanese transport, 537

Niizuki, Japanese destroyer, 472

Nikki Maru, Japanese transport, 571

Nikkin Maru, Japanese freighter, 683

Nikko Maru, Japanese transport, 843

Nimitz, Chester William, 222, 223, 249, 250, 262, 263, 268, 330, 361, 367, 369, 431, 437, 451, 550, 672, 673, 814, 841, 859, 867; before World War I, 35; in World War I, 43; Commander in Chief, Pacific Fleet, 125, 204; after Pearl Harbor attack, 204–5; and Battle of Coral Sea, 220; and Battle of Midway, 234, 239, 245–46, 248–49; and Alaska patrols, 269, 271–72; and Truk patrols, 307, 308, 344; and Makin commando raid, 316; replaces Ghormley with Halsey, 329; Casablanca Conference decisions on strategy, 398–99; conflict with MacArthur on strategy, 422, 557, 693–95; and deactivation of Mark VI, 430, 504; in Gilbert Islands invasion, 505, 506; in Marshall Islands invasion, 557–58, 560; in New Guinea campaign, 607; in Marianas invasion, 620, 642–43, 664; in Palaus invasion, 722–24; use of reserve officers encouraged, 818; invasion of Japan planned, 824; in Iwo Jima invasion, 824; and Loughlin's court-martial, 838–40; and sinking of Russian ship, 864, 865; cease-fire message, 870; in surrender ceremonies, 871, 872; postwar career, 879, 880

Nimitz, Chester William, Jr., 497, 784–85; in *Sturgeon,* 128, 166, 304, 344; in *Bluefish,* 490–92; Mark VI exploder, modifications recommended, 610, 614, 616, 618; in *Haddo,* 616–19; patrols, 637, 639, 717; and last patrol of *Harder,* 717–19; postwar career, 884

Nippo Maru, Japanese freighter, 684, 781

Nippon Maru, Japanese tanker, (former whale factory), 435, 484

Nishimura, Vice Adm. Shoji, 749; in Battle of Leyte Gulf, 758, 759, 767

Nissen Maru, Japanese tanker (former whale factory), 448

Nisshin Maru, Japanese tanker, 87, 355, 624

Nissho Maru, Japanese freighter, 581

Nittai Maru, Japanese freighter, 616

INDEX

Nittetsu Maru, Japanese freighter, 741
Nittoku Maru, Japanese ship, 587
Noisemaker, decoy device to confuse sonar, 787
Nokaze, Japanese destroyer, 846
Norfolk, Va., 690; Navy Yard, 56, 205
Norfolk Maru, Japanese transport, 718
North Africa, Allied invasion of, 263–65, 398
North Carolina, battleship, 301, 302, 361, 553
Northampton, cruiser, 339
Norway, patrols near, 266
Noshiro, Japanese cruiser, 506
Noumea, 257, 295, 329, 369n, 462, 474
Nowell, Byron Horne, in *Paddle,* 585, 737
Numakaze, Japanese destroyer, 543

O-6, 604
O-8, 481
Oakley, Thomas Benjamin, Jr.: in *Growler,* patrols and wolf packs, 646, 651, 674–75, 706–8, 711, 783; lost, 783
O'Brien, destroyer, 302
Obry, Ludwig, torpedo design, 25
Ocean Islands, 341
Octopus (C-1), 30n, 54
Office of Naval Communications (ONC), 53, 260–63
Office of Naval Intelligence (ONI), 260–61; codebreaking before World War II, 52–53, 87
Office of Strategic Services (OSS), 690n
Ofuma, Japanese prison, 420, 576
Ogura Maru II, Japanese tanker, 706
Oi, Japanese cruiser, 685
Oita Maru, Japanese freighter, 731
Oite, Japanese destroyer, 567
O'Kane, Richard Hetherington, 315, 333, 469, 470, 493, 517, 540, 770, 804, 808; in *Wahoo,* patrols, 381–83, 407, 408, 426, 427; in *Tang,* support of air strike on Truk, 567–68; support of air strike on Saipan, 571, 573; patrols, 602, 609, 682–83, 699–701, 730–31, 746–48; lifeguarding at Truk, 609, 818; last patrol and loss of *Tang,* 767–69; captured, 768–69; medals, 769; sinking record revised, 878
Okikase, Japanese destroyer, 336
Okinami, Japanese destroyer, 591
Okinawa, 18, 463, 660, 662, 747, 794; patrols and wolf packs near, 543, 590, 603–5, 660, 662, 698, 747, 794, 807, 870; strategy for recapture, 557; air strikes on, 745; FM sonar test at, 790, 829, 857; U.S. invasion of, 824, 827, 828 (map), 829–30, 832–33, 842
Okinawa Maru, Japanese freighter, 643
Okinoshima, Japanese minelayer, 222
Okitsu Maru, Japanese seaplane tender, 562
Oklahoma, battleship, 99
Okuni Maru, Japanese freighter, 707
O'Leary, Forrest Marmaduke, 83, 210, 339; criticizes Joyce's patrol, 211–12; in Mark XIV controversy, 226–27
Olongapo, 130
Olsen, Eliot, 215, 266, 397; in *Grayling,* patrols, 209–10, 309; in Battle of Midway, 245
Olsen, Hjalmar E., 580n
Olsen, Robert Irving: in *Angler,* rescues civilians from Panay, 580–81; patrols, 630–31, 649
Ommaney Bay, jeep carrier, 792
Omurosan Maru, Japanese tanker, 799
O'Neill, Guy Edward, Jr.: in *Bonefish,* 496; in *Gunnel,* 785
ONC, *see* Office of Naval Communications
ONI, *see* Office of Naval Intelligence
Operation Barney (Sea of Japan penetration), 858
Operation Catchpole (Eniwetok invasion), 560

Operation Desecrate (air attack on Palaus), 561, 602
Operation Detachment (Iwo Jima invasion), 824
Operation Flintlock (Marshall Islands invasion), 557
Operation Forager (Marianas invasion), 642
Operation Galvanic (Gilbert Islands invasion), 505, 506, 508, 520, 525, 552n
Operation Hailstone (air strike on Truk), 560, 567
Operation Hotfoot (proposed carrier attack on Japan), 790–91
Operation Iceberg (Okinawa invasion), 829
Operation King Two (Leyte invasion), 744–45
Operation Olympic (proposed invasion of Japan), 824
Operation Stalemate II (Palau Islands invasion), 723, 724
Operation Torch (North Africa invasion), 263, 265–66
Operation Watchtower (Guadalcanal landing), 296
Oppenheimer, J. Robert, 869
O'Regan, William Vincent ("Mickey"), 813; commands wolf pack, 677–78
Orica (K-3), 36
Orion, submarine tender, 609, 617, 673
Oroluk, 524
Osaka, bombing of, 827
Osake Maru, Japanese transport, 647
Osmeña, Sergio, 174
OSS, see Office of Strategic Services
Otasamu, 866
Otoriyama Maru, Japanese tanker, 686
Otowasan Maru, Japanese tanker, 799
Otto, Nikolaus, engine, 29
Otus, submarine tender, 82, 130, 164, 176, 185n; at Cavite in Japanese attack, 132; withdrawn from Philippines, 155; in Australia, 191, 197, 389–90

Owen-Stanley Range, New Guinea, 222, 294, 302
Oyodo, Japanese cruiser, 748, 761, 792, 800, 868
Ozawa, Adm. Jisaburo, 643, 649; reinforcement of Biak, 634, 641; in Battle of Philippine Sea, 649–55, 657, 659, 660; retreat after battle, 660, 661 (map), 662; counteroffensive before Leyte invasion, 748–49; in Battle of Leyte Gulf, 758–59, 763 (map)

P class of submarines, 64–66, 76, 77, 82, 83
Pace, Leo Leander, 813
Pacific Fleet, 78–79, 81, 85, 129, 135; Japanese plans for attack, 85, 128; operations after Pearl Harbor attack, 204–5; 1943 additions to, 422–24
Paddle, 526, 585; patrols and wolf packs, 734, 737, 751, 769, 796–98, 800
Page, Walter H., 41
Paine, Roger Warde, Jr., in *Wahoo,* 381, 384, 385, 427, 469–70
Paint, color for submarines, 570n
Palau Islands, 17, 128, 135, 137, 158, 178, 180, 209, 211, 340, 372, 431, 634, 649; Japanese fleet concentrated in, 175–76; Japanese base, 305–6, 425, 472; 1942 patrols to, 353; Japanese convoy route, 386–87, 480, 482; 1943 patrols to, 405, 409, 411, 423, 439, 440, 453, 458, 474, 513, 530, 536–37, 553; strategic plans on, 557, 558; Japanese fleet transferred to, 560, 563; air strike on, 561, 578 (map), 602; submarine support of air strike, 562, 569–71, 574–77, 579–80, 609; 1944 patrols to, 585, 600–602, 605, 647, 697; Japanese reinforcements for, 620; invasion planned, 693, 695; U.S. invasion of, 722–24, 726 (map), 818; submarine support of invasion, 724–25, 727–28, 734–35

INDEX

Palau Maru, Japanese ship, 310
Palawan, 491, 741; Japanese prison camp, 687–88; survivors of *Flier* on, 715
Palawan Passage, 290, 741, 751, 752, 755, 756, 759, 780, 786
Palembang, 178
Palembang Maru, Japanese tanker, 846
Palmer, Robie Ellis, 336, 454
Paluan Bay, 717
Pampanito, 859; support of air strike on Palaus, 574, 577; patrols and wolf packs, 662, 706, 708–9, 711, 769, 847
Panama, 43, 48, 217–18, 270, 271, 365, 447, 450, 475, 592, 665, 706
Panama Canal, 46, 47, 80; minefield, 322–23; Japanese plan to bomb, 872
Panay, 174, 784; guerrillas landed on, 393, 397; civilians rescued from, 580–81
Paracel Islands, 777
Paramushiro, 417, 422, 425
Parche, patrols and wolf packs, 597–99, 679–81, 746, 830
Pargo, 568; patrols and wolf packs, 543–46, 585, 735, 738, 846, 847, 865
Parham, William Brownlee, in *Gabilan,* 852–53, 868–69
Parks, Lewis Smith, 211, 249, 319, 458, 667, 813, 883; in *Pompano,* patrols, 107, 114–15, 122, 205, 206; commands wolf pack, 679–81; in Loughlin's court-martial, 839*n*, 840; in surrender ceremonies, 872
Pasalong Bay, 705
Patrol Boat 39, Japanese, 449
PCO (Prospective Commanding Officer) pool, 251–52*n*, 321, 344, 376, 407, 456, 457, 488, 492, 497, 610, 807
Pearl Harbor, 58, 63, 76, 77, 80, 219; fleet moved to, 70; submarines at, in November 1941, 82–83; Japanese plans for attack, 85–86, 89–90, 128; Japanese approach to (map), 93; Japanese attack, 97–102, 103 (map), 106; submarine training at, 156; as submarine base, advantages, 203; January–June 1942 patrols from, 204–16, 223–30, 251–55; submarine command changes, 213, 223, 249–52, 254–55; Fremantle submarines exchanged with, 223–24, 251, 285, 290, 310, 312, 486, 580–85; Squadron Eight submarines arrive, 223–24; July–December 1942 patrols from, to Truk, 307–10, 311 (map), 312–18, 326, 329–34, 337; July–December 1942 patrols from, 318–26, 335–37; submarine operations, 1942, summarized, 359–62; January 1943 command changes, 366–68; submarines returned to, from Brisbane, 380; Joint Intelligence Center, 400; Lockwood's survey of submarine performance, 400–404; January–August 1943 patrols from, 404–15, 423–71; senior and junior officers at, 509–10; first wolf packs from, 509, 541–48, 551; September–December 1943 patrols from, 510–48; command changes, end of 1943, 548–50; January–April 1944 patrols from, 562–605; 1944 wolf packs from, 597–600, 643–46, 665–68, 674–81, 701–11, 721, 724–25, 727–31, 746–48, 764–65, 767, 769–77, 788, 801–4, 807–11; May–June 1944 patrols from, to Marianas, 642–47, 649; June–August 1944 patrols from, 665–69, 674–84, 695–711; Roosevelt's alleged responsibility for attack, 690–92; submarines in support of Palau Islands invasion, 724–25, 727–28; September–December 1944 patrols from, 731–34, 767–80, 801–11; end-of-1944 command changes, 812–15; Lockwood's headquarters moved to Guam, 814, 833; code-

Pearl Harbor (*cont.*)
  breaking unit, *see* Codebreaking, Hypo; FRUPAC
Pelelieu, 647, 649, 695; U.S. invasion of, 723–24
Pelias, submarine tender, 83, 224, 236–37, 282, 303, 368, 475, 609, 610, 617; in Pearl Harbor attack, 99, 106; in Exmouth Gulf, 389–90
Penang, 395, 396
Pennsylvania, battleship, 99
Perch, 64*n,* 77, 82*n,* 151, 164, 177, 179, 183, 213, 320, 789; patrol from Manila, 141, 145; defense of Java, 184–85; lost, 188
Perch II, 599, 731, 746
Percifield, Willis Merritt, 78*n,* 154, 155
Periscope, night, 787
Perkins, William Beckwith, Jr., in *Burrfish,* 568, 695, 791
Permit, 64*n,* 77, 82*n,* 155, 164, 165, 187, 285, 591, 594, 666*n;* patrol from Manila, 141, 145; in Lingayen Gulf, 147, 150, 151; evacuates personnel from Corregidor, 193–94, 218; 1942 patrols, 290; 1943 patrol, 466–69; support of Marshall Islands invasion, 563–64; 1944 patrol, 609; retired, 818*n*
Perth, 191, 192, 197, 274, 283, 284, 303, 312, 389, 673, 716, 815; *see also* Fremantle
Perth, Australian cruiser, 185, 186
Peru, Naval Mission, 341
Pescadores, 128, 135, 138, 747, 748
Peterson, George Edmund, 813; commands wolf pack, 597, 599
Peterson, Richard Ward, 524; in *Sunfish,* 335, 407, 455–56; in *Icefish,* 730, 748, 770
Peto: in cooperative attack, 482, 485; in wolf packs, 599–600, 772–74
Philippine Sea, Battle of, 649–55, 656 (map), 657–60, 661 (map), 662, 744
Philippines, 17, 63, 361; in Plan Orange, 46; MacArthur in, before World War II, 77; plans for defense, 81–82, 128–30; Japanese plans for attack, 85, 128; Japanese capture, 127–35; U.S. forces leave, 153–55; loss of, analyzed, 155–60; guerrillas and supplies landed in, 321, 356, 357, 359, 393, 397, 497–98; strategy for recapture of, 398–99, 557, 693–95; refugees evacuated from, 498, 580–81, 624–25; Japanese reinforcements for, 620, 622, 627, 767, 769, 770, 773, 774, 777, 818; air strikes on, 722, 725, 734, 735, 739, 744–47, 782; Toyoda's plan for counterattack, 744, 747, 749, 751; U.S. forces return to, *see* Leyte; Luzon; Mindoro; recaptured, 794; in planned invasion of Japan, 824
Photography from submarines, 114, 520, 526
Phra Ruang, Thai destroyer, 719
Pich, German submarine commander, 743
Pickerel (F-3), 35
Pickerel, 64*n,* 77, 82*n,* 107, 151, 155, 164–66, 189, 285; patrol to Camranh Bay, 139; defense of Timor, 180–81; lost, 408–9, 552*n,* 780
Picuda, 770; wolf packs, 599, 600, 702, 703, 705, 772–74, 808–10
Pieczentkowski, Herman Arnold ("Pi"): in *Sturgeon,* 304; patrols, 305, 344, 433; in torpedo tests, 437, 438
Pierce, George Ellis, 373; in *Tunny,* patrols and wolf packs, 706, 707, 829, 859, 861, 863–65
Pierce, John Reeves, 267, 706; in S-23, 267–68; in *Argonaut,* Makin raid, 317, 318; lost, 372–73
Pigeon, submarine rescue vessel, 134
Pike (A-5), 30*n*
Pike, 64*n,* 66, 77, 82*n,* 151, 155, 164, 165, 177, 186, 190, 273, 282, 456, 609, 702; patrol to Hong Kong, 138–39; defense of Timor,

180–81; in Battle of Midway, 236n; patrol in Japanese waters, 335–37; 1943 patrols, 410, 435; retired, 552n
Pillsbury, destroyer, 689–90
Pilotfish, patrols and wolf packs, 643–46, 660, 731, 840
Pintado: patrols and wolf packs, 643–46, 660, 698–99, 730, 761, 770–71, 847; in Battle of Leyte Gulf, 761, 762
Pipefish, 646–47, 652
Piper, 825, 865, 871
Piranha, patrols and wolf packs, 677–79, 725, 727, 788, 801
Pitt, William, the Younger, 24
Plaice, patrols and wolf packs, 649, 697–98, 801, 833, 834
Plan A-Go, Japanese, 620–21, 634, 641, 649–50
Plan Black, World War I, 42
Plan Kon, Japanese, 634, 636–38, 641, 649–51
Plan Orange against Japan, 46–48, 51, 57, 81, 129; *see also* Rainbow Five
Plan Position Indicator, *see* PPI
Platter, George, 346
Plunger (A-1), 30n, 35
Plunger, Holland's first submarine, 28, 29, 30n
Plunger, 64n, 83n, 122, 123, 224, 251, 330, 345, 541, 666n; in Pearl Harbor attack, 100–101; patrols in Japanese waters, 107, 113–14, 120, 121, 253; in Battle of Midway, 236n, 246; patrol with SJ radar, 331; patrols in Sea of Japan, 466–71; supports Gilbert Islands invasion, 525–26; 1944 patrols, 587–88, 649; retired, 818n
Pogy, patrols, 433–35, 530, 590, 731, 842, 865
Poland: in World War II, 70; S-25 loaned to, 217n, 341
Polar circuits, patrols and wolf pack, 593–96, 665–68, 697, 806
Polaris submarines, 882

Pollack, 64n, 83n, 123, 211, 212, 224, 231, 233, 330, 360n, 407; in Pearl Harbor attack, 100–101; patrols in Japanese waters, 107, 112–13, 121, 335, 336; in Battle of Midway, 236n; 1943–1944 patrols, 454–55, 649, 697; retired, 818n
Pomalaa, 670
Pomfret, patrols, 668–69, 728–30, 746, 825
Pompano, 64n, 83n, 122, 210, 211, 427, 458; in Pearl Harbor attack, 100–101; patrols to Marshalls, 107, 114–15, 122, 205, 206; East China Sea patrol, 224–26; in Battle of Midway, 236n; patrol off Honshu, 319–20; 1943 patrols, 407, 412, 461, 498–99; lost, 461, 552n, 780
Pompon, 649, 697, 842
Ponape, 506, 524, 568
Pope, destroyer, 91n
Porpoise (A-6), 30n
Porpoise (British submarine), 742
Porpoise, 64n, 66, 77, 82n, 155n, 157, 166, 189, 273, 282, 466; in Lingayen Gulf, 147, 150–51; at Balikpapan, 168; in Battle of Midway, 236n; patrol in Japanese waters, 335, 336; 1943 patrols, 410, 456–57; withdrawn from combat, 457, 552n
Port Moresby, 339, 348, 622; Japanese invasion planned, 219–20, 222, 294; invasion defeated, 302; MacArthur's headquarters, 303–4
Porter, George Egbert, Jr., 497; in *Bluefish,* 490–93; joint patrol with *Rasher,* 492–93; joint patrol with *Cod,* 491–92; in *Sennet,* 825
Porter, destroyer, 330
Porthos, French liner, 615
Portsmouth, N.H., Navy Yard, 40, 49, 53, 72, 223, 411, 423, 479, 593, 765
Poseidon missile, 883
Post, Wiley, 52
Post, William Schuyler, Jr., 533, 615, 883; in *Argonaut,* 104–5; in

Post, William Schuyler, Jr. (cont.)
Thresher, 350–51; in Gudgeon, 392–94, 514; attack on Unyo, 547–48; in Spot, 835–36
Potshot (Exmouth Gulf), proposed advance base, 284–85, 389–90
Potter, E. B., 248
PPI (Plan Position Indicator), 448, 565
Pratas, 856
Prince of Wales, British capital ship, 135
Princeton, aircraft carrier, 399n, 422, 506, 759
Prisoners (POWs) in Japanese ships, 708–10, 737, 769
Proteus, submarine tender, 871–72
Pryce, Roland Fremont, 151, 155n, 166, 168, 266, 564n; in Spearfish, patrol to Camranh Bay, 139–40; in defense of Java, 179, 183–84; and Mark XIV torpedo tests, 277
PT-109, 392
PT boats at Corregidor, 193
Puffer, 580, 684, 687; patrols and wolf packs, 499–501, 614–16, 706, 711, 807; support of air strike on Surabaya, 629, 632, 633
Purnell, William Reynolds ("Speck"), 218, 274
Pye, John Briscoe, 807
Pye, William Satterlee, 123, 125
Pyle, Ernie, 827

Q-ships: in World War I, 38, 45; Japanese, 534
QLA, see FM sonar
Quebec, strategic planning conference, 723
Queen Elizabeth, British battleship, 629
Queenfish, wolf packs, 706–7, 709, 710, 772–73, 808–10, 835–36
Quelpart Island (Cheju Do), 844
Quezon, Manuel, 77, 153; leaves Corregidor with his family, 174
Quincy, cruiser, 296
Quincy, Mass., Navy Yard, 40

R-1, 492, 739
R-4, 498
R-12, 552n, 573, 817
R-13, 597
Rabaul, 295, 296, 306, 339–41, 346, 369, 370, 399, 574; U.S. raids, 205, 215–16; patrols near, 297, 316, 344–45, 481; Japanese convoy route, 386–87, 474, 480, 482; U.S. air attacks, 472, 474, 476; U.S. attack on Japanese cruisers, 506; bypassed in New Guinea campaign, 606
Raborn, Albert, 702; in Picuda, 599–600
Radar, 72; SD, 113, 322; SJ, trials on patrol, 321–22, 331; PPI, 448; APR, 833–34
Radio direction finding, see RDF
Raeder, Adm. Erich, 70
Raguet, Conde LeRoy, in Barbel, lost, 849
Rainbow Five (formerly Plan Orange), 76, 84, 267
Rainer, Gordon Benbow ("Dizzy"), 98, 99, 143; in Dolphin, patrol to Marshalls, 107, 115–16, 121–22, 205
Rainer, Mrs. Gordon B., 98
Raleigh, cruiser, 61
Ramage, Lawson Peterson ("Red"), 329, 337, 360, 434, 830; in Trout, Truk patrol, 312–13; in Battle of Guadalcanal, 344; criticizes torpedo performance, 354–55, 391–92; patrols from Fremantle, 354–57, 391–92; in Parche, wolf packs, 597–99, 679–81; Medal of Honor, 681; 1944 patrols, 746; postwar rank, 884
Ramon Maru, Japanese freighter, 321
Ramsey, Robert P., 264, 266
Rangoon, 395
Rasher; joint patrol with Bluefish, 492–93; patrols and wolf packs, 615–18, 629, 632, 633, 636–37, 703–4, 706, 721, 840; record for tonnage sunk, 849

INDEX

Raton: in cooperative attack, 482, 484; patrols and wolf packs, 615–16, 629, 631–32, 703, 712, 718, 740, 781–83

Ray, 616, 687; in cooperative attack, 482, 485; patrols and wolf packs, 497, 626, 633, 636, 717–18, 781–83

Raymond, Reginald Marbury, 458–60, 732; death, 489

Rayuko Maru, Japanese transport, 708

Razorback, 725*n*, 736; patrols and wolf packs, 725, 727, 803, 840

RDF (radio direction finding): in World War I, 38, 44; Japanese, 63; U.S. adopts, 63; British, in World War II, 71, 72, 75–76

Rector, Darrell Dean, 291–92

Redfin, 617; patrols and wolf packs, 610–11, 619, 637, 641, 650, 715, 784–85, 800, 868

Redfish, 818; patrols and wolf packs, 702, 705, 775–77, 801–3

Redman, John Roland, in ONC, 260–63

Redman, Joseph Reasor, in ONC, 260–62

Reed, John Ward, in *Sunfish,* 844

Refo, Miles Permenter, III: in *Jack,* 583; in *Hoe,* collision with *Flounder,* 850

Reich, Eli Thomas, 588, 884; memorandum on Mark XVIII, 402–4; in *Lapon,* 466, 469; in *Sealion II,* patrols and wolf packs, 682–83, 706–9, 711, 775–77; sinks *Kongo,* 776

Reno, cruiser, 765

Renown, British cruiser, 629

Repulse, British capital ship, 135

Requin, 677

Rescue equipment, 65–66, 768*n*

Reynolds, James Richard, in S-37, 184, 186, 297, 299

Reynolds, W. L., 714, 715

Rhymes, Cassius Douglas, Jr., 140, 141, 341; on Mark XIV torpedo tests, 170; "The Fearless Skipper," poem, 199–200, 326; in S-38, 461–62; in *Chub,* 854

Rice, Robert Henry, 231, 254, 309, 326, 327; in *Drum,* 227–28; in *Paddle,* 526; in Bureau of Personnel, 526, 567, 593; Lockwood's feud with, 812

Rice, Mrs. Robert H., 310

Richardson, George Floyd, 527

Richardson, Gill MacDonald, codebreaker, 89, 607

Richardson, James Otto, 70

Richelieu, Free French battleship, 629

Richmond, cruiser, 417

Rickover, Hyman George, 882

Riefkhol, Frederic Louis, 296

Rimmer, Hugh Raynor, in *Albacore,* lost, 780

Rindskopf, Maurice Herbert, in *Drum,* 730, 748, 769, 770

Ringgold, destroyer, 522

Risser, Robert Dunlap: in *Seawolf,* 449, 450; in *Flying Fish,* 1944 patrols, 603, 647, 649, 651, 657; 1945 wolf pack, 860, 861, 863; report on Japanese fleet in Philippine Sea, 651–53

RO class, Japanese submarines, 495, 508, 564, 662, 736, 765

RO-30, 229; RO-41, 736; RO-45, 602; RO-46, 833; RO-49, 825; RO-56, 835; RO-112, 833, 834; RO-113, 833, 834; RO-115, 833

Roach, John Paul ("Beetle"), 443, 553, 825; in *Haddock,* wolf packs, 546–47, 730, 761, 770–72; salvage of papers from Japanese ship, 603–5; in Battle of Leyte Gulf, 761

Robalo, 581, 617, 737, 789, 814, 817*n*; Manning Kimmel commands, 626; last patrol and death of Kimmel, 687–88, 714, 715, 721

Robbins, Orme Campbell ("Butch"): in *Sterlet,* 732, 765; patrols and wolf packs, 745, 747, 791; in Battle of Leyte Gulf, 762, 764

Robertson, Edward Dunbar, 502

Roby, Harry B., 343

Rochefort, Joseph John, codebreaker, 88, 91–92, 219, 227, 260–63, 268, 370, 881; after Pearl Harbor attack, 117–18, 123, 125; and Battle of Midway, 234, 239, 248–49, 262; and security leak on Battle of Midway, 256; removed from position, 262–63
Rock, 591, 780; patrols, 679, 751, 757, 780
Rockwell, Francis Warren ("Skinny"), 218, 283
Roi, 229
Roko Maru, Japanese freighter, 700
Rongelop, 116
Ronquil: patrols, 730, 746, 749, 791; in Battle of Leyte Gulf, 762, 764
Rooney, Roderick Shanahan, in *Corvina,* 523
Roosevelt, Franklin D., 87, 175, 253–54; Assistant Secretary of the Navy, 36; naval construction program, 64; orders fleet moved to Pearl Harbor, 70; preparations for war, 72, 75, 78–80; changes in navy high command, 125; and security leak on Battle of Midway, 258; orders submarines sent to Scotland, 263; Casablanca Conference, 398, 399; alleged responsibility for Pearl Harbor attack, 690–92, 881; in strategic planning, 694–95; Quebec Conference, 723; unconditional surrender of Japan wanted, 823; death, 839
Roosevelt, Franklin D., Jr., 249
Roosevelt, James, 317, 318
Roosevelt, Theodore, 29, 47
Root, Elihu, 51, 52, 59
Roper, Clifford Harris ("Stoney"), 83, 250, 307, 328–29; commands Squadron Eight, 223; in Battle of Tassafaronga, 339
Roseneath, Scotland, 263, 265
Ross, Philip Harold: in *Halibut,* 337, 433, 547; in *Golet,* 667
Rossel Island, 300
Rota, 650

Rowell (*Richard M. Rowell*), destroyer, 736
Royal Oak, British battleship, 71
Ruble, Harold Eustace, in *Piranha,* 677–79, 725, 788
Ruhe, William James: describes life in S-37, 297; in *Crevalle,* 493–95
Runner, 409, 460; lost, 460–61, 552*n*, 780
Runner II, 868
Russell, George Lucius, 791, 813, 881
Russia: submarines before World War I, 33, 33–34*n*, 36; in World War II, 398, 823; possible invasion of Japan, 416; declares war on Japan, 869–70
Russian ships: sunk by *Sawfish,* 405, 468; in La Pérouse Strait, 464; trawler sunk by *Permit,* crew rescued, 467–68; sunk by *Sandlance,* 594; *Tambor* attacks, 697; sunk by *Spadefish,* 863–65
Russillo, Michael Peter, in *Muskallunge,* 647, 714
Russo-Japanese War, 46, 650*n*; submarines in, 33–34*n*
Rutter, Royal Lawrence, 115; in *Dolphin,* 251, 252, 321; in *Kete,* 807
Ryoei Maru, Japanese tanker, 846
Ryoyo Maru, Japanese ship, 596
Ryuho, Japanese aircraft carrier, 335, 337, 662, 744, 748, 766, 868
Ryujin Maru, Japanese freighter, 215
Ryujo, Japanese aircraft carrier, 268, 301, 315, 399*n;* lost, 301, 302
Ryukyu Islands: U.S. bombing of, 745, 833; minefield near, 837
Ryusei Maru, Japanese freighter, 615
Ryuyo Maru, Japanese freighter, 501
Ryuzan Maru, Japanese freighter, 454

S-boats, 47, 52, 77, 78, 80, 125, 157, 176; Lake and Holland designs, 40; maneuvers in 1921, 47–48; in Asiatic Fleet, 82; loaned to Britain, 217*n;* sent from Atlantic to Brisbane, 217–18; in Alaska, 267–68, 272, 418, 420–21; patrols from

INDEX

Brisbane, 296–301, 305, 340, 345; returned to U.S., 302, 305, 345; torpedoes on, 304–5; patrols, 1943, 461–62; retirement, 551*n*
S-1, 54*n*, 217*n*
S-14, 706
S-18, 267, 459
S-20, 444
S-23, 267, 317
S-25, 217*n*, 341
S-26, 498, 817
S-27, 268–69, 497, 603
S-28, 420, 459, 592, 818
S-30, 420, 540, 614
S-31, 269*n*, 272, 461, 462
S-32, 325
S-33, 523
S-35, 272, 420
S-36, 141, 144–45, 155; lost, 169, 171
S-37, 137–38, 155, 166, 177–78, 184, 186, 297, 299, 493, 595, 623; lost, 272
S-38, 137–38, 147–48, 155, 165, 186, 187, 222, 298, 299, 461–62, 466, 493
S-39, 136, 137, 155, 169, 177, 178, 183, 186–87, 503; lost, 300–301
S-40, 137–38, 147, 149–50, 299, 300, 420*n*
S-41, 155, 157, 166, 177–79, 183, 299, 420, 724
S-42, 222, 402, 420*n*, 421
S-43, 299, 301
S-44, 222, 297–99, 304, 334, 360, 372, 462, 497, 581, 595; lost, 420, 552
S-45, 297, 420*n*, 421
S-46, 297, 420*n*, 421
S-47, 222, 420*n*, 421
S-48, 882*n*
Sackett, Earl LeRoy, 197
Sado, Japanese frigate, 718
Sado Maru, Japanese freighter, 214
Safford, Laurence Frye, codebreaker, 219, 370; before World War II, 53, 63, 73, 75, 87; in Negat unit, 260–61

Sagami Maru, Japanese transport, 353
Sagami Nada, 336
Sagara Maru, Japanese seaplane tender, 445
Saigon, 616
Saigon Maru, Japanese transport, 739
Sailfish (formerly Squalus), 67, 82*n*, 151, 164, 165, 187, 190, 195, 273, 303, 307, 308, 796; 1942 patrols, 141, 143, 305; command change, 304, 463; 1943 patrols, 462–64, 527–30, 553; command problems, 462–64, 593; 1944 patrol and wolf pack, 701–2, 745–46; retired, 818*n*
Sainei Maru, Japanese ship, 678
St. Angelo, Augustus Robert ("The Saint"), 515; in Snapper, 341, 380
St. George's Channel, 299
St. Lo (Midway), jeep carrier, 736, 738, 765
St. Louis, cruiser, 472, 813
St. Vincent, Earl, 24
Saipan, 17, 105, 398, 411, 412, 435, 513, 553, 558, 567, 568, 642, 646, 649; air strikes on, 561, 646; submarine support of air strikes, 571, 573–74; Japanese reinforcements for, 590–91, 600–602, 644, 663; patrols near, 595, 643; U.S. invasion of, 652–54, 664–65, 669; submarine base, 673, 695, 705, 708, 710, 721, 729, 730, 746, 765, 771, 772, 777, 816, 842; aircraft based on, 824
Saipan Maru, Japanese transport, 453
Sakhalin, 416, 464, 866
Sakito Maru, Japanese transport, 591
Salajar Strait, 352, 612, 670–71
Salmon (D-3), 30*n*
Salmon, 64*n*, 76*n*, 82*n*, 164, 187, 198*n*; 201, 229, 496, 521, 772, 867; in Lingayen Gulf, 147, 149, 150; in defense of Java, 184; 1943 patrols, 289–90, 428; 1944 patrols, 730, 746, 747; in Battle of Leyte Gulf, 762, 764, 765; retired, 765, 818*n*

1056

Salmon class of submarines, 64–65, 67, 76, 82, 83
Salt Lake City, cruiser, 417
Samar, 736, 737, 782
Samidare, Japanese destroyer, 622, 697
Samoa, 63, 204, 219
San Bernardino Strait, 136, 137, 164, 649–52, 657, 724, 746, 749, 758, 759, 761, 767
San Diego, 76, 77, 346, 789
San Diego, cruiser, 711
San Jacinto, aircraft carrier, 399*n*
San Juan, cruiser, 330
Sandlance, 622; patrols, 594–95, 643, 712–13
Sands, Eugene Thomas, 463; in *Sawfish,* sinks Russian ships, 405, 468, 594, 864; patrols, 427–28, 510–11
Sangley Point, 130
Santa Cruz, Battle of, 329–30, 338
Santa Fe, cruiser, 522
Santee, jeep carrier, 765
Santos, Chief Justice of Philippines, 174
Sanyo Maru, Japanese seaplane tender, 633
Sanyo Maru, Japanese tanker, 810
Saratoga, aircraft carrier, 57, 123, 204, 296, 330, 361, 399, 422, 423; damaged, 301–2, 553; repaired, 369*n*; in Gilbert Islands invasion, 505, 506; in Surabaya air strike, 627, 629; at Iwo Jima, 827
Sargo, 64*n*, 82*n*, 160, 169, 174, 176, 192, 193, 198*n*, 210, 285; patrol to Camranh Bay, 139, 140; Mark XIV torpedo tests, 170; bombed by Australian airplane, 185; 1942–1943 patrols, 286–87, 432, 457; support of air strike on Palaus, 570–71; 1944 patrol, 731; retired, 818*n*
Sargo, nuclear-powered submarine, 882
Sarmi, 620
Sasebo, 843
Saunders, Willard Arthur: in *Grayback,* 212, 287–88; torpedo tests, 437–38

INDEX

Saury, 64*n*, 82*n*, 164, 168, 183, 198*n*, 360*n*, 438, 458; patrol near Luzon, 141, 143; in Lingayen Gulf, 147–50; Mark XIV torpedo tests, 277; 1943 patrols, 288–89, 341, 450–51; attack on *Unyo,* 547–48; 1944 patrols, 731, 745, 746, 791; retired, 791, 818*n*
Savadkin, L., 768
Savo Island, 299
Savo Island, Battle of, 294–96. 298
Sawfish, 463, 668; sinks Russian ships, 405, 468, 594; 1943 patrols, 427–28, 510–11; 1944 patrols and wolf packs, 679, 730, 746, 748, 769–70
Sayre, Francis B., 153, 174–75
Sazanami, Japanese destroyer, 484
Scabbardfish, patrols and wolf packs, 697, 698, 777–78, 833, 834, 860
Scamp, 506, 553, 567; 1943 patrols, 475–76; in cooperative attack, 484; 1944 patrols, 579–80, 731; lost, 780, 817*n*
Scanland, Francis Worth, Jr., in *Hawkbill,* patrols and wolf packs, 725, 727–28, 795, 852
Schacht, Kenneth George, 189
Schade, Arnold Frederic, 884; in *Growler* disaster, 374–75; in *Bugara,* 855
Scherer, Donald Arthur, in *Permit,* 609
Schleck, Walter Frederick, Jr., experiments on underwater escape, 768*n*
Schmidt, Maximilian Gmelich, 589
Schneider, Earle Caffrey, 552*n*
Schoeni, Walter Paul, in *Apogon,* 523, 677
Schratz, Paul Richard: in *Scorpion,* 458–60; in *Sterlet,* 732, 764*n*, 765
Schwab, Ernest Louis, Jr., in *Darter,* 752, 756
Scorpion, 463, 732; patrols, 458–60; lost, 589 817*n*

INDEX

Scotland, submarines ordered to, 263–65, 401, 481
Scott, John Addison, 427, 627, 702; in *Tunny*, 1943 patrols, 412–13; support of air strike on Palaus, 574–75; 1944 patrols, 595, 643, 646
Sculpin, 64n, 67, 83n, 169, 192, 303, 304, 514, 576, 616, 725n; patrol from Manila, 135, 137; in defense of Java, 177, 179; 1942 patrols, 305, 345; 1943 patrols, 428–29, 435, 524–25; lost, 525, 552; survivors, 525, 526, 529
SD radar, 113
Sea Devil, 801, 840
Sea Dog: 1944 patrols and wolf pack, 731, 746, 804; in Battle of Leyte Gulf, 762; 1945 patrol and wolf pack, 830, 843n, 859–61, 863, 864
Sea Fox: 1944 patrols and wolf packs, 732, 746, 769; crew members killed on Guam, 835; 1945 wolf pack, 835–36, 838
Sea of Japan, 405, 819; 1943–1944 patrols in, 464, 465 (map), 466–71, 511; FM sonar in, 857–61; 1945 patrols in, 858–61, 862 (map), 863–65, 870, 871
Sea of Okhotsk, 319, 321, 468, 667, 865
Sea Owl: test of Cutie torpedoes, 788; patrol and wolf pack, 801, 834–35
Sea Poacher, 788, 801, 833, 834
Sea Robin, 804, 846, 868
Seadragon, 64n, 78n, 82n, 155n, 160, 176, 185, 192, 193, 198n, 343, 361; at Cavite in Japanese attack, 132, 134; at Camranh Bay, attack on Japanese ships, 170–71, 212; at Corregidor, evacuates personnel and delivers supplies, 173–74, 194–95, 218; in earthquake, 195; 1942 patrols, 291, 344–45; 1944 patrols and wolf packs, 746, 748, 769; retired, 818n
Seadragon, nuclear-powered submarine, 882
Seahorse: 1943 patrols, 457–58, 518–20; support of action on Palaus, 569–70, 725; 1944–1945, patrols and wolf packs, 600–602, 609, 651, 674–77, 725, 730, 858–59
Seal (*G-1*), 35n, 66
Seal, 64n, 76n, 82n, 144, 151, 155, 164, 183, 187, 198n, 288, 351, 765, 814; 1942 patrols, 290–91, 354; supports Gilbert Islands invasion, 525–26
Sealion, 64n, 78n, 82n, 154, 308, 403; at Cavite in Japanese attack, 132, 134; destroyed, 134, 160, 171
Sealion II, patrols and wolf packs, 682–83, 706–9, 711, 769, 775–77
Searaven, 64n, 78n, 82n, 151, 155, 164, 165, 171, 176, 177, 183, 187, 189–90, 195, 273, 493; 1942 patrols, 138, 178; fire in, 196; rescues Australians from Timor, 196; 1943 patrols, 433, 524; support of Gilbert Islands invasion, 524; support of air strike on Truk, 568
Seawolf (*H-1*), 35
Seawolf, 64n, 78, 82n, 151, 156, 164, 186, 360n, 481, 510, 603, 646, 711, 725n, 738, 808, 869; patrol from Manila, 135, 136; leaves Philippines, 155; at Corregidor with supplies, 172–73; defense of Bali, 180; defense of Java, 184; voyage from Java to Australia, 190–91; 1942 patrols, 290, 353–54; 1943 patrols, 448–50, 510, 531–33; 1944 patrols, 647, 649, 736–37; lost, 737, 770n, 817n
Segundo, 725, 803
Seiki Maru, Japanese freighter, 420
Seisho Maru, Japanese transport, 774
Seiyo Maru, Japanese tanker, 662
Selby, Frank Gordon: in *Billfish*, 487–88; in *Puffer*, 501; patrols, 614–16, 632–34, 641, 706, 711
Seligman, Morton Tinslar, of *Lexington*, and security leak, 256–60

Sellars, Robert Frederick; in *S-31*, 272, 462; in *Blackfish*, 621, 730, 748, 833
Sendai, Japanese cruiser, 474
Sennet, 825, 865
Settsu, Japanese cruiser, 868
Seventh Fleet, 504, 638
Seymour, Jack Murray, in *Balao*, 480
Shad, 264–66, 589; patrols and wolf packs, 541–43, 775, 776, 802
Shadwell, Capt. L. M., British commander, 742, 743
Shane, Louis, Jr.: in *Shark*, 137–38, 164; lost, 165
Shanghai, 208, 447; Japanese convoy from, 622, 624; patrols near, 683, 772, 775, 802
Shark (A-7), 30n
Shark, 64n, 66, 77, 78, 82n, 164, 270, 447; patrol from Manila, 137–38; takes Admiral Hart from Manila, 153; lost, 165, 171, 271
Shark II, 790; in wolf packs, 643–46, 730, 746, 748, 769–70; lost, 770, 817n
Sharp, George Arthur: in *Spearfish*, 432; in *Florikan*, 592; in *Nautilus*, 593, 758
Shea, Maurice William ("Mike"), 350, 392, 610; in *Raton*, patrols and wolf packs, 703, 712, 718, 740–41, 781–83
Shelby, Edward Ellis, 552n; in *Sunfish*, support of air strike on Saipan, 573–74; wolf packs, 772, 774, 775, 801, 840
Shelton, destroyer, 736, 738
Shepard, Evan Tyler ("Ty"): in *Picuda*, 770; wolf packs, 772–74, 808–10
Sheridan, Martin, war correspondent, 841–42
Sherman, Frederick Carl, of *Lexington*, 256–58
Shibertoro, 867
Shienei Maru, Japanese freighter, 712
Shigemitsu, Mamoru, 873
Shigure, Japanese destroyer, 759, 846

Shikinami, Japanese destroyer, 708
Shikoku, 869
Shikuka, 866
Shima, Vice Adm. Kiyohide, 792; in counterattack before Leyte invasion, 746–48; in Battle of Leyte Gulf, 758, 759, 767
Shimoda, Kantora, 839
Shimonoseki Strait, 843
Shimotsuki, Japanese destroyer, 794
Shimpo Maru, Japanese tanker, 711
Shinano, Japanese battleship, later aircraft carrier, 245–46n, 766; sunk, 778–80
Shiniyo Maru, Japanese transport, 737
Shinki Maru, Japanese freighter, 731
Shinyo, see *Jinyo*
Shinyo Maru, Japanese freighter, 810
Shinyubari Maru, Japanese freighter, 574
Shirakumo, Japanese destroyer, 596
Shiranuhi, Japanese destroyer, 270
Shirataka, Japanese minelayer, 622, 707
Shiritori, 867
Sho 1, Japanese plan for counterattack, 744, 747, 749, 751
Shoho, Japanese aircraft carrier, 220, 230, 399n
Shojin Maru, Japanese ship, 450
Shokaku, Japanese aircraft carrier, 191, 211, 258, 269, 301, 330, 331, 338, 351, 353, 407, 417, 515, 547; in Battle of Coral Sea, 220, 222; hunt for ("wounded bear") 230–31, 232 (map), 233; *Swordfish* attacks, 535; sunk, 657–58, 662
Shokaku class, Japanese aircraft carriers, 433, 619, 658, 773
Shoken Maru, Japanese tanker, 643
Shoko Maru, Japanese ship, 451
Shonan Maru, Japanese freighter, 228
Shosei Maru, Japanese gunboat, 643
Shozan Maru, Japanese ship, 678
Shriver, R. Sargent, 713
Shun Yuan, Japanese ship, 739

INDEX

Siberote, Dutch ship, 169
Sibutu Passage, 488, 633, 637, 638, 650, 711, 714, 751
Sieglaff, William Bernard ("Barney"), 535, 808, 883; in Pearl Harbor attack, 99, 106; in *Tautog,* patrols from Fremantle, 352–53, 392; on polar circuit, 595–96; in *Tench,* 840–41; Operation Barney, 858; in surrender ceremonies, 872
Silversides, 227, 228, 424, 480, 487, 490, 518, 536, 804; sent to Brisbane by way of Truk, 330; patrols from Brisbane, 346–47, 480–81, 485; patrol, Pearl Harbor to Brisbane, 451–53; in Palaus, 530; 1944 patrols and wolf packs, 585, 643–44, 730, 746, 747, 791, 807; in Battle of Leyte Gulf, 762, 764; 1945 wolf pack, 830, 832
Simmons, George Stuart, III, in *Gurnard,* 623
Simpson, H. S., in *Bashaw,* 846, 847, 849
Sims, William S., 42, 43
Sims, destroyer, 220
Singapore, 81, 85, 128, 135, 395, 399, 613, 614, 616, 684, 698, 743, 758, 794, 796, 797; Japanese drive toward, 163, 170, 175; surrender of, 178; strategy for recapture, 557; Japanese naval movement to, 561, 610, 724, 739; Japanese naval movement from, 621, 625, 641, 708, 747–49, 751; Japanese ships in, 846, 853; British midget submarines in raid, 854–55
Sisler, Vincent Ambrose, Jr., 420
Skate (F-4), 35
Skate, 622, 627; lifeguarding at Wake Island, 520, 521; 1943 patrols, 521, 526–27, 530–31, 552, 567; 1944–1945 patrols and wolf packs, 731, 746, 747, 859–61, 863
Skate, nuclear-powered submarine, 882
Skipjack (E-1), 35, 43

1059

Skipjack, 64n, 76n, 82n, 164, 177, 189, 198n, 273, 274, 360n, 503; patrol from Manila, 135, 137; defense of Java, 179; Mark XIV torpedo tests, 276; support of Marshall Islands invasion, 562–63; retired, 818n
Skjonsby, Verne Leslie, 470
Small, Walter Lowry, 407, 603; in *Batfish,* 869
Smart, J. E., in *XE-1,* 855
Smith, Arthur Chester, in *Trutta,* 830
Smith, Chester Carl, 199, 206, 284, 380, 389, 390, 410, 751; in *Swordfish,* 1942 patrols, 139, 164, 171, 176, 195, 288, 343; attack on Japanese force in Celebes, 165–66; evacuates officials from Corregidor, 174–75; moves to Subic Bay, 845
Smith, Holland M., 508, 665
Smith, Robert Holmes, 365n
Snapper (C-5), 30n, 35
Snapper, 64n, 67, 76n, 82n, 151, 164, 176, 185, 192, 196, 380, 394, 466, 515, 581, 725n; delivers supplies to Corregidor, 194–95; in earthquake, 195; 1942 patrols, 285–86, 341–42; 1944 patrols, 647, 731; retired, 818n
Snook, 550, 600; 1943 patrols and wolf pack, 447–48, 543–45; in East China Sea, Triebel's last patrol, 586–88; 1944 patrols and wolf packs, 745, 746, 769; lost, 835
Soembawa, 852
Sofu Gan, *see* Lot's Wife
Solomon Islands, 219, 295, 303, 324, 331, 340, 359, 361, 388, 411, 422, 505, 607, 865; patrols in, 304–6; Japanese reinforcements and supplies for, 307, 312, 357, 372, 386, 391, 405, 411, 423; battles of Esperance and Santa Cruz, 329–30, 338; Japanese submarines in, 330; naval conflicts in, 369, 372; strategy in, 398, 399; surface-force

Solomon Islands (*cont.*)
engagements in, 472, 473 (map), 474
Solomon Islands, Eastern, Battle of, 301–2
Somerville, Adm. Sir James, 629
Sonar, 18, 57, 79, 84; ASDIC, 49, 71; in Fleet Exercises, 66–67; Japanese, 113; FM (QLA), 787, 789–90, 829; FM guidance in Sea of Japan, 857–61
Sonsorol, 621, 649
Sorong, 638
Soryu, Japanese aircraft carrier, 123, 176, 252, 399; in Battle of Midway, lost, 237, 238, 244, 245
South China Sea, 792, 794, 804; patrols, 201, 285, 286, 288, 491, 492, 512, 583, 612, 626, 687, 714, 751, 794, 841; wolf packs, 684–87, 727, 767, 785, 835
South Dakota, battleship, 330, 813
Southerland, Richard, 304
Soyo Maru, Japanese submarine tender, 530
Spadefish: 1944 wolf packs, 702–5, 772–74; bombed by U.S. aircraft, 842; FM sonar tests, 858; 1945 wolf pack, 859, 860, 863
Spark, British submarine, 852, 853, 855
Spearfish, 64*n*, 82*n*, 155*n*, 166, 168, 186, 193, 198*n*, 564*n*, 571, 577, 592, 623, 725*n*; patrol to Camranh Bay, 139–40; defense of Java, 179, 183–84; at Corregidor, evacuates personnel, 196–97; 1943 patrols, 432, 435, 525–26; supports Gilbert Islands invasion, 525–26; 1944 patrols, 806–7; retired, 807, 818*n*
Spence, destroyer, 792
Sperry, submarine tender, 249, 330–32, 339, 371, 372, 561, 791, 805
Sperry Gyroscope Company, 280
Spikefish, 870
Spot, 835–36, 869
Springer, F. H., 730

Spruance, Edward Dean: in *Tambor*, 105, 215; in Battle of Midway, 246, 250; in *Lionfish*, 830, 832
Spruance, Raymond Ames, 105, 250, 794, 830, 832; in Battle of Midway, 234, 246, 247, 249, 660; invasion of Marianas, 642–43, 652; in Battle of Philippine Sea, 652–55, 660, 662; in Iwo Jima invasion, 824–25, 827
Squalus, 64*n*, 480, 529, 807; disaster, 67; see also *Sailfish*
Staley, Joseph Jarlathe, in *Mingo*, 582
Stalingrad, Battle of, 398
Stark, Harold Raynsford, 75, 77, 78, 80, 82, 87, 125; warning of Japanese attack, 91, 129, 158
Statesman, British submarine, 853
Steelhead, 547, 680*n*, 706, 868; 1943 patrols, 433–35, 536, 552; 1944 wolf pack, 679–81
Steffanides, Edward Frank, Jr., in *Tuna*, 730, 761, 849
Steffen Strait, 452
Steinmetz, Everett Hartwell: in *Pollack*, 697; in *Crevalle*, 830, 859, 860, 863
Stephan, Edward Clark, in *Grayback*, 342–43
Sterlet, 812, 818; 1944 patrols and wolf packs, 731, 732, 745–47, 791; command friction, 732, 764*n*, 765; in Battle of Leyte Gulf, 762, 764, 765; 1945 patrols, 825, 827, 829
Sterling, Forest J., *Wahoo* patrols described, 381, 383–86, 425
Stevens, Clyde Benjamin, Jr., in *Plaice*, 649, 697–98, 801
Stevens, James Edward: in *Flounder*, patrols and wolf packs, 785–86, 847; collision with *Hoe*, 849–50
Stevenson, Harry Clinton, in *Aspro*, 539–41
Stevenson, William Alfred: in *S-30*, 420; in *Aspro*, 539–41; patrols, 647, 649, 741

INDEX

Stickleback, 765, 865
Stimson, Paul Cecil, in *Sea Robin,* 804, 846, 868
Stingray (C-2), 30n
Stingray, 64n, 76n, 82n, 155, 159, 165, 166, 168, 171, 176, 185, 192, 193, 285, 330, 332, 360n, 577; in Lingayen Gulf, 145–47; bombed by Allied aircraft, 474, 477; 1944 patrols, 600, 646–47, 654, 736; retired, 818n
Stockton, Vard Albert, in *Snook,* 447, 448, 586–88
Stone, Hamilton Laurie, 341; in *Snapper,* 1942 patrols, 151, 164, 176, 185, 192–93, 196, 285; delivers supplies to Corregidor, 194–95
Stone, Lowell Thornton, in *Lapon,* 582–83, 625, 631–32
Stoner, Howard Fletcher, 457, 562
Storage batteries, 26, 65
Stormes, destroyer, 460
Stovall, William Shirley, Jr., 394; in *Gudgeon,* patrols, 310, 312, 343–44, 356–57; in *Dace,* 568–69, 579
Strategic Bombing Survey, 503–4, 694, 879
Street, George Levick, III, 871; in *Tirante,* patrols, 842–44, 866; Medal of Honor, 844
Strong, destroyer, 472
Stump, Felix Budwell, of *Lexington,* 521–22
Sturgeon (E-2), 35
Sturgeon, 64n, 67, 76n, 82n, 127, 130, 151, 155, 176, 185, 192, 193, 283, 299, 303, 437, 581, 747n; 1942 patrols, 138, 145, 166, 168, 305, 344; command change, 304; 1943 patrols, 433; retired, 818n
Sturr, Henry Dixon, 795; in *Becuna,* 725, 728, 796, 846
Styer, Charles Wilkes ("Gin"), 83, 106, 145, 216, 307, 328, 330, 332, 339, 348, 372, 456, 460, 511, 538, 548, 840; in Pearl Harbor attack, 98; and 1942 patrols, 205; and Battle of Midway, 234; returned to U.S., 249, 550; command changes, 812–13; postwar career, 880
Styer, Charles Wilkes, Jr., 332
Stygian, British submarine, 854, 885
Styles, Ralph Emerson, in *Sea Devil,* 801, 840
Subic Bay, 141, 145, 155, 640, 717, 855; U.S. landing in, 792; Brisbane unit moved to, 814, 845–46; Fife's headquarters moved to, 850; patrols from, 851–56
Submarine Officers' Conference, 68, 403
Submarines: early developments, 23–31; European, before World War I, 32–36; diesel power adopted, 33–36; in World War I, 36–45, 47, 48; in international politics and conferences, 49–52, 58–60; *see also* Germany, submarines; Japanese submarines
Submarines, U.S.: first bought by U.S. government, 29–30; diesel power adopted, 34–36; letters and numbers, 36, 39–40, 43–44, 47, 59n, 73; in World War I, 39–44; between World Wars, 46–69; names, 56n, 64n; London conference on limitation of, 58–60; preparations for World War II, 72–73, 76–85; in Pacific, October–November 1941, 82–85; command, selection by "class year," 107n; defense of Philippines analyzed, 156–60; report by Wilkes and Fife to Admiral King on, 198–201; commanders (skippers), qualities of, 199–201; summary of 1942 operations, 359–62; Lockwood's survey of performance, 400–404; new in 1943, 423–24; cooperative efforts, 482–85, 487–93, 504, *see also* Wolf packs; 1943 additions and losses, 551–52n; summary of 1943 operations, 551–54; new inventions

Submarines, U.S. (cont.)
for, 787–90; summary of 1944 operations, 816–19; 1944 losses and retirements, 817–18; command, shortage of officers, 818; final records of performance, 877–79; postwar models, 882–83; officers' postwar lives, 883–85
Subtle, British submarine, 853
Suffolk, British cruiser, 629
Sukukaze, Japanese destroyer, 562
Sullivan, John, Navy Secretary, 880
Sulu Archipelago, 639
Sulu Sea, 164, 173, 196, 501, 503, 619, 625, 627, 650, 714, 718, 740
Sumatra, 128, 163, 226, 292, 340; Japanese invasion, 178; tankers from, as targets, 486–87
Sumatra Maru, Japanese freighter, 394
Summers, Paul Edward, 332; in Pampanito, 577; 1944 wolf pack, 706, 708–9, 711; 1945 patrol, 847
Sunda Strait, 186, 187, 190, 350–52, 617, 629, 630
Sunfish, 335, 407, 457, 524; 1943 patrols, 455–56; support of air strike on Saipan, 573–74; 1944 wolf packs, 772, 774, 775, 801; 1945 patrol, 844
Surabaya, 153, 164, 165, 172–74, 176, 177, 179, 183, 184, 186, 199, 201, 351, 392, 394, 454, 466, 493, 613, 615, 616, 711, 743, 785, 852, 853; submarines withdrawn to, 154–55; Japanese naval retreat to, 561, 610; air strike on, 620, 627, 628 (map), 629; submarine support of air strike, 629–32; German submarine at, 743
Surigao Strait, 646, 650, 651, 758, 767
Sussex, British packet, 39
Suzukaze, Japanese destroyer, 177
Suzutzuki, Japanese destroyer, 747
Sweeney, Charles W., 870

Swinburne, Edwin Robinson, commands wolf pack, 706, 707, 709
Swordfish, 64n, 82n, 164, 174, 176, 195, 273, 380, 410, 751, 806; patrol to Hainan, 139; leaves Philippines, 155; attack on Japanese force in Celebes, 165–66; 1942 patrols, 288, 343; 1943 patrols, 380–81, 533–36; 1944 patrols, 649, 807; lost, 807, 817n, 829
Swordfish, nuclear-powered submarine, 882
Syverson, Douglas Neil ("Red"), 450

Taei Maru, Japanese freighter, 225
Taeusch, Frederick Leonard, in Permit, 467, 563
Taigen Maru, Japanese freighter, 225
Taihin Maru, Japanese freighter, 740
Taiho, Japanese aircraft carrier, 655, 657–59, 662, 702n
Taijima Maru, Japanese transport, 623
Taijin Maru, Japanese ship, 590
Taiko Maru, Japanese ship, 461
Taikyo Maru, Japanese ship, 810
Taiman Maru I, Japanese freighter, 842
Taimei Maru, Japanese passenger freighter, 658
Taito Maru, Japanese transport, 647
Taiwan, see Formosa
Taiyo (Otaka), Japanese aircraft carrier, 230, 313, 329, 337, 412, 413, 435, 702–5
Taiyo Maru, Japanese passenger ship, 226, 230n
Taka Bakang reef, 169
Takachiho Maru, Japanese transport, 406
Takagi, Vice Adm. Takeo, 565, 662
Takaika Maru, Japanese freighter, 645
Takao, Japanese cruiser, 506, 754–58, 766, 817, 846, 855
Takao Maru, Japanese ship, 426
Takasaki, Japanese tanker, 633

INDEX

Takashima Maru, Japanese transport, 668
Taketoyo Maru, Japanese transport, 718
Takima Maru, Japanese trawler, 605
Takimasu Maru, Japanese ship, 451
Takunan Maru, Japanese freighter, 732
Talaud, 495, 636
Tama, Japanese cruiser, 417, 748, 761, 762, 766
Tamagawa Maru, Japanese transport, 173
Tamahime Maru, Japanese freighter, 645
Tamatsu Maru, Japanese transport, 704
Tambor, 68n, 79–80, 83n, 84, 98, 213, 215–16, 312, 327, 581, 759n, 864n; at Wake Island, 105, 106, 123; in Battle of Midway, 236n, 245–47, 250; patrols from Fremantle, 351–52; 1944 patrols, 697, 732, 791; retired, 791, 818n
Tambor class of submarines, 67–69, 72, 79–80, 83, 126
Tanaga Bay, 271
Tanahmerah, 607
Tang, 574, 808, 818; support of air strike on Truk, 567–68; support of air strike on Saipan, 571, 573, 574; 1944 patrols, 602, 609, 682–83, 699–700, 730–31, 747; last patrol, lost, 767–69, 770n, 817n
Tang (1951), 882
Tang class, postwar submarines, 882
Tango Maru, Japanese freighter, 615
Tanikaze, Japanese destroyer, 123, 247, 638
Tantalus, British submarine, 847
Tarakan, 166, 178, 192, 290, 487, 637
Tarantula (B-3), 30n
Tarawa, 398, 422, 454–55; U.S. landing on, 318; Japanese reinforcements, 454–55, 457; U.S. invasion of, 505, 506, 515, 520, 522, 523, 543, 558

1063

Target Bearing Transmitter, see TBT
Tarpon (C-3), 30n
Tarpon, 64n, 66, 77, 82n, 164, 177, 185, 330, 444, 490, 646, 730, 884n; patrol from Manila, 136, 137; defense of Timor, 180–81; aground, 181; returned for overhaul, 192; in Battle of Midway, 236n; patrol near Truk, 331–32; 1943 patrols, 405–6, 513–14, 518; retired, 818n
Tarushima Maru, Japanese freighter, 532
Task Force 38, 642, 722, 744, 745, 790, 792, 794, 804, 824, 868, 870, 871
Task Force 42, 339, 367
Task Force 51, 274n, 303
Task Force 58, 642–43, 646, 652, 653, 655, 824, 825, 827, 829, 830, 832
Tassafaronga, Battle of, 339, 369
Tatekawa Maru, Japanese tanker, 634
Tatsuaki Maru, Japanese ship, 773
Tatsuju Maru, Japanese freighter, 767
Tatsuta, Japanese cruiser, 594, 622
Tatsuta Maru, Japanese passenger ship, 406, 615
Tautog, 68n, 83n, 122, 224, 285, 361, 487, 535, 738, 780, 834; in Pearl Harbor attack, 99; patrols to Marshalls, 107, 116, 121, 229; in pursuit of *Shokaku,* 230–31, 233; patrols from Fremantle, 351–53, 392; on polar circuit, 595–96; last patrol and retirement, 807, 818n; ships sunk by, 808
Tawi Tawi, 158, 582; Japanese naval retreat to, 561, 610; Japanese fleet at, 621, 625–27, 629, 634, 641, 649, 650; patrols to, 632–34, 637–40, 669, 674
Taylor, A. Hoyt, 63
Taylor, Arthur Howard, 337, 580, 673; in *Haddock,* trial of SJ radar, 321–22; "Squat Div One," poem in "subversive literature" in-

1064

Taylor, Arthur Howard (*cont.*) cident, 326–29; torpedo tests, 437, 438
Taylor, Rufus Lackland, codebreaker, 89, 195, 607, 881
TBS (Talk Between Ships) radio, 542
TBT (Target Bearing Transmitter), 565
TDC (Torpedo Data Computer), 65, 67n, 68, 79, 198–99, 357, 565
Teibi Maru, Japanese transport, 496
Teibo Maru, Japanese freighter, 286
Teifuku Maru, Japanese freighter, 336
Teihoku Maru, Japanese transport, 870
Teiko Maru, Japanese transport, 615
Teikon Maru, Japanese tanker, 711
Teiryu Maru, Japanese ship, 679
Teisen Maru, Japanese freighter, 627
Teishun Maru, Japanese freighter, 322
Tench, 840–41, 866
Tennessee, battleship, 99
Tenryu, Japanese cruiser, 334, 337, 360, 378
Tenshinzan Maru, Japanese freighter, 623
Terushima Maru, Japanese freighter, 454
Thailand, 85
Thames Maru, Japanese freighter, 499
Theobald, Robert Alfred, 268
Third Fleet, 642, 722, 744, 824, 867
Thomas, William Bismarck, 733
Thomas, Willis Manning, 427, 458; in *Pompano*, patrol to Honshu, 319–20; 1943 patrols, 407, 412; lost, 461
Thomis, Wayne, 257, 258, 260
Thompson, William Calhoun, Jr.: in *Bowfin*, 487–88, 490; in *Cabrilla*, 617; patrols, 633, 634, 741
Thrasher (G-4), 35n
Threadfin, 843n; wolf pack, 830, 832, 843

INDEX

Thresher, 68n, 83n, 210, 213, 251, 349, 360n, 499, 731, 787; in Pearl Harbor attack, 101–2; patrol to Marshalls, 107, 116, 121, 122; supports Tokyo bombing raid, 214–15; patrols from Fremantle, 350–51, 391; supports Gilbert Islands invasion, 523; patrol from Midway, 538–39; 1944 patrol, 677–78
Tibbets, Paul W., Jr., 869
Tichenor, Murray Jones, 341, 368, 501, 610, 612, 672, 717, 813; on *Harder* for patrol, 637, 670; in investigation of loss of *Flier*, 716; postwar career, 884–85
Ticonderoga, aircraft carrier, 794
Tiedeman, Carl, 339; in *Snapper*, 192, 285; in *Guavina*, 713–14, 785, 786, 798
Tigrone, 593, 835, 865–66
Tilefish, 679
Timor, 128, 163, 176–78, 273, 284, 612, 672; Japanese capture, 180, 181; Australian Air Force men rescued from, 196; guerrillas rescued from, 356–57
Tinian, 105, 380, 558, 642, 869, 870; air strike on, 561; U.S. invasion of, 664; aircraft based on, 824
Tinosa, 646, 687, 797n, 857; 1943 patrols, 433–35, 536–37; torpedo failure, 435–38; 1944 patrols and wolf pack, 597–99, 682, 683; FM sonar tests, 789–90, 858; 1945 wolf pack, 860, 861, 863
Tirante, 842–44, 866
Tirpitz, Adm. Alfred von, 33, 37
Tirpitz, German battleship, 854, 855
Titus, Jack Clarence, in *Narwhal*, 737–38
Tjilatjap, 176, 177, 179, 183, 185, 186
Toan Maru, Japanese freighter, 702
Toba Maru, Japanese freighter, 196
Toho Maru, Japanese freighter, 644
Tojo, Gen. Hideki, 76, 85, 665
Tokai Maru, Japanese freighter, 380

INDEX

Tokaia Strait, 775
Tokiwa Maru, Japanese ship, 440
Toko Maru, Japanese transport, 742
Tokushima Maru, Japanese ship, 706
Tokyo: Doolittle bombing raid, 205, 214–15, 220, 335, 359, 790; 1945 bombing of, 824–25, 827, 868
Tokyo Bay: patrols near, 211–12, 214, 335, 336, 406, 429–30, 468–69, 534, 553, 732, 733, 746, 777–78, 780, 825, 859; Japanese fleet assembles in, 417, 425, 427; lifeguarding in, 825, 827, 842; surrender ceremonies, 871–73
Tokyo Maru, Japanese tanker, 226
Toman Maru, Japanese freighter, 426
"Tombstone promotion," 122n, 884–85
Tomioka, Rear Adm. Sadatoshi, 873
Tonan Maru, Japanese whale factory, 316, 320
Tonan Maru II, Japanese tanker, 516, 699
Tonan Maru III, Japanese tanker (former whale factory), 432, 436, 437, 457, 536, 624
Tone, Japanese cruiser, 123, 506, 846, 868
Toowoomba, rest camp, 371
Toro, 869
Torpedo Data Computer, *see* TDC
Torpedo exploders: contact, 361, 437–39, 508; hair-triggered, 480; *see also* Magnetic exploder; Mark VI
Torpedoes: early developments, 19–20, 25, 30–31; in World War I, 41; research and experiments, 53–56, 61–62; production, 69, 120–21; firing technique, 111–12; failure, 169–70, 192, 198, 304–5, 354–55, 391–92, 401–2, 412–15, 588, *see also* Mark XIV; aerial, failure, 238; tests, 275–79; oxygen, 279, 279–80n, 486; electric, 279–81, 348, 694n; German, electric, 280; Japanese, oxygen and electric, 279–82n, 486; production difficulties, 348, 401; defects isolated, 435–39, 553; Japanese man-guided, (*kaitens*), 663, 765–66, 824, 869, 872; performance satisfactory, 694; Cutie (electric acoustical), 787–89, 825, 843, 867; in 1944, summary, 818–19; and revised sinking records, 879; postwar models, 882
Torsk, 865, 870
Tosan Maru, Japanese transport, 686
Tosei Maru, Japanese ship, 498
Totai Maru, Japanese ship, 529
Toten Maru, Japanese ship, 668
Toun Maru, Japanese freighter, 767
Townsville, 300, 301, 339
Toyama Bay, 863
Toyo Maru, Japanese freighter, 411, 412
Toyoda, Adm. Soemu, 561, 653, 662, 664; preparations for Allied attack (A-Go battle plan), 620–21; plan for counterattack (Sho 1), 744, 747, 749, 751; counterattack against air strikes, 745, 746, 748; and *Yamato*'s last sortie, 830
Toyooka Maru, Japanese transport, 707
Transbalt, Russian freighter, 864
Transport No. 5, Japanese, 733
Trenchant, British submarine, 854
Trepang, 732, 803–4, 825, 827
Trident Conference, 422, 472
Trident submarines, 883
Triebel, Charles Otto ("Chuck"), 270, 373, 450, 451, 550, 600, 677, 885n; in *Snook,* patrols and wolf packs, 447–48, 543–46, 586–88; criticizes torpedo performance, 588; in Bureau of Ordnance, 588; postwar rank, 883
Trigger, 380, 697, 725, 732, 806, 842; in Battle of Midway, 236n, 246–48; Alaska patrols, 269, 271; minelaying patrol, 335, 336; 1943 patrols, 428–30, 435, 517–20; 1944 patrols and wolf packs, 564–65, 600–603, 730, 745–47, 791; in Battle of Leyte Gulf, 762, 764, 765; lost, 829–30, 843n

Trigger (1951), 882
Triton, 68*n*, 83*n*, 84, 98, 205, 208, 360*n*, 361, 579; at Wake Island, 105, 120, 123; command change, 224; East China Sea patrol, 224–25, 254; Alaska patrol, 269, 270; sent to Brisbane, 334; last patrol, lost, 375, 552*n*
Trout, 68*n*, 83*n*, 84, 123, 205, 213–14, 316, 360*n*, 553, 584, 593, 597; in Midway attack, 102, 104; at Corregidor, 206, 216; in Battle of Midway, 236*n*, 245; in Truk patrol, 312–13; in Battle of Guadalcanal, 344; patrol from Fremantle, 354–57; lost, 591, 817*n*
Trout (1951), 882
Truk, 116, 175, 205, 212, 213, 335, 340, 341, 359–61, 372, 386, 417, 431, 484, 558, 602, 614, 621, 624, 647; January–April 1942 patrols to, 209–10, 215, 224, 229; *Shokaku* at, 230–31, 233; Japanese base, 305–6, 339, 423, 425, 432, 434, 472, 474, 476, 484, 506, 526; July–September 1942 patrols to, 307–10, 311 (map), 312–18, 326, 329, 337; October–December 1942 patrols to, 330–34, 337, 344, 345, 347; strategic plans on, 399, 557; January–June 1943 patrols to, 405, 406, 409–12, 423, 432–35, 439, 456, 457; June–December 1943 patrols to, 474, 478, 481, 508, 515–17, 523, 524, 526, 530, 536; Japanese tankers bound for, as targets, 486–87, 503; Japanese fleet withdrawn from, 560, 563, 570–71, 610; air strikes on, 560, 561, 566 (map), 607; submarine support of air strikes, 562–65, 567, 607, 609, 818
Truman, Harry S., 869, 879
Trumbull, Robert, 424
Trutta, 830, 864, 884*n*
Tsugaru Strait, 464
Tsukushi Maru, Japanese transport, 701
Tsushima, Battle of, 650

Tsushima Maru, Japanese transport, 698
Tsushima Strait, 405, 464, 511, 731, 857, 858, 859, 864
Tsuyama Maru, Japanese transport, 730
Tucker, Joseph Robbins, 463
Tulagi, 220, 222, 297, 568; U.S. forces on, 295, 296; submarine supply depot, 475, 483
Tullibee: patrol and wolf pack, 434, 546–47; support of air strike on Palaus, 574–76; lost, 576, 817*n*
Tuna (G-2), 35*n*
Tuna, 68*n*, 83*n*, 205, 206, 208, 250, 387, 539, 643, 725; East China Sea patrol, 225; in Battle of Midway, 236*n*; Alaska patrol, 269, 271; sent to Brisbane by way of Truk, 331; 1943–1945 patrols and wolf packs, 498, 604–5, 730, 770, 772, 847, 849; in Battle of Leyte Gulf, 761; retired, 818*n*
Tunny, 427, 627, 702, 857; 1943 patrols, 412–13; support of air strike on Palaus, 574–75; 1944–1945 patrols and wolf packs, 595, 643, 646, 660, 859–61, 863, 864
Turbot (G-3), 35*n*
Turner, Vernon Clark, in *Billfish,* 701
Turtle, submarine in American Revolution, 23
Twatem, Japanese cruiser, 868
Tyler, M. H., 521
Tyree, Alexander Kelly, in *Bowfin,* 827, 829, 858–60, 863
Tyree, John Augustine, Jr., 446, 884; in *Finback,* 453–54, 593, 609

U-168, German submarine at Surabaya, 786*n*
U-183, German submarine, 853
U-505, German submarine, captured, 689–90
U-537, German submarine, sunk, 785–86
U-boats, class, *see* Germany
Uchide Maru, Japanese transport, 571

INDEX

Ugaki, Rear Adm. Matome, 755
Ulithi, 567, 647, 649, 658, 745, 794, 805, 827; air strike on, 561; U.S. capture of, 723; Japanese human torpedoes at, 766
Ultra messages: definition of, 87; security precautions on, 259, 304
Umikaze, Japanese destroyer, 567
Underwood, Gordon Waite, in *Spadefish*, 702–6, 772–74, 842
Unryu, Japanese aircraft carrier, 766, 771, 802–3
Unyo, Japanese aircraft carrier, 417, 432–33, 435, 506, 574; *Sculpin* survivors on, 525, 526; attacks on, 547–48, 553; sunk, 710
Urakaze, Japanese destroyer, 123, 775
Ural Maru, Japanese transport, 740
Uyo Maru, Japanese freighter, 529
Uzan Maru, Japanese freighter, 214

V-boats, 49, 52, 56–58, 60, 83
Valiant, British cruiser, 629
Van Buskirk, Beverly Robinson, 188–89
Van Gordgen, K. R., 536–37
Van Hook, Clifford Evans, 755, 757, 814, 815
Van Leunen, Paul, Jr., in *Peto*, 599–600
Vella Gulf, 474
Vella Lavella, 474
Verde Island Passage, 138, 147
Verne, Jules, *Twenty Thousand Leagues under the Sea*, 25
Vickers, Limited: torpedoes, 30–31; submarine engines, 34
Vigan, 141, 143, 153, 159, 164, 176
Villamor, Major, 356
Vincennes, cruiser, 296
Vinson, Carl, Congressman, 64
Viper (B-1), 30n, 66
Vireo, tug, 239
Virgin Islands, 80
Visayan Sea, 650
Visayas, 765
Vistula River, 823
Vladivostok, 215, 405, 464

Voge, Richard George, 199, 249, 298, 303, 354, 401, 403, 462, 550, 673, 711, 843n; at Cavite in Japanese attack, 132, 134; in *Sailfish*, 1942 patrols, 144, 151, 164, 165, 187, 191, 195, 196; operations officer at Pearl Harbor, 304, 307–8, 326, 813; and 1943 patrols from Pearl Harbor, 406, 407, 409, 411, 412, 432, 433, 511, 519, 528, 531, 532, 554; and patrols in Sea of Japan, 464, 466, 469, 511; and 1944 patrols from Pearl Harbor, 564, 594, 595, 679, 708, 731, 770, 780; and *Awa Maru* incident, 837, 839; and 1945 operations, 849, 857; postwar career, 880–81
Volcano Islands, 824

Wahlig, Frederick Henry, in *Grouper*, 724, 840
Wahoo, 360n, 453, 460, 584, 770, 857; in Truk patrol, 315–16; sent to Brisbane by way of Truk, 331, 333; patrol from Brisbane to Pearl Harbor, 380–86, 402; 1943, patrols from Pearl Harbor, 407–8, 425–27, 469–71; patrol in Sea of Japan, 469–71; last patrol, lost, 510–11, 552n
Wahoo (1951), 882
Wainwright, Jonathan, 197
Wakatake Maru, Japanese freighter, 767
Wakde, 620
Wake Island, 76, 97, 114, 119, 204, 247, 334, 410, 412, 540, 604, 622, 835; simulated attack on, 84; Japanese approach to (map), 92; Japanese attack, 105–6, 120; Japanese capture, 122–23, 124 (map), 125, 128, 135; U.S. raids, 205, 505; *Skate* in lifeguarding operation, 521
Wales, George Herrick, in *Pogy*, 433–34, 530
Walker, Lt. Comdr., in Mark XIV torpedo test, 170
Walker, Edward Keith, 234, 249

INDEX

Walker, Francis David, Jr., 138, 165; in *Crevalle*, 493, 495, 496; patrols and wolf packs, 624–25, 630, 641, 684–87, 735–36
Walker, William Warren, in *Snapper*, 647
Wallace, Lewis, 444; in *Tarpon*, patrol from Manila, 136, 137; 1942 patrols, 164, 185, 192; in defense of Timor, 180–81
Wallach, Mrs. Charles, 365–66
Walling, John Franklin: in *Flying Fish*, 314, 332, 333; in *Snook*, lost, 835
Walrus (K-4), 36
Ward, Norvell Gardiner ("Bub"), 344; in *Seadragon*, 134, 171, 292; in *Gato*, 376; in *Guardfish*, 484, 567, 677–80
Ward, Robert Elwin McCramer ("Bob"): in *Gurnard*, 265, 440–42; in *Sailfish*, 527–30, 553, 701–2, 745–46
Warder, Frederick Burdette, 199, 206, 298, 301, 350, 448, 450, 463–64, 512, 581, 711–12, 737; in *Seawolf*, patrol from Manila, 136, 137; 1942 patrols, 151, 155, 164, 186; at Corregidor with supplies, 172–73; in defense of Bali, 180; in defense of Java, 184; voyage from Java to Australia, 190–91; patrols from Fremantle, 290, 353–54; commands wolf pack, 543, 545, 546; in Submarine School, 814; postwar rank, 883
Wasatch, Kinkaid's flagship, 815
Washington, George, 23
Washington, battleship, 56, 302, 330
Washington, D.C., arms limitation conference, 1921–1922, 50–52, 58
Wasp, aircraft carrier, 64, 295, 399; lost, 301–2, 361, 553
Wasp, aircraft carrier (new, 1943), 399*n*, 829
Watkins, Frank Thomas, 549*n*, 884; in *Flying Fish*, 431–32

Waugh, Richard Albert, 432; in *Saury*, 745, 791
Weddingen, Otto, 37
Weinel, August Frederick, 503
Weiss, Donald Frederick, 789; in *Tinosa*, 537; patrol and wolf pack, 597–99, 682, 683
Wenger, Joseph Numa, codebreaker, 261, 881
Wenneker, Vice Adm. Paul H., 664
West Virginia, battleship, 99
Westbrook, Edwin Monroe, Jr., in *Cod*, 855
Westinghouse Electric & Manufacturing Company, 281, 402, 403, 787
Wewak, 453, 569, 607, 609; *Wahoo* at, 382–83, 386, 402; U.S. attacks, 472
Whale: 1942 patrol, 325; 1943 patrols, 409–10, 434, 435, 532; 1944 patrols, 662, 725
Whale factories, Japanese, 289–90, 290*n*
Wheland, Karl Raymond, in *Gabilan*, 730, 749
Whelchel, David Lee, 486, 547; in *Steelhead*, patrols and wolf packs, 433, 434, 536, 553, 679–81, 868
Whitaker, Reuben Thornton, 127–28, 166, 282–83, 298, 795, 849; in *S-44*, 299; Fife's character described, 372; on Donaho's discipline, 380; in *Flasher*, 581; patrols and wolf packs, 627, 629, 684–87, 739–40; postwar rank, 883
White, David Charles, 253, 345, 466; in Pearl Harbor attack, 100–101; in *Plunger*, patrols in Japanese waters, 107, 113–14, 120, 121, 253; *Conte Verde* incident, 253–54; patrol with SJ radar, 331; in *Cero*, 541–42
Whitehead, Robert, torpedo design, 25, 30, 41
Whiting, George Harris, 395
Whitmore, William F., 420
Widgeon, submarine rescue vessel, 438
Wiggin, Bruce Eastman, 212

INDEX

Wilhelm II, Kaiser, 37–39
Wilkes, John, 78, 82, 165, 166, 169, 171, 173, 196, 275, 282, 292, 348, 362; commands new Squadron Five, 77; and Japanese attack on Philippines, 130–32, 134; and patrols from Manila, 131, 135, 138, 139, 141, 143–45; and "battle" of Lingayen Gulf, 145–47, 149, 150; and loss of Manila, 153–60; orders attack on Davao, 164; in controversy on Mark XIV torpedo, 169–70; sends aid to Corregidor, 172, 194, 195; and defense of Java, 176–81, 183–85; leaves Java for Australia, 186; in Australia, 191, 192, 197, 218, 223; criticizes Chapple, 194; report to Admiral King, 197–201; Admiral King's orders to, 201–3; replaced, returned to U.S., 273–74; postwar career, 880
Wilkin, Warren Dudley, 813; commands wolf pack, 679
Wilkins, Charles Warren ("Weary"), 107, 210–12, 315, 321, 460, 526; in Pearl Harbor attack, 97–98, 106; in *Narwhal*, 319; in *Seahorse*, 676–77; support of Palau Islands invasion, 725; commands Squadron Twelve, 813; postwar rank, 883
Wilkinson, Eugene ("Dennis"), 752
Wilkinson, Theodore Stark, 260–61
Will, John Mylin ('Dutch"), 282, 390, 498, 605, 610, 813, 881
Williams, Jack, radio intelligence expert, 118
Williams, Joseph Warford, Jr., in *Spearfish*, 525–26
Williams, William Wadsworth, 374
Williamson, Delbert Fred, in *Drum*, 523–24
Williamson, Thomas Fort, 269*n*
Willingham, Joseph Harris, 808, 834; in *Tautog*, patrols to Marshalls, 107, 116, 121, 229; pursuit of *Shokaku*, 231; patrol from Fremantle, 352; in *Bowfin*, joint patrol with *Billfish*, 487–88

Willoughby, Charles A., 304
Willson, Russell, 227
Wilson, William Ritchie ("Ike"), 91*n*
Wilson, Woodrow, 39, 41–42
Winton engine, 61, 64, 67, 68*n*, 79, 157, 198, 266, 446
Withers, Thomas, Jr., 83–84, 123, 156, 250, 268, 362; in Pearl Harbor attack, 98, 100–102; and first wartime patrols from Pearl Harbor, 106–7, 109–10, 112, 115–16, 119–22; and January–March 1942 patrols, 205–12, 216; in Mark VI controversy, 213, 216, 227; in Mark XIV controversy, 216; commands Portsmouth Navy Yard, 223
Wogan, Thomas Lincoln, 490, 518, 520, 615, 853; in *Tarpon*, patrol near Truk, 331–32; 1943 patrols, 405–6, 513–14; in *Besugo*, 730, 746–49; in Battle of Leyte Gulf, 762
Woleai, 432, 436, 457, 574, 647; air strike on, 561, 576; submarine support of air strike, 576–77
Wolf packs, 509; German submarines, 84; beginning of, in Pacific, 387; first from Pearl Harbor, 541–48, 551; in 1944, 562, 597–600, 643–46, 660, 665–68, 674–81, 694, 701–11, 721, 724–25, 727–31, 739–42, 746–48, 764–65, 769–77, 781–86, 788, 795–96, 798, 801–4, 807–11; in 1945, 830, 832–34, 840, 852–53, 858–61, 863–65
World War I: submarines in, 36–45, 47, 48; Japan with Allies in, 46; German submarines, sinking records, 878*n*
World War II: beginning of, 70–72; U.S. preparations for, 72–73; U.S. strategy, advance plans, 78–85; Japanese plans, 85–86, 89–90, 128; summary of 1942 operations, 359–62; Casablanca Conference decisions on strategy, 398–99; Trident Conference on strategy, 422; 1943 Allied counteroffensive, 472, 473

World War II (cont.)
  (map), 474; summary of 1943 operations, 551–54; 1944 strategy, 557, 693–95; summary of 1944 operations, 816–19; in 1945, last months, 823; 1945 strategy, 824; Japanese surrender, 870–73
Worthington, Robert Kemble: in *Silversides*, 452, 480; in *Balao*, 840
Wotho, 116
Wotje, 115, 122, 454; U.S. invasion of, 558
"Wounded Bear," see *Shokaku*
Wright, Wesley Arnold ("Ham"), codebreaker, 74, 88, 117, 401
Wright, William Harry, in *Archerfish*, 649
Wright, William Leslie ("Bull"), 127, 151, 176, 185, 193, 298, 299, 303, 581; in *Sturgeon*, patrol near Formosa, 138, 145; attacks on Japanese in Borneo, 166, 168; returns to U.S., 304; command change, 813
Wylie, William Naylor, 457; in *Scorpion*, 458–60

XE-1, British midget submarine, 855
XE-3, British midget submarine, 855

Yahagi, Japanese destroyer, 830, 832
Yalu River, 407
Yamagumo, Japanese destroyer, 524–25
Yamaika Maru, Japanese freighter, 683
Yamakaze, Japanese destroyer, 252–53
Yamakuni Maru, Japanese freighter, 534
Yamamizu Maru, Japanese tanker, 619
Yamamoto, Adm. Isoroku, 85, 90, 191, 269, 369; Midway invasion plans, 219, 222; and Battle of Midway, 234, 246–48; and Battle of Santa Cruz, 329; and Battle of Guadalcanal, 338–39; death, 370, 561
Yamashimo Maru, Japanese freighter, 573

Yamashiro class, Japanese battleships, 734
Yamato, Japanese battleship, 245–46n, 247n, 506, 539, 560, 563, 586, 724, 766, 771, 778, 785, 800, 825, 829; *Skate* attacks, 530–31; in Biak reinforcement, 638–39; in Battle of Philippine Sea, 650, 651; and Leyte invasion, 749, 755; in Battle of Leyte Gulf, 759; last sortie, 830, 831 (map), 832, 843; sunk, 832
Yamato Maru, Japanese ship, 448
Yangtse River, 447
Yap, 574, 649, 650, 658, 695, 724; air strikes on, 561, 697
Yardley, Herbert Osborne, 52
Yasukuni Maru, Japanese submarine tender, 565
Yawata, Japanese transport, 114–15, 122
Yeager, Robert, 735–36
Yellow Sea, 407–8, 440, 447, 459–60, 683, 772, 788, 819, 833, 840, 858, 867
Yoho, Jud Francis, Jr., 460
Yokohama, U.S. bombing of, 827
Yokosuka Naval Base, 872
Yorktown, aircraft carrier, 64, 204, 222, 234, 399; in Battle of Coral Sea, 220; in Battle of Midway, lost, 238, 239, 361, 553
Yorktown, aircraft carrier (new, 1943), 399n, 422, 568, 829
Yoshida Maru I, Japanese freighter, 623
Yoshino Maru, Japanese transport, 681
Yubari, Japanese cruiser, 289, 434, 621–22, 641, 649, 713
Yukikaze, Japanese destroyer, 633
Yunagi, Japanese destroyer, 705, 706
Yura, Japanese cruiser, 305, 306
Yuzan Maru, Japanese ship, 459

Zabriskie, David, Jr., 665–67
Zamboanga, 634, 639
Zinto class, Japanese cruisers, 138

Zuiho, Japanese aircraft carrier, 269, 330, 331, 338, 506, 744; battle with *Skate* and *Gunnel*, 526–27; sunk, 759, 766

Zuikaku, Japanese aircraft carrier, 191, 211, 258, 301, 330, 351, 353, 506, 744; in Battle of Coral Sea, 220, 222; returns to Japan after battle, 230, 233; in Alaskan waters, 269; in Battle of Philippine Sea, 659, 662; sunk, 759, 766

Zuikaku class, Japanese aircraft carriers, 316

Zuiyo Maru, Japanese tanker, 741

Zwaardvisch, British-built submarine with Dutch crew, 743, 786*n*

About the Author

Clay Blair, Jr., was born in Lexington, Virginia, in 1925. He served in the U.S. Navy in World War II, volunteering for submarine service. He attended submarine school (including a cruise on an S-boat) and was attached to the tender *Sperry* for four months at the advance submarine base, Apra Harbor, Guam. In 1945 he made the last two long war patrols of *Guardfish*, the first off Honshu, February to April, the second off Honshu and Hokkaido during May and June. Rising to the rank of Quartermaster 2nd Class, he qualified in submarines and was decorated with the Submarine Combat Insignia and the Asiatic-Pacific Theater medal with three battle stars. After the war, Mr. Blair joined a submarine reserve unit, making a summer cruise in a newer fleet submarine.

As a Washington journalist for Time-Life and the *Saturday Evening Post* from 1950 to 1960, Mr. Blair followed submarine developments closely and came to know many wartime submarine skippers with whom he spent many hours "diving the boats" and analyzing the submarine war. He was the first journalist to go to sea on the new *Tang*-class submarine *Trigger*, the guided missile submarine *Barbero*, and the first to write about the nuclear-powered submarine *Nautilus*, and her "father," Captain Hyman G. Rickover. He led a successful journalistic crusade to retain Rickover in the navy and subsequently was one of the first journalists to make a sea voyage on *Nautilus*. In later years he inspected and wrote about nuclear-powered Polaris submarines and the new nuclear-powered attack submarine *Guardfish*.

Mr. Blair has published three previous books on submarines: *The Atomic Submarine and Admiral Rickover*; *Nautilus 90 North*, the best-selling account of the *Nautilus* voyage beneath the Arctic ice cap, which was published in twenty-six countries; and *Pentagon Country*, a novel centering on the controversy over the navy's submarine weapons system of the near future, Trident.